D0226047

ACG 4401
UCF
UNIVERSITY BOOKSTORE
1 $61.75

6TH EDITION

Accounting
Information Systems

Barry E. Cushing
University of Utah

Marshall B. Romney
Brigham Young University

Addison-Wesley Publishing Company
Reading, Massachusetts ■ Menlo Park, California ■ New York
Don Mills, Ontario ■ Wokingham, England ■ Amsterdam ■ Bonn
Sydney ■ Singapore ■ Tokyo ■ Madrid ■ San Juan
Milan ■ Paris

Executive Editor: *Barbara Rifkind*
Senior Sponsoring Editor: *Julia Berrisford*
Associate Editor: *Kim T.M. Kramer*
Senior Production Supervisor: *Loren Hilgenhurst Stevens*
Production Services: *Barbara Gracia*
Copy Editor: *Carol Beal*
Proofreaders: *Elizabeth Andrews and Joyce Grandy*
Text Designer: *Loren Hilgenhurst Stevens*
Cover Designer: *Eileen R. Hoff*
Illustrator: *George Nichols*
Senior Marketing Manager: *David Theisen*
Manufacturing Supervisor: *Roy Logan*

Materials from uniform CPA Examination Questions and Unofficial Answers, copyright © 1956, 1962, 1963, 1964, 1969, 1971, 1973, 1978, 1979, 1980, 1983, 1984, 1985, 1986 by the American Institute of Certified Public Accountants, Inc., are reprinted with permission.

Materials from the Certificate in Management Accounting Examinations, copyright © 1973, 1974, 1977, 1978, 1979, 1980, 1981, 1982, 1983, 1984, 1985, 1986, 1987, 1988, 1989, 1990, 1991 by the National Association of Accountants, are reprinted or adapted with permission.

Materials from the Certified Internal Auditor Examination Questions and Suggested Solutions, copyright © 1974, 1976, 1977, 1979, 1980, 1983, 1985, 1986, 1988, 1989 by The Institute of Internal Auditors, Inc., 249 Maitland Avenue, Altamonte Springs, Florida 32701 U.S.A. Reprinted with permission.

Materials from the Society of Management Accountants of Canada Examinations, copyright © 1976, 1979, 1981, 1982, 1983, 1984, 1985, 1987, 1988 by the Society of Management Accountants of Canada, are reprinted or adapted with permission.

Library of Congress Cataloging-in-Publication Data
Cushing, Barry E.
    Accounting information systems: a comprehensive approach / Barry E. Cushing, Marshall B. Romney.—6th ed.
       p.   cm.
    Includes bibliographical references and index.
    ISBN 0-201-58025-X
    1. Accounting—Data processing. 2. Information storage and
retrieval systems—Accounting. I. Romney, Marshall B. II. Title.
HF5679.A34 1993   93-6598
657'.0285—dc20   CIP

Reprinted with corrections, April 1994.

Copyright © 1994 by Addison-Wesley Publishing Company, Inc. All rights reserved. No part of this publication may be reproduced, stored in a retrieval system, or transmitted, in any form or by any means electronic, mechanical, photocopying, recording, or otherwise, without the prior written permission of the publisher. Printed in the United States of America.

4 5 6 7 8 9 10-DO-97 96 95 94

PREFACE

Today, professional accountants work in an exciting and complex environment that is constantly changing. Progress in information technology is occurring at an ever-increasing rate. Business organizations are changing their methods of operation and their management structures to meet the demands of an increasingly competitive environment. The economic and legal environment that accountants work in is also changing in unpredictable ways. All of these environmental changes require that today's accounting students be better prepared than ever before to enter the challenging world of the accounting profession.

A central feature of accounting in today's business world is the interaction of accounting professionals with computer-based information systems. As primary users of information systems in organizations, accountants must participate in their design and understand their operation. Accounting managers must measure and evaluate the performance of information systems. Internal and external auditors must assess the quality of information processing and evaluate the accuracy of information input and output. The major share of the work of accounting consultants is in the design, implementation, and evaluation of information systems.

This book is intended for use in a one-semester course in accounting information systems at the advanced undergraduate or graduate level. Introductory financial and managerial accounting courses are necessary prerequisites, and an introductory course in data processing that covers a computer language or software package is helpful. The book can also be used as the main text in graduate or advanced undergraduate courses in management information systems.

As with the first five editions, the purpose of this text is to help prepare students for a career in the accounting profession. Today's accounting students will become tomorrow's users, auditors, and managers of computer-based information systems. To be successful in pursuing an accounting career, students must possess a basic knowledge of computer-based information systems and their role in performing the accounting function in contemporary business organizations. Thus students must

■ understand the flow of accounting data and information in business organizations;

- be familiar with the tools of accounting systems work, such as data flow diagrams and flowcharting;
- understand how computer technology is used in information processing;
- understand how information systems are developed, implemented, and maintained;
- have a thorough knowledge of control principles and their application in information systems and various organizational contexts;
- understand the five major business and accounting cycles in which an organization's transactions are processed.

This book is written to help students acquire the understanding and knowledge of accounting information systems that they must have to succeed in their chosen field.

MAJOR CHANGES IN THE SIXTH EDITION

Each new edition of this text has responded to the rapidly changing environment of business and accounting, and the sixth edition is no exception. A number of major changes have been made to this edition in response to recent developments in the field and in the teaching of accounting information systems courses.

New Features

Three new chapters have been added to the book. Chapter 3 consolidates into one chapter all of the systems development and documentation techniques that are needed and used by information systems developers and users. Chapter 11 discusses alternative approaches to the traditional systems development life cycle, such as purchasing software, prototyping, and outsourcing. It also discusses reengineering business processes. Chapter 14 discusses computer fraud and how it can be deterred and detected.

Most of the other 17 chapters have been substantially revised. In fact, we estimate that over 50% of the book has been rewritten. In revising the chapters, we made every effort to update the text and problem material to include the most current information technology and applications.

Each chapter begins with a realistic case problem raising many issues covered in the chapter. This case problem is integrated throughout the chapter, and a description of how the case is resolved appears at the end of each chapter.

Focus boxes are included in each chapter to provide current real-world examples of the concepts, techniques, and practices described in the text. In addition, numerous shorter examples of real-world situations and applications are incorporated into the text throughout every chapter.

An appendix has been added to the book containing four comprehensive cases. Each case has a list of requirements relating the case to material covered in most chapters in the book. Instructors can use one or more of these in a cumulative manner by making assignments from the same case after covering a chapter.

Each chapter has at least two end-of-chapter cases. One is the Anycompany case, which gets the students out into the community working with a local company. During visits to this company students are asked to discuss the concepts covered in the chapter with company employees and management and to investigate how the company has handled or would handle the issues discussed in the chapter.

Each chapter has a set of assignment materials designed to help students develop and test their knowledge. Included are over 1000 short review questions, discussion questions, problems of short and moderate length, and cases that are longer and integrate material from various parts of the chapter. Many new problems and cases have been added, and many others have been revised to reflect changes made in the text. Among the problems and cases are many items selected from professional examinations, including the CPA, CMA, CIA, and SMAC exams. Many new real-world problems and cases have been added to the assignment material. They were developed from reports in current periodicals and draw upon the experiences and problems faced by actual companies.

The text contains over 380 figures, diagrams, flowcharts, tables, and photographs that illustrate important concepts: Most of them are new to this edition.

At the end of the book is an extensive bibliography, by chapter, that should help students or instructors locate additional current readings and background material in order to pursue selected topics in greater depth.

The glossary at the back of the book, which contains definitions of key terms used in the text, has been revised extensively.

An overview of the sixth edition

The Introductory Chapters

Part I, "Conceptual Foundations of Accounting Information Systems," consists of three chapters that review the underlying concepts fundamental to an understanding of accounting information systems. Chapter 1 has been significantly revised and stresses how information systems add value to businesses. The chapter on organization in the fifth edition has been eliminated, and the more important material from that chapter has been integrated into other chapters. Chapter 2 on transaction processing emphasizes the data processing cycle. It also describes the key elements of accounting information processing cycles. Chapter 3 is a new chapter on systems development and documentation techniques. Data flow diagrams, systems flowcharts, document flowcharts, structure charts, and structured English are some of the design tools reviewed in this chapter.

Information Technology

Part II, "The Technology of Information Systems," includes Chapters 4 through 7 and focuses on the technology used to design and operate computer-based information systems. These chapters emphasize the concepts that drive the progress of technology, rather than the specific features of current technology, which tend to become quickly outdated. Chapter 4 is a review of hardware and software. Chapter 5, which discusses personal computers, has been rewritten to provide an end-user orientation. Chapter 6, which discusses telecommunications, has been updated, and a greater emphasis was placed on local area networks. Chapter 7, the data base chapter, has been revised; relational data bases are now emphasized.

All chapters in this section reflect the latest developments in information systems technology. Numerous examples have been incorporated into these chapters to provide a real-world setting. By explaining both the fundamentals of information systems (IS) technology and the present direction of technological developments, these chapters should enable students to appreciate technological change and how it affects IS possibilities.

The Systems Development Process

Part III, "The Systems Development Process," consists of Chapters 8 through 11. It focuses on the definition, development, and implementation of information systems. The four life cycle chapters from the fifth edition have been condensed into three chapters and revised to incorporate more current material. Chapter 8 emphasizes the steps that must be performed throughout the analysis and design of a new information system, including the planning and management of systems development, behavioral aspects of system change, and feasibility analysis, with an emphasis on economic feasibility. Chapter 9 covers the process of systems analysis and examines conceptual systems design. It also discusses computer-aided software engineering (CASE) tools. Chapter 10 discusses physical systems design as well as the steps involved in implementing a new system. Chapter 11 is a new chapter that explains some of the recent approaches to systems development, including reengineering, prototyping, and outsourcing. It also discusses the systems acquisition process in detail. Numerous real-world examples have been added to all four chapters to increase reader interest.

Control and Audit of Information Systems

Part IV, "Control and Audit of Accounting Information Systems," includes Chapters 12 through 15. This section has been extensively modified to incorporate more current material, including numerous examples to provide a real-world basis. Chapter 12 is organized around a discussion of a firm's internal control structure, consisting of its control environment, control procedures, and accounting systems. To reflect significant developments in recent accounting literature, this chapter also includes an analysis of the costs and benefits of internal control. Chapter 13 examines management control and internal control in computer-based information systems. A new chapter on computer fraud (Chapter 14) has been added to this section. This new chapter discusses how and why fraud occurs, explains how to prevent and detect fraud, and provides many problems and cases that cover actual incidents of computer fraud. Chapter 15 reviews principles and techniques for audit evaluation of internal control in computer-based systems and discusses techniques for using the computer in the audit of accounting information systems.

Application of Accounting Information Systems

Part V, "Accounting Information Systems Applications," consists of five chapters that integrate the material in the first four parts of the book by taking a detailed look at how accounting information systems are applied within typical business organizations. This section describes the information processing requirements of the five major accounting cycles: the revenue cycle (Chapter 16), the procurement cycle (Chapter 17), the production cycle (Chapter 18), the personnel/payroll cycle (Chapter 19), and the financial management and reporting cycle (Chapter 20). Each chapter explains the accounting processes, data bases, and internal control procedures associated with a cycle.

In Part V all five chapters were completely revised. Descriptions of manual systems were replaced with generic descriptions of the primary functions and procedures performed within each of the major processing cycles. Almost all of the systems flowcharts and sample documents and reports were revised, and the related narratives modified, to better reflect the nature of contemporary accounting systems applications. In place of the previous emphasis on batch processing systems, the sixth edition emphasizes and explains the growing dominance of on-line systems in leading-edge organizations. The role of information systems in establishing a competitive advantage is stressed. And numerous real-world examples are incorporated throughout these chapters.

INSTRUCTIONAL SUPPLEMENTS

From the beginning, our guiding objective in preparing this textbook has been to simplify the teaching of accounting information systems by freeing instructors from the burden of locating, assembling, and distributing teaching materials, allowing them to concentrate on classroom presentation and discussion. We view this book and the related materials available from Addison-Wesley not as a textbook but as a teaching system. The major elements of this teaching system are described next.

Instructor's Manual

An *Instructor's Manual* is available to instructors who adopt this textbook. This manual begins with suggested syllabi for using the textbook in a one-semester or one-quarter course. The first section of the manual consists of 20 chapters corresponding to the chapters in the text. Each of these chapters contains a one-page outline of major topics covered in the chapter, suitable for reproduction as a transparency. It also contains learning objectives for the chapter material; detailed teaching notes discussing how to present the chapter material to students; alternative lecture examples; references to key figures and discussion questions, problems, and cases; and alternative discussion questions, problems, and readings, where appropriate. The second section of the *Instructor's Manual* is a test item file containing approximately 2000 objective questions and their solutions for use in preparing examinations. This test bank is also available in computerized form for an IBM PC. The final section of the *Instructor's Manual* contains over 110 transparency masters of key tables and charts in the textbook.

Solutions Manual

A separate *Solutions Manual* is also available to those who adopt the text. It contains guidelines for leading class discussions based on each discussion question in the text, and it has suggested solutions for each of the text problems and cases.

Software Supplement

The book *Spreadsheet and Database Applications for Accounting Information Systems,* by Professors Roy Johnson of Roosevelt University and Denise Nitterhouse of DePaul University (Addison-Wesley, 1990), is also available. It is intended to supplement this book with coverage of spreadsheet and database software packages and with exercises designed to provide students with hands-on experience in applying accounting information systems concepts in a computer environment.

Supplementary Book of Readings and Cases

The book *Accounting Information Systems: A Book of Readings with Cases,* by James R. Davis and Barry E. Cushing (Addison-Wesley, 1987), is intended to supplement this book with outside readings organized according to a similar topical outline and with more complex and comprehensive cases.

By offering these supplements, we have attempted to develop a comprehensive teaching package that will make the teaching of accounting information systems courses an enjoyable experience for both new and seasoned instructors.

ACKNOWLEDGMENTS

We wish to express our appreciation to Professor Paul J. Steinbart of Memphis State University for preparing the *Instructor's Manual* and computerized test bank to accompany this edition. We also thank Martha M. Eining of the University of Utah and Carol F. Venable of San Diego State University for preparing the comprehensive cases included in this edition.

We appreciate the help of Nina Whitehead in typing and preparing the various copies of the book and the *Solutions Manual*. We also wish to thank Andrew Knighton, Alan Lyon, and Eric Peterson, masters candidates at Brigham Young University, for their assistance in reviewing problems and problem solutions for this edition. Finally, we are grateful to Iris Vesey for her contributions to the problem material.

We are indebted to numerous faculty members throughout the world who have adopted the earlier editions and who have been generous with their suggestions for improvement. We are especially grateful to those who participated in reviewing the sixth edition as it was being developed:

Ronald Barden, Georgia State University
Jan Gillespie, University of Texas at Austin
Severin Grabski, Michigan State University
Dan Norris, Iowa State University
George Peek, Western Illinois University
Bob Phillips, Radford University
Steve Rockwell, University of Florida
Arjan Sadhwani, University of Akron
Carol Venable, San Diego State University
Gemma Welsch, DePaul University
Chris Wolfe, Texas A&M University

We are grateful for permission received from four professional accounting organizations to use problems and unofficial solutions from their past professional examinations in this book. Thanks are extended to the American Institute of Certified Public Accountants for use of CPA Examination materials, to the Institute of Certified Management Accountants of the National Association of Accountants for use of CMA Examination materials, to the Institute of Internal Auditors for use of CIA Examination materials, and to the Society of Management Accountants of Canada for use of SMAC Examination materials.

In addition, we would like to thank Kim Kramer, development editor; Loren Hilgenhurst Stevens, production supervisor; Barbara Gracia, production packager; Carol Beal, copy editor; and others on the staff at Addison-Wesley Publishing Company for their efforts in helping us to make this a better book.

Suggestions and comments from users on the text and the related materials are welcome.

Salt Lake City, Utah   B.E.C.
Provo, Utah   M.B.R.

TABLE OF CONTENTS

PART I CONCEPTUAL FOUNDATIONS OF ACCOUNTING INFORMATION SYSTEMS 1

Chapter 1 Accounting Information Systems: An Overview 1

Integrative Case: S&S, Inc. 1
What Is an Information System? 2
Types of Information Systems 12
The Role of the Accounting Information System 16
Business and Accounting Cycles 20
Information Systems and Business Organization 21
Why Study Accounting Information Systems? 25
How Information Systems Add Value to Businesses 26
Case Conclusion: An Example of an Accounting Information System— S&S, Inc. 29
The Future of Accounting Information Systems 32
A Preview of the Book's Contents 35
Summary 36
Key Terms 36
Discussion Questions 37
Problems 38
Case 1.1: Anycompany, Inc.—An Ongoing Comprehensive Case 45
Case 1.2: Ackoff's Management Misinformation Systems 46

Chapter 2 Transaction Processing: Elements and Procedures 51

Integrative Case: S&S, Inc. 51
Introduction 53
Transaction Processing 53
Data Input 59
Data Storage 61
Data Processing 66
Information Output 77
Coding Techniques 78
Case Conclusion: Processing Transactions at S&S Inc. 85
Summary 86
Key Terms 87
Discussion Questions 87
Problems 89
Case 2.1: Anycompany, Inc.—An Ongoing Comprehensive Case 96
Case 2.2: S&S, Inc. 97

Chapter 3 Systems Development and Documentation Techniques 99

Integrative Case: S&S, Inc. 99
Introduction 100
Data Flow Diagrams 102
Flowcharts 113
Decision Tables 128
Structured English 130
HIPO Charts 131
Case Conclusion: Understanding the System at S&S, Inc. 132
Summary 133

Key Terms   134
Discussion Questions   135
Problems   136
Case 3.1: Anycompany, Inc.—An
   Ongoing Comprehensive Case   141
Case 3.2   142

PART II THE TECHNOLOGY OF INFORMATION SYSTEMS   144

Chapter 4 A Review of Computer Hardware and Software   144

Integrative Case: S&S, Inc.   144
Introduction   145
Section A: Computer Hardware   147
Computers: History and Classifications   147
Central Processing Unit   155
Secondary Storage Devices and Media   159
Input Devices   162
Computer Output Devices   168
Section B: Software   170
Levels of Computer Languages   170
Systems Software   179
Application Software   182
Case Conclusion: Understanding
   Hardware and Software Concepts at
   S&S, Inc.   183
Summary   185
Key Terms   186
Discussion Questions   187
Problems   189
Case 4.1: Anycompany, Inc.—An
   Ongoing Comprehensive Case   192
Case 4.2: Information Systems and the
   Manufacturing Industry   193

Chapter 5 Personal Information Systems: Microcomputers and End-User Decision Support Systems   194

Integrative Case: S&S, Inc.   194
Introduction   195
An Introduction to Microcomputers   198
End-User Computing (EUC)   203
Microcomputer and End-User
   Software Tools   211

Case Conclusion: Implementing a
   Microcomputer-Based System at
   S&S, Inc.   232
Summary   233
Key Terms   234
Discussion Questions   234
Problems   236
Case 5.1: Anycompany, Inc.—An
   Ongoing
   Comprehensive Case   241
Case 5.2: Selecting a Small Business-
   Oriented Computer   242

Chapter 6 Data Communications Systems   244

Integrative Case: S&S, Inc.   244
Introduction   246
Data Communications System Model   248
Data Communications Hardware   249
Data Communications Software   250
Communications Channels   252
Communications Network Organization   261
Data Communications Network Types   266
Data Communications Applications   274
Case Conclusion: Implementing a Data
   Communications System at S&S, Inc.   285
Summary   285
Key Terms   286
Discussion Questions   287
Problems   288
Case 6.1: Anycompany, Inc.—An
   Ongoing Comprehensive Case   295
Case 6.2: J.C. Penney   295
Case 6.3: A Move to Cooperative
   Computing   297

Chapter 7 Data Base Systems   299

Integrative Case: S&S, Inc.   299
Introduction   301
The File-Oriented Approach Versus the
   Data Base Approach   301
Data Base Management Systems   308
Tree and Network Data Structures   314
Relational Data Base Structure   317
File and Data Base Design
   Considerations   329

Impact of Data Base Systems on
  Accounting   333
Case Conclusion: Implementing a Data
  Base System at S&S, Inc.   334
Summary   335
Key Terms   336
Discussion Questions   336
Problems   338
Case 7.1: Anycompany, Inc.—An
  Ongoing Comprehensive Case   341
Case 7.2: Wekender Corporation   341

PART III THE SYSTEMS DEVELOPMENT PROCESS 343

Chapter 8 The Systems Development Process: An Overview 343

Integrative Case: Shoppers Mart   343
Introduction   344
Change: The One Constant in
  Information Systems   345
The Systems Development Life Cycle   347
Planning and Managing Systems
  Development   350
Behavioral Aspects of Change   356
Feasibility Analysis   363
Case Conclusion: Beginning the Systems
  Development Process at Shoppers
  Mart   369
Summary   372
Key Terms   373
Discussion Questions   373
Problems   375
Case 8.1: Anycompany, Inc.—An
  Ongoing Comprehensive Case   384
Case 8.2: Audio Visual Corporation   384

Chapter 9 Systems Analysis and Conceptual Systems Design 386

Integrative Case: Shoppers Mart   386
Introduction   387
Systems Analysis   387
Conceptual (General) Systems Design   409
Computer-Aided Software Engineering
  (CASE)   414

Case Conclusion: The Systems Analysis
  and Conceptual Systems Design
  Process at Shoppers Mart   419
Summary   420
Key Terms   421
Discussion Questions   421
Problems   422
Case 9.1: Anycompany, Inc: An Ongoing
  Comprehensive Case   427
Case 9.2: Citizen's Gas Company   428

Chapter 10 Systems Design, Implementation, Operation, and Management 429

Integrative Case: Shoppers Mart   429
Introduction   431
Physical (Detailed) Systems Design   432
Implementation and Conversion   440
Operation and Maintenance   455
Case Conclusion: Systems Design,
  Implementation, and Operation at
  Shoppers Mart   458
Summary   459
Key Terms   460
Discussion Questions   460
Problems   461
Case 10.1: Anycompany, Inc.—An
  Ongoing Comprehensive Case   470
Case 10.2: Newton Manufacturing   471

Chapter 11 Alternative Approaches to Systems Development 472

Integrative Case: Alternative
  Development Strategies at Shoppers
  Mart   472
Introduction   474
Systems Acquisition   475
Outsourcing   490
Prototyping   496
Reengineering Business Processes   503
Case Conclusion: Systems Development
  at Home Improvement Center   510
Summary   512
Key Terms   513
Discussion Questions   513
Problems   515

Case 11.1: Anycompany, Inc.—An
   Ongoing Comprehensive Case   522
Case 11.2: Widget Manufacturing
   Company   523

PART IV CONTROL AND AUDIT OF ACCOUNTING INFORMATION SYSTEMS   525

Chapter 12 Control and Accounting Information Systems   525

Integrative Case: Springer's Northwest
   Lumber & Supply   525
Introduction   526
The Control Environment   537
Control Procedures   542
The Accounting System   550
Analysis of the Costs and Benefits of
   Internal Control   558
Case Conclusion: Investigating the
   Internal Control System at Springer's
   Northwest Lumber & Supply   565
Summary   566
Key Terms   567
Discussion Questions   568
Problems   568
Case 12.1: Anycompany, Inc.—An
   Ongoing Comprehensive Case   576
Case 12.2: The Greater Providence
   Deposit and Trust Embezzlement   577

Chapter 13 Internal Control in Computer-Based Information Systems   579

Integrative Case: Seattle Paper Products   579
Introduction   580
Organization of the Information Systems
   Function   582
Management Control of the Information
   Systems Function   589
Other General Controls   600
Application Controls   615
Case Conclusion: Correcting Computer

Control Problems at Seattle Paper
   Products   634
Summary   635
Key Terms   636
Discussion Questions   637
Problems   638
Case 13.1: Anycompany, Inc.—An
   Ongoing Comprehensive Case   643
Case 13.2: The State Department of
   Taxation   644

Chapter 14 Computer Fraud   645

Integrative Case: Northwest Industries   645
Introduction   646
What Is Fraud?   648
Computer Fraud   651
Why Fraud Occurs   659
Deterring Computer Fraud   664
Case Conclusion: The Differences in
   Withholdings at Northwest Industries   674
Summary   675
Key Terms   676
Discussion Questions   677
Problems   679
Case 14.1: Robert T. Morris—A Worm
   Run Amok   685
Case 14.2: Kevin Mitnick—The Dark-
   Side Hacker   687
Case 14.3: David L. Miller—Portrait of a
   White-Collar Criminal   688

Chapter 15 Auditing of Computer-Based Information Systems   691

Integrative Case: Seattle Paper Products   691
Introduction   692
The Nature of Auditing   693
Information Systems Audits   702
Financial Audits and Computer Audit
   Software   731
Operational Audits of Computer-Based
   Information Systems   741
Case Conclusion: Resolving Audit Issues
   at Seattle Paper Products   743
Summary   744

Key Terms   744
Discussion Questions   745
Problems   745
Case 15.1: Anycompany, Inc: An
  Ongoing Comprehensive Case   751
Case 15.2: Preston Manufacturing
  Company   752

PART V ACCOUNTING INFORMATION SYSTEMS APPLICATIONS   753

Chapter 16 The Revenue Cycle: Sales and Accounts Receivable   753

Integrative Case: Electronics
  Incorporated   753
Introduction   754
The Marketing Management Function   755
Basic Revenue Cycle Functions and
  Procedures   760
The Sales Order Processing System   770
Case Conclusion: Improving Marketing
  Information Systems at Electronics
  Incorporated   792
Summary   793
Key Terms   793
Discussion Questions   793
Problems   794
Case 16.1: Anycompany, Inc.—An
  Ongoing Comprehensive Case   804
Case 16.2: Elite Publishing Company   805

Chapter 17 The Procurement Cycle: Purchases, Inventories, and Accounts Payable   806

Integrative Case: Electronics
  Incorporated   806
Introduction   807
The Purchasing and Inventory
  Management Function   808
Basic Procurement Cycle Functions and
  Procedures   813
The Purchasing and Inventory Data
  Processing System   824
Case Conclusion: Improving

Procurement Cycle Information
  Systems at Electronics Incorporated   851
Summary   852
Key Terms   853
Discussion Questions   853
Problems   854
Case 17.1: Anycompany, Inc.—An
  Ongoing Comprehensive Case   862
Case 17.2: Blackwell Industries   863

Chapter 18 The Production Cycle   864

Integrative Case: Electronics
  Incorporated   864
Introduction   865
The Production Management Function   867
Basic Production Cycle Functions and
  Procedures   877
The Production Information System   889
Case Conclusion: Improving Production
  Cycle Information Systems at
  Electronics Incorporated   918
Summary   919
Key Terms   920
Discussion Questions   920
Problems   921
Case 18.1: Anycompany, Inc.— An
  Ongoing
  Comprehensive Case   926
Case 18.2: The Powerflow Corporation   927

Chapter 19 The Personnel/Payroll Cycle   929

Integrative Case: Electronics
  Incorporated   929
Introduction   930
The Personnel Management Function   932
Basic Personnel/Payroll Cycle Functions
  and Procedures   937
The Personnel/Payroll Data Processing
  System   950
Case Conclusion: Improving Personnel
  Information Systems at Electronics
  Incorporated   972
Summary   974

Key Terms   975
Discussion Questions   975
Problems   976
Case 19.1: Anycompany, Inc.—An
   Ongoing Comprehensive Case   983
Case 19.2: Darwin Department Store   983

**Chapter 20   The Financial Management and
                Financial Reporting Cycles   985**

Integrative Case: Electronics
   Incorporated   985
Introduction   986
The Financial Management Function   987
The Financial Management and Financial
   Reporting Cycles: Basic Functions and
   Procedures   997
The Financial Information System   1012

Case Conclusion: Improving Financial
   Information Systems at Electronics
   Incorporated   1040
Summary   1042
Key Terms   1043
Discussion Questions   1043
Problems   1044
Case 20.1: Anycompany, Inc.—An
   Ongoing Comprehensive Case   1050
Case 20.2: Transinternational
   Distribution Company   1052

Appendix: Comprehensive Cases   A-1
Glossary   G-1
References   R-1
Index   I-1

PART I

CHAPTER 1

Accounting Information Systems: An Overview

LEARNING OBJECTIVES

After studying this chapter, you should be able to:

- Explain what constitutes information and how to determine the value of information, explain what is meant by a system, and explain what an information system is and what its components are.
- Describe the basic features of accounting and management information systems, and distinguish between the two.
- Explain the role of accounting information systems in organizations, and discuss how they meet the needs of both external and internal information users.
- Describe the five basic business cycles and their relationship to each other.
- Explain why the study of accounting information systems is an important part of your educational program.

INTEGRATIVE CASE: S&S, INC.

After working for several years as a regional manager for a national retailing organization, Scott Parry decided to open his own business. Susan Anderson, one of his district managers, had also expressed a desire to go into business for herself. Together they formed a company, S&S Inc., to sell home appliance products to the public. The product line at S&S will include refrigerators, freezers, electric and gas ranges, microwaves, washers, dryers, television sets, VCRs, radios, stereos, CD players, air conditioners, and vacuum cleaners. They have rented a large and attractive building in a heavy–traffic pattern area of town.

Scott and Susan have arranged for all of the major manufacturers to supply them with appliances. Because of limited funds, they will initially sell only a few models of each appliance in their showroom. The manufacturers will also supply parts, since S&S wants to provide full service for everything it sells. Scott and Susan figure that they will need to employ from 10 to 15 persons—2 or 3 as office personnel, 2 or 3 in delivery, 2 or 3 in service and repair, and 4 to 6 in sales. They will soon begin the process of hiring employees to perform these various functions.

Scott and Susan have set the grand opening of their store for five weeks from tomorrow. Although they have completed many of the arrangements for their opening, they are still uncertain about how to resolve the following problems:

1. Deciding their pricing policy and grand-opening sales promotion strategy.
2. Determining the appropriate product mix for their limited showroom space. The appliances vary widely in terms of price, quality, reputation, and reliability. The manufacturers also vary in terms of delivery reliability and sales terms.
3. Deciding whether to extend credit, and in what amounts, to potential customers.

How would you suggest that Scott and Susan address these problems? ■

WHAT IS AN INFORMATION SYSTEM?

What Scott and Susan need is more information. And they cannot get it until they have an information system. But just what is an information system? Before that question is answered, let's first discuss what information is and what a system is. Once we understand these two concepts, we can gain a better understanding of an accounting information system (known as an AIS).

What Is Information?

Information refers to processing output that is organized, meaningful, and useful to the person who receives it. A distinction is generally drawn between data and information. Data can be thought of as random facts that are accepted as input to an information system and are stored or processed. Data usually represent observations or measurements of events that are of importance to information system users. For example, items of data concerning a sale may be the identification number of the salesperson, an identifier of the item sold, and the amount of the sale. When many such data elements are organized and analyzed, they become information for marketing directors attempting to evaluate their sales forces.

Data is processed into information so that decision makers can make better decisions. This is shown graphically in Fig. 1.1. As a general rule, the more information a decision maker has and the better the information, the better the decision that is made.

Characteristics of Information. For information to be useful, it must possess several characteristics. Information must be reliable, relevant, timely, complete, understandable, and verifiable.

Information is *reliable* when it is free from error or bias. In other words, it must accurately represent the events or activities of the organization. For example, a report showing that S&S sold 98 micro-waves when it actually sold 198, does not contain reliable information. Errors such as these may result from erroneous or incomplete input data or a processing error.

Information is *relevant* when it will make a difference to the decision maker. It can do this by reducing uncertainty or by adding increased knowledge or value to the decision maker. For example, a report showing the number of cars sold in the United States is not relevant to S&S's decision of whether or not to change its supplier of refrigerators.

Information is *timely* when it is provided in time to affect the decision-making process. For example, assume that S&S prepares a report listing the accounts payable that offer a 2% discount if paid within 10 days. This report is not timely if the disbursements clerk receives it after the 10-day period has expired.

Information is *complete* when it includes all relevant data. That is, it must not omit important data that a user would expect it to contain. For example, a report showing S&S's sales is not complete if the sales for one department is not included.

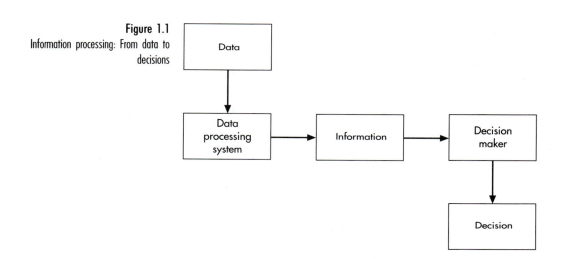

Figure 1.1
Information processing: From data to decisions

Information is *understandable* when it is presented in a form that is useful and intelligible to the user. For example, a report prepared for Susan Anderson of S&S, though it may be complete, is not understandable if she cannot locate the information she needs.

Information is *verifiable* if two knowledgeable people can independently produce the same information. For example, the weekly pay of an employee is verifiable if two separate payroll clerks calculate the same pay for the week.

Value of Information. The objective of an information system is to transform data into information of value to decision makers. But how do we determine the value of information? The **value of information** is the difference between the benefit produced by the information (usually in the form of an improved decision) and the cost of producing it. This can be expressed by the following formula:

$$\text{value of information} = \text{benefit} - \text{cost.}$$

Perhaps this idea is best illustrated by an example. Suppose that Scott and Susan are trying to decide between three sales prices for a popular new line of microwaves. They believe they can achieve the following monthly sales volume (expected sales), contribution margin (selling price less variable costs), and total profit at the sales prices listed.

Sales Price	Expected Sales	Contribution Margin	Total Profit
$349	70	49	$3430
379	50	79	3950
399	30	99	2970

If they price their microwaves on the basis of this information, they will sell them at $379 in order to maximize their profits. Unfortunately, there is at least one problem with their analysis: The expected sales are guesses. Therefore, they really do not know how many microwaves they could sell at each price.

Now suppose that a market research firm tells them that for $1000 the firm can provide them with perfect information. That is, the firm can tell them with 100% certainty how many units they can sell at each price. If you were Scott or Susan, would you "buy" the information by hiring the research firm?

One problem they face in making this decision is that they do not know the value of the information they will receive. They can identify its cost ($1000), but they do not know the benefits that the new information will bring. If the information merely confirms that $379 is the price that will maximize their profits, what have they gained? They have removed some uncertainty, and they will have a better idea of just how many units they can expect to sell. This information will help them in terms of planning and scheduling. But is it worth $1000? Its worth will depend on how much benefit they get out of the information.

Unfortunately, it is often difficult to quantify the benefits received from a reduction of uncertainty and better planning and scheduling.

On the other hand, suppose that the market research shows a resistance to microwaves that cost over $350 but a receptiveness to quality microwaves priced at $349. Based on the research, the firm presents S&S with these revised estimates:

Sales Price	Expected Sales	Contribution Margin	Total Profit
$349	90	49	$4410
379	40	79	3160
399	20	99	1980

On the basis of the revised sales figures, is the information worth its cost? Most certainly. If Susan and Scott do not spend the money for the information, they will sell the microwave ovens for $379 and will have total profits of $3160, instead of the $3950 they had previously estimated. If they buy the information and sell microwaves for $349, they can make $4410. Therefore, the benefit of the information is $1250 (4410 − 3160). The value of the information is $250 (1250 − 1000). By spending the $1000, they will be able to increase sales by $1250 each month. The cost of the information will easily be paid for in the first month of operation.

Unfortunately, making decisions about the value of information is never as simple as in this example. However, the example points out that information is valuable because it reduces uncertainty (although it is rarely possible to know something with 100% certainty, as in the example). By reducing uncertainty, information improves the quality of decisions. The more inexperienced and uninformed people are, the more likely the information is to help them.

However, there are some practical problems with analyzing the value of information in this manner. First, it is often difficult to determine the value of information before it has been produced and utilized. For example, Scott and Susan have no idea how useful the information will be until they have it and use it to make their decision. Second, the costs and especially the benefits of information are very difficult to quantify. Nevertheless, the value of information should be analyzed as effectively as possible before a firm attempts to produce it. Otherwise, information might be produced whose costs exceed its benefits.

Now that we have explored the meaning of information, let's discuss the meaning of the word *system*. Then we can put the two concepts together and discuss what an information system is.

What Is a System?   A *system* is an entity consisting of two or more interrelated components or subsystems that interact to achieve a goal. One of the simplest systems is the thermostat and the heating unit in a home. Its goal or objective is to keep the house at a specified temperature, say between 68 and 72 degrees. The input to the system is the temperature inside the home. The thermostat monitors the temperature until it falls to

68 degrees. At that time, the thermostat causes the heater to start (the system output). Again, the thermostat monitors the temperature that is input into the system until it reaches 72 degrees, at which time the heater is shut off.

A system relevant to accounting tasks is the **computer-based system**, which refers to the equipment, programs, data, and procedures for performing a set of related tasks on a computer.

In any system, alternative courses of action must be evaluated from the standpoint of the system as a whole, rather than from that of any single subsystem or set of subsystems. This is referred to as the **systems concept**. The systems concept encourages **integration**, the combining of previously separated subsystems. Integration has made data processing more efficient by eliminating duplication of recording, storage, reporting, and other processing activities within an organization. For example, formerly companies performed the preparation of customer statements, the collection of cash, and the maintenance of accounts receivable records separately; now these functions are combined in a single application.

Information Systems

We can combine the concepts of information and systems to define an information system. An **information system** is an organized means of collecting, entering, and processing data and of storing, managing, controlling, and reporting information so that an organization can achieve its objectives and goals. The importance of having a quality information system is illustrated in Focus 1.1.

1.1 FOCUS

So That's Why They Keep Spending...

What happens to a government when it can't monitor its own money? It keeps spending and spending. Just ask the Red Lake Band of the Chippewa Indians. For years the Chippewa Indians in northern Minnesota prospered from timber, mineral, and fishing resources. As much as $500,000 a year of revenues poured into a government trust fund managed by the Bureau of Indian Affairs (BIA). However, a 1982 audit discovered that years of sloppy bookkeeping by the BIA has actually left the tribe more than $800,000 short. Two years ago the BIA deducted an additional $1.2 million from the fund for accounting errors. At that point the Chippewas had had enough and filed suit against the federal government for mismanagement of funds. Apparently, the BIA problems are only the tip of an enormous iceberg of faulty accounting systems in the federal government.

In the 1950s, the federal government was on the cutting edge of information systems. But years of underinvestment and budget-slashing have gutted

Formal and Informal Systems. Information systems can be formal or informal. A formal information system is one that has an explicit responsibility to produce information. Accounting, production, and marketing information systems are three examples of formal information systems used in most business organizations. In contrast, an informal information system is one that arises out of a need that is not satisfied by a formal channel. It operates without a formal assignment of responsibility. The "grapevine" is a familiar informal channel of information common to all organizations. As organizations grow in size, it is natural for some informal channels to become formalized.

Manual, Automated, and Computer-Based Systems. Information systems can also be classified according to their level of automation. Information systems in which most of the data processing load is carried by people are called manual information systems. The major advantages of people as data processors are their abilities to perform all the various functions of a data processing system and to adapt to unfamiliar situations. The major disadvantages are their lack of reliability and speed.

An automated system is one in which most data processing activities are handled by machines. If a computer is used as the data processor, the system is referred to as a computer-based system. The advantage of computer-based systems is that they can perform many processing functions without human intervention. These activities are carried on at incredibly fast speeds with great accuracy. However, computer systems also tend to be less flexible and adaptable than manual sys-

---

back-office spending for most government agencies. The result: Most federal agencies lack adequate technology to monitor revenues, expenditures, and cash resources. For example, the Air Force currently has over 130 separate accounting information systems, many of them antiquated. Auditor attempts to balance Air Force books are a good lesson in futility.

As a result of poor training and inadequate information systems, the books of many agencies, including the BIA, haven't been balanced in half a century. The BIA has two computer systems to monitor fund accounts, yet most staffers still record entries by hand. As a result, payments often go to incorrect accounts and to the wrong people. To balance the books, financial clerks routinely plug in fake accounting entries. According to a General Accounting Office (GAO) investigator, the BIA is like a bank that doesn't know how much money it has.

Government inefficiency is costing taxpayers dearly, perhaps masking the true scope of the annual budget deficit. According to GAO audits, most government agencies pay their bills too early or too late, costing taxpayers millions in unearned interest and late fees. Other tax-

payer costs of poor information systems include poor tax collection procedures, limited defense inventory controls, and inadequate monitoring of government loans to individuals.

Changes are still a long way off as politicians reconcile their differences and search for solutions. However, one thing is certain: The spending will continue unabated and uncontrolled until adequate information systems reestablish fiscal accountability.

Source: Adapted from Dean Foust, "Uncle Sam Can't Keep Track of His Trillions," *Business Week* (September 2, 1991): 72–73.

tems, and the cost of the initial design and acquisition effort is often enormous.

Note that automation does not mean that manual processing is always eliminated from the business or even from every transaction cycle. Some organizations, especially smaller ones, have a mix of automated systems and manual systems, because it is not always desirable or feasible to automate all functions. For example, a company may not need an automated fixed asset system if it has few fixed assets with little asset turnover. Likewise, a small company with a cash-only sales policy would not need to purchase an accounts receivable software module for a personal computer-based accounting system. In both cases, the number of transactions within the particular cycle does not justify automation.

Computer-based systems have a wide range of capabilities and features. In recent years two types of computer systems have evolved: large-scale computer systems, which serve many users through a central mainframe computer, and small-scale systems, which use many personal computers distributed among the users. Large-scale systems have a larger storage capacity, have more processing power, and can process higher volumes of data. Small-scale systems are more flexible, are easier to use, and provide programs that are more readily adaptable to solving the problems of computer users. Large-scale systems are typically operated and managed at a centralized location within the organization by computer specialists; small systems are operated and managed by end users and are located at various end-user sites spread throughout the organization. In many business organizations both large-scale and small-scale computer systems are utilized, each for those applications to which it is best suited.

The relationship between processing costs and the volume of data items processed can be used to compare manual and automated data processing systems. Consider the case of S&S. If transactions are processed manually, there are no significant equipment costs. The only major cost is human labor costs, and each transaction will cost about the same as any other. In other words, most data processing costs in a manual system are variable relative to volume. As processing volume increases, total processing costs increase proportionately, and the cost per item processed stays relatively constant.

Now suppose that S&S leases a large mainframe computer to process its transactions. The fixed costs of the equipment and the related facilities represent a significant portion of the cost of processing the transactions. However, the computer can handle many more transactions than a person can. Therefore, fewer people are needed to process the transactions. So as processing volume increases, total processing costs do *not* increase proportionately, and the cost per item processed actually declines.

Finally, consider a third scenario: a small computer to process S&S's transactions. The fixed costs of the equipment are not as high,

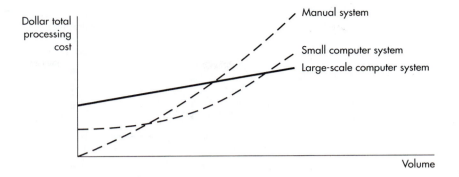

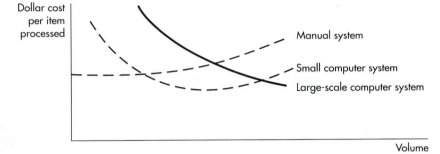

Figure 1.2
Relationship of processing costs to processing volume in manual and automated data processing systems

but S&S will need more people to handle the processing. In other words, the firm will incur a combination of fixed and variable costs that falls somewhere between the two extremes of a manual system and a large-scale computer system.

These relationships are illustrated in Fig. 1.2. The curves represent relative values rather than actual figures. These graphs help to explain why manual systems are suited to very low volume operations, small computer systems to low- to moderate-volume operations, and large-scale computer systems to high-volume operations. In a growing organization the increasing volume of data processing work represents one of the major pressures that have led all but the very smallest organizations to move from a manual to an automated system. The vertical lines connecting the two graphs represent break-even points between, first, manual and small computer systems and, second, small- and large-scale computer systems.

Components of an Information System

The process of turning data into information is often referred to as **data processing** or **information processing**. The data processing cycle has four stages: data input, data processing, data storage, and information output. These stages are shown in Fig. 1.3. The data processing cycle is covered in depth in Chapter 2.

Several components are characteristic of information systems for all businesses. These components and their relationships to each other are shown in Fig. 1.3 and are explained in this section.

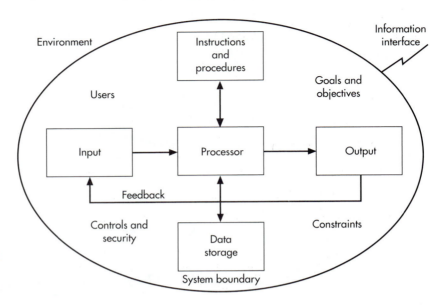

Figure 1.3
Components of an information system

Goals and Objectives.   Each information system is designed to accomplish one or more goals or objectives. These objectives reflect the driving force behind the system and the reasons the system exists. The principle objective of S&S's information system, for instance, will be to provide all the information that decision makers need to properly and profitably operate the business.

Inputs.   Data is gathered by the system or by users of the system. This data is entered as **input** into the system. For example, some of the data S&S will need to enter into the system it develops is data on prices, quality, and reliability of suppliers of the appliances it will be selling.

Outputs.   The information produced by the system is called the **output**. Output from the system is sometimes entered back into the system as input. This input is then referred to as **feedback**. One output of S&S's system will likely be some sort of vendor report that will help it decide which vendors have the best combination of price, quality, and reliability.

Stored Data.   Data that is input or processed by the system is often needed later by a system user or by the information system and becomes **stored data** maintained within the system. S&S, for example, will have to store data about each customer's accounts receivable balance and creditworthiness. Stored data must be updated frequently to keep it current. This update process is called **file maintenance** and is discussed in Chapter 2. Most stored data is maintained electronically by computer systems.

Processor.   The data entered into the system is either processed and sent to the users as information or stored for later use. Most business organizations of any size use computers as their data processors. As we will see in later chapters, S&S will acquire a computer-based information system.

Instructions and Procedures. An information system does not possess its own innate intelligence. It cannot process data and produce information without being told what to do. Hence, the system must store detailed **instructions and procedures.** Computer software is written to instruct computers how to process data. Instructions and procedures for humans are typically placed in procedures manuals. S&S will also need to acquire software to help it process its transactions.

Boundaries. Every system has physical limits. A **boundary** separates the elements of a system from its environment. An **environment** is everything that surrounds a system.

Constraints. Each system has internal or external limitations that constrain the system. For example, the **constraints** may restrict the size of the system, the number of users, or the methods that can be used to input, process, store, or output data or information. One constraint that S&S faces is limited resources.

Users. The people that interact with the system and use the information produced by the system are referred to as **users.** In a business organization these users include those who participate in the transactions and record the data, those who use or manage the system, and those who are involved with system controls and security. Those who use information from the system are often referred to as **end users.** Scott, Susan, their new employees, and their customers and suppliers will be the users of the system that is developed for S&S.

Security Measures. The information produced by a system must be accurate and free of errors. It must also be protected from unauthorized access. **Security measures** (also referred to as controls) are built into an information system to ensure accurate information. For example, one control that S&S could use to prevent unauthorized access to its computer-based system is a password that users must enter.

Information Interfaces. Information must pass between users, between machines and users, between an organization and other entities in its environment, between subsystems of the information system, and so forth. These shared boundaries, or points at which this information passes, are referred to as **information interfaces.** For example, in order for S&S to electronically deposit the paychecks of its employees into their bank accounts, the systems from each organization must have a means of exchanging information.

Subsystems. Information systems are almost always composed of smaller systems, called **subsystems.** Many systems are themselves part of a larger system. A college bookstore, for example, is a system. It is composed of different departments (texts, clothing, school supplies, etc.) that are subsystems. Yet the bookstore is often a subsystem of the university or of a company that controls other bookstores across the country. Each subsystem performs a specific function that is important to and supports the system of which it is a part. The important subsystems in an accounting information system are discussed briefly later in the chapter and more fully in Chapters 16–20.

TYPES OF INFORMATION SYSTEMS

This section briefly discusses several different types or classifications of information systems that have been developed to meet specific information needs of organizations. These classifications are not exact, inasmuch as the categories overlap somewhat. In addition, with technology changing so fast, these classification schemes are constantly evolving. These information systems are summarized in Table 1.1.

Table 1.1
Types of information systems

Type of System	Descripton of System
Management information system (MIS)	Collects and processes the data needed to produce the information managers need to plan, control, and manage an organization
Accounting information system (AIS)	Subsystem of MIS that handles transaction processing and other financial data Often the most widely used information system in a business Often referred to as the transaction processing system
Decision support system (DSS)	Develops models to help make decisions in unstructured environments where there is a high degree of uncertainty Includes what-if analysis which allows exploration of various alternatives Most frequently used on an ad hoc basis
Executive information system (EIS)	Provides executives with the information they need, at the needed level of detail and in an easy-to-understand and easy-to-use format Often makes use of graphics Used for strategic planning and for identifying problems and opportunities
Expert system (ES)	Puts the expertise and knowledge of experts in a specific area in the hands of users Used to solve problems and make decisions Produces consistent decisions and ensures that important decision criteria are considered
Office automation system (OAS)	Uses computer technology to improve productivity of office workers Helps with the creation, revision, storage, retrieval, and distribution of documents, messages, and other communications Draws upon a wide variety of software packages
End-user system (EUS)	Developed to meet specific operational and managerial information needs of users Usually is a microcomputer and user-oriented DSS and OAS software Used for information retrieval, application development, and personal productivity

Management Information Systems

The basic functions of management are planning and control. **Planning** includes such activities as setting objectives, establishing policies, choosing management personnel, deciding on capital expenditures, making decisions on products and their promotion, and developing operating budgets and plans for the future. **Control** involves implementing policies, evaluating the performance of subordinates, taking action to correct or improve performance, and taking action to adjust to changing environmental conditions.

The major purpose of a **management information system (MIS)** is to facilitate the management of an organization. It is responsible for collecting and processing the data needed to produce information for planning and controlling the activities of the organization. It encompasses all levels of administration in an organization, from top management (responsible for the overall success or failure of the organization) to operating management (responsible for the day-to-day operation of a single department). Depending on the size of the organization, there may be one to several layers of management between these two extremes.

Management information systems are an integral part of the four activities that are referred to as the **management cycle**. These four activities are shown in Fig. 1.4. First, managers develop operating plans at the beginning of a time period, such as a month or a year. They use information from the MIS and store the plan in the system; hence the two-way arrows in Fig. 1.4. Second, throughout the period they execute the plan. They also monitor the plan by capturing transaction data on the results of operations and feeding it into the MIS. The data entered into the system is processed and fed back to the managers of the system. Exception reports are often prepared to identify areas of the operation where corrective action is required. Third, managers take corrective action as needed to control the operation, and these

Figure 1.4
Relationship of a management information system to the management cycle.

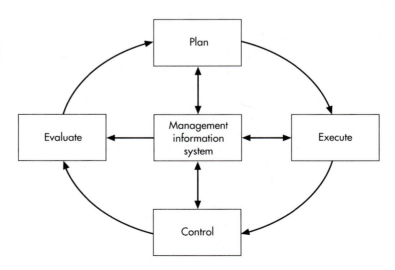

changes are fed back into the system. Fourth, at the end of the period the results are evaluated and compared with the plan set up at the beginning of the period. These evaluations are an essential part of the planning process for the next period.

Accounting Information Systems

An **accounting information system (AIS)** supports day-to-day operations by collecting and storing data about an organization's transactions. These systems help ensure that an organization's data is processed consistently. It is typically used by those who process the transactions and those who use information from the system to make decisions. The information produced by the AIS is made available to all levels of management for use in planning and controlling an organization's activities.

Accounting information systems possess all the characteristics of management information systems. The major difference between the two is one of scope. The management information system encompasses all data entering the organization. In contrast, the accounting information system is concerned with financial information and information generated from processing transaction data. As a result, accounting information systems are often referred to as transaction processing systems. An accounting information system is a subsystem of the management information system.

The accounting information system is often the most widely used and the largest of the information subsystems in a business organization. In some organizations the accounting information system is the only formally designated information system and is thus, in effect, the management information system. In organizations with a formal management information system accountants play a key role in system administration and operation. Thus an understanding of accounting information systems is essential to the study of management information systems, and vice versa.

Decision Support Systems

A **decision support system (DSS)** helps users make decisions in unstructured environments where there is a high degree of uncertainty. A DSS is a tool or model used to solve ad hoc processing requirements rather than to support an ongoing process. As a result, it is usually built by the user rather than by a professional programmer. It is most frequently used in interactive sessions to manipulate business-related data. It allows the user to explore various alternatives, to ask what-if questions, to deal with constantly changing business problems, and to make decisions in situations that arise unexpectedly. It is also used, where possible, to automate clerical chores, which allows the user to focus on real business problems.

Accounting and management information systems are best suited to well-structured problems where predefined reports are required. In contrast, a DSS is best suited to problems where there is uncertainty and ill-defined reporting requirements. Decision support systems are discussed in greater depth in Chapter 5.

Executive Information Systems

The purpose of an executive information system (EIS) (also called an executive support system) is to provide executives with immediate and easy access to information in a highly interactive format. An EIS is designed to provide executives with the information they need to make strategic plans, to control and operate the company, to monitor business conditions in general, and to identify business problems and opportunities.

An EIS is designed to accept data from many different sources; combine, integrate, and summarize the data; and display it in an easy-to-understand-and-use way. To avoid overloading executives with unnecessary details, an EIS presents data at the highest level of aggregation. However, when the details underlying the aggregated data are needed, they are easily accessible. Because an EIS must be very easy to use, it is often graphically oriented and makes use of pointing devices and touch screens.

An EIS can be better understood by comparing it with the other types of information systems. Management and accounting information systems generate standard reports at predefined intervals. They help monitor a predefined set of ongoing company operations over a period of time. In contrast, an EIS is designed to help executives sift through a multitude of information sources (including that produced by the MIS and the AIS) to find the information they need and to produce it at the level of detail needed and in the form that is most easy to understand and use. A DSS is a model of a business problem that allows users to make more informed decisions. In contrast, an EIS is an information consolidation and retrieval system that allows top management to spot problems and monitor an organization's progress.

Kraft, Inc., installed an EIS to help executives monitor over five hundred different products that it sells to over thirty-three thousand grocery stores. Every morning they are able to pull up on their computer screens a wide variety of data about the previous day's sales. They can use this data to spot problems, monitor the sales of individual items, make comparisons to previous periods, and examine a wide variety of other sales data. Prior to the implementation of the EIS, executives had to pour through thick stacks of paper reports that were not available until midafternoon. The EIS frees them from the data-gathering and summarization task and allows them to focus on business decisions and problems.

Expert Systems

An expert system (ES) is a computerized system that supports users that need expertise in a well-defined area. The system contains as much of the stored expertise of a set of experts as possible. The expertise and knowledge in the information system is made available to users, who use it as an "expert consultant" to help them solve problems and make decisions. Use of an expert system guides the decision process, produces more consistent decisions, and ensures that important decision criteria are considered. Expert systems are discussed in more detail in Chapter 5.

Office Automation Systems

An **office automation system (OAS)** is the use of computer and information technology to increase the productivity of information workers. OAS has also reduced the costs and the time involved in the creation, review, revision, storage, retrieval, and distribution of documents, messages, and other forms of communication among individuals, work groups, and organizations. Office automation systems use a variety of technologies, including word processing, spreadsheets, data bases, desktop publishing, electronic mail, facsimile transmission, voice mail and other telephone systems, electronic conferencing, desktop organizers, image processing, project management, and telecommunications. The technologies used in office automation are discussed in more detail in Chapters 5–7.

End-User Systems

An **end-user system (EUS)** is an information system developed by the users themselves to meet their own operational and managerial information needs. In contrast, many of the other types of information systems are developed by professionals in the information systems (IS) department. An EUS draws upon the transaction processing system and other information systems, the corporate data bases, and information maintained by the system itself to meet users' information needs. It usually consists of a microcomputer workstation and several software packages. Users often utilize decision support and office automation system tools to develop their end-user systems. There are many reasons why an EUS is developed, including information retrieval, personal productivity, and application development. End-user systems are discussed in more detail in Chapter 5.

THE ROLE OF THE ACCOUNTING INFORMATION SYSTEM

The modern business organization is a very complex institution. It may employ thousands of people in tasks ranging from the development and engineering of new products to the management of a large sales force. How can the modern business organization plan, coordinate, and control the multitude of activities that it undertakes? How can it supply information to the many people and institutions that are interested in its activities? The accounting information system plays a vital role in accomplishing these tasks. Figure 1.5 shows the relationship of the accounting information system to the business organization and to the environment in which the business organization is a part.

The accounting information system serves two categories of users— those external to the business organization and those internal to it (management). The subset of accounting that is concerned with the information needs of external users is known as **financial accounting**. Many of their needs for information are met by general-purpose financial

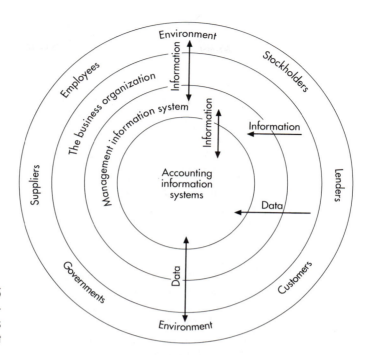

Figure 1.5
Relationship of the accounting information system to the business organization and its environment

statements, such as the income statement and the balance sheet. **Management accounting** is the subset of accounting concerned with internal information needs. The information needs of internal users reflect a common objective—to maximize the economic well-being of the business organization.

External Information Requirements

There are many external users that need information about business organizations. Six of the more important external user groups are indicated in Fig. 1.5. For each group one or more of the information needs that an accounting information system can satisfy are now explained. These information requirements are not intended to be all-inclusive; they are merely examples.

Customers. The customers of a business organization need routine information about what they have purchased or what is available for purchase. In addition, credit customers require periodic information concerning the status of their accounts, including the amount owed, the discount available, and the date payment is due.

Suppliers. Each time a business buys something, the supplier requires certain information. For example, the supplier needs to know the item desired and the quantities to be purchased. If the goods shipped are not acceptable to the buyer, information must be exchanged concerning adjustments in sale terms or the return of the goods.

Stockholders. A company's stockholders are vitally interested in all phases of its operations. They wish to evaluate past performance and predict future performance. Stockholders also need routine information concerning the execution of their stock transactions and the receipt of dividend payments.

Employees. Employees expect periodic receipt of wages and salaries, accompanied by detailed information concerning deductions such as income taxes, Social Security taxes, insurance premiums, and union dues. They are also interested in general financial information, such as average wage levels, fringe benefit costs, and profits.

Lenders. Financial institutions supply a business with capital. They are very interested in the business's ability to meet its financial obligations and its prospects for future success.

Governments. Many agencies of federal, state, and local governments require information about the business. The Internal Revenue Service (IRS) requires information concerning the company's profits, the taxes the company owes to the government, and the amount of employee taxes withheld. The Social Security Administration requires information on the amount of wages earned and Social Security taxes withheld. If the company is in a regulated industry, such as railroads or insurance, one or more federal or state agencies is likely to desire information about its operations.

Many other groups also desire information about a business entity. These include credit agencies such as Dun & Bradstreet, which publish information about a company's credit standing; industry and trade associations, which publish information about a particular industry; and financial analysts, who advise clients interested in making investments.

For the most part, the information supplied to external users is either mandatory or essential. An example of **mandatory information** is a report to the government on taxable income and tax withholdings. Another is financial statements, which must be issued to stockholders by all publicly traded corporations. Examples of **essential information** include product information, billings sent to customers, and credit capacity information sent to lenders.

Internal Information Requirements

In contrast to external information is internal or **discretionary information**. *Discretionary* means that choices must be made regarding this information: what should be made available, to whom, how frequently, and so forth. Most managerial decisions require more detailed information than is needed for external reporting. There are also many more ways to approach the reporting of the information to internal users than there are to external users. Because of the many requirements and the options available, the area of internal information presents a much greater challenge to those who design accounting information systems than does the area of external reporting. The primary consideration in satisfying mandatory and essential information requirements is to minimize costs while (1) meeting minimum standards of reliability and usefulness and (2) meeting regulatory requirements. With discretionary information the primary consideration is that the benefit obtained from the information exceed the cost of supplying it.

Accounting information plays two major roles in management decision making. First, it provides a stimulus for management decision making by indicating the existence of a situation requiring management action. For example, a cost report that indicates a large variance of actual costs over budgeted costs might stimulate management to take corrective action. Second, by reducing uncertainty regarding the merits of various alternatives, accounting information provides a basis for choosing among possible alternative actions. For example, accounting information is often used as a basis for setting prices or for choosing which capital assets to purchase.

As shown in Fig. 1.5, the accounting information system receives data not only from sources outside the business but also from internal sources. For example, product cost information in a manufacturing firm is generated in part from data on materials usage and labor usage that are collected within the factory. The accounting information system prepares information for management by performing certain operations on all the data it receives. The management of the business organization then utilizes this information when making decisions. Management decisions in turn affect the internal operation of the business organization, including the accounting information system, and the relationship of the business organization to its environment.

All levels of management in a business organization—including marketing, purchasing and inventory control, production, personnel, and finance—require information. Just a few of the informational requirements of these internal users are presented as illustrative of the information that management needs the accounting information system to produce.

Marketing Management.   Marketing is responsible for selling the products the company produces. To do so, it needs the information necessary to make the following types of decisions: How much should the company charge for each item it sells? What should the company's discount, credit terms, and warranty policies be? How much should the company spend on advertising and promotion campaigns and on research studies?

Purchasing and Inventory Control Management.   Managers in these functional areas must have the information necessary to make the following kinds of decisions: How much inventory or raw materials should the company purchase? How should the company decide how much to purchase? When should they purchase it? Which vendors should the company use? What combination of price, reliability, product styling, brand, and quality should be purchased?

Production Management.   Production managers need information to decide what products to produce, as well as what style, color, and size to produce. They must also decide when to produce it and how much of each item to produce. In addition, they need to decide what production method to use and what materials are necessary to produce each product.

Personnel Management.   Personnel managers need information on how much to pay each employee and what to deduct from each employee's paycheck. They also need information on the skill and experience of each employee, trends in hours worked, efficiency, turnover, and absenteeism.

Financial Management.   Financial managers are responsible for ensuring that a steady flow of capital is available to the company. Thus they need information on cash inflows and outflows and on sources of capital funds. They also need to plan for capital expenditures and adequate insurance coverage and to establish credit and collection procedures.

BUSINESS AND ACCOUNTING CYCLES

The five functional areas just mentioned are the main interrelated business cycles of a typical business organization. Figure 1.6 illustrates the relationship between these business cycles. Each of the business cycles has one or more accounting cycles. For example, the accounting cycles in the financial management business cycle include the cash receipts, cash disbursements, capital expenditures, and financial reporting cycles. The business and accounting activities in each cycle are very much interdependent in terms of both operations and information. A brief overview of each business cycle is presented here to introduce the concepts of the cycles and their functions. Each of the business cycles and their related accounting cycles are discussed in much greater detail in Chapters 16–20.

The revenue cycle, discussed in Chapter 16, encompasses the business activities and related data processing operations that provide products and services to customers in exchange for revenue. These business activities include soliciting customer orders, executing sales transactions, and delivering products and services in exchange for revenue. The expenditure cycle, covered in Chapters 17 and 19, consists of two related cycles. The procurement cycle involves the purchase of materials and services. The personnel/payroll cycle involves the payment of employees for their services. The production cycle, discussed in Chapter 18, is concerned with the manufacture of products. The finance cycle, discussed in Chapter 20, deals with the management of the organization's financial resources and includes such activities as cash collections and disbursements, capital investment, and financial statement preparation. Some of the information needs of

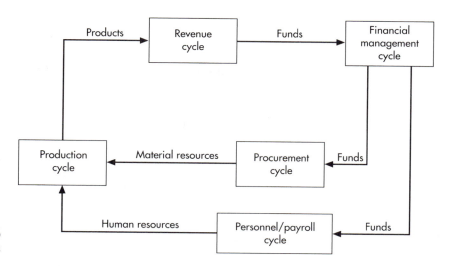

Figure 1.6
Relationships among business cycles

each of these applications were discussed previously in the section on internal information needs.

Each of these applications performs a vital function in the organization. But an application that meets the needs of an organization does not just happen. It is a very time-consuming and difficult task to design information systems that meet the needs of a particular group of users. The next section provides us with a brief overview of the relationship between information systems and business organizational structures.

INFORMATION SYSTEMS AND BUSINESS ORGANIZATION

The distribution of authority and responsibility within a business entity is indicated by its organizational structure. An understanding of the patterns of authority and distribution of responsibility is essential for the assessment of information needs within an organization. In turn, information needs define the required structure of data collection and processing activities within the accounting information system. Therefore the structure of data collection, processing, and reporting activities within an accounting information system must closely parallel the organizational structure of the entity it serves. An understanding of the concept of organization thus provides a foundation for the study of accounting information systems.

Most business organizations define their primary goal as the maximization of long-run profits. Two forms of organization are commonly used to divide this overall goal into subgoals. The first is the functional organizational structure, under which employees with the same or similar occupational specialties, such as marketing, production, and accounting, are grouped together within organizational subunits of the business. The second is the divisional organization structure, under which the organization is partitioned into several divisions, each of which is relatively independent of the others and operates almost as a separate, smaller company.

In a manufacturing business organized along functional lines the overall goal of profit maximization might be divided into subgoals through the use of the following organizational subunits: marketing, with the goal of maximizing sales revenue; production, with the goal of minimizing the production cost per unit; finance, with the goal of providing the resources required for operation of the business at minimum expense; and accounting, with the goal of measuring the success of the organization in achieving its goals. These goals may be broken down further into additional sets of subgoals assigned to lower-level units.

A familiar means of illustrating patterns of authority delegation is the organization chart. Figure 1.7 shows a partial organization chart for a typical single-plant manufacturing company organized along functional lines. Each box represents an organizational unit supervised by a manager. Each line connecting a manager to a lower-level manager represents the delegation of authority to a subordinate and the corresponding responsibility of the subordinate to report to the superior. A manager is responsible for all the activities that appear under the manager's control on the chart—that is, for the performance of all managers to whom a portion of that manager's authority has been delegated. The hierarchical structure of the organization is clearly apparent.

Although the chart omits reference to the information systems function, in many modern organizations this function has achieved status as a major department on the same level as production, marketing, and accounting. The information systems function is discussed in greater detail in subsequent chapters.

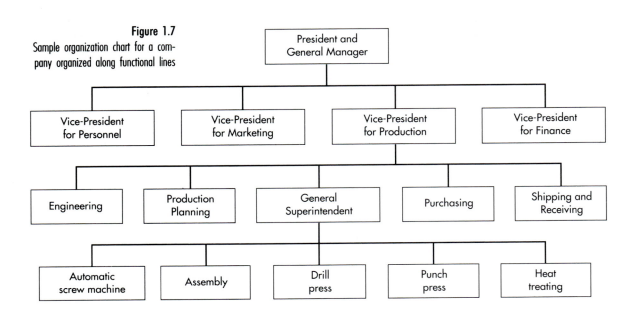

Figure 1.7
Sample organization chart for a company organized along functional lines

The functional organizational structure provides the advantages of greater functional effectiveness due to specialization, centralized control, and economies of scale. However, as a business organization grows by adding new product lines or new plants, or even by diversifying into other lines of business, the pure functional organizational structure may prove ineffective in coordinating and motivating employees to achieve the overall goal.

Under the divisional organization structure each division has virtually the same primary goal—that is, maximization of long-run profits —as the organization as a whole. An example of a business organization using a divisional structure appears in Fig. 1.8. Notice that even though the divisional structure is used at the higher levels of the organization, the functional structure is still used at the lower levels. Some vestiges of the functional structure may also appear at the top of the organization in the office of the Executive Vice-President for Administrative Services, which coordinates such functions as personnel, accounting, finance, and systems.

Figure 1.8
Sample organization chart for a company organized along divisional lines

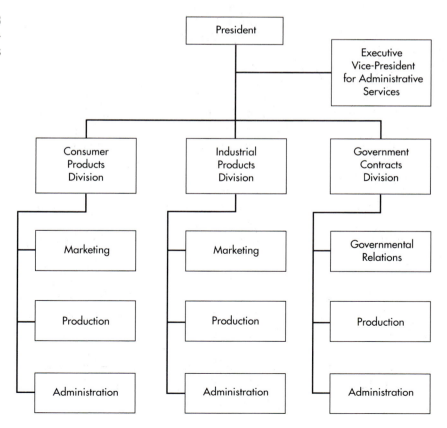

If an organization can divide its overall goal into subgoals in such a way that all employees working to achieve their assigned subgoals are also contributing to the optimal achievement of the overall goal, **goal congruence** is said to exist. The larger the organization becomes, the more difficult it is to achieve goal congruence and the more likely it is that **goal conflict** will arise, in which a decision or action consistent with one subgoal is at variance with a decision or action dictated by another subgoal. This is true regardless of the form of organization chosen. For example, in a business organized along functional lines the marketing subgoal of maximizing sales revenue may suggest offering a highly diverse product line, whereas the production subgoal of minimizing per-unit production costs suggests offering a limited product line. Goal conflict can occur in divisionalized companies when a raw material or component produced by one division is used as input by another division. The producing division will maximize its profits by selling to the consuming division at a specified price, whereas the consuming division may be able to maximize its profits by buying the input from another source at a lower price.

An organization's choice of organizational structure has significant implications for accounting information systems that provide the financial information each organizational unit needs to plan and control its operations. The information required by any particular organizational unit is a function of its assigned subgoal. Planning information must assist the unit manager in making decisions and taking actions to achieve subgoals. Making such decisions is difficult when a manager supervises several departments with conflicting goals. Control information must include measures of financial performance relative to goals. To provide planning and control information, system designers must understand the structure of the organization, the way the overall goal has been divided into subgoals, the decisions and actions necessary to achieve the various subgoals, and the information needed to make those decisions and take those actions.

The degree of centralization of decision-making authority within an organization is another relevant organizational issue. In a highly centralized organization authority is concentrated at the higher management levels, with lower levels having a minimum of decision-making power. In a highly decentralized organization a significant amount of decision-making authority may be delegated to lower levels. The concept is relative, and most organizations fall well within the two extremes. Even within the same organization authority may be highly centralized in one functional area, such as production, and highly decentralized in other functional areas.

There is no general method of organization that is superior for all types of businesses. If decision making is highly centralized, an organization will, theoretically, be better able to coordinate and control its activities in order to achieve optimal results with respect to its overall goal. However, decentralization of decision-making authority to the divisional level generally causes divisional managers to be more highly motivated to achieve maximum levels of performance. Furthermore, information failures may occur in the reporting of information from the divisions to a central location, and these failures can cause centralized decision makers to receive poor information and make poor decisions. Whichever of these strategies is adopted by a business organization, the accounting information system must be designed to provide the necessary planning and control information to the appropriate managers on a timely basis. It must also be designed to match the unique needs and characteristics of the business organization of which it is a part.

WHY STUDY ACCOUNTING INFORMATION SYSTEMS?

There are several reasons why a student's knowledge of accounting is not complete without an understanding of accounting information systems. In most other accounting courses the student is placed in the role of an information producer or user (making journal entries, preparing or reading financial statements or other reports, etc.). Certain information is assumed to be available to the student, and the student addresses such questions as how to account for the information, how to report the information, or how to audit the information.

These questions are certainly relevant, but there is another very relevant question: Where did the information come from? The answer is, of course, that it is produced by an information system. This answer raises a number of other questions:

- Who decides what information is relevant for a particular purpose?
- How is that decision made?
- Who is going to use the information, and who is going to develop it?
- What steps are required in order to obtain the relevant information and make it available to the users?
- What resources (people, machines, money, etc.) are consumed in obtaining the information and making it available?
- What is the most cost-effective way of coordinating the necessary resources to perform the required steps?
- Is the value of the information worth the cost of producing it?
- How can the organization ensure that the information is available on a timely basis?
- How can the organization ensure that the information is accurate and reliable?

These are the kinds of questions that are addressed by a course in accounting information systems. Virtually all organizations must find answers to these questions—and in most organizations the accountant plays a central role in finding them.

The accounting student of today may tomorrow become an auditor, accountant, manager, business owner, or management consultant. Each of these positions requires a close involvement with the information system. One of the auditor's main objectives is to evaluate the accuracy of information, and one of the approaches most commonly used by auditors is to assess the reliability of the information system. The accountant—whether in auditing, industry, government, or a non-profit organization—is likely to play a major role in evaluating and improving existing information systems and designing new ones. Accountants at the managerial level are often directly responsible for managing the information systems department. Finally, many accountants become management consultants because of the opportunity to employ their expertise more effectively in the design, evaluation, and management of information systems.

The ongoing revolution in information technology has had a profound effect on information systems. The driving force behind this revolution is, of course, the computer. In virtually all organizations the computer is responsible for processing accounting transactions and preparing accounting reports. As computers become smaller, faster, easier to use, and less expensive, the computerization of accounting work will continue. This development makes it even more essential for accounting students to understand accounting information systems.

Therefore a course in accounting information systems that emphasizes the role of the computer is an essential element in a student's preparation for a career in accounting. Most undergraduate accounting and business curricula have incorporated computer education for many years. Although general course work dealing with computers and electronic data processing is important and useful, accounting students also need to know how modern information technology relates to accounting. This book is written to provide a solid foundation of knowledge for future accounting graduates who will participate in the evaluation, design, use, audit, control, and management of accounting information systems.

A final reason to study information systems is to understand how they can add value to business organizations.

HOW INFORMATION SYSTEMS ADD VALUE TO BUSINESSES

In recent years a great deal has been written about the importance of creating value and the way in which information systems provide value to organizations. Two of the first people to espouse this idea were Michael Porter and Victor Millar. According to Porter and Millar, the ultimate goal of any business is to provide value to its customers. The value a business creates is measured by the price buyers pay for its products or services. The business will be profitable if the value it creates is greater than the costs of its products or services. In like manner, the main purpose of information technology is to add value to a business. It can do this by producing information that gives the company a competitive advantage.

The authors state that a company's activities can be divided into technologically and economically distinct activities. These value activities can be linked together in what they call a value chain, which is shown in

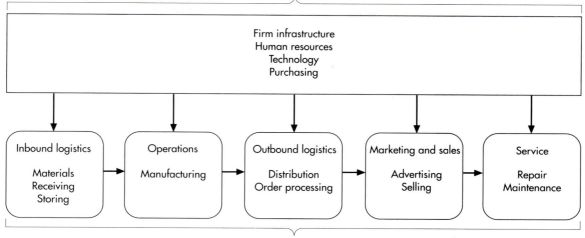

Figure 1.9
Value chain
(*Source:* Michael E. Porter and Victor
E. Millar, "How Information Gives
You Competitive Advantage," *Harvard
Business Review* 63 (4) (July/August
1985): 151.)

Fig. 1.9. As shown in the figure, a company has nine interconnected value activities, and they fall into two main categories: primary activities and support activities. A company's **primary activities** are those in which they create a product, market it, deliver it to buyers, and then service and support it. **Support activities** allow the primary activities to take place and include the firm's infrastructure, human resource management, technology development, and purchasing.

The five primary activities are described as follows:

- **Inbound activities** consist of receiving, storing, and distributing materials and other items that serve as inputs to the products or services of the organization. For example, an inbound activity is the receipt and handling of the steel, rubber, and glass that an automobile manufacturing plant needs to produce a car.

- **Operation activities** transform the inputs into final products or services. For example, the assembly line in an automobile manufacturing plant converts parts into a finished car.

- **Outbound activities** facilitate the distribution of finished products or services to buyers. For example, shipping an automobile to a dealer is an outbound activity.

- **Marketing and sales activities** facilitate the purchase of products or services by buyers. For example, the ads and promotions seen on TV for new cars are marketing and sales activities.

- **Service activities** provide all the repair and maintenance activities needed to continue producing products or services. For example, the people who repair machines on the automobile assembly line are performing a service activity.

The four support activities are described as follows:

- **Firm infrastructure** refers to the firm's organizational support activities and functions that support the entire chain. They include information systems, accounting, finance, the legal department, and general management.
- **Human resources** refers to activities such as recruiting, hiring, training, and providing employee compensation and benefits.
- **Purchasing** refers to the procurement of the resources needed for the primary activities. This activity includes the purchasing of materials, supplies, machinery, and buildings.
- **Technology** refers to the broad range of activities created to improve a product or service. Technology includes things such as research and development, implementing new computer technology, and product design.

As products or services are created, value is added throughout the chain. In other words, each activity adds value to the product or service and thus adds a margin of value (profit) to the company. For example, value is added as raw materials are turned into a final product. For a business to be competitive, it must be able to perform its value activities at a lower cost or a higher quality than its competitors.

Accountants, analysts, and managers should use the value chain to determine where and how information systems can add value to an organization. To do so, they should identify the activities in the chain and the linkages between the activities, determine the cost and the value of each activity and its linkages, and analyze where and how the information system could be used to add value. Identifying the activities and linkages helps users understand the business and the relationships between the activities. Once the cost and the value of each activity and linkage have been determined, users can get a clear picture of how an information system can add value to the organization.

Information systems can provide value in many ways. Here are three of the more common ones.

1. *An information system can improve products or services.* Products and services can be improved by increasing quality, reducing costs, or adding features the customer wants. For example, an information system can add value by monitoring the machinery that produces a product and notifying an operator when defects start to occur so that the machines can be recalibrated.

2. *An information system can increase efficiency.* There are any number of ways that an information system can increase efficiency in an organization. To illustrate, suppose that a company is experiencing delays on an assembly line because the manufacturing department is running out of raw materials, even though there are sufficient raw materials available in the warehouse. An information system could add value by keeping track of raw materials on hand in the manufac-

Figure 1.10
Value System
(*Source:* Michael E. Porter and Victor E. Millar, "How Information Gives You Competitive Advantage," *Harvard Business Review* 63 (4) (July/August 1985): 151.)

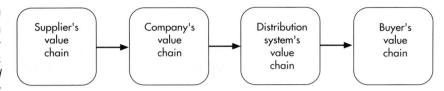

turing area and automatically sending an order to the warehouse when raw materials are needed.

3. *An information system can improve the management process.* The role of managers in a business is to plan, control, and evaluate an organization's activities. In doing so, they must provide the company with a vision of what it is and where it is going. They must also provide a balance between the needs of an organization and its constraints. Problem solving and decision making are two of the most important things managers do. An information system can add value by providing managers with the timely and reliable information they need to reduce the risks of decision making and to improve the decisions that are made.

Focus 1.2 describes some of the ways in which Wal-Mart uses information technology to add value to their company.

An organization's value chain is a part of a larger series of activities known as the **value system**. The value system, as shown in Fig. 1.10, is composed of the value chains of a company, its suppliers, its distributors, and its customers (i.e., the buyers of the company's products). By paying attention to the intercompany linkages in the value system, a company can add value not only to itself but also to its suppliers, distributors, and buyers. For example, a just-in-time inventory system that links S&S with its suppliers can reduce S&S's handling and storage costs. The suppliers of S&S benefit by having increased information about S&S sales and orders, which helps them plan production and reduce inventories.

CASE CONCLUSION: AN EXAMPLE OF AN ACCOUNTING INFORMATION SYSTEM AT S&S, INC.

At the beginning of the chapter S&S, Inc., a company that Scott Parry and Susan Anderson had recently organized, was profiled. Scott and Susan had three questions and the reader was asked to make suggestions. The chapter shows that an accounting information system could answer these questions. The chapter also showed that there are many other questions that S&S will need to answer and that a system could answer. One of several approaches to an accounting information system is presented here to reinforce many of the points made in the chapter. The AIS presented is not intended to be comprehensive; it is merely representative of ways the company can process some of its accounting information.

1.2 FOCUS

The Use of Information Technology at Wal-Mart

Wal-Mart Stores is one of the most successful and fastest-growing retail stores in history. In part, this success is due to the many ways Wal-Mart uses information systems to add value in distribution, inventory control, communications, purchasing, and management.

Between 1985 and 1987 Wal-Mart installed the nation's largest satellite communication network. This network, which is the heart of its information system, allows two-way voice and data communication and one-way video communication between headquarters, distribution centers, suppliers, and stores. The overall costs of this communication network are less than the previous telephone network. This network is used in a variety of ways. First, the video system allows management to speak with all employees at once or to hold meetings with the managers from each store. Second, data is transferred between stores, headquarters, distribution, and suppliers. Third, Wal-Mart is linked to about seventeen hundred vendors who supply about 80% of the goods that Wal-Mart sells. Electronic purchase orders and instant data exchange are used to simplify the ordering process. Fourth, credit card authorizations, which take only five seconds, are handled through the network. Fifth, management is provided with detailed figures on nearly every aspect of Wal-Mart's operations.

Wal-Mart has a history of using information systems to add value. In 1974 the company started using computers to control inventory on an item-by-item basis in distribution centers and stores. Then in 1983 it began using point-of-sale (POS) scanners, which reduced the time customers waited at the checkout by 25% to 30%. When a product is sold, a POS terminal records the sale and reduces the inventory level. Because the system is integrated throughout the Wal-Mart network, management knows at any time the specific inventory level of any product in any of its stores.

Recently, Wal-Mart established a just-in-time ordering and delivery system with one of its major suppliers, Procter & Gamble (P&G). When the stock of a P&G product reaches a re-

---

The most significant accounting transactions S&S will engage in are in the areas of (1) sales, including cash sales, credit card sales, installment sales, sales of trade-ins, and sales of parts and service; (2) purchases of inventory; (3) payroll; (4) expenses, including utilities, advertising, supplies, insurance, and taxes; (5) cash receipts on account; and (6) cash disbursements. S&S needs to determine how to input, process, store, and output the information regarding these transactions. Most small retail businesses use a computer-based system designed especially for the retailing industry.

In modern retail systems sales information is usually collected and input at the point of sale and entered into the system through a cash register that is tied into the system's computer. The data that must be collected includes customer information, terms of sale, items and quantities sold, prices and total charges, and delivery, if any. Where

order point, a computer automatically sends an electronic purchase order by satellite to the nearest P&G factory. P&G's information system checks its inventory, notifies its distribution system of the order, and then automatically ships more product directly to the store. The purchase and payment of products is all done electronically. This system saves days or even weeks over the time it would normally take to order and receive a product. The information system is a win-win situation because both Wal-Mart and P&G end up with lower costs.

For products that are not shipped directly to the stores, Wal-Mart uses a centralized distribution system. Boxes of merchandise are placed on a conveyor system. Boxes move on the conveyor belt to a central merge, where an operator releases cartons onto a sorting system. A laser scanner then reads a bar code on the box and tells the automatic sorter where

the boxes should go. The boxes are then diverted to the appropriate shipping doors. Because an information system controls the distribution system, more products can be shipped and distribution costs are lower.

Wal-Mart's distribution system provides a significant cost advantage over that of Sears or Kmart, as shown by the following data.

	1988 Sales (in millions)	Distribution Costs (in millions)	Distribution Costs (as percent of sales)
Wal-Mart	$20,649	$ 263	1.3
Kmart	27,301	956	3.5
Sears	50,251	2513	5.0

Wal-Mart also uses its information system to control the climate in every store. The lighting, heating, and air-conditioning controls in all Wal-Mart stores are connected via computer to Wal-Mart's headquarters. This reduces costs by centrally managing the use of energy and freeing store management and

personnel from having to control the utility costs.

Wal-Mart's use of modern technology and information systems have given it both a technological and a competitive advantage over most other discounters. Through the use of information systems technology, Wal-Mart has increased productivity, increased profitability, helped fuel its explosive growth, and driven costs down.

Source: Arthur A. Thompson, Jr., and A. J. Strickland III, *Strategic Management— Concepts and Cases*, 6th ed. (Boston: Irwin Publishing, 1992), 955–987.

appropriate, multiple copies of a sales invoice are prepared, including one for the customer and one for delivery. For the service work order, which is also prepared in multiple copies, data must be collected relating to the customer, product, work performed, parts sold, and amount collected.

S&S will need to maintain inventory and accounts receivable records. The inventory data base should contain data on the cost, list price, quantity on hand, quantity on order, and pattern of past sales of each inventory item. It must be updated when sales are made and when orders are placed or items are delivered. The accounts receivable data base should contain data on each credit customer, including the amount due, credit terms, and customer addresses. New installment sales and customer payments are posted to these records. Other significant accounting files should include an accounts payable file, a payroll file, and the general ledger, which has as records the balance sheet and income statement accounts.

Scott and Susan will need to receive information from the system in order to make management decisions. One of the most important decisions involves inventory. They will need to be able to determine what is on hand at any point in time, what should be purchased and when, what each appliance should sell for, what trade-in allowances should be provided, the relative profitability of each product line, and so forth. System output should be designed so that this information is provided to Scott and Susan on a regular basis, perhaps in the form of a daily or weekly report, or upon demand. They should also be able to go into the system and access the stored data to answer specific questions not answered in their periodic reports. They will also want to have information on things such as advertising and promotion, credit and collection of receivables, and the performance of their employees. Reports can also be designed to provide them with this information.

A significant part of any accounting system is the set of control procedures followed in processing accounting data. At the end of each day the amount of cash in the registers should be compared with totals taken from the cash registers and the sales documents. A similar comparison is made of service work orders and cash received for parts and services. Service workers and delivery people should have the customer sign one copy of a work order to acknowledge receipt of goods or services. To ensure control over company assets, either Scott or Susan should open all mail, total all checks received, sign all outgoing checks, and prepare a monthly bank reconciliation. A periodic review of accounts receivable records should be made in order to identify customers who are behind in their payments. These customers should be sent letters encouraging them to keep their accounts current. Inventory stocks should be reviewed periodically to determine what items should be ordered. At the end of each month various accounting tasks should be done: adjusting entries, a trial balance, and, finally, a balance sheet and an income statement for the month.

Later chapters will examine many other examples of accounting information systems. All such systems, however, contain the same basic set of components: people, equipment, transactions, input, stored data, output, documents, and procedures. ■

THE FUTURE OF ACCOUNTING INFORMATION SYSTEMS

Change is inevitable in society, and in today's society the rate of change seems to be accelerating. Change will bring new problems and new challenges to designers of accounting information systems. It will bring new technology and new ways of doing things. What might some of these changes be? We can speculate about what change may occur for Scott and Susan as S&S develops over the next five years.

Imagine that Susan and Scott saw all of the wholesale clubs sprouting up and decided to open a huge warehouse appliance store that sold very high volume and low-markup appliances. The store was an instant success, and they rapidly expanded nationwide.

S&S now has regional warehouses that supply their wholesale appliance clubs. Each evening inventory is taken in each warehouse by a robot that uses lasers to scan the universal product code on all merchandise. It then inputs this into the warehouse's computer. The computer reconciles the prior day's inventory figures, the current day's shipments and receipts, and the new inventory count. Any discrepancies are sent to the inventory manager's computer for him to investigate the next day. The company also uses a version of just-in-time inventory. The computer analyzes inventory on hand, average daily use, historical and seasonal trends, economic order quantities, and delivery times. Then it automatically orders the goods needed from approved vendors and schedules the arrival of the goods. A summary of all orders is sent to the inventory manager's computer for him to review the next morning. It also reviews all store orders received and schedules delivery of the appliances to the stores. Where appropriate, it arranges for goods to be sent directly from the suppliers to the individual stores. A similar system operates in the stores and is linked to the warehouse computer. All of these tasks are done electronically; there are no paper documents.

S&S encourages its customers to pay electronically using debit cards. This strategy provides instant access to a customer's cash but eliminates the problems of handling large amounts of currency. The company also pays all of its bill electronically. When merchandise is delivered, funds are electronically transferred from S&S's accounts to the suppliers' accounts. Employees are also paid by electronically transferring funds to their accounts. Most of the other bills are paid the same way. For instance, the utility company sends an electronic notice showing energy consumption. It is checked for reasonableness by the computer; and if the bill is within acceptable parameters, the funds are transferred the same day to the utility company. Once again, there is no paper work in the system. Everything is handled electronically.

One of S&S's competitive advantages is that it subscribes to a personalized information service. This service has developed software that learns a company's or a person's need for information. The service remembers what each subscriber likes and doesn't like to read and the preferred format for receiving it. It combs all known information sources looking for information that will appeal to or is needed by each individual subscriber. The service then produces a personalized, electronic newspaper for each subscriber. By providing the service with feedback, the system is, over time, able to hone in on each individual subscriber's needs and wants. S&S has used this service to keep it up to date on all developments affecting its business and industry. S&S is connected to the service 24 hours a day, and one of the first things Scott and Susan do every day is to read their personal newspaper. Articles they want to store are filed by the service, and items they want to act on are transferred to the personal productivity software (a combination spreadsheet, decision support system, presentation graphics package, and word processing all rolled into one).

Susan was recently elected vice-president of the Appliance Vendors Association. On a Monday night of a recent extended business trip, she used her laptop computer to access the electronic mail system at S&S. There she found a message from the president of the association telling her that a member of Congress was proposing import quota restrictions on several countries that were key suppliers of appliances. He asked her to prepare a special report for a key meeting he had with the congressman on Friday. Rather than cancel her trip, she used her computer to access her files at S&S and download the information she needed onto her computer. She found that she was missing data on the number of imports from several of the countries and on the pricing differences between their products and comparable U.S. products. She accessed a public data base, found what she wanted, and downloaded it onto her computer.

Over the next several nights, she used her personal productivity software to prepare her report. At one point she found it necessary to access the expert system developed for use by members of the association. From her hotel room she had her computer call the association, identify herself as an authorized user, and access the system. She used the expert system to help her make a critical decision regarding the purchase of a particular appliance. She needed to determine where several lines of appliances could be purchased most cheaply when cost, freight, import duties, and several similar factors were involved. She included the decision and the logic used by the expert system in her report.

When her report was finished, she used a special audiovisual room at the hotel to film a videotape presentation she wanted to make to the congressman. Susan then electronically sent a copy of her report and presentation to the computer at her office and directed that the report be printed and placed on her desk and that the presentation be stored on videotape. Then she sent a message out over the local area network at S&S scheduling a meeting with her buyers for the day after her return. Finally, she sent a copy of the report and the visual presentation to the association president's computer so that he could view the video and print the report out on his system the next day. She also left him a note in his electronic mail telling him where she could be reached for the remainder of the trip.

Two days later when she checked into a new hotel, the clerk told her that she had electronic mail waiting for her and that he would transfer it to the computer in her room. She found a copy of her report with requests for some minor changes. She made the corrections on the hotel's computer, sent a copy to the president and to her office computer, and stored a copy on her laptop computer.

Does all this sound farfetched? It shouldn't. Most of the technology required for such a scenario is already in place. It is just a matter of designing new information systems to take advantage of the technology. Remember that the personal computer is just a little more than 12 years old. Think of all the progress that has been made since then. And think about what could happen in the next 12 years. If technology advances as fast in the next 12 years as it has in the last 12, what will accounting information systems look like?

It is not at all unlikely that you will have on your desktop or carry in your briefcase or hand a computer that is more powerful than the current supercomputers. There are even companies that are designing computers that you can wear like clothing. These wearable computers will be made of soft plastic and strapped on with Velcro. The hardware of the future may include in one machine all the functions of our current personal computers (PCs), telephones, fax machines, printers, copiers, and VCRs. They may even include the capabilities of cameras and satellite transmitters. Some have even gone so far as to predict that we will have computers more powerful than today's workstations that are the size of a cuff link.

These computers will be controlled by an integrated software package that combines all of the functions now performed by a spreadsheet, word processor, graphics package, data base, expert system, and much more. We will be able to interact with the system by dictating to it, writing on it, or typing in ideas. It is likely that we will be able to verbally ask our computer a question and it will be able to automatically figure out what it is we need and search our own data bases and a global network of electronic libraries to find the information to meet our needs. Our computers will be linked with computers from all over the world, and they will constantly communicate with each other. As time passes, these computers will probably become as common and as essential to us as a telephone is today.

A PREVIEW OF THE BOOK'S CONTENTS

Part 1 contains a discussion of the conceptual foundations of accounting information systems. Chapter 2 discusses the data processing activities used by all systems to keep their information current. Chapter 3 discusses the techniques that are used in systems development and documentation. The concepts explained in Part 1 apply to all kinds of accounting systems, from the simplest systems used by small businesses to the most advanced computer-based systems employed by multinational corporations.

Part 2 discusses the computer technology available to designers of accounting information systems. Part 3 describes the accounting information systems' development life cycle. Part 4 focuses on internal control, computer fraud, and the audit of accounting information systems. Part 5 explains the application of information systems concepts and techniques to specific business cycles, including the revenue cycle, the procurement cycle, the production cycle, the payroll cycle, and the finance cycle.

SUMMARY

An information system takes data or facts and processes them to produce information for decision makers. Information is not produced unless users believe that the benefit they receive will exceed the cost of producing the information. Most information systems are computer-based because of the speed and reliability of computers.

The accounting information system in an organization is a subset of the management information system. A management information system is responsible for producing the information management needs to plan and control an organization. An accounting information system deals with financial information and information obtained from the collection and processing of transaction data.

Accounting information systems in business organizations provide information useful to internal as well as external users. Internal users are many and varied, but most are involved with the management of marketing, purchasing and inventory control, production, personnel, and finance. These are referred to as the major systems applications, subsystems, or cycles. External users include customers, suppliers, stockholders, employees, lenders, and government agencies.

Because of the central role of information systems in modern business organizations, the study of information systems is an important part of a student's preparation for a career in accounting or business.

The purpose of this book is to develop an understanding of accounting information systems—the elements they contain, the ways in which they are designed, and the role they play in supplying information to those requiring it, both within the business organization and outside it.

KEY TERMS

Define the following terms.

information	output	control
data	feedback	management information
value of information	stored data	system (MIS)
system	file maintenance	management cycle
computer-based system	instructions	accounting information system
systems concept	procedures	(AIS)
integration	boundary	decision support system (DSS)
information system	environment	executive information system
formal information system	constraints	(EIS)
informal information system	users	executive support system
manual information systems	end users	expert system (ES)
automated system	security measures	office automation system (OAS)
data processing	information interfaces	end-user system (EUS)
information processing	subsystems	financial accounting
input	planning	management accounting

mandatory information	goal congruence	marketing and sales
essential information	goal conflict	service activities
discretionary information	value activities	firm infrastructure
business cycles	value chain	human resources
accounting cycles	primary activities	purchasing
functional organizational	support activities	technology
structure	inbound activities	value system
divisional organization	operation activities	
structure	outbound activities	

Discussion Questions

1.1 Should an accounting information system be structured to meet the needs of external or internal users? To what extent are the needs of these two categories of users similar, and to what extent are they different?

1.2 How do the information systems of nonprofit organizations or governments differ from those of business organizations? In what ways are they similar?

1.3 Would you ever produce information if you did not think its benefit would outweigh its costs? If so, give several examples of when you would and why you would produce this information.

1.4 Most information systems seem to have the same basic components, yet each system is different. For example, the system used by American Airlines is different from that used by a developer of software such as Microsoft. Compare and contrast these two systems.

1.5 An information system that S&S might use in five years from now was described in the chapter. What elements of that system are technologically possible now? What parts do you personally think will not be possible in five years? What else do you believe the system could do that is not mentioned?

1.6 Accountants have significant involvement with accounting information systems, both as users and as designers. Accounting graduates become auditors, management accountants, management consultants, business managers, and business owners. Compare and contrast these professions in terms of their use of and their involvement in the design of an AIS.

1.7 A well-designed computer-based accounting information system must be able to ensure that the data and information are accurate. How can you ensure that the data input into an AIS is accurate? How can you ensure that the data entered into the system is processed properly? How can you ensure that the output is accurate?

1.8 You are the new controller at the Management Training Center (MTC). MTC specializes in executive training courses that run from three to eight weeks. You are struggling to learn your job and are looking for information to help you. You find that you can get information from MTC's computer in three ways: a microcomputer that sits on your desk, a daily printout of the prior day's activities, and a monthly report. Compare and contrast each report based on the six characteristics of information discussed in the chapter.

1.9 The chapter discussed 12 components of an information system. Give an example of each of the information system components for the following companies.

a. An automobile dealership
b. A small manufacturer of plastics
c. A developer of software products for microcomputers
d. A multilevel marketing company like Avon or Amway
e. A CPA firm
f. A hotel chain
g. A retail jewelry store
h. An insurance broker
i. A major league sports franchise

1.10 Why must users participate in the design of a new system's output? How can they ensure that they are involved? When should they become involved? What should their involvement be?

1.11 Financial statements are a key output of an accounting information system. Describe how the balance sheet and income statement for a midsized manufacturing firm can be helpful to each of the following users.

a. Customers
b. Suppliers
c. Stockholders
d. Managers
e. A bank that has lent them money
f. The Securities and Exchange Commission
g. Prospective investors

1.12 After S&S had been open for a year, it decided to expand its operations. One of the expansion ideas was to add a line of Japanese appliances. In order to reduce costs, S&S decided to buy directly from two of the Japanese manufacturers. Scott is close to finalizing the contracts. He has encountered a number of problems: language difficulties, legal questions, tight cash flow, deciding which vendors to buy from, determining pricing for each product, determining the most cost effective shipping routes, import regulations, currency fluctuation, and how much and how often to order. An accounting information system could provide information to help solve which of these problems? How could the accounting information system be helpful?

1.13 In an interesting twist some economists now say that more information isn't always better. In two separate studies researchers have found evidence suggesting that contrary to expectations, computers don't always increase productivity. Too much information, contend scientists, leads to decision paralysis. People lack standards for determining how much information is enough. In the end, people devote far too much time to further data analysis and forgo decision making.

Researchers also cite that the strategic benefits of computerization are exaggerated. Computers seldom provide a company with competitive advantage because every company in the industry responds to technology trends. In fact, the studies revealed that computerization tended to reduce productivity growth and, as an investment, was less efficient than other capital spending.

When is more information not always better?[1]

1.14 Ricky Hatch is the president of a company that manufactures footwear. Because of rapid growth over the past five years, the sales department has been complaining that orders are not being filled correctly, shoes are being returned because of defects, pricing is not competitive, and stockouts have been common. Ricky is considering installing an information system to solve these problems. How can an information system add value to Ricky's company? What tools are available to assist with evaluating how an information system can add value?

1.15 Your manager is trying to determine the value that a particular information system might add to the business. She wants to use a value chain to assist in the analysis, but she is unclear about what primary and support activities are. You have been asked to explain the five primary and four support activities. Be sure to explain what each activity consists of, how activities are linked, and the importance of the links between activities.

Problems

1.1 Joan Anderson manages the accounting department of a small company. She regularly uses the formal communication system (e.g., memoranda from her and other company managers) to inform employees of changes in company policy and other matters that should be called to their attention. She also uses the informal communications network that exists in the company to inform her employees. For

---

[1] *Source:* G. Pascal Zachary, "Computer Data Overload Limits Productivity Gains," *Wall Street Journal* (November 11, 1991): B1.

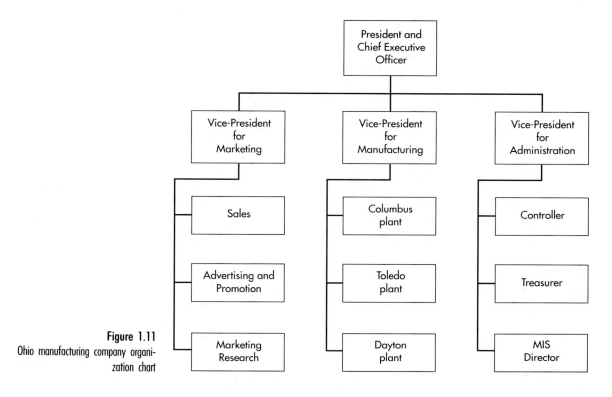

Figure 1.11
Ohio manufacturing company organization chart

example, she will make sure that certain employees overhear selected conversations with other departmental supervisors.

Required

a. Discuss the differences between formal and informal communication systems with respect to each of the following features of a communication system.

1. The accuracy of communication
2. The speed of communication
3. The influence the communication has on the employee.

b. Can an informal communication system be beneficial to the management process? Explain your answer. (CMA Examination, adapted)

1.2 A partial organization chart for the Ohio Manufacturing Company is shown in Fig. 1.11. Draw another chart showing how the organization might be structured if it were to adopt a divisional rather than a functional organization structure.

1.3 Suppose you have just inherited $3000 and have decided to invest it. You have identified three

investments: stock in Companies A, B, and C. You estimate the following investment returns.

Investment	Expected Return
Company A	$320 per year
Company B	400 per year
Company C	250 per year

If you had to make a decision on only this much information, you would probably select investment B.

Required

a. Suppose an investment advisory firm told you that it could guarantee, with 100% certainty, what the return will be. How much would you pay this person for the information? Would you pay $100, more than $100, or less than $100? Why?

b. Suppose that you paid the $100 and the firm predicted the following returns on investment. These returns turned out to be the actual returns. Was your decision to spend the $100 for that information a wise one? Why? What was the value of the information to you?

Investment	Actual Return
Company A	$320 per year
Company B	240 per year
Company C	420 per year

c. Suppose, instead, that the information you purchased produced the following returns. What is the value of this information?

Investment	Actual Return
Company A	$390 per year
Company B	340 per year
Company C	220 per year

d. The return shown in c above is an annual return. What would the value of the information be to you after the second year (ignore the time value of money)?

1.4 Wooster Company is a beauty and barber supplies and equipment distributorship servicing a five-state area. Management generally has been pleased with the overall operations of the company until now. The present purchasing system has evolved through practice rather than having been formally designed. Consequently, it is inadequate and needs to be redesigned.

A description of the present purchasing system is as follows: Whenever the quantity of an item is low, the inventory supervisor phones the purchasing department with the item description and the quantity to be ordered. A purchase order is then prepared in duplicate in the purchasing department. The original is sent to the vendor, and the copy is retained in the purchasing department and filed in numerical order. When the shipment arrives, the inventory supervisor sees that each item received is checked off on the packing slip accompanying the shipment. The packing slip is then forwarded to the accounts payable department. When the invoice arrives, the packing slip is compared with the invoice in the accounts payable department. Once any differences between the packing slip and the invoice are reconciled, a check is drawn for the appropriate amount and is mailed to the vendor with a copy of the invoice. The packing slip is attached to the invoice and is filed alphabetically in the paid invoice file.

Wooster Company intends to redesign its purchasing system from the time an item needs to be ordered until the time payment is made. The system should be designed to ensure that all of the proper controls are incorporated into the system.

Required

a. Identify the internally and externally generated documents that would be required to satisfy the minimum requirements of a basic system, and indicate the number of copies of each document that would be needed.

b. Explain how all of these documents should interrelate and flow among Wooster's various departments, including the final destination or file for each copy. (CMA Examination, adapted)

1.5 Denny Daniels is production manager of the Alumalloy Division of WRT Incorporated. Alumalloy has limited contact with outside customers and has no sales staff. Most of its customers are other divisions of WRT. All sales and purchases with outside customers are handled by other corporate divisions. Therefore, Alumalloy is treated as a cost center for reporting and evaluation purposes rather than as a revenue or profit center.

Daniels perceives the accounting department as a historical number-generating process that provides little useful information for conducting his job. Consequently, the entire accounting process is perceived to be a negative motivational device that does not reflect how hard or how effectively he works as a production manager. Daniels tried to discuss these perceptions and concerns with June Scott, the controller for the Alumalloy Division. Daniels told Scott, "I think the cost report is misleading. I know I've had better production over a number of operating periods, but the cost report still says I have excessive costs. Look, I'm not an accountant, I'm a production manager. I know how to get a good-quality product out. Over a number of years, I've even cut the raw materials used to do it. But the cost report doesn't show any of this. Basically, it's always negative, no matter what I do. There's no way you can win with accounting or the people at corporate who use those reports."

Scott gave Daniels little consolation. Scott stated that the accounting system and the cost reports generated by headquarters are just part of the corporate game and almost impossible for an individual to change. "Although these accounting reports are pretty much the basis for evaluating the efficiency of your division and the means corporate uses to determine whether you have done the job they want, you shouldn't worry too much. You haven't been fired yet! Besides, these cost reports have been used by WRT for the last twenty-five years."

Daniels perceived from talking to the production manager of the Zinc Division that most of what Scott said was probably true. However, some minor cost reporting changes for Zinc had been agreed to by corporate headquarters. He also knew from the trade grapevine that the turnover of production managers was considered high at WRT, even though relatively few were fired. Most seemed to end up quitting, usually in disgust, because of beliefs that they were not being evaluated fairly. The following are typical comments of production managers who had left WRT:

Corporate headquarters doesn't really listen to us. All they consider are those misleading cost reports. They don't want them changed and they don't want any supplemental information.

The accountants may be quick with numbers but they don't know anything about production. As it was, I either had to ignore the cost reports entirely or pretend they were important even though they didn't tell how good a job I had done. No matter what they say about not firing people, negative reports mean negative evaluations. I'm better off working for another company.

A recent copy of the cost report prepared by corporate headquarters for the Alumalloy Division follows. Daniels does not like this report because he believes it fails to reflect the division's operations properly, thereby resulting in an unfair evaluation of performance.

ALUMALLOY DIVISION COST REPORT			
for the Month of April, 19XX (000 omitted)			
	Master Budget	Actual Cost	Excess Cost
Aluminum	$ 400	$ 437	$37
Labor	560	540	(20)
Overhead	100	134	34
Total	$1060	$1111	$51

Required

a. Comment on Denny Daniel's perception of the following.

1. June Scott, the controller
2. Corporate headquarters
3. The cost report
4. Himself as a production manager
5. The accounting information system

b. Discuss how these perceptions affect his behavior and probable performance as a production manager and employee of WRT.

c. Identify and explain three changes that could be made in the cost information presented to the production managers that would make the information more meaningful and less threatening to them. (CMA Examination, adapted)

1.6 General Hardware Industries (GHI) is a large manufacturer of hardware for home and industrial use. GHI is organized along divisional lines, with each of its three major plants being a separate division. The divisions are the Power Tools Division (St. Louis), the Hand Tools Division (Omaha), and the Specialty Tools Division (Kansas City). A partial organization chart for GHI is shown in Fig. 1.12.

GHI has recently completed the acquisition of Kimball's Lawn Management, Inc. (KLM), a manufacturer of lawn and garden equipment and chemical sprays and fertilizers. KLM has five major plants located in the Midwest and specializing in the following product lines.

Chicago plant (company headquarters)	Fertilizers
Springfield plant	Weed and bug sprays
St. Paul plant	Garden tools (hoes, rakes, shovels, etc.)
Sioux Falls plant	Sprinkler systems
Milwaukee plant	Power mowers, tillers, spreaders, etc.

KLM is organized along functional lines, as shown in Fig. 1.13.

Required

a. Draw an organization chart for the new company assuming that it will use a functional organization structure. Discuss the arguments that could be made for organizing the newly merged company along functional lines.

b. Draw an organization chart for the new company assuming that it will use a divisional organization structure. Discuss the arguments that could be made for organizing the newly merged company along divisional lines.

1.7 The annual report is considered by some to be the single most important printed document that companies produce. It provides information used in making both economic investments and business decisions. The content of the annual report has expanded considerably in recent years in an effort to satisfy a growing audience that includes not only shareholders but also financial analysts, investors,

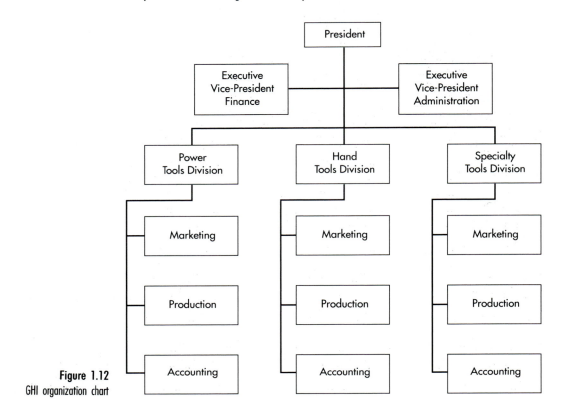

Figure 1.12
GHI organization chart

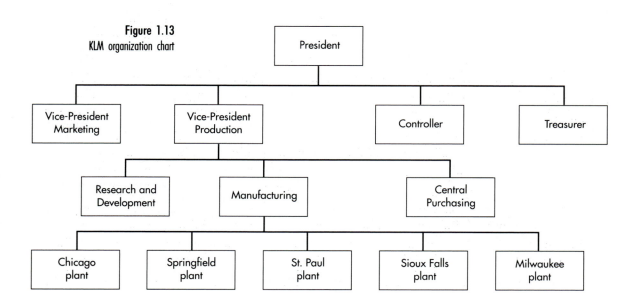

Figure 1.13
KLM organization chart

and customers. The future of most companies depends on acceptance by the investing public and by its customers; therefore companies should take this opportunity to communicate well-defined corporate strategies.

Required

a. Describe four types of information found in an annual report, other than the financial statements and accompanying footnotes, that are useful to the users of annual reports.

b. Discuss at least two advantages and two disadvantages of stating well-defined corporate strategies in the annual report.

c. Evaluate the effectiveness of annual reports in fulfilling the information needs of the following current and potential users.

    1. Shareholders   3. Employees

    2. Creditors   4. Customers

(CMA Examination, adapted)

1.8 The Garrison Corporation has an Internal Audit Department that reports to the Audit Committee of the Board of Directors. This department has re-

---

December 15, 199X

To the Audit Committee:

    During an audit of the Purchasing Department, it was determined by a check of the numerical sequence of purchase orders that two purchase orders were missing during the month of July 199X, indicating a weakness in internal controls. The Purchasing Department should be more diligent in controlling the sequence of purchase orders, since these documents commit funds of the company, and misuse can make the company vulnerable to fraud.

    The Purchasing Department has been appropriately attaching receiving reports to the original purchase orders; however, some receiving reports have not been completed. Also, some of the purchase orders have not had appropriate authorization signatures. These controls need to be reevaluated.

    During a walk-through of the Purchasing Department, some rumors were heard that illegal or unethical acts have been occurring. Some people stated that the purchasing agents are taking bribes; others think that the purchasing agents are "greasing the palms" of their friends. Management should distribute a statement about its position on the Foreign Corrupt Practices Act and develop a code of ethics for the Purchasing Department employees to alleviate any internal control weaknesses in this area.

---

cently completed an audit of Garrison's Purchasing Department. The following memo presents portions of the audit report, which will be discussed with the Vice-President of Purchasing and then forwarded to the Audit Committee.

Required

a. In order to be an effective communication device, an internal audit report should have several attributes. Describe each of the following attributes as they apply to internal audit reports.

    1. Timeliness

    2. Clarity

    3. Conciseness

    4. Objectivity

    5. Constructiveness

b. Evaluate the internal audit report presented in terms of the attributes listed in requirement a.

(CMA Examination, adapted)

1.9 Many management accountants are included among an expanding group of middle managers who are experiencing changes in the definition of their jobs and in the roles they play in the organization. The management accountant's primary function of monitoring and controlling operations began to diminish with the computerization of data. The initial thrust of computerization was to displace or replace some clerical functions. Middle management's role and work remained unchanged due to the remoteness of the computer. The only changes were the amount of information generated, the quality of that information, and the speed with which it was generated. Middle management still monitored activities, interpreted data, and controlled operations. Thus middle management was the link between information generation and top management.

    Top management now has direct access to the generated data through improved computer output and desktop computers that allow not only passive monitoring but also immediate, on-line interactive capacity.

Required

a. Discuss the effect that these changes in computer technology and computerized information systems have on the following.

    1. The role and work of middle managers

    2. Line and staff structures

b. The refining of computerized information systems and its effects have been termed a technological revolution. Compare this technological

revolution to the industrial revolution with respect to the impact on the human element of the business organization.
(CMA Examination, adapted)

1.10 It used to be that Japanese cars sold themselves. Customers would walk onto a car lot and take whatever was available. Now customers are demanding different specifications and specific options, but they don't want to wait very long for the car to arrive from the factory. Nissan Motor Company has been looking at how it can change to meet its customers' needs.

In the current distribution system a customer orders a car from a local dealer. The order must then go from the dealer to a regional manager, then to corporate headquarters, and finally to the factory. The car is then manufactured and shipped to the dealer. The problems with the current system are that the process takes too long and the dealer does not know exactly when the car will arrive.

Nissan's management has agreed to listen to your proposal for an integrated order entry system that electronically links individual dealers directly to corporate headquarters and factories in Japan. This linkage would allow dealers to order cars directly from the factory. The key to management's funding the project is your ability to show them how the information system will benefit the customer and thereby add value to the company.[2]

Required

a. Prepare a diagram of the value chain for a Nissan assembly plant. Include the five primary activities and the four support activities. Also, prepare a diagram of the value system of which Nissan is a part (from Nissan's suppliers to the dealers who sell Nissan's cars).

b. Describe in detail how an integrated order entry system could add value to Nissan.

1.11 You have recently hired a full-time employee to assist you in the opening of Katie's Flower Shop.

Because you anticipate that the majority of company sales will be made over the phone and on account, collection of accounts is likely to be a critical problem in your business. To help solve this problem, you have asked your newly hired assistant to design a form that can be used to record sales transactions. Your assistant has just completed the form shown in Fig. 1.14 and has asked you to review her work.

Required

a. What do you like and find functionally appropriate about the form your assistant has completed?

b. What changes in the form might increase the success of collecting the accounts?

1.12 Suppose you have $100 to invest and you have identified the following alternative investments with the expected payoffs shown. Which investment would you choose?

Investment	Payoff
A	$20
B	30
C	15

a. Suppose I could do a market study or investment analysis and tell you with 100% certainty what the real payoff will be. How much would you pay me for my information?

b. Suppose I find the following payoffs, which turn out to be the actual payoffs in the market. How much was my information worth?

Investment	Payoff
A	$22
B	24
C	34

c. Suppose I had told you that the payoffs were as listed next, which were again an accurate prediction of the market. How much was my information worth?

Investment	Payoff
A	$20
B	29
C	27

---

[2] *Source:* Clinton Wilder, "Value Judgement",
Computerworld (March 2, 1992): 69–70.

| KATIE'S FLOWER SHOP | | No. 1234 |
| 123 Elm St.   456-7890 | | |

Sold to:

Order Date _____

Terms:
_____ **Paid**
_____ **30 Day Account**
_____ **C.O.D.**

Deliver to:

Delivery Date _____

Delivered By _____

Quantity	Description	Amount

Goods Received By _____

Tax	
Total	

Figure 1.14

CASE 1.1: ANYCOMPANY, INC.—AN ONGOING COMPREHENSIVE CASE

One of the best ways to learn is to immediately apply what you have studied. The purpose of this case is to allow you to do that. You will select a local company that you can work with. At the end of most chapters you will find an assignment that will have you apply what you have learned using the company you have selected as a reference. This case, then, may become an ongoing case study that you work on throughout the term.

Visit several small- to medium-sized businesses in the local community. Explain that you will be doing a term-long case, and ask for permission to use the company as the firm you are going to study. Explain that you will need to meet with people in the company several times during the term to get the information you need. However, you will not need a great deal of their time or be a disruption to them. Offer to share any observations or suggestions that you can come up with as a way of allowing the firm to feel good about helping you.

Once you have lined up a company, answer the following questions.

1.   Does the company have a management information system? An accounting information system? What subsystems does the company have in place? Describe the information system in place in the company.

2.   Who are the major external users of information produced by the company? The major internal users? What information is produced for each set of users?

3.   Identify two users of information in the company. For each user, identify two outputs of the system that provide the user with decision-making information. For each output, identify the decision(s) that is made, the data that must be input into the system to produce the information, the way the data is processed to produce the information outputs, the manner in which data is stored, and the way that instructions and procedures are given to the system and to the users. For each output, use the characteristics of information (reliable, timely,

etc.) to evaluate the usefulness of the information provided.

4.   What information does the company not have that it would like to have? For one of these items of information, make a best estimate of calculating the value of that information. What are some of the constraints that limit the company's ability to produce the information it desires?

5.   Identify one informal information system in the business, and contrast its effectiveness and usefulness with one of the formal systems.

6.   Does the company use a functional organization structure or a divisional organization structure? Draw an organization chart for the company. Does the company use a centralized or decentralized approach?

7.   How does the information system add value to the organization? Briefly explain each of the company's primary and support activities.

8.   What does the company envision its information system being in 5 years? In 10 years?

9.   How effective do you think your study of the company has been? Why?

CASE 1.2: ACKOFF'S MANAGEMENT MISINFORMATION SYSTEMS

The following case is adapted from one of the classic information systems articles entitled "Management Misinformation Systems." It was written by Russell L. Ackoff and appeared in *Management Science*. In the article Ackoff identified five common assumptions about information systems and then explained why he did not agree (contentions in the case) with the assumptions.

Read each of the five assumptions and contentions and Ackoff's explanation. For each of the five, decide whether you agree or disagree with Ackoff's contentions. Defend the stand you take by preparing a report that explains why you believe the way you do. Also, be prepared to defend your beliefs in class.

Assumption 1: Management Needs More Information

Assumption 1:   Most MISs are designed on the assumption that the critical deficiency under which

most managers operate is the lack of relevant information.

Contention 1:   I do not deny that most managers lack a good deal of information that they should have, but I do deny that this is the most important informational deficiency from which they suffer. It seems to me that they suffer more from an overabundance of irrelevant information.

This is not a play on words. The consequences of changing the emphasis of an MIS from supplying relevant information to eliminating irrelevant information is considerable. If one is preoccupied with supplying relevant information, attention is almost exclusively given to the generation, storage, and retrieval of information: Hence emphasis is placed on constructing data banks, coding, indexing, updating files, access languages, and so on. The ideal that has emerged from this orientation is an infinite pool of data into which managers can reach to pull out any information they want. If, on the other hand, one sees the manager's information problem primarily, but not exclusively, as one that arises out of an overabundance of irrelevant information, most of which was not asked for, then the two most important functions of an information system become filtration (or evaluation) and condensation. The literature on MISs seldom refers to these functions, let alone considers how to carry them out.

My experience indicates that most managers receive much more data (if not information) than they can possibly absorb even if they spend all of their time trying to do so. Hence they already suffer from an information overload. They must spend a great deal of time separating the relevant documents. For example, I have found that I receive an average of 43 hours of unsolicited reading material each week. The solicited material is usually half again this amount.

I have seen a daily stock status report that consists of approximately six hundred pages of computer printout. The report is circulated daily across managers' desks. I've also seen requests for major capital expenditures that come in book size, several of which are distributed to managers each week. It is not uncommon for many managers to receive an average of one journal a day or more. One could go on and on.

Unless the information overload to which managers are subjected is reduced, any additional information made available by an MIS cannot be expected to be used effectively.

Even relevant documents have too much redundancy. Most documents can be considerably condensed without loss of content. My point here is best made, perhaps, by describing briefly an experiment that a few of my colleagues and I conducted on the operations research (OR) literature several years ago. By using a panel of well-known experts, we identified four OR articles that all members of the panel considered to be "above average" and four articles that were considered to be "below average." The authors of the eight articles were asked to prepare "objective" examinations (duration 30 minutes) plus answers for graduate students who were to be assigned the articles for reading. (The authors were not informed about the experiment.) Then several experienced writers were asked to reduce each article to two-thirds and one-third of its original length only by eliminating words. They also prepared a brief abstract of each article. Those who did the condensing did not see the examinations to be given to the students.

A group of graduate students who had not previ-

ously read the articles were then selected. Each one was given four articles randomly selected, each of which was in one of its four versions: 100%, 67%, 33%, or abstract. Each version of each article was read by two students. All were given the same examinations. The average scores on the examinations were compared.

For the above-average articles there was no significant difference between average test scores for the 100%, 67%, and 33% versions, but there was a significant decrease in average test scores for those who had read only the abstract. For the below-average articles there was no difference in average test scores among those who had read the 100%, 67%, and 33% versions, but there was a significant increase in average test scores of those who had read only the abstract.

The sample used was obviously too small for general conclusions, but the results strongly indicate the extent to which even good writing can be condensed without loss of information. I refrain from drawing the obvious conclusions about bad writing.

It seems clear that condensation as well as filtration, performed mechanically or otherwise, should be an essential part of an MIS, and that such a system should be capable of handling much, if not all, of the unsolicited as well as solicited information that a manager receives.

Assumption 2: Managers Need the Information They Want

Assumption 2: Most MIS designers "determine" what information is needed by asking managers what information they would like to have. This is based on the assumption that managers know what information they need and want.

Contention 2: For a manager to know what information he needs, he must be aware of each type of decision he should (as well as does) make and he must have an adequate model of each. These conditions are seldom satisfied.

Most managers have some conception of at least some of the types of decisions they must make. Their conceptions, however, are likely to be deficient in a very critical way, a way that follows from an important principle of scientific economy: The less we understand a phenomenon, the more variables we require to explain it. Hence managers who do not understand the phenomena they control play it "safe" and, with respect to information, want "everything." The MIS designer, who has even less understanding of the relevant phenomena than the manager, tries to provide even more than everything. She thereby increases what is already an overload of irrelevant information.

For example, market researchers in a major oil company once asked their marketing managers what variables they thought were relevant in estimating the sales volume of future service stations. Almost 70 variables were identified. The market researchers then added about half again this many variables and performed a large multiple linear regression analysis of sales of existing stations against these variables and found about 35 to be statistically significant. A forecasting equation was based on this analysis. An OR team subsequently constructed a model based on only one of these variables, traffic flow, which predicted sales better than the 35-variable regression equation. The team went on to explain sales at service stations in terms of the customers' perception of the amount of time lost by stopping for service. The relevance of all but a few of the variables used by the market researchers could be explained by their effect on such a perception.

The moral is simple: One cannot specify what information is required for decision making until an explanatory model of the decision process and the system involved has been constructed and tested. Information systems are subsystems of control systems. They cannot be designed adequately without taking control into account. Furthermore, whatever else regression analyses can yield, they cannot yield understanding and explanation of phenomena. They describe and, at best, predict.

Assumption 3: Giving Managers the Information They Need Improves Their Decision Making

Assumption 3: It is frequently assumed that if managers are provided with the information they need, they will then have no problem in using it effectively.

Contention 3: Operation research (an academic subject area dealing with the application of mathematical models and techniques to business decisions) stands to the contrary.

For example, give most managers an initial tableau of a typical "real" mathematical programming, sequencing, or network problem and see how close they come to an optimal solution. If their experience and judgment have any value, they may not do badly, but they will seldom do very well. In most management problems there are too many possi-

bilities to expect experience, judgment, or intuition to provide good guesses, even with perfect information.

Furthermore, when several probabilities are involved in a problem, the unguided mind of even a manager has difficulty in aggregating them in a valid way. We all know many simple problems in probability in which untutored intuition usually does very badly (e.g., What are the correct odds that 2 of 25 people selected at random will have their birthdays on the same day of the year?). For example, very few of the results obtained by queuing theory, when arrivals and service are probabilistic, are obvious to managers; nor are the results of risk analysis where the managers' own subjective estimates of probabilities are used.

The moral: It is necessary to determine how well managers can use needed information. When, because of the complexity of the decision process, they can't use it well, they should be provided with either decision rules or performance feedback so that they can identify and learn from their mistakes.

Assumption 4: More Communication Means Better Performance

Assumption 4: One characteristic of most MISs is that they provide managers with better current information about what other managers and their departments are doing. Underlying this provision is the belief that better interdepartmental communication enables managers to coordinate their decisions more effectively and hence improves the organization's overall performance.

Contention 4: Not only is this not necessarily so, but it seldom is so. One would hardly expect two competing companies to become more cooperative because the information each acquires about the other is improved.

For example, consider the following very much simplified version of a situation I once ran into. The simplification of the case does not affect any of its essential characteristics. A department store has two "line" operations: buying and selling. Each function is performed by a separate department. The Purchasing Department primarily controls one variable: how much of each item is bought. The Merchandising Department controls the price at which it is sold. Typically, the measure of performance applied to the Purchasing Department was the turnover rate of inventory. The measure applied to the Merchandising Department was gross sales; this department sought to maximize the number of items sold times their price.

Now by examining a single item, let us consider what happens in this system. The merchandising manager, using his knowledge of competition and consumption, set a price which he judged would maximize gross sales. In doing so, he utilized price-demand curves for each type of item. For each price the curves show the expected sales and values on an upper and lower confidence band as well. (See Fig. 1.15.) When instructing the Purchasing Department about how many items to make available, the merchandising manager quite naturally used the value on the upper confidence curve. This minimized the chances of his running short, which, if it occurred, would hurt his performance. It also maximized the chances of being overstocked, but this was not his concern, only the purchasing manager's. Say, therefore, that the merchandising manager initially selected price P1 and requested that amount Q1 be made available by the Purchasing Department.

In this company the purchasing manager also had access to the price-demand curves. She knew that the merchandising manager always ordered optimistically. Therefore, using the same curve, she read over from Q1 to the upper limit and down to the expected value, from which she obtained Q2, the quantity she actually intended to make available. She did not intend to pay for the merchandising manager's optimism. If merchandising ran out of stock, it was not her worry. Now the merchandising manager was informed about what the purchasing manager had done, so he adjusted his price to P2. The purchasing manager in turn was told that the merchandising manager had made this readjustment, so she planned to make only Q3 available. If this process (made possible only by perfect communication between departments) had been allowed to continue, nothing would have been bought and nothing would have been sold. This outcome was avoided by prohibiting communication between the two departments and forcing each to guess what the other was doing.

I have obviously caricatured the situation in order to make the point clear: When organizational units have inappropriate measures of performance that put them in conflict with each other, as is often the case, communication between them may hurt organizational performance, not help it. Organizational structure and performance measurement must be taken into account before opening the floodgates and permitting the free flow of information between parts of the organization.

Assumption 5: Managers Only Need to Understand How to Use a Systems

Assumption 5: A manager does not have to understand how an information system works, only how to use it.

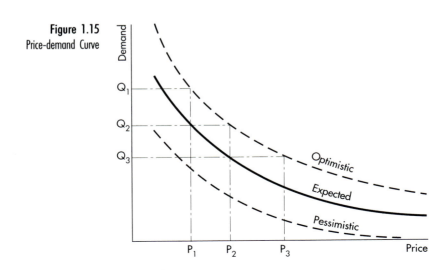

Figure 1.15
Price-demand Curve

Contention 5: Managers must understand their MIS or they are handicapped and cannot properly operate and control their company.

Most MIS designers seek to make their systems as innocuous and unobtrusive as possible to managers, lest they become frightened. The designers try to provide managers with very easy access to the system and assure them that they need to know nothing more about it. The designers usually succeed in keeping managers ignorant in this regard. This leaves managers unable to evaluate the MIS as a whole. It often makes them afraid to even try to do so, lest they display their ignorance publicly. In failing to evaluate their MIS, managers delegate much of the control of the organization to the system's designers and operators—who may have many virtues, but managerial competence is seldom among them.

Let me cite a case in point. A chairman of the board of a medium-size company asked for help on the following problem. One of his larger (decentralized) divisions had installed a computerized production inventory control and manufacturing manager information system about a year earlier. It had acquired about $2 million worth of equipment to do so. The board chairman had just received a request from the division for permission to replace the original equipment with newly announced equipment that would cost several times the original amount. An extensive "justification" for so doing was provided with the request. The chairman wanted to know whether the request was really justified. He admitted to complete incompetence in this connection.

A meeting was arranged at the division, at which I was subjected to an extended and detailed briefing. The system was large but relatively simple. At the heart of it was a reorder point for each item and a maximum allowable stock level. Reorder quantities took lead time as well as the allowable maximum into account. The computer kept track of stock, ordered items when required, and generated numerous reports on both the state of the system it controlled and its own "actions."

When the briefing was over, I was asked if I had any questions. I did. First I asked if, when the system had been installed, there had been many parts whose stock level exceeded the maximum amount possible under the new system. I was told there were many. I asked for a list of about 30 and for some graph paper. Both were provided. With the help of the system designer and volumes of old daily reports I began to plot the stock level of the first listed item over time. When this item reached the maximum "allowable" stock level, it had been reordered. The system designer was surprised and said that by sheer "luck" I had found one of the few errors made by the system. Continued plotting showed that because of repeated premature reordering the item had never gone much below the maximum stock level. Clearly, the program was confusing the maximum allowable stock level and the reorder point. This turned out to be the case in more than half of the items on the list.

Next I asked if they had many paired parts, ones that were only used with each other; for example, matched nuts and bolts. They had many. A list was produced and we began checking the previous day's withdrawals. For more than half of the pairs the differences in the numbers recorded as withdrawn were very large. No explanation was provided.

Before the day was out it was possible to show by some quick and dirty calculations that the new computerized system was costing the company almost $150,000 per month more than the hand system that it had replaced, most of this in excess inventories.

The recommendation was that the system be redesigned as quickly as possible and that the new equipment not be authorized for the time being.

The questions asked of the system had been obvious and simple ones. Managers should have been able to ask them, but—and this is the point—they felt themselves incompetent to do so. They would not have allowed a hand-operated system to get so far out of their control.

No MIS should ever be installed unless the managers for whom it is intended are trained to evaluate and hence control it rather than be controlled by it.

Source: Reprinted by permission of Russell Ackoff, "Management Misinformation Systems," *Management Sciences* 14 (4) (December 1967). Copyright © 1967, The Institute of Management Sciences, 290 Westminster Street, Providence, RI 02903.

CHAPTER 2

Transaction Processing: Elements and Procedures

LEARNING OBJECTIVES

After studying this chapter, you should be able to:

- Describe and give examples of the basic activities that take place in transaction processing cycles and in the data processing cycle.
- Explain how data is captured and entered into a data processing system.
- Explain how data is stored in computer-based systems, and describe the different types of files and their uses.
- Explain how data files are maintained and the approaches used to maintain them.
- Explain how information can be organized and presented to users to help them fulfill the responsibilities they have been given.
- Design coding systems for simple data processing applications.

INTEGRATIVE CASE: S&S, INC.

The grand opening of S&S, Inc. (see the introductory story in Chapter 1), is two weeks away. Scott and Susan are working long hours to make the final arrangements for the store opening. They are hiring salespeople, both to work in the store and to call on outside businesses such as builders, apartment complexes, and others who may need large volumes of appliances. The training for both sets of salespeople is scheduled to begin next week. Several people experienced in appliance repair are also being hired.

Susan has ordered an adequate inventory of appliances for the first month. The store is being remodeled and will have a bright, cheery decor. All seems to be in order. All, that is, except the accounting records.

Like many entrepreneurs, Scott and Susan have not given as much thought to their accounting records as they have to other parts of their business. They recognize that they need qualified accounting help, and they hired Ashton Fleming as their full-time accountant. Scott and Susan feel Ashton is perfect for the job because of his two years of experience with a national CPA firm and his desire to help build a company from the ground up. When they hired Ashton, Susan and Scott explained that they are entrepreneurs who do not know much about accounting and plan to lean heavily on him to help them decide how to run the accounting end of the business.

On Ashton's first day on the job Scott shows Ashton where he placed all the invoices for the inventory he and Susan purchased. He explains that the employees are paid by the hour and are paid every two weeks, with the first paychecks due next week. He also pulls out several folders. One contains the documentation on their bank loan, and the first payment is due several days after the grand opening. The others contain information on rental payments, utilities, and several other expenses.

Ashton asks Scott where the computer is that will help with the accounting. Scott replies that with all the challenges they have had in opening up the business, they just have not had time to tackle that yet. Scott does say that getting a computerized system is his number 1 priority after the store opens and business stabilizes. That could take several months, though, so for now Ashton will have to keep the books by hand. Scott wants Ashton to begin the planning and organizing, though, so that when the system is acquired, S&S can immediately move to it.

After Scott leaves, Ashton begins to wonder why he ever accepted the job. Although Ashton has audited companies, he has never organized a company's books and is unsure how to go about it. Nor does he really understand how to plan for a computer-based accounting information system. A million questions run through his head. Here are just a few of them.

1. What do I do now? Where do I start? How am I going to organize things? How am I going to process all the different types of transactions?

2. How am I going to figure out how to use a computerized system when I don't really know how one works? How do you process transactions using a computer? How do you enter and store data? How do you generate reports, and what reports are needed?

3. How do I go about setting up a chart of accounts to keep track of the different types of transactions? ■

INTRODUCTION

Based on the introductory story, we can conclude that Ashton, as the new accountant of S&S, needs to decide how to process all of S&S's transactions. He needs to organize a system that will record transactions as they take place and process the data until it is presented as summary-level information in the financial statements or in other reports. This chapter introduces you to the activities that take place as accounting transactions are processed.

The main objective of an accounting information system is to produce the information needed to properly manage and control a company. Chapter 1 discussed the nature of information and the data from which it is produced. This chapter provides a brief introduction to how accounting transactions are processed in a manual system. It also discusses the data processing cycle, which is the process of entering, processing, storing, and reporting data in a computer-based information system. The final section of the chapter discusses the procedures used to code data for input, storage, and retrieval.

TRANSACTION PROCESSING

A **transaction** is an agreement between two entities to exchange goods or services or any other economic event that can be measured in economic terms by an organization. In the case of S&S, for example, both the purchase and the sale of inventory are transactions. External transactions take place between a business organization, such as S&S, and an external party, such as their customers or suppliers. An example is S&S's purchase of appliances from the manufacturer. Internal transactions take place within an organization, such as between departments or divisions of the company. Examples include paying company employees or transferring goods from one department to another.

Transaction Processing Cycles

The process that begins with capturing transaction data and ends with an informational output such as the financial statements is called **transaction processing**. A typical business entity will engage in a large volume of transactions. However, a great majority of these transactions fall into one of the five basic business cycles introduced in Chapter 1. Within each cycle most of the transactions are very similar. For example, in the payroll cycle each employee will be paid at the end of a specified time period, such as a week or month. That means that S&S will repeat the same type of transaction over and over again. The same is true for the other cycles. Each cycle typically handles high volumes of a limited number of different transactions. These cycles and the manner in which they process transactions are the subject of the five chapters in Part 5 of this book.

Table 2.1 summarizes the major components of the five business cycles. The first column lists the seven elements found in each cycle. The next five columns show examples of the elements for each of the five cycles. A more detailed description of these and other business cycle elements is provided in Part 5 of this book.

Cycle Elements	MANUFACTURING COMPANY TRANSACTION PROCESSING CYCLES				
	Revenue	Procurement	Production	Personnel	Financial
Transaction	Sale	Purchase	Assembly	Employee services rendered	Cash receipts and disbursements
Source document	Invoice	Purchase requisition	Production order	Employee time card	Journal voucher
Transaction file	Sales journal	Purchases journal	Job time records	Payroll transactions	General journal
Master file	Accounts receivable	Inventory ledger	Work-in-process file	Payroll file	General ledger
Report	Sales analysis	Vendor performance	Production cost summary	Payroll register	Trial balance
Output document	Customer statement	Purchase order	Quality inspection record	Employee paycheck	Disbursement check
Query response	Customer balance	Order status	Production job status	Employee qualifications	Account status

Table 2.1
Examples of elements of primary business cycles

In each of the five transaction processing cycles certain basic activities take place. To facilitate the explanation of these activities, we use the revenue cycle of S&S as an example. The example assumes that a manual system is in place at S&S. Computerized systems are discussed later in the chapter.

Processing Revenue Cycle Transactions at S&S

In order to organize S&S's books, Ashton decided to study the way the store is to operate. He decided to walk a sales transaction through all the steps that would be needed to take it from when it occurs to its inclusion in the financial statements. That way he felt he could get the big picture and see how everything fits together. The step-by-step approach that Ashton used is summarized in Fig. 2.1.

The *first* step in processing transactions is to capture the data for each transaction that takes place. The most frequent transaction in the revenue cycle is a sale, either for cash or for credit. Other revenue cycle transactions include the return of merchandise that was sold and the writing off of uncollectible credit sales.

After some thought Ashton concluded that at S&S a sale can be initiated in one of two ways: when a customer in the store makes a purchase or when a customer requests that goods be shipped or that services be performed. S&S has purchased sophisticated, state-of-the-art cash registers that can capture sales data and produce receipts for customers. They are also designed to be linked into a computer system. To handle the customers that call in, S&S will use a sales invoice that lists customer data such as name and address and the items,

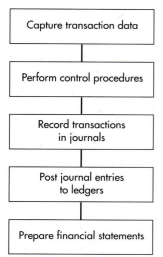

Capture transaction data

Perform control procedures

Record transactions
in journals

Post journal entries
to ledgers

Prepare financial statements

Figure 2.1
Processing sales transactions at S&S

quantities, and prices of the appliances that are sold. To record service activities, such as appliance repair, it will use a service record or invoice to record the services performed, the time spent performing them, and the parts that are used.

The *second* step in processing transactions is to perform certain control functions. Ashton wants to be sure that the data that are captured are correct and complete. S&S also does not want to agree to sell and immediately deliver items that it does not have. Thus Ashton must come up with a means of inventory control. Nor does S&S want to sell on credit to people who are poor credit risks. To prevent that, Ashton decides that S&S needs to set up procedures for approving customers for credit and deciding on how much credit to grant them. After a customer has been approved, procedures need to be set up to ensure that they do not exceed their credit limit.

The *third* step in processing transactions is to record them in journals. In the double-entry system of accounting, each time a transaction takes place, a journal entry is prepared showing the accounts and the amounts that are to be debited and credited. These entries are entered into a journal. The **general journal** is used to record seldom-encountered transactions and end-of-period adjustments. Since most transactions (such as sales, cash receipts, and purchases) are repetitive, similar accounting transactions are entered chronologically into a **specialized journal**.

Ashton decided to set up a sales journal to record all of the sales that take place. Each entry in the sales journal will represent a credit to sales and a debit to either accounts receivable or to cash. So that the amount of the accounts receivable can be posted to the proper customer, the entry in the sales journal will contain the name of the person or company making the purchase, as well as the amount, the date, and other relevant data.

The *fourth* step is to post the journal entries to ledgers. A **ledger** contains detailed information about the dollar balances in specific company accounts. A **general ledger** contains summary-level financial data about all of the asset, liability, equity, revenue, and expense accounts of a firm. When the amount of data for any one general ledger account is large, a special ledger, called a **subsidiary ledger**, is used to record data for that account. The sum of all the accounts in a subsidiary ledger should equal the amount in the corresponding general ledger account. Each general ledger account that is supported by a subsidiary ledger is called a **control account**. Subsidiary ledgers are often used for accounts receivable, accounts payable, inventory, and fixed assets.

When the number of specialized transactions becomes large, it is sometimes not practical to record each transaction individually in a specialized journal and then again in the subsidiary ledger accounts. In these situations accountants can use a form called a **journal voucher** to summarize a group of transactions. The documents recording the transactions are gathered and totaled, and an entry is put on the journal voucher that summaries the documents. These daily summary totals are then posted to the general ledger and, where appropriate, to the subsidiary ledger. In essence, a journal voucher and the supporting documents are equivalent to a specialized journal.

Ashton decided to set up a general ledger and an accounts receivable subsidiary ledger. To give Scott a brief and simple explanation of the journalizing and posting process that will be used for sales, Ashton created Fig. 2.2. It shows that each sale is to be recorded in the sales journal. Then each individual sale is posted to the specific customer's account in the accounts receivable subsidiary ledger in the same way that the KDR Vending account is handled. Then the total debit to accounts receivable from the sales journal is debited to the accounts receivable control account in the general ledger. Likewise, the total amount of credit sales is posted to the sales account in the general ledger. The posting references and document numbers will provide what is known as an **audit trail**, which is a way to move backward in the document flow to trace where a number came from.

There are several other entries that are needed in the revenue cycle. If the perpetual method of inventory is used, the following journal entry is required to recognize the cost of the product inventory that was sold to the customer:

(2)	Cost of Goods Sold	xxx	
	Inventory or Finished Goods		xxx

Merchandise that is returned is recorded as follows:

(3)	Sales Returns & Allowances	xxx	
	Accounts Receivable		xxx
	Inventory of Finished Goods	xxx	
	Cost of Goods Sold		xxx

Not all customers who buy on credit pay their bills. When an account is deemed uncollectible, it is written off as follows:

(4)	Bad Debt Expense (or Allowance for Doubtful Accounts)	xxx	
	Accounts Receivable		xxx

In a similar way, the transactions from each of the business cycles are processed and entered into journals and ledgers. The general ledger becomes the highest-level summary of an organization's accounting transactions.

The *fifth* and final step is preparing financial reports. To prepare statements, Ashton will organize and display the general ledger accounts in a **trial balance**. It is so named because one of its purposes is to ensure that the debit and credit accounts in the ledger are in balance. After Ashton makes any necessary closing entries and adjustments to

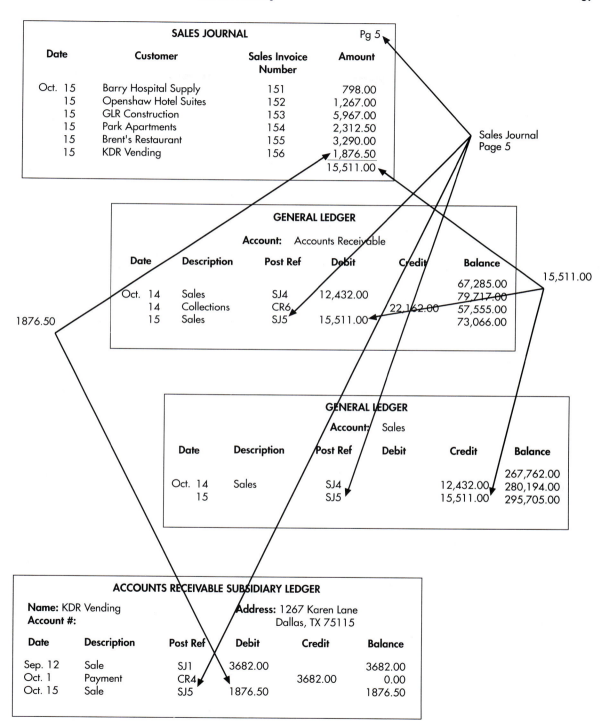

Figure 2.2 Recording a credit sale in a sales journal and posting it to the sales and accounts receivable control account in the General ledger and to the customer's account in the accounts receivable subsidiary ledger

the general journal account balances, he will prepare financial statements. This financial reporting process is repeated each accounting period.

Other output is also prepared from the transactions that are processed, such as sales analysis, sales forecasts, and inventory status reports. Some of the reports that are prepared from the accounting records are discussed later in the chapter in the "Information Output" section.

This section of the chapter discussed how accounting transactions are processed in a manual system. The way that transactions are processed in a computerized system is discussed in the next major section.

The Data Processing Cycle

In non-computer-based systems the journals and ledgers are maintained on paper. In computer-based systems transactions are processed by computers. For computer processing, transaction data must be translated into machine-readable form, processed, stored in computer-readable form, and then converted back into human-readable form for system users. The operations performed on data in computer-based systems in order to generate meaningful and relevant information are referred to collectively as the **data processing cycle**. As shown in Fig. 2.3, the data processing cycle has four stages: data input, data processing, data storage, and information output. As also shown in Fig. 2.3, the data processing cycle makes use of three main resources: software, hardware, and people. The next four sections of the chapter discuss data input, data storage, data processing, and information output in more detail. Focus 2.1 describes how an efficient data processing system can save a company a great deal of money.

The relationship of the data processing cycle to the documents, journals, ledgers, and files used in processing transactions is shown in Fig. 2.4.

Figure 2.3
The data processing cycle

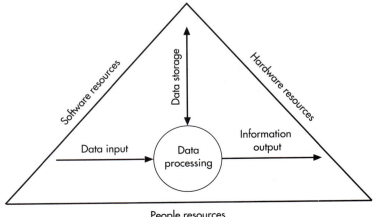

People resources

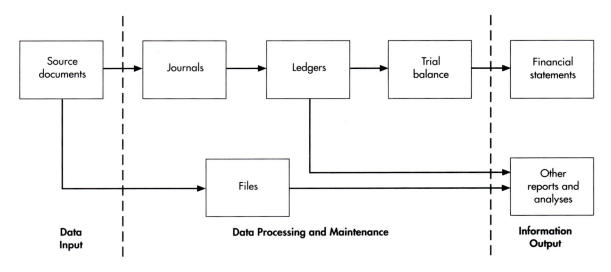

Figure 2.4
The data processing cycle in accounting

DATA INPUT

In the data input stage transaction data are collected and entered into the system. However, during data input a number of operations may need to be performed on data in order to facilitate subsequent processing. Data may need to be *classified* by assigning identification codes (account number, department number, etc.) to data records based on a predetermined system, such as a chart of accounts (discussed in more detail later in this chapter). Data are usually *verified* to ensure their accuracy prior to submitting them for processing. It is much less costly and much more effective to prevent errors from entering a system than it is to try and detect and correct the errors once they have entered the system. In some cases data need to be *transmitted* from one location to another. For example, a branch office may capture transaction data and forward them to the main office for processing.

Data can be collected and entered into the system in several ways. One way of capturing data is to use a **source document**, a form (usually preprinted) on which an initial record of transaction data is entered. Examples of source documents generated internally include sales orders, purchase requisitions, receiving reports, and employee time cards. External source documents include invoices from suppliers and checks and remittance advices from customers. Source documents are usually accumulated and organized into batches before they are transcribed into machine-readable form. This transcription is done by scanning the documents or by keying the information onto a magnetic medium such as tapes, disks, or diskettes. The devices that do this are described in Chapter 4.

2.1 FOCUS

Information Systems Can Reduce Health Care Costs

Health care costs in the United States are rising at an alarming rate. One way that they can be cut is by using more efficient data processing systems.

At the Lake Charles Memorial Hospital more than twelve thousand claims errors occurred when claims were misplaced, mailed to the wrong office, or returned by Medicare or insurance companies due to inaccurate information on payment forms. Two years later more than 90% of the billing errors at the hospital had been eliminated by a new medical claims system. At Miami's Baptist Hospital a more efficient system cut in half the 30 to 35 days it took to receive reimbursements for medical services from government agencies.

Most the country's six thousand hospitals have a hospital information system (HIS) that collects and processes information internally. However, the ways that hospitals move patient information from their HIS to the billing department and then to the health care payees differ greatly. Many insurance com-

Data can also be input using a turnaround document. A **turnaround document** is a record of company data that is sent to an external party and then returned to the system as input. They are prepared in machine-readable form to facilitate their subsequent processing as input records. An example is the bill that utilities send to their customers. When it returns with the payment, the bill is read by a special scanning device.

Data can also be entered by keying it into an on-line terminal or a microcomputer. Banks and credit unions are examples of firms that use these keying devices. Tellers key in the customer account code for each customer they attend and then the deposit or withdrawal amount. In some automated systems data is input directly into the system and then a hard (paper) copy of the transaction is printed and used as a source document.

There are several ways to increase the accuracy, completeness, and speed of data entry when keying devices are used. One way is to use computer or terminal screens that are preformatted with the information that the user needs to enter into the system. Often these screens resemble source documents, such as sales invoices and purchase orders. Users fill out the screen in the same way they would a paper source document.

Another keying aid is a series of prompts that ask the user questions until the system has all the data it needs. Often the nature of a succeeding question depends on the answer to a previous question. For example, consider a system built to help automobile insurance agents update

panies print the billing data from their HIS and drop it in the mail. The health care payees must then key the data into their system and process the claim. The printing, mailing, and rekeying process takes a great deal of time, slows down the payment cycle, and introduces errors into the process. Less than 5% of the estimated 3.5 billion health care claims filed each year are done so electronically.

With respect to their billing and collection systems, hospitals face a number of problems. They often must use different methods of billing depending on who is billed and how they want their bills sent. The result is a great deal of confusion and a high rate of errors. Another problem is interfacing their systems with those of the payees. Some people claim that the interface between the HIS and the payment organizations is still in the Dark Ages. Another problem is that the systems developers at hospitals have so much to do in terms of running the hospital and providing patients with adequate health care that the billing and collection areas of the hospital system take a backseat.

So what can be done? A major problem is that there are no electronic standards for medical bills. A number of health care providers and payees are hammering out a set of standards for electronic billing and payments. Once the standards have been developed, they need to be consistently applied across the industry. Thus health care providers will have to place a high priority on improving their billing and collection systems. The hospitals mentioned earlier have already proven that such efforts can yield a high payback.

Source: Charles Pelton, "IS Operations Make for a Healthy Cash Flow," *InformationWeek* (December 11, 1989): 33, 36.

---

their client's insurance. A "No" response to the question "Is the insured adding a new driver?" will result in no further questions about a new driver. A "Yes" response will result in a series of questions to capture the needed data about the new driver.

Many on-line data entry devices do not require keying. These devices are referred to as **source data automation** devices because they capture transaction data in machine-readable form at the time and place of their origin. Familiar source data automation devices are the automatic teller machines (ATMs) used by banks and the optical scanners used in grocery and other retail stores. These and other data input devices are described in more detail in Chapter 4. Focus 2.2 describes how one insurance company is using scanning technology to input data into their computer.

DATA STORAGE

A company's data is one of its most important resources. Without it, few corporate decisions could be made and most organizations would cease to exist. However, the mere existence of a great deal of relevant data does not guarantee that it can be put to good use. An organization's data must be maintained in a way that allows the company ready and easy access to the critical data it needs to function properly. Accountants are the primary guardians of an organization's data. As a result, they need to understand how data is organized and stored in computer-based systems and how it can be accessed. In essence, they need to know how to manage data for maximum corporate use. The

2.2 FOCUS

Insurance Company Is Eliminating Paperwork

Insurance underwriters at Central Life Assurance Company (CLA) were drowning in paper. For 96 years CLA handwrote insurance applications and associated documentation, which generated enormous amounts of paperwork. These handwritten insurance applications were then given to data entry personnel to enter into the data processing system. Several problems existed with this paper system. Documents were frequently misplaced, misfiled, or mixed up with outdated documents. The filing cabinets that held the documents took up valuable floor space. Because of the large amount of paperwork, it was difficult to find a document that was being processed.

CLA is solving its paper glut by moving to a paperless system that captures data as it is received in the office. When documents are received, they are

data storage concepts necessary to understand data management are discussed now.

Fundamental Data Storage Concepts and Definitions

Imagine how hard it would be to read a textbook if it were not organized into chapters, sections, paragraphs, and sentences. Also imagine how hard it would be for an organization to find anything if its data were randomly dumped into file cabinets. Fortunately, most textbooks and company files are organized in such a way that information can be retrieved easily. Likewise, information in computer-based systems can be organized so that it can be stored and retrieved efficiently. This section explains basic data storage concepts and definitions using accounts receivable information as an example.

An **entity** is an item about which information is stored. Examples of an entity include employees, inventory items, and customer accounts. Each entity has **attributes**, or characteristics of interest, that need to be stored. The pay rate of an employee and the address of a customer are examples of attributes. For the various entities each attribute has a **data value**. For example, P.O. Box 7 (the data value) is the address (an attribute) of XYZ Company (the entity). Generally, all entities of the same type possess the same set of attributes. For example, all employees possess an employee number, a pay rate, a home address, and so on. The specific data values for those attributes, however, will differ among entities—for example, one employee's pay rate might be $8.00, whereas another's might be $8.25.

scanned in the mail room, and an image of the document is stored on a magnetic disk. Each document is indexed and checked for accuracy as it is scanned. After documents are scanned, they are routed to the proper department based on the index number assigned.

Scanned underwriting files contain all the information about a specific account: applications, financial reports, medical information, photographs, and so on. Because each scanned image (document) is indexed, the system places all the images together by case. Agents can then access this information at any time from a PC on their desk through a fiber optics network. So agents can quickly view any application without having to sort through a pile of papers. After a case is closed, the images are archived on an optical disk instead of in a filing cabinet.

The new system has affected CLA in several ways. Customer service has improved, because applications can be processed faster and more accurately. In the past, when a customer would call an agent about a claim, the agent would have to look up the necessary information and call the person back. Now agents can access the information instantly while the customer is on the phone. The voluminous amounts of paperwork have been eliminated, and the new system is much more organized and easier to use. The result is better service and more efficient processing at significant cost savings.

Source: James Daly, "Insurer Sees Future in Imaging Strategy," *Computerworld* (January 6, 1992): 41.

Data in EDP (electronic data processing) systems are stored by organizing smaller units of data into larger and more meaningful units of data. This data hierarchy, beginning with characters (the smallest element) and ending with data bases (the largest), is shown in Fig. 2.5. A **character** is a number or letter and is the smallest element of data that is meaningful to a user. Characters are combined to form data values (such as P.O. Box 7). Data values are stored in **fields**, which are grouped together to form records. Thus a **record** is a collection of data values that describe specific attributes of an entity. In Fig. 2.6, for example, each row represents a different record, and each column represents an attribute. The intersection of each row and column is a field. Each field contains a data value that describes the particular attribute and the record to which it pertains.

Similar records are grouped together to form a **file**. For example, all receivable records are stored together in an accounts receivable file. In recent years files containing related data have been combined to form what are called **data bases**. These files are stored so as to facilitate both updating of the data and user access to the data. For example, the accounts receivable file might be combined with the customer, sales analysis, and other related files to form a customer data base.

The two alternative approaches to computer-based data management rely on files and data bases. The use of files as the primary structure for storing data is referred to as the **file-oriented approach**. It is also referred to as the traditional approach and the applications approach.

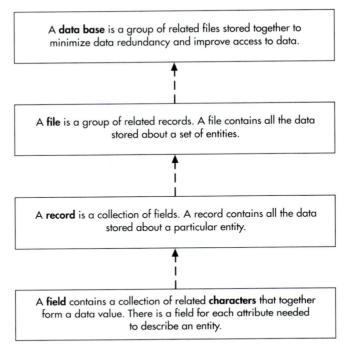

Figure 2.5
Hierarchy of Data Elements

A **data base** is a group of related files stored together to minimize data redundancy and improve access to data.

A **file** is a group of related records. A file contains all the data stored about a set of entities.

A **record** is a collection of fields. A record contains all the data stored about a particular entity.

A **field** contains a collection of related **characters** that together form a data value. There is a field for each attribute needed to describe an entity.

Figure 2.6
Accounts receivable file

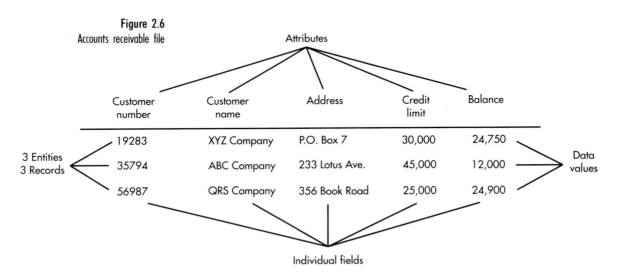

This accounts receivable file stores information about three separate entities: XYZ Company, ABC Company, and QRS Company. As a result, there are three records in the file. Five separate attributes are used to describe each customer: customer number, customer name, address, credit limit, and balance. There are, therefore, five separate fields in each record. Each field contains a data value that describes an attribute of a particular entity (customer). For example, the data value 19283 is the customer number for the XYZ Company.

In this approach the primary focus is on individual applications, such as processing accounts payable. Each application has one or more files that support the application, such as an accounts payable file. Where more than one file is needed to support an application, the files are independent and physically separate from each other.

The use of data bases as the primary data storage structure is referred to as the **data base approach** or the data base management system approach. The focus in data base systems is data integration and sharing. The objectives are to try to eliminate data redundancy by storing data just once and to make that data available to all authorized users. The data base approach is explained in more detail in Chapter 7.

Types of Files

Files exist to store data for organizations. Since there are many kinds of data and many purposes for storing data, there are different kinds of files. This section explains the types of files.

A **master file** is a permanent file of records that reflect the status of items relevant to the business, such as inventory or customer accounts. A master file is permanent in that it will exist indefinitely, even though individual records within it may frequently be inserted, deleted, or changed. Master files are the most common types of files maintained in accounting and business information systems. A master file is similar in concept to the subsidiary ledger discussed earlier in the chapter. Examples of master files include a payroll master file, an accounts receivable master file, and a fixed assets master file.

When a master file is created, it must contain all the data that a company needs about the item of interest. For example, in an accounts receivable file the company needs to know the customer name, address, balance due, terms, and the like. The current status of items such as the balance due changes as sales are made and receivables are collected. Accordingly, master files are continually updated as transactions occur. Master files are also frequently queried by users to find out current balances or to extract information for analysis. Most company reports are prepared by printing out information contained on master files.

A **transaction file** contains a number of similar transactions that have been grouped together for processing purposes, such as updating a master file. For example, a transaction file containing sales data that is used to update the accounts receivable master file would contain the customer number, the amount of the sale, the date of the sale, and other similar data.

As data is entered on a transaction file, it must be edited for accuracy and completeness. Periodically, the transaction file is used to update the master file. Generally, a transaction file will contain one record for each source document. Examples of typical business transaction files include a file of inventory issue and receipt transactions, a file of sales transactions, and a file of employee timekeeping records. A transaction file is similar in concept to the special journal discussed earlier in the chapter.

A **table file** contains reference data that is retrieved during data processing to facilitate calculations or other tasks. Examples are payroll tax withholding tables, sales tax tables, and freight rate tables. These files must be updated whenever their data change.

A **history file** contains transactions that have already been processed. They are retained for reference purposes and are often a source of useful management information. For example, a sales history file may be analyzed to provide summary and trend information on total sales by region, by salesperson, by customer, by product, and so forth.

A **backup file** is a duplicate copy of a current file. They are maintained in order to protect the organization from the consequences of the partial or complete loss of a current file.

A **suspense file** contains records that are erroneous or of uncertain status that have been temporarily removed from regular processing so that they can be investigated and corrected. An example is a credit sale transaction for which there is no accounts receivable record.

A **report file** is a temporary file containing information that is to be printed out at a later date.

DATA PROCESSING

During data processing data is manipulated to create information. This processing often includes many different activities. *Calculating* encompasses any form of mathematical manipulation. *Comparing* involves the simultaneous examination of two or more items of data, such as an inventory balance on hand and a reorder point, as a basis for subsequent action. *Summarizing* is a very important processing activity involving the aggregation of bits of data into meaningful totals or condensations. A related activity is *filtration,* which is the screening out of extraneous data from subsequent processing. Still another processing activity is *retrieval,* which is the fetching of data items from storage for use in processing or for output purposes.

Another data processing activity is file maintenance. The periodic processing of transactions against stored data to make the data current is referred to as **data maintenance** or **file maintenance**. Data maintenance is the most common task performed in virtually all data processing systems.

There are four different types of data maintenance. Record *additions* are insertions of entire new records into the file. Record *deletions* are extractions of entire records from the file. Record *updates* involve revising a current master file balance, generally by adding or subtracting an amount from a transaction record. Record *changes* involve such operations as revising credit ratings and changing addresses.

A specific example of a data maintenance application in accounting is shown in Fig. 2.7. This simple illustration shows the updating of an accounts receivable record for a sales transaction. The transaction data is matched against the correct record using a record identifier—in this case, the account number. The amount of the sale ($360) is then added to the account balance ($1500) to get the new current balance ($1860).

TRANSACTION DATA

Account Number	Transaction Type	Transaction Date	Document Number	Transaction Amount
0123	Sale	02/19/87	9876	$360.00

MASTER FILE RECORD

Account Number	Credit Limit	Previous Balance	Current Balance
0123	$2000.00	$1000.00	$1500.00

File update process
• Verify data accuracy
• Match primary key (account number)
• Add transaction amount to current balance
• Compare new balance to credit limit
• Repeat for all transactions
• Print summary reports

UPDATED MASTER FILE RECORD

Account Number	Credit Limit	Previous Balance	Current Balance
0123	$2000.00	$1500.00	$1860.00

Figure 2.7
File updating example

Note in Fig. 2.7 that even for this very simple example involving only one type of transaction (an update), the process contains several steps.

All computer systems must have some formalized means of organizing and accessing the data that is stored. The data must be organized and stored on the physical devices in such a way that it can be accessed easily and efficiently. The ways that files are organized and accessed are discussed next.

File Organization and Access

File organization refers to the way data is stored on the physical storage media. The data may be stored in sequential order or randomly. These methods are referred to respectively as sequential and direct (or random) file organization.

File access refers to the way the computer finds, or retrieves, a record it has stored. File access methods are a way of logically organizing the records in a file; thus they are referred to as methods of logical file organization. With sequential access the records are read, one by one, in the sequential order in which they are stored. With direct access the computer must have some means of locating the desired record without searching each record in the file. Several direct-access approaches are commonly used to locate records: individual keys, pointers, indexes, and randomized calculations. These methods are explained later in the chapter.

Records are typically stored and retrieved using a record identifier called a key. The basic purpose of the primary key is to uniquely identify

Record Type	Primary Key
Payroll	Employee number
Customer	Account number
Parts inventory	Stock number
Work in process	Job number
Finished goods	Product number
General ledger	Account code
Fixed assets	Asset number
Accounts payable	Vendor number

Table 2.2

Examples of record keys for typical business records

each record. This facilitates such data processing activities as retrieving specific records from a file, storing records, and updating records to reflect transactions. Sequential files are generally maintained in sequence according to their primary key. Table 2.2 lists some common data records in a business organization and identifies the primary key most commonly used for each.

A **secondary key** is another field used to identify a record in a file. However, it is usually not unique. Secondary keys can be used to sort records in a file into a specific order. For example, consider a professor's computerized grade rolls. For most uses of the file, such as recording grades, the file may need to be in alphabetical order by last name. At other times, such as analyzing final grades, the professor may want to see the file in the order of total points earned in the class or by the grade earned. In this example the unique identifier, the last name, is the primary key, and the total points earned and the grade earned are secondary keys.

It is not necessary for accountants to understand the technical details of the storage process. However, they must understand how files are organized and accessed in order to (1) understand the constraints that may be imposed on the data by organization and access methods and (2) be able to select the approach that best meets their needs.

Data can be processed in sequential order or randomly as it occurs. In addition, transactions can be grouped and processed in batches, or they can be processed as they occur. Transactions can be processed on-line and in an on-line, real-time mode. Each of these methods is explained next.

Sequential File Processing

Records in **sequential files** are stored in numeric or alphabetical order according to the record key (e.g., customer numbers from 00001 to 99999). The sequence of the records in the file can be changed by sorting the file according to a new key (e.g., by customer name rather than customer number). To access a sequential file record, the system starts at the beginning of the file and reads each record until the desired record is located. Because the search process is so inefficient, it is impractical for applications that require immediate access to records.

In **sequential file processing** the master and transaction files are processed in the same predetermined order. For example, in the processing of sales transactions to update the accounts receivable master file, the files would usually be processed in customer account number order. To illustrate the sequential updating process, consider the example shown in Table 2.3. This table presents a master file, a transaction file, and an updated master file. The only fields shown are the identifier (customer account number) and the balance and transaction amounts. A positive transaction amount indicates a sale, and a negative one indicates a payment on account. For ease in reading, each step in the update process is numbered.

FILES BEFORE UPDATE				
MASTER FILE			**TRANSACTION FILE**	
Account #	Balance		Account #	Amount
101	1000		101	+ 700
102	600		101	− 1000
104	1900		103	+ 500
			104	+ 1600

UPDATE PROCESS					
		MASTER FILE		**TRANSACTION FILE**	
Step	Action	Acct #	Balance	Acct #	Balance
1	Read master file record	101	1000		
2	Read transaction file record			101	700
3	Match & update	101	1700		
4	Read transaction file record			101	-1000
5	Match & update	101	700		
6	Read transaction file record			103	500
7	No match; write 101 to new master file	—	—		
8	Read master file record	102	600		
9	No match; write 102 to new master file	—			
10	Read master file record	104	1900		
11	No match; write 103 to error file	—			
12	Read transaction file record			104	1600
13	Match & update	104	3500		

FILES AFTER UPDATE				
MASTER FILE			**ERROR FILE**	
Account #	Balance		Account #	Amount
101	700		103	500
102	600			
104	3500			

Table 2.3
Sequential file updating example

During sequential file processing the computer reads a master (step 1) and transaction record (step 2). Since the account numbers match, the master file record is updated (step 3); the balance for customer 101 is now $1700. Since a master record may have more than one update, a new transaction record is read (step 4). The account numbers are again compared; since they match, customer 101's master file record is updated again (step 5) and the balance is now $700. A new transaction record is read (step 6). Since the account number of the master file record is smaller than that of the transaction record, there are no further updates for the master file record, and the master file record is written back out to the master file (step 7). A new master file record is read (step 8). The match (step 9) shows that there is no update to master file record 102, so it is written to the new master file. Another master file record is read (step 10). A match (step 11) shows that the transaction record is now smaller than the master record. Thus either an error has occurred (record 103 has been lost from the master file), or transaction record 103 is an addition to the master file. Assuming the former, record 103 is written to a special error file. A new transaction record is read (step 12), and customer 104's master record is updated (step 13). The system would continue to alternate the reading of the master and transaction files as needed until the records in the master file had all been updated.

Sequential file organization is a simple, fast, and efficient method of file organization when a large volume and a reasonably high percentage of records are processed periodically in a file that does not need frequent updates. In addition, it is very efficient for batch processing operations. For example, a university that pays all employees monthly could easily process the file sequentially.

Direct-Access File Processing

In direct-access processing, transactions can be processed as they occur. Thus the master file records and the transaction data can be in any order. When a transaction occurs, the computer system uses an identifier in the transaction data (such as account number) to search the master file for the desired record. When found, it is retrieved into computer memory, updated, and written back out on the master file.

If files are constantly accessed or queried, need frequent updates, or must be up to date at all times, direct-access processing is appropriate. For example, airline reservation systems must constantly be up to date, so they are updated using direct-access processing. Direct-access methods must be used when it is not practical or possible to anticipate the sequence in which records will be processed or queried.

A program flowchart illustrating a generalized, direct-access file update appears in Fig. 2.8. When users of the system wish to update a record, they notify the system (step 1) of their intentions and the process begins. The system then prompts the user to enter the transaction data (step 2), and the user enters the requested data (step 3). When the requested data has been entered, the system will take the record identifier from the transaction data and use it to search the computer files for the corresponding master record (step 4). If the record cannot be found (step 5), the user is sent an error message (step 6) informing him or her of the error and requesting the user to reenter the data or abort the update. The user is able to immediately correct the error and reenter the data or abort the update until the transaction can be corrected.

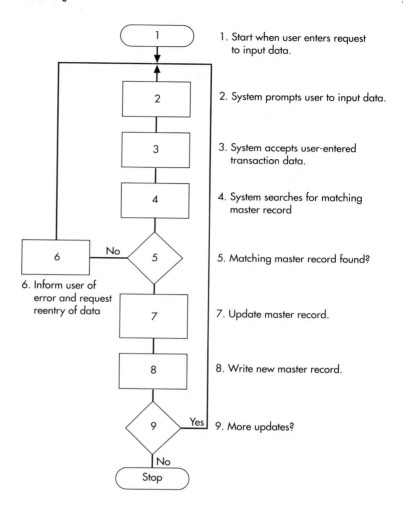

1. Start when user enters request to input data.

2. System prompts user to input data.

3. System accepts user-entered transaction data.

4. System searches for matching master record

5. Matching master record found?

6. Inform user of error and request reentry of data

7. Update master record.

8. Write new master record.

9. More updates?

Figure 2.8
Generalized direct-access file processing program flowchart

If the master file record is found (step 5), the data from the transaction is used to update the record (step 7). The updated record is then written back out (step 8) to its original physical location on the direct-access storage medium. Since the "new" (updated) record is written over the "old" record, the old record is lost unless it is first written to a separate file. The system then queries the user to find out whether there are any more updates (step 9). If there are, then the program returns to step 2, and the system requests that new transaction data be entered. If there are no more updates, file processing is terminated.

A major concern in implementing the direct-access approach is determining where to store records and how to find and retrieve them after they are stored. This search process (in step 4) is more complicated than it appears on the surface. Several different methods of record storage and access are used to achieve direct-access capabilities. Three of these methods, randomizing, indexed file, and multi-attribute search file organization, are now briefly discussed.

Randomizing.   Randomizing uses an algorithm, or mathematical formula, to convert a record key into a storage address. The record is stored at that address, and the same randomizing procedure is performed on the key when the record is to be retrieved.

Indexed File Organization.   A second way to access records directly is to have the computer create a separate file called an index file. The **index file** contains the record key and the location (physical address) where the record is stored. An index file is used the same way a card catalog in a library is used. To find a book in the library, you go to the card catalog, determine the approximate physical location of the book, proceed to the shelf that holds the book, and search that shelf for the book. In a similar fashion, an index file can be used to find a record in a data file. The user requests a specific record by specifying its key, the key is looked up in the index, and the computer uses the address obtained from the index file to find and retrieve the desired record.

Indexed-Sequential-Access Method (ISAM).   The most popular indexing approach is the **indexed-sequential-access method (ISAM)**. With this approach records are stored in sequential order by their primary key on a direct-access storage device. Because records are stored sequentially, the file can be used like any other sequential file. However, an index file is also created and used with the file. This means that the file can also be accessed randomly. In other words, an ISAM file has the advantages of both sequential and direct file organization. Either file processing method can be chosen, depending on the specific business needs.

The ISAM approach does have drawbacks. It requires more storage space, because of the index. In addition, creating, storing, and maintaining the indexes can be costly. Finally, large quantities of new records cannot be added easily to the file. As an aid in solving the problem of additions and deletions, the file can be reorganized periodically.

Figure 2.9 is an example of an indexed-sequential file. In this example 25 customer records numbered from 1478 to 1502 are stored in blocks of 5 in five storage addresses numbered from 4061 to 4065. The index contains five entries, one for each address. Each index entry contains the key of the last customer record in the block and the address of that block.

Multiattribute Search File Organization.   The three file organizations previously described allow the file to be accessed by the primary key, but they do not facilitate the access of data records based on one or more secondary keys. When file access by secondary keys is desired, a multiattribute search file organization is used. Two methods are discussed here: linked lists and inverted lists (also called inverted files).

In a **linked list**, each data record has a **pointer** field containing the address of the next record in the list. Thus all related records are linked

Index	
Key	Address
1482	4061
1487	4062
1492	4063
1497	4064
1502	4065

Data Storage Area

Address No. 4061	Customer No. 1478	Customer No. 1479	Customer No. 1480	Customer No. 1481	Customer No. 1482
Address No. 4062	Customer No. 1483	Customer No. 1484	Customer No. 1485	Customer No. 1486	Customer No. 1487
Address No. 4063	Customer No. 1488	Customer No. 1489	Customer No. 1490	Customer No. 1491	Customer No. 1492
Address No. 4064	Customer No. 1493	Customer No. 1494	Customer No. 1495	Customer No. 1496	Customer No. 1497
Address No. 4065	Customer No. 1498	Customer No. 1499	Customer No. 1500	Customer No. 1501	Customer No. 1502

Figure 2.9
An Indexed-sequential file

together by pointers. A group of records "connected" by pointers is referred to as a list or a chain. Table 2.4 illustrates the use of embedded pointers to chain together parts records having the same secondary keys. The links in each chain are pointers contained in the fields labeled "Next S" and "Next PL." Each of these fields "points to" the storage address of the next record having the same value for supplier and product line, respectively. For example, the chain for all parts supplied by ABC Company contains the records at machine addresses 11, 16, 17, 21, and 30.

Whereas linked lists use pointers embedded within the records, **inverted lists** use pointers stored in an index. An **inverted file** is one in which inverted lists are maintained for some of the attributes. Table 2.5 shows inverted lists for the secondary keys "supplier" and "product line," created from the sample data records in Table 2.4. There is one list for each value of each attribute, and each list contains the machine addresses of all records having that value. Using these inverted lists, any or all records containing a particular supplier or product line can be easily and quickly accessed.

Table 2.4
Parts records chained on
two secondary keys using
embedded pointers

Address	Part #	Supplier	Next S	Product Line	Next PL
11	125	ABC Co.	16	Widget	17
12	164	XYZ Inc.	14	Doodad	16
13	189	GHI Corp.	18	Clavet	15
14	205	XYZ Inc.	24	Lodix	18
15	271	RST Mfg.	19	Clavet	22
16	293	ABC Co.	17	Doodad	20
17	316	ABC Co.	21	Widget	23
18	348	GHI Corp.	20	Lodix	19
19	377	RST Mfg.	22	Lodix	21
20	383	GHI Corp.	23	Doodad	24
21	451	ABC Co.	30	Lodix	25
22	465	RST Mfg.	25	Clavet	27
23	498	GHI Corp.	26	Widget	*
24	521	XYZ Inc.	28	Doodad	26
25	572	RST Mfg.	*	Lodix	28
26	586	GHI Corp.	27	Doodad	29
27	603	GHI Corp.	29	Clavet	*
28	647	XYZ Inc.	*	Lodix	30
29	653	GHI Corp.	*	Doodad	*
30	719	ABC Co.	*	Lodix	*

* End of chain.

As mentioned earlier, transactions can be processed using either a sequential file organization or a direct-access organization. In addition, transactions can be processed by grouping them into batches or by processing them as they occur. Discussions of both batch and on-line processing follow.

Batch Processing

Processing similar transactions in groups, or batches, is referred to as **batch processing**. This processing usually takes place at given time intervals (such as daily or weekly) or whenever a manageable number (e.g., 50 or 100) of source documents have been gathered. It is most appropriate for processing common transactions that occur in large numbers, such as payroll and accounts payable. Batched transactions can be processed sequentially or with direct-access file processing techniques. Batch processing is illustrated in Fig. 2.10.

Table 2.5
Inverted lists for the
secondary keys of Table 2.4

Supplier	Addresses	Product Line	Addresses
ABC Company	11, 16, 17, 21, 30	Clavet	13, 15, 22, 27
GHI Corporation	13, 18, 20, 23, 26, 27, 29	Doodad	12, 16, 20, 24, 26, 29
RST Manufacturing	15, 19, 22, 25	Lodix	14, 18, 19, 21, 25, 28, 30
XYZ Inc.	12, 14, 24, 28	Widget	11, 17, 23

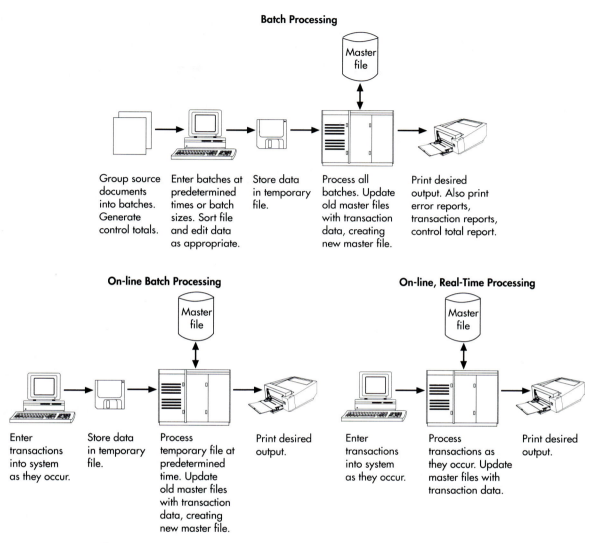

Figure 2.10
Batch and on-line processing

One way of assembling transactions for batch processing is called **remote batch processing**. This approach involves accumulating transaction records for batch processing at locations geographically separated from the central processing site. Usually, such records are recorded on a machine-readable medium and transmitted to the central processing site electronically.

In batch processing the inputs to the file maintenance process include the old master file and the transactions. Before the transactions are entered into the system, several things may need to be done first: transcribing source documents onto magnetic medium, sorting the transaction file into the same order as the master file, editing the transaction file for errors and incomplete data, and generating **control** totals for each batch. Examples of control totals are the total number of transactions and the total dollar amount of updates. These totals are calculated during subsequent processing steps and compared to the original totals to ensure that all data is processed.

Batch processing output includes a new master file and any reports desired by system users. The reports needed by external and internal users to fulfill their responsibilities are discussed later in the chapter. However, we note at this point that several reports that help control the update process are usually produced as a result of data processing. For instance, an exception report lists any errors detected by the system during processing, like an unmatched transaction record. A transaction report lists each transaction that was processed and summary totals.

On-Line Processing

When individual transactions are captured on equipment (such as on-line terminals or microcomputers) that is connected to the computer—as opposed to capturing it on source documents—the procedure is referred to as **on-line processing**. On-line processing can take one of two forms: on-line batch or on-line, real-time. Both are illustrated in Fig. 2.10.

In on-line batch processing data is entered directly into the computer system, but it is stored electronically and processed at a later date. For example, a bank or a credit union may capture all its data using terminals connected to the computer, but it may not process all those transactions until it has closed for the day.

An **on-line, real-time processing** system is able to process data immediately after it is captured and provide updated information to the user on a timely basis. On-line, real-time processing usually entails one of two forms of processing: on-line updating and inquiry processing. **On-line updating** is a form of data maintenance in which individual transactions are processed as they occur to update a master file. In on-line updating each individual transaction is edited for accuracy and completeness as it is entered and immediately processed.

In **inquiry processing** the computer system receives queries from users about information in the data files. The system locates the desired information and displays it in the format specified by the user. Examples of on-line, real-time systems are airline reservation systems and the New York stock exchange quotation system.

Batch Versus On-Line

Batching transactions for input rather than keying them in on-line offers the advantages of economies of scale and increased productivity. Employees whose only job is data entry are more productive than those who only intermittently enter data as transactions occur. However, on-line entry is more timely, since transactions are captured as they occur. It is also more accurate, because the system can refuse transactions that are not complete or that contain errors. In addition, it eliminates the need for data preparation activities such as transcribing and sorting. Source data automation is a more efficient means of data entry than keying, because keying data is time-consuming, error-prone, and expensive. As a result, whenever technically and economically feasible, companies are trying to capture and input data using source data automation.

The advantage of on-line updating of master files is that all records are always up to date. As a result, any user can obtain up-to-date information in response to a query. This capability is very useful in dealing with customers, in monitoring production processes, and in decision making. With batch processing, files are up to date only immediately after the processing of a batch of transactions, which may be only once a day.

INFORMATION OUTPUT

The final step in the data processing cycle is making information available to the user. Because there are so many types of users and so many and varied uses of information, there are literally thousands of different types of reports. It would be virtually impossible to discuss all the different types of reports here. Instead, information output is discussed in terms of the format of the output, the purpose of the output, and the user's responsibilities.

Forms of information output

Information output is usually presented in one of three forms: a document, a report, or a response to a query. Documents, such as checks, invoices, and purchase orders, may be transmitted to external parties, or they may be used internally in other data processing activities. Documents utilized as transaction records are an essential form of information system output. Examples include purchase orders, customer statements, and employee paychecks. Documents such as these that are generated as a result of transaction processing activities are sometimes called operational documents in order to distinguish them from the source documents that arise at the beginning of transaction processing.

Reports of all kinds are prepared for both external and internal users. Reports are often produced on a regular basis (daily, weekly, or monthly). Examples include quarterly and yearly financial statements, weekly or monthly inventory stock status reports, weekly or monthly sales analyses, and a monthly aged accounts receivable trial balance. Reports are also produced on an exception basis to call attention to unusual conditions. For example, a system could be programmed to produce a report when product defects in a production process exceed a certain percentage. Finally, reports can be produced on demand, when needed. An example is an employee performance report.

Reports are used by employees to control the operational activities of the business organization and by managers to make decisions and design strategies for the business. External users need reports for a wide variety of reasons, such as to evaluate the company's profitability and to judge creditworthiness. Report design considerations are discussed further in Chapter 10.

Increasingly, the information needs of managers and accountants cannot be met by documents or periodic formal reports. Instead, management and accountants need quick answers to their questions. In addition, problems constantly arise that need rapid action and resolution. To answer these questions and to resolve these problems, users make queries to the system through personal computers or terminals tied to the system. The information needed is retrieved, displayed on the monitor, and analyzed as needed by the software in use. When reports and answers to queries are printed on a monitor, they are referred to as ''soft copy'' (as opposed to ''hard copy'' or paper) reports.

Purpose of the Information

Reports are prepared for both external and internal users. Reports such as financial statements are produced for external users to meet stewardship requirements. Reports such as income tax returns and 10-K filings with the Securities and Exchange Commission are produced to comply with legal requirements.

Reports are also produced for internal users, those who manage a company. All organizations are faced with limited resources and must make the best use possible of these scarce resources and plan for their future. Reports such as budgets, sales forecasts, and projected cash flow statements help them in this planning process. A wide variety of reports projecting the revenues and estimating the costs of new products, capital acquisitions, or investment projects are also useful for planning purposes.

Managers must also operate the company on a day-to-day basis. To do so effectively, they need information on past events and trends, current operations, and what will be expected of them in the future. They need information that will allow them to make and implement decisions and to complete their assignments. Reports such as inventory stock status reports, accounts receivable aging, production and delivery schedules, and open purchase orders help corporate personnel accomplish these tasks.

Internal users must also control the organization they are managing. The organization must constantly monitor its progress so that problems that arise can be corrected as soon as possible. Often, monitoring is done by devising standard or expected performances and then comparing them with actual performance. These differences are called *variances*. When the variances get too far out of line, management takes corrective action to bring them back within an acceptable range. Examples of control reports include those that compare standard and actual production error rates, materials use, equipment use, labor efficiency, profitability, and sales.

CODING TECHNIQUES

Coding techniques are an essential aspect of the design, processing, and control of business records. Virtually all data processing systems, whether manual or automated, use codes. Coding is the systematic assignment of numbers or letters to items to classify and organize them. Codes are essential to such data processing activities as sorting, summarizing, storage, reporting, and retrieval. This section describes and illustrates some of the codes used in an accounting information system.

Basic Coding Concepts There are two different types of codes: alphanumeric and numeric. Alphabetic codes have two primary advantages over numeric codes. First, an alphabetic code can be mnemonic, or suggestive of the name of the item it represents. For example, an airline can use DFW to represent the Dallas–Fort Worth airport. Second, a single position in an alphabetic code can represent up to 26 different possible categories, as opposed to only 10 in a numeric code.

Many different types of codes are used in business and accounting applications. With **sequence codes** items are numbered consecutively, to ensure that there will be no gaps in the sequence. This enables the user to account for all the items, because any missing items will cause a gap in the numerical sequence. Examples of sequence codes include the prenumbering of checks, invoices, and purchase orders.

With a **block code** blocks of numbers within a numerical sequence are reserved for categories having meaning to the user. Consider a manufacturer of home appliances with four basic product lines, each with a variety of models. For example, S&S could reserve a specific range of code numbers for each major product category, as shown below.

Product Code	Product Type
1000000–1999999	Electric range
2000000–2999999	Refrigerator
3000000–3999999	Washer
4000000–4999999	Dryer

With this scheme a user familiar with the code can readily identify the type and model of item by code number alone. Other examples include ledger account numbers (blocked by account type), employee numbers (blocked by department), and customer numbers (blocked by region).

Group codes are often used in conjunction with the block code. In group codes two or more subgroups of digits are used to code the item. If S&S uses a seven-digit product code number, for example, the group coding technique might be applied as follows.

Digit Position	Meaning
1–2	Product line, size, style
3	Color
4–5	Year of manufacture
6–7	Optional features

There are four subcodes within the product code, each conveying a different meaning. This type of code allows one to sort, summarize, and retrieve information by using one or more of the subcodes. This technique is often applied to general ledger account numbers.

The Chart of Accounts

The chart of accounts is a coded listing of all balance sheet and income statement accounts used by a business. Since the codes are account numbers, they allow transaction data to be coded, classified, and entered into the proper accounts. Coding techniques are frequently used in the development of a chart of accounts. Most charts of accounts use numeric codes with a combination of group coding and block coding techniques. An example of a group coding scheme for account numbers follows.

Digit Position	Classification
1–2	Division, plant, or office
3–4	Department
5–7	Major account

The first two digits indicate the division, plant, or office location to which the transaction relates, and the second two digits indicate the specific department within that division, plant, or office. The major account code identifies broad account classifications, such as cash or selling expenses.

Block coding is usually applied to the major account codes and often to the divisional and departmental codes as well. One possible block coding scheme for a chart of accounts follows.

Major Account Code	Major Account Type
100–199	Current Assets
200–299	Noncurrent Assets
300–399	Liabilities
400–499	Capital
500–599	Revenue
600–699	Cost of Goods Sold
700–799	Selling Expenses
800–899	General & Administrative Expenses
900–999	Nonoperating Income & Expenses

A simplified chart of balance sheet accounts consistent with this block coding scheme appears in Table 2.6. A corresponding chart of income statement accounts appears in Table 2.7. These charts are simplified in that many of the accounts represent general categories that can include a number of more detailed accounts. For example, the cash account could include cash on hand, petty cash funds, demand deposits, savings accounts, and certificates of deposit. The degree of detail required will vary with the size of the organization and its needs. The level of detail shown in the tables might be adequate for a very small company, whereas a large company might require hundreds of separate accounts.

Account Code	Account Name	Account Code	Account Name
100–199	Current Assets	300–399	Liabilities
100	Cash	300	Accounts Payable
110	Marketable Securities	310	Accrued Wages & Salaries
120	Accounts Receivable	320	Accrued Taxes
125	Allowance for Doubtful Accounts	330	Accrued Interest
130	Notes Receivable	340	Dividends Payable
140	Inventory—Raw Materials	350	Notes Payable
150	Inventory—Work in Process	360	Bonds Payable
160	Inventory—Finished Goods	370	Other Liabilities
170	Prepaid Expenses		
200–299	Noncurrent Assets	400–499	Capital Accounts
200	Land	400	Capital Stock
210	Buildings	410	Preferred Stock
215	Allowance for Depreciation—Buildings	420	Paid-in Surplus
220	Equipment	430	Retained Earnings
225	Allowance for Depreciation—Equipment		
230	Office Fixtures		
235	Allowance for Depreciation—Office Fixtures		
240	Long-Term Investments		
250	Intangible Assets		
260	Other Assets		

Table 2.6
Simplified balance sheet
chart of accounts

The chart of accounts is an extremely useful tool for processing accounting data in organizations of all types and sizes. It facilitates the recording and posting of transactions, and it simplifies the preparation of financial statements and a variety of other summary reports. Even a very small single-location business like S&S can obtain substantial benefits from the use of a chart of accounts.

Coding Design Considerations

The most obvious consideration in the design of a coding system is that the codes chosen be consistent with their intended use. Thus the code designer must determine the types of system outputs desired by users prior to selecting the code. For example, the existence of a responsibility accounting system certainly requires that accounting transactions be coded by organizational unit. Similarly, if sales analyses by salesperson are important to the evaluation of sales performance, then sales transactions should include the salesperson code.

Another consideration in code design is that the designer should allow sufficient latitude in the code for growth in the number of items to be coded. For example, a three-digit employee code is inadequate for an organization with 950 employees. In addition, the coding system should be as simple as possible, in order to minimize costs, facilitate memorization and interpretation of coding categories, and ensure employee acceptance. Also, the coding systems selected by different

Account Code	Account Name	Account Code	Account Name
500–599	Operating Revenues	700–799	Selling Expenses
500	Sales Revenue	700	Sales Commissions
510	Sales Discounts	710	Advertising
520	Sales Returns & Allowances	720	Entertainment
530	Miscellaneous Revenue	730	Delivery
		740	Warrantee
		750	Other Selling Expenses
600–699	Cost of Goods Sold		
600	Cost of Goods Sold		
610	Direct Materials	800–899	General & Administrative Expenses
620	Direct Labor	800	Payroll Control
630	Factory Overhead Control	810	Wages & Salaries
631	Indirect Labor	820	Legal & Consulting
632	Supplies & Small Tools	830	Travel
633	Supervision	840	Depreciation—Office Fixtures
634	Depreciation—Plant	850	Stationery & Supplies
635	Depreciation—Equipment	860	Postage
636	Heat, Light, & Power	870	Communications
637	Taxes & Insurance	880	Interest
640	Applied Factory Overhead	890	Taxes
		895	Other Administrative

Table 2.7
Simplified income statement
chart of accounts

areas of an organization should be consistent in order to facilitate subsequent integration of data processing activities. Finally, the coding system must be consistent with a company's organizational structure—that is, the number of product lines, for example, and the number of divisions, departments, or plants.

Organizational Codes and Responsibility Accounting

In many companies it is generally very useful for the chart of accounts to incorporate subcodes indicating not only the division or branch responsible for the transaction but also the department within that division or branch. In the group coding scheme for accounts shown earlier, for instance, the first two digits represent the division, and the third and fourth digits represent the department. The advantage of these codes is quite simple: They greatly facilitate the accumulation, analysis, summarization, and reporting of accounting information according to responsibilities. In other words, codes are an essential part of a responsibility accounting system.

Responsibility accounting involves reporting financial results on the basis of managerial responsibilities within an organization. There are three major factors in a responsibility accounting system: initial assignment of managerial responsibilities; translation of these responsibilities into a formal set of goals expressed in financial terms; and reports showing how actual performance compares with the established goals. Responsibility accounting—particularly as it relates to the second and third factors—is one of the more vital functions of the accounting information system. The latter two functions of responsibility accounting are now discussed.

When a formal statement of the goals or plans of an organization is expressed in financial terms, it is called a **budget**. The structure of the budget corresponds to the organization structure; that is, the overall budget of the business is made up of a hierarchy of smaller budgets, each representing the financial plan of a division, department, or other unit of the organization. The most common budget in organizations is an operating budget, which is an estimate of an organization's revenues and expenses for normal operations for a given time period, usually a month or a year.

Whereas the budget is the primary vehicle of financial planning in a business organization, the **performance report** is the primary vehicle of financial control. A performance report is a summary of budgeted revenues, costs, and expenses; the corresponding actual dollar amounts; and the variances, which are the differences between budgeted and actual dollar amounts for each item. The budget and the financial performance report, which are the cornerstones of a responsibility accounting system, are vital elements of management control within a business organization.

In general, all costs and expenses incurred by an organization should be charged to an account coded to indicate the department for which the cost or expense is controllable. All sales should be coded to reflect the department that generated the sale. Asset accounts such as inventories or fixed assets may be coded to indicate the department having custodial responsibility for the asset. Most other accounts are general or control accounts, such as cash, accounts payable, or payroll, and need not contain any specific departmental code.

Organizational codes facilitate several data processing activities related to responsibility accounting. For example, cost and expense data can be sorted by department code and summarized for each department to generate reports of controllable costs for all departments. Budgeted data can be similarly coded and processed to facilitate the preparation of performance reports indicating budget variances. The codes perform a filtration function, separating out uncontrollable costs for each department so that they are not included in the performance summary. The organizational codes also serve as a partial index for storing cost and expense data. This simplifies the retrieval of data for purposes of comparing and analyzing past trends within and among departments.

Because the performance report is essentially an extension of the budget, the performance reporting system within a business organization will, like the budgeting system, possess a hierarchical structure. This point is illustrated in Fig. 2.11, which shows performance reports for managers at four different organizational levels. Note that each report shows actual costs and variances (the amount budgeted is not

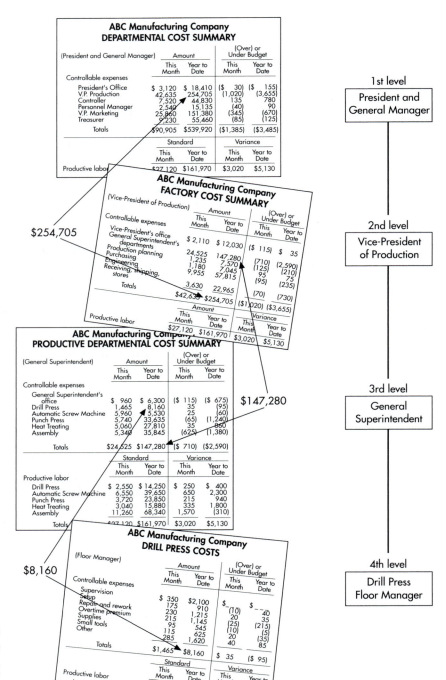

Figure 2.11
Hierarchy of performance reports
(*Source:* Adapted with some
revisions from John A. Higgins,
"Responsibility Accounting,"
Arthur Andersen Chronicle 12 (2)
(April 1952): 1–17.)

shown) for the current month and the year to date, but only for those items that are controllable at that level. The hierarchical nature of performance reporting is evident in the information reported: The total cost of each department below the top level becomes a single line item on the performance report of the manager at the next higher level. Thus as you move up the organizational ladder from the level of an individual department to the level of the organization as a whole, each report becomes less detailed and more summarized. The reports at the lower levels of an organization are sometimes referred to as detailed reports; the reports at the upper levels of management are referred to as summary reports.

Another important concept closely related to responsibility accounting is the principle of **management by exception**. If the performance report shows actual costs at less than, or only slightly greater than, the budgeted figures, a manager can assume that the item is under control. On the other hand, if actual costs are significantly higher than budgeted costs, management is made aware of an item of cost that may be out of control. The exception triggers a study of the situation and, if needed, action to correct the problem.

CASE CONCLUSION: PROCESSING TRANSACTIONS AT S&S INC.

The immediate need at S&S is to develop an accounting system that can function until a computer can be purchased. To do so, Ashton identified the transactions that the company will face. He considered each of S&S's five business cycles, and he identified the activities that S&S will engage in and the entries needed to record those events. Then Ashton designed source documents to capture the transaction data for each activity. He built controls into the system to ensure that the data is accurate and complete and that transactions are processed as desired. Specialized journals were prepared to record similar transactions, and a general journal was set up to handle the others. A general ledger as well as subsidiary ledgers were also set up. A chart of accounts was developed, and a coding scheme was devised to allow S&S to post its transactions.

However, Ashton realized that the manual system he designed will not be adequate in the long run. So he began to work on convincing Scott and Susan to automate the system as soon as possible. And in the meantime he must plan for the computerized system. He realized that one decision that S&S must make is how to enter and process transaction data. After careful consideration he came up with several recommendations. He believes that critical data such as sales must be captured in electronic form, using source data automation. This technique will allow S&S to process the sales as they occur and always keep inventory files up to date. Other data such as inventory receipts, accounts payable, accounts receivable collections, and purchasing can

be keyed into the computer as they occur for either immediate processing or nightly batch processing. He will wait to decide between on-line
batch processing and immediate processing until S&S selects software
and designs the system for each cycle. Other data files, such as payroll,
can be handled with time cards as the source document and can be
processed sequentially in batch mode.

Ashton knows that he wants to store as much of the company's data
on the computer-based system as possible and in such a way that it is
easily accessible. Therefore, he plans to investigate the data base
packages on the market. He must also find accounting software that
will process all of S&S's transactions. In addition, the software must
allow S&S to produce the output Ashton will need to handle his
accounting duties as well as the information that Scott and Susan will
need to manage the company. Ashton is not yet sure just what
computer equipment and programs he will need, but he is sure that
with a little more study (see Chapters 4–7) he will be able to handle this
aspect of the system. ■

SUMMARY

Transaction processing encompasses several steps. Transaction data is
collected, edited for accuracy and completeness, and entered into
specialized journals and ledgers. It is then entered into the general
journal and ledger. From these summary documents financial statements are prepared.

The data processing cycle in computer-based systems has four
stages: data input, data maintenance, data processing, and information
output. Data can be entered into the system by using batch or on-line
entry. Data is processed in batch or on-line processing mode. Data can
be processed sequentially or randomly as transactions occur.

In computer-based systems data is stored in fields, records, files,
and data bases. Two of the most important files are the transaction file
and the master file. A key task in any accounting system is file maintenance, the updating of accounting data to reflect recent transaction
activity. Many organizations use a file-oriented approach to data storage. However, a more advantageous approach to data storage is a data
base system. It provides easy access to data and allows users much
more freedom in terms of data retrieval and analysis.

Information is presented in documents, reports, and inquiry responses. Information is prepared to help users plan, control, and
operate a system. Effective reporting and utilization of information by
persons in an organization is critical. A central part of this process is a
responsibility accounting system, which reports financial results associated with the responsibilities assigned to managers and employees
within the organization.

Coding of records and files is a central feature of accounting information systems. All records have a primary key, which serves as a
unique record identifier. They may have secondary keys, which facili-

tate processing and retrieval. The chart of accounts is an example of a business coding system. The design of coding systems that facilitate efficient processing and reporting of business data is an important skill for information systems specialists.

KEY TERMS

Define the following terms:

transaction	master file	linked list
transaction processing	transaction file	pointer
general journal	table file	chain
specialized journal	history file	inverted lists
ledger	backup file	inverted file
general ledger	suspense file	batch processing
subsidiary ledger	report file	remote batch processing
control account	data maintenance	control totals
journal voucher	file maintenance	on-line processing
audit trail	file organization	on-line, real-time processing
trial balance	file access	on-line updating
data processing cycle	logical file organization	inquiry processing
source document	sequential access	documents
turnaround document	direct access	reports
source data automation	key	queries
entity	primary key	coding
attributes	secondary key	sequence codes
data value	sequential files	block code
character	sequential file processing	group codes
fields	direct-access processing	chart of accounts
record	randomizing	responsibility accounting
file	index file	budget
data bases	indexed–sequential-access	performance report
file-oriented approach	method (ISAM)	management by exception
data base approach		

DISCUSSION QUESTIONS

2.1 The following data items comprise an accounts receivable record that is to be incorporated into a data base system.

Customer account number (primary key)
Customer name
Customer address
Location code
Credit rating code
Credit limit
Beginning account balance
Current transactions
Transaction type
Document number
Transaction date
Amount
Current balance

Identify the data items within this record that are good candidates for secondary keys. Explain each of your choices.

2.2 Identify some of the master files and file processing procedures you would be likely to encounter in the following organizations.

a. A university
b. A hospital
c. A bank
d. An insurance company
e. A stockbrokerage
f. An advertising agency

Select one master file and discuss the type of coding system that would be appropriate for records in that file.

2.3 In theory, a business organization should not use any procedure or technique unless its benefits exceed its costs. Discuss the benefits and costs of a chart of accounts.

2.4 Computer data processing is based on the logical organization of data into files, records, and fields. State whether each of the following is a file, a record, or a field.

a. All information on one customer
b. Accounts receivable subsidiary ledger
c. Employee number
d. Amount owed a particular vendor
e. General ledger
f. Accounts payable subsidiary ledger
g. Information on a particular vendor
h. The name of one vendor
i. All information on one inventory item

2.5 For each of the following data processing applications, indicate whether (a) batch processing or (b) on-line, real-time processing would be the more appropriate mode of processing. Explain your answers.

a. Weekly processing of employee time cards to prepare paychecks
b. Processing of customer reservation requests by a motel chain
c. Processing of credit checks by a retail credit bureau
d. Preparation of monthly customer bills by a utility company
e. Processing of customer transactions occurring at teller windows by a bank

f. Scheduling of material and labor activity in an automated factory
g. Preparation of monthly financial statements
h. Processing of cash receipts on account from customers
i. Reordering of merchandise inventory in a high-volume retail store

2.6 The Wong-Lee Restaurant uses customer checks with prenumbered sequence codes. A waitress prepares the customer's check, which the customer then presents to the cashier. Waitresses are told not to destroy any checks; if a mistake is made, the waitress is to void the check and prepare another. All voided checks are given to the manager daily. Explain the role of sequence codes in controlling cash receipts in this situation.

2.7 Suppose you were designing a computer-based transaction processing system and needed to identify all the data, information, and other items that would make up the system. Where would you begin? Which stage of the data processing cycle would you concentrate on? Data input, data processing, data storage, or information output? Why?

2.8 The increased reliance by management upon factual data has resulted in the development and implementation of coding systems. In a computerized environment these coding systems are an essential tool in accumulating and organizing the basic information used in day-to-day operations. Outline the characteristics of a well-designed code structure. Identify two principal advantages of an alphabetic code structure over a numeric code structure: What role should the accounting department play in the design of a coding system? (SMAC Examination, adapted)

2.9 A large resort hotel recently computerized its front-desk system. During the design stage the controller recommended to the software designer that the new system should include a "management by exception" reporting system. As a result, the software house included the report presented in Table 2.8 in the front-desk software package. What is meant by a "management by exception" reporting system? How would the report shown in Table 2.8 be used and by whom? (SMAC Examination, adapted)

2.10 Responsibility accounting is widely used by many companies of all sizes and in almost all industries. Exactly what is responsibility accounting?

Table 2.8
Resort hotel: Room rate versus
standard rate report

Room #	Guest's Name	Room Type	Number of Guests		Room Rate		Comments
			Adults	Child	Charged	Standard	
1701	J. J. Doe	Spec.	2	1	65.00	75.00	Corp rate
1723	Prime Minister	Suite	1	0	0	500.00	Complimentary
1602	John Smith	Stand	2	3	80.00	70.00	—

What are the advantages a company attains through the use of responsibility accounting? How is the use of responsibility accounting advantageous to the managers of a company? (CMA Examination, adapted)

PROBLEMS

2.1 As an accountant for Radiotronics Corporation, a manufacturer and distributor of radios, you have been asked to design a sales analysis code. Some facts relevant to this task follow.

■ The company has four major product lines: portable radios, cassette and CD players and radios, clock radios, and citizens band (CB) radios. The numbers of styles available in each product line are 12, 4, 10, and 5, respectively.

■ The company has divided its sales area (which covers most of the United States and part of Canada) into nine regions. Each region is divided into 6 to 12 districts, each of which is assigned to a salesperson.

■ The company sells to seven major categories of customers and has approximately 1500 separate customer accounts.

Required
Design a group coding system for assigning sales analysis codes to sales transactions. Indicate the meaning and usefulness of each digit position or group of digit positions within the code.

2.2 Forward Corporation is a progressive and fast-growing company. The company's Executive Committee consists of the president and the four vice-presidents who report to the president–marketing, manufacturing, finance, and systems. The company has ordered a new computer for processing its financial information. Because the computer acquisition required a substantial investment, the president wants to make certain that the computer is employed effectively. The new computer will enable Forward to revise its financial information system so that several departments will get more useful information. This new system should be helpful especially in marketing, because its personnel are distributed widely throughout the country.

The Marketing Department is organized into nine territories and 25 sales offices. The Vice-President of Marketing wants the monthly reports to reflect those items for which the department is responsible and can control. The Marketing Department also wants information that identifies the most profitable products; this information is used to establish a discount policy that will enable the company to meet competition effectively. Monthly reports showing performance by territory and sales office also would be useful.

The Vice-President of Finance has recommended that the accounting system be revised so that reports can be prepared on a contribution margin basis. Furthermore, only those cost items controlled by the respective departments should appear on their reports. The monthly report for the Manufacturing Department should compare actual production costs with a budget containing the standard costs for the actual volume of production. The Marketing Department should be provided with the standard variable manufacturing cost for each product so it can calculate the variable contribution margin of each product. The monthly reports to the Marketing Department should reflect the variable contribution approach; the reports should present the net contribution of the department calculated by deducting standard variable manufacturing costs and marketing expenses (both variable and fixed) from sales.

A portion of Forward Corporation's chart of accounts follows.

Account Number	Description
2000	Sales
2500	Cost of sales
3000	Manufacturing expenses
4000	Engineering expenses
5000	Marketing expenses
6000	Administrative expenses

The company wants to retain the basic structure of the chart of accounts to minimize the number of changes in the system. However, the numbering system will have to be expanded in order to provide the additional information that is desired.

Required

The coding structure now in effect must be modified to satisfy the needs of Forward Corporation's management. Using the marketing areas as the example, devise an account number coding system that will permit the preparation of the contribution reports for the Marketing Department. In the presentation of the account number coding system, include the following items.

a. Add additional accounts to the chart of accounts as needed.

b. Provide flexibility in the coding structure so that it would not have to be revised completely should Forward Corporation expand or restructure its sales area.

c. Explain and justify the coding structure presented.

(CMA Examination, adapted)

2.3 Universal Floor Covering is a manufacturer and distributor of carpet and vinyl floor coverings. The home office is located in Charlotte, North Carolina. Carpet mills are located in Dalton, Georgia, and Greenville, South Carolina; a floor covering manufacturing plant is in High Point, North Carolina. Total sales last year were just over $250 million.

The company manufactures over two hundred different varieties of carpet. The carpet is classified as being for commercial or residential purposes and is sold under five brand names with up to five lines under each brand. The lines indicate the different grades of quality; grades are measured by type of tuft and number of tufts per square inch. Each line of carpet can have up to 15 different color styles.

Just under two hundred varieties of vinyl floor covering are manufactured. The floor covering is also classified as being for commercial or residential use. There are four separate brand names (largely distinguished by the type of finish), up to eight different patterns for each brand, and up to eight color styles for each pattern.

Ten different grades of padding are manufactured. The padding is usually differentiated by intended use (commercial or residential) in addition to thickness and composition of materials.

Universal serves over two thousand regular wholesale customers. Retail showrooms are the primary customers. Many major corporations are direct buyers of Universal's products. Large construction companies have contracts with Universal to purchase carpet and floor covering at reduced rates for use in newly constructed homes and commercial buildings. In addition, Universal produces a line of residential carpet for a large national retail chain. Sales to these customers range from $10,000 to $1 million annually.

There is a company-owned retail outlet at each plant. The outlets carry overruns, seconds, and discontinued items. This is Universal's only retail sales function.

The company has divided the sales market into seven territories, with the majority of concentration on the East Coast. The market segments are New England, New York, Midatlantic, Carolinas, South, Midwest, and West. Each sales territory is divided into five to ten districts, with a salesperson assigned to each district.

The current accounting system has been adequate for monitoring the sales by product. However, there are limitations to the system because specific information is sometimes not available. A detailed analysis of operations is necessary for planning and control purposes and would be valuable for decision-making purposes. The accounting systems department has been asked to design a sales analysis code. The code should permit Universal to prepare a sales analysis that would reflect the characteristics of the company's business.

Required

a. Account coding systems are based upon various coding concepts. Briefly define and give an example of the following coding concepts.

1. Sequence coding
2. Block coding
3. Group coding

b. Identify and describe factors that must be considered before a coding system can be designed and implemented for an organization.

c. Develop a coding system for Universal Floor Covering that would assign sales analysis codes to sales transactions.

1. For each portion of the code, explain the meaning and purpose of the position.
2. For each portion of the code, identify and justify the number of digits required. (CMA Examination, adapted)

2.4 Ollie Mace has recently been appointed controller of a family-owned manufacturing enterprise. The firm, S. Dilley & Company, was founded by Mr. Dilley about 28 years ago, is 78% owned by Mr. Dilley, and has served the major automotive companies as a parts supplier. The firm's major operating divisions are Heat Treating, Extruding, Small-Parts Stamping, and Specialized Machining. Sales last year from the several divisions ranged from $150,000 to over $3 million. The divisions are physically and managerially independent except for Mr. Dilley's constant surveillance. The accounting system for each division has evolved according to the division's own needs and to the abilities of individual accountants or bookkeepers. Mr. Mace is the first controller in the firm's history to have responsibility for overall financial management. Mr. Dilley expects to retire within six years and has hired Mr. Mace to improve the firm's financial system.

Mr. Mace soon decides that he will need to design a new financial reporting system that will accomplish the following goals.

■ It should give managers uniform, timely, and accurate reports on business activity. Monthly divisional reports should be uniform and available by the tenth of the following month. Companywide financial reports also should be prepared by the tenth.

■ It should provide a basis for measuring return on investment by division. Divisional reports should show assets assigned to each division and revenue and expense measurement in each division.

■ It should generate meaningful budget data for planning and decision-making purposes. The accounting system should provide for the preparation of budgets that recognize managerial responsibility, controllability of costs, and major product groups.

■ It should allow for a uniform basis of evaluating performance and a quick access to underlying data. Cost center variances should be measured and reported for operating and nonoperating units, including headquarters. Also, questions about levels of specific cost factors or product costs should be answerable quickly.

A new chart of accounts, Mr. Mace thinks, is essential to getting started on other critical financial problems. The present account codes used by divisions are not standard.

Mr. Mace sees a need to divide asset accounts into six major categories, such as current assets and plant and equipment. Within each of these categories he sees a need for no more than 10 control accounts. From his observations to date, 100 subsidiary accounts are more than adequate for each control account.

No division now has more than five major product groups. Mr. Mace foresees a maximum number of six cost centers within any product group, including operating and nonoperating groups. He views general divisional costs as a non–revenue-producing product group. Altogether, Mr. Mace estimates that about 44 natural expense accounts plus about 12 specific variance accounts would be adequate.

Mr. Mace is planning to implement the new chart of accounts in an environment that at present includes manual records systems and one division that is using an EDP system. Mr. Mace expects that in the near future most accounting and reporting for all units will be automated. Therefore the chart of accounts should facilitate the processing of transactions manually or by machine. Efforts should be made, he believes, to restrict the length of the code for economy in processing and convenience in use.

Required

a. Design a chart of accounts coding system that will meet Mr. Mace's requirements. Your answer should begin with a digital layout of the coding system. You should explain the coding method you have chosen and the reason for the size of your code elements. Explain your code as it would apply to asset and expense accounts.

b. Use your chart of accounts coding system to illustrate the code needed for the following data.

1. In the Small-Parts Stamping Division $100 was spent on cleaning supplies by Foreman Bill Shaw in the polishing department of the Door Lever Group. Code the expense item using the code you developed.

2. A new motorized sweeper has been purchased for the Maintenance Department of the Extruding Division for $3450. Code this asset item using the code you developed. (CMA Examination, adapted)

2.5 The Argon County Hospital is located in the county seat. Argon County is a well-known summer resort area. The county population doubles during the vacation months (May–August), and hospital activity more than doubles during these months. The hospital is organized into several departments. Although it is a relatively small hospital, its pleasant surroundings have attracted a well-trained and competent medical staff.

An administrator was hired a year ago to improve the business activities of the hospital. Among the new ideas he has introduced is responsibility accounting. This program was announced along with quarterly cost reports supplied to department heads.

Previously, cost data were presented to department heads infrequently. Excerpts from the announcement and the report received by the laundry supervisor are presented below.

The hospital has adopted a responsibility accounting system. From now on you will receive quarterly reports comparing the costs of operating your department with budgeted costs. The reports will highlight the differences (variations) so you can zero in on the departure from budgeted costs. (This is called management by exception.) Responsibility accounting means that you are accountable for keeping the costs in your department within the budget. The variations from the budget will help you identify what costs are out of line, and the size of the variation will indicate which ones are the most important. Your first report accompanies this announcement.

The annual budget for 1973 was constructed by the new administrator. Quarterly budgets were computed as one-fourth of the annual budget. The administrator compiled the budget from analysis of the prior three years' costs. The analysis showed that all costs increased each year, with more rapid increases between the second and third year. He considered establishing the budget at an average of the prior three years' costs, hoping that the installation of the system would reduce costs to this level. However, in view of the rapidly increasing prices, he finally

Table 2.9 Argon County Hospital: Performance Report—Laundry Department July-September 1973	Budget	Actual	(Over) Under Budget	Percent (Over) Under Budget
Patient days	9,500	11,900	(2,400)	(25)
Pounds processed—laundry	125,000	156,000	(31,000)	(25)
Costs				
Laundry labor	$ 9,000	$12,500	$(3,500)	(39)
Supplies	1,100	1,875	(775)	(70)
Water, water heating, & softening	1,700	2,500	(800)	(47)
Maintenance	1,400	2,200	(800)	(57)
Supervisor's salary	3,150	3,750	(600)	(19)
Allocated administration costs	4,000	5,000	(1,000)	(25)
Equipment depreciation	1,200	1,250	(50)	(4)
	$21,550	$29,075	$(7,525)	(35)

Administrator's comments: Costs are significantly above budget for the quarter. Particular attention needs to be paid to labor, supplies, and maintenance.

chose 1972 costs less 3% for the 1973 budget. The activity level measured by patient days and pounds of laundry processed was set at 1972 volume, which was approximately equal to the volume of each of the past three years.

Required

a. Comment on the method used to construct the budget.

b. What information should be communicated by variations from budgets?

c. Does the report effectively communicate the level of efficiency of this department? Give reasons for your answer.

d. Explain the purposes of a responsibility accounting system.

(CMA Examination, adapted)

2.6 This problem involves tracing the operations performed on a hypothetical set of master and transaction records through the sequential updating process shown in Table 2.3. Assume that a new master file is created to replace the old master file and that any unmatched transaction records represent errors. Assume that the master file and the transaction file are composed of the following record numbers in the sequence given.

MASTER FILE	
Account #	Balance
011	1400
013	700
014	250
015	2950
016	1725
017	885
018	1150
019	2780
EOF (End of File)	

TRANSACTION FILE	
Account #	Balance
011	+ 570
012	+ 700
014	+ 1400
014	− 250
016	+ 275
018	− 350
EOF	

Required

a. Construct a table like Table 2.3 and show how the transactions would be processed. Alternate between reading master file records, reading transaction file records, updating master file records, and writing records to the new master file, as necessary. Number the steps as shown in Table 2.3. Continue until you have traced all records through the program.

b. Suppose that there was a transaction record with the account number 020 with a + 625 balance after record number 018 and in front of the end-of-file record. Beginning at the point at which this change would first make a difference, trace the records through the program to the finish, recording the actions in your table as described in part a.

2.7 The first few days of sales at S&S were excellent. Consumer demand for appliances exceeded all initial expectations. However, Scott has come to the accounting office in a state of alarm. Apparently, the strong demand has rapidly diminished the stocks of S&S's most popular items. In fact, this afternoon a customer left the store quite upset that S&S would have to place a special order for an advertised appliance that wouldn't be delivered for several weeks.

Scott is concerned with his inability as a manager to monitor the level of inventory on hand as sales are transacted. Scott encourages you to focus on the inventory problem and draft a potential solution aimed at integrating an inventory processing system into the future information system.

Required

a. What problem is S&S facing? What are the underlying causes of S&S's inventory situation?

b. Describe the relationship between the sales and the inventory/warehousing function. What major transactions affect the physical flow of inventory at S&S?

c. What information does Scott need to facilitate the flow of inventory? What impact does timeliness have on the value of information?

d. How effective would a manual system be in helping solve the inventory problem?

e. As you design a computerized information system, what data input and data processing methods can be used to deal with the inventory problem? Justify your selection.

f. Will an automated inventory control system solve all of S&S's inventory problems?

2.8 On a day-to-day basis, students are involved with a number of transaction processing systems. On a college campus transactions occur in the Administration Office, in the bookstore, and at the local pizza place.

Required

Identify three transaction processing systems that you were involved in over the past month.

a. Note the outputs produced from each system. Are any coding systems employed in the production of the output?

b. Identify the potential inputs involved with each system. What input methods are employed? What role do source documents play in the data collection and input process for the information system?

c. What data processing and storage techniques are being used in each example?

d. Based on current technology, what potential improvements could be made in each information system? What benefits would such improvements bring to the owners of the system?

2.9 Ron Black, Controller of Kessler Corporation, has been working with the Systems Department to revise and implement a data entry and data retention system for computer files used by the various departments that report to him. The departments involved and details of their data processing activities follow.

General Accounting

- Daily processing of journal entries submitted by various departments
- Weekly updating of file balances with subsystem data from areas such as payroll, accounts receivable, and accounts payable
- Sporadic requests for account activity and balances during the month, with increased activity at month-end

Accounts Receivable

- Daily processing of receipts for payments on accounts receivable
- Daily processing of sales to customers
- Daily credit limit checks on the customers
- Daily identification of orders in excess of $20,000 per customer
- Daily requests for customer credit status
- Weekly reporting to the general accounting file

Accounts Payable

- Processing of payments to vendors three times per week

- Weekly expense distribution update to the general accounting file

Budget Planning and Control

- Updating of flexible budgets on a monthly basis
- Quarterly budget revisions based on sales forecast and production schedule changes
- Monthly inquiries for budget balances

Mary Crandall, Manager of the Systems Department, has explained to Black and his staff the concepts of batch processing versus real-time processing (on-line processing), as well as off-line versus on-line file retention. Crandall has indicated that batch processing, along with off-line file retention, is the least expensive combination of techniques. A rough estimate of the cost of each of the other possible combinations of techniques is listed next.

Data Entry/File Retention Techniques	Cost in Relation to Batch/Off-line Processing
Batch/on-line	1.5 times
Real-time/on-line	2.5 times

Required

a. Define and discuss the major differences between the following techniques for data entry.
  1. Batch processing
  2. Real-time processing

b. Define and discuss the major differences between the following techniques for file retention.
  1. Off-line
  2. On-line

c. For each of the four departments that report to Black at Kessler Corporation, identify and explain (1) the type of data entry technique and (2) the type of file retention that should be used. Assume that the volume of transactions is not a key variable in the decision.

d. From a managerial perspective Black feels that the Budget Planning and Control Department should be more effective in assisting operations with controlling costs. Of the data entry techniques identified in part a, which technique will best help Black achieve this objective. Explain your answer. (CMA Examination adapted)

2.10 Advanced technologies are changing the way companies are doing business. Improvements in imaging applications and real-time processing methods are providing managers with reliable, up-to-the-minute information. Such information plays a critical role in the daily operations of Central Life Assurance Company, a billion-dollar underwriter in the Midwest.

Required

Using the material in Focus 2.2, answer the following questions.

a. Identify the data processing elements in the advanced system adopted by Central Life Assurance Company (CLA).

b. What problems was CLA having with its older automated system? In what ways is imaging technology improving the quality of data processed at CLA?

c. How does the customer benefit from the implementation of up-to-date technology by CLA? How could the improved system effect CLA's biggest competitors?

d. As a system's consultant, would you recommend an imaging system to a client? Why or why not?

2.11 Indicate whether the following data would appear on a master file, a transaction file, or both.

a. Date	j. Customer address
b. Account balance	k. Invoice number
c. Account number	l. Credit limit
d. Amount of payment	m. Vendor name
e. Customer name	n. Quantity on hand
f. Location of a sale	o. Amount of sale
g. Phone number	p. Vendor number
h. Product number	q. Quantity received
i. Product description	

2.12 Referring to the inverted lists in Table 2.5, describe the process the system would follow to answer the question, "Which parts supplied by RST Manufacturing are used in the Lodix product line?" Retrieve the appropriate part numbers from Table 2.4.

2.13 Assume that the hypothetical inventory records in Table 7.4 are stored sequentially at machine addresses numbered from 1 to 9, and that we wish to use embedded pointers to chain together all items having the same color.

Required

a. Prepare a table with column headings "Machine Address," "Stock Number," "Color," and "Next C" (for the pointer to the next item of the same color). Fill in this table according to the specifications.

b. Using an index, invert this file on the secondary key "color."

2.14 The MASI Corporation has decided to store its records using the indexing approach known as ISAM. Assume that 50 records with key values numbered sequentially from 500 to 549 are stored in blocks of 5 at 10 machine addresses numbered sequentially from 200 to 209. Each entry in the index contains the key of the last record in a block, as well as the address of that block.

Required

a. Prepare an index for this file segment.

b. Assuming an indexed-sequential file organization, explain how the system would access record number 522.

2.15 Using "company" and "agent" as secondary keys, chain together the independent insurance broker records shown in Table 2.10. Set up a pointer field for each secondary key that contains the address of the next logical record in the list. (*Hint:* See Table 2.4.) Independent of your answer above, prepare an inverted list for the secondary keys. (*Hint:* See Table 2.5)

2.16 Canam Transportation Company is an international trucking company operating in the northeastern United States and in the provinces of Ontario and Quebec. The company is primarily a transporter of bulk lubricating oil.

The company's fleet consists of 20 large trucks. The company owns 10 and has a capital lease on the remainder. Each truck is identified uniquely by a three-digit number. This number is recorded on all supplier invoices and on all driver pay reports. Both the driver and the customer are paid or billed on the basis of the kilometers driven for a specific delivery.

Here are some other items that affect costs.

■ Waiting time for loading and unloading incurs a cost. Both the driver and the customer are paid or billed at a standard hourly rate. The rate charged to the customer is twice the amount paid to the driver.

■ In the United States highway tolls are often incurred. These costs are charged directly to the customer without a markup.

■ Both provinces and each state charge an annual truck permit fee.

■ Highway and fuel taxes are also incurred and are based upon the kilometers driven and the amount of diesel fuel consumed by the vehicles within each jurisdiction. These taxes are calculated and paid quarterly. The rate of fuel tax varies by jurisdiction.

■ There is a fuel tax refund based upon the number of liters of diesel fuel consumed by the truck engines to pump the product on and off the tanker trailers. The rate of consumption is 0.7 liter of diesel fuel to

Table 2.10
Insurance broker records

Address	Policy #	Insured	Company	Agent
50	999	Joseph	ABCDE	Kathy
51	888	Elizabeth	FGHIJ	Kevin
52	777	Peter	KLMNO	Jeri
53	666	Heidi	ABCDE	Dee
54	555	Paul	QRSTU	Kevin
55	444	Julie	KLMNO	Kathy
56	333	James	FGHIJ	Jeri
57	222	Teresa	QRSTU	Kevin
58	111	John	ABCDE	Jeri
59	100	Carolyn	KLMNO	Dee
60	90	Mark	FGHIJ	Kathy
61	80	Anna	QRSTU	Dee

pump on or off 100 liters of products. A report for this refund is done quarterly.

The President of Canam Transportation Company does not feel that a special fixed asset subledger is necessary to maintain the expenses and revenues for each truck. He feels that the general ledger system using a computerized spreadsheet package should be adequate to provide this information as well as to facilitate the financial statement preparation. Furthermore, he requires a periodic analysis of each truck's cost per kilometer driven,

showing both fixed and variable costs and each component of these costs.

The President has requested that you, as the Management Accountant for Canam Transportation Company, design the following.

1. A chart of accounts for the company
2. The report that will be used to analyze each truck's cost per kilometer driven (SMAC examination, adapted)

CASE 2.1: ANYCOMPANY, INC.—AN ONGOING COMPREHENSIVE CASE

One of the best ways to learn is to immediately apply what you have studied. The purpose of this case is to allow you to do that. You will select a local company that you can work with. At the end of most chapters you will find an assignment that will have you apply what you have learned using the company you have selected as a reference. This case, then, may become an ongoing case study that you work on throughout the term.

If you have not already done so, visit several small- to medium-sized businesses in the local com-

munity. Explain that you will be doing a term-long case, and ask for permission to use the company as the firm you are going to study. Explain that you will need to meet with people in the company several times during the term to get the information you need. However, you will not need a great deal of their time or be a disruption to them. Offer to share any observations or suggestions that you can come up with as a way of allowing the firm to feel good about helping you.

Once you have lined up a company, answer the following questions.

1. How many business cycles does the company have? Does it have all five covered in Chapters 16–20? Does it have any others? Select any two cycles and trace how transactions are processed by explaining what happens in each of the activities shown in Fig. 2.1. List the major transactions that take place in each of the two cycles you selected.

2. Describe the data input processes of the company. How is data entered into the company's computer? Does the company use batch input or on-line data entry? If it uses a combination, explain what data is entered using batch entry and what data is entered on-line. Explain the company's use of any of the following: source documents, turnaround documents, batch totals, and source data automation.

3. Describe the data storage procedures the company uses. Does the company use the file-oriented approach or the data base approach to data storage? If it uses a combination, explain what each approach

is used for. How large are the company's data bases or files? How many records are in each file or data base? How many of the different files described in this chapter does the company use? How often are files updated?

4. Describe the data processing procedures the company uses. Does the company use batch processing or on-line processing? Sequential or direct-access processing? If it uses on-line processing, describe its on-line updating and inquiry processing.

5. What are the major information outputs of each transaction cycle? What are the main outputs for planning, control, and operation? For each output, explain the format that communicates the information to its users. Describe the company's use of responsibility accounting.

6. Describe the coding techniques the company uses. As appropriate, explain how it uses primary and secondary keys and sequence, block, and group codes. Describe and evaluate the company's chart of accounts. Explain the company's use of organizational codes.

CASE 2.2: S&S, INC.

You are a student accountant that S&S has hired to help with its accounting system. Ashton is beginning the process of designing a computer-based system for S&S. Although Ashton has not yet purchased a computerized system, he feels the need to do some advance-planning and design work. At the present time Ashton is trying to analyze the input, storage, and output needs of S&S. Ashton would like you to prepare the following for your next meeting with him.

1. Ashton would like a list of all of the different reports and documents that you think S&S needs to ensure that the business is properly managed. He also needs to know how you feel the data should be organized and stored on the computer. Therefore you have decided to make a list of all the following items.

a. Reports, documents, and other informational

output (whether they be on paper or displayed on a terminal or computer screen) that you feel S&S will need to properly manage its business

b. Input "forms" that you feel S&S will need to collect transaction and other input data; these inputs may take the form of source documents, preformatted screens, or user prompts

c. Files that you think S&S will need to store all the data it will process

2. Ashton would also like to have an idea about what data and information you feel would need to be collected, processed, and reported. A complete list of all data elements for every single output, input, and file would be too much information for Ashton to assimilate. Therefore, you have decided to provide him with some representative examples. You have decided to list all of the data items (specific items of information such as company name, date,

amounts) that should appear on the following output reports and documents to make them fully functioning system output.

a. Purchase order
b. Sales invoice (for sales on credit)
c. Stock status report (a report of inventory on hand)

You will also list the data that should be captured on each of the following documents (whether it be a source document, preformatted screen, or user prompt).

d. Receiving report
e. Employee time card for hourly employees

Finally, you will list the data that should be stored in the following data base.

f. Sales/accounts receivable

3. Scott would like to see what some of these system inputs and outputs will look like. He has asked you to design the following items.

a. Sales invoice
b. Receiving report

(*Hint:* You may want to refer to Chapters 16–20 for ideas.)

CHAPTER 3

Systems Development and Documentation Techniques

LEARNING OBJECTIVES

After studying this chapter, you should be able to:

- Prepare and utilize data flow diagrams to understand, evaluate, and design information systems.
- Describe the uses of document, system, and program flowcharts, and be able to use them to understand, evaluate, and design information systems.
- Prepare and utilize decision tables.
- Describe the uses of structured English and HIPO charts.

INTEGRATIVE CASE: S&S, INC.

What a month it has been for Ashton Fleming! It was hectic beginning his new job and at the same time getting ready for the week-long grand opening of S&S (see Chapters 1 and 2). Then he was swamped processing all the transactions from the highly successful grand opening. To top it all off, he became confused and discouraged because of his experience at Computer Applications (CA), a local computer company.

On an impulse, he had stopped at CA on his way back from lunch. Kimberly Serra, the manager of CA, was very bright and helpful. However, Ashton was unprepared for some of the questions she asked. She asked what S&S's system requirements were and just exactly what they needed the system to do. She explained that CA sold or could develop systems that ranged from a simple general ledger system to highly integrated software that handled a wide variety of accounting applications, including accounts receivable and payable, inventory, payroll, cost accounting, fixed assets, and cash receipts and disbursements. Ashton really had not thought that through very well, so he was unable to respond adequately.

Another question Kimberly asked was how the current system at S&S worked. That question Ashton could answer. Ashton told Kimberly how all the different company documents were used and where they all went. However, Ashton felt he got carried away with his explanation. Kimberly seemed unable to follow the flow of information very well. Ashton got the feeling that some of what he told her was helpful and some was not really relevant to the issue at hand.

Ashton came away impressed by CA and Kimberly. Kimberly offered to come and study how S&S works so that she could help Ashton decide what S&S needed in terms of a system. However, Scott and Susan have not given Ashton the go-ahead yet to begin work on a new system. Besides, Ashton got the distinct impression that S&S was not yet ready to develop or acquire a system. What Ashton had to do first was to understand S&S better so that he knew what information he really needed and what he wanted the system to do for S&S.

From his days as an auditor, Ashton is aware of how important good system documentation is in helping someone unfamiliar with the system to both understand the system and to evaluate it. It seems to him that good system documentation would be a big help to him and Kimberly as they work toward a new system. It would also help Scott and Susan evaluate the current and proposed system.

Ashton discussed his experience and conclusions with Susan and Scott. They agreed with Ashton and told him to take the lead in moving toward a new system. They seemed very interested in Ashton's proposal to document the current and proposed systems. They were especially interested in diagrams or charts that would help them to quickly grasp how the system worked. They gave Ashton the assignment to determine:

1. What tools and techniques S&S should use to document their existing system so that they are easy to understand and evaluate?

2. What development tools and techniques S&S should use to design their new computer-based information system. ■

INTRODUCTION

The first three chapters of this book lay the foundation for the remainder of the text. One very important part of that foundation is an understanding of the basic tools and techniques that are used to develop, document, and evaluate accounting information systems.

System users and designers work together to develop a new system. Accountants function as both users and designers, since they are heavy users of the system and are often members of the design team. To develop a system, users and designers must gain an understanding of the current system before they design the new one. The tools and techniques discussed in this chapter are used to document and explain an existing system. They are also the tools and techniques used both to design a new system and to document it.

Accountants are also responsible for evaluating accounting information systems. Both internal and external auditors must first understand a system before they can audit and evaluate it. The tools and techniques presented in this chapter are often used by accountants as they evaluate information systems.

Documentation consists of all the narratives, flowcharts, diagrams, and other written material that explain how a system works. That explanation will cover the *who*, *what*, *when*, *where*, *why*, and *how* of data entry, data processing, data storage, information output, and the controls that protect the system. In other words, documentation is a complete description of the system and how it operates.

Documentation can take many forms. Because of the old adage, "a picture is worth a thousand words," one popular means of documenting a system is to develop diagrams, flowcharts, tables, and other graphical representations of information. Graphical representations are supplemented by narrative descriptions of the system. A **narrative description** is a written, step-by-step explanation of system components and how these components interact. Graphical representations can convey in one page what would take many pages of narrative description to explain. They convey more information more efficiently, in less time, and with less effort. One reason for their efficiency is that many people are visually oriented and can grasp things better if they see a model or graphical representation.

In this chapter the most common systems documentation tools and techniques are explained. Data flow diagrams are discussed. So are document flowcharts, system flowcharts, and program flowcharts. Finally, decision tables, structured English, pseudocode, and HIPO charts are discussed. Student accountants need to understand these tools, as well as learn how to use them, prepare them, and evaluate them, for several reasons.

First, accountants must understand how these development and documentation tools are used in the workplace. Depending upon their job function, accountants will need varying levels of understanding. Some will only have to read the documentation in order to understand how a system works. Others will be involved as users in specifying their needs to systems developers. They will need to understand the tools well enough to evaluate the systems that are proposed. Others will need to understand the tools well enough to use them to evaluate the system as part of an auditing team. Finally, some accountants will actually be a part of a design team and will have to use the tools and prepare the documentation.

Second, an understanding of these tools is necessary because they are used throughout this book. Systems flowcharts, for example, are used extensively to show how systems work and how data and information flow. Third, these tools and techniques are so important that they are often tested on professional examinations— as you can see by noting the number of questions in the book that are adapted from these exams. Learning about the tools and techniques of documentation will better prepare you for these examinations.

Finally, these tools add value to an organization. In systems development time is money, in that the less time it takes to develop a system, the less costly it is. These tools save both time and money.

DATA FLOW DIAGRAMS[1]

A data flow diagram (DFD) is a graphic description of the flow of data within an organization. These diagrams are used to document existing systems and to plan and design new systems. They emphasize the logical view of data rather than the physical view. The logical view of data is the way users conceptually organize, view, and understand the relationships between data items. The physical view refers to how, where, and by whom data are physically arranged and stored on disks, tapes, and other storage media. In other words, a logical view of data shows what the system does with data—that is, where data comes from, the processes that are performed on the data, where it is stored, and what happens to the processed data. It is not concerned with the physical aspects of the system such as hardware, software, data structure, or file organization.

According to a study by Kievit and Martin, data flow diagrams and systems flowchats are the two most frequently used development and documentation tools. Their study shows that 62.5% of information systems professionals use data flow diagrams (27.5% always, 33.8% most of the time, and 1.2% occasionally). Systems flowcharts are used by 97.6% (33.7% always, 36.3% most of the time, and 27.5% occasionally). An impressive 92.5% of these users were either very satisfied or satisfied with the use of data flow diagrams. The comparable percentage for systems flowcharts is 92.6%.

This chapter explains how to draw a data flow diagram, and Chapters 9–10 describe their use in systems analysis and design.

Elements in a Data Flow Diagram

A data flow diagram is made up of four basic elements: data sources and destinations, data flows, transformation processes, and data

---

[1] Parts of this discussion were adapted from Tom DeMarco, *Structured Analysis and System Specification* (Englewood Cliffs, N.J.: Prentice-Hall, 1979). DeMarco has been at the forefront of structural analysis and design techniques and is a well respected authority on the subject.

Symbol	Name	Explanation
□	Data sources and destinations	The people and organizations outside the system that send data to and receive data from the system are represented by square boxes. Data destinations are also referred to as data sinks.
↗	Data flows	The flow of data into or out of a process is represented by curved or straight lines with arrows.
○	Transformation processes	The processes that transform data from inputs to outputs are represented by circles. They are often referred to as bubbles.
⌐	Data stores	The storage of data is represented by an open-ended rectangle.

Figure 3.1
Data flow diagram symbols

stores. Each of these items is represented on a DFD by one of the symbols shown in Fig. 3.1.

These four symbols can be combined to show how data is processed. For example, the data flow diagram in Fig. 3.2 shows that the input to process C is data flow B, which comes from data source A. The outputs of process C are data flows D and E. Data flow E is sent to data destination J. Process F uses data flows D and G as input and produces data flow I as output. Data flow G comes from data store H. Data flow I is sent to data destination K.

While Fig. 3.2 shows the uses of the four elements of a DFD, it does not relate to anything meaningful. Fig. 3.3 is the same as Fig. 3.2, except that the data flows, data sources and destinations, data stores, and processes each have a specific name. A close examination of the DFD shows that it represents the customer payment process in a company like S&S. Figures 3.2 and 3.3 will be used to examine the four basic elements of a DFD in more detail.

Data Sources and Destinations. Data flow diagrams show the sources of data entering the system and the destinations of data leaving the system. A source or destination symbol is used to represent an organization or individual outside the system that sends or receives data used or produced by the system. An outside entity can be both a source and a destination. **Data sources** and **data destinations** are represented by squares, as illustrated by items A (customer), J (bank), and K (credit manager) in Fig. 3.3.

Data flows. A **data flow** represents the flow of data between processes, data stores, and data sources and destinations. When data flows

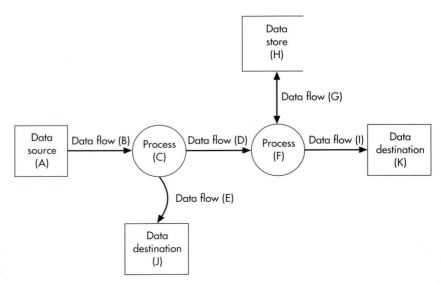

Figure 3.2
Basic data flow diagram elements

between data stores and either a data source or destination, it must go through some form of data processing—that is, through a transformation process.

Regardless of which of the other components the data flow connects, the method of illustrating the data flow (a straight or curved line with an arrow at one end) does not change. Data flow arrows differ from flowchart arrows in that they are labeled to indicate the type of data being passed from one step to the next. The reader thus knows exactly what information is flowing; no inferences are required (as in

Figure 3.3
Data flow diagram of customer payment process

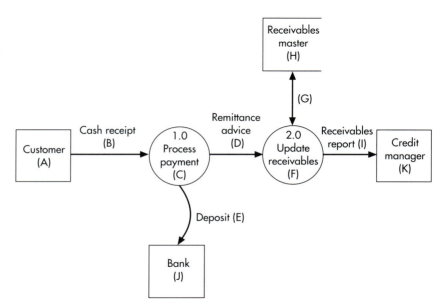

the case of flowcharting). Data flows are represented in Fig. 3.3 by items B (cash receipt), D (remittance advice), E (deposit), G (unlabeled; it represents file data), and I (receivables report).

A data flow can consist of one or more pieces of datum. For example, consider data flows B (cash receipt), D (remittance advice), and E (deposit). Data flow B, a payment received from the customer, consists of two parts: the check itself and the remittance advice. Process 1.0, entitled "Process payment," splits up these two data elements and sends them in different directions. The remittance advice (D) flows to another process, where it is used to update accounts receivable records. The check (E) is sent to the bank with a deposit slip.

Since data flows may be composed of more than one data element, how do you know whether to show one line or more than one? The determining factor is whether the data elements always flow together. For example, if customers sometimes send inquiries about the processing of their payments, the DFD could be revised as shown in Fig. 3.4. Two lines are shown in Fig. 3.4 because customer inquiries, though interacting with the same elements of the DFD, do not always accompany the payment. The two data elements have different purposes, and the customer inquiry occurs less frequently. If they were represented by the same data flow, the separate elements would be obscured, and the DFD would be more difficult to interpret.

A number of DFD conventions have been developed over the years. First, different data flows cannot have the same name, and the names chosen should represent the data and what is known about the data. Second, data flows that move into and out of data stores (such as item G) do not require names; the data store name is sufficient to identify the data flow. All other data flows should be named. Third, a DFD does not show the reason why a process begins, such as a date (month-or year-end), an inventory falling below a certain value (causing a purchase order to be issued), or a receivable being overdue (causing overdue notices to be sent). Finally, data flows can move in two directions, as shown in item G of Fig. 3.3. Data flow out of the file to facilitate the update and to produce the receivables report. Data flow back to the file in the form of updated receivables balances.

Processes. Processes represent the transformation of data. Fig. 3.3 shows that the payment process takes the payment information and splits it into the remittance advice and the deposit (which includes the checks and a deposit slip created within the payment process). The updating

Figure 3.4
Splitting customer
payments and inquiries

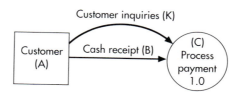

process takes the remittance advices and the receivables master file balances and updates the master file, producing an updated master file and a report listing current customer balances.

The name of each process should be as descriptive as possible so that the reader knows what happens in the process. Action verbs such as *update*, *edit*, *prepare*, *reconcile*, and *record* should be used to name the processes. Most processes receive their names from the data flows that move in and out of them (hence the names *process payment* and *update receivables*). In a completed DFD, as shown in Fig. 3.3, each process is given a number. These numbers are references that help readers move back and forth between the different levels of DFDs (these levels are explained later). The numbers assigned to the processes depend on how they interrelate, as will be explained later.

Data Stores.   A **data store** is a temporary or permanent repository of data. Unlike document flowcharts, DFDs do not show the physical storage medium (disks, tapes, paper, etc.). The rationale for ignoring the type of device used is that from a managerial viewpoint users should be indifferent to how the data are actually stored. Their only concern should be that data are available. Therefore, the person developing the DFD should concentrate on determining which data should be stored rather than how they should be stored. As with the other DFD elements, data store names should be as descriptive as possible so that the reader will understand what the store contains. As shown in Fig. 3.3, item H, DFD data stores are represented by open-ended rectangles, with the data store's name inside.

Data Dictionary.   Data flows and stores are typically collections of data elements. For example, a data flow labeled "employee information" might consist of a number of data elements such as employee name, employee address, and employee birth date. All the data elements, stores, and flows in a system are defined and described in a **data dictionary**. The data dictionary contains descriptions of the storage data, the processing data, the documents, and the physical items such as inventory. Typically, a master copy of the data dictionary is maintained in one place to ensure consistency and accuracy throughout the development process.

Guidelines for Drawing a DFD

There is no best way to develop a DFD. The more experienced people become in drawing DFDs, the more they realize that different problems call for different methods. However, the following general approach has been recommended by DeMarco, one of the pioneers of the DFD approach.

1. Determine system boundaries.
2. Determine system data flows and relationships.
3. Label DFD elements.
4. Repeat the process.

Determine System Boundaries. The procedure of determining a system's inputs, outputs, and processes depends a great deal on the development effort giving rise to the data flow analysis. The objective is to include everything relevant to the development effort and to exclude everything irrelevant. Since anything excluded will not be considered in developing the system, data elements should be included until a definitive decision can be made to exclude them. Once the system boundary has been determined, all data flows entering or leaving the boundary should be identified.

Determine System Data Flows and Relationships. This step emphasizes *actual* data flows and relationships, not what *should be* happening. An understanding of how the system actually works can be obtained by observing the flow of information through an organization and by interviewing the individuals who use and process the data. It is usually best to construct a DFD by concentrating first on data flows, rather than on processes or data stores. DeMarco has described this process as follows:

> *Look for the major pipelines of data moving about the operation. Suppose you identify a significant set of information that the user treats as a unit (i.e., it arrives together, it is processed together, and he thinks of it as a whole). That is certain to end up as a data flow on your DFD. Enter it on your diagram, and try to connect it with the data flows on the periphery. Put bubbles wherever some work is required to transform one data flow or set of data flows into another. Don't worry yet about naming these processes; leave them blank.*
>
> *Look inside the blank processes that are starting to appear on your DFD. Can you imagine any internal data flows that might be used within the process? Check with the user to see if they do indeed exist. If so, replace the single process by two (or three or four) and put the identified data flow between them.*
>
> *For each data flow, ask the questions: What do I need in order to build this item? . . . Where do these components come from? Can any of the incoming data flows be transformed into any of these? What intervening processes will be required to effect the transformation?*
>
> *Enter files on your DFD to represent the various data repositories that the user tells you about. Make sure you know the contents of each file in enough detail that you can figure out flow into and out of it.*
>
> *Be prepared to go back and modify the context boundary. You may have forgotten an input that is required as a key component of one of your data flows; add it in. You may have an incoming data flow that vanishes—is of no use to anything inside the context; take it out.*[2]

Determining how the system starts and stops is usually deferred to a later stage in the DFD development process, as are the details of

---

[2] Tom DeMarco, *Structured Analysis and System Specification* (Englewood Cliffs, N.J.: Prentice-Hall, 1979), 64–65.

unimportant error paths. Important error paths, such as those that require previous entries to be reversed, should be included in the DFD. A final guideline is to diagram flows of data, not control processes or control actions.

Label DFD Elements.   The names given to DFD elements have a significant impact on the quality and readability of the diagram. If an element is improperly or incompletely named, the diagram will not communicate effectively. The reader will end up with either an incomplete or an improper understanding of the system.

Since the main emphasis of a DFD is the flow of information through a system, all the data flows should be named first. The naming of stores and processes can wait until all data flows have been named. This approach forces the person developing the DFD to concentrate on data flows, rather than on the processes or stores. Once the data flows have been labeled, naming the processes should be relatively easy, since the flow of the data through the system is already understood and processes typically take their names from the data inflows or outflows.

Several guidelines should be followed in naming the different data elements of the DFD. First, be sure to name all DFD elements. Second, make sure that the names describe all the data or the entire process. If a name cannot completely describe the data or process, then decompose the flow or process further. Third, avoid names like *input data* or *update process* that are not fully descriptive. Instead, choose active and descriptive names like *daily inventory update* and *validate transaction*. Fourth, do not combine unrelated items into a single data flow or process. If data do not flow together naturally or are not processed together, separate them.

Repeat the Process.   Many times, those who develop DFDs are able to develop only a general concept or idea in the first pass through a DFD. As a result, they must work through the data flows of an organization many times. Each subsequent pass through the process helps refine the diagram and identify the fine points. In every instance the person developing the DFD should plan to make more than one pass through the flow of data.

Just as several passes through the data are needed to capture all the relevant data flows and tie up loose ends, several levels of DFDs are often needed to fully explain the data flows of an organization. Usually required are a summary-level DFD and then a DFD that breaks each summary-level process into smaller parts. This subdivision process, which can continue for several levels, is discussed next.

Subdividing the DFD   Data flow diagrams are subdivided into successively lower levels in order to provide greater amounts of detail, since few systems can be adequately diagramed on one sheet of paper. Also, users have differing needs, and the differing levels can better meet users' needs for details about the system.

The highest-level DFD is referred to as a context diagram or a context-level diagram. A **context diagram** provides the reader with a summary-level view of a system. It shows a data processing system, the inputs and outputs of the system, and the external entities that are the sources and destinations of the system's inputs and outputs.

Figure 3.5 is an example of a context diagram. It is one of the data flow diagrams that Ashton Fleming drew as he was analyzing the payroll processing procedures at S&S. It shows that the payroll processing system receives time cards from the different departments in S&S and employee data from the personnel department. When these data are processed, the system produces tax reports and payments for governmental agencies, employee paychecks, a check to deposit in the payroll account at the bank, and payroll reports for management.

Ashton finds the context diagram useful, but he also wants to diagram the details of the system. To do so, he decides to decompose the context diagram into successively lower levels, each with an increasing amount of detail. In preparation for this task he wrote the narrative description of S&S's payroll processing procedures shown in Table 3.1. Read the narrative carefully and determine how many major data processing activities are involved. Then identify the data inputs and outputs of each activity. Ignore all references to people, departments, places where documents are forwarded to or filed, and the disposition of all duplicate copies.

We identified five main data processing activities in payroll processing (you may have noted more or fewer, depending on how you

Figure 3.5
Context diagram for S&S payroll processing

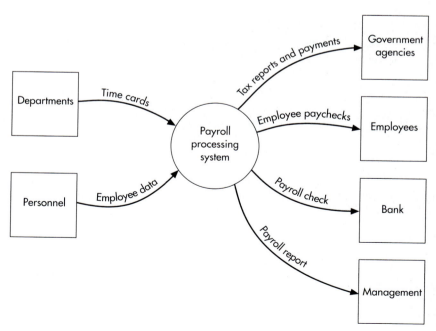

When employees are hired they fill out a new employee form. When there are changes to an employee's payroll status, such as a raise or a change in the number of exemptions, personnel fills out an employee change form. A copy of these forms is sent to payroll. These forms are used to create or update the records in the employee/payroll file and are then stored in the file. Employee records are stored alphabetically.

Some S&S employees are paid an annual wage, but most are hourly workers who record the times they work on time cards. At the end of each pay period department managers send the time cards to the payroll department. The payroll clerk uses the time card data, data from the employee file (such as pay rate and annual salary), and the appropriate tax tables to prepare a two-part check for each employee. The clerk also prepares a two-part payroll register showing gross pay, deductions, and net pay for each employee. The clerk updates the employee file to reflect each employee's current earnings. The original copy of the employee paychecks are forwarded to Susan. The payroll register is forwarded to the accounts payable clerk. The time cards and the duplicate copies of the payroll register and the paycheck are stored by date in the payroll file.

Every pay period the payroll clerk uses the data in the employee/payroll file to prepare a payroll summary report for Susan so that she can control and monitor labor expenses. This report is forwarded to Susan along with the original copy of the employee paychecks.

Every month the payroll clerk uses the data in the employee/payroll file to prepare a two-part tax report. The original is forwarded to the accounts payable clerk, and the duplicate is added to the tax records in the payroll file. The accounts payable clerk uses the tax report to prepare a two-part check for taxes and a two-part cash disbursements voucher. The tax report and the original copy of each document are forwarded to Susan. The duplicates are stored by date in the accounts payable file.

The accounts payable clerk uses the payroll register to prepare a two-part check for the total amount of the employee payroll and a two-part disbursements voucher. The original copy of each document is forwarded to Susan, and the payroll register and the duplicates are stored by date in the accounts payable file.

Susan reviews each packet of information she receives and approves and signs the checks. She forwards the cash disbursements vouchers to Ashton, the tax reports and payments to the appropriate governmental agency, the payroll check to the bank, and the employee checks to the employees. She files the payroll report chronologically.

Ashton uses the payroll tax and the payroll check cash disbursement vouchers to update the general ledger. He then cancels the journal voucher by marking it "posted" and files it numerically.

Table 3.1
Narrative description of payroll processing at S&S

identified the activities). The first is updating the employee/payroll master file as described in the first paragraph of the narrative. The second is paying the employees, which is discussed in the second, fifth, and sixth paragraphs. (We will later break this activity into smaller parts in a lower-level DFD.) A third is the generation of management reports, as described in the third paragraph. A fourth is the payment of taxes, as described in the fourth paragraph. A fifth activity is posting all the entries to the general ledger, as described in the last paragraph. Each of these activities has data flowing into and out of it. All the data inflows and outflows, as well as the five activities, are summarized in Table 3.2.

These data processing activities and the data that flow into and out of them form the basis of a DFD. Using the information in Table 3.2, Ashton exploded his context diagram and created the DFD shown in Fig. 3.6. Notice that not all the data inputs and outputs are shown on the DFD. The data coming from the personnel department were grouped together and called "employee data". In process 2.0 the data inflows and outflows (tax tables and payroll register) that are not

Activities	Data Inputs and Outputs	
Update employee/payroll file	In:	New-employee form
		Employee change form
		Employee/payroll file
	Out:	Updated employee/payroll file
Pay employees	In:	Time cards
		Employee/payroll file
		Tax tables
	Out:	Employee checks
		Payroll register
		Updated employee/payroll file
		Payroll check
		Payroll cash disbursements voucher
Prepare reports	In:	Employee/payroll file
	Out:	Payroll report
Pay taxes	In:	Employee/payroll file
	Out:	Tax report
		Tax payment
		Payroll tax cash disbursements voucher
		Updated employee/payroll file
Update general ledger	In:	Payroll tax cash disbursements voucher
		Payroll cash disbursements voucher
	Out:	Updated general ledger

Table 3.2
Activities and data flows in payroll processing at S&S

related to an external entity or to another process are not shown. These data flows are internal to the ''pay employees'' activity and are shown on the next DFD level.

Ashton was still not satisfied with the level of detail he had captured, so he exploded process 2.0 (pay employees). The DFD he created is shown in Fig. 3.7. It provides more detail about the data processes involved in paying employees. It includes the tax tables and the payroll register data flow that were left out of Fig. 3.6. In a similar fashion, each of the processes shown in Fig. 3.6 could be exploded to show a greater level of detail.

There are tools other than DFDs that can be used to document and design information systems. The next most common tool is a flowchart. The next section discusses the differences between a DFD and a flowchart.

Differences Between Data Flow Diagrams and Flowcharts

A DFD emphasizes the flow of data, whereas a flowchart emphasizes the flow of documents or records containing data. In other words, a DFD is a representation of the logical flow of data, whereas a flowchart represents the physical flow of data. Data flow diagrams concentrate

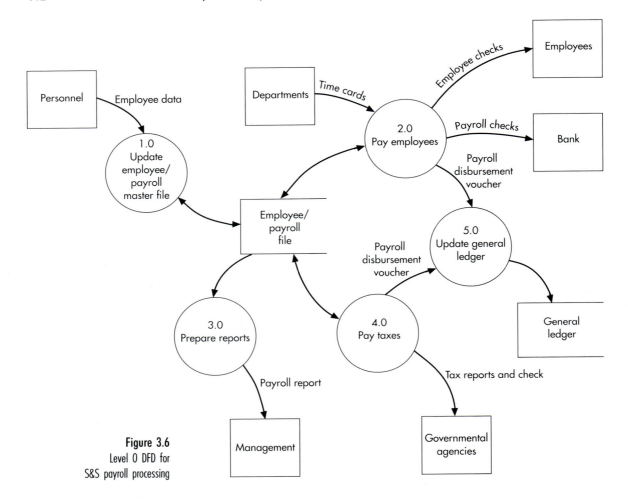

Figure 3.6
Level 0 DFD for
S&S payroll processing

on what is happening in a system. In flowcharts a description of how things happen sometimes gets in the way of a description of what is happening.

Data flow diagrams make use of only four symbols. Flowcharts, on the other hand, make use of many different symbols, as is shown later. A larger variety of symbols allows flowcharts to pictorially show more than DFDs. Therefore those who draw DFDs must make sure that the labels on a DFD and the verbal descriptions that accompany it effectively communicate what is happening.

A flowchart shows the sequence of processes and data flows. Data flow diagrams do not. Nor do DFDs convey the timing of events, as a flowchart can. These distinctions are discussed in more detail in the next section.

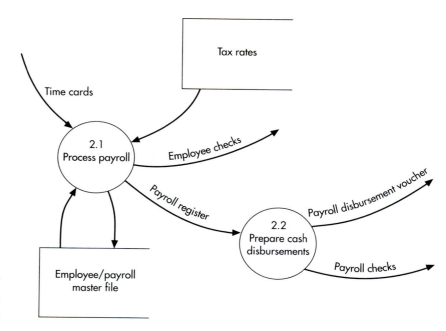

Figure 3.7
DFD for process 2.0 in
S&S payroll processing

FLOWCHARTS

A **flowchart** is an analytical technique used to describe some aspect of an information system in a clear, concise, and logical manner. Flowcharts use a standard set of symbols to pictorially describe the transaction processing procedures used by a company and the flow of data through a system. The use of flowcharts at St. Francis Hospital is described in Focus 3.1.

The process of preparing flowcharts is facilitated through the use of several recently developed software packages. These packages allow you to create a flowchart on a computer screen. The flowchart can be stored electronically for future use as well as printed out on paper. These packages speed the development of the initial flowchart of a process. Editing and making changes to the system is also greatly facilitated by the software.

There are two basic types of flowcharts. A **systems flowchart** is a graphical representation of an information system. It shows the inputs to an information system, the data stored and maintained by the system, the procedures used to process the data, and the output from the system. It can also show the flow of documents through a system. A **program flowchart** shows the logic used in computer programs. The relationship between systems and program flowcharts is shown in Fig. 3.8. A detailed explanation of the symbols used in flowcharting follows.

Flowchart Symbols

The American National Standards Institute (ANSI) publishes a list of **flowcharting symbols**; the most common are shown in Fig. 3.9. Each symbol

3.1 FOCUS   Flowcharts, Hospitals, Flowcharts, and the Health Care Crisis

In recent years health care costs have climbed dramatically. Though the public is inclined to blame health care professionals for the outrageous increases, health care facilities contend that they too are feeling squeezed by fewer free dollars and increasing government regulation. One solution to the problem is the use of flowcharts.

In Tulsa, Oklahoma, administrators at St. Francis Hospital have introduced a strict diet of flowcharts to assist department personnel in using their resources more wisely. These flowcharts give the user an objective written plan for development of new services, programs, or facilities by providing step-by-step guidelines. Such

a plan insures that major expenditures are thoroughly considered before any dollars are spent.

The flowchart method at St. Francis is simple. Using a preliminary flowchart, department heads develop a proposal identifying a desired project. The proposal outlines the scope of the project and justifies the need for the project. The proposal is

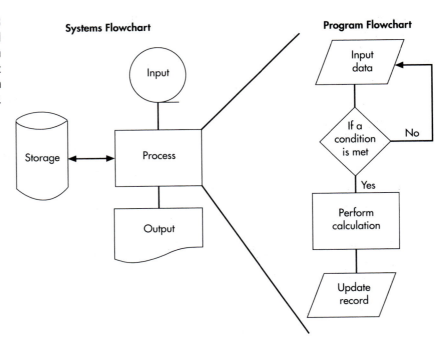

Figure 3.8
Relationship between systems and program flowcharts. A program flowchart describes the specific logic to perform a process shown on a systems flowchart.

then submitted to hospital administration for review. If the proposal is approved, the planner then moves to a second flowchart that covers in detail the seven actual planning steps. These seven steps help the planner develop a well-thought-out report that outlines the specific recommendations and a plan of action for the completion of the proposed project.

Administrators see a number of benefits to using flowcharts in the planning phases of any major project. The flowchart approach prevents health care planning personnel from reacting hastily to requests, thereby assuring careful decision making. Decentralized planning creates an awareness of cost containment among personnel by involving all levels of management in the planning process. The flowcharts also provide uniformity among departments, ensuring that inconsistencies are spotted early.

St. Francis Hospital has used the flowcharting process for remodeling pediatrics and maternity, building a new intensive care unit, constructing 14 new labor delivery/recovery rooms and three Cesarean section rooms, and expanding the bone marrow transplant program to include allogeneic transplants. In addition, the flowcharts are used in the diagnostic radiology department to determine the need for additional scanning equipment.

The bottom line, supporters argue, is cost. By using flowcharts, managers make better, more informed decisions that save the hospital money and allow it to offer a greater number of services to patients at more reasonable rates.

Source: Juanita C. Quinn, "Flow Chart Eases Planning Process for Hospitals," *Health Care Strategic Management* (April 1991): 16–18.

has a special meaning that is easily conveyed by the shape. The shape indicates the operations performed; the hardware devices used; and the input, output, processing, and storage media employed. The symbols also describe the operations performed in a system and the sequence of those operations. The symbols are drawn by a software program or with a flowcharting template, a piece of hard, flexible plastic on which the shapes of the symbols have been cut out.

Flowcharting symbols, as shown in Fig. 3.9, can be divided into four categories: input/output, processing, storage, and data flow and miscellaneous. The hardware that performs these functions is explained in Chapter 4.

Input/output symbols represent either devices or media that provide input to or record output from processing operations. Eight input/output symbols are shown and explained in Fig. 3.9. The most frequently used symbols are the document, display, and manual input symbols. Together the display and manual input symbols are used to represent CRT terminals and microcomputers. The input/output symbol is used frequently in program flowcharts and occasionally in document flowcharts. The punched card and punched tape symbols are rarely used. The transmittal tape symbol is most frequently used in batch processing applications.

There are four processing symbols shown in Fig. 3.9. The processing symbol is used frequently in systems and program flowcharts. The

Symbol	Name	Explanation
INPUT/OUTPUT SYMBOLS		
	Document	A document or report; the document may be prepared by hand or printed by a computer
	Multiple copies of one document	Illustrated by overlapping the document symbol and printing the document number on the face of the document
	Input/output	Any function of input and output; also used to represent accounting journals and ledgers
	Display	Information displayed by an on-line output device such as a CRT terminal or microcomputer monitor
	Manual input	Data entry by on-line devices such as a CRT terminal or microcomputer; the display and manual input symbols are used together to represent CRT terminals and microcomputers
	Punched card	Data stored on cards; seldom used anymore
	Punched tape	Data stored on punched paper tape; seldom used anymore
	Transmittal tape	Manually prepared control totals; used for control purposes to compare to computer-generated totals

Figure 3.9
Common flowcharting symbols

Symbol	Name	Explanation
PROCESSING SYMBOLS		
	Processing	A computer-performed processing function; usually results in a change in data or information
	Manual operation	A processing operation performed manually
	Auxiliary operation	A processing function done by a device that is not a computer
	Keying operation	An operation utilizing an off-line keying device (e.g., key to disk, cash register)
STORAGE SYMBOLS		
	Magnetic disk	Data stored on a magnetic disk
	Magnetic tape	Data stored on a magnetic tape
	Magnetic diskette	Data stored on a magnetic diskette
	On-line storage	Data stored in a temporary on-line file in a direct-access medium such as a disk
N	File	File of documents manually stored and retrieved; inscribed letter indicates file-ordering sequence: N = numerically A = alphabetically D = by date

Figure 3.9
(Continued)

Symbol	Name	Explanation
FLOW AND MISCELLANEOUS SYMBOLS		
⟶	Document or processing flow	Direction of processing or document flow
┄┄┄▸	Information flow	Direction of information flow
(communications link symbol)	Communications link	Transmission of data from one location to another via communication lines
◯	On-page connector	Connects the processing flow on the same page; its usage avoids connecting lines criss-crossing a page
(off-page connector symbol)	Off-page connector	An entry from, or an exit to, another page
(flow of goods symbol)	Flow of goods	Physical movement of goods; used primarily with document flowcharts
(terminal symbol)	Terminal	A beginning, end, or point of interruption in a process or program; also used to indicate an external party
◇	Decision	A decision-making step; used in a computer program flowchart to show branching to alternative paths.
(annotation symbol)	Annotation	Addition of descriptive comments or explanatory notes as clarification

Figure 3.9
(Continued)

manual operations symbol is used in document flowcharts and in systems flowcharts. The auxiliary operation symbol is used in systems flowcharts and occasionally in document flowcharts. The keying operation symbol is used most frequently in systems flowcharts.

A computer must store electronically all the data that it is not currently using. The most common storage devices are magnetic disks, tapes, and diskettes. Businesses also must store paper documents for further use; these are typically stored in a file cabinet. The five storage symbols shown in Fig. 3.9 represent these storage mediums. The file symbol is used frequently in document flowcharts. The other four are most frequently used in systems flowcharts.

A number of symbols are used to indicate data flow on a flowchart. Straight lines with arrows attached indicate document or processing flow. Dashed lines with arrows attached indicate the flow of information. If there is insufficient room on one page for a complete flowchart, an off-page connector is used to show the links between separate pages. Both of these symbols are used in all flowcharts. The communications link symbol is used in systems flowcharts to indicate when data are transmitted over data communication lines. In document flowcharts a wheelbarrow symbol is used to show goods moving between departments. The terminal symbol is often used in document and program flowcharts to show where a process begins or ends. The decision symbol is used in program flowcharts to indicate a branch in program logic. When a flowchart is prepared, a label is inserted into each symbol describing the data or operations represented by that symbol. If there is insufficient room for the label, the annotation symbol may be used to provide a more complete explanation.

General Guidelines for Preparing Flowcharts

Flowcharts would be difficult to read and understand if they were always drawn differently and were inconsistent. To avoid these problems, people who prepare flowcharts can use the guidelines that follow. When these guidelines are used, flowcharts are more readable, more clear and concise, and more understandable. However, even with these guidelines, some differences are bound to occur, because flowcharting is more of an art than a science. The important thing for preparers to remember is to be consistent.

The following guidelines promote consistency and enhance readability in flowcharts. These guidelines were used to construct the flowcharts in this chapter.

1. Understand a system before flowcharting it. Interview users, developers, auditors, and management, or have them fill out a questionnaire; read a narrative description of the system; observe the system; or walk transactions through the system.

2. Identify the entities, such as departments, job functions, or external parties, that are to be flowcharted. Identify documents and information flows in the system as well as the activities or processes performed on the data. (For example, when reading a description of the system, the preparer could draw a box around the entities, a circle around the documents, and a line under the activities.)

3. When several entities need to be shown on a flowchart, divide the flowchart into columns, label each column, and flowchart the activities of each entity in its respective column.

4. Flowchart only the normal flow of operations, making sure that all procedures and processes are in the right order. Identify exception procedures by using the annotation symbol.

5. Design the flowchart so that flow proceeds from top to bottom and from left to right.

6. Give the flowchart a clear beginning and a clear ending. Show where each document originates. Show the final disposition of all documents so that there are no dangling ends that leave the reader wondering what happened.

7. Use standard flowcharting symbols, and draw them with a template or with a computer.

8. Clearly label all symbols. Write a description of the input, process, or output inside the symbol. If the description will not fit in the symbol, use the annotation symbol. Print neatly, rather than writing in freehand.

9. Place document numbers in the top right-hand corner of multiple copies of documents. The document number should accompany the symbol as it moves through the system.

10. Precede each manual processing symbol by an input and an output. Do not directly connect two documents, except when moving from one functional area to another. When a document is moved to another functional area (another column), show the document in both functional areas.

11. Use on-page connectors sparingly. Use off-page connectors to move from one flowchart page to another. Clearly label all connectors to avoid confusion.

12. Use arrowheads on all flow lines. Do not assume that the reader will know the direction of the flow.

13. Try to use only one page per flowchart. When that is not possible, clearly label the pages 1 of n, 2 of n, and so on.

14. Show documents or reports first in the functional area (column) in which they are created. They can then be shown moving to another column for further processing. A manual process is not needed to show the documents being forwarded.

15. Show all data entered into or retrieved from a computer file as passing through a processing operation (a computer program) first.

16. Use a line from the document to a file to indicate that it is being filed. A manual process is not needed to show a document entering a file.

17. Draw a rough sketch of the flowchart as a first effort. In this way you can worry about content rather than about getting the drawing right. Few systems can be flowcharted without going through more than one draft of the flowchart.

18. Verify the flowchart's accuracy by reviewing it with people who are familiar with the system. Make sure that all uses of flowcharting conventions are consistent.

19. Redesign the flowchart to avoid clutter and a large number of crossed lines. Draw a final copy of the flowchart.

20. Place the name of the flowchart, the date it was prepared, and the preparer's name on each page of the flowchart.

Types of Systems Flowcharts

There are several different types of systems flowcharts. A flowchart that traces the flow of paper documents through a system, from their origination to their final destination, is referred to as a **document flowchart**. A **computer configuration flowchart** shows the different hardware devices in a computer system. A **computer system flowchart** shows the inputs to a computer system or program, the program modules that process the data, and the output from the system. Each of the three flowcharts is used to document various aspects of the system. Sometimes the flowcharts are referred to by their specific names and sometimes they are simply referred to as systems flowcharts. A discussion of each type of flowchart follows.

Document Flowcharts

A document flowchart illustrates the flow of documents between areas of responsibility within an organization. Document flowcharts trace a document from its cradle to its grave. That is, the flowchart shows where each document originates, its distribution, the purposes for which it is used, and its ultimate disposition. Everything that happens to the document is indicated on the flowchart.

A document flowchart is particularly useful in analyzing the adequacy of control procedures in a system, such as internal checks and separation of functions. Flowcharts that describe and evaluate internal controls are often referred to as **internal control flowcharts**. The document flowchart can also be used to reveal weaknesses or inefficiencies in a system, such as inadequate communication flows, an unnecessary complexity in document flows, or procedures responsible for causing wasteful delays. Document flowcharts may also be prepared as part of the systems design process and should be included in the documentation of an information system.

The first step in document flowcharting is to divide a blank page into vertical columns. A column is reserved for each entity, and the column is labeled with the name of the entity. Next, the origination and final disposition of each document is shown in the departments or entities within which the document's flow begins and ends. The flow of data and documents through the system is also indicated. In this step the name of each document and the description of each operation or procedure that is performed is inscribed within the appropriate symbol. When multiple copies of a given document are prepared, multiple document symbols are drawn on the flowchart and numbered to facilitate the tracing of the subsequent flow of each separate copy.

The document flowchart that Ashton developed for the payroll process at S&S, as described in Table 3.1, is shown in Fig. 3.10.

Computer Configuration Flowchart

Flowcharting symbols may also be used to represent an equipment configuration. For example, Fig. 3.11 illustrates a configuration that Ashton might consider recommending to Scott and Susan if they set up an administrative office away from the store. It consists of a minicomputer, a magnetic disk (an external hard disk), a printer, and a microcomputer that would be located in the accounting department. It also

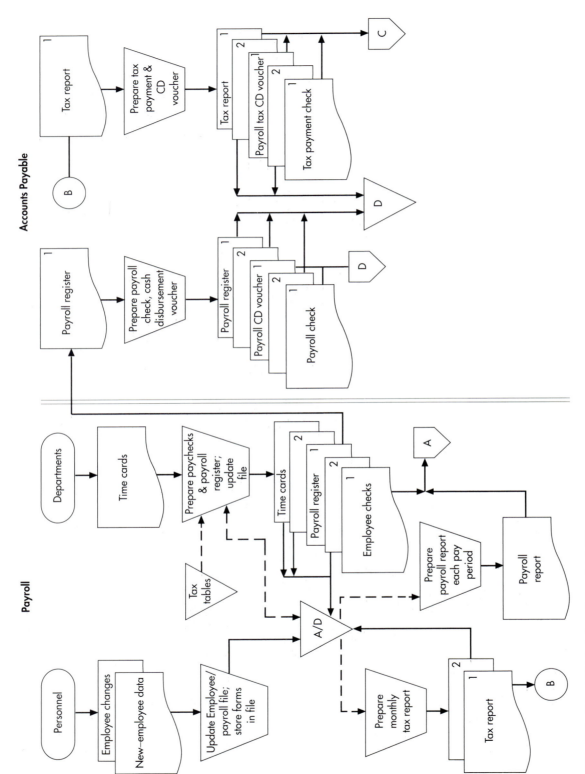

Figure 3.10 Document flowchart of payroll processing at S&S

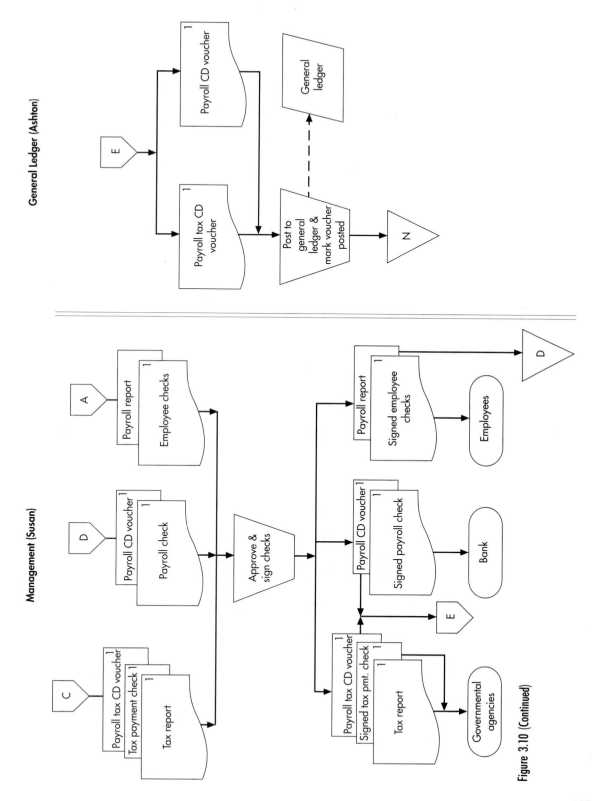

General Ledger (Ashton)

Management (Susan)

Figure 3.10 (Continued)

123

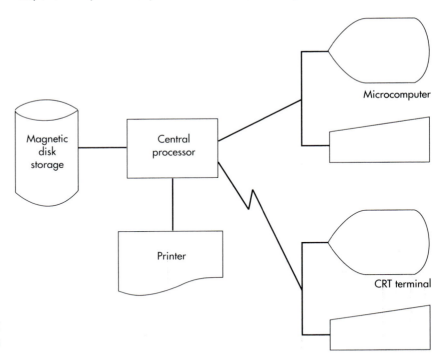

Figure 3.11
Simple computer system configuration

includes a sales terminal in the store. While the flowchart only shows one of each device, the flowchart could easily be expanded to show multiple terminals and multiple microcomputers.

Notice in Fig. 3.11 that the communications link symbol is used to indicate that the CRT is geographically remote from the central processor, connected to it through a telephone hookup. In contrast, the straight line connecting the printer and the microcomputer to the central processor indicates that they are located at the same site as the processor. Also note that this illustration uses combinations of symbols to represent the terminal and the microcomputer. There is no single flowcharting symbol for representing a microcomputer or a CRT display terminal. However, because they have both a monitor and a keyboard, they can be represented by a combination of the on-line keyboard and the information display symbols. Note that a printer is illustrated with the document symbol.

A more sophisticated computer configuration flowchart is shown in Fig. 3.12. This figure shows a computer system that includes two tape drives, three disk drives, a microcomputer, a CRT terminal, an optical character reader, a printer, and a central processing unit (CPU) with an on-line console keyboard. Of course, this is only another simple illustration. Many organizations will have a more complex configuration, with multiple devices of many different varieties. Many of the chapters in this book present computer configuration flowcharts.

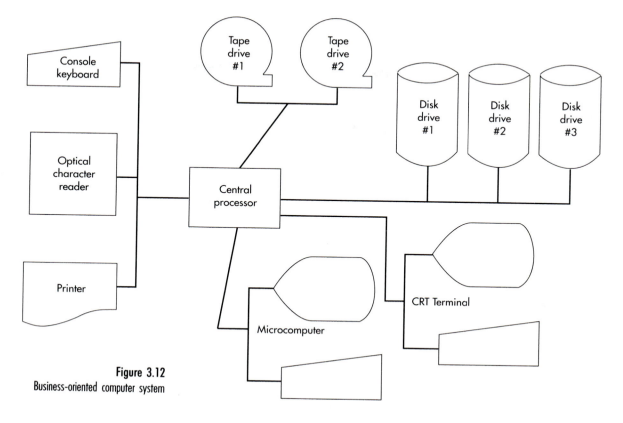

Figure 3.12
Business-oriented computer system

Computer System Flowcharts

Computer system flowcharts depict the way data is processed in an information system. They have three essential components: input, processing, and output. One purpose of the flowchart is to show the relationship between these system components.

A computer system flowchart begins by identifying what inputs enter the system and where they come from. The input can be new data entering the system or data stored for future use or both. The input is followed by the processing portion of the flowchart; which shows what processing steps are performed on the data. The logic used by the computer to actually perform the processing task is shown on a program flowchart, which was illustrated in Fig. 3.8. The new information that results is the output component. The output can either be stored for later use, be displayed on a screen, or be printed on paper for appropriate users. In many instances the output from one process is an input to another process, and the components repeat themselves.

As part of his plan for a computer system, Ashton Fleming drew the sales processing system flowchart in Fig. 3.13. His proposal is to capture sales data using state-of-the-art sales terminals. These terminals will edit the sales data (e.g., to ensure that all necessary sales data is collected) and print out a customer receipt. All sales data will be

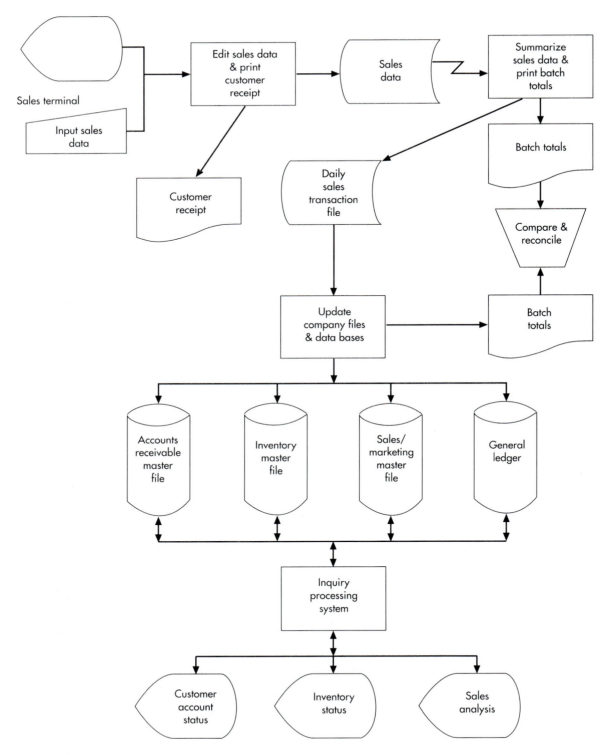

Figure 3.13 Systems flowchart of on-line batch processing of sales transactions at S&S

stored in a sales data file on a disk. At the end of each day the data will be forwarded to S&S's computers, where the data will be summarized and batch totals will be printed. The summary data will then be processed, and batch totals will again be generated and printed. These batch totals will be compared with the batch totals generated before processing, and all errors and exceptions will be reconciled. As part of the update process, the accounts receivable, inventory, and sales marketing master files and the general ledger will be updated. The various users of the data will be able to access the files at any time by using an inquiry processing system. The inquiry processing system will produce standard reports and allow the user to access the data needed for special analyses.

Systems flowcharts are an important tool of systems analysis, design, and evaluation. They are universally employed in systems work and therefore provide a ready form of communication among systems personnel. Because the systems flowchart is an excellent vehicle for describing document flows and procedures within an information system, it is used extensively to describe accounting systems in Part 5 of this book, which deals with accounting applications. Each chapter in Part 5 has one or more flowcharts like Fig. 3.13.

Program Flowcharts   A program flowchart illustrates the sequence of logical operations performed by a computer in executing a program. Flowcharts employ a subset of the symbols shown in Fig. 3.9. As shown in Fig. 3.14, the flow line connects the symbols and indicates the sequence in which operations are performed. The processing symbol represents a data movement or arithmetic operation, such as the performance of a calculation. The input/output symbol represents either the reading of input or the writing of output. The decision symbol represents a comparison of one or more variables and the transfer of flow to alternative logic paths. All points where the flow begins or ends are represented by the terminal symbol. Connectors, labeled with a digit or a capital letter, represent the continuation of the logic flow at a different location. Several exit connectors may have the same label, but there can be only one entry connector with a given label. Once designed and approved, the program flowchart serves as the blueprint for coding the computer program.

The flowchart in Fig. 3.14 shows a very simple example of the logic that a computer at S&S could use to process credit orders. The first step after starting is to enter a sales order. The next step is to determine if the customer has been approved for credit. If credit has not been approved, the order is rejected. If credit has been approved, the system determines if there is enough inventory on hand to fill the order. If not, the order is held until sufficient inventory arrives to fill the order. If there is enough inventory, the system tests to see if the order is for more than 500 units. If it is not, the order is filled. If the order is for more than 500 units, a 20% discount is given and the order is filled.

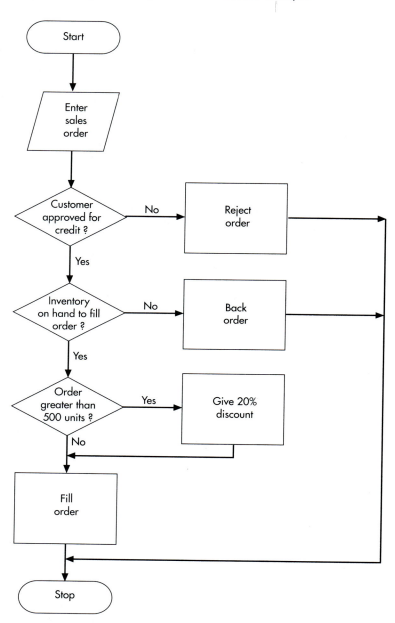

Figure 3.14
Simple program flowchart for processing credit orders

DECISION TABLES

A **decision table** is a tabular representation of decision logic. For any given situation a decision table lists all the conditions (the *if*s) that are possible in making a decision. It also lists the alternatives (the *then*s) that are possible. Each unique "*if* this condition exists, *then* take this action" relationship between the conditions and alternatives is referred to as a decision rule. Decision tables are used by systems personnel to represent the often complex logic of a computer program. The decision rules focus on the decision choices that are inherent in most data processing programs and the corresponding courses of action to be taken by the program for each unique combination of logic.

Auditors can use decision tables to evaluate a client's application programs. If a decision table already exists, the auditor can review it for completeness and accuracy. If it does not, the auditor can create a decision table and then review the logic. This review may point out weaknesses or errors in the computer program. Some studies have shown that up to 70% of application programs contain logic or syntax errors. Using the decision table, an auditor can create transaction data that can be processed by the system on a test basis. One or more transactions can be developed to test each separate decision rule to see whether the transactions are actually processed as they should be. These tests give the auditor assurance that the program actually does what it is supposed to do.

The general form of the decision table is illustrated in Table 3.3. Table 3.4 is a decision table that illustrates the decisions and actions that S&S could take in filling credit orders. It corresponds with the program flowchart in Figure 3.14.

A decision table has four parts: the condition stub, the condition entry, the action stub, and the action entry. The condition stub contains the various logic conditions for which the input data are tested. For example, there are three entries in the condition stub in Table 3.4. Note that they correspond to the three decision symbols in the program flowchart in Fig. 3.14.

The condition entry consists of a set of vertical columns, each representing a decision rule in which the entries must be either yes (Y), no (N), or a dash (–). The dash indicates that the result of the condition test makes no difference. For example, when credit is not approved, it

Table 3.3

General form of a decision table

STUB		ENTRY								
		CONDITION RULE NUMBER								
Condition		1	2	3	4	5	6	7	8	9
(Specific conditions)										
		ACTION RULE NUMBER								
Action		1	2	3	4	5	6	7	8	9
(Specific actions)										

	a	b	c	d
Credit approved	N	Y	Y	Y
Order ≤ inventory on hand	—	N	Y	Y
Order> 500 units	—	—	N	Y
Reject order	X			
Back order		X		
Fill order			X	X
Give 20% discount				X

Table 3.4
Simple decision table for processing credit orders

does not matter if there is enough inventory on hand or if the order exceeds 500 units.

The action stub contains the steps that the program should take. In Table 3.4, four actions can be undertaken: reject the order, back order, fill the order, or give a discount. The action entry columns are used to indicate when an action is to be taken. An X indicates that the action described in that row is performed if the input data meet all the condition tests. A blank indicates that the action is not performed.

The primary advantage of decision tables is that they indicate clearly all possible logical relationships among the input data. As a result, the program can be prepared to recognize and respond properly to each possible decision rule. The primary disadvantage is that decision tables do not reflect the sequence in which operations are to be performed within the program. Furthermore, they may become unmanageably large if the program is complex. Many organizations use both program flowcharts and decision tables to help design and code computer programs. Another tool that programmers and designers use is structured English, which is described next.

STRUCTURED ENGLISH

During systems analysis and design systems designers must determine what outputs, inputs, and stored data are needed by the system. They must also determine what each must contain. Once this step has been done, designers must determine how outputs are to be produced, how files and data bases are to be updated, and how inputs are to be processed. To do so, designers must divide the system into distinct and manageable modules or programs, each with a distinct beginning and end. Designers must then communicate to the computer programmer the logic processes needed in each distinct program module. One popular tool for this step is structured English.

Structured English—also called **pseudocode**, because of its similarity to program code—uses the three basic logic structures that are used to solve computable problems. These structures are (1) sequential structures, (2) decision logic in the form of IF–THEN or ELSE–THEN, and (3) loops or repeating structures such as REPEAT UNTIL or DO

Line Number	Instructions
1	Access accounts receivable file and transaction records
2	REPEAT UNTIL all accounts receivable transactions have been processed
3	Read transaction record
4	Access corresponding customer record
5	IF transaction is a sale
6	THEN add amount of sale to balance due
7	ELSE transaction is a payment
8	THEN subtract amount of payment from balance due

Table 3.5
Example of structured English

WHILE. These three logic structures are shown in Table 3.5. This table is a simplified version of an accounts receivable updating routine. The eight instruction lines have been numbered for reference purposes.

A sequential structure consists of a series of processing steps that are to be executed in the specified sequential order. In Table 3.5, for example, lines 3 through 5 are executed in sequential order. IF–THEN decision logic causes one of any number of actions to be taken, depending on a condition tested by an IF statement. If the condition exists, one action is taken. If it is not, a different action is taken. Lines 5 through 8 represent a conditional structure. A repeating structure is used to REPEAT a step or series of steps UNTIL some specified condition is met. Line 2 begins a repeating structure; it tells the computer to repeat all indicated lines (3 through 8) until all accounts receivable records have been processed.

Structured English has a number of advantages. It is easy to understand, which allows users to review the intended program logic for accuracy. It also makes writing programs easy, because it uses the same basic patterns as structured programming. Use of structured English significantly reduces the amount of time required to code a program.

HIPO CHARTS

A technique that has become increasingly popular in recent years is the **HIPO chart**, also known as a structure chart. The acronym HIPO, a name given to the technique by IBM, stands for *h*ierarchy plus *i*nput *p*rocess *o*utput. The technique involves analyzing a system and defining users' needs by diagraming the functions performed. Each block in the diagram represents a separate function. The individual blocks are linked by straight lines in a hierarchical structure, much like an organization chart. Lower-level blocks in the hierarchy represent more detailed breakdowns of the functions within the higher-level blocks. A simple

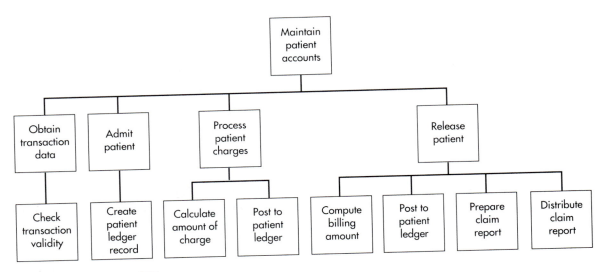

Figure 3.15

Structure chart of hospital patient accounting process

example of a structure chart, representing the process of accounting for patient charges in a hospital, appears in Fig. 3.15.

There can be any number of levels within a structure chart, and some branches may have more levels than others. The block at the top level represents the overall process, whereas the blocks at the second level represent the major functions necessary to accomplish the process. Blocks at the third and lower levels represent specific processing steps at increasingly finer levels of detail. The simplest structure chart may have only three levels, whereas a more complex and detailed chart may have seven or more levels.

HIPO charts provide a blueprint for the preparation of computer program code and serve as a replacement for, or a supplement to, the program flowchart. An advantage of HIPO charts over program flowcharts is that HIPO charts show the system in terms of clear-cut modules that can be related to the flows of information within the organization. This modular approach is especially helpful when a designer is trying to focus on particular areas or assign specific tasks to individuals or teams. Another advantage of HIPO charts is that they are easy to read and create because they represent the logical representation of the system and don't try to represent the physical (such as disk drives and other hardware) implementation.

CASE CONCLUSION: UNDERSTANDING THE SYSTEM AT S&S, INC.

Ashton prepared the data flow diagrams and flowcharts of S&S's payroll processing system (Figs. 3.6 and 3.10) to document the existing system and to explain how it operated. After he had completed the diagrams and flowcharts, he showed them to Scott and Susan. He was pleased to see that Scott and Susan were able to grasp the essence of the system from the documentation. The data flow diagrams gave them an idea about the logical flow of data, and the flowcharts showed them the physical dimensions of the system—that is, where each document came from, what happened to it in each department, and the final disposition of each document.

Susan and Scott agreed with Ashton's recommendation that he document the remainder of the system. They felt that the documentation would help all three of them not only understand the current system but also improve it. In fact, the payroll documentation had already helped them identify a few minor changes they wanted to make in their system. Susan picked up on the fact that only one copy of the payroll report was prepared. (See Fig. 3.10.) She now understood why the payroll clerk sometimes had to come to her and borrow the payroll report. She thus recommended that a second copy of the report be made and kept in the payroll department. Susan also questioned the filing of all the payroll records in the employee/payroll file. Too many different things were being filed together. As time passed, she felt that the file would become unwieldy and difficult to use. She recommended that the file be broken up into three different files: the personal data on each employee, the documentation for each pay period, and the payroll tax data. A discussion with the payroll clerk verified that this approach would make payroll processing easier and more efficient.

Over the next few weeks Ashton was able to document the rest of the accounting cycles. He found that this process helped him identify inefficiencies and unneeded reports; he also found that some documents in the system were not adequately controlled. In addition, he got several ideas about how an automated system could help him reengineer the business processes at S&S—that is, eliminate unneeded processes and procedures to make the system more effective and use technology to perform tasks previously performed by people.

When Ashton had completed his analysis and documentation of the current system, Susan and Scott asked him to take the lead in moving the company from a manual to a computerized system. To do that, Ashton will need to gain a thorough understanding of the information needs of the various people in the company. He will then need to design a new system using the tools, such as data flow diagrams and flowcharts, that were explained in this chapter (systems development is discussed in Chapters 8–11). He will also need to begin investigating the hardware and software options that are available to S&S (information technology is discussed in Chapters 4–7). ■

SUMMARY

Information systems are in constant need of improvement and change. Those who use, evaluate, or design them need tools to develop information systems and to document them as they are developed, changed and improved. The systems development and documentation tools discussed in this chapter are data flow diagrams, document flowcharts, systems flowcharts, program flowcharts, decision tables, structured English, and HIPO charts.

A data flow diagram is a graphic description of the flow of data within an organization. A data flow diagram is made up of four basic elements: transformation processes, data flows, data stores, and data sources and destinations. Businesses are increasingly using data flow diagrams because they are able to effectively represent the logical or conceptual flow of data.

A flowchart describes an information system in a clear, concise, and logical manner. Guidelines presented in the chapter can assist those who prepare flowcharts. When these guidelines are used, flowcharts are more readable, more clear and concise, and more understandable.

There are three types of systems flowcharts. Document flowcharts show the flow of paper documents through a system, from their origination to their final destination. A computer configuration flowchart shows the different hardware devices in a computer system. Computer systems flowcharts show how data is processed in computerized information systems.

A computer systems flowchart shows the inputs to an information system, the data stored and maintained by the system, the procedures used to process the data, and the output from the system. It can also show the flow of documents through a system.

A program flowchart illustrates the sequence of logical operations performed by a computer in executing a program. Once designed and approved, the program flowchart can serve as the blueprint for coding the computer program.

Flowcharts are prepared by using a set of specialized symbols. Each symbol has a unique meaning that is easily conveyed by the shape. The shape indicates the operations performed and the input, output, processing, and storage media employed. The symbols are drawn using computer software or a flowcharting template.

A decision table is a tabular representation of the logic of a computer program. It indicates the combinations of alternative logic conditions in the program and the corresponding courses of action taken for each unique combination of logic.

Structured English, or pseudocode, is used to communicate to the computer programmer the logic processes needed in each distinct program module. HIPO charts are used to analyze a system and to define users' needs by diagraming the functions performed. Each block represents a separate function, and blocks are linked in a hierarchical structure much like an organization chart.

KEY TERMS   Define the following terms.

documentation	data store	computer configuration
narrative description	data dictionary	flowchart
data flow diagram (DFD)	context diagram	computer system flowchart
logical view	flowchart	internal control flowcharts

physical view
data sources
data destinations
data flow
processes

systems flowchart
program flowchart
flowcharting symbols
document flowchart

decision table
structured English
pseudocode
HIPO chart

DISCUSSION QUESTIONS

3.1. Your management consulting team has reached an impasse about whether to use flowcharts or structured analysis and design techniques such as data flow diagrams and HIPO charts on your current project. The partner in charge is growing impatient with your team's lack of progress and has given you the responsibility of making the final decision and presenting it to the team. Prepare arguments for and against each of the following design tools—flowcharts, data flow diagrams, and HIPO charts—and determine when each tool should be used on a project.

3.2 Identify the data flow diagram elements in the following narrative: A customer purchases a few items from a local grocery store. The salesclerk enters the transaction in the cash register and takes the customer's money. When the day ends, the salesclerk gives the cash in the till and the register tape to the manager.

3.3 Discuss the following statement: "Use of any one of the systems documentation procedures discussed in the chapter, such as a data flow diagram, is adequate to fully document a given system." Do you agree? Explain.

3.4 At St. Francis Hospital in Tulsa, Oklahoma, flowcharting techniques are bringing about real cost savings for hospital administrators by formalizing the planning process (see Focus 3.1). How do flowcharting procedures provide the hospital with real cost savings? What other benefits come from using formal flowcharting procedures during the planning process?

3.5 Which documentation procedures are most useful in assisting each of the following individuals?

a. Controller
b. Systems analyst
c. Systems designer
d. A computer programmer
e. An external auditor

3.6 Your roommate has asked you to explain flowcharting conventions using real-world examples. Draw each of the major ANSI flowchart symbols from memory, placing them into one of five categories: input, output, processing, storage, data flow, and miscellaneous. For each symbol, discuss several ways each symbol can be used.

3.7 The text suggests that flowcharting is more of an art than a science. Discuss the implications of this statement as it relates to the development of formal documentation methods.

3.8 In discussing documentation techniques at a company meeting, several participants question you about their departmental problems. Respond to their questions by identifying which systems documentation method is most appropriate for handling each problem. Justify your answer.

a. "For the last six months, I've been unable to reconcile our bank statement with the books. I'm concerned that someone may be stealing company funds. How can I uncover the source of the problem?"

b. "We're planning on purchasing a local area network (LAN) for use by all human resources personnel. How can I best describe our hardware needs to a local vendor?"

c. "For the past three years auditors have been unable to locate shipping documents when they perform their annual audit. How can I determine the location of these missing documents?"

3.9 Compare the guidelines for the preparation of flowcharts and of data flow diagrams. What general design principles are common to both documentation techniques? What are the limitations common to both documentation methods?

Problems

3.1 Prepare systems flowcharting segments for each of the operations described.

a. Processing of transactions on magnetic tape on the computer to update a master file stored on magnetic tape

b. Processing of transactions on magnetic tape on the computer to update a master file stored on a disk

c. Off-line conversion of source documents to magnetic tape using an optical character reader (OCR)

d. On-line processing of OCR documents to update a master file on magnetic disk

e. Reading data from a disk file into the computer to be listed on a printed report

f. Keying of data from source documents to magnetic tape using an off-line, key-to-tape encoder

g. Manual sorting and filing of invoices

h. Online processing of source data using a CRT terminal from a remote location to a central computer system for updating a magnetic disk master file and also for recording the source data on a magnetic tape file

3.2 The Happy Valley Utility Company uses turnaround documents in its computerized customer accounting system. Meter readers are provided with preprinted forms prepared by the computer, each containing the account number, name, address, and previous meter readings of a customer. Each of these forms also contains a formatted area in which the customer's current meter reading may be marked in pencil. After making their rounds, meter readers turn in batches of these documents to the Computer Data Preparation Department, where they are processed by a mark-sense document reader that transfers their contents to magnetic tape.

The magnetic tape file containing the customer meter readings is then sent to the computer center, where it is used as input for two computer runs. The first run sorts the transaction records on the tape into sequential order by customer account number. On the second run the sort transaction tape is processed against the customer master file, which is stored on a magnetic disk. Outputs of this second run are (1) a printed report listing summary information and any erroneous transactions detected by the

computer and (2) customer bills printed in a special OCR-readable font. The bills are mailed to the customers with the request that the stub portion be returned with the customer's payment.

Customer payments are received in the mail room, where they are checked for agreement with the returned stubs. Customer checks are then sent to the cashier's office. The mail room provides the Computer Data Preparation Department with three sets of records: (1) stubs for which the amount received agrees with the stub amount, (2) stubs for which the amount received differs from the stub amount, and (3) a list of amounts received from customers who did not return their stubs. For the latter two types of records data preparation personnel use a special typewriter to prepare corrected stubs. All the stubs are then processed by an OCR document reader that transfers their contents onto magnetic tape.

The magnetic tape containing the payment records is then sent to the computer center, where it is sorted on the computer into sequential order by customer account number and processed against the customer master file to post the payment amounts. Two printed outputs from this second process are a report listing erroneous transactions and summary information and a report listing past-due customer balances.

Required

a. Draw a systems flowchart of the billing operations, commencing with the computer preparation of the meter reading forms and ending with the mailing of bills to customers.

b. Draw a systems flowchart of the processing of customer payments, starting with the mail room operations and ending with the computer run that posts the payment amounts to the customer master file.

c. Prepare a list of the minimum equipment needed in the company's hardware configuration to accomplish all the operations described.

3.3 Prepare a program flowchart and a decision table for the following program: Input to the program consists of an accounts receivable file containing (among other things) the amount due, due date, and credit limit for each customer. The program checks the due date of each customer record against the current date and prepares an aging schedule. Each customer's record is listed on a separate line of the aging schedule, with the amount due printed in one of three columns: (1) less than 60 days past due; (2) 61–180 days past due, and (3) over 180 days past due.

The program next compares the amount due with the customer's credit limit. Customer records that both are over 180 days past due and have an amount due in excess of the credit limit are printed on a "Bad Debts Report" for possible write-off by the credit manager. Other accounts that have an amount due in excess of the credit limit are printed on a "Credit Review Report" that goes to the treasurer. After the last record in the accounts receivable file is processed, the program is halted.

3.4 The Andy Dandy Company is a retailer in the business of buying goods from wholesalers and re-selling these goods to the public. The company wishes to make its purchases from the most reliable wholesaler. The following information was compiled and is now available to the computer.

- A quality rating from 1 to 4 for each wholesaler (1 is considered the highest)
- Percentage of times each wholesaler has been late in delivering each Andy Dandy Company order
- Whether each wholesaler's prices have been stable or unstable
- Whether each wholesaler is in an economically rich area or a depressed area
- Whether or not each vendor has suggested new products from time to time

Purchasing personnel have established the following criteria to be used in wholesaler selection.

- If the quality rating is 1, award the wholesaler 20% of the business.
- If the quality rating is 2 and the wholesaler is not more than 10% late, award that vendor 15% of the business.
- If the quality rating is 2 and the wholesaler is more than 25% late, reject the wholesaler.
- If the quality rating is 2 and the wholesaler is between 10% and 25% late, award that vendor 10% of the business, but only if prices have been stable.
- If the quality rating is 3 and the wholesaler is not more than 5% late, award that vendor 10% of the business, but only if the vendor is in a depressed area and has been good at suggesting new products.
- If the quality rating is 4, reject the wholesaler.

Required

Prepare a decision table to show the computer logic

that is needed to write a program for vendor selection for the Andy Dandy Company. (SMAC Examination, adapted)

3.5 The Dewey Construction Company processes its payroll transactions to update both its payroll master file and its work-in-process master file in the same computer run. Both the payroll master file and the work-in-process master file are maintained on disk and accessed randomly.

Data to be input to this system are keyed onto a tape using a key-to-tape encoder. The tape is then processed to update the files. This run also produces a payroll register on magnetic tape, employee paychecks and earnings statements, and a printed report listing error transactions and summary information.

Required

Prepare a systems flowchart of the process described.

3.6 Ferraro Corporation's computer program to maintain its parts inventory records has five major modules, which operate as follows:

1. The "obtain transaction data" module updates a transaction summary log and checks the transaction's validity, either accepting it as valid or writing an error message.
2. The "process new item" module creates a new-parts inventory master file record.
3. The "process issue transaction" module deducts the issue amount from the quantity on hand and computes the amount to be reordered, if any.
4. The "process receipt transaction" module adds the receipt amount to the quantity on hand, deducts the receipt amount from the quantity on order, and updates the supplier record.
5. The "prepare outputs" module writes the updated master record, prepares the stock status report, and prepares purchase orders.

Required

Prepare a structure chart (HIPO) of Ferraro Corporation's parts inventory file maintenance process.

3.7 From the following description of processing of casualty claims by an insurance company, prepare a document flowchart.

The process begins with the receipt by the Claims Department of a notice of loss from a claimant. The Claims Department prepares and sends the claimant four copies of a proof-of-loss form on which the claimant must detail the cause, amount, and other aspects of the loss. The Claims Department also initiates a record of the claim, which is sent with the notice of loss to Data Processing, where it is filed by claim number.

The claimant must fill out the proof-of-loss forms with the assistance of an adjustor, who must concur with the claimant on the estimated amount of loss. The claimant and adjustor each keep one copy of the proof-of-loss form. The claimant sends the two remaining copies of the proof-of-loss form to the Claims Department. Separately, the adjustor submits a report to the Claims Department confirming the estimates on the claimant's proof-of-loss form.

The Claims Department authorizes a payment to the claimant, forwards a copy of the proof-of-loss form to Data Processing, and files the original proof of loss and the adjustor's report alphabetically. The Data Processing Department prepares checks in payment of claims and mails them to the customers, files the proof of loss with the claim record, and prepares a list of disbursements, which it transmits to the Accounting Department.

3.8 Beccan Company is a discount tire dealer that operates 25 retail stores in the metropolitan area. Both private-brand and name-brand tires are sold by Beccan. The company operates a centralized purchasing and warehousing facility and employs a perpetual inventory system. All purchases of tires and related supplies are placed through the company's central Purchasing Department to take advantage of quantity discounts. The tires and supplies are received at the central warehouse and distributed to the retail stores as needed. The perpetual inventory system at the central facility maintains current inventory records, designated reorder points, optimum order quantities, and continuous stocktaking for each type and size of tire and other related supplies.

The documents employed by Beccan in their inventory control system and their use are described next.

■ *Retail stores requisition:* This document is submitted by the retail stores to the central warehouse whenever tires or supplies are needed at the stores. The shipping clerks in the Warehouse Department fill the orders from inventory and have them delivered to the stores

■ *Purchase requisition:* The inventory control clerk in the Inventory Control Department prepares this document when the quantity on hand for an item falls below the designated reorder point. The document is forwarded to the Purchasing Department.

■ *Purchase order:* The Purchasing Department prepares this document when items need to be ordered. The document is submitted to an authorized vendor.

■ *Receiving report:* The Warehouse Department prepares this document when ordered items are received from vendors. The receiving clerk completes the document by indicating the vendor's name, the date the shipment is received, and the quantity of each item received.

■ *Invoice:* An invoice is received from vendors, specifying the amounts owed by Beccan.

The departments involved in Beccan's inventory control system are described next.

■ *Inventory Control Department:* This department is responsible for the maintenance of all perpetual inventory records for all items carried in inventory. This inventory includes current quantity on hand, reorder point, optimum order quantity, and quantity on order for each item carried.

■ *Warehouse Department:* This department maintains the physical inventory of all items carried in inventory. All orders from vendors are received (receiving clerk) and all distributions to retail stores are filled (shipping clerks) in this department.

■ *Purchasing Department:* The Purchasing Department places all orders for items needed by the company.

■ *Accounts Payable Department:* Accounts Payable maintains all open accounts with vendors and other creditors. All payments are processed in this department.

Required

Prepare a document flowchart to show how these documents should be coordinated and used among the departments at the central facility of Beccan Company to provide adequate internal control over the receipt, issuance, replenishment, and payment of tires and supplies. You may assume that the documents have a sufficient number of copies to ensure that the perpetual inventory system has the necessary basic internal controls. (CMA Examination, adapted)

3.9 For situations 1–4, perform these two steps.

a. Determine what type of hardware the company will need.

b. Draw a computer systems flowchart of the system described. See Fig. 3.11 and 3.12 for examples of computer systems flowcharts.

1. U-Bag-M Groceries maintains an electronic inventory system and has computerized the

receipt, sales, and ordering of merchandise. When a shipment is received, the cases are run along specialized conveyer belts. A scanner that is attached to the store's central computer is located on each side of the conveyer. The scanner reads the universal product code on each package as it passes and updates the inventory records for the items received. When merchandise is sold, the customer's purchase is scanned as it passes through the checkout stand and the appropriate inventory levels are credited for the sales that take place. When the on-hand quantity of a stock item falls below the reorder point, the computer system prints a copy of the order form. All receiving and sales transactions that cannot be handled by the scanners are entered manually.

2. Higher Education University has a computerized registration system. Prior to the beginning of classes, students can register 24 hours a day from anywhere in the country using a Touch-Tone phone. Once classes begin, the telephone registration is shut down, and the adding or dropping of a class is handled by registration employees who process registration queries and requests through an on-line terminal. Prior to the beginning of class the computer generates a class confirmation form that is mailed to the student. A report for each class section is also prepared and distributed to the professors who are teaching the class.

3. Quick Snack Incorporated distributes its snack food items through grocery stores and vending machines. Route personnel deliver items, stock the shelves, and collect out-of-date products from client stores. The route personnel use small laptop computers to help them record the sales and the out-of-date pulls made at each store. The route personnel also provide the store managers with printed bills and receipts. At the end of the day the data stored in the laptop computer are transferred to the company's centralized computer. For stocking vending machines the company's computer prepares a card on each machine to be serviced on a given day. The vendor then services the machine and records the stock information on the card. The vendor returns the card to the main office, where the cards are pro-

cessed nightly by the computer. Management can access the corporate data through on-line queries and through the use of the periodic, scheduled reports prepared by the computer.

4. U-Dial Phone Company maintains branch offices as well as a corporate office. Owing to the large number of customers, U-Dial staggers both monthly billing dates and payment deadline dates. When a customer billing date comes, an itemized bill (including a payment form) is prepared by the computer and mailed to the customer. A customer can either mail the payment to the corporate office or pay the bill in person at a branch office. When a customer mails in the payment, it is supposed to be accompanied by the payment form. Each day the preprinted forms are read and transferred onto a tape that is used to update the customer master file stored on disk. If a customer pays in person, a teller updates the customer's files online.

3.10 As the internal auditor for No-Wear Products of Hibbing, Minnesota, you've been asked by your supervisor to document the company's current payroll processing system. From your documentation No-Wear Products hopes to develop a plan for revising the current information system to eliminate unnecessary delays in the processing of paychecks. Your best explanation of the system came from an interview with the head payroll clerk:

The payroll processing system at No-Wear Products is fairly simple. Time data is recorded in each department using time cards and a time clock. Sometimes it's annoying, however, when people forget to punch out at night and we have to record their time information by hand. At the end of the period our payroll clerks enter the time card data into a payroll file for processing. Our clerks are pretty good—though I've had to make my share of corrections when they mess up the data entry.

Before the payroll file is processed for the current period, the personnel department sends us data on personnel changes, such as increases in pay rates and new employees. Our clerks enter this information into the payroll file so it is available for processing. Usually, when mistakes get back to us, it's because the people in personnel are recording the wrong pay rate or an employee has quit and they forget to remove the record.

The data is then processed and employee paychecks are generated for each employee. Several important reports are then generated for manage-

ment—though I don't know exactly what they do with them. In addition, the government requires regular federal and state withholding reports for tax purposes. Currently, the system generates these reports automatically, which is nice.

Required

a. Design a context diagram for the current payroll processing system at No-Wear Products.

b. Develop a data flow diagram to document the payroll processing system at No-Wear Products.

3.11 Ashton Fleming has decided to analyze the accounts payable process at S&S. His intent is to document how the system works so that it will be easier for S&S to move to a computerized system. He is also concerned that there may be weaknesses in the system, and he wants to make improvements to it. He has written the following narrative to explain what happens at S&S.

Before a vendor invoice is paid by S&S, it must be matched against the purchase order used to request the goods and the receiving report prepared by the Receiving Department. Since all three of these documents come into the Accounts Payable Department at different times, a separate alphabetical file is kept for each type of document. The purchase orders that are forwarded from purchasing are stored in a purchase order file. The receiving reports are stored in a receiving report file. When vendor invoices are received, the accounts payable clerk records the amount due in the accounts payable ledger and then files the invoices in the vendor invoice file.

The policy at S&S is to make sure that all accounts are paid within 30 days so that it can take advantage of the early-payment discounts that suppliers offer. When it comes time to pay a particular bill, the accounts payable clerk retrieves the vendor invoice and attaches the purchase order and the receiving report. These matched documents are forwarded to Ashton Fleming.

Ashton reviews the documents to ensure that they are complete and prepares a two-part check. The checks as well as the other three documents are forwarded to Susan for her approval and signature. Ashton records the amount of the check in the cash receipts journal.

Susan reviews the documents to ensure that they are valid payables and signs the checks. She forwards the check to the vendor and returns the documents as well as the second copy of the check to the accounts payable clerk. The clerk files the documents alphabetically in a paid invoice file.

At the end of every month the accounts payable clerk uses information from the accounts payable ledger to prepare an accounts payable report. This

report is forwarded to Susan for her review. After she is finished with the report, Susan files it chronologically.

Required

a. Prepare a data flow diagram to document accounts payable processing at S&S.

b. Prepare a document flowchart to document accounts payable processing at S&S.

3.12 Since opening its doors in Hawaii two years ago, Oriental Trading has enjoyed tremendous success. As a wholesaler, Oriental Trading purchases textiles from Asian markets and resells the textiles to local retail shops. To keep up with the strong demand for textiles in the Hawaiian Islands, Oriental Trading is expanding its local operations. At the heart of the expansion is the introduction of a new information system to handle the tremendous increase in purchases.

You have conducted several interviews with supervisors in the departments that interact with the acquisition/payment system. The following is a summary of your discussions.

A purchase requisition is sent from the inventory system and is received by Sky Ishibashi, a clerk in the Purchasing Department. Sky prepares a purchase order from information in the vendor and inventory files and mails it to the vendor. The vendor returns a vendor acknowledgment to Sky indicating the receipt of the purchase order. Sky then sends a purchase order notification to Elei Mateaki, a clerk in the Accounts Payable Department.

When the Receiving Department accepts vendor goods, the inventory system sends Elei a receiving report to notify him that the goods have been received. Elei also receives the invoices that are mailed in by the various vendors. Elei matches the invoices with the purchase order notification and the receiving report and updates the accounts payable master file.

Elei then sends a payment authorization to the Accounting Department. In the Accounting Department Andeloo Nonu prepares and mails a check to the vendor. When the check is issued, the system automatically updates the accounts payable master file and the general ledger.

Required

Develop a context diagram and a data flow diagram of the acquisition/payment system at Oriental Trading.

3.13 Ashton Fleming has worked furiously for the past month trying to completely document the major business information flows at S&S. Upon completing his interviews with the people involved with cash receipts, Ashton asks you to develop a comprehensive data flow diagram for the cash receipts system. The narrative of the system that Ashton developed follows.

Customer payments include cash received at the time of purchase as well as payments on account received in the mail. At the end of the day all checks are endorsed by the Treasurer, and a deposit slip is prepared for the checks and the cash. The checks, cash, and deposit slips are then deposited daily at the local bank by a clerk.

When checks are received as payment for accounts due, a remittance slip is included with the payment. The remittance slips are used to update the accounts receivable file at the end of the day. The remittance slips are stored in a file drawer by date.

Every week a cash receipts report and an aged trial balance are generated from the data in the A/R ledger. The cash receipts report is sent to Scott and Susan. A copy of the aged trial balance by customer account is sent to the Credit and Collections Department.

Required

Develop a context diagram and a data flow diagram for the cash receipts system at S&S.

3.14 A mail-order company advertises products in magazines. Most orders are initiated by magazine subscribers who fill in and send coupons to the mail order company. The company also takes orders over the phone, answers enquiries about products, and handles payments and cancellations of orders. Products that have been ordered are sent either directly to the customer or to regional offices of the company that handle the required distribution. The mail-order company has three basic data files that retain customer mailing information, product inventory information, and billing information based upon invoice number. During the next few years, the company expects to become a multimillion-dollar operation. Recognizing the need to computerize much of the mail order buisiness, the company has begun the process by calling you.

Required

Draw a context diagram and at least two levels of logical data flow diagrams for the above operations.

3.15 A student completes a registration request form and mails or delivers it to the registrar's office. A clerk enters the request into the system. First, the accounts receivable subsystem is checked to ensure that no fees are owed from the previous quarter. Next, for each course, the student transcript is checked to ensure that the course prerequisites are completed. Then, class position availability is checked and the student's social security number is added to the class list.

The report back to the student shows the result of registration processing as follows: If fees are owing, a bill is sent to the student and no registration is done. If prerequisites for a course are not filled a note is sent to the student and that course is not registered. If the class is full, the student request is marked with 'course closed'. If a student is accepted into a class, the day, time, and room are printed next to the course number. Student fees and total tuition are computed and printed on the form. Student fee information is interfaced to the accounts receivable subsystem. Course enrollment reports are prepared for the instructors.

Required

Prepare a context diagram and at least two levels of logical data flow diagrams for the above operation.

CASE 3.1: ANYCOMPANY, INC.—AN ONGOING COMPREHENSIVE CASE

One of the best ways to learn is to immediately apply what you have studied. The purpose of this case is to allow you to do that. You will select a local company that you can work with. At the end of most chapters you will find an assignment that will have you apply what you have learned using the company you have selected as a reference. This case, then, may become an ongoing case study that you work on throughout the term.

Visit several small- to medium-sized businesses in the local community. Explain that you will be doing a term-long case, and ask for permission to use the company as the firm you are going to study. Explain that you will need to meet with people in the company several times during the term to get the information you need. However, you will not need a great deal of their time or be a disruption to them. Offer to share any observations or suggestions that you can come up with as a way of allowing the firm to feel good about helping you.

Once you have lined up a company, perform the following steps.

1. Select one of the business cycles in the company for study. Examine all available documentation of the cycle's information system.

2. Prepare a report as follows:

a. Describe who is involved in processing the data in the system. Include in your report a partial organization chart that shows the relationships between the people that are involved.

b. Describe the different information that flows through the organization. Include in your report a context diagram and as many levels of data flow diagram as you need to show the flow of information in the cycle.

c. Explain what documents are used in the system. Include in your report a document flowchart showing the main documents used in processing transactions in the cycle, from origination to final destination. Also include a sample of the documents used in the system.

d. Explain what master files are in use in the company, and describe how and when they are updated. Include in your report a systems flowchart showing all inputs to the computerized system, all processing performed, and all output of the system.

e. Describe any other development tools used to create and document the system.

3. Select one of the software programs or applications in use by the company. You want to make sure that you do not get anything too complex or difficult to understand. Therefore you may want to select only a portion of a program. As directed by your instructor, do one or more of the following steps.

a. Draw a program flowchart showing the logic used in the program.

b. Create a decision table that shows the conditions tested in the program and the actions to be taken when each unique condition is met.

c. Convert the logic used in a portion of the program to structured English.

d. Develop a HIPO chart that shows the different functions performed in the program.

4. Assignments 2 and 3 had you use the techniques and tools with a system that already existed. As an alternative to those assignments, analyze a system that is currently being developed.

CASE 3.2

You are the systems analyst for the Wee Willie Williams Widget Works (also known as Dub 5, which is a shortened version of 5 W's). Dub 5 produces the keys that are used in making typewriter and computer keyboards. The company supplies many of the typewriter and computer manufacturers, but its biggest customer is IBM. It has been producing keys for IBM for over 20 years, and several years ago it signed a 10-year contract to provide the keys for all of IBM's personal computers.

As the systems analyst, you have been assigned the task of developing a data flow diagram for Dub 5's order processing system. You have gathered all the information you feel you need to develop the first-pass DFD and have just sat down to try and complete the diagram.

Customer orders, which are all credit sales, come in from customers by mail and by phone. When an order is processed, a number of other documents are prepared. You have diagramed the overall process and the documents produced, as shown in Fig. 3.16. The following documents are created.

■ A packing slip is prepared by the Order Processing Department and then used by the Warehouse Department to fill the order. The packing slip accompanies the goods shipped from the warehouse.

■ A customer invoice is prepared and mailed to the customer after the goods are shipped.

■ A monthly customer statement is mailed to the customer.

■ An order rejection is sent to the customer with an explanation of why the goods cannot be shipped.

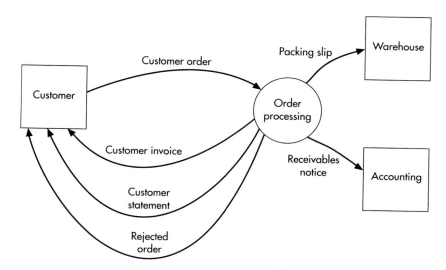

Figure 3.16
Overall process for Dub 5

■ A receivables notice, which is a copy of the customer invoice, is sent to the Accounting Department so that the accounts receivable records can be updated.

In reviewing your notes, you write the following narrative summary.

When an order comes in, the clerk in order processing looks up the customer in the company's credit file to determine whether the customer lacks credit approval or has exceeded the credit limit. If either of these conditions is true, the order is sent to the Credit Department. When an order has been approved for credit, the order is entered into the system on a standard order form. The information on the form is used to update the company's customer file (in which the name, address, and other information is stored), and the form is then placed in the company's order file.

When a rejected order is received by the Credit Department, the clerk first determines why the order has been rejected. If the company has exceeded its credit limit, it is sent a personalized copy of a standard letter informing the company that its credit limit has been exceeded and that the merchandise

will be shipped as soon as Dub 5 receives a payment from the customer. If the company has not been approved for credit, a credit application is sent to the company along with a letter informing the company that the order will be shipped as soon as credit approval is granted.

Before preparing a packing slip, the order processing employee checks the inventory records to determine whether the company has the products ordered on hand. If the items are on hand, a packing slip is prepared for every order form that is completed.

Once notification is received that the goods have been shipped, a customer invoice is prepared. One copy of the customer invoice is kept by the Order Processing Department, one copy is sent to the customer, and one copy is sent to the Accounting Department so that the receivables file can be updated. The receivables file contains all account information except name and address. A note is made in the customer file that the invoice has been sent. Every month customer statements are sent by Dub 5.

From the information just discussed, complete a DFD for Dub 5.

PART II

CHAPTER 4

A Review of Computer Hardware and Software

After studying this chapter, you should be able to:

- Explain why accountants must understand computer concepts.
- Differentiate between supercomputers, mainframes, minicomputers, and microcomputers.
- Explain how the three components of a CPU function and how data are represented in a computer.
- Compare and contrast the secondary storage devices used in computer systems.
- Compare and contrast the input and output devices used in computer systems.
- Compare and contrast the different levels of hardware and computer languages.
- Identify the functions and purposes of the different types of systems and application software.

**INTEGRATIVE CASE:
S&S, INC.**

Scott Parry is delighted that progress is finally being made toward acquiring a computerized system for S&S, Inc. (see Chapters 1–3). That is evident by the way he talks about the meeting he and Ashton had with Kimberly Serra, the manager of a local computer firm. Ashton set up the meeting with Kimberly after he was given the assignment to begin investigating a computerized information system. Ashton planned to take both Scott and Susan, the other owner of S&S. However, at the last minute Susan was unable to go.

It is evident to Scott that Ashton has a very good grasp of how S&S operates. For the past several weeks Ashton has used every spare minute analyzing S&S's needs for information and documenting its current system. In the meeting Ashton explained S&S's system to Kimberly and identified what he would like the system to do for S&S. Kimberly pointed out several things that the system might do for S&S that Ashton had not considered. Scott and Ashton left the meeting with a list of ideas and things to investigate.

The next day Scott calls Ashton into his office. He says that it is apparent to him that he needs to be more involved in the acquisition process. He confides he was initially reluctant to get involved because he knows so little about computers. His only exposure to them was a class in college a number of years ago.

Scott comments that he understood much of what went on in the meeting, but when Ashton and Kimberly began talking about computers, it was like they had switched to a foreign language. Scott asks Ashton to bring him some material that will help him get up to speed on computer technology so that he is better able to understand computer concepts. Scott also has the following questions that he would like Ashton to answer for him.

1. What size of computer system does S&S need: a mainframe, a minicomputer, or a personal computer?

2. What kind of storage medium should S&S use: hard disks, optical disks, tapes, or floppy disks? What kind of input and output devices?

3. What do all the acronyms that he and Kimberly used stand for—terms like CPU, ROM, RAM, MIPS, POS, UPC, 4GL, and DBMS? How much is a megabyte? How fast is a nanosecond?

4. What is the difference between system software and application software?

5. What kinds of software does S&S need, and what does each of the software programs do? ■

INTRODUCTION

Many accountants are like Scott Parry. They think people are speaking a foreign language when they begin to talk about computers. When accountants do not understand the terminology of computers, or the "computer language," it is more difficult to understand information systems.

The chapters in Part II provide accounting students with an understanding of systems terminology and technology. This chapter is intended as a review of the fundamental computer concepts of hardware and software. It also is intended as an introduction to computers for those who have had little background in computer technology. Its emphasis is on *what* computers are and *how* they work. The intent is to help students learn to speak "computerese."

Chapters 5 through 7 concentrate on the uses of computer technology. Chapter 5 explains microcomputers and end-user computing and discusses their impact on accounting information systems. Chapter 6 discusses data communications and advanced systems. Chapter 7 explores data base concepts.

Accountants need a basic understanding of computer technology. Although accountants do not need to be technical experts, most, like Ashton Fleming of S&S, need to understand what computers are, what they are composed of, how they operate, and how they store and process data. This understanding helps them to use, develop, evaluate, and manage their information systems.

One very important reason why accountants need to understand computer concepts is the role they play as users of the system. As technology advances and as computer equipment becomes more cost-effective to use, more and more accountants are taking advantage of the power of computers. Accountants are often provided with personal computers and powerful, easy-to-use software. This software allows them to access corporate data, download it into their personal computer, and analyze the data to produce the information they need. Accountants are also using their desktop computers as stand-alone systems by entering and maintaining all the data they need.

As a result, more users are able to satisfy their own information needs on a timely basis, without having to wait for the assistance of their programming staff. This allows the programming staff to concentrate on the complex, multiuser information systems that are needed by most large organizations. It has also put computer power within the reach of those who do not have access to programming staffs. "Taking computer power to the people" has resulted in an explosive growth in the area of microcomputers and personal productivity tools (discussed in the next chapter).

A second reason why accountants need to understand computer concepts is the accountant's role in systems design. Like Ashton of S&S, accountants are often members of the team that is responsible for hardware acquisition and software design or acquisition. An understanding of hardware and software concepts is essential in determining system requirements.

A third reason relates to the accountant's role as an information system evaluator. Both internal and external auditors are called upon to assess the strengths and weaknesses of information systems. In doing so, they must evaluate systems on the basis of criteria such as the adequacy of internal controls in the information system and the effectiveness and usefulness of the system. It is difficult to assess systems effectively without an understanding of hardware and software concepts.

A fourth reason is that accountants often have managerial positions with responsibilities for managing computer resources. They may oversee the purchase of the systems, supervise those who use them, and evaluate the use of computer resources.

This chapter is divided into two main parts. The first part discusses hardware, which is the physical equipment and devices that comprise a computer system. The second part discusses software, which is the instructions, procedures, or algorithms that direct the operation of computer hardware.

Section A: Computer Hardware

Computer hardware comprises all the physical equipment necessary to carry out the electronic data processing (EDP) tasks of a computer system. It includes the information processor, called the central processing unit (CPU). It includes devices that prepare data for input, as well as input, output, and storage devices. It also includes telecommunications devices that are used to transmit data from one location to another. The input, output, storage, and telecommunication devices are called **peripherals**.

As Ashton began to investigate the hardware choices that were available to S&S, he found many different hardware options. Figure 4.1 shows the different hardware devices he found for data preparation, input, processing, storage, data communications, and output.

Hardware will be discussed in five main sections. The first discusses the history and size classifications of computers. The second discusses the central processing unit. The third section discusses the various secondary storage devices and media. The fourth and fifth sections discuss the input and output devices common to computer-based systems.

COMPUTERS: HISTORY AND CLASSIFICATIONS

A Short History of Computers

The speed, power, and storage capacities of computers have increased dramatically since they were first introduced. At the same time, their size and cost have decreased dramatically. For example, the first computers were able to process hundreds of instructions per second. Current computers can process hundreds of millions of instructions per second. Storage capacity has gone from thousands of characters of storage to billions. The cost to execute a million instructions has fallen from about $10 to less that a tenth of a cent. Early computers filled a whole room; modern computers can fit in the palm of your hand.

These technological improvements have been so significant that they have been used to classify computers into four distinct generations. In Table 4.1 several important characteristics of computers are compared across the four generations. There are many that expect a fifth generation of computers to be introduced in the 1990s.

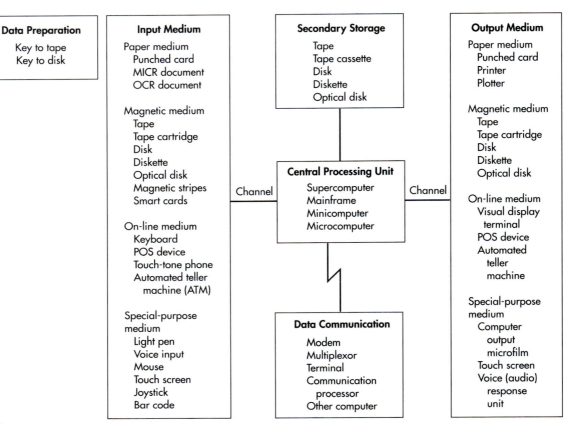

Figure 4.1
Computer hardware

The *first generation* of computers, of the late 1940s to late 1950s, were used in scientific applications at government and university sites. They utilized vacuum tubes to process and store information. These computers consumed a great deal of energy, produced a great deal of heat, occupied a great deal of space, and had very limited storage and memory capabilities. Even so, these machines gained widespread use, with the IBM 650 being the most popular.

It is interesting to note that the essential features of the modern computer were proposed in 1834 by Charles Babbage, a mathematical genius. However, in 1842 the British government, which initially had provided grants, refused further support for the analytical engine. The prime minister at the time, Sir Robert Peel, stated that the calculating machine was worthless to science. In 1991 the British spent nearly $600,000 to build the engine from Babbage's original design to prove that the analytical engine would have worked. In contrast to today's pocket calculators, Babbage's machine is 6 feet high and 10 feet long, contains 4000 parts, and tips the scale at 3 tons.

Second-generation computers were introduced in the late 1950s, when transistors and printed circuitry replaced vacuum tubes. These

	COMPUTER CHARACTERISTICS				
Generation of Computer	Computer Circuitry	Main Memory	Secondary Storage	Input Medium	Output Medium
First	Vacuum tubes	Magnetic drum	Magnetic tape Magnetic drum	Punched cards Paper tape	Punched cards Printed reports
Second	Transistors	Magnetic core	Magnetic tape Magnetic disk Magnetic drum	Punched cards Paper tape	Punched cards Printed reports

Third	Integrated circuits	Magnetic core
		Large-scale
		  integrated (LSI)
		  circuits
			Magnetic tape
			Magnetic disk
				Punched cards
				Keyboard entry
				Key to tape
				Key to disk
				Optical character
				  reader
				Magnetic ink
				  character reader
				Automatic teller
				  machine
				Point-of-sale
				  terminal
					Printed reports
					Video display
					Computer output
					  microfilm
					Plotter
					Point-of-sale display
					Automatic teller
					  machine

Fourth	Very large scale
	  integrated (VLSI) circuits
		VLSI circuits	Magnetic tape
			Tape cartridge
			Magnetic disk
			Diskette
			Optical disk
				Keyboard entry
				Key to tape
				Key to disk
				Optical character
				  reader
				Magnetic ink
				  character reader
				Point-of-sale
				  terminal
				Automatic teller
				  machine
				Voice
				Mouse
				Touch screen
				Light pen
					Printed report
					Video display
					Computer output
					  microfilm
					Plotter
					Audio response
					Point-of-sale display
					Touch screen
					Automatic teller
					  machine

Table 4.1

Comparison of the four generations of computers

advances led to smaller, faster, less expensive, and more reliable computers that used less energy, produced less heat, and had significantly more storage capacity. Magnetic cores (small doughnut-shaped devices strung together on wires) were used for internal storage. Magnetic disks and tapes were introduced for external storage. The most popular computers of the generation were IBM's large 7000 series of computers and the smaller computers of the 1400 series.

The *third generation* of computers, introduced in the mid-1960s, used integrated circuits, which had thousands of tiny transistors printed onto silicon chips. This again led to computers that were much smaller, faster, and more powerful than anything that preceded them. Sophisticated operating systems were developed to automate the control of computer operations. Computer languages became much more like the English language and therefore were easier to use and understand. This put the power of the new generation of computers in the hands of many more people. The most popular third-generation computers were the IBM series 360 and 370.

Computers entered a *fourth generation* when very large scale integration (VLSI) semiconductor circuits were introduced in the 1970s. With VLSI technology over a million circuits can be put on a chip the size of a fingernail. This again reduced the size of computers and increased their speed, power, and storage capacities. The fourth generation also saw the arrival of microprocessors, a computer on a thumbnail-size silicon chip. These microprocessors are used everywhere, from automobiles to toys to watches.

Computer Classifications: From Supercomputers to Microcomputers

The first computers were large, general-purpose machines designed to meet the processing needs of an entire organization. Only the largest organizations could afford to buy these mainframe computers. As technology improved and costs fell, smaller and less costly computers were developed. As computers began to proliferate, they were classified into four main categories: supercomputers, mainframes, minicomputers, and microcomputers. These classifications are based upon the size and power of the computer. Power is measured by such things as speed, memory capacity, computational power, and the number of users and peripherals that can be supported.

Ashton developed a table to compare the speed, storage capacity, and price of these broad classifications. It is shown in Table 4.2.

Supercomputer. Supercomputers are the largest and most powerful computers built. They have enormous storage capacities and are up to 10 times faster than mainframes. Most supercomputers are used for high-speed, number-crunching military and scientific tasks. Their uses include weapons research, weather forecasting, government research, large time-sharing networks, and very complex engineering applications. The leading manufacturer, Cray Research, has installed over two hundred of their machines worldwide.

Table 4.2
Comparison of supercomputers, mainframes, minicomputers, and microcomputers

	RAM Memory	MIPS*	Price
Supercomputer	500 MB to over 10 GB	Up to 1 TIPS†	$100,000–$35 million
Mainframe	100 MB to over 6 GB	Up to 500 MIPS	$60,000–$30 million
Minicomputer	Up to 200 MB	Up to 200 MIPS	Up to $500,000
Microcomputer	Up to 32 MB	Up to 100 MIPS	Up to $15,000

* Millions of instructions per second, a measure of computer speed.
† Trillions of instructions per second, a measure of computer speed.

Supercomputers achieve their high performance levels by using parallel processing (also referred to as multiprocessing). In parallel processing multiple processors work on the same problem at the same time by breaking the problem into pieces. Recently, very powerful microprocessors have been developed that are, in effect, mainframes on a chip. These chips have been used to produce mini-supercomputers that cost about $100,000, are small enough to sit by a desk, and have half the speed of the Cray computers costing millions of dollars.

Mainframe Computer. Mainframe computers have huge memories, have very fast processors, and are very powerful. They can process hundreds of different programs, handle massive amounts of data, respond to hundreds of different users, and coordinate hundreds of different peripherals all at the same time. They are used to solve scientific and military problems requiring many calculations, such as those in aircraft manufacturing and petroleum engineering. They are extensively used in business because they can process millions of transactions a day. They are used by banks to process checks, deposits, and other account information; by airlines for reservation systems; by universities for registration and scheduling; and by large organizations to handle customer inquiries and transaction processing.

The complexity of mainframes often requires a professional staff of programmers, operators, and analysts. The mainframe and all the peripherals such as disk and tape drives are housed in the **data processing center.** To ensure the security of the system, access to the data processing center is controlled. The computer system depicted in Fig. 4.2 is representative of the mainframes commonly used by large organizations and housed in a data processing center.

Much smaller computers are now available that are capable of doing many of the tasks that previously were performed only on mainframes. This has led many organizations to downsize their systems. **Downsizing** is shifting data processing and problem solving from mainframes to smaller computer systems. Downsizing can save organizations a great deal

Figure 4.2
ES/9000 mainframe computer
(*Source:* Photo courtesy of IBM.)

of money. It also allows the end user to become more involved in processing the data. This trend is accelerating, and some accountants feel that as much as 75% of the processing of accounting data will be done by desktop computers in the next few years. As the trend toward downsizing and networking continues, mainframes will increasingly be used as hosts to many smaller systems. They will coordinate and facilitate the interchange of data within a network of powerful microcomputers. In the future mainframes will have to become smaller and much less expensive to compete with other computers on the market.

Minicomputer. Minicomputers (also referred to as midrange computers) are larger and more powerful than microcomputers and smaller and less powerful than mainframes. The differences between minicomputers and microcomputers and mainframes is fuzzy. The largest microcomputers are now more powerful and less expensive than the smaller minicomputers. Likewise, the smaller mainframes are squeezing out the high end of the minicomputers. Many manufacturers of minicomputers have experienced declining sales recently as users move down to powerful microcomputers or up to smaller mainframes.

Minicomputers and mainframes often come in what is called a family of computers: computers that are compatible with each other and differ mainly in size and capacity. A computer family allows a company to start off small and move upward within the family as its needs increase. This upgrading is relatively painless, since the data and software work on all machines in the family. In a family of minicomputers, the smallest is comparable to the most powerful microcomputers, and the largest is comparable to the smallest mainframes.

4.1 FOCUS

Future Fashion in Personal Computing Is Intimate "Hardwear"

If a 2-pound laptop sounds like the last word in computing style, I have news for you. The next wave is intimate computing; and the ultrahip won't carry their computers, they will wear them. A coming "hardwear" revolution will deliver everything from goggle/display combinations to chips embedded in our clothes. These devices will delight consumers and become important business tools.

So why would anyone wear a screen on his face? Imagine you are an aircraft mechanic working in the wheel well of a 747, and you need to refer to a wiring sequence depicted in a manual sitting in your office on the other side of the airport. Instead of getting in your jeep, you flip a small head-mounted display over one eye, and talking into a small

Minicomputers generally function in an ordinary office environment. They do not need air-conditioning, special wiring, environmental controls, or a specialized staff of computer experts, as do mainframes. Most are designed for multiusers and can handle multiple terminals or workstations. Minicomputers are often used for specialized tasks such as computer-aided design and manufacturing (CAD/CAM). They are frequently used in universities, factories, and research labs. They can be connected to mainframes to help with time-consuming input and output tasks and are used in telecommunications networks. Many organizations use them to handle all their data processing tasks.

Microcomputer. For accountants the **microcomputer** is the most important of the four computer classifications, because most accountants use them on an almost daily basis. Their popularity stems from their ease of use, tremendous versatility, small size, low cost, and considerable power. For instance, the largest and most powerful of the microcomputers available today sits on a desktop (or fits inside a briefcase), has the computational power of a third-generation computer in use during the 1970s, and is sold for a fraction of the cost.

Microcomputers [also referred to as personal computers (PC) or as micros] come in a wide assortment of sizes and have a wide variety of uses. Microcomputers have been classified according to size or use: pocket, hand-held, pen-based, notebook, laptop, portable, transportable, desktop, and floor standing. They have also been classified according to where and how they are used: home, personal, professional, workstation, and multiuser, the latter being very powerful microcomputers designed to support several users at a time. Focus 4.1 discusses another classification, referred to as "wearable" computers.

---

boom microphone, you call up an image from an optical disk spinning in a Walkman-size computer on your belt. Thanks to peculiarities in our binocular vision, you can still see your work even as the image hangs in space the size of a normal screen viewed from reading distance.

Everything in this vision can be done today with off-the-shelf hardware. Reflection Technology introduced its Private Eye display in 1989 and is partnering with various companies from Hughes Aircraft to Sun Micro-

systems to build hardware systems and enhance the underlying technology. One start-up, Reddy Systems, has already mocked up the CD ROM unit described previously.

Wearable computers will appear first on the belts of field maintenance professionals and then spread into other deskless, information-intensive jobs. For example, NEC is reportedly developing a belt-mounted inventory computer for grocery stock clerks.

Wearing a computer may

sound like a strange thing to do, but we already do it today with electronic watches and tiny pagers. A decade from now executives may feel naked without their electronic "information exoskeletons," and softwear goggles will be de rigueur accessories for fashion-conscious teens.

Source: Paul Saffo, "Future Tense," *InfoWorld* (December 9, 1991): 66.

Perhaps the most important distinction between microcomputers is between those that are used on desktops and moved infrequently and those that are designed to be moved from location to location. Movable microcomputers (from pocket to portable) have a great deal of appeal because they can be used almost anywhere. Some industry experts expect the sales of portable computers to overtake those of desktops by 1996. The sales of desktop computer are expected to grow only from 14 to 16 million a year between 1992 and 1996. However, the sales of hand-held and portable computers together are expected to increase from 4 million in 1992 to almost 20 million in 1996. Figure 4.3 shows a desktop and a portable microcomputer.

A new type of hand-held computer, called a **personal digital assistant (PDA)**, is expected to have an especially big impact. For example, Prudential Insurance bought 10,000 of Sony's Wizard for its agents. Another recent advancement is a pen-based computer that for the first time allows the user to interface with the computer without using a keyboard or a mouse. Instead, data are entered and manipulated by writing directly on the screen with a penlike device called a stylus. Dataquest, a market research organization, has predicted a worldwide market for pen-based computers of $13 billion by 1995.

Microcomputers are used in two major ways: as stand-alone computers and as a part of a network of computers. As stand-alone computers, they allow individuals or organizations to maintain their own data and use their own software for tasks such as word processing, spreadsheets, graphics presentations, and accounting. As part of a network of interrelated computers, they allow documents, mail, transaction data, and other business data to be transmitted electronically to other users in the network. Peripheral devices (such as printers and disk drives), data, and computer files can be shared. These networks

Figure 4.3
Microcomputers: desktop and portable
(*Source:* Photos courtesy of IBM.)

offer the end user the best of both worlds. On the one hand, people can use their microcomputers independently of the network as stand-alone devices. On the other hand, the user has access to all the data and programs that are stored in the system. For example, when users need data stored on a mainframe data base, they can access the appropriate computer files and **download** the data from the mainframe to their micro-computer. There they can manipulate and analyze it to meet their own information needs. They can then upload the data to the system or send it to someone else in the network or to someone outside the network, using telecommunications technology.

As Ashton investigated the hardware options available to S&S, he realized that rapidly changing technology was blurring the distinction between the different sizes of computers. In his own mind he began to classify computers as personal computers, servers (larger microcom-puters or minicomputers that coordinate networks of computers), de-partmental computers, corporate computers, and research computers. However, he realized that regardless of how computers are classified, they all have common ingredients. One of those, the central processing unit, is discussed next.

CENTRAL PROCESSING UNIT

Processing functions in a computer are performed by the **central processing unit (CPU)**. The CPU has three main components: the arithmetic-logic unit, the control unit, and the primary memory. The **arithmetic-logic unit** carries out all the arithmetic calculations and logical comparisons (such as comparing the values of two data items). The **control unit** interprets program instructions. It also controls and coordinates the input, out-put, and storage devices in the system. The data and instructions used by the system are stored in the **primary memory**. The relationships of these three components to each other and to computer input, output, and storage are illustrated in Fig. 4.4.

There are two types of internal, or primary, memory: read-only and random-access. The contents of **read-only memory (ROM)** may be read but usually may not be altered by other program instructions. ROM con-tains information that is permanently stored in the computer, such as the most fundamental of the systems programs, including all or part of the operating system. Computers store programs, data, and instructions temporarily in their internal **random-access memory (RAM)**. Any memory location in RAM can be directly accessed by the computer, and RAM can be erased and reused as needed. A **semiconductor**—a tiny silicon chip inscribed with a number of miniature circuits—is the most common form of RAM. Semiconductor memory chips are small, inex-pensive, and very fast.

Peripheral devices connected to the CPU by cables, telephone lines, and so forth, are called **on-line devices** because they directly access the CPU and carry out input/output processes as needed. **Off-line devices**, on the other hand, are not connected directly to the CPU and are usually

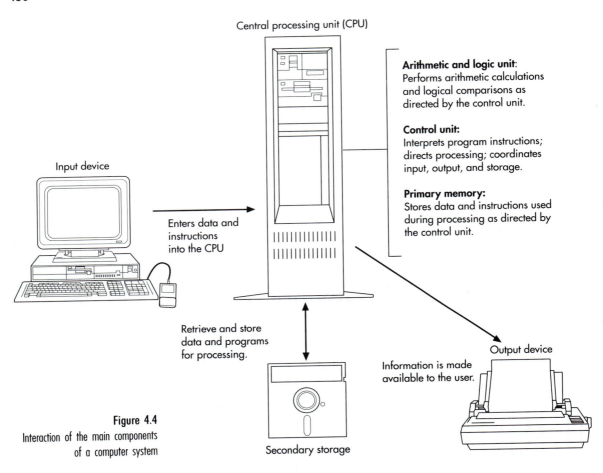

Central processing unit (CPU)

Arithmetic and logic unit:
Performs arithmetic calculations
and logical comparisons as
directed by the control unit.

Control unit:
Interprets program instructions;
directs processing; coordinates
input, output, and storage.

Primary memory:
Stores data and instructions used
during processing as directed by
the control unit.

Input device

Enters data and
instructions
into the CPU

Retrieve and store
data and programs
for processing.

Output device

Information is made
available to the user.

Figure 4.4
Interaction of the main components
of a computer system

Secondary storage

used to prepare data for input into the system or to prepare output for distribution.

Storage Measurements

Computers execute and store data in internal memory in what are called **bits** (short for "binary digit"). A bit is a storage location capable of assuming one of two possible states ("on" or "off," "0" or "1"). A group of 8 bits, called a **byte**, is used to represent a character of data. Because each bit can be either "on" or "off," there are 256 (2 to the eighth power) possible combinations of the 8 bits. Each combination represents a different character, such as a number or a letter of the alphabet.

As shown in Table 4.3, memory capacity is also expressed in terms of a **kilobyte** (K or KB). Although 1K actually represents 1024 bytes or characters, it is usually referred to as 1000 characters of memory. Therefore 640K represents approximately 640,000 characters of storage. Memory is also expressed in terms of **megabytes** (M or MB, a million characters of data), **gigabytes** (G or GB, a billion characters of storage),

Time Measures	Storage Measures

Millisecond = 1000th of a second
Microsecond = 1,000,000th of a second
Nanosecond = 1,000,000,000th of a second
Picosecond = 1,000,000,000,000th of a second
Megahertz = millions of cycles per second
   (measurement of processing speed of micro-
   computers)
MIPS = million of instructions per second
   (measurement of speed of computers)
	Bit = storage location that is on or off
	Byte = 8 bits that represent one character
	Kilobyte = 1000 characters
	Megabyte = 1,000,000 characters
	Gigabyte = 1,000,000,000 characters
	Terabyte = 1,000,000,000,000 characters

Table 4.3
Measuring computer speeds and capacities

and **terabytes** (TB, a trillion characters of storage). Common internal memory storage capacities of the different sizes of computers are shown in Table 4.2. Common secondary memory storage capacities are shown in Table 4.4.

Ashton's investigations convinced him that the future promises to bring big advancements in storage capacities. For example, he read that Peter Rentzepis, a chemistry professor at University of California at Irvine, has patented a three-dimensional storage media the size of a sugar cube that is capable of storing as much as 6.5 TB of data. The storage, which is very inexpensive and fast, is still a number of years away from commercial applications.

Speed Measurements

The speed of a CPU is measured in terms of MIPS (millions of instructions per second) and TIPS (trillions of instructions per second). Typically, the measurement used to compare two CPUs is the MIPS for each CPU. All else being equal, the greater the MIPS, the better the system. Representative MIPS speeds of the different sizes of computers are shown in Table 4.2.

When one computer is compared with another, some of the more important measures of CPU performance include access time and execution time. **Access time** refers to the time required to retrieve data from memory. **Execution time** refers to the time required to perform a computer instruction, such as add, multiply, or compare. These times are measured in very small fractions of a second. As shown in Table 4.3, the terminology used to refer to these fractions is **millisecond** (thousandth), **microsecond** (millionth), **nanosecond** (billionth), and **picosecond** (trillionth). To get an idea of the magnitude of these speeds, consider this

Table 4.4
Comparison of secondary storage media

	Access Time	Data Transfer Speed	Storage Capacity
Magnetic disk	10–100 milliseconds	200,000–5 million bytes per second	10 million–15 billion bytes
Floppy disk	100–600 milliseconds	10,000–30,000 bytes per second	360,000–4 million bytes
Magnetic tape	Not applicable	50,000–3 million bytes per second	Up to 1 billion bytes
Optical disk drive	100–400 milliseconds	150,000–500,000 bytes per second	Up to 3 billion bytes

example: If people took one step per nanosecond, they could circle the earth 20 times in 1 second. Representative access times of the various storage devices is shown later in the chapter in Table 4.4.

Microcomputer Hardware

The central processing unit (CPU) in a microcomputer is called a microprocessor. A microprocessor is a large-scale integrated circuit on a silicon chip. Other silicon chips constitute the computer's primary memory, where both instructions and data are stored. Still other chips govern the input and output of data and carry out control operations. Many of the recent microcomputers contain several processors. For example, an arithmetic processor, called a coprocessor, can be used to complete calculations up to two hundred times faster than the main processor.

Microprocessor chips are often identified by a number (e.g., 6502, Z80, 68000, 8080, 8088, 8086, 80286, 80386, and 80486). The 80486 chip from Intel contains 1.2 million transistors, and it cost more than $250 million and took 450 work-years to develop. In 1992 Intel, a leading chip manufacturer, broke with tradition and named its new microprocessor chip the Pentium. If it had not broken with tradition, the chip would have been referred to as the 80586 chip. The Pentium, which was first produced in 1993, is the newest Intel chip on the market, and many microcomputer manufacturers are now designing new machines using this chip. It is 67 times as fast as the 286 chip and can process 100 million instructions per second. Intel started work on the 686 chip in 1990 and will soon start work on the 786. By the year 2000 Intel hopes to have a chip that will have 1000 million transistors and execute 2 billion instructions a second.

The chips are mounted on a heavy plastic circuit board called the main circuit board or motherboard. Most personal computers have expansion slots on the motherboard that allow the user to add additional capabilities (such as increased memory or modems) and additional communication ports.

Communications between the computer's electrical components are in the form of digital electronic pulses. They travel along a data bus, which connects the various components of the microcomputer. Figure 4.5 shows a data bus and the hardware components of a microcomputer system that are hooked to it.

There are three important measures of the speed and computational power of a microprocessor. The first measure is word size, or the number of bits processed at one time. Computers move data internally using a group of bytes that is referred to as a word. Generally, a computer moves one word at a time to and from its storage locations. Although word sizes vary among computers, the most common word size in large computers is 32 bits. With a 32-bit chip a computer can work with 4 billion pieces of data in memory at the same time. The first generation of microcomputers had 4- or 8-bit microprocessors. The second generation was built with 16-bit chips. Now 32-bit microprocessor chips are widely available. A number of companies are

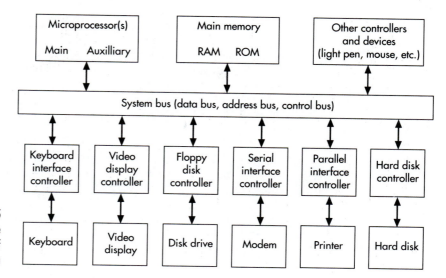

Figure 4.5
Diagram of a data bus and the
hardware components of
a microcomputer system

working on 64-bit chips that will make 20 quintillion (2 followed by 19 zeros) pieces of data available.

The second measure of a microprocessor is the frequency of the processor's electronic clock—how many steps a computer can execute per second. Microcomputer clock frequency speeds have improved from 1 **megahertz** (1 million cycles per second), common just a few years ago, to over 60 megahertz.

The third measure is the bus size, or the number of bits that can, at one time, be transmitted from one location in the computer to another. The trend is toward larger word and bus sizes and a higher frequency. As the word and bus sizes increase, an operation can be completed or transferred in fewer machine cycles. As the frequency of the internal clock increases (there are more cycles per second), computer operations can be completed faster.

SECONDARY STORAGE DEVICES AND MEDIA

Computer systems make extensive use of **secondary storage** to store data not currently needed by the system. Commonly used secondary storage devices include magnetic tape, magnetic disks, diskettes (also referred to as floppy disks), and optical disks. Magnetic tape is the most frequently used sequential-access medium. The other three are the most frequently used random-access media. Ashton compiled the access times, data transfer speeds, and storage capacities for each of these four secondary storage media. They are lised in Table 4.4. Each of these four storage media is discussed next.

Magnetic Tape

Magnetic tape is the oldest secondary storage medium still in common use. As shown in Fig. 4.6, tapes come in two different forms: tape reels and

Figure 4.6
Comparison of magnetic tape reels and tape cartridges and the devices that read and write to them (*Source:* Photos courtesy of IBM.)

the more recently developed tape cartridges. A reel of magnetic tape generally has nine horizontal rows, called tracks, on which data are recorded in the form of magnetic bits. A tape cartridge stores data in 18 tracks. Both types need a tape drive for reading and writing purposes.

There are three advantages of magnetic tapes: They can hold a lot of data, they are inexpensive, and they take up little storage space. Their biggest disadvantage is their inflexibility. They must be read sequentially, and records cannot be added, deleted, or updated without processing the entire file. Tape cartridges are much faster, store more information, take up less space, and are more convenient to use than traditional tape reels. Tapes are used for backup purposes, for data that are not needed frequently by the system, and for data that do not require direct access.

Magnetic Disks   Currently, **magnetic disks** are the dominant direct-access storage device because they provide the optimal trade-off among such factors as cost, access time, storage capacity, and flexibility. A magnetic disk is similar in appearance to a stack of phonograph records, except that there is space between each adjoining pair of disks for one or more read/write heads. Data are recorded on both sides of each disk.

The biggest advantage of disks is their direct-access capability, which allows greater flexibility in processing data. The computer does not have to read an entire file to find the record desired because the read/write head can move directly to any physical storage location. As a result, the system can readily locate the record needed and access it directly. Thus accessing, deleting, and updating a single piece of data in a record can be accomplished much more efficiently than if the data were stored on magnetic tape. This direct and fast access makes disks the most popular secondary storage medium.

The disadvantages of disks are their cost and their bulkiness. Even though more data can be stored on a disk than on a single tape, disk storage is still significantly more expensive than tape storage. Magnetic disks take up as much as 10 to 15 times more space than tapes storing the same amount of data.

A special type of magnetic disk, called a **hard disk**, is used in minicomputers and microcomputers. The hard disk shown in Fig. 4.7, for example, is one used on minicomputers. A hard drive comes in a clean, airtight, sealed box. Inside are one or more hard disks and the accompanying access mechanisms. Because of its protective environment, hard disks can be operated at higher speeds and can pack data closer together. Thus large quantities of data can be stored in a small space and accessed quickly. Common storage capacities for these hard drives are from 20 MB to over 3.5 GB. Common sizes are $2^{1}/_{2}$, $3^{1}/_{2}$, and $5^{1}/_{4}$ inches.

Diskettes

A **diskette**, or **floppy disk**, is a circular piece of flexible magnetic film enclosed in a protective cover. It comes in various sizes, with the most common being $3^{1}/_{2}$ and $5^{1}/_{4}$ inches. Its greatest advantages are its compactness as a storage medium and its relatively low cost. Diskettes have a much smaller storage capacity and a slower access time than do hard disks. The diskette is commonly used for secondary storage only in smaller computer systems and as a data entry medium.

Optical Disks

A recent innovation in secondary storage is the **optical disk**. Optical disks use laser technology to burn microscopic holes in a disk's recording surface. Laser beams also read the stored information. Most optical disks are **WORM (write-once, read-many)** devices. As a result, they are often

Figure 4.7
Hard disk (left) and optical disks (right)
(*Source:* Photos courtesy of IBM.)

referred to as **CD ROM (compact disk, read-only memory)**. Some optical disks can be rewritten on. However, it is difficult to rewrite on the disks, and there is a modest limit to the number of rewrites that can be done.

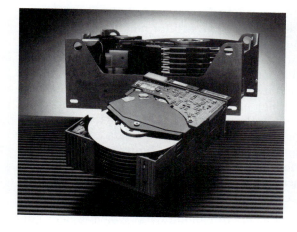

There are significant advantages to laser optical disks. First, they can hold much more data (up to 680 MB) than magnetic disks of similar size. For example, Groliers has published its 21-volume *Academic American Encyclopedia* on a single optical disk. Second, laser disks can be removed from their drives, so the disk unit can read or write to an almost unlimited number of disks. Third, recorded disks can be mass-produced easily and inexpensively. Like other storage media, they have some disadvantages, one of which is access time. Currently, access time for these disks is longer than for magnetic disks. Second, it is not possible to alter the data stored on CD ROM disks.

Ashton came across many references to accountants' using optical disk technology. For example, he found that Price Waterhouse was one of the first CPA firms to use optical disks. It uses them to provide each office with a portable resource library on accounting pronouncements and the firm's policy on accounting issues. In addition, he found that the Research Institute of America recently gave tax accountants the opportunity to receive their tax service on an optical disk.

A **videodisk** is a special type of optical disk that can store audio and video as well as text data. The disk can be accessed a frame at a time for motionless viewing or can be played like a videotape for moving action and sound. Any frame of the disk can be accessed in three seconds or less. These disks have many uses, including interactive training and marketing products, such as shoes, home furnishings, real estate, and vacation resorts.

INPUT DEVICES

Business data processing systems are characterized by high volumes of input and output and relatively simple computations. Input and output device speeds, however, are much slower than those of central processors. As a result of this mismatch in speeds, business systems are often referred to as being **input/output-bound**. This reduces **throughput**, which is the total amount of useful work performed by a computer system during a given period of time. Most approaches to increasing throughput focus on circumventing the basic mismatch between CPU and input/output speeds. One popular approach for mainframe computers is to have all input/output instructions performed by hardware devices (minis, micros, etc.) that act as communication interfaces between the mainframe CPU and all input/output devices.

Data entry costs often outweigh the cost of processing the data once captured. Entry costs are high because of the large volume of accounting data that is entered and the frequent need for human intervention in capturing data. Therefore it is important to utilize data entry methods that minimize human interaction and that maximize the use of high-speed computer input devices.

Ashton found that there are several different approaches to entering data into a system. Here are the options he identified.

1. *The use of source documents* to capture data, which is later converted into machine-readable form: This approach is time-consum-

ing, costly, and error-prone, and it requires several steps involving several people. It also utilizes two different forms of data media (paper, then tape or disk).

2. *The use of turnaround documents:* Since turnaround documents are produced by the system, their use reduces the input preparation work load and the possibility of input errors. Although the devices that read turnaround documents are relatively slow, they are faster than people keying information into the system. Unfortunately, this approach is often not possible, since much of the input to a system is not a direct result of system output.

3. *The use of an on-line terminal* or a microcomputer to key the data directly into the computer. This approach still requires significant effort to key in the data and may require that the data be captured on paper before being keyed into the system.

4. *The use of source data automation devices* to automate the data capture and entry process. This approach decreases the time, effort, and errors associated with the first and third approaches.

5. *The use of* electronic data interchange, which is essentially one computer talking to another, such as a buyer sending a purchase order to a supplier electronically. Like the fourth alternative, this approach is very attractive in terms of cost, speed, minimal human effort, and accuracy. Electronic data interchange is discussed in detail in Chapter 6.

Ashton concluded that there is not always a "right" answer about which method should be used in a particular situation. Instead, there are choices between alternatives, each with its own set of advantages. The best method is often the best combination of reliability, cost, speed, and accuracy. As a general rule, however, the more automated the process, the more effective it will be.

The hardware devices that are used in these five alternatives are discussed next. Table 4.5 shows Ashton's compilation of the speeds of some of the more frequently used input and output devices.

Data Preparation Devices

The key-to-tape encoder is used to record data on tape, for subsequent processing by the system. In a key-to-disk encoder several keying stations are linked to a minicomputer that has an attached disk memory. Data may be entered simultaneously from each of the keying stations and pooled on the disk file. The computer edits and sorts the data when all the records have been entered and then stores it for subsequent processing on the mainframe computer.

On-line Entry Devices

A visual display terminal (VDT) (also often referred to as a cathode ray tube, CRT) is an input/output device that can enter data directly into the computer and receive output directly from the computer. It uses a keyboard for input, and the output is displayed visually on a monitor. *VDTs* are still popular today, but increasingly, microcomputers are

I/O Device	Typical I/O Speed
Video display terminals (output)	250–500,000 characters per second
Printers (output)	Character printer: 10–600 characters per second Line printer: 200–3000 lines per minute Page printer: 10–200 pages per minute
Optical character recognition (OCR) scanners (input)	100–3600 characters per second
Magnetic ink character recognition (input)	700–3200 characters per second 180–2400 documents per minute

Table 4.5
Comparison of input/output
device speeds

Source: James O'Brien, *Management Information Systems* (Homewood, Ill.: Irwin, 1990): 147.

used to perform these input functions. Microcomputers can do everything that the terminals can do, and in addition, they can be used as a personal computer when not functioning as a data input device.

Ashton found that on-line data entry devices have significant advantages. First, the editing of transaction data for accuracy is greatly facilitated because the computer can perform various logic and reasonableness tests on each data item. The computer can also notify the user of any errors, thereby allowing the errors to be corrected before they are entered into the system. Second, they can be placed in remote locations, so transaction data can be entered into the system from their place of origin as they occur.

Both VDTs and microcomputers require that data be keyed in, which can be slow and tedious. As a result, there is a move toward a more user-oriented interface. Several different approaches are being taken, including the use of an electronic mouse, light pens, joysticks, and touch-sensitive screens. A **mouse** is a small device with push buttons that can be used to point to icons, or pictures, on the screen that represent functions. Pushing a button on the mouse, referred to as clicking, causes the activity that the icon represents to take place. **Light pens** use photoelectric circuitry to enter data through the VDT screen. Their principal use is in graphics applications. With the appropriate software they can draw, fill, or color shapes on the screen. They can also move the cursor and make menu selections. A **joystick** looks like a gearshift lever and is used to move the cursor on the screen. Joysticks are especially popular for controlling video games and for computer-assisted design. **Touch-sensitive screens** allow users to enter data or select menu items by touching the surface of a sensitized video display screen with a finger or a special pointer. Figure 4.8 shows a touch-sensitive screen.

Source Data Automation Devices

Ashton was especially interested in how organizations were using technology to capture input data. He found that most organizations are moving toward **source data automation (SDA)** devices that collect input in machine-readable form at the time when and the place where the data originate. This technique significantly decreases human involvement,

Figure 4.8
Input devices: A touch
sensitive screen (left) and
a voice input system (right)
(*Source:* Photos courtesy of IBM.)

resulting in greater accuracy and considerable time and cost savings. It also results in more timely data input, and it avoids the bottlenecks that often occur with slower input methods.

Magnetic ink character recognition (MICR) devices read characters encoded on documents in a special magnetic ink. The most significant use of MICR is in the banking industry, where it is used to encode account numbers and amounts on customers' checks and deposit slips. A blank check has the bank number, account number, and check number encoded on the lower left portion of the check. When a check is processed, the amount of the check is inscribed in the lower right corner.

Optical character recognition (OCR) devices read documents containing type-written, computer-printed, or hand-printed characters. Turnaround documents, which are output from a computer that are later returned to the company and read as input, are read by an OCR reader. OCR devices are commonly used in business. For example, American Express installed OCR equipment that is able to read 60% of the handwritten numbers on the 900,000 charge slips that it processes every day. The system, which cost more than $10 million dollars when installed in 1992, will pay for itself in four years. The IRS now reads handwritten 1040EZ forms and by the year 2000 hopes to be able to read all tax forms electronically. Other common uses include insurance company premium notices and utility company billings.

Originally, a **point-of-sale (POS)** recorder was just an electronic cash register linked to a centralized computer and its data files. However, technological advancements have turned POS recorders into intelligent and multifunctional networked workstations.

Many POS recorders utilize devices that read price or product code data. One example is the optical scanner commonly used in grocery stores to read the **universal product code (UPC)**. The UPC is one of the many different types of **bar codes** that are now standard on many products. The scanners can be built into a counter or can be hand-held wands. The scanner reads the bar code by emitting an intense light. The scanner

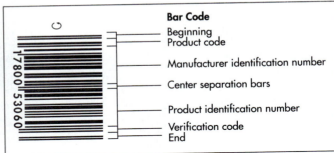

Bar Code
Beginning
Product code

Manufacturer identification number

Center separation bars

Product identification number

Verification code
End

Figure 4.9
Data collection terminal capable of
reading bar codes and magnetic
stripes

recognizes the pattern of bars and spaces and translates it into electronic impulses that are sent to the computer. The computer recognizes the product, retrieves the price of the item sold, and sends it back to the cash register to display and to print on a receipt. The computer can also update the quantity sold and the inventory balance stored in the file. For credit sales a clerk can enter the customer's account number and have the system check the customer's credit, as well as update the accounts receivable record. The automatic performance of these and similar functions greatly enhances the productivity of retail sales clerks. Figure 4.9 shows a UPC bar code and a data collection terminal that reads the bar code.

The use of bar codes has moved beyond the grocery store. They are now used in general merchandise retailing, hospitals, libraries, military and other government operations, transportation facilities, and the automotive industry. **Two-dimensional (2-D) bar codes** (it reads the whole

FOCUS

"Active Badges" Keep Silent Tabs on Employees' Whereabouts

George Orwell's Big Brother is watching more keenly than ever at the Olivetti Research Laboratory and the computer laboratory at Cambridge University in Cambridge, England. Employees

there are sporting experimental infrared tracking devices called "active badges" that allow a computer network to silently keep tabs on each person's whereabouts.

The small clip-on badges hanging from shirt pockets and dangling from belts are equipped with transceivers that emit uniquely coded signals every few seconds. The signals are picked

surface area of the bar code, rather than just the pattern of lines) have been developed that can store the equivalent of two pages of text in the same space as a UPC. These codes can tell the scanning device where a product came from, where it should be sent, and how it should be handled during shipping. One of the first uses of the code was in handling barrels of hazardous toxic waste.

The use of bar codes has spawned other automatic identification systems. Most credit, ID, and banking cards have a **magnetic stripe** that contains up to 125 characters of information, such as name, address, and account number. When the card is used for a purchase, a POS terminal reads the information on the stripe, transmits it to the bank, and verifies that the credit card is valid. **Smart cards** extend the capabilities of magnetic stripes. These cards have an embedded 64K chip that can contain a minibiography about you. Smart cards can be used to keep track of your medical history, employment information, interests, and so on.

Many manufacturing plants use **machine vision** to inspect products or equipment. Sensing equipment, such as a video camera, allows a computer to "see" an object. The computer, which has been programmed to know what a normal product looks like, is then able to detect defects. Machine vision is also used in the biotechnology industry to locate diseased cells in a culture.

Radio frequency identification tags are a way to track data from one location to another. These tags send and receive a radio signal that identifies the objects attached to them. Radio frequency identification tags are used to track products such as Federal Express or UPS packages as they are shipped across the country.

Another type of identification, called an active badge, is explained in Focus 4.2.

An approach to source data automation that has made great strides

---

up by infrared sensors located in each room and transferred to workstations and personal computers that serve as nodes on a distributed computer network. When telephone calls come in to the facility, the receptionist can call up the system, locate the individual, and transfer the call to the nearest telephone.

The practical benefits of active badge tracing have turned some initial doubters into be-lievers, according to Mark Chopping, a research engineer at the Olivetti lab. "We find we don't miss phone calls anymore," he said. "A lot of the people who refused to wear the badges at first came back after two months and asked for one."

In addition to enhancing physical security in corporate buildings, this automatic tracing system can be used to track objects such as luggage or even children at airports.

One potential stumbling block is that the system responds to the badge, not the individual. Whoever wears that uniquely coded badge can assume the identity of the proper owner. Solving the authentication problem is the target of a related Olivetti/DEC research project.

Source: Maryfran Johnson, "Wherever You Go, They Will Follow," *Computerworld* (July 15, 1991): 19.

in recent years is **voice input**. At a minimum a voice input system needs a voice recognition unit, a microphone, and a terminal to display the recorded input. Figure 4.8 shows a voice input device that understands spoken words and transmits them into a computer.

There are a number of voice input systems currently in use. The airline and parcel delivery industries, for example, use voice input systems to route packages. The U.S. Postal Service also uses them to help sort mail. In 1992 AT&T replaced six thousand operators with a computer that understands speech and forwards phone calls almost as well as humans. AT&T's word-spotting technology picks out certain words, such as *collect call*, and forwards the call. Speaking in an accent, stammering, stuttering, and even singing do not affect the accuracy of the system. IBM researchers are developing a voice recognition system that currently recognizes over sixty thousand words. It allows you to dictate information, such as a letter, instantly review it, correct errors, and it learns from its mistakes.

Emergency room physicians at Holy Name Hospital in Teaneck, New Jersey, use voice recognition systems to quickly and accurately fill out emergency room medical charts. The $27,000 system, which paid for itself in four months, consists of a PC and a phone receiver. It is able to factor out the noises of the emergency room and record only what the doctors say. It uses an expert system and a built-in knowledge base that interacts with the doctors to help them check for symptoms they may have missed. This system has greatly strengthened the hospital's cases against malpractice suits.

COMPUTER OUTPUT DEVICES

The previous section discussed the devices by which information is entered and stored in a computer system. This section describes four output devices that are not directly related to any specific form of computer data entry: video display units, printers and plotters, voice response units, and computer output microfilm.

Visual Display and Audio Response Units

One of the most popular output mediums is a visual display terminal, or a monitor. A CRT is a device that displays phosphorous characters on the screen. In recent years a flat-panel display that uses liquid crystal or gas discharge technology has also been introduced, particularly for small, portable systems. Monitors are either monochrome (limited to one color) or multicolor. Display units vary widely in price and quality. The more expensive monitors usually have high-quality color and better resolution. **Resolution** refers to how small an element the display hardware can manipulate to produce letters, numbers, or graphs. This element is called a **pixel**, which is short for "picture element." The more pixels per square inch, the higher the resolution. With high resolution the screen will be sharper, diagonal lines will be straighter, filled-in areas will be darker, and graphics will be clearer.

Audio response units generate "voice" responses from a computer. They are most useful when the desired response is relatively short and when no documentation is necessary. Accounting applications include verifying a customer's credit and answering inquiries about a customer's bank balance. A typical voice response unit contains a collection of recorded words and phrases representing its vocabulary. The computer determines the sounds needed to generate the necessary message and transmits the message to the user.

Printers, Plotters, and Microfilm

A **printer** produces paper output, often referred to as **hard copy**. Printers vary widely in terms of print quality, speed, graphics capabilities, and cost, which is directly affected by the first three elements. Color printing is also available, but at significant additional cost. Some color printers are so sophisticated that they can produce photographic-quality images on paper or on transparencies.

Ashton found that printers can be classified in several ways:

1. *By printing capacity:* Character printers print one character at a time, line printers print one line at a time, and page printers print one page at a time. The speeds of these printers are shown in Table 4.5.

2. *As impact or nonimpact:* **Impact printers** strike an embossed character against an inked ribbon positioned in front of a piece of paper. The most popular impact printer is the dot matrix printer, which forms characters by using a group of small wires to form dots. **Nonimpact printers** transfer images without actually striking the paper. One of the most widely used, the laser printer, reflects laser beams off a rotating disk that contains the available characters. The reflected laser beam is projected onto the paper, where it forms an electrostatic image. The paper is then passed through a toner to produce high-quality images. Nonimpact printers are generally more reliable than impact printers. However, impact printers have historically been less expensive.

3. *By type of interface:* Printers are connected to computers by either a cable or a data communications line. If the computer sends the data needed to generate a character along a single cable one bit at a time, the printer must use a **serial interface**. If the computer sends the bits needed to generate a character simultaneously along parallel cables, the printer must have a **parallel interface**. Serial transmission is slower but can be used over longer distances.

A **plotter** is a special type of printer that produces a graphical output on paper by moving a writing arm across a paper surface. Modern plotters can produce three-dimensional and multicolored drawings. The growing interest in computer graphics as a tool for management decision making has led to increased use of plotters for preparing management reports.

Computer output microfilm (COM) devices use a photographic process to place computer output on microfilm. COM is an extremely fast output technique that, relative to paper, reduces storage space requirements by 95% to 99%. It permits faster document retrieval and is a less expensive storage medium than paper. Microfilm is used by businesses to store their noncurrent accounting records and copies of company documents. Examples of common applications include the copies of depositors' checks held by banks and the documents held by retail or industrial firms.

Section B: Software

The hardware devices discussed in this chapter are worthless without good software. **Software** is the detailed instructions that control the functions of the different hardware devices. A specific set of detailed instructions that tell the computer how to accomplish a particular task is called a **computer program**. The process of writing software programs to accomplish a specific task or set of tasks is called **computer programming**. Software programs are written in a **programming language**.

Ashton found that software programs can be divided into two separate categories: application software and systems software. **Application software** is written to perform various clerical functions and to support users. Examples include programs to keep the accounts receivable, accounts payable, inventory, and payroll records up to date. **Systems software** interprets the application program instructions and tells the hardware how to execute them. The diagram shown in Fig. 4.10 illustrates this relationship.

Software concepts are covered here in three main sections. In the first section programming languages and the different levels or generations of languages are examined. The next two sections discuss systems and application software.

LEVELS OF COMPUTER LANGUAGES

For the computer to carry out a processing task, it must have a set of instructions. This instruction set, or computer program, may be written in any of the over two hundred programming languages in active use. Each has its own unique vocabulary, grammar, and rules for usage. Languages are often classified as high-level or low-level. The closer the language is to the language used by the computer, the lower the level of the language. The closer the language is to English and the easier it is to use, the higher the level.

Figure 4.10
Application and systems software: interfaces between users and hardware

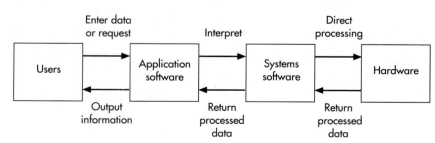

Language	Instruction
Machine language	0101100000100000000100001110000 0101101000100000000100001110001 0101000000100000000100001110010
Symbolic assembly language	L 2,A A 2,B ST 2,C
Procedure-oriented language	ADD SALARY, COMMISSION, GIVING TOTALPAY
Fourth-generation language	COMPUTE THE TOTALPAY OF ALL EMPLOYEES BY ADDING THEIR SALARY AND COMMISSION.

Table 4.6
Typical instructions in the four levels of programming languages

This section briefly addresses four levels of languages (from lowest to highest): machine language (first-generation), symbolic languages (second-generation), high-level languages (third-generation), and very high level languages (fourth-generation). These language generations are similar to the hardware generations discussed earlier in the chapter. Table 4.6 shows an example of the code, or program statements, that can be used in each of the four language levels to give instructions to the computer. Note that first-generation languages use binary-coded digits (0s and 1s). Second-generation languages use symbolic-coded instructions. Third-generation languages use English-like statements and arithmetic notation. Fourth-generation languages use natural and nonprocedural statements.

Machine-Level Languages

Each computer has its own machine language, which is a binary code (a string of 0s and 1s) that can be interpreted by the internal circuitry of the computer. Programming in machine language is extremely difficult, time-consuming, and error-prone. It is not used anymore because higher-level languages are available.

Symbolic Languages

A more understandable alternative to machine language is symbolic language. In a symbolic language each machine instruction is represented by symbols that bear some relation to the instruction. For example, the symbols L, A, and ST might represent the LOAD, ADD, and STORE instructions, respectively. A symbolic language program is converted to machine language by a special program called an assembler. In this conversion process the symbolic language program, called the source program, and the assembler are input to the CPU. The machine language program, called the object program, is the output. Assembler programs are not easy for most people to learn or use and are not common in business data processing.

High-Level Languages

The use of macroinstructions—instructions that are translated into multiple machine language instructions—is one reason third-generation languages were initially referred to as high-level languages. High-level languages are **machine-independent languages**, which means that the same language can be used on many types of computers.

High-level languages are generally easier to learn, have less rigid rules, and are more flexible than symbolic languages. As a result, they are less error-prone and easier to use. However, they are less efficient than symbolic languages. Table 4.7 lists some of the more popular high-level languages and their uses.

Table 4.7
High-level languages

Name and Original Name	Description and Uses
COBOL (COmmon Business Oriented Language)	Designed specifically for business applications involving large amounts of record processing and file updating. The most common programming language for business applications. English-like and self-documenting.
FORTRAN (FORmula TRANslation)	The first high-level language to be widely used and accepted. Designed to solve scientific problems that can be expressed in terms of mathematical formulas. The most common programming language for applications in science and engineering.
BASIC (Beginner's All-purpose Symbolic Instruction Code)	Designed to be very simple to learn so that non-programmers could easily learn it. Similar to FORTRAN, but simpler and easier to learn. Widely used on microcomputers and by on-line time-sharing services.
C (previous versions were called A and B)	Used extensively in developing software packages, especially for microcomputers. Has the executional efficiency of an assembly language, yet has some of the ease of use and machine independence of high-level languages.
ALGOL (ALGOrithmic Language)	Like FORTRAN, a language designed primarily for scientific and mathematical problems. Used internationally in place of FORTRAN.
PASCAL (named after mathematician Blaise Pascal)	Designed to allow a structured, modular approach to programming. Has a powerful data structuring and data manipulation feature. Very flexible and self-documenting. Used in both large computers and microcomputers.
APL (A Programming Language)	A symbolic interactive programming language. Designed for efficient interactive programming of analytical business and scientific applications. Especially popular for time-sharing.

Name and Original Name	Description and Uses
ADA (named after Augusta Ada Byron)	A recent, very sophisticated multipurpose language. Designed for the U.S. Department of Defense. Resembles PASCAL. Written to replace COBOL and FORTRAN.
PL/1 (Programming Language 1)	Highly flexible modular language oriented toward applications that require a significant number of computations and that process large amounts of data records.
RPG (Report Program Generator)	Originally designed to produce reports. Has evolved into a powerful, prompt-driven programming language.
LISP (LISt Process)	Procedure-oriented language designed to manipulate symbols that are grouped into ordered lists. Widely used in artificial intelligence and expert system applications.
PROLOG	Artificial intelligence language especially suited to symbol manipulation. Is nonprocedural. Widely used in Japan for artificial intelligence.

Table 4.7
(Continued)

Compilers are used to convert high-level languages into machine language. A systems flowchart showing the process of compiling and executing a high-level program appears in Figure 4.11. The compiler and the source program are input into the system. The compiler translates the source program into a machine language object program. Two other outputs are possible: a report listing the source program and diagnostic messages. **Diagnostic messages** inform the programmer of **syntax errors**, which are errors in the use of the language rather than logic, or programming, errors. **Logic errors** occur when the instructions given to the computer do not accomplish the desired objective. If there are no significant syntax errors, the object program and the input are read into the computer. The program is executed, and a printed report and a data file are written out.

A translation program called an **interpreter** is used in some high-level languages. An interpreter takes each programming instruction and, one at a time, checks it for syntax errors, translates it into machine language, and executes it. In contrast, a compiler translates all instructions into machine language and then executes them. Since the interpreter translates and executes instructions one at a time, neither object programs nor diagnostics are produced. The BASIC language used in microcomputers is usually an interpreted language.

Fourth-Generation Languages

As computers have become more common, **fourth-generation languages (4GLs)** were developed that are nonprocedural and more conversational. In

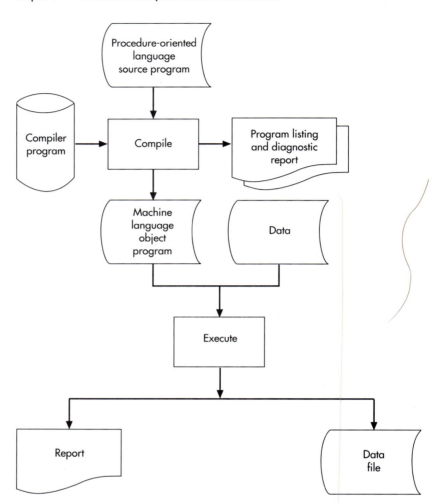

Figure 4.11
Compiling and executing a procedure-
oriented language program

prior generations programmers had to concentrate on telling the
computer the exact procedures to follow to produce the information
desired. When users needed information, they had to specify their need
to an analyst, who translated it to a programmer, who produced the
information, anywhere from days to months later. By the time the
users got the information, it was often too late to be of any value.

With 4GL users specify the results they want, leaving the 4GL to
determine the sequence of instructions needed to achieve the results.
The approach is to specify *what* information the user wants instead of
how (multiply this, compare that, do this if some condition exists, etc.)
to produce it. The result is a much simpler and more efficient programming process. The programs are much shorter; are easier to write,
maintain, read, and understand; and are more often free from errors.
As a result, they offer tremendous cost and time savings. Some of the
4GLs so closely resemble English that they are referred to as **natural**

END-USER-ORIENTED TOOLS			
Query Languages and Report Generators		**Decision Support, Financial Modeling**	
ADRS II	Intelect	Express	Spreadsheets (1-2-3,
Answer/DB	Oracle	FCS	Excel, Quatro Pro,
Clout	QMF	IFPS	etc.)
Datatrieve	Query-by-Example	Info Center/1	SPSS
Easytrieve Plus	RPG III	Metaphor	Strategem
HAL	Structured Query	Model	System W
Honeywell PDQ	Language	SAS	
Inquire			
Graphics Generators		**Application Generators for End Users**	
BPS Graphics	SAS Graph	CA-Universe	Mapper
Graph Plan	Tell-A-Graph	dBASE IV	Nomad 2
Harvard Graphics	VP Graphics	Focus	Powerhouse
		Fusion	Ramis II
		Ingres	TIF
4GL FOR PROFESSIONAL PROGRAMMERS: APPLICATION GENERATORS			
ADF	Ideal	Mimer	Rapid/3000
ADS/Online	INFO	Mitrol	Relate/3000
Application Factory	LINC II	Model 204	Speedware
CSP	Mantis	Natural 2	Telon
GENER/OL	Mark V	Pacbase	UFO
	Millenium		

Table 4.8
Fourth-generation languages

languages. Table 4.8 shows the list that Ashton prepared of some of the more popular 4GLs, organized by their principal uses.

Many 4GLs can be used by end users and professionals alike. These languages allow the user to make queries of a data base, to format and produce reports, to prepare graphical presentations, to provide decision support and financial modeling capabilities, and to develop other application programs. Thus unsophisticated users can interact with the system to get immediate responses to their information needs. In other words, with minimal training users can now satisfy many of their information needs in a few minutes.

Other 4GLs are sufficiently complex and powerful that they are used mainly by professional analysts and programmers. These are full-function, general-purpose languages that are intended to replace 3GLs rather than just supplement them. They are used instead of COBOL and other 3GLs to develop application programs. Many who use them claim tremendous productivity gains. One reason for the gains is that a program that would take hundreds of lines of COBOL code requires only 5 to 10 lines in a 4GL program.

The drawback to 4GLs is that they are less efficient than 3GLs. They take longer to execute and use more memory and system resources. They are not as powerful as 3GLs, but they are continually being improved and are overcoming some of these limitations. The following subsections briefly discuss some of the functional categories of 4GLs. Table 4.9 compares 3GLs and 4GLs and summarizes some of the differences between them.

Data Base Query Languages.   Information users often need to produce reports or to receive quick responses to questions they have. For example, a savings and loan officer might need to determine the amount owed on a mortgage, or an accounts receivable supervisor might need to know whose account is both 60 or more days past due and in excess of $1000. Data base query languages allow users to search a data base and retrieve the needed information to meet these information requests, or ad hoc queries. Many query languages have an update feature that allows users to update the data in the data base. However, strict controls are maintained over updates to prevent unauthorized updates to the data base files. Query languages are discussed in greater depth in Chapter 7.

Report Generators.   To produce reports, a programmer must place titles on the page, specify page numbers and page breaks, group similar data,

Table 4.9
Major differences between 3GLs and 4GLs

Third-Generation Languages (3GLs)	Fourth-Generation Languages (4GLs)
Intended for use by professional programmers	May be used by a nonprogramming end user as well as a professional programmer
Require specification of *how to perform task*	Require specification of *what task* to perform (system determines how to perform the task)
All alternatives must be specified	Default alternatives are built in; an end user need not specify these alternatives
Require large number of procedural instructions	Require far fewer instructions (less than one-tenth in most cases)
Code may be difficult to read, understand, and maintain	Code is easy to understand and maintain because of English-like commands
Language developed originally for batch operation	Language developed primarily for on-line use
Can be difficult to learn	Many features can be learned quickly
Difficult to debug	Errors easier to locate because of shorter programs, more structured code, and use of defaults and English-like language
Typically file-oriented	Typically data base–oriented

Source: James A. Senn, *Information Systems in Management* (Belmont, Calif.: Wadsworth 1990): 218.

calculate various levels of totals, specify the number and width of columns, and perform other procedures to select and format data. Because these steps are fairly standard, **report generators** were developed to make the process easier and faster. These programs can access one or more files or data bases, select the data desired, aggregate or manipulate it, and print it in the desired format. Thus users can produce customized reports that are not available with existing application programs.

Application Generators. An **application generator** produces a set of programs to accomplish a specific set of tasks based on user specifications. Sophisticated application generators include a special programming language, a code generator to produce 3GL program code, and a library of commonly used modules of program code. They also contain tools for creating files and data bases and a data dictionary to coordinate the use of data among applications. In addition, they have a screen-painting feature to develop input and output layouts, a query language, and a graphics and report generator.

Ashton found some interesting examples of the power and the time-saving benefits of application generators. For instance, IBM claims to have achieved a 27:1 improvement in productivity when ADF, its report generating program, was used instead of COBOL or IDS (a data base program) to write programs. At another company it took six months to write a management reporting system. That same program was created in half a day using an application generator called FOCUS.

Graphics languages. People are often able to understand data more easily when it is presented in picture or graphical form rather than tabular form. **Graphics languages** display numerical data in the form of line charts, bar charts, pie charts, scattergrams, and other graphical forms. Some packages can also manipulate data and perform calculations. Most only require the user to specify the data to be graphed and the type of graph. As shown in Table 4.8, there are several stand-alone graphics packages, both for larger systems and for microcomputers. Many spreadsheets also have graphics capabilities.

Decision Support Systems and Financial Modeling Packages. A **decision support system (DSS)** is an interactive software package that helps users make better decisions than they could on their own. One of the most important capabilities of a DSS is to allow the user to ask what-if questions. By examining all the ramifications of a decision (the what-ifs), the user is able to make a more informed decision. Decision support systems are discussed in Chapter 5.

A **financial modeling system** is a DSS that uses mathematical, statistical, and forecasting procedures to facilitate decision making. The defining characteristic of modeling software is that the user creates and manipulates a decision model and does not just manipulate input to a determined model. Of importance are statistical applications involving correlation and regression, analysis of variance, statistical sampling, time series analysis, operations research models, linear programming, inventory or queuing models, PERT and critical path analysis, cash flow discounting, and cost-volume-profit analysis.

Beyond Fourth-Generation Languages

In this section a number of new language approaches are discussed that some people view as fifth generation and others as fourth. The important thing is not what generation they are, but that we understand what they are and how we are impacted by them.

Object-Oriented Programming. The first **object-oriented language** was Smalltalk, introduced in the 1960s. Acceptance of object-oriented languages grew slowly at first, but now they are very popular programming alternatives, because they are icon- and graphics-oriented. Users can create programs by pointing to or moving a simple picture, called an **icon**, around on the screen. This programmer-machine interface is more natural, powerful, and easy to understand and use than that of a 3GL.

An object-oriented language has two main components: an object and a message. An **object** is an element of data and a set of instructions that specify the actions to be performed on the data. A **message** is an instruction given to an object or a communication between objects. To write a program, you create or select objects instead of writing procedural code. Everything you create exists as an object that can be modified, reused, or copied, just like a cell in a spreadsheet. These objects are then sent messages telling them what to do. The object decides how to do the task requested. For example, an object could be an icon that looks like a fax machine. Selecting it could mean that data should be sent to someone else by fax.

In **structured programming** a problem is broken down into self-contained modules that perform a specific task. A program module is written to accomplish each task. These modules are called *reusable code* and are saved in a library for future use. Then when programmers want to write a program, they do not, so to speak, have to reinvent the wheel. They merely select prewritten program modules, called objects, and link them together. The process is more like assembling a program than writing one. While structured techniques and programming can be used with any language, an advantage of **object-oriented programming (OOP)** is its dependence on structured programming concepts and its use of reusable code.

The advantages of OOP are its graphical interface, its ease of use, and its tremendous productivity. With OOP computer users can, with a little training and practice, write programs to meet their individual needs. Its disadvantage is that it produces programs that are larger, and therefore slower, than 3GL programs. As a result, it does not use memory and other computer resources as effectively. However, hardware is much less expensive than programmers, and the increase in productivity usually makes up for the increased system resources used.

The most common object-oriented language is C + +. Other popular languages are Smalltalk, Actor, and Objective C.

Expert Systems. In an **expert system** the knowledge of one or more experts is reduced to a set of decision rules. In an interactive mode the user responds to the questions asked by the expert system and the system then proposes a solution. Expert systems are discussed in Chapter 5.

SYSTEMS SOFTWARE

Systems software controls the use of the hardware, the application software, and other system resources used in executing data processing tasks. It also prepares user programs for execution by translating them into machine language. As shown in Fig. 4.12, Ashton identified several different types of systems software: operating systems, data base management systems, utility or service programs, language translators, and communications software. Some of the systems software, such as the operating system and the translators, comes with the hardware. Some, like data base management system software, is purchased from independent software houses.

Figure 4.12
Types of software: systems and application

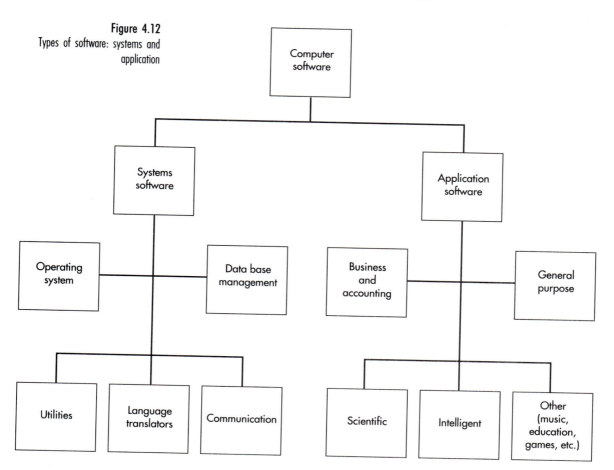

Operating Systems   The **operating system** (OS) is the most important and indispensable type of systems software. It is a group of related programs that manage the processing operations and the input, output, and storage functions of the computer system. It resides in main memory or in an on-line storage device readily accessible to main memory.

Ashton investigated the various microcomputer, minicomputer, and mainframe operating systems on the market and prepared Table 4.10, which lists and briefly describes some of the most common operating systems in use.

The principal objective of an operating system is to manage system resources in order to maximize the effectiveness and efficiency of a computer system. The operating system performs administrative functions such as scheduling jobs, allocating primary memory space, keep-

Table 4.10
Operating systems (OS)

Operating System	Description
Microcomputers	
CP/M	Developed in 1975; the first disk-based, eight-bit OS. Became the early standard. CP/M-86 is an expanded version for 16-bit microcomputers.
PC-DOS	Operating system developed for the IBM personal computer.
MS-DOS	Very similar to PC-DOS. Developed for IBM PC-compatibles. Because IBM PC clones are the most popular microcomputers, it is the industry leader. Developed by Microsoft.
OS/2	Developed for the IBM Personal System 2 (PS/2) family of microcomputers. Can handle 32-bit chip technology, supports multitasking, and runs programs that require more than 640K of RAM. Developed by IBM and Microsoft.
Windows NT	Graphical user interface (GUI) OS developed for IBM PC-compatibles. Each application runs in its own window, allowing multiple applications to be running at the same time. Provides multitasking and 32-bit access, and allows programs to use more than 640K of RAM. Runs both Windows and DOS programs. Developed by Microsoft.
UNIX	Used on very powerful microcomputers, workstations and minicomputers. Supports multitasking, multiuser processing, and networking. Very portable (can be carried to other machines). Developed by Bell Labs.
XENIX	A UNIX-like OS developed by Microsoft.
Apple-DOS	OS for Apple's microcomputers.
PICK	Multiuser, multitasking OS used with minicomputers and microcomputers. Very portable.
Mainframes and Minicomputers	
ULTRIX	OS for Digital Equipment Corporation's (DEC) computers.
MVS, VM	OS for IBM mainframes.
CPF, SSP	OS for IBM's System/3 minicomputers.
VAX/VMS	OS for DEC's VAX family of minicomputers.
UNICOS, COS	OS for Cray's supercomputers.

ing track of all application programs and systems software, maintaining operating statistics, communicating with equipment operators, and coordinating input/output devices and operations.

Prior to the advent of multiprogramming, operating systems were relatively simple. In a multiprogrammed system, however, several jobs can be processed on the computer at the same time. The operating system must be very sophisticated in order to switch the hardware and data back and forth among a number of different programs and keep the input/output devices for all the programs working at peak speed.

In a virtual memory system on-line secondary storage is used as an extension of primary memory. The operating system continually switches pages (or blocks of memory, anywhere from 2K to 4K bytes) back and forth between primary and secondary memory. This process, called paging, makes the system appear to have virtually an unlimited amount of primary memory. The virtual memory technique increases the number of programs the system is able to process at one time, thereby increasing the efficiency of the system.

A recent development is the operating environment. In essence this is a software program that sits on top of the operating system and provides a system with desirable enhancements. Windows, a program produced by Microsoft, is an example of a graphical user interface operating environment. In a graphical user interface (GUI) a mouse or trackball is used to point at icons and menu selections. This technique replaces, either fully or partially, the commands entered by using a keyboard. Most GUIs allow for the screen to be divided into several windows so that the user can work with several different programs.

Data Base Management Systems

A data base is a collection of related files and records stored together and accessible to multiple users. A data base management system (DBMS) is a specialized set of computer programs that manages data bases. The DBMS acts as the interface between the data in a data base, the related application programs, and the operating system. As data base software becomes more common and as more people use it to develop and run application software on personal computers, data base software has moved into the realm of application software. Accordingly, we list it as one of the types of general-purpose software in the application software section of the book. Data bases are discussed in Chapter 7.

Utility or Service Programs

Utility programs handle common file, data manipulation, and housekeeping tasks that most computer systems perform on a regular basis. Program debugging aids help a user correct programs. Text editors allow on-line users to modify the contents of data files and computer programs. Sort/merge programs either sort a file into a specific order or merge two or more sorted files into one file. Media conversion programs transfer data from one medium to another (cards to tape, tape to disk, etc.). Utilities are generally easy to use, efficient to operate, and inexpensive to acquire.

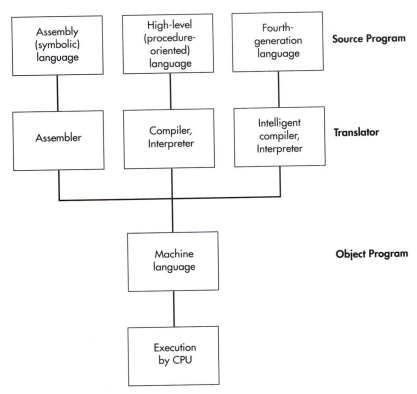

Figure 4.13
Language translators

Language Translators   Language translators are software programs, such as the assemblers, compilers, and interpreters discussed earlier in the chapter, that convert programming language instructions into the computer's machine language. These translators are summarized in Fig. 4.13.

Communications Software   Most EDP users transmit data electronically over communication lines. They transmit data between computers and between terminals and computers, and they access corporate and public data bases to extract information. Communications software control and support all data communications activities. These programs connect and disconnect communications links and terminals, automatically poll terminals or other computers for input/output activity, prioritize communication requests, and detect and correct data transmission errors. Communications software is discussed in Chapter 6.

APPLICATION SOFTWARE

Application software performs the specific data processing tasks required by a company. It is by far the most important type of software for accountants. As illustrated in Fig. 4.12, application software can be divided into five categories:

1. *General-purpose programs* handle tasks common to many users. They include word processing, spreadsheets, graphics, and data bases. They also include software packages that some of the major accounting firms have developed to assist in auditing work.

2. *Business programs* update master files to include the effects of transactions as they take place. They also support the various business functions of a company: accounting, marketing, production, finance, personnel, and management.

3. *Intelligent applications* focus on expanding the role of the computer beyond the traditional data processing functions. Examples include decision support software, expert systems, and artificial intelligence.

4. *Scientific programs* perform the research and development tasks needed in such disciplines as mathematics, the sciences, and engineering. These programs are beyond the scope of this book.

5. *Other*. This catchall category of the arts, medicine, entertainment, and education is beyond the scope of the book.

Since there are hundreds of different types of businesses, each with many unique processing needs, there are thousands of different application programs in use. It would be impossible to discuss all of these uses here. Instead, much of the remainder of this book discusses application software in one way or another. Chapter 5 discusses microcomputer software, Chapter 6 discusses telecommunications software, and Chapter 7 discusses data base software. Chapters 8–11 discuss the development, purchase, and implementation of application software. Chapter 13 discusses the use of controls in application software, and Chapter 15 discusses the software used in auditing applications. Finally, Chapters 16–20 discuss the application software used in the five different business and accounting cycles.

CASE CONCLUSION: UNDERSTANDING HARDWARE AND SOFTWARE CONCEPTS AT S&S, INC.

Several weeks after Ashton began his study of hardware and software, he presented his reports, tables, and diagrams to Scott. Scott read the material and is excited about what he read. He was also surprised at all the technological advancements that had taken place since his college course in computers. He calls Ashton into his office and comments:

> *You know, it seems to me as though there is nothing so constant as change in computer technology. I know that sounds strange, but people just keep demanding more and more out of their information systems. They want instantaneous access and processing, infinite storage, unlimited communication between computers, and ease of use. And because of their demands, software developers are requiring hardware that is faster, smaller, less expensive, and more powerful. And that means that*

*hardware manufacturers are having to continually push back the fron-
tiers of technology. The result has been a technological explosion. And I
don't see it slackening anytime soon. I can see that we have only just
begun to learn about computers. It seems to me that just trying to keep
abreast of all technological advancements that are taking place will
require a lot of effort on our part.*

Ashton agrees with Scott, and together they begin to plan a
computer system for S&S. They decide on three guiding principles.
First, S&S will pursue aggressive growth and will grow as fast as is
financially feasible. Second, they will develop an information system
plan for the future that makes maximum use of technology. The intent
is to use technology to do everything possible and to eliminate human
intervention wherever possible. Third, the plan will be modular. It
must allow them to implement what they can currently afford and grow
into their final design.

At some point S&S will eventually need a mainframe computer and
powerful microcomputers that link all the stores together. However,
their current needs can be met with a microcomputer system for their
one store. To forestall the technological and functional obsolescence
that is sure to come with advancing technology, they decide to buy the
fastest and most advanced system available. Thus they want a Pentium
microprocessor, a large amount of primary memory, a large hard disk,
and a system that can be expanded as their needs grow. Additional
storage can be provided by floppy disks and tape cartridges. They also
want their computer system to have one or more high-speed laser
printers. Scott asks Ashton to investigate these systems more so that
they can determine exactly what they need.

Ashton discovered that the Appliance Vendors Association, which
Scott and Susan recently joined, disseminates information about products and prices using CD ROM technology. It will soon be using
videodisks. Therefore the new system should have the ability to handle
these storage mediums. Ashton also found that the association recommends a number of accounting software packages that it has tested and
evaluated.

Scott suggests they capture as much of their input data as possible
by using source data automation devices. They want to use POS
devices with audio response units at all their customer checkouts.
They plan to use UPC or some other form of bar coding to capture
sales data as well as for other tasks, such as taking inventory.

They want to encourage their customers to pay with credit cards or
some other form of noncash payment such as smart cards. In this way
they can handle all sales payments electronically and avoid the problems of bad checks, extending credit, cash overages and shortages, and
theft of cash. They also want to hook up the POS devices to their
system so that they can have up-to-date inventory records. They want
their system to automatically recognize that inventory is needed and to
electronically communicate with their suppliers to order the items
needed.

As S&S expands, Susan wants to print 10–20 separate versions of a customer catalog, each with a different format and product mix. Susan wants to keep track of every purchase made by every customer so that she can select the best catalog for each. She also wants to customize the catalog cover by mentioning a previous purchase or mentioning the company's line of business. Furthermore, this data base of customer data will allow her to target particular customers for special deals.

With respect to software they decide to go with a GUI operating environment such as Windows. They also want to get a utility software package as well as communication software. They will also need a data base package, a graphics package, a spreadsheet, and a word processing package.

Scott and Ashton are both excited about their proposed system by the time they finish their preliminary plan. Scott wants Ashton to do some more investigation before they make any final decisions. He asks Ashton to conduct an in-depth study of microcomputer systems and the software available for them (see Chapter 5). He also asks him to check out the area of telecommunications (see Chapter 6) and to investigate data base technology (see Chapter 7). ■

SUMMARY

Accountants need to have a basic understanding of computer technology. They need to understand what computers are, what they are composed of, how they operate, and how they store and process data. This understanding helps them to use, develop, evaluate, and manage their information systems.

The improvements in computer technology have been so dramatic that they are used to classify computers into four distinct generations. We are currently in the fourth generation, and many are predicting a fifth generation in the 1990s. Computers are divided into four main categories: supercomputers, mainframes, minicomputers, and microcomputers. These classifications are based upon the size, speed, memory capacity, computational power, and the number of users and peripherals that can be supported.

A CPU has three main sections: a control unit, an arithmetic-logic unit, and memory. Memory can be either read-only (ROM) or random-access (RAM). The computer stores data in binary form, called bits. Bits are aggregated into even larger groups called bytes. Memory is most frequently expressed in terms of thousands of characters, called kilobytes (K), or millions of characters, called megabytes (M).

Secondary storage devices are either sequential or direct-access devices. The most common sequential medium is magnetic tape. The most common direct-access devices are magnetic and optical disks and diskettes.

Data are sometimes prepared for input into a system by using data preparation devices such as key-to-tape and key-to-disk encoders. Alternatively, data can be input using terminals, microcomputers, light pens, touch-sensitive screens, or a mouse. Data is also entered using source data automation devices such as MICR, OCR, and POS devices. The most common output devices are video display units, printers, plotters, voice response units, and computer output microfilm (COM).

Software is the computer program that controls a hardware device. Writing programs is called computer programming and is done in a programming language. Software languages have progressed through several different generations: machine-level, symbolic (assembler), high-level (3GL), and 4GL. Each succeeding generation has been more English-like and easier to learn and use.

Software programs can be divided into two separate categories: systems software and application software. Systems software controls the system and tells the computer how to operate or perform routine tasks. Systems software consists of operating systems, data base management systems, utility or service programs, language translators, and communications software. Application software is written to accomplish specific information or transaction processing needs. There are three types of applications software of interest to accountants: business, general-purpose, and scientific.

KEY TERMS

Define the following terms:

computer hardware	MIPS	throughput
peripherals	TIPS	electronic data interchange
mainframe computers	access time	key-to-tape encoder
data processing center	execution time	key-to-disk encoder
downsizing	millisecond	visual display terminal (VDT)
minicomputers	microsecond	mouse
microcomputer	nanosecond	light pens
personal digital assistant (PDA)	picosecond	joystick
download	microprocessor	touch-sensitive screens
central processing unit (CPU)	motherboard	source data automation (SDA)
arithmetic-logic unit	data bus	magnetic ink character recognition (MICR)
control unit	word	optical character recognition (OCR)
primary memory	megahertz	
read-only memory (ROM)	secondary storage	point-of-sale (POS) recorder
random-access memory (RAM)	magnetic tape	universal product code (UPC)
semiconductor	magnetic disks	bar codes
on-line devices	hard disk	two-dimensional (2-D) bar codes
off-line devices	diskette	magnetic stripe
bits	floppy disk	smart cards
byte	optical disk	machine vision
kilobyte	WORM (write-once, read-many)	Radio frequency identification
megabytes	CD ROM (compact-disk, read-only memory)	voice input
gigabytes	videodisk	resolution
terabytes	input/output-bound	

pixel	object program	message
audio response units	macroinstructions	structured programming
printer	machine-independent	object-oriented programming
hard copy	languages	(OOP)
impact printers	compilers	expert system
nonimpact printers	diagnostic messages	operating system (OS)
serial interface	syntax errors	multiprogramming
parallel interface	logic errors	virtual memory
plotter	interpreter	operating environment
computer output microfilm	fourth-generation languages	graphical user interface (GUI)
(COM)	(4GLs)	data base management system
software	natural languages	(DBMS)
computer program	ad hoc queries	utility programs
computer programming	report generators	language translators
programming languages	application generator	communications software
application software	graphics languages	
systems software	decision support system (DSS)	
machine language	financial modeling system	
symbolic language	object-oriented language	
assembler	icon	
source program	object	

Discussion questions

4.1 Each new generation of computers has revolutionized the computer industry. These revolutions have changed our society. What effects do you believe the fifth generation of computers will have on the computer industry, and more importantly, what effect do you see it having on our society?

4.2 Source data automation devices are becoming increasingly popular. Some futurists envision a day when a person will not use any cash, checks, or credit cards. Rather, a person will use a card on which his or her personal identification number is inscribed. Do you believe this system will help or hinder the individual and facilitate or complicate business transactions? What are the advantages and disadvantages of moving the data entry process closer to the point at which data originates?

4.3 Accountants in all specialty areas are increasingly exposed to computers. Accountants use computers in their work both at the office and at the client's location. Also, accountants' clients are increasingly using computers. Discuss how accountants in each of the functional areas of tax, audit, and MAS (management advisory services) use computers and what they need to be aware of in regard to a client's computer system.

4.4 Researchers at IBM have demonstrated a tiny switch that depends on the motion of a single atom, making it the smallest electronic device in existence. While any practical application is likely to be more than a decade away, the new ''atom switch'' raises the possibility that electronic circuits may someday be built with parts measuring only an atom or molecule across. The atom switch is measured in nanometers (billionths of a meter). By comparison, the circuitry in today's top-performance computer chips is measured in microns (millionths of a meter).

Professor Rentzepis of the University of California at Irvine has developed and patented a three-dimensional data storage device the size of a sugar cube that is capable of storing as much as 6.6 terabytes. For storing data a laser beam is split into two beams, which are aimed at the cube at right angles. The data is stored at the point where the two lasers meet. The cube is very inexpensive and very fast and has no moving parts, which increases its reliability. The greatest potential use of the technology is in massively parallel computing. A prototype of the technology may be ready within the decade.

It will take several years for these technologies to be refined. But once they are, what are the implications for accounting systems? What will these technologies allow us to do with computer technology?

4.5 Laboratories put bar codes on containers of blood and urine samples for accurate identification. Alamo Rent-a-Car bar codes its 60,000-car fleet in preparation for a new inventory system. Airlines have standardized bar codes for making sure luggage gets to the right city. Recently developed bar codes carry more data and will even store computer programs. How will technological developments in bar codes and computers affect accounting information systems? The way companies do business in the future?

4.6 Tired of going through boxes of disorganized old photos? If so, Eastman Kodak may have the answer for you with a recent product innovation: the photo CD player. Photographers using CD technology continue to take pictures with their regular cameras and then take in their film and have the pictures stored on a photo compact disk. The disk is then viewed by using a special CD player developed to show photographs on a TV screen. As more pictures are taken, they can be added to the CD. In the coming years Kodak plans to add other capabilities, including audio narration features, music, graphics and text.[1]

What uses could business find for photo CD technology?

4.7 In an effort to trim the high cost of cutting trees, Detroit Edison Company is equipping its line clearance group and private tree trimmers with the latest in portable technology. Using a hand-held electronic work pad and pen, inspectors for Detroit Edison fill out electronic work orders as they inspect the company's power lines for overgrown trees. The work orders are stored on memory cards and returned to the main office, which distributes the work orders to independent contractors. The work orders detail the necessary work assignments, including job location, the type of power lines involved, and the branches that the contractor must trim back.

When the work is complete, the contractor uses an electronic pen and notepad to record an invoice detailing the work completed and the total cost of the project. The memory disk with the original work order and the contractor's invoice is returned to the utility company, which processes the invoice and makes payment.

Personnel at Detroit Edison really like the new technology because it saves them time and they don't get bogged down in paperwork. Most inspectors had never used PCs and the expected resistance never materialized.[2]

Discuss the benefits of portable computer technology. How is new computer technology improving user acceptance of new information systems?

4.8 New computer technology knows few boundaries. At Olivetti Research Laboratory researchers have developed an "active badge" tracking device that silently monitors an employee's whereabouts by using sensors spread throughout an organization (see Focus 4.2).

The introduction of the new technology raises a number of legal and ethical issues. Critics argue that the new technology sacrifices individual privacy for convenience and efficiency. Some employees wearing active badges may feel like house arrest victims whose bracelets trigger an alarm when they leave home. Some people feel it is great technology in the right hands, but a bad manager may make life miserable for the wearer.

What boundaries, if any, should society set on the use of this new employee-tracking technology? Should minimum legal or ethical standards be set to govern all new technology? What safeguards must be developed to make active badge technology more palatable to the public?

---

[1] *Source:* Walter S. Mossberg, "Personal Technology," *Wall Street Journal* (May 21, 1992): B1.

[2] *Source:* Neal Boudette, "Pen PCs Help Utility Trim Costs," *PC Week* (August 10, 1992): 19.

Problems

4.1 Identify which input, output, or storage medium or device best fits each of the following descriptions.

a. Many modern department stores use this device to ring up a customer's sales and to post the information from that sale directly to accounts receivable and inventory records.

b. When making a professional graphics presentation, a high-level manager would want to use this device to produce the highest-quality hard copy output.

c. A large university could store its payroll information on this sequential magnetic medium and then use the medium, in batch processing mode, to update the payroll file and print employee paychecks.

d. When his bank is closed, Joe uses this device to get $20 to buy gas and to go to the movies.

e. Credit unions use this device to read the checks written by their members so that the amounts can be deducted from their accounts.

f. When making reservations, airline personnel use this device extensively to access the computer system and get information about the status of a specific flight.

g. This storage device is used by brokerage companies so that a customer's record can be accessed immediately, without processing any other records.

h. S&S could use this device to electronically send purchase orders to their suppliers.

i. This recently developed storage device is used to store historical and other permanent information. Only very recently has it been made an erasable medium.

j. Large insurance companies use this device to prepare form letters and hard copies of other computer-generated documents.

k. This device is used by utility companies to read turnaround documents received from customers.

l. A hand-held computer that helps people organize their schedule and personal affairs.

m. This device is used by modern grocery stores to read the UPC of food items. By interpreting the UPC, the system can extract the price of the product from the computer's memory.

n. This device is used by the parcel industry to route packages to their appropriate destinations. Background noises need to be controlled so that the device does not become confused.

o. This device is used by large industrial corporations to condense historical data by up to 99% for storage on rolls of film.

p. This device is used by telephone companies to give people the telephone numbers they are seeking when they dial directory assistance.

q. Tags such as those used by Federal Express track data from one location to another.

4.2 The Western Oil Company processes an average of 8500 charge sales documents per business day. To process these transactions, the company is considering two alternatives: an optical character recognition (OCR) system and a shared-processor, key-to-disk system.

The OCR system rents for $1500 per month. It would require an operator who would receive a monthly salary of $1800. It could be expected to read successfully between 97% and 98% of all charge sales documents. For those documents it rejects, the operator would manually enter the correct data from a console. Even considering the time required to deal with rejected documents, this system would have more than enough capacity to handle Western's current and projected volume of charge sales.

If the key-to-disk system were acquired, the shared processor would rent for $1000 per month, and each keying station would rent for $120 per month. Each keying station would be operated by a data entry clerk, who would receive a monthly salary of $1600 and could be expected to achieve a net productivity rate of 9600 keystrokes per hour. During each 8-hour day, the clerks would spend approximately 6 hours and 40 minutes working at the keyboard. Each charge sale document has 15 characters that must be keyed.

Required

a. If the key-to-disk system were acquired, how

many keying stations and operators would be required, assuming all work is done on the day shift?

b. From an economic standpoint, which of the two alternatives is most attractive? Show computations.

c. Identify additional factors that should be considered in deciding between the two alternatives?

4.3 Pinta Company is a regional discount department store chain headquartered in Salt Lake City, Utah. Its stores are scattered throughout the Southwest and sell general merchandise. The firm is thinking about buying a point-of-sale (POS) system for its stores. There are a number of POS systems available, but the President believes that the type using a light pen to scan the universal product code on merchandise is the most suitable.

The company is concerned about a number of potential security problems. It worries that the POS terminals may be a security risk because of the many operators and the close proximity to customers. It also is concerned that the data collected by the system could be lost or destroyed. A final concern is that there might be unauthorized changes to the prices and other data stored in the computer.

Required

The President has asked you to prepare a report that does the following:

a. Explains the functions and operation of a POS system, including its use in credit checking and electronic transfers of funds.

b. Identify the advantages and disadvantages of the POS system described in part a.

c. Identify the controls and security measures that could effectively counteract their security concerns. (CMA Examination, adapted)

4.4 A recent article on bar coding states:

Management accountants are under intense pressure to modernize internal accounting systems and to provide timely, accurate, and relevant reports to users. In response to this pressure, increasing numbers of them have focused on the key-entry process, which increases both errors and the time that users must wait for reports. The desire for better and faster data leads to technologies that capture data in real-time at the point of origin. Bar coding is considered the most popular and cost effective of these technologies.[3]

a. Do you agree? Why? Why not?

b. In what activities of an organization is bar coding most useful? Least useful?

c. What are the benefits to an organization of using bar coding? Even if the benefits of a bar-coded data entry system do not outweigh its costs, why might a company still implement the system?

d. What technical problems might someone using bar coding expect to encounter? What behavioral problems might a company experience in converting to a bar-coded data entry system?

e. Assume that the company for which you are the comptroller is considering the implementation of a bar-coded data entry system. In what way should you or your accounting staff be involved in the design and implementation of the system? What concerns might you have about implementing the system?

4.5 Visit two or more of the larger computer stores in your area and make a list of the computers, peripheral devices, and systems and application software available for sale. Develop a list of criteria that you can use in selecting a computer, peripherals, and two different software packages for a business with which you are familiar. Make a recommendation about what you feel would best meet the business's needs.

4.6 Select one of the topics discussed in the chapter and research the topic to determine what developments have taken place since this textbook was written. There are a number of ways to research the topic, including visiting computer stores and reading recent issues of computer magazines (like *PC Week* or *Personal Computing*). Write a report that covers your findings. Alternatively (or in addition), your instructor may ask you to present your findings to the class.

4.7 The Fleming Furniture Company (FFC) in High Point, North Carolina, uses a medium-sized computer to process sales orders. FFC is one of the largest wholesale distributors of furniture in the nation. It has purchasing agreements with all the furniture manufacturers in North Carolina. It sells furniture by mailing out catalogs of its furniture and

---

[3] From Arjan T. Sadhwani and Thomas Tyson, "Does Your Firm Need Bar Coding?" *Management Accounting* (April 1990): 45–48.

by displaying its merchandise at quarterly furniture fairs across the country. Its sales force uses WATS lines to contact customers and writes up the orders on company order forms.

Periodically during the day order forms are picked up from the salespeople and taken to the data entry department. There they are batched and entered using a key-to-disk-to-tape system linked to a minicomputer. At the end of the day the orders that have been entered and stored on the disk are sorted and transferred to tape. The tape is then used as input to the order processing program. The output is a sales order containing the data on the order form.

The firm is investigating the possibility of placing terminals on the salespersons' desks and having them enter sales orders directly into the computer. A local company has proposed a hardware configuration that costs $13,000 per month. The proposed system includes all the hardware (terminals, CPU, printer, etc.) needed to process the orders. In order to determine whether or not to switch, FFC has asked you, its accountant, to calculate the cost of the current system. You have gathered the following information.

- There are an average of 20 working days in each month.
- An average of 900 sales orders are processed each day, except after the quarterly furniture fairs, when the number of orders processed increases.
- Each sales order contains an average of 125 characters of data.
- Each preprinted, multicopy sales order costs $0.20. The order forms cost $0.10 each.
- The internal pricing mechanism used by the company allocates costs for the current medium-sized computer at $250 per hour, which includes the cost of the CPU, the peripherals, and the operator.
- The multiple-station, key-to-disk-to-tape encoder is rented from a local company for $35 per operator-hour. It is used to enter data for several different functions, including order entry.
- The data entry clerks who operate the encoder work 7.5-hour days and are paid $1050 a month.
- Data entry clerks can enter an average of three order forms every two minutes.
- The tape drive reads 60,000 characters per minute.
- It takes the computer 15 minutes per day to read the 900 sales orders and generate the sales orders.

- It takes the encoder six minutes per day to sort the records.

Required

a. Compute the monthly costs of the old system according to the following categories:

   1. Equipment   3. Materials
   2. Labor   4. Total cost

b. Should the company rent the new system or stay with the old system? What factors other than cost should the company consider?

4.8 The basic elements of an information system include the following:

a. Input   c. Processing   e. Data
b. Storage   d. Output   communication

Classify each of the following items into one of the five previous categories. For some items more then one answer is possible.

1. Primary memory
2. Keyboard
3. 3½-inch floppy disk
4. CD ROM drive
5. Terminal
6. Math coprocessor
7. Pentium chip
8. Turnaround document
9. Modem
10. Bar code
11. Automated teller machine
12. Personal digital assistant
13. Semiconductor
14. ROM
15. Audio response unit
16. Serial interface

4.9 Selecting the right operating system to handle your desktop applications is easy, right? Not necessarily. Even though your operating system decision boils down to three common operating environments—DOS, OS/2, and UNIX—the issues surrounding the selection of the right operating system are far more complex.

The prime determinant in making a selection of operating systems is the overall corporate environment. Gary Moeller, manager of information resources for the city of San Antonio agrees: "When we decided to standardize on the UNIX operating system, we had to examine not just what would save us the most money, but what kind of work each department did and what kind of work they might be doing in the future. It wasn't an easy task."

Changing an operating system impacts the organization as a whole and each individual employee. For instance, at Travelers Insurance, managers decided to shift from the current DOS environment to the OS/2 environment, a simple switch considering that Travelers' 15,000 PCs are IBM products. Nevertheless, the shift to OS/2 was a slow one so as to prevent a sudden disruption in the way the company currently operates.

Switching operating systems isn't a simple matter of changing programs. UNIX operating systems and OS/2 systems have distinct differences that a business must consider. For example, the multitasking feature, which is common to both environments, allows for concurrent processing and switching among a number of applications operating simultaneously. The UNIX systems handle multitasking best in a multiuser environment, while the OS/2 can run multitasking operations on a single-user micro-

computer or in a networking environment.[4]

Required

a. What is an operating system? What role does the operating system play in the operation of a computer?

b. Describe the general features and functions of a standard operating system. Why is the selection of an operating system a complex task?

c. Research the differences between the OS/2 and the UNIX operating systems. How do these differences affect the selection of an operating system?

d. What is an operating environment? How does an operating environment like Windows support an operating system?

Case 4.1: ANYCOMPANY, INC.—AN ONGOING COMPREHENSIVE CASE

One of the best ways to learn is to immediately apply what you have studied. The purpose of this case is to allow you to do that. You will select a local company that you can work with. At the end of most chapters you will find an assignment that will have you apply what you have learned using the company you have selected as a reference. This case, then, may become an ongoing case study that you work on throughout the term.

Tour the computer facilities of the business you selected and write a report that discusses the following:

1. The kinds of computers the company uses and the size classifications they fall into

2. The hardware devices the company uses for input, output, processing, storage, and data commu-

nications (if applicable); include items such as equipment, speed of the devices used, storage capacities, and prices (if possible)

3. The systems and application software used by the organization

4. Your overall impression of the facility, the personnel who operate and manage it, and the controls used to safeguard the system

5. Your views about how the visit has helped you get a better grasp of the material covered in the chapter.

---

[4] *Source:* Bob Francis, "Desktop Tug of War: OS/2 vs UNIX," *Datamation* (February 15, 1989): 18–19.

Case 4.2: INFORMATION SYSTEMS AND THE MANUFACTURING INDUSTRY

The U.S. manufacturing industry has undergone tremendous change in the past 20 years. Once the mainstay of American business, the manufacturing sector has struggled with aggressive global competition, changing consumer tastes, and a shift in prod-

uct allegiances. Now after years of mergers, consolidations, and bankruptcies, the survivors are reemerging leaner, stronger, and ready to take on the competition. The source of their confidence is information technology.

Ford Motor Company

At Ford Motor Company the use of information technology has helped it become more efficient and sensitive to customer needs. "Our ten mainframes are the lifeblood of our business," says Jerry Peterson, Director of Technical systems at Ford. "They're used for our mainstream business systems from order processing to engineering and manufacturing to material logistics."

One of Ford's primary goals is to make technology accessible to every employee. PCs and workstations will play a larger role. PCs provide Ford with access to mainframe computer resources and data, engineering computers, and process control systems, as well as standard automation services. Ford is looking to distributed applications to help their employees use information more effectively.

Computer-aided engineering analysis is also supporting competitive advantage in the design processes at Ford. Previously it took five years from design to the assembly line. Ford is now reducing that to three years with process reengineering and tools such as computer modeling and simulation.

Peterson notes: "We constantly want to be ahead of the competition. We use our mainframe and our PCs heavily to spot potential problems and to provide our employees with a shared library of information that enables them to work as a team to improve quality."

Burroughs Wellcome and Company

For this pharmaceutical concern data processing is decentralized, with systems built upon specific needs, including research, regulatory compliance, and environmental control. Burroughs uses a variety of computer hardware, from large systems to PCs to networks, to handle information problems.

For most pharmaceutical manufacturers a product takes at least 10 years to enter the market. During the development time the computers at Burroughs Wellcome are used to develop and store critical data, including safety evaluation, development, and manufacturing data. According to the company's Senior Vice-President of Production Engineering, "We have an enormous manufacturing documentation system built to meet government regulations that require hundreds of thousands of pages of data a year. Such a system is a vital contribution to our business."

Bio-Met Inc.

Bio-Met prefers smaller systems. The Indiana-based manufacturer of orthopedic implants uses midrange systems for generalized business processing, controls, and materials planning—with a lot of workstations to collect data.

At Bio-Met the workstations are the backbone of the business. Using computer workstations or PCs, an engineer tests design specifications using CAD/CAM software. Once the design is complete, the software application instructs a numerical-control machine tool to develop the product. Using computer technology eliminates much of the guesswork that goes into designing orthopedic implants for individual patients.

Bio-Met's Director of MIS justifies the firm's position: "We have enough computing ability without using mainframes. We are heavily oriented to making our system more efficient, more aligned with our operations. They are central to our business."

Rockwell International Corporation

Most aerospace manufacturers use mainframes to store vast amounts of data used in the design and construction of aircraft and parts. At Rockwell large mainframes support a data center for storing product specifications for millions of parts. For a given airplane design specifications may include over three hundred thousand parts.

In addition, Rockwell uses workstations in the development of new aerospace products. Currently, researchers are using workstations in the design of a new high-maneuverability aircraft. Such systems also allow for the exchange of design information with international and domestic partners. In the future Rockwell hopes to shift to a distributed system to make better use of existing computer capacity.

1.   Business leaders argue that the decision to acquire an information system is a business decision, not a systems decision. Do you agree? Why or why not? Use examples from the companies described in this case to support your conclusion.

2.   What role does competitive advantage play in the acquisition of an information system?

3.   No one system works for every company. What issues enter into a company's decision to select a computer system from among a variety of computer classifications (e.g., minicomputer, PCs)? For each computer classification, discuss its specific advantages and disadvantages.

4.   Will information technology alone sustain the manufacturing industry in the years ahead? Discuss.

CHAPTER 5

Personal Information Systems: Microcomputers and End-User Decision Support Systems

LEARNING OBJECTIVES

After studying this chapter, you should be able to:

■ Explain why accountants need to be able to understand and use microcomputer technology.

■ Explain the importance of end-user computing, its risks and benefits, and how to manage and control it.

■ Identify and describe the capabilities, benefits, and uses of the different types of microcomputer and end-user software.

INTEGRATIVE CASE: S&S, INC.

Scott Parry and Susan Anderson have worked hard to get their new business established. S&S had a very successful grand opening a few months ago, and Susan's marketing campaign has established them as a major force in the appliance business. However, they are not content to have a single, strong store, and Susan has developed an aggressive growth and expansion plan for the next three to five years.

With the business on its feet Scott knows it is time to develop an information system to provide them with the information they need to manage their business, achieve the growth they desire, and make sound business decisions. Ashton Fleming, their accountant, has developed an adequate manual system and has been investigating a computerized system. Ashton has also been helping Scott get a better understanding of current technology. Scott has read the material on computer hardware and software that Ashton gave him (Chapter 4). He has also accompanied Ashton on several visits to a local computer firm. Scott and Ashton are convinced that S&S needs a microcomputer-based system.

Scott has spent some time thinking about the new system. At their next meeting he presents Ashton with the following list of questions and concerns and asks him to investigate a microcomputer-based system for S&S.

1. How many employees will need a microcomputer? How will they use the computer in their jobs?

2. How involved should the employees (the end users) be with the system? What are the benefits and risks of their involvement in the system? How can the risks be minimized and the benefits maximized?

3. What kind of accounting software do they need? Can they buy one package that meets all their needs, or do vendors sell accounting software in pieces? And if they sell it in pieces, can the different pieces communicate with each other?

4. What other software will they need? A spreadsheet and word processor seem obvious, but do they need a data base system? A graphics package? Income tax software? What other types of microcomputer software are there, and will they need any of them?

5. How involved should he and the other employees be in developing systems using spreadsheets, data bases, and so on? ■

INTRODUCTION

During the early days of computers information systems were usually centralized. An organization had one or a few computers supporting large numbers of users. Data was stored centrally, and anytime users wanted an information system developed or needed additional information from the existing system, they had to submit a development request to the information systems department. If the request was approved, one or more systems analysts would meet with the users to determine their needs and then develop the new system. Unfortunately, there were a number of problems with this approach:

■ In some cases up to 70% of information systems resources were spent just maintaining existing systems. Since most organizations have limited resources, there was never enough computer capacity, people, or money to meet all user needs on a timely basis. This resulted in a backlog of unfulfilled systems requests of two to five years. This backlog discouraged users from making additional requests, resulting in a hidden backlog of information needs.

■ The development process was very lengthy, which meant that the response to users needs was very slow. Development and maintenance requests had to be prepared, approved, and prioritized. Systems people had to interview the users, try to understand their needs, and develop the system. The analysts had to explain the system requirements to the programmers who had to write the programs and test them. Once the system was tested, the new system had to be presented to the users for approval and modification. Finally, there was a lengthy implementation process.

- Information needs are continually changing and evolving and existing systems become inadequate. Oftentimes, user needs changed before a system could be developed.

- Systems analysts and users had a hard time communicating. Analysts did not understand the needs of users, and users did not understand computer technology.

The result was a general sense of frustration. Users did not get the information they needed, when they needed it, and in the form they needed it. Systems developers found it difficult to develop systems that met the true needs of the users. Users often did not know their true information needs and would frequently change their information requests. In addition, it was hard to develop a system that met the needs of all users when their needs were so diverse.

In response to these frustrations, IBM of Canada in the late 1970s set up an information center to help employees gain access to corporate data using high-level languages. This strategy allowed them to bypass the normal systems development process, thereby avoiding the long delays. By accessing corporate data themselves, they were able to meet their own information needs on a timely basis. Thus was born end-user computing.

End-user computing (EUC) is the hands-on development, use, and control of computer-based information systems by end users (EU). In other words, end users make use of computer technology to meet their own information needs rather than having to rely on professionals in the information systems (IS) department. The information systems staffers usually still develop the transaction processing systems and maintain companywide data bases of information. They also provide technical advice and operational support to the end users. However, it is the end users who draw upon the transaction processing system, the corporate data bases, and other information systems to meet their information needs.

An example of end users' meeting their own information needs is provided by a savings and loan in California. The S&L wanted a system that would keep track of loan reserve requirements. The Information Systems Department told the Loan Department that the system would take up to 18 months to develop. Rather than wait, the people in the Loan Department decided to produce the information themselves. Using a microcomputer and Paradox, a data base program, they developed a functional program in a single day. Adding enhancements to the program took anywhere from a few hours to a few days to complete. Not only did the Loan Department cut the development time from

18 months to a few days, it also ended up with exactly what the department needed because its staff developed it themselves.

The trend toward end-user computing was already established when microcomputers were introduced in the early 1980s. With the advent of inexpensive micros and a wide variety of powerful and inexpensive software, the trend toward end-user computing accelerated significantly. Users began to develop their own systems on their personal computers. They created and stored their own data, accessed company data and downloaded it into their personal computers, and began sharing data and computer resources in networks. As end users began to meet their initial needs, two things happened. First, the users realized that the computers could be used to meet more and more existing information needs. Second, they found that the increased information created many new uses and needs for information. The result has been a tremendous growth in end-user computing, a growth that is expected to continue to accelerate.

The growth in end-user computing has significantly altered the role of the IS staff, which has had to assume the additional role of information facilitator. As such, they try and make as much information available to the authorized people as possible. The result is a decentralization of control over computer resources and end users' meeting many of their own information needs. While this situation has resulted in more work for the IS staff, it has been counterbalanced by a lessened demand for their services, since more users meet their own needs. As the trend continues, it is expected that end-user computing will represent 75% to 95% of all information processing by the turn of the century.

What Scott and Ashton realized after they had studied computer systems for a while was that there are basically three types of information systems in organizations. The first two involve end-user computing. The first type is called a **personal information system**. In this system individuals use a personal computer, data they have created and stored themselves, and corporate data to meet their own personal information needs. This chapter discusses personal information systems. The second type is called a **group information system**. In this system a group, such as a department, links its personal computers together and uses its own and corporate data to meet the information needs of the group. The technology used in group information systems is discussed in Chapter 6. The third type is called an **enterprise information system**. This is the system that provides and maintains the programs and data used by the organization as a whole. Enterprise information systems are discussed throughout the book and especially in Chapters 16–20.

Two developments that began independently, end-user computing and microcomputers, have converged to revise the way we use computers in today's world. Each has made the other a more powerful influence in today's business environment. This chapter will discuss each development independently and then blend the two to show how we are computing today. The first part of this chapter discusses micro-computers and their impact upon accounting and systems. The second part discusses end-user computing. The last part of the chapter discusses microcomputer and end-user software tools.

AN INTRODUCTION TO MICROCOMPUTERS

Microcomputer hardware concepts were discussed in Chapter 4. The software that operates on microcomputers is discussed later in this chapter. This section provides a historical perspective by discussing some of the early developments in microcomputers. It also discusses the tremendous impact computers have had on the accounting profession and the uses of micros by accountants.

A Brief Historical Perspective

The first microcomputer was the Altair 8800. It was marketed to hobbyists by a small electronic company called Micro Instrumentation and Telemetry Systems. It was introduced in 1975 and sold for $650 ($395 in kit form). Sales were mediocre until it was featured on the cover of *Popular Electronics*. The feature story resulted in thousands of orders from people who wanted their own personal computer.

Other companies were quick to note the potential for microcomputers. In April 1977 Steve Jobs and Steve Wozniak introduced their Apple II computer. Their company, Apple Computer, was instrumental in making microcomputers available to the general public. Apple was so successful that within seven years it was one of the largest five hundred companies in America. Also in 1977 Commodore introduced its Pet computer and Tandy released its TRS-80. From 1977 until 1982 these three companies were the leading sellers of microcomputers.

For the first few years microcomputers were used principally by hobbyists and by those familiar with programming languages. Then in 1979 three major software products were introduced that significantly increased the attractiveness of the microcomputer. The first, an electronic spreadsheet named VisiCalc, was introduced by a Harvard Business School student and a programmer friend. VisiCalc allowed users to perform calculations on rows and columns of numbers. Although it was crude and lacking in power by today's standards, it was an impressive tool when it was introduced. VisiCalc was a very popular software product, and thousands of people bought the Apple computer just to be able to use it.

The second software product was an Ashton-Tate program called dBase II. This data base program allowed users to create and maintain their own data bases. The third product was WordStar, a word processing package that allowed users to create, edit, store, and manipulate text. Users now had a computer that could fit on top of their desks and software that would allow them to process columns of numbers, to process written text, and to store and retrieve data in an organized fashion. Suddenly, micros were no longer just toys for hobbyists but powerful and functional business tools.

The success of the early players in the personal computer market made other companies sit up and take notice. Among them was IBM, which announced its IBM personal computer (PC) on August 12, 1981. IBM officials privately estimated that they could sell 250,000 personal computers over a five-year period. Instead, they sold 800,000 in 1982, and by 1983 they were making and shipping as many as 250,000 in a single month. The IBM PC was a huge success and became the standard for the personal computer industry. In 1984 IBM had a 63% share of the personal computer market. In recent years numerous IBM clones (or compatibles) have flooded the market. The clones are usually either less expensive, more powerful, or have more features than IBM's products. In addition, Apple has introduced a number of popular products, including the Macintosh and a very popular notebook computer called the PowerBook. As a result, IBM currently only has a small share of the personal computer market.

A summary of milestones in the development of microcomputer systems is presented in Table 5.1.

The power of microcomputers has grown dramatically in the past decade. Ads in computer magazines state that if the automobile industry had made the same progress the computer industry had, a Mercedes-Benz would cost $2.50 and get two million miles per gallon. In a similar vein, if the aircraft industry had evolved as spectacularly as the computer industry had, a Boeing 767 would cost $500 and would circle the globe in 20 minutes on 5 gallons of fuel. These figures reflect reductions in cost, increases in speed, and decreases in energy consumption analogous to that undergone by computers. The result is that today's personal computers have as much raw processing speed as a 1980s mainframe costing millions of dollars.

The Microcomputer Revolution

Microcomputers are truly one of the more important technological developments in the last hundred years. They have spawned a virtual revolution in the way we do business. They have impacted the vast majority of business workers; an estimated 75–80% of them use personal computers in their work. To illustrate their impact, consider these statistics: In 1981 there were about 2 million micros in use; by 1994 it is estimated that there will be over 100 million in use all over the world. In 1995 it is estimated that another 15 million will be sold and that sales will grow at about 10–15% per year. Purchasing all of this computer power is not inexpensive. American and Canadian businesses spend $35 billion a year on personal computing equipment, software, and services. There are over one hundred microcomputer manufacturers. Thousands of other companies provide support by developing software; manufacturing peripheral devices; selling system components; and providing training, service, maintenance, consulting, and a myriad of other products and services. So great has been their impact that some people claim that micros will eventually have a greater effect than the industrial revolution. While that may or may not

Table 5.1
Important events
in microcomputer history

Year	Hardware Developments
1974	Intel introduces 8080 microprocessor
1975	Altair 880 marketed to computer hobbyists
1977	Apple II, Commodore Pet, and TRS-80 microcomputers introduced
1978	Intel introduces 8086 microprocessor
1979	Intel introduces 8088 microprocessor
1981	IBM PC announced; Osborne 1, the first portable PC, introduced
1982	Intel introduces 80286 microprocessor
1984	Apple introduces Macintosh and sells 100,000 in first six months
	Laser printers introduced
1985	Intel introduces 80386 microprocessor
1986	Compaq introduces Deskpro 386, the first 32-bit PC
	Clones pass IBM PCs in market share
1987	Apple introduces Macintosh II; IBM introduces PS/2
1988	Notebook-size PCs appear
1989	Palmtop PCs and pen computers introduced
1990	Intel introduces 80486 microprocessor
1992	Intel announces pentium (80586) chip

Year	Software Developments
1976	CP/M operating system developed
1979	Spreadsheet (VisiCalc), data base (dBase II), and word processor (WordStar) introduced
1981	MS-DOS operating system developed
1982	WordPerfect word processing program introduced
1983	Lotus 1-2-3 ships 60,000 copies its first year
1985	Microsoft Excel shipped
	Desktop publishing becomes popular
1988	IBM ships DOS 4.0
1990	Windows 3.0 introduced (GUI becomes popular)
1991	Apple introduces System 7 operating system
	Microsoft introduces DOS 5.0
1992	IBM OS/2 2.0 and Microsoft Windows 3.1 shipped

be true, microcomputers have certainly become one of the most common personal and professional productivity tools.

Microcomputers come in all shapes and sizes, ranging from those that occupy a desktop to those that can fit in the palm of your hand. Enormous sums are spent on research and development, and new products with improved technology are announced regularly. The result is an industry that reinvents itself every 18 months. Any microcomputer purchased today will be technologically (but not functionally) obsolete in 6–12 months. Each new generation of computers seems to be smaller, faster, more powerful, more functional, and less expensive; to have greater storage capacity; and to be more user-friendly. Many are also more portable and more easily linked to other computer systems. What is astounding is to think about what the next 15 years hold for us, considering that technology has come so far in the past 15 years. Truly, the microcomputer revolution has just begun.

During his investigation of microcomputer-based systems Ashton ran across an article in *Fortune* magazine that talked about the future of the PC. The brief summary of the article he prepared for Scott and Susan is shown in Focus 5.1.

The Use of Microcomputers by Accountants

The tools that accountants need to succeed have changed. They can no longer rely on calculators and pencil and paper as their principal tools. They now must have and use powerful micros and local and wide area networks. Recent studies show that the majority of the companies that employ accounting graduates expect new employees to have PC skills when they graduate. They want graduates to have at least a working knowledge of operating systems, electronic spreadsheets, data base management systems, word processing, and methods of transferring data between programs. They also want the graduates to have some familiarity with general ledger programs, graphics software, networking, and downloading from a mainframe. About the only skill that most companies do not require at least some familiarity with is programming skills. Many of these firms also make computer literacy a requirement for promotion. As time passes, microcomputer competence as a condition for employment and advancement will increase.

Microcomputers are revolutionizing the world of accounting and auditing by significantly increasing the productivity of those who use them. Accountants in industry have found a multitude of uses for micros, from running an entire accounting system to downloading data from the company's mainframe to their PC to analyze corporate data and make decisions. They also use the PC for developing their own information systems, for office automation, and for a wide variety of analysis and decision-making tasks.

The what-if capabilities of the software significantly improve a tax accountant's ability to view the consequences of different tax-planning strategies. The microcomputer can also be used to enter, process, and prepare individual and corporate tax returns in a matter of minutes. Since the early years of micros, tax accountants have been among the heaviest users of microcomputers.

Management consultants use the micros for decision support. The microcomputer software assists them as they help clients to decide whether to build, buy, or lease a building; manufacture a product; acquire another company; divest themselves of a line of business; or take any number of other important actions.

Auditors use micros to reduce clerical activities and to improve audit quality and productivity. Auditors use micros for doing audit planning, risk analysis, engagement management, statistical sampling, and audit tests; for accessing mainframe data; for preparing audit

5.1 FOCUS

Memorandum

TO: Scott and Susan
FROM: Ashton
RE: Summary of a Fortune Magazine Article Discussing the Future of the PC

Every once in a while a new product is introduced that changes the way businesses operate. For example, the automobile, the telephone, the fax machine, the copy machine, and the airplane have all had a tremendous impact on business practices. In 1977 the personal computer (PC), was introduced. Little did people realize that this "utilitarian, ivory-colored metal box of chips, wires, and motors" would "reshape organizations, build enormous personal fortunes, and redraw the rules of the computer industry." The PC spawned an industry that now has sales in excess of $100 bil-

lion a year. This new invention "rendered the typewriter nearly extinct, turned secretaries into word-processing experts, pulled small businesses into the information age, and inspired man-machine love affairs every bit as passionate as automobiles have."

Fortune magazine recently interviewed a number of PC experts and asked for their predictions for the 1990s.

- *Razzle-dazzle technology will emerge faster than ever.* In 1981 a basic IBM PC cost just over $2600. Adjusted for inflation, that purchase price now "buys a computer with 35 times the processing power, 1,200 times the disk capacity, a high-quality color monitor, and more." Special chips "manipulate and exchange photographic images, video,

and sound, as well as numbers and text." Soon computers will read handwriting and display and edit video images. The makers of semiconductors, the brain of the computer, will "cram practically an entire personal computer on a single chip no bigger than a dime."

- *Data networks will come of age.* You will be able to send and receive almost any type of document or image, including still and moving photos, documents, recordings, and spreadsheets. You will be able to see the person you are conversing with. Employees in offices all over the world will share documents and communicate throughout the day by using a computer rather than a telephone or a fax machine.

- *Users could confront a bewil-*

reports; and for doing research using on-line data bases. Audit software is discussed in more detail later in this chapter.

Most organizations need someone who is experienced in the field of microcomputers and who understands their business, their information system, and the way they operate. They want someone who can communicate with corporate management and who can determine their business needs, translate them into "computerese," and communicate them to the computer industry. To provide the needed assistance, CPA and consulting firms have organized special groups in their consulting or audit staffs, and large organizations have set up microcomputer support staffs. As microcomputer use continues to grow, the need for microcomputer consultants will also grow. As this field increases in

dering array of choices. Hundreds of organizations are producing a baffling number of products from which to choose. For example, recently introduced notepads (clip-board-size computers that read handwriting) will put "digital devices in the hands of tens of millions of salespeo-ple, delivery people, construction workers, and even executives who have never before touched a computer." IBM and Apple recently joined forces to de-velop personal computers that electronically send and re-ceive "living documents—fascinating amalgams of im-ages, sounds, numbers, and text that carry with them all the software needed to make them work. The recipient will not only view the material on his or her screen but will be able as well to fiddle with the spreadsheets, edit the text, and dictate comments that the computer will record."

■ *Japan's electronics companies will become more of a force.* They will create entirely new markets with creative devices that combine aspects of computers and inexpensive electronic gadgets. For exam-ple, "digital readers will show up soon in the U.S.—book-size devices that display pub-lished material. So will small portable 'personal communi-cators' that combine a cellular phone, a fax, and a PC that keeps track of phone num-bers, memos, and the like."

■ *Computers will change the na-ture of organizations and office work.* In the past de-cade there has been little measurable increase in the productivity of office workers. A major reason is that the PC was used to automate old ways of working. The real payoff in using computers is in changing the nature of orga-nizations and in reengineering office work.

"Technology has reinvented the corporation again and again. The modern company is the child of reliable post and telegraph sys-tems. The modern headquarters is the product of the telephone which made it possible to sepa-rate management from the factory. As computers become a primary means of communica-tion, companies will transport work to the workers instead of transporting workers to the work."

This is not in reference to "telecommuting—white-collar workers toiling over keyboards at home—but business travel, everything from flying across America to walking to the con-ference room down the hall. Computers are evolving into the ultimate communication de-vice—beyond telephones, cellular phones, faxes, even live video hookups. As your computer takes over from such devices, the way you work will change. You'll be less likely to head for the airport, wait on a fax, or even leave your desk for a meeting—unless you want to. That could streamline work and bring a surge in office produc-tivity to greet the new century."

Source: Adapted from Brenton R. Schlender, "The Future of the PC," *Fortune* (August 26, 1991): 40–48.

importance, it should offer a career path to students familiar with accounting and with microcomputers.

No matter which career path in accounting students choose, the chances are that if they want to succeed, they will be required to have a significant understanding of how to use microcomputer hardware and a variety of computer software products.

END-USER COMPUTING (EUC)

After the automobile was introduced, a famous sociologist predicted that the size of the automobile market was 2 million cars. A major factor in his calculation was his belief that only 2 million people would be willing to serve as chauffeurs. Instead, most people in industrialized nations today learn to drive themselves, and the market is in the tens of millions of cars sold annually. It was also once predicted that the telephone system would collapse because the geometric growth in calls would require everyone to be telephone operators. Instead, equipment was developed that automated many of the functions performed by operators.

Since the introduction of the computer, the demand for information systems has grown astronomically. Many companies have backlogs and hidden backlogs of development requests that will take them years to meet. Some companies have even gone out of business because they could not meet their information needs fast enough. If a company wanted to eliminate all its information backlogs, it would need hundreds of thousands of additional programmers. In some companies almost everyone would then have to become a programmer. Doesn't this sound like the automobile and the telephone examples? What is the solution? End users meeting their own information needs. As with telephones, technology will be developed to automate much of the process for us. Just as most people learn to drive automobiles, increased computer literacy and easier-to-use programming languages will allow almost everyone to operate powerful computers.

It is essential that accountants understand end-user computing concepts, since they will be end users or have a significant involvement with end-user computing no matter where they go to work. This section of the chapter is designed to help accounting students get a better understanding of end-user computing. The first two topics discussed are the skill levels of end users and end-user development and use. The next two are the benefits and the risks of end-user computing. The section ends with a discussion of how to manage and control end-user computing.

Skill Levels of End Users

In terms of their expertise and skill with computers, Ashton found that end users can be divided into three categories: nonskilled, semiskilled, and skilled. **Nonskilled end users** are not computer-literate and have little experience with computer systems. They are not able to develop their own programs and must use systems developed by others. They are usually restricted to simple data entry or selection tasks, such as entering data on the screen or choosing among options. As a result, they are usually guided by detailed, on-screen instructions or by detailed menus. They need a great deal of assistance and must rely entirely on others for technical help.

Semiskilled end users are moderately experienced computer users and have typically received formal training on the computer. They are able to use basic spreadsheet, word processing, and data base features. Some are able to use common fourth-generation languages to query corporate data bases and to produce their own ad hoc reports. They have some troubleshooting skills and can resolve some of the technical problems they face. However, they still need to be supported by more experienced users.

Skilled end users have extensive experience and training in computers and in software use and development. They are familiar with and use many of the advanced features of software packages (such as macros). Often they are able to program in languages such as BASIC, C + +, or COBOL. They develop sophisticated programs and simple systems for themselves and others.

End users can function individually or in groups. In individual end-user computing users meet their own individual needs. In group end-user computing users are linked together using networks and other special software and work together toward a common goal. For example, people from several different sites that are linked together and to corporate and outside data bases can work together to prepare a proposal for a client. They can thus work on the proposal simultaneously, rather than having one person read it and then pass it on to another for review, comment, and updating. The result is a proposal in hours or one or two days rather than weeks. The use of groupware, the software that allows this group work, is discussed more fully in Chapter 6.

Appropriate End-User Development and Use

When information users develop an application on their own, rather than using the IS department, the result is **end-user development**. The development work is performed by people in traditional business roles, such as managers, accountants, and internal auditors. Full-time computer specialists act as advisors but do not actually do the development work.

Ashton found that end-user computing is not a substitute for traditional transaction processing systems. It is beyond the scope and ability of end users to develop complex systems, such as those that process a high level of transactions or update records in multiple files or data bases. Therefore, it is not appropriate for the routine processing of payroll, accounts receivable, accounts payable, general ledger, or inventory transactions. Ashton found that end-user development is appropriate for the following tasks:

- Retrieving information from existing company data bases to produce simple reports or to answer one-time queries
- Performing what-if analyses on data the user maintains or on data extracted from company data bases; performing sensitivity analysis, statistical analysis, or mathematical modeling
- Developing data management applications using prewritten software such as a spreadsheet or a data base system
- Preparing and processing documents using word processing and electronic mail
- Preparing schedules and lists, such as depreciation schedules, accounts receivable aging, and loan amortizations
- Preparing data for enhanced presentations, using graphics and special fonts

The query or report is only needed once or infrequently, and the data is available in existing files or data bases.

Application data, content, logic, calculations, or report formats will change frequently.

End-user tools are available and adequately supported.

A heavy and direct involvement of the user in the development process is required to identify application requirements.

The application can be developed and maintained easily by the user.

The application must be developed quickly and IS personnel are unavailable.

The application will not update or change any data in the files or data base.

The application is not critical to the success of the organization.

The application does not require a high level of security.

The application development cost is minimal.

The application is intended for a single user or a small group of users, rather than the entire organization.

Standards exist to guide the development and use of end-user computing and to minimize the potential negative effects.

The system is self-documenting or requires a low level of documentation.

Table 5.2
Conditions favoring end-user application development

Some of the conditions that make end-user development more appropriate are listed in Table 5.2 Many of the tools used in end-user computing are presented later in the chapter.

Benefits of End-User Computing

One of the reasons end-user computing has increased so significantly is that it offers tremendous advantages. Most of the benefits relate to the ability of users to create, control, and implement their own information systems. These benefits are summarized next.

User Creation, Control, and Implementation.   In end-user computing accountants are able to control their own information instead of being controlled by the IS department. They can decide for themselves what information needs are important and whether or not a system should be developed.

Timeliness.   With end-user-created applications much of the lengthy delay inherent in the traditional system development process is avoided. End users usually don't have to go through expensive and time-consuming cost-benefit analyses, detailed requirements definitions, and committees that are a part of traditional systems development. Nor do they have to wait on others or wait for time on the mainframe computer. Instead, they can develop the system they want when they want to develop it.

Improved Productivity, Performance, and Creativity.   End users improve personal productivity by reducing or eliminating tedious, time-consuming, and repetitive tasks. This improves the quality of their work and allows them to handle more complex tasks. It frees them for more creative, thought-oriented activities and for planning and control activities. It also results in better, faster, and more accurate decisions.

Freeing Up of IS Resources.   The more information needs that users can meet, the more time IS personnel have to spend on other information and maintenance needs. This reduces both the visible and the invisible backlog of systems development projects.

Reduced Communication Problems.   End-user-developed systems avoid the user-analyst-programmer communication problems inherent in traditional program development since the users develop the system.

Technological Literacy.   Working in an end-user computing environment improves the computer literacy of users. This allows them to make better use of current technology and technological advancements.

Versatility and Ease of Use.   Most end-user computing software is easy to understand and use. With it users can meet most of their information needs. They can change the information they produce or modify their application anytime their requirements change. With portable micros an end user's office can be at work, at home, on a plane, or almost anywhere else.

Ownership.   People are more interested in and take better care of things that they own. With end-user computing the system becomes *my* system, not *the* system. This empowerment or sense of ownership makes users better workers and better decision makers.

Risks of End-User Computing

There also are some significant drawbacks to end-user computing and to eliminating analyst/programmer involvement in systems creation. Some of the more important of these are discussed next.

Logic and Development Errors.   Because many end users have little experience in systems design and development, they are more likely to make errors and less likely to recognize that an error has occurred. There are many different kinds of errors. The user-developer may solve the wrong problem, poorly define the nature of the problem, or inadequately define the requirements of the system. The user may apply an inappropriate analytical method to the right problem or use the wrong software. The user may also use incomplete or outdated information. Often the error is caused by faulty logic or by incorrectly using formulas or software commands.

Perhaps the problems inherent in applications created by users can best be illustrated with the following episode, reported by columnist Jim Seymour in *PC Week.*

An oil and gas company was looking at a proposed acquisition. One member of the team analyzing the deal developed several sophisticated spreadsheet models. When the models showed that the company should proceed with the acquisition, consultants from their CPA firm were brought in to examine the results. The CPAs examined the spreadsheet and decided the data looked good.

An aide, wanting to be ready for tough questions from the board of directors, made his own examination of the spreadsheet data the day before the special board meeting. He discovered that something was very wrong with the numbers. A panicky afternoon and evening followed. The working group was hastily reassembled. The accounting firm's local managing partner came over with the two partners who'd approved the work. They called for a half-dozen colleagues.

There was no pitch to the board. The deal would have been a disaster. A few sloppy formulas in the spreadsheets had skewed the projections of what could be gotten from spinning off properties, what a restatement of reserves would mean, and what would happen when a consolidated balance sheet was prepared for the combined entities. The spreadsheet developer was fired. That CPA firm no longer does any special work for the company and won't have the company as an audit client much longer.[1]

Inadequately Tested Applications.   Users are not as likely to rigorously test their applications, either because they are not cognizant of the need to do so or because of the difficulty of or the time needed for the testing process. One result is an application with the types of errors mentioned previously.

Inefficient Systems.   Most end users are not programmers and have not been trained in systems development. Often the systems they develop, while getting the job done, are not done very efficiently. Inefficient systems also result when users do not have the necessary resources to do the job right.

Poorly Controlled Systems.   Many end users fail to implement controls to protect their system. Applications are developed without regard to organizational standards or objectives. They are developed without sufficient input, output, or processing controls. Controls over data access and manipulation, including controls over the downloading and uploading of information, are also lacking. Likewise, security, audit trail, and backup and recovery controls are not instituted and followed.

System Incompatibilities.   Some companies add end-user equipment as they can afford it, buying the least expensive or the most powerful equipment available. As a result, some companies have a diversity of hardware and software that is very hard to support or to network.

Poorly Documented Systems.   User-created systems are often poorly documented. Documentation is not viewed as important by many end users, nor is it a naturally interesting thing to do. Most users do not consider that others might have to understand the system and how it works, and so they don't bother with documentation.

---

[1] Adapted from Jim Seymour, "Left Unchecked, Spreadsheets Can Be a What-If Disaster," *PC Week* (August 21, 1984): 37. Copyright © 1984, Ziff Communications Company.

Duplication of Systems and Data and Wasted Resources. Most end users are not aware that other users may have similar information needs. The result is a lot of duplication of effort. Inexperienced users also may take on more than they are able to accomplish. Often it is only after having expended significant time and resources that they realize they will never be able to complete their application. They end up wasting effort and resources.

Increased Costs. While buying one microcomputer is not very expensive, buying them for hundreds or thousands of workers is costly. And updating the hardware and software every few years is also expensive. End-user computing also has a high opportunity cost. Developing end-user systems keeps users from doing other things with their time and may divert their attention from their primary job. In addition, end-user computing makes increased demands on the company mainframe for time and data and on IS people for support and assistance. Supporting PCs and end users can be expensive. Surveys have showed that it costs from $600 to $2000 per end user and PC, depending on the size of the company.

Dysfunctional Behavior. Some users go overboard in developing end-user systems, resulting in a variety of dysfunctional behaviors. End users may develop information systems as a means of enhancing their power, position, or reputation. They may develop information "just in case" they may need it. They may get so caught up in end-user development that they neglect their other duties. They may get to the point of analysis paralysis, in which they analyze data to death and are still not able to make a decision. They may develop systems so that they can slant things toward a position they want to support.

Ashton learned that as the complexity and sophistication of information systems increase, so does the likelihood of a problem. Many of the risks occur because of the lack of systems analyst involvement and the inexperience of the users developing the system. The risks have to be put into perspective, however, and viewed in light of the benefits to be achieved. Most organizations want the benefits of user-created systems and do not want to curb their development. At the same time, however, they want to minimize the risks. This balance can be achieved by providing systems analysts as advisers and reviewers and by requiring that user-created systems be reviewed and documented before they are used. In addition, users can be trained in the systems analysis process so that they can identify and adequately meet their needs and can review the work of other users.

Managing and Controlling End-User Computing

Ashton discovered that organizations use several different approaches to manage and control end-user computing. The **monopolist approach** centers power and control over end-user computing in the IS department, which discourages the growth of end-user computing. Unfortunately, this approach denies the organization most of the benefits of end-user computing and is not in the best long-term interests of the company. The **laissez-faire approach** openly encourages end-user computing and lets end users do whatever they want. There are no controls over what end-user computing tools are purchased or how they are used. Chaos is often the result, and supporting the system is next to impossible. The **controlled-growth approach** tries to provide enough guidance and standards to adequately control the system yet allow users the flexibility they need. The controlled-growth approach is the most common and advantageous approach to managing end-user systems.

The controlled-growth approach often makes use of an **information center (IC)**. The role of the information center is to facilitate, coordinate, and control end-user activities and supports. Here are some of the specific duties of the information center.

- It serves as a clearinghouse for end-user information, coordination, and assistance.
- It sets standards for, and assists end users with, application development and maintenance. The IC helps an end user meet minimal standards for control and security.
- It provides a quality control function over user applications by requiring users to adequately control and test applications.
- It sets standards for hardware and software purchase and use, and it evaluates new end-user hardware and software products that come on the market.
- It assists end users with hardware and software selection. This function helps ensure compatibility among system components, reduces costs through quantity purchases, limits maintenance and support problems, and facilitates the transfer of data within an organization.
- It provides technical support for the hardware and software authorized and supported by the company.
- It trains end users in basic computer education and in how to use specific hardware and software.
- It facilitates access to data so that end users can meet their data access needs with minimal IS help.
- It restricts end-user access to only that data they need and are authorized to have.
- It helps control corporate data. Data and data bases should not be duplicated, and users with similar needs should be able to access the same data. So that data errors are reduced, all end users should be required to download corporate data rather than allowed to rekey it into their end-user systems. Uploads of data for an end-user system should be strictly controlled to ensure that errors are not introduced into the system.
- It develops and implements standards to reduce or eliminate fraud, software piracy, viruses, and other potential problems.

■ It sets documentation standards and helps end users follow them.

■ It provides hot-line assistance to help end users resolve problems that arise with their systems.

MICROCOMPUTER AND END-USER SOFTWARE TOOLS

As explained in Chapter 4, software can be classified as systems software or application software. Application software can be classified as (1) special-purpose (accounts receivables, general ledger, inventory, etc.) and (2) general-purpose (spreadsheets, data bases, etc.). Good application software is so important that many companies eventually invest more money in end-user software than in hardware.

Much is said in today's world about being computer-literate. However, even more important than knowing *about* computer hardware and software is knowing *what* software tool to use and *when* to use it. End users must be able to determine the problem they face, how it can be solved, and if they can use computer technology to solve it. If they can, they need to know *which* end-user software tool is most appropriate for the particular problem they face. In other words, they need to know *how* to apply modern technology to their job functions. This section discusses some of the general-purpose software that is most frequently used by end users and when its use is most appropriate. It also discusses accounting and tax packages, audit software, spreadsheets, data bases, word processors, desktop publishing, business graphics, image processing, desktop organizers, project management, decision support systems, expert systems, and artificial intelligence. Telecommunications software is discussed in Chapter 6.

Accounting Software

Users of microcomputer-based accounting packages have widely varying needs. Since it would not be possible for a software package to meet the needs of all users, micro-based accounting software often comes in modules. The modules are designed to handle the various kinds of transactions that a company faces. In that way users can purchase the modules that meet their needs. The most popular accounting module is the general ledger, which is the financial reporting system for most accounting software. Other popular software modules are accounts receivable, accounts payable, inventory management and control, fixed assets, payroll, and order entry and processing. However, there are many other software modules, including bill of materials, job and product costing, materials requirement planning, scheduling, purchase order, point of sale, and sales order. All the modules are integrated so that they can pass information back and forth between themselves. The general ledger module serves as the central, unifying module. The other modules feed it summary information.

Each module is designed to accept data and edit it for correctness and validity. It also processes the data, updates all relevant master files and data bases, and produces the needed reports and documents. The modules are designed to be flexible so that users can adapt the package to their individual needs. They are also designed to be user-friendly. They make use of simple menus, screen prompts, and easy-to-adapt report formats; and they come with easy-to-read documentation. They are also designed with control issues in mind. They have extensive audit trails and features that force all transactions and accounts to balance. Error messages and help features assist those who make mistakes or are uncertain about how to proceed.

Microcomputer-based accounting software is especially popular among smaller organizations, because it allows companies to computerize their manual systems and to provide better and more prompt information. A number of larger firms are also beginning to move their accounting systems from mainframes to local area networks. One reason they are able to do so is the power of existing micro-based software. For example, the general ledger module from Armor Systems can generate income statements for 1200 different departments, handle 32,700 employees, and process an almost infinite number of journal entries. And all of this power and flexibility can be purchased for $200 to $1000 per module.

Income Tax   Tax laws are becoming increasingly more complex and difficult to master. This difficulty, combined with the power and flexibility of new tax software, has resulted in significant growth in the use of tax preparation packages. An estimated 25 million individual 1991 returns were prepared by using income tax preparation software, as were over 3 million 1991 corporation and partnership returns. About 80% of all returns filed by tax preparers were prepared on in-house computers using tax preparation software. Most tax planning is also done using micros and income tax–planning software. Therefore, an understanding of microcomputers and tax-planning and preparation software is a must for anyone considering a career in taxation.

About eighty companies sell tax preparation software. Each package has unique features that are appealing. This wide variety of software and features makes it difficult to select software. Ashton identified the following features as among the most important in selecting income tax software.

- The software company should be strong, stable, and financially sound, and it should support its software. Telephone support is essential, with electronic bulletin board, fax, and on-line support desirable.
- The package should be easy to learn and use.
- The package should contain all of the tax forms needed.
- The package should make all complex calculations, such as passive losses and the alternative minimum tax.
- The package should have the ability to carry forward information from prior years.

■ The company should ensure timely delivery of its products. The package will be needed in time to learn the new features prior to tax season.

■ The package should allow for electronic filing, since the number of returns filed electronically is growing rapidly.

■ The package should support networking, since local area networks that link tax preparers together are very popular.

■ Because time is money, the package should make calculations and print very quickly.

■ The package should have the ability to be integrated with other software, such as word processing and client billing.

Audit Personal computing has revolutionized the auditing profession. It used to take auditors hours to prepare and foot a manual trial balance, post adjustments, prepare and foot an adjusted trial balance, and prepare financial statements. Then if another adjustment was discovered or a change was made, the entire footing and preparation process had to be repeated. Nowadays, trial balance software allows auditors to input the working trial balance, handle all types of adjusting and reclassification entries, and automatically compute the adjusted trial balance. It also facilitates the completion of the financial statements, footnotes to those statements, and information for tax returns. Going one step further, many or all of the working papers that support the numbers in the financial statements can be automated and tied to the trial balance.

Auditors can use a **generalized audit software package (GASP)** to perform many auditing tasks. For example, a GASP can access a customer master file, test-foot the balance, select a statistical sample of the accounts, and print both the working paper control sheet and the confirmation letters. Here are several other examples of how auditors use microcomputers.

■ *Analytical reviews:* Ratios comparing this year's results to the prior 10 years' results can help auditors spot problem areas that need to be investigated in more depth.

■ *Engagement planning:* A comparison of last year's budgeted and actual time spent on audit tasks can result in a better-planned and more efficient audit.

■ *Engagement management:* Software is available to help auditors manage their time, schedule audits, and so on.

■ *Statistical sampling:* Software can help in the selection and evaluation of audit samples.

■ *Clerical tasks:* Time-consuming clerical processes like keeping track of confirmations, writing memos and reports, preparing budgets and time reports, and developing and managing audit programs can be automated.

- *Audit tests:* Audit tests such as testing depreciation or amortization and testing tax estimates are easily performed.

- *Downloading data:* The microcomputer can be used to access corporate data, download it to a micro, and analyze it.

- *Research:* There are far too many accounting, auditing, and tax standards and rules for anyone to remember. A microcomputer can be used to research major auditing issues.

- *Decision support:* A decision support system can help auditors make decisions such as the scope of the audit and the nature and timing of evidence collection.

The use of microcomputer systems has led to significant cost savings by both external and internal auditors. The ability to use word processing and spreadsheets to document systems has produced savings. Even greater cost savings come from the ability to quickly and effectively update the documentation when changes occur. Cost savings also are realized as a result of improved risk analysis, better planning and control of the audit, better report content and presentation, and enhanced creditability. Finally, savings result from auditors' ability to communicate with their offices and others by using telecommunications technology.

Spreadsheets　　Electronic spreadsheets have played a major role in the personal computer revolution. For many businesses they have eliminated the need for paper, pencil, eraser, and calculator in the production of work sheets and reports. Electronic spreadsheets are extremely diverse; almost anything involving mathematical relationships can be done quickly and accurately on them. Their use is widespread in a variety of functional areas in businesses of all sizes.

An **electronic spreadsheet** is a matrix of columns and rows containing blank cells. Many spreadsheets have more than 8000 rows and 250 columns, or more than 2 million cells. Cells can hold alphabetic or numeric data, formulas, and references to other cells. Cells are referred to by their column letter and row number. Since all cells cannot be viewed simultaneously, only a small section of the matrix, called a window, is displayed on the screen at any one time. Directional (arrow) keys are used to scroll through the work sheet, exposing different portions of the matrix.

An electronic spreadsheet is used the same way a regular work sheet is used, except that the computer does all the calculating. Labels can be put along the top, down the side, or wherever they are desired. For example, a company's income statement can be set up as shown in Table 5.3. Column A contains the trial balance account names, and columns B through G contain the trial balance, the adjustments, and the postadjustment balances. Each cell can contain a number or a formula that the computer can use to calculate a value. Cell G4, for example, shows 195,000, which is derived from the formula C4 − D4 + E4.

A		B	C	D	E	F	G
1 Account		Trial balance		Adjustments		Ending balance	
2		DR	CR	DR	CR	DR	CR
3							
4 Sales			200,000	5000			195,000
5 Cost of Goods Sold							
6 Beginning Inventory		20,000				20,000	
7 Purchases		140,000				140,000	
8 Goods Available		160,000				160,000	
9 Ending Inventory		30,000			3000	33,000	
10 Cost of Goods Sold		130,000				127,000	
11 Operating Expenses		40,000			2000	42,000	
12							
13 Net Income			30,000				26,000

Table 5.3
An income statement prepared on a spreadsheet

The most impressive feature of an electronic spreadsheet is its ability to answer what-if questions. Data can be changed, added, or deleted, and the effect of these changes are quickly calculated. For example, we can change any of the data in Table 5.3 and immediately see the impact on net income. This immediate, automatic recalculation provides a what-if feature that has made spreadsheets an essential tool for many business applications.

Once a particular spreadsheet has been created with appropriate headings, formulas, and functions, the spreadsheet logic can be saved and reused. A reusable spreadsheet is called a **template**. A template can be created, for example, to calculate depreciation on fixed assets that are purchased. It can then be used over again for each new asset purchased. The reusable nature of the spreadsheet and its what-if capability help managers select the best decision alternative by allowing them to interact with a computerized model that compares alternative solutions to the problem.

Spreadsheets have a **macro** command capability. The user can store a series of keystrokes in a macro and then activate the macro each time the keystrokes must be repeated. Spreadsheets also provide macro programming commands that allow the user to write programs. Macro functions allow users to create their own menus so that they can customize their templates. An entirely new programming industry has arisen in which programmers develop and sell specialized templates to a wide variety of unsophisticated users. Users then have access to all the power of spreadsheets without having to learn all the sophisticated commands and functions.

Software that integrates two or more of the major productivity tools (spreadsheets, word processing, data base, graphics, and telecommunications) is referred to as **integrated software**. By dividing the screen into two or more windows, the user can view displays from several of

POPULAR SPREADSHEET SOFTWARE		POPULAR INTEGRATED PACKAGES	
Windows Spreadsheets	**Vendor**	**DOS Integrated Software**	**Vendor**
Excel	Microsoft	Framework	Borland International
Lotus 1-2-3	Lotus Development	Lotus Works	Lotus Development
Quattro Pro	Borland International	Microsoft Works	Microsoft
		Smartware II	Informix Software Inc.
DOS Spreadsheets	**Vendor**	Symphony	Lotus Development
Javelin Plus	Javelin Products Group	**Windows Integrated Software**	**Vendor**
Lotus 1-2-3	Lotus Development	Microsoft Works	Microsoft
Multiplan	Microsoft		
PlanPerfect	WordPerfect	**Macintosh Integrated Software**	**Vendor**
Quattro Pro	Borland International	AppleWorks	Apple
SuperCalc	Computer Associates International	Claris Works	Claris
Macintosh Spreadsheets	**Vendor**		
Excel	Microsoft		
Lotus 1-2-3	Lotus Development		
Resolve	Claris		
Wingz	Informix Software Inc.		

Table 5.4
Spreadsheet software

the applications at the same time. In an integrated package users only have to enter data into one package, rather than into each separate stand-alone package. However, the components are sometimes not as powerful, fast, or flexible as single-function packages. Table 5.4 lists some of the most frequently used spreadsheets and integrated packages.

Many companies have taken the available spreadsheet packages and enhanced them with **add-ins**. Add-ins perform useful functions and tasks that the software itself does not do or does not do as well. Table 5.5 lists some of the add-ins available for Lotus 1-2-3.

Data Bases   In **data bases**, which are discussed in detail in Chapter 7, data are organized and stored electronically in such a way that they can be easily located, updated, and retrieved. A powerful software program called a **data base management system (DBMS)** is required to manipulate and store the data. Just a few years ago, these sophisticated software products were available only on mainframe computers and cost up to $100,000. Today, however, there are many quality data base software packages for micros that cost less than $700.

Data bases differ in their capabilities and range from simple to very complex. However, most quality micro-based data base management systems allow the user to perform a number of basic functions. For example, they allow the user to create, update, and delete records in a file and to sort the data base according to one or more key fields. They facilitate searching, or querying, the data

@BASE	Adds more powerful data base management functions
@Functions	Provides about 45 additional functions
@RISK	Provides risk analysis and financial modeling
101 Macros	Contains 101 macros that perform common functions
Cambridge Spreadsheet Analyst	Helps the end user find common errors in 1-2-3 spreadsheets
Noteworthy	Documents a spreadsheet
Project 8-9-10	Helps an end user monitor and control small projects
SeeMore	Allows more of a spreadsheet to be displayed on the monitor
Sideways	Prints a spreadsheet sideways
Statplan III	Adds significant statistical features currently not a part of 1-2-3
What IF Solver	Allows the end user to solve optimization problems, integer programming, and some linear and nonlinear programming problems
XYZ: Consolidate	Consolidates information from different spreadsheets

Table 5.5

Examples of spreadsheet add-ins using Lotus 1-2-3 as the example

base for specific records or for records containing certain data. They allow users to print reports that are formatted according to their needs. They perform mathematical and logic operations, and they make use of business and scientific functions to calculate totals and averages. Many have security features, network connectivity, and the ability to present material in a graphical form. They can easily pass information back and forth between spreadsheets, word processors, and other end-user software. They have programming languages that allow users to develop a wide variety of applications. Some of the more popular DBMS packages on the market are listed in Table 5.6.

Table 5.6

Common data base software for microcomputers

Windows Data Base	Vendor	DOS Data Base	Vendor
Access	Microsoft	Clarion Professional Developer	Clarion Software
Approach	Approach Software	DataEase	DataEase International
DataEase Express	DataEase International	Dataflex	Data Access
dBase	Borland International	dBase	Borland International
Paradox	Borland International	Foxpro	Microsoft
SuperBase	Software Publishing	Knowledge Man	Micro-Database System
		Paradox	Borland International
Macintosh Data Base	**Vendor**	Rbase	Microrim
		Revelation	Cosmos
4th Dimension	Acius		
FileMaker Pro	Claris		
FoxBASE	Microsoft		
Helix Express	Helix Technologies		
nuBASE Pro	New Era Software Group		
Omnis	Blyth Software		

Word Processing

Because of its flexibility, ease of use, and timesaving features, a word processor is one of the most popular microcomputer software packages. Most people who use word processing never willingly return to using a typewriter. **Word processing** is the computer-assisted creation, editing, correcting, manipulation, storage, and printing of textual data. Documents can be stored on a hard disk or a diskette for later use or printed on paper. A stored document can be retrieved at a later date, and the editing, changing, storing, and printing of the data can be repeated as often as desired. Word processors have the following common features:

- Text can be easily edited, inserted, deleted, copied, or moved.
- Data can be formatted (boldfaced, italicized, underlined, centered, double-spaced, indented, etc.) as needed.
- Text can be searched for a particular word or combination of words, and if desired, the located text can be replaced with different text (i.e., 1994 can replace 1993 in a report).
- A speller can check a document for correct spelling and can simplify the correction process. A grammar checker can test for poor grammar and syntax. A thesaurus can find synonyms or antonyms.
- Indexing and outlining features can prepare tables of contents, alphabetical indexes of terms, and outlines.
- A help feature assists with problems or explains features.
- Mathematical functions make simple calculations in documents.
- Two or more documents can be worked on simultaneously by switching back and forth between them.
- Footnotes and end notes can be prepared.
- A sort feature can sort data.
- Pages can be numbered; headers and footers can be added to desired pages.
- Text can be printed in a wide variety of fonts.

Accountants can use word processing in a number of ways. They can use them to type letters, memos, proposals, reports, manuals, product catalogs, price lists, brochures and sales literature, newsletters, billings, and financial statements. Many word processors can be integrated with data base, graphics, and spreadsheet software. For example, the user can merge a list of customer names and addresses in a data base with a letter prepared by the word processor. In this way a form letter can be customized so that it looks as if it were a personal letter. Word processors also allow a spreadsheet analysis or a graph to be included in the body of a word processing text. Thus a word processor is a very powerful tool that is almost indispensable today in business organizations. Some of the most popular word processing packages on the market are listed in Table 5.7.

Windows Word Processors	Vendor	DOS Word Processors	Vendor
Ami Pro	Lotus Development	Ami Pro	Lotus Development
Microsoft Word	Microsoft	DOS Word Processors	Vendor
Signature	XyQuest		
WordPerfect	WordPerfect	MultiMate Advantage	Borland International
WordStar	WordStar International	Microsoft Word	Microsoft
		WordPerfect	WordPerfect
Macintosh Word Processors	**Vendor**	WordStar	WordStar International
		XyWrite	XyQuest
MacWrite	Claris		
Microsoft Word	Microsoft		
WordPerfect	WordPerfect		

Table 5.7

Common word processing packages for microcomputers

Word processing systems are one of the primary components of an office automation system. **Office automation (OA)** is the use of computer and information technology to increase the productivity of information workers. Office automation reduces the costs of and shortens the time for the creation, review, revision, storage, retrieval, and distribution of documents, messages, and other forms of communication among individuals, work groups, and organizations.

The technologies used in office automation are discussed in more detail in the following sections of this chapter and in Chapter 6.

Desktop Publishing

To illustrate the accounting uses of desktop publishing, consider the following example. The CPA firm of Miles and Park was trying to build its tax practice and to better serve its clients. It decided to put out a special year-end, tax-planning newsletter. The partners considered using their word processing software, but they felt that the newsletter would look unprofessional. They investigated getting the newsletter printed professionally, but the printers in town were expensive and required long lead times. By the time they analyzed the tax law changes, got into the printer's queue, waited for the newsletter to be printed, and got it into the hands of their clients, the tax year would be over. In addition, once they handed the copy to the printer, they could not make changes of any kind. Stumped, they considered abandoning the project.

Then one of their staff suggested desktop publishing. They were able to get a high-quality system that enabled them to produce a typeset-quality product by themselves. They were able to prepare, produce, and print the newsletter in a very timely fashion. Last-minute changes were quickly and easily made, and they had greater control and flexibility than they would have had if the newsletter had been printed professionally. The product worked so well that they started using it for their financial statements, audit reports, and bids on new jobs. They even used it to prepare an informational brochure that outlined their services. They figured the package paid for itself in a year.

Windows Desktop Publishers	Vendor	DOS Desktop Publishers	Vendor
Express Publisher	Power Up Software	Avagio	Unison World Software
Microsoft Publisher	Microsoft	Express Publisher	Power Up Software
PageMaker	Aldus	GEM Desktop Publisher	Digital Research, Inc.
Publish-It	Timeworks, Inc.	PageMaker	Aldus
PagePlus	Serif, Inc.	Publish-It	TimeWorks, Inc.
QuarkXpress	Quark	Ventura Publisher	Ventura Software, Inc.
Ventura Publisher	Ventura Software, Inc.		

Macintosh Desktop Publishers	Vendor		
PageMaker	Aldus		
Publish-It	Timeworks, Inc.		
QuarkXpress	Quark		
Springboard Publisher	Springboard Software		

Table 5.8
Popular desktop publishing packages

Desktop publishing (DTP) provides an end user with the ability to design, develop, and produce professional-quality printed documents containing text, charts, pictures, graphs, spreadsheets, photographs, and illustrations. A DTP package takes the complicated and expensive commercial-typesetting process, simplifies it, and places it in a desktop computer. Using today's DTP packages, authors can cut the publishing process from 6–18 months to as few as 6 days. Some of the popular desktop publishing packages are listed in Table 5.8.

As shown in Fig. 5.1, desktop publishing involves four steps. The first step is to enter the data. Since word processors have better text preparation and editing features than DTP packages, text material is often prepared by a word processor and entered into the DTP. Data can also be entered from data bases, spreadsheets, graphics packages, and other software. Artwork can be entered in one of three ways. First, a graphics package can create it. Second, clip art—a collection of predrawn images—can be used. Third, pictures, photographs, and drawings can be scanned and stored electronically by using image processing (explained later in the chapter).

The second step is to format the pages. In this step the user specifies the number and width of columns. Also, the user creates headers, footnotes, captions, borders, backgrounds, and other formatting items. The user can select from a wide variety of font types and styles.

The third step is to merge the text and illustrations into the page format that was created. The software will automatically flow the text into the columns and wrap it around the illustrations. The artwork and other images can be edited and scaled to the size desired. The software allows the user to see on the screen an exact image of what the printed page will look like, called WYSIWYG (what you see is what you get).

The last step is to store and print the finished product. There are several ways to prepare copies of the final document. If only a few

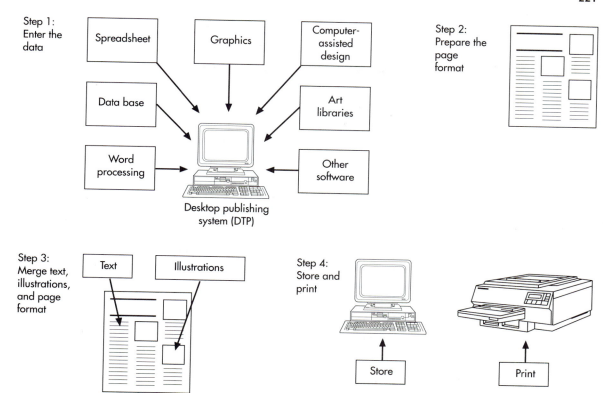

Figure 5.1
Desktop publishing: The
four-step process

copies are needed, they can be produced on a laser printer. Alternatively, a high-speed copier can be used to make a number of copies. The highest-quality copy is made by taking a copy of the stored document on disk to a professional printer for typesetting and professional printing.

Graphics Software

It is said that a picture is worth a thousand words. In computer terms, one might say that a graph is worth a thousand spreadsheet cells. The concept is the same: Data presented in graphic or pictorial form is much easier to understand than data presented in textual or numerical form. In addition, Ashton determined that graphics packages have the following benefits:

- Graphics presentations are more persuasive than verbal presentations. The right graphics are able to get right to the point, generating an impact that is not easily forgotten.

- Graphics presentations shorten meetings. The same information can be presented in less time using graphics.

- Graphics aid decision making and reduce the decision-making process. They help managers spot trends, interrelationships, problems, and opportunities earlier; and they help them in analyzing and interpreting data.

Windows Presentation Graphics	Vendor	DOS Presentation Graphics	Vendor
Aldus Persuasion	Aldus	Harvard Graphics	Software Publishing
CA-Cricket	Computer Associates International	Hollywood	Claris
		Presentations	WordPerfect
Charisma	Macrografx Inc.	**Macintosh Presentation Graphics**	**Vendor**
Freelance Graphics	Lotus Development		
Harvard Graphics	Software Publishing	Aldus Persuasion	Aldus
PowerPoint	Microsoft	DeltaGraph Professional	DeltaPoint
Presentations	WordPerfect	PowerPoint	Microsoft
Stanford Graphics	3-D Visions	Quicktime	Apple

Table 5.9

Popular presentation graphics software packages for microcomputers

■ Graphics make a good impression, capture a person's attention, and improve retention. People using graphics are perceived as being better prepared; as being able to make clearer and more interesting presentations; and as being more effective, credible, and professional. People remember more of what is presented when graphics and other visual aids are used.

Placing these packages in the hands of users has several distinct advantages. First, the users get exactly what they need because they are producing it. Second, it saves time, since users can produce the graphics very quickly whenever they desire. Finally, it costs much less than having graphics prepared professionally.

Many software packages, such as spreadsheets and data bases, contain a graphics capability. These packages are used to analyze and store data, and a graph is an extension of that analysis. Graphics are also produced by dedicated or stand-alone graphics packages that cost less than $1000. These packages are capable of producing some very impressive presentation graphics, including computer-generated presentations on TVs and computer monitors. Graphics can be printed on paper or displayed on color transparencies, slides, and photos. Among the most popular graphics are bar, pie, and line graphs. Each can be accompanied by graph titles, labels, and legends. The user can also create and store original graphics. Some of the more popular graphics packages are listed in Table 5.9.

What-if analysis, which is so popular with spreadsheets, is also possible with graphics packages. What-if graphing allows the user to view, in graph form, the effects of various alternatives. This improves users' productivity and enhances the quality of their analysis and decision making. Packages in which the screen can be divided into more than one window allow graphs to be viewed at the same time as text or spreadsheet data. Thus users can change data in the spreadsheet and see the results of those changes graphically. Figure 5.2 shows some examples of graphic output.

Image Processing   In **image processing** various scanning and photographic techniques are used to capture the exact image of a document. The scanning device con-

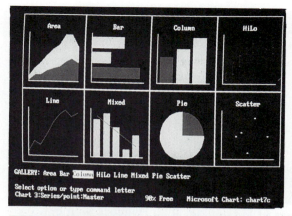

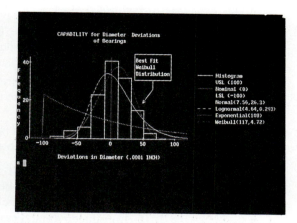

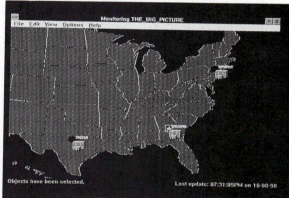

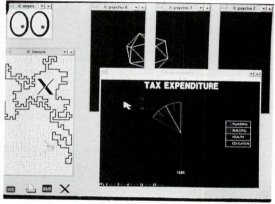

Figure 5.2
Examples of computer graphic output

verts the text and pictures into digitized electronic code and stores it on laser optical disks. An exact replica of the document is easily produced on the computer's monitor or on paper. A copy can be transmitted to another computer over telephone lines. Image processing could well have the impact in the 1990s that word processing had in the 1980s.

Ashton discovered that there are several advantages to image processing:

■ Vast amounts of data can be stored in very little space. One 12-inch removable optical disk platter can store up to 40,000 documents. For increased storage 20–100 optical disk platters can be stored in devices called jukeboxes (because of their resemblance to the old music jukeboxes).

■ Stored data can be retrieved at fantastic speeds. Documents that are stored can be coded or indexed in several different ways so that they can be retrieved using any number of identifying labels, attributes, or keywords or phrases.

■ When large volumes of data are stored and processed, the cost per document stored is quite inexpensive. As a result, the costs to file, retrieve, and refile documents are reduced significantly.

- Handwritten or typed text data can be added to the image, as can voice messages. The document can be added to a word processing package, or the data from the document can be included in a spreadsheet or data base.

- Document security is enhanced, since various levels of security clearance can be assigned to documents to restrict access to authorized users.

- Documents can be accessed by more than one person at a time and can be routed to more than one person for simultaneous review.

Companies that have installed image processing systems have reaped significant benefits. One system at Blue Cross and Blue Shield reduced insurance claims processing from seven days to two days and produced annual savings of $10 million. John Hancock won new business because of the tremendous improvements in customer service it was able to provide. Additional benefits are having less paper to process and store, doing more work with a smaller staff, and reducing transcription errors and the number of lost documents. The image processing systems installed at UPS and Union Bank are explained in Focus 5.2

S&S decided to use image processing to automate the selection and purchase of new appliances for its stores. S&S arranged to receive vendors' catalogs as images on an optical disk. The product information and specification images on the disk are accessible for simultaneous review by salespersons and service personnel at different locations. The information on the disks is discussed electronically by the different departments using written and voice messages. Product

---

5.2 FOCUS

Signing On-line Yields Productivity Benefits

UPS. The old saying "sign on the dotted line" may soon be replaced by "sign on-line." In the summer of 1990 United Parcel Service (UPS), equipped all 60,000 of its drivers with delivery information acquisition device (DIAD) units. The DIAD units are small computers about the size of a clipboard that contain special image-capturing software. The signer uses a stylus (a penlike rod) to sign on a pressure-sensitive pad. The imaging software displays the signature on the pad and records it electronically. At the end of each day drivers use special hardware and an information network to transmit the delivery data to the UPS Enterprise System/9000 mainframe in Mahwah, New Jersey. The entire system cost UPS about $350 million.

information and specifications, including handwritten margin notes or drawings that point out various items of interest, are passed between the two groups.

When a new product is selected, an electronic purchase order is prepared. Modifications to the product specifications, drawings, and spoken messages can be electronically attached to the purchase order. The entire package—purchase order, product specification modifications, notes, comments, drawings, and so on—is sent to Susan for approval. Susan will send the entire package electronically to the vendor's computer.

Desktop Organizers

Desktop organizer (or personal information management) software helps end users organize their daily activities. Ashton discovered that the typical desktop organizer contains the following components:

- A calendar to keep track of appointments and meetings; many notify the user when it is time for a meeting or appointment
- A calculator for mathematical computations
- An electronic notepad on which to jot down ideas and notes
- A card file (an electronic name-address system) and an automatic telephone-dialing feature
- Features of other programs, such as electronic mail and word processing
- A tickler file, or to-do list

Many desktop organizers are memory-resident; that is, they stay in memory at all times and, by pressing a single key, can be called up

---

The new system has a number of important benefits. Drivers are able to check out much faster at the end of the day. A great deal of paperwork is eliminated. In addition, tracking packages is much faster and more accurate. When a call for package information is received at customer service, the ES/9000 data base is searched for proof of delivery by an automated retrieval system. The proof of delivery is then printed and sent to the client. In the future, this printed copy will be eliminated.

UPS will expand its imaging system and install a delivery information automated lookup system (DIALS) that will let UPS clients dial in and search for the package information themselves.

Union Bank. Union Bank in San Diego installed an image recognition system that allows tellers at its 176 California branches to access 1.4 million customer signature cards stored on the bank's mainframe in Monterey Park. Tellers can quickly match the signatures on checks that are being cashed with the signatures stored electronically in the mainframe. This is especially beneficial to customers who cash checks at branch offices other than their home branch. Under the old system it took up to a week to match the signature on a check with the signature stored on microfiche at the customer's home branch. The new system reduced check forgery losses by 50% in 1991.

Source: Kim S. Nash, "Signing On-line Yields Productivity Benefits", *Computerworld* (November 18, 1991): 29, 37.

Desktop Organizers	Vendor	Desktop Organizers	Vendor
Act!	Conductor Software	Packrat	Polaris Software
Agenda	Lotus Development	Primetime Personal	Primetime Software
Current	IBM	Sidekick	Borland International
Grandview	Symatec Corporation	Total Manager	Bartel Software
Instant Recall	Chronologic Corporation	Who-What-When	Chronos Software
Memory Mate	Broderbund Software Inc.		

Table 5.10
Popular desktop organizers

without disturbing the application that is currently running. For example, you could check your personal calendar while you were working on a spreadsheet and then return to the spreadsheet without having to exit and reenter the various programs. Some of the more popular desktop organizers are listed in Table 5.10.

Project Management

Accountants are often a part of or head up teams assigned to complete complex, multistep projects. One way to plan, schedule, track, and control those projects to ensure that they are completed within the budget and on time is to use **project management software**. With this software a complex project must be broken down into smaller and simpler tasks for which time, cost, and resource requirement estimates are established. These estimates are fed into the project management software along with task interrelationships (which tasks have to be completed before another task can begin). The software schedules the tasks and identifies which cannot be delayed without delaying the whole project. Users can perform what-if analyses to try out different work plans and schedules and to see how slippage in one task will affect other tasks. Some of the more popular project management software package on the market are Harvard Total Project Manager, MacProject, Microsoft Project, Super-Project Plus, and Time Line.

Decision Support Systems

A **decision support system (DSS)** helps managers make decisions in unstructured and semistructured problem situations where there may not be a "correct" answer. These decisions require that judgment, experience, and intuition be used. A computer-based DSS makes use of decision models, the decision maker's knowledge and experience, and quick and efficient data access and retrieval methods to help users formulate problems and channel their thinking so that the best possible decision can be made. Figure 5.3 illustrates the elements of a decision support system and their relationships to one another.

The key element of any decision support system is the decision maker the system is designed to support. The system designer must fully understand the decision process from both a quantitative and a behavioral perspective and must establish a combination of models, data bases, and software systems that can effectively supplement (rather than replace) the manager's judgment in making the decision. The key element of the software system is the user interface, which pro-

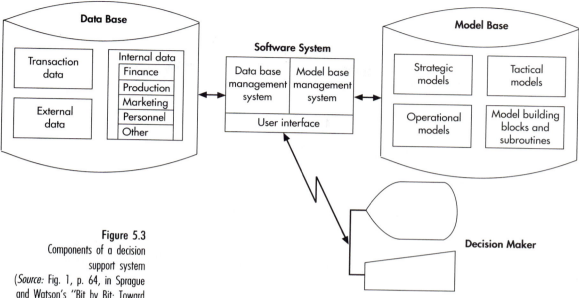

Figure 5.3

Components of a decision support system

(*Source:* Fig. 1, p. 64, in Sprague and Watson's "Bit by Bit: Toward Decision Support Systems," © Copyright (1979) by the Regents of the University of California. Reprinted from *California Management Review*, volume xxii, no. 1, by permission of the Regents.)

vides the user with a set of commands (verbs such as FIND, DISPLAY, and GRAPH) that may be used to access and manipulate all the other elements of the system. The user interface must be human-oriented rather than system-oriented in order to accommodate managers who lack the knowledge or inclination to deal with standard computer languages.

Ashton identified several common abilities of DSS software:

- *What-is capabilities:* DSS can be used to answer questions like these: What is S&S's best-selling appliance? Who are the top salespeople at S&S? How does this year's sales of a product compare to last year's. To the sales goal?

- *What-if capabilities:* DSS can be used to answer questions like these: What effect would a 10% increase in S&S's store sales have on gross profit? What effect would a new incentive sales program for all salespeople have on net income?

- *Goal seeking:* DSS can be used to determine what would have to be done to achieve a specified goal. For example, "What sales and expense levels would S&S have to have to reach a certain net income goal?

- *Simulation:* These packages use different probabilities and expectations to simulate a particular situation.

To illustrate the types and uses of a DSS, we briefly explain two different systems. American Airlines developed a DSS named An Analytical Information Management System (AAIMS). It is used by airlines, engine and aircraft manufacturers, consultants, and financial analysts. It supports planning, operations, marketing, and finance functions such as seating capacity and utilization, load factors, aircraft utilization, traffic and capacity growth, market share, operating statistics, and revenue and profitability. Citibank developed Managerial Analysis for Profit Planning (MAPP) to help bank managers make decisions about financial planning and budgeting. It also helps them to define banking products, identify the costs of providing the products, decide how to price them, and decide how to shift resources around among bank products and services.

Historically, a DSS was available only on a large computer. Some of the most popular DSSs available for large systems are IFPS, EXPRESS, and SYSTEM W. A number of excellent DSS packages are now available for microcomputers as well. There is also a great deal of software that makes it easy for a microcomputer to electronically access data contained in other systems and download it to microcomputer-based files. These two advancements have allowed DSS to become micro-based. There are dozens of micro-based DSS currently on the market, including Encore! Plus, Expert Choice, IFPS/Personal, SAS/PC, Javelin Plus, and MicroPROPHIT. In addition, most electronic spreadsheets, data bases, and graphics packages can be used for decision support purposes.

Group Decision Support Software (GDSS). Most readers have had the experience of working in a group and are familiar with some of the difficulties encountered in groups. Some people tend to dominate a group discussion or decision. Others are reluctant to contribute or defer to others in the group. Often the discussion will bounce around among topics, and by the time it is your turn to make a comment, the discussion has already shifted to another topic. Some people have axes to grind and return to the same topic repeatedly.

Group decision support software (GDSS) helps overcome many of these group dynamics problems by allowing and encouraging everyone to participate in the decision-making process. It also provides other significant benefits such as timesavings. Many managers spend up to 70% of their time in meetings, leaving them little time to implement or manage decisions that are made. Another benefit is bringing together people with different experiences, expertise, points of view, areas of responsibility, and backgrounds. Together, these people often make better decisions that individuals acting alone can.

A GDSS brings a group of people together to do things such as share information, exchange ideas, explore differing points of views, examine proposed solutions, arrive at a consensus, and vote on a course of action. There are three different types of GDSS:

1. *A face-to-face session* in a **decision room** (sometimes referred to as a war room): This room is equipped with workstations connected to a coordinating computer; a large screen for displaying information such as tables, graphs, charts, and video and for recording ideas and information developed by the group; and other special equipment to

support decisions. Seating is usually in a semicircle or a horseshoe so that everyone can see everyone else.

2. *A configuration of two or more decision rooms:* In this approach several decision rooms are linked together so that several groups can participate in the decision.

3. *A remote network* of independent workstations: Instead of using a special room for a face-to-face meeting, this approach uses networking technology and **groupware** software to link individual users together with a data base and GDSS tools. An advantage of this approach is that the users do not all have to make use of the system at the same time. In fact, the decision-making process may last several days or more as users at their convenience respond to comments made by others.

Expert Systems and Artificial Intelligence

Susan has a great idea for expanding market share and profitability at S&S. She wants to begin targeting recent college graduates and young married couples who do not yet have an established credit rating and cannot afford to pay cash for their household furnishings. Currently, most of these people have few options when it comes to furnishing their apartments and homes. She feels that S&S, by offering them credit in-house, can capture most of this untapped market. She has one concern, though: that this group is a high-risk group, and if credit is granted to too many poor credit risks, it could end up costing S&S a great deal of money. She asks Ashton if there is some way that S&S can use computers to screen applicants right in the store as they apply for credit. Ashton responds that yes, there is a way to determine whether customers are a good credit risk. The answer lies in using artificial intelligence or an expert system.

A comparatively recent innovation in computer software is artificial intelligence. **Artificial intelligence (AI)** (also referred to as knowledge-based systems and intelligent systems) is software that tries to emulate aspects of human behavior, such as reasoning, communicating, seeing, and hearing. AI software can use its accumulated knowledge to reason and, in some instances, learn from experience and thereby modify its subsequent reasoning. There are several types of AI, including natural language, visual recognition, robotics, voice recognition, neural networks, and expert systems. Except for expert systems, AI has yet to have a significant impact on accounting information systems.

An **expert system** is a computerized information system that allows nonexperts to make decisions that are comparable to those of an expert in the problem area. In the design of an expert system a process known as **knowledge engineering** is used to develop a knowledge base. This knowledge base represents the data, knowledge, rules of thumb, and decision rules that experts use to make decisions. Alternatively, the knowledge base can contain the facts and results of many similar cases. The software allows the nonexpert user to interact with the knowledge base and make the same decision that an expert would make. Expert systems usually apply to a narrow, specific subject area and are typically most beneficial for complex or ill-structured tasks that require experience and specialized knowledge.

Ashton found numerous instances of companies using expert systems and other means of artificial intelligence. For example:

- The IRS uses an expert system to analyze and classify tax returns and to determine which returns should be passed on to tax fraud investigators.
- Kerr Steamship cut its staff by one-third when it introduced an expert system to discover the cheapest means of transporting inland cargo.
- Mrs. Fields Cookies uses an expert system to gather weekly data from all of its stores. It also uses an expert system to keep track of rental expenses at its more than eight hundred stores.
- Xerox uses an expert system for financial planning. Planning is done for the next three years, and the system continually analyzes actual results against the forecast and updates it as needed.
- Some accountants are using expert systems to support their work as expert witnesses—for example, to project revenues at companies that are shut down by natural or man-made disasters.
- Spiegel uses an expert system to determine which people on a mailing list are most likely to buy its mail-order products.
- Safeguards and Security Enhancements is an expert system that uses data gathered by a building's security system to detect incidents of physical security violations.

Expert systems typically contain the following four components:

1. **Knowledge base**: The data, knowledge, rules of thumb, and decision rules used by experts to solve a particular type of problem
2. **Knowledge base management system**: The software that manages the knowledge base
3. **Inference engine**: The program containing the logic and reasoning mechanisms that simulate the logic process of the expert; uses data obtained from the knowledge data base and from the user to draw conclusions
4. **User interface**: The program that allows the user to communicate with the expert system

Expert systems provide several gradations of expertise. Some function as assistants or aides. They perform routine analysis and call the user's attention to the tasks that require human expertise. Other expert systems function as colleagues or peers. The user "discusses" a problem with such a system until they both agree on a solution. When a user can accept the system's solution without question, the expert system can be referred to as a true expert. Developers of expert systems are still striving to create a true expert; most current systems function at the assistant or colleague level.

Expert systems can be classified according to the type of inference engine used. In an example-based system the developer enters the facts and results of a large number of cases. Through induction the expert system converts the examples to a decision tree. The system then uses the decision tree to match the case at hand with those previously entered in the knowledge base. Rule-based systems are created by obtaining the data and decision rules used by experts and putting them in the form of complex conditional logic expressed in terms of if–then rules. The system operates by asking the user a series of questions and applying the if–then rules to the answers in order to draw conclusions and make recommendations. Rule-based systems are appropriate when a history of cases is unavailable or when a body of knowledge can be structured in a set of if–then rules. In a frame-based system all the information (data, descriptions, rules, etc.) about a topic is organized into logical units called frames, which are similar to records in data files. The frames are linked together by using software "pointers." Rules are then established about how the frames are assembled or interrelated to meet the user's needs.

Ashton found that expert systems offer the following benefits to nonexpert users:

- They can provide a cost-effective alternative to human experts.

- In some cases they can outperform a single expert because they have the expertise of many experts and also because they are faster, more consistent, and do not get distracted, overworked, or stressed out.

- They enable users to produce better-quality and more consistent decisions. Users can identify potential problems with their decisions and increase the probability of making correct decisions.

- They can greatly increase the speed with which an "expert" decision is made.

- They can increase productivity. For example, Westinghouse claims to have increased the volume of its business by more than $10 million per year using an expert system. Likewise, Texas Instruments has achieved a 10% increase in semiconductor production using an expert system.

- They are a good way to preserve the expertise of an expert leaving the organization.

Although expert systems have many advantages and great promise, they also have a number of significant problems that currently limit their use:

- They can be costly and time-consuming to develop. Some large experimental systems have required up to 15 years to develop and have cost millions of dollars.

- It can be difficult and costly to obtain the knowledge needed for the system from expert users. Experts often have difficulty specifying exactly how they make decisions.

- Unfortunately, designers have not been able to program common sense into current systems. As a result, rule-bound systems tend to break down when presented with a situation they are not programmed to handle.

- Until recently, developers have encountered a somewhat skeptical market. This skepticism was due partly to the poor quality of the first expert systems produced and partly to users' expecting the system to do too much.

As technology advances, some of these problems will be overcome, and expert systems will play an increasingly important role in accounting information systems. Some of the most popular expert systems currently used by accountants are Expert Ease, TI Personal Consultant, Rule Master, VP Expert, auditMASTERPLAN, AUDITPLANNER, AY/ASQ, Loan Probe, and ExperTAX.

CASE CONCLUSION: IMPLEMENTING A MICROCOMPUTER-BASED SYSTEM AT S&S, INC.

Scott and Ashton met several times to hammer out policies and plans for their new system. They reached three conclusions:

1. Their success depended, in part, on their ability to use technological advancements to increase efficiency and productivity, to improve customer service, and to achieve the growth they desired.

2. The benefits to S&S of end-user computing significantly outweighed the risks. Therefore they wanted all of their employees to be at least semiskilled and to be significantly involved in end-user development.

3. They should restrict hardware and software purchases to the standards they set to ensure compatibility and connectivity.

With some help from Kimberly Serra, the manager of Computer Applications (CA), S&S acquired several microcomputers and some software. Ashton and Scott narrowed the accounting software down to three packages, all of which were equally acceptable. They decided to buy Great Plains software, principally because it could be run on a network and because CA was very familiar with it and could easily give them the support they needed. Kimberly trained Ashton and a few members of the office staff and helped them install the software and convert all the data over to the computer. Ashton knew the first month or two of using the software would be difficult as they completed their learning by actually using the software and creating all the reports they needed to operate the business. However, he knew that Kimberly and the customer support group at CA would help them through any difficulties they faced.

S&S also purchased several copies of the Quatro Pro spreadsheet and WordPerfect and one copy of Harvard Graphics. Ashton and his staff initially plan on using the spreadsheet to develop budgets and forecasts. They also want to develop a cash flow management template to help them avoid the cash crunch that so often accompanies rapid growth. The word processing package will handle all their correspondence, memos, financial statements, and price lists. The graphics package will be used to produce the charts and graphs they will need when they try to raise money for expansion. Susan wants to significantly expand their sales in the next few months by aggressively granting credit. To help them manage the credit-granting task, she wants to buy an expert system to predict creditworthiness.

S&S considered other software but decided against buying it until the company can absorb what it has already purchased. High on the list for the future is networking software and a data base package, but Scott and Ashton both feel they need to know more about the topics before they make a decision. They are also interested in a desktop organizer. They are intrigued by the capabilities offered by desktop publishing and image processing, but they do not feel that their business is large enough to invest in either at the present. They decided against audit and income tax software and will hire a local CPA to perform the services they need. They also decided against any specialized decision support or project management software, since they think their spreadsheet can adequately satisfy their current needs.

To improve the skill level of its employees, S&S decided to encourage those that need it to enroll at courses at the local community college or to attend several one- or two-day seminars. Either way, S&S agreed to pay the bill. It also decided to make microcomputer literacy a requirement for all employees regardless of their job. Ashton found out that one of his staff has an interest and significant experience in computers and will assign him, on a part-time basis, to provide support to the other employees.

Scott and Susan are pleased with the progress they have made with computerizing their business. However, both realize they have much to learn, and they want to investigate linking their computers together and linking their computer to those of their supplies. Scott has already begun to make a list of the questions he needs answered before they can decide whether networking and a data base are appropriate for S&S. (See Chapters 6 and 7.) ∎

SUMMARY

The use of microcomputers by accountants has skyrocketed in the past few years, and it will continue to increase in the future. One reason use has grown so significantly is the tremendous increase in end-user computing.

Microcomputers have come a long way since they were introduced to hobbyists in 1975. Their use has revolutionized the way we do business and the way accountants work. Auditors, tax specialists, consultants, and management accountants all use microcomputers extensively in their work.

The computer skill level of end users ranges from almost no understanding to very knowledgeable. The most knowledgeable are the ones involved in the development of end-user systems. The benefits of end-user computing include user creation and control of programs and ease of use. The risks of having end users create their own applications for microcomputers include logic errors, inefficient systems, and poor control over the programs developed. In order to maximize benefits and minimize risks, organizations should establish an information center to facilitate, coordinate, and control end-user computing.

Many microcomputer and end-user tools are discussed in the chapter. They include accounting and tax packages, audit software, spreadsheets, data bases, word processors, desktop publishing, business graphics, image processing, desktop organizers, project management, decision support systems, expert systems, and artificial intelligence.

KEY TERMS

Define the following.

end-user computing (EUC)
personal information system
group information system
enterprise information system
nonskilled end users
semiskilled end users
skilled end users
end-user development
monopolist approach
laissez-faire approach
controlled-growth approach
information center (IC)
generalized audit software
    package (GASP)

electronic spreadsheet
template
macro
integrated software
add-ins
data bases
data base management system
    (DBMS)
word processing
office automation (OA)
desktop publishing (DTP)
image processing
desktop organizer
project management software

decision support system (DSS)
group decision support software (GDSS)
decision room
groupware
artificial intelligence (AI)
expert system
knowledge engineering
knowledge base
knowledge base management system
inference engine
user interface

DISCUSSION QUESTIONS

5.1 Employers of newly graduated accountants want their new employees to have a working knowledge of business-related computer applications. However, many of the employers do not feel that a knowledge of computer programming is as impor-

tant. Explain what you feel the reasons are for the differences in emphasis.

5.2 More and more companies are automating their offices. Experts predict that in the near future business offices will be totally automated and integrated. What advantages do you see in this automation? What disadvantages do you see coming from office automation?

5.3 Microcomputers have emerged as an efficient source of data processing. However, the uncontrolled proliferation of microcomputers throughout an organization may create problems, such as increased maintenance costs and nonstandard documentation. Briefly state three additional problems that may arise if microcomputers are allowed to proliferate throughout an organization. In addition, briefly describe three steps that an organization can take to control the proliferation of microcomputers and their effects. (CIA Examination, adapted)

5.4 To operate an automobile, you only need to know how to drive. How much do you think microcomputer users need to know about computers? For example, do they need to know how to operate them, how to repair them, and how all their components work? Do you think these needs will change in the future?

5.5 If you were the owner of a business that was considering buying a microcomputer, what resources might you draw upon to determine whether to acquire a microcomputer? To determine what your micro-based system should accomplish? To determine which model would best meet your needs?

5.6 A wide variety of companies are now using microcomputers. Identify several specific ways the following types of firms could use microcomputers.

a. The banking industry
b. Manufacturing companies
c. Retail firms
d. Governmental units
e. Universities and colleges
f. Service firms (CPAs, attorneys, etc.)

5.7 Skilled end users present companies with both a tremendous opportunity and a significant risk. Explain the opportunities and the risks, and discuss how they should be managed.

5.8 One way to maximize the benefits and minimize the risks of end-user development is to establish development standards. What specific issues should end-user development standards cover?

5.9 Assume that you have been asked to debate the question, "Are paperless offices possible?" Prepare material to support both the affirmative and the negative sides to the question. Come to class prepared to defend both positions.

5.10 Motivated by a four-year backlog of mainframe application requests, Harley-Davidson, Inc., "migrated" from mainframes to Applications System/400s minicomputers and personal computers. According to the Milwaukee-based manufacturer, the new computers are saving as much as 35% in processing costs over the old mainframe system. The smaller systems are easier to develop and 8–10 times cheaper than mainframe systems. Setting up the smaller systems also trains employees in understanding the nature of the automated processes they work with and encourages user innovation.[2]

Why are companies moving from mainframe computing to microcomputer networking? What advantages and disadvantages does end-user computing provide over traditional mainframe applications?

5.11 In March 1991 Bridgestone Tire piloted a project called Bridgestone Information Network (Bisnet) with 14 of its poorest-performing sales representatives. With the aid of laptop computers programs were developed that took advantage of demographic data to improve customer service. Salespeople in the field used the laptops to access the company mainframe computer and provide dealers with information to tailor product lines and promotions to regional buying patterns.

The success was encouraging. "We saw a fairly substantial increase in sales," insists John Moore, Manager of Sales/Marketing Systems at Bridgestone Tire. The objective of the project was to empower the field sales force with information to meet the changing needs of customers and to provide direct sales support without delays in information. Because of the success of the project, Bridgestone now has all of its salespeople "on-line".[3]

Why are laptop computers so popular? How are laptops changing computer applications in business?

5.12 No one understood paperwork like Pizza Hut, Inc. In a given month Pizza Hut handled about 175,000 invoices, with only 75,000 hooked up to an electronic data interchange (EDI) system. The remaining invoices were opened manually, coded, and then keyed into the accounting system. However, the problem was recently solved when Pizza Hut installed an electronic document imaging system to handle the flow of paperwork.

---

[2] *Source:* Clinton Wilder, "Users: Downsizing Gain Is Worth the Pain," *Computerworld* (October 14, 1991): 4.

[3] *Source:* Michael Fitzgerald, "Laptops Make Sales Force Shine," *Computerworld* (August 12, 1991): 35.

Under the new approach incoming invoices arrive as faxes that go directly into the image system using a personal computer. The information is coded electronically and then referenced with the master supplier data base where the invoice is recorded. Using the imaging strategy, Pizza Hut is able to capture another 50,000 invoices without paper at a 25% improvement in productivity. Payback on the $1.6 million investment is expected in under three years.[4]

How do electronic imaging systems work? What benefits do electronic imaging systems provide to businesses? What other possible uses are there for electronic imaging systems?

5.13 Sears, Roebuck and Company recently announced plans to install new point-of-sale (POS) terminals in 868 of its retail stores. The new terminals aren't typical cash registers but, rather, personal computers driven by a 16-megahertz I386SX microprocessor and linked to the Sears information network.

The new technology is predicted to cut expenses by as much as $50 million a year through improved efficiency. Using PC computers will enable salespeople to issue Sears charge cards and gift certificates, access customer information, and ring up orders from one terminal. Training time will be reduced from 3 to 4 hours on old terminals to about 45 minutes on the new PCs.[5]

How will personal computers change the computing environment at Sears? What advantages will the personal computer network provide?

5.14 J.C. Penney Company, a popular retail chain, is considering the implementation of an expert system in its catalog telemarketing sector. The company employs roughly four thousand operators in 14 separate centers throughout the United States. When peak calling hours hit, Penney struggles to keep its 800 number open for customers. Using an expert system, Penney hopes to reroute incoming customer phone calls from busy operators to operators that are free.[6]

What is an expert system? How do expert systems help businesses like J.C. Penney increase productivity?

PROBLEMS

5.1 Larsen & Larsen is a local CPA firm with about five hundred small clients. The firm's winter work consists of doing individual, partnership, estate, trust, and small-corporation tax returns. During the summers and the rest of the year the firm does tax planning, prepares quarterly financial statements and tax returns for clients, and does write-up and consulting work. The firm consists of two partners and two staff accountants as well as two secretaries.

Required

Propose a computer system that would serve Larsen & Larsen's needs. Include in your proposal the following features:

a. How a microcomputer system could benefit Larsen & Larsen

b. Some of the drawbacks of a microcomputer system

c. The software that Larsen & Larsen would most likely need

d. The hardware needed to make the system effective

5.2 The U-Fix-It auto parts company sells foreign and domestic auto parts in Pasadena, California. Sam Turner started the company six years ago, with his son Bob working as a salesclerk. The company has since blossomed into one of the larger auto parts stores in Pasadena. Sam is now semiretired, Bob has

---

[4] *Source:* Ellis Booker, "Pizza Hut: Making It Great with Imaging, EDI," *Computerworld* (January 27, 1992): 67, 72.

[5] *Source:* Ellis Booker, "Sears Selects Compuadd for $53M POS Project," *Computerworld* (January 13, 1992):7.

[6] *Source:* Patricia Keefe, "Penney Cashes in on Leading Edge," *Computerworld* (June 20, 1988): 1, 62–64.

been promoted to General Manager, and the company employs a total of 50 people.

Company sales exceeded $1.5 million last year. Of the sales, 30% are at wholesale prices to local garages and mechanics who have the option of purchasing on credit. When a credit sale takes place, a three-part invoice is prepared. One copy is sent to the customer. A second is used to update the company's inventory records. The third copy is used to help the company keep track of the accounts receivable records of its 500 credit customers. The remaining sales (70%) are made at retail to customers who pay either with cash or with bank cards.

Because Sam dislikes computers, no computer system has been used in the company. Bob does not share his father's views about computers; in fact, he feels computers are necessary if U-Fix-It is to remain competitive. Bob is looking for a computer system that will meet the company's present as well as future needs.

Bob would like the system to keep track of the company's inventory of 2000 parts. He would like to store information such as part description, quantity on hand, economic order point, retail price, supplier information, and part cost. U-Fix-It purchases its inventory on credit from about a dozen suppliers.

When a customer comes in or calls the company to purchase a part, the salesclerk should be able to access the inventory status and sales information on the part. If the customer is buying on credit, the system should produce a sales invoice.

Bob also wants to be able to use the computer to spot sales trends and to make sales and cash flow projections. He would like to have reports dealing with sales, accounts receivable, and accounts payable. He feels that he could make better decisions if data could be represented graphically. Finally, Bob wants the system to process the company's correspondence.

Required

a. How would a microcomputer system benefit U-Fix-It? What disadvantages might a microcomputer have for U-Fix-It?

b. List the application software that will be required to meet U-Fix-It's needs. Also, describe the systems software that will be needed.

c. List the microcomputer hardware that will be needed for the system Bob has in mind.

5.3 Master's Clothier operates a chain of men's clothing stores in the Seattle, Washington, area. The store offers its own credit card to preferred customers. The store's accounts receivable department is located at corporate headquarters in downtown Seattle. The accounts receivable function is handled manually by a supervisor and five employees. Three of the employees are full-time (40 hours a week), and the other two employees are part-time (20 hours a week). The supervisor is paid $30,000 a year, full-time employees are paid $7.50 per hour, and part-time employees are paid $6.00 per hour.

The company has been studying the feasibility of computerizing the accounts receivable department. The computer system being considered consists of two 486 microcomputers, each with a 120-MB hard disk and two floppies, two printers, and all the software needed by the company. This system would provide 30% excess capacity on each machine.

The system would reduce the number of employees needed in the department. With the computerized system there would be a supervisor, two full-time employees, and two part-time employees working 15 hours a week. Owing to the increased skills needed, salaries for the hourly employees would increase to $10 an hour for full-time employees and $7.50 an hour for part-time employees. The supervisor is a salaried employee, and her salary would not be affected.

The cost for the hardware, which has an estimated useful life of four years, and for the software follows.

Computer	$5200	each
Printer	1700	each
Software	1500	each
	$8400	each

Yearly expenses would also be incurred for the computerized system. Yearly expenses would include maintenance contracts costing $300 for each computer. Software updates would cost $300 per year per machine. Office supplies under the old system run $1500 per year. With the new system office supplies are estimated to be $1100 per year. Money is worth 10% a year to Master's Clothier.

Required

a. Compare the net present value of the yearly savings generated by the proposed computer system with the purchase price of the proposed system. Ignore the tax benefits of the purchase in making your calculations. Show your computations.

b. What factors besides the costs shown would influence the computer acquisition decision?

c. Would you recommend the purchase of the

computer system to Master's Clothier? Would your answer change if the system had a three-year useful life?

5.4   Tom Rasmussen is a manager with a medium-sized CPA firm. His most important client is High-fees, Unlimited. Before beginning his audit of High-fees, Tom went to lunch with Charlie Curtis, Highfees's Controller. During lunch the following conversation took place.

CC: Tom, I've been talking to some of my customers and they say Ajax Manufacturing, my biggest competitor, is buying a microcomputer-based system and will be able to give them better service than I can. I'm worried. Do you think I need a computer system also?

TR: Oh, sure you do. You have to keep up with the competition. Why, their having a computer system could put you at a serious disadvantage.

CC: Yeah, I agree I need one, but I'm just not sure which microcomputer system I need. What do you think? Which system do you think I should buy?

TR: I think you are best protected by going with the largest, most secure supplier. I think I'd go with IBM if I were you. You can't go wrong by buying from IBM. They aren't really very expensive—I've seen them advertised in the *Wall Street Journal* for $1695.

CC: One of the things I want to do with the micro-computer I buy is spreadsheet analysis with a program like 1-2-3. That IBM personal computer you mentioned comes with 512K. Do you think that will be enough, or should I get more memory?

TR: I think 512 million bytes should be plenty. Most micros have 512K, and they run spreadsheet packages just fine.

CC: I was thinking about using prepackaged software, but I've heard that you have a hard time finding a package that fits your needs just right. The vendor I talked to said I could learn to program in just a few weeks. He said that after just a few weeks of experience, I would be able to write whatever software was needed to exactly meet my needs. What do you think I should do?

TR: I certainly wouldn't use prepackaged software. It takes a lot of time to find the package that comes closest to your needs. By that time you could have learned to program. In the same amount of time you could have picked up a new skill, and with a little more time you could have exactly what you want, rather than some approximation of your needs.

CC: You know, another thing I need is a printer. For what I want to do, I'll have to print a lot of reports. I'm not sure whether I should get a dot matrix printer or a laser printer.

TR: Is a dot matrix printer the one that prints those characters that look like a bunch of dots?

CC: Yes.

TR: Gee, I think those characters look terrible. The character quality is really poor. I'd go with a laser printer.

CC: How about secondary storage? Should I get as large a hard disk as possible to go along with two floppy disk drives?

TR: Hard drives are expensive. I'd save money by getting a smaller-capacity hard disk. Floppies are only a few cents each, and they hold a lot of data. You can use as many as you want for very little cost.

CC: Well, you've been very helpful. I think I'll buy the IBM system you recommended and install it. I should have everything up and running by the time you want to start the audit next month.

TR: You should be okay now. Selecting the micro-computer and writing the software is the hard part. From there it is all downhill.

Required

a.   Identify and explain the inaccuracies in Tom's comments.

b.   What can you learn from this conversation?

5.5   Rent-A-Fridge (RAF) is a two-year-old company located in Boulder, Colorado. It is owned by two enterprising accounting students who realized that there was a need for a company that rented refrigerators to students during the school year. Although the owners started by renting refrigerators, they have now expanded to renting stereos, televisions, telephones, VCRs, and microwaves. The company employs three full-time people and a dozen part-time people who work mostly at the beginning and end of the school year. The owners plan to expand their business to other college towns when they graduate.

As accounting students, the owners understand the importance of an efficient and effective information system. To produce the information they need, they have decided to buy a microcomputer. They feel the computer will allow them to process their transactions promptly, keep their files up to date, produce correspondence, assist in planning, and allow them to easily and quickly retrieve the large quantities of information they need.

Required

a. Draw and label a diagram of the hardware configuration that you feel would be most suitable for RAF.

b. List several applications that you feel would be most suitable for RAF's microcomputer system.

c. Briefly describe the system software that would likely be suitable for use by RAF's microcomputer system.

d. Suppose that RAF grows to four stores and 60 employees. Will a single microcomputer system be sufficient for its needs? If not, what alternative systems might RAF consider?

5.6 The scene is all too typical. You've put off preparation of the earnings analysis report until the last minute. As you search for an available machine to write up the report, you find that employees are using all the Macintosh machines and you have to use an unfamiliar IBM-compatible PC. As you turn on the machine, you're greeted by a strange C> prompt. After several failed attempts to call up the word processing program, you pull out a dusty typewriter and begin your work, wondering all along why software is so hard.

Software designers argue that's all changing. Current trends in software design and performance reveal that customers are seeking less customer assistance. Graphical user interface (GUI) technology is also making software use easier. Research indicates that users with GUI technology pick up computing concepts faster and are more inclined to improve existing software skills.

Peripheral technology is also simplifying software applications by removing the keyboard and replacing it with an electronic pen that writes directly on the screen. In the more distant future designers insist users will handle computer operations with vocal commands. Currently, emergency room doctors use voice technology to dictate information into an expert system that helps doctors make an immediate diagnosis. Such applications don't replace the doctor's judgment but do provide the physician with an additional opinion.

In spite of trends to simplify the use of software, critics argue that designers have a long way to go. Software is frustrating because different applications use entirely separate commands. With each application the user must remember the proper routines while avoiding the dangers of pressing the wrong button. For example, one program may use the F7 key to print a document, and another program may use the same key to erase the screen.

Easy-to-use software packages sometimes leave the user frustrated by the limited applications available. After taking several hours to learn the program, the user discovers that the program does not have sufficient power to handle the needed applications. The sales price of easier programs also is much lower, discouraging manufacturers from developing "simplified" technology.

Computer designers are also to blame for user frustrations. Designers continue to reinforce illogical system designs in upgraded technology to avoid confusing current users. Designers also fail to consider the users' lack of technical education. Designers have no design step that requires them to "put an idiot in front of the screen" and evaluate his or her response. Perhaps that's just what the designers need to do.[7]

Required

a. Why is software technology so hard to use?

b. What changes in the software industry are necessary before software technology can address user frustrations?

c. Describe the recent changes in technology that are making software applications easier to use.

5.7 As computing technology grows more affordable, computer companies are scrambling to provide for a profitable but neglected segment—the small business. According to a survey by the National Federation of Independent Business, computer use among small firms has increased 55% in the past five years. Currently, about two-thirds of all small businesses own computer technology. But are computers helping? The final tally is still out, and users are sending in mixed reviews for a number of reasons.

Small companies lack the expertise to operate a computer and the payroll to finance the help. Companies struggle finding a system that meets their needs, training employees, and, perhaps the greatest problem of all, getting competent, affordable help. OCI Inc., a gas distribution company in Connellsville, Pennsylvania, spent $55,000 on computer consultations and software. In the end the advice was ineffective and the software was full of serious

---

[7] *Source:* William F. Bulkeley, "Technology, Economics, and Ego Conspire to Make Software Difficult to Use," *Wall Street Journal* (May 20, 1991): R7–R8.

flaws. According to Bill Biggs, the disgruntled company President, "You almost have to become an expert yourself; it's a frustrating experience."

Training employees is another challenge. On limited budgets computer training is too expensive for most businesses. The result is lower productivity and increased errors. "People just plop a computer in an office and assume you know what's going on, and we didn't, other then to turn it on," says Jane Tribby, an Office Manager for a Northern Virginia chiropractor. "I feel comfortable with the system now, but it's been a year." Employees must also stay abreast of changes in the computer industry with industry magazines and newsletters.

If small firms are to survive the information age, business owners can't afford to remain discouraged. Managers must work to integrate computer applications into all areas of their business to compete with the bigger players.[8]

Required

a. Why is computer use growing among small businesses?

b. What challenges are small-business owners facing as they employ computer technology in the workplace?

c. Assume that you are the owner of a small business and you are seeking to purchase a small computer system for your office. Discuss:

1. What role should you take as the owner in purchasing the system?

2. How can you help your employees adapt to the computer system?

3. Will you seek outside assistance to help with the purchase? Why?

5.8   End-user computing isn't a new idea at Alaska Air Group, Inc., the Seattle-based holding company of Alaska Airlines. In fact, Alaska Air transformed its information system almost 10 years ago to meet the needs of end users and to save money.

Under the Alaska Air network most levels of employees and management are linked to the corporate mainframe and to each other through Apple and IBM PCs located throughout the business. By focusing on the skills of end users, the company took the IS group out of the operations cycle, reducing the IS backlog.

The reasons information is so accessible are simple. Alaska Air hires only competent, skilled computer users as employees. With that competence the IS staff has been trimmed dramatically at a significant cost savings to the company. Available information also helps employees participate directly in improving efficiency and frees IS personnel to focus on applications development and other strategic projects.

The approach has worked well at Alaska Air, where IS costs have been held to under $10 million, thanks largely to the end-user focus. At the same time, passenger-revenue-miles—the barometer of airline passenger business—has increased by more than 50%. "IS isn't growing as fast as the airline, yet we're still putting in more applications. The moves we've made so far have brought phenomenal productivity," says Leif Haslund, Assistant Vice-President of Administrative Services at Alaska Air. "We'll stay on this course."[9]

Required

a.   What benefits does end-user computing provide businesses such as Alaska Air? What threats does end-user computing pose?

b.   As the CEO of a major corporation, would you consider end-user computing as a means of controlling IS costs? Why or why not?

5.9   No invention in the past decade has had a more profound effect upon business than the personal computer. The growth of personal or end-user computing is reshaping the structure of organizations, the nature of business transactions, and the scope of information available to the decision maker. Surprisingly enough, as Focus 5.1 reveals, the best is yet to come.

Required

a.   What predictions are futurists making for the next 10 years in the computer industry? Do you agree? Why or why not?

b.   How will computers force a complete reorganization of work over the next 10 years?

c.   What hardware devices will the future bring to business?

d.   What personal predictions do you have for the coming decade in the microcomputer industry?

---

[8] *Source:* Jeanne Sadler, "Small Businesses Tap into the Power of Computers," *Wall Street Journal* (July 1991): B1.

[9] *Source:* Julia King, "Buck Bangers: Users Help Alaska Air Soar," *Computerland* (December 23, 1991/January 2, 1992): 16.

5.10 With the rise of personal computers and laptops in the workplace, many companies are considering the move to an automated internal audit. The Singer Company, a defense contractor, has pioneered electronic auditing by integrating data processing into virtually all phases of the audit. The result: a paperless internal audit.

Initially, Singer employed the microcomputer for administrative purposes, such as preparing audit risk analysis and time budgets. With encouragement from the internal audit staff the company made the big move to the paperless audit.

Initial problems with automation came from backlogs in the EDP Department. Auditors were forced to draw information from mainframe systems that were controlled and administered by the EDP staff. Internal audit needs were always given low priority and were never completed as needed. The situation forced auditors to work during times when technical support was not available. In addition, an EDP support person was needed at all times to handle technical problems. Clearly, the audit staff needed its own computer system.

The Internal Audit Department purchased its own integrated minicomputer, which doubled as a file server for a small network. The manufacturer provided training support for the auditors, and the system was operational in three weeks. Problems with implementation included auditors at different levels of end-user training, incompatibilities with the existing mainframe system, and user resistance.

As a result of the automation, Singer employs only 18 government contract auditors (down from 36) to handle all of Singer's U.S. audits. Access to the information on the network allows auditors at a number of isolated sites to communicate information and ideas, reducing staff travel time. The networking system allows the immediate transfer of files between audit managers and the field, allowing timely feedback on work paper reviews and job variances.[10]

Required

a. What are the benefits of the new paperless audit at Singer Company?

b. Discuss the initial challenges Singer Company had with the mainframe system and the EDP Department. Why are these problems common when using centralized data processing systems?

c. When Singer introduced the new end-user technology, several problems developed. List each problem and discuss potential solutions. Should such problems prevent the implementation of the new network system?

d. Is the systems evolution at Singer Company common in business today? Explain.

CASE 5.1: ANYCOMPANY, INC.—AN ONGOING COMPREHENSIVE CASE

One of the best ways to learn is to immediately apply what you have studied. The purpose of this case is to allow you to do that. You will select a local company that you can work with. At the end of most chapters you will find an assignment that will have you apply what you have learned using the company you have selected as a reference. This case, then, may become an ongoing case study that you work on throughout the term.

Visit the local business you selected. Study how the company uses microcomputers, and determine the extent to which it makes use of end-user computing. Prepare for your visit by making a list of questions to ask and a list of items to check on while you are there. Prepare a report that explains the following:

1. The extent to which microcomputers are used in the company and your perception of how skilled the users are

2. The benefits they have achieved and the risks they face from end-user computing: Also explain

---

[10] *Source:* Jonathan B. Schiff, "Towards the Paperless Audit," *Internal Auditor* (June 1989): 30–35.

how they are managing end-user computing to maximize the benefits and minimize the risks they face

3. The company's software tools and how they are utilized

4. Your recommendations about to how they

could make better use of the software discussed in the chapter, including new uses of software they already have and how they might use software that they are not now using

---

CASE 5.2: SELECTING A SMALL, BUSINESS-ORIENTED COMPUTER

Cathy Daniels had just returned home to Minneapolis from the annual Retail Hardware Business National Convention. Cathy felt that the most impressive session of the conference was Thursday's computer display on the latest computer technology for small businesses. The conference was clearly worth the cost just to see the opportunities available for today's small-business owners.

Cathy spent the remainder of her ride home thinking about how she could use a computer in her store. Cathy's first thought was an inventory application. Cathy carried 4200 inventory items from over 50 separate vendors. The information she needed to store for each inventory item consisted of 480 characters of data, each identified by a 12-digit product code. Inventory had been troubling Cathy for some time; she knew that if she didn't get control of the crisis, she might eventually go bankrupt because of her high carrying costs and the large quantities of slow-moving products. A computer would solve all these problems.

Cathy also recognized the need for some general application software that her employees could use, particularly spreadsheet and word processing programs. Cathy didn't have the cash for a large system, but she felt that a budget of $10,000 was a good round number to work from. On her first morning back at work, Cathy called in Andrew Knight, her accountant. Andrew was just out of college and had a special knack for electronics. Cathy felt confident that Andrew could handle the selection and operation of the new system with a little direction.

Buying the Hardware

Andrew was elated with the opportunity to select a new system for the office and he began with a call to his good friend, Anne Larsen, who had just opened

a new computer store in town. Over lunch, Andrew discussed the needs of the hardware store with Anne. Anne impressed Andrew not only with her knowledge of computer systems but also with her recent successes and experience in the field. Anne had spent two years on the audit staff of a national Big 6 CPA firm and had become intrigued with computers. When a local computer store was put on the market, Anne borrowed $40,000 and opened the store. Recently, Anne attended a four-week school where she learned all about the three lines of computers that she carries in the store.

A few days after their luncheon Andrew stopped by Anne's store to ask a few questions. Anne was very competent and understood his needs. In fact, Anne knew exactly what computer hardware the store would need. After some discussion Anne invited Andrew into her office to discuss specific financial terms. They were able to work out a deal that was mutually advantageous. For a reduction in the hardware price Andrew would allow Anne to use the computer system as a showcase of her ability to help clients computerize their business. Andrew also got a break on the price of the system, which was on sale. Anne assured Andrew of the 80386 SX model's success over the past four years. Though a new model would soon replace the existing 80386 SX model he was buying, many of the people using the new models were having problems with them, and she felt that the manufacturers needed at least six months to work out all the bugs in the hardware. Andrew was aware that a common mistake among first-time buyers was to purchase equipment that the business would outgrow in a few years. According to Anne, the 80386 SX computer could be expanded by as much as 20% to meet future growth needs.

Installing the Hardware

The next morning at work, Andrew received the following fax copy of the computer system Anne felt would work well for the hardware store:

(3) Model 386SX computers	$6000
(3) Color monitors and VGA graphics adapters	1500
(2) 24 pin dot matrix printers	1000
Showcase discount	(500)
Total price	$8000

Anne also promised Andrew immediate delivery of the computers because she had several in stock. Although the total package cost might exceed the budgeted amount for hardware, Cathy was pleased with Andrew's success in finding a system and encouraged Andrew to accept the proposal promptly.

Anne delivered the computer the following week and helped Andrew install the three machines. Installing the computers was fairly simple, although the installation cost was an additional $500 for extra cables and the operating system software. In the course of two hours the system was ready to go. Cathy and Andrew were pleased with the machines and invited a number of friends in to show them their new microcomputer system. Andrew explained that each computer had 1 MB of internal RAM memory and two 5¼-inch drives and a hard drive with 20 MB of storage space. The dot matrix printers were also impressive as state-of-the-art printing technology. Besides, getting the dot matrix printers saved them almost $1500 over the cost of laser printer technology.

Buying the Software

With the hardware in place Andrew returned to the computer store several days later to discuss software needs. Anne had spent some time considering the software needs that Andrew discussed and referred him to a friend who offered a broad range of accounting software. Andrew visited the store, Sophisticated Organizational Software (SOS), that afternoon and discussed his needs with the Store Manager. The Manager indicated that in the next week SOS would release its most powerful integrated accounting package ever, Accounting Plus 1.0. Besides handling routine inventory transactions, the program could also handle receivables and payables functions, as well as fixed asset utilization and depreciation. The program also came with financial modeling capabilities and optimization software for decision making. The program even handled routine word processing. The software was perfect for the hardware store's needs because it was designed to operate on solitary PCs. The Manager admitted that the program was a little more expensive, but for all the extras, the program was well worth it.

Andrew spent the remainder of the day testing the demonstration model of the Accounting Plus package. The inventory subprogram was quite versatile, allowing for a 10-digit product number, a 35-digit vendor or customer address, and plenty of additional fields for special codes and balances. The package would also handle up to 600 transactions a day. Besides, if the program didn't meet all of the hardware store's needs, SOS would easily modify the program. The Store Manager indicated that after some further testing Andrew could have the software package as early as next week. However, the documentation on the software would still take a few more weeks to complete. As soon as the program was available, SOS would install the program at no additional cost. The package also came with a free training seminar at the SOS headquarters in Milwaukee, Wisconsin. The seminar would last five days and discuss a host of applications for the new software. The hardware store could purchase additional training for a nominal fee. Feeling comfortable with his decision, Andrew paid the modest $3000 price for the software package and signed the vendor's purchase and maintenance contract.

The next day, Andrew reported his progress to Cathy. Including the software and the maintenance package, the total cost was only $11,000. In addition, they had the ability to expand in the future and to add other applications at a minimal cost. To top it all off, Andrew felt confident that he could handle the inventory-related items by himself, freeing others to take on additional tasks. Cathy and Andrew were pleased with their progress to date and were looking forward to next week when the software would be available for installation. Installation and start-up would take another day or two, and then the system would be fully operational. Andrew had done such a good job that Cathy decided to give him a raise out of all the money the company would now save by using a computer.

Identify and briefly discuss the weaknesses, errors, and misconceptions in the thinking of both Andrew and Cathy.

CHAPTER 6

Data Communications Systems

LEARNING OBJECTIVES

After studying this chapter, you should be able to:

■ Explain the fundamental concepts of data communications systems.

■ Identify the hardware and software typically found in data communications systems, and explain how they operate.

■ Compare and contrast alternative communications channels, communications channel configurations, and data communications carriers.

■ Compare and contrast centralized and distributed processing data communications networks.

■ Explain the features and uses of local area networks, wide area networks, value-added networks, and telephone networks.

■ Describe a number of common data communications applications, and explain how the data communications model elements are combined to meet the user's needs.

INTEGRATIVE CASE: S&S, INC.

The telephone call from Dominican Electric (DE), one of S&S's new suppliers, surprised Scott Parry. Ramon Lantigua, a corporate accountant with DE, explained that DE has for years been moving toward a paperless office. Many of its customers use electronic data interchange (EDI) to order goods electronically. DE then sends the customers an electronic invoice, and the customer transfers funds to DE electronically. Lantigua explained that EDI saved DE over a million dollars last year. As both an incentive and as a means of helping its customers foot the cost of going to EDI, DE was offering all non-EDI customers a 5% discount on all merchandise purchased for the first year each customer uses EDI.

A week ago, the cover article of a national news magazine had sparked Scott's interest in data communications. The article discussed telecommunications advancements and stated that it would soon be almost impossible for businesses to compete without networking capabilities. So when Lantigua called, Scott tried to learn as much as he could about DE's new system. Lantigua offered to arrange a visit to DE's headquarters in Atlanta and Scott accepted. Scott and Ashton were intrigued by what they found:

- DE has three main manufacturing sites and six central warehouses spread all over the United States, Canada, and Mexico. At each site all microcomputers are a part of a local area network (LAN) that allows users to share high-speed printers and disks and to access the site's main computer. The LAN at each location is part of a wide area network (WAN); that is, each LAN is connected to DE's central computer in Atlanta. Each user is able to communicate electronically with everyone else on either the LAN or the WAN. The LAN and WAN connections are made using a mixture of telephone lines, cables, satellites, and microwave transmissions.

- Most formal communication at each site and between sites is done by using electronic mail. A voice mail system is used to record and store voice messages. Periodic meetings are conducted with key personnel at different sites using teleconferencing. DE is also connected to several public data bases that allow them to search and retrieve critical accounting, marketing, and business data.

- Most major customers and suppliers are linked electronically to DE's computers. All inquiries from customers regarding the availability of goods are received and answered electronically. When purchase orders are received electronically, the system automatically sends a delivery order to the appropriate warehouse and schedules the delivery of goods. When the goods are shipped, a shipping order is sent electronically to the customer.

- The information from the purchase orders is used by DE to plan and schedule inventory. The system monitors on-hand supply and future demand and schedules production of each appliance for the coming week. The system also monitors the supply of parts and raw materials on hand and, based on scheduled production, orders the parts and raw materials needed for the next week. This instant communication allows DE to use just-in-time inventory.

- Most funds in and out of the company are handled with electronic funds transfer (EFT).

The visit to DE helped Scott realize several things. First, he wanted S&S to be on the cutting edge technologically, and so he needed to spend time learning about networks. Second, he wanted all the PCs at S&S to be able to talk to each other and to share data, hardware, and software. Furthermore, he and Susan were going to open several more stores in the next few months, and he wanted them to be able to talk to each other. Third, he wanted to see if he could lower his costs and improve both his customer service and his decision making by using EDI and other advanced telecommunications capabilities.

On the return flight Scott asked Ashton to find material to help him understand the fundamentals of data communications. Scott wanted to know what hardware and software was involved, how data is transferred between communication devices, the different types of networks in use, and how other organizations are using networks. Scott also asked Ashton to investigate the following questions.

1. How should S&S link its PCs so that they can talk to each other? What devices should they hook up to their network and share? How should they manage and control the sharing of the data?

2. How should S&S link its internal network to outside networks, such as DE's, so that it can use EDI and EFT? How will S&S communicate with the other networks? By telephone? By satellite?

3. What hardware and software should S&S acquire to develop a data communications system? Would S&S need another computer? Specialized communications equipment? Special communications software?

4. Should the system S&S develops when it expands be centralized or distributed? What does S&S need to consider now, in terms of telecommunications, in its expansion plans?

Ashton was overwhelmed with his new assignment. He was not sure he had the experience or the expertise necessary to lead S&S into the world of networking. His final thought as the airplane taxied up to the terminal was, "Why didn't I learn more about these essential data communications concepts when they were discussed in my accounting information systems class?" ■

INTRODUCTION

Businesses need to be able to make quick and efficient decisions based on timely and accurate information. As businesses become more complex and more geographically dispersed, the problems of data collection, processing, and communication increase, yet the need for information intensifies. For most organizations communication by letter or even by telephone no longer meets their needs. Instead, they use computers and communications technology to form **data communications networks**. These systems bridge geographical distances, giving authorized users immediate access to a company's computerized data. Business communications is currently one of the fastest-growing segments of the computer industry. This is illustrated by industry estimates that total costs for telecommunications products and services will grow from $505 million in 1990 to $1.8 billion in 1995.

Here are some examples of business communications uses.

- The president of a manufacturing company uses a microcomputer tied into an electronic data base called Dow-Jones News/Retrieval to monitor changes in the firm's stock price. Meanwhile, a vice-president is using a micro to compose the strategy memo she plans to relay to all manufacturing sites via the firm's electronic mail system.

- Late at night, when phone rates are lowest, microcomputers in the offices of mortgage brokers nationwide exchange data with a mainframe in Chicago. The microcomputers receive data on additions or changes to available loan products, whereas the mainframe receives data on new loan applications and changes in existing applications.

- An auditor working in a client's office wants to double-check a recent accounting pronouncement. Rather than go back to her office, she uses her microcomputer to query a data base maintained in New York. Within minutes the pronouncement and the firm interpretation are stored electronically in her microcomputer files.

- A large retail store transmits data on sales volume and products sold from every store to its headquarters on a daily basis. The main office, thousands of miles away from some of the stores, uses the data to determine what is selling and what isn't and to respond quickly to changed market conditions. Customers at these stores use credit cards issued from banks thousands of miles away to make purchases. Within seconds the retail store's computer can be connected electronically with the credit card insurer to perform a credit check.

These activities depend on the fast and reliable communication and the transmission of data between geographically separated points. **Data communications** is the transmission of data from a point of origin to a point of destination. Data communications systems, which typically transmit data over communications lines or by satellite, have evolved gradually. In the early days of computers, control, efficiency, personnel considerations, and economies of scale led many organizations to consolidate their systems into one large **centralized data processing system**. As organizations became larger and more diversified, centralization often proved inconvenient. Data had to be transported to the data center, entered into the system, and processed; and then the output had to be returned to the user.

When minicomputers were introduced, they were placed in remote locations within an organization and linked to a centralized computer to form a **distributed data processing (DDP) system**. DDP systems provide organizations with a great deal of flexibility. Each remote computer can meet the specific processing needs of the remote location and communicate summary results to the centralized (host) system; or it can be a self-contained system.

Microcomputers have further fueled the trend toward DDP systems. They have also resulted in the development of local area networks. A LAN allows individual users to use a micro to meet their own personal needs; to share common resources such as data, printers, and storage; and to communicate with everyone else in the LAN and in other networks that can be accessed by the LAN. Microcomputers have also fueled the trend toward wide area networks, value-added networks, and telephone networks. These networks are discussed later in the chapter.

Data communications technology is important in the development and operation of accounting information systems. Accountants must understand data communications fundamentals, such as the hardware and software used, how the different components of a data communications system interface, the types of data communications systems, and how data communications systems are used. This chapter provides a basic understanding of these topics, which are becoming increasingly important to accountants as they use, audit, and help select data communications systems.

DATA COMMUNICATIONS SYSTEM MODEL

Before specific data communications configurations, approaches, and uses can be discussed, certain communications concepts must be understood. Perhaps the most important of these concepts is the data communications model. As shown in Fig. 6.1, a data communications system consists of five major components: (1) the sending device, (2) the communications interface device, (3) the communications channel, (4) the receiving device, and (5) communications software. The figure also lists some common devices and communications channels.

A data communications system transmits data from one location (the source) to another (the receiver). For example, a remote microcomputer (or terminal) transmits data to a centralized computer for processing. The data to be transmitted, called the **message**, is entered into the sending device and stored. When the micro (or terminal) is ready to transmit the message, a communications interface device such as a modem converts the input message to signals that can be transmitted over a communications channel such as a telephone line. At its destination another communications interface device converts the message back to internal computer code and forwards it to the receiving computer. When the receiving unit sends a message back to the source to verify that the message has been received, the communications process is reversed. Communications software controls the system and manages all communication tasks.

Now that the elements of the data communications model have been identified, we can discuss each one. The next section discusses the hardware devices—that is, the computers that send and receive the

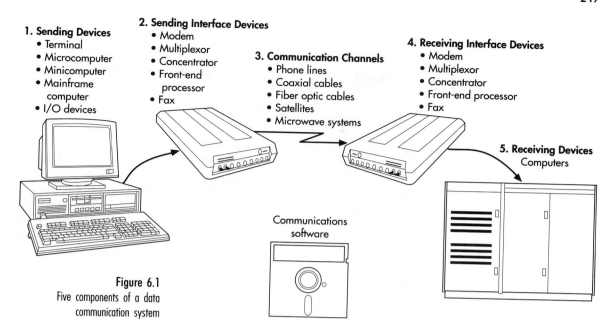

1. Sending Devices
- Terminal
- Microcomputer
- Minicomputer
- Mainframe computer
- I/O devices

2. Sending Interface Devices
- Modem
- Multiplexor
- Concentrator
- Front-end processor
- Fax

3. Communication Channels
- Phone lines
- Coaxial cables
- Fiber optic cables
- Satellites
- Microwave systems

4. Receiving Interface Devices
- Modem
- Multiplexor
- Concentrator
- Front-end processor
- Fax

5. Receiving Devices
Computers

Communications software

Figure 6.1
Five components of a data communication system

data and the communications interface devices. Then data communications software is considered. The topic is completed with a discussion of the communications channels used in data communications.

DATA COMMUNICATIONS HARDWARE

The data communications model has five elements, three of which are hardware devices. Of the three, only communications interface devices are discussed here. The hardware devices that can send or receive data, such as microcomputers, minicomputers, and mainframe computers, dumb and intelligent terminals, and source data automation devices are discussed in Chapters 4 and 5. Four different communications interface devices are discussed here: modems, multiplexors, concentrators, and front-end processors.

Communications Interface Devices

A **modem** (*modulator/demodulator*) converts (modulates) a computer's digital signals to analog (telephone line) signals and then demodulates the signals at the destination. Modems can be classified as internal (mounted on an expansion board within the micro) or external (a freestanding unit that fits under a telephone, as shown in Fig. 6.1, and is connected to the computer through a serial interface). External modems provide greater flexibility, since they can be used with more than one type of computer. Pocket modems that weigh a pound or less have become quite popular with travelers.

The **baud rate** is the speed at which a modem transmits and/or receives data. The higher the baud rate, the lower the transmission costs but the higher the modem cost. There are currently three common speeds to choose from: 1200, 2400, and 9600 baud. While 2400 is the current standard, the industry is fast moving to 9600 baud. A modem's character-per-second speed is roughly a tenth of its baud rate. Therefore, a 2400-baud modem can transmit about 240 characters per second.

Slow-speed devices, such as terminals, do not use the full capacity of high-speed transmission lines. In such cases a **multiplexor** can be used to combine signals from several slow-speed devices and transmit them over a high-speed communications channel. A multiplexor on the other end separates the signals back to the individual messages. This increases transmission speeds and reduces costs, because only one communications channel is needed for several terminals. The cost savings may be partially offset by the cost of the multiplexors and the more expensive communications channels needed for multiplexing. Some multiplexors have built-in modems and others do not. Figure 6.2 shows a data communications system without and with multiplexing.

When the volume of data transmission is high, a computer called a **front-end processor (FEP)** is used to relieve the CPU of time-consuming data communications coordination and control functions. An FEP performs communications tasks such as handling input and output messages and restricting access to authorized users. It can also edit data, detect and correct errors, poll terminals to determine if they are ready to send or receive data, store data until called for by the CPU, and preprocess data prior to transmitting it to the central computer. The main advantage of an FEP is that it frees the CPU for data processing tasks. Its main disadvantages are extra cost and the increased system complexity that results.

DATA COMMUNICATIONS SOFTWARE

Special **communications software** has been developed to manage data communications activities such as linking devices and transferring data between them. The communications software may be executed either by the main computer or by a front-end processor. The communications software performs the following main functions.

- *Access control:* These functions link the devices that send and receive data. They include automatic telephone dialing and answering; restricting access to users with appropriate account codes, passwords, or other security codes; linking the different devices; establishing communications parameters such as speed, mode, and direction of transmission; and disconnecting the devices.

- *Network management:* These function perform "traffic control." They include polling sending devices to see if they are ready to send/receive data, queueing input awaiting processing and output waiting to be sent, determining system priorities and executing them accordingly, routing messages to their proper destination, and logging network activity, use, and errors.

Without Multiplexing

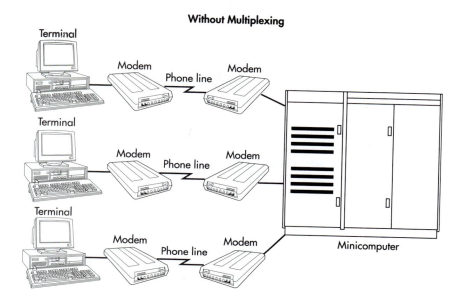

With Multiplexing

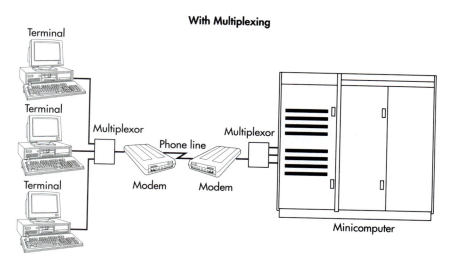

Figure 6.2
Data communication

- *Data and file transmission:* These functions control the transfer of data, files, and messages between the various devices.
- *Error detection and control:* These functions ensure that the data sent was the data received.
- *Data security:* These functions protect the data during transmission from unauthorized access.

Many different companies sell communications software. Some of the more popular communications software packages for micros are listed in Table 6.1.

DOS		WINDOWS		MAC	
Software	Vendor	Software	Vendor	Software	Vendor
ProComm	Datastorm Technologies	Smartcomm	Hayes	Smartcomm	Hayes
CrossTalk	DCA	ProComm Pluss	Datastorm Technologies	Quick Link	Smith Micro Software
Mirror	SoftKlone	Quick Link	Smith Micro Software		
PC-Talk	Headlands Press	Cross Talk	DCA		
Carbon Copy	Microcomm	DynaComm	Future Soft Engineering		
Qmodem	Mustang Software Inc.				
Quick Link	Smith Micro Software				

Table 6.1

Popular communication software for microcomputers

One of the difficulties organizations face in building a data communications system is that it is composed of many different hardware devices, from a wide variety of manufacturers, that do not communicate easily with each other. As a result, communications software is written to work with one or more protocols. A **protocol** is a set of rules and procedures governing the exchange of data between systems. These rules establish how the systems identify themselves, how data are to be transferred, when the transfer should start and stop, what devices should be involved, and how errors should be handled. Key elements of a protocol are the format of the data, the type of signal to be used, control information for coordination and error management, procedures for matching the speeds of systems devices, and the proper sequence of data.

COMMUNICATIONS CHANNELS

A **communications channel** is the line or link that connects the sender and the receiver in the data communications network. This connection can be a line that physically connects the two devices, like a coaxial cable, a standard telephone line, or a fiber optics cable. The connection can also be made by terrestrial microwaves, by satellite microwaves, or by cellular radio. However, as shown in Fig. 6.3, a communications network often makes use of several different transmission media. This figure illustrates how Lantigua's request for Scott's visit to Atlanta was forwarded from his office on the West Coast to the corporate controller in Atlanta.

This section discusses various characteristics of data communications channels, the different types of channels, channel configurations, and the companies that market communications links.

Data Communications Channel Characteristics

Messages can be transmitted in a number of ways, depending on the hardware and the data communications system configuration in use. Transmission signals may be analog or digital; serial or parallel; asynchronous or synchronous; or simplex, half-duplex, or full-duplex. Channels are either narrowband, voiceband, or wideband. These channel characteristics are discussed next.

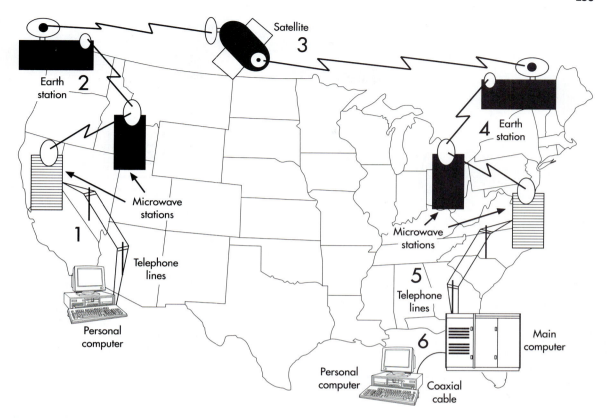

A West Coast corporate accountant for DE uses his PC to send electronic mail to the corporate controller on the East Coast.

1. Lantigua's electronic mail message is sent over phone lines to a microwave transmitter.
2. The message is forwarded by several microwave stations to a satellite earth station.
3. The West Coast earth station forwards the message to a satellite, which relays the message to an earth station on the East Coast.
4. The East Coast earth station forwards the message by microwave stations.
5. The last microwave station forwards the message by telephone wire to DE's main computer in Atlanta.
6. The host forwards the message by coaxial cable to the corporate controller's personal computer.

Figure 6.3

Typical communication network using cables, telephone wires, microwaves, and satellites

Digital Versus Analog. Computers store data internally in discrete, or **digital**, form as the presence or absence of an electronic pulse. Telephone lines were originally built to carry voice transmissions that are in **analog** (or wave) form. Therefore data transmitted over ordinary telephone lines must be converted into analog signals using a modem. To improve data transmission, telephone companies developed digital lines that allow data to be transmitted in digital form. Digital transmission is faster and more efficient, is less error-prone, and does not require a modem, since the modulation/demodulation process is unnecessary. A comparison of analog and digital signals is shown in Fig. 6.4.

Serial Versus Parallel. Data transmission can be either serial or parallel, depending on the hardware and the communications channel used.

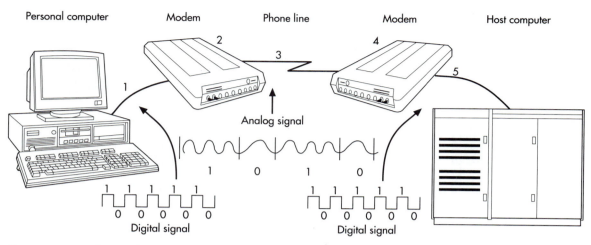

Computers store data in digital form. The steps involved in sending data over a normal phone line follow.

1. The sending device sends a modem a digital signal.

2. The modem translates the digital signal to an analog signal.

3. The analog signal is sent to the receiving modem.

4. The receiving modem translates the analog signal back to a digital signal.

5. The modem sends the digital signal to the receiving device.

Phone companies are currently installing digital lines that do not require modems to make the digital-to-analog-to-digital translation. However, it will take time to replace existing lines with digital lines.

Figure 6.4
Digital and analog signals

With **serial transmission** bits are transferred one at a time. With **parallel transmission** two or more bits are transferred at the same time over separate communications channels. Transferring an eight-bit byte serially is like having eight cars travel on a single-lane highway. Transferring the bits eight at a time is like having all eight cars travel abreast down an eight-lane highway. Parallel transmission is used when increased speed is more important than the added cost of parallel transmission. Figure 6.5 illustrates serial and parallel transmission.

Asynchronous Versus Synchronous. When electronic signals are sent over a communications channel, both the sending and the receiving unit must be in synchronization so that the signals can be interpreted properly. With **asynchronous transmission** (or start/stop transmission) each character is transmitted separately and is preceded by a start bit and followed by a stop bit. With **synchronous transmission** a block of characters is transmitted, with start and stop bits only at the beginning and end of each group of characters. The decision about which method to use usually involves a trade-off among speed, efficiency, and cost. Asynchronous transmission is inexpensive and simple and allows for irregular transmission of data. Synchronous transmission is much faster and more efficient but also more expensive. Asynchronous transmission is usually used for low-speed transmissions, and synchronous is used for high-speed transmissions. PCs usually use asynchronous transmission to commu-

Serial Transmission

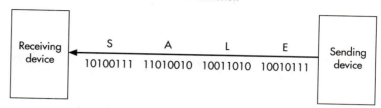

The eight bits representing each character are sent in single file.

Parallel Transmission

Figure 6.5
Serial and parallel transmissions

There are eight separate channels, each carrying one of the eight bits that represent a character.

nicate, while minicomputers and mainframes usually use synchronous transmissions. Figure 6.6 illustrates asynchronous and synchronous transmission.

Simplex Versus Duplex. Communications channels provide for three different options with respect to the direction of transmission. A **simplex channel** can either send or receive signals, but it cannot do both. **Half-duplex channels** allow for data transmission in both directions, but only one

Figure 6.6
Asynchronous and synchronous transmission

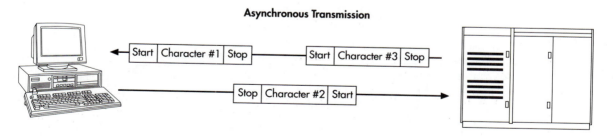

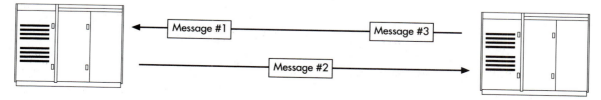

direction at a time. These channels are sufficient for low-speed data transmission, for telephone service, or for use when an immediate response is not necessary. **Full-duplex channels** allow the system to transmit data in both directions at the same time. These channels are used for high-speed data transmission between computers or when real-time processing (immediate responses to data inquiries) is necessary. Figure 6.7 shows the three directional transmissions.

Bandwidth. Communications channels are also classified by their **bandwidths**, which is the difference between the highest and the lowest frequencies that can transmit data. The wider the bandwidth, the more frequencies there are, and therefore more data can be transmitted.

Narrowband lines are not suitable for transmitting audible or voicelike signals. **Voiceband lines** are used for voice or data communications. They are typically telephone lines and are commonly used to communicate with microcomputers and CRT terminals. Three voice-grade telephone services are available. **Leased lines** are dedicated exclusively to the use of a single customer. A **switched line** is an ordinary long-distance telephone line. A **WATS line** is a special long-distance telephone service where the user pays a fixed fee for a certain number of hours use and then pays a lower charge for additional use.

Ashton prepared Table 6.2 to help him compare the three types of lines. He also analyzed and graphed the relationship between monthly cost and use for the three types of lines (see Fig. 6.8).

Broadband lines are used for high-speed data transmission between computer systems. Coaxial and fiber optics cables, terrestrial microwave systems, and satellites are usually used because of their greater reliability and fewer interferences.

Alternative Communications Channels

The communications channel selected can have a significant impact on system reliability, cost, and security. Therefore accountants should understand the various communications channels that are available and their characteristics, advantages, and disadvantages. This section

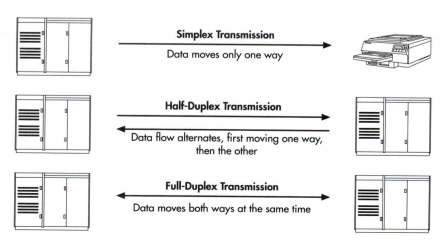

Figure 6.7
Simplex, half-duplex, and full-duplex data transmission

Simplex Transmission
Data moves only one way

Half-Duplex Transmission
Data flow alternates, first moving one way, then the other

Full-Duplex Transmission
Data moves both ways at the same time

	Leased Line	Switched Line	WATS Line
Use	Exclusive use of line Always connected, no connection time	Ordinary long-distance telephone lines Requires dial-up and connection	Ordinary long-distance telephone lines Requires dial-up and connection
Cost	Fixed, based upon distance Least costly for high-volume use	Varies depending upon distance, time of day used, and amount of use Least costly for low use	Fixed monthly fee for a specific number of hours Beyond minimum, cost varies depending on amount of use Least costly at moderate levels of use
Advantages	Lower error rate Faster rates of transmission Increased privacy	Any telephone can be used for data transmission Any system can be reached by the line	Any telephone can be used for data transmission Any system can be reached by the line

Table 6.2
Comparison of leased,
switched, and WATS lines

provides the perspective needed by those managing or designing a data communications system. Table 6.3 lists some of the more important characteristics of the alternatives.

Standard Telephone Lines. Most telephone lines consist of two insulated copper wires, called twisted pairs, that are arranged in a spiral pattern. Large numbers of these pairs are bundled together in large cables wrapped in protective sheaths. Although used primarily for voice, twisted pairs can be used to transmit both analog and digital signals. Telephone lines are the most convenient communications channel because large numbers of them are already installed.

Figure 6.8
Sample economic comparison of
leased lines, switched lines, and
WATS lines for S&S

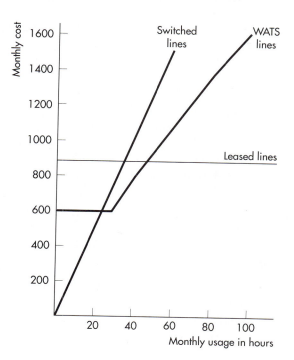

Type of Channel	Cost	Transmission Quality	Relative Speed	Relative Carrying Capacity	Ease of Installation	Ease of Maintenance	Bandwidth
Twisted-pair telephone lines	Low	Poor	1	1	Easy	Easy	Voice
Coaxial cable	Medium	Good	25	1,000	Medium	Medium	Broad
Fiber optics	High	Excellent	2000	1 trillion	Difficult	Easy	Broad
Microwave	Medium	Good	20	10,000	Difficult	Easy	Broad
Satellite	Medium	Good	20	50,000	Difficult	Easy	Broad

Table 6.3
Comparison of
communications channels

Coaxial Cable. A coaxial cable is a group of copper and aluminum wires that are usually buried underground or placed on the ocean floor. Coaxial cable is used in long-distance telephone networks; a single cable can carry as many as fifteen thousand calls simultaneously. Local area networks use coaxial cable because it can support a large number of devices having a variety of data and traffic types. Coaxial cable can transmit both analog and digital signals. It can be used at higher frequencies and data rates than can twisted pairs and is less susceptible to interference and cross talk.

Fiber Optics. A fiber optics cable consists of thousands of tiny filaments of glass or plastic that transmit data using light waves. The light waves, which are generated by lasers, are very concentrated and of high frequency. Fiber optics cables are much faster, smaller, lighter, and less expensive than coaxial cables. A transmission that takes an hour on copper wires can be accomplished in less than a second using fiber optics. A fiber optics cable can contain up to ten times more channels and weigh up to ten times less than a coaxial cable. Optical fibers are practically immune to noise and cross talk and therefore have a lower error rate. Fiber optics cables have a very high resistance to wiretaps and offer much higher levels of security. They operate at temperatures that would melt copper cables.

Microwave Systems. Terrestrial microwave is frequently used for long-distance data or voice transmission. It does not require the laying of expensive cable; instead, long-distance dish or horn antennas with microwave repeater stations are placed approximately 30 miles apart. Each transmitter station receives a signal, amplifies it, and retransmits it to the next station.

Communications Satellites. Satellite transmission is similar to microwave transmission except that the signal is transmitted to a satellite in space rather than to another nearby microwave dish antenna. The satellite acts as a relay station and sends the transmission back to an earth station. There are several dozen of these communications satellites currently in use. They transmit signals at a rate of several hundred million bits per second. Unlike costs of most other media, the cost of satellite transmissions is independent of the distance the message must be transmitted.

Chevron Oil is using source data automation devices and satellite technology to improve customer service and to automate the collection of sales data. Customers at service stations can now pay for their gasoline without any human interaction. Before filling up, motorists pay for the gasoline by running their credit cards through a credit card reader at the pump. This reader passes the information to a satellite dish on top of the service station. The data is beamed by satellite to computers that check the motorist's credit. The approval process takes only five seconds.

Cellular Radio and Telephone. By using **cellular radio**, companies can take greater advantage of the number of radio frequencies available. If the area normally covered by a single powerful transmitter is divided into small sections called cells, each with a transmitter, each frequency can be used by different companies in each cell. In this way up to 25 times more people can use the radio frequencies. A powerful central computer and sophisticated interface equipment coordinate and control the transmission between cells. Microwave, satellite, and cellular transmission are compared in Fig. 6.9.

Figure 6.9
Four examples of wireless transmission
(*Source:* Adapted from Steve Alter, Information Systems: A Management Perspective, Addison-Wesley, 1991, p. 346.)

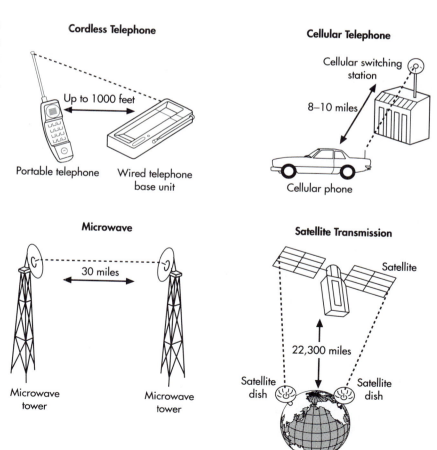

Cordless Telephone

Up to 1000 feet

Portable telephone   Wired telephone base unit

Cellular Telephone

Cellular switching station

8–10 miles

Cellular phone

Microwave

30 miles

Microwave tower   Microwave tower

Satellite Transmission

Satellite

22,300 miles

Satellite dish   Satellite dish

Communications Channel Configurations

The communications channels that connect the various points in a data communications system may be configured in a number of ways. The three basic configurations, point-to-point, multidrop, and line-sharing, are illustrated in Fig. 6.10. The simplest configuration uses **point-to-point lines**, or one line from each remote device to the central processor. **Multidrop lines** link the devices to each other, with only one or a few terminals linked directly to the CPU. The use of a **line-sharing device** allows data from several terminals to be combined for transmission on a single line. A large data communications network often contains a combination of all three approaches. The network designer does not simply choose one of the three approaches for the entire network. Instead, the relative advantages and disadvantages of each configuration are evaluated, and the best approach for each individual terminal connection is chosen. The comparison of the three approaches that Ashton developed is presented in Table 6.4.

Figure 6.10

Data communications network using point-to-point lines, multidrop lines, and a line-sharing device

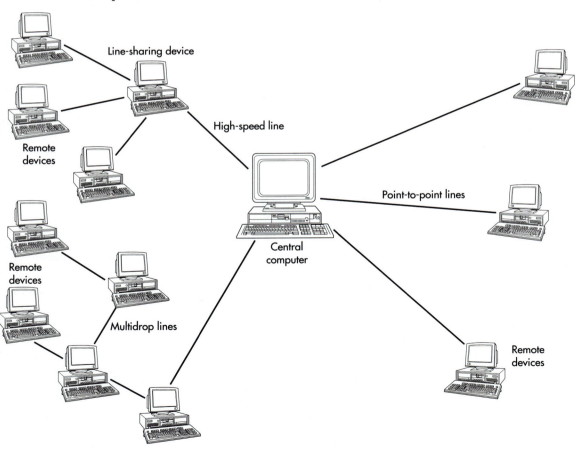

	Point to Point	Multidrop	Line Sharing
Type of line	Leased, switched, or WATS	Leased	Leased, switched, or WATS for connecting lines Shared line is leased
Advantages	Simple hardware requirements Availability to users No waiting for tied-up lines Line failure affects only one user	Reduces line mileage Reduces cost	No waiting for tied-up lines Reduces line mileage Reduced line charges
Disadvantages	Maximizes line mileage Most costly	Only one terminal can transmit at a time Line failure can affect several users Little flexibility in network	Increased cost for line-sharing equipment More expensive high-speed line required Line failure can affect several users

Table 6.4 Comparison of point-to-point, multidropped, and line-sharing configurations

COMMUNICATIONS NETWORK ORGANIZATION

An information system may consist of a stand-alone computer that does not need to communicate with other computers. Most information systems, however, consist of one or more computers, a number of other hardware devices, and communications channels linking the devices together to form a **communications network**. Each device in the network is referred to as a **node**. The network can take so many forms that most networks in use today are unique. This section of the chapter explains two organizational approaches to networks: centralized and decentralized.

Centralized and Decentralized Data Processing Networks

In a **centralized network** data processing is done at a centralized processing center using sophisticated software. User terminals, microcomputers emulating terminals, and source data automation devices are linked to the host computer. These devices send data to the host computer for processing. Processed data is returned to the devices as needed.

Centralized networks provide a number of advantages. Among them are economies of scale, better control, more experienced personnel, and elimination of duplicate functions. Among the disadvantages are greater complexity, higher communications and software costs, and significantly less flexibility. Another problem with centralized processing is that one system is trying to meet the requirements of a large number of users, many of whom have unique needs. The larger the system, the greater the likelihood is that the users will feel that the centralized system is not meeting their needs.

Some of these disadvantages can be overcome by implementing a **decentralized system**, in which there is an independent CPU and a data processing manager at each site. Decentralized systems, however, may

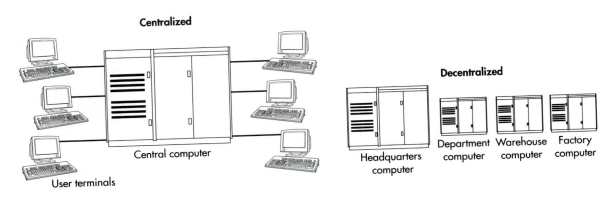

Centralized

Central computer

User terminals

Decentralized

Headquarters computer

Department computer Warehouse computer Factory computer

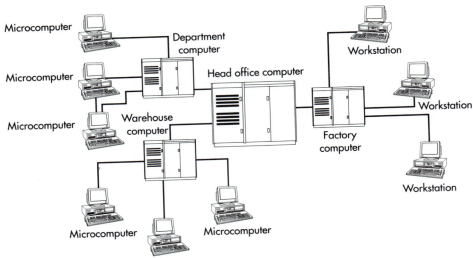

Distributed

Microcomputer

Microcomputer

Microcomputer

Department computer

Warehouse computer

Head office computer

Factory computer

Workstation

Workstation

Workstation

Microcomputer

Microcomputer

Microcomputer

Figure 6.11

Comparison of centralized, decentralized, and distributed data processing

be lacking in such areas as communication between systems, amount of information available, and ability to control the various organizational entities. An approach that achieves many of the advantages yet eliminates many of the disadvantages of both centralized and decentralized processing is known as distributed data processing. Figure 6.11 compares centralized, decentralized, and distributed data processing approaches.

Distributed Data Processing Networks

In a **distributed data processing (DDP)** system processing and management tasks are distributed to the different company locations, which are connected electronically to form a DDP network. Each location has its own computer, its own storage and input/output devices, and often its own data. Each local system is capable of processing its own data and thus has most of the advantages of decentralized processing. Because each local system is part of a network of interconnected processors, data can be transferred electronically between locations. Often, a large computer serves as the host computer, and local systems pass data to the host for summarizations and for preparation of top-management reports. This setup gives the company many of the benefits of centralized processing. The result is a user-oriented (decentralized) as well as a top-management-oriented (centralized) architecture.

There are a number of system components that can be distributed. Here are two of the most important.

1. *Processing capability:* Some locations may have their own computers and software, others may only have data preparation and data entry equipment, and still others may have some intermediate processing capability.

2. *Data base:* The data base can be divided up and partitioned out to the individual locations. This avoids data redundancy but requires more complex data communications to permit other locations to find and access the data they need. Alternatively, the data base can be stored at a central location and copies of the data needed by each location can be maintained locally. This has the advantage of a centralized data base and simpler data communications. It does, however, result in data redundancy.

There are a number of significant advantages to DDP systems. DDP allows users to have control over the local system yet have access to a more powerful system as needed. DDP usually meets users' needs better than centralized systems, because processing is done at or closer to the local level. Users can tailor a system to their needs and improve the quality of the information generated. DDP allows faster and more accurate data entry and correction, since data entry and processing are closer to the source and the time of the actual event. Local processing usually provides faster responses, since communication delays are eliminated, and there is usually less competition for system resources. Communications costs are often less, since most processing is done at local levels. Network computers can provide backup for each other, and there is less risk of catastrophic loss since data processing resources are in multiple locations. Finally, each local system can be treated as a module that can easily be added, upgraded, or deleted from the system.

There are also a number of disadvantages to a DDP system. A DDP system may be more expensive than a centralized system. In addition, it is more difficult to coordinate the system and maintain hardware, software, and data consistency as each location tries to meet its own unique needs. There may be significant data duplication owing to multiple locations, each with a data base. Multiple locations and communications channels often make it harder to achieve adequate security controls and separation of duties. Also, the relatively unsophisticated operating systems of smaller computers in the network make the introduction of elaborate security features and controls difficult. There is less on-site expertise, since the expertise possible with a centralized system cannot be duplicated at each site. It may be more difficult to standardize documentation and control, since authority and responsibility are also distributed.

In the design and implementation of a DDP system several factors should be kept in mind. Since most DDP systems are complex, the system should be designed to ensure reliability. The more complex the system, the more things there are that can go wrong and therefore the greater is the need for reliability. The system should be easy to use, since the more difficult the system is to use, the less likely people are to use it. The system should be properly controlled to ensure data integrity and security. The system should be responsive to the user. If the system is slow and cumbersome, it will not be able to respond to users in a timely fashion and therefore will not be used. The system should also be flexible. It should be capable of handling a wide range of tasks and of efficiently meeting the varied needs of users. The system probably should not be installed unless it will pay for itself through cost savings or increased revenues.

DDP Network Configurations.   Network devices in a distributed network can be linked together in several ways. These network configurations, referred to as the star, ring, bus, and hierarchical topologies, are illustrated in Fig. 6.12. In these figures the nodes labeled A through G stand for devices such as computers, printers, and disk storage that are part of the network.

In a **ring network** the data communications channels form a loop or a circular pattern as they link the local processors together. Each computer communicates with its neighbor and passes any message not intended for it around the ring to the appropriate computer.

In a **star network** all devices in the network are linked to a host computer. Each distributed computer or device routes all data and messages through the central computer, which forwards them to the proper location (this process is called **network switching**). A star network has the same configuration as a point-to-point centralized processing system. Thus a centralized system can be changed to a DDP system by substituting microcomputers or minicomputers for the remote terminals and shifting some of the processing to the micros or minis.

In a **bus network** all devices are attached to a main channel called a bus. Each network device can access the other devices by sending a message to its address. Each device reads the address of all messages sent on the bus and responds to the messages sent to it. Bus networks are easily expanded since they only have to be attached to the main channel and do not affect other devices. However, system performance decreases as more devices are attached to the channel and as more messages are sent.

A **hierarchical network** is a variation of the star network. It is so named because it looks and acts like a hierarchical organization chart. It

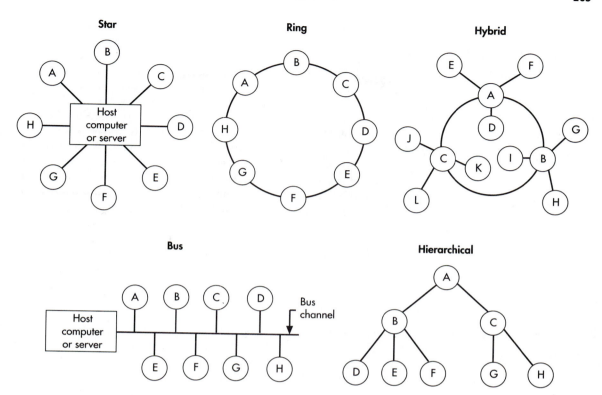

Figure 6.12
DDP network configurations

consists of several levels of computers, all tied to a central or host computer. For example, a company might have a large computer to service the central office and top-management needs. It might be connected to medium-sized computers at each regional office, each of which in turn is linked to small computers in each branch location. Each level processes its own data and passes upward the summary data needed at the higher level. In addition, any job that is too large to be handled at the current level is passed upward. Data are likewise transferred from the top level down to lower levels.

There is no simple answer to the question of which approach is best. That decision is usually based on the distance between the points in the network, the amount of data to be transmitted, the speed with which the message must be communicated, and the ability of each location in the network to handle messages. The decision also depends on the organization's needs and the specific circumstances of the situation. In practice, most organizations use some combination of approaches. For instance, they might use a **hybrid network**—one that contains several of the different basic patterns. In a hybrid network several large systems might be linked together in a ring configuration, while each also serves as the center of a star configuration consisting of smaller systems.

DATA COMMUNICATIONS NETWORK TYPES

The recent information systems trend in organizations all over the world has been toward downsizing. In a business sense downsizing means restructuring into a leaner and more competitive organization by cutting staff and increasing productivity. With respect to information systems **downsizing** is moving from large mainframes and centralized data bases to networks of personal computers and workstations. In a survey of *Fortune* 500 companies the Meta Group, Inc., a research firm, found that 90% of the respondents planned to move some mainframe applications to smaller platforms with the next 24 months. Almost 23% said that they planned to eliminate mainframes altogether and move to minicomputer-based servers. Why are so many organizations deciding to downsize their information system? Because downsizing results in several very powerful benefits: It cuts cost, speeds application development, increases information access, and empowers users.

When organizations downsize, they often move to local area networks linked to a larger wide area network. This section discusses these two types of networks as well as value-added networks and telephone networks.

Local Area Networks

A **local area network (LAN)** electronically connects computers of all sizes, workstations, terminals, disk drives, printers, modems, and other equipment located within a limited proximity, such as a building or a group of buildings. The most common LAN configuration is a group of microcomputers and shared peripherals such as printers and storage devices. Local area networks are fast becoming the most popular corporate computing platform. Many organizations are replacing their mainframe and minicomputer systems with LANs. In one study 98% of the companies surveyed had a LAN. In addition, about 40% of all PCs used in business are connected to a network.

LANs are used in a number of ways to make organizations more effective and efficient.

- *Electronic messages:* Users can send mail, messages, documents, files, announcements, and so on, electronically instead of on paper. For example, Microsoft uses a network that includes most of the company's over five thousand employees. All major decisions and changes in company policy are announced on the network, and any employee is free to send William Gates, the Chairman, an electronic message regarding the decision.

- *Shared resources:* A LAN reduces the investment required in hardware since users can, for example, share a high-quality printer. Nor does every user need a separate copy of a software package. Instead, a company can buy a **site license**, which allows everyone on the network or at a particular location to use the software. Upgrading software is much easier since only one copy needs to be replaced.

■ *Shared data:* Multiple users can access a common data base. For example, several accounts payable clerks can process payments and answer vendor questions by accessing the same data base. This resolves the problems of inconsistent data and having to maintain duplicate copies of data.

■ *Remote access:* From the LAN users can access other networks outside the local network.

An example of a LAN configuration using a bus topology (a ring or star topology is also possible) is shown in Fig. 6.13. As shown in the figure, a LAN is composed of the following six major components:

1. *Hardware:* This component includes computers, printers, and disk drives.

2. *Cables* that connect the network devices: Coaxial cables are most common, although fiber optics cables are also used. Telephone lines are not used. A LAN generally has a bus or ring topology and a high bandwidth.

3. *LAN interface:* Each hardware device that is to be connected to the network cable needs an interface device to send and receive messages.

4. *Communications interface devices*, such as a gateway and a router: A **gateway** allows the LAN to be connected to dissimilar networks such as a wide area network. Gateways allow the LAN to communicate with computers almost anywhere in the world and to draw on

Figure 6.13
Example of a LAN configuration

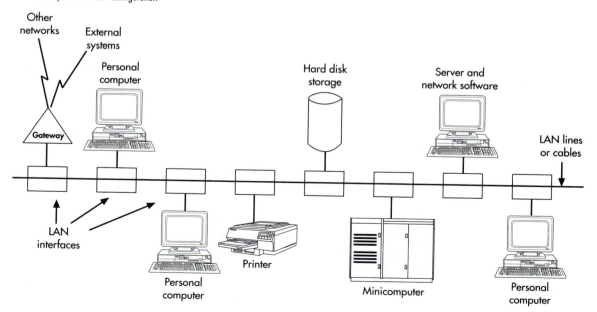

LAN Operating Software	Vendor
Appleshare	Apple
LAN Manager	Microsoft
LAN Server	IBM
OS/2 LAN	IBM
Pathworks	Digital Equipment Company (DEC)
PC LAN	IBM
NetWare	Novell
Vines	Banyan

Table 6.5
Popular LAN operating software

the greater computing power and storage capacity of larger systems. A router connects two LANs of the same type.

5. *Network software:* This component is the brain or intelligence of the LAN. It acts as a traffic manager to route data between the hardware and to prevent and detect data "collisions." A number of companies have developed LAN operating system software. A list of some of the most popular software is shown in Table 6.5.

6. *Network server:* A LAN does not have a host computer. Instead, it has one or more specialized, high-capacity computers called a **server**. The server contains the network software, and together they handle the communication, storage, and resource-sharing needs of the other computers in the network. The sever also contains the application software. It stores data common to users, such as information on customers and vendors. It can store an individual user's information so that it can later be shared with other users.

Servers are used in two different ways. When a computer in the LAN requests data from a **file server**, it sends an entire file at a time. In a **client/server** system, on the other hand, the server processes data as much as possible before the data are transmitted. Suppose, for example, that Ashton wanted to know how many of S&S's accounts receivable (A/R) balances were both over $5000 and over 60 days past due. As shown in Fig. 6.14, the file server would send the entire accounts receivable file to Ashton's PC, and he would have to use the file to find the answer. In a client/server, on the other hand, the server would determine which accounts met the criteria and send them to the Ashton's PC.

The client/server approach to LANs is very popular. For example, Price Waterhouse recently revised its entire technological approach and has moved to a client/server software environment based entirely on a graphical user interface (GUI). United Airlines estimates it saved $4 million dollars when it moved a crew-scheduling application from a mainframe to a Unix-based client/server application. The client/server application doubled available processing capacity and resulted in better performance and more efficient crew scheduling. BC Gas, a Cana-

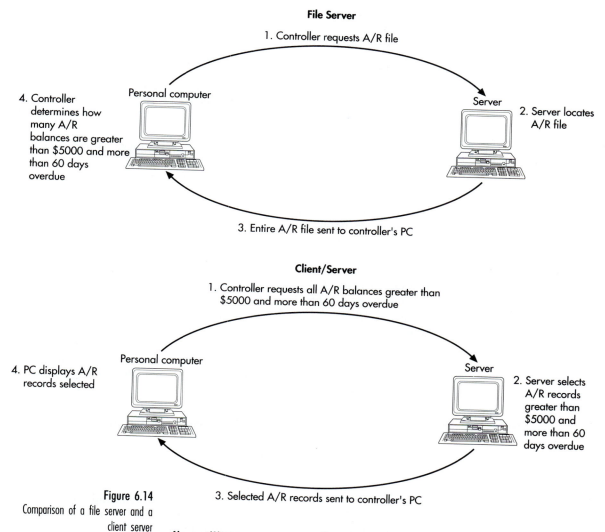

Figure 6.14
Comparison of a file server and a client server

dian utility, expects to realize annual savings of $1.4 million by moving to a client/server system.

A LAN must have some way to put messages on the network and to take them off. The two most common ways to do this are referred to as Ethernet and Token Ring. **Ethernet,** a bus configuration, allows LAN devices to listen to the line. When a device is ready to send a message over the LAN, it breaks the message down into packets of data. Each packet is assigned a code that identifies the sending and the destination location. The sending station then "listens" to the line, and when it is free, the message is placed on the line. The message is carried along the LAN line to its destination. Each station listens for packets addressed to it and removes them as they arrive. When transmission has been completed and the message has been removed from the line, the receiving station sends an acknowledgment back to the sending station.

The token ring approach passes a token around the ring configuration. This token indicates that the network is free to transmit a message. When a node wants to send a message, it captures the token, thereby preventing anyone else from sending a message on the line. The node then sends its message. When the transmission is completed, the token is released to the network so that some other node can capture it and use it to send a message.

A LAN has a number of significant advantages. First, a LAN system is quite flexible. With a LAN you can coordinate, control, and share resources, yet individuals are free to meet their own needs. Second, a LAN is less expensive than other systems, since it does not require a central computer system and it can easily share equipment like laser or color printers. For example, Niagara Mohawk Power estimates that it saves $2000 annually for every mainframe user that is switched to a networked PC. Third, LANs are easily installed anywhere they are needed. General Electric, for example, has hundreds of installed LANs. Fourth, hardware devices can easily be added to or deleted from a LAN, and breakdowns in particular devices have no effect on other system devices. Fifth, a LAN is able to handle large volumes of data at very high transmission speeds. Niagara Mohawk estimates that users can access data 10%–25% faster from a network data base than from a mainframe data base. Sixth, a LAN can create backup files easily and regularly, a task that is difficult to get users to do on their individual PCs.

Financial Guaranty Insurance Company (FGIC), a municipal bond insurer with $1.2 billion in assets, was one of the first companies to downsize completely from a mainframe to a PC-based network, beginning in 1987. It took the firm 18 months to install Compaq Computer PCs on a Novell, Inc. NetWare 386 token ring network, write all new applications using Fox Software's Foxbase, and eliminate its IBM 4381 mainframe. The improvements were marked. Instead of spending about $6 million per year on a mainframe system that was not adequately serving the growing company, FGIC now has a budget of $2.5 million. The information systems staff size shrunk from 70 to about 20. Development backlog, once a "generation" behind, has been shortened so that when the department delivers a program, it's still useful.

As popular and useful as LANs are, they do have some disadvantages. Because the technology is so young, uniform standards for LANs are not very well developed. There are still a lot of products that do not communicate well with each other. Second, computer security methods are also not as well developed as they are with larger systems. Third, LANs require specially trained staff to manage and support them. For example, St. Paul Company, an international insurance agency, has 26 LANs, each with an administrator and an assistant.

Ability to access WANs, other computer networks and platforms
Availability of and need for a menu structure
Availability of and need for a graphical user interface
Backup and recovery abilities
Cost
Ease of installation
Ease of management and administration
Ease of use
Extent and quality of vendor support
Printing capabilities
Security
Speed and performance
Upgrade and enhancement options

Table 6.6
LAN selection considerations

Each must understand application software, LAN software, how to troubleshoot, and how to deal with frustrated users.

Ashton found that there are a number of things to consider when choosing a LAN for an organization. Some of the more important considerations are listed in Table 6.6.

Wide Area Networks

A **wide area network (WAN)** is a telecommunications network that covers a large geographic area. That area can be as small as a few cities or can span the globe. A WAN uses telephone lines, cables, microwaves, satellites, or a combination of these communications channels. They often connect a wide variety of hardware devices in many different locations. Many users design their own systems by selecting from services offered by common carriers. **Common carriers** are organizations authorized by the Federal Communications Commission or state agencies to provide public communications services. Some well-known common carriers are AT&T, Western Union, MCI, U.S. Sprint, and General Telephone and Electric.

Companies develop WANs for many different reasons. One of the most common reasons is for distributed data processing. Other uses include electronic mail, electronic data interchange, electronic funds transfer, product development by teams in multiple locations, taking orders or reservations, tracking inventory shipments or the location of express or overnight packages, and consolidating corporate data.

Many large organizations have developed extensive WANs. For example, Texas Instruments has developed an extensive WAN that includes 23 mainframes, over 2000 minicomputers, and almost 70,000 terminals and microcomputers at 50 sites. Engineers in 18 different countries use it for product development. CIGNA insurance spends over $75 million a year (3% of its revenues) running its own network. CIGNA feels that its network provides it with higher reliability and lower transaction costs than its competitors have. Merrill Lynch has an extensive network linking over 650 offices all over the world.

Value-Added Networks

WANs are usually developed so that scattered offices and sites in the same company can communicate with each other. These companies also want to be able to communicate with other organizations. One of the difficulties in doing so, however, is that companies have different hardware and software, thereby complicating communications between different organizations' networks. One solution to this problem is a **value-added network (VAN)**, which is a public network that adds value to the data communications process.

VANs offer specialized hardware, software, and data handling techniques that improve transmission effectiveness and decrease costs. For example, suppose S&S wants to send purchase orders electronically to all its vendors. Rather than try to create interfaces with all the different hardware and software of its vendors, it could use a VAN. The orders could be sent to the VAN with instructions about to whom the information should be forwarded. Ford Motor, for instance, only has to worry about linking its system to one other system, the VAN, instead of to hundreds of vendors. The VAN handles the difficult task of interfacing with all of the different types of hardware and software used by the vendors.

One of the most important services offered is access to public data bases. **Public data bases** are electronic libraries containing millions of items of data that can be reviewed, retrieved, analyzed, and saved. Almost any information that a user might need is available, including some that is not even in print. As a result, electronic libraries have begun to replace regular libraries. Over three hundred vendors supply more than two thousand data bases to over 30 million people, who spend millions of dollars to access the data bases. Some of the most popular data bases are Dow-Jones News/Retrieval, CompuServe, Compustat, LEXIS, NEXIS, NAARS, The Source, Quotron, Prodigy, Dialog, and Value Line Data Base II.

All that is needed to access these data bases is a PC, a modem, communications software, a telephone, and an account with the public data base vendor. The communications software is loaded into the PC, and the vendor's telephone number is dialed. The communications software helps the two devices communicate, and the vendor's software sends a menu to the computer. From a series of menus, the user selects the desired service and identifies the tasks to be performed and any criteria the software needs to perform the task. When the task is finished, the communications software logs the user off the system. Search costs run from $5 to $200 an hour and vary depending on the time of day. In addition to the search charge, there are communications network charges and local telephone charges. A typical data base search takes from 8 to 18 minutes and, depending on the data base searched, costs between $5 and $20.

The major advantage of such a system is obvious: instant access to a large amount of data. The main disadvantage is the difficulty of learning how to access the different public data base services and how to search them effectively. The costs of the searches are reasonable given the information retrieved. It would often take hours of painstaking research to find the same information in a nonelectronic library.

A **bulletin board system (BBS)** is designed to let computer users meet, get to know each other, and share ideas and information. Except for long-distance telephone charges, most BBS systems are free. Most cater to some sort of specialized interest such as investing, law, accounting, education, games, and music. In addition, a great deal of public domain software is available free from different BBSs. There are an estimated fifty thousand bulletin boards worldwide. Some of the more popular are run by The Boston Computer Society, EIES, Citinet, FidoNet, and The Whole Earth 'Lectonic Link (WELL).

There are also large, privately owned organizations that sell computing services and information to the public for a fee. A **time-sharing service** sells users small slices of time on large mainframes. A company can rent hardware time, software programs, or both. Users can send data to the service electronically, have it processed, and then have it returned to them. A **service bureau** is an organization that provides data processing services on its own equipment to users for a fee. Because many users share the computer facilities of the service bureau, the cost to each user is only a portion of the total cost of a computer system.

Telephone Networks

A **private branch exchange (PBX)** is special-purpose computer that manages a company's telephone network. Originally, the PBX only handled the switching of incoming and outgoing calls to and from the telephone company line to the company's internal line. In this way a company could have 100 internal phones but only need 10–20 outside lines. Now, however, a PBX is able to handle both voice and digital data, turning it into a local network capable of handling data communication tasks.

The primary advantage of a PBX as a local area network is that it does not need special wiring. All users have to do is plug their PCs into a telephone jack. Then by using a modem and the telephone, users can send information (such as electronic mail, a data file, or a document) to other users. The user can be on the same PBX or on some other network accessible by telephone lines. The primary disadvantage is that a PBX is limited to telephone lines. Telephone lines are slower and not as capable of handling large volumes of data as other communication channels.

Most current telephone lines are analog, while computers are digital devices. The industry is slowly converting to digital phone lines. The goal is to have an extensive digital network that conforms to certain standards. This network, called the **integrated services digital network (ISDN)**, will have built-in intelligence and will permit all types of data (voice, data, images, facsimile, video) to be sent over telephone lines. In essence, it will allow all communications devices to communicate with each other directly.

There are a number of advantages to ISDN. First, it will greatly expand the types of data that can be sent over regular telephone lines. Second, it will greatly increase the speed of those transmissions. Third, it will reduce equipment costs and make equipment more effective. Fourth, it will permit the simultaneous transmission of voice and text data, so that several people could, for example, both see and discuss the same spreadsheet at the same time. Unfortunately, there are still bugs that must be worked out of ISDN before it will be fully operational. Some critics of ISDN say that it will be obsolete by the time it can be fully operational.

DATA COMMUNICATIONS APPLICATIONS

Although data communications systems are generally more costly and complex than conventional data processing systems, their utilization has increased sharply in recent years. This increase reflects their potential as a profitable management tool. This section discusses just a few of the many uses for data communications systems in today's businesses.

Computer-Based Message Systems

Data communications systems are used to transmit electronically a wide variety of items, including documents, memos, pictures, graphics, mail, and voice messages. For example, an extensive network at Microsoft Corporation is used for almost all intercompany communications to its employees.

Facsimile (fax) transmission allows documents, pictures, graphics, and signatures to be sent over a data communications system. A facsimile machine at the sending station translates the different shades of light and dark on a page into signals that can be sent over the communications links. A similar machine on the receiving end translates the signals back into the proper images and reproduces them on a piece of paper. In today's business environment a business is not complete unless it has a fax machine.

Electronic mail (E-mail) systems allow a person to send, receive, or forward a message to or from anyone else who has a "mailbox," or electronic storage location, in the system. As soon as a message is sent, the intended receiver is notified that an E-mail message has arrived and who it is from. If the recipient is not able to respond to the message, it is stored until the person can "open" the mail and read the electronic message. If a recipient's computer is off, he or she is notified of the E-mail when the person next logs onto the system. In most systems the sender can include files (such as spreadsheets, documents, or reports) with the message. The system can be used to send messages internally or, using gateways to public E-mail services, to other organizations. By setting up predefined distribution lists, users can avoid having to reenter names each time a message is sent to the same group.

E-mail is an ideal way to conduct many forms of communication and can at least partially replace the telephone and the regular mail system. One major advantage of the system is that the messages are sent instantly, rather than taking days by either external or internal mail systems. Another advantage is that it eliminates games of "telephone tag," in which people who are unable to reach each other keep leaving messages on their answering machines. Another advantage is that a recipient can store a message, save it, print it, erase it, edit it, or forward it to someone else.

The volume and the different types of E-mail messages being sent are increasing exponentially. There are currently over 16 million LAN-based E-mail users operating from more than 3 million systems. By 1995 there may be almost 36 million systems. One reason for this increase is that companies are moving from mainframe-based E-mail systems (such as IBM's Profs and DEC's All-IN-One) to LAN-based systems, which are more flexible and less expensive. In addition, LAN E-mail vendors are expanding their programs by developing a variety of interfaces for their systems. The interfaces include converting the E-mail message into a fax, telex or, telegram for recipients who do not have an E-mail system; integrating voice messages with the E-mail message; sending a hard copy of the message using a mailing system; and using radio frequencies to allow portable computer users to send and retrieve messages.

Ashton and Scott were both very interested in an E-mail package. Ashton made a list of some of the more popular LAN E-mail vendors and public E-mail services, which is shown in Table 6.7.

Voice mail (V-mail) is a computerized method of sending spoken messages to other people. It combines the storage feature of the answering machine with the accessing, editing, and forwarding capabilities of E-mail. A V-mail system records a spoken message and converts it into a digital message that can be stored in the receiver's electronic mailbox for future retrieval. The biggest advantage that V-mail has over E-mail is that telephones are more widely available than computers linked to networks. Therefore V-mail systems are more flexible. However,

Table 6.7
Providers of electronic mail services

LAN E-Mail Software	Vendor	Commercial E-Mail Services	Vendor
Beyond Mail	Beyond, Inc.	Dialcom	BT Tymnet, Inc.
cc:Mail	Lotus Development	EasyLink	AT&T
DaVinci eMail	DaVinci Systems Corporation	Infoplex	CompuServe
Lotus Notes	Lotus Development	MCI Mail	MCI
Microsoft Mail	Microsoft	Notice	Infonet
Office	WordPerfect	Quick-Comm	GE Information Service
QuickMail	CE Software Inc.	Sprint Mail	U.S. Sprint

V-mail is not very good for conveying long, complicated, or technical messages or data. Another disadvantage of V-mail is that recipients must listen to all the V-mail messages that may precede the one they are looking for. In E-mail the list of messages can be scanned, and recipients can go directly to a specific message.

Voice mail systems have a variety of storage and forwarding capabilities that notify the recipient when a message is waiting. When the recipient is ready to listen to the message, it is retrieved, converted into audio form, and played back. People can access their V-mail systems and listen to their voice mail from almost any telephone in the world. As with E-mail, a recipient can store the message, erase it, or forward it to someone else. A V-mail message can also be sent to more than one person at a time. To illustrate the uses of V-mail, consider John Wentworth, President of the Wentworth Company, who uses voice mail extensively. When he is not at his desk to get a phone call, his voice mail answers, takes the message, and then pages him. When he wants to get a message out to a group of his employees, he leaves a message with voice mail and tells the system to broadcast it. The system then finds the people, pages them, and tells them that they have a message waiting.

Teleconferencing is a way of using telecommunications technology to conduct a "meeting" with people in separate locations. There are three types of teleconferencing: audio, video, and computer. All three save travel time and costs.

Audio teleconferencing is simply a conference call, in which several locations are linked together so that they can hear each other.

In video conferencing the participants can both see and hear each other. Since video conferencing requires complex video equipment, it is much more expensive that audio conferencing. Video conferencing requires high-speed communications channels that allow the transmission of the massive amounts of data necessary to integrate voice, data, and images. Thus participants in a video conference usually gather in specially equipped rooms designed for that purpose. AT&T, for example, has set up teleconferencing rooms where conferees can gather and conduct a conference with multiple users at multiple locations. Many organizations have set up their own video conferencing rooms. Mellon Bank estimates that video conferencing saves it about $400,000 dollars a year. J.C. Penney and Merrill Lynch also use video conferencing to communicate with their stores and offices.

In computer conferencing conference participants use personal computers and typewritten messages to communicate with each other. Each participant types in comments, questions, and ideas, and they are forwarded to all participants. There is a great deal of flexibility with this approach. Anyone can join the conference at any time because a complete history of everyone else's comments is maintained by the system. Likewise, a participant can leave the conference to attend to other duties and return at his or her convenience. Participants can direct their comments to a specific person, attach their comments to comments already on the screen, or edit someone else's ideas or comments. The conference can be extended for an indefinite amount of time so that others can input their ideas and think about all the ideas presented. People can say exactly what they want and when they want, instead of having to be recognized to make a comment.

Groupware programs have been designed using computer teleconferencing as the basis. End users have found groupware ideal for holding computer conferences, deciding when to hold meetings, making a calendar for a department, collectively brainstorming on creative endeavors, managing projects, designing products, and creating documents. Focus 6.1 explains how the Massachusetts Society for Prevention of Cruelty to Children used groupware to develop a federal grant.

Computer-based transmission of messages has a number of important advantages. Messages can be distributed very quickly, and the sender does not have to worry about busy signals or unanswered phones. In addition, since most systems are capable of informing the sender that the message was placed in the receiver's mailbox, the sender has fewer worries about whether a message was received. The cost of communication is quite reasonable. A further advantage is that the user and the receiver can send or read their mail at any time simply by accessing the system.

Transportation and Travel Reservations

Firms in the travel industry, notably the airlines and major motel chains, were among the first to implement data communications systems to process and confirm customer reservations. Data terminals or microcomputers are located at each reservations counter or motel lobby. On-line file storage devices contain a record of the availability of services, such as seats on airline flights or rooms at motels in a chain. A customer may request a reservation in person or by phone. The reservation is entered into the system, and if the requested seat, room, or other service is available, the file record is updated and the reservation is immediately confirmed to the customer.

Holiday Inn has a companywide PC network linking its 1600 hotels and related properties to a centralized reservation system. Within each hotel anywhere from 2 to 20 PCs are connected over IBM token ring networks running Novell's NetWare. A satellite link connects the LANs to the company's reservation system. The system also transfers data directly from the hotels to corporate headquarters for use in market research. The system substantially reduces the time it takes hotel staff to book rooms, determine occupancy levels, and establish rates. The reservation system response time is now 1 to 3 seconds, compared with the 8 to 15 seconds needed previously. A reservation transaction now costs 43¢; the industry standard is more than three times that rate. The cost-effectiveness aspect of the system led to an Excellence in Enterprise Networking award.

In an airline reservations system several functions may be performed in addition to maintaining records of seat availability and

6.1 FOCUS

Groupware Helps Win Federal Grants

By the time the Massachusetts Society for Prevention of Cruelty to Children learned it qualified to win federal grants worth $600,000, it only had three weeks to prepare three different 150-page proposals. To make matters worse, the society had to collect information from five different regional offices. Before the installation of its groupware software, the agency would have considered itself fortunate to complete just one of the proposals. This time, however, the five offices used their PC network to simultaneously prepare, review, and edit the proposals. The groupware network eliminated the need for preparing separate drafts, faxing to the other offices, and patching together a final copy.

Groupware allows workers with special skills to help each other and to merge their expertise. Groupware brings the power of computer networks together with the creative benefits of a face-to-face brainstorming session. It allows individuals at widely scattered locations to use their PCs to work on the same problem at the same time. The information entered into the groupware system or the

processing reservations. These functions include calculating fares, updating sales and accounts receivable records, responding to customer requests for reconfirmation, and processing passenger checkins. In a motel room reservations system functions such as calculation of room charges, guest checkin and checkout, and revenue accounting are generally performed at each local unit rather than by the data communications system.

Banking Systems

Banks were also among the first institutions to use data communications systems. In a banking system various customer functions are performed at teller windows and automated teller machines (ATMs). A primary function is checking a customer's account to determine whether the balance is large enough to cover a withdrawal being made by the waiting customer. In addition, deposits and withdrawals may be posted to customer accounts through the system. Hardware requirements include a data terminal for each teller window, ATMs at various locations, and on-line file storage to maintain a record of each customer's account.

The banking system can make an up-to-date record of each customer's account available to every teller and ATM, even those located some distance from the main bank. These systems enable banks to provide faster and more convenient service to customers, while reducing the number of tellers required to wait on customers.

Many banks have since expanded their applications into other areas, such as mortgages, commercial loans, consumer loans, and credit files.

changes made to the data in the system are immediately made available to others on the network. They can easily respond to the data entered or to the changes made, and everyone else can see and react to their input.

The primary objective of a groupware package is to automate tasks involving groups. One time-consuming task in working in groups is scheduling meetings. Often it requires multiple phone calls, E-mail messages, or memos to find a time when everyone can meet. Software, such as Meeting Maker from On Technology, automatically finds common

meeting times by checking participants' schedules. Other groupware, such as Instant Update from On Technology, makes it possible for groups to simultaneously work on a document. Instant Update stores a master copy of a document on a central computer. The coordinator of the project instructs the groupware to send everyone involved in the project a copy of the document and their assignment. As individuals complete their tasks and as changes are made by those reviewing the assignments, the groupware tags each segment so that it can keep track of who does what. Whenever required, team members

can ask the system to display a copy of the current status of either the entire document or some part of the document.

One very powerful groupware product is Lotus Development's Lotus Notes. It coordinates all groupware applications on a computer network, including writing group documents, meeting scheduling, and E-mail. Its purpose is to make available all the information a person needs for the job, thereby eliminating most management positions related to information transfer and control.

Source: Andrew Jenks, "Groupware Fosters Shared Info, Ideas," *USA Today* (October 21, 1991): 10E.

In recent years the practice of having one large data communications system to handle all banking transactions has evolved. Retail merchants can be tied into the banking network through point-of-sale terminals and microcomputers, and sales transactions can be immediately charged to the consumer's bank account and simultaneously credited to the merchant's account. Transactions among corporations and other institutions can be handled electronically rather than by check. Deposit of paychecks to the bank accounts of employees by their employers can also be done electronically. Using microcomputers and modems, individuals can access the bank's system and pay all their bills electronically. This practice has become known as **electronic funds transfer (EFT)**.

The ATM provides bank customers with banking services 24 hours a day. All they have to do is find an ATM, insert their specially coded plastic bank card, and type in a **PIN (personal identification number)**. The PIN is a confidential code known only to the bank's customer and the computer. Using the bank's data communications network, the ATM checks the PIN to see whether it matches the account number on the bank card. If it does, the user can withdraw or deposit funds. With the proper ATM and data communications links the user can also purchase a variety of other items, such as stamps, airline tickets, and movie and theater tickets.

Retail Sales   Many retail organizations such as S&S use data communications systems to collect and summarize sales data and to perform credit-checking and inventory control functions. Electronic cash registers and point-of-sale recorders serve as data terminals for these applications. They capture, at the point of sale, such information as the item sold, the quantity, and the price. Also, a customer's credit standing may be checked at the time a credit transaction is initiated. As shown in Fig. 6.15, credit is checked by forwarding the credit card number to the bank's computer, which electronically determines the credit standing and amount of credit that can be granted. If the credit sale is authorized or if the sale is for cash, the inventory file is accessed and updated for the specific merchandise sold. In addition to maintaining an up-to-date record of all inventory items, the system can originate inventory reordering as needed. Up-to-date sales and inventory totals can be obtained by management through on-line data base queries. The system also can maintain the price of the item purchased and automatically ring up the amount. Many systems use audio response units to inform the customer of the amount.

Sales Order Processing   A sales order processing system is similar in many respects to a retail sales system. Companies such as S&S can gain a significant competitive advantage by using a data communications system to reduce the time between the receipt of customer orders and their delivery. The system can maintain a finished goods inventory file on-line and can have data terminals or microcomputers distributed throughout the sales territory. Salespeople can call orders in to a regional center at which the terminals or computers are located; alternatively, each salesperson can be equipped with a small portable terminal or computer to enter orders directly from the customer's plant or office. The system can access the finished goods inventory file to confirm the availability and quantity of each item ordered, and this information is be relayed to the salesperson immediately. The finished goods inventory file is updated as the orders are placed. All appropriate journal entries are made immediately in the general ledger, and the invoice is immediately posted to an on-line accounts receivable ledger. If inventories are stored in a network of warehouses, delivery can be initiated by electronically transmitting a shipping order to the warehouse closest to the point of delivery.

In addition to speeding up the sales order delivery cycle, the system has several other useful features. With the accounts receivable file online, a salesperson can answer customer inquiries about the status of the customer's account. The credit-checking process also can be accomplished on-line as part of the order entry process. In addition, a sales analysis master file can be updated as orders are placed. This file can be used by marketing executives to generate up-to-date information on sales trends, thus facilitating management control of the sales function. Furthermore, as the finished goods inventory balances are updated, the updated balance of each item can be checked to determine whether reordering or additional production is necessary to replenish the stock.

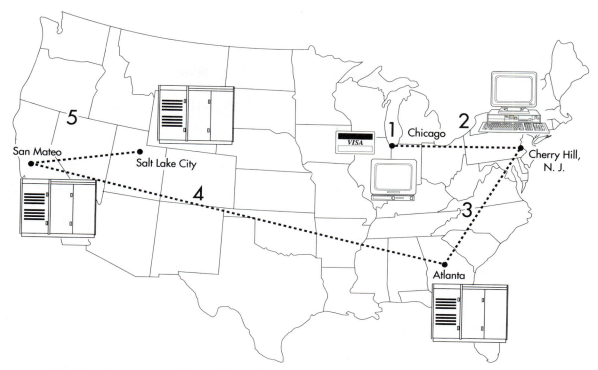

All data in the system travels by satellite, microwave, or telephone lines. The system determines the least expensive route as the approval request is processed.

1. A customer purchases a new $1500 TV in Chicago using a VISA credit card. The local merchant uses a POS device supported by National Data Corporation to read the credit card. The credit approval process takes about 15 seconds.

2. The credit request is sent to National Data Corporation's computers in Cherry Hill, New Jersey.

3. NDC's computer in Cherry Hill sends the request to NDC's computer in Atlanta, which, because of the size of the credit approval, turns it over to VISA's minicomputer.

4. VISA's minicomputer forwards the query to VISA's mainframe in San Mateo, California.

5. The San Mateo mainframe forwards the request to the bank in Salt Lake City that issued the VISA card. The Salt Lake City bank verifies that credit is available. The credit approval retraces its path back to Chicago where the purchase is finalized.

Figure 6.15

Credit approval process in a retail organization

(*Source:* Adapted from *Business Week* (October 8, 1990): 144.)

The advantages of this system are the confirmation of sales orders in real time and the complete integration of the accounting function. One entry of data results in the updating of all accounting records affected by the data and initiates the preparation of all documents necessary for processing the transaction. A more extensive discussion of this system is given in Chapter 16.

Many companies have made their sales order systems more responsive to customer needs. Focus 6.2 discusses the changes Bell Atlantic, for example, is making to its system.

Electronic data interchange, discussed in the following section, takes sales order processing one step further—customers enter their own orders.

FOCUS

Bell Atlantic Automates Sales Service System

Even though Bell Atlantic has 6500 customer service representatives, it is struggling to meet the needs of its 12.8 million customers. When a customer calls one of its 169 business offices to inquire about a new service, it can take a representative up to 20 minutes to find out what the customer wants, look through huge manuals for pricing information or technical specifications, and log on to one or more unfriendly mainframe systems.

Bell Atlantic hopes to solve the problem by replacing its antiquated and poorly linked service order systems with a new Sales Service Negotiation System (SSNS). The dumb terminals currently used will be

---

Electronic Data Interchange

Imagine that you are a manager in an organization currently struggling with three problems regarding the processing of transactions with both suppliers and customers. First, the current manual system is very slow, often requiring one to two weeks to complete a transaction agreed on over the telephone in a matter of minutes. Second, because the processing of transactions involves a number of people, the cost of processing each transaction is rather high. Third, clerical errors on the part of the people entering transaction data into the system and processing it are common and result in even longer processing times, strained relations with both suppliers and customers, delayed production, and so forth.

One potential solution to these problems is the use of **electronic data interchange (EDI)**. EDI is the direct, computer-to-computer transmission of business documents between two separate organizations. Rather than physically exchanging a purchase order, invoice, or bill of lading, the participants transmit the information on these documents electronically; this system eliminates paper flow between the two organizations. Because the information is in electronic form, human intervention is limited to transaction verification, with no human transaction processing. The proper processing of transactions is facilitated by standards established by the two organizations. The flow of transaction data, with and without EDI, is illustrated in Fig. 6.16.

EDI is fast becoming the standard means of processing transactions between customers, suppliers, and manufacturers in a number of industries, both domestically and internationally. There are currently over fifteen thousand firms using EDI, and that number is expected to double annually for the next several years. In many companies, such as Ford, General Motors, K Mart, J.C. Penney, and Dow Chemical, most

replaced with a network of intelligent workstations. Human judgment will give way to artificial intelligence. A new on-line data base will allow Bell Atlantic to replace the 19 million pages of documentation it now sends every year to its order takers with electronic messages and updates. The main objective of the system is to provide better customer service by quickly and efficiently meeting the customers' needs.

Designing and implementing the SSNS will not be an easy task. Several hundred people will work on it for five years at a cost of between $70 and $130 million. It will consist of the following components:

- LANs at all 169 business offices

- 8000 workstations from Sun Microsystems

- An IBM 3090 mainframe and multiple Sun servers

- Support software that prompts the order taker to ask questions based on customer requests and responses

- An expert knowledge-based sales tool to help order takers match customer profiles with available services and options

- Data bases of text and product data to replace reference manuals

- An interface module that translates orders into the formats needed by the various local telephone company order systems

Source: "May I Take Your Order?" Computerworld (October 7, 1991): 29.

documents that enter their system are produced as output from another system.

EDI has several advantages. One is the speed of data transmission. This eliminates information float, which is the delay caused by printing out information, moving it through the mail system, and reentering it in the recipient's computer. With EDI, a purchase order that is created today can be received and processed by a supplier that same day. Another advantage is the reduction in clerical errors, since most human interaction is eliminated. A third is the cost savings that result: EDI eliminates data entry, which accounts for about 25% of the cost of processing a transaction. EDI also protects a company's markets by making it easier for customers to order from that company than from a competitor that does not use EDI. EDI reduces inventory levels and carrying costs because orders can be placed and processed faster. A supplier's computer can also instantaneously respond to a purchase order, letting a customer know if the items ordered are in stock. A final advantage is survival: Many companies today will only do business with vendors and suppliers that use compatible EDI systems.

Motorola Codex recently completed a three-year project that eliminates paper from its business dealings with key suppliers. The communications equipment manufacturer began by using an integrated EDI and EFT system to connect itself with Texas Instruments (TI), one of its main suppliers. In doing so, it became one of the few companies to have an electronic "closed loop," from initial production plan to final payment, with EDI transactions integrated into its existing manufacturing, purchasing, and financial applications. Codex transacts about 40% of its purchase orders through EDI, but TI was the first of its EDI-linked suppliers to receive its payments electronically. As soon as

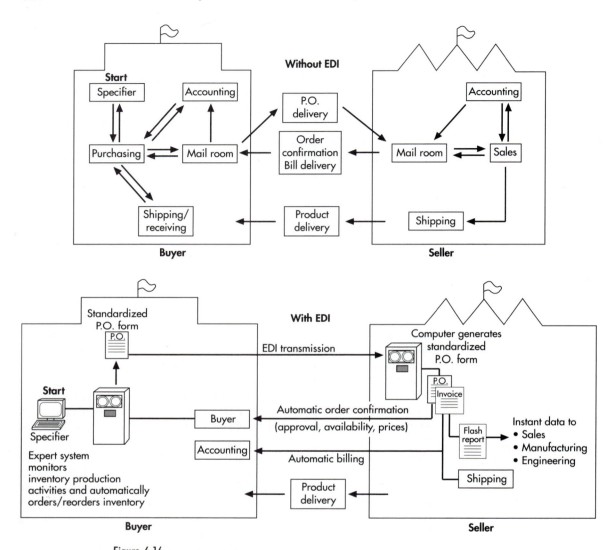

Figure 6.16

Flow of transaction data with and without EDI

(Source: Willie Schatz, "EDI: Putting the Muscle in Commerce and Industry," *Datamation,* (March 16, 1988): pp. 56–64. Reprinted with permission.)

Codex receives goods from TI, the system sends an electronic payment authorization to its bank, which sends the payment to TI's collection bank. Codex expects costs savings in reduced product cycle time, supply inventories, paperwork, and filing.

EDI is not without its problems. One difficulty is communication among the different computers. Solving this problem can involve considerable effort and expense. So most new adopters of EDI use a value-added network that allows them to overcome most of this problem. Other disadvantages include the lack of standardized product and service codes and transmission protocols. The benefits of EDI seem to far outweigh the disadvantages, however. Given the ability of EDI to address significant problems businesses face in processing transactions with other organizations, its use can only be expected to increase.

CASE CONCLUSION: IMPLEMENTING A DATA COMMUNICATIONS SYSTEM AT S&S, INC.

After their visit to DE's headquarters, Scott and Ashton both spent as much time as they could spare learning about data communications. They soon realized that they needed outside help and hired Data Connections (DC), a firm specializing in data communications systems for small businesses.

After helping S&S assess their needs, DC proposed that S&S install a LAN. Each LAN would connect all of the PCs at each location using token ring technology. The LAN would allow users to share a number of resources, such as top-of-the-line laser printers and a wide variety of software, including accounting, spreadsheet, and word processing. As S&S expands, each location will have a LAN installed, and the LANs can be linked together in a WAN. The LAN should give them all the advantages of a decentralized processing system, and the WAN will give them the benefits of a centralized system. The LAN also would give them E-mail capabilities, and the WAN would give them corporatewide E-mail.

The LAN would be designed so that it connects to DE's VAN. Using the VAN eliminates a variety of problems relating to the compatibility of the connections between S&S's and DE's equipment.

To implement the system, S&S needs to purchase a client/server to manage the system and store the data that system users will share. The LAN will also require modems, a LAN interface, and a gateway to connect the LAN to the VAN. With respect to software S&S will need a LAN operating system, such as NetWare from Novell. It will also need to buy the network version of the application software it wants to use.

All the LAN devices will be connected by coaxial cable. The VAN has a local number that S&S can call so that S&S will not have to incur long-distance telephone charges while using the EDI system. The VAN uses a combination of leased lines, telephone lines, satellites, and microwave transmission. It has sophisticated software that optimizes line use and minimizes communications channel costs.

Scott, Susan, and Ashton liked the system proposed by DC, as did the rest of the employees at S&S. So Scott hired DC to install the system and train S&S employees in the use of the system. DC also trained a recent information systems graduate to maintain and support the system. She will take on those duties on a part-time basis until the system grows large enough to require a full-time position. ■

SUMMARY

A data communications system consists of five major components: the sending device, the communications interface device, the communications channel, the receiving device, and communications software.

A number of hardware devices can be attached to a communications channel and used to send data to or receive data from a computer. These devices include terminals; microcomputers, minicomputers, and mainframe computers; and source data automation devices. Communications interface devices, such as multiplexors, concentrators, and front-end processors, allow slow-speed data communications devices to take advantage of high-speed transmission lines.

Data communications systems software is usually more complex than conventional systems software. The software accomplishes several major tasks, including access control, network management, data and file transmission, error detection and control, and data security.

A communications channel connects the sender and receiver in a data communications network. Signals in a data communications system may be analog or digital; serial or parallel; asynchronous or synchronous; simple, half-duplex, or full-duplex. Communications channels are classified according to their information-carrying capacity: narrowband, voiceband, and wideband. Data communications devices can be connected with coaxial cables, standard telephone lines, fiber optics cables, terrestrial microwave systems, satellites, or cellular radios. Three voice-grade telephone line services are available: leased lines, switched lines, and WATS lines. Communications channels may be configured in three basic ways: point to point, multidrop, and line sharing.

Communications channels link a variety of hardware devices to form a communications network. The networks can take one of the following forms: centralized, decentralized, or distributed data processing. A DDP network can have a ring, star, bus, hierarchical, or hybrid topology. There are several different types of networks: local area networks, wide area networks, value-added networks, and PBX and ISDN telephone networks.

There are many different computer-based message systems, including fax, electronic mail, voice mail, and teleconferencing. Groupware is an especially popular use of teleconferencing.

This chapter discussed several uses of data communications: transportation and travel reservations, banking (including electronic funds transfer), retail sales, sales order processing, and electronic data interchange. EDI is fast becoming a common means by which businesses exchange transaction data.

KEY TERMS
Define the following.

data communications networks	message	protocol
data communications	modem	communications channel
centralized data processing system	baud rate	digital
	multiplexor	analog
distributed data processing system	front-end processor (FEP)	serial transmission
	communications software	parallel transmission

asynchronous transmission
synchronous transmission
simplex channel
half-duplex channel
full-duplex channel
bandwidths
narrowband lines
voiceband lines
leased lines
switched line
WATS line
broadband lines
coaxial cable
fiber optics cable
terrestrial microwave
satellite
cellular radio
point-to-point lines
multidrop lines
line-sharing device
communications network
node

centralized network
decentralized system
distributed data processing
   (DDP)
ring network
star network
network switching
bus network
hierarchical network
hybrid network
downsizing
local area network (LAN)
site license
gateway
router
server
file server
client/server
ethernet
token ring
wide area network (WAN)
common carriers

value-added network (VAN)
public data bases
bulletin board system (BBS)
time-sharing service
service bureau
private branch exchange (PBX)
integrated services digital network (ISDN)
facsimile (fax) transmission
electronic mail (E-mail)
voice mail (V-mail)
teleconferencing
audio teleconferencing
video conferencing
computer conferencing
groupware
electronic funds transfer
PIN (personal identification
   number)
electronic data interchange
   (EDI)

Discussion questions

6.1 At some future date all households and merchants may possess a microcomputer that serves as an on-line terminal to a communitywide data communications computer system. Discuss some of the ways members of a household might use such a system. How could they use the microcomputer on a stand-alone basis?

6.2 Communication is vital to any organization. It is especially vital to a multidivisional company that is spread over a wide geographic area. Corporate structure is often aligned along communication lines. Discuss the organizational structure that might conform to the star, ring, or hybrid network configuration. Could organizational difficulties arise if an improper configuration were chosen?

6.3 Public data bases are increasingly popular. They are used by accountants, doctors, lawyers, and other professional and private groups. Public data base systems are changing the way people think about information. Some people feel that data bases will eventually replace books and libraries. Discuss the extent to which you feel public data base sys-

tems will replace traditional information-gathering techniques. Also, discuss the implications of rapid information retrieval.

6.4 Discuss how a data communications system might be usefully applied within the following organizations.

a. A university
b. A life insurance company
c. A hospital
d. A construction company

6.5 Scott Parry is not sure whether or not he should implement a centralized, decentralized, or distributed data processing system. He has asked you to briefly define and list the advantages and disadvantages for each approach. He has also asked you to outline the special control factors required in a distributed processing system. Prepare a one-page memo that summarizes the information Scott needs.   (SMAC Examination, adapted)

6.6 Corporate America is using tools such as electronic mail and computer bulletin boards to improve communications and reduce paperwork. For instance, Microsoft Corporation is run largely through a computer network linked to its over 5000 employees. Decisions of all types are announced through the network, and any employee is free to send a message to Microsoft's Chairman William Gates.

Motorola recently announced a nationwide service that allows laptop and palmtop computer users to use radio waves to receive up to 56 E-mail messages at one time. Radio waves and satellites are used to send the message from the sender's location to the recipient's computer. If the recipient's computer is off, it will store the incoming messages until they can be read.[1]

Why is E-mail growing exponentially in popularity? How is it changing the face of corporate business? What advantages will remote E-mail provide for businesses? What potential problems could arise from the use of computer communication networks?

6.7 Downsizing computer applications is a recent trend among organizations, as exemplified by the Industrial Bank of Japan's Los Angeles branch. High maintenance costs and limited applications are forcing the bank to abandon its outdated Hitachi mainframe in favor of a network handled with a 486 server. Integrating the new network system was painless. Within weeks the network system was installed at about a tenth of the cost of a mainframe with similar capabilities. "You just can't justify those costs anymore when you compare it to a client/server environment," says Paul Bryant, Systems Administrator. Since its implementation, the network has only gone down once and was restored in less than one hour. According to Bryant, "Being a bank, we're extremely concerned with performance, reliability, and security. [The network system] has more than met our needs."[2]

What is downsizing? How are downsizing trends affecting the use of network applications? What advantages do client/server systems provide over traditional mainframe applications?

Problems

6.1 The management of Cross Country Company is currently considering a change from centralized data processing to either decentralized or distributed data processing.

Required

a. Briefly define each of the following:
1. Centralized data processing
2. Decentralized data processing
3. Distributed data processing

b. Each of these data processing approaches has advantages and disadvantages when compared with one or both of the other two approaches. Match the advantages and disadvantages in column 2 with the processing approaches shown in column 1. The items in column 2 may be used more than once. (SMAC Examination, adapted)

Column 1	Column 2
Processing Approaches	Advantages or Disadvantages
1. Centralized	a. Reduces the risk of loss or destruction to hardware and critical data
2. Decentralized	b. Gives no opportunity for a distributed network
3. Distributed	c. Depends on one computer
	d. Permits the use of the data base approach and minimizes the duplication of common data
	e. Makes maintaining the overall security of data difficult
	f. Provides no method for coordinating or exchanging data during processing

6.2 The directors of Colorgraph Printing are reviewing a proposal to acquire Puball Publishers. Puball's operations are located in an urban area about 300 miles from Colorgraph's headquarters.

---

[1] *Source:* Ellis Booker, "Motorola to Provide Remote E-Mail," *Computerworld* (November 4, 1991): 18.

[2] *Source:* Karyl Scott, "NetWare on Downsizing Fast Track," *InfoWorld* (February 10, 1992): S61–S64.

Colorgraph's success in recent years, according to its management, has been due in large part to its computerized management information system. Puball, however, has used a computer only for financial accounting applications such as payroll and inventory records.

In considering the acquisition, Colorgraph's Board of Directors focused on two options for developing a computerized management information system that would include Puball: (1) a centralized system or (2) a distributed system.

Required

a. Indicate how intelligent terminals or microcomputers may be used with a centralized system, a distributed system, or with both types of systems.

b. Compare the degree of information detail likely to be transmitted from a site location to headquarters in a centralized system and in a distributed system.

c. Explain briefly why Puball's management would be more likely to be involved in and concerned with data processing in a distributed system than in a centralized system. Assume Puball would be organized as a separate profit center.

d. Explain briefly why a distributed system would be less subject to a complete system breakdown. (CIA Examination, adapted)

6.3 The Illinois Wholesale Liquor Corporation utilizes a real-time invoicing, inventory, and accounts receivable system. All sales orders are received in a central sales order department, where they are entered into the system by clerks utilizing CRT terminals. The system immediately transmits a shipping order to one of several warehouses, each of which has a teleprinter on-line to the system to receive these orders. It also prepares six copies of a customer invoice for each order and updates accounts receivable and finished goods master files. The firm's Vice-President of Finance utilizes a CRT terminal for an occasional inquiry into the system. Periodic reports generated by the system include an inventory reorder report (daily) and an accounts receivable aging schedule (monthly).

Required

Prepare a systems flowchart of the system.

6.4 The Widget Manufacturing Company is planning to install a LAN at its San Francisco regional sales office that will be on-line to its computer center in Los Angeles 400 miles away. One decision that must be made is whether to lease a line, obtain a

WATS line, or use switched public lines. The monthly cost of a leased line includes a service charge of $83.50 plus mileage charges based on the following rates.

In the computation of total monthly mileage charges using these rates a separate calculation is needed for each individual mileage segment, with the results then added to obtain a total cost. For example, a line of 300 miles includes a fixed cost of $83.50 plus mileage charges of $2.82(100) + $1.48(150) + $0.79(50), for a total of $627.00 per month.

Mileage	Rate/Mile
0–100	$2.82
101–250	$1.48
251–300	$0.79
Over 300	$0.26

The charge for a WATS line includes $30.50 per month for the service charge plus $18 per hour for the monthly use charge. Public telephone rates are $0.57 for the first minute and $0.34 for each additional minute. Estimated time for entering a transaction over the terminal will average two minutes.

Required

a. Compute the monthly cost of the leased line.

b. At what average monthly volume of transactions will the total cost of the leased line be equal to the cost of using (1) the WATS line and (2) the switched public lines? (Make each computation separately.)

c. Assume that an average volume of 810 transactions per month is expected. Which of the three alternatives will be least expensive? Show all supporting calculations.

d. Assume that the transactions will be entered in groups of three so that the extra rate for the first minute will be avoided for two-thirds of all transactions if switched public lines are used. How will this step affect your answer to part c?

6.5 The Texas Machinery Distributing Company, a wholesaler of a variety of machinery products, has its headquarters and a central warehouse in Houston, Texas. Sales offices are located in Dallas, Waco, Austin, San Antonio, Laredo, Corpus Christi, and Abilene. The company has decided to install a real-time data communications system for processing sales orders. The computer center is located in Houston, and one or more microcomputers that will also function as terminals will be located in each sales office.

A major concern of the company in the design of a real-time system is the cost of the data communications network. The company is considering four alternative configurations:

1. Seven voice-grade leased lines, from Houston to each sales office
2. A wideband line from Houston to Austin and a communications processor in Austin to service six voice-grade leased lines from the other six sales offices
3. Dial-up service from each sales office to Houston
4. A wideband line from Houston to Austin and a communications processor in Austin to service dial-up lines from the other six sales offices

Monthly cost figures for voice-grade leased lines follow.

Mileage	Rate/Mile
0–50	$2.20
51–150	$1.40
Over 150	$1.05

There is a monthly charge of $98.50 for each voice-grade line.

Monthly cost figures for wideband leased lines follow.

Mileage	Rate/Mile
0–50	$2.40
51–150	$1.60
Over 150	$1.20

In addition, there is a $165.20 monthly charge for each wideband line. (*Note:* For an explanation of how these rates are used, see problem 6.4.)

The following table shows the distance in miles from Houston to the seven sales offices and from Austin to the other six sales offices.

	Houston	Austin
Waco	181	106
Austin	164	—
Dallas	244	198
San Antonio	195	79
Laredo	312	233
Corpus Christi	208	194
Abilene	349	217

The following table shows the cost of a two-minute long-distance call from Houston to the seven sales offices and from Austin to the other six sales offices.

	Houston	Austin
Waco	$0.88	$0.82
Austin	0.85	—
Dallas	0.91	0.88
San Antonio	0.88	0.76
Laredo	0.94	0.91
Corpus Christi	0.88	0.88
Abilene	0.94	0.91

It is assumed that each call will consume approximately two minutes.

The following table shows the expected average monthly volume of calls from each of the seven sales offices.

Office	Monthly Volume
Waco	200
Austin	450
Dallas	650
San Antonio	500
Laredo	150
Corpus Christi	350
Abilene	200

If either alternative 2 or 4 is chosen, the communications processor will cost $500 per month.

Required

Determine the total monthly cost of the data communications network under each of the four alternatives. Based on cost, which alternative should the company select?

6.6 Classy Videos is a chain of eight video rental stores located in Chicago. Classy rents videocassettes of the most popular movies and VCRs. Each store has between 4000 and 5000 videos in stock, as well as 100 to 150 video machines. Last year, the chain had its best year ever, with rental revenue in excess of $9 million.

Classy Videos rents only to members of the Classy Video Rental Club. A person can become a member by filling out an application and paying a $100 deposit. The company requires the application information and deposit because it has experienced problems with cassettes and machines being stolen by customers. Once a customer has rented items and promptly returned them six times, the $100 deposit is returned.

Each cassette and VCR has its own identification number and checkout card. When club members want to check out a movie or VCR, they select its checkout card from the rental catalog and give the card to a clerk on duty. The clerk then pulls the customer's file and enters the rental information. A club member may also reserve a movie or machine by calling the store and having the clerk pull the identification card. If a store does not have the desired movie in stock, the movie can be acquired on loan from another store.

When Classy Videos consisted of a few stores, the system just described was adequate. Now, however, problems exist. Two of the biggest problems are lost identification cards and lengthy lines of customers waiting for service, especially during peak hours. Additional problems include an inability to determine which movies and VCRs are available for rental and which have been rented, movies and VCRs being checked out to the wrong customers, members finding out that the movie they reserved has been checked out to someone else, and keeping track of transferred inventory.

Classy is in the process of reviewing computer systems that will help solve some of the problems mentioned as well as provide for future expansion. The company is trying to choose among (1) stores connected by dumb terminals to a minicomputer at a central store, (2) microcomputers at each store that can communicate with each other on demand, and (3) microcomputers at each store and a minicomputer at a control store.

Required

a. Identify the hardware needed for each approach, and explain the advantages and disadvantages of each of the three alternatives.

b. Select the configuration that you feel will best meet Classy's needs, and support your decision.

c. Irrespective of your decision in part b, draw and label the configuration for option 3.

d. Describe the files that Classy will need to maintain in order to store the information it needs.

e. Would a computer system solve all of Classy Video's problems? Explain why or why not.

6.7 The Savings Bank of California (SBC) is a large bank headquartered in Los Angeles. A strong selling point for the bank is a customer's ability to conduct his or her banking at offices throughout the state. SBC has regional offices in San Diego, Orange County, southern Los Angeles, northern Los Angeles, and San Francisco. Each region consists of between five and eight local banks.

SBC has established its own statewide real-time computer system. Each regional office maintains a

data base for its local savings, checking, and loan customers. This data base can be accessed by the banks in that particular region, by other regional offices, and by corporate headquarters. Each local bank has 4 to 12 terminals that tie into a minicomputer. The minicomputers at each local bank are linked directly to computers located at SBC's regional offices. The lines between the local banks and the regional offices have fairly heavy use because of the number of transactions handled each day by the banks. Each regional computer is tied to two other regional computers, so that if one computer goes down, information can be rerouted around the computer that is down. In addition to being tied to two other regional computers, each regional computer is tied directly to a mainframe computer at corporate headquarters.

Both the regional computers and the headquarters mainframe use front-end processors to help manage the data communications process. The regional computers are used during the day to process checks, bank card payments, and other transactions to customer accounts. Periodically during the day the regional computers update the mainframe data bases for the transactions processed during the day. The mainframe computer at corporate headquarters coordinates the activities of the regional computers and maintains SBC's companywide records. The headquarters mainframe also handles all funds transfers with the bank's office in New York. Communication between corporate headquarters and the New York office is through microwave transmission.

When a customer goes to a local bank, the teller, through a terminal, uses the local bank's minicomputer to access the regional computer data base. If the customer is a member of the region, his or her account is updated for the transaction. If the customer's account is not maintained by the local region, the correct regional data base is accessed and updated. Funds from the local region are then transferred from or to the accessed region to cover the transaction.

Required

a. What type of communications network is SBC using: centralized, decentralized, DDP, LAN, VAN, PBX, or ISDN? Explain your answer, stating how you know that the other networks are not what SBC is using.

b. Draw the communications network configuration used by SBC. Is this network a star, ring, hybrid, or hierarchical network?

c. What kinds of communications channels can SBC use in its data communications system?

d. The communications channels that connect the local banks and the regional offices can be either point to point, multidrop, or line sharing. When is each most appropriate, and what are the advantages and drawbacks of each?

e. Should the channels that connect the local banks and the regional centers be narrowband, voiceband, or wideband?

6.8 The corporate office of Chancy's Inc., located in Portland, Oregon, handles the billings, collections, accounting, and projections for the company. Currently, all computer processing is done on the company's mainframe computer using terminals. Because of the heavy demands placed on the system, it is often overtaxed. Users sometimes have to wait in long queues to gain access. Once the system has been accessed, response time is often slow because of the number of jobs being run on the mainframe. This overloading causes the system to periodically malfunction. The malfunctions and poor response time have had a negative effect on company productivity; for example, billings are often late, and the collection process is very slow.

The company has purchased a number of microcomputers in the past few years in an attempt to improve productivity. The micros have allowed Chancy's people to significantly increase the quality of their projections, forecasts, and other planning tools. The company is currently thinking about installing a LAN that would allow users to process and share data locally. It would also allow users to access Chancy's mainframe data base using their personal computers.

Required

a. What is the advantage of installing a LAN?

b. What risks would the company be taking by installing a LAN?

c. What controls should Chancy implement to minimize its risk?

6.9 For each of the cases described, first diagram the configuration described, and then determine the following.

1. Whether the configuration is a centralized, decentralized, or distributed processing system

2. Whether a star, ring, hierarchical, or hybrid configuration is used

3. Whether the lines used in the configuration are point to point, multidrop, or line sharing

a. Mountain West Milk Producers process milk and milk products for consumers in Utah. The association's headquarters is in downtown Salt Lake City. Milk is processed at a plant 10 miles west of downtown. Ice cream is made 30 miles south of Salt Lake City, and cheese is cured 60 miles north of Salt Lake City.

Each morning, drivers collect raw milk from the association's milk producers and transport it to storage tanks at the processing plant. Information on the amount of milk collected and the amount of fat content is keyed into the processing plant's microcomputer. The types of products produced, their cost, sales data, and transfers are also kept on the micro. The processing plant prints out daily reports to meet its information needs. Similar information is also collected at the ice cream and cheese processing plants.

The information from the three locations is transferred by modem to a front-end processor linked to the mainframe computer at company headquarters. The information gathered is stored on disk and used by headquarters to prepare payroll, invoices, payment checks to milk producers, and financial statements.

b. The Nevada Department of Motor Vehicles (DMV) has an office in the state capital and offices in each major city in the state to register motor vehicles and license drivers. The capital office has a number of microcomputers that are linked to a front-end processor. Upon receipt of a registration form in the mail, processing clerks at the state office use the vehicle's serial number to update the vehicle record in the DMV's data base. As people come in to the local offices to be licensed or to register their vehicles, the clerks use the micro to update the local division data base. At the end of each working day the capital's mainframe pulls the day's update information from the division minicomputers and updates the state's data bases. Receipts are printed at both the local and state offices and given or mailed to the appropriate people.

Besides being linked to the capital mainframe, the local minicomputers are linked to the computers of two other divisions. As a result, all the division minis are linked together to provide quicker access to local information as well as to provide system backup. Computerization of the system has helped state, county, and local police to quickly obtain driver's license and registration information. These agencies are tied by modem to the local and state data bases.

c. Rollo Community Bank in Rollo, North Dakota, is an independently held and operated bank. The bank makes business, car, farm, and mortgage loans. Because of its close proximity to the Canadian border, the bank handles currency exchanges for a small fee. The bank employs three officers and seven tellers. The tellers operate five terminals that are tied to a minicomputer. The tellers handle all monies coming into or going out of the bank. The three officers have access to the minicomputer through the terminals but do not have the authorization to conduct transactions. When the loan officer approves a loan, the debtor presents the loan papers to a teller, who issues a check for the loan amount. The bank also uses the minicomputer to communicate with a currency exchange data base in New York. Up-to-date exchange rate information is vital, especially in times of rapid currency rate fluctuation.

d. Luxury Cars International is a worldwide manufacturer and distributor of automobiles headquartered in Kansas City. Its U.S. operations include 4 production plants, 20 regional warehouses, and 300 franchise distributors. The company's production efforts are driven by demand, so accurate distribution information is vital to ensure proper inventory levels.

The franchise dealerships keep their inventory records on a microcomputer. Car orders are generated in two ways: (1) a customer makes a special order for an automobile that the dealer does not have in stock, or (2) the dealer estimates the demand for makes and models, compares this demand with inventory levels, and generates orders as needed. The dealerships are tied by modem to a minicomputer at a regional warehouse. When the dealer has a special order, the microcomputer is used to access the regional data base. This data base stores the warehouse inventory as well as the inventory levels of dealerships in the region. If the desired car is not in the regional data base, an order is sent to a minicomputer in St. Louis that controls inventory for the entire company. This computer polls the other regional computers to try to find the desired car. If the desired car is found, the computer decides whether it is better to have the car transferred to the desired location or to special-order the car. If the decision is

to have the car transferred, the appropriate regional warehouse is notified.

If a special order is to be placed, the computer in St. Louis calls a minicomputer in Chicago that controls production for the company. The production computer then forwards the order to the plant that makes the desired car, and the order is processed. Each of the four plants makes a different line of automobiles. The plants use a mainframe computer to process the order requests and to control the production process. A regular order (nonspecial order) is processed in the same fashion, except that the other dealerships in the region and the other regions are not scanned.

The franchises periodically forward summary data to the regional minicomputer, which summarizes them and produces regional reports. The various regions pass summary-level information to the St. Louis minicomputer that coordinates the company's inventory. There the data are summarized, and corporate-level sales and inventory reports are produced. The production plant computers produce information to help production plant management. They also send summary-level information to the computer in Chicago, which summarizes the data and produces corporate-level production reports. The Chicago and St. Louis computers pass information to the headquarters computer in Kansas City, which prepares corporate financial statements.

6.10 Luana's Clothing Distribution, Inc., has installed a mainframe computer at its headquarters building. All 12 branch offices will be linked to the mainframe and have access to the company's online data base. The diagram that follows shows the locations of the branches with respect to the corporate headquarters. The headquarters mainframe is labeled by HQB in the diagram. Branch locations are labeled BR and the branch number.

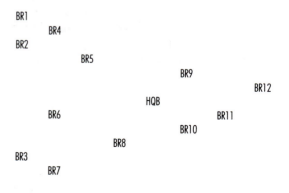

Required

a. Join the various branch locations to form a centralized computer network with each of the following configurations. Assume that the branch locations are using terminals.

1. Point to point
2. Multidrop
3. Multiplexed or line sharing

b. Assume that one of the branches in each of the three clusters has a minicomputer and the others have a microcomputer. Each cluster will have its own distributed processing system. Draw this distributed processing system using the following configurations.

1. Star   2. Ring   3. Hybrid

6.11 The past two decades has witnessed a transition from a centralized mainframe computer environment to a distributed network, where an organization has the ability to share computer processing. One of the fastest-growing segments of the computer industry is LAN, which is said to be the wave of the future. LANs permit the transfer of information between microcomputers, word processors, data storage devices, printers, voice devices, and telecommunication devices. Current opinion states that the flow of organizational communications has been enhanced by the transition from the optimization of computers experienced in the traditional distributed network to the optimization of human resources in the LAN environment.

Required

a. Describe the reasons why an organization would choose a distributed network over the traditional centralized computer environment.

b. Compare and contrast the characteristics of a traditional distributed computer network with those of a LAN as they relate to the following.

1. Utilization of computer hardware.
2. User interaction and the sharing of electronic information

c. Identify and explain three problems that can result from the use of LANs.

d. Explain the hardware characteristics associated with a computer modem as it relates to distributed information processing.

(CMA Examination, adapted)

6.12 An integrated services digital network (ISDN) found an experimental home in an unlikely location: Harrah's Hotel and Casino in Reno, Nevada. Using ISDN technology, Harrah's hoped to speed a customer's hotel checkin so that the customer would be free to immediately go to the gambling tables.

The system they installed works like this: Upon reaching the Reno International Airport, a Harrah's customer goes to a kiosk in the airport lobby and uses a screen menu to enter a request for a room. A hotel clerk appears on a large monitor and converses with the customer. The customer communicates with the clerk using a telephone attached to the kiosk. Payment for the room is made by credit card using a magnetic card reader. A camera in the kiosk takes a picture of the customer, which is faxed through the network to the hotel. The doorman, with fax in hand, then greets the customer personally at the door, hands him a key to his room, and takes the customer's bags. This advance checkin is designed to save customers time and allow them to proceed straight to the casino.

The process rarely worked—but not because of the technology. The system scared people. Only about 10 people of the 70 or 80 a day that tried to use the kiosk were not frightened away. The rest of the customers who activated the system ran away as soon as the hotel clerk appeared on the screen. Since the system could not be cost-justified for only 10 people a day, it was finally removed.

However, Harrah's management remains convinced that ISDN technology is still the wave of the future. Sometime in the next few years it expects to try other uses of the technology.[3]

Required

a. What is ISDN? What do developers hope to accomplish with it?

b. What advantages can ISDN provide over traditional communications devices? What are the drawbacks of ISDN technology? How can users respond to these problems?

c. Discuss three potential applications for ISDN technology in business.

---

[3] *Source:* Alan Radding, "Small Wagers Can Pay Off, But Don't Bet the Farm," *Computerworld* (November 20, 1989): 85–91.

CASE 6.1: ANYCOMPANY, INC.—AN ONGOING COMPREHENSIVE CASE

One of the best ways to learn is to immediately apply what you have studied. The purpose of this case is to allow you to do that. You will select a local company that you can work with. At the end of most chapters you will find an assignment that will have you apply what you have learned using the company you have selected as a reference. This case, then, may become an ongoing case study that you work on throughout the term.

Once you have lined up a company, perform the following steps.

1.   Successful businesses use data communications tools to improve productivity and increase the flow of information in an organization. Using your selected company, gather the following information.

a.   What is the general structure of the company's data communications network? Is processing and control centralized, decentralized, or distributed? Why?

b.   Identify the data communications hardware and software the company employs.

c.   Identify the data communications channels the company uses by determining what the principal characteristics of each channel are and what channel configurations are used.

d.   Identify any network systems by determining what local area networks (LANs) the company utilizes, how they are configured, what servers are used to regulate the systems, and what other networks the company employs.

e.   What other data communications applications does the company employ? How do these applications assist the company in carrying on business?

2.   Develop a comprehensive diagram of the data communications systems employed by your company.

a.   Identify general strengths and weaknesses of the systems.

b.   Discuss any recommendations aimed at improving the existing systems.

CASE 6.2: J.C. PENNEY

With respect to information technology, the retail firm of J.C. Penney is on the leading edge. For the past 20 years J.C. Penney has been hard at work innovating and updating computer technology in all stores to improve efficiency and to create a competitive advantage. It seems that the strategy has paid off. Steady sales growth and the maximization of revenue per employee has made J.C. Penney a leader in retail sales.

The reasons for Penney's success with technology begins at the top. Management has made the implementation of technology a top priority in order to give the retail chain an edge against the competition. Better end-user technology has reduced the demands upon the MIS staff, allowing Penney to reduce the number of staff. Remaining MIS personnel focus their efforts on developing custom applications for Penney and providing technical backup for end-user applications.

J.C. Penney has further honed its information strategy over the past years in the following ways.

■ *Network applications:* Penney was one of the earliest adopters of the IBM System Network Architecture (SNA) and remains a firm believer in networks and distributed processing. The network was conceived to operate as a utility so that end-users can access the network from virtually anywhere. In a given year the national network handles 350 million credit authorizations and 300 million transactions a year. Custom software secures the network and a built-in, menu-driven interface allows first-time users easy access throughout the system. The network also provides access to a variety of corporate information including stock quote data, office automation software, and development tools.

■ *POS systems:* Using optical character recognition (OCR) devices, Penney monitors every piece of inventory from purchase to final sale. On a given day a store's transactions are stored on a computer for nightly transmission to a host processor in one of Penney's six major data centers, where the information is assimilated and returned within 24 hours. This information is invaluable in helping Penney discern changing consumer trends in regional areas. With such information Penney can respond instantly by redirecting warehouse merchandise to profitable regions and by directing the efforts of corporate buyers.

■ *EDI:* Penney relies upon electronic data interchange (EDI) to handle transactions with over two hundred suppliers. On a daily basis suppliers can dial into the Penney system and access orders for delivery the following morning. Use of EDI saves Penney time and money by eliminating a host of manual procedures.

■ *Corporate TV:* Using corporate teleconferencing, Penney maintains the largest business TV network of any U.S. retailer. Prior to the start of a new buying season corporate buyers select their seasonal lines. Using corporate TV, the corporate buyers then display their products for selection by store buyers, who choose merchandise for their local store using a corporate computer program.

■ *Strategic applications:* Penney uses expert systems in its catalog telemarketing sector. Penney employs 4000 operators in 14 centers to handle telephone orders. During peak hours the pace is intense. An expert system assists operators by redirecting telephone calls from busy operators to those that are free.

■ *Software development:* With routine tasks handled by end users the MIS staff is free to devote time to custom applications and software development. With prototyping methods software development is very successful. The MIS staff reports that they've never had to spend millions of dollars to implement and then scrap a project.

■ *Productivity center:* A final key to Penney's success is a center designed for the benefit of all end users. The productivity center is a place where employees can come to address end-user problems and tinker with new software. Staffers assist end users by answering questions and addressing specific user problems.[4]

1.   Why is an information strategy important? How can an effective information strategy create competitive advantage for Penney? Why do you think Penney has been so successful in implementing its strategy?

2.   Discuss the various information system strategies employed by Penney in terms of the information provided and how the strategy contributes to the success of the business.

3.   What role does the MIS staff play in the strategy? What are the advantages of such a strategy?

---

[4] *Source:* Alan Alper and James Daly, "Penney Cashes in on Leading Edge," *Computerworld* (June 20, 1988): 1, 61–63.

Case 6.3: A Move to Cooperative Computing

TO: All Department Heads, Student
           Affairs
FROM: Jim Brady, Network Applications
           Division
DATE: January 7, 199X
SUBJECT: Unification of Department Servers

Recent trends toward centralizing network applications are changing the way networks are employed in meeting business needs. Network operating systems are becoming more powerful, allowing a single server to accommodate more users. Managing a LAN is now a full-time responsibility as additional services become essential. Finally, as networks are employed in more serious applications, organizationwide standards are needed to regulate data integrity, security, and reliability.

The Role of the Student Affairs Division

As you know, the student affairs division provides a number of student services through several departments, including career planning, job placement, student employment, counseling, and testing. When networks were introduced in 198X, each department established an autonomous network to handle departmental information. As time has passed, these individual networks have expanded to the point where they do not operate very efficiently. To handle the problem, we propose the use of a single server for all of the network applications in the division.

A Single-Server System

Our recommendation is to install a single-server system to meet the needs of the entire division. Such a system will provide several advantages, including the following:

- End users will see improved performance with the use of more advanced 486-based server technology.

- A single server will allow the LAN administrator to focus efforts on improving network applications and developing new network services.

- The switch will bring significant cost savings in the long run, with a greater variety of applications.

Implementation

Implementing the plan will require the cooperation of all department heads as well as a number of support organizations.

- We want to get your old servers out as soon as possible so that we can install the new server immediately.

- Implementation of the single-server system will begin in September, with installation scheduled for completion in two weeks.

Conclusion

Our division's evolution from mainframes to minis to PCs to networks represents a shift from centralized to decentralized to cooperative computing. Implementing the single server for our division is a step in the right direction and will require your full support. Thank you.[5]

1.   As a department head, how would you evaluate Jim Brady's suggestion to integrate department servers into a single division server?

   a.   What are the risks of such an approach?

---

[5] *Source:* Dave Molta, ''Save Time, Energy and Money: Consolidate Your Servers,'' *Network Computing* (August 1991): 85–86.

b. What are the advantages of a single server?

c. What concerns do you have over the implementation of the new server?

d. Do you support this idea? Why?

2. Discuss the evolution of computing from centralized systems to cooperative systems. Is this consistent with national trends? Which approach do you think is best? Why?

3. Why is network computing considered by many as "cooperative computing"? Why are network systems increasing in popularity?

4. How do network configurations fit in with general changes in organizational structure and management style?

CHAPTER 7

Data Base Systems

LEARNING OBJECTIVES

After studying this chapter, you should be able to:

- Compare and contrast the file-oriented and data base approaches to data storage.
- Explain the difference between the logical and physical views of data.
- Explain what a data base management system (DBMS) is, what it does, and what it is composed of.
- Compare and contrast DBMS functions and users.
- Compare and contrast various file and data base organization and access methods.
- Explain how a relational data base operates.
- Explain the role of accountants in data base design.
- Explain the impact of data base systems on accounting.

INTEGRATIVE CASE: S&S, INC.

Susan Anderson is frustrated. Over the past few years she has spent a great deal of time managing the four stores that she and Scott opened. She has just gotten the sales figures for October and sales are down at three of the four stores for the third month in a row. Although she cannot put her finger on the data just now, she thinks sales are down in comparison with sales over the last two years as well. Things do not look good, and she is trying to figure out what is wrong and what she can do to reverse the trend by increasing sales.

For example, the stores ran a special promotion in October on televisions, and her impression is that it was not as successful as other promotions have been in the past. She believes that if she is able to compare the TV promotion with prior promotions, she can get some answers. But the problem is that the data she needs just aren't available in the form she needs them. Each store processes its accounting data using the Great Plains software. But the software doesn't provide some of the information she needs to make strategic decisions—information such as individual customer tastes and preferences, special discounts and promotions run by S&S's numerous suppliers, and national economic trends that affect purchasing patterns. Another problem is that the information from the individual stores is not being effectively combined and summarized.

Susan's thoughts are interrupted by a telephone call. It's an old friend, Denise Ainge, who has made several recent purchases. She is having problems with one of the appliances and has a question about her account. Denise does not have the invoice number of the sale and only knows she bought the appliance in October. Susan knows it will take time to track down the appropriate invoice. Since she has a meeting in just a few minutes with Scott and Ashton, she tells Denise she will have one of her staff call her back after they have found the information needed to answer her question.

During the meeting with Scott and Ashton, Susan expresses her frustrations and wants to know how S&S can gather and store the types of data she needs. She wants to be able to compare the performances of the monthly promotions. Susan explains her experience with Denise Ainge and says that she wants that type of information available and at her fingertips, instead of having to search for it and then return a phone call. In addition, she is sure that in the future she will have other information needs, and she wants to be able to ask a variety of unstructured questions to meet those needs.

Ashton thinks that many of Susan's needs can be met with data base software and explains what he knows about it to Scott and Susan. Scott comments that he has heard that relational data bases are very popular. Susan asks Ashton to investigate data bases and her need for information. She asks him to find information relating to the following questions:

1. How can S&S store the data it needs and make it readily available to those who need it?

2. What data base software is available for a network of microcomputers?

3. What is a relational data base, and how does it work?

4. What factors does a company need to consider in designing and using a data base? ■

INTRODUCTION

An accounting information system is designed to produce information for a wide variety of users. These users need information for record keeping, planning and evaluation, and decision making. To produce this information, an organization must process and store records of the events, activities, and transactions that occur. Thus the management and storage of data is one of the most critical functions of an accounting information system.

Accountants have a significant role to play in the data management and storage process. For example, they must interact with systems analysts to help the organization answer questions such as the following: What data should be stored by the organization, and who should have access to them? Which data storage approach should be used: manual, file-based, or data base? How should the data be organized, updated, stored, accessed, and retrieved? How can both scheduled and unanticipated information needs be met? To answer these questions and others like them, accountants must understand the data management and storage concepts explained in this chapter.

The first section of this chapter compares the file-oriented and the data base approaches to data storage. The section emphasizes the shortcomings of the file-oriented approach and the advantages of the data base approach. The second section looks at the software that makes the data base approach possible and the people who typically use data base systems. The third section discusses tree and network data structures. The fourth section discusses the most important type of data base organization, the relational data base. Finally, the last two sections discuss the role of accountants in data base design and the potential impact of data base systems on accounting.

THE FILE-ORIENTED APPROACH VERSUS THE DATA BASE APPROACH

Many companies have developed their information systems piecemeal by adding new applications as the need arises. These new application programs were designed to meet the specialized needs of a limited number of users. The result is a proliferation of individual computer applications and a significant increase in the number of master files required to support their data storage needs. The data thus stored "belong" to, and are managed by, the department or organizational entity that created it, and each set of files is independent of every other set. This approach is known as the file-oriented approach.

As the number of applications and master files increased, organizations recognized the need for a data storage approach that was oriented toward the organization as a whole. The data base approach views data as organizational resources that should be used by and managed for the entire organization, not just the creating department or function. This is achieved by combining related application files into larger "pools" of data, which can then be accessed by many different application programs. A data base is a set of interrelated, centrally coordinated data files. The data in the data base are independent of both the computer

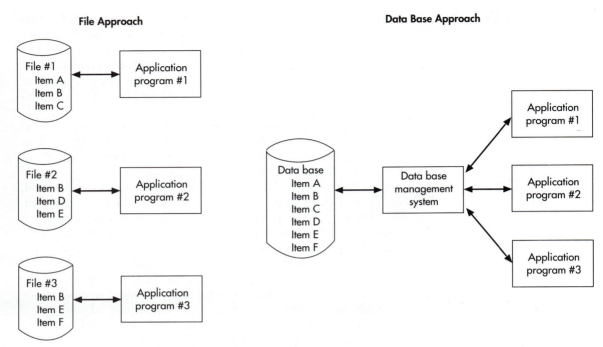

Figure 7.1
File-oriented approach versus
data base approach

programs using them and the secondary storage devices in which they are stored. An example is an employee data base that consolidates data formerly segregated in separate files, such as a payroll file, a personnel file, and a job skills file. Figure 7.1 illustrates the differences between the file-oriented approach to data processing and the data base approach.

The specialized computer program that manages and controls the data and interfaces between the data and the application programs is the **data base management system (DBMS)**. The combination of the data base, the DBMS, and the application programs that access the data base through the DBMS is the **data base system**. The person responsible for creating, updating, maintaining, and controlling the data base is the **data base administrator (DBA)**.

Logical and Physical View of Data

Most file-oriented data storage techniques require the programmer to know the actual physical location and layout of the data records used in the application program. Figure 7.2 shows a **record layout** of an accounts receivable file. Suppose that a programmer needs to produce a credit report showing the customer number, credit limit, and current balance. To write the program, the programmer must usually understand the technical characteristics of the hardware, how the data are stored, the location of the fields needed for the report (i.e., record positions 1 through 10 for customer number), the length of each field, the format of each field (alphanumeric or numeric), and so forth. The process becomes more complex if the programmer needs to access several files to obtain the data needed for the report.

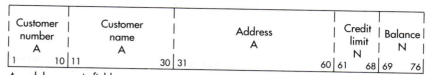

Customer number A	Customer name A		Address A	Credit limit N	Balance N
1 10	11 30	31	60	61 68	69 76

Figure 7.2
Accounts receivable file record layout

A = alphanumeric field
N = numeric field

Data base systems overcome this problem by separating the storage of data elements from the use of those data elements. In other words, the data base provides two separate views of the data: the physical view and the logical view. Figure 7.3 shows accounts receivable data and the two views of the data.

The **logical view** is the way users conceptually organize, view, and understand the relationships between data items. When a system supports a logical view of data, users can access, make queries of, or update the data stored in the customer data base without reference to how or where the data are stored. With the data base approach, a user can produce the monthly statement in Fig. 7.3 without understanding the details of how the data on the report are physically stored. The user or analyst is responsible only for defining the logical data requirements of the application.

Separating how data are used from how they are stored and accessed means that users can change their logical view (the data items needed) without making changes in the physical view (the physical storage of the data). Likewise, the data base administrator can change the physical storage of the data without the user's having to change the application programs.

A model of the overall logical organization of a data base is referred to as the conceptual **schema** (plural: *schemata*). The schema describes the types of data elements in the data base (fields, records, files, etc.), the relationships between the data elements, and the structure or overall logical model used to organize and describe the data. A subset

Figure 7.3
Logical and physical views of data in a customer data base

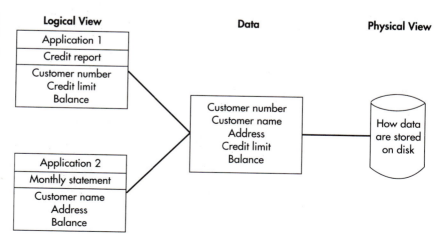

of the schema that includes only those data items used in a particular application program or by a particular user is referred to as a **subschema** (or user schema or view). The subschema is more than just the data items in an application; it is also the way the user defines the data and the data relationships. It is therefore a part of the conceptual schema that defines the entire data base.

The schema for the sales/cash receipts cycle for S&S, for example, would contain data about customers, sales, cash receipts, salespersons, cash, and inventory. From a given schema several subschemata may be derived—one for each of the programs or queries that access the data base. The subschema, or user view, that Susan might use to answer Denise Ainge's question would include the data about customers and sales. The subschema that Susan would use to analyze monthly promotions would include data about sales, salespersons, and inventory.

The **physical view** is bits- and bytes-oriented and refers to how and where data are physically arranged and stored on disks, tapes, and other media. EDP personnel use this view to make efficient use of storage and processing resources. The data base administrator is responsible for physically storing the data in a way that will allow the logical requirements to be met. Programmers and users, however, generally do not need to understand the physical view, since they are only interested in using the data, regardless of how it is stored.

Shortcomings of the File-Oriented Approach

Problems with the file-oriented approach arise when users need information contained in two or more files. If an existing application program cannot provide the information needed, satisfying the information request can be very costly and time-consuming. The inability of the system to meet simple requests for information in such situations can be frustrating to management and other users.

Ashton identified the following shortcomings of the file-oriented approach.

- *Data redundancy:* The same item of data often is stored in more than one place. Duplication is costly and inefficient, and it requires that multiple files be updated each time the duplicated data change.

- *Data inconsistencies:* When duplicate data are stored on separate files, data inconsistencies arise when an item is not updated on all files.

- *Lack of data integration:* Because data are spread over different files, it is difficult to respond to unanticipated information requests on a timely basis without writing a new computer program.

- *Large number of data files:* Each file requires periodic updates, backups, cataloging, and other processing. Data organization and management often becomes time-consuming and expensive.

- *Program/data dependence:* File-oriented programs typically contain references to the specific format and location of data stored on files.

Changes to the data usually require that changes be made to all programs that use the files. Thus program maintenance can consume a significant amount of time.

■ *Lack of data compatibility:* Because each application file is independent, there usually is little standardization of field names or lengths, attribute values, data representation, and so forth.

■ *Lack of data sharing:* This problem occurs when the "owner" of data is unwilling to share the data or when an entity developing a new application is not aware of the data's existence elsewhere in the organization.

Because of its disadvantages, the file-oriented approach is seldom used today for new applications. Instead, most new information systems are developed using the data base approach.

Advantages of the Data Base Approach

In file-oriented systems, generating special-purpose reports involving data from two or more separate applications is difficult because a new computer program has to be written. This can take so long that the report would not be timely or useful. Data base systems have substantially fewer limitations. For example, with a data base system S&S can get quick answers to these questions: "Which appliances are supplied by DE Corporation?" "Which deliveries are past due?" A data base also can be used to identify entities possessing more than one specified attribute. Answers to questions such as "Which employees in the Sales Department speak Spanish?" and "Which vendors supply microwave parts?" fall into this category. These inquiries are possible because the DBMS software is an interface between the data and the inquiry or application program. In other words, the DBMS software is capable of searching and finding the data needed.

The reporting capabilities of a data processing system are substantially enhanced by data base capabilities. Report formats can be revised easily in response to managerial needs. Reports can be generated on an as-needed basis as well as on a regular weekly or monthly schedule. By using the interactive capability of a data base system, a manager can browse through the data base to search for the underlying causes of problems highlighted on an exception report or to obtain detailed information underlying a summary report. The interactive feature of the system also enables the manager to formulate new questions based on the system's response to previous questions.

Data base systems support "cross-functional" data analysis much more readily than file-oriented systems do. Cross-functional analysis is analysis of data relating to different functional areas of the business, such as marketing and accounting. Many data relationships are cross-functional in nature, such as the association between dollar sales and marketing regions, or between selling costs and promotional campaigns. A file-oriented system is typically capable of maintaining only a few such relationships among data elements. In a data base system most or all of these relationships may be explicitly defined and used in the preparation of management reports. A greater variety of reports in terms of content and format is thus possible. Furthermore, the system is more capable of responding to unforeseen managerial requests of an unusual nature that arise on short notice.

Here are some additional advantages of the data base approach:

- *Minimal data redundancy:* Because data items need to be stored only once, unless duplication is necessary to enhance system performance, **data redundancy** is eliminated or minimized.

- *No data inconsistencies:* Since each data item is stored only once, the data inconsistency inherent in file-oriented systems is eliminated.

- *No duplicate processing:* With data stored only once, data only need to be entered once and updated once.

- *Standardized data:* With no duplicate data there is no problem with different data names, field lengths, and formats.

- *Data independence:* Because data are stored independently of the programs that use them, the data base approach provides **data independence**. Application programs need not be aware of the physical details of data storage. This allows the user to concentrate on the use of the data.

- *Lack of data ownership:* When the organization owns the data, no group has special rights over them. They can be shared by all authorized users.

7.1 FOCUS

Chase Data Base Improves Customer Service

Michael Dacey recently had a client call about an obscure company in Finland. It used to take up to a week to research a request of this nature and forward the information to the customer. This time, Dacey was able to answer the request in a few minutes without even leaving his desk. Before the phone call was completed, Dacey had used his desktop system and the Chase Information Exchange (CIX) to retrieve reports on the company from one of Chase Manhattan Bank's data bases, print a hard copy, and fax it to the impressed client. In the late 1980s Chase decided to leave behind the mainframe-based environment of the 1980s. The decision to change was made when Chase realized it had many platforms that didn't communicate and many products that were incompatible. It had data but no information.

In place of the mainframes Chase is installing a desktop-dominated architecture tied to a

- *Central management of data:* A data base administrator is typically responsible for coordinating, controlling, and managing data as a firmwide resource. As a result, data management and coordination usually are more efficient.
- *Security:* Many DBMS software packages have built-in controls that help ensure data integrity. For example, passwords can be used to limit access to authorized users. Security is often better with data bases because a data base administrator ensures the security of the data base.

Focus 7.1 discusses some of the advantages that Chase Manhattan Bank is reaping from data base technology.

Disadvantages of the Data Base Approach

Data bases have disadvantages that make their use inappropriate in certain situations. One disadvantage is the cost of more expensive hardware and software and the highly trained personnel usually required for a data base system. A DBMS adds an additional layer of systems software and increases storage requirements. Data base systems can be difficult to design and implement. Since a DBMS is highly integrated and concentrated, it is more vulnerable to hardware and software failures. In the file-oriented approach the loss of a file affects only a few application programs. In a DBMS loss of the data base renders inoperable all the applications using the data base. Likewise, in a file-oriented system an erroneous update affects only a few programs; in a DBMS it can affect many applications.

---

worldwide network of information. Its new strategy is intended to provide managers with self-sufficiency at the desktop. The intent at Chase is to give employees easy access to information to help them be more competitive and less technophobic. CIX is a key element of the $1.8 million development effort that combined data from a variety of different Chase systems and external news and information sources. After a massive integration effort the information can now be presented to the user on desktop systems in a standard, consistent format.

Chase uses Lotus Notes, a groupware package, for much of its internal communications. Notes also allows widely dispersed locations to work together. Among the many numerous Notes-based applications at the bank are a client-tracking system. The system maintains information on accounts. In addition, an account manager can create a document outlining a recent conversation with a client and pass it to co-workers for their comments. This information can be shared with the client in a later discussion.

The bank is moving toward

Microsoft's Windows environment as its graphical user interface. The Windows selection helps Chase achieve its goal of a consistent, user-friendly front end. The bank will continue with three main desktop operating environments, including Microsoft's DOS, IBM's OS/2, and Unix.

Source: Rosemary Hamilton, "Chase Banks on 'Info' Access," *Computerworld* (January 27, 1992): 6.

Despite these weaknesses, most organizations use data base technology so that they can reap the rewards it offers. Over 90% of all mainframe computer sites were estimated to be using data base technology in the early 1990s. Data base use in microcomputer systems is also growing rapidly. Today, nearly all new computer-based information systems are being implemented with a data base approach.

This section explained the two different approaches to data management and storage. The organization and access methods used in file-oriented systems were explained in Chapter 2. The next section discusses data base management systems in detail.

DATA BASE MANAGEMENT SYSTEMS

Although users may have their own logical view of the data, the system stores the data in only one way. Data base management system (DBMS) software provides the link between the actual organization of the data on file storage media and the various logical views of the data in the minds of the users. In some cases the physical data organization that optimizes data storage factors, such as access time and capacity utilization, may differ from the logical data organization best suited to the needs of data users. Data items such as customer account balance, name, address, and credit history may be stored in separate locations or on separate devices, even though users perceive a close logical relationship between them. It is the responsibility of the DBMS to manage the data base in such a way that users can work effectively with logical sets of data items, without being aware of the complexities involved in the physical organization of those sets of data items. Ideally, to each user, the system should appear to behave as if the data were physically stored in exactly the way that user logically views them.

One of the most significant differences between the processing of traditional files and the processing of data bases is that traditional files are processed by only a small number of programs, each doing its work at a separate time, whereas data bases can be processed by several programs, some working on the same data base concurrently. In this situation errors may be introduced into the data base when different programs attempt to use or modify the same data items simultaneously. Data base management systems must have the capability to deal with multiple concurrent updates.

Most DBMS packages contain a number of different languages and interfaces. Although each package is different, there are some common components of a DBMS, which the next section describes.

DBMS Languages and Interfaces

The **data definition language (DDL)** ties the logical and physical views of the data together. It is used to initialize or create the data base, to describe the schema and each individual subschema, and to describe all the records and fields in the data base. The DDL is also used to specify any security limitations or constraints that are imposed on records or fields in the data base.

The **data manipulation language (DML)** is used to update, replace, store, retrieve, insert, delete, sort, and otherwise manipulate the records and data items in the data base. Because of the DML, a user can accomplish these manipulations by using data names rather than by referring to the physical storage locations of the items. The DML also provides an interface to the programming languages used by the application programmers.

The **data query language (DQL)** is a high-level language used to interrogate the data base. Most DQLs contain a fairly powerful set of commands that are easy to use yet provide a great deal of flexibility. They allow users to satisfy many of their information needs without having to involve an application programmer. An example of a DQL is the Structured Query Language (SQL), a package produced by IBM. Table 7.1 illustrates the SQL language.

The query language is typically available to all users. Use of the data base definition language and the data manipulation language is often confined to the data base administrator and the application programmer, respectively. Restricting these languages to their respective users helps maintain proper control.

Report writers are similar to DQLs. All the users need to do is specify the data elements to be printed and the desired output. The report

Table 7.1
Examples of a data query language

Structured Query Language (SQL) query:

SELECT	NAME,EXPERIENCE
FROM	PER. RECORDS
WHERE	DEPT = DP AND EXPERIENCE > 7
	AND LANGUAGE = SPANISH
ORDER BY	EXPERIENCE,DESC

Sample output:

NAME	EXPERIENCE
Carter, V.	30
Sheide, G.	23
Nielson, G.	21
Wilson, M.	19
McMahon, J.	17
Young, S.	15
Bosco, R.	13
Detmer, T.	8

This query selects (the SELECT command) the fields named Name and Exerience for all records in the file PER.RECORDS (the FROM command) that meet specified criteria (the WHERE command). The stated criteria are that they work in the data processing department, that they have more than 7 years of experience, and that they speak Spanish. The selected fields from the records are printed out in descending order (the ORDER BY and the DESC commands) based on their number of years of experience.

writer searches the data base, extracts the desired items, and prints them out in the user-specified format.

DBMS Functions and Users

The functions of a DBMS may be divided into three broad categories: creation, maintenance, and interrogation. Data base creation includes defining, organizing, and creating the content, relationships, and structure of the data needed to build a data base. Data base maintenance involves adding, deleting, updating, changing, and controlling the data in the data base. Data base interrogation is querying the data base in order to access the data needed to support information retrieval and report generation. The three DBMS functions are related to the three different types of users who typically interact with the data base, as illustrated in Fig. 7.4.

Data Base Administrator. The DBA is responsible for coordinating, controlling, and managing the data in the data base. The DBA can be thought of as the human equivalent of the DBMS. That is, the DBA not only must be aware of users and their data requirements but also must understand how the DBMS operates and how data are stored and processed. In other words, the DBA must understand both the users and the technical data storage side of the system to ensure that the system meets the needs of users.

A DBA has the following major responsibilities:

■ To help establish the data models that describe the relationships among the data used in the organization

■ To establish data standards and specifications

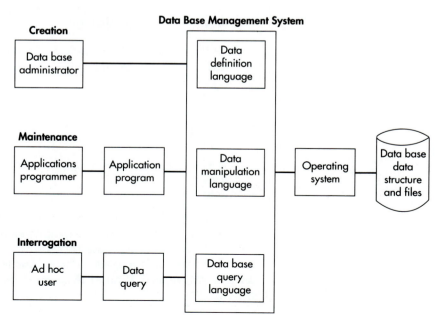

Figure 7.4
Data base users and how they interface with the data base system

- To specify the content, relationships, and structures of the data base
- To provide for creating, updating, and otherwise maintaining the data base
- To approve changes to the data base
- To develop retrieval methods to meet the needs of the data base users
- To specify and maintain the physical structure of the data base
- To maintain a data dictionary
- To provide for adequate control over the data base (The DBA function is itself a form of control, since the responsibility for data is taken from users and programmers and entrusted to the DBA.)

Application Programmers. The programs that process the data stored in the data base are developed by application programmers. **Application programmers** formulate a logical method, or user view, of the data to be processed. Then they write an application program, using a programming language. The application programs interact with the DBMS, which refers to the appropriate subschema to determine the internal physical schema of the data requested. The DBMS requests the operating system to retrieve the required data, and the DBMS then turns them over to the application program for processing. When processing has been completed, the data are turned back to the DBMS, which instructs the operating system to store them.

DBMS software has greatly expanded the ability of application programmers to handle complex data structures. It has also simplified the tasks of application programmers and ad hoc users. As a result, a broader range of timely reports can be produced for users with a smaller investment in programming time and with less difficulty.

Users. Users are those who receive periodic and scheduled reports, who run the application programs written by programmers, or who query the data base as desired. Users who make unscheduled, as-needed inquiries of the data base are often referred to as **ad hoc users**. Ad hoc users can receive an immediate response to their query in the form of a screen display or a printed report formatted to meet their specific needs. Data bases have significantly increased the ease and speed with which users can produce reports. Only a few short statements are needed to get answers to questions about company operations.

The Data Dictionary

A data base system cannot be successfully implemented in an organization unless the implementers have a thorough understanding of the data elements used within the organization, where they come from, and how and by whom they are used. For this reason, taking an inventory of data elements is one of the first steps in the process of implementing a data base system. The information collected during the inventory is recorded in a special file called a **data dictionary**. The data dictionary contains information on both the types of data and the uses for the data.

The data dictionary is a centralized source of data about data. For each data element used in the organization there is a record in the data dictionary that contains data about that data element. For example, each data dictionary record might contain the name of the data element, its description, the name of the record(s) in which it is contained, the name of the source document from which it originates, its size or field length, and its field type (numeric, alphanumeric, etc.). It might also contain the names of all programs that use it, the names of all output reports in which it is used, the names of people (programmers, managers, etc.) who are authorized to use it, and any data names from other files or systems that are applied to the same data element. Table 7.2 is a sample data dictionary that Ashton developed for S&S.

The data dictionary is usually maintained automatically by the DBMS. In fact, this is often one of the first applications of a newly implemented data base system. Inputs to the data dictionary include

Table 7.2

Example of a data dictionary

Data Element Name	Description	Records in Which Contained	Source	Field Length	Field Type	Programs in Which Used	Outputs in Which Contained	Authorized Users	Other Data Names
Customer number	Unique identifier of each customer	A/R record, customer record, sales analysis record	Customer number listing	10	Alphanumeric	A/R update, customer file update, sales analysis update, credit analysis	A/R aging report, customer status report, sales analysis report, credit report	No restrictions	None
Customer name	Complete name of customer	Customer record	Initial customer order	20	Alphanumeric	Customer file update, statement processing	Customer status report, monthly statement	No restrictions	None
Address	Street, city, state, and zip code	Customer record	Credit application	30	Alphanumeric	Customer file update, statement processing	Customer status report, monthly statement	No restrictions	None
Credit limit	Maximum credit that can be extended to customer	Customer record, A/R record	Credit application	8	Numeric	Customer file update, A/R update, credit analysis	Customer status report, A/R aging report, credit report	R. Drummond W. Francom H. Heaton	CR__limit
Balance	Balance due from customer on credit purchases	A/R record, sales analysis record	Various sales and payment transactions	8	Numeric	A/R update, sales analysis update, statement processing, credit analysis	A/R aging report, sales analysis report, monthly statement, credit report	O. Cherrington J. Hansen K. Stocks	Cust__bal

records of any new or deleted data elements, as well as changes in names, descriptions, or uses of existing data elements. Outputs include a variety of reports useful to programmers, data base designers, and users of the information system. Sample reports include a list of all programs in which a data item is used, a list of all synonyms for the data elements in a particular file, a list of all data elements used by a particular user, and a list of all output reports in which a data element is used. Reports of this type are extremely useful in the design and implementation of a data base system, as documentation of the system, and as an audit trail.

The accountant has a very good understanding of the data elements that exist in a business organization, where they originate, and where they are used. This knowledge is a result of the accountant's role in the design of information systems and in the processing of financial data. Therefore an experienced accountant should play a key role in the development of the data dictionary.

Commercially Available DBMS Packages

Few organizations attempt to write their own DBMS software, because the complex and sophisticated programming involved makes it cost-ineffective. Instead, they purchase or lease one of the commercially available data base packages. Although data base packages are available for most models and makes of computers, the packages can be divided into two categories: mainframe and microcomputer packages. They sell for as little as $99 for microcomputer data bases or up to $100,000 for mainframe data bases. In general, the larger the computer and the more expensive the package, the more powerful, flexible, and versatile the package is. Table 5.6 lists some of the more popular microcomputer data bases. Table 7.3 lists some of the more popular mainframe packages. As with any other software, users who are selecting a data base package should carefully evaluate the available packages to ensure that they select the package that best meets their needs.

Table 7.3
Commonly used DBMS software for mainframe data bases

Package	Vendor
Adabas	Software AG
CA-Datacom	Computer Associates International
DMS 1100	Unisys
DB2	IBM
FOCUS	Information Builders, Inc.
HP Image/SQL	Hewlett-Packard
IDMS	Cullinet Corporation
IMS	IBM
Model 204	Computer Corporation of America
Oracle	Oracle
Supra	Cincom Systems, Inc.
SQL/DS	IBM
TOTAL	Cincom Systems, Inc.

United Parcel Service developed its Delivery Information Automated Lookup System (DIALS) using IBM's DB2 data base. Containing 1.1 terabytes of data, it is one of the largest DB2 implementations in the United States. It is used to confirm the delivery of more than 13 million packages every day. It can provide proof of delivery within an hour of a customer's making an inquiry.

TREE AND NETWORK DATA STRUCTURES

Modern data base relationships fall into different categories called logical data structures or logical models. The logical model selected by users depends on their conceptual view of the data and what they want to accomplish. There are three basic logical models: tree (or hierarchical), network, and relational. The first two are discussed in this section. The relational model, which is the most important and the most frequently used, is discussed in the next section of the chapter.

Tree (Hierarchical) Data Base Structure

A tree is a data structure in which relationships between data items are expressed in the form of a hierarchical structure. A customer file in which data relationships are represented in the form of a tree structure appears in Fig. 7.5. This tree consists of four nodes, which are the record types: customer data, credit transactions, invoices, and invoice line items. The uppermost record type, which in this case contains the customer data, is referred to as the root of the tree. One characteristic of a tree is that each node other than the root is related to one and only one other node at a higher level, which is called its parent. Each node,

Figure 7.5
Customer accounts data in a tree structure

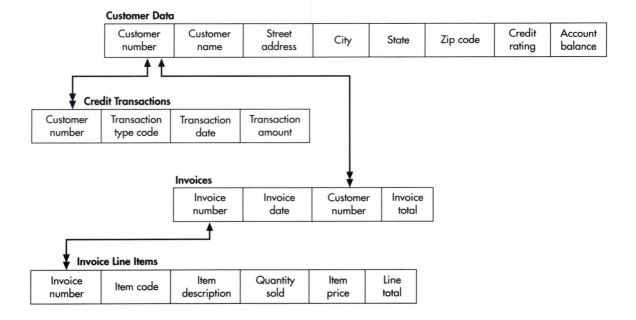

however, may have one or more nodes related to it at a lower level, and these are called its **children**. The tree structure is implemented and controlled using pointers and chains.

The arrows in Fig. 7.5 show the data relationships. In the diagram each line between a parent and child has one arrow pointing to the parent and two arrows pointing to the child. This indicates that each represents a **one-to-many relationship** (1:M)—each child has only one parent, but each parent may have several children. For example, each invoice is associated with only one customer, but each customer may have several invoices. Also, each line item belongs to a single invoice, but a given invoice may have several line items. In a one-to-many relationship the child record is referred to as a **repeating group**. Such relationships are common in accounting records. For example, a company can have several sales offices, each sales office can have several salespeople, each salesperson can have several customers, each customer can make several purchases, and each purchase can include several items.

Network Data Base Structure

In traditional business systems, relationships too complex to be expressed in the form of trees are represented in a network. A **network** is a data structure involving relationships among multiple record types such that (1) each parent may have more than one child record type (as in a tree) and (2) each child may have more than one parent record type (not possible in a tree). For example, in Fig. 7.6 "Credit transactions" has more than one parent: general ledger accounts and customer data.

Each data relationship in Fig. 7.6 is a one-to-many relationship. A network structure may also contain one or more **many-to-many relationships** (M:M), in which a child record type may be owned by one or more parent records. For example, consider the relationship among vendors and products in Fig. 7.7. A vendor may sell S&S several products, and a product may be purchased from several vendors. Therefore it is a many-to-many relationship, as shown by the double arrows pointing in both directions. A network in which all the data relationships are one-to-many, as in Fig. 7.6, is referred to as a **simple network**. One in which some or all the relationships are many-to-many, as in Fig. 7.7, is

Figure 7.6
Accounting data files in a network structure

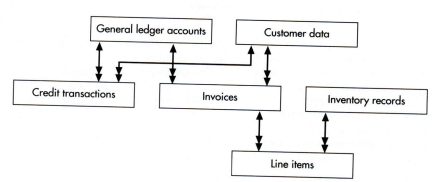

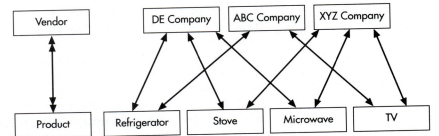

Figure 7.7
Network involving
many-to-many relationships

referred to as a **complex network**. As shown later in this chapter (see Fig. 7.9), a complex network (M:N relationships) is usually converted to a simple network structure (a series of 1:M relationships) before it is actually implemented.

The advantage of networks is that many limitations of tree structures can be avoided. More complex logical relationships between records can be represented if many-to-many relationships are allowed. The disadvantages of networks are their complexity and difficulty of use. In most network systems the user must have specialized training in data processing (including a detailed knowledge of the relationships represented in the network and the physical storage structure used) in order to query or update the network. Networks seem to be best suited for applications that are recurring and voluminous and in which there are relatively few user queries. Correspondingly, a network structure is least useful for applications in which users frequently query the data base.

7.2 FOCUS

New Information System at Coke Based on Relational Data Base

By the year 2000 the Coca-Cola Bottling Company of New York plans to have a new information system installed. Its plan to migrate its financial applications to a relational data base (RDBMS) will move the company from an outdated system based on overnight batch processing and computer printouts to a state-of-the-art, on-line system.

The bottling company began planning the move to the RDBMS in 1989. In April 1990 the company installed the Oracle RDBMS on its IBM 3090 mainframe. On January 1, 1991, after almost another year of planning, Coke installed Oracle's general ledger package. It was followed by a human resources package in September. The second financial application package, accounts payable, went on-line in November. To ensure that there was a proper conversion between the old and the new systems, the

RELATIONAL DATA BASE STRUCTURE

The relational data base model was developed by Dr. E. F. Codd in 1970 as a way of simplifying the complex data relationships used in tree and network structures. Tree and network data structures afford little processing flexibility, since all data relationships must be planned and defined in advance. Often, however, relationships develop that were not anticipated when the data base was organized. As a result, when new relationships are needed, the entire data base may have to be redesigned. The problem of handling unanticipated, or ad hoc, data relationships is largely solved by using the relational model.

Virtually all DBMSs written for the PC market and most new mainframe DBMSs are relational data bases. They are conceptually simple and therefore much easier for the nonprofessional to understand, implement, and use. Relationships between data need not be predefined, and the data base can evolve to meet changing relationships. These factors facilitate end users' building their own data bases and accessing them in any way they choose.

Since relational data bases are built using flat files, they are discussed first. Then an example for S&S is used to illustrate practical relational data bases. Focus 7.2 discusses how Coca-Cola Bottling of New York is migrating its financial applications to a relational data base.

Flat File Structure

A flat file is a file structure in which each record is identical to every other record in terms of attributes and field lengths. A simple example of a flat inventory file that S&S could use appears in Table 7.4. Notice that each record maintains data on an identical set of attributes—stock number, description, color, vendor, quantity on hand, and price. Also,

---

company processed its data by using the new Oracle financial systems as well as the older applications for two months.

One of the problems that Coca-Cola faces is that data from the older applications have to be integrated into the three Oracle applications. Special programs are written to make the translation from the IBM VSAM files of the older applications to the Oracle data base tables.

Every three months the firm plans to convert another application to the Oracle RDBMS. Because Coca-Cola has dozens

of custom applications that must be rewritten, it will take many years to complete the migration.

The migration will have a number of benefits. One of the most important is a reduction in processing time. For example, processing time during some month-end closings takes only 3 hours instead of the 12 hours it used to take. Another benefit is fast response times to company queries. For example, it takes only 10 seconds instead of 30 minutes to search the 750,000 rows of data in the Oracle RDBMS to find a single journal

entry. Development times have also been shortened. Another benefit of the system is that it will provide the company with a better understanding of how its Coke products compare with competing products. A final benefit is that the 150 users of the system now have the option of doing ad hoc reports whenever they want them.

Source: Jean S. Bozman, "Coke Plans to Add Life with Relational Database Move," *Computerworld* (January 13, 1992): 35.

Stock Number	Description	Color	Vendor	On Hand	Price
1036	Refrigerator	White	Gibman	12	$349.99
1038	Refrigerator	Yellow	Gibman	07	$359.99
1039	Refrigerator	Copper	Gibman	05	$379.99
2061	Range	White	Hotspot	06	$489.99
2063	Range	Copper	Hotspot	05	$499.99
3541	Washer	White	Whirlaway	15	$349.99
3544	Washer	Yellow	Whirlaway	10	$359.99
3785	Dryer	White	Whirlaway	12	$249.99
3787	Dryer	Yellow	Whirlaway	08	$259.99

Table 7.4
Flat file

the field size available for each attribute is identical for each record. These characteristics are typical of many accounting files.

A significant advantage of a flat file is that it can be viewed as a table in which the rows are records and the columns are attributes. Records can easily be selected by establishing selection criteria for one or more attributes (columns). Flat files are frequently used as the basic physical implementation approach for the relational model.

S&S Sales Invoices: An Illustration of a Relational Data Base

Relational data base concepts will be explained by using an example for S&S, Inc. Figure 7.8 is a simplified sales invoice that outlines the essential information S&S captures when it makes a sale.

In a manual system S&S captures sales information by filling in the sales invoice. This paper copy becomes S&S's logical view of the data collected. And in a manual system physically storing the sales invoice data is easy. S&S simply stores one or more copies of this invoice in a file cabinet. For example, one copy may be filed by sales invoice number so that the company has a chronological record of sales. Another copy may be filed by customer so that S&S can easily find out what a particular company had purchased.

When S&S stores the data on a computer, the problem is a little more complex. Suppose, for example, that S&S has five sales invoices (numbers 101 to 105) that it wants to store electronically. On several of these invoices S&S records that the customers bought more than one item (a television and a refrigerator, for example). How would S&S go about storing this information electronically? Trying to store all the data together causes problems, such as how to record the sale of different products without storing redundant data or having wasted storage space.

One method S&S can use is to simply store the data in a table, shown in Table 7.5. The problem with this approach to data storage is the amount of redundant data that has to be stored. For example,

| | | S&S, INC. | | |
| INVOICE | | | | |

Invoice No.   Date

                                                        Salesperson No.

Sold To: Customer No.
           Customer Name
           Street
           City   State

Item #	Quantity	Description	Unit Price	Amount
			Total	

Figure 7.8
Simplified sales invoice for S&S, Inc.

examine sales invoice 102 in Table 7.5. The invoice and customer data (the first nine columns) have to be stored three times, since there are three separate inventory items sold. Likewise, inventory descriptions and unit prices are repeated each time an item is sold. Because sales volume can be fairly high in a retail store (this table represents only five invoices), redundancy can make file maintenance unnecessarily time consuming and highly susceptible to errors.

Another approach to storage is to record the sales invoice and customer information in the first nine columns only once but to add additional columns to handle situations where more than one item number is sold on an invoice. This strategy is illustrated in Table 7.6. The problem with this approach is that S&S must decide how many item numbers it should leave room for in the record. Should S&S leave room for 3 items, 5 items, or 10 items? If it leaves room for only 3 items and sells 4 items, where can it record the sale of the fourth item? If S&S leaves room for the sale of 10 items and only sell 1, there is a lot of wasted space. For example, notice the wasted space in Table 7.6 for sales invoices 103 and 104.

The relational model avoids these problems by storing all data elements in the data base in two-dimensional tables called **relations**. These tables are, in effect, flat files in which each row is a record. Each column represents a field where the record's attributes are stored. In these tables the relationships among data are reduced to their simplest forms. As an illustration of reducing data to its simplest form, the sales

Sales Invoice #	Date	Salesperson	Customer #	Invoice Total	Customer Name	Street
101	10/15/93	J. Buck	151	1447	D. Ainge	123 Lotus Lane
101	10/15/93	J. Buck	151	1447	D. Ainge	123 Lotus Lane
102	10/15/93	S. Knight	152	4394	G. Kite	40 Quatro Road
102	10/15/93	S. Knight	152	4394	G. Kite	40 Quatro Road
102	10/15/93	S. Knight	152	4394	G. Kite	40 Quatro Road
103	10/28/93	S. Knight	151	898	D. Ainge	123 Lotus Lane
104	10/31/93	J. Buck	152	789	G. Kite	40 Quatro Road
105	11/14/93	J. Buck	153	3994	F. Roberts	401 Excel Way
105	11/14/93	J. Buck	153	3994	F. Roberts	401 Excel Way
105	11/14/93	J. Buck	153	3994	F. Roberts	401 Excel Way

Table 7.5
Storing sales invoice data by duplicating sales invoice data

invoice data in Tables 7.5 and 7.6 are broken down into the four relational tables shown in Table 7.7.

Constructing Relational Tables. How do you go about designing relational tables and deciding how to reduce data to its simplest form? A complete explanation of how to design relational data bases is beyond the scope of this text. However, two important guidelines are presented here to provide a background in relational data base design. The *first guideline* is that a separate data table should be used for each type of entity. In Table 7.7, for example, the invoice table contains only information that describes the invoice record—its number, date, the salesperson who sold the merchandise, the customer number, and the amount of the invoice. Similarly, the customer table contains only information relating specifically to each customer (i.e., number, name, and address). The line item table contains information only about each item sold, including the sales invoice number where it was sold, the item number, the quantity, and the extended amount. Finally, the inventory table contains only information about inventory items, including the item number, the unit price, and its description. In contrast, Table 7.5 contains information regarding four separate objects of interest: invoices, customers, items sold, and inventory. The result in Table 7.5 is data redundancy.

Table 7.6
Storing sales invoice data by adding additional columns for more items

Sales Invoice #	Columns 2–9	Item #	Quantity	Description	Unit Price	Extended Amount
101		10	2	Television	499	998
102		10	1	Television	499	499
103		50	2	Microwave	449	898
104		40	1	Range	789	789
105		10	3	Television	499	1497

City	State	Item #	Quantity	Description	Unit Price	Extended Amount
Phoenix	AZ	10	2	Television	499	998
Phoenix	AZ	50	1	Microwave	449	449
Mesa	AZ	10	1	Television	499	499
Mesa	AZ	20	3	Freezer	699	2097
Mesa	AZ	30	2	Refrigerator	899	1798
Phoenix	AZ	50	2	Microwave	449	898
Mesa	AZ	40	1	Range	789	789
Chandler	AZ	10	3	Television	499	1497
Chandler	AZ	20	1	Freezer	699	699
Chandler	AZ	30	2	Refrigerator	899	1798

Another weakness of the combined table in Table 7.5 is that customer and inventory data are not maintained independently of inventory item data. If, for example, a customer address changes and S&S needs to change it on the sales records, the clerk would have to go through the data base and change the address on each invoice record. Instead, if the customer file is separate, the address only has to be changed once, in the customer table.

A *second guideline* is that each table should be designed so that every row is unique. This can be accomplished by ensuring that at least one column (or combination of columns) contains a different value for each row so that it can serve as the *primary key* for the table. For example, the primary key of the inventory table is the "Item #" column. In this instance each item number, which uniquely identifies each item of inventory, also uniquely identifies a row in the table. Thus each row contains information pertaining to a specific item of inventory. In the line item table there is no single column that contains unique row values. In this instance the "Sales Invoice" and "Item #" columns, taken together, constitute the primary key. That is, the combination of values in the two columns, which uniquely identifies a relationship between a sales invoice and an inventory item, uniquely identifies each row. This key is called a **concatenated key**.

Item #	Quantity	Description	Unit Price	Extended Amount	Item #	Quantity	Description	Unit Price	Extended Amount
50	1	Microwave	449	449					
20	3	Freezer	699	2097	30	2	Refrigerator	899	1798
20	1	Freezer	699	699	30	2	Refrigerator	899	1798

INVOICE TABLE				
Sales Invoice #	Date	Salesperson	Customer #	Invoice Total
101	10/15/93	J. Buck	151	1447.00
102	10/15/93	S. Knight	152	4394.00
103	10/28/93	S. Knight	151	898.00
104	10/31/93	J. Buck	152	789.00
105	11/14/93	J. Buck	153	3994.00

LINE ITEM TABLE			
Sales Invoice #	Item #	Quantity	Extended Amount
101	10	2	998.00
101	50	1	449.00
102	10	1	499.00
102	20	3	2097.00
102	30	2	1798.00
103	50	2	898.00
104	40	1	789.00
105	10	3	1497.00
105	20	1	699.00
105	30	2	1798.00

CUSTOMER TABLE				
Customer #	Customer Name	Street	City	State
151	D. Ainge	123 Lotus Lane	Phoenix	AZ
152	G. Kite	40 Quatro Road	Mesa	AZ
153	F. Roberts	401 Excel Way	Chandler	AZ

INVENTORY TABLE		
Item #	Unit Price	Description
10	499.00	Television
20	699.00	Freezer
30	899.00	Refrigerator
40	789.00	Range
50	449.00	Microwave

Table 7.7
Relational tables for S&S's
sales invoice data

Relational data bases are stored on direct-access devices using a complex addressing scheme that the user need not be aware of or understand. Physical implementation, which is hidden from the user, often involves indexes, inverted lists, and pointers.

Querying the Data Base.   A relational data base is, in reality, a collection of tables. The tables serve as the building blocks from which more complex relationships can be created. In other words, updates are accomplished and queries answered by using a relational DBMS to select or combine data elements from one or more tables. Since the data can be selected and combined in a variety of ways, the relational model provides a very powerful access capability. Three fundamental operators are used to process the tables:

■ PROJECT creates a new table (or relation) by selecting specified columns from the original table. In other words, the new table that is created does not contain the unneeded columns from the original table.

■ SELECT creates a new table by selecting from the original table those rows that meet specified conditions. In other words, the new table that is created does not contain the unneeded rows from the original table.

■ JOIN creates a new table by selecting the columns needed from two or more tables and then selecting the rows that meet specified conditions. JOIN is used frequently, since a single relation often does not contain all the data necessary to satisfy a user inquiry.

The data in Table 7.7 will be used to show how S&S can query the data base. Several different queries will be made that will extract data from one or more of the tables.

Query 1: What are the dates and invoice totals for all sales in October? This query is made by using the PROJECT operator to select the two appropriate columns (date and invoice total) and the SELECT operation to select all sales in October. The relational DBMS software making the query will create a temporary file containing the data that meets the query requirements. The invoice table and the query response is shown in Table 7.8. The query response can also be printed out in a report.

Query 2: What are the invoice numbers of all sales to D. Ainge, and who made the sale? The results of this query are shown in Table 7.9. The DBMS uses the PROJECT and JOIN operators to select the "Sales Invoice #" and "Salesperson" columns from the invoice table and the "Customer Name" column from the customer table and to join them in a temporary table. The customer number field, which is common to both the invoice table and the customer table, is used by the DBMS to link the two files together, thereby allowing the customer name field to be retrieved and added to the columns from the invoice table. The SELECT operator is used to select the sales to D. Ainge, and the result is as shown in Table 7.9. To illustrate how the software and the operators work, Table 7.9 shows the temporary table as it would look if the PROJECT and JOIN operators were used prior to the SELECT operator selecting the sales to D. Ainge. This table would not appear on your screen if you were running the query in a relational DBMS.

Query 3: How many televisions were sold in October, and when were they sold? The results of this query are shown in Table 7.10. As in

Table 7.8
Query 1: What are the dates and invoice totals of all sales in October?

INVOICE TABLE						QUERY RESPONSE	
Sales Invoice	Date	Salesperson	Customer #	Invoice Total		Date	Invoice Total
101	10/15/93	J. Buck	151	1447.00		10/15/93	1447.00
102	10/15/93	S. Knight	152	4394.00		10/15/93	4394.00
103	10/28/93	S. Knight	151	898.00		10/28/93	898.00
104	10/31/93	J. Buck	152	789.00		10/31/93	789.00
105	11/14/93	J. Buck	153	3994.00			

Query response: The dates and invoice totals of all October sales.

PROJECT selects the "Date" and "Invoice Total" columns. SELECT selects October invoices (101 to 104).

INVOICE TABLE				
Sales Invoice #	Date	Salesperson	Customer #	Invoice Total
101	10/15/93	J. Buck	151	1447.00
102	10/15/93	S. Knight	152	4394.00
103	10/28/93	S. Knight	151	898.00
104	10/31/93	J. Buck	152	789.00
105	11/14/93	J. Buck	153	3994.00

PROJECT selects the "Sales Invoice #" column and the "Salesperson" column from the invoice table and the "Customer Name" column from the customer table. Customer number, the common field in both the invoice table and the customer table, is used to move between tables.

CUSTOMER TABLE				
Customer #	Customer Name	Street	City	State
151	D. Ainge	123 Lotus Lane	Phoenix	AZ
152	G. Kite	40 Quatro Road	Mesa	AZ
153	F. Roberts	401 Excel Way	Chandler	AZ

TEMPORARY TABLE AFTER PROJECT AND JOIN COMMANDS		
Sales Invoice #	Salesperson	Customer Name
101	J. Buck	D. Ainge
102	S. Knight	G. Kite
103	S. Knight	D. Ainge
104	J. Buck	G. Kite
105	J. Buck	F. Roberts

This is what the temporary table looks like after the PROJECT and JOIN commands are executed. However, this table would not appear on the screen; it is shown for illustrative purposes only. The SELECT operator selects the shaded rows.

QUERY RESPONSE		
Sales Invoice #	Salesperson	Customer Name
101	J. Buck	D. Ainge
103	S. Knight	D. Ainge

The completed query looks like this. The customer name column can be deleted, if desired.

Table 7.9

Query 2: What are the invoice numbers of all sales to D. Ainge, and who made the sale?

query 2, the PROJECT operator is used to select the appropriate columns from the three tables. Common fields in the tables are used to link the tables and allow the DBMS to move back and forth between the tables needed to answer the query. The SELECT operator eliminates any rows that do not meet the query's criteria. The query response appears as shown in Table 7.10.

Query 4: Display the names and addresses of all customers buying televisions in October. The answer to this query is shown in Table 7.11. The answer to the query is only two lines, but the relational DBMS must use all four tables to answer the query. The inventory table is used to identify televisions as product 10. The item number field links

INVOICE TABLE

Sales Invoice #	Date	Salesperson	Customer #	Invoice Total
101	10/15/93	J. Buck	151	1447.00
102	10/15/93	S. Knight	152	4394.00
103	10/28/93	S. Knight	151	898.00
104	10/31/93	J. Buck	152	789.00
105	11/14/93	J. Buck	153	3994.00

This query needs information from the invoice, line item, and inventory tables. The PROJECT operator selects the columns needed (the shaded columns). The JOIN operator combines the columns in a temporary table. The SELECT operator selects the rows that meet the query criteria. Common fields in the files are used to link the tables, as shown by the arrows.

LINE ITEM TABLE

Sales Invoice #	Item #	Quantity	Extended Amount
101	10	2	998.00
101	50	1	449.00
102	10	1	499.00
102	20	3	2097.00
102	30	2	1798.00
103	50	2	898.00
104	40	1	789.00
105	10	3	1497.00
105	20	1	699.00
105	30	2	1798.00

Common fields in the files are used to link the tables, as shown by the arrows.

INVENTORY TABLE

Item #	Unit Price	Description
10	499.00	Television
20	699.00	Freezer
30	899.00	Refrigerator
40	789.00	Range
50	449.00	Microwave

QUERY RESPONSE

Date	Quantity	Description
10/15/93	1	Television
10/15/93	2	Television

The query response looks like this (the "Description" column could be left out when the query is displayed, if desired).

Table 7.10
Query 3: How many televisions were sold in October, and when were they sold?

INVOICE TABLE

Sales Invoice #	Date	Salesperson	Customer #	Invoice Total
101	10/15/93	J. Buck	151	1447.00
102	10/15/93	S. Knight	152	4394.00
103	10/28/93	S. Knight	151	898.00
104	10/31/93	J. Buck	152	789.00
105	11/14/93	J. Buck	153	3994.00

This query only displays data taken from the customer table. However, data from all four tables are used to answer the query. The data used in each table are shaded. The "Description" column in the inventory table is used to decide what item # relates to televisions (10). The "Item #" column in the line item table is used to identify on what invoice numbers televisions were sold (101, 102, and 105). The "Date" column in the invoice table is used to narrow television sales to October sales (invoices 101, 102).

CUSTOMER TABLE

Customer #	Customer Name	Street	City	State
151	D. Ainge	123 Lotus Lane	Phoenix	AZ
152	G. Kite	40 Quatro Road	Mesa	AZ
153	F. Roberts	401 Excel Way	Chandler	AZ

Sales invoices 101 and 102 correspond to customers 151 and 152. Those names and addresses are retrieved from the customer table and displayed as shown below.

LINE ITEM TABLE

Sales Invoice #	Item #	Quantity	Extended Amount
101	10	2	998.00
101	50	1	449.00
102	10	1	499.00
102	20	3	2097.00
102	30	2	1798.00
103	50	2	898.00
104	40	1	789.00
105	10	3	1497.00
105	20	1	699.00
105	30	2	1798.00

INVENTORY TABLE

Item #	Unit Price	Description
10	499.00	Television
20	699.00	Freezer
30	899.00	Refrigerator
40	789.00	Range
50	449.00	Microwave

QUERY RESPONSE

Customer Name	Street	City	State
D. Ainge	123 Lotus Lane	Phoenix	AZ
G. Kite	40 Quatro Road	Mesa	AZ

Table 7.11   Query 4: Display the names and addresses of all customers buying televisions in October

the inventory table and the line item table. The line item table is used to identify all of the sales invoices (101, 102, and 105) where item 10 was sold. The sales invoice number field is used to link the line item and invoice tables. The "Date" column in the invoice table is used to narrow sales of televisions to the month of October. The only sales invoices showing that televisions are sold in October are 101 and 102, sold to customers 151 and 152. The customer number field is used to link the invoice table to the customer table. Customers 151 and 152 are identified in the customer table, and their names and addresses are printed out as shown in Table 7.11.

Query 5: Which salesperson has the highest sales volume? This query involves only the invoice table, but it is different than the other four queries in that it does more than just retrieve information; this query makes a calculation. The relational DBMS adds all of the sales (the invoice total field from the invoice table) for each salesperson and displays the result shown in Table 7.12.

Advantages and Disadvantages of the Relational Data Base

From the S&S example it is apparent that a relational DBMS can provide users with direct and immediate access to a readily understandable data base. The relational data base approach provides data bases that are easier to work with, more flexible, and more easily modified than any other type of data base. The essence of a well-designed relational data base is that it can provide users with the particular information they want, when they want it.

Here are some of the advantages to the relational data base model:

- It often is the most flexible and useful approach for unplanned, ad hoc queries. In a relational data base access paths are not predetermined; creating new relations simply requires joining tables. In contrast, in a tree or network approach new connections and access paths must be established if a new relationship is to be added.

- The DDL and DML are usually simple and user-oriented, and maintenance and physical storage are fairly simple. In contrast, the preestablished relationships of the tree and network structures usually require a more complex DDL and DML, and maintenance often is more difficult.

- It provides a clear and conceptually simple design and view of complex data relationships but at the same time offers a set of powerful data manipulation capabilities.

Table 7.12
Query 5: Which salesperson has the highest sales volume?

QUERY RESPONSE	
Salesperson	Sum of Invoice Total
J. Buck	6230.00
S. Knight	5292.00

The DBMS sums the invoice total for each salesperson.

- The data base is very flexible, since each relation within the data base can serve as a point of entry.
- Data can be easily added, deleted, or modified.
- Data are maintained in table form, which is more consistent with the human mental process and is very familiar to business-oriented users. This makes the model easier for unsophisticated computer users to master and use.

A disadvantage of relational data bases is that they are sometimes less efficient than a nonrelational DBMS. They can occupy more memory, take longer to update, and be slower in retrieving data. These problems usually make them less effective for high-volume data bases that are infrequently accessed. However, this problem has become less of an issue since computer speeds have increased dramatically. Another disadvantage is that the indexes used in the relational model, which must be created and maintained along with the records themselves, can be very large and cumbersome.

Since the advantages greatly outweigh the disadvantages for most applications, the relational approach has experienced rapid growth. It is now the dominant data base approach, so accountants should understand the model, how it works, and its advantages and disadvantages. An application of the model is provided in Focus 7.3, which describes how Occam Research is combining the power of a relational data base

7.3 FOCUS

A Mac and a Relational Data Base Provide Instant Information

Managers at Colgate-Palmolive Company are using a network of Apple Macintoshes and Muse, a data analysis application from Occam Research, to access data from a wide variety of sources. It is almost as if the managers' personal computers think for them.

Muse combines the power of a personal computer and a rela-tional data base with integrated analytical tools. The system is able to search a wide variety of sources for information, includ-ing obscure sources that the managers would probably never consider accessing. The Muse system is able to gather and in-teractively analyze financial and market data about hundreds of consumer products sold in 160 countries. The system also has the ability to graph the data for instant ad hoc analysis.

This system allows managers to see trends and pinpoint oppor-tunities for growth in just a few minutes, rather than having to dig for the information. Prior to the installation of Muse the man-agers had to wade through thousands of spreadsheets to lowith integrated analytical tools to provide its employees with instant ad hoc analysis capabilities.

FILE AND DATA BASE DESIGN CONSIDERATIONS

Ashton discovered that when an organization decides to implement a data base, eight important steps must be performed:

1. Take an inventory of data elements used in the organization.
2. Design schemata for initial data base applications.
3. Survey available DBMS software, and select the package that best meets the organization's requirements.
4. Define subschemata for specific applications.
5. Write new application programs or modify existing ones.
6. Load the data into the data base.
7. Process transaction data to update the data base.
8. Maintain the schemata, subschemata, and application programs.

These tasks can be categorized into four different phases: requirements definition, conceptual design, physical design, and implementation and operation.

Requirements Definition

In the first phase the data requirements, or logical views, of the individual users and applications are determined. There are at least two

---

cate the widely scattered sales data they needed. When they finally did find the data they needed in the spreadsheets, they had to cut and paste them together to consolidate the information. Because of the quantity of information, it could often take hours to find and prepare the data they needed.

One significant advantage of Muse is that it is easy to use, since it understands commands in plain English. For example, to find out how many tubes of toothpaste were sold in France in the first quarter, you simply ask the system to provide you with that information in simple

English. The data used in Muse is collected electronically from global subsidiaries and placed on an IBM mainframe. Users access Muse-related information through a series of Macintoshes running over a 3Com Corporation twisted-pair network.

The data that the system uses is organized in multiple tables of data. The tables are joined automatically so that a large number of them can be referenced at once. Suppose that a manager requests sales data for a particular region for the prior three years. If she notices that sales are rising, she can ask the system to determine what the rise is

attributable to. Of special assistance are the what-if reporting features that, because of the data access problem, could not be done with a spreadsheet. This allows users to locate information and investigate relationships that they had never considered before.

Source: James Daly, "Stumped? Ask Your Mac," *Computerworld* (March 9, 1992): 37.

different types of system requirements: those arising from processing and recording transactions and events, and those arising from users' information needs.

Several different strategies exist for developing system requirements. One is to organize existing applications and files into a data base and then let the data base evolve as new applications are needed and new queries arise. This approach works well for data bases that do not change very much or very often. Another approach is to do a detailed study of the data requirements for all current applications and then combine them to form the data base. A third approach, often referred to as conceptual data modeling, is to try to identify all current and anticipated needs. This approach is based on the argument that data and the relationships between them are the foundation of an information system. It calls for developing a conceptual model of an organization and its components (people, resources, events). By modeling all entities within the organization and the relationships between those entities, one anticipates present and future data requirements.

No matter which approach is used, the end result should be a listing of the data required in an organization's data base. Determining data requirements is covered in greater depth in Chapter 9.

Conceptual Design

If one is designing a data base system, certain design objectives should be kept in mind. These objectives are summarized in Table 7.13. Unfortunately, all of these objectives cannot be maximized. As in all

Table 7.13
Data base design objectives

Completeness	The data base should contain all the data (and the relationships between the data) needed by its various users. There should be proper integration and coordination of all users and suppliers of data. The data contained in the data base should be recorded in the data dictionary.
Relevance	Only relevant and useful data should be captured and stored.
Accessibility	Stored data should be accessible to all authorized users on a timely basis.
Up-to-dateness	Stored data should be kept current and up to date.
Flexibility	The data base should be flexible enough that a wide variety of users can satisfy their information needs.
Efficiency	Data storage should be accomplished as efficiently as possible. As few resources as possible should be used to store the data. Data base update, retrieval, and maintenance time should be minimized.
Cost-effectiveness	Data should be stored in such a way that desired system benefits can be achieved at the lowest possible cost.
Integrity	The data base should be free from errors and irregularities.
Security	The data base should be protected from loss, destruction, and unauthorized access. Backup and recovery procedures should be in place so that the data base can be reconstructed if necessary.

areas of systems design, certain trade-offs are required. For example, cost-effectiveness is usually at odds with other objectives like flexibility, efficiency, accessibility, integrity, and security. The key is to achieve the best possible balance so that each objective is maximized, given the restraints imposed by the other objectives.

A critical step in implementing a data base is the design of data base schemata. Most organizations use separate data bases for major functional areas rather than a single comprehensive data base for the entire organization. Thus the first step in schema design is to determine which data elements to include in which schema. To resolve this problem, designers must identify "clusters" of files and programs that are closely related to each other in terms of processing and use but are not closely related to files and programs in other clusters. These cluster often are the accounting cycles explained in Chapters 16–20. For example, the sales–accounts receivable–cash collections data base would contain all the data related to these functions.

Once the data elements to be included within a particular schema have been identified, the designer must specify the relationships that exist between them. Those data elements having a one-to-one relationship with each other are candidates for inclusion within the same record. Each entity within a schema may be related to one or more other entities, and each relationship may be either one to many or many to many. All relationships that are relevant, either to the processing of transactions against the data base or to the retrieval of information from the data base in response to specific user needs, should be explicitly recognized in the data base schema.

Another important aspect of schema design is designating which data elements will serve as keys. The appropriate primary key for each record is generally obvious—for example, customer number for the customer file and invoice number for the invoice file. The careful selection of secondary keys, however, is significant, because it can enhance data base processing efficiency and facilitate information retrieval. The most appropriate secondary keys generally are those data elements that identify certain properties held in common by groups of records. Examples include invoice due date, employee department number, and inventory location code.

An important objective in the design of a data base schema is simplifying the data structure. The more complicated data structures such as networks (especially complex networks) are more difficult for DBMS software packages to work with than simpler data structures such as trees and flat files. In fact, the schema definition techniques used by some DBMS software packages do not allow network data structures to be specified explicitly.

By introducing limited redundancy into a data base schema, however, designers can represent a network data structure as a series of tree structures. As shown in Figure 7.9, a complex network can be represented by tree structures (four in this case). Although there is

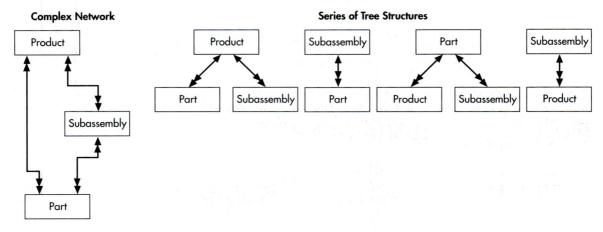

Figure 7.9

Complex network structure involving many-to-many relationships converted to a series of tree structures

redundancy in the record types appearing in this schema, this does not necessarily mean that there will be redundancy in the physical data stored in this data base.

Many data base specialists feel that it is desirable to simplify schemata further by reducing all data base files to two-dimensional tables or flat files. As explained earlier, this type of data base is called a relational data base. Any type of data base structure can be reduced to a relational form. For example, Fig. 7.10 shows the tree data structure from Fig. 7.5 converted to relational form. Notice that each of the relations represented by arrows in Fig. 7.5 is represented in Fig. 7.10 by data elements that are contained within the same record. For example, the customer number field is the link between the customer table and the credit transactions and invoice tables. The item code is the field that links the invoice line item table with the inventory item table.

Accountants, like Ashton at S&S, should play a key role in the design of data base schemata. The accountant's familiarity with record content and data relationships endows him or her with the perspective necessary to ensure that schema designs adequately satisfy all user requirements. Other management personnel should also be involved in the design of schemata that relate specifically to their areas of responsibility.

Physical Design and Implementation

Physical design consists of taking the conceptual design and converting it into physical storage structures. Physical data base design is seldom of concern to accountants and is therefore beyond the scope of this book.

The implementation phase consists of converting the current system to the data base approach and getting it up and running properly. Implementation concerns are covered in Chapter 10.

Record Type

Record Content

Customer	Customer number	Customer name	Street address	City	State	Zip code	Credit rating	Account balance

Credit Transaction	Customer number	Transaction type code	Transaction date	Transaction amount

Invoice	Invoice number	Invoice date	Customer number	Invoice total

Invoice Line Item	Invoice number	Item code	Quantity sold	Line total

Inventory Item	Item code	Item description	Item price

Figure 7.10
Relational data base

IMPACT OF DATA BASE SYSTEMS ON ACCOUNTING

Within most large organizations accounting data are now stored in data base systems. This has some interesting implications for accounting. One of them—the need for accountants to be involved in the process of designing and implementing data base systems—has already been examined. At the organizational level another significant issue is the impact of data base systems on internal control. The centralization of data storage and integration of data processing brought about by data base systems require that emphasis be placed on matters such as the accuracy of input data, the preservation of audit trails, the control of access to the data, and the maintenance of backup copies of data files. In essence, the organization's data base is an asset that must be safeguarded just as cash, inventories, and equipment are.

At a more general level data base technology may have a profound impact on the fundamental nature of accounting. For example, the accounting process traditionally begins with recording transactions from source documents onto journals. This step is followed by posting from the journals to ledgers, balancing ledger accounts, and ultimately generating financial statements. When the accounting system is converted to a data base, all the accountant needs to do is enter source document data into the data base. Because of predefined data linkages within the accounting data base, the posting and balancing steps are accomplished automatically and immediately as the source data are entered. Financial statements and other accounting reports may then be generated at any time in response to a user request.

Even more important, data base technology could lead to the abandonment of the double-entry accounting model. The basic rationale for the double-entry model is the use of redundancy to provide a check on the accuracy of data processing. Every transaction generates equal debit and credit entries, and the equality of debits and credits is checked and rechecked at numerous points in the accounting process. Data redundancy, however, is the antithesis of the data base concept. If the amounts associated with a transaction are entered into a data base system correctly, it is necessary to store them only once, not twice. Computer data processing is sufficiently accurate to make the elaborate system of checks and double checks, which characterizes the double-entry accounting model, unnecessary.

Thus data base technology could possibly do away with the need for the double-entry model. This has not happened yet because alternative accounting models that are more consistent with data base concepts are not widely used. Furthermore, the double-entry model is so firmly entrenched in accounting that it may never change—rather, it may just be implemented on data base systems with little or no modification, in spite of the apparent inconsistencies. On the other hand, the data base approach could be implemented properly and reports generated with the appropriate debits and credits to satisfy accountants that need to see the double-entry model.

CASE CONCLUSION: IMPLEMENTING A DATA BASE SYSTEM AT S&S, INC.

Scott and Susan have ambitious plans to expand S&S into a nationwide chain of stores specializing in home appliance products. Realizing their objectives will require them to make excellent decisions, because competition is tough and margins are low. Thus access to the proper information and state-of-the-art computer technology is critical.

The Great Plains software they have used for the past few years has served them well and will continue to do so in the near future. However, to develop the competitive edge they seek, they decide to develop their own customized system using a relational data base. With this system they not only will have the accounting data provided now by their software but also will be able to incorporate the additional information they need.

Steve and Ashton investigate the various data base options available and decide upon the Oracle data base. They decide to have just one corporate data base. That way they have to capture data just once, the data do not have to be entered into different data bases, and all the programs at the company will be able to talk to each other. They decide that anything a computer can do, it should do. That will free their employees to concentrate on more creative and people-oriented tasks such as meeting customer needs, selling merchandise, and adding value to both S&S and to the customer.

It took Steve, Susan, and Ashton many months to develop the

system they wanted. When they finished, they had a corporatewide data base that gave them almost instant access to a wealth of data at all of their stores. Data are captured at each store using electronic cash registers and microcomputers. This information is passed on the LAN to a back-office computer and is summarized. Every night, the mini-computer at S&S's headquarters automatically dials each store, retrieves the summary information from each store, and enters the data into S&S's relational data base.

Everyone who has a regular need for information has a set of one or more queries that were prepared especially for that person. Employees use these on-line queries and their microcomputers to retrieve from the data base the information they need to perform their jobs. For example, Susan checks the sales figures and the inventory levels at each store every morning. She is also able to produce an income statement for any store or group of stores for any time period she specifies. Each morning, she also runs a query to produce an exception report that flags any unusual activity at any of the stores. Any unusual or ad hoc need for information can easily be produced using the data base's data query language.

Each night, the system automatically updates the inventory levels for each store and determines if inventory should be ordered for the store. If an order is needed, a suggested order is forwarded to the store and is there awaiting store managers when they open the next morning. They have the option of changing the order or simply confirming it. Once the order is returned to headquarters, the computer at S&S uses EDI to place the orders with the appropriate suppliers.

Developing the system at S&S was not easy. It required a great deal of time and effort to determine the needs of users and to ensure that the system would meet those needs. The process of designing and developing systems is explained in Chapters 8–11. Chapters 16–20 discuss the different business cycles and the information that a data base must contain for each cycle. ■

SUMMARY

There are two principal approaches to data storage: file-oriented and data base. The file-oriented approach works well in many situations but has a number of significant disadvantages, including data redundancy, lack of data independence, and inability to satisfy many types of information requests. The data base approach overcomes many of these disadvantages.

In the data base approach there are two data views: logical and physical. The logical view is how users perceive the data to be organized. The physical view is how data are actually stored on disks or tapes. The separation of the two views, called data independence, is one of the reasons data base technology is so powerful.

The data base management system is a sophisticated software program that handles translation between the two data views. It consists of a number of different languages, including data definition, data manipulation, and data query languages. There are three types of DBMS users: data base administrators, application programmers, and users. Data elements stored in the data base are recorded in a data dictionary.

Data base organization and access methods include the flat file, tree, network, and relational structure. The relational data base is regarded as the easiest to understand and is the most frequently used in business today.

Data base design consists of four phases: requirements definition, conceptual design, physical design, and implementation. This chapter discusses the first two phases, and Chapter 10 discusses implementation issues. The third, physical design, is typically of little concern to accountants.

Since accountants are among the individuals most familiar with their organization's data, they should assume a significant role in data base design. To fulfill that role, they must understand and be able to apply the concepts explained in this chapter.

KEY TERMS

Define the following terms.

file-oriented approach	data definition language (DDL)	parent
data base approach	data manipulation language (DML)	children
data base		one-to-many relationship
data base management system (DBMS)	data query language (DQL)	repeating group
	report writers	network
data base system	application programmers	many-to-many relationship
data base administrator (DBA)	ad hoc users	simple network
record layout	data dictionary	complex network
logical view	logical data structures	relational data base
schema	logical models	flat file
subschema	tree	relations
physical view	nodes	concatenated key
data redundancy	root	conceptual data modeling
data independence		

DISCUSSION QUESTIONS

7.1 What are the advantages and disadvantages of integrating all of an organization's data into a single comprehensive data base? Would you favor such an approach? Explain.

7.2 A data base allows two distinct views of data—a logical view and a physical view. How does this differ from a file-oriented approach? Contrast the two views, and discuss why separate views are necessary in data base applications. Describe which perspective is most useful for each of the following employees: a programmer, a manager, and an internal auditor. How will understanding logical data structures assist accountants in designing and using data base systems?

7.3 As companies downsize from centralized mainframes to distributed networks, many firms are also implementing sophisticated data base applications. One company doing so is Chase Manhattan Bank (see Focus 7.1). What motivated Chase Manhattan Bank's shift to the Chase Information Exchange (CIX)? How is the CIX data base empowering employees at Chase Manhattan? How has the data base concept changed the nature of computer use by companies?

7.4 Discuss the role of the data dictionary in the development of an accounting data base. What information is included in a data dictionary? In what ways is a data dictionary used?

7.5 Differentiate between a data base and a data base management system (DBMS). How does the separation of the information from the application program provide advantages over the traditional file-oriented approach?

7.6 What are the advantages and disadvantages of the relational data base approach? How is this approach changing the type of users of DBMS? The foundation of a relational data base is a series of two-dimensional tables that designate relations. What is a data relation or relationship? Describe the process by which the user employs relational tables to draw needed information from the relational data base.

7.7 The use of a relational data base, combined with integrated analytical tools, is changing the way users conduct business at the Colgate-Palmolive Company (see Focus 7.3). How does the relational data base make data more accessible to users? What advantages does the relational data base provide over traditional file-oriented structures?

7.8 Discuss the potential impact of data base technology on the fundamental nature of accounting. Do you believe that this potential impact will ever be realized? Why or why not?

7.9 A new data base designed and operated by Equifax is revolutionizing the auto insurance industry. To combat fraudulent applications for auto insurance, over three hundred insurance companies use the Comprehensive Loss Underwriting Ex-

change data base to share information about potential customers. The data base contains all auto insurance claims made by a customer against any insurance company in the past three to five years. It also contains the current status of the claims and the cost of the claims to the insurer. With such information available at a low cost insurance companies have improved the effectiveness of the applicant-screening process, which keeps insurance premiums down.

The way the system works is simple. Companies pay an annual fee to subscribe to the data base service and a fee of $2.25 for each application check. More than 1.8 million data base searches have been done, turning up prior claims 20% of the time. Of these additional claims 90% were unreported by the insurance applicant. Any information that the check turns up that is not on the application can cause a company to raise premiums or even to cancel a policy. To ensure fairness, customers can gain access to a copy of their report and can challenge the accuracy of findings.[1]

What advantages does this data base technology provide insurance companies and auto insurance applicants? What are the possible risks of this data base system?

7.10 Organizing the vast amounts of U.S. Census Bureau information on welfare recipients was a seemingly impossible task. In spite of the information's usefulness for welfare workers the information remained unaccessible in antiquated government computers for years. In 1983 things finally changed.

Researchers at the University of Wisconsin's Institute for Research on Poverty developed a prototype system called SIPP Access to aid them in conducting a U.S. Census Bureau study called the Survey of Income and Program Participation (SIPP). The new system was specifically designed to organize and access large volumes of data.

Using a relational data base management system (RDBMS), developers reduced storage requirements for the data by 75% without losing any information. As a result of the efficiency of the relational data base, data retrieval has become extremely rapid. Information that used to take researchers sev-

---

[1] *Source:* Diane Levick, "A New Weapon for Car Insurers: Database Allows Companies to Check Drivers' Records," *New York Newsday* (February 20, 1990): 49.

eral years to uncover can now be gathered in hours. With such information researchers hope to improve the efficiency of the current welfare system.[2]

How has the Census Bureau benefited from the new relational data base? How could a relational data base reduce storage requirements by over 75%?

PROBLEMS

7.1 The need for a more coordinated approach to the management of data has resulted in the development of data base management systems.

Required
Describe briefly each of the following aspects of data base management systems.

a. Advantages of using data base management systems

b. Problem areas when data base management systems are in use

(CIA Examination, adapted)

7.2 Changes in the design and development of computer-based accounting information systems have been impressive in the past two decades. Traditionally, computer-based data processing systems were arranged by departments and applications. Computers were applied to single, large-volume applications such as inventory control or customer billing. Other applications were added once the first applications were operating smoothly.

As more applications were added, problems in data management developed. So businesses looked for ways to integrate data processing systems to make them more comprehensive and shorten response times. As a consequence, the data base system was composed of the data base itself, the data base management system, and the individual application programs.

Required
a. Explain the differences between the traditional (file-oriented) approach to data processing and the use of the data base system in terms of the following:
1. File structure
2. Processing of the data

b. Many practitioners have asserted that security is of greater importance in a data base system than in traditional systems.
1. Explain the importance of security and the problems that may arise in implementing security in a data base system.
2. Identify special control features a company should consider incorporating in its data base system.

c. Identify and discuss the favorable and unfavorable issues other than security that a company should consider before implementing a data base system.

(CMA examination, adapted)

7.3 Susan wants to develop a data base to handle S&S's expenditures cycle, including inventory purchases, accounts payable, and cash disbursements.

a. Identify the steps that the management of S&S must consider when designing a data base system. Discuss the importance of each step in the overall development of the data base.

b. What role should design objectives play in the development of the data base schema for the expenditures cycle? Will all objectives be satisfied in the development of the data base?

c. What role should the accountants at S&S play in the development of the data base schemata for the expenditures cycle?

7.4 The following schema was developed for a personnel data base to be used in the QRS Manufacturing Company. The data are to be accessed by a number of corporate users. Identify three potential users, and design a subschema for each.

Employee number	Salary
Employee name	Social Security tax withheld
Job title	Federal tax withheld
Department number	State tax withheld
Department name	Pay period

---

[2] *Source:* Sharon Baker, "University Scientists Crack High-Tech Welfare Data Shell," *Computerworld* (May 22, 1989):

Company #	Company Name	Commission Rate	Revenue
10,000	SNIOZ Corp.	25%	$ 10,000
20,000	TSRIF Corp.	35%	100,000
30,000	SEOJ Corp.	75%	230,000
40,000	Aseret Corp.	20%	481,000
50,000	LLAM Corp.	68%	23,000
60,000	Oidar Corp.	19%	770,000
70,000	POTA Corp.	55%	999,000
80,000	Oisac Corp.	13%	99,999
90,000	MBI Corp.	92%	38,000

Table 7.14
Revenue table

7.5 Use Table 7.14 to satisfy the relational data base user inquiries. (*Hint:* See Table 7.1.)

Required

a. What records would be displayed in response to the following inquiry?

```
SELECT      COMPANY NAME, REVENUE
FROM        REVENUE TABLE
WHERE       REVENUE > $200,000
ORDER BY    REVENUE, DESC
```

b. What records would be displayed in response to the following inquiry?

```
SELECT      COMPANY NAME, COMMISSION
            RATE, REVENUE
FROM        REVENUE TABLE
WHERE       COMMISSION RATE > 30% AND
            REVENUE < $100,000
ORDER BY    COMMISSION RATE, DESC
```

c. Design a relational data base query similar to those in parts a and b that would select all companies that have commission rates of less than 50% and revenues exceeding $250,000. Have the records displayed in ascending (ASC) order by commission rate. Show the records that would be displayed in response to this query.

7.6 You are to design a schema for a purchasing data base. This data base will encompass the data in five types of records that are presently maintained on magnetic disk files. These types of records and their content are as follows:

1. Supplier record—supplier number, supplier name, supplier address, shipment terms, billing terms

2. Purchase order record—order number, supplier number, order date, buyer name

3. Purchase order line item record—order number, part number, part description, quantity ordered, quantity received, price, line total, requested delivery date

4. Parts inventory record—part number, part description, standard cost, quantity on hand, quantity on order

5. Parts quotation record—part number, supplier number, quoted price

Required

a. Prepare a diagram of your schema, using a format similar to that of Fig. 7.5. For each relationship between a pair of records, indicate by means of arrowheads whether the relationship is one to one, one to many, or many to many.

b. Prepare a diagram (using the Fig. 7.5 format) showing the subschema that would be used by a program that adds new purchase order records to the data base.

c. Prepare a diagram (using the Fig. 7.5 format) showing the subschema that would be used by a program that enters records of receipts of parts on order into the data base.

d. Prepare a diagram (using the Fig. 7.5 format) showing the subschema that would be used by a program designed to generate a report that shows quotations and related supplier information for a specified part.

7.7 The Paradise Hotel is a 1000-room, 50-story resort hotel in San Diego. The hotel is very popular with tourists and with business conventions. A convention center was built next to the hotel to meet the needs of the business clientele.

The number of rooms rented at the Paradise fluctuates because of seasonal cycles, business convention schedules, and special promotions offered by the competition. Business is heaviest during the tourist season, when reservations must be booked several months in advance to ensure room preferences and availability. Even though most business conventions are held during the off-season, advance notice of nearly a year must be made for business conventions in order to have a large enough block of rooms available. In the off-season, reservations are not as important for nonconvention guests.

If the Paradise Hotel charged the same room rate over the entire year, the hotel would be empty during the off-season and overcrowded during the tourist season. So that demand can be controlled, low rates are charged during the off-season, premium rates are charged during the peak tourist season, and regular rates are charged the rest of the year. When people making reservations identify themselves as members of an approved convention, they are extended a special rate. A group reserving a large block of rooms is extended an even lower rate. In addition to varying by season, convention, and group, room prices vary according to floor and size.

Staffing and managing a complex as large as the Paradise Hotel and its convention center is a formidable task. The work force must be kept low in the off-season, and additional help must be hired for the peak season. Employees must be assigned to departments and scheduled so that adequate help is always on hand. Meal planning and preparation vary according to how many guests are anticipated. Smaller conventions need to be planned around the large conventions, and all convention participants must be given adequate information. Throughout the entire process adequate information must be kept for the accounting function.

Since most of the hotel's clientele come through travel agencies, the hotel works closely with them. Travel agencies make their reservations by using the hotel's toll-free number to call service representatives, who record the reservations.

Required

a. How could Paradise use a data base to improve the effectiveness and efficiency of its operation?

b. What other types of computer applications do you foresee Paradise having? Discuss their importance to Paradise.

7.8 Mariposa Products, a textile and apparel manufacturer, acquired its own computer in 1978. The first application to be developed and implemented was production and inventory control. Other applications that were added in succession were payroll, accounts receivable, and accounts payable.

The applications were not integrated owing to the piecemeal manner in which they were developed and implemented. Nevertheless, the system proved satisfactory for several years. Generally, reports were prepared on time, and information was readily accessible.

Mariposa operates in a very competitive industry. The combination of increased operating costs and the competitive nature of the industry has had an adverse effect on profit margins and operating profits. Ed Wilde, Mariposa's President, suggested that some special analyses be prepared in an attempt to provide information that would help management improve operations. Unfortunately, some of the data were not consistent among the reports. In addition, there were no data by product line or by department. These problems were attributable to the fact that Mariposa's applications were developed piecemeal, and as a consequence, duplicate data that were not necessarily consistent existed on Mariposa's computer system.

Wilde was concerned that Mariposa's computer system was not able to generate the information his managers needed to make decisions. He called a meeting of his top management and certain data processing personnel to discuss potential solutions to Mariposa's problems. The consensus of the meeting was that a new information system that would integrate Mariposa's applications was needed.

Mariposa's Controller suggested that the company consider a data base system that all departments would use. As a first step, the Controller proposed hiring a data base administrator on a consulting basis to determine the feasibility of converting to a data base system.

Required

a. Identify the components that comprise a data base system.

b. Discuss the advantages and disadvantages of a data base system for Mariposa Products.

c. List the factors that Mariposa Products should consider before converting to a data base system.

d. Describe the duties of a data base administrator.

e. Explain the basic difference between a file-oriented system and a data base management system. (CMA, Examination, adapted)

7.9 Most DBMS packages contain a data definition language (DDL), a data manipulation language (DML), and a data query language (DQL). For each of the following examples, indicate which language would be used and why.

a. The data base administrator (DBA) defines the physical structure of the entities and relationships within the data base.

b. The controller requests a cost accounting report containing a list of all employees being paid for more then 10 hours overtime in a given week.

c. A programmer develops a program to update the fixed assets records stored in the data base.

d. The personnel manager requests a report noting all employees who are retiring within five years.

e. The inventory serial number field is extended in the inventory records to allow for recognition of additional inventory items with serial numbers containing more then 10 digits.

f. A user develops a program to print out the company's payroll checks.

g. An additional field is added to the fixed asset records to record the estimated salvage value of each asset.

CASE 7.1: ANYCOMPANY, INC.— AN ONGOING COMPREHENSIVE CASE

One of the best ways to learn is to immediately apply what you have studied. The purpose of this case is to allow you to do that. You will select a local company that you can work with. At the end of most chapters you will find an assignment that will have you apply what you have learned using the company you have selected as a reference. This case, then, may become an ongoing case study that you work on throughout the term.

Visit the business you have chosen and write a report covering your visit. Include the following information in your report.

1. The name of the DBMS the company uses

2. The way the data base is used

3. How the data base is controlled

4. Resources needed to implement, operate, and maintain the data base

5. Any problems encountered in using the data base

6. Advantages to the company from using the data base

7. Documentation on the system (e.g., include a page from the data dictionary)

CASE 7.2: WEKENDER CORPORATION

Wekender Corporation owns and operates 15 large departmentalized retail hardware stores. The stores carry a wide variety of merchandise, but the major thrust is toward the weekend "do-it-yourselfer." The company has been successful in this field, and the number of stores in the chain has almost doubled since 1980.

Each retail store acquires its merchandise from the company's centrally located warehouse. Consequently, the warehouse must maintain an up-to-date

and well-stocked inventory to meet the demands of the individual stores.

The company wishes to maintain its competitive position with similar types of stores. Therefore Wekender Corporation must improve its purchasing and inventory procedures. The company's stores must have the proper goods to meet customer demand, and the warehouse, in turn, must have the necessary goods available. The number of company stores, the number of inventory items carried, and the volume of business all are creating pressure on the company to change from a manual data processing system to a computerized data processing system. Recently, the company has been investigating two different approaches to computerization—a computer with batch processing and a computer with on-line, real-time processing. No decision has been reached on the approach to be followed.

Top management has determined that the following items should have high priority in the new system.

- Rapid ordering to replenish warehouse inventory stocks with as little delay as possible (Wekender buys from over fifteen hundred vendors)
- Quick filling and shipping of merchandise to the stores (this process involves determining whether sufficient stock exists)
- Some indication of inventory activity (over eight hundred purchase orders are prepared each week)
- Perpetual records in order to permit management to determine inventory level by item number quickly (Wekender sells over seventy-five hundred separate items)

A description of the current warehousing and purchasing procedures is given in the paragraphs that follow.

Stock is stored in bins and is located by inventory number. The numbers are supposed to be listed sequentially on the bins to facilitate locating items for shipment; frequently, this system is not followed, and as a result, some items are difficult to locate.

Whenever a store needs merchandise, a three-part merchandise request form is completed—one copy is kept by the store and two copies are mailed to the warehouse. If the merchandise requested is on hand, the goods are delivered to the store together with the third copy of the request. The second copy is filed at the warehouse.

If the quantity of goods on hand is not sufficient to fill the order, the warehouse sends the quantity available and notes the quantity shipped on the request form. Then a purchase memorandum for the shortage is prepared by the warehouse. At the end of each day all the memos are sent to the Purchasing Department.

When ordered goods are received, they are checked at the receiving area and a receiving report is prepared. One copy of the receiving report is retained at the receiving area, one is forwarded to accounts payable, and one is filed at the warehouse with the purchase memorandum.

When the purchase memorandums are received from the warehouse, purchase orders are prepared. Vendor catalogs are used to select the best source for the requested goods, and the purchase order is filled out and mailed. Copies of the order are sent to accounts payable and the receiving area; one copy is retained in the Purchasing Department.

When the receiving report arrives in the Purchasing Department, it is compared with the purchase order on file. Both documents are compared with the invoice before the invoice is forwarded to accounts payable for payment.

The Purchasing Department strives to periodically evaluate vendors for financial soundness, reliability, and trade relationships. However, because the volume of requests received from the warehouse is so great, this activity currently does not have a high priority.

Each week a report of the open purchase orders is prepared to determine whether any action should be taken on overdue deliveries. This report is prepared manually by scanning the file of outstanding purchase orders.

1. Wekender is considering a batch processing system and an on-line, real-time computer system. Which system would better meet the needs of Wekender Corporation? Explain your answer.

2. Briefly describe the hardware components Wekender needs for the system recommended in step 1. Sketch a configuration of this system.

3. Identify the data files that would be necessary, and briefly indicate the type of information that would be contained in each file.

4. Specify how each of the files identified in requirement 3 should be organized and accessed.

5. How might Wekender benefit from using a data base rather than a file-oriented approach?

6. Which data base organization and access method would you recommend to Wekender? Why?

7. Regardless of your answer in requirement 6, design a relational data base table for vendor data.

PART III

CHAPTER 8

The Systems Development Process: An Overview

LEARNING OBJECTIVES

After studying this chapter, you should be able to:

- Explain the steps in the systems development life cycle.
- Discuss the objectives and techniques of planning and managing information systems development.
- Explain why behavioral problems occur during changes, describe what form resistance to change takes, and discuss how to avoid behavioral problems.
- Discuss the various types of feasibility analysis, and calculate economic feasibility.

INTEGRATIVE CASE: SHOPPERS MART

Several months ago Ann Christy was promoted to the position of Controller of Shoppers Mart (SM), a small but rapidly growing regional chain of discount stores. Since her promotion she has been trying to determine how well her people are serving other areas of the company and what the accounting function could do to better serve them. She has held meetings with the President and CEO of the company and with all of the key managers at the headquarters office. She has also spent several weeks on the road visiting some of the stores, talking to store managers and employees.

After the interviews were completed, she summarized her results. Here are some of her more important findings.

1. Many store managers cannot get the information they need to make decisions unless the information needed is in one of the preformatted reports that are produced periodically. As soon as information is needed from several different functional areas, the system bogs down.

2. The Purchasing Department cannot get timely information about what is selling and what is not selling in the stores. As a result, stores are often out of popular items and overstocked with items that do not sell well.

3. Top management is concerned that SM is losing market share to larger rivals who are able to beat it on price and selection. The current system is not capable of giving management the information it needs to analyze and solve the problem.

After analyzing the situation, Ann is convinced that what Shoppers Mart needs is a new information system—one that is flexible, efficient, and responsive to users' needs. Ann knows that a new system will never be successful unless it has the complete support of top management. Therefore, in preparation for her pitch to company management to ask for approval, support, and funding for the new system, Ann has scheduled a meeting with the head of systems development. In preparation for this meeting she lists some of the questions she wants to ask.

1. What is the process that the company needs to go through to design and implement the information system? What specific steps are involved, and what takes place in each step?

2. What types of planning are necessary to ensure success? Who will be involved, and how? Do any special committees need to be formed? What resources need to be planned for? How should all of the planning be documented?

3. How are people going to react to a new information system? What types of problems might the change to a new system cause? What steps should the company take to minimize the problems?

4. How is a new system justified and sold to top management? How can expected benefits and costs be quantified to determine if the system is economically viable and if it will pay for itself? ■

INTRODUCTION

This chapter provides an overview of the systems development process. It begins by discussing why information systems need to be changed. The process by which this change has traditionally been managed is called the systems development life cycle. The second section of the chapter introduces and previews this life cycle.

The main focus of the chapter is a discussion of three topics that are applicable to all phases of the systems life cycle. The first is planning and managing systems development. The second is behavioral problems faced in implementing systems changes. The last is feasibility analysis, which is an activity that is conducted at various stages in the life cycle.

The five phases of the systems development life cycle are discussed in more detail in Chapters 9 and 10. Chapter 9 deals with systems analysis and conceptual system design. Chapter 10 discusses physical systems design, implementation, and operation. Chapter 11, discusses other development approaches that have become quite popular in the past few years.

CHANGE: THE ONE CONSTANT IN INFORMATION SYSTEMS

Because we live in a highly competitive and ever-changing world, organizations are continually faced with a need for new, faster, and more reliable ways of obtaining information. To meet this need, an organization's information system must continually undergo changes, ranging from minor adjustments to major overhauls. Occasionally, the changes are so drastic that the old information system is scrapped and replaced by an entirely new information system. Change is so constant and so frequent that at any given time almost all organizations are involved in some level of system improvement or change. The result is that the development of most organizations' information systems is never completed.

Organizations like Shoppers Mart change their information system for a number of reasons. But most system changes are the result of one of the following events:

- *Changes in the business or nature of the organization:* Increased competition, business growth or consolidation, mergers and divestitures, new regulations, or changes in regional and global relationships can alter an organization's structure and purpose. In order to remain responsive to the needs of the organization, the information system must change as the organization changes.

- *Changes in the needs of people:* As people gain experience or take on new responsibilities, their information requirements often change.

- *Technological changes:* Typically, human and organizational needs exceed the available technology or the resources of the organization. As technology advances and becomes less costly, an organization can obtain a system that is much more responsive to the needs of its information users.

- *Competitive advantage:* If a company has more or better information and receives it faster than its competitors, it has a competitive advantage. This advantage may allow it to offer a better product, a better service, or a lower cost. For example, retailers such as Wal-Mart have spent heavily on technology to provide themselves with more information about their customers and what they purchase in order to increase sales. Bell Atlantic plans to invest $2.1 billion in the 1990s to develop a new information system. The system was approved by management because of its ability to increase revenues, which represented a shift in management focus, since previously 90% of new systems were approved to automate labor and reduce expenses.

■ *Productivity increases:* Computers allow many clerical and repetitive tasks to be automated. Expert systems and artificial intelligence allow the knowledge of experts to be used by many others. Systems improvements can also significantly decrease the time needed for certain tasks.

■ *Growth:* Companies often outgrow their information systems and either need to upgrade the capacities of their current system or need to replace it with a new system.

■ *Downsizing:* In recent years there has been a movement to downsize businesses to make them more competitive and more responsive to customer needs. There has been a corresponding movement to downsize from centralized mainframes to networked microcomputers to take advantage of the plunging price/performance ratios they offer. The downsizing movement has placed both the decision making and the information to make the decisions as far down the organization chart as possible.

■ *Improve quality:* Many organizations involved in total quality management (TQM) find it difficult to improve quality without first improving the information system that generates the data needed to measure and evaluate quality. In 1989 Carrier Corporation faced eroding market share owing to difficulties in servicing customers effectively. For example, a manual order entry system was plagued with a 70% error rate. Carrier started a TQM program and today an expert system coordinates everything from sales to manufacturing, resulting in fewer errors, lower costs, and happier customers.

■ *Reengineering:* When organizations first computerized their businesses, the common practice was to take manual procedures and automate them. Then as technology advanced, organizations tried to integrate the new technology into the system. But they ended up with business procedures and systems that are not as efficient as they could or should be. As a result, many companies have begun to completely redesign the way they do business in order to streamline their procedures. This process, called reengineering, seeks to use technology to simplify company operations and information systems as much as possible. Reengineering is discussed in depth in Chapter 11.

The Accountant's Role in Changing the Information System

In most business organizations accountants play a key role in the process of systems change. Ann Christy, the Controller for Shoppers Mart, is an accountant involved in systems change, for example. An accountant's involvement can take many forms, such as using, managing, auditing, or developing the system. In some firms the accounting and information systems' functions are the same. In these cases accountants are directly responsible for performing systems work. In most firms accountants are primary users of the information system and therefore must become involved in its design. Thus accountants should have a broad-based understanding of the process used to design or change an information system.

The functions of systems analysis and design in an organization have traditionally been performed by systems analysts. **Systems analysts** are responsible for developing and implementing information systems that satisfy the needs of users, such as accountants. Analysts study existing systems, design new computer applications, and prepare specifications for computer programming. The analyst deals with people, organizations, and systems technology in order to successfully bridge the gap between the user and technology. Like the accountant, the systems analyst is a central figure in the systems life cycle, playing a leading role in systems analysis, design, and implementation.

THE SYSTEMS DEVELOPMENT LIFE CYCLE

Ann Christy asked the Manager of Systems Development to explain the process Shoppers Mart would go through to design and implement a new information system. This process, known as the **systems development life cycle (SDLC)**, has five phases—systems analysis, conceptual design, physical design, implementation and conversion, and operation and maintenance. In each of these phases the activities shown in Fig. 8.1 are performed.

In addition, certain activities are performed throughout the life cycle. These include planning, managing behavioral reactions to change, and assessing the ongoing feasibility of the project.

Systems Analysis

During the **systems analysis phase** information relevant to the purchase or development of a new system is gathered. The analysis phase begins when a problem is perceived or a need for new information is identified. Because people and organizations are always trying to improve their information systems, requests for systems development are numerous. Since systems development projects are expensive and time-consuming, these requests must be screened carefully in order to save an organization's limited resources for the most worthwhile projects. This screening process is referred to as an initial investigation. A systems analyst conducting an initial investigation must gain a clear picture of the nature of the problem or need, determine the project's viability and expected costs and payoffs, make an initial evaluation of the extent of the project and the nature of the new system, and make recommendations about whether the development project should be initiated as proposed, modified, or abandoned.

Projects that pass this initial screening proceed to the systems survey where an extensive study of the current system is undertaken. The objectives of the survey are to further define the nature and scope of the project, gain a thorough understanding of the existing system's strengths and weaknesses, and make preliminary assessments of the

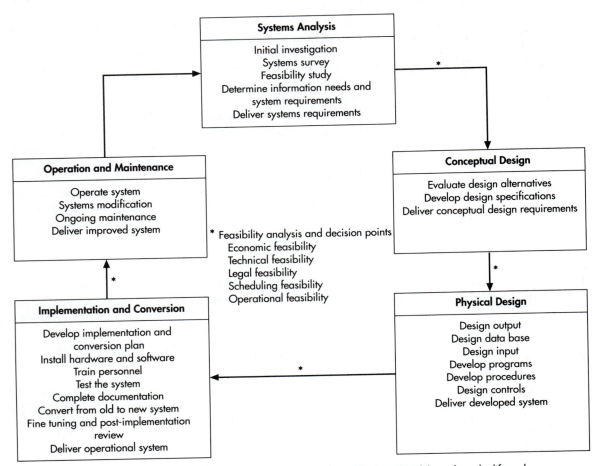

Planning must be done and behavioral aspects of change must be considered throughout the life cycle.

Figure 8.1

Developing information system solutions: the systems development life cycle

organization's current and future processing needs. Information can be gathered by interviewing system users and managers, gathering and analyzing current system documentation, preparing and distributing questionnaires, and observing system users and activities.

An in-depth study of the feasibility of the proposed system is usually conducted before corporate resources are committed. The project must be examined to ensure that expected system benefits exceed costs; the hardware, software, and personnel needed to solve the problem or information need are available; the system will be used by those whom it is intended to serve; the system is in compliance with all applicable laws and regulations; and the system can be developed in a timely manner.

If a project is feasible, the company identifies the information needs of system users and managers and develops and documents the requirements that the system must fulfill. These system requirements are used to select a prewritten system or to develop a new system. The analysis phase is brought to a close when a systems analysis report is prepared and submitted to management.

Conceptual Design

The first step in designing a system to meet the needs of users is referred to as the **conceptual**, or general, **systems design phase**. The first task in conceptual design is to identify and evaluate design alternatives that will meet the needs of the users. Once one of the design alternative has been selected, the systems developers must prepare detailed specifications outlining what the system is to accomplish and how it is to be controlled. This phase is completed by summarizing the conceptual design activities and presenting them to management.

Physical Design

During the **physical design phase** the company determines *how* the conceptual design is to be implemented. Physical design translates the broad, user-oriented requirements of the conceptual design into a detailed set of specifications that is used to code and test the computer programs. During this phase input and output documents are designed, computer programs are written, files are created, procedures are developed, and controls are built into the new system.

Implementation and Conversion

The **implementation and conversion phase** brings all the different elements and activities of the system together. An implementation and conversion plan should be developed and followed to coordinate the many implementation activities and minimize the difficulties of installing the new system. New employees may need to be hired and trained, or existing employees may need to be relocated. New processing procedures must be tested and new equipment must be installed and tested. Standards and controls for the new system must be established. System documentation—descriptions of procedures, charts, instructions for employees, and other descriptive material—must be completed.

When the new system is ready to begin functioning, it may be operated simultaneously with the old system for a brief period, so that the company can compare the output of the two systems to ensure that the new system has no major defects. The final step in this phase is the dismantling of the old system and complete conversion to the new one.

Operation and Maintenance

After the new system has been operating on its own for a short while, follow-up studies are usually conducted to detect and correct the inevitable design deficiencies that were not apparent at the point of conversion. Throughout its lifetime the system will be subject to periodic review. Minor modifications will be made as problems arise or as new needs become evident. This period is referred to as the **operation and maintenance phase**. Eventually, a major modification or replacement of the system will be necessary, and the systems development life cycle will begin all over again.

PLANNING AND MANAGING SYSTEMS DEVELOPMENT

Imagine that Jane and John Smith build a two-bedroom house. Several years later they add a bedroom: then they add another bedroom and a bathroom. Over the years they also add a family room, a recreation room, a deck, and a two-car garage; in addition, they expand the kitchen and the dining area. When they first build the house, if they give no thought to what they will eventually want in their home, the house probably will end up being a poorly organized patchwork of rooms surrounding the original structure. In addition, the cost of the house can end up greatly exceeding its value.

This scenario can also apply to information systems if they are not properly planned. The end result of poor systems planning is a costly and poorly integrated system that is difficult to operate and maintain.

Planning is important for a number of reasons.

- Planning helps ensure that the system will be consistent with the overall strategic plan of the organization.
- Planning facilitates efficient systems development, provides for coordination between information system subsystems, and provides a sound basis for selecting new applications for development.
- Planning helps an organization keep on top of the ever-present changes in information technology.
- Planning helps keep costs down; avoids duplication, wasted efforts, and cost and time overruns; and produces systems that are not costly or difficult to maintain.
- Planning facilitates management approval and helps developers meet users' and the organization's needs.
- Planning helps management prepare for future resource needs and prepare employees for the changes that will occur.

When development efforts are not well planned, organized, and managed, there is a frequent need to return to a prior phase and correct errors and design flaws, as illustrated in Fig. 8.2. This process is very costly and results in delays, frustration, and low morale. One way to minimize efforts is to do a good job of planning the development effort. For example, systems planning at MCI has been one important factor in that company's success, as explained in Focus 8.1.

The People Who Plan, Manage, and Develop Information Systems

Many people have a significant role in planning, managing, and developing an information system. They include management, the steering committee, and the project development team. The role each plays in system development is discussed next.

Management.   One of the most important factors in successful systems planning is obtaining the full support and involvement of top management. Nothing is quite as effective in generating support for a system as a clear signal from the top level of the organization that involvement in the systems function is important. In addition to supporting systems

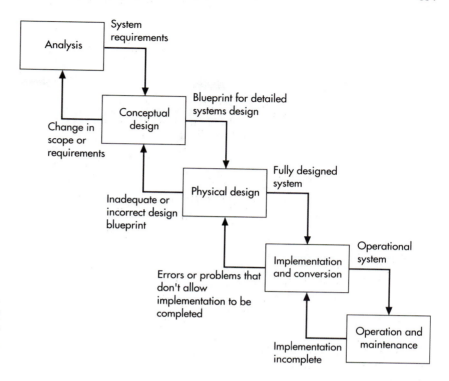

Figure 8.2
Reasons for returning to a prior systems development life cycle phase

projects, top management should establish the goals and objectives of the information system and integrate long-range systems plans with those of the organization; participate in major decisions relating to the systems function, such as hiring key personnel, acquisition of major equipment, and selection of major systems projects; review the performance of the systems department and its key management personnel; and establish policies relating to project selection, organizational structure, and career paths for systems personnel.

The principal roles of user management are to help determine information requirements for projects within their departments, cooperate with systems analysts in estimating the costs and benefits of proposed systems applications, assign key members of their staff to participate in systems development projects, and make a financial commitment in their departmental budgets to support the development and operation of new systems.

Information Systems Steering Committee.   Because information systems span functional and divisional boundaries, most organizations establish an executive-level **steering committee** to plan and oversee the IS function. The committee consists of management from the systems department, the controller, and other management affected by the information systems function. The steering committee is responsible for the policies that govern the organization's information system.

8.1 FOCUS

Planning Helps MCI Cope with Popular New Service

When MCI's Friends & Family service was introduced, order entry transaction volume soared 70% in three months. Fortunately, MCI was able to keep response times for the order en- try system within acceptable bounds. One reason MCI was prepared was because it does a lot of planning. Computer capac- ity planning and performance management are critical activ- ities at MCI, where double-digit annual growth is the norm and computing does not just support the business—it is the business. Five-year plans are updated an- nually, annual plans are revised

---

Steering committees provide several advantages. They help ensure the right level of top-management participation, guidance, and control of the information systems function. They also facilitate coordination and integration of information systems activities among departments and functions, thereby increasing goal congruence and reducing goal conflict.

Project Development Team.   Each development project is managed by a **project team** consisting of systems specialists, management, and users affected by the change. The team develops a project's plan and directs it through the steps of the systems life cycle. The team monitors the project to ensure its timely and cost-effective completion, makes sure that proper consideration is given to the human element in the system, and communicates the status of the project to top management and the steering committee. Team members should communicate frequently with users and hold regular meetings to consider ideas and discuss progress so that there are no surprises upon completion of the project. A team approach produces more effective results and facilitates the acceptance of the results by all parties concerned.

Systems Objectives and Constraints

An important step in planning an information system is to determine system objectives so that the analysis team can focus on the elements that are most vital to its success. Some of the most important objec- tives are shown in Table 8.1. It is difficult for any system to satisfy all these objectives. For example, the problem of maintaining adequate internal control must be viewed as a trade-off between the objectives of economy and reliability. Similarly, the problem of cutting clerical costs must be analyzed in terms of a trade-off between the objective of

quarterly, and quarterly plans may change biweekly. MCI's capacity planning staff has such a good track record that top management will accept, with little question, a recommendation to spend millions on a system.

The planning process takes input from three sources. Sales projections go into a computer model developed by MCI, as do service-level objectives such as response time. Out of the model flows capacity requirements for each of MCI's five data centers, indicating the need for hardware resources such as off-line and on-line storage and main memory and processor power. Capacity planners also factor in advance notice of new software coming from MCI's applications developers and forecasts of new technology from industry research firms and vendors.

Once applications are in production, MCI uses a variety of automated tools to spot abnormal patterns, looming bottlenecks, and other trouble spots. When they are found, the consulting group works with users and software developers to fine-tune applications or to smooth work loads.

Source: Gary H. Anthes, "Planning Spells Results at MCI," *Computerworld,* (January 27, 1992): 31.

Table 8.1
Information system objectives

Objective	Description
Usefulness	The information produced by the system should help management and users in decision making.
Economy	The benefits of the system should exceed the cost.
Reliability	The system should process data accurately and completely.
Availability	Users should be able to access the system at their convenience.
Timeliness	Critical information should be produced on a timely basis and less critical items processed as time permits.
Customer service	Courteous and efficient customer service should be provided.
Capacity	The system should have sufficient capacity to handle periods of peak operation and to handle future growth.
Ease of use	The system should be user-friendly.
Flexibility	The system should be sufficiently flexible to accommodate operating or system requirement changes of a reasonable magnitude.
Tractability	The system should be designed so that it can be easily understood by users and designers. Tractability facilitates problem solving and future systems development.
Auditability	The auditability of a system can be maximized if it is considered at the very beginning of systems development.
Security	The system should include safeguards so that only authorized users can access or change data.

economy, on the one hand, and the objectives of capacity, flexibility, and customer service, on the other.

The project team must realize that the success of a system often depends on its ability to cope with the constraints under which the organization is operating. Some common constraints are requirements imposed by an external unit such as a governmental agency, management policies and guidelines, lack of sufficiently qualified people, the capabilities and attitudes of system users, available technology, and limited financial resources. It is the responsibility of all concerned with the system to find ways to minimize the effects of these constraints on systems design.

Strategies for Systems Development

Systems change is handled best when an organization takes a systems approach. The systems approach recognizes that every system must have an objective, a set of components, and a set of interrelationships among the components. The system objectives form a framework for the analysis of problems and opportunities. With the systems approach problems and alternatives are viewed from the standpoint of the entire organization, rather than from that of any single department or interest group.

Organizational constraints usually make it impossible to develop all parts of a new information system simultaneously. Therefore, organizations divide the system into smaller subsystems, or modules, that are analyzed, developed, and installed independently. Great care should be taken to ensure that the system's modules are properly integrated into a workable system. Then when changes are made to the system, only the affected module needs to be changed.

Systems analysis and design strategies are of two basic types: bottom-up and top-down. In the bottom-up approach individual applications are designed and developed as needed. The integration of the various independent modules is then addressed as the need for integration arises. Often the process of integration is difficult, and various modules must be redesigned to achieve integration.

The top-down approach begins with a definition of the organization's objectives and strategies. Next, information requirements for the organization as a whole are determined. The information system is viewed as a fully integrated system, rather than as a collection of loosely coordinated subsystems. Top management participates directly in the analysis and design process. This approach tends to build management knowledge and support, which often results in a greater willingness to commit resources. One potential problem is that an organization may attempt to apply the approach on too broad a scale, in search of the elusive total information system. This can lead to a dramatic failure.

The best procedure is a combination of the two approaches. It is essential that the needs and suggestions of lower-level employees be solicited and considered (information flow from bottom to top). Management can then develop a system that meets the organization's needs, using the top-down approach.

Information Systems Plans

For the information system at Shoppers Mart to be successfully designed and implemented, the company will need to develop two different types of plans: individual project plans prepared by project teams and a master plan developed by the information system steering committee.

Project Development Plan.   The basic building block of information systems planning is the **project development plan**. Each plan contains an analysis of the benefits and costs of the proposed application; a list of the developmental and operational requirements of the new application or system, including requirements for personnel, hardware and software resources, and financial resources; and a schedule of the activities required to develop and operate the new application or system.

The Master Plan.   All existing application and individual project planning requirements can be summed together to project total information system resource requirements. The **master plan** should be more than just an aggregation of the individual project plans. It should be a long-range planning document that specifies what the system will consist of, how it will be developed, who will develop it, how needed resources will be acquired, and where the information system is headed. The master plan should also give the status of projects in process, prioritize planned projects, describe the criteria used for prioritization, and provide timetables for development. The projects with the highest priority should be the first to proceed to the systems analysis phase. The importance of this decision dictates that it be made by top management and not by computer specialists.

In her study of company operations, Ann Christy obtained a copy of the table of contents of the master plan used at Shoppers Mart. It is shown in Table 8.2.

A planning horizon of approximately five years is reasonable for any master plan. The plan should be updated at least once each year. MCI, which uses a five-year plan, updates parts of its master plan as often as biweekly.

Documenting the Systems Development Process

Documentation provides detailed information on how a system works so that it can be operated, maintained, and audited. It also helps ensure that all relevant decisions and actions have taken place during each phase of the project. In addition, it facilitates management and supervisory review and control.

Documentation standards should be established for the methodology to be used in the development, to report and monitor progress, and to review and approve procedures. These standards should specify the documents to be generated, the format for each document, and the individuals responsible for each document. A separate group is sometimes organized to monitor and collect the documentation generated by each development project. Some of the documentation generated during systems development is shown in Table 8.3.

```
Organizational goals and objectives
     Company mission statement and organization goals
     Strategic plan: how the IS can help Shoppers Mart reach its goal
     Organizational constraints
     Organizational approach to information systems
     Organization and information system priorities
Assessment of current capabilities
     Inventory and assessment of current systems
     Inventory and assessment of approved systems
     Inventory and assessment of current hardware
     Inventory and assessment of current software
     Inventory and assessment of current personnel
     Assessment of current strengths and weakness
Status of systems being developed
Analysis of proposed systems and their priorities
     Systems approved for developmental activities
     Proposals for development under consideration
     Timetables and schedules of systems development
Forecast of future developments affecting plan
     Forecasts of future organizational information needs
     Forecasts of technological developments
     Forecasts of environmental/regulatory changes
     Audit and control requirements
     Government or other external user needs
```

Table 8.2
Components of the systems master
plan at Shoppers Mart

Control and Audit Considerations

All information systems should contain sufficient controls to ensure the accurate and complete processing of data. They should also be easy to audit. Auditability and control of a system can be maximized if these concerns are considered at the very beginning of systems development. Trying to achieve auditability and control after an information system has already been designed is much more inefficient, time-consuming, and costly. For this reason auditors should be involved in the design of the system. Their responsibility should be to design controls into the system, to verify that these controls are implemented in the system, and to monitor and test the system periodically after it is running. (Control and audit issues are discussed in depth in Chapters 12–15.)

BEHAVIORAL ASPECTS OF CHANGE

The saying that "there is nothing so constant as change" is particularly applicable to information systems. Change in an organization's information system may lead, in turn, to both formal and informal changes within the organization. Formal changes may affect department boundaries, communication channels, divisions of responsibilities, and working relationships between line and staff groups. Informal changes may

Life Cycle Phase	Documentation
Systems analysis	Data dictionaries
	Data flow diagrams
	Document and system flowcharts
	Feasibility study
	Interview and observation notes
	Input, output, file, and data base layouts and descriptions
	Proposal to conduct systems analysis
	Questionnaires, responses, and analysis
	System requirements report
	Systems survey report
	Systems analysis report
	User requirements
Conceptual systems design	Conceptual design report
	Control and security specifications
	Data flow diagrams
	Document and system flowcharts
	File or data base specifications
	HIPO charts (hierarchy plus input process output)
	Input and output specifications
	Structured English program specifications
Systems acquisition	Benchmark rankings and documentation
	Point-scoring analysis
	Request for proposals (RFP) and responses
	Requirements costing documentation
	Systems acquisition report
	Vendor, software, and hardware selection criteria
Physical design	Control and security descriptions and documentation
	Data entry procedures
	Procedures and manuals for operators and users
	Program flowcharts and documentation
	Training plans and materials
Implementation and conversion	Implementation and conversion plan
	Testing plan
Operation, maintenance, and control	Audit plans
	Maintenance schedules
	Operating schedules

Table 8.3
Documentation of the systems
development process

affect the working and social relationships of people, their group work norms, and their status. The less visible informal changes are generally a by-product of a formal change. Systems designers often fail to consider the informal changes, which to many employees are more important than the formal changes.

Individuals involved in systems development are agents of change. They must interact with users, management, and others to gather data about the existing system, develop system requirements, and propose and design changes to the system. In doing so, they are continually confronted with how humans react to and deal with change. These behavioral aspects of change are critical, because the best system will fail if it does not have the support of the people it is intended to serve. Those involved in system development should expect to meet resistance to change. Niccolo Machiavelli, in his book *The Prince*, discussed resistance to change some four hundred years ago. He said:

> *It must be considered that there is nothing more difficult to carry out, nor more doubtful of success, not more dangerous to handle, than to initiate a new order of things. For the reformer has enemies in all those who could profit by the old order, and only lukewarm defenders in all those who could profit by the new order. This lukewarmness arises partly from fear of their adversaries, who have the laws in their favor, and partly from the incredulity of mankind, who do not truly believe in anything new until they have had an actual experience of it.*[1]

Those involved in change should employ sound principles of human relations; that is, they should be sensitive to and consider the feelings and reactions of persons affected by the change. They should also be aware of potential problems and seek to avoid them.

This section considers why problems occur when changes are made in an organization, how people typically react to changes, and how problems resulting from behavioral changes can be minimized or eliminated.

Why Behavioral Problems Occur

Each new system or change in an existing system is intended to improve the system and make it more efficient. Those affected, however, may not view the change in the same light. Individuals will usually view a change as good or bad depending on how they are personally affected by it. Management, for example, will view a change positively if it increases profits or performance or reduces costs. An employee, on the other hand, will view the same change as bad if his or her job is terminated or adversely affected.

To minimize or eliminate adverse behavioral reactions to change, one must first understand why resistance takes place. Some of the more important factors affecting the acceptance of change are described in the following list.

- *Personal characteristics and background:* Generally speaking, the younger people are, the fewer years they've been with the company, and the more highly educated they are, the more likely they are to

---

[1] Nicollo Machiavelli, *The Prince*, translated by Luigi Rice, revised by E. R. P. Vincent (New York: New American Library, 1952).

accept change. Likewise, the more positive the outlook people have about automation, the less likely they are to oppose change.

■ *Manner in which change is introduced:* Resistance is often a reaction to the methods of instituting change rather than to change itself. For example, the rationale used to sell the system to top management may not be appropriate for lower-level employees. The elimination of menial tasks and the ability to advance and grow are often more important to users than increasing profits or reducing costs.

■ *Experience with prior changes:* If employees have had a bad experience with prior changes, they tend to be more reluctant to cooperate with planned changes.

■ *Top-management support:* If employees sense a lack of top-management support, they may think, "If top management doesn't support it, why should I?"

■ *Communication:* Employees often do not know why changes are made. Unless management makes it clear that a change is not an indication of poor performance, they may react negatively to it.

■ *Biases and natural resistance to change:* People often have emotional attachments to their duties or to the people they work with, and they simply don't want to change.

■ *Disruptive nature of the change process:* Requests for information and interviews are disruptive of the normal routine and place additional burdens on people. These requests can thus create negative feelings toward the system.

■ *Fear:* Many people fear the unknown, the uncertainty accompanying change, loss of their jobs, loss of respect or status, failure, technology, and automation.

How People Resist Change

Behavioral problems may begin as soon as people find out that a change is being made. Initial resistance is often subtle; it may be manifested by arriving late for work, performing duties sluggishly, or failing to provide information to systems analysts. Major behavioral problems often occur after the new system has been implemented—that unpleasant possibility the employee was trying to ignore is now a reality. Major resistance often takes one of three forms: aggression, projection, or avoidance.

Aggression.   Aggressive behavior is usually intended to destroy, cripple, or lessen the effectiveness of a system. **Aggression** may take the form of increased error rates, disruptions, or deliberate sabotage. One organization, for instance, introduced an on-line information system in one of its branches, only to discover soon thereafter that the data input devices were inoperable. Some devices had honey poured into them, others had been mysteriously run over by forklifts, and still others had paper clips rather than badge cards inserted in them. The system was also plagued with errors in the data input.

More subtle forms of aggression may subvert the purpose for which the system was designed. When one organization installed an information system to collect work hours in different workstations on a daily basis, some workers used the system to gang up on an unpopular foreman. Workers were supposed to clock in and out each time they moved from one station to another. Instead, they would punch in at the unpopular foreman's area and then work in a different area. This adversely affected the unpopular foreman's performance, as he was charged for hours that did not belong to his operations.

Projection.   Projection involves blaming anything and everything on the new system. For example, missing and incorrect data, which were present but simply undetected in the manual system, are initially blamed on an automated system until the actual cause is determined. In essence, the system becomes the scapegoat for all real and imagined problems and errors. Like a snowball moving downhill, the system can gather more and more negative comments from people as time passes. If these criticisms are not controlled or answered, the effectiveness of the system can be damaged or even destroyed.

Avoidance.   Dealing with problems through avoidance is a common human trait. For example, if a person cannot decide between two job offers, he may delay the decision until one company withdraws its offer and the decision is made for him. Likewise, if people have a problem with an information system, they may just avoid using the system. These people are hoping that the problem (the system) will either go away or resolve itself.

Preventing Behavioral Problems

Some people think that the human element is the most significant problem a company encounters in designing, developing, and implementing an information system. There is no one best way to overcome behavioral problems. However, systems development personnel can improve people's reactions to a system by observing the following guidelines when designing and implementing the system.

- *Meet the needs of the users.* It is essential that the form, content, and volume of system output be designed to satisfy the needs of the users.
- *Keep lines of communication open.* Managers and users should be fully informed of system changes as soon as possible. They should be told what changes are being made and why, and they should be shown how the new system will benefit them. The objective here is to allow employees to identify with the company in its efforts to improve the system. This policy helps prevent employees from feeling that the company has goals and plans separate from, or even opposed to, those of the employees. Open communication also

helps prevent damaging and inaccurate rumors and misunderstandings.

- *Provide a proper atmosphere.* It is critical that everyone affected by systems development have an attitude of trust and cooperation. If employees become hostile, it will be very difficult to change their attitude or to successfully implement the system.

- *Get management support.* Top management should fully support the system and make it clear that everyone else is expected to support the system. Where possible, a powerful owner or champion, who can provide resources for the system and motivate others to assist and cooperate with systems development, should be found.

- *Allay fears.* Systems designers should provide assurances, to the degree possible, that there will be no major changes in job responsibilities or loss of jobs. These goals can often be achieved through relocation of displaced personnel, normal attrition, and early retirement. If employees must be terminated, severance pay and assistance in obtaining new positions should be provided. These policies may be expensive, but the decline in morale caused by the lack of such policies can be even more expensive. Likewise, individuals who implement the change should provide assurances that they are genuinely concerned with making life better for those involved in the system. This should help the employees affected to remain relaxed and productive during the change.

- *Have users participate.* Those who will use or otherwise be affected by the system should participate in its development by providing data, making suggestions, and helping make decisions. Participation is ego enhancing, challenging, and intrinsically satisfying, and it builds self-esteem and security. Users who participate in developing a system are more knowledgeable about the technical aspects of the system and are better trained to use it. They are also more committed to the system and therefore more likely to use it. In addition, the new system is usually better if users participate in its development, because users know more about the old system and their needs than systems developers do. Although user participation is critical, designers must be careful not to require too much time from users during development, since this would disrupt their normal activities.

- *Provide honest feedback on user suggestions.* Users should be encouraged to provide suggestions to improve the system. However, if they make suggestions that are not implemented and are not given an explanation about why they were not used, bad feelings may result. To avoid misunderstandings, developers should tell users which suggestions are being used and how they are being implemented, which suggestions are not being used and why, and which suggestions will be incorporated at a later date and why they are not being incorporated at the present time.

- *Make sure users understand the system.* Effective use or support cannot be obtained if users are confused about or do not understand the system. Generally, much more explanation is needed than systems designers, who have a working knowledge of computers, think is necessary.

- *Humanize the system.* Acceptance of the system is not likely if individuals believe, rightly or wrongly, that the computer is controlling them or has usurped their positions.

- *Describe new challenges and opportunities.* Systems analysts should attempt to discover and emphasize important and challenging tasks that can be performed with the new system. They should point out that the system may provide greater job satisfaction and increased opportunities for advancement.

- *Reexamine performance evaluation.* Employees will resist a new system if it causes them to be evaluated on the basis of something over which they have no control. Management should reexamine performance evaluation criteria and the reward system to ensure that they are satisfactory for all those affected by the system.

- *Test the system's integrity.* The system should be properly tested prior to implementation to minimize initial bad impressions.

- *Avoid emotionalism.* When logic vies with emotion, logic doesn't stand a chance. Emotional issues should be sidestepped, allowed to cool, or otherwise handled in a nonconfrontational manner. Employees should not be forced into taking a stand on the basis of emotion; that stand may be very hard for them to abandon.

- *Sell the system properly.* Advantages of a system such as reduced operating costs, streamlined operations, and reduced head count are not likely to appeal to lower-level employees. These employees are generally more interested in how the change will affect them personally. They must be sold on the system by arguments that address their concerns.

- *Control the users' expectations.* At times a system is sold too well and users have unrealistic expectations of the system and what it will be able to do. Be realistic when describing the merits of the system.

- *Keep the system simple.* Avoid complex systems that cause radical changes. Make the change seem as simple as possible by conforming to existing organizational procedures where possible.

Observing these guidelines is both time-consuming and expensive. As a result, there is a tendency to skip the more difficult steps (like maintaining open communication) in order to speed up systems development and installation. However, ignoring behavioral considerations often has very serious consequences. It is usually better to spend the extra time and money to ensure that a system is well accepted and well designed.

FEASIBILITY ANALYSIS

Development of a new system can cost millions of dollars and take many years to complete. Because of the significant dollar and time costs, management is understandably reluctant to start a new systems project without studying its feasibility. A feasibility study (also referred to as a business case) is intended to provide the objective information management needs to determine whether or not to start a new development project or to continue a project already in development. The extent and duration of feasibility studies vary, depending on the size and the nature of the system to be implemented. For example, the feasibility study for a large-scale system is generally quite extensive. On the other hand, the study for a desktop system might be conducted very informally.

As with any systems study, the study team should include both people with technical knowledge and people with knowledge of and experience in the operations of the business. If people with technical knowledge are not available within the organization, consultants familiar with the company or the industry can be hired. Representatives should also be obtained from top management and from internal control or internal auditing. User involvement is critical, since only users can supply much of the effort, knowledge, and experience required.

Feasibility studies are initially performed before a project is undertaken. Then as the project proceeds, the feasibility analysis is updated so that the viability of the project can be continually assessed. The purpose of updating and reassessment is to avoid wasting time and money on projects that are doomed to fail or that are not worthwhile. As project development unfolds, things sometimes come to light to show that a project originally deemed feasible is actually not a good idea. The farther into a development project, the less likely it is to cancel the project if a proper feasibility study has been prepared and updated. Although it is not common, systems have been scrapped after the design is completed and prior to implementation.

Of course, projects can also be scrapped after they are implemented, either because they do not work or because they do not meet an organization's needs. Bank America, for example, hired a software firm to replace a 20-year-old batch system used to manage billions of dollars in institutional trust accounts. In 1987, after two years of development, it was implemented despite warnings that it was not adequately tested. Ten months later the system of 2.5 million lines of code was scrapped, the bank's top systems and trust executives had resigned, and the company had taken a $60 million write-off to cover expenses related to the system. During the 10 months the system was in place the company lost 100 institutional accounts with $4 billion in assets. As another example, Focus 8.2 describes a project at Blue Cross and Blue Shield that was scrapped after 6 years of work and $120 million dollars of expense.

As a project progresses, more information becomes available, allowing a more accurate decision to be made regarding feasibility. Therefore each level of feasibility analysis is more detailed and extensive

FOCUS 8.2

Blue Cross Abandons Runaway

Blue Cross and Blue Shield of Massachusetts hoped that its new information system would usher in a new era at Blue Cross. However, after six years and $120 million the project was behind schedule and significantly over budget. The project was canceled, and Blue Cross turned its computer operation over to Electronic Data Systems Corporation, an outside contractor.

While information system failures of this magnitude are rare, they happen more often than one would expect. According to a KPMG Peat Marwick survey, 35% of all major information system projects become a "runaway"—a project that is millions of dollars over budget and months or years behind schedule. Other surveys show that almost every *Fortune 200* company has had at least one runaway.

One major reason for the de-

than the prior level. Evaluating a proposal at increasing levels of detail during the various phases of the life cycle and continually reassessing the project's viability help to ensure that projects are not pursued unless they appear to be in the company's best interests. This process of preparing, updating, and using feasibility analyses is summarized in Fig. 8.3.

Feasibility documentation should include all relevant information gathered during the study. If several different alternatives are being considered, the report should document each of the alternatives. The documentation should contain descriptions of the project, the system's performance requirements, and the proposed system solutions. It should contain explanations of why the project is being undertaken and the critical assumptions on which the study is based. It should also contain a listing of the expected tangible and intangible costs and benefits of the proposed solution.

Types of Feasibility Analysis

Several dimensions should be evaluated during a feasibility study, including technical, economic, operational, legal, and scheduling feasibility.

With **technical feasibility** the basic question is, Can the planned system be developed and implemented in the organization using existing technology?

Several questions may arise for **operational feasibility**. Does the organization have access to people who can design, implement, and operate the

velopment problems was Blue Cross's failure to properly supervise the project. Blue Cross hired an independent contractor to develop the software and failed to appoint someone to coordinate and manage the project. Top management did not set a firm set of priorities stating which features of the system were essential and which applications should be developed first.

When the developers presented the claims processing software to Blue Cross, they thought it was a finished product. The managers and users at Blue Cross had other ideas. They were not happy with the software and requested numerous changes. As a result, the whole project was delayed. This led to ever-increasing cost overruns. By the time System 21 was launched, Blue Cross had fallen way behind its competitors in its ability to process an ever-swelling load of paperwork. In fact, between 1985 and 1991 it lost a million subscribers and came close to bankruptcy. It also had a poorly integrated system—nine different claims processing systems running on hardware dating back to the early 1970s.

The lesson that Blue Cross learned with System 21 was a painful one. The system it spent six years working on was abandoned, and it turned its hardware over to EDS. Fortunately, although the system died, the patient survived.

Source: Geoffery Smith, "The Computer System that Nearly Hospitalized an Insurer," *Business Week* (June 15, 1992): 133.

proposed system? Can and will the system be used by those within the organization whom it is intended to serve? The answers depend on an organization's environment, its existing procedures, how motivated its personnel are to support the system, and the behavioral issues discussed earlier in the chapter.

A major question for **legal feasibility** is: Will there be any conflict between the system under consideration and the organization's ability to discharge its legal obligations? The proposed system should comply with all applicable federal and state statutes and administrative agency regulations, as well as all contractual obligations by which the company is bound.

Scheduling feasibility must answer the question of whether the system can be developed and implemented in the time allotted. If it cannot, the system will have to be modified, a different alternative selected, or the date of implementation postponed. However, adding development resources does not always reduce development time. Adding staff who cannot be used effectively may even impede development.

Two questions must be answered for **economic feasibility**. First, will the benefits from the proposed system justify the time, money, and other resources and costs required to implement it? Second, does the organization have the funds necessary to develop and implement the system, given the requirements of other capital projects within the organization? In order to answer these questions, developers must investigate and analyze the various costs and benefits associated with each alter-

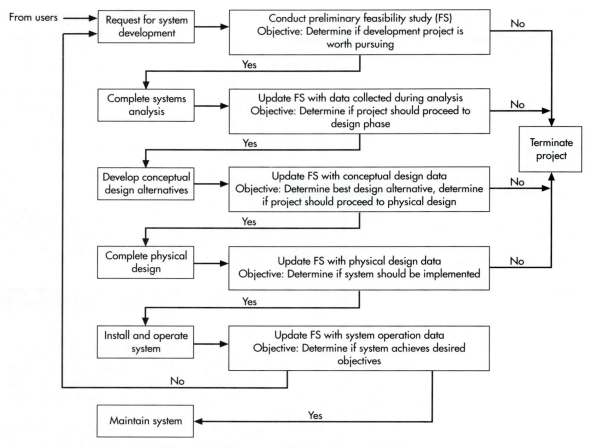

The viability of system development projects must be continuously assessed.

Figure 8.3
Preparation, update, and use of feasibility studies (FS)

native. Economic feasibility, which is the most important and fre-quently used of the five dimensions, is discussed in greater depth in the following section.

Economic Feasibility: Calculating Costs and Benefits

Determining economic feasibility requires a careful investigation of the costs and benefits of a proposed system. Because accountants are familiar with cost concepts, they can make a significant contribution to this evaluation. The basic framework for feasibility analysis is the **capital budgeting model**. This model requires that dollar estimates be made of the initial outlay costs, operating costs and other cash outflows, and cost savings and other benefits. The benefits are then compared with the costs to determine if the system is cost-beneficial.

The benefit and cost estimates must be made for each year that the system will be in use. It is usually not too difficult to develop estimates of the initial outlay and operating costs for a computer system. In contrast, making reliable estimates of the expected cost savings and other benefits can be a formidable task. If a number of alternatives are available, planners can choose the one that has the highest net present value, the highest internal rate of return, or the fastest payback.

Initial Outlay Costs. Equipment costs represent an initial outlay cost if the system is purchased or an operating cost if the system is rented or leased. Equipment costs vary from personal computer systems that sell for less than $2000 to enormous mainframes costing millions of dollars. Many people mistakenly think that the cost of the computer system itself is the major expense. In reality, the cost of acquiring the software and of maintaining, supporting, and operating the system is almost always more than that of the equipment.

Software acquisition costs include the cost of acquiring the operating system, utility routines, compilers, application programs, and so forth, as well as the time and effort required to design, program, test, and document the users' application software. The personnel costs associated with hiring, training, and relocating personnel may be substantial. Site preparation costs may be incurred for large computer systems. There are costs involved in installing the new system and converting files to the storage media used by the new system. A significant element of this cost arises from the need for a period of parallel operation of the old and new systems prior to the final changeover. These costs are summarized in Table 8.4.

Operating Costs. The primary continuing operating cost is that of maintaining the system. Studies have shown that between 65% and 75% of an organization's systems efforts are spent in maintaining current information systems. In addition, there may be significant annual cash outflows for equipment replacement and expansion and software updates. Personnel costs include the salaries of systems analysts, programmers, operators, data entry personnel, and management. Costs are also incurred for supplies, overhead, and financial charges.

Benefits. The following list identifies some of the tangible and intangible benefits a company might obtain from a new system.

- Cost savings from reducing the number of clerical personnel. However, these savings may be offset by the costs of staffing the computer system.

- Improved customer service. Increased inventory control, for example, means fewer stockouts, and more efficient customer order handling means fewer errors and faster delivery.

- Improved productivity. The use of spreadsheet programs, for example, significantly reduces the time required to perform routine analytical and clerical functions.

- Improved management decision making. With more timely, more comprehensive, and more reliable information, managers can make critical decisions more effectively.

Hardware
  Central processing unit (mainframe, mini-
    computer, or microcomputer)
  Peripherals (hard and floppy disk drives,
    printers, terminals, etc.)
  Communications (networks, modems, tele-
    phone lines, fax machines, and
    instruments)
  Data preparation equipment
  Input and source data automation devices
  Specialized output devices (voice response,
    microfilm, etc.)

System upgrade costs
  Processor expansion or upgrade
  Additional storage capacity
  Updated version of software

Software
  Application software design, programming,
    and testing
  Program and system documentation
  Application software purchase costs
  System software (Operating system, lan-
    guage translators, and utilities)
  General purpose software (DBMS, Spread-
    sheets, word processors, etc.)
  Communications software (E-mail, voice
    mail, etc.)

Documentation
  System documentation
  Training program documentation
  Operating standards and procedures

Personnel
  Supervisory personnel
  Recruiting and training
  Input (data conversion) personnel
  Computer operators
  Consultants
  Systems analysts and programmers

Site preparation
  Air-conditioning, humidity, dust controls
  Physical security (access)
  Additional floor space
  Fire and water protection
  Cabling, wiring, and outlets
  Furnishing and fixtures

Installation
  Freight and delivery charges
  Setup and connection
  Rearrangement of existing furniture and
    fixtures

Conversion
  Systems testing
  File and data conversions
  Parallel operations

Supplies
  Forms modification and design
  Data storage devices (tapes, disks,
    floppies)
  Computer supplies (paper, preprinted forms,
    ribbons, toner, etc.)

Overhead
  Utilities and power

Maintenance/backup
  Hardware/software maintenance
  Backup and recovery operations
  Power supply protection

Financial
  Finance charge
  Legal fees
  Insurance
  Sales and property taxes

Table 8.4
Initial outlay and operating costs

- Better management control, as a result of programs that spotlight the extremes of good and bad performance in the organization.

- More accurate data processing, resulting in fewer errors and better control over the processing of data.

- Reduced operating costs, increased processing capability, and improved job satisfaction and employee morale.

Capital Budgeting. During conceptual systems design several alternative approaches to meeting the stated objectives and requirements of the system are generally developed. Various feasibility measures are then used to narrow the list of alternatives. After this initial culling, the primary basis for subsequent analysis becomes the relative economic merits of the remaining alternatives. One of the best frameworks for making this decision is capital budgeting techniques.

Capital budgeting techniques deal only with quantitative factors. Unquantifiable factors can be included by estimating costs or benefits, assigning probability estimates to each, and then including the expected values in the analysis. If unquantifiable factors are excluded, they should at least be listed and their likelihood and expected impact on the organization evaluated. Bases of comparison in capital budgeting techniques include payback period, net present value, and internal rate of return.

The **payback period** is the number of years required for the net savings to equal the initial cost of the investment. When several projects are compared, the one with the shortest payback period is selected. When one project is evaluated, its payback period is compared with a minimum standard to determine acceptance or rejection.

In the **net present value** (NPV) method all estimated future cash flows are discounted back to the present, using a discount rate that reflects the time value of money to the organization. The initial outlay costs are deducted from the discounted cash flows to obtain the net present value. A positive net present value indicates that the alternative is economically feasible. When several projects are compared, the one with the highest positive net present value is accepted.

The **internal rate of return** (IRR) is the effective interest rate that equates the present value of the total costs to the present value of the total savings. When only one project is evaluated, its rate of return is compared with a minimum acceptable rate to determine acceptance or rejection. When several projects are compared, the proposal with the highest effective internal rate is selected.

CASE CONCLUSION: BEGINNING THE SYSTEMS DEVELOPMENT PROCESS AT SHOPPERS MART

The months since Ann Christy had met with the Manager of Systems Development had passed quickly. The meeting had helped her understand the development process (or life cycle) that the company would need to follow to design and implement the system.

One of the first things she did was to prepare her presentation to top management. Her first task was to decide the type of system that would give Shoppers Mart a competitive advantage. To do so, she used her interview notes, studied the systems used by competitors, and had several more discussions with the Systems Development staff.

Ann concluded that the corporate office should use satellite technology to gather sales data from each store on a daily basis. Analyzing the prior day's sales for each store would help Shoppers Mart minimize stockouts and overstocking. Making this sales data available to suppliers would help them respond more quickly to Shoppers Mart's need for merchandise.

Coordinating buying at the corporate office would help Shoppers Mart negotiate lower wholesale prices. Stores could send in orders electronically the day they are prepared. On the basis of store orders, the analysis of each store's sales of the prior day, and current warehouse inventory levels, Shoppers Mart could use electronic data interchange to send purchase orders to suppliers. The suppliers could process the order and send the goods the day they received the order.

Ann also wanted to coordinate purchasing so that inventory levels were minimized. She wanted to have suppliers deliver merchandise to regional warehouses the same day they were to be shipped to the stores. At the same time, she wanted to allow each store the flexibility to order locally to respond to local sales trends and conditions. She also wanted to centralize most accounts payable so that the firm could make payments electronically.

Each store would have a local area network connected to the corporate data bases. The LAN could be used to meet the store's individual information needs. Access to the corporate data base would allow the store to access the corporate data it needs for decision making. These two features would allow the stores to meet their information needs.

Ann reviewed the proposed system with the legal department and her own staff and was assured that the system complied with all legal considerations. Ann discussed it with the systems people at Shoppers Mart, and they assured her that the system was possible technologically. Freeing up personnel and scheduling them to work on such a massive system was another matter. That was a decision that would have to be made by top management and communicated to the systems people.

To assess the economics of the project, Ann did a preliminary feasibility study and found that the project appeared to be an excellent use of funds. Ann estimated that the new system would cost $5 million. The company would depreciate the computer hardware over its expected six-year life. Ann also estimated the system's recurring operating costs and the cost savings from installing the system. A 34% tax rate applies to the company, and the company's cost of capital is 10%. According to her calculations, the system would pay for itself in the fourth year. With an interest rate of 10% the project would generate a return, adjusted for the time value of money, of over $3 million. The internal rate of return calculation shows that the project will earn a return of 25% over its six-year life. The details of Ann's feasibility study are shown in Table 8.5.

Ann presented the proposed system to top management and described its objectives. She also presented the preliminary feasibility study she had prepared by handing out a hard copy and by projecting it onto a screen. All challenges to her initial estimates were plugged into the model and management could instantly see what effect the changed

	Initial Outlay	Year 1	Year 2	Year 3	Year 4	Year 5	Year 6
Initial outlay costs							
Hardware	$2,000,000						
Software	400,000						
Training	200,000						
Site preparation	200,000						
Initial systems design	2,000,000						
Conversion	200,000						
Total initial outlays	$5,000,000						
Recurring costs							
Hardware expansion			$260,000	$300,000	$340,000	$380,000	$400,000
Software			150,000	200,000	225,000	250,000	250,000
Systems maintenance		60,000	120,000	130,000	140,000	150,000	160,000
Personnel costs		500,000	800,000	900,000	1,000,000	1,100,000	1,300,000
Communication charges		100,000	160,000	180,000	200,000	220,000	250,000
Overhead		300,000	420,000	490,000	560,000	600,000	640,000
Total costs		$960,000	$1,910,000	$2,200,000	$2,465,000	$2,700,000	$3,000,000
Savings							
Clerical cost savings		$600,000	$1,200,000	$1,400,000	$1,600,000	$1,800,000	$2,000,000
Working capital savings		900,000	1,200,000	1,500,000	1,500,000	1,500,000	1,500,000
Profits from sales increases			500,000	900,000	1,200,000	1,500,000	1,800,000
Warehousing efficiencies			400,000	800,000	1,200,000	1,600,000	2,000,000
Total savings		$1,500,000	$3,300,000	$4,600,000	$5,500,000	$6,400,000	$7,300,000
Net savings (costs)		540,000	1,390,000	2,400,000	3,035,000	3,700,000	4,300,000
Less income taxes (34% rate)		(183,600)	(472,600)	(816,000)	(1,031,900)	(1,258,000)	(1,462,000)
Cash savings (net of tax)		$356,400	$917,400	$1,584,000	$2,003,100	$2,442,000	$2,838,000
Savings on taxes due to depreciation deduction		340,000	544,000	326,400	195,500	195,500	98,600
Net savings	($5,000,000)	696,400	1,461,400	1,910,400	2,198,600	2,637,500	2,936,600

Payback occurs in the fourth year when the savings net of taxes of $6,266,800   exceed the costs of $5,000,000

Net present value (interest rate of 10%):

(5,000,000)	(5,000,000)
696,400 × 0.9091 =	633,097
1,461,400 × 0.8265 =	1,207,847
1,910,400 × 0.7513 =	1,435,284
2,198,600 × 0.6830 =	1,501,644
2,637,500 × 0.6209 =	1,637,624
2,936,600 × 0.5645 =	1,657,711
Net present value	3,073,206
Internal rate of return is	25.04%

Depreciation on initial investment of $5,000,000
Taxrate   34%

Year	MACRS rate	Depreciation	Tax savings
1	20.00%	1,000,000	340,000
2	32.00%	1,600,000	544,000
3	19.20%	960,000	326,400
4	11.50%	575,000	195,500
5	11.50%	575,000	195,500
6	5.80%	290,000	98,600

Table 8.5   Economic feasibility study for Shoppers Mart's new information system

assumptions would have on the return. Even when the stiffest challenges to Ann's numbers were plugged into the model, the system showed a very positive return. As a result of this meeting, top management was very supportive and enthusiastic about the new system. The managers requested that a number of changes be made to the system and gave Ann approval to begin the systems analysis phase of the project. The managers requested another meeting with Ann and her team at the conclusion of the analysis phase, when they would decide whether to proceed to the design phases. In the meantime, Ann was to update the feasibility study as she gathered more information.

Ann soon found that the enthusiastic support of management was critical to the success of the new system. Several employees who had vested interests in the old system were very critical of her ideas. Most felt that the current system was adequate and that her new ideas just would not work. Some employees remembered the problems Shoppers Mart had when the current system was implemented a number of years ago. Ann and her staff concluded that those who were resistant to the new system were afraid of the change and how it would affect them personally. To counter the negative behavioral reactions, Ann took great pains to explain the new system to all employees. She also tried to sell the system by explaining how it would benefit not only the company as a whole but also the individual employees. With management approval she assured employees that they would not lose their job with the company and that all affected employees would be retrained. She got the two most vocal opponents involved in planning the system, and they were soon two of its biggest advocates.

Ann set up a steering committee and was granted approval to put the managers (or their assistants) of all affected departments on the committee. A master plan for developing the system was formulated, and the system was broken down into manageable projects. The projects were prioritized, and project teams were formed to begin work on the highest-priority projects. Documentation standards were developed and approved. ■

SUMMARY

Information systems are constantly undergoing change because of technological improvements, new regulations, growth, problems that must be solved, and the need to improve or replace old or inefficient information systems. The process of change is well defined and is referred to as the systems analysis and design life cycle. Accountants play a significant role in information systems development.

The likelihood that system changes will be made successfully are improved by proper planning and management. Problems and alternatives should be viewed from the standpoint of the entire organization. Systems objectives and constraints should be identified and taken into account. Management support is critical to the success of the changes. The steering committee (a group of executive-level people) should oversee and supervise all information systems design activities. The system can be designed using a top-down or a bottom-up approach, but a combination of the two is usually best. The overall approach to systems planning is referred to as the master plan. A basic ingredient of the master plan is a project development plan. All system changes should be properly documented and controlled.

If the changes made to the information system are not handled properly, adverse behavioral reactions can occur. People resist change by aggressively attacking the system, by blaming it for any and all corporate ills, and by avoiding it. Behavioral problems can be minimized through procedures such as maintaining open and honest communication.

Before a system is implemented, its feasibility should be measured. There are five types of feasibility: technical, economic, operational, legal, and scheduling. The most important is usually economic; expected system benefits should exceed system costs. Capital budgeting techniques are often used in feasibility analysis.

KEY TERMS

Define the following terms:

reengineering	steering committee	avoidance
systems analysts	project team	feasibility study
systems development life cycle (SDLC)	systems approach	technical feasibility
	bottom-up approach	operational feasibility
systems analysis phase	top-down approach	legal feasibility
conceptual systems design phase	project development plan	scheduling feasibility
	master plan	economic feasibility
physical design phase	behavioral aspects of change	capital budgeting model
implementation and conversion phase	aggression	payback period
	projection	net present value
operation and maintenance phase		internal rate of return

DISCUSSION QUESTIONS

8.1 The approach to long-range information systems planning described in this chapter is obviously important for large organizations having extensive investments in computer facilities. Should small organizations—in which the computer department employs fewer than, say, ten persons—attempt to implement such planning programs?

8.2 Assume that you are a systems consultant advising a firm's management on the design and

implementation of a new computer system. Management has decided not to retain several employees after the system is implemented. Some of these employees have many years of service in the firm. How would you advise management to communicate this decision to its employees?

8.3 While reviewing a list of benefits from a computer vendor's proposal, you note an item that reads "improvements in management decision making—

$50,000 per year.'' How would you interpret this item? What influence should it have on the economic feasibility and the computer acquisition decision?

8.4 You are a member of the feasibility study team for the JKL Company, which is considering the acquisition of its first computer system. The company's management has decided that a warehouse adjoining the main plant should be used to house the computer system if it is acquired. This warehouse was built only five years ago, but the company has not used it since discontinuing a major product line three years ago. The warehouse was rented briefly to another firm but is not presently in use for any purpose. You feel that the warehouse would make an excellent location for a new computer facility. In the feasibility analysis, how should the cost of space for the computer facility be determined?

8.5 Your friend and fellow systems analyst Joe Doakes has said, ''Systems analysts do not have to be psychologists or be concerned with people problems in their work. Their main function is to determine the proper facilities, computer or otherwise, for performing the data processing functions of an organization. When this has been done, they establish job specifications for employees in the system. Analysts can perform these functions with a minimum of contact with people in the organization.'' Do you agree with this statement? If not, what line of argument would you use in response to your friend?

8.6 This chapter suggested that an organization should make special efforts to ease fears among its employees about potential loss of jobs or seniority. One advantage of the mechanization of a system, however, is the reduction of clerical costs, which may mean a reduction in jobs. Are these two concepts inconsistent? What policies should be consistent with both concepts?

8.7 Some executives believe that it is extremely important to manage ''by the numbers.'' This form of management requires that all employees with departmental or divisional responsibilities spend time understanding the company's operations and how they are reflected by the company's financial reports. Because of managers' increased comprehension of the financial reports and the activities that they represent, their subordinates will become more attuned to the meaning of financial reports and the important signposts that can be detected in these reports. Companies utilize a variety of numerical

measurement systems, including standard costs, financial ratios, human resource forecasts, and operating budgets. Discuss the behavioral implications of management by exception. Explain how employee behavior could be adversely affected when ''actual to budget'' comparisons are used as the basis for performance evaluation. (CMA Examination, adapted)

8.8 The company President is perplexed by requests for computers from three different areas of the firm. The EDP Manager wants $4.5 million to upgrade the mainframe computer. The Vice-President of Engineering wants $450,000 to replace a minicomputer. The Vice-President of Finance wants $200,000 to purchase microcomputers.

Rapid growth is putting a strain on computer resources, keeping profits down. Payroll, accounting, inventory, and engineering functions are computerized; other tasks are manual. The firm is organized by business functions, with vice-presidents for manufacturing, marketing, engineering, finance, personnel, and services. The President wonders if a steering committee is needed.

Discuss the objectives, responsibilities, and composition of an information systems steering committee. Justify your recommendations concerning its membership and the selection of a chairperson. (CIA Examination, adapted)

8.9 In which phase of the systems development cycle would each of the following positions be most actively involved? Justify your answers.

a. Managerial accountant
b. Programmer
c. Systems analyst
d. Financial vice-president
e. Information systems manager
f. Auditor

8.10 For each task, specify in which stage of the systems life cycle developers normally perform the activity. Use the following five stages of the system life cycle.

1. Systems analysis
2. Conceptual (general) system design
3. Physical (detailed) systems design
4. Implementation and conversion
5. Operation and maintenance

More then one answer may apply for each activity.

a. Write operating procedures manuals
b. Develop program and process controls
c. Identify alternative systems designs

d. Develop a conceptual model of the system
e. Identify external and administrative controls
f. Test the system
g. Train personnel
h. Evaluate the existing system
i. Analyze the achievement of systems benefits

j. Modify and alter programs
k. Analyze TQM performance measures
l. Conduct a feasibility analysis
m. Align IS development plans with business objectives

Problems

8.1 For 20 years Conroy Company had been the industry leader in the manufacture and sale of office equipment. Over the past 3 years, however, the company's position at the forefront of the industry had gradually declined to a current-year ranking of seventh. Jim Graham, President and owner of Conroy, believes that this decline was due to intensified competition and shrinking profit margins. After an industry convention, Todd Bridges, Manager of the Production Division, reported to Jim that several competitors had successfully computerized their operations. The managers of these companies felt that computerization had brought better operational control and increased profit margins. Todd maintained that computerization was the only factor standing between Conroy and its return to industry dominance.

After several discussions with the company controller, Jim decided that for future profitability and control it would be necessary for Conroy to computerize its operations. Jim knew that computerization would be no small chore, given the size of Conroy's operations and the high level of divisional interdependence among the marketing, accounting, production, and finance divisions. In addition, Jim knew that gaining the support of top division managers would also present difficulties, because the company had operated with a manual system for so many years.

Because of these obstacles and Conroy's limited number of employees with a systems background, Jim has hired you as a systems consultant. Your first assignment is to outline a plan for systems development that will get the company moving back into position as the industry leader.

Required

a. Outline the steps Conroy should go through in planning and managing the new system's development.

b. Why should Conroy use the systems approach to change? What approach to systems development should Conroy use?

c. Explain how Jim could effectively gain the support of the remaining members of top management and increase their confidence in and desire to utilize the new system.

8.2 Steve Gates has seen the future, and so far he wants no part of it. The offices at Sierra Manufacturing Company, where Gates is Vice-President, have just been automated. Sitting at his desk in Sacramento, Gates can push buttons on the keyboard of a computer terminal and staff memos will appear on the screen. He can respond with his own memos, which will instantly be sent to colleagues, either for immediate viewing or for storage and later retrieval. By pressing a few other buttons, he can view company financial data stored in the corporate computer.

Gates can do all that and more, but instead he has unplugged the terminal. "I think most managers, including me, are talkers," he states. "I would much rather talk than write."

Gates's resistance exemplifies the reaction of many professionals and executives who are being forced to make major psychological and behavioral adjustments as they begin to move into a paperless world.

Required

a. What do you believe is the real cause of Gates's resistance to the computer system?

b.   As a colleague of Gates, how could you help him realize the benefits of computerization and overcome his computer phobia?

8.3   Mary Smith is the bookkeeper for Dave's Distributing Company, a distributor of Coke and Sprite. Because the company is rather small, for many years Mary performed all of the daily accounting tasks by herself. Dave, the President and owner of the company, supervised the warehouse/delivery people and the front office, but he also spent much of his time jogging and skiing.

For several years profits were good and sales grew faster than industry averages. Although the system was working well, Dave was being pressured by bottlers to computerize his accounting system. With strong encouragement from them and a little guidance from a CPA friend, Dave bought a new microcomputer and accounting software to accompany it.

Only one day was required to set up the hardware, install the software, and convert the files. Mary seemed surprised the morning the vendor installed the new computer, but she only complained a little as they rearranged her office to make room for it. Although the software company provided two days of training on the system, Mary seemed to have a hard time learning how to run the computer and enter the data. As a result, Dave decided that she should run the manual and computer systems in parallel for one month to verify the accuracy of the new computer system.

Things did not go well during the month of parallel processing. Mary continually complained that she did not have enough time to run both systems by herself and that she did not understand how to run the computer system. To keep accounts up to date, Dave spent two to three hours a day running the new system himself.

One problem Dave found was that much of the time he spent running the system was devoted to identifying discrepancies between the computer and manual results. When the error was located, it was almost always in the manual system. Therefore, Dave's confidence in the new system increased significantly.

At the end of the month Dave was ready to scrap the manual system and go entirely with the computer system, but Mary said she was not ready. Dave went back to skiing and jogging, and Mary went on with the manual system. When Dave saw that the computer system was falling behind, he again spent time catching it up. He also spent time with Mary to make sure she understood how to run the computer system.

After a few more months of operation Dave had spent many more hours keeping the computer system up to date and making sure Mary understood what she was supposed to do. Dave was at the height of frustration. "I know Mary knows how to run the system, but she doesn't seem to want to do it. I can do all the accounting work on the computer in two or three hours a day, but she can't even do it in her normal eight-hour workday. What shall I do?"

Required

a.   What actions and lack of actions may have contributed to the system's failure?

b.   In retrospect, how should Dave have handled the computerization of the accounting system?

c.   At what point in the decision-making process should Mary have been informed? Should she have had some say in whether the computer was purchased? If Mary had not agreed with the decision to acquire the computer, what should have been done? Exactly what should have been the nature of her input?

d.   A hard decision needs to be made about what to do with Mary. Significant efforts have been made to train her, but they have not been successful. What would you recommend at this point? Should she be fired or moved somewhere else in the business, or should more efforts be made to train her to do her job?

8.4   Wright Company employs a computer-based data processing system to maintain all company records. The present system was developed in stages over the past five years and has been fully operational for the past 24 months.

When the system was being designed, all department heads were asked to specify the types of information and reports they would need for planning and controlling operations. The systems department attempted to meet the specifications of each department head. Company management specified that certain other reports be prepared for department heads. During the five years of system development and operation there have been several changes in the department head positions due to attrition and promotions. The new department heads often made requests for additional reports based on their specifications. The systems department complied with all of these requests. Reports were discontinued only upon the request of a department head, and then only if the report was not required by top management. As a result, few reports were, in fact, discontinued. Consequently, the data processing system was generating a large number of reports each reporting period.

Company management became concerned about the quantity of information being produced by the system. The internal audit department was asked to evaluate the effectiveness of the reports generated by the system. The audit staff determined early in the study that more information was being generated by the data processing system than could be used effectively. They noted the following reactions to this information overload.

■ Many department heads would not act on certain reports during periods of peak activity. The department heads would let these reports accumulate in the hope of catching up during a subsequent lull.

■ Some department heads had so many reports that they did not act at all on the information, or they made incorrect decisions because of misuse of the information.

■ Frequently, action was not taken until the department head was reminded by someone who needed the decision. Department heads did not appear to have developed a priority system for acting on the information produced by the data processing system.

■ Department heads often would develop information they needed from alternative, independent sources, rather than utilize the reports generated by the data processing system. This was easier than searching among the reports for the needed data.

Required

a. Indicate whether each of the observed reactions is a functional or dysfunctional behavioral response. Explain your answer in each case.

b. Recommend procedures the company could employ to eliminate dysfunctional behavior and to prevent its recurrence.

(CMA Examination, adapted)

8.5 The controller of Tim's Travel, a rapidly growing travel corporation, is preparing a proposal for the executive committee regarding the feasibility of either upgrading the company's existing computer system or replacing it with a new MANTIS XIT-470.

The present system is eight years old and requires immediate rehabilitation or replacement. It is estimated that rehabilitation would cost $97,500 and would extend the useful life of the system another seven years. The book value of the present system is $19,500, although it would bring $24,000 if sold.

Rehabilitation of the current system would result in a reduction of one employee at an average salary of $19,400; there will be a reduction of two employees if Tim's goes with the MANTIS. Annual operating costs are expected to be $15,950 per year. Because of the expansion possibilities at Tim's Travel, rehabilitation is expected to increase profits 3.5% above last year's level of $553,000.

The BetaTech Company, a local computer outlet, has quoted a price of $224,800 for the new MANTIS XIT-470, which carries a useful life of seven years. Operating costs for the MANTIS are estimated to be $14,260. One of the attractive features of the MANTIS is that its average processing speed is 12% faster than that of other systems in its price range. The increase in processing could increase the current year's profits by as much as 4.5%.

Assume that Tim's present tax rate is 35% and that money is worth 11%. Also assume that after seven years the salvage value, net of tax, would be $12,000 for the MANTIS and $7500 for the present system. The cost recovery percentages for a five-year asset are as follows.

Year	Percent
1	15.0
2	22.0
3	21.0
4	21.0
5	21.0

Required

Perform an economic feasibility analysis to determine whether Tim's Travel should rehabilitate the old system or purchase the MANTIS. As part of the analysis, compute the after-tax cash flows for years 1 through 7 and the NPV and the IRR of each alternative. If a spreadsheet package is available, use it to make the calculations.

8.6 Rossco Incorporated is considering purchasing a new Z-660 computer to maximize office efficiency. The proposal outlining the new system estimates that initial systems design would cost about $84,000; hardware, $104,000; and new software, $55,000. A net reduction of four employees, at an average salary of $21,500 per year, is expected if the new machine is acquired; however, system training costs are expected to be $11,000. A special study that was just completed found that computerization could decrease average yearly inventory by $154,000. In addition, computerization could decrease accounts receivable collection time by 15 days. Average yearly accounts receivable are $2,400,000.

An additional $35,000 would be required for installation of the system and $16,000 for conversion of files. Annual operating costs for the new computer, other than employee wages, are expected to be $21,000 per year higher than those for the current manual system. The expected life of the machine is seven years, with an estimated salvage value of zero. The effective tax rate is 35%, and the accelerated cost recovery system (ACRS), using a five-year life, is being used for both book and tax purposes. The cost recovery percentages for a five-year asset follow:

Year	Percent
1	15.0
2	22.0
3	21.0
4	21.0
5	21.0

Required

Analyze the desirability of the proposal (on a spreadsheet if available), using the net present value and internal rate of return methods. Assume that money is worth 11% and that all cash flows are at the end of the year. (*Hint:* Figure the yearly opportunity cost savings for both inventory and accounts receivable. Assume that there are 365 days in a year.)

8.7 XYZ Conglomerate Company has completed a feasibility study to upgrade its computer system. Management asked for a detailed schedule of the benefits of this new system. Table 8.6 presents the document that was provided.

Required

As financial officer of the company, which of the benefits would you accept as relevant to the cost justification of the system? Defend your answer. (SMAC Examination, adapted)

8.8 The Perry Corporation has four new computer applications under development or scheduled to begin development shortly. The monthly requirements of these development projects for computer time and for systems analyst/programmer time over the next two years are indicated in Table 8.7.

Operational requirements for the company's existing applications total 400 computer system hours and 200 analyst/programmer hours. These requirements increase by 10% at the end of each six-month period.

The firm presently employs six analyst/programmers who work 8 hours per day for an average of 22 days each month. A total of 720 hours of computer time are available per month (30 days × 24 hours per day). However, of each hour of computer time used, an average of only 80% is used for productive work, with the other 20% being used for equipment maintenance, reruns, and so forth.

Required

a. At what point will a significant increase in the capacity of Perry's computer system become necessary? Why?

b. Assume that a new computer system is to be acquired and that the conversion to this new system will be complete as of the first day of month 13. Further assume that one analyst/programmer will work full-time on implementing this conversion during the six months preceding the first day of month 13. How many full-time analyst/programmers must Perry employ during each of the 4 six-month periods?

c. Assume that (1) the monthly salary of an analyst/programmer is $2000; (2) the monthly hardware rental and all other fixed costs for the present system total $10,000 and will total $15,000 after the new system is implemented; (3) upon implementation the new system will exactly triple throughput (i.e., work formerly taking three hours on the computer will now take one hour); and (4) all variable costs relating to the operation of both the old and new systems, during both productive and nonproductive use, total $20 per hour. Prepare a financial projection of the monthly total of these costs for each month over the two-year period.

8.9 The Alkin Chemical Company manufactures and sells chemicals for agricultural and industrial use. The company has grown significantly over the past five years. However, the company's accounting information system is the original system that the former president's son developed and installed while he was at the university. Many of the managers feel that much of the information generated by the system is not relevant and that more appropriate and timely information is required.

The Controller is concerned that the actual monthly cost data for most production processes are compared with the actual costs of the same processes for the previous year. However, the production supervisors contend that the system is adequate because it allows for the explanation of discrepancies. The current year's costs seldom vary from the previous year's costs when adjusted for inflation. Thus, they feel that costs are under control.

The Vice-President of Manufacturing has found that she must spend days compiling information

Table 8.6
Benefits to be derived
from the new system

1. Production
   a. Marketing forecasting is presently in dollars per product line. Cal-
      culation of units by product line takes an estimated two man-
      days, a total of $80. This saving would be repeated each time
      the market forecast was updated, presumably monthly. The pro-
      gram to calculate the forecast in units would be more accurate
      than the present method of applying factors to dollar value. $ 960
   b. More effective inventory control would permit an overall reduction
      in inventory. The ability to quickly establish total requirements
      would help to overcome parts stockout situations. For this calcu-
      lation we estimate a 10% inventory reduction. The cost of capital
      at XYZ Conglomerate Company approximates 20%, and the bene-
      fit then approximates 20% of $100,000. $20,000
   c. Evaluation of changes to plans will be possible in detail. This is
      not so under our manual system. Parts explosions are time-con-
      suming and can only be done monthly. The impact here would
      be increased production flexibility and the reduction of sales
      losses due to finished goods stockouts. We estimate that this
      can be valued as the equivalent of hiring two clerks. $15,000 $35,960

2. Engineering
   a. Use of the computer in filing and updating bills of material
      would save 40% of the industrial engineer's time. $ 4,000
   b. The improved updating of files, which includes the bills of mate-
      rial and product structure files, which affect many areas, should
      save a minimum 25% of one clerk (if we took all areas, this
      would probably be closer to 50%. $ 1,500
   c. Estimated clerical savings in labor calculations, rates, and bonus
      detail is two days per week, or 40% of one person. $ 2,000 $ 7,500

3. Sales
   a. Improved reporting will enable sales staff and sales management
      to react more quickly to prevailing conditions. The implied bene-
      fit would be sales increases, especially during promotions, and a
      better sales/expense ratio. We are assuming an improvement in
      sales of only $1000 per person, for a total of $5000. $ 5,000

4. Marketing
   a. Revised reports and an improved forecasting system will help in
      establishing sales trends and will help the Production Department
      in flexibility and inventory control.

5. Accounting
   a. Standard costing of all bills of material, and in fact, the side ef-
      fect of being able to cost new products quickly, can be
      expressed as the equivalent of saving 30%–40% of the plant ac-
      countant's time. $ 3,000
   b. A revised incentive earnings and payroll system installed on the
      computer should reduce the Payroll Department clerical labor from
      three days to one day—possible benefit of 40% of one clerk. $ 2,400 $ 5,400

                                                            Total $53,860

	PROJECT A		PROJECT B			PROJECT C		PROJECT D	
Months	System hours	Analyst-programmer hours	System hours	Analyst-programmer hours	Months	System hours	Analyst-programmer hours	System hours	Analyst-programmer hours
1–6	20	240	30	352	1–6	25	264	—	—
7–12	75	380	30	400	7–12	30	280	—	120
13–18	80	100	100	550	13–18	30	300	20	380
19–24	88	110	150	120	19–24	100	500	30	410

Table 8.7

found on the many reports generated by the current system to prepare the simplest cost analysis. She feels that the system should be flexible enough for each manager to develop quickly his or her own recurring reports.

As a result of these concerns, the new President has appointed a committee to review the system. This committee is to determine management's information needs for cost control and decision purposes, and to ensure that the behavioral needs of the company and its employees are met. The Vice-President of Finance and Administration is to head this committee.

Just after the President announced the formation of this new committee, the Vice-President of Finance and Administration overheard one of the cost accountants say, "I've been doing it this way since the company began and now this committee plans to make my job redundant." Several employees in the General Accounting Department also felt that their positions were going to be eliminated or changed significantly. Several days later, the Vice-President of Finance and Administration overheard one of the production managers state that he believed the system was in need of revision because the most meaningful information that he was receiving came from a junior salesman.

Required

a. Identify the behavioral implications of having an accounting information system that does not appear to meet the needs of management.

b. Identify and explain the specific problems the company appears to have with regard to the perception of the employees concerning both the accounting information system and the firm.

c. Identify the policies or practices the company could follow during systems implementation to achieve consistency with the objective of reducing costs and to ensure that no employee is laid off. (SMAC Examination, adapted)

8.10 In recent years there has been an explosive growth in electronic communication. Computers, copying machines, facsimile machines, word processing equipment, electronic mail, teleconferencing, and sophisticated management information systems have changed and altered the way information is received, processed, and transmitted. With the decreasing costs of computer equipment and the increasing power in automation, the full impact of computerization has not yet been felt. Although the development of computer applications is directed at being user-friendly or user-oriented, the integration of computers into the organization has had both positive and negative effects on the employee.

Required

a. Describe the benefits that companies and their employees can receive from electronic communication.

b. Discuss the impact on an organization caused by the introduction of an electronic communication system.

c. Explain (1) why an employee might resist the introduction of electronic communication systems and (2) the steps an organization can take to alleviate the employee's resistance to electronic communication. (CMA Examination, adapted)

8.11 A savings and loan association has decided to undertake the development of an in-house computer system to replace the processing it currently purchases from a time-sharing bureau. The internal auditors have suggested that the systems development process be planned in accordance with the systems development life cycle concept.

The following nine items have been identified as major systems development activities that will have to be undertaken.

1. System test
2. User specifications
3. Conversion
4. System planning study
5. Technical specifications
6. Postimplementation planning
7. Implementation planning
8. User procedures and training
9. Programming

Required

a. Arrange the nine items in the sequence in which they should logically occur.

b. One major subactivity that will occur during system implementation is the conversion of data files from the old system to the new system. Indicate three types of documentation of a file conversion work plan that would be of particular interest to an auditor.

(CIA Examination, adapted)

8.12 PWR Instruments is a manufacturer of precision nozzles for fire hoses. The company was started by Ronald Paige, who has an engineering background and who serves as PWR's President. This closely held corporation has been very successful and has experienced steady growth.

Reporting to Paige are six vice-presidents representing the company's major functions—marketing, production, research and development, information services, finance, and personnel. The Information Services Department was established during the fiscal year just ended when PWR began developing a new computer-based information system. The new data base system employs a minicomputer as a central processing unit with several terminals and microcomputers in each of the six departments connected to the central processing unit. The microcomputers are capable of both downloading data from and uploading data to the main computer. For example, analysts in the Finance Department are able to access the data stored on the main computer through the microcomputers and use the microcom-

puters as smart terminals on a stand-alone basis. PWR is still in the process of designing and developing new applications for its computer system.

Paige has recently received the management letter prepared by the company's external audit firm at the conclusion of the annual audit, and he has called a meeting with his vice-presidents to review the recommendations. One of the major items that Paige wants to discuss with his management team is the recommendation that PWR form an information systems steering committee.

Required

a. Explain why the external auditor would recommend that PWR Instruments establish an information systems steering committee, and discuss the specific responsibilities of an information systems steering committee.

b. Identify the individuals at PWR Instruments who would be most likely to serve on the information systems steering committee.

c. Explain several advantages that PWR Instruments might realize from the establishment of an information systems steering committee.

d. An information systems steering committee must be familiar with the system development life cycle. Identify the steps in the system life cycle.

(CMA Examination, adapted)

8.13 Over four hundred years ago, Machiavelli wrote in *The Prince*, ''It must be considered that there is nothing more difficult to carry out, nor more doubtful of success, nor more dangerous to handle, than to initiate a new order of things.'' This statement is as applicable today as it was in 1520.

Implementing organizational change is one of the most demanding assignments faced by any executive. It has been suggested that every change requires three steps; ''unfreezing'' the current situation, the change itself, and finally ''refreezing'' the effected change. This view, however, lacks the specific details needed by an operating manager who must effect a change.

Required

a. Identify and describe the specific steps a manager must take to implement an organizational change.

b. Suppose an organization does make a change that affects employees directly or affects how they conduct their operations.

1. Explain why employees generally resist change.
2. Outline and describe the ways a manager can reduce the resistance to change. (CMA Examination, adapted)

8.14 Don Richardson, Vice-President of Marketing for the JEM Corporation, has just emerged from another strategic planning session aimed at developing a new line of business. The company's management team has been discussing these plans for several months, since major organizational changes will be required to implement the strategic plan. Rumors about the plans have been circulating the office for months, and Richardson has already been confronted by several employees who are anxious about the expected changes. His only response has been to tell them that an official announcement of this new business plan is expected shortly.

When he returns to his office, Richardson is met by an ad hoc committee composed of his department managers. The Sales Manager, Susan Williams, has been the most vocal of the group and, as expected, is acting as spokesperson. "Mr. Richardson, it is imperative that we speak to you right away. The employees are becoming very apprehensive about the proposed changes, and lately their job performance has slacked off."

"That's right," adds George Sussman, Promotions Manager. "My subordinates are asking me all sorts of questions concerning this new line of business, and I don't have any answers for them. They won't hold still for that 'official announcement' any longer. I suspect that some of them are already looking for jobs in the event that department 'changes' phase out their positions."

Required

a. Describe the general steps in the decision-making process that a company should follow before choosing to implement a major organizational change.

b. Explain why employees generally resist organizational change.

c. Discuss ways JEM Corporation can alleviate employee resistance to change.
(CMA Examination, adapted)

8.15 Remnants, Inc., is a large company that manufactures and markets designer clothing throughout the United States. From its St. Louis headquarters, Remnants has developed a regional system for marketing and servicing its products. Each region functions as a profit center because of the authority given regional managers within their territories.

Each regional organization consists of an accounting and a budget department, a personnel and training department, and several area offices which market and service the products. Each of the area offices consists of sales, service, and administrative departments headed by managers who report to the area manager.

The New York area office departed from the standard organizational structure by establishing a branch office to market and service the firm's products in the Boston area. The local office is headed by a branch manager who reports directly to the area manager.

In recent years the Boston branch manager has encouraged the area manager to consider a new information system for the local branch to handle the branch's growing information needs. The New York area manager and the eastern regional manager have concluded that they should establish a project team with people from the regional office, the area office, and the branch office to assess the information needs at the Boston branch office and develop system recommendations, if necessary. The regional manager appointed the following people to the project team, with Keith Nash as chairperson:

Eastern Region Office
Kurt Johnson, Budget Supervisor
Sally Brown, Training Director

New York Office
Keith Nash, Administrative Director

Boston Branch
Heidi Meyer, Branch Manager and Sales Manager
Bobby Roos, Assistant Branch Manager and Service Manager
Matthew Knight, Salesperson
Tara Jolly, Serviceperson

a. A project team, similar to the one organized at Remnants, Inc., is a group of individuals organized to contribute their skills to accomplish a given objective. Characteristics of members of the group can influence the functioning and effectiveness of it. Identify some of these characteristics.

b. What sources of conflict can you see arising among the members of this group because of its composition? Do you think the group will succeed in its objective to develop an information system for the Boston branch office?

c. What contribution would a person who holds a position as budget supervisor make in a project team such as this one?

8.16 Managers face a continual crisis in the systems development process: IS departments develop systems that businesses can't use. At the heart of the problem is a proverbial "great divide" that separates the world of business from the world of information systems. Few departments seem able or ready to cross the gap.

A major reason for the crisis in information systems development is many large systems handling corporate information needs are seriously out of date. As a result, companies are looking for ways to improve existing systems or to build new systems.

Another reason for the crisis is the widespread use of PC-based systems that have spawned a high level of user expectation that is not being met by IS departments. As computer education increases, users are seeking more powerful applications that are not available on many older systems.

The costs of the "great divide" can be devastating for unprepared companies. An East Coast Chemical Company spent more than $1 million on a budgeting and control system that was never used by anyone. The Systems Department created an administrative budgeting system; the company's expertise was technical excellence, not budgets. As a result, the new system completely missed the mark when it came to meeting business needs.

Another example of poor systems development comes from a midwestern bank. It used an expensive computer-aided software engineering (CASE) tool to develop a system that users ignored because there had been no design planning. According to Michael Miller, a senior analyst for Franklin Savings Association, "They built the system right; but, unfortunately, they didn't build the right system."

So what is the solution? The first step in effective systems design is a thorough business analysis, not a systems analysis. A business analysis includes a thorough review of how a business operates and how the functions of the business relate. Only with this understanding can systems professionals and business managers communicate effectively in developing an integrated system.

In addition, businesses are seeking managers that have a systems background, because they provide a liaison between the systems department and the finance and accounting departments, helping business managers to clearly communicate their needs.

What's still missing is more involvement between systems people and end users. Systems designers must take more time to interact with end users. In addition, business managers must provide their employees with the training time they require to make the system work right.[2]

Required

a. What is the "great divide" in the systems development process? What are the reasons for the gap?

b. What are the suggested solutions to the information crisis? How will the systems approach to development help?

c. Discuss the role that a systems designer, a business manager, and an end user can take to narrow the "great divide."

d. Who plays the most vital role in the effective development of the system?

---

[2] Adapted from Susan Janus, "Managers Face a Crisis in Systems Development," *PC Week* (January 2, 1989): 1, 8.

CASE 8.1: ANYCOMPANY, INC.—AN ONGOING COMPREHENSIVE CASE

One of the best ways to learn is to immediately apply what you have studied. The purpose of this case is to allow you to do that. You will select a local company that you can work with. At the end of most chapters you will find an assignment that will have you apply what you have learned using the company you have selected as a reference. This case, then, may become an ongoing case study that you work on throughout the term.

Visit several small- to medium-sized businesses in the local community. Explain that you will be doing a term-long case, and ask for permission to use the company as the firm you are going to study. Explain that you will need to meet with people in the company several times during the term to get the information you need. However, you will not need a great deal of their time or be a disruption to them. Offer to share any observations or suggestions that you can come up with as a way of allowing the firm to feel good about helping you.

Once you have lined up a company, perform the following steps.

1. Schedule a visit with a member of the information systems staff. With help, identify the most significant revision in the company's information system (for some, this may mean the initial design and implementation). Discuss the following issues.

   a. What groups were organized to oversee systems design/revision and implementation? How was the implementation strategy developed?

   b. What problems did the company run into when it was developing/revising its system? How did the company handle the problems?

   c. What personnel were affected by the change in the information system? In general terms, how did employees react to the changes? What did the project development team do to minimize potential negative affects of the system change?

   d. If the company was starting the project over again, what would it do differently? Why?

2. Review the following.

   a. Review the documentation covering system design/revision and implementation. Take a few moments to review any project development plans and the master plan, if available.

   b. If appropriate, ask to review the feasibility analysis surrounding the implementation of the information system.

3. From your interview and your observations, write a brief report summarizing your findings. Consider the following issues:

   a. How well did the company organize the design/revision and implementation of the information system?

   b. What suggestions would you provide the company to improve its development and implementation procedures in the future? Why?

CASE 8.2: AUDIO VISUAL CORPORATION

Audio Visual Corporation manufactures and sells visual display equipment. The company is headquartered near Boston. The majority of sales are made through seven geographical sales offices located in Los Angeles, Seattle, Minneapolis, Cleveland, Dallas, Boston, and Atlanta. Each sales office has a warehouse located nearby that carries an inventory of new equipment and replacement parts. The remainder of the sales are made through manufacturers' representatives.

Audio Visual's manufacturing operations are conducted in a single plant, which is highly departmentalized. In addition to the assembly department, there are several departments responsible for various components used in the visual display equipment. The plant also has maintenance, engineering, scheduling, and cost accounting departments.

Early in 1993 management decided that its information system (IS) needed upgrading. As a result, the company installed a mainframe at corporate headquarters, and local area networks at each of the seven sales offices.

The integration of the new computer and the LANs into the Audio Visual information system was carried out by the IS staff. The IS Manager and the four systems analysts who had the major responsibility for the integration were hired by the company in the spring of 1994. The department's other employees—programmers, machine operators, and keypunch operators—have been with the company for several years.

During its early years Audio Visual had a centralized decision-making organization. Top management formulated all plans and directed all operations. As the company expanded, some of the decision making was decentralized, although the information processing was still highly centralized. Departments had to coordinate their plans with the corporate office, but they had more freedom in developing their sales programs. As the company expanded, information problems developed, and the IS Department was given the responsibility to improve the company's information processing system when the new equipment was installed.

The IS analysts reviewed the information system in existence prior to the acquisition of the new computer and identified weaknesses. They then designed new applications to overcome the weaknesses. During the 18 months since the acquisition of the new equipment the following applications have been redesigned or developed and are now operational: payroll, production scheduling, financial statement preparation, customer billing, raw material use in production, and finished goods inventory by warehouse. The operating departments of Audio Visual affected by the systems changes were rarely consulted or contacted until the system was operational and the new reports were distributed to the operating departments.

The President of Audio Visual is very pleased with the work of the IS Department. During a recent conversation with an individual who was interested in Audio Visual's new system, the President stated, "The IS people are doing a good job and I have full confidence in their work. I touch base with the IS people frequently, and they have encountered no difficulties in doing their work. We paid a lot of money for the new equipment and the IS people certainly cost enough, but the combination of the new equipment and new IS staff should solve all of our problems."

Recently, two additional conversations regarding the computer and the information system have taken place. One was between Jerry Adams, Plant Manager, and Bill Taylor, the IS Manager; the other was between Adams and Terry Williams, the new Personnel Manager.

Taylor-Adams Conversation

Adams: Bill, you're trying to run my plant for me. I'm supposed to be the manager, yet you keep interfering. I wish you would mind your own business.

Taylor: You've got a job to do, but so does my department. As we analyzed the information needed for production scheduling and by top management, we saw where improvements could be made in the work flow. Now that the system is operational, you can't reroute work and change procedures, because that would destroy the value of the information

we're processing. And while I'm on that subject, it's getting to the point where we can't trust the information we're getting from production. The documents we receive from production contain a lot of errors.

Adams: I'm responsible for the efficient operation of production. Quite frankly, I think I'm the best judge of production efficiency. The system you installed has reduced my work force and increased the work load of the remaining employees, but I don't see that this has improved anything. In fact, it might explain the high error rate in the documents.

Taylor: This new computer cost a lot of money, and I'm trying to be sure that the company gets its money's worth.

Adams-Williams Conversation

Adams: My best production assistant, the one I'm grooming to be a supervisor when the next opening occurs, came to me today and said he was thinking of quitting. When I asked him why, he said he didn't enjoy the work anymore. He's not the only one who is unhappy. The supervisors and department heads no longer have a voice in establishing production schedules. This new computer system has taken away the contribution we used to make to company planning and direction. We seem to be going way back to the days when top management made all the decisions. I have more production problems now than I used to. I think it boils down to a lack of interest on the part of my management team. I know the problem is within my area, but I thought you might be able to help me.

Williams: I have no recommendations for you now, but I've had similar complaints from purchasing and shipping. I think we should get your concerns on the agenda for our next plant management meeting.

1. Apparently the development of and transition to the new computer-based system has created problems among the personnel of Audio Visual Corporation. Identify and briefly discuss the apparent causes of these problems.

2. How could the company have avoided the problems? How could such problems be avoided in the future? (CMA Examination, adapted)

CHAPTER 9

Systems Analysis and Conceptual Systems Design

LEARNING OBJECTIVES

After studying this chapter, you should be able to:

- Discuss the key issues and steps in systems analysis.
- Explain the steps that are followed in conducting a systems survey.
- Discuss how systems analysts identify users' information needs and specify system requirements.
- Explain the conceptual systems design processes, and describe the activities undertaken in conceptual design.
- Explain how computer-aided software engineering tools can help developers analyze and design information systems.

INTEGRATIVE CASE: SHOPPERS MART

The day after Ann Christy received permission from top management at Shoppers Mart to proceed with systems analysis, she sat in her office planning her approach to developing the new system. She realized that in preparing for the presentation she had made to management, she had merely conducted an initial investigation into the proposed system. Management had conditionally approved the system based on that limited investigation. A further approval to proceed with the conceptual design of the system would be needed after the analysis phase was complete. It was now time to conduct a more complete analysis of the proposed new system.

Ann feels that the analysis phase is of critical importance to the success of the system. She has heard that most of the errors and mistakes that plague new systems originate during the analysis phase of the development life cycle. She wants to avoid a faulty analysis, especially from an inadequate determination of user needs and system objectives. She also wants to make sure that Shoppers Mart develops a sound plan and approach for the new information system. She scheduled a meeting with the head of Systems Development to discuss the following questions:

1. Should Shoppers Mart's current system be analyzed to determine its weaknesses and strengths so that the design of the new system can be improved?
2. How will system developers determine exactly what the system should try to accomplish and what information the users will need to better serve the customer and to make better decisions?
3. Does the preliminary feasibility study need to be updated with the information gathered during analysis?
4. Should she develop two or three approaches to meet Shoppers Mart's needs that she can propose to management?
5. Is there software that can help automate the systems development process and help the designers be more effective? ∎

INTRODUCTION

This chapter discusses, in detail, the first two steps of the traditional systems development life cycle (SDLC) introduced in Chapter 8 and diagramed in Fig. 8.1: systems analysis and conceptual design. Chapter 10 discusses the other three steps: physical systems design, implementation and conversion, and operation and maintenance. This chapter also explains computer-aided software engineering (CASE) technology, which systems designers use to help them analyze and design systems.

SYSTEMS ANALYSIS

Systems analysis is the first phase of the traditional analysis and design life cycle. This phase is typically conducted by a project team composed of systems analysts and user representatives such as management accountants. It begins with a request for development and ends with the submission of a systems analysis report summarizing the findings of the analysis phase. The five steps in the analysis phase and their objectives are shown in Fig. 9.1.

Development requests come from users, management, or an information system planning function. They also result from attempts to take advantage of technological changes, satisfy an external regulation, handle growth, solve a particular problem, or implement broad systems improvements. As discussed in Focus 9.1, Nashua, a manufacturer of computer products and office supplies, recognized the need to change when it began to lose customers because of an unresponsive system.

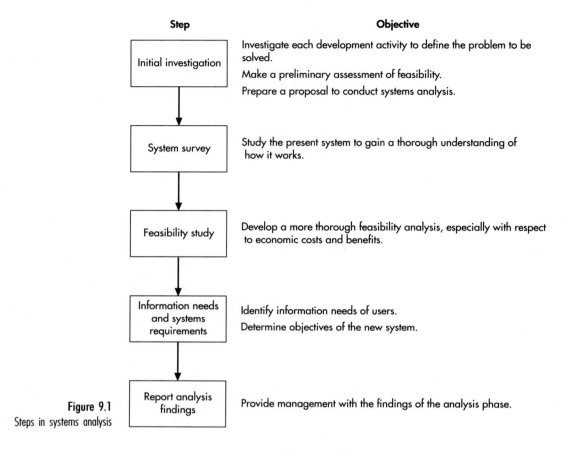

Figure 9.1
Steps in systems analysis

Step	Objective
Initial investigation	Investigate each development activity to define the problem to be solved. Make a preliminary assessment of feasibility. Prepare a proposal to conduct systems analysis.
System survey	Study the present system to gain a thorough understanding of how it works.
Feasibility study	Develop a more thorough feasibility analysis, especially with respect to economic costs and benefits.
Information needs and systems requirements	Identify information needs of users. Determine objectives of the new system.
Report analysis findings	Provide management with the findings of the analysis phase.

9.1 FOCUS

Nashua Reduces Order Taking from 2 Days to 3 Minutes

Nashua used to have two different sets of information systems. The centralized system was only capable of processing data common to all divisions. That meant that local systems were needed to handle the unique requirements of each division and augment the centralized system.

The two types of systems caused a great deal of customer and employee frustration and dissatisfaction. When a customer called to place an order, the employee taking the order had to take the information from the customer and tell him he would call back. He then had to access

When a request for a new system or for major improvements to an existing system is made, a written **request for systems development** is usually prepared. The table of contents of the request that Ann prepared for Shoppers Mart is shown in Table 9.1. The request describes the goals and objectives of the proposed change, why the change is being requested, and the anticipated benefits and costs of the proposed system.

Initial Investigation

When a request for systems development is received, an **initial investigation** is conducted to verify the nature of the problem and the needs of the users and to gather the information needed to evaluate the feasibility of the request. The steps in the initial investigation are summarized in Fig. 9.2.

Although it is not an easy task, the exact nature of the problem needs to be determined during the initial investigation. Often the information user will recognize that something is wrong and will identify some of the effects but will not know the exact cause. In some instances the reasons for initiating systems analysis are poorly defined by the initiators. In other instances what the requester thinks is the cause is not the real source of the problem. For example, a manager of a government agency once asked a consultant to help him set up an accounting system to produce information on fund expenditures and funds available that he did not have. Further investigation showed that the agency's system provided the information but that the manager did not understand the reports he was receiving.

Sometimes a new information system is not the solution to the problem. Organizational problems, such as having too many people reporting to a single individual, cannot usually be corrected by a new

---

the centralized system, verify customer information, and do a credit check. He then had to exit the centralized system and log onto the local system using a personal computer. The local system was used to calculate pricing, which was unique to each division. The employee then had to call the customer back with pricing information. If the customer still wanted to place an order, the employee had to access another central system to determine inventory availability. If no problems surfaced during this complex process, it took two days to take the order—that is, if the customer had not lost interest or gotten frustrated and gone to a competitor.

Nashua recognized a need to change its system and launched a five-year strategic plan for IS decentralization. The plan has been successful. Where it used to take two days to process a telephone order, clerks are now able to process orders in three minutes. And that time includes quoting prices on available inventory and mentioning volume discounts or special orders when applicable.

Source: Catherine Marenghi, "Nashua Keeps Quality Flame Burning in Customer Service," *Computerworld* (January 6, 1992): 61.

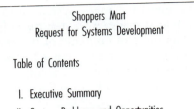

Table 9.1
Typical table of contents for a request for systems development

Shoppers Mart
Request for Systems Development

Table of Contents

I. Executive Summary
II. System Problems and Opportunities
III. Goals and Objectives of Proposed System
IV. Anticipated Costs and Benefits
V. Recommendations

Figure 9.2
Initial investigation process

User recognizes need for change,
prepares request for systems development

Determine
nature of
problem or
need

Conduct
preliminary
feasibility
analysis

} Initial investigation of request by
   systems department

Reject request,
inform
requestor   ←No— Approve request

} Steering committee approval,
   prioritization of project

Yes

Prepare proposal
to conduct
systems analysis

} Systems Department summarizes
   development project objectives and
   approach

Forward to project development
team for system survey

information system. If a decision maker lacks organization skills and cannot make use of the information currently available, a new information system may be a waste of time and money. Similarly, if control problems are caused by a failure to enforce procedures, a new system may not help. A new system is most useful when the problems are a result of lack of information, inaccessibility of data, and inefficient data processing.

An important part of problem definition is determining exactly what the project should and should not accomplish. This is referred to as the **scope of the system** and should be broad enough that the project can solve the problem and make a meaningful contribution, but narrow enough that the project is manageable. The scope is affected by the tasks to be accomplished and by the time, funds, and personnel available. Setting the scope of the system is sometimes referred to as determining the **system boundaries**.

The problem cannot be adequately defined without significant involvement on the part of the users. Therefore the users who initiated the request and who will be affected by the request will need to be involved in the investigation. The users are in the best position to elaborate on any problems with the system and are often the source of very creative ideas about how the problems can be resolved and how other users in the company can be involved to improve the system.

Enough information about estimated system costs and benefits is gathered to allow the steering committee to weed out invalid requests and to ensure that only those that are compatible with the organization's long-range plans are developed. They also prioritize the projects so that the ones with the highest expected payoffs are developed first. If a development request is not undertaken, the users should be informed of the reasons for the decision. If the request is approved, a proposal to conduct systems analysis is prepared, the project is added to the system master plan, and the development team begins the survey of the existing system.

A **proposal to conduct systems analysis** is prepared for those projects that are to be undertaken. The table of contents for the proposal that Ann prepared for Shoppers Mart is shown in Table 9.2. As the table shows, a proposal to conduct systems analysis builds on the request for systems development. The data gathered in the initial investigation is added to the original request to give it greater depth. In addition, the scope of the system is defined, those who will participate in the development are identified, and the tasks to be accomplished are set forth along with a plan for accomplishing them.

The proposal serves as a guide for the later phases of the development life cycle. As the investigation progresses, the analyst will modify, add to, and delete from the original report as more information becomes available. The original requestor of the system can use the report to evaluate whether the analyst clearly understands what is desired.

```
┌─────────────────────────────────────────────────────┐
│                  Shoppers Mart                      │
│           Proposal to Conduct Systems Analysis       │
│                                                       │
│   Table of Contents                                   │
│                                                       │
│      I.  Executive Summary                            │
│     II.  System Problems and Opportunities            │
│    III.  Goals and Objectives of Proposed System      │
│     IV.  Project Scope                                 │
│      V.  Anticipated Costs and Benefits               │
│     VI.  Participants in Development Project           │
│    VII.  Proposed Systems Development Tasks and Work Plan │
│   VIII.  Recommendations                              │
└─────────────────────────────────────────────────────┘
```

Table 9.2

Typical table of contents for a proposal to conduct systems analysis

Systems Survey

Gathering facts about an existing information system is referred to as the **systems survey**. The survey process may take several days or many months, depending on the complexity and scope of the system, the nature of the problem or change, the size of the project team, and how meaningful a study of the existing system is. The project team is usually made up of representatives of user groups, management, and the information systems function.

One objective of the survey is to understand the existing system. This includes an understanding of the company's operations, policies, and procedures; its data and information flow; and the interrelationships among organizational entities. The project team must find out what information is entered, stored, and produced by the system. The team must identify the system's weaknesses and decide how to correct them. The team also should identify the system's strengths so that they can be retained in the new system.

A second objective is to establish a working relationship with system users in order to build acceptance of, support for, and commitment to the system. A third is to collect the data needed to identify users' needs, conduct a feasibility analysis, determine the new system's requirements, and make a recommendation to management.

The benefit of a systems survey is that it determines the extent and nature of the changes needed and provides the development team with design ideas. Another benefit is that it identifies the hardware, software, personnel, and supplies available to the project development team. A major disadvantage is that the process is time-consuming and expensive. In addition, the more familiar project members become with the system, the more likely they are to lose some of their objectivity. They may get so close to the old system that they cannot step back and determine how the new system ought to be structured.

Gather Data. Data about the current system can be gathered internally from company employees. It can also be gathered from organizational and system documentation such as organization charts, procedures manuals, financial reports, and other company documents. External sources include marketers of similar systems, consultants, customers and suppliers, industry associations, and government agencies. The advantage of external sources is that they may provide ideas, concepts, techniques, or expertise not available within the company. Disadvantages are the time and costs required to find the right information.

Whether the sources are internal or external, four methods are commonly used to gather data about a system: interviews, questionnaires, observations, and document collection. The advantages and disadvantages of each are summarized in Table 9.3.

An **interview** is usually a very productive fact-finding technique. Users' experience with the system enables them to offer valuable opinions regarding existing problems and the feasibility of suggested solutions. It is especially useful in gathering answers to important ''why'' questions: Why is there a problem? Why does the system work

Table 9.3
Advantages and disadvantages of the different data gathering methods

Advantages	Disadvantages
INTERVIEW	
Can be used to answer "why" questions Interviewer can probe and follow up Questions can be clarified Builds positive relationships with interviewee Builds acceptance and support for new system	Time-consuming Expensive Personal biases or self-interest may produce inaccurate information
QUESTIONNAIRE	

Can be anonymous
Not time-consuming
Inexpensive
Allows more time to think about responses
	Doesn't allow for in-depth questions or
	   answers
	Can't probe or follow up on responses
	Questions can't be clarified
	Impersonal; doesn't build relationships
	Often ignored or completed without much
	   thought

OBSERVATION	
Can verify how system *actually* works, rather than how it *should* work Results in greater understanding of system	Time-consuming Expensive Difficult to interpret observations properly Observed people may alter behavior
SYSTEM DOCUMENTATION	
Describes how system should work Written form facilitates review and analysis	Time-consuming May not be available or easy to find

this way? Why is this information important? However, an interviewer must take care to ensure that an interviewee's personal biases, self-interest, or a desire to say what he thinks the interviewer wants to hear does not produce inaccurate information.

Ann Christy felt that the interviews she conducted during her analysis of the system were very successful, largely because of the way she approached the participants and the amount of preparation that went into each interview. Ann made an appointment with the person to be interviewed, explained the purpose of the interview beforehand, indicated the amount of time she would need, and made sure she was on time. Before each interview she studied the interviewee's responsibilities, made a list of the points she wanted to cover, and added them to the questions she asked everyone. During the interview she made the interviewee feel at ease by being friendly, respectful, courteous, and tactful. Her questions dealt with the person's responsibilities, how the person interacted with the system, how the system might be improved, and what information the person needs to do the job. A list of some of the questions she asked everyone is shown in Table 9.4. She let the interviewee do most of the talking, and she paid special attention to nonverbal communication, since subtle overtones and nuances can be as significant as direct responses to questions. She took notes and augmented the notes with detailed impressions shortly after the interview. In especially important interviews she asked permission to tape the interview.

Questionnaires are most useful when the amount of information to be gathered is small and well defined, when the information must be obtained from many people or from people who are physically removed from the analyst, or when the information is intended to verify similar information gathered from other sources. Questionnaires take relatively little time for an analyst to administer, but developing a

Table 9.4
Sample questions used by Ann Christy during her interviews

1. In what ways does the current information system meet your needs?
   a. What information is especially useful?
   b. How do you use the information?
   c. What decisions do you make using the information?
   d. Where do you see this information coming from?

2. In what ways does the information system not meet your needs?
   a. What information would you like to have that you don't now have?
   b. How would you use the information?
   c. What decisions would you make using the information?

3. How could the current information system be improved?
   a. Are there any procedures of processing activities that are not needed?
   b. Are there any that you need but do not have?
   c. How could the system be more responsive, faster, and more efficient?

quality questionnaire that captures the information needed can be challenging and can require significant amounts of time.

Observation is often used to verify information gathered using other approaches. It is also used to determine how the system actually works, rather than how people or the documentation indicate it should work. It is difficult to always interpret observations properly. People may change their normal behavior if they know that they are being observed. They may make mistakes they normally would not make or do things as they should be done rather than as they usually do them.

To maximize the effectiveness of observations, the analyst should identify beforehand what is to be observed and estimate how long it will take. The analyst should obtain permission and explain to the people being observed exactly what will be done and why. The observer should refrain from making value judgments, and notes and impressions should be formally documented as soon after the observation as possible. The findings and conclusions should be reviewed with those observed and their immediate supervisor.

Another important source of facts about an information system is the organization's **documentation**. Table 9.5 contains a list of the documents that an analyst may want to gather as the system is analyzed. If documentation is unavailable or incomplete, it may be worthwhile to develop it in rough form. Documentation describes how the system is intended to work; it gives the analyst a frame of reference for analyzing how the system actually works. Throughout the systems survey the project team should be alert to differences between the intended operation of a system and its actual operation. These differences provide important insights into problems and weaknesses.

Table 9.5
Examples of documentation gathered during the systems survey

Budgets	Record layouts
Charts of account	Retention policies for input, output, and stored data
Financial statements	
Source documents	
Data flow diagrams	System flowcharts
Document flowcharts	Corporate minutes
File and data base layouts and descriptions	Job descriptions
	Organization charts
Input forms, documents, and specifications	Policy statements
	Procedures manuals
Output documents, reports, and specifications	Reference manuals
	Strategic plans
Program listings, flowcharts, and operating instructions	Training materials

Document Findings and Model the Existing System. The information gathered during the analysis phase will be used throughout the systems development project. Therefore it must be documented and made available to those who need it during the different development stages. Documenting is done in a variety of ways, including copies of questionnaires, interview notes, memos summarizing interview and observation findings, and copies of documents. Another way of documenting an existing system is to model it.

As shown in Fig. 9.3, four different models can be used to analyze and design a new system. Two of these models deal with the physical aspects of the current and proposed systems, and the other two deal with the logical aspects of the current and proposed systems. The **physical model** concentrates on illustrating *how* a system functions. It might describe the flow of documents, the computer processes performed, the people performing the process, the equipment used, or any other physical elements of the system. The **logical model** concentrates on illustrating *what* is being done, such as the essential activities and the flow of information in the system, irrespective of how that flow is actually accomplished. The logical model focuses on managerial information and on the process of gaining this information, not on the physical processes of transforming and storing data.

Systems analysts can prepare a physical model of the old system, a logical model, or both to help them understand the existing system. When preparing both models, analysts usually create a physical model of the old system first and then a logical equivalent of the physical model. It is usually not wise to spend a great deal of time modeling and documenting a physical system that is to be thrown out. Analysts sometimes spend too much time on the current physical system because it is in place and easy to work on. It is much more important to understand the conceptual model (or what happens) of the existing system.

In designing a new system, analysts first design a new conceptual, or logical, model. This model adds all of the new activities and flows of

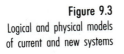

Figure 9.3
Logical and physical models of current and new systems

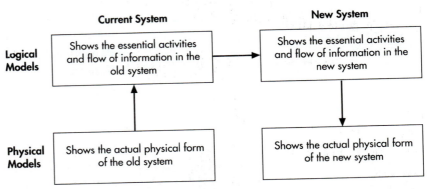

	Current System	New System
Logical Models	Shows the essential activities and flow of information in the old system	Shows the essential activities and flow of information in the new system
Physical Models	Shows the actual physical form of the old system	Shows the actual physical form of the new system

information to those retained from the old system. Once the logical model has been designed, a new physical model can be designed showing how the essential activities and information flows of the logical model will be implemented physically. The logical model is designed so that it can be physically implemented on any computer system, using any of a number of computer languages. The conceptual model is developed during conceptual systems design, which is discussed later in the chapter. After analysts determine what should happen in the new system, they can worry about how it should happen when they design the physical model of the new system. Physical systems design is discussed in Chapter 10.

Flowcharts are among the first and most widely used tools for analyzing systems. The principal advantage of flowcharts is that they make it fairly easy to trace the logic of processing, flag control points, analyze system strengths and weaknesses, and determine any corrections that need to be made. Flowcharts are most useful in understanding how current systems work. They are not as useful in designing systems because they force the designer to concentrate too soon on the physical aspects of the system (whether something should be done manually or by a computer, what electronic device should be used, etc.).

Flowchart ideas have been refined and extended for use in structured systems analysis and design. Some of the more common tools used in structured analysis and design include data flow diagrams, HIPO charts, and structured English. **Structured systems analysis** identifies the logical or conceptual relationships among the desired systems output, the data used in the system, and the system inputs. A top-down approach can be used, where very high level functions and their activities and relationships are investigated first. Each of these very high level functions is broken down into smaller functions, which are then investigated. This process continues until the development team has worked down to the lowest level of activity. The result is an upside-down tree, with each lower level containing the logical components of the higher-level activity.

A significant advantage of structured analysis and design techniques such as data flow diagrams is that they do not tie an analyst to a particular physical implementation. The development team can concentrate on what should be done without having to worry about how it should be done. For example, consider a process that inputs data into the system. A data flow diagram allows the development team to concentrate on what data are to be collected and entered without worrying about which type of input device should be used to enter the data.

There are other analysis and design tools and techniques used by systems developers to create logical and physical models. Table 9.6 lists the tools used most frequently and the chapter where each is discussed in this text.

Table 9.6
Systems analysis and
design tools and techniques

CASE (Chapter 9)	Organization charts (Chapter 2)
Coding (Chapter 10)	Program flowcharts (Chapter 3)
Data flow diagrams (Chapter 3)	Prototyping (Chapter 11)
Decision tables (Chapter 3)	Record layouts (Chapter 10)
Document flowcharts (Chapter 3)	Report layouts (Chapter 10)
Forms design checklist (Chapter 10)	Systems flowcharts (Chapter 3)
HIPO charts (Chapter 3)	

Analyze the Existing System. When data gathering is completed, the survey team needs to evaluate its findings. An evaluation of system strengths and weaknesses can help the team develop preliminary ideas about how the new system might be designed and structured. Strengths should be retained and weaknesses should be corrected. For example, if output is being duplicated, a consolidation of reports might produce cost savings. Similarly, a lack of control might be corrected by changing data collection procedures or by prenumbering documents. Design ideas will be developed further during conceptual design.

Prepare a Systems Survey Report. The systems survey culminates with the development of a systems survey report that describes the current system. Table 9.7 shows the table of contents for the Shoppers Mart report. As the table shows, the survey report describes current systems operations. The report should be supported by documentation such as memos to users and management, interview and observation notes, questionnaire data, file and record layouts and descriptions, descriptions of all inputs and outputs, and copies of all documents collected. It may also be supported by flowcharts or data flow diagrams.

Feasibility Study   The information gathered during the systems survey is used to conduct a more thorough feasibility analysis than the cursory analysis done during the initial investigation. This detailed study is used by the steering committee to decide whether to terminate the project, proceed unconditionally, or proceed only if specific problems, such as inadequate resources or information, can be resolved. Although the project can be terminated later in the systems life cycle, the go/no-go decision made here is critical, because subsequent steps in the life cycle require major commitments of time and money.

There are many different ways to produce the needed outputs and meet the objectives of the required system. Therefore the feasibility analysis should consider several different conceptual approaches to systems design to ensure that the most practical approaches are recommended. The study must also identify the system's scope, its probable

Shoppers Mart
Systems Survey Report

Table of Contents

I. Executive Summary

II. System Goals and Objectives

III. System Problems and Opportunities

IV. Current System Operations

    A. Policies, Procedures, and Practices Affecting System

    B. Systems Design and Operation (Intended and Actual)

    C. System Users and Their Responsibilities

    D. System Outputs, Inputs, Processes, and Data Storage

    E. System Controls

    F. System Strengths, Weaknesses, and Constraints

    G. Costs to Operate System

V. User Requirements Identified During Survey

Table 9.7
Typical table of contents for a systems survey report

characteristics, and its costs. Finally, it is essential that users be represented on the team that conducts the study to provide data, make their needs and desires known, and be apprised of the findings.

Information Needs and System Requirements

The objective of this step in the analysis phase of the SDLC is to define and document the information needs of the users and the requirements of the new system. Based on these needs, a thorough definition of what the system will do can be produced. Determining information needs may not be easy because of the sheer quantity and variety of information that must be specified, even for a relatively simple information system. A second reason is that people may not know what their information needs are or may identify them incorrectly. Figure 9.4 somewhat humorously illustrates the problems in systems communications, including the difficulty in determining what it is that users really need.

As an example showing the importance of accurately determining system requirements, consider Corning Corporation. In 1988 Corning began looking at the quality of the ophthalmic pressings that it manufactures and sells to the makers of prescription lenses. It found that 35% of the drafting documents used to make the pressings had errors in them. It also found that at each step of the manufacturing process the drafting errors became increasingly expensive to correct. Correction cost $250 if the error was discovered before the toolmakers cut the

As proposed by user management

As sold to top management

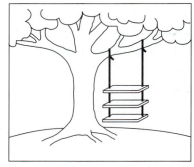

As designed by the senior analyst

As written by the applications programmers

Figure 9.4
Communications problems in systems
analysis and design

tools, $20,000 if discovered before the assembly line began production, and up to $100,000 after the pressing was sent to the customer. As a result of the study, a number of corrective actions were undertaken that reduced the error rates from 35% to 0.2%.

The same type of cost relationship exists in IS development. As shown in Fig. 9.5, the cost to correct an error increases as development proceeds through the life cycle phases. Compounding this problem is the fact that the earlier the phase, the more frequent and more severe the errors are. The implications of this graph are that a company should not skimp on systems analysis and should make every effort to ensure quality from the very beginning of the development process.

Strategies for Determining Requirements.   There are four strategies for determining information systems requirements: asking the user, studying currently developed systems, studying the use of currently developed systems, and experimentation or prototyping. The best strategy for a particular situation depends on the type of system to be developed.

The primary determinant of strategy is the amount of uncertainty associated with successfully developing a system. A well-known framework for measuring uncertainty—and thereby determining the appropriate requirements analysis strategy—was developed by Nau-

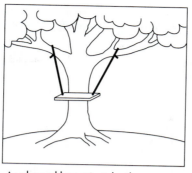

As planned by project development team

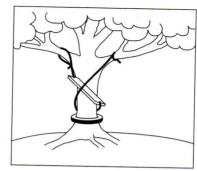

As approved by the steering committee

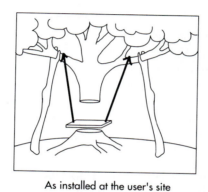

As installed at the user's site

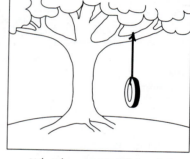

What the users actually needed

Figure 9.4
(Continued)

Figure 9.5
Relative occurrence of errors and
relative costs to fix them
during systems development

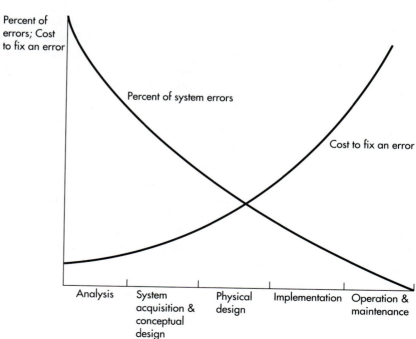

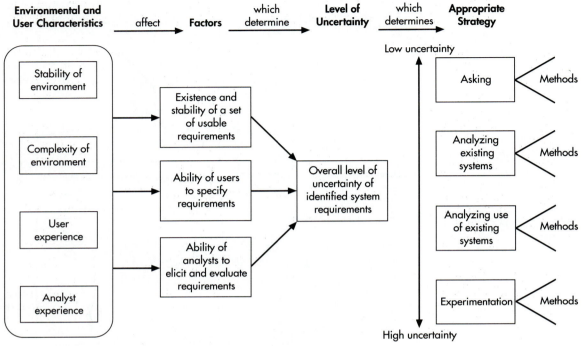

Figure 9.6
Requirements analysis
strategy selection

mann, Davis, and McKeen.[1] They suggest that the uncertainty associated with the systems development process is contingent on various characteristics. Figure 9.6 illustrates the elements of **contingency theory** as it relates to selection of a strategy for requirements analysis. The four characteristics listed on the left side of Fig. 9.6 determine the levels of three factors that, in turn, determine the overall uncertainty. The overall level of uncertainty of the project then determines which strategy would most likely provide a well-defined set of system requirements.

The four characteristics of a project that affect the three factors determining the overall level of uncertainty are described in the following list.

■ *Stability of the environment:* This characteristic encompasses the stability of the organization itself, of the industry in which it operates, of the technology required for the system, of management and staff, and of the maturity of the organization in using information systems. The less stable the environment, the less likely the analyst or users are to be able to identify a set of usable requirements.

---

[1] J. David Naumann, G. B. Davis, and J. D. McKeen, ''Determining Information Requirements: A Contingency Method for Selection of a Requirements Assurance Strategy,'' *Journal of Systems and Software*, Vol. **1** (19xx): 227.

- *Complexity of the environment:* Complexity depends primarily on whether the system will provide clerical support or decision support and the degree to which information used throughout the organization will be integrated. The more oriented the system is to decision support or the greater the desired integration, the greater the uncertainty is in all three of the factors determining the overall uncertainty.

- *User experience:* Typically, the less experience users have with the current system and with information systems in general, the less likely they are to be able to specify system requirements.

- *Analyst experience:* Analyst experience refers to the experience of the analyst with the current and the proposed systems. Because systems development projects can be quite different, general experience cannot compensate totally for lack of experience with the specific type of system at hand.

Taken together, these four characteristics determine (1) the existence and stability of a set of usable requirements, (2) the ability of users to specify their requirements, and (3) the ability of analysts to elicit and evaluate users' requirements. As the level of any of these three factors decreases, the overall level of uncertainty associated with establishing a set of requirements increases.

A particular project's level of uncertainty, represented by its position on the vertical line in Fig. 9.6, determines which strategy is most likely to be successful. Often more than one strategy may be used, especially if the proposed system involves both clerical and decision support applications.

The simplest and fastest strategy is to simply ask users what their information needs are. The main disadvantage of this approach is that the people either may not realize or may not understand their true needs. Though they may know how to do their job, they may not be able to break that job down into the individual information elements they use.

A second strategy is to analyze existing systems, both internal and external to the organization, to determine exactly what information is being used. The idea behind this approach is that one should investigate the possibility that a partial solution to the problem already exists, so as to avoid "re-creating the wheel."

A third strategy is to examine the utilization of the existing system. This strategy differs from the second approach in that it takes into account the fact that users may not use the existing system as intended. There may be modules that are not used as intended, are augmented by manual tasks, or are avoided altogether. This approach helps analysts determine whether a system can be modified or must be wholly replaced.

A fourth approach is an iterative approach called **prototyping**. This approach is used when analysts realize from the start that they are unlikely to be able to identify a usable set of requirements. Therefore they quickly rough out a system for users to critique. The idea here is that once the users see something on the screen, they can begin to identify what they like and dislike. Prototyping is discussed in greater detail in Chapter 11.

One of the main reasons for developing an application is to support decision-making functions. Therefore we briefly discuss decision making next.

Framework for Studying Decision Making.   A useful framework for studying management decisions is provided by Anthony,[2] who classifies management activities into three broad categories: strategic planning, management control, and operational control. **Strategic planning** involves determining organization objectives, changes in those objectives, and policies that govern the acquisition, use, and disposition of resources for attaining the objectives. **Management control** is the process by which managers ensure that resources are obtained and used effectively and efficiently in the accomplishment of the organization's objectives. **Operational control** ensures that specific tasks are carried out effectively and efficiently. To clarify these definitions, Anthony presents a table, reproduced here in Table 9.8, listing several types of decision-making activities that fall under each heading.

Keen and Scott Morton[3] identify a second dimension by which management decisions may be characterized—the degree of structure they possess. **Structured decisions** are repetitive, routine, and well enough understood to be delegated to clerks or to be automated on a computer. They are decisions for which a decision model is already built. **Unstructured decisions** are nonrecurring and nonroutine—no framework or model exists for solving them. The decision maker must rely primarily or exclusively on judgment and intuition. Unstructured decisions are often supported by a decision support system.

Semistructured decisions may be partially but not fully automated, because they require subjective assessments and judgments in conjunction with formal data analysis and model building. Keen and Scott Morton propose that their three-way classification of decisions be merged with Anthony's framework to produce a two-dimensional taxonomy of decisions. They illustrate this taxonomy by means of a table, reproduced here in Table 9.9, that contains an example of each of nine different categories of decisions.

A rough correspondence exists between managers' level in the organization and the nature of their decision-making responsibilities. Top management generally faces unstructured or semistructured decisions that involve strategic planning issues. Middle-level managers

---

[2] Robert N. Anthony, *Planning and Control Systems: A Framework for Analysis* (Boston: Graduate School of Business Administration, Harvard University, 1965), 16–18.

[3] Peter G. W. Keen and Michael S. Scott Morton, *Decision Support Systems: An Organizational Perspective* (Reading, Mass.: Addison-Wesley, 1978), 85–86.

Strategic Planning	Management Control	Operational Control
Choosing company objectives	Formulating budgets	
Planning the organization	Planning staff levels	Controlling hiring
Setting personnel policies	Formulating personnel practices	Implementing policies
Setting financial policies	Working capital planning	Controlling credit extension
Setting marketing policies	Formulating advertising programs	Controlling placement of advertisements
Setting research policies	Deciding on research projects	
Choosing new product lines	Choosing product improvements	
Acquiring a new division	Deciding on plant rearrangement	Scheduling production
Deciding on nonroutine capital expenditures	Deciding on routine capital expenditures	
	Formulating decision rules for operational control	Controlling inventory
	Measuring, appraising, and improving management performance	Measuring, appraising, and improving workers' efficiency

Source: Robert N. Anthony, *Planning and Control Systems: A Framework for Analysis* (Boston: Graduate School of Business Administration, Harvard University, 1965), 19. Copyright © 1965 by the President and Fellows of Harvard College. Reprinted by permission.

Table 9.8
Examples of activities in a business organization included in major framework headings

generally deal with semistructured decisions concerning management control. Supervisors and employees at the lowest organizational levels typically face semistructured or structured decisions involving operational control. It is important to examine the types of decisions for which a manager is responsible as a first step in designing an information system to support that manager's activities. The decision taxonomy presented in Table 9.9 provides a useful framework for doing so.

Identifying the information requirements of lower-level managers is often not an easy task. Precise identification of the decision responsibilities and information requirements of top-level managers engaged in strategic planning is even more difficult. The functions of top-level managers may be defined by such vague phrases as "setting objectives," "establishing policies," and "devising market strategies." The information required for these unstructured or semistructured decisions is primarily external information dealing with the product markets, the economy, the company's competitors, the availability of resources, and other environmental factors. Such information generally must encompass a broad time horizon, deal with a large number of variables, and be future-oriented. Top-level managers may need to have large quantities of data summarized. Demands for information may arise on an irregular or infrequent basis. Because of these factors, a top-level manager may find it difficult to specify information requirements.

Type of Decision	MANAGEMENT ACTIVITY			Support Needed
	Operational Control	Management Control	Strategic Planning	
Structured	1 Inventory reordering	4 Linear programming for manufacturing	7 Plant location	Clerical, EDP, or management science models
Semistructured	2 Bond trading	5 Setting market budgets for consumer projects	8 Capital acquisition analysis	Decision support systems
Unstructured	3 Selecting a cover for *Time* magazine	6 Hiring managers	9 R&D portfolio management	Human intuition

Table 9.9
Keen and Scott Morton's
decision taxonomy

Source: Peter G. W. Keen and Michael S. Scott Morton, *Decision Support Systems: An Organizational Perspective* (Reading, Mass.: Addison-Wesley Publishing Company, 1978), 87. Reprinted by permission.

Documentation of User Requirements.   The end result of the information identification step is a set of detailed system requirements for the new system. This report concentrates on what should be produced by the system. It leaves the "how it is to be produced" to the design phase of the life cycle. System requirements should include items such as those listed in Table 9.10.

In addition to the detailed listing of requirements, a management summary written in nontechnical language is often prepared for management. It should concisely summarize important user requirements and development efforts to date. When possible, the requirements list should be supported by sample record layouts, sample outputs, or graphs. These visuals make it easier for readers to conceptualize the system.

User and Management Approval.   Once user requirements have been determined and documented, the project team must meet with the users, explain the requirements, and obtain their agreement and approval. The system is usually explained by using oral presentations, the management summary of system requirements, and selected documentation of the requirements. Time should be allotted in these meetings to answer questions, accept recommendations, and discuss potential modifications to the requirements. It is important that the project team

Processes	A description of all processes in the new system, including what is to be done and by whom
Data elements	A description of the data elements needed, including their name, size, format, source, and significance
Data structure	A preliminary data structure, showing how the data elements will be organized into logical records
Outputs	A copy of system outputs, and a description of their purpose, frequency, and distribution
Inputs	A copy of system inputs, and a description of their contents, source, and who is responsible for them
Documentation	A description of how the new system and each subsystem will operate
Constraints	A description of constraints such as reporting deadlines, operating schedules, security requirements, space and staffing limitations, and statutory or regulatory requirements
Controls	Controls to ensure the accuracy and reliability of inputs, outputs, and data processing
Reorganizations	Organizational reorganization needed to meet the users' information needs, such as increasing staff levels, adding new job functions, restructuring jobs, or terminating existing positions or jobs

Table 9.10
Possible contents of
system requirements

be responsive to the questions, comments, suggestions, and concerns of users. When an agreement is reached, user management should sign the system requirements documents to indicate approval. The review and approval process can consume a significant amount of time, but it is essential if the user commitment necessary for successful development and implementation is to be obtained.

Systems Analysis Report

The systems analysis and design phase is concluded by preparing the systems analysis report, which summarizes and documents the findings of the analysis activities. The comprehensive report and its accompanying backup documentation serve as a repository of data from which systems designers can draw. The table of contents of the systems analysis report prepared for Shoppers Mart is presented in Table 9.11. It shows the information typically contained in this report.

A go/no-go decision may be made as many as three times during systems analysis: during the initial investigation, at the end of the feasibility study, and at the completion of the analysis phase.

The critical importance of the systems analysis phase of the SDLC is summarized very well by Focus 9.2. It emphasizes that no matter what approach a company uses to implement a new system, one of the most important keys to success is an effective systems analysis to ensure that the company correctly defines the business problem.

```
┌─────────────────────────────────────────────────────────────────────┐
│                            Shoppers Mart                              │
│                        Systems Analysis Report                        │
│                                                                       │
│   Table of Contents                                                   │
│                                                                       │
│        I.  Executive Summary                                          │
│       II.  System Goals and Objectives                                │
│      III.  System Problems and Opportunities                          │
│       IV.  Project Scope                                              │
│        V.  Relationship of Project to Overall Strategic Information Systems Plan │
│       VI.  Current System Operations                                  │
│      VII.  User Requirements                                          │
│     VIII.  Feasibility Analysis                                       │
│       IX.  System Constraints                                         │
│        X.  Recommendations for New System                            │
│       XI.  Proposed Project Participants and Work Plan               │
│      XII.  Summary                                                   │
│     XIII.  Approvals                                                 │
│      XIV.  Appendix of Documents, Tables, Charts, Glossary of Terms  │
└─────────────────────────────────────────────────────────────────────┘
```

Table 9.11
Typical table of contents for a systems analysis report

9.2 FOCUS

Are Systems Analysis Techniques Outdated?

The failure of IS professionals to meet user needs in a timely manner has contributed to the users' desire to acquire their own PCs and "do it themselves." At the same time, many firms have stopped developing their own systems and have purchased one of the many software packages produced by major software vendors.

If companies are going to purchase systems that someone else has already developed, why do we need professional systems employees? Is there still a place for sound systems analysis techniques, tools, and methodologies in a world of end-user computing and third-party systems? What happens to old-fashioned systems analysis practices in the face of new approaches to systems development? Should the timeworn approaches be discarded because the end result has failed to meet the needs of the business? The answer is an emphatic "no."

What is needed is for software developers to better execute the approaches they have. As developers feel the

CONCEPTUAL (GENERAL) SYSTEMS DESIGN

The objective of conceptual systems design is to take user requirements and develop a general framework for their implementation. The development team must consider all the data gathered during systems analysis, including a description of the current system, how it operates, and its problems and weaknesses; an evaluation of the information needs of system users; and a set of systems requirements. Using these data as a base, the development team decides on the approach to resolving the problems and to satisfying the information requirements.

Conceptual design often follows a top-down pattern. The designer begins with higher-level functions within the system and moves downward through a series of functions and subfunctions, adding depth and detail at each level. For example, Ann and the development team at Shoppers Mart could begin with the five business cycles discussed in Chapters 16–20. They could then take each cycle and break it down into smaller business processes. For example, the revenue cycle can be broken down into sales order preparation, credit checking, checking inventory availability, filling and shipping the product, billing, receiving cash, and processing accounts receivable. Each of these activities can in turn be broken down into smaller activities.

With business processes thus decomposed into their most fundamental activities, the design team can begin to specify how the needs of systems users can be met. The result is a detailed conceptual structure of the proposed system and all its parts, with all major processes, inputs, outputs, and data requirements specified.

---

pressure to perform system miracles, they find it easy to skip the basics of systems analysis and design and begin by writing code. This only leads to disaster: They develop nice, well-structured systems that do not meet user needs and have nothing to do with the business problem they were trying to solve. Effective systems analysis is needed to ensure that developers are correctly defining the business problem and that they design the appropriate solution.

A Peat Marwick survey shows that 35% of all major IS projects are "runaways" that are hopelessly incomplete and over budget. An American Management Systems study revealed that 75% of all large systems are either not used, not used as intended, or generate meaningless reports. Many of these problems can be attributed to ineffective or incomplete systems analysis efforts.

Effective systems analysis is a critical phase in the development life cycle. It begins with problem recognition, feasibility analysis, and a study and documentation of the existing system. This information is used to define the requirements of the new system or the system change. The goal of systems analysis is to determine the requirements for any proposed system. Whether the end user is going to use a fourth-generation language to develop an end-user system, or the systems department is going to recommend a third-party system for users, an effective systems analysis effort is needed to ensure that the system meets business requirements and takes the organization where it really wants to go.

Source: Charlene A. Dykman and Ruth Robbins, "Organizational Success Through Effective Systems Analysis," *Journal of Systems Management* (July 1991): 6–8.

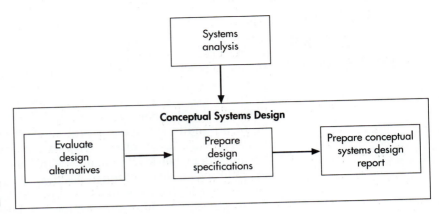

Figure 9.7
Steps in conceptual systems design

There are three steps in conceptual systems design: evaluating design alternatives, preparing design specifications, and preparing a conceptual systems design report. These three steps are shown in Fig. 9.7 and are discussed in the subsections that follow.

Evaluate Design Alternatives

When people are considering making a change to their home, they have many options. They can add on to or remodel their current home, buy a different house, buy and remodel a house, or have one custom-built. Similarly, alternatives for systems design range from making minor modifications to the current system to developing a completely new system.

In designing a custom-built house, a homeowner knows that she needs a kitchen, a dining area, a family room, bedrooms, and bathrooms, and a garage. However, she has to make decisions about how many stories or levels to have, how to best arrange the rooms, and what appliances and features to have. System designers must also make decisions. They must answer questions like these: Should the company mail hard copy purchase orders to vendors or use EDI? Should they have a large centralized mainframe and data base, or should they distribute computer power throughout the company using minicomputers, microcomputers, distributed data bases, LANs, and WANs? Should data entry be through keyboard, OCR, POS, EDI, or some combination?

The design team should identify, document, and describe a variety of available design alternatives. The team should then evaluate each alternative with respect to (1) how well it meets the stated objectives of the organization and the information system, (2) how well it meets the users' information needs, (3) whether it is economically, operationally, legally, and technically feasible, and (4) its advantages and disadvantages. Table 9.12 shows some of the design considerations for conceptual and physical design, along with available alternatives.

The design alternatives should be presented to the steering committee in sufficient detail to allow the committee to make an intelligent and

Design Consideration	Design Alternatives
Communications channel configuration	Point-to-point, multidrop, or line-sharing
Communications channels	Telephone lines, coaxial cable, fiber optics, microwave, or satellite
Communications network	Centralized, decentralized, distributed, or local area
Data storage medium	Tape, floppy disk, hard disk, or hard copy
Data storage structure	Files or data base
File organization and access	Random or sequential
Input medium	Keying, OCR, MICR, POS, EDI, or voice
Operations	In-house or outsourcing
Output frequency	Instantaneous, hourly, daily, weekly, or monthly
Output medium	CRT, hard copy, voice, or turnaround document
Output scheduling	Predetermined times or on demand
Printed output	Preprinted forms or system-generated forms
Processing	Manual, batch, or real-time
Processor	Micro, mini, or mainframe
Software acquisition	Canned, custom, or modified
Transaction processing	Batch or on-line
Update frequency	Instantaneous, hourly, daily, weekly, or monthly

Table 9.12
Design considerations and alternatives

informed decision. The steering committee must evaluate the alternatives and select the one that appears to best meet the organization's needs.

Prepare Design Specifications

Once a design alternative has been selected, conceptual design specifications are developed. Since the information system is being designed to meet users' information needs, output specifications should be prepared first. For example, Shoppers Mart needs to evaluate the sales in each of its stores. One way to do that is with a sales analysis report. Shoppers Mart must make decisions regarding how often to produce the sales report (daily or weekly), what the report should contain (store number, sales volume, etc.), what the report should look like, and whether users need a hard copy or screen output (or both).

Because the system must store all the elements needed to produce the sales report, data storage (file and data base) specifications are usually developed next. Some of the development decisions include what data elements must be stored to produce the sales report (store number, sales volume, etc.), whether the data should be stored in sequential or random order, what type of file or data base to use, and what field size to use for the data items.

Next come specifications for the input. Design considerations for Shoppers Mart, for example, include what sales data need to be entered into the system (salesperson, location of sale, amount of sale, etc.), and where, when, and how to collect the data.

The fourth set of specifications is for processing procedures and operations. Design considerations for Shoppers Mart, for example, include how to process the input and stored data to produce the sales report and the sequence in which the processes must be performed. The order in which the design specifications are usually prepared is shown in Fig. 9.8.

The conceptual design specifications should contain the name and purpose of each output, data base, processing program, or input. The specifications should also include a description of the controls and error-handling procedures and of the volume and frequency of processing or preparation. A summary of some of the more important elements to be included in the specifications appears in Table 9.13.

Systems Acquisition

At some point the organization must decide whether to develop software for the new system or to buy it. Data for this make-or-buy decision are gathered throughout the analysis phase. For example, an important part of the feasibility study is identifying whether software is already available for the proposed system. The decision to make or to buy should be made after system requirements have been determined but before planners are too far into conceptual design, because much of the design phase can be omitted if software is purchased. Once system requirements are known, they can be used to determine which package most closely fits the requirements or can be modified to fit the requirements.

Prepare the Conceptual Systems Design Report

At the end of the conceptual design phase the project development team prepares and submits a conceptual systems design report to the steering committee for review and approval. This report serves as a guide to physical systems design, it communicates to management and users how the system will meet their information and data processing needs, and it is used by the steering committee to assess the ongoing feasibility of the system.

The conceptual systems design report should contain a description

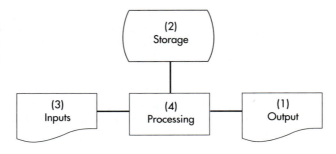

Figure 9.8
Order of specifications preparation
(numbers represent order)

	Output	Data Base	Processing	Input
Name	X	X	X	X
Purpose	X	X	X	X
Controls description	X	X	X	X
Error-handling procedures	X	X	X	X
Frequency	X	X	X	X
Volume	X	X	X	X
Content	X	X		X
Format	X	X		X
Medium	X	X		X
Layout	X	X		X
Sequential or random order		X	X	X
Distribution	X			
Trigger or cause	X			
Response time	X			
File type and size		X		
Record size		X		
File organization		X		
Data structure		X		
Specific operation to perform			X	
Sequence of operation			X	
Calculation performed			X	
Source				X
Collection method				X

Table 9.13
Design specifications

of why the project is being undertaken, a list of project objectives, an outline of the expected costs and benefits, and a brief summary of the results of the project to date. The main component of the report is a description of one or more recommended designs for the new system. This description should contain (1) a description and a listing of the contents of each system output, data base, and input; (2) the general flow of processing and the relationships among the major programs, files, inputs, and outputs; (3) hardware, software, and other resource requirements; and (4) audit, control, and security processes and procedures. Any critical assumptions or unresolved problems that may affect the final systems design should also be discussed. The table of contents of the conceptual systems design report prepared for Shoppers Mart is shown in Table 9.14.

Shoppers Mart
Conceptual Systems Design Report

Table of Contents

I. Executive Summary of Conceptual Systems Design

II. Overview of Project Purpose and Summary of Findings to Date

III. Recommended Conceptual Design(s) of Proposed System

    A. Overview of Recommended Design(s)

    B. Objectives to Be Achieved by Design(s)

    C. Impact of Design(s) on Information System and Organization

    D. Expected Costs and Benefits of Design(s)

    E. Audit, Control, and Security Processes and Procedures

    F. Hardware, Software, and Other Resource Requirements

    G. Processing Flows: Relationships of Programs, Data Bases, Inputs, and Outputs

    H. Description of System Components (Programs, Data Bases, Inputs, and Outputs)

IV. Assumptions and Unresolved Problems

V. Summary

VI. Appendixes, Glossary

Table 9.14
Table of contents for a conceptual systems design report

COMPUTER-AIDED SOFTWARE ENGINEERING (CASE)

Software developers have often been compared to the shoemaker's children who had to go barefoot. Software developers spend all their time developing software to make other people's tasks easier, yet they seldom turn their attention to developing software to make their own work easier. That has changed in the past few years with the development of several powerful computerized development tools that speed up the SDLC. Dataquest, a market research firm, estimates that companies spent $12 billion on computer-aided software engineering tools in 1993.

Computer-aided software (or systems) engineering (CASE) technology consists of an integrated package of computer-based systems development tools that automate important aspects of the software development process. CASE tools are used to plan, analyze, design, program, and maintain information systems. They are also used to enhance the efforts of managers, users, and programmers in understanding the information needs of the organization. Some of the more popular CASE tools are listed in Table 9.15.

There are two different types of CASE tools: front-end and back-end. **Front-end (or upper) CASE** tools support the early stages of the SDLC, such as systems analysis and design. For example, these CASE systems help developers produce complete and consistent system specifi-

Tool	Vendor
Analyst/Designer Toolkit	Yourdon
CA-Telon	Computer Associates International
DesignAid II	Transform Logic
EasyCASE Pro	Evergreen CASE Tools
Excelerator	Intersolv
Foundation	Arthur Andersen & Company
Freeflow	Iconix
Information Engineering Facility	Texas Instruments
Information Engineering Workbench	KnowledgeWare
Maestro II	Softlab
MicroSTEP	Syscorp International
OpenSelect	Meridian Software
System Architect	Popkin
Teamwork	Cadre Technologies
Visible Analyst Workbench	Visible Systems Corporation

Table 9.15
Popular CASE Tools

cations; develop graphic models of systems, such as data flow diagrams, structure charts, and entity relationship diagrams; develop data dictionaries; and document the system. Front-end CASE tools are more popular and more well developed than back-end tools.

Back-end (or **lower**) **CASE** tools support the later phases of the SDLC. For example, programmers use back-end tools to generate structured program code from data base specifications and from screen and report layouts. They also use them for testing and maintenance activities. Many back-end tools allow the programmer to use a simple fill-in-the-blanks interface to input the information and get back executable code from the CASE tool. The programmer can then refine and adapt the code as needed. Because they are used to develop code, back-end tools are sometimes referred to as **computer-aided programming tools**.

A **data repository** or **CASE encyclopedia** stores and manages project data dictionaries using a relational or object-oriented data base. The data repository contains all the information about the system being developed. This information includes record and data elements; data details; systems processes, modules, and functions; and definitions of report designs, screen designs, and data entry forms. It also includes system development plans, program code, and project management information. All data stored in the repository is cross-referenced to all other system components such as data bases, programs, files, and input and output screens. Stored data can be reused on subsequent projects, providing developers with increased flexibility and productivity.

The latest generation of CASE tools brings upper and lower CASE tools together into an **integrated** (or **customized**) **CASE** package that is linked by the data repository. The day will soon come when the analyst will simply enter the specifications of what exists, what is wanted in addition, the high-level logic (structured English), and the input and output forms. The CASE tool will do the rest. And some day, if developers of CASE tools have their way, development environments will allow nontechnical users, familiar with particular business or decision needs but ignorant of the technical workings of the computer, to give their specifications to the computer and let it do the physical designing.

CASE Tools   CASE tools do not replace skilled designers. Rather, CASE technology provides a host of well-integrated tools that give developers effective support for all phases of the SDLC. An integrated CASE product has the following components.

- *Strategic planning tools:* Strategic planning CASE tools assist top-level managers and designers in identifying business information needs and in determining which projects are the most important to a company's strategic health and therefore should receive priority treatment.

- *Project management tools:* These tools help managers plan, schedule, organize, manage, control, and report the progress of the overall SDLC. They include programs to schedule systems development tasks, budget expenditures, and allocate resources such as personnel and time. The software can also be used to assess the risk of various projects and to monitor planned performance against actual performance.

- *Data base design tools:* These tools generate a working data base design from the data descriptions stored in the data repository. This data base is a starting point for systems designers who complete the design. The software also develops a data dictionary to support the data base and entity relationship diagrams to show relationships between data tables.

- *Diagramming tools:* These tools are used to draw, modify, manipulate, and store data flow diagrams, entity relationship diagrams, flowcharts, hierarchical structure charts, organizational charts, and other diagrams and charts used in systems design.

- *Screen layout tools:* This CASE tool allows developers to quickly and easily design the format, features, content, and physical layout of input and output screen displays. Users can easily see the screens that they will be working with and give feedback about format and content.

- *Report layout tools:* This tool allows users to design the format, features, content, and physical layout of printed outputs.

- *Automatic code generators:* This software uses the system specifications to write application code for the target hardware/software environment. Typical program generators can generate between 50% and 75% of a program's source code. The more complex programming steps are handled by the programmer.

■ *Validation design tools:* This CASE tool runs internal consistency checks on the data stored in the data repository. It checks all diagrams, specifications, and data bases to make sure that they are complete and consistent. Problems within the repository, such as logic errors, incomplete data, and inconsistent data elements, are flagged for the system designer.

■ *Word processing and graphics tools:* Many CASE tools include internal word processing and graphics capabilities to facilitate the documentation process. They allow users to modify the write-up and graphical description of the system when changes are made to the system.

■ *Systems management tools:* Systems management tools help systems specialists configure controls over programs and data base structures, correct errors, and adapt to changing systems environments.

Advantages and Disadvantages of CASE Technology

CASE tools have several important advantages over unautomated development processes. There are also a number of drawbacks to their use. The advantages of CASE are discussed next.

■ *Improved productivity:* Companies using CASE tools report significant increases in speed of development and productivity. For example, Sony Corporation and Du Pont both reported productivity increases of over 600% in the development of some applications. One reason for the improved productivity is that bug-free code can automatically be generated from system specifications. At Baptist Medical System a programmer using an integrated CASE tool developed, in one week, a system to control child care benefits that would have taken two programmers two months each to complete.

■ *Improved program quality:* CASE tools make it easier for structured development standards to be enforced, which improves the quality of development and reduces the threat of serious design errors. The use of a single design repository to correlate design components leads to more internally consistent development and tighter controls over the information used in the development process. CASE tools also have the ability to check the internal accuracy of the design and detect inconsistencies.

■ *Cost savings:* Savings of 80%–90% over unautomated development approaches are possible. At Du Pont an application that would have required 27 people-months at a cost of almost $270,000 was finished in 4 people-months at a cost of $30,000. Du Pont was able to generate over 90% of the code directly from design specifications. Du Pont has now installed CASE tools at most of its sites and has used it on numerous applications.

- *Improved control procedures:* CASE tools encourage the development of system controls and security measures early in the design process. They also encourage and facilitate the development of system auditability and error-handling procedures.

- *Documentation:* CASE tools automatically document the system as the development process progresses.

- *Reduced maintenance requirements:* The increase in program quality leads to significantly lower system maintenance efforts once the system is operational.

- *Automation of repetitive tasks:* CASE software can automate repetitive tasks, such as drawing diagrams and charts, creating logical models, converting a logical model into an efficient data base, and documenting the system. This frees the developer to concentrate on more creative and interesting tasks.

- *Limited what-if analysis of design alternatives:* Just as a change in a number is carried throughout the affected areas of a spreadsheet, a change in the design of a system is carried through the CASE software.

- *Sharing of design data:* With design data stored in the data repository, it becomes much easier for members of the development team to share design details and to review and modify the work of others. It also improves communication among team members and users.

CASE tools are proving very helpful to systems developers and programmers. However, CASE tools still remain largely untested. Some of the problems with CASE technology are noted next.

- *Inflexibility:* CASE tools are most appropriate to the development of new systems, which accounts for only about 20% of all systems projects.

- *Incompatibility:* CASE tools lack programming standards that allow different CASE tools to interact effectively. In addition, some CASE tools are not compatible with data base programs or fourth-generation languages (4GLs).

- *Cost:* CASE technology is relatively expensive, with some packages in excess of $300,000. Additional costs are incurred to develop CASE standards and methodologies and to train systems developers to use CASE tools effectively. Some companies spend $2 on training and standardization for every $1 they spend on CASE software. As a result, most smaller companies aren't able to use integrated CASE tools.

- *Limited capabilities:* CASE technology is still in its infancy, and much work must be done to make CASE tools more powerful and versatile. Hopefully, at some point general cradle-to-grave CASE support will be available, as will automatic programming capabilities (developing final programming code from data flow diagrams and data dictionaries).

In spite of its limitations, CASE technology provides systems programmers and designers with a host of support tools to aid in the systems development process. As CASE tools continue to improve, they will have even more of an impact on the analysis and design of systems.

CASE CONCLUSION: THE SYSTEMS ANALYSIS AND CONCEPTUAL SYSTEMS DESIGN PROCESS AT SHOPPERS MART

The information Ann Christy collected during the interviews she conducted led her to propose and receive permission to develop a new system for Shoppers Mart. In consultation with management she decided to tackle the sales processing portion of the system first. She gave the project development team the data she had collected and assigned it the task of surveying the existing system and of studying the business processes involved in managing and controlling sales data. She met weekly with the team to review and supervise its progress.

Members of the team began the survey by reviewing all available documentation to gain a better understanding and perspective of the current system. They supplemented and validated this information by interviewing users and observing how the system was actually used. They were interested not only in how the current system actually worked but also in how the users thought it ought to work. The team presented its findings in a systems survey report (see Table 9.7 for the table of contents). The team documented its results by preparing data flow diagrams showing how the current system operates.

The most difficult part of the systems analysis was determining the needs of system users. Some information had been gathered by Ann, and the team had picked up more information during the survey. That information was supplemented by in-depth interviews with a cross section of current information system users at all levels of the organization. To get a broader breadth of information, the team also prepared a questionnaire, which it sent to system users. Ann had stressed the importance of user involvement, and the team was careful to include users in all that it did. The process was time-consuming; but when the team had completed its work, both Ann and the users felt very comfortable with the user specifications that were developed. The table of contents of the report the team turned into Ann is shown in Table 9.11.

Ann used the data provided by the team to update her feasibility analysis and presented the updated analysis to management. The team findings validated Ann's initial findings, and management gave approval to proceed with the project.

As soon as Ann received permission to proceed with conceptual systems design, the development team began identifying all possible approaches to meeting system requirements. Team members visited several retail chains that had similar operations to get more ideas. The approaches identified were discussed with users, management, and the steering committee and finally narrowed down to the approach Ann proposed in her initial pitch to top management.

The team then developed conceptual design specifications for the output, input, processing, and data storage elements of the system. The team reviewed the information needs of all users and identified the nature and types of reports they would need. The company decided to use technology whenever it could by having as much of the output as possible screen-based. Then the design team identified all the files and data bases that would be needed to store the data needed to meet system requirements. The team decided to capture as much data as possible electronically. The team made sure that all of the data required as output was either captured as input or calculated/generated during the processing of the data. The table of contents for the conceptual systems design report the team developed is shown in Table 9.14.

With systems analysis and conceptual design completed, Ann can now turn her attention to the physical design of the new system and to implementation, conversion, and operation issues. ■

SUMMARY

This chapter discusses two important phases of systems development: systems analysis and conceptual systems design.

Systems analysis consists of five steps: (1) initial investigation, (2) systems survey, (3) feasibility study, (4) identification of information needs and systems requirements, and (5) preparation of the systems analysis report. The initial investigation screens users' requests for systems development so that resources are not wasted on projects that are not worthwhile.

The systems survey analyzes the existing system to identify its strengths and weaknesses. The feasibility study investigates a project's economic, technical, operational, scheduling, and legal feasibility. If the system appears feasible, the information needs of users are identified and system requirements are developed. The purpose and requirements of systems can range from performing clerical processes to supporting management decision making. Contingency theory is a means of identifying an appropriate requirements analysis strategy. The analysis phase is concluded by summarizing all findings in a systems analysis report.

There are three steps in conceptual systems design. The first is to evaluate the available design alternatives and select the most appropriate design. The second is to prepare conceptual design specifications for the new system. The last step is to prepare the conceptual systems design report.

Key Terms

Define the following terms.

systems analysis	logical model	conceptual design specifications
request for systems development	structured systems analysis	conceptual systems design report
initial investigation	systems survey report	
scope of the system	contingency theory	computer-aided software (or systems) engineering (CASE)
system boundaries	prototyping	
proposal to conduct systems analysis	strategic planning	front-end (or upper) CASE
	management control	back-end (or lower) CASE
systems survey	operational control	computer-aided programming tools
interview	structured decisions	
questionnaires	unstructured decisions	data repository or CASE encyclopedia
observation	semistructured decisions	
documentation	systems analysis report	integrated (or customized) CASE
physical model	conceptual systems design	

Discussion Questions

9.1 The discussion of systems analysis in this chapter has been oriented toward a business organization. What significant differences in objectives and approaches would you expect in a systems investigation by (a) a public school system, (b) a university, (c) a hospital, and (d) a government agency?

9.2 Describe some examples of decisions in systems analysis that involve a trade-off between each of the following pairs of objectives.

a. Economy and usefulness
b. Economy and reliability
c. Economy and customer service
d. Simplicity and usefulness
e. Simplicity and reliability
f. Economy and capacity
g. Economy and flexibility

9.3 Aligning information management goals with long-term business plans can reap significant dividends. Discuss the business problems that Nashua faced as described in Focus 9.1. How has a well-developed system at Nashua solved these problems? What are the long-term benefits of Nashua's new system?

9.4 According to Focus 9.2, 35% of all systems development projects are "runaways"—hopelessly over budget and incomplete. Why are they? What can companies do to prevent runaway project development costs? What are the potential costs of a runaway system?

9.5 Jerry was concerned. For years his dairy production facilities had led the state in total sales volume. Recent declines in sales left Jerry wondering what the company was doing wrong. Jerry asked several customers how they felt about his product. Generally, they are satisfied, but they noted several areas of concern. Among their concerns were the dairy company's record of late deliveries and its incomplete orders. Further discussion with some of the company's production employees (not the cows) revealed several problems, including bottlenecks in milk pasteurization and homogenization owing to a lack of coordination in job scheduling, mix-ups in customer orders, and improperly labeled products. How would you suggest Jerry begin addressing the company's problems? What types of data gathering techniques would be helpful at this time?

9.6 The following problem situations could arise

in any manufacturing firm. Discuss what questions the consultant should ask in order to understand the problem.

a. Poor product quality is increasing customer complaints.

b. The Accounting Department sees an increase in the number and the dollar value of bad debt write-offs.

c. Operating margins have risen steadily over the past four years owing to higher-than-expected production costs from idle time, overtime, and the re-working of products.

9.7 For each of the independent cases listed, discuss which data gathering method(s) are most appropriate and why they are most appropriate.

a. Surveying the adequacy of internal controls in the purchase requisition procedure

b. Identifying the information needs of the company controller

c. Determining how the cash disbursements process is actually performed

d. Surveying the opinions of employees concerning the move to a total quality management program

e. Investigating a significant rise in uncollectible accounts

9.8 When designing a new system, the systems analyst can develop or study four different models—two depicting the physical aspects of the system and two depicting the logical aspects of the system. Clearly distinguish between these two types of models. Also, describe how all four models are used by systems analysts to understand and design the system. Explain the rationale for this approach.

9.9 While developing a new accounting system for Magix, Inc., you call Bev Ware, the company's Controller, to arrange an interview to discuss specific information needs. Your conversation goes something like this:

You: Hi Bev. I'm developing the new information system for Magix and would like to arrange an appointment with you to address your specific information needs. Do you have some time?

Bev: This project is Jim's idea, isn't it? A lot of people are opposed to this project. I happen to be one of them. I told him quite clearly I don't have time to play computer games with anyone. You'll have to get your information somewhere else. Sorry.

What alternative actions should system designers take when users are unwilling to participate in the development process?

PROBLEMS

9.1 As a systems consultant of wide repute, you have been invited to the executive offices of Consolidated Adhesives Corporation for an interview with the Controller. The Controller has indicated to you that she is concerned about the operation of the company's payroll processing system. Recent expansion of the company has placed a strain on the system, and frequent overtime is necessary for regular processing to be completed.

The payroll and cost distribution sections of the company perform their functions manually. In addition to requiring frequent overtime, the system lacks the ability to produce useful management reports and may be weak in internal controls. The Controller is considering two possible alternatives: hiring additional employees in the payroll and cost distribution sections and installing a computer system.

The Controller has assured you that the President and other top executives of Consolidated Adhesives agree that a systems study should be conducted by a qualified outsider. You have been introduced to the Assistant Controller, who performs internal auditing functions, and have been told that he is available to assist you full-time if necessary.

You have agreed to accept this assignment and have decided to send two of your assistants to complete the initial work while you finish another project. You direct your assistants to complete a preliminary evaluation of possible alternatives, which you will use in making a final decision and preparing recommendations.

Required

Prepare a schedule of activities to guide your assistants in performing their assignment. Be fairly explicit regarding the kind of information they might expect to find, how they should go about collecting it, and how they should proceed in analyzing it. Note that you are being asked not to give a solution to the problem but only to describe, with reference to the particular situation, how a systems analyst would proceed with the initial phases of a systems investigation.

9.2 Joanne Grey, a senior consultant, and David Young, a junior consultant, were assigned by their firm to conduct a systems analysis for a client. The objective of the study was to consider the feasibility of integrating and automating certain clerical functions. Grey had previously worked on jobs for this client, but Young had been hired only recently.

On the morning of their first day on the job Grey directed Young to interview a departmental supervisor and learn as much as he could about the operations of the department. Young went to the supervisor's office, introduced himself, and made the following statement: "Your company has hired my firm to study the way your department works and to make recommendations about how its efficiency could be improved and its costs lowered. I would like to interview you to determine what goes on in your department."

Young questioned the supervisor for about 30 minutes but found him to be uncooperative. He then gave Grey an oral report on how the interview had gone and what he had learned about the department.

Required

Describe several flaws in the approach taken to obtain information about the operation of the department under study. How should this task have been performed?

9.3 Business organizations are required to modify or replace a portion or all of their financial information system in order to keep pace with their growth and take advantage of improved information technology. The process involved in modifying or replacing an information system requires a substantial commitment of time and resources. When an organization undertakes a change in its information system, a systems analysis takes place.

Required

a. Explain the purpose and reasons for analyzing an organization's existing system during a system study.

b. Identify and explain the general activities and techniques that are commonly used during systems analysis.

c. System analysis is often carried out by a project team composed of a system analyst, a management accountant, and other persons in the company who would be knowledgeable and helpful in the system study. What would be the role of the management accountant in systems analysis?
(CMA Examination, adapted)

9.4 The Glass Jewelry Company is a manufacturer of costume jewelry. You have just been hired as the management accountant in charge of the accounting and control functions. During your introductory meeting with the President he outlined your first project: the design and implementation of a new accounting information system for the company. He stated that the new system must be fully implemented within 6 months. Total company sales for the most recent year were $10 million. Sales are expected to double within the next 18 months.

Required

a. As the management accountant, outline the procedures you would follow to complete your assigned project. Your response should include a description of the following:

1. The various sources of information
2. The methods of documenting the information collected
3. The methods of verifying the information collected

b. One of the subsystems that you plan to design is the accounts payable system. This system will contain a number of programs; two of them are the following:

1. Enter invoices
2. Print payable checks

For each of these programs, describe the purpose of the program, and outline the application control considerations.
(SMAC Examination, adapted)

9.5 The Ski Manufacturing Company, located in Saint Laurent, Quebec, is one of the leading manufacturers of both downhill and cross-country skis. As a result of the sudden decrease in the value of the Canadian dollar, the company is anticipating rapid growth in its export markets.

Currently, the company uses a system developed 15 years ago to process its accounts receivable. Customer records are kept in computer files in account number sequence. Each customer account contains the customer account number, customer name and address, previous balance due, date of last payment, and date the account was established. A

```
┌─────────────────────────────────────────────────────────────────────┐
│                    APPLICATION FOR CHARGE ACCOUNT                      │
│                                                                       │
│                                              Date:                    │
├──────────────────────────────────┬────────────────────────────────── │
│  Customer:                        │  Account No.:                     │
│                                   │                                   │
├──────────────────────────────────┼────────────────────────────────── │
│  Address:                         │  Buyer's Name:                    │
│                                   │                                   │
│                                   │  Salesperson:                     │
├──────────────────────────────────┼────────────────────────────────── │
│  Estimated Volume:                │  Payment Terms:                   │
├──────────────────────────────────┼────────────────────────────────── │
│         Product Type              │          Price Code               │
├──────────────────────────────────┼────────────────────────────────── │
│                                   │                                   │
│                                   │                                   │
├──────────────────────────────────┴────────────────────────────────── │
│  Shipping Information:                                                 │
│                                                                       │
│                                                                       │
│                                                                       │
└─────────────────────────────────────────────────────────────────────┘
```

Figure 9.9
Application form

new customer is added to file when an application for charge account form (see Fig. 9.9) is received.

A transaction file, consisting of sales slips, credit slips, and payment memos, is created daily. Each new record in the transaction file is created by typing data from an input document into the system. The transaction file is then sorted into account number sequence. Once a day the transactions are processed to create an accounts receivable register (see Fig. 9.10). During this processing a daily accounts summary file is created.

An accounts receivable summary report is created weekly from the master file. At the month's end individualized customer statements (see Fig. 9.11) are produced from all the month's transactions.

As a result of the anticipated growth, the president feels that the current system will not be adequate. He foresees accounting, credit granting, and collection problems relating to both the handling of sales to new offshore companies and the increased export sales volumes.

Required
Evaluate the given system by identifying five weaknesses, explaining why each is a weakness, and recommending a corrective procedure for each. (SMAC Examination, adapted)
Use the following format:

Weakness	Explanation of Why It Is a Weakness	Recommendation

9.6 Selling goods to a manufacturer that employs a just-in-time (JIT) inventory system requires immediate and reliable information from a company's information system—just ask Sony Corporation of America. The need for faster information is partially a result of a shift in business strategies at Sony. Over the past decade Sony has increased market penetration by supplying electronic parts to computer manufacturers. However, the information systems at Sony were built for the consumer market.

ACCOUNTS RECEIVABLE REGISTER			
			Date:
Account No.:	Sales	Payment	Net Change in Account Balance

Figure 9.10
A/R register

STATEMENT			
Account No.:		Date:	
Customer:			
Date	Charges	Payments	Balance

Figure 9.11
Customer statement

The system was simply not prepared to handle this shift in information needs.

The problems with the system were readily apparent. One of the biggest problems Sony has is that it does not get the information it needs when it needs it from its factories. As a result, it can't provide good delivery information to its customers. And that causes a big problem, because if Sony isn't responsive to its customers' needs, someone else will be—and Sony will lose them.

To speed system development, the MIS organization at Sony is employing a computer-aided software engineering (CASE) tool from Texas Instruments. The tool lets systems designers use local workstations linked to a mainframe. The tool uses artificial intelligence features to develop program code.

To use the CASE tool, the designer enters statements that describe the data the company will use and the relationships between the data files that will store the data. The CASE tool checks the data relationships to ensure that they are consistent. After any inconsistencies have been cleared up, the CASE tool produces code that describes the relationships. The information is then stored in a global encyclopedia of corporate information. This process continues until a model of how the company operates is developed. The CASE tool allows this model to be updated and altered as relationships change.

Sony is finding several advantages to using CASE technology. For instance, use of CASE technology requires developers to possess a certain business expertise; this expertise makes designers more effective in translating business problems into systems solutions. The CASE system is also boosting productivity tremendously. Recent smaller development projects at Sony have seen sixfold increases in programming productivity. CASE tools also require significant planning long before any source code is written. Such planning minimizes wasted programming time and the possibility of a "runaway" system.[4]

Required

a. What are the benefits of CASE technology? How does CASE technology improve the systems development process?

b. Discuss reasons why CASE technology may not be used in systems development.

9.7 For U.S. Sprint 1987 was a year of tough decisions. With the deregulation of the telephone industry and the breakup of "Ma Bell" in the early eighties, Sprint found itself growing at unplanned rates of 30%–40% per year.

The first casualty of Sprint's tremendous success was its aging billing system. The data processing system at Sprint was prepared to handle 1 million customers. By 1987 Sprint had almost 11 million customers and was growing daily!

By mid-1987 the MIS department had reached a crisis point. During the years of growth Sprint had developed a hybrid system to handle information processing. The system was developed largely by combining piecemeal hardware and software applications as needs arose. The system was not accurate, and the MIS people couldn't get into the system. They reached a point where they could only react to the system, rather than being able to act to solve the problem.

The system had two main problems. First, the billing system lacked the necessary computing power and storage space. Second, the system's data base was unable to handle the hundreds of simultaneous requests for information. It soon became apparent to the company that it didn't just have a data processing problem—it had a business problem that showed up first in the billing system.

To combat the problems, Sprint stabilized its two main data processing centers in Sacramento and Dallas. Team members analyzed the situation and configured hardware and software requirements to meet the rapidly growing needs for information. In addition, team members focused on long-range planning implications and identified operational, tactical, and strategic issues within the business according to the level of management responsibility.

Management at Sprint believes that problems developed because managers focused their efforts on operational needs with no thought given to tactical or strategic thinking. The problem was solved by training management personnel to focus their planning on meeting short-term needs while retaining a vision of the corporation's long-term objectives.

By the end of 1988 the results were impressive:

- 95% of all transactions were processed in under five seconds.
- 97% of all callers were getting through to a Sprint representative to handle billing concerns.

Looking ahead, MIS team members plan to implement a strategic information architecture built upon "quality information" to support Sprint's primary goal of becoming the market leader in the telecommunications industry.[5]

Required

a. Discuss the business and information problems at U.S. Sprint in 1987. When do information system problems become business problems?

b. What systems development approach had U.S. Sprint employed to handle its information problems in the past? Was the approach successful? Explain.

c. How did tactical and strategic planning aid Sprint in analyzing system needs? How would Sprint's approach have differed if it had adopted a systems approach to development?

9.8 The Masco Company is a manufacturer of building and home improvement products operating within central Canada. In the past three years the company has had an annual growth rate of 100%.

The company's major product lines include the following: ten different lines of kitchen and bathroom faucets, four lines of bath and shower units, a complete line of plumbing supplies, and various specialty products.

The company has 36 commissioned salespersons who operate in 10 different sales regions. Each region has a sales manager. Some of the responsibilities of the sales manager include the supervi-

[4] *Source:* David Gabel, "A Yen for Just-in-Time Decisions Aids Sony's Drive for Coprocessing," *Computerworld* (April 10, 1989): SR/5.

[5] *Source:* "U.S. Sprint Readies for its Run into the 90's," *IBM Update* (March/April 1989): 8.

sion of sales staff, consultation with the construction industry, provision of sales forecasts, and performance of variance analysis. The salespersons are not simply order takers but are responsible for educating the users and for collecting all overdue accounts. The sales staff distribute the products almost exclusively through wholesalers, who then sell to plumbers, builders, and remodelers. However, in the past two years an increasing proportion of the faucets and plumbing supplies have been sold directly to department stores and other retail outlets.

Approximately 40% of the company's products are used in new construction, 45% in the replacement market, and 15% in commercial, institutional, and industrial construction.

In order to accumulate data, the Marketing and Sales Department employs a staff of 25 clerical workers. Unfortunately, statistics are usually tabulated 45 days after the month's end.

The Vice-President of Sales and Marketing has requested that one of the company's management accountants propose a number of reports that a new computerized sales analysis system should produce.

Required

As the management accountant assigned to prepare this proposal, identify three reports that could be generated by the new computerized sales analysis system. For each report, provide the following:

a. A title for the report and a description of the report's content

b. Purpose of the report

c. Who should use the report

Prepare your response in the following format. (SMAC Examination, adapted)

Report Title	Report Content	Purpose	User

CASE 9.1 ANYCOMPANY, INC.: AN ONGOING COMPREHENSIVE CASE

One of the best ways to learn is to immediately apply what you have studied. The purpose of this case is to allow you to do that. You will select a local company that you can work with. At the end of most chapters you will find an assignment that will have you apply what you have learned using the company you have selected as a reference. This case, then, may become an ongoing case study that you work on throughout the term.

Visit several small- to medium-sized businesses in the local community. Explain that you will be doing a term-long case, and ask for permission to use the company as the firm you are going to study. Explain that you will need to meet with people in the company several times during the term to get the information you need. However, you will not need a great deal of their time or be a disruption to them. Offer to share any observations or suggestions that you can come up with as a way of allowing the firm to feel good about helping you.

Once you have lined up a company, perform the following steps.

1. With a member of the IS staff, discuss the procedures the company follows in analyzing general system requirements.

a. Does the company conduct preliminary investigations when considering a change in the information system? What systems survey methods does the company employ?

b. What strategies does the company employ in determining systems requirements? How does the company determine when a request for an IS change is appropriate?

c. When a decision is made to change an existing system, how does the company approach conceptual systems design? What are the outputs from conceptual systems design?

2. Summarize the results of your findings in a memo report. Include your evaluation of:

a. How effective are the company's analysis and conceptual system design procedures?

b. How can the company improve its existing procedures to be more effective?

CASE 9.2 CITIZEN'S GAS COMPANY

Citizen's Gas Company is a medium-size gas distribution company that provides natural gas service to approximately 200,000 customers. The customer base is divided into three revenue classes. Data by customer class follow.

Class	Customers	Sales in Cubic Feet	Revenues
Residential	160,000	80 billion	$160 million
Commercial	38,000	15 billion	25 million
Industrial	2,000	50 billion	65 million
		145 billion	$250 million

Residential customer gas use is primarily for residential heating purposes and, consequently, is highly correlated to the weather. Commercial and industrial customers, on the other hand, may or may not use gas for heating purposes, and consumption is not necessarily correlated to the weather.

The largest 25 industrial customers from the total of 2000 account for $30 million of the industrial revenues. Each of these 25 customers uses gas for both heating and industrial purposes and has a consumption pattern that is governed almost entirely by business factors.

The company obtains its gas supply from ten major pipeline companies. The pipeline companies provide gas in amounts specified in contracts that extend over periods ranging from 5 to 15 years. For some contracts the supply is in equal monthly increments, whereas for others the supply varies in accordance with the heating season. Supply over and above the contract amounts is not available, and some contracts contain take-or-pay clauses—that is, the company must pay for the volumes specified in the contract, whether or not it can take the gas.

To assist in matching customer demand with supply, the company maintains a gas storage field. Gas can be pumped into the storage field when supply exceeds customer demand; likewise, gas can be obtained when demand exceeds supply. There are no restrictions on the use of the gas storage field except that the field must be filled to capacity at the beginning of each gas year (September 1). Consequently, whenever the contractual supply for gas for the remainder of the gas year is less than that required to satisfy projected demand and replenish the storage field, the company must curtail service to the industrial customers (except for quantities that are used for heating). The curtailments must be carefully controlled so that an oversupply does not occur at year-end. Similarly, care must be taken to ensure that curtailments are adequate during the year to protect against the need to curtail commercial or residential customers in order to replenish the storage field at year-end.

In recent years the company's planning efforts have not provided a firm basis for the establishment of long-term contracts. The current year has been no different. Planning efforts have not been adequate to control the supply during the current gas year. Customer demand has been projected only as a function of the total number of customers. Commercial and industrial customers' demand for gas has been curtailed. This has resulted in lost sales and caused an excess of supply at the end of the gas year.

In an attempt to correct the problems of Citizen's Gas, the President has hired a new Director of Corporate Planning and has instructed the Director to present him with a conceptual design of a system to assist in the analysis of the supply and demand of natural gas. The system should provide a monthly gas plan for each year for the next five years, with particular emphasis on the first year. The plan should provide a set of reports that assists in the decision-making process and that contains all necessary supporting schedules. The system must provide for the use of actual data during the course of the first year to project demand for the rest of the year and the year in total. The President has indicated to the Director that he will base his decisions on the effect on operating income of alternative plans.

1.   Discuss the criteria that must be considered in specifying the basic structure and features of Citizen's Gas Company's new system to assist in planning its natural gas needs.

2.   Identify the major data items that should be incorporated into Citizen's Gas Company's new system to provide adequate planning capability. For each item identified, explain why the data item is important, and describe the level of detail that would be necessary for the data to be useful.
(CMA Examination, adapted)

CHAPTER Systems Design, Implementation, Operation, and Management

LEARNING OBJECTIVES

After studying this chapter, you should be able to:

- Discuss the physical systems design processes.
- Describe the activities undertaken in physical systems design.
- Describe the steps in the systems implementation and conversion process.
- Describe the steps in the systems operation and maintenance process.

**INTEGRATIVE CASE:
SHOPPERS MART**

Ann Christy feels drained, but that does not dampen her enthusiasm. She has just returned from a meeting with top management, where she presented the conceptual design for the new information system at Shoppers Mart. The steering committee had already accepted the design, and top management just gave her final approval to proceed to the physical design stage.

Each store is to have one or more local area networks that link all the microcomputers in the store together and connect them to a local data base. Each store will use state-of-the-art cash registers that capture all of the sales data electronically at the point of sale and feed it to the local store data base. Each store will be linked electronically to the central office. All sales data, store orders for merchandise, and other summary-level information will be uploaded to the corporate data base daily. The corporate data base will also download any information needed to manage the store on a daily basis. The central office will use electronic data interchange technology to order goods and to pay supplies.

Ann knows what the system is to accomplish and how it is to operate. Now all she and her development team have to do is to complete the design and implement the system. Ann knows that the physical design stage is where the company gets down to specifics and decides what each report should look like, decides what each data base should contain, and begins to write all the computer code. She is also aware that the implementation stage is where all the pieces are put together and the system is prepared for actual operation.

Ann is concerned because many development projects bog down during the physical design and implementation stages. She certainly does not want to have a runaway project on her hands that she cannot control. She wants to make sure that Shoppers Mart does things right. She decides to schedule another meeting with the head of systems development to discuss the following questions.

1. What is the development team going to do to make sure that system output will meet user needs? What does the team need to consider when it designs the output desired?
2. When and how should system input be captured? Who should capture it? How can data input errors be minimized or reduced?
3. How and where should system data be stored? What type of data base should be used, and how should the data be organized and accessed?
4. How can the company be sure that the software that is developed is bug-free?

10.1 FOCUS

STARS Saves Virginia $80 Million

Hundreds of thousands of Virginia taxpayers now get tax refunds within a week of filing instead of the two to three months it used to take. They owe the quick turnaround to Jane Bailey, Director of IS at the Department of Taxation. Bailey managed the development of the State Tax Accounting and Reporting System (STARS), a multisystem project that took nine years to complete. STARS has been so successful that the IRS, 27 states, and a Canadian province have sent teams to Richmond to see if a little magic might rub off on their own systems development efforts.

The state's central information technology group strongly recommended that the department engage outside contractors for the job, saying Bailey's six-person staff was far too small and unsophisticated to overhaul the vast and motley collection of manual and batch systems in place at the time. But Bailey insisted that it be an inside job. She convinced management to let her do it because once it was developed, she would have to

5. What does the company need to do to prepare its employees to use the new system?

6. How should Shoppers Mart convert from its current system to the new system? Should it operate both the current system and the new system simultaneously and compare the results until it is sure the new system functions properly? Or should it just convert to the new system immediately?

7. How much time and effort will be needed to maintain the system once it has been developed? ■

INTRODUCTION

Chapter 8 presented an overview of the traditional systems development life cycle (SDLC) and discussed three things that are done throughout the life cycle: planning, feasibility analysis, and behavioral considerations. Chapter 9 discussed systems analysis and conceptual system design.

This chapter completes the discussion of the traditional SDLC by discussing physical design, implementation and conversion, and operation and maintenance. Physical systems design is discussed in the first major section of the chapter, systems implementation and conversion in the second, and operation and maintenance in the third section.

The state of Virginia has been especially successful in designing and implementing its information system. In fact, it serves as a model for other governmental agencies. Focus 10.1 describes the improvements the state has made.

---

maintain it and respond quickly to tax law changes.

Bailey's staff eventually swelled to 45 people. She insisted on getting first-rate people; if she could not hire the experts and specialists she needed, she retained them as consultants and then used the consultants to train her existing staff. In addition, she recruited five management analysts to redesign business processes, write user documentation, and train users. Ten people out of her 40-member staff are management analysts who work full-time on user procedures and issues. Seeing user involvement as crucial,

Bailey succeeded in getting six managers from user areas assigned full-time to the project.

Over the years STARS's scope has expanded to encompass more functions and more users, and its budget climbed from its original $3 million to $11 million. A major new piece of software was installed every three to six months. Users had to adapt, often getting 15 new screens at a time. The megaproject eventually involved putting together 1500 COBOL programs, 40 IBM IMS data bases, and 350 on-line screens in 25 applications for 1800 users.

"They asked for a Chevrolet,

and they got a Cadillac. They didn't realize what an on-line system could do for them. Once they saw that first piece of data on-line, their eyes lit up, and they wanted more," Bailey says.

The payoff has been impressive. STARS users estimate that it saved the state $80 million over five years, most of it from added collections from would-be tax cheats.

Source: Gary H. Anthes, "Triumph over a Taxing Project," *Computerworld* (November 4, 1991): 65–69.

PHYSICAL (DETAILED) SYSTEMS DESIGN

Once the conceptual design has been approved, the project progresses to physical systems design. The conceptual design established the outputs, processes, inputs, and storage structures as viewed by those who will operate and use the system. **Physical systems design** translates the fairly high level, user-oriented requirements of the conceptual design into a detailed set of specifications that are used to code and test the programs.

Like conceptual systems design, physical systems design begins with the specifications of the required system outputs. Next is the determination of the content and format of system files and inputs. Following these steps comes the design of programs, procedures, and controls. These steps are shown in flowchart form in Fig. 10.1.

Output Design

The objective of detailed output design is to determine the nature, format, content, and timing of all printed reports and documents and all screen displays. Tailoring the output to meet users' needs requires cooperation between those who will use the output and those who design it (the systems development team). Some of the more important considerations in output design include the following:

■ *Use:* Who is going to use the output, why do they need it, and what decisions are they going to make with it?

■ *Medium:* Should the output be on paper, on a screen, voice response, a diskette, an archival medium such as microfilm, or some combination of these?

■ *Format:* Should the output appear in table, narrative, or graphic form? The format that conveys the most information in the clearest

Figure 10.1
Physical systems design

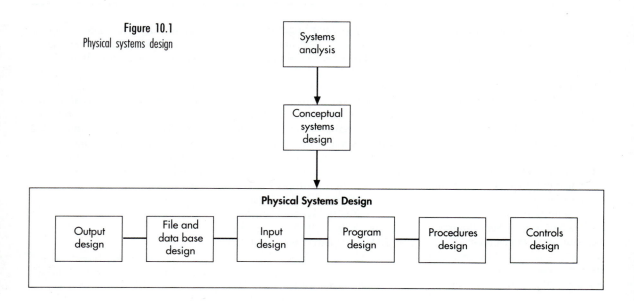

form should be selected. For example, large volumes of data can often be condensed into a few pages of graphic reports that can be interpreted more quickly and more meaningfully than long tabular reports.

- *Preprinted:* Should paper output be on a preprinted form (such as a check or purchase order) or on blank paper? Preprinted output is usually more suitable for external users, while blank paper is often more suitable for internal users.
- *Location:* Where should the output be sent?
- *Access:* Who should have access to a hard copy of the output, and who should be able to access the output on their computer screen?
- *Detail:* What level of detail is needed? Lengthy output should be preceded by an executive summary and a table of contents. Headings and legends should be used to organize the data and highlight important items. Detailed information should go in an appendix.
- *Timeliness:* How often should the output be produced?

With respect to when they are produced, reports may be divided into four categories: scheduled reports, unscheduled special-purpose analyses, triggered exception reports, and demand reports. **Scheduled reports** have a prespecified content and format and are prepared on a regular basis. Examples include monthly departmental performance reports, weekly sales analyses, and annual corporate financial statements. **Special-purpose analyses** (or ad hoc reports) have no prespecified content or format and are not prepared according to any regular schedule. They are prepared in response to a management request to investigate a specific problem or opportunity.

Triggered exception reports have a prespecified content and format but are prepared only when abnormal conditions trigger the reporting process. Excessive absenteeism, cost overruns, inventory shortages, and other situations requiring immediate corrective action might trigger such reports. **Demand reports** also have a prespecified content and format but are prepared only in response to a request from a manager or other employee. Both triggered exception reports and demand reports can be used effectively to facilitate the management process.

In designing the output, the development team should prepare a sample copy of the report or screen and ask the user whether the information on the report and the format are acceptable. For example, users should see and approve the sample layout for a store inventory report for Shoppers Mart that is shown in Fig. 10.2.

Users should be allowed sufficient time to study the suggested output in order to make sure that it contains all that is needed, that no extraneous data are included, and that the output is in the most useful form. If the output is unacceptable, the development team must modify it and allow users to review it again. This process should be repeated until the output is acceptable to users. This step is so important that

| SHOPPERS MART | | | | | | | |
| STORE INVENTORY REPORT 12-31-9X | | | | | | | Page XX of XX |
Item Number	Description	Location Code	Quantity on Hand	Unit Cost	Quantity on Order	Unit Cost	Total Quantity
999,999	XXXXXXXXXX	9999	999,999	99,999.99	999,999	99,999.99	999,999
999,999	XXXXXXXXXX	9999	999,999	99,999.99	999,999	99,999.99	999,999
999,999	XXXXXXXXXX	9999	999,999	99,999.99	999,999	99,999.99	999,999
999,999	XXXXXXXXXX	9999	999,999	99,999.99	999,999	99,999.99	999,999
999,999	XXXXXXXXXX	9999	999,999	99,999.99	999,999	99,999.99	999,999
999,999	XXXXXXXXXX	9999	999,999	99,999.99	999,999	99,999.99	999,999
999,999	XXXXXXXXXX	9999	999,999	99,999.99	999,999	99,999.99	999,999
Sub total(s)							999,999
Total							999,999

Figure 10.2
Possible layout for a store inventory report

many organizations require users to sign a document stating that the form and content of the proposed reports are acceptable to them. Companies follow this procedure to avoid the expense and time delays resulting from a change made later in the life cycle. For example, when the users at Shoppers Mart reviewed the report layout in Fig. 10.2, they requested that the description column be larger so that a more complete description of the item could be shown. They also suggested that the location code be changed to a 9999-99 format, where the first four digits represent store number and the last two represent location within the store.

File and Data Base Design

An information system's data storage requirements can be met in a number of ways. Existing files and data bases can be used if they were designed with the needs of the new application in mind or if they can be modified. If the existing files and data bases cannot be used, new ones will have to be developed. Here are some of the more important considerations in file and data base design.

- *Medium:* Should files and data bases be stored on magnetic disk, diskettes, optical disk, or magnetic tape?
- *Organization and access:* Should sequential, indexed-sequential, or random-access methods be used to store and access the data?
- *Processing mode:* Should records be processed in batch mode or in real-time?
- *Maintenance:* What procedures are needed to maintain the files and data bases, and how are they most effectively accomplished?
- *Size:* What is the expected size of each record in the data base? How many records will be stored in the data base, and how fast is the number of records expected to grow?

■ *Activity level:* What percentage of the records will be added or deleted over a year's time? What percentage of the records will be updated at a time?

In many instances building a prototype data base has several advantages. First, it allows all access paths through the data base to be tested to make sure they function as designed. Second, it allows operational characteristics such as access and processing times to be tested for acceptability. Third, a prototype data base can be used during application program development and testing.

A **record layout**, such as the one shown in Fig. 10.3, is a form on which the content, position, format, and other characteristics of the data fields within a record are entered. Once record layouts have been completed for all input and file records, they can be used in the process of coding the computer program.

Input Design   In designing input, the development team and the users must identify the types of input data and the means of entering them into the system. Considerations in input design include the following:

■ *Medium:* Should data be entered using key-to-disk methods; a keyboard; source data automation, such as an OCR, an MICR, or a POS terminal; or voice input?

■ *Source:* Where is the data coming from: another computer, an employee, a customer, a remote location, or a document? How does that affect its entry into the system?

■ *Format:* What format (source document, turnaround document, screen) most efficiently captures the data with the least amount of effort and cost?

■ *Type:* What is the nature of the data?

■ *Volume:* How much data is to be entered?

■ *Personnel:* Who is entering the data, and what are their abilities, functions, and level of training? Is there a need to instruct users on

Figure 10.3
Record layout

Field Name	Account Number	Customer Name	Customer Address
Characteristics	Numeric; Key	Alphanumeric	Alphanumeric
Position	01–08	09–32	33–104

Region Code	Type Code	Salesman Name	Credit Rating
Numeric	Numeric	Alphanumeric	Alphanumeric
105–107	108–110	111–122	123–125

Credit Limit	Date of Last Sale	Account Balance
Money	Date	Money
126–134	135–140	141–149

how to enter the data? Which input method would be easiest for them to understand and use?

- *Frequency:* How often does the data need to be entered into the system?

- *Cost:* How can data entry costs be minimized without forfeiting efficiency and accuracy?

- *Error detection and correction:* What errors are possible under each option, and how can they be detected and corrected?

Screen and Forms Design

Both the input and the output of data rely heavily on the use of computer screens and on preprinted forms. As a result, it is important to understand how to efficiently design screens and forms.

Designing Computer Screens.   A computer screen should be laid out so that data can be entered quickly, accurately, and completely. As much information as possible should already appear on the screen or should be retrieved by the system. For example, inputting a customer number could automatically cause the system to retrieve the customer's name, address, and other important information. This minimizes the amount of information the data entry person has to type.

Data should be entered in the same order as it is displayed on any paper form that may be used to capture the data. The screen should be filled out from left to right and top to bottom. Logically related data should be grouped together. Users should be able to jump from one data entry location to another using a single key or to go directly to any portion of the screen to enter data. Users should have a means of always knowing where they are on the screen. The system should acknowledge all of the users' actions and all keying and screen commands should be consistent across all screens in the system.

Errors in data entry are frequent and can be very costly. Therefore, users should be able to correct mistakes. There should be a Help feature to provide on-line assistance. Clear and explicit error messages should appear when errors are made and should be consistent across all screens.

The screen should not be cluttered. Restricting the amount of data on a screen is the best way to avoid clutter. Another way is to limit the number of menu options on a single screen. Since human factors are very important, they should outweigh technical factors if the two clash.

Designing Preprinted Documents and Business Forms.   Many transactions are initially recorded or printed on business forms. A form is a preprinted document with headings and spaces for the insertion of data. In a computerized system a form may consist of a preprinted image on a computer terminal screen. Figure 10.4, a sample credit memorandum form, illustrates many of the principles of forms design that are discussed here.

The introduction at the top of the form should contain the title, the form number, and the name and address of the organization using the

```
Copy Distribution:                    SHOPPERS MART
    Blue-Customer                    1123 ORWEL DRIVE
    Yellow-Accounting              ORLANDO, FLORIDA 32806
    Pink-Data Proc.
                                          CREDIT MEMO                    No. 36082

        ┌                    ┐     Reason for return codes:
                                      1. Damaged in transit.
    To                                2. Does not meet specifications.
                                      3. Item not ordered.
        └                    ┘        4. Other — insert explanation below.
```

Invoice Number	Invoice Date	Invoice Total	Salesperson
Customer Acct. No.	Return Date	Receiving Rept. No.	Received By

Item Number	Reason for Return	Quantity	Price	Total

Approved by _____ Date __/__/__
Authorized Signature

Sales Tax	
Total	

Figure 10.4
Sample credit memorandum form

form. The form should contain instructions on how to use the form and on the appropriate distribution of completed copies of the form.

In the main body of the form logically related information should be grouped together. Boxes and columns should be used to organize and provide sufficient room to record the data. For example, a sales invoice has blank rows to record the item number, description, quantity, and price of the item sold. The sequence of the data should be consistent with the sequence in which the data is gathered or the sequence in which the data will be transcribed to some other medium. This is especially critical when it is a source document from which data are keyed into a computer. Common explanations or statements should be preprinted so that the user can simply check off a box next to it.

The space at the bottom of the form is used to record the final disposition and/or final approval of the transaction, including an approval signature, date, and dollar total.

A number of important principles regarding forms design are summarized in the checklist in Table 10.1. This checklist serves as a useful tool for both the evaluation of existing forms and the design of new ones.

Program Design

Application programs that are developed must meet the detailed specifications prepared by the project development team. Program development is usually one of the most time-consuming activities in the entire life cycle. As a result, program development should be as efficient and effective as possible. Here are some procedures for improving program development.

- *Modules:* Subdivide the program into small, relatively well defined modules. This reduces program complexity and enhances reliability and modifiability.

Table 10.1
Forms design checklist

General considerations
1. Are preprinted data used to the maximum extent feasible?
2. Is the weight and grade of paper appropriate for the planned use?
3. Are bold type, double-thick lines, varying colors, and shaded areas used appropriately?
4. Is the form a standard size?
5. Is the form large enough for its intended purpose?
6. Is the size of the form consistent with requirements for filing, binding, or mailing?
7. Can the form be used in a window envelope?

Introductory section
8. Does the name of the form appear in bold type?
9. Are successive copies of the form prenumbered consecutively?
10. If the form is externally distributed, is the company's name and address preprinted on it?
11. Do all introductory data appear at the top of the form?

Instructions
12. Is it clear how the form is to be filled out?
13. Is the routing of the form indicated?
14. Is the distribution of completed copies indicated?

Main body
15. Is logically related information grouped together?
16. Are boxes and columns used appropriately?
17. Is there sufficient room to record each data item?
18. Is the ordering of the data items consistent with the sequence in which they are recorded or transcribed?
19. Are standardized explanations preprinted so that codes or checkoffs can be used instead of written user entries?

Conclusion
20. Is space provided to record data concerning final disposition of the form?
21. Is space provided for a signature or signatures indicating final approval?
22. Is space provided to record the date of final disposition or approval?
23. Is space provided for a dollar or other numeric total?
24. Do all concluding data appear at the bottom of the form?

- *Common routines:* Use a set of basic coding structures for common routines such as input, output, and file maintenance.

- *Standards:* Develop and use programming standards, which are a set of rules for writing programs. These standards contribute to consistency of programming styles among programmers, which makes programs easier to maintain.

- *Walk-through:* Conduct a structured program walk-through to find incorrect logic, errors, omissions, or other problems with the program.

- *Team approach:* Use a team consisting of, say, a chief programmer, assistant programmers as needed, and a programming secretary. The chief and assistant programmers work together to produce code. The programming secretary performs clerical functions and is responsible for preparing all program documentation.

Procedures Design

Procedures should be developed for everyone who interacts with the newly designed system. The procedures should answer the who, what, when, where, why, and how questions related to all system activities. Procedures should cover issues such as input preparation, transaction processing, error detection and correction, controls, reconciliation of balances, data base access, output preparation and distribution, and computer operator instructions. These procedures may take the form of system manuals, user instruction classes or training materials, or on-line Help screens. The procedures may be written by the development teams, by the users, or by teams representing both groups.

Controls and Standards Design

A common saying in the computer industry is, "Garbage in, garbage out." This adage emphasizes that if the input, processing, and data base functions of an information system are not properly controlled, the information it produces will be of little value. Therefore controls must be built into a system to ensure its effectiveness, efficiency, and accuracy. The controls should be designed to prevent errors from occurring, to detect them when they do occur, and to correct those that are detected. In this area the accountant must play a critical role. Some of the more important control concerns that must be addressed in system design are listed here. Controls are discussed in greater detail in Chapters 12–14.

- *Validity:* Are all interactions with the system valid? For example, how can the system ensure that cash disbursements are made only to legitimate vendors?

- *Authorization:* Are all input, processing, storage, and output activities authorized by the appropriate authority? For example, how can the system ensure that an addition to the payroll file has been authorized by personnel?

- *Accuracy:* Has input to the system been verified to ensure that it is mechanically accurate? Have all data passed between processing

```
┌─────────────────────────────────────────────────────┐
│                    Shoppers Mart                      │
│              Physical Systems Design Report           │
│                                                       │
│      Table of Contents                                │
│                                                       │
│       I. Executive Summary of Physical Systems Design │
│      II. Overview of Project Purpose and Summary of   │
│          Findings to Date                             │
│     III. Major Physical Design Recommendations        │
│          A. Output Design                             │
│          B. Input Design                              │
│          C. Data Base Design                          │
│          D. Software (Processing) Design              │
│          E. Hardware Design                           │
│          F. Controls Design                           │
│          G. Procedures Design                         │
│      IV. Assumptions and Unresolved Problems          │
│       V. Summary                                      │
│      VI. Appendixes, Glossary                         │
└─────────────────────────────────────────────────────┘
```

Table 10.2
Typical table of contents for a physical systems design report

activities been controlled to ensure that none are lost in processing? For example, how can the system be protected from keying errors during input?

■ *Access:* Is access to system data adequately controlled? For example, how can hackers be denied access to corporate data files?

■ *Numerical control:* Are all documents used in the system prenumbered or uniquely identified to prevent errors or intentional misuse? For example, are all checks prenumbered so that all disbursements can be recorded and traced?

■ *Audit trail:* Can all transaction data be traced from source documents to final output (and vice versa)? For example, when a customer calls with a question about her account, can the transaction details be accessed so that the issue can be resolved?

Physical Systems Design Report

At the end of the physical design phase a **physical systems design report** is prepared for management review and approval. This report is usually the basis for management's decision about whether or not to proceed to the implementation phase. As an example, the table of contents of the physical systems design report prepared at Shoppers Mart is shown in Table 10.2

IMPLEMENTATION AND CONVERSION

Systems implementation is the process of installing hardware and software and getting the system up and running. Systems implementation generally consists of a fairly well defined set of activities, including planning and scheduling the installation process, developing and testing soft-

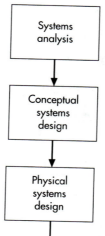

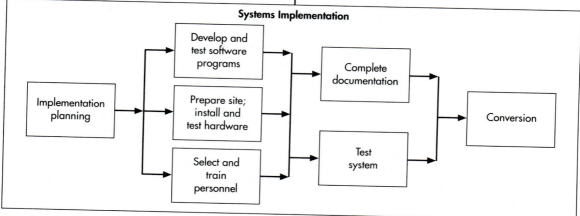

Figure 10.5
Systems implementation
and conversion

ware programs, preparing the site and installing and testing the hardware, selecting and training personnel, completing documentation, testing the system, and converting from the old to the new system. These activities are shown in Fig. 10.5 and are discussed in detail in this section.

Implementation Planning

Implementation and conversion planning begins well before the implementation phase begins; strategies must be considered at each SDLC stage. Detailed implementation plans, however, cannot be finalized until management has approved the design of the new system. Implementation planning is the responsibility of an **implementation team** composed of users, management, and systems personnel. The implementation plan should be reviewed by the steering committee, appropriate users, and systems management before implementation actually begins.

An **implementation plan** should identify and describe the following for each major implementation task: a timetable for its completion, who is responsible for it, estimates of its cost, and task milestones that mark the end of the task. The implementation team should also identify a clear point at which the entire project is deemed completed. Both users and EDP management should agree that when this termination point is reached, the system will be considered operational; any further changes will be classified as maintenance rather than continuing development. If agreement is not reached, users may refuse to accept the new system until all the modifications and changes they identify after implementation have been made. This can prolong a project almost indefinitely.

The implementation team should identify in advance the risk factors that decrease the likelihood of successful implementation. These factors may include nonexistent or unwilling users, large numbers of users, inability to specify use patterns in advance, inability to predict and cushion the impact of the system on all parties, lack or loss of management support, and lack of experience with similar systems. Implementation strategies should be devised to cope with each risk factor. Possible strategies are testing prototype systems, using an evolutionary approach, simplifying the system, obtaining user participation or commitment, obtaining management support, providing training, providing for ongoing user assistance, and tailoring the system to the users' capabilities.

Planning Techniques.   Two techniques for scheduling and monitoring the progress of the implementation effort are PERT and the Gantt chart. PERT (program evaluation and review technique) is used to plan projects by determining every distinct activity required to complete a project and all of the precedent and subsequent relationships among the activities. These activities and their relationships are used to draw a PERT diagram, which is a network of arrows and nodes. The arrows represent project activities that require an expenditure of time and resources. The nodes represent the competition of one or more activities and/or the initiation of one or more subsequent activities. An estimate of the time needed to complete each activity is made, and the critical path through the diagram—the path requiring the greatest amount of time—is determined. The project is managed to ensure that none of the activities on the critical path are delayed, since that would mean that the whole project would be delayed. If possible, resources are shifted to work on critical path activities to try and reduce the total amount of time needed to complete the project. An example of a PERT diagram is shown in Fig. 10.6. The critical path through this network proceeds through activities B, C, F, H, I, J, K, and M, and the total time required to complete the project is 83 weeks.

A **Gantt chart** is a bar chart in which project activities are listed on the left-hand side of the chart and units of time (days or weeks) are shown across the top. For each activity a bar is drawn from the scheduled starting date to the ending date, thereby defining the time period over

Activity	Time (weeks)	Predecessor Activities	Activity Description
A	36	None	Physical preparation (including vendor lead time)
B	4	None	Organizational planning
C	2	B	Personnel selection
D	2	A	Equipment installation
E	10	C	Personnel training
F	15	C	Detailed systems design
G	9	F	File conversion
H	4	F	Establishing standards and controls
I	9	H	Program preparation
J	9	I	Program testing
K	20	D,E,G,J	Parallel operations
L	8	I	Finalizing system documentation
M	20	K,L	Follow-up

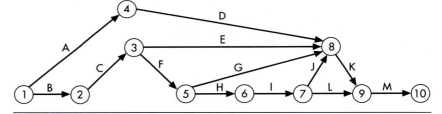

Figure 10.6
PERT network of the computer implementation process

which that activity is expected to be performed. A sample Gantt chart appears in Fig. 10.7.

The completion of each activity should be recorded on the Gantt chart as a project proceeds. In Fig. 10.7 the amount of space within each bar that is filled in corresponds to the degree of completion of each activity. Thus at any time, it is possible to determine quickly which activities are on schedule and which are behind schedule. The capacity to show, in graphic form, the entire schedule for a large, complex project, including progress to date and current status, is the primary advantage of the Gantt chart. Gantt charts, however, are limited in that they do not show the relationships among various project activities.

Some tips for the process of implementation planning are listed in Table 10.3.

Developing and Testing Software Programs

As shown in Fig. 10.8, seven steps are usually followed when one develops software programs. Although accountants usually need not be experienced computer programmers, they should understand the development cycle typically used in creating a computer program. The time required for program preparation may range from a few days to a few years, depending on the complexity of the program.

PROJECT PLANNING CHART

Project Number	01 - 650
Project Name	Labor Cost Anaylsis Module
Project Leader	J. Flaherty

Page 1 of 1
Prepared by S. Doe
Date 11 / 10 / 9X

ACTIVITY		WEEK STARTING

No.	Name	11/17	11/24	12/1	12/8	12/15	12/22	12/29	1/5	1/12	1/19	1/26	2/2	2/9	2/16	2/23	3/2	3/9	3/16	3/23	3/30					
1-1	Organize implementation team	██																								
1-2	Prepare system support procedures		████																							
1-3	Develop conversion plan		████																							
1-4	Develop testing plan				██																					
2-1	Prepare program specifications				████																					
2-2	Revise system documentation				██																					
2-3	Perform programming tasks																									
3-1	System test																									
4-1	Install system support procedures																									
5-1	Acceptance test																									
6-1	Conversion																									

Figure 10.7
Sample Gantt chart

The first step in new program development is to determine user needs. The result of this process should be an agreement between the development team and the users about the detailed requirements to be met by the new software.

The next step is to develop a plan to achieve the desired objectives. Programming tools such as flowcharts, decision tables, structured English, HIPO charts, and data flow diagrams are available to the system development team. These tools are explained in Chapter 3.

The third step is to write the program instructions in a computer language, a process referred to as **coding**. A program can usually be coded relatively easily when structured English, a program flowchart, or a decision table is used as a reference. Care should be exercised to ensure that all programming language rules are followed.

Table 10.3
Implementation planning tips

Start as soon as the development project begins.

Finalize plans as soon as implementation is approved.

Get approval of plans before beginning implementation.

Identify major tasks, timetables, responsibilities, and their point of completion.

Determine and agree to the point of project completion.

Identify implementation risk factors and strategies to cope with each one.

Use Gantt charts to monitor progress.

Use PERT to identify critical tasks.

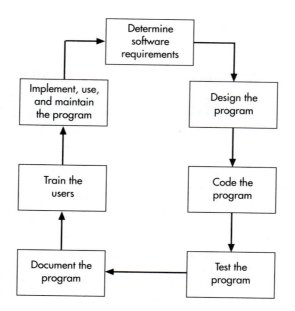

Figure 10.8
Software program life cycle

Program complexity is reduced and reliability and modifiability are increased when programs are composed of **modules**, which are well-defined program segments that perform separate logical functions. For example, in a file maintenance program that processes several different types of transactions, there could be a separate module for each transaction type. Each module should have only one entry point and one exit point, to facilitate testing and modification.

Generally, these modules should have no interaction with each other but should interact primarily with the program's control module or central logic section. The control module is responsible for determining the type of each transaction, directing program control to the appropriate module, and passing data between modules. This modular approach to programming is generally referred to as **structured programming**.

Modularity should begin in the program design phase. A popular method for designing a complex program is to first determine the overall approach that the program should take. Once the approach has been determined and related program steps have been identified, each program step can be planned in greater detail. This process of designing a program from the top level down to the detail level is often referred to as **hierarchical program design**.

Modularity facilitates both program design and utilization. Program preparation is made easier in many ways: Program logic design is simplified; coding is made easier and may be split, with different programmers working on different program modules; documentation is made easier; and debugging is facilitated because errors in one module should not affect any other module. Modularity makes a program

10.2 FOCUS

Software Flaws Take Costly Toll

An $18.5-million rocket explodes seconds after lift-off. Telephone networks mysteriously crash in three cities, leaving 10 million customers without local service. A nuclear plant in Ontario releases hundreds of gallons of radioactive water near Lake Huron.

These three seemingly unrelated events have one disturbing thing in common: They all were caused by computer software bugs, tiny errors buried in the programs that run computers. The name *bug* was coined during World War II when a researcher, puzzled by the shutdown on a computer, removed a moth stuck between two electric relays. Lately, these electronics pests have been on a rampage.

■ Without warning, people living in and around Washington, D.C., Los Angeles, and Pittsburgh lost local phone service on several days almost at the

same time each morning. The culprit? Three missing digits in several million lines of programming that controls the phone companies' call-switching computers.

■ During the Persian Gulf War a software error prevented a Patriot missile from firing at an incoming Iraqi Scud missile. The Scud crashed into an Army barracks, killing 28 people.

■ The nation's largest airline reservations system, operated by American Airlines, shut down for almost 12 hours, crippling 14,000 travel agencies nationwide. The bug forced American's reservations agents to write tickets by hand.

■ A bug in the software that runs a linear accelerator—a device that uses X rays and electron beams to treat cancer victims—caused the accelerator to deliver a radiation

overdose, killing one patient and leaving two others deeply burned and partly paralyzed.

Software bugs also have devastated some companies: Ashton-Tate, once a powerhouse in personal computer software, never recovered after it shipped bug-filled software to customers. DSC Communications, a small maker of call-switching computers, spent weeks in the glare of bad publicity because three missing digits in its computers' software caused phone outages.

Where do these software bugs come from? They are created by human hands. To create a software program, a programmer writes millions of lines of code. Despite the most painstaking preparation, one incorrect letter or punctuation mark in a line of code—even a missing period—can cause a computer to issue an incorrect command or no com-

easier to review and understand, because the control module provides a capsule summary of the entire program. Program maintenance is also easier to accomplish.

The fourth step in program development is to completely test the program. Focus 10.2 discusses the difficulty of accomplishing this step. It also discusses the consequences of releasing software with undetected errors (it can result in fatal injuries).

Debugging is the process of discovering an error in a program and eliminating it. Programmers test the programs they write in different

mand at all. For instance, the flaw in DSC's call-switching computers caused them to send out hundreds of erroneous messages to other DSC computers, asking for help in rerouting calls. In fact, no help was needed. However, the flood of messages caused the computers to shut down and gave callers the busy signals for hours.

Software bugs exist in most computer software, and they're almost impossible to get rid of. A program containing bugs can work just fine for quite some time. But then, one day with no warning—zap—the bug triggers something and the computer suddenly goes haywire.

Programmers go to great pains to detect bugs and eliminate them long before the software is shipped to customers. But no company has the time or the money to find each and every bug—or to simulate the exact situations the computer program will encounter in the real world.

"If you could perform 1000 tests a second on a program with a couple of hundred instructions, it would take 3000 years to completely and exhaustively test it," says Roger Pressman, author of

a forthcoming book entitled *Software Shock*. "None of us would be around to see the result."

Instead, software is tested with assumptions about how it will be used. Only a certain amount of information—for instance, the number of paychecks to be sent out each Friday—is used to test the program. No one can predict that a few enterprising customers will add more information than the software can handle.

Software developers also can't predict whether the people using computers will simply work faster than the software itself. The linear accelerators that killed one cancer patient and maimed two others were controlled by an operator who typed extremely fast. She accidentally selected the X-ray mode and then switched to the electron beam. But the computer's software wasn't quick enough to recognize the change. It appeared that the adjustment had been made, but it hadn't been. The machine beamed radiation at full power to a tiny spot on the patients' bodies. The bug was so subtle that it took programmers nearly a year to detect it and eliminate it.

The sheer volume of software code needed to create a complex program makes it easy for bugs to hide. There are some 2.5 million lines of code in systems that check for cracks in the engine wheel of a space shuttle, 12 million lines in a call-switching computer used by the nation's phone companies. Experts say finding a flaw in this code is as difficult as looking for one misspelled name in the entire New York City telephone book.

Computer users worried about bugs have at least one consolation. The increasing number of bug-related catastrophes has spawned firms that use special software to find flaws in code and exterminate them. Some have developed diagnostic software that allows users to ask the computer questions about its software. Then the software tells a user where the problem—and the bug—might be located. Even with this help, though, predicting when or where a software bug will strike is at best a guessing game.

Source: John Schneidawind, "Getting the Bugs Out," *USA Today* (August 29, 1991): 1–2. Copyright 1991, USA Today. Reprinted with permission.

ways. One method is desk checking, which is a visual and mental review of the program to discover keying or programming errors. A second test phase, program compilation, detects any syntax errors that have been made in writing the program. Any errors identified during program compilation must be investigated and corrected before the program can be run.

Once the program has been successfully compiled, the next step is to test the program for logic errors. Program testing often utilizes test data that simulate as many real processing situations or input data combinations to which the program may be exposed as possible. Test data should include all valid transactions and all possible error conditions. The response of the program to each test case is observed in order to detect improper responses, which indicate that the program contains some flaw or bug. For example, improper responses are the program's failing to process a valid transaction properly or failing to detect an error condition.

Large programs are often tested in three stages. In the first stage each individual program module is tested for internal consistency and correctness. In the second stage program modules are linked together and tested to see that they interface properly. The error detection process is simplified if modules are linked one at a time or a few at a time. This method minimizes the number of places in which errors could be occurring and is more efficient than linking all modules together at once. The third stage is testing the program together with any other programs it must interface with. In other words, the program is tested as a part of the entire system.

The fifth step in program development is to document how the program works. This step helps the programmer and anyone who follows to understand what the program does so that errors can be corrected and modifications made. Attention should be given to this step throughout the program preparation process. For example, during program coding descriptive remarks may be inserted into the program where appropriate. Structured English, systems flowcharts, record layouts, program flowcharts, decision tables, and related items used in creating the program should be prepared according to prescribed standards and retained as part of the program documentation. When the program is completed, the program documentation should also be complete and ready to be organized into a meaningful documentation manual.

The sixth step in development is to train the program users. Training may take place during the later portion of the test phase. The program documentation is often used to train users.

The last step is install and use the system. During the time it is being used, any number of factors may require program revisions. The process of revising programs once they are in use is referred to as program maintenance. Factors that may necessitate a specific change include requests from managers for new reports or for revisions in old reports; changes in program input or file content; changes in values, such as tax rates, that are part of the program; detection of a previously undiscovered bug; and conversion to new system hardware.

The utilization period of business data processing programs varies widely but usually is not longer than six or seven years. A program may be made obsolete by business growth, by a change in information needs within the business, or by changes in system hardware or software. At this point its life cycle has come to an end, and the program is discarded, replaced, or substantially revised.

Site Preparation

As soon as the company knows what hardware configuration will be used in the system, site requirements can be determined and work can begin on the selection and preparation of the site. Space is needed for the equipment, for storage and supplies, and for the offices of systems personnel. Site selection should also consider the possibility of future expansion of the system. Since site selection and preparation can be a lengthy process, it should begin well in advance of the date when the hardware is actually to be installed.

A micro- or minicomputer usually requires very little in the way of physical site preparation. However, installation of a larger system may be quite costly and may require extensive physical changes, such as additional electrical outlets, data communications facilities, raised floors, humidity controls, special lighting, and air-conditioning. Security measures, such as fire protection and an emergency power supply, may also be necessary. Once the site is prepared and the hardware is delivered, the system can be installed and thoroughly tested.

If a company does not need to make major modifications to the hardware used in the system, site preparation may not be necessary.

Personnel Administration and Training

Systems in organizations are made up of two interdependent parts—a technical system and a social system. The technical system consists of the tasks, processes, and technologies required to accomplish the organizational objective, such as converting inputs to outputs. The social system involves the skills, attitudes, values, and interrelationships of people as well as the incentive and authority structures within which they work. The performance of the system as a whole depends on the smooth interaction of these two systems. Many implementation failures can be attributed to an organization's concentrating on the technical system without devoting adequate attention to the social system. Tips on how to deal with the social system are listed in Table 10.4.

Table 10.4
Personnel administration tips

Let users know early what is required during implementation.
Remember that systems fail if inadequate attention is paid to the social system.
Recognize and plan for changes to the organizational structures.
Remember that open and honest communication avoids many behavioral problems.
Emphasize the positive aspects of change.
Reassure affected employees that they will be taken care of.
Improve morale by giving displaced employees jobs elsewhere in the company.
Train all employees on how to use the new system.
Plan and schedule training well in advance.
Train users just prior to system testing and conversion.

A change in information systems may require adjustments to a company's organizational structure. New departments may have to be staffed, departments may have to be eliminated, or staff in a department may have to be reduced. Jobs that may need to be established and defined include analyst, programmer, LAN manager, and end-user support staff. The structure and status of the data processing department itself may change.

As an example of the impact of a new system on organizational structure, consider the case of Blue Cross and Blue Shield of Wisconsin. It contracted for a new $200-million system that was to handle all aspects of its business. The system—which was initiated by members of the technical staff who did not understand the company's business requirements—did not work properly. It sent hundreds of checks to a nonexistent town, made $60 million in overpayments, and resulted in the loss of 35,000 clients. When the failure was analyzed, analysts discovered that one of the reasons for the failure was that the implementation of the system should have included a restructuring of the organization. Three layers of management were later removed.

Communication with Employees. A policy of communicating openly and honestly with employees prior to and during implementation is critical. Employees should be made aware that the organization will undergo a major systems change and that sacrifices, inconveniences, and increased time commitments will be necessary. Users will actually have to make the changes required by the system, rather than just talk about them. Management and the development team should watch for serious problems such as deterioration in employee morale and should be prepared to deal with the problems. Plans relating to relocation of displaced personnel, staffing new positions, and training programs should be announced long before the installation process begins.

The positive aspects of the change, such as employees' being freed from routine functions to spend more time on the creative aspects of their jobs, should be stressed. Throughout the entire employee relations effort the interest and concern of top management should be made apparent.

Personnel Selection and Training. Employees for the new system can be hired from outside the company or transferred internally. Giving employees who are displaced by the system positions with the new system builds employee loyalty and morale, is less costly than hiring new people, and is more effective, since the employees already understand the firm's operations.

Although an effective training program is time-consuming and therefore expensive, it is a key to the successful implementation of any new information system. Employees at all levels of an organization need to be oriented to the policies and operations of the new system. They also need to be taught how to interact with the system to obtain information. Even those employees who initially will have no interaction with the new system should be given orientation sessions to help them understand the new system and what it can accomplish for them.

Training should be planned and scheduled well in advance. It should take place just before systems testing and conversion. Training too early is ineffective since the information may be forgotten. And if users are not trained until after implementation, they may develop erroneous or ineffective methods of working with the new system before the training occurs.

There are many different types of effective training programs. Vendors and training specialists provide technical training, self-study manuals, or computer-assisted instruction. Employees often do a good job of training fellow employees. Other training approaches include videotaped presentations, role playing, case studies, and experimenting with the system under the guidance of an experienced user.

Boots the Chemists, a London-based international pharmacy chain with over a thousand stores, came up with a novel approach to training. Store employees were nervous about computers, so they were invited to a party at a store where the POS system had been installed. They were asked to try and harm the system by doing things such as pushing the wrong buttons or fouling up a transaction. Employees quickly found that they could not harm the system and that it was, in fact, easy to use.

Finalizing Documentation

Someone once said that "you aren't finished until the paperwork is done." That saying is certainly true with respect to systems development. A great deal of documentation must be prepared when a new system is developed. Three major categories are described next.

1. *Development documentation* describes all aspects of the new system. It includes a description of the system; copies of all outputs, inputs, and file and data base layouts; program narratives and charts; test results; conversion results; and user acceptance forms.

2. *Operations documentation* explains the operation of the system. It includes an operating schedule; files and data bases accessed; equipment required; and printing, security, and file retention requirements.

3. *User documentation* teaches users how to operate the system. It includes a procedures manual and all necessary training materials.

Testing

Before a newly designed system is implemented, it is essential that it be thoroughly tested. For example, one of the reasons why the system at Blue Cross and Blue Shield did not work was that it was not adequately tested. The developers underestimated the complexity of the system and promised an overly optimistic delivery time of 18 months. One of the shortcuts they made to meet that deadline was to deliver an untested system.

Documents and reports, user inputs, operating and control procedures, processing procedures, and computer programs should all be given a trial run in realistic circumstances. In addition, the capacity limits and the backup and recovery procedures of the system should be tested.

There are three common forms of testing: walk-throughs, processing test transactions, and acceptance testing. Each type is discussed in the paragraphs that follow.

A **walk-through** is a detailed, step-by-step review of system procedures or program logic. Walk-throughs during the early stages of systems design are generally attended by members of the development team and other system users. The focus is on the inputs, files, outputs, and data flows of the organization. Walk-throughs during later stages are generally attended by programmers and deal with the logic and structure of program code. To be most effective, walk-throughs should occur on a regular basis throughout the systems design process.

The purpose behind the **processing of test transactions** is to determine if a program operates as it should. Appropriate controls and error routines are incorporated into all programs. Hypothetical test transactions are developed to represent all valid processing and to represent all conceivable errors. These transactions are run through the system to see if valid transactions were processed properly and to see if errors were detected and handled appropriately. For each test transaction the correct system response must be specified in advance in order to evaluate the test results. Whenever the test results indicate that a significant change must be made in a program, the proposed change should be reviewed and approved by system users.

For an **acceptance test**, test transactions and acceptance criteria are developed by system users. The tests are run, and the users review the test results and decide whether the system is acceptable. Acceptance testing generally follows the processing of test transactions by the systems development team and immediately precedes the conversion process. Rather than using hypothetical transaction and file records, an acceptance test generally uses copies of real transaction and file records. Users may participate in some steps, such as preparing records for computer input, reviewing computer outputs, and processing computer-generated documents. Any final decisions to accept the system or to require specific modifications are the responsibility of the users.

Conversion

Conversion is the process of changing from the old system to the new. Many systems elements must be converted: hardware, software, data files, and procedures. It is during conversion that all these system elements must come together to produce an effective information system. A formal conversion plan should be developed and approved prior to the implementation phase. The conversion plan is similar to the implementation plan in that tasks, responsibilities, and expected completion dates should be specified for all activities. Conversion is complete when the new system has become a routine, ongoing part of the organization's information system.

Conversion Approaches. Four approaches that are frequently used to convert from an old system to a new system are the direct, parallel, phase-in, and modular approaches. These approaches are illustrated in Fig. 10.9.

Direct conversion (also referred to as "burning the bridges" or "cold turkey") means discontinuing the old system when the new system is introduced. For example, Shoppers Mart could discontinue its old system on a Saturday night and begin to use its new system on Monday morning. Direct conversion is most appropriate when the old system has no value or the new system is so different that comparisons between the systems would be meaningless. The approach is inexpensive, but it leaves no backup system in case of a problem. Unless the system has been carefully developed and properly tested, direct conversion has a high risk of failure.

Parallel conversion means operating the old system and the new system simultaneously (in parallel) for a period of time. For example, Shoppers Mart could process all its transactions with both the old and the new systems. The outputs of the two systems could then be compared, differences reconciled, and problems with the new system corrected. After a month or so, when the new system had proven itself, Shoppers Mart could discontinue the old system. Parallel processing protects companies from failure and errors caused by the new system, but it is costly and stressful to process all transactions twice. But because

Figure 10.9
Comparison of conversion methods

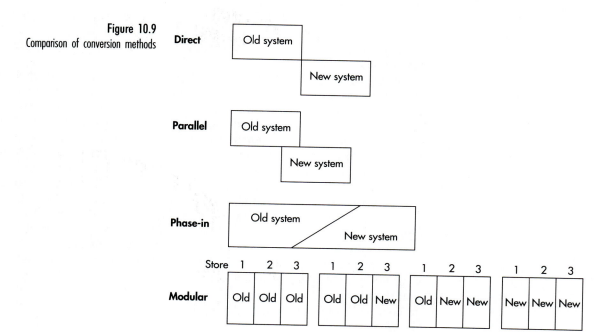

many organizations experience problems in implementing a new system, parallel processing has gained widespread popularity.

In **phase-in conversion** the old system is gradually replaced by elements of the new system. For example, Shoppers Mart could implement first its inventory system, then its disbursements system, then its sales collection system, and so forth, until the whole system was functional. One advantage of this method is that drastic changes are avoided. Since only gradual changes are made, data processing resources can be acquired gradually over time. Another advantage is that the costs of converting old data files are minimized. The disadvantages are the cost of creating the temporary interfaces between the old and the new systems and the time required to make the gradual changeover.

In **modular conversion** a new system is implemented in only a portion of the organization, such as one of the company's locations. For example, Shoppers Mart could install its new POS system at one of its stores using a direct, parallel, or phase-in approach. Once it resolves any problems at that one store, it could implement it at the remaining locations. This approach localizes conversion problems and allows users and operators to be trained in a live environment. The disadvantages are the long conversion time and the need for interfaces between the old and the new systems, which coexist until all locations have been converted.

Data Conversion.   One of the most important conversion activities is **data conversion**. Existing files may need to be modified in three different ways. The data may need to be moved to a different storage medium (e.g., disks rather than tapes), the content of the data may need to be changed (e.g, fields or records added or deleted), or the format of files may need to be changed. Data conversion can be time-consuming, tedious, and expensive. The difficulty and magnitude of the task can be easily underestimated.

The data conversion process is shown in Fig. 10.10. The first step is to decide which data files need to be converted to the new system. Then the files that are to be converted must be checked for completeness and data inaccuracies and inconsistencies removed. If special programs need to be written to transfer data from the old storage structure and medium to the new, they must be thoroughly tested so that they do not introduce errors into the system during conversion.

The actual conversion of the data, which involves loading the data into new files or data structures, comes next. It is followed by the validation of the new files. Control totals, such as record counts, hash totals, and financial totals, should be generated as the data are converted to the new system. These totals should be reconciled with the same totals generated by the old system in order to ensure that data were not lost during conversion.

If the file conversion process takes much time, the new files must be updated with the transactions that take place during data conversion. Once all files and data bases have been converted and tested for

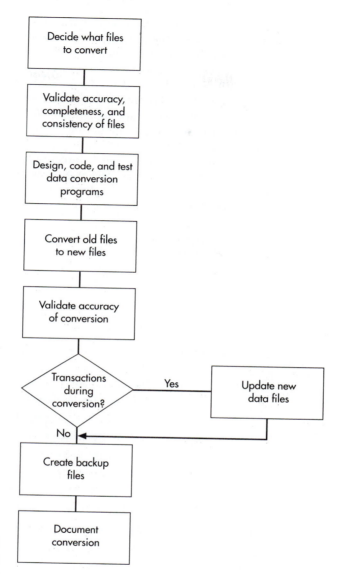

Figure 10.10
Data conversion process

accuracy, the new system can begin to function. The system should be monitored for a period of time to make sure it runs smoothly and accurately. The final two activities are to make sure that backup copies of the new files are created and properly stored (in case discrepancies or problems appear later) and to document the conversion activities.

OPERATION AND MAINTENANCE

After a new system has operated for a brief period, it should be evaluated. This evaluation is referred to as a **postimplementation review**. This review is essential, since no matter how well changeover activities are planned, numerous unforeseen incidents and problems usually arise. During the review the project development team should verify that the new system is meeting its planned objectives. Additionally, the team should assess the adequacy of system standards and controls and correct all errors detected by the system. Major differences between actual and expected performance should be brought to the attention of management and necessary adjustments made. Factors to consider and questions to answer in conducting a postimplementation review are listed in Table 10.5.

After the review has been completed, a **postimplementation review report** should be prepared by representatives from the user group and the systems department. As an example, the table of contents of the report prepared at Shoppers Mart is shown in Table 10.6. It is representative of what the report should contain.

The report should be presented to all affected user groups. Acceptance of the report is the concluding activity in the systems develop-

Table 10.5

Factors and questions to investigate during postimplementation review

Factors	Questions
Goals and objectives	Does the system help the organization meet its goals, objectives, and overall mission?
Satisfaction	Are the users satisfied with the system? What would they like changed or improved?
Benefits	How have users benefited from the system? Were the expected benefits achieved?
Costs	Are actual costs in line with expected costs?
Reliability	Is the system reliable? Has the system failed? If so, what caused its failure?
Accuracy	Are the data the system produces accurate and complete?
Timeliness	Does the system produce information on a timely basis?
Compatibility	Are the hardware, software, data, and procedures compatible with existing systems?
Controls and security	Is the system safeguarded against unintentional errors, fraud, and unauthorized instrusion?
Errors	Do error-handling procedures exist, and are they adequate?
Training	Are systems personnel and users adequately trained to support and use the system?
Communications	Is the communications system adequate?
Organization changes	Are any organizational changes brought about by the system beneficial or harmful? If harmful, how can they be resolved?
Documentation	Is system documentation complete and accurate?

Table 10.6
Table of contents for a
postimplementation review report

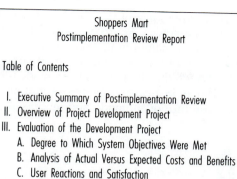

Shoppers Mart
Postimplementation Review Report

Table of Contents

I. Executive Summary of Postimplementation Review
II. Overview of Project Development Project
III. Evaluation of the Development Project
    A. Degree to Which System Objectives Were Met
    B. Analysis of Actual Versus Expected Costs and Benefits
    C. User Reactions and Satisfaction
IV. Evaluation of Project Development Team
V. Recommendations
    A. Recommendations for Improving the New System
    B. Recommendations for Improving the System
       Development Process
VI. Summary

ment process. When the report is accepted, control of the system is passed to the data processing department of the organization.

Handing control of the system over to the systems department only signifies the end of the formal development process. It does not end the work associated with the newly developed system. In fact, the work has just begun. Studies have shown that over the life of a typical system, only about 20%–30% of the work takes place during development. The other 70%–80% of the effort is spent maintaining the system. Most of these maintenance costs relate to software modifications and updates. This relationship is illustrated in Fig. 10.11.

Figure 10.11
Software maintenance costs
over the life of a system

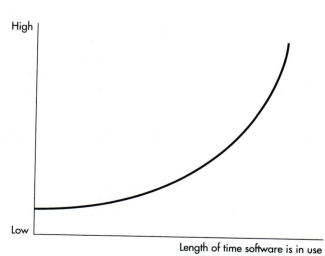

Annual software
maintenance costs

High

Low

Length of time software is in use

The experience of the Hartford Insurance Group illustrates the cost of maintenance. Approximately 70% of its personnel resources are devoted to maintaining existing systems. Hartford must maintain an inventory of 34,000 program modules containing 24 million lines of COBOL code. The job has been made more difficult because over time changes in insurance regulations and business strategies have reduced the structure of the code and increased its complexity.

CASE CONCLUSION: SYSTEMS DESIGN, IMPLEMENTATION, AND OPERATION AT SHOPPERS MART

Ann Christy met with the head of systems development and developed a strategy for physical systems design and implementation. The development team took each report identified in conceptual design and, depending on what form the output was to take, either designed the screen format or the hard copy format. The format of one of the screen-based reports, the store inventory report, is shown in Fig. 10.2. The reports were shown to representatives of all affected users groups and reworked until all involved were satisfied with them. In Fig. 10.2, for example, the users requested room for a more complete description of each inventory item and a more complete location code.

The development team then designed each file and data base needed by the system as well as all of the input screens. Next came the detailed design of the software programs needed to collect the data, process it, and produce the output. The team also developed new procedures for handling data and operating the system, where appropriate. The accountants and the internal audit staff were especially helpful during the design of the controls needed to protect the system against errors and fraud. The table of contents for the physical systems design report that was developed is shown in Table 10.2.

Ann and her staff started planning for implementation early in the development process. A location for the new mainframe that headquarters had approved was identified early, and approval was obtained to begin site preparation during the design phase. The hardware manufacturer was notified to ship the mainframe, and it was installed and tested. Then the software programs that had been developed and tested individually were installed, and the entire system was tested. The new system was staffed almost exclusively from existing employees, and they were trained as the system was tested. The documentation of the system was completed after the training and testing were completed and while data from the old system were being converted to the new system.

Ann and her staff decided to use a variety of conversion approaches. Corporatewide data stored on the centralized computer was so important and sensitive that the company could not afford for mistakes to be made. As a result, Ann decided on a parallel conversion strategy. The current and the new systems were operated together for a month and the results compared. When the bugs in the new system were ironed out, the old system was discontinued. A modular approach was used for the store information system. The system was installed at several stores and tested and all bugs were ironed out before the system was installed at the remainder of the stores. The conversion process was not easy, and it required a fair amount of overtime and duplicate processing; but the process was finally completed. After a few months Ann and her staff did a postimplementation review, and plans were made to make the adjustments needed to enhance the already high user acceptance and satisfaction of the new system.

Ann made her final presentation to top management after the system was installed and operating. She was widely congratulated and even heard the President mention to an Executive Vice-President that she was worth keeping an eye on and that they needed to target her for even more responsibility within the organization. ■

SUMMARY

This chapter discussed three phases of the SDLC: physical systems design, implementation and conversion, and operation and maintenance.

Six systems elements must be designed during the physical design phase: output design, data base design, input design, program design, procedures design, and controls design. The design of computer screens and preprinted forms as well as the various tools used in physical design were discussed.

Systems implementation is the process of converting the product of systems analysis and design into an effectively operating information system. The first step in implementation is planning. Two planning techniques commonly used in systems implementation are the Gantt chart and PERT. The Gantt chart is a form of bar chart in which scheduled and completed activities are displayed against a time line scaled in weeks or days. PERT involves diagramming the sequence of activities comprising a project by means of a network in which arrows represent activities and nodes represent events. Both techniques provide a framework for scheduling, coordinating, expediting, and monitoring the progress of the implementation effort.

Other steps in implementation are developing and testing software programs, preparing the site, installing and testing the hardware, communicating with employees, selecting and training personnel, finalizing documentation, testing the system, and converting to the new system.

After conversion is completed, a postimplementation review should be conducted to assess user satisfaction and to evaluate the system. When users accept the system, the development project is completed. The system is turned over to the systems department, which maintains it until it is replaced.

KEY TERMS

Define the following terms.

physical systems design	Gantt chart	acceptance test
scheduled reports	coding	conversion
special-purpose analyses	modules	direct conversion
triggered exception reports	structured programming	parallel conversion
demand reports	hierarchical program design	phase-in conversion
record layout	debugging	modular conversion
form	technical system	data conversion
physical systems design report	social system	postimplementation review
systems implementation	walk-through	postimplementation review
implementation team	processing of test transactions	report
implementation plan		
PERT (program evaluation and review technique)		

DISCUSSION QUESTIONS

10.1 Rhonda Grubbs, President of Italian Imports Unlimited, has recently engaged your firm to design and implement a new computerized sales system. So that she will better understand the work you will be doing, she has asked you to give her a brief overview of the systems design process. Discuss the differences between conceptual (general) systems design and physical (detailed) systems design. Also, outline and briefly describe the tasks that will be undertaken during each of these phases.

10.2 An important aspect of output design is determining how often reports are generated. Some reports are prepared on a daily basis, whereas others are prepared only upon request. Describe in some detail the various categories of reports commonly found in businesses. Be sure to discuss the timing, content, and format of each. Give several examples of each.

10.3 Jan Jamison, President of Future Designs, Inc., has decided to carry out a major restructuring of the company, involving both departmental and management changes. The restructuring will coincide with the implementation of a new information system. Jan's rationale is that it will be easier and less time-consuming to make all the changes at one time. As

a systems consultant working with the company, respond to Jan's decision.

10.4 Prism Glass Company is currently in the process of converting from a manual data processing system to a computerized system. To expedite the implementation of the system, the President of Prism has asked your consulting team to postpone establishing standards and controls until after the system is fully operational. How should you respond to the President's request?

10.5 When a company converts from one system to another, many areas within the organization are affected. Explain how conversion to a new system will affect the following, both individually and collectively.

a. Personnel
b. Data storage
c. Operations
d. Policies and procedures
e. Physical facilities

10.6 Now that you've completed your study of the traditional systems development life cycle, identify the significant reports developed by systems designers during the systems life cycle. What role do these reports play in the development of the information system?

10.7 Discuss the relationship between the technical system and the social system in the development life cycle. Identify the actions management can take to ensure that the two systems coalesce during the implementation of a new information system.

10.8 As a receivables clerk for a large corporation, you are excited to discover that the network system the company has been developing for years is finally operational. Since you have little practical knowledge of the system, you boot up your station and begin browsing through the screen menus and attempt to call up information. You punch a few buttons that sound right, and you get a rather ominous error message. You try everything you can think of to return to your menu, all to no avail.

Why are user procedures necessary for a new system? Assume that management wants to develop a systems manual to outline user procedures. What issues should the manual cover? How should it be developed?

10.9 The following notice was posted in the employee cafeteria on Monday morning.

TO: All Accounting and Clerical Employees
FROM: I.M. Krewel, President
SUBJECT: Termination of Employee Positions

Effective Monday morning of next week, all accounting and clerical employees not previously contacted will be terminated. Our new computer system eliminates the need for most accounting and clerical functions. We're grateful for the loyal service you've rendered as employees and wish you success.

Pick up your final checks on Friday before you go.

Discuss the President's approach to personnel administration. What are the possible repercussions of such an approach? Assuming that job termination is the best alternative available, how would you approach the situation?

10.10 Testing new software is critical in reducing the incidence of programming errors, known as bugs (see Focus 10.2). What is a software bug? Can effective software testing eliminate the threat of bugs altogether? How are software developers dealing with the risk of bugs in their software?

Problems

10.1 An inventory record has the following data elements, each containing the number of characters indicated.

Part number	7
Description	20
Location code	4
Unit cost	8
Vendor code	5
Vendor name	20
Quantity on hand	5
Quantity on order	5
Reorder point	5
Order quantity	5

Required
Prepare a record layout for this record.

10.2 Benjamin and Watson Enterprises has decided to acquire a new computer system and is presently entering a 12-month implementation period. A schedule of activities is shown in Table 10.7. The monthly costs attached to these various implementation activities are shown in Table 10.8. In addition, the future site of the computer is presently being rented out at $1000 per month.

Required
Prepare an implementation cost schedule for the 12-month implementation period. Show each cost as a one-line item, and show the total cost incurred during each of the 12 months. Also show the total cumulative cost as of the end of each month.

10.3 The list that follows gives project activities, the scheduled starting time, and the completion time of each activity.

Activity	Starting Date, Monday, Week of	Ending Date, Friday, Week of
A	Jan. 5	Feb. 9
B	Jan. 5	Jan. 19
C	Jan. 26	Feb. 23
D	Mar. 2	Mar. 23
E	Mar. 2	Mar. 16
F	Feb. 2	Mar. 16
G	Mar. 30	Apr. 20
H	Mar. 23	Apr. 27

Required

a. Using a format similar to that illustrated in Fig. 10.7, prepare a Gantt chart for this project.

b. Assume that today is February 16 and that activities A and B have been completed, activity C is half completed, activity F is a quarter completed, and the other activities have not yet commenced. Record this information on your Gantt chart. Is the project behind schedule, on schedule, or ahead of schedule? Explain.

c. Discuss the relative merits of the Gantt chart and PERT as tools for project planning and control.

Table 10.7
Schedule of activities

Beginning of	Activity
Month 1	A data processing manager-programmer is hired. This person is responsible for final systems design and program flowcharting.
Month 5	A programmer is hired. The coding process is begun.
Month 6	A data entry operations supervisor is hired and immediately assumes responsibility for keying the programs.
Month 7	Program testing is begun, which requires rental of outside facilities. The rental contract with the company currently using the future computer site is terminated. The remodeling of the site in preparation for installation is begun.
Month 10	Two data entry operators are hired. The file conversion process begins.
Month 11	Site remodeling, program testing, and file conversion are completed. The computer is installed, and two computer operators are hired. Parallel operation begins.
Month 13	Parallel operation is completed, and final changeover to the new system is achieved.

Table 10.8
Monthly costs

Nature of Cost	Cost per Month
Salaries	
Data processing manager-programmer	$2500
Programmer	1700
Data entry operations supervisor	1200
Data entry operator	900
Computer operator	1200
Overtime during parallel operation	3000
Rental of time for program testing	600
Remodeling of site	2000
Computer rental	6000
Miscellaneous overhead after system is installed	1000

10.4 Refer to the PERT network of the computer implementation process shown in Fig. 10.6. Using months as the basic unit of time, prepare a Gantt chart for the project represented in Fig. 10.6. Assume that each activity is scheduled to begin immediately following the scheduled completion of any preceding activities. To simplify your analysis, you may assume that four weeks equal one month.

10.5 Chaotic order processing at Wang Laboratories had long been accepted by Wang customers as the cost of doing business with the computer giant. The tremendous growth of Wang throughout the 1970s left the company with a serious revenue tracking problem: Customers would often wait months for Wang to fill their order and process the invoice. Repeated attempts by Wang's understaffed MIS department to solve the problem always met with failure.

Finally, in 1980 Wang Laboratories hired a small consulting organization to solve its revenue tracking problems and expedite prompt receipt of payments. The 18-month project turned into a three-year nightmare. After three years and $10 million, the consultants were dismissed from the unfinished project.

The reasons for the project failure were clear. First, the project was too large and far too complex for the appointed consulting team. According to one consultant, the systems development process was so dynamic that the failure to complete the project quickly was self-defeating, as modifications took over the original design.

Second, management had no clear vision of the new MIS system and lacked a strong MIS support staff. As a result, a number of incompatible tracking systems sprung up throughout the company's distributed computer system.

Third, the consulting firm had little experience with the desired technology: a complex data base that represented the heart of the new system.

Finally, the project had too many applications. Interdependencies among subprograms and subroutines left consultants with few completed programs. Every program was linked to several subprograms, which in turn were linked to several other programs. Programmers would begin an initial program only to find that several subroutines were necessary. Programmers eventually found themselves lost in a myriad of subroutines with no completed program.

Wang's ultimate solution to the crisis came from the internal MIS department. After much effort the internal staff developed a troubled revenue tracking system that suffered quality problems for years.[1]

Required

As a member of the MIS staff, the President of Wang Laboratories has asked you to write a memo explaining the failure of the systems development project.

a. Outline the specific reasons for the development failure. What role did the consultants play in the project's failure?

b. Identify the organizational issues that management must address in the future.

c. Recommend any steps the company could take in the future to guarantee the quality of consulting services.

10.6 Tiny Toddlers Company, a large multinational manufacturer of children's toys and furniture, is planning the design and implementation of a distributed data processing system to assist its sales force. The company has 10 sales offices in Canada and 20 sales offices in the United States. The company's sales departments have been set up in a regional structure: Each sales office maintains its own customers and is responsible for granting credit and collecting receivables.

The proposed system will not only permit inquiries but also allow entry of daily sales and maintenance of the customer master file. Reports used by each sales office to maintain the customer master file and to enter the daily sales orders are shown in Figs. 10.12 and 10.13.

Required

a. Identify and describe the structure of the required data files. (*Hint:* Two of the files that are needed are a customer master file and a sales order transaction file.) For each file, include the following information.

    1. File name
    2. Contents (field names)
    3. Access key (record key)

b. Evaluate the reports shown in Figs. 10.12 and 10.13, which are to be used by the regional sales offices of Tiny Toddlers Company. Use the format that follows. For each report, indicate the weak-

---

[1] *Source:* Glen Rifkin and Mitch Betts, "Strategic Systems Plan Gone Awry," *Computerworld* (March 14, 1988):1, 104–105.

CUSTOMER MAINTENANCE FORM	
New Customer?	☐ Yes _____ ☑ No 24671
Name	The Little Ones Furniture Store
New Address	5 St. Antoine Street N. Quebec City
Old Address	305 St. Antoine Street S. Quebec City
Salesperson #	02
Requested Credit Limit	50,000
Sales Office	Eastern Canada
Pricing Code	25
Estimated Sales	300,000
Credit Limit	10,000
Currency	U.S.A. ☐, Canada ☐
Bank	Canadian Credit Bank 50 St. Antoine Street Quebec City
Bank Line	_____
Rating	Satisfactory
_____ Sales Manager	
_____ Credit Manager	

Figure 10.12
Customer maintenance form
for Tiny Toddlers

ness, explain the weakness, and recommend how the weakness may be corrected.
(SMAC Examination, adapted)

Report Weakness	Explanation of the Weakness	Recommendation(s)

10.7 Sullivan Sport is a large distributor of all types of recreational equipment. All sales are made on account, with terms of net 30 days from the date of shipment. The number of delinquent accounts as well as uncollectible accounts has increased significantly during the past 12 months. Customers frequently complain of errors in their accounts. Management believes that the information generated by the present accounts receivable system is inadequate and untimely.

The current accounts receivable system was developed when Sullivan began operations in 1983. A new computer was installed 18 months ago. The

SALES ORDER FORM		
Customer: 24671 The Little Ones Furniture Store 5 St. Antoine Street N. Quebec City		Date:

Product Code	Description	Quantity
24571	Crib	4
M0002	Mattress	102
HG730	High chair – white	32
HG223	High chair – natural wood	22
CT200	Change table	300
D0025	Desk – modern design	2
C9925	Chair – modern design	5
BP809	Bumper pads	1200

Salesperson No.:

Entered by:

Figure 10.13
Sales order form for Tiny Toddlers

accounts receivable application was not revised at that time because other applications were considered more important. Management has now asked the Systems Department to design a new accounts receivable system to satisfy the following objectives.

■ Produce current and timely reports about customers that will (1) aid in controlling bad debts; (2) notify the Sales Department of delinquent customer accounts (those that should lose credit privileges); and (3) notify the Sales Department of customers with uncollectible accounts (accounts to be closed and written off).
■ Notify customers on a timely basis regarding (1) amounts owed to Sullivan and (2) changes in account status (loss of charge privileges).
■ Minimize the chance for errors in customers' accounts.

Input data for the system will be taken from four source documents: credit applications, sales invoices, cash payment remittances, and credit mem-

oranda. The accounts receivable master file will be maintained by customer account number.

The conceptual design of the new accounts receivable system has been completed by the Systems Department. A brief description of the proposed reports and other output generated by the system are detailed below.

■ *Accounts receivable register:* This report is a daily alphabetical listing of all customers' accounts that shows the balance as of the last statement, activity since the last statement, and the current account balance.
■ *Customer statements:* These monthly statements for each customer show activity since the last statement and the new account balance; the top portion of the statement is to be returned with the payment and serves as the cash payment remittance.
■ *Activity reports:* These monthly reports show (1) customers who have not purchased any merchandise for 90 days; (2) customers whose account balances exceed their credit limit; and (3) customers

who have current sales on account but are delinquent.

■ *Delinquency and write-off register:* This report is a monthly alphabetical listing of delinquent or closed customers' accounts.

Required

a. Identify the data that Sullivan Sport should capture and store in the computer-based accounts receivable file records for each customer.

b. Review the proposed reports to be generated by Sullivan Sport's new accounts receivable system, and discuss whether these reports are adequate to satisfy the objectives designated by management.

c. Recommend changes, additions, and/or deletions that should be made to the proposed reporting structure to be generated from Sullivan Sport's new accounts receivable system.

(CMA Examination, adapted)

10.8 Mickie Louderman is the new Assistant Controller of Pickens Publishers, a growing company with sales of $35 million. She was formerly the controller of a smaller company in a similar industry, where she was in charge of accounting and data processing and had considerable influence over the entire computer center operation. Prior to Louderman's arrival at Pickens, the company revamped its entire computer operations center, placing increased emphasis on decentralized data access, microcomputers with mainframe access, and on-line systems.

The controller of Pickens, John Richards, has been with the company for 28 years and is near retirement. He has given Louderman managerial authority over both the implementation of the new system and the integration of the company's accounting-related functions. Her promotion to controller will be dependent on the success of the new accounting information system (AIS).

Louderman began to develop the new system at Pickens by using the same design characteristics and reporting format that she had developed at her former company. She sent details of the new accounting information system to the departments that interfaced with accounting, including inventory control, purchasing, personnel, production control, and marketing. If they did not respond with suggestions by a prescribed date, she would continue the development process. Louderman and Richards determined a new schedule for many of the reports, changing the frequency from weekly to monthly. After a meeting with the Director of Computer Op

erations, she selected a programmer to help her with the details of the new reporting formats.

Most of the control features of the old system were maintained to decrease the initial installation time, while a few new ones were added for unusual situations; however, the procedures for maintaining the controls were substantially changed. Louderman appointed herself the decisive authority for all control changes and program testing that related to the AIS, including screening the control features that related to batch totals for payroll, inventory control, accounts receivable, cash deposits, and accounts payable.

As each module was completed by the programmer, Louderman told the department to implement the change immediately, in order to incorporate immediate labor savings. There were incomplete instructions accompanying these changes, and specific implementation responsibility was not assigned to departmental personnel. Louderman believes that operations people should "learn as they go," reporting errors as they occur.

Accounts payable and inventory control were the initial areas of the AIS to be implemented; several problems arose in both of these areas. Louderman was disturbed that the semimonthly runs of payroll, which were weekly under the old system, had abundant errors and, consequently, required numerous manual paychecks. Frequently, the control totals of a payroll run would take hours to reconcile with the computer printout. To expedite matters, Louderman authorized the payroll clerk to prepare journal entries for payroll processing.

The new inventory control system failed to improve the carrying stock level of many items, causing several critical raw material stockouts that resulted in expensive rush orders. The primary control procedure under the new system was the availability of ordering and use information to both inventory control personnel and purchasing personnel by direct-access terminals so that both departments could issue purchase orders on a timely basis. The inventory levels were updated daily, so the previous weekly report was discontinued by Louderman.

Because of these problems, system documentation is behind schedule, and proper backup procedures have not been implemented in many areas. Louderman has requested budget approval to hire two systems analysts, an accountant, and an administrative assistant to help her implement the new system. Richards is disturbed by her request since her predecessor had only one part-time employee as his assistant.

Required

a. List the steps Louderman should have taken during the design of the accounting information system to ensure that end-user needs were satisfied.

b. Identify and describe three areas where Louderman has violated the basic principles of internal control during the implementation of the new accounting information system.

c. Refer to Louderman's approach to implementing the new accounting information system.

   1. Identify and describe the weaknesses.

   2. Make recommendations that would help Louderman improve the situation and continue with the development of the remaining areas of the accounting information system at Pickens Publishers.

(CMA Examination, adapted)

10.9 Each month the department heads of the National Association of Trade Stores receive a financial report of the performance of their departments for the previous month. The report is generally distributed around the sixteenth or seventeenth of the month. Although the association is a not-for-profit trade and educational association, it does attempt to generate revenues from a variety of activities to supplement the member dues. The association has several income-producing departments: research, education, publications, and promotion consulting services. As a general rule, each department is expected to be self-supporting, and the department head is responsible for both the generation of revenue and the control of costs for the department. As an example of the monthly department report, the March 1977 report of the Education Department is presented in Table 10.9, along with the comments of the Accounting Department.

The annual revenue target that becomes the revenue budget is established by the Executive Director and the association's Board of Directors. The annual and monthly expenses budgets are then developed at the beginning of the year by the department heads for all costs except rent, utilities, and janitorial services; equipment depreciation; and allocated general administration. The amounts for these accounts are supplied by the Accounting Department. The monthly budget figures for revenues are also determined by the department heads at the beginning of the year. The monthly budget amounts

for revenues and expenses are not revised during the year.

For example, the following changes in operations have taken place but the monthly budgets have not been revised: (1) a new home study course was introduced in February, one month earlier than scheduled; (2) a number of the week-long courses were postponed in February and March and rescheduled for April and May; and (3) the related promotion effort—heavy direct-mail advertising in the two months prior to a course offering—was likewise rescheduled.

Required

Identify and briefly discuss the good and bad features of the monthly report of the Education Department as a means of communication in terms of the following:

a. Its form and appearance in presenting the operating performance of the Education Department

b. Its content in providing useful information to the department head for managing the Education Department

Include in your discussion the changes you would recommend to improve the report as a communication device. (CMA Examination, adapted)

10.10 An important step in the systems implementation phase is to decide which systems conversion approach should be used.

Required

a. Identify and define three different systems conversion approaches that the management accountant could use when converting a manual system to a computerized system.

b. Outline the advantages and disadvantages of each of the systems conversion approaches identified in part a.

c. Outline the tasks, other than the systems conversion task, that should be performed during the systems implementation phase.

(SMAC Examination, adapted)

10.11 The McCann brothers have decided to open an auto repair shop. John will be in charge of machine work, stocking of parts and supplies, and accounting. Ted will be the head mechanic and supervise the auto repair work. Arrangements have been made to lease a suitable building, and three qualified auto mechanics have been hired.

The shop will maintain an inventory of the most commonly used parts and accessories. Other parts and accessories can be obtained as needed from

	BUDGET			ACTUAL			VARIANCE		VARIANCE AS % OF BUDGET	
	Person Days or Units	$	%	Person Days or Units	$	%	Person Days or Units	$	Person Days or Units	$
Revenue										
Week-long courses	1500	225,000	71.4	1250	187,500	66.4	(250)	(37,500)	(16.6)%	(16.6)%
One-day seminars	50	15,000	4.8	17	5,100	1.8	(33)	(9,900)	(66.0)	(66.0)
Home study courses	1000	75,000	23.8	1100	89,700	31.8	100	14,700	10.0	19.6
Total revenues		315,000	100.0		282,300	100.0		(32,700)		(10.4)%
Expenses										
Salaries		174,000	55.2		167,000	59.1		$7,000		4.0%
Course material		35,500	11.3		34,670	12.3		830		2.3
Supplies & telephone		4,000	1.3		4,200	1.5		(200)		(5.0)
Rent, utilities, & janitorial services		7,000	2.2		7,000	2.5		—		—
Equipment depreciation		700	0.2		700	0.2		—		—
Allocated general administrative		5,000	1.6		5,000	1.8		—		—
Temporary office help		5,000	1.6		3,750	1.3		1,250		25.0
Contract employees		15,000	4.8		18,500	6.6		(3,500)		(23.3)
Travel		12,000	3.8		11,500	4.1		500		4.2
Dues & meetings		500	0.2		500	0.2		—		—
Promotion & postage		32,000	10.1		36,500	12.9		(4,500)		(14.1)
Total expenses		290,700	92.3		289,320	102.5		1,380		0.5%
Contribution to the association		24,300	7.7		(7,020)	(2.5)		(31,320)		(128.9)%

Comment: The department did not make its budget this month. There was a major shortfall in the week-long course revenues. Although salaries were lower than budget, this saving was entirely consumed by overexpenditure in contract employees and promotion. Further effort is needed to increase revenues and to hold down expenses.

Table 10.9 National Association of Trade Stores, Education Department: Report for the Month of March 1977

local parts wholesalers. A separate room in the shop has been equipped with shelving to serve as a parts storeroom. The McCanns wish to minimize their investment in inventories but also hope to avoid making frequent trips to buy unstocked parts.

As customers bring their autos in for repairs, a service work order detailing the work to be done will be prepared. At this time many customers will ask for an estimate of the repair cost and when the work will be completed. As the work is performed, the cost of parts and labor will be recorded on the service work order. When the customer returns to pick up the repaired vehicle, a copy of the service work order will serve as a bill. Customers may pay their bill with cash, check, or credit card. The McCanns will guarantee their work for 30 days.

The McCanns have asked you for assistance in designing a service work order for their business.

Required

a. At a minimum, what information should the sales invoice contain?

b. Design a service work order document. How many copies of this document should be prepared? What will the copies be used for?

10.13 Columbia Corporation is a medium-sized, diversified manufacturing company. Ryon Pulsipher has been promoted recently to Manager of the company's Property Accounting Section. Pulsipher has had difficulty in responding to some of the requests from the individuals in other departments of Columbia for information about the company's fixed assets. Five of the requests and problems Pulsipher has had to cope with follow.

1. The Controller has requested schedules of individual fixed assets to support the balance in the general ledger. Pulsipher has furnished the necessary information, but he has always been late. The manner in which the records are organized makes it difficult to obtain information easily.

2. The Maintenance Manager wishes to verify the existence of a punch press that he thinks was repaired twice. He has asked Pulsipher to confirm the asset number and location of the press.

3. The Insurance Department wants data on the cost and book values of assets to include in its review of current insurance coverage.

4. The Tax Department has requested data that can be used to determine when Columbia should switch depreciation methods for tax purposes.

5. The company's internal auditors have spent a significant amount of time in the Property Accounting Section recently attempting to confirm the annual depreciation expense.

The property account records that are at Pulsipher's disposal consist of a set of manual books. These records show the date the asset was acquired, the account number to which the asset applies, the dollar amount capitalized, and the estimated useful life of the asset for depreciation purposes.

After many frustrations Pulsipher realized that his records are inadequate and that he cannot supply the data easily when they are requested. He has decided to discuss his problems with the Controller, Gig Griffith.

Pulsipher: Gig, something has to give. My people are working overtime and can't keep up. You worked in property accounting before you became controller. You know that I can't tell the tax, insurance, and maintenance people everything they need to know from my records. Also, the internal auditing team is living in my area and that slows down the work pace. The requests of these people are reasonable, and we should be able to answer these questions and provide the needed data. I think we need an automated property accounting system. I would like to talk with the information systems people to see if they can help me.

Griffith: Ryon, I think you have a great idea. Just be sure you are personally involved in the design of any system so that you get all the information you need. Keep me posted on the project's progress.

Required

a. Identify and justify four major objectives Columbia Corporation's automated property accounting system should possess in order to provide the data that are necessary to respond to requests of information from company personnel.

b. Identify the data that should be included in the computer record for each asset included in the property account.   (CMA Examination, adapted)

CASE 10.1: ANYCOMPANY, INC.—AN ONGOING COMPREHENSIVE CASE

One of the best ways to learn is to immediately apply what you have studied. The purpose of this case is to allow you to do that. You will select a local company that you can work with. At the end of most chapters you will find an assignment that will have

you apply what you have learned using the company you have selected as a reference. This case, then, may become an ongoing case study that you work on throughout the term.

Visit several small- to medium-sized businesses

in the local community. Explain that you will be doing a term-long case, and ask for permission to use the company as the firm you are going to study. Explain that you will need to meet with people in the company several times during the term to get the information you need. However, you will not need a great deal of their time or be a disruption to them. Offer to share any observations or suggestions that you can come up with as a way of allowing the firm to feel good about helping you.

Once you have lined up a company, perform the following steps.

1. With a member of the IS staff, discuss the procedures the company follows in designing and implementing changes in the company's information system.

a. What methods does the company use in the conceptual design of an information system? Who determines which design alternatives are selected?

b. How does the company handle the physical design procedures involved in the development of the system? If available, view any documentation or flowcharts used in the development of a prior system.

c. What implementation strategy does the company employ? What conversion procedures does the company find most effective in making the transition from an old system to a newer one?

2. Obtain the documentation manual for one of the company's software programs. Evaluate the effectiveness of the documentation, and identify any strengths and weaknesses. What could you do to improve the documentation?

3. Summarize the results of your findings in a memo report.

a. How effective are the company's design and implementation procedures?

b. How can the company improve its existing procedures to be more effective?

CASE 10.2: NEWTON MANUFACTURING

Newton Manufacturing was a company on the go. Regular increases in sales volume left the company's aging information system struggling to meet the strategic information needs of management. Based in Newton, Iowa, Newton Manufacturing was doing $48 million in annual sales as a promotional goods distributor. With future growth looking promising, the company was clearly at a crossroad.

Newton's first step in developing a new system was to begin a three-year intensive feasibility study to assess the information needs of the company and to design the most effective system to meet the company's needs. With the help of consultants MIS experts at Newton organized a feasibility team to examine existing configurations in a number of areas, including the following:

- Hardware
- Operating system software
- Application software
- System development methodology
- Application development methodology

- Project management methodology
- Backup and recovery
- Maintenance
- Employee education

Newton's systems manager planned to assess each area's needs based on an open-systems approach. The study would focus on the possibility of shifting from a hierarchical mainframe environment to a more flexible and open client/server data base.

Setting a Feasibility Study Plan
Newton's management developed a five-year strategic business plan prior to investigating the feasibility of an open-systems model. With a strategic plan in place researchers developed a work plan for assessing current hardware and software configurations. The structured work plan developed by the feasibility team included a detailed schedule outlining milestones, responsibilities, and contingency plans.

Planning also included defining the roles of the individual team members. The project manager began by overseeing the initial needs assessment, including formulating objectives, determining critical success factors, and defining project requirements.

Assessing Current Hardware Needs

The shift from a mainframe to a large, integrated data base necessitated a close look at numerous departments—accounts payable, accounts receivable, order entry, and so on. The analysts then developed a specific plan to study each area. Upon studying response time, disk capacity, and applications, the researchers determined that the system was adequate at current levels of customer demand. However, if demand was to increase, the system could not handle the additional work load.

Through interviews with users and employee surveys analysts discovered several other important insights.

- Response time did not hinder operating areas.
- Expanded use of PCs meant that processing requirements were already being dispersed to individual machines.
- Demands for additional applications were usually requests for functions that users could perform on available applications, such as word processing.
- Current records had little data redundancy.

On the basis of these initial findings, support for an open system grew.

Assessing Operating Software

To test the feasibility of shifting from a hierarchical to a relational data base, the analysts completed a reexamination of the existing file structure. They also reviewed Newton's current systems development methodology and developed a new set of de-velopment standards to reflect the radical change in the data base environment.

A review of the existing applications revealed both on-line and batch programs written in COBOL. The analysts realized that all software would have to be converted when a new configuration was developed by the software engineers.

Assessing Education Needs

To control behavioral problems associated with the new system, researchers evaluated the current level of computer education among users. With the help of senior management an education plan was established for each department that would coincide with the installment of equipment.

Creating a New Operating Environment

Upon presenting the results of the systems survey to Newton's Board of Directors, a team of systems engineering consultants were brought in to oversee the design and implementation of a new system. In addition, the consultants spent time confirming the studies done by the first research group.[2]

With the completion of the implementation phase, Newton will possess one of the most effective information systems in the industry. Discuss the elements that made the analysis, design, and implementation of the system successful.

---

[2] *Source:* Dan Schneider, "The Feasibility of Converting to an Open Systems Architecture," *Journal of Systems Management* (June 1991): 28–30.

CHAPTER 11

Alternative Approaches to Systems Development

LEARNING
OBJECTIVES

After studying this chapter, you should be able to:

- Describe how organizations acquire application software, vendor services, and hardware.
- Evaluate competing vendor proposals to supply information systems resources.
- Explain why organizations use outsourcing companies to process their data, and discuss the benefits and risks of using them.
- Describe how prototypes are used to develop information systems, and discuss the advantages and disadvantages of doing so.
- Explain the principles of reengineering and the obstacles faced by those who begin reengineering projects.

INTEGRATIVE CASE:
ALTERNATIVE
DEVELOPMENT
STRATEGIES AT
SHOPPERS MART

Several months after the new system for Shoppers Mart was completed, Ann Christy is summoned to the office of Scott Miles, the President of Shoppers Mart. Scott informs Ann that Shoppers Mart is interested in expanding and diversifying. Its first move is the acquisition of a chain of home improvement stores that will be owned by Shoppers Mart but will be operated independently of the parent company. The Board of Directors believes that the home improvement market is poised for explosive growth. They want to utilize the company's expertise in retailing to capture a sizable portion of the market.

Home Improvement Center, the chain to be acquired, was once one of the market leaders. Recently, however, it has fallen on hard times and can be acquired at a very good price. The Board of Directors feels that there are two reasons for the company's problems. One is that since it grew faster and larger than the company could manage, it is overstaffed and inefficiently operated. The second is that the company is not effectively determining and meeting its customers' needs. The current management of Home Improvement Center believes that customer tastes and preferences do not change very often in the home improvement market. As a result, their information system does not provide them with the information they need to judge customer demands. Nor does it help them to respond quickly when a change in customer tastes and preferences is detected.

The board's acquisition strategy has two parts. The immediate step is to downsize the operation and dramatically improve operational efficiency. Unprofitable stores will be closed, and staff at the stores and the central office will be reduced. This will solve the immediate profitability problems, but it will not provide Shoppers Mart with the strategic advantage it needs to capture a commanding share of the market.

The second part of the strategy is to develop an information system that not only captures—and even anticipates—customer tastes and preferences but also allows Shoppers Mart to respond more rapidly than its competitors to those changes. This is where Ann comes in. The board members feel that they can use the expertise Ann and her people have gained to design and implement a new system for Home Improvement Center. The board wants Ann to head up the team that will design the new system. Speed is of utmost importance, because competition in the home improvement market is intensifying and the window of opportunity to increase market share will not last long.

Ann accepts the challenge. She schedules a tour of some of the Home Improvement Center stores for the following week and immediately begins planning her strategy. She is especially concerned about the need to quickly develop a quality information system. She has a number of questions that she wants to answer during the tour or immediately thereafter.

1. Can development time be reduced by adapting some of the software now used at Shoppers Mart or by buying software from an outside vendor? What other resources, such as hardware and maintenance services, will the new company need to be effective?

2. Can an outside company be hired to process some of the non-strategic data processing functions, thereby freeing her people to concentrate on the portion of the system that will provide them with a competitive advantage?

3. Can the traditional development process be speeded up? What is the

fastest way to get a working model of the new system into the employees' hands so that they can evaluate it?

4. Are the company's business processes and procedures sound, or does she need to completely reshape organizational work practices and information flows before developing the information system? ■

INTRODUCTION

Users and developers have experienced a number of difficulties using the traditional systems development life cycle (SDLC):

■ Systems development projects can be backlogged for up to two to three years (and even longer for invisible backlogs). For example, the Pentagon estimates that unless there are significant productivity gains in developing application software, about 60 million software workers will be required by the year 2010 at the current rate of growth in software demand.

■ Information systems fail to meet users needs. This problem is often not discovered until after a lengthy development process. It is usually not until a system is implemented and users see the final product and begin to use it that they realize that it does not meet their needs. This problem arises even when users are involved in the design, review the proposed system, and approve the design. One reason this problem occurs is that users are not able to visualize what the system will look like or how it will operate by reviewing the design documentation.

■ Users are unable to adequately specify their needs. Often they do not know exactly what they need; and even when they do, they sometimes cannot communicate their needs to systems developers.

■ Changes cannot be made in a system after systems requirements have been "frozen." If users were able to keep changing their requirements, then the system would never be finished, and the costs would skyrocket each time the system was reworked.

In today's fast-changing world many software developers find themselves in Ann Christy's position. They need development tools and approaches that are both faster and more efficient and at the same time less cumbersome and costly than those of the traditional life cycle. A number of approaches have been developed to solve the problems of the SDLC or to make that approach more efficient and effective. Four are discussed in this chapter:

1. Purchasing prewritten software

2. Hiring someone else (outsourcing) to operate all or part of your information system

3. Prototyping

4. Reengineering business processes

Ann Christy decided to conduct an in-depth investigation of these four approaches to systems development. She knew enough about them to realize that several of the approaches can be used together. For example, prototyping can be used in the reengineering process. In addition, an organization that outsources its information systems functions could also reengineer its business practices. Ann decided to investigate the purchasing of prewritten software and other system acquisitions first.

SYSTEMS ACQUISITION

One of the most popular alternatives to developing software in-house is to purchase prewritten software. Many companies write software to sell to others. Some of these developers specialize in a particular industry; others offer a complete package of software, hardware, and service. For example, a number of very good systems are geared to doctors, dentists, and others in the medical fields. There are also systems for automobile repair and service, full-service restaurants, fast-food outlets, video rentals, and other similar retail stores.

The decision to make or buy software should be made after system requirements have been determined but before planners are too far into conceptual design, because much of the design phase can be omitted if software is purchased. Once system requirements are known, they can be used to determine which package fits the requirements. If a prewritten package does not fit the requirements, the package may be able to be modified to fit the company's requirements. Data for this make-or-buy decision is gathered during systems analysis. For example, an important part of the feasibility study is identifying whether software is already available for the proposed system.

The decision to make or to purchase prewritten software can be made independent of the decision to acquire other system resources, such as hardware, service, and maintenance. Likewise, the other resources can be purchased independent of the software. Often, though, the hardware and vendor decisions are dependent upon the software decision. The flowchart in Fig. 11.1 summarizes the systems acquisition process.

This section discusses some basic considerations in selecting software, hardware, and vendors. Then it discusses how to request and evaluate vendor proposals for systems. Finally, it considers the issue of financing systems acquisitions.

Selecting Application Software

One can obtain application software by developing it internally, by buying a "canned" or "off-the-shelf" software package, or by buying a software package and modifying it. The advantages and disadvantages of each of these approaches are discussed below.

Custom Software. In the early days of computers almost all organizations designed and wrote their own application software, called **custom software**.

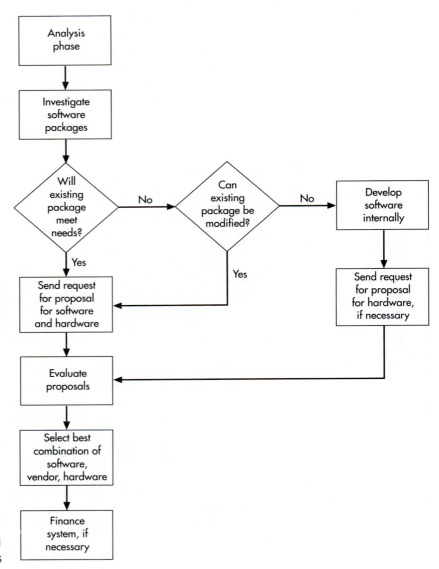

Figure 11.1
Systems acquisition process

Although a great deal of canned software is available, many organizations feel that their needs are unique or that their organizations are so
large and complex that the only way their needs can be met is by
developing custom software.

Custom software is usually developed and written in-house. Alternatively, an organization can engage a company (such as Andersen
Consulting or EDS) to custom-write an application package. Such
outsiders can sometimes assemble a customized package from their
inventory of program modules or components. These modules may be

adapted, added to, combined, and organized to form a customized product that meets a company's specific needs.

Developing custom software is a difficult and error-prone process that consumes a great deal of time and resources. End users must define their requirements, and an analyst must interpret these requirements and fashion them into a structure of programs, data files, inputs, and outputs. The analyst must work with users to determine the exact format of all output reports and terminal screen formats. Together they must identify all system inputs, the specific data elements required for each input, and the data to be retained in the files. The analyst must also develop detailed descriptions of all the internal processing logic necessary to produce the desired system output. These program specifications must then be interpreted and coded by a programmer.

Because of the many and varied tasks that must be accomplished, the entire process requires a significant amount of discipline and management supervision. A company must carefully control the development process, especially when contracting with personnel outside the organization. A company should also carefully choose a software developer. The software developer should have an in-depth understanding of how the company conducts business. A contract should be signed that places responsibility for meeting the company's requirements on the developer and that allows the company to discontinue the project if certain conditions are not met. All aspects of the software project should be designed in detail, and there should be frequent checkpoints for monitoring the project. The relationship between the company and the developer should be rigorously defined, and there should be frequent communication between them. Costs should be controlled tightly, and cash outflows should be minimized until the project has been completed and accepted.

Canned Software.   Written by computer manufacturers or software development companies, **canned software** is sold on the open market to a broad range of users with similar needs. Some developers combine their software with hardware and sell them as a package. These combinations are called **turnkey systems,** because the vendor installs the entire system and the user only has to "turn the key on" to get the system to function.

Producing custom software is labor-intensive and therefore quite expensive. As a result, more and more people are turning to the much less costly prepackaged, or canned, software. They see no reason to continually write programs that are available commercially. In fact, estimates indicate that as many as 80% of those installing computers today are either using or considering canned software packages. For example, many companies develop and market accounting software packages.

In the future it is likely that application systems will be developed in-house only by very large organizations and organizations that have

Table 11.1
Advantages and disadvantages
of custom, canned, and
modified software

Advantages	Disadvantages
Custom Software Approach	
A program can be tailored to meet exact needs.	The approach is costly and labor-intensive; even the smallest application may cost thousands of dollars.
The company can operate the way it wants, with no canned program limitations.	It usually takes months, or years, to develop.
The software is more compatible and integrated more easily with the organization's other software.	Few programs are bug-free when installed.
The company can manage and control the program development process.	Significant management time and stringent controls are required.
Employees may have a greater loyalty to a system they helped develop.	Standards for programming, development, and documentation must be developed.
A competitive advantage is possible by building a unique AIS.	There are many people concerns: availability, salary, promotion, supervision, etc.
	The development process can be frustrating; developers must analyze needs, develop the system, revise it, test it, debug it, revise it, etc.
	It is difficult for users to specify their needs or for developers to understand users' needs.
	The in-house staff may lack the specialized experience needed for the project.

unique requirements. However, even today many large organizations purchase software from outside suppliers. For example, Dun & Bradstreet Software recently signed two substantial contracts to lease its General Ledger software system. One was with San Francisco–based Pacific Gas & Electric Company, which awarded a $750,000 contract to D&B. The agreement calls for the license and installation of D&B's General Ledger software at the utility company to replace the existing in-house-developed general ledger system. Another was with Lockheed Aeromod Center, Inc., an aircraft maintenance services subsidiary of Lockheed Corporation. Lockheed signed a $1 million contract with D&B Software for the General Ledger system and related professional services. The software will be used to track direct and indirect expenses and determine project-specific revenue figures.

Modified Canned Software.   Some people feel that the best of both worlds can be achieved by customizing a canned package to meet users' specific needs—that is, by creating **modified canned software**. Modifications can be made by the creator of the software, by internal programmers,

Table 11.1
Continued

Advantages	Disadvantages
Canned Software Approach	
It is the least costly approach.	The software may not fit the company's needs. The changes required to use the software may not be in the company's best interests.
There is little delay; the software is ready to run.	An evaluation of the packages is time-consuming and costly.
The buyer can reduce risk by test-driving software and talking to other users.	Often the software is not as efficient as custom or modified software.
Users can select the package that best meets their needs.	No in-house expertise is available for solving software problems.
Programs are more likely to be bug-free.	The developer may go out of business or fail to maintain and update the package.
Updates are inexpensive.	
Highly specialized packages are difficult or expensive to duplicate.	
Better user documentation is provided.	
Modified Software Approach	
The software meets company needs and preferences better than canned software does.	Modification is difficult.
The company can operate the way it wants to, without canned program limitations.	Many vendors do not allow their programs to be modified. Unauthorized modification is not supported or updated.
The software is less costly and time-consuming than a custom program.	Documentation of changes may be nonexistent or incomplete.
The best mix of custom and canned benefits can be achieved.	Significant modifications may cost as much as a custom-written program.
	Modification may introduce program logic errors, control problems, etc.

by a third-party software vendor, or by other users of the same package.

Which Approach Is Best?   Because situations and conditions differ, there is no best approach. Each situation must be considered separately and evaluated on the basis of the relative advantages and disadvantages of the three approaches. A list of advantages and disadvantages is presented in Table 11.1.

As a general rule, canned software tends to be best when a package can be located that adequately meets an organization's needs or when the organization can adapt its needs to the capabilities of the package. This is especially true in cases where systems are small and company needs are not overly complex. As the size and complexity of the system or its requirements increase, there is less likelihood that the company will be able to find canned software that meets its needs or can be adapted to or modified. Many people believe that a company should never attempt to write custom software unless in-house, experienced programming personnel are available and the job cannot be done more cheaply on the outside. In the final analysis, an organization has to look at its specific needs and the software available on the market and decide what is best for it.

Selecting a Vendor

Any organization in the market for an information system must choose a vendor. There are many different types of vendors in the computer industry. Vendors can be found by looking in the phone book, getting referrals, scanning computer or trade magazines, attending conferences, or using search organizations. A list of the different types of vendors is presented in Table 11.2. An organization considering computer acquisition will find it worthwhile to consider the services of firms in several of these industry segments.

A number of organizations evaluate vendors as well as hardware and software products. Some, like Datapro, Computerworld Buyers Guide, and Auerbach, offer subscription services for an annual fee. Monthly magazines like *PC World* and *PC Magazine* and weekly newspapers like *InfoWorld* and *PC Week* also evaluate computer products and services and publish the results.

The computer industry is very competitive. Many hardware and software vendors have flourished for a while and then gone out of business. For example, Ashton-Tate was once the supplier of the best-selling data base package. Due to product development problems and economic hardships, it sold out to Borland. Osborne Computers produced the first portable PC, but it, too, fell on hard times and went out of business. There are also many people who offer computer services but who have little experience and little capital. As a result, it is important to be very selective when choosing a vendor.

Selecting Hardware

Many first-time buyers of computers are perplexed by the question "Which computer should I buy?" Obviously, the answer to this question depends on a user's specific needs and circumstances, but there will probably be a number of computers that can meet those needs. Often the right answer to this question is to first select the software that meets your needs and a vendor that will give you quality service. Then eliminate all of the computers that do not run the software that you need. Finally, choose the one that has the best combination of low cost, reliability, and dependable service.

Preparing Requests for Proposals

Once system requirements have been defined, the organization is ready to purchase the hardware and software it needs. If a company only needs a microcomputer, a word processor, and a spreadsheet, it usually can do its own research and make its selection.

	Vendor Type	Products and Services
Table 11.2 Vendors of hardware, software, and related services	Mainframe manufacturers	Manufacture and sell a wide range of general-purpose mainframe computer systems. Mainframes are most likely to be used by large organizations and governmental agencies. Many of these companies also provide software, maintenance, and other services. Examples include IBM, DEC, and Unisys.
	Minicomputer manufacturers	Manufacture smaller, less powerful computers that have many of the features and capabilities of the mainframes. Most mainframe manufacturers also produce minis.
	Microcomputer manufacturers	Manufacture microcomputers (also called personal or desktop computers). Most mainframe and minicomputer manufacturers also produce microcomputers.
	Peripheral equipment manufacturers	Manufacture a variety of input, output, and memory devices. Usually offer price and performance advantages over computer manufacturers.
	Computer leasing companies	Lease computers to users on a long-term basis.
	Turnkey suppliers	Purchase hardware from manufacturers and package it with application software that is tailored to that equipment and to the needs of specific customers. Called turnkey suppliers because the delivered systems are (theoretically) ready to be turned on and operated.
	Software vendors	Develop and sell application, general-purpose, utility, data base management, and other software programs for all sizes of computers.
	Supplies vendors	Produce items such as tapes, disks, diskettes, and forms.
	Outsourcers	Can manage an organization's in-house data processing facilities for a fee, operating under guidelines and schedules established by the user. Can provide data processing services on their own equipment for a fee; data may not be as secure as those processed in-house.
	Time-sharing vendors	Provide computer processing, on-line storage, and access to data banks to users for a fee. Users access computers interactively through remote terminals and telecommunication lines. Charges depend on time and other resources used or number of items accessed.

When a company is buying larger and more complex systems, the people making the selection often invite vendors or consultants to propose hardware and software that meet the organization's needs. At this point the company can decide to work with just one vendor or to ask two or more companies to propose systems. A company will consider only one vendor when it does not have the expertise, desire, or time to evaluate competitive proposals; when its needs can only be met by a single vendor; or when it wishes to reduce the conversion and training costs required to switch vendors. Usually, however, it is better to request various vendors to propose systems for consideration. This gives a company various options from which to choose and puts it in a better bargaining position.

When the decision is to consider more than one vendor, potential vendors are usually screened to determine which have products that appear to meet the company's needs. Vendors passing the initial screening are each sent a formal document called a **request for a proposal** (RFP) asking them to submit a proposal by a specified date. The proposals that are submitted are evaluated, and the best one or two systems are identified. These systems are then investigated in-depth to verify that they do indeed meet the company's needs.

A formalized approach to acquiring system resources, such as using an RFP, is important for a number of reasons. First, it saves time because the same information is given to all vendors, eliminating repetitive interviews and questions. Second, it simplifies the decision-making process, because all responses are written in the same format and based on the same information. Third, it reduces errors, because the chances of overlooking important factors are reduced. Fourth, it lessens the chances of disagreements and lawsuits, because the vendor knows what to expect and everything is in writing.

An RFP can be prepared through one of two approaches. One approach is to give exact hardware and software specifications. In response, vendors submit proposals specifying the cost at which they would supply the system described. The advantages of soliciting specific proposals are that total costs are usually lower and less time is required for vendor preparation and company evaluation. This approach, however, does not permit the vendor to recommend technology unknown to the requesting company, thereby placing total responsibility for determining the optimal system on the requesting company.

A second approach is to use a generalized RFP that contains a problem definition and requests a system that meets specific performance objectives and requirements. This approach forces the vendor to propose a solution. It allows the requesting company to leave the technical issues to the vendor, which generally will have highly experienced personnel prepare the proposal. The disadvantages of this approach include the greater difficulty of evaluating proposals and the potential for higher bids.

Generally speaking, the more information a company can provide to vendors, the better vendors will be able to specify a system that will meet the company's needs. Much of the information in an RFP can be drawn from the documentation produced during systems analysis. It is especially important that a company provide the vendors with the detailed specifications for the new system. This description of the proposed system should include the required applications, inputs and outputs (including their content and frequency), files and data bases, frequency and methods of file updating, and frequency of inquiry. It is also essential that the company distinguish between mandatory requirements and desirable requirements so that a vendor can determine if it can meet the company's essential needs.

After her tour of the administrative offices of Home Improvement Center and several of the stores, Ann Christy was convinced that the company needed to upgrade its computer hardware. In order to shorten the development time, she also wanted to investigate the possibility of purchasing at least some of the software needed by Home Improvement Center. She assigned several members of her staff to do a preliminary analysis of the company's needs. Using the results, she and her staff prepared an RFP and sent it out to several vendors. Table 11.3 shows the table of contents of the RFP that Ann and her team developed. It is representative of the information an RFP usually contains.

Table 11.3

Typical table of contents for a request for proposal

Home Improvement Center
Request for Proposal

Table of Contents

I. Executive Summary
II. Background Information
   A. History and Description of Company
   B. Overview of Existing Hardware and Software
   C. Summary of System Problems/Needs
III. Proposed System
   A. Objectives and Scope of Proposed System
   B. Description of Proposed System
   C. Implementation Schedule
   D. Cost Constraints
IV. Requirements
   A. Software
   B. Data Base
   C. Hardware
   D. Data Communications
   E. Training
   F. Maintenance
V. Instruction to Vendors
   A. Proposal Format
   B. Criteria for Evaluating Proposals
   C. Proposal Submission and Vendor Evaluation Dates
   D. Required References
VI. Summary

Evaluating Proposals and Selecting a System

After the vendors' proposals have been received, they must be evaluated. This evaluation can involve several passes, each requiring a greater level of detail. In the preliminary evaluation proposals that do not provide all the information requested in the RFP or that are ambiguous should be eliminated or returned for additional information. In addition, all proposals should be evaluated against the organization's mandatory requirements. If a proposal does not meet certain minimum requirements, it should be eliminated. The intent at this level is not to select the best system or vendor but to eliminate from further consideration those vendors whose proposals are inadequate.

Table 11.4 shows the list that Ann Christy used to perform her first pass through the vendor proposals she received. The proposal from Vendor 5 was returned with a request to provide the missing data. The vendor will be reconsidered if it submits the data needed and the proposed system meets the mandatory requirements. Vendor 4 was rejected since the system it proposed did not meet two of the mandatory requirements.

The second pass requires a detailed study of each proposal and an evaluation of the system. Each proposal should be read carefully and

Table 11.4

Home Improvement Center: Preliminary screening of vendor proposals

Evaluation Criteria	Vendors				
	1	2	3	4	5
Was all data needed to evaluate the proposal sent?	Y	Y	Y	Y	N
Is the proposal clear and unambiguous?	Y	Y	Y	Y	N
Does the proposed system meet the mandatory hardware requirements?					
Hardware is compatible with the vendor's next largest system.	Y	Y	Y	Y	?
Hardware can process data at speeds exceeding X MPS.	Y	Y	Y	Y	Y
Internal and external memory are both expandable.	Y	Y	Y	Y	Y
Hardware is not on the verge of technological obsolescence (introduced more than two years ago).	Y	Y	Y	Y	Y
Does the proposed system meet the mandatory software requirements?					
Software is compatible with existing software and proposed hardware.	Y	Y	Y	N	?
Software has on-line inquiry capabilities.	Y	Y	Y	Y	Y
Software contains adequate input, output, storage, and processing controls.	Y	Y	Y	Y	Y
Software has been installed elsewhere and the users are satisfied.	Y	Y	Y	Y	Y
Software documentation is adequate.	Y	Y	Y	Y	?
Software is easily maintained, and vendor updates it regularly.	Y	Y	Y	Y	Y
Software has LAN and WAN networking capabilities.	Y	Y	Y	N	Y

fully understood by those making the evaluation. The solution proposed by each vendor should be assessed to determine its feasibility and desirability. The proposals should be compared against the proposed system's requirements and against each other. The system should also be evaluated to determine what it can do and to validate the vendor's claims. The evaluation should measure the system's performance, determine if it actually meets all mandatory requirements, and determine how many of the desirable requirements it meets. The vendor should be asked to demonstrate the hardware and the software using company-supplied data. Sometimes vendors feel that it is too much of a bother and do not want to use the company-supplied data. This is a strong indicator that the vendor might not be very willing to provide the support needed after the sale is made. If the system cannot handle the company's data, the system should be eliminated from consideration. Table 11.5 presents a list of the criteria that can be used to evaluate hardware, software, and vendors.

There are several ways to compare vendor proposals. One popular means of comparing the performance of computer hardware and software is to use a **benchmark problem**—a data processing task with input, processing, and output jobs typical of those the new computer system will be required to perform. The times required to process the tasks on each system are then calculated and compared. The system having the lowest time is judged to be the most efficient.

A second approach is to use mathematical models to simulate the performance of each proposed system with respect to the complete processing requirements of the user. **Simulation analysis** can be very revealing, but it requires a detailed understanding of the proposed system's performance parameters. Unless an analyst feels very confident that the proposed system performance parameters are well understood, simulation should not be utilized.

A third approach is **point scoring**. The point-scoring approach that Ann and her team used at Home Improvement Center is shown in Table 11.6. Ann took the mandatory criteria listed in Table 11.4 and assigned each one a weighting factor based on its relative importance. Then each vendor was assigned a score for each criterion based on how well its proposal measured up to the ideal for that criterion. Summing the weighted scores gave Ann an overall score that she can use to compare the various vendors. From the point-scoring approach Vendor 3 offers the best system. Its system scored 190 points more than Vendor 2, the next closest vendor.

Point scoring provides an overall view of vendor proposals and how they compare. It allows the user to convert a mixture of factors into a common unit, a weighted rank. This focuses attention on the factors relevant to the decision process. However, care must be taken to avoid placing too much emphasis on the outcome of the point-scoring technique. This approach does not recognize that the factors being evaluated may interact in ways that are not taken into account. Nor does it

Table 11.5

Hardware, software, and vendor evaluation criteria

Hardware Evaluation
Is the cost of the hardware reasonable based on its capabilities and features?
Can the hardware run the desired software?
Are the CPU's processing speed and capabilities adequate for the intended use?
Are the secondary storage capabilities adequate?
Are the input and output speeds and capabilities adequate?
Does it have adequate communication capabilities?
Is the system expandable?
Is the hardware based on the most recent technology or on technology that is out of date or soon to be out of date?
Is the hardware available now? If not, when?
Is the system under consideration compatible with existing hardware, software, and peripherals?
How do evaluations of the system's performance compare with those of its competitors?
What is the availability and cost of support and maintenance?
What guarantees and warranties come with the system?
Are financing arrangements available? (If applicable.)

Software Evaluation
Does the package meet all mandatory specifications?
How well does the package meet desirable specifications?
Will program modifications be required to meet company needs?
Does the software contain adequate controls?
Is the performance (speed, accuracy, reliability, etc.) adequate?
How many other companies use the software?
Are other users satisfied with the package?
Is the package well documented?
Is the software compatible with existing corporate software?
Is the software user-friendly?
Can the software be demonstrated and test-driven?
Does it have an adequate warranty?
Is it flexible and easily maintained?
Is on-line inquiry of files and records possible?
Will the vendor keep the package up to date?

Table 11.5
Continued

Vendor Evaluation
How long has the vendor been in business?
How large is the vendor?
Is the vendor financially stable and secure?
How much experience does the vendor have with the product?
How well does it stand behind its products? How good is its guarantee?
Does the vendor regularly update its products?
Does the vendor have financing?
Will it put its promises in writing in a contract?
Will the vendor supply a list of customers in order to assess their satisfaction with the system?
Does the vendor have a reputation for reliability and dependability?
Does the vendor provide hardware and software support and maintenance?
Does it provide implementation and installation support?
Does it have high-quality, responsive, and experienced personnel?
Does it provide training?
How responsive and timely is the vendor support?

Table 11.6
Home Improvement Center:
Point-scoring evaluation
of vendor proposals

Criterion	Weight	Vendor 1 Score	Vendor 1 Weighted Score	Vendor 2 Score	Vendor 2 Weighted Score	Vendor 3 Score	Vendor 3 Weighted Score
Hardware compatibility	60	6	360	7	420	8	480
Hardware speed	30	6	180	10	300	5	150
Memory expandability	60	5	300	7	420	8	480
Hardware not obsolete	30	9	270	9	270	6	180
Software compatibility	90	7	630	7	630	9	810
On-line inquiry capabilities	40	9	360	10	400	8	320
Controls	50	7	350	6	300	9	450
Satisfied installed base	40	10	400	8	320	6	240
Documentation	30	9	270	8	240	7	210
Easily maintained; updated regularly	50	7	350	8	400	9	450
LAN and WAN capabilities	50	8	400	7	350	8	400
Vendor support	70	6	420	9	630	10	700
Total	600		4290		4680		4870

evaluate the effects of a particular weakness on other factors or assess compensating strengths. In addition, since both the weights and the points are assigned subjectively, the margin for error is sizable.

A fourth technique for evaluating the relative merits of proposed systems is known as requirements costing. In this approach a list is made of all the features required for the new system. If any feature is not present in a particular system, an estimate is made of the cost of purchasing or developing that feature for that system. The total cost for each system is computed by adding its acquisition cost to the cost of purchasing or developing any additional required features. The resulting sums represent the total costs for systems having all the required features and thus provide an equitable basis for comparing alternative systems.

Neither requirements costing nor point scoring is totally objective. A disadvantage of point scoring is that it does not incorporate dollar estimates of costs and benefits. Requirements costing partially overcomes this problem but generally overlooks intangible factors such as system reliability and vendor support. In any event, the final choice among vendor proposals is not likely to be a clear-cut decision. The decision cannot rest solely on objective criteria but must rely to some extent on subjective factors and cost considerations.

Once the best system has been selected, it should be investigated in even greater depth. The software should be test-driven more thoroughly, other users of the system should be contacted and interviewed or questioned, vendor personnel should be evaluated more thoroughly, and proposal details should be completely verified. In essence, the company wants to verify that the system that appears to be the best on paper actually is the best. The problems that Geophysical Systems Corporation had (see Focus 11.1) when it selected a company to

11.1 FOCUS

A Computer Runaway

Geophysical Systems Corporation developed a device that uses sonar to analyze the production potential of oil and gas discoveries. The company hired

Seismograph Service Corporation to create a $20-million computer system that would process its sonar-generated data. To its dismay, Geophysical found

that the Seismograph system could not accurately process the massive volume of data and perform the complex computations needed. When this became ap-

develop a system illustrate the importance of a thorough evaluation of the system. When the best system has been identified, the contract can be negotiated, financing arranged if necessary, and the system acquired.

Financing Systems Acquisition

Once a system has been selected, it must be financed by purchasing, renting, or leasing the system. A rental contract may generally be terminated with a few month's notice, whereas a leasing contract usually covers a fixed period of two to ten years. Rental payments are higher than lease payments for the equivalent hardware. Lease contracts usually allow the user to purchase the system at a specified price at the conclusion of the lease term. Under both plans the manufacturer provides maintenance of the equipment, and the charge for this service is included in the monthly payment. The terms of equipment purchase from a computer manufacturer are relatively straightforward. Equipment maintenance is handled by a separate contract payable on a monthly basis.

The relative advantages and disadvantages of purchasing, leasing, and renting are listed in Table 11.7.

It used to be that companies made the decision to acquire or upgrade a system somewhat independently of other financing decisions. That is, the feeling was that you *had* to have a computer system, so the expected return on investment was not as important as it was for other things. In recent years organizations have been much more selective, though. Information systems have to compete with other areas of the company for scarce financial resources. If the proposed system does not provide a greater return than other uses for funds, it does not get funded. That is one of the reasons why companies have begun to hire others to operate their information systems and process their data.

---

parent, Geophysical's clients canceled their contracts. As a result, the company went from sales of $40 million and profits of $6 million a year to filing for bankruptcy two years later.

Geophysical sued Seismograph, claiming that the supplier's system failed to perform as promised. In addition, it claimed that Seismograph knew the system would not be able to

perform as desired before it began the development project. The jury agreed, awarding Geophysical over $48 million as compensation for lost profits and the cost of the computer system. (Seismograph has appealed on the basis that its system did work and that Geophysical's sales decline resulted from a slump in oil prices.)

Geophysical's experience is

not uncommon; there are many runaway systems development projects. Therefore it is essential that companies carefully evaluate the feasibility of their purchase and the vendors that will supply it.

Source: Jeffrey Rothfeder, "Using the Law to Rein in Computer Runaways," *Business Week* (April 3, 1989): 70–76.

Table 11.7
Advantages and disadvantages
of purchasing, leasing, and
renting a computer

Advantages	Disadvantages
Purchasing	
The cumulative cash outflow is the lowest.	Up-front cost of purchasing ties up the company's capital.
The computer often has residual value at the disposal date.	Ownership has risks and responsibilities.
There are ownership advantages, such as total user control.	The equipment may become technologically obsolete or be outgrown.
The company can sell the computer at any time.	Maintenance services are not included in the price.
	Expenses such as taxes and insurance are incurred.
Leasing	
No up-front cost to purchase is incurred.	Cumulative cash outflow is higher than it is with purchasing.
It is less expensive than renting.	There is no ownership interest.
There is no risk of technological obsolescence.	It is less flexible than renting.
An option to purchase equipment is possible.	It involves a longer time commitment than renting.
It is more flexible than purchasing.	A fee is required if the lease is terminated early.
Renting	
There is no up-front purchase cost.	The cumulative cash outflow over the life of the computer is highest.
There is no long-term financial investment.	There is no ownership interest.
It is more flexible than leasing or purchasing.	Extra charges are possible if the computer is used more than a predetermined number of hours.
There is no risk of technological obsolescence.	
It minimizes risks, which is especially beneficial for inexperienced buyers.	
Maintenance charges are included in rental payments.	

OUTSOURCING

Another alternative to using the traditional SDLC to develop in-house applications is outsourcing. **Outsourcing** is the practice of hiring an outside company to handle all or part of the data processing activities. The extent to which a company's data processing is outsourced can range from routine assistance with a single application, such as payroll, to the entire information system. A company can outsource only its nonessential computing operations or it can outsource all operations, including systems development projects. The nature and extent of outsourcing agreements vary. Most outsourcing contracts are signed for five to ten years. The cost of the agreement depends on the extent of the outsourcing and can range from thousands to millions of dollars a year.

Outsourcing is a viable option for many organizations. A brief description of some of the largest outsourcing agreements that have been signed in the last few years is given in Table 11.8.

Under the more elaborate outsourcing agreements outsourcers buy their client's computers and hire all or most of their employees. They then operate and manage the entire system on the client's site, or they migrate the system to the outsourcer's computers. For example, natural gas producer Enron signed a $750-million agreement with EDS to outsource its entire information system. EDS bought Enron's computers, software, and transmission network. It also hired all 550 of Enron's information systems staff at comparable wages and benefits. Enron pays EDS a fixed annual fee, plus additional fees based on processing volume. During the 10-year life of the contract Enron expects to save $200 million, which is almost 25% of its computing costs.

The Growth in Outsourcing Applications

Outsourcing was initially used for standardized applications such as payroll, accounting, and purchasing. However, in 1989 Eastman Kodak surprised the business world by hiring three different companies to

Table 11.8
Sample of some of the largest outsourcing agreements

Organization	Agreement
Chase Manhattan Bank	Turned over an undisclosed portion of its IS operations to IBM's Integrated Systems Solutions Corporation (ISSC); savings of 30% on IS related expenses.
Continental Airlines	Signed a $2.1-billion outsourcing contract with EDS.
Continental Bank	Signed a $700-million, 10-year outsourcing contract with EDS. EDS will handle the company's computer and network operations. Applications development and maintenance has been subcontracted to Ernst and Young.
Eastman Kodak	Signed a $500-million, 5-year outsourcing contract with IBM.
Enron Corporation	Signed a $750-million outsourcing contract with EDS.
First American Bankshares	Signed a $400-million outsourcing contract with Perot Systems.
First City Bancorp.	Signed a $600-million outsourcing contract with IBM.
First Fidelity Bancorp.	Signed a $500-million outsourcing contract with EDS.
General Dynamics	Outsourced its entire IS operations, including applications development, to Computer Sciences Corporation (CSC) on a 10-year contract worth $3 billion.
National Car Rental	Signed a $500-million outsourcing contract with EDS.

operate its computer systems. Kodak sold its mainframes to IBM and outsourced its data processing operations to it. It outsourced its telecommunications functions to DEC and its PC operations to Businessland. Kodak continues to perform its own information systems strategic planning and systems development, but implementing and operating the systems is the responsibility of the three outsourcers. The results have been dramatic. Capital expenditures for computers have fallen 90%. Operating expenses have decreased between 10% and 20%. Over the 10-year period of the agreement Kodak expects the annual information systems savings to be about $130 million.

Kodak's decision led other organizations to consider outsourcing. Over 30% of IBM mainframe users are considering or actively pursuing outsourcing. Information systems consultants say that half of the corporations they work with will investigate outsourcing all or part of their information systems operations. The result, according to Stephen McClellan, a Merrill Lynch analyst who follows computer services and software, is that outsourcing has become the biggest trend in computing since the PC.

Current statistics support that statement. Outsourcing revenues were $5.9 billion in 1989 and are expected to grow about 27% a year and approach $21 billion by 1996. Only 3% of the $394 billion spent in the United States on information systems was spent on outsourcing in 1991. By 1995 that percentage is expected to be close to 8%. The 1990 Index Consulting Survey revealed that one-third of the businesses surveyed had turned over some aspect of their MIS operations to a third party. Dennie Welsh, president of IBM's ISSC subsidiary, says that IBM expects outsourcing to grow faster than any other part of the data processing industry.

In 1991 the *Vision 2000 Study* released by Arthur Andersen and the Bank Administration Institute predicted that the number of U.S. banks will fall by 25% over the next decade due to consolidation. As consolidations increase, banks will work to downsize operations and lower costs through outsourcing IS operations to third parties. Several major banks have already jumped on the outsourcing bandwagon, and many more are expected to follow. For example, NationsBank, the nation's largest superregional bank, entered into a 10-year outsourcing contract with Perot Systems valued at $200 million. Perot Systems will hire a number of the bank's employees to handle the newly acquired data centers throughout the South. Though already highly profitable, NationsBank sought lower IS costs by outsourcing the IS functions of a number of acquired companies.

Most companies that try outsourcing are satisfied with the results. Executive Insight Group conducted a survey of 103 *Fortune* 500 firms in 1991. Sixty of the firms surveyed were using outsourcers and 80% of them were satisfied with outsourcing.

The largest outsourcers in the world, sometimes referred to as the Big Five, have roughly 50% of the worldwide market for outsourcing.

The Big Five are EDS (with about 21% of the market), IBM (13%), Andersen Consulting (6%), Digital Equipment (6%), and Computer Sciences Corporation (5%). Most major computer manufacturers, computer consultants, and accounting firms also provide outsourcing services to clients.

The Benefits: Why the Outsourcing Trend Is Growing

There are a number of reasons why organizations are choosing to outsource all or some of their information systems functions. The benefits of outsourcing are explained in depth in this section. The risks of outsourcing are discussed in the next section.

An Attractive Business Solution. Outsourcing has become a plausible business solution, rather than just an information systems solution. Kodak and Enron both believe that outsourcing is a viable approach, strategically and economically. Kodak believes that it should focus on its ''core competencies,'' such as selling film, cameras, and its other products, which is what it does best. It feels that it should leave the data processing business to the computer companies, who are more qualified in that field. Kodak believes that its information systems are essential; it just does not feel that it needs to operate them itself. Instead, Kodak treats its outsourcers as partners and works closely with them to meet Kodak's strategic and operational data processing needs.

Some organizations that are reluctant to outsource their entire information system downsize them to core activities and outsource the nonessential and maintenance activities. For example, Copperweld Corporation, a tube maker in Pittsburgh, turned over its routine data processing to Genis Enterprises. Outsourcing reduced its information systems budget from $9 million to $4 million and its staff from 100 to 20. The 20 who remained were then free to concentrate on developing strategic information systems that will give the firm a competitive advantage in the marketplace.

Asset Utilization. Many organizations have millions of dollars tied up in information systems technology. Because information technology is changing so fast, the information systems function can drain cash as the company pours millions more into its data processing centers to keep up with the advancements. To alleviate this cash drain, more and more companies are trying outsourcing.

Health Dimensions, a hospital management company in San Jose, California, outsourced the data processing functions of its four hospitals. Outsourcing allowed it to use its limited monetary resources for equipment and people that increase revenues rather than in capital outlays for more computers.

There is also a great deal of cash value in data centers that companies can capitalize upon. They can improve their cash position in two ways: by selling those assets to an outsourcer for cash and by reducing their annual expenses. For example, when General Dynamics outsourced its information systems, it sold its data centers and other facilities to Computer Sciences Corporation for $200 million.

Access to Greater Expertise.   As systems technology becomes more complex and confusing, businesses are seeking the expertise and special services provided by outsourcers. Many of these companies simply cannot find people to manage and develop the increasingly complex networks required in today's businesses. Business changes (such as downsizing and reorganization) and growth (such as expanding the number of locations at which they do business) also lead companies to consider outsourcing.

Continental Bank turned to outsourcing because the cost and the time of the people required to keep the company at the cutting edge of technology was going up almost exponentially. Washington Water Power Company opted for outsourcing when the prospect of upgrading its system and replacing an obsolete computer seemed too daunting a task.

Economic Difficulties.   Cost pressures and a difficult economic climate force companies to consider staff reductions, cutbacks on employee training, data center consolidations, budget and resource cutbacks, and other reductions in overhead and costs. For many, outsourcing is an attractive way to resolve many economic problems. For instance, Foremost Insurance Company, a $374-million firm, was faced with spending $1.5 million to upgrade its system. It turned to outsourcing because it felt that outsourcing allowed the company to "move to the next level" of computing at a very reasonable cost.

Lower Costs.   Outsourcing is cost-effective for many firms, especially those that utilize their information systems resources inefficiently. Companies that outsource can benefit from the economies of scale the outsourcers achieve from standardizing users' applications, buying hardware at bulk prices, splitting development and maintenance costs between projects, and operating at higher volumes. Outsourcers pass along some of these savings, and most companies that outsource achieve savings of 15%–30% of their information systems costs. For example, Continental Bank will save about $100 million (20% of current information technology costs) over the next 10 years.

Using outsourcers also helps companies stabilize their costs. Companies typically pay outsourcers a set fee per month and an additional fee based on the number of items processed. These fees can all be charged off in the year incurred for income tax purposes, instead of having to depreciate computer equipment over a number of years.

Improved Development Time.   When systems development projects are outsourced, the company benefits from the skills of trained industry specialists who have installed many systems. Outsourcers often specialize in particular industries with unique computing needs. Outsourcers provide help with anything from assisting with development and design to handling the complete design and installation of a new system, including the selection of hardware and software. The steep learning curve for systems development allows the outsourcer to develop and implement a system faster and more efficiently than many companies can in-house. Outsourcers are also able to help a company cut through much of the company politics surrounding systems development.

Eliminating Use Peaks and Valleys.

Many organizations have seasonal businesses that require heavy computer use for part of the year and very light use the rest of the year. These companies need to have enough computer power to handle the peaks, but this power sits idle for the remainder of the year. The heavy fixed costs associated with meeting the peak uses can significantly eat into profits. Outsourcing can be used to solve this problem.

For example, from January to March W. Atlee Burpee & Company processes mail-order and wholesale requests for its seeds and gardening products. During this period its IBM 4381 mainframe operated at 80% capacity; it worked at 20% the rest of the time. Yet, the company had the same monthly leasing cost for the busy months as it had for the lean months. In addition, it had to pay the salary of five operators and managers for the whole year, even though they were underutilized most of the year. In November of 1992 Burpee hired an outsourcer, Computer Science Corporation, and it now pays the outsourcer according to how much it uses the system. Burpee will spend $1.8 million in processing fees during the five-year contract, which is half of what its mainframe system would have cost.

Facilitates Downsizing.

Companies that downsize can be left with an information systems function that is much too large for their needs. An example is General Dynamics, which in the early 1990s was forced to downsize dramatically due to reduced spending in the defense industry. When cutting a thousand information systems jobs did not solve its information systems problem, the company decided to outsource its IS operations. Outsourcing allowed General Dynamics to liquidate a huge IS function that was a liability in the downsized company. General Dynamics sold all of its data centers to Computer Sciences Corporation for $200 million and transferred 2600 employees to CSC. It signed a $3-billion, 10-year outsourcing contract. General Dynamics made this change even though its IS function was rated number 1 in the aerospace industry in 1989 and 1990.

The Risks of Outsourcing

In spite of the benefits and the high satisfaction associated with outsourcing, companies that outsource often experience one or more of the following drawbacks.

Inflexibility.

Most outsourcing contracts require a company to commit to services for an extended period of time, with 10-year agreements being the most common. If problems arise during this period, or if the company is not satisfied, it can be difficult to break the contract. In addition, outsourcing contracts are sometimes vague about how differences are to be resolved.

Any company entering into an outsourcing agreement should ensure that the contract clearly defines its requirements and specifies the means for resolving disputes. The company should seek a mutually beneficial arrangement that allows it to get out of the outsourcing agreement if certain conditions are not met. The company should also seek a contract that ties cost increases to improved company performance. That way, the outsourcer has additional motivation to help a company succeed.

Loss of Control.   When a company outsources significant portions of its information system, it runs the risk of losing control over its system. In addition, when an external company processes its business data, the company is exposed to possible abuse.

Reduced Competitive Advantage.   Over the long run there is a possibility that the company will lose a fundamental understanding of its own information system needs and how the system can provide it with competitive advantages. If a company's system does not continue to evolve and improve, it does not add value to the company and help it achieve its objectives.

Locked In.   Once a company makes the decision to outsource, it, in a sense, become locked into outsourcing. If a company outsources its entire information system and sells its data processing centers to the outsourcer, a return to processing its own data becomes very expensive and difficult. If the company is not able to buy back the data processing facilities from the outsourcer, it will have to buy new buildings and equipment and hire a new data processing staff. The costs and effort involved are often prohibitive.

Outsourcing is not a viable information systems approach for everyone. Of the companies that investigate outsourcing, only half will select outsourcing as a business strategy. However, for those companies that do elect to outsource, the benefits can be impressive. Outsourcing provides companies with a cost-effective alternative to developing and maintaining their own information systems resources. Before committing to outsourcing, though, management should thoroughly analyze the benefits *and* the drawbacks of this innovative approach.

PROTOTYPING

Prototyping is an approach to systems design in which a simplified working model, or **prototype**, of an information system is developed. The word *prototype* comes from the Greek words *protos* and *topos*, meaning "first model" or "first type." In essence, a prototype is a scaled-down, experimental version of the system requested by the users. This "first-draft" model is quickly and inexpensively built and given to users so that they can try it out. Experimenting with the prototype allows users to determine what it is that they would actually like the system to accomplish and what they like and don't like about the system. From their reactions and feedback the developers modify the system and again present it to the users. This iterative process of trial use and modification continues until the users are satisfied that the system adequately meets their needs.

The basic premise of prototyping is that it is much easier for most people to express what they like or dislike about an existing system (the prototype) than it is to imagine what they would like in a system. In other words, if users can work with an application, they will know immediately if it is what they want. Even a simple system that is not fully functional demonstrates the features of the system far better than do diagrams, drawings, verbal explanations, or volumes of documentation.

UNUM Life Insurance, the world's largest disability insurance carrier, used prototyping to show managers how a new system using image processing would work. UNUM realized that the systems it developed in the seventies and eighties merely automated its manual and paper processes. It wanted to use new technologies, such as image processing, to link UNUM's system with all external and internal systems and their users. However, top management had a hard time getting middle managers to envision how they wanted to use image processing and to understand the issues involved in the change. To help them understand, UNUM designed a prototype. When the managers saw the concept, they caught on to its possibilities and the issues they would have to deal with to make the change. Up until that point all image processing meant to them was replacing file cabinets; but after seeing the prototype, they realized the business potential.

Steps in Developing a Prototype

As shown in Fig. 11.2, four steps are involved in developing a prototype. The first step is to identify the basic requirements of the system. To do this, the developer meets with the user to agree on the size and scope of the system and to decide what should be included and what should be excluded from the system. They must also determine the outputs the user needs for decision making and for transaction processing as well as the inputs and data needed to produce these outputs. The emphasis is on *what* output should be produced rather than on *how* it should be produced. The developer must make sure that the user's expectations are realistic and that the user's basic information requirements can be met. From the general requirements identified during the meeting with the user, the designer develops cost, time, and other feasibility estimates for several alternative information system solutions that allow the user to determine whether to proceed with the project. Since only general requirements are identified for the initial prototype, the process of determining system requirements for the prototype is less formal and time-consuming than it is in the traditional SDLC approach. Detailed system requirements are developed by the users as they interact with the prototype.

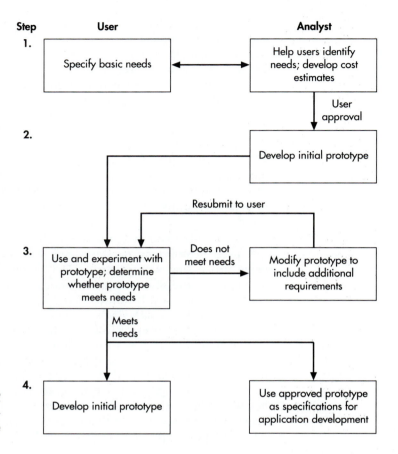

Figure 11.2
Steps followed in developing a system from a prototype

In the second step the analyst develops an initial prototype that meets the agreed-upon requirements. In building the prototype, the analyst emphasizes speed and low cost rather than efficiency of operation. The goal is to implement the prototype within a short time period, perhaps days or weeks. Nonessential functions, system controls, exception handling, validation of input data, processing speed, and efficiency considerations may be sacrificed in the interests of simplicity, flexibility, and ease of use. It is critical that users be able to see and use tentative versions of data entry display screens, menus, input prompts, and source documents. They also need to be able to respond to prompts, make inquiries of the system, judge response times, and issue commands.

A number of tools help system designers develop prototypes. These tools are efficient, are easy to use, and can create files, screens, reports, and program code much faster and with much less effort than conventional programming languages. They include fourth-generation languages, CASE tools, data bases, high-level query languages, generalized report writers, and various application software packages.

When the prototype is finished, the developer returns to users and demonstrates how to use the system. It is turned over to users with the understanding that the prototype is incomplete and will need to be modified. Users are instructed to experiment with the system and to write down everything that they do not like and want changed and everything that the system does not do that they would like it to do. When they have completed the list, they are to let the developer know so that the desired changes can be made.

The third step is an iterative process in which users identify changes, developers make changes, and the system is again turned over to users for evaluation and experimental use. This iterative process continues until the users are satisfied with the system. A typical prototype will go through four to six iterations.

The fourth step is to use the system approved by the users. As shown in Fig. 11.2, an approved prototype is typically used in one of two ways. Sometimes, the prototype becomes an operational system. Other times, the incomplete prototype serves as the specifications for a more complete systems development.

About half of the prototypes that are developed are turned into fully functional systems referred to as operational prototypes. To make the prototype operational, the developer must make any changes in the system that are required to incorporate needed controls, improve operational efficiency, provide backup and recovery, and integrate the prototype with the systems with which it interfaces. Changes must also be made, if necessary, so that the system will accept real input, access real data files, process data and make the necessary computations and calculations, and produce real output.

In many instances it is not practical to modify the prototype to make it a fully functional system. These prototypes are referred to as non-operational or throwaway prototypes and can be used in several ways. The prototype may be discarded, and the system requirements identified during the prototyping process can be used to develop a new system. The system development life cycle is followed to develop the system, with the prototype as the model for development. The prototype can also be used as the initial prototype for an expanded system designed to meet the needs of many different users. Finally, if the user and the developer decide that the system under consideration is not practical, the prototype can be discarded completely. The user learns that the system is not useful or desirable and the company has saved itself years of development work and a lot of money by avoiding the much more costly traditional SDLC process.

Advantages of Prototyping

The advantages of prototyping are described in detail in the following subsections.

Better Definition of User Needs. Because prototyping requires intensive end-user involvement, it almost always results in a better definition of user needs and requirements than does the traditional approach. It produces clear, concise functional specifications in situations where users find it hard to generate a complete and correct set of requirements before development starts or where requirements change significantly during development. Many users find that systems developed using prototypes do not have to be modified for quite some time because they were done "right." When significant changes are needed, it is usually because the business requirements have changed.

Higher User Involvement and Satisfaction.   Because prototype systems better meet users' requirements, they result in a much higher level of user satisfaction. This significantly reduces the risk that the implemented system will not be used. It also improves the productivity of the users and the designers, since they are better able to communicate with each other. Early user involvement also helps to build a climate of acceptance rather than skepticism and criticism about the new system.

Faster Development Time.   It only takes a few days or weeks to get a prototype system up and running. For instance, John Hancock Mutual Life Insurance developed the prototype of an executive information system in only one month, as described in Focus 11.2. This short development time allows users to immediately evaluate significant changes in the way business is transacted, because the user can see the results right away. In contrast, it may take a year or more under the traditional approach before the new system can be evaluated. During

---

11.2 FOCUS

Prototyping: The Third Dimension

An architect develops two-dimensional blueprints that show what a custom home will look like. But that is not the same as walking through a model of the proposed home. That third dimension, walking through the home, lets you actually see the rooms and get a feel for the layout. Creating customized software provides a similar

challenge. Users must try to visualize the look and feel of their software from written specifications. Prototypes are very helpful to users who have ideas or plans but do not know how to turn them into reality as well as to users who have a problem but don't know how to begin solving it. A prototype lets them "walk through" the proposed system

and experiment with its look and feel before committing to the expense of application development.

   John Hancock Mutual Life Insurance Company was dissatisfied with the traditional development process: determining user specifications (getting information from high-level executives was especially difficult),

that time the system approach being developed may no longer be useful, and enough time has passed for user resistance to build.

Fewer Errors. Because the user experiments with and uses each version of the prototype, errors are detected early in the development process and eliminated. As a result, the systems are more reliable and less costly to develop. In addition, it is much easier to identify and terminate an infeasible system before a great deal of time and expense have been incurred.

More Opportunity for Changes. In the traditional approach to systems development the design team must correctly identify system requirements the first time around, because at some point the requirements have to be frozen so that the team can complete the system. With prototyping, however, users continue to suggest changes to the system until it is exactly what they want. It is much easier and cheaper to change a prototype than it is to change the real system once it is in place.

Less Costly. Several studies have shown that some prototype systems can be developed for 10% to 20% of the cost of traditional systems. For example, one utilities company on the East Coast used prototyping to develop 10 major applications. It claimed a 13-to-1 improvement in development time over traditional methods using COBOL.

---

writing them up, developing the system, and presenting it to the end users. The typical reaction from a user was, "I may have said that is what I wanted, but it isn't what I want."

To counter these problems, Hancock used a prototyping approach to develop an executive information system (EIS). The EIS was needed because the company was very dissatisfied with its inability to get data easily and quickly from the existing system.

A team was formed. It included systems development personnel from IBM, user representatives, systems analysts, and programmers. The prototyping process was very interactive, and the continual involvement of the end users eliminated a great deal of misunderstanding. The programmers on the team started programming almost immediately. They prepared sample screens for the first interview session with users. The development people sat down with the users and showed them how the system would work. The users were then given a chance to try the screens. Almost immediately, users could determine whether what they said they wanted was really what they needed.

The result was a prototype for an executive information system that took only one month to build. The prototype allows top management at Hancock to access and query current and historical financial data and measurements. Top managers who had been skeptical when the project began were impressed by how much the team was able to accomplish in one short month.

Disadvantages of Prototyping

There are also some disadvantages to the prototyping process, and they are described in detail next.

Significant User Time.   The prototyping approach can be successful only if users are willing to devote a significant amount of time to working with the proposed system and providing the developer with feedback and suggestions. This may require a greater involvement and commitment than busy key users are willing to give.

Less Efficient Use of System Resources.   The shortcuts that make rapid prototyping iterations possible sometimes do not use computer resources very efficiently. As a result, systems design and programming may not be as sound for these prototype systems as they would be when the traditional system development is used. The result is poor performance and reliability and high maintenance and support costs. However, because systems are becoming cheaper and faster, this operational efficiency limitation is not as important as it used to be.

Incomplete Systems Development.   In some cases, such as large or complex systems, prototyping does not lead to a comprehensive and thorough requirements analysis. For example, a prototype may meet the needs of the immediate user but may fail to take into account the needs of those who feed information into the system or who use information produced by the system.

Inadequately Tested and Documented Systems.   Because prototypes are used heavily before acceptance, developers are often tempted to short-change the testing and documentation process. The lack of testing can make these systems error-prone, and the lack of documentation can make them hard to maintain.

Negative Behavioral Reactions.   When a prototype is a throwaway, users must be informed so that problems do not arise when they want to use the prototype instead of waiting for the final system to be developed. Users may also become dissatisfied if developers are unable to accommodate all their demands for improvements. In addition, dissatisfactions and impatience occur when users have to go through too many iterations. Finally, when people know that they are part of an experiment, their behavior may change, which may bias the prototype.

Never-Ending Development.   When prototyping is not managed properly, the prototype may never be completed, since business needs are constantly evolving and are continually being revised. In addition, unending iterations and revisions of the system may be proposed during prototyping because changes are so easy to make.

When to Use Prototyping

Although prototyping has a number of significant advantages, it is not necessarily the best systems development approach in all cases. In general, prototyping is appropriate when there is a high level of uncertainty about the system, when it is unclear what questions to ask, when

Table 11.9
Conditions that favor the
use of prototyping

Users do not understand their needs very well, or their needs change rapidly.
System requirements are hard to define.
Inputs and outputs of the system are not known.
The task to be performed is unstructured or semistructured.
Designers are uncertain about what technology to use.
The system to be developed is critical and needed quickly.
The risk associated with delivering the wrong system is high.
The users' reactions to the new system are important development considerations.
Many different design strategies must be tested.
The development staff is experienced with 4GL and other prototyping tools.
The design staff has little or no experience in developing the type of system or application under consideration.
The system will be used infrequently (and therefore processing efficiency is not a major concern).

the final system cannot be clearly visualized because the decision process is still unclear, when speed is an issue, or when there is a high likelihood of failure.

Systems that are especially good candidates for prototyping are decision support systems, executive information systems, expert systems, and information retrieval systems. It is also appropriate for systems that involve experimentation and trial-and-error development or where the requirements evolve as the system is used. Prototyping is not usually appropriate for large or complex systems that serve major organizational components or cross a number of organizational boundaries. Nor are they often used for developing standard accounting information systems such as accounts receivable, accounts payable, or inventory management.

In most cases prototyping supports the SDLC rather than replacing it entirely. Prototyping is not a substitute for careful requirements definition, structured design methodology, or thorough documentation. Nor can prototyping totally replace traditional development methodologies and tools.

A summary of the conditions that make prototyping an appropriate design methodology is presented in Table 11.9.

REENGINEERING BUSINESS PROCESSES

Between 1982 and 1992 almost a trillion dollars was spent on information technology. Notwithstanding that enormous investment, the productivity of the average American worker during that 10-year period did not increase significantly. In some cases it actually declined. Many management gurus, such as Michael Hammer, claim that one reason productivity did not increase significantly is that businesses kept their manual and paper flow processes and procedures and merely used computers to speed them up. As a result, businesses failed to make use of the processing capabilities of computers. By automating existing processes, companies just became more efficient at doing things the wrong way.

Most of the ways we do business today date back to earlier days when there were no computers and work was based on economies of scale and the specialization of labor. Work was organized as a sequence of separate tasks. Jobs were narrowly defined and structured so that a person did the same thing repeatedly. Work flowed between a number of such specialists. These workers did not have to do a lot of thinking or reasoning; they just had to carry out their assigned tasks as efficiently as possible.

Tracking mechanisms were introduced to track the progress of the workers and the tasks performed. Controls, such as checks and balances and approvals, were introduced to ensure and maintain high quality. An organizational structure was put in place that often had several layers of management and workers who checked the work of others. This approach was appropriate for boom times when demand was high and efficiency, standardization, control, and making and meeting goals were paramount.

In recent years the work environment has changed drastically. Increases in manufacturing capabilities have improved much more than demand has increased. Instead of having a limited supply of goods and services, we now have limited demand. Companies find themselves with too many manufacturing plants and employees. Many will have to downsize, some quite drastically, to survive. For example, General Motors and IBM have had to shut down production facilities and lay off hundreds or thousands of employees. Competition for sales is keen; the customer is king and demanding the greatest amount of value possible for his dollar. The world in general, and business in particular, is more complex, and companies are scrambling to change and adapt to the new environment. Companies have found that an attitude of "business as usual" is a sure formula for a shrinking market share, lower profitability, and, ultimately, financial ruin.

Current systems and data processing approaches are not designed to handle the flood of new information made available and to assimilate and take advantage of the steady stream of new technological advancements. What is needed is a new approach to business that dramatically increases key performance measures. Cutting fat, downsizing, and automating existing procedures is not sufficient. What is needed is an approach that is more flexible, innovative, customer-focused, and oriented toward quality, service, and speed.

With the advent of networks of powerful desktop computers, portable computers, and other advancements we have the technical capability to do things much differently than previous generations. With powerful data bases and almost unlimited storage we also have access to more and better information than we ever had before. In summary, an approach is needed that instead of paving cowpaths, blazes new trails.

What management gurus advocate is radical change—what they refer to as business process reengineering. **Reengineering** is the thorough analysis and complete redesign of all business processes and information systems to achieve dramatic performance improvements. It is not an evolutionary process or a process of making marginal improvements. Rather, it is a revolutionary process that challenges all of the old organization structures, rules, assumptions, work flows, job descriptions, management procedures, controls, and organizational values and culture that make businesses underperform.

Reengineering seeks to reduce a company to its essential **business processes**. It focuses on why those processes are done rather than on the details of how they are done. It then completely reshapes organizational work practices and information flows to take advantage of technological advancements. The objectives are to simplify the system, to make it more effective, and to improve a company's quality, service, and speed.

Some may argue that reengineering is not really an alternative to the SDLC, since many of the steps of the traditional cycle may be followed. For example, there must be an analysis as well as a conceptual and physical design phase. In addition, the system must be implemented and operated. However, the approach to reengineering—challenging everything about the system and radically redesigning it—is sufficiently different from the traditional approach that we have chosen to include its discussion in this chapter.

The Principles of Reengineering[1]

It is easy for someone to talk about what reengineering is and how it can benefit a company. But can those benefits be measured and quantified? CSC Index, an information systems consulting group, states that benefits can be measured in three ways: cost savings, time savings, and the reduction in defects. It measured these three aspects before and after helping 15 clients complete reengineering efforts. CSC found that fundamentally changing a business process produced an average improvement of 48% in cost, 80% in time, and 60% in defects.

Organizations have also measured the benefits they received. When Citibank reengineered a credit analysis system, its employees were able to spend 43% (instead of 9% previously) of their time recruiting new business instead of completing paperwork on closed deals. Profits increased by over 750% for a two-year period. Datacard Corporation reengineered its customer service operations and its sales increased sevenfold. A process that used to take up to a full day and five phone calls was replaced with one that took an hour. A reengineering effort at

---

[1] The source for much of this section is Michael Hammer, ''Reengineering Work: Don't Automate, Obliterate,'' *Harvard Business Review* (July/August 1990): 104–112.

CIGNA RE speeded up document processing even though the number of employees was reduced almost by half. American Express is currently engaged in 57 different reengineering efforts, each expected to save the company from $0.5 million to $50 million.

What are the secrets to reengineering? How can a company minimize the cost of reengineering and maximize the benefits received? Michael Hammer, one of the leading proponents of reengineering, has set forth what he calls the principles of reengineering. These guidelines, which have helped organizations successfully reengineer their business processes and find new ways to work, are discussed in the following subsections.

Organize Around Outcomes, Not Tasks.   In a reengineered system the traditional approach of dividing up the work required to complete a particular process and assigning different parts of the process to different people is not appropriate. This approach, with its numerous handoffs, results in delays and errors. Instead of subdividing a process, reengineering gives one person responsibility for the entire process, wherever possible. Each person's job is designed around an objective or an outcome, such as a finished component or a completed process, rather than one of many tasks necessary to produce the finished component or complete the process.

For example, at Mutual Benefit Life, an insurance company, approving an insurance application used to include 30 different steps performed by 19 people in 5 different departments. Handing the paperwork from one person to another resulted in an approval process of anywhere from 5 to 25 days. When MBL reengineered the application process, it did away with existing job descriptions and departmental boundaries. It now assigns all applications to a case manager, who has the power to perform all tasks necessary to approve the application. Case managers are supported by a number of automated information systems, including an expert system. They can also call on specialists for help with particularly difficult applications. Because one person is in charge of the entire process, files do not change hands, there are fewer errors, costs have decreased substantially, and turnaround time has improved dramatically. Case managers now handle more than twice the volume of new applications, allowing the company to eliminate 100 field positions. A new application can be processed in as little as 4 hours, and the average turnaround is now only 2–5 days.

Have Output Users Perform the Process.   The owners and managers of companies often split their companies into separate departments and have them specialize in specific tasks. Each department does its work and passes its ''product'' off to someone else. As a result, each department is a customer of another department. For example, accounting does only accounting, and purchasing does only purchasing. This system may work well when expensive items are being purchased, but consider the problem when accounting wants to order nonstrategic or inexpensive things, such as office supplies. It has to requisition the supplies from purchasing, which must select suppliers and order the goods. This system is slow and cumbersome, and it can actually cost more than the supplies themselves cost.

One large manufacturer had this exact problem before reengineering its business processes. The manufacturer took advantage of information technology and set up a computerized data base of approved vendors (maintained by purchasing), developed an expert system for purchasing nonstrategic items, and linked everyone together using a network. The new process allows users, with the help of the expert system and the data base, to order their own supplies. The purchasing process is now faster, simpler, and less costly, because the department that uses the supplies orders the supplies.

Have Those Who Produce Information Process It.   Most organizations process their acquisition/payment information like Ford Motor Company used to. Before reengineering Ford had its purchasing department prepare a multicopy purchase order. One copy was sent to the vendor, another was sent to accounts payable, and the third was kept by purchasing. When goods were received, the receiving department prepared a multicopy receiving report, sent one copy to accounts payable, and kept the other. The vendor prepared a multicopy invoice and sent one copy to accounts payable. Accounts payable processed all three documents and had to match 14 different data items on the three documents before a payment could be made. Accounts payable spent most of its time trying to reconcile all of the mismatches. Payments were delayed, vendors were unhappy, and the process was time-consuming and frustrating. It took more than 500 people in North America to process Ford's accounts payable.

In Ford's reengineered acquisition/payment system the people who produce the information also process it. Purchasing agents create and process their purchase orders by entering them into an on-line data base. Vendors ship the goods but send no invoice. When goods arrive, the receiving clerk enters three items of data into the system: part number, unit of measure, and supplier code. The computer matches the receiving information with the outstanding purchase order data to see if they correspond. If they do not match, the goods are returned. If they do match, the goods are accepted and the computer prepares a check for the vendor. The check is sent to the vendor by accounts payable. The reengineered system saves a significant amount of money, much of it by reducing staff in accounts payable by 75%.

Centralize and Disperse Data.   To achieve economies of scale and to eliminate bureaucracy and redundant resources, companies centralize operations. To be more responsive to their customers and to provide better service, companies decentralize operations. With current technology companies no longer have to choose between these two approaches. Corporatewide data bases can centralize data. Telecommunications technology can disburse data to the various locations. In effect, companies can have the advantages of both approaches.

Hewlett-Packard had a decentralized purchasing system that served the needs of the 50 different manufacturing units very well. However, HP could not take advantage of its extensive buying power to negotiate quantity discounts. So HP reengineered its system and introduced a Corporate Purchasing Department. This department developed and maintained a shared data base of approved vendors. Each plant continued to meet its unique needs by making its own purchases from the approved vendors. However, the corporate office tracked the purchases of all 50 plants and used that data to negotiate quantity discounts, win other concessions from the vendors, and resolve problems with vendors. The result was a significantly lower cost of goods purchased, a 50% reduction in lead times, a 75% reduction in failure rates, and a 150% improvement in on-time deliveries.

Integrate Parallel Activities.   Certain processes, such as product development, are performed in parallel and then integrated at the end. For example, Chrysler had many different teams, each working on the design of different parts for a new car. One team worked on the engine, another on the transmission, another on the frame, and so forth. Unfortunately, the teams often did not communicate as well as they should have. At the integration and testing phase they often found that the components did not fit together properly. As a result, they had to be redesigned, at considerable expense.

Chrysler reengineered its product development process and put people from each area on a team. Each team was in charge of a particular automobile. As a result, Chrysler was able to significantly reduce its product development time and reduce costly redesigns. This principle of reengineering also helped a large electronics company shorten its product development cycle by more than 50%.

Empower Workers, Use Built-In Controls, and Flatten the Organization Chart.   Most organizations have a layer of personnel that do the work and several layers of personnel that record, manage, audit, or control the efforts of others. The logic behind this structure is that the people doing the work are not able to make correct decisions or are not able to monitor and control the process themselves, or both. According to the empowerment reengineering principle, though, the people who do the work should be given decision-making responsibilities. This results in faster responses to problems and increases the quality of the task performed. Information technology, such as expert systems, can help workers make correct decisions and avoid mistakes. This reengineering principle also states that controls should be built into the process itself. For example, the system can be programmed to not proceed until all relevant data have been entered and edited by the system for validity, correctness, and reasonableness.

When Mutual Benefit Life empowered its case managers with decision-making ability, it was able to eliminate several layers of managers. Those who were retained changed their focus from supervision and control to support and facilitation.

Capture Data Once, at Its Source. Historically, each functional area of an organization designed and built its own information system. As a result, a particular piece of information was entered into several different applications. For example, a vendor number was entered in the accounts payable system and into the purchasing system. Each department had to collect the same piece of information (usually on different forms), enter it into its system, and store it. This process is both inefficient and expensive. In addition, there are discrepancies in the information between departments as a result of data capture and data entry errors.

However, in today's world we do not have to live with these problems. EDI and source data automation devices such as bar coding allow data to be captured electronically at its source. The data captured can be entered once in an on-line data base and made available to all who need it. This approach reduces errors, eliminates data processing delays, and reduces clerical and other costs.

A few years ago, management at Sun Microsystems became alarmed that its information systems could not easily communicate with each other. Some data had to be entered as many as 10 times into different incompatible systems. The system was reengineered, and now data entered into any system anywhere in the world is entered only once and made available to whoever needs it.

Underlying each of these seven principles is the efficient and effective use of the latest in information systems technology. In fact, reengineering would not be feasible at all if it were not for the many recent technological advances. Future advances will allow even more powerful and far-reaching reengineering efforts. For instance, imagine the impact that radio and satellite-based communication technology, coupled with very powerful hand-held computers, will have on the way companies do business in the future. Another new technology that should have a major impact on reengineering efforts is image processing. Paper documents can only be in one place at a time, but electronic images of a document can be used by multiple users simultaneously. "Active" documents that, when created, automatically know where to go will also have an impact. For example, suppose that you order a mail-order computer. After the salesclerk creates the active order, it will automatically be sent to shipping, inventory control, sales and marketing, your credit card company, and your customer record. With an active document the decision about where the information on the document is to go needs to be made only once. From then on, all orders are automatically sent to the appropriate location.

Challenges Faced by Reengineering Efforts

Reengineering business processes is challenging, and companies that begin reengineering projects can expect to face many obstacles. An understanding of the challenges and obstacles that companies face will help those undertaking a reengineering project have a better chance of succeeding. Here are some of the challenges that companies must face.

- *Tradition:* The inefficient business processes that are reengineered often are decades old, and traditional ways of doing things do not die easily. The traditional way of doing things often is a part of the culture of the organization. Thus the culture and beliefs held by individuals will also have to change.

- *Resistance:* Change, especially radical change, is always met with a great deal of resistance. Throughout the process those in charge of the project will need to continually reassure and persuade those affected that the changes will work and are needed.

- *Time requirements:* Reengineering is a lengthy process, almost always taking two or more years to complete.

- *Cost:* It is costly to thoroughly examine the way business is handled and to question the way everything is done in order to find a faster and more efficient way of accomplishing it.

- *Lack of management support:* Reengineering is still in its infancy. Since few companies have completed reengineering projects, many top managers have not yet been converted to its benefits. Many are afraid of the "big hype, few results" syndrome. Without top management support, reengineering has little chance of succeeding, because information systems management does not have enough power and influence to push through a reengineering project.

- *Risk:* Information systems management is aware that supporting a reengineering project can be a risky career move. If it is a success, they will be looked upon with great favor in the organization. If it is not, they may be looking for a new job.

- *Skepticism:* Some in the information systems community are skeptical about reengineering. Some view it as traditional systems development, but in a brand new wrapper with a fancy name. Others don't believe it can be done at all. One of the biggest obstacles to reengineering is outlasting the nonbelievers and the cynics who say it cannot be done.

- *Retraining:* In many reengineering projects the way work is done changes dramatically. Thus workers have to be retrained, which is time-consuming and expensive.

CASE CONCLUSION: THE SYSTEMS DEVELOPMENT PROCESS AT HOME IMPROVEMENT CENTER

Ann wasted no time in getting started on the new system for Home Improvement Center. She immediately assigned members of her staff to analyze the needs of the company. She assigned others to begin investigating prototyping, reengineering, outsourcing, and the acquisition of software and hardware. She took a tour of the administrative offices of Home Improvement Center and several of the stores.

The findings of the development team supported the beliefs of the Board of Directors. The existing system was antiquated and out of date. It did not take advantage of recent advancements in information technology. The system depended heavily on paper documents. For example, a great deal of paper shuffling was required to authorize the ordering of inventory, to place the order, and to pay vendors. Ann's team made the recommendation to top management that the entire system be reengineered.

The board was concerned about the amount of time that it would take to reengineer the system, but it realized that reengineering was the best way to gain the competitive advantage it wanted. Ann informed the board that several things could be done to decrease the development time. Perhaps the most important was to make use of some of the system developed at Shoppers Mart. The board gave her the approval to proceed.

In reengineering the system, Ann made use of the latest technological advancements. She required all vendors to bar-code all merchandise they sold to Home Improvement. Bar codes and point-of-sale (POS) devices are used to capture all sales data. Company service representatives in each store were instructed to enter into the computer all items the customers request that the store does not stock. The sales and not-in-stock data are fed into a centralized data base, and a program tracks and anticipates buying trends. When a buying trend is detected, either at an individual store or at a regional or national level, the stores are notified so that they can respond quickly. Each store is free to order goods electronically from the central warehouse or directly from approved buyers, depending on which is closer and which can provide the fastest service. When goods are received, they are matched with an approved purchase order, and an electronic payment is sent to the vendor. Corporate buyers monitor the individual store purchases and negotiate quantity discounts for the company.

To determine their needs, Ann had team members interview the users. From the data gathered in the interviews and from other data gathered during systems analysis, the team members developed a prototype of the system desired. The iterative process of presenting the prototype to the users, soliciting their feedback, and making revisions was followed until the system met the needs of users. The prototype then served as the systems requirements for that part of the system.

Ann considered the software that the vendors proposed. She also considered outsourcing a portion of the system. She decided against both approaches. Instead, wherever possible, she used elements of the system she developed at Shoppers Mart. Sometimes she was able to use elements of the system without having to adapt them. At other times she used elements of the system as a prototype to serve as a point of departure for determining user needs. However, Ann did use the vendor proposals to select and purchase the hardware she needed for the stores and the central office.

Ann and her team are able to reengineer the information system at Home Improvement Center and still meet the deadlines set for them. They find prototyping to be an invaluable tool. They also find that modifying the software written for Shoppers Mart is a big timesaver. After the system is developed, it is installed, and the company converts from the old system to the new one.

As time passes, the wisdom of the Board of Directors becomes evident. The system that Ann and her team designed does indeed provide the company with a competitive edge. It is not long before Home Improvement Center is not only the market leader but also very profitable. Nor does it take long for the company to decide to acquire other retail businesses and repeat their successes. ■

SUMMARY

There are a number of problems in the traditional systems development life cycle. They include backlogs of system development projects of up to two to three years, systems that do not meet users' needs, users who do not adequately specify their needs, and the difficulty of making changes to a system once systems requirements have been frozen. Several development approaches can help overcome these problems: purchasing prewritten software, outsourcing, prototyping, and reengineering business processes.

One alternative to developing custom software is to purchase canned software or to modify canned software. Companies will also need to acquire other system resources, such as hardware, service, and maintenance. Hardware and software are often purchased by sending vendors a request for a proposal. Vendor proposals are evaluated, and the system that best meets the users' needs is selected.

Outsourcing is another alternative to the traditional SDLC. In outsourcing, an organization hires an outside company to handle data processing activities. Outsourcing was initially used for standardized applications such as payroll, accounting, and purchasing. However, in recent years companies have begun outsourcing all aspects of their information systems. Most companies who try outsourcing are satisfied with the results. The organizations that are the leaders in providing outsourcing services are EDS, IBM, Andersen Consulting, Digital Equipment, and Computer Sciences Corporation.

Prototyping is developing a scaled-down version of a system so that users can experiment with it. Experimentation helps users determine what they like and don't like about the system. Four steps are followed in developing a prototype: (1) Identify the basic requirements of the system; (2) develop an initial prototype to meet the agreed-upon requirements; (3) identify and make changes to the prototype; (4) use the system. Some of the prototypes become fully functional operational prototypes. The rest are throwaway prototypes, but the system requirements identified during the prototyping process are used to develop a new system.

Reengineering is the analysis and redesign of business processes and information systems to achieve dramatic performance improvements. Reengineering reduces a company to its essential business processes and reshapes organizational work practices and information flows to take advantage of technological advancements. There are seven principles of reengineering: (1) Organize around outcomes, not tasks; (2) have output users perform the process; (3) have those who produce information process it; (4) centralize and disperse data; (5) integrate parallel activities; (6) empower workers, use built-in controls, and flatten the organization chart; and (7) capture data once, at its source. Underlying each of these seven principles is the efficient and effective use of the latest in information systems technology.

KEY TERMS

Define the following terms.

custom software	simulation analysis	operational prototypes
canned software	point scoring	nonoperational or throwaway
turnkey systems	requirements costing	prototypes
modified canned software	outsourcing	reengineering
request for a proposal	prototyping	business processes
benchmark problem	prototype	

DISCUSSION QUESTIONS

11.1 Large computer manufacturers generally employ very competent personnel who will assist a customer in designing a system at no charge or for a relatively small fee. Being good businesspeople interested in repeat sales, representatives of a computer manufacturer will consider the needs and objectives of the customer. Why, then, should a firm contemplating the acquisition of a computer system for the first time consider employing the relatively expensive services of an EDP consultant? What is the role of the accountant in the computer acquisition process. Should the accountant play an active role, or should all the work be left to computer experts? In what aspects of computer acquisition might the expertise of the accountant produce a useful contribution?

11.2 A city in the Midwest, with a population of 45,000, purchased a minicomputer from a major mainframe vendor and set about developing application programs with an in-house staff of programmers. Four years later, an analysis of the system showed that only one new major application system had been developed. Further analysis showed that the one program was neither complete nor functioning properly. Moreover, none of the application software running on the system met the minimum requirements of users. The system, both the hardware and the application software, frequently failed.

The analysis also showed that purchase of a similarly configured system, fully programmed with prewritten software, would have saved the city nearly half a million dollars. Moreover, the city's annual DP costs exceeded the annual costs of a brand-new turnkey system with packaged software.

Why would the city have been better off purchasing canned software? Do you think the city would have been able to find software to adequately meet its needs? Why do you think the city was unable to produce quality, workable systems?

11.3 Programs can be custom-made, prewritten and purchased, or prewritten and modified. All three alternatives have advantages and disadvantages. In this age of increasing computerization, which do you feel will become predominant? Do you feel that any of the methods will be phased out? Does your response vary depending on the type and size of user organization being considered?

11.4 Some organizations have a policy of acquiring all hardware and software from a single vendor. Discuss the advantages and disadvantages of this approach. (SMAC Examination, adapted)

11.5 You are a systems consultant for Cooper, Price, and Arthur, CPAs. During your country club's annual match play tournament, your second-round opponent is Frank Fender, owner of a large automobile dealership. During the course of the round Fender describes a proposal he has recently received from Turnkey Systems Corporation to install a computer in his dealership. The computer would take over data processing for inventories, receivables, payroll, accounts payable, and general ledger accounting. Turnkey personnel would install the system and train Fender's employees. The proposed system is to cost $70,000. Fender asks your opinion of this proposal. Without going into too much detail, identify the major themes you would try to touch upon in responding to his inquiry. Identify the advantages and disadvantages of using a turnkey system to operate the organization's accounting system.

11.6 Eastman Kodak is said to be the first major company to outsource its information system operations to another company. Kodak entered an approximate $500-million, ten-year contract with IBM, DEC, and BusinessLand to outsource Kodak's data processing. Some analysts expect that Kodak may cut its data processing budget by as much as 50%. Explain why Kodak would want to outsource. When a company outsources, should it give complete control of its information systems to the outsourcer?

11.7 Suppose that you are a Chief Information Officer (CIO) of a large company like Sony or Wal-Mart and that you are in charge of writing the contract for an eight-year, $750-million outsourcing contract with IBM. What kind of precautions would you take in writing the contract?

11.8 Sara Jones is the owner of a rapidly growing department store and faces stiff competition from similar businesses. The department store is using an old and out-of-date information system, and every day the store is getting further behind in processing its information. Lack of timely and efficient information processing is causing poor customer service, late or error-prone billing, and inefficient accounting of inventory. If Sara's department store is going to continue growing and successfully competing, the company must upgrade its system. Time is of the essence. However, the company is not exactly sure what it wants in its new information system. Sara has heard about a concept called prototyping, but she doesn't know what prototyping is and why it would or would not help her. What would you tell Sara if she asked you to define prototyping and to explain how it is done? Also include an explanation of the advantages and disadvantages of prototyping and the circumstances in which prototyping would be most appropriate.

11.9 Clint Grace is the owner of a chain of regional department stores. Grace has been in the department store business for over 30 years. He has definite ideas about how department stores should be run. He is financially conservative and is reluctant to make expenditures that do not have a clear financial payoff.

In recent years the stores' profitability has declined sharply. Customer dissatisfaction is at an all-time high. A store never knows exactly how much inventory is on hand and when purchases are needed until a shelf is empty. Grace asks you to study the reason for the sharp decline in profitability and to recommend a solution. During your research you find that the information system in place is inefficient and unreliable. You also find that the business processes and procedures the company uses are old and out of date.

You believe that the solution is to reengineer the business processes at the department stores and in the central office. What are some of the challenges you might face as you reengineer the business processes in Grace's department stores? With what you know about Grace's personality, how will you approach making the recommendation?

11.10 In the later part of 1992 CSC Index conducted a major survey called Critical Issues of Information Systems Management. CSC asked 407 top-level managers in North America and Europe to identify the greatest challenges they face in using and managing technology in 1993. Respondents of the survey listed reengineering as their number 1 challenge. Discuss the possible reasons for this response.

PROBLEMS

11.1 Don Otno is confused. He has been looking into software for several months but cannot decide which of three alternatives to choose. He has come to you for help.

Computers Made Easy (CME), a computer store located in Otno's office complex, was where Otno started his search. He almost wished he hadn't looked any further. Steve Young, the manager of CME, appeared to be very knowledgeable and listened attentively as Otno explained his problems, needs, and concerns. The manager asked Otno some hard questions, a number of which he couldn't answer. At the end of that first visit Young asked Otno to find out the answers to the questions he couldn't answer and to return the next day. Young felt he had the solution to Otno's problem.

The next day, Otno went back with the answers; and after discussing them, Young stated that he had a series of software packages that would, with a few exceptions, come fairly close to meeting Otno's needs. The packages would run on either of two high-powered microcomputers that Young carried. He could fix Otno up with a complete package, and Otno could start implementing the package almost immediately. The price for the whole system was unexpectedly reasonable.

Otno was impressed but cautious. He had heard too many stories about bad vendor choices when the buyer didn't shop around. His next visit was to Custom Designed Software (CDS), a company that sells hardware and writes customized software for its clients. This time Otno was prepared for all their questions, and after three hours he left convinced that CDS could produce a program that was exactly what he needed. Cost and time estimates hadn't been established, but CDS assured him that the cost would be reasonable and that the programs would only take a few months to complete.

Seeking a third opinion, Otno called a friend who had computerized several years ago. The friend recommended he visit Modified Software Unlimited (MSU). The MSU representative was very persuasive. She said customized packages were very good but expensive. Packaged software was inexpensive,

she said, but rarely met all your needs. The best of both worlds could be obtained by having MSU modify the package that came closest to meeting Otno's needs. The resultant software would, like the custom software, meet Otno's needs better than the packaged software but would be cheaper than the custom software.

On his way back to his office Otno stopped by CME and tactfully asked Young's opinion of customized software and modified packages. Steve expressed enough concerns about both types that Otno came full circle; he began thinking that packaged software was best.

Late that night Otno realized that he really wasn't qualified to make the decision. He was swayed by whichever vendor he was talking to at the time. The next morning he called you for help.

Recognizing the opportunity to render an important service, you agreed to counsel him. At Otno's request you undertook to conduct a study and submit a report showing the advantages and disadvantages of each vendor's approach. The report is to conclude with your recommendation.

Required

a. Outline the report contents, identifying the advantages and disadvantages of each approach.

b. Recommend the course of action that you feel would be best for Otno, and support your decision.

11.2 One unhappy federal agency recently spent almost $1 million on a software development contract that produced no usable software, the General Accounting Office (GAO) reported. The million-dollar boondoggle resulted from an agency contract to design an integrated personnel/payroll system originally contracted out for $445,158 and 15 months. The agency terminated the contract after 28 months with nothing to show for an expenditure of $970,000.

When it issued the request for proposals for the software, the agency was still in the initial stages of systems development. It had not fully developed user requirements or system specifications for any of the proposed software. The agency awarded a fixed price contract requiring phased software development, but it did not require agency approval of a completed phase before work continued. The contract did not contain acceptance testing procedures and did not identify quality criteria for documentation. Delivery dates, the scope of work, and costs were revised several times. The contractor complained of extensive changes requested and inexcusable delays caused by the agency. Agency officials acknowledged that some of the changes requested were not clearly identified in the contract and that others were obviously outside the scope of work.

The contractor further maintained that the agency took too much time to review products submitted for approval. The agency admitted the delays, but it blamed those delays on the poor quality of the documentation under review. The contractor did not clearly understand the software systems the agency desired because the contract did not specify system requirements or performance criteria. Both agency and contractor staff agreed that the contract was not specific, that the terminology was vague, and that many systems requirements were not clearly identified. The contractor did not wait for approval of completed phases before proceeding. When the agency rejected the general system design, the contractor had to scrap work already done on detailed system work.

User requirements were never adequately defined and frozen, and changes delayed completion schedules, increased contract costs, and caused the agency and the contractor to disagree about whether the new requirements were included in the original scope of work. The contract was amended 13 times to provide for additional work to be done to add or delete requirements and to reimburse the contractor for the extra costs resulting from agency-caused delays. The amendments increased the cost of the contract to $1,037,448.

The agency eventually became convinced that the contractor could not deliver at an acceptable time and cost, canceled the contract, and tried to withhold payment for poor performance. A negotiated settlement price of $970,000 was agreed upon. None of the software was ever used by the agency.[2]

Required

a. What went wrong in this particular case? Whose fault was it?

b. How could the agency have done a better job of managing the systems development project? Could the contractor?

c. Can we generalize from this case that organizations and governmental agencies should not try to have custom software written for them? Why or why not?

11.3 You are an accountant employed by the Argus Corporation. You are serving as a consultant on a software evaluation and selection project. The choice has been narrowed down to three software packages, and you have decided to use requirements costing to make the final choice.

You have gathered the following information.

■ Argus has identified five features, A, B, C, D, and E, that it would like the system to have.

■ Package 1 costs $100,000 and possesses all the desirable features except E. An optional routine that incorporates E can be purchased for an additional $20,000.

■ Package 2 costs $80,000 and possesses all features except B and E. Feature B can be developed at a cost of $25,000, and feature E can be developed for $10,000.

■ Package 3 costs $80,000 and possesses all features except B and D. For this package feature B can be constructed for $25,000 and feature D for $15,000.

Required

a. Determine the total cost required to acquire each package, with all desirable features included. Which package looks best?

b. Suppose that you could develop feature E for package 1 for $10,000, which would mean that you would not have to buy the optional subroutine associated with this feature. How would this change (if at all) your answer to part a?

c. Suppose that the project team decided that feature D was an unnecessary luxury that need not be developed. How would this change (if at all) your answer to part a? (*Note:* Ignore the changes in assumptions mentioned in part b.)

d. List some factors other than package features and costs that might affect your choice among these three packages.

11.4 The Schulte Corporation has recently decided to replace its computer system with a larger, more advanced model. Proposals have been received from three vendors. As chair of the evaluation committee, you have prepared a list of nine criteria for

---

2 Adapted from Jake Kirchner, "GAO Tells a $970,000 Horror Story," reprinted with permission from *Computerworld* (December 3, 1979): 12. Copyright 1979 by CW Communications/Inc., Framingham, Mass. 01701.

comparing these proposals and have ranked each vendor on a scale of 1 to 10 on each criterion. The criteria and assigned ranks are as follows.

Criterion	Vendor A	Vendor B	Vendor C
Hardware performance	9	8	6
Software capability	8	6	7
System reliability	7	9	6
Rental cost	7	6	9
Ease of use	7	8	7
Ease of conversion	8	9	6
Modularity	8	9	5
Vendor support	6	9	7
Documentation	8	7	6

You have prepared a tentative set of weightings for the nine criteria as follows: hardware performance, 50; software capability, 50; system reliability, 30; rental cost, 30; ease of use, 50; ease of conversion, 20; modularity, 20; vendor support, 50; documentation, 20. Upon reviewing these weights with the Manager of Information Systems, you receive the following reaction: "These weights are generally fine, except that vendor support isn't that critical to us anymore. We have an experienced and capable staff. I'd give that a weight of only about 20. On the other hand, software capability is extremely critical. How good is the operating system? What kind of utilities, data management packages, and compilers are they offering? I think that ought to rate a 70."

Required

a. Prepare a point-scoring analysis of the three vendor proposals using your tentative set of weights.

b. Prepare a point-scoring analysis using the weights as adjusted by the Manager of Information Systems.

c. What conclusions can you reach as a result of this analysis? Discuss.

11.5 A multinational engineering company that operates in 25 states and three countries was faced with a critical decision: choosing a network operating system to support the distributed structure of the enterprise. Selecting the right network operating system was vital. The operating system plays the biggest role in determining the functionality, manageability, and acceptance of the system by end users.

In order to choose from the many systems available to it, the company developed and followed a four-step approach:

Step 1: Develop and rate the evaluation criteria.

Step 2: Define the current and future operating environment.

Step 3: Identify and evaluate the network alternatives.

Step 4: Test and prototype target products.

With a plan in place the company set out to find the right network operating system.

Step 1: Develop the evaluation criteria. The company organized an evaluation committee and gave it a charge to develop proper evaluation criteria. Committee members spent several weeks interviewing the intended users to gather information about the features they were most interested in. A list of specific criteria follows.

Menu or graphical user interface
Ease of use
Scope of vendor support
Ease of LAN management and administration
Cost, speed, and performance
Wide area communications abilities
Ability to access other computing platforms
Security
Fault tolerance and recovery abilities
Ability to connect workstations to the LAN
Global naming services
Printing capabilities
Upgrade and enhancement options
Stability of vendor

The company then organized the criteria into four categories and prioritized them. The four categories are as follows:

1. *Business criteria* refer to overall business, economic, and competitive issues.

2. *Operational criteria* refer to tactical issues and operating characteristics.

3. *Organizational criteria* refer to people issues such as the impact of the LAN on the IS structure.

4. *Technical criteria* refer to hardware, software, and communications issues.

The evaluation committee then used a weighting scale of 1 to 5, with 5 as the highest, to select the top three evaluation criteria for each category. Criteria vital to short-term and long-term business goals were given a 5. "Wish list" criteria that were less important were usually weighted 3. Inapplicable criteria were given a 1. From this list of 12 criteria the company could then evaluate alternatives.

Step 2: Define the operating environment. A number of different data gathering techniques were used to gather data about the intended system. From this information the designers developed a model of the information system. The model revealed that the company needed to share accounting, sales, marketing, and engineering data at three organizational levels: the district, the division, and the home office. In addition, district offices needed access to centralized financial information to handle payroll. From these needs for data the company decided it needed a distributed LAN architecture that allows users throughout the organization access to company data.

Step 3: Identify the operating alternatives. Analyzing the myriad of alternate vendors and products took a lot of time and patience. The company used a number of methods to evaluate vendors and products. Using the criteria developed in step 1, the company evaluated each package on the basis of the most important criteria selected by the committee. Each committee member established personal matrixes for each product, and then the committee members compared notes during a roundtable discussion.

Step 4: Test and prototype products. The highest-scoring products were then tested further using prototypes. Finally, the company selected the product that "fit" the organization's needs most completely.[3]

Required

a. Discuss the role of the evaluation committee in the selection process. How should members of the committee be selected? What advantages come by using a committee to make the selection? What problems may arise?

b. What data gathering techniques could the engineering company use to assess user needs?

c. What is the benefit of analyzing the operating environment before selecting a LAN operating system? What data gathering techniques should a company employ in understanding the operating environment?

d. Discuss the data gathering methods available to the company in selecting a vendor.

e. In selecting a system using the point-scoring

method, how should the committee resolve scoring disputes? List at least two methods.

f. Assume that the point scoring approach narrowed the process to three candidates. Should a purchase decision be made on the point-scoring process alone? What other procedure(s) should the committee employ in making the final selection?

11.6 Mark Mitton is the accountant acting as liaison to the Information Systems Department for a medium-sized retail firm in Salem, Oregon. His boss has been investigating several small-business computer systems and has narrowed the selection down to three turnkey systems. Lacking the experience to make the final evaluation, he asked Mark to review the three systems and make a final recommendation.

Mark carefully reviewed each system, talked to other users of the system, and interviewed representatives of each system. Prior to his investigation Mark developed a shopping list of features he felt the system should have. Using a point-scoring system, Mark assigned weights to each factor to coincide with his evaluation of the importance of each factor in the overall selection process.

Mark developed a table to help him select from the three available turnkey systems (see Table 11.10). In evaluating each system, Mark considered the hardware and software the system provided and the vendor that supplies the entire package.

Required

Using a spreadsheet program, develop a point-scoring matrix to determine which of the three systems Mark should select.

a. On the basis of cumulative point totals, which of the three systems should Mark recommend?

b. Mark's co-worker, Susan Shelton, didn't agree with Mark's weighting of the selection criteria. Susan suggested that Mark adopt the following changes:

Flexibility	60	Reputation and reliability	50
Quality of support utilities	10	Graphics capability	10

On the basis of the changes, which vendor should Mark now recommend?

c. Mark made the adjustments suggested by Susan and submitted the information to his manager. His manager suggested the following changes to the current weighting scale:

Reputation and reliability	90	Training assistance	65

---

[3] *Source:* Robert Lem, "The Choice Is Yours," *Computerworld* (November 18, 1991): 85–86.

Table 11.10	Selection Criteria	Weight	System 1	System 2	System 3
Software, Vendor, and Hardware Selection	**Software**				
	Meets business needs	100	6	8	9
	Accepted in marketplace	30	6	7	6
	Quality of documentation	50	7	9	8
	Quality of warranty	50	4	8	7
	Ease of use	80	7	6	5
	Control features	50	9	7	9
	Flexibility	20	4	5	9
	Security features	30	4	4	8
	Modularity	30	8	5	4
	Integration with other software	30	8	9	6
	Quality of support utilities	50	9	8	5
	Vendor				
	Reputation and reliability	10	3	9	6
	Experience with similar systems	20	5	5	6
	Installation assistance	70	9	4	6
	Training assistance	35	4	8	6
	Timeliness of maintenance	35	5	4	4
	Hardware				
	Internal memory size (RAM)	70	5	6	8
	Diskette capacity	40	9	9	5
	Graphics capabilities	50	7	7	8
	Processing speed	30	8	8	5
	Overall performance	40	9	4	4
	Expandability	50	7	2	5
	Support for LAN technology	30	3	4	7

Experience with similar systems	40	Internal memory size	10
		Installation assistance	40

Will the manager's changes affect the decision about which system to buy?

d. What can you conclude about point scoring from the changes made by Susan and by Mark's manager? From your review of Mark's selection criteria, develop your own weighting scale to evaluate the selection of the three software packages. Justify your answers.

e. What are the weaknesses of the point-scoring method?

11.7 The following list outlines the activities a company may perform in the process of reengineering its business. Match each activity with one of the seven principles of reengineering.

Reengineering Activities

a. One person processes an employment application from beginning to end.

b. The department manager who will be using the yearly budget is the one who prepares the budget.

c. The Purchasing Manager has the authority to handle every aspect of making a purchase.

d. Each plant issues its own purchase orders, while

a new corporate department coordinates purchasing across all the plants.

e. All customer service representatives share a corporatewide data base that contains the sales data for each customer.

f. A salesclerk enters a customer's order into a computer terminal. The order is then automatically sent over the LAN to shipping, inventory control, and the Credit Manager. In addition, the master file is updated immediately.

g. Employee responsibilities are redesigned to allow engineers to manage and design their own projects.

h. An insurance claims adjuster goes directly to the scene of an accident and settles the claim immediately.

i. The person who does the preliminary research on a new product also uses the information to develop the product.

j. Each department in a large corporation orders its own supplies from an approved vendor list instead of having the Purchasing Department order the supplies.

k. The Receiving Department processes and prepares its own receiving reports instead of having the Accounting Department prepare the reports.

l. One person performs all the steps between selling and installing a computer system instead of having a different person perform each step.

Seven Principles of Reengineering

1. Organize the business and information system around outcomes, not individual tasks.

2. Have those who are going to use the output from the process perform the process.

3. Have those who produce information process it.

4. Use information technology to achieve the benefits of both centralization and decentralization of data.

5. Integrate parallel processes instead of performing them separately and trying to integrate them at the end of the process.

6. Flatten the organization chart by giving workers the power to make decisions and by controlling the process with built-in controls.

7. Capture data only once, at its source, using source data automation techniques.

11.8 Nielsen Marketing Research USA (NMR), with operations in 29 countries, is the recognized world leader in the production and dissemination of marketing information. Nielsen was a pioneer in the development of the decision support information business and has been the primary supplier of this information for over 70 years. Perhaps NMR's most recognizable product is the Nielsen ratings for television programs.

Nielsen is one of the largest users of computer capacity in the United States. Its information system has consistently been ranked above average in efficiency for its industry. However, it has recently commissioned IBM's Integrated Systems Solutions Corporation (ISSC) to evaluate the option of outsourcing NMR's information processing. NMR wants to know if outsourcing will allow it to concentrate on giving its customers value-added services and insights and if outsourcing can increase its flexibility, promote rapid growth, and provide it with more real-time information.[4]

Required

What are the benefits and risks to NMR of outsourcing? Do you think the benefits of outsourcing outweigh the risks? Why or why not?

11.9 The Pedaler, one of the largest bicycle manufacturers in the world, has grown significantly in the 20 years since it was formed. Eighteen years ago the company began using a computer to handle its data processing needs. During those 18 years several million dollars were spent on computer hardware and software. The company now employs over two hundred people to handle all the data processing needs.

For the past several years the data processing department has been very effective in handling the needs of the company. During the slow season data processing employees have light schedules, and many work on special projects for the company. During the peak season each employee averages five hours of overtime per week. Each year in the off-season most data processing employees spend one to two weeks at company-sponsored training seminars, where they learn about the latest data processing technology.

Recently, The Pedaler has grown so fast that the Data Processing Department is having a hard time keeping up with all its processing needs. Management realizes the tremendous benefit a data processing department provides but has been wondering

---

[4] *Source:* "Nielsen Commissions First-Ever Study to Explore Outsourcing Its Information Processing," *PR Newswire* (February 1, 1993).

whether it is worth expanding the Data Processing Department. This expansion will cost over $1 million in new equipment and office space over the next three years. The company is currently growing so fast that it has had to borrow money to fund the growth. Investing in a new data processing system will slow the growth or add significantly to debt.

At the last board of directors meeting outsourcing was suggested as a possible solution. Brian Cycle, the President of the company, has asked you, an independent consultant specializing in information system strategies, for your advice.

Required

Write a one-page memo explaining outsourcing and summarizing the benefits and drawbacks of outsourcing The Pedaler's data processing functions. Address the issues of whether outsourcing can save The Pedaler money and whether outsourcing can effectively meet the needs of a growing company.

11.10 Meredith Corporation publishes books and magazines, owns and operates television stations, and provides a real estate marketing and franchising service. Meredith is dissatisfied with its ability to retrieve correct and timely inventory information from its information system. Each division either developed its own inventory system or already had a system when it was acquired by Meredith. As a result, Meredith has 11 different systems to track inventory, and the systems are unable to communicate with each other. Meredith recognizes that it needs a single inventory system that all divisions use and that ties the different parts of the company together. The systems must be ready to use within a short period of time. Because of the time constraints and the diverse needs of the different divisions, Meredith has decided to use prototyping to develop the new system.

Management is already aware of some of the company's needs. Management wants to know at a moment's notice how many books of any given title are on hand and where they are being stored. It also wants to know how much inventory is on hand, in process, and available for sale, and whether or not any back-order problems exist. In summary, it wants to tie the different systems together and have one consistent inventory pool from which to extract the information needed for making good business decisions.

Required

a. List three questions that you could use when interviewing Meredith's personnel to determine the basic requirements of the system. Explain why you would ask that question, and describe the information you hope to receive by asking it.

b. From the description of Meredith, what do you think some of its information needs are?

c. Explain how the prototyping process would work at Meredith. What you would do during the iterative process step. How many iterations would be realistic for this prototype? Why would you want the fewest iterations possible?

d. As you develop the prototype, what do you want to ignore, and what do you feel is critical in order to quickly develop a good production-tracking system?

e. What types of tools will you want to consider using while designing your prototype? Why would you use these tools instead of conventional programming languages?

f. Would you want this prototype to be operational or nonoperational? Why? If it were an operational prototype, what would have to happen? If it were a nonoperational prototype, how would the prototype be used?

g. Suppose that the result of the prototyping process is that the company decides that the system is not practical. It abandons the system and takes some other approach to solving its inventory problem. Does that mean that prototyping is not a valid systems development approach?

11.11 The management of Quickfix would like to decrease costs and increase customer service by reengineering its computer repair procedures. Currently, when a defective or broken computer needs servicing, the customer calls one of five regional customer service centers. A customer service representative manually records information about the customer and what needs to be repaired in a log. The customer service representative then searches through a list of qualified technicians to find the one closest to the customer. That technician is then called on the phone to see if he or she can handle the repair. If the technician is unable to work the repair into the schedule, the representative looks for the next closest technician and calls him. When a technician who can perform the service is located, he is given the customer information over the phone and told what needs to be repaired. The technician then calls the customer and makes arrangements to pick up the broken computer and replace it with a loaner while the broken one is being fixed. Making these arrangements takes one to two days and sometimes more if technicians are not available and do not promptly return phone calls.

The broken computer is sent to a repair depot. Typically, the entire repair process takes another four to seven days. Overall, it can take up to three weeks for an item to be repaired.

When a customer calls to see if the item is repaired, the customer service representative tells the customer that she will check on the repaired item and call the customer back. The customer service representative then calls the technician, finds out the status of the item, and calls the customer back. Throughout the entire repair process usually five phone calls take place between the customer, the customer service representative, and the technician.

There are three main problems with this process: (1) it is time-consuming; (2) it is an inconvenience for customers to have their computer removed, a new one installed, and then the old one reinstalled when fixed; and (3) customer service representatives do not have immediate access to information about items currently being repaired.

Required

a. Identify the most basic activities that occur when an item is repaired and that the reengineered process should be developed around.

b. Describe how the current repair process can be reengineered to achieve the goal of more timely repair and increased customer service.

c. What will be the specific benefits of reengineering the repair process?

Case 11.1 ANYCOMPANY, INC.: AN ONGOING COMPREHENSIVE CASE

One of the best ways to learn is to immediately apply what you have studied. The purpose of this case is to allow you to do that. You will select a local company that you can work with. At the end of most chapters you will find an assignment that will have you apply what you have learned using the company you have selected as a reference. This case, then, may become an ongoing case study that you work on throughout the term.

Visit several small- to medium-sized businesses in the local community. Explain that you will be doing a term-long case, and ask for permission to use the company as the firm you are going to study. Explain that you will need to meet with people in the company several times during the term to get the information you need. However, you will not need a great deal of their time or be a disruption to them. Offer to share any observations or suggestions that you can come up with as a way of allowing the firm to feel good about helping you.

Once you have lined up a company, perform the following steps.

1.   With a member of the information systems staff, discuss the following issues.

a.   What procedures does the company follow in determining the hardware and software resources needed? How does the company select software, hardware, and a vendor?

b.   Does the company now outsource any of its data processing activities? If so, what benefits is it now deriving, and what risks is it exposed to? Does the company think the decision was a good one? If the company does not now outsource, has it considered the option? If it considered outsourcing and rejected it, why did it reject the option? If it has not considered outsourcing, explain outsourcing, and ask how viable it thinks the option would be.

c.   Does the company use prototyping? If it has, what benefits did it derive from the prototype? What were the disadvantages with respect to the prototype? Has the company continued to use prototypes, or has it discontinued their use? If it has not used a prototype, has it considered the approach? If the company considered prototyping and rejected it, why did it reject prototyping? If it has not considered prototyping, explain prototyping, and ask the company if it thinks the approach can benefit it.

d.   Is the company familiar with the reengineering process? Has it ever attempted a reengineering project? If so, how did it benefit? What problems did it experience with the project? Will it continue to reengineer its business processes? If the company is not familiar with reengineering, explain the principles of reengineering and describe the difficulties faced by those who reengineer. Ask the company how feasible it thinks the approach would be for it.

2.   Summarize your findings in a report.

CASE 11.2 WIDGET MANUFACTURING COMPANY

The Widget Manufacturing Company is a major producer of widgets, with total sales of $50 million annually. Its Information Systems Department currently has an ABC Model 115 computer, which operates 12 hours per day, five days per week, processing payroll, general accounting, inventory control, and accounts receivable in batch mode. This equipment also supports an on-line order entry system with four workstations located in the Sales Department. This application processes an average of 240,000 transactions per year.

The company prepared a two-year information systems plan. D. MacTavish, the Director of Information Systems for Widget, determined that the present computer could absorb any additional workload caused by rapidly increasing sales. This increase could be handled by scheduling a full second shift and possibly a third shift. The present computer would not have sufficient memory or be fast enough, however, to handle a new production-scheduling system that was planned and that would require more workstations be added in the Production Planning Department and at several locations throughout the plant. This new system would increase the number of workstation transactions by approximately 720,000 per year but would require approximately one year to develop and implement following the availability of a new system.

After a presentation to the President and Executive Committee, MacTavish was authorized to prepare the hardware and software specifications for a system that would meet the needs of Widget for the next two years. Also, because the company was expanding so quickly, the President asked MacTavish to include the cost of renting space in a nearby office building in which the entire Information Systems Department could be located. This would provide space in the Widget head office building for additional staff that were needed by other company departments. The Widget Information Systems Department currently occupies approximately 3300 square feet of space in the basement of the Widget head office building. MacTavish was asked to prepare a financial summary showing the cost of the present and proposed systems for presentation to the company's Board of Directors.

MacTavish prepared the specifications for the new systems and sent them to the ABC Computer Company, the supplier of the present computer. He also invited the PQR Company to submit a proposal for its equipment and software, and he decided to ask XYZ, an outsourcing company, to respond with the prices it would charge to process Widget's information. Included in the specifications were all processing volumes and transaction rates for existing and proposed applications. Also included was the fact that Widget uses 75 magnetic tapes for backup storage of important disk files. This figure was expected to increase to 100 tapes with the implementation of the production-scheduling system.

The important facts from each of the three proposals MacTavish received follow.

The ABC proposal: The ABC representative recommended a Model 138 computer that leased for $273,478 per year. This system would have sufficient memory and be fast enough to handle all current applications plus the new system. Since it is also a member of the same "family" of computers as Widget's Model 115, it would use the same software as the 115 and therefore require the same amount of training as was needed on the present equipment. He pointed out, however, that the larger 138 could use a new series of workstations that ABC had recently announced and would enable Widget to acquire the additional workstations it needed to replace its present terminals at a total cost of $14,100 per year for the two years. This new system would require the same space as the present Model 115.

The PQR proposal: The PQR Company recommended a Model 906 system. The equipment that would be located in the Widget computer center would cost $213,660 per year, and all of the necessary workstations would be supplied at a cost of $9468. PQR's marketing policy differed from that of ABC in that all software and staff training costs were included in the price of the equipment. It also was willing to provide a discount of $66,000 during the second year if Widget would sign a two-year lease for the equipment. The PQR proposal indicated that its equipment would fit into an area equivalent to that occupied by the present computer.

The XYZ proposal: The XYZ outsourcing proposal involved the installation of a minicomputer at the Widget computer center that would be used for editing and balancing all batch input. The data would be sent over a telephone line several times a day to a large computer located at the outsourcing company, where it would be processed. Output would be returned to Widget over the same communications line to the minicomputer, where it would be stored on a disk until it could be printed out and distributed. The on-line order entry system and the new production-scheduling system would use workstations connected to the large computer at XYZ, and any printed output from these systems would be sent by telephone line to the minicomputer for printing and distribution. The cost to Widget for leasing the minicomputer would be $32,724 per year, and workstations would be leased for $11,000 annually. The cost of the communications line between the minicomputer at the Widget offices and the large system at XYZ would be $21,420 each year, with an installation charge the first year of $4020.

On the basis of benchmark tests using existing Widget programs, XYZ estimated that the cost of running all batch programs would be $132,000 per year. The cost of storing the backup tapes for Widget would be $1 per tape per year.

XYZ used a price schedule for on-line applications based on the number of transactions entered through the workstations. Its price was quoted at 10¢ per transaction. Software charges were included in the prices quoted. As an incentive to Widget, XYZ offered a volume discount of $109,800 during the second year and agreed to provide all necessary training of Widget staff during the first year of the agreement at no cost. Widget would have to pay for training during the second year. Since XYZ used an ABC computer, Widget staff could take the same courses and at the same cost as they would have required had the larger ABC machine been selected.

In the opinion of XYZ, the installation of a minicomputer by Widget would reduce the computer center space requirements by 450 square feet.

During negotiations for a nearby office building MacTavish was able to negotiate the lease of space for his department at a rate of $10 per square foot per year, the amount of space dependent on the alternative selected by Widget's Board of Directors.

Present computer costs are as follows:

Central site hardware (per month)	$16,764.00
Software (per month)	1,516.00
Workstations (per month)	1,292.50
Training costs (total annual cost)	7,000.00

Note: All hardware and software is leased. The company follows the policy of capitalizing lease payments for financial statement purposes.

As MacTavish, write a report to the Board of Directors recommending which proposal to accept. Include the quantitative and qualitative aspects of each proposal. Indicate what impact, if any, the decision regarding the development of the proposed production-scheduling system would have on your recommendation.   (SMAC Examination, adapted)

PART IV

CHAPTER 12

Control and Accounting Information Systems

LEARNING OBJECTIVES

After studying this chapter, you should be able to:

■ Explain the basic concepts of control in business organizations.

■ Describe the major elements in the control environment of a business organization.

■ Describe several of the control policies and procedures most commonly used in business organizations.

■ Evaluate a system of internal accounting control, identify its deficiencies, and prescribe modifications to remedy those deficiencies.

■ Perform a quantitative analysis of internal control risks and exposures.

INTEGRATIVE CASE:
SPRINGER'S
NORTHWEST LUMBER
& SUPPLY

Jason Scott is thrilled to be starting his new job. After completing his bachelor's degree in accounting at Idaho State, Jason has been hired as an internal auditor for Northwest Industries, a large and diversified forest products company involved in logging, production of lumber and paper products, and wholesale and retail distribution of lumber and building materials. After a week of training he has been assigned to the audit of Springer's Northwest Lumber & Supply, a large building materials outlet in Bozeman, Montana, that is 90% owned by Northwest Industries. For his first assignment his supervisor, Susan Lee, has asked him to trace a sample of purchase transactions through an entire accounting cycle, from purchase requisition to cash disbursement, to verify that proper control procedures have been followed.

However, by midafternoon Jason is becoming frustrated. The purchasing system is poorly documented, so Jason has discussed how it works with Ed Yates, the Accounts Payable Manager. But he keeps finding transactions that have not been processed as Yates had described. Purchase requisitions are missing for several items. Yates pointed out that these had been personally authorized by Bill Springer, the Purchasing Vice-President. Some vendor invoices have been paid without supporting documents such as purchase orders or receiving reports. Prices charged for some items seem unusually high to Jason, and he notices a few discrepancies in item prices between the vendor invoice and the corresponding purchase order. Yates seems to have a logical answer for every question raised, culminating with his advice to Jason that the real world is not always as tidy as the world portrayed in college textbooks.

At dinner that evening Jason discusses his findings with Susan Lee. He is surprised to learn that she also has some concerns. According to Susan, Springer's Northwest is the largest building materials supplier in the Bozeman area, having a near monopoly on the business. Management authority is concentrated in the company President, Joe Springer, and his two sons Bill (the Purchasing VP) and Ted (the Controller). Several other relatives and friends of the family are on the payroll. Lines of authority and responsibility within the company are loosely defined and hard to understand, according to Susan. While the company has always been one of Northwest Industries' best-performing retail outlets, Susan feels that Ted Springer may have engaged in "creative accounting" in order to keep that record intact.

While returning to his room after dinner, Jason reflects on his first day on the job. In particular, he ponders the following issues:

1. Since Ed Yates had a logical explanation for every unusual transaction that Jason found, should Jason describe these transactions in his audit report?

2. Is a violation of proper control procedures acceptable if it has been authorized by management?

3. Susan Lee's concerns about Springer's loosely defined lines of authority, possible use of "creative accounting," and so on, are matters of management policy. What do these matters have to do with the proper application of control procedures? ∎

INTRODUCTION

In an abstract sense, control is the process of exercising a restraining or directing influence over the activities of an object, organism, or system. Assisting management in the control of a business organization is one of the primary objectives of accounting information systems.

The accountant can help achieve this objective by designing effective control systems and by auditing (or reviewing) control systems that are in place to ensure that they are operating effectively. The four chapters in Part 4 of this text focus on the control and audit of accounting information systems in business organizations.

The goal of control is to prevent losses to the organization arising from several possible hazards:

1. Wasteful and inefficient use of resources
2. Poor management decisions
3. Unintentional errors in recording or processing data
4. Accidental loss or destruction of records
5. Loss of assets through employees' carelessness or pilferage
6. Lack of compliance by employees with management policies or government regulations
7. **Embezzlement**, which is the theft or misappropriation of assets by employees, accompanied by the falsification of records in order to conceal the theft
8. Other illegal acts by employees, such as the taking of a bribe

Such hazards are often referred to as **threats**. The dollar amount that could be lost if a particular threat became a reality is referred to as the **exposure** from the threat, and the likelihood that the threat will actually come to pass is referred to as the **risk** associated with the threat.

This chapter explains the general principles of control in business organizations and describes key control procedures most suitable for typical accounting information systems. Chapter 13 describes how the general principles of control apply to computer-based information systems and explains the control procedures most applicable to computer-based accounting information systems. Chapter 14 provides an in-depth examination of the causes and remedies for computer fraud, one of the most substantial threats faced by modern control systems. Finally, Chapter 15 examines the processes and procedures used in auditing computer-based accounting information systems.

OVERVIEW OF CONTROL CONCEPTS

A host of different control concepts—including internal control, management control, feedback control, and preventive control—can be used to describe the principles of control in business organizations. This section explains these and related control concepts in order to set the stage for the subsequent description of control principles and procedures.

A Brief History

Accountants often use the term **internal control** to refer to control within business organizations. The term was first defined in 1949 by a committee of the American Institute of Accountants (now named the American Institute of Certified Public Accountants, or AICPA), as follows:

> *Internal control comprises the plan of organization and all of the coordinate methods and measures adopted within a business to safeguard its assets, check the accuracy and reliability of its accounting data, promote operational efficiency, and encourage adherence to prescribed managerial policies.*[1]

After 1949 the AICPA published a number of extensions and clarifications of this definition. For example, a 1958 pronouncement drew the following distinction between **accounting controls** and **administrative controls**

> Accounting controls *comprise the plan of organization and all methods and procedures that are concerned mainly with, and relate directly to, the safeguarding of assets and the reliability of the financial records. . . .* Administrative controls *comprise the plan of organization and all methods and procedures that are concerned mainly with operational efficiency and adherence to managerial policies.*[2]

In 1972, an AICPA pronouncement provided the following clarifications of these definitions.

> *Administrative control includes, but is not limited to, the plan of organization and the procedures and records that are concerned with the decision processes leading to management's authorization of transactions. Such authorization is a management function directly associated with the responsibility for achieving the objectives of the organization and is the starting point for establishing accounting control of transactions.*
>
> *Accounting control comprises the plan of organization and the procedures and records that are concerned with the safeguarding of assets and the reliability of financial records and consequently are designed to provide reasonable assurance that*
>
> a. *Transactions are executed in accordance with management's general or specific authorization.*
>
> b. *Transactions are recorded as necessary (1) to permit preparation of financial statements in conformity with generally accepted accounting principles or any other criteria applicable to such statements and (2) to maintain accountability for assets.*
>
> c. *Access to assets is permitted only in accordance with management's authorization.*

---

[1] Committee on Auditing Procedure, American Institute of Accountants, *Internal Control* (New York: AICPA, 1949), 6. Copyright © 1949 by the American Institute of Certified Public Accountants, Inc., and reprinted with permission.

[2] Committee on Auditing Procedure, American Institute of Certified Public Accountants, *Statement on Auditing Procedure No. 29* (New York: AICPA, 1958), 36–37. Copyright © 1958 by the American Institute of Certified Public Accountants, Inc., and reprinted with permission.

d. The recorded accountability for assets is compared with the existing assets at reasonable intervals and appropriate action is taken with respect to any differences.[3]

In this pronouncement the AICPA emphasized that the primary concern of the independent auditor in examining a company's financial statements is to evaluate its accounting controls. Of course, the internal accountant responsible for the design of accounting information systems is concerned with all aspects of internal control, including both accounting and administrative controls.

The Foreign Corrupt Practices Act

In 1977 shock waves reverberated through the accounting profession when the United States Congress incorporated language from the AICPA's 1972 pronouncement into the Foreign Corrupt Practices Act. Specifically, all publicly owned corporations subject to the Securities Exchange Act of 1934 are now legally required to

(A) make and keep books, records, and accounts, which, in reasonable detail, accurately and fairly reflect the transactions and dispositions of the assets of the issuer; and (B) devise and maintain a system of internal accounting controls sufficient to provide reasonable assurances that—

    i. transactions are executed in accordance with management's general or specific authorization;

    ii. transactions are recorded as necessary (1) to permit preparation of financial statements in conformity with generally accepted accounting principles or any other criteria applicable to such statements, and (2) to maintain accountability for assets;

    iii. access to assets is permitted only in accordance with management's general or specific authorization; and

    iv. the recorded accountability for assets is compared with the existing assets at reasonable intervals and appropriate action is taken with respect to any differences.[4]

These provisions were designed to make corporations more accountable with respect to the primary purpose of the act, which was to prevent the bribery of foreign officials in order to obtain business. In essence, however, the effect of the act was that corporations are now required by law to maintain good systems of internal accounting control! Needless to say, this requirement has generated tremendous inter-

---

[3] Committee on Auditing Procedure, American Institute of Certified Public Accountants, *Statement on Auditing Procedure No. 54* (New York: AICPA, 1972), 239–240. Copyright © 1972 by the American Institute of Certified Public Accountants, Inc., and reprinted with permission.

[4] *Foreign Corrupt Practices Act of 1977, U.S. Code,* 1976 edition, Supplement II, Volume One (Washington, D.C.: U.S. Government Printing Office, 1979), 862.

est among management, accountants, and auditors in the design and evaluation of internal control systems.

The Internal Control Structure

In a pronouncement issued by the AICPA's Auditing Standards Board in 1988, an attempt was made to further clarify and broaden the concept of internal control.[5] According to this pronouncement, all business entities have an **internal control structure** consisting of the policies and procedures established to provide reasonable assurance that the organization's specific objectives will be achieved. The pronouncement identifies three elements of an organization's internal control structure: the control environment, the accounting system, and control procedures. The control environment is the general framework within which specific control policies and procedures operate. The accounting system consists of the records and procedures used to record, process, and report an organization's transactions and to maintain accountability for the related assets and liabilities. Control procedures are specific steps carried out to minimize the risk of particular control threats. Table 12.1 summarizes the primary factors associated with these three elements of the internal control structure.

Management Control

Prior to the 1980s virtually all pronouncements on internal control emanated from the AICPA and thus reflected the perspective of independent auditors. Specifically, the AICPA's pronouncements on internal control have focused on those aspects of control that are most important to the preparation of an independent opinion on the fairness of a company's financial statements. However, corporate managers and internal accountants have a different perspective on internal control than independent auditors do and have long felt that the AICPA's view of internal control is too narrow.

For example, according to a 1981 study published by the Research Foundation of the Financial Executives Institute (FEI), corporate managers view control more broadly than the public accounting profession does, seeing it as "a means of motivating, encouraging, and assisting officers and employees to achieve corporate goals and to observe corporate policies."[6] The study refers to this concept as **management control** and concludes that it has three essential features. First, management control is an integral part of management responsibilities associated with the goals and purposes established for the organization by management. Second, management control is broader than internal accounting control in that it encompasses both measures designed to reduce errors and irregularities *and* positive activities directed toward the achievement of organizational goals. Third, management control is

---

[5] Auditing Standards Board, American Institute of Certified Public Accountants, *Statement on Auditing Standards No. 55* (New York: AICPA, 1988).

[6] R. K. Mautz and James Winjum, *Criteria for Management Control Systems* (New York: Financial Executives Research Foundation, 1981), 2.

Control Environment	Accounting System	Control Procedures
The control environment represents the collective effect of various factors on establishing, enhancing, or mitigating the effectiveness of specific policies and procedures. Such factors include the following.	The accounting system consists of the methods and records established to identify, assemble, analyze, classify, record, and report an organization's transactions and to maintain accountability for the related assets and liabilities. An effective accounting system gives appropriate consideration to establishing methods and records that will function as follows.	Control procedures are those policies and procedures in addition to the control environment and accounting system that management has established to provide reasonable assurance that specific organizational objectives will be achieved. Generally, they may be categorized as procedures that pertain to the following.
Management's philosophy and operating style		Proper authorization of transactions and activities
The organization structure	Identify and record all valid transactions	Segregation of duties that reduce the opportunities to allow any person to be in a position to both perpetrate and conceal errors or irregularities in the normal course of duties— assigning different people the responsibilities of authorizing transactions, recording transactions, and maintaining custody of assets
The functioning of the board of directors and its committees, particularly the audit committee	Describe on a timely basis the transactions in sufficient detail to permit proper classification of transactions for financial reporting	
Methods of assigning authority and responsibility	Measure the value of transactions in a manner that permits recording their proper monetary value in the financial statements	
Management's control methods for monitoring and following up on performance, including internal auditing	Determine the time period in which transactions occurred to permit recording of transactions in the proper accounting period	Design and use of adequate documents and records to help ensure the proper recording of transactions and events
Personnel policies and practices	Present properly the transactions and related disclosures in the financial statements	Adequate safeguards over access to and use of assets and records
Various external influences that affect an organization's operations and practices, such as examinations by bank regulatory agencies		Independent checks on performance and proper valuation of recorded amounts

Source: Adapted from Auditing Standards Board, AICPA, *Statement on Auditing Standards No. 55*, (New York: AICPA, 1988), paragraphs 9–11. Copyright © 1988 by the American Institute of Certified Public Accountants, Inc., and reprinted with permission.

Table 12.1

Elements of the internal control structure.

personnel-oriented; that is, it seeks to facilitate the success of the organization's employees in attaining the organization's goals within the constraints of organizational policy.[7]

In an attempt to integrate these diverse views and provide a common ground for mutual understanding of internal control, the AICPA, FEI, and various other organizations sponsored a joint study of internal control in 1989. This study, known as the "COSO study" after the Committee on Sponsoring Organizations that issued it, was published in 1992. It puts forward the following definition.

---

[7] *Ibid.*, 14.

Internal control is a process, effected by an entity's board of directors, management and other personnel, designed to provide reasonable assurance regarding the achievement of objectives in the following categories:

Effectiveness and efficiency of operations.

Reliability of financial reporting.

Compliance with applicable laws and regulations.[8]

According to the COSO study, internal control is a *process* in the sense that it permeates an organization's operating activities and is an integral part of the basic management processes of planning, executing and monitoring. It is effected by *people* in that people establish the organization's objectives, put control mechanisms in place, define responsibilities and limits of authority, and thereby affect the actions of other people. Moreover, internal control provides *reasonable assurance* regarding achievement of the organization's objectives, rather than absolute assurance, because the possibilities of human failure, collusion by two or more people, and management override of the internal control system all make absolute assurance an impossible goal.[9]

The heart of the COSO report's description of internal control consists of five interrelated components derived from the way management runs a business and integrated with the management process. Table 12.2 summarizes the study's description of each of these five components. These components relate to each of the three internal control objectives listed in the definition. Finally, both the internal control objectives and components apply to the entire enterprise as well as to its parts, such as subsidiaries, divisions, business units, functional activities, and operating cycles.[10] More information about the COSO study is given in Focus 12.1.

Key aspects of these various contributions to the historical development of the concept of internal control are summarized in Table 12.3. It is interesting to note how the concept has evolved from its origins as a way of helping external auditors determine the most efficient method of planning an independent audit. Now internal control is viewed as a central principle of good management, and its importance is underscored by a federal statute requiring U.S. corporations to maintain good systems of internal accounting control.

---

[8] Committee of Sponsoring Organizations of the Treadway Commission, *Internal Control—Integrated Framework* (New York: Committee of Sponsoring Organizations of the Treadway Commission, 1992), 9.

[9] *Ibid.*, 10–11.

[10] *Ibid.*, 12–16.

Component	Description
Control environment	The core of any business is its people—their individual attributes, including integrity, ethical values and competence—and the environment in which they operate. They are the engine that drives the organization and the foundation on which everything rests.
Risk assessment	The organization must be aware of and deal with the risks it faces. It must set objectives, integrated with the sales, production, marketing, financial and other activities so that the organization is operating in concert. It must also establish mechanisms to identify, analyze, and manage the related risks.
Control activities	Control policies and procedures must be established and executed to help ensure that the actions identified by management as necessary to address risks to achievement of the organization's objectives are effectively carried out.
Information and communication	Surrounding the control activities are information and communication systems. These enable the organization's people to capture and exchange the information needed to conduct, manage, and control its operations.
Monitoring	The entire process must be monitored, and modifications made as necessary. In this way the system can react dynamically, changing as conditions warrant.

Table 12.2
Five interrelated components of internal control.

Other Control Concepts

The concepts of internal control, administrative control, accounting control, and management control are all broad in scope, aimed at describing entire control systems. The specific control procedures used in these systems may be described as either preventive, detective, or corrective. In addition, control processes may be characterized as being based on feedback or feedforward control. These concepts are briefly reviewed here.

Preventive controls are designed to deter problems before they arise. Many potential control problems can be prevented by hiring highly qualified accounting and data processing personnel, by appropriately segregating the duties assigned to these personnel, by effectively controlling physical access to facilities, by utilizing well-designed documents, and by establishing suitable procedures for authorizing transactions. Note that such control techniques are generally designed to operate from *within* the process being controlled. As such, they are the kind of control procedures that are perhaps most consistent with the original meaning of the term *internal* control.

12.1 FOCUS

The COSO Report on Internal Control

A three-year study to define internal control and provide practical guidance companies can use to assess and improve their control systems was issued in 1992 by the Committee of Sponsoring Organizations (COSO), a private-sector group consisting of the American Accounting Association, the AICPA, the Institute of Internal Auditors, the Institute of Management Accountants, and the FEI. The international accounting firm of Coopers & Lybrand conducted the study and prepared the report.

"It is our intention that this report establish an understanding of internal control and enable companies to review or strengthen their controls against a common backdrop," said COSO Chairman Robert L. May.

Detective controls are designed to discover control problems soon after they arise. They include such procedures as duplicate checking of calculations, preparing periodic performance reports that highlight variances between actual and standard costs, reporting past-due accounts and out-of-stock inventory items, preparing bank reconciliations, verifying the proper use of all prenumbered documents, and preparing monthly accounting trial balances. Because not all potential control problems can be prevented, detective control procedures are a necessary part of any effective control system.

Corrective controls are procedures designed to remedy problems discovered through detective controls. Corrective controls include procedures taken to identify the cause of a problem, correct any errors or difficulties arising out of the problem, and modify the processing system so that future occurrences of the problem may be minimized or eliminated. One such procedure is the maintenance of backup copies of key transaction and master files so that the original copies may be restored in the event that they are damaged or destroyed. Also included are procedures for correcting any errors found during the data verification process and for resubmitting the related transactions for subsequent processing. In addition, a log of these errors may be maintained to facilitate follow-up procedures and ensure that proper corrective action is taken.

Control processes are sometimes classified as being based on either feedback or feedforward controls. Feedforward controls are primarily preventive in nature, whereas feedback controls are detective. **Feedback controls** measure some aspect of the process being controlled and adjust

"It will also help companies that issue reports on internal control do so against the COSO standard, which should vastly improve communications to stakeholders," May said. "Finally, legislators and regulators can look to the report to get a thorough understanding of what internal control actually is and what it can and cannot do."

The study took three years and involved tens of thousands of hours of research, discussion, analysis, and due process and in-

volved hundreds of people including members of the five COSO organizations, chief executives and board members, legislators and regulators, lawyers, consultants, auditors, and academics. Comments from an Exposure Draft issued 18 months ago were considered in preparing the final report.

Undertaken in 1987, the report spells out the responsibilities everyone in an organization has for proper functioning of controls and describes the exter-

nal auditor's role in assessing controls. The report goes well beyond financial controls to incorporate all of the controls management uses in running the company.

Source: from "Accounting Groups Issue Report on Internal Control," *Management Accounting* (December 1992): 62. Reprinted with permission of the Institute of Management Accountants.

the process when the measure indicates that it is deviating from plan. A responsibility accounting system, for example, measures the cost of a business process. When this cost is substantially in excess of a budget or standard, management is notified through a performance report. Management then identifies the source of the problem and initiates steps to correct it. The term **feedback** refers to the information generated by the measurement system that is used to identify the problem and initiate corrective action. In a responsibility accounting system feedback is contained within the performance report. Other examples of feedback control systems include standard cost accounting systems, systems for reviewing the payment history of credit customers, quality control systems, and the internal audit function.

Feedforward controls monitor both the operation of a process and the process inputs in an attempt to predict potential problems before they occur so that adjustments may be made to avert the problems. For example, a cash budgeting system monitors both a company's cash flows and the operations that cause cash flows, and it produces a forecast of future cash flows. If this forecast indicates a future cash deficiency, steps may be taken to arrange for a line of credit that will cover the deficiency. Another example of a feedforward control system is an inventory control system that predicts when each inventory item will be out of stock and initiates reorders that will replenish the stock before it runs out.

The various types of control overlap in many instances. For example, many management controls are also administrative controls, and they may incorporate feedback or feedforward control concepts. Most

Table 12.3
Overview of the historical
development of internal
control concepts.

Year	Source	Contribution
1949	American Institute of Accountants (now AICPA) monograph on internal control	Promulgates first definition of internal control as having four objectives, which are to safeguard assets, check the accuracy and integrity of accounting data, promote operational efficiency, and encourage adherence to prescribed managerial policies.
1958	AICPA, *Statement on Auditing Procedure No. 29*	Introduces the distinction between accounting controls, or controls concerned mainly with safeguarding assets and the reliability of financial records, and administrative controls.
1972	AICPA, *Statement on Auditing Procedure No. 54*	Further clarifies the distinction between accounting controls and administrative controls, and specifies four objectives of accounting controls.
1977	U.S. Congress, Foreign Corrupt Practices Act	Codifies the AICPA's 1977 definition of internal accounting control as a legal requirement for public corporations subject to the Securities Exchange Act of 1934.
1981	Research Foundation of the Financial Executives Institute (FEI)	Introduces a definition of management control and draws a distinction between internal accounting control and management control.
1988	AICPA, *Statement on Auditing Standards No. 55*	Introduces the concept of internal control structure, consisting of the control environment, accounting system, and control procedures.
1992	Committee of Sponsoring Organizations of the Treadway Commission (includes AICPA and FEI)	Proposes a broad definition of internal control as a process designed to achieve objectives relating to operating effectiveness and efficiency, reliability of financial reporting, and compliance with laws and regulations. Five interrelated components of internal control are identified, encompassing both management control and accounting control considerations.

organizations have preventive, detective, and corrective accounting controls. The nature of a particular control procedure is less important than whether it effectively accomplishes its objective, which is to prevent losses to the organization that arise from a particular threat or hazard. In the analysis of controls within an organization it is important to first determine what the organization's control objectives are and then establish whether there are effective control procedures (of any type) that accomplish these control objectives.

The remainder of this chapter describes internal control concepts, policies, and procedures that are most relevant to the design of accounting information systems. For this purpose the AICPA's concept of the internal control structure provides a useful framework. Accordingly, the next three major sections of this chapter examine the three key elements of the internal control structure, beginning with the control environment, and followed by control procedures and the accounting system.

THE CONTROL ENVIRONMENT

The most critical aspect of an organization's control environment is management's attitude toward internal control and the emphasis it places on internal control in the organization. Through management's statements, policies, and actions, its attitude toward internal control becomes apparent to other members of the organization. If it is obvious that management considers internal control to be of great importance, other members of the organization are likely to strive harder to adhere to specific control policies and procedures in order to better accomplish the organization's objectives. On the other hand, if management shows little concern for internal control, other members of the organization are not likely to be as diligent or as effective in achieving specific control objectives.

For example, consider the findings of Susan Lee and Jason Scott during their internal audit of Springer's Northwest Lumber & Supply. Susan found that lines of authority and responsibility within the company were loosely defined, and she suspected that Springer's management may have engaged in "creative accounting" to show its performance in the best light. Meanwhile, Jason found evidence of poor internal control practices in the purchasing and accounts payable function. It is quite possible that these two conditions are related—that is, that a loose attitude toward sound management practices on the part of Springer's management has contributed to a lack of attentiveness to good internal control practice in the purchasing area.

The control environment of an organization encompasses a variety of factors that collectively affect the specific control policies and procedures established by the organization and the effectiveness of these policies and procedures. As listed in Table 12.1, the factors identified by the AICPA are (1) management's philosophy and operating style, (2) the organization structure, (3) the functioning of the board of directors and the audit committee, (4) management's methods of assigning authority and responsibility, (5) management's methods of monitoring and following up on performance, including internal auditing, (6) personnel policies and practices, and (7) various external influences, such as government regulation. Each of these factors is discussed in detail in the remainder of this section.

Management's Philosophy and Operating Style

The management of any business organization strives for profitable operations, growth, and other indicators of business success. But there are often differences in *how* managements attempt to achieve their goals for a business organization. For example, does management take undue business risks to achieve its objectives, or does it act prudently in assessing potential risks and rewards prior to committing the organization to a course of action? Does management attempt to manipulate measures of business performance such as net income in order that its performance will be seen in a more favorable light? Does management put pressure on its employees to achieve results regardless of the methods required, or is management concerned that employees behave in an ethical manner? Does management work toward long-term organizational objectives, even if it means temporary setbacks in achieving short-term objectives? Is the organization dominated by one or a few individuals, or is responsibility shared among members of a management team? Collectively, the answers to these questions reflect management's philosophy and operating style. The more responsible management's philosophy and operating style is, the more likely it is that employees will also behave responsibly in working to achieve the organization's objectives.

Organization Structure

Another key element of a company's control environment is its organization structure, which defines the lines of authority and responsibility within the company and provides the overall framework for planning, directing, and controlling its operations. The organization structure of a business may be represented formally by an organization chart depicting the reporting relationships among the various units of the business. The aspects of organization structure that are most relevant from the standpoint of internal control in accounting information systems are the degree of centralization or decentralization of authority, the relative use of functional versus divisional organization structure, the way in which the allocation of organizational responsibilities affects the information requirements of managerial personnel throughout the organization, and the specific organization of the accounting and information systems functions.

The Audit Committee

An important element of the control environment of a publicly held corporation is the functioning of its board of directors, whose members act as representatives of the shareholders in directing the business and affairs of the corporation. Much of the board's work is performed through its various committees, and one particularly important committee from a control standpoint is the audit committee. The audit committee is responsible for overseeing the corporation's internal control structure, its financial reporting process, and its compliance with related laws, regulations, and standards. The audit committee works closely with the corporation's external auditors as well as with its internal auditors. Rapid growth in the use of audit committees began in the 1970s at the urging of the AICPA and the Securities and Exchange Commission (SEC). Since June of 1978, corporations whose shares are traded on the New York stock exchange have been required to have an audit committee consisting of solely of outside directors—that is, directors who are not also members of management. At the present time most large public corporations have an audit committee.

The audit committee's purpose is to enhance the accountability of corporate managers to stockholders. An audit committee, particularly one consisting primarily or exclusively of outside directors, provides an independent review of the actions of corporate managers on behalf of corporate shareholders. This review serves as a check on the integrity of management, improves the quality of the financial reporting process, and increases the confidence of the investing public in the propriety of financial reporting and the securities markets.

Methods of Assigning Authority and Responsibility

Management's methods of assigning authority and responsibility have an important influence on the control environment. Authority and responsibility may be assigned through formal job descriptions, written policy and procedures manuals, computer systems documentation, employee training, and operating plans, schedules, and budgets. Of particular importance is a formal company code of conduct addressing such matters as standards of ethical behavior, acceptable business practices, regulatory requirements, and conflicts of interest.

A policy and procedures manual is an important tool for assigning authority and responsibility in many organizations. Such a manual often includes job descriptions detailing the responsibilities of each position in the organization. It spells out management policy with respect to handling specific transactions, and it documents the systems and procedures employed to process each transaction. It includes a detailed listing of the organization's chart of accounts, along with sample copies of forms and documents. It should feature a copy of the company's code of conduct. A policy and procedures manual encompassing these elements serves as a helpful on-the-job reference for employees and a useful tool in training new employees.

Methods of Monitoring Performance

The control environment is also affected by management's control methods for monitoring and following up on performance. Key methods of monitoring performance include effective supervision, responsibility reporting, and internal auditing. Effective supervision involves assisting employees engaged in operating or data processing tasks, monitoring the effectiveness with which employees carry out their assigned tasks, and safeguarding assets by watching over employees who have access to assets. Supervision is an especially important means of control in organizations that are too small to be able to afford elaborate responsibility reporting schemes or adequate separation of duties for internal control purposes.

Responsibility accounting systems are described in detail in Chapter 2. Their key elements include formal plans in the form of budgets, quotas, schedules, standard costs, and quality standards; performance reports that compare actual with planned performance and highlight significant variances; and procedures for investigating significant variances and taking timely action to correct the conditions leading to such variances.

Internal Auditing. While external auditors are engaged to render an opinion on a company's financial statements, internal auditors are employed within and by companies to provide an independent appraisal of the effectiveness of internal controls and of the quality of managerial performance in carrying out assigned responsibilities. Internal auditing involves reviewing the reliability and integrity of financial and operating information, reviewing the controls employed to safeguard assets, assessing employees' compliance with management policies and procedures and with any applicable laws and regulations, and evaluating the efficiency and effectiveness with which management carries out its responsibilities and achieves organizational objectives. In order to perform these duties effectively, the internal audit function must be organizationally independent of accounting and operating functions, so that internal auditors can be as objective as possible in evaluating managerial performance. Accordingly, the head of the internal auditing function should report to the company president, the board of directors, and the audit committee.

Both internal and external auditors share a concern with internal accounting controls. However, internal auditors also place great emphasis on a company's administrative or management controls. Examples of the kinds of management control problems that the internal audit function can often detect are failure to pay accounts in time to earn discounts, excess overtime, underused assets, obsolete inventory, padded travel expense reimbursements, excessively loose budgets and quotas, failure to adhere to prescribed policies and procedures, poorly justified capital expenditures, and production bottlenecks. By providing feedback on the existence and nature of such problems, internal auditors enable management to take corrective action to maintain effective management control of the organization.

Personnel Policies and Practices An organization's personnel policies and practices are still another key element of its control environment. Policies and practices dealing with hiring, training, evaluating, compensating, and promoting employees can have an important effect on the organization's ability to accomplish its goals and objectives as well as its ability to minimize the risks and exposures associated with internal control threats.

Employees should be hired and promoted on the basis of a comparison of their qualifications to the requirements of the position. A written job description sets forth the job requirements. Résumés, reference letters, and background checks are important means of evaluating the qualifications of job applicants. Qualifications required for responsible positions generally include experience, intelligence, character, dedication, and capacity for leadership. Training programs should be planned carefully to familiarize new employees with their responsibilities and with the organization's policies and procedures. Finally, an organization's policies with respect to working conditions, compensation, job incentives, and career advancement can be a powerful force in encouraging efficiency and loyal service.

The importance of performing thorough background checks on the qualifications of job candidates is underscored by numerous case histories. For example, in 1985 Philip Crosby Associates (PCA), a highly successful consulting and training firm, underwent an exhaustive search to select a finance director for its new international unit. The person hired was John C. Nelson, an MBA and CPA with a glowing reference from his former employer. In reality, however, both the CPA and the reference were phony, and John C. Nelson was really Robert W. Liszewski, alias Bruce Fox, who had recently served an 18-month jail sentence for embezzling $400,000 from a bank in Indiana. By the time PCA discovered this, Liszewski had embezzled $960,000 from PCA using wire transfers to a dummy corporation supported by forged signatures on contracts and authorization documents.[11]

For employees in positions of trust who have access to cash or other property, additional control policies are appropriate. One such personnel practice is a requirement that all employees who have custody of assets or who are responsible for sensitive record-keeping or authorization functions must take an annual vacation, during which time their functions are performed by someone else. Many employee frauds are discovered when the perpetrator is suddenly forced by illness or accident to take time off. Periodic rotation of duties among key employees is another policy that may achieve the same results. Of course, the very existence of such policies acts to deter fraud and thus enhance internal control. Finally, fidelity bond insurance coverage of key employees is also important. A **fidelity bond** is a contract under which the bonding company is liable for losses arising from deliberate fraudulent acts committed by a bonded employee.

External Influences   Numerous external influences may affect the operations and practices of a business organization and hence its control environment. They include requirements on financial reporting and related matters imposed by stock exchanges, by the Financial Accounting Standards Board (FASB), and by the Securities and Exchange Commission. They

---

[11] Joshua Hyatt, "Easy Money," *Inc.* (February 1988): 91–96.

also include requirements imposed by regulatory agencies for specific industries, such as those for banks, utilities, and insurance companies. Examples of external influences include the internal control provisions of the Foreign Corrupt Practices Act, which are enforced by the SEC, and periodic audits of financial institutions by auditors from the Federal Deposit Insurance Corporation. External requirements often heighten management's awareness of the importance of internal control policies and procedures.

While the control environment sets the tone for effective internal control, good control procedures are essential to ensure that an organization achieves its specific internal control objectives. Accordingly, the next section of the chapter describes a variety of control procedures that may be applied at various levels of an organization.

CONTROL PROCEDURES

Control procedures are management policies and rules regarding employee behavior that are designed to provide reasonable assurance that management's control objectives are achieved. Generally, control procedures fall into one of five categories:

1. Proper authorization of transactions and activities
2. Segregation of duties
3. Design and use of adequate documents and records
4. Adequate safeguards over access to and use of assets and records
5. Independent checks on performance

This section describes control procedures within each of these categories.

Authorization

An organization's employees typically perform tasks and make decisions that can affect the safety of assets within the organization and the exchange of assets with external parties. For example, a retail salesclerk handles cash and may also carry out procedures for approving sales to customers on account. In all but the very smallest organizations management does not have the time to supervise the performance of such activities by all its employees or to approve all the basic decisions that its employees make in carrying out routine operating tasks. Instead, management establishes general policies regarding the appropriate actions or decisions for specific situations and then empowers specific employees to perform those activities and/or make those decisions. This empowerment is called **authorization**. The policies and practices that management prescribes for performing, documenting, and monitoring the authorization function are an important part of an organization's control procedures.

One or more employees may be designated as authorized to perform a particular function or approve a specific type of transaction. The act of authorization must be documented, generally by having the authorizer enter his or her signature, initials, or authorization code on the document that is used to record the transaction. Employees involved in all subsequent stages of processing the transaction should review this document to verify that the appropriate authorization(s) are present.

The absence of appropriate documentation of the authorization act is often an important indicator that a control problem exists. For this reason, both internal and external auditors will often review samples of various kinds of transactions to verify that they have been properly authorized. Thus Jason Scott was assigned to review a sample of purchase transactions during the audit of Springer's Northwest Lumber & Supply. And, indeed, Jason did discover that some purchase transactions had not been properly authorized through the use of purchase requisitions but had instead been "personally authorized" by Springer's Purchasing Vice-President. In addition, Jason found that payment of some vendor invoices had been authorized without proper supporting documents, such as purchase orders and receiving reports. If Jason includes an accurate description of these findings in his audit report, it will give his superiors cause for concern about the adequacy of Springer's internal control procedures.

Certain activities or transactions may be of such consequence to an organization that its management does not delegate full responsibility for them to regular employees. For example, the organization might require management review and approval of all sales orders in excess of $20,000, capital expenditures in excess of $10,000, or write-offs of uncollectible accounts in excess of $5000. In such cases the usual policy is for the employee to bring the transaction to management's attention for special approval, or **specific authorization**. In contrast, when regular employees are authorized to handle routine transactions without special approval, this procedure is referred to as **general authorization**.

Management should have written policies on general and specific authorization for each of the major classes of transactions in which the organization engages. Some examples of authorization functions within the major categories of business transactions are shown in Table 12.4.

Segregation of Duties   Another critical set of control procedures relates to the effective segregation of duties. When a transaction processing system is established, management is responsible for allocating various tasks among the employees who will process the transactions and carry out any related operating activities. In such cases good internal control demands that no single employee be given too much responsibility. Specifically, no employee should be in a position to both perpetrate and conceal irregularities (intentional diversions of the organization's assets for personal gain) or unintentional errors. Effective segregation of duties for this purpose is referred to as **organizational independence**.

For each major type of transaction three general categories of functions must be separated in order to achieve effective segregation of duties: (1) the authorization function, (2) the recording function, and (3) the function of maintaining custody of the related assets. The

Transaction Types	Examples of Authorization Functions
Sales orders	Approval of customer credit Approval of shipment Approval of sales returns and allowances
Purchases	Authorization to order goods or services Authorization of capital expenditures Selection of vendors Acceptance of delivered products
Production	Approval of products and quantities to be produced Approval of raw materials issued for use in production Approval of production schedules Approval of completed products
Personnel/payroll	Hiring of new employees Approval of increases in employee compensation Approval of records of time worked Approval of payroll withholdings
Cash receipts	Endorsement of checks for deposit in bank Write-offs of uncollectible accounts
Cash disbursements	Approval of vendor invoices for payment Approval of checks written to settle accounts payable Approval of replenishment of petty cash fund

Table 12.4
Examples of authorization functions.

recording function involves preparing source documents; maintaining journals, ledgers, or other files; preparing reconciliations; and preparing performance reports. Custody of assets may be direct, as in the case of handling cash or maintaining an inventory storeroom, or indirect, as in the case of receiving customer checks in the mail or writing checks on the organization's bank account.

If, for a specific type of transaction, any two of these three functions are the responsibility of a single person, problems may arise. For example, in September 1982 the former City Treasurer of Fairfax, Virginia, was convicted of embezzling at least $600,000 from the city treasury. Her scheme, carried out between 1976 and 1981, worked as follows: When residents used currency to pay their real estate and personal property taxes, she would keep the currency. She would record the tax collections on her property tax records but would not report them to the City Comptroller. Eventually, an adjusting journal entry would be made to bring her records into agreement with those of the comptroller. In addition, when currency was received to pay for business license fees, court fees, and so on, it would be recorded on a cash register and deposited at the end of each day. She would steal portions of this currency but then make up any discrepancy in the bank deposit by substituting miscellaneous checks she had received in the mail that would not be missed when they were not recorded.[12] In this example one person was responsible both for the *custody* of cash receipts and for the *recording* of those receipts, and she was able to divert some cash receipts and falsify the accounts to conceal the diversion.

Consider another example where one employee was responsible for *authorizing* transactions and also had *custody* of cash. In January 1992 the Utilities Director of Newport Beach, California, was charged with embezzling $1.2 million from the city between 1981 and 1992. His alleged scheme worked in the following way. First, he would forge invoices or easement documents authorizing payments to a real or fictitious city property owner, for example, for the rights to put a water line through that person's land. City Finance Department officials would hand him the checks to deliver to the property owners. He would then forge signatures, endorse the checks to himself, and deposit them in his own accounts.[13] The control weakness in this case was that the Utility Director was given physical custody of checks relating to transactions that he had also authorized, which enabled him to authorize fictitious transactions and divert the related city payments.

Finally, suppose that an employee is responsible for both *authorization* and *recording* functions. In August of 1987 the former Payroll Director of the Los Angeles Dodgers Baseball Club pleaded guilty to embezzling $330,000 from the team between 1983 and 1985. His scheme involved several other Dodgers employees. He would credit these employees for hours not worked and then receive a kickback of around 50% of their extra compensation. He also added the names of these employee's girlfriends and other fictitious names to the Dodgers payroll and split their paychecks with his coconspirators. This fraud was discovered when the Payroll Director became ill and another employee took over his duties.[14] In this case, since the perpetrator was responsible both for authorizing the hiring of new employees and for recording employee hours worked, he did not need to also prepare or handle the paychecks. The Club Treasurer would simply deliver the paychecks to the other conspirators or mail them to an address specified by the Payroll Director.

In a system that incorporates an effective separation of duties among employees, it should be almost impossible for any single employee to commit embezzlement successfully. Collusion, or conspiracy of

---

[12] John W. Coughlan, "The Fairfax Embezzlement," *Management Accounting* (May 1983): 32–39.

[13] James M. Gomez and Eric Bailey, "Newport Says $1.2 Million Missing in Embezzlement," *Los Angeles Times* (January 16, 1992): B-1.

[14] Terry Pristin, "Ex-Dodger Worker Gets Prison for Grand Theft," *Los Angeles Times* (August 22, 1987): part 2, p. 3.

two or more persons to commit fraud, may still be possible, although a well-designed system can also minimize the chances of successful collusion.

Documents and Records

A third important set of control procedures involves the design and use of adequate documents and records to help ensure the proper recording of transactions and events. Transaction source documents should be designed to facilitate the collection of all relevant information relating to the transaction. Documents that initiate a transaction should contain a space for the signature of the person authorizing the transaction. Documents used to record the transfer of responsibility for assets from one person or department to another within the organization should include a space for the signature of the receiving party, acknowledging receipt of the asset. The form and content of documents and records should be as simple as possible to facilitate efficient record keeping, to minimize the likelihood of recording errors, and to facilitate review and verification of recorded information. Documents and records that are well designed and effectively used can contribute greatly to the achievement of management's internal control objectives.

In the area of document design an important practice for control purposes is the sequential prenumbering of all documents. This practice makes it possible to account for and review every document used in a process. The removal of any documents will cause a number to be missing in the sequence. Prenumbering reduces the likelihood of fraudulent use of documents by dishonest employees.

The record-keeping system throughout a business organization should be well coordinated in order to facilitate the tracing of individual transactions through the system. The path that a transaction takes through a data processing system, from source document to summary reports and account balances, is referred to as the **audit trail** or **transaction trail**. The audit trail consists of reference numbers, codes, dates, and other cross-referenced data that are recorded in files, ledgers, and journals to facilitate the tracing of records to source documents or to records in other files. Good audit trails facilitate the correction of errors and the verification of output information in a system.

Safeguarding of Assets

A fourth category of control procedures involves safeguards over access to and use of assets and related records. Assets must be protected from such threats as theft, unauthorized use, and vandalism on the part of dishonest employees, shoplifters, or burglars. Effective supervision and segregation of duties play an important role in safeguarding assets. The maintenance of accurate records of assets on hand is also very important, since it may be difficult to determine that a loss of assets has occurred and to ascertain the extent of the loss unless accurate records are available specifying the assets that should be on hand.

Measures designed to restrict physical access to assets, and thereby limit the chances of loss, play a central role in safeguarding assets. For example, cash registers, safes, lockboxes, or safety deposit boxes are used to limit access to cash, securities, and other paper assets. Restricted storage areas may be used to protect inventories of raw materials, parts, supplies, and small tools. Access to restricted areas may be controlled by providing only one or two access points and by requiring that authorized personnel properly identify themselves prior to entry, using a security badge or machine-readable access card. Alarm systems and closed-circuit TV systems may be used to monitor access to restricted areas or protect against shoplifting or employee pilferage. Security personnel are generally responsible for the development and enforcement of procedures for the physical safeguarding of assets.

In addition to restricting access to assets such as cash and inventories, an organization should also protect and control access to records and documents. Important records should be protected through the use of fireproof storage areas and the maintenance of backup copies stored at a separate location. Access to vital records should be restricted by locking them in desks or file cabinets when not in use. Access to blank checks and forms such as purchase orders and disbursement vouchers should be limited to authorized personnel. As one example of what might happen when access to vital documents is not adequately restricted, consider what recently happened to the city of Inglewood, California. A janitor was charged with stealing 34 blank checks while cleaning the city Finance Office, forging the names of city officials on the checks, and cashing them for amounts ranging from $50,000 to $470,000.[15]

Independent Checks

A fifth set of control procedures involves independent checks on the performance of transaction processing functions within an accounting system and on the accuracy of data files maintained by the system. The term *internal check* is often used to describe such procedures. Internal check procedures should be "independent" because they are generally more effective if performed by someone other than the person responsible for the original operation.

One type of internal check is the reconciliation of two independently maintained sets of records. For example, a bank reconciliation confirms agreement between a company's record of the amount of cash in its bank account and the bank's record. Another example of an internal check is the periodic totaling of subsidiary ledgers, such as the accounts receivable ledger or the fixed asset ledger, for comparison with the corresponding general ledger control account balances.

Another type of reconciliation is the comparison of actual quantities of assets to recorded amounts. The amount of cash in a cash register drawer should be reconciled at the end of each shift with the amount recorded on the cash register tape. Inventories should be counted at periodic intervals and the counts compared with perpetual inventory

---

[15] "In Wake of Theft, City Shifts Banks," *Los Angeles Times* (October 4, 1991): B-5.

records of quantities on hand. Such a check should be done for all inventory items at least once annually and more frequently for items having a high dollar value.

The double-entry accounting maxim that debits must equal credits provides numerous opportunities for internal checks in processing accounting data. For example, in any accounting journal the totals of the debit and credit columns should always be equal, and this equality should be verified before the journal entries are posted to the general ledger. Another example is provided by the trial balance, which is prepared at the conclusion of each accounting period (prior to the preparation of financial statements) to verify that the total of all debit balances in the general ledger accounts is equal the total of all credit balances. Any discrepancy in these checks indicates the presence of one or more errors. When a discrepancy is found, it is necessary to search for the specific error or errors and initiate correction procedures before further processing steps are performed.

Payroll processing provides another good opportunity for this form of internal check. Debits in a payroll entry are allocated to numerous inventory and/or expense accounts by the cost accounting department. Credits are allocated to several liability accounts for wages and salaries payable, taxes withheld, employee insurance, union dues, and so on, by the payroll department. At the conclusion of these two complex operations the comparison of total debits to total credits provides a powerful check on the accuracy of both processes.

When records are processed in batches, internal checks are often accomplished by means of **batch totals** (also called **control totals**), which are sums of a numerical item accumulated from all records in a batch. Batch totals are typically established when a batch of records is initially formed and then checked against comparable totals computed at subsequent stages of processing. The discovery of a discrepancy at any point indicates that an error occurred during the previous processing stage. Such errors should be located and corrected before processing continues.

An example of the use of batch totals is provided by Sarah Robinson, who runs a small mail-order business selling imported candies from her home in Salt Lake City, Utah. Sarah's husband, Craig, is a CPA and has established a record-keeping system for Sarah's business that includes accounts receivable and general ledger files. Once each week, Sarah processes the batch of all customer payments that have been received on account through the mail during the past week (see Fig. 12.1). First, she prepares a list of all receipts, including the customer name and amount received. She also computes a batch total of the dollar amount of all checks received and notes this total on the receipts list, which she then gives to Craig. Then she prepares a bank deposit slip for the batch of checks and deposits them in the bank. To verify the accuracy of the bank deposit, she compares the bank-validated copy of the deposit slip with her original batch total. From Sarah's list of payments received Craig posts credits to the appropriate

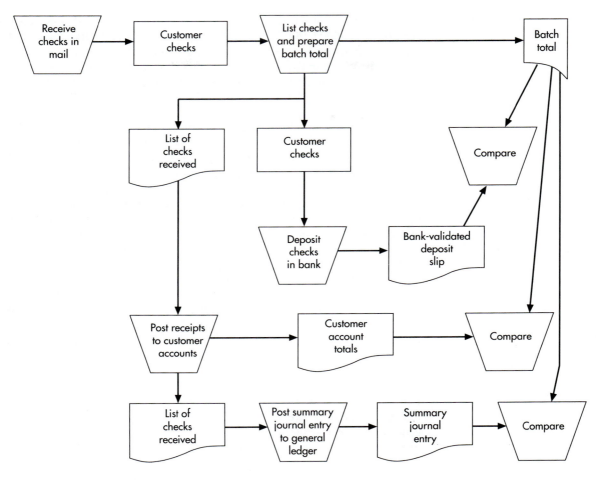

Figure 12.1
Example of the use of batch totals
in processing cash receipts.

customer account records and updates each customer's balance due.
He then computes the new total balance of the accounts receivable file,
determines the difference between the old and new file totals, and
verifies that this difference agrees with Sarah's batch total. Finally,
Craig prepares a summary journal entry and posts it to the general
ledger, again verifying that the amount of this entry is equal to Sarah's
batch total. Thus at each step of the process the batch total provides an
independent check on the accuracy of the related processing steps.

If a discrepancy is discovered between total debits and total credits
or between two batch totals, the amount of the difference can often
provide clues about which entry or record contains the error. For
example, if the difference is equal to the amount of one transaction,
that transaction may have been omitted from a posting process or a
batch total computation. If the difference is divisible by 9 with no
remainder, the likely cause is a **transposition error**, in which the column
positions of two adjacent digits were inadvertently exchanged (for

example, 46 for 64). If the amounts differ by only one digit other than zero (such as 5000, 200, 10, or 0.08), there may have been a transcription error, in which one digit was transcribed incorrectly during processing (for example, a 4 in the tens column may have been transcribed as a 9, which would cause an error of 50 in the amount). If none of these conditions is present, the error might be located by dividing the difference by 2 and looking for a transaction amount exactly equal to the result; if such an amount is found, it may have been incorrectly debited instead of credited or added instead of subtracted. Of course, if more than one error is made in processing a group of accounting journal entries or a batch of transaction data, these shortcuts will not be as helpful in identifying the specific errors made.

Internal checks should be used in conjunction with the segregation of duties. Generally, segregation results in two or more persons being involved in the processing of any transaction. Those involved in each processing stage subsequent to the initiation of a transaction should perform at least a limited review of prior work. The presence of authorization signatures on source documents should be checked. Documents supporting disbursements, loan approvals, account write-offs, and similar transactions should be reviewed by persons other than those who initiated the transactions. The accuracy of critical data items, including prices, quantities, and extensions on documents such as invoices and purchase orders, should be reviewed by a person not involved in preparing the documents.

The maintenance of accurate accounting records is not the only benefit derived from the prevention, detection, and correction of errors in accounting data. Records produced by the accounting system are a crucial part of transactions with employees, customers, vendors, and other important constituents of a business organization. Frequent errors in record keeping may erode the organization's credibility with these groups and thereby undermine management's efforts to achieve its objectives for the organization. Internal checks and other internal control procedures thus play an important role in the effective management of a business organization.

Given an understanding of the nature and operation of specific accounting procedures, we must now consider the specific contexts in which those procedures operate. Those contexts consist of the various accounting systems that exist within a business organization to process accounting transaction data. These accounting systems are examined in the next section.

THE ACCOUNTING SYSTEM

An organization's accounting system consists of the records and procedures established to record, process, and report the results of its transactions and to maintain accountability for its assets and liabilities. According to the AICPA:

An effective accounting system gives appropriate consideration to establishing methods and records that will—

a. Identify and record all valid transactions.

b. Describe on a timely basis the transactions in sufficient detail to permit proper classification of transactions for financial reporting.

c. Measure the value of transactions in a manner that permits recording their proper monetary value in the financial statements.

d. Determine the time period in which transactions occurred to permit recording of transactions in the proper accounting period.

e. Present properly the transactions and related disclosures in the financial statements.[16]

These may be viewed as the primary objectives of all accounting systems.

In any accounting system there is a regular cycle of data processing procedures that must be performed. As described in Chapter 2, these procedures are as follows:

- Recognizing an accounting transaction and capturing the relevant transaction data
- Performing control procedures such as editing and verifying the transaction data
- Recording the transaction in one of several journals
- Posting the journal entries to ledgers, including the general ledger and often a subsidiary ledger
- Preparing financial statements

As explained in Chapter 1, this sequence of activities is often referred to as the accounting cycle.

Accounting systems generally consist of several accounting subsystems. Each subsystem is designed to process transactions of a particular type. While they differ with respect to the type of transactions processed, all accounting subsystems are similar with respect to the sequence of procedures followed in processing the transactions. Thus the procedures followed within each accounting subsystem may also be referred to as accounting cycles. In Chapter 1 five of these individual accounting cycles were identified and given names reflecting their related transaction types. Briefly, these key accounting cycles are (1) the revenue cycle, (2) the procurement cycle, (3) the production cycle, (4) the personnel/payroll cycle, and (5) the financial management cycle. These five accounting cycles and their related control objectives and procedures are described in detail in the five chapters that comprise Part 5 of this book (Chapters 16–20). However, to enhance our

---

[16] *Statement on Auditing Standards No. 55*, 6.

understanding of how control procedures are employed to achieve control objectives, this section provides a brief description of the primary internal controls associated with each of these five accounting cycles.

The Revenue Cycle

The revenue cycle involves a set of activities associated with the exchange of products and services for revenues. These activities include receiving customer orders, checking customer credit, delivering products and services to customers, and preparing invoices and accounts receivable records reflecting the amounts due from customers.

The primary internal control objectives in the revenue cycle are to ensure that all sales are properly authorized and accurately recorded, to safeguard finished goods inventories, and to facilitate the collection of revenues. To these ends, shipments of goods should not be approved until the creditworthiness of the customer has been evaluated and approved. Transfer of goods from the finished goods storeroom to the shipping department must be authorized by documents evidencing a sale. Shipping personnel must acknowledge receipt of the goods and notify billing personnel once the shipment has been made. Billing personnel then prepare the invoice based on the original sales order and the documentation supplied by shipping. After the invoices are prepared and copies are mailed to the customer, the accounts receivable records must be updated, with batch totals being used to control the accuracy of posting. In addition, accounts receivable personnel often prepare and send to each customer a periodic statement of account. Segregation of duties within the revenue cycle is accomplished by separating the authorization functions (credit approval and shipping authorization) from the recording function (preparation of sales orders and customer bills, and maintenance of accounts receivable records) and from the custodial function (inventory storeroom and shipping department).

A common embezzlement scheme within the revenue cycle involves selling and delivering products or services to an unauthorized or fictitious customer, from whom payment is never collected. For example, an FBI investigation into alleged embezzlement at the National Bank of Washington was reported in August 1990. The perpetrator apparently constructed a phony loan on the bank's books and routed the money to himself.[17] Proper segregation of the authorization and custodial functions should minimize the risks of such employee frauds.

The Procurement Cycle

The procurement cycle includes various activities associated with the purchase of raw materials, merchandise, supplies, and services. These activities include identifying and documenting a need for procurement, preparing a purchase order, receiving and documenting inventory de-

---

[17] Michael Hedges, "FBI Probes 2 Thefts by NBW Employees," *Washington Times* (August 10, 1990): C-3.

liveries, maintaining inventory records and records of transactions with suppliers, and paying suppliers for goods and services received.

The three basic objectives of internal control in the procurement cycle are as follows:

1. To ensure purchase of all needed inventories and other assets and services at reasonable prices
2. To protect inventories from damage, theft, or unauthorized use
3. To ensure that all purchase transactions are accurately recorded and processed

To ensure that only necessary items are purchased, management should direct that a clerk initiate a purchase order only upon receipt of a formal requisition by an employee responsible for stores keeping or production planning. To ensure that reasonable prices are paid, management should adopt a formal process for selecting the supplier that offers the best combination of price, quality, service and reliability. To safeguard inventories, management should direct receiving personnel to prepare a report listing the quantity and condition of each item received. This report should be signed by a stores-keeping employee to acknowledge the secure transfer of inventories from the receiving area to stores.

Accounts payable personnel perform the most significant control function in a purchasing system, in that they are responsible for authorizing payment of supplier invoices. Such authorization is granted only after a review of the purchase order, to ensure that the products or services were actually ordered and that prices charged are consistent with order prices, and of the receiving report, to ensure that inventories were received in good condition and securely transferred to the stores-keeping area. Organizational independence in this process is achieved by separating the authorization functions (requisitioning, supplier selection, and supplier invoice approval) from the custodial functions (the receiving and stores-keeping departments) and from the recording functions (record keeping for accounts payable and inventories).

A common embezzlement scheme within the procurement cycle involves an employee who purchases goods and services at inflated prices and then receives a kickback from the supplier. A variation of this scheme involves purchasing overpriced goods and services from a bogus company set up by the perpetrator. For example, in 1985 a purchasing employee at Kapiolani Women's and Children's Medical Center in Honolulu was indicted for conspiring with two nonemployees to buy building maintenance equipment at wholesale prices, sell it to Kapiolani at highly inflated prices, and retain the profits, which were estimated at around $500,000 by the time the fraud was discovered.[18]

---

[18] Linda Kephart, "Cracking Down on White Collar Crime," *Hawaii Business* (October 1985): 21–28.

Proper segregation of the requisitioning, supplier selection, and supplier invoice approval functions should minimize the risks of this type of employee fraud.

The findings of Jason Scott on the audit of Springer's Northwest Lumber & Supply suggest the clear possibility of this type of fraud. Jason observed missing purchase requisitions, payment of supplier invoices in the absence of supporting documents, and item prices that seemed unusually high. When Jason's report is read by an experienced internal audit manager at Northwest's headquarters, it is likely that alarm bells will sound. Susan Lee's report on the loose control environment at Springer's will further heighten headquarter's concerns. It is very likely that another audit team will be sent to Bozeman to take a closer look at the situation there.

The Production Cycle

The production cycle is a set of activities associated with the manufacture of a product. These activities include designing and engineering the product; planning the quantity, timing, and scheduling of production; supervising and recording the flow of inventories through the production process; and monitoring the efficiency and quality of production operations.

The four primary objectives of internal control in the production cycle are as follows:

1. To ensure production of only required products
2. To prevent loss of inventories
3. To ensure that all production activity is accurately recorded
4. To uphold high standards of production efficiency and quality

To ensure production of only required products, a production planning department decides what products to manufacture and in what quantities, on the basis of outstanding customer orders, current sales trends, and current finished goods inventory balances. To prevent loss of inventories, management institutes a program to maintain the physical security of the factory premises.

Control over goods in production begins with the transfer of raw materials from stores keeping to the factory. This process is controlled by documents initiated by the production planning department authorizing the transfer. Production planning and cost accounting personnel must keep strict documentary control over each batch of work in process as it moves through the factory. Maintaining a record of quantities involved in each transfer of goods from one factory department to another makes it possible to trace any shortage to the specific department responsible. The final step in the production process is the transfer of goods to the finished goods storeroom, which is evidenced by a document signed by the finished goods custodian, acknowledging receipt of the goods.

Organizational independence with respect to production work in process is achieved by separating the custodial functions (raw material stores, factory departments, and finished goods stores) from the recording function (cost accounting) and from the authorization function (production planning). Note that the custody of inventories is effectively controlled by requiring signed acknowledgment of every transfer of inventories from one department to another. In addition, control over production efficiency and quality is provided by effective supervision on the part of factory supervisors and by a responsibility accounting system that reports on production quality and costs for each factory department.

A common internal control problem in the production area involves theft of inventories by factory employees. The risk of theft can be minimized by maintaining current and accurate records of production inventories, by encouraging diligence on the part of factory supervisory personnel, and by providing an effective security program for the factory premises. Another critical internal control problem involves failure to maintain high levels of manufacturing efficiency and quality. This problem is addressed through sound engineering design, competent supervision, and an effective responsibility accounting and reporting system.

The Personnel/Payroll Cycle

The personnel/payroll cycle is a set of activities associated with hiring and compensating employees. These activities include collecting information on job applicants; selecting applicants to be hired; training, assigning, and evaluating employees; calculating employee compensation and benefits; and disbursing employee paychecks.

The primary objectives of internal control in the personnel/payroll cycle are to ensure that (1) all payroll transactions are properly authorized and accurately recorded and (2) wages and salaries are paid in appropriate amounts for services rendered. A key control procedure is to document the need to hire any new employee through formal requests initiated by supervisory personnel, approved by higher-level managers, and processed through a personnel department. Formal procedures should also be required to establish or change the level of compensation paid to any employee.

An accurate record of hours worked should be collected for employees paid on an hourly basis. This record may be obtained using a mechanical device such as a time clock or badge reader that records the time that each employee arrives and departs the work location. In addition, supervisory personnel are often required to prepare a record of the time spent by each employee on specific job assignments or perhaps to verify such records prepared by the employees themselves. These two independently prepared records of employee hours should be reconciled with each other as an initial step in payroll processing.

The data processing function is responsible for maintaining records of employment, pay rates, and authorized deductions for each employee. All changes in these records, including new hires and terminations as well as pay rate changes, should be authorized through the personnel department. Internal check procedures should be built into the payroll calculation process to ensure that employee compensation is accurately determined. Special procedures should be used to ensure that each paycheck is disbursed to the appropriate employee. Organizational independence in payroll processing is achieved by separating the authorization functions (supervisory employees and the personnel department) from the custodial functions (preparation and distribution of paychecks) and from the recording functions (timekeeping and payroll record keeping). A separate bank account for payroll is also a desirable control feature, because it greatly simplifies the record keeping associated with the organization's regular bank account.

Perhaps the most common payroll frauds involve overstating employee hours, hiring unauthorized employees, and inserting the names of fictitious employees on the payroll. All of these techniques were used in the embezzlement scheme perpetrated by the Los Angeles Dodgers' Payroll Director, as described earlier in the chapter. In addition, corporate managers sometimes abuse their authority by hiring relatives or friends who would not otherwise be employed. For example, while carrying out the audit at Springer's Northwest Lumber & Supply, Susan Lee noticed that numerous relatives and friends of management were on the payroll, which suggests the possibility of irregularities and deserves closer examination. Control procedures that minimize the risk of these types of employee fraud include separating the functions of hiring authorization, personnel and payroll record keeping, paycheck preparation, and paycheck distribution; independently verifying the accuracy of employee hours; and carefully controlling the process of distributing paychecks to employees.

The Financial Management Cycle

The financial management cycle is a set of activities directed at securing a steady flow of financial resources into and through an organization. These activities include establishing credit policies, managing the collection of receivables, obtaining equity and debt capital, planning capital expenditures, preparing financial and operating budgets, controlling cash flows, processing cash receipt and disbursement transactions, and administering the financial reporting process. For purposes of this brief discussion we focus on the role of internal control in processing cash receipt and disbursement transactions.

The basic objectives of internal controls for processing cash receipts and disbursements are (1) to ensure that all cash-related transactions are properly authorized and recorded and (2) to prevent the loss of cash. In this section four distinct cash processing functions are briefly reviewed: receipt of cash in payment for merchandise in a retail store, receipt of customer checks through the mail, cash disbursements by check, and the maintenance of a petty cash fund.

Important controls over the sale of merchandise for cash by a retail store include effective supervision, the use of sequentially prenumbered sales documents so that all sales documents can be accounted for, and the use of a cash register. Cash registers have such control features as optical scanners that accurately read item prices, automatic calculation and display of the correct amount of change to be returned to the customer, and an internal log of each recorded sale that cannot subsequently be altered. At the end of each cashier's shift the internal record of cash received should match the amount of cash accumulated in the employee's cash drawer. The receipt of cash over the counter is a particularly vulnerable process from an internal control standpoint, as illustrated by the case of a parts manager in an automobile dealership who would steal cash paid by customers for auto parts and destroy the duplicate copies of the invoice to conceal the theft.[19] The use of a cash register, together with sequentially prenumbered sales documents that are regularly checked to discover any missing documents, should minimize the risk of this kind of theft.

Customer payments on account are usually made by check through the mail. Control over these receipts typically begins in a mail room, where they are opened, recorded, and batched. Customers should be instructed to return a copy of an invoice or remittance document indicating the amount of the payment enclosed, to provide an independently prepared record of each payment. Close supervision provides additional control over the mail-opening function.

After the mail has been opened and a batch of checks collected, a separate employee (such as the company treasurer or senior cashier) should be responsible for endorsing the checks and depositing them in the bank. The bank should be instructed that no checks made out to the company should be cashed and that all must be deposited directly into the company's account. The remittance documents are used as the basis for posting the payments to customer account records. The batch total established in the mail room provides a control over the accuracy of both of these processes (see Fig. 12.1). Additional control is provided by the preparation of a bank reconciliation. Organizational independence is achieved by separating the functions of opening incoming mail, posting to customer accounts, endorsing and depositing checks in the bank, and preparing the bank reconciliation.

For control over cash disbursements it is essential that the functions of authorizing payment and recording accounts payable be separated from the function of writing checks. Many firms use a system in which the assembly of documents supporting a disbursement is followed by the preparation of a **voucher**, a document that summarizes the data relating to the disbursement and represents final authorization of payment. The person writing checks should examine the voucher and other supporting documents prior to preparing the check and should stamp "paid" or some other notation on the supporting documents to prevent them from being used more than once. Further control is provided by having a second employee examine the supporting documents and sign the checks. The function of preparing the bank recon-

---

[19] United States Fidelity & Guaranty Company, *The Forty Thieves* (Baltimore: USF&G Companies, 1970), 25.

ciliation should also be performed independently of authorizing payment and signing checks.

The potential for embezzlement by employees responsible for processing cash disbursements is illustrated by the case of a man employed as an assistant bookkeeper by a paint dealer. This employee would prepare one check for payment of an invoice and have it signed by one authorized company official. He would then prepare another check for payment of the *same* invoice and have it signed by a different official. He would cash the second check and keep the proceeds. Over a number of years he stole more than $53,000 in this manner.[20] This type of fraud can be prevented by separating the check preparation and check distribution functions and by requiring that all documents used to support cash disbursements be clearly marked as "paid" to preclude their reuse in this manner.

Many organizations like to be able to make some small disbursements in cash in order to avoid the delay and inconvenience of the voucher and check preparation procedure. In such cases it is often appropriate to establish a petty cash fund from which small disbursements of cash may be made. For control purposes it is best to limit the size of disbursements that may be made from the fund and to require the fund custodian to obtain a receipt for every disbursement made. The total amount of the fund should be maintained at a constant sum so that the total of all receipts and cash on hand is equal to the fund total at all times. Responsibility for the fund should be assigned to one person only and not separated. Checks to replenish the fund should pass through the regular voucher procedure, and supporting documentation in the form of all petty cash receipts should be required for replenishment. This procedure for setting aside a limited amount of funds for a specific purpose, to be periodically reimbursed from the company's general account, is called an **imprest system**.

This chapter so far has examined the internal control structure, including the control environment, the control procedures, and the accounting system. However, no internal control procedures are worthwhile unless their benefits exceed their costs. This raises the important issue of cost-benefit analysis of internal control, which is examined in the next section.

ANALYSIS OF THE COSTS AND BENEFITS OF INTERNAL CONTROL

No internal control system can ever provide an organization with foolproof protection against all internal control risks. The cost of a foolproof system would be prohibitively high. Therefore, the objective in designing an internal control system is to provide "reasonable assurance" that no control problems will arise. This means that the benefit of any internal control procedure must exceed its cost.

---

[20] *Ibid.*, 33.

The costs of an internal control system are much easier to measure than the benefits. The primary element of internal control cost is personnel cost, including the personnel time required to perform control procedures and the costs of hiring additional personnel in order to achieve effective segregation of duties.

The benefits of additional internal control procedures stem from reductions in the risk of loss. Any measure of loss must incorporate both the exposure, or amount of potential loss associated with a control problem, and the risk, or probability that the problem will occur. One such measure is **expected loss**, computed as the mathematical product of risk and exposure:

$$\text{expected loss} = \text{risk} \times \text{exposure}.$$

The expected loss from any potential control problem can be calculated, given estimates of exposure and risk. To evaluate the viability of a new control procedure, one must compute the expected loss both without the new procedure and with the new procedure. The estimated benefit of the new internal control procedure will be equal to the reduction in estimated expected loss resulting from its implementation. This measure must then be compared with the incremental cost of the new control procedure. Though such calculations are necessarily subjective and therefore susceptible to error, they are still useful in many cases as a rough guide.

An example of this method of cost-benefit analysis is provided by Joseph D. Hogg, an Audit Advisor at Atlantic Richfield in Los Angeles.[21] Consider a payroll system that prepares 12,000 checks biweekly. Occasionally, data errors occur that require reprocessing the entire payroll, at a cost of $10,000. Consideration is given to adding a data validation step that would reduce the risk of such data errors from 15% to 1%. This validation step would cost $600 per pay period. Should the validation step be employed? The analysis required to answer this question is shown in Table 12.5. To summarize, the expected loss without the validation step is 15% of $10,000, or $1500. With the validation step the expected loss is 1% of $10,000, or $100. Thus the validation step provides an expected benefit of $1400. Since it costs only $600, the validation step should clearly be implemented.

In evaluating the costs and benefits of internal control, management must employ good judgment and consider factors other than those reflected in the simple expected benefit calculation. For example, if the exposure is so large as to threaten the continued existence of the organization, management should be willing to implement internal control procedures having a cost higher than the simple reduction in expected loss. That is, it may be worthwhile to spend a little more than indicated by the cost-benefit analysis in order to minimize the possi-

---

[21] Joseph D. Hogg, "How Much Does an Error Cost—And How Much Does It Cost to Prevent It?" *Internal Auditor* (August 1992): 67–69.

	Without Validation Procedure	With Validation Procedure	Net Expected Difference
Cost to reprocess entire payroll	$10,000	$10,000	
Risk of payroll data errors	15%	1%	
Expected reprocessing cost ($10,000 × risk)	$1500	$100	$1400
Cost of validation procedure	$0	$600	$(600)
Net expected benefit of validation procedure			$800

Table 12.5
Cost-benefit analysis of payroll validation procedure.

bility that the organization will perish. This extra cost can be viewed as an insurance premium to protect the organization against catastrophic loss.

It has been suggested that risk can be factored into two components: inherent risk and control risk.[22] **Inherent risk** is the susceptibility of a set of accounts or transactions to significant control problems in the absence of internal control. For example, cash and inventories are inherently more susceptible to theft than are prepaid expenses and fixed assets. **Control risk** is the risk that a significant control problem will not be prevented or detected by the internal control system. Although this distinction has intuitive appeal, in practical settings internal control will never be completely absent, and therefore any measure of inherent risk will be of no value. In the evaluation of either an existing internal control system or a proposed system a *single* risk measure should be assessed. The assessment should take into account both the possibility that a control problem will arise (a possibility that will probably be reduced if the control system is improved, because good internal controls tend to discourage employees from being careless or dishonest) and the likelihood that the internal control system will prevent the problem or detect and correct it, if it does arise.

In evaluating the benefits of internal control procedures, management should consider both the effectiveness of the control procedure and its timing. All other factors being equal, a preventive control is superior to a detective control. By the time a control problem is identified by a detective control, a certain amount of control loss may already have been sustained, and additional cost may be required to correct the problem. By definition, preventive controls are designed to avoid such loss. On the other hand, if preventive controls fail and a control problem arises, detective controls are essential to discover the problem and recover from it. Thus preventive and detective controls

---

[22] AICPA, *Statement on Auditing Standards No. 55*, 13.

Figure 12.2
Steps in a controlled process.
(*Source:* Barry E. Cushing,
"A Mathematical Approach to the
Analysis and Design of Internal
Control Systems," *Accounting Review*
(January 1974): 24–41.
Reprinted by permission.)

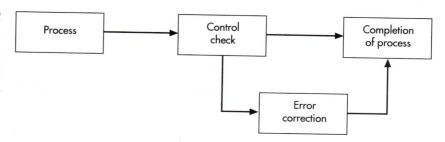

complement each other, and a good internal control system should employ both.

Reliability Analysis   Perhaps the most difficult aspect of internal control cost-benefit analysis is the assessment of risk, because it seems to be highly subjective. However, for many years engineers have utilized highly sophisticated techniques to measure the reliability of automated systems, including systems that involve a combination of human and machine processes. The reliability of a system or process is the probability that it will be completed without error. Since risk is the probability that error will occur, risk and reliability are mathematical complements; that is,

$$risk = 1 - reliability.$$

This suggests that by adapting the techniques of reliability engineering to the analysis of internal control systems, an organization may be able to derive more objective measures of the risks associated with an internal control system—and hence more satisfactory assessments of the benefits of internal control.

One well-known method of assessing the reliability of an internal control system in processing a particular transaction or set of transactions was developed by Cushing.[23] This technique assesses the effectiveness of a specific control procedure (such as the use of a control total in posting a batch of transactions to an account) in detecting and correcting a specific type of error (such as an error in posting one or more transaction amounts). Internal control procedures of this kind may be viewed in terms of a series of steps, including the initial process, the control check (or detection step), and the error correction step (see Fig. 12.2).

In Cushing's reliability model the system reliability measure is computed from a series of reliability measures for the individual components of the process. Completion of the process with no errors will

---

[23] Barry E. Cushing, "A Mathematical Approach to the Analysis and Design of Internal Control Systems," *Accounting Review* (January 1974): 24–41.

occur when any two of the three steps preceding process completion (see Fig. 12.2) are correctly performed. The individual reliability measures required are the following probability estimates.

P = the probability that the original process (such as posting) will be correctly executed.

D = the probability that the control check (such as comparison of control totals) will detect and signal an error, given that one exists.

N = the probability that the control check will not signal an error if no error exists.

C = the probability that the error correction process will find and correct an error, given that one exists and has been signaled.

F = the probability that, in the event that the control check signals an error when none exists, this mistake will be discovered and the original process results allowed to stand.

Note that each of the parameters represents the probability of a correct system action, and that for each one there is a complementary probability of error. For example, $1 - P$ is the probability that the original process will be incorrectly executed.

Reliability (indicated by R) is equal to the sum of three probabilities:[24]

$$R = (P \times N) + [P \times (1 - N) \times F] + [(1 - P) \times D \times C],$$

where

$(P \times N)$ = the probability that the process will be executed correctly and the control step will not signal an error,

$[P \times (1 - N) \times F]$ = the probability that the process will be executed correctly and the control check will erroneously signal an error, but that the control error will be discovered and the process results will not be changed,

$[(1 - P) \times D \times C]$ = the probability that an error in the process will be made but that the control check will signal an error and the proper correction will be made.

Table 12.6 shows the calculation of system reliability for a set of hypothetical component reliability estimates.

The following example shows how measures of internal control reliability may be incorporated into a cost-benefit analysis of internal control. Assume that the exposure associated with a particular internal

---

[24] In these calculations the joint probabilities of successful process completion are mathematical products of the marginal probabilities associated with individual steps in the process. A necessary assumption is that the marginal probability values are statistically independent.

Hypothetical Estimates	Calculations			
$P = 0.8$	(1) $P \times N$		$= (0.8)(0.9)$	$= 0.7200$
$D = 0.95$	(2) $P \times (1 - N) \times F$	$= (0.8)(0.1)(0.99)$		$= 0.0792$
$N = 0.9$	(3) $(1 - P) \times D \times C$	$= (0.2)(0.95)(0.98)$		$= \underline{0.1862}$
$C = 0.98$				$R = 0.9854$
$F = 0.99$				

Table 12.6
Illustrative reliability calculations.

control problem is $10,000, and that the internal control system that deals with this problem has a reliability of 90%. This means that the risk is 10% (1.00 − 0.90) and the expected loss is $1000 (10% of $10,000). Now suppose that an additional internal control procedure costing $500 has been proposed that would improve system reliability to 98%. This improvement would reduce the risk to 2% (1.00 − 0.98) and the expected loss to $200 (2% of $10,000). The benefit of this proposed internal control procedure may be measured by the $800 reduction in expected loss ($1000 − $200). This estimated benefit exceeds the cost of $500, suggesting that the new control procedure should be implemented.

The reliability model provides a framework for collecting information about data processing systems and their associated internal control procedures. Management may use it simply to evaluate the effectiveness of existing internal control procedures or to decide whether to implement additional controls. It may be used by itself or in conjunction with the expected loss model. It may be extended to systems incorporating multiple control procedures and to systems in which several different kinds of errors may occur, with each type of error having its own probability of occurrence. It may be applied to internal control procedures that are performed by people or to those executed by computers. The reliability model is thus a useful technique with a variety of applications.

Compliance with the Foreign Corrupt Practices Act

Cost-benefit analysis provides management with a framework for evaluating and documenting its compliance with the internal control provisions of the Foreign Corrupt Practices Act of 1977. As described earlier in this chapter, these provisions require all publicly held corporations to maintain good systems of internal accounting control. Although most executives would contend that their systems of internal accounting control were good prior to passage of this act, most also deem it necessary to take specific steps to demonstrate that their corporations are in compliance with the act's internal control provisions.

The first step in such a compliance program is to document the corporation's existing internal accounting control systems. Documentation may include narrative descriptions of internal control objectives and procedures; document flowcharts and systems flowcharts delineating data and information flows; and organization charts, job descriptions, and other explanations of assigned responsibilities within the organization. Many authorities have suggested that this process can be facilitated by considering the internal accounting control system as consisting of a series of systems, one for each of the organization's major accounting cycles. Each accounting cycle then becomes the focal point of a separate analysis and documentation effort.[25]

The second step in a compliance program is to evaluate the quality of the internal accounting control system. Because the law stipulates that the control system must provide "reasonable assurances" that certain control objectives are being met, this evaluation may be based on a cost-benefit analysis. All significant control threats within each accounting cycle should be identified, and estimates of the exposure and risk associated with each threat should be developed. Any control threats for which expected loss exceeds a minimum threshold (determined by management) represent potential control weaknesses that require further analysis.

The third step is to evaluate the costs and benefits of instituting controls to deal with each potential control weakness. Costs include direct expenditures to implement control procedures and possible indirect effects such as reductions in employee morale or delays in transaction processing. Benefits include estimates of reductions in expected loss and other factors such as increased management confidence in the system and prevention of losses having potentially catastrophic effects on the organization. Many of these cost and benefit estimates must necessarily be made subjectively.

The final step is to weigh the costs and benefits and make a prudent judgment about whether more control is needed. If the benefits of a control procedure (both quantitative and subjective) outweigh the related costs, that control procedure should be implemented. If proposed internal control procedures do not provide benefits that exceed their costs, the existing internal control system should be retained.[26] By undertaking a careful review and evaluation of this kind, management demonstrates that it has obtained "reasonable assurances" that any potential control weaknesses have been identified, evaluated, and dealt with appropriately.

Compliance with the internal control requirements of the Foreign Corrupt Practices Act is a continuous process—not simply a one-year project—of reviewing and evaluating control systems. The primary responsibility for this process rests with management, which in turn

---

[25] See, for example, Arthur Andersen and Company, *A Guide for Studying and Evaluating Internal Accounting Controls* (Chicago: Arthur Andersen, 1978); or American Institute of Certified Public Accountants, *Report of the Special Advisory Committee on Internal Accounting Control* (New York: AICPA, 1979).

[26] This evaluation procedure is described in greater detail in Price Waterhouse & Company, *Guide to Accounting Controls: Establishing, Evaluating and Monitoring Control Systems* (New York: Price Waterhouse & Company, 1979), 24–48.

must rely on the assistance of accounting systems designers and internal and external auditors. The corporation's board of directors and its audit committee are also responsible for ensuring that management adopts the policies and processes involved in compliance. Many corporations have discovered that regardless of the legal requirements a compliance program that continuously monitors the effectiveness of internal accounting controls makes good business sense.

CASE CONCLUSION: INVESTIGATING THE INTERNAL CONTROL SYSTEM AT SPRINGER'S NORTHWEST LUMBER & SUPPLY

After spending three days in Bozeman, Jason Scott and Susan Lee returned to the main office of Northwest Industries in Portland, Oregon, and filed a report of their findings at Springer's Northwest Lumber & Supply. One week later, they were each summoned to the office of Roger Sawyer, Northwest's Director of Internal Auditing, to explain their findings in greater detail. Shortly thereafter, a high-level internal audit team was dispatched to Bozeman to take a closer look at the situation at Springer's.

After the audit team returned, Jason and Susan were curious about what they had found. They made inquiries but were told that the situation was still under investigation. Six months later, they had heard nothing new. Then a company newsletter included a short announcement that the Springer family had sold their remaining 10% interest in the Bozeman lumber and supply business to Northwest and had resigned from their management positions there. Two Northwest executives from other locations were being transferred to Bozeman to replace them. Still, there was no word on the audit findings.

Jason and Susan did not find out what had happened until two years later, when they were assigned to a job supervised by Frank Ratliff, who had been one of the members of the high-level internal audit team sent to Bozeman to investigate Springer's. After-hours one evening, Ratliff swore them to secrecy and then told them the story. On the basis of the reports prepared by Jason and Susan, the investigation team had examined a large sample of purchasing transactions and all employee timekeeping and payroll records over a 12-month period, and it had also taken a detailed physical inventory. The team discovered that the problems identified by Jason—including missing purchase requisitions, missing purchase orders and receiving reports to support payments to vendors, and excessive item prices—were widespread among the purchasing transactions it examined. Team members also found that these problems occurred almost exclusively among transactions with three large vendors from whom Springer's had purchased several million dollars worth of inventories and supplies. Members of the team discussed the unusually high item prices with representatives of these vendors, but they did not receive a satisfactory explanation. However, a check of the county business licensing bureau revealed that Bill Springer held a significant ownership interest in each of these three vendors. Thus by authorizing the payment of excessive prices to companies he partially owned, Bill Springer would have earned a share of several hundred thousand dollars of excessive profits, all at the expense of Northwest Industries.

The investigation team had also found evidence that several employees who were on Springer's payroll had received paychecks either for not working at all or for working fewer hours than could be documented according to timekeeping records. Finally, the team determined that Springer's inventory account was materially overstated. The physical inventory revealed that a significant quantity of the inventory recorded in the books did not exist, and that other portions of the recorded inventory were unsalable. The adjusting journal entry required to write down Springer's inventory to a satisfactory value wiped out a substantial portion of the outlet's reported profits over the past three years.

When they confronted the Springers with these findings, team members received vehement denials that any laws had been broken. They had considered going to the authorities to seek a formal investigation of fraud and embezzlement, but they became concerned that their case might not be strong enough to prove in court. They were also worried that adverse publicity might damage the company's strong position in the Bozeman market. So after a few months of negotiation with the Springers they agreed to the settlement that had been reported in the newsletter. Part of the settlement was that no public statement would ever be made about any alleged fraud or embezzlement involving the Springers. According to Ratliff, this was not unusual. In many cases of likely or obvious fraud or embezzlement settlements are reached quietly, with no legal action being taken, so that the company can avoid adverse publicity. ■

SUMMARY

One of the primary functions of the accounting information system is to assist management in the control of business operations and activities. This function is embodied in the concept of internal control, which has been defined by the AICPA as comprising "the plan of organization and all of the coordinate methods and measures adopted within a business to safeguard its assets, check the accuracy and reliability of its accounting data, promote operational efficiency, and encourage adherence to prescribed managerial policies." Since its promulgation in 1949 this definition has been embellished numerous times in AICPA literature. The language of one AICPA pronouncement was incorporated by the U.S. Congress into the Foreign Corrupt Practices Act of 1977, which requires publicly held corporations to maintain systems of internal accounting control that meet certain minimum standards.

According to recent AICPA literature, an organization's internal control structure consists of three elements. The first is the control environment, which is the general framework within which specific control policies and procedures operate. The second is the accounting system, which consists of records and procedures used to record, process, and report the organization's transactions and to maintain accountability for the related assets and liabilities. The third is specific control procedures, including proper authorization of transactions, segregation of duties, design and use of adequate documents and records, adequate safeguards over access to and use of assets and records, and independent checks on performance. The concept of the internal control structure provides a useful framework for understanding the nature of internal control systems in business organizations.

No internal control system is foolproof. At best, an internal control system provides only reasonable assurance that control threats and risks are being minimized. Thus the costs and benefits of control must be considered. Although the incremental costs of control procedures can often be estimated, control benefits are harder to quantify. One approach to quantifying benefits involves estimating the expected loss from a particular control threat as the mathematical product of the risk and the exposure associated with the threat. The risk variable may be calculated using a model that considers the reliability of the various components of the internal control system.

Control and accounting are inexorably intertwined. Indeed, it may be said that control is the central concept and purpose of accounting and that accounting is the primary vehicle of control in business organizations.

KEY TERMS

Define the following terms.

embezzlement	feedback controls	batch totals
threats	feedback	control totals
exposure	feedforward controls	transposition error
risk	fidelity bond	transcription error
internal control	authorization	voucher
accounting controls	specific authorization	imprest system
administrative controls	general authorization	expected loss
internal control structure	organizational independence	inherent risk
management control	collusion	control risk
preventive controls	audit trail	reliability
detective controls	transaction trail	
corrective controls	internal check	

Discussion questions

12.1 Consider the internal control problems encountered by Jason Scott and Susan Lee during their audit of Springer's Northwest Lumber & Supply, as described at the beginning and end of the chapter. Discuss the following questions.

   a. What deficiencies existed in the control environment at Springer's?

   b. Do you agree with the decision to reach a settlement with the Springers rather than to prosecute them for fraud and embezzlement?

   c. Should Jason and Susan have been told about the final outcome of the case? Explain.

   d. What lessons may be learned from this episode and from the way it was resolved?

12.2 For each of the control activities listed, discuss whether the activity contains elements of a preventive control, a feedback control, and/or a feedforward control. (*Note:* Some may contain elements of two or all three.)

   a. Audit of a governmental agency by the General Accounting Office

   b. Tabulation and review of customer complaints by a manager

   c. Review of sales statistics indicating the impact of various advertising techniques on consumers' buying behavior

   d. Review of trends in the number of passengers on various routes by an airline

   e. Analysis of résumés of potential employees by a manager responsible for hiring

   f. Reporting of student grades in a university

   g. Analysis of accident statistics in a factory

12.3 Effective segregation of duties is sometimes not economically feasible in a small business. What other elements of internal control should be given greater emphasis in a small business in order to compensate for the lack of effective segregation of duties?

12.4 Refer to Fig. 12.1 and the related discussion of cash receipts processing by Sarah and Craig Robinson. Note that all of the procedures described are performed manually. Craig has just purchased a personal computer for his home and intends to computerize the records for Sarah's business. Discuss the effect that this will have on the use of batch totals in cash receipts processing.

12.5 Some people feel that controls in business organizations are dysfunctional, in that they create resentment and loss of morale without producing much benefit. Discuss this position.

12.6 You are an executive with the Superwidget Corporation. In recent years Superwidget's external auditors have given clean opinions on its financial statements and favorable evaluations of its internal control systems. Discuss whether it is necessary for your corporation to take any further action to comply with the Foreign Corrupt Practices Act.

Problems

12.1 You are an audit supervisor who has recently been assigned to a new client, Go-Go Corporation. You recently visited Go-Go's corporate headquarters to become acquainted with key personnel and to conduct a preliminary review of the company's accounting policies and systems. During this visit, the following events occurred.

- You met briefly with Go-Go's audit committee, which consists of the corporate Controller, Treasurer, Financial Vice-President, and Budget Director.

- You recognized the corporate Treasurer as a former aide to John Boatsky, who was convicted of fraud in an insider-trading scandal three years ago.

■ At another meeting management explained its plans to change its method of accounting for depreciation from the accelerated method to the straight-line method. Management implied that if your firm does not concur with this change, Go-Go will employ other auditors.

■ You learned that the Financial Vice-President serves as the manager of a staff of five internal auditors.

■ You noted that all management authority seems to reside with three brothers, who serve as Chief Executive Officer, President, and Financial Vice-President.

■ You were told that the performance of divisional and departmental managers is evaluated on a subjective basis, because Go-Go's management believes that formal performance evaluation procedures are "counterproductive."

■ You learned that the company has reported increases in earnings per share for each of the past 25 quarters. However, earnings during the current quarter have leveled off and may decline.

■ You reviewed the company's policy and procedures manual, which consisted of descriptions of policies for dealing with customers, vendors, and employees.

■ Your preliminary assessment is that the accounting systems are well designed and employ effective internal control procedures.

Required

The information you have obtained suggests possible problems relating to one or more of the elements of Go-Go's internal control structure. Identify these possible problems, and explain each problem in relation to internal control structure concepts.

12.2 The first column in Table 12.7 is a list of amounts from source documents that have been summed to obtain a batch total. You may assume that these amounts and the batch total are correct.

Columns (a)–(d) contain batch totals computed from the same amounts after these source documents were processed in a subsequent processing step. In each of these four cases one processing error was made. In each case you are to (1) compute the difference between the batch total obtained after processing and the correct batch total shown on the left, (2) explain specifically how this difference is helpful in discovering the processing error, and (3) identify the processing error.

12.3 Explain how the principle of organizational independence is being violated in each of the following situations.

Table 12.7 Amounts from source documents	(a)	(b)	(c)	(d)
$3,630.62	$3,630.62	$3,630.62	$3,630.62	$3,630.62
1,484.86	1,484.86	1,484.86	1,484.86	1,484.86
2,164.67	2,164.67	2,164.67	2,164.67	2,164.67
946.43	946.43	946.43	946.43	946.43
2,626.28	− 2,626.28	2,626.28	2,626.28	2,626.28
969.97	969.97	969.97	969.97	969.97
2,772.42	2,772.42	2,772.42	3,772.42	2,772.42
934.25	934.25	934.25	934.25	934.25
1,620.94	1,620.94	1,620.94	1,620.94	1,620.94
4,566.86	4,566.86	4,656.86	4,566.86	4,566.86
1,249.32	1,249.32	1,249.32	1,249.32	1,249.32
1,070.27	1,070.27	1,070.27	1,070.27	1,070.27
2,668.51	2,668.51	2,668.51	2,668.51	2,668.51
1,762.62	1,762.62	1,762.62	1,762.62	873.26
873.26	873.26	873.26	873.26	$27,578.66
$29,341.28	$24,088.72	$29,431.28	$30,341.28	

a. A payroll employee recorded a 40-hour work-week for an employee who had quit the previous week. He then prepared a paycheck for this employee, cashed it by forging the signature, and kept the cash.

b. While opening the mail, the cashier set aside two checks payable to the company on account and later cashed these checks and pocketed the cash.

c. The cashier prepared a fictitious invoice from a company having the name of his brother-in-law and wrote a check in payment of the invoice, which the brother-in-law later cashed.

d. An employee of the finishing department walked off with several parts from the storeroom and recorded the items in the inventory ledger as having been issued to the assembly department.

e. The cashier cashed a check from a customer in payment of an account receivable, pocketed the cash, and concealed the theft by properly posting the receipt to the customer's account in the accounts receivable ledger.

12.4 McClain's Lumberyard uses the following procedures in selling lumber to customers.

■ The customer informs a clerk in the office of the sizes and quantities of lumber to be purchased.

■ The clerk records the items on a sales document, calculates the total cost, and collects payment from the customer.

■ A yard worker obtains the lumber from the yard and assists in loading it onto the customer's car or truck; or if the purchase is large and the customer wishes, McClain's will deliver the order.

Required

Explain several aspects of the design and use of the sales document that will facilitate control of cash receipts and inventories by McClain's.

12.5 The Y Company, a client of your firm, has come to you with the following problem: It has three clerical employees who must perform the following functions.

1. Maintain the general ledger
2. Maintain the accounts payable ledger
3. Maintain the accounts receivable ledger
4. Prepare checks for signature
5. Maintain the disbursements journal
6. Issue credits on returns and allowances
7. Reconcile the bank account
8. Handle and deposit cash receipts

Assuming that there is no problem about the ability of any of the employees, the company requests that you assign these functions to the three employees in such a manner as to achieve the highest degree of internal control. Assume that these employees will perform no other accounting functions than the ones listed, and that any accounting functions not listed will be performed by persons other than these three employees.

Required

a. List four possible unsatisfactory pairings of the functions.

b. State how you would distribute the functions among the three employees. Assume that with the exception of the nominal jobs of the bank reconciliation and the issuance of credits on returns and allowances, all functions require an equal amount of time.

(CPA Examination)

12.6 The Future Corporation is a small manufacturing concern in Aggie, Texas. It operates one plant and employs 50 workers in its manufacturing facility. Employees are paid weekly. Each week the department supervisors supply the payroll clerk with signed time sheets and also with a list of any employees hired or terminated by the supervisor. The payroll clerk compares the time sheets with the time cards and prepares and signs payroll checks. The paychecks are then given in sealed envelopes to the supervisors, who in turn give them to the respective employees.

Required

Identify several weaknesses in internal control over Future's payroll system. For each weakness, describe how internal control could be improved.

12.7 You are auditing the Alaska Branch of Far Distributing Company. This branch has substantial annual sales, which are billed and collected locally. As a part of your audit, you find that the procedures for handling cash receipts are as follows:

Cash collections on over-the-counter sales and COD sales are received from the customer or delivery service by the Cashier. Upon receipt of cash the Cashier stamps the sales ticket "paid" and files a copy for future reference. The only record of COD sales is a copy of the sales ticket, which is given to the Cashier to hold until the cash is received from the delivery service.

Mail is opened by the secretary to the Credit Manager, and remittances are given to the Credit

Manager for review. The Credit Manager then places the remittances in a tray on the Cashier's desk. At the daily deposit cutoff time the Cashier delivers the checks and cash on hand to the Assistant Credit Manager, who prepares remittance lists and makes up the bank deposit that the manager also takes to the bank. The Assistant Credit Manager also posts remittances to the accounts receivable ledger cards and verifies the cash discount allowable.

You also ascertain that the Credit Manager obtains approval from the executive office at Far Distributing Company, located in Chicago, to write off uncollectible accounts, and that the Manager has retained in custody as of the end of the fiscal year some remittances that were received on various days during the last month.

Required

a. Describe the irregularities that might occur under the procedures now in effect for handling cash collections and remittances.

b. Give procedures that you would recommend to strengthen internal control over cash collections and remittances.

(CPA Examination)

12.8 ConSport Corporation is a regional wholesaler of sporting goods. The systems flowchart in Fig. 12.3 and the following description present ConSport's cash distribution system.

1. The Accounts Payable Department approves for payment all invoices (I) for the purchase of inventory. Invoices are matched with the purchase requisitions (PR), purchase orders (PO), and receiving reports (RR). The accounts payable clerks focus on vendor name and skim the documents when they are combined.

2. When all the documents for an invoice are assembled, a two-copy disbursement voucher (DV) is prepared, and the transaction is recorded in the voucher register (VR). The disbursement voucher and supporting documents are then filed alphabetically by vendor.

3. A two-copy journal voucher (JV) that summarizes each day's entries in the voucher register is prepared daily. The first copy is sent to the General Ledger Department, and the second copy is filed in the Accounts Payable Department by date.

4. The vendor file is searched daily for the disbursement vouchers of invoices that are due to be paid. Both copies of disbursement vouchers that are due to be paid are sent to the Treasury Department, along with the supporting documents. The Cashier prepares a check for each vendor, signs the check, and records it in the check register (CR). Copy 1 of the disbursement voucher is attached to the check copy and filed in check number order in the Treasury Department. Copy 2 and the supporting documents are returned to the Accounts Payable Department and filed alphabetically by vendor.

5. A two-copy journal voucher that summarizes each day's checks is prepared. Copy 1 is sent to the General Ledger Department, and Copy 2 is filed in the Treasury Department by date.

6. The Cashier receives the monthly bank statement with canceled checks and prepares the bank reconciliation (BR). If an adjustment is required as a consequence of the bank reconciliation, a two-copy journal voucher is prepared. Copy 1 is sent to the General Ledger Department. Copy 2 is attached to Copy 1 of the bank reconciliation and filed by month in the Treasury Department. Copy 2 of the bank reconciliation is sent to the Internal Audit Department.

Required

ConSport Corporation's cash disbursement system has some weaknesses. Review the cash disbursement system.

a. For each weakness in the system, identify where the weakness exists by using the reference number that appears to the left of each symbol in Fig. 12.3.

b. Describe the nature of the weakness.

c. Make a recommendation about how to correct the weakness.

Use the following format in preparing your answer.

Reference Number	Nature of Weakness	Recommendation to Correct Weakness

(CMA Examination)

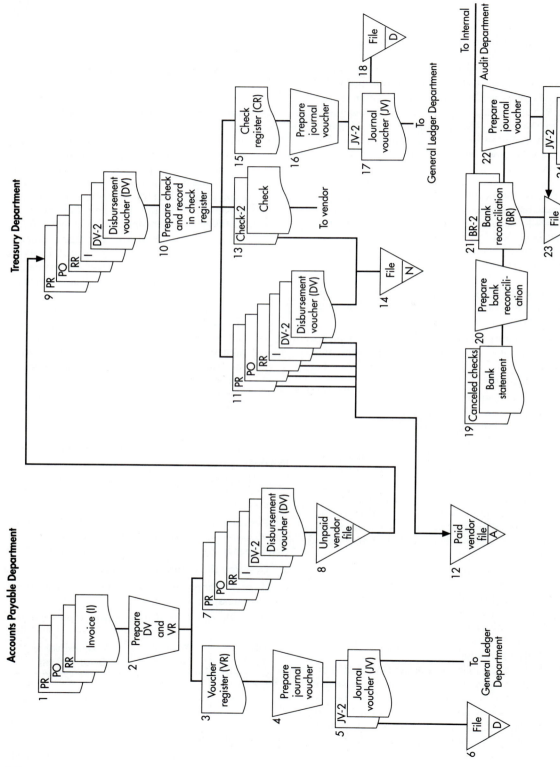

Figure 12.3 Cash distribution system for ComSport corporation

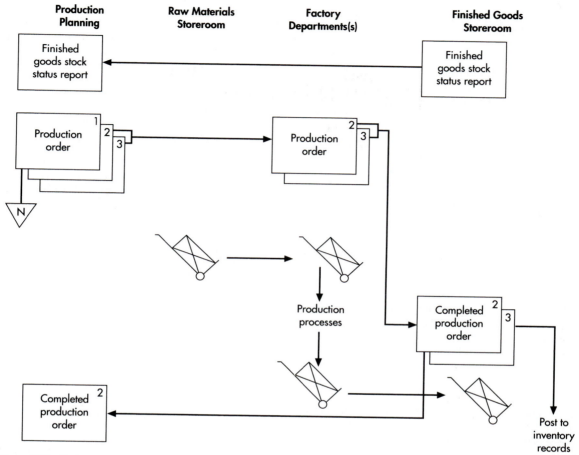

Figure 12.4 Production operations document flows for April Manufacturing

12.9 Figure 12.4 is a document flowchart prepared by a clerk to document data flows relating to production operations for the April Manufacturing Company.

Required

a. Describe several deficiencies in internal control in the system shown in Fig. 12.4. For each deficiency, indicate an error, manipulation, or inefficiency that may result.

b. Indicate the best means of remedying each deficiency described in part a.

12.10 The Kowal Manufacturing Company employs about 50 production workers and has the following payroll procedures.

The Factory Supervisor interviews applicants and, on the basis of the interview, either hires or rejects the applicants. The applicant who is hired prepares a W-4 form (Employee's Withholding Exemption Certificate) and gives it to the Supervisor. The Supervisor writes the hourly rate of pay for the new employee in the corner of the W-4 form and then gives the form to a payroll clerk as notice that the worker has been employed. The Supervisor verbally advises the Payroll Department of rate adjustments.

A supply of blank time cards is kept in a box near the entrance to the factory. All workers take a time card on Monday morning, fill in their names, and note in pencil on the time card their daily arrival and departure times. At the end of the week the workers drop the time cards in a box near the door to the factory. The completed time cards are taken from the box on Monday morning by a payroll clerk. Two payroll clerks divide the cards alphabetically between them, one taking the A to L section of the payroll and the other taking the M to Z section. Each clerk is fully responsible for a section of the payroll. The clerk computes the gross pay, deductions, and net pay, posts the details to the employee's earnings records, and prepares and numbers the payroll checks. Employees are automatically removed from the payroll when they fail to turn in a time card.

The payroll checks are manually signed by the Chief Accountant and given to the Supervisor. The Supervisor distributes the checks to the workers in the factory and arranges for the delivery of the checks to the workers who are absent. The payroll bank account is reconciled by the Chief Accountant, who also prepares the various quarterly and annual payroll tax reports.

Required

List your suggestions for improving the Kowal Manufacturing Company's system of internal control for the factory hiring practices and payroll procedures.   (CPA Examination)

12.11 The flowchart in Fig. 12.5 depicts the activities relating to the shipping, billing, and collecting processes used by Smallco Lumber, Inc.

Required

Identify weaknesses in the system of internal accounting control relating to the activities of (a) the warehouse clerk, (b) bookkeeper 1, (c) bookkeeper 2, and (d) the collection clerk.   (CPA Examination)

12.12 The accounting and internal control procedures relating to purchases of materials by the Branden Company, a medium-sized concern manufacturing special machinery to order, have been described by your junior accountant in the following terms.

After approval by Manufacturing Department supervisors, materials purchase requisitions are forwarded to the Purchasing Department Supervisor, who distributes such requisitions to the several employees under his control. These employees prepare prenumbered purchase orders in triplicate, account for all numbers, and send the original purchase order to the vendor. One copy of the purchase order is sent to the Receiving Department, where it is used

as a receiving report. The other copy is filed in the Purchasing Department.

When the materials are received, they are moved directly to the storeroom and issued to the supervisors on informal requests. The Receiving Department sends a receiving report (with its copy of the purchase order attached) to the Purchasing Department and forwards copies of the receiving report to the storeroom and to the Accounting Department.

Vendors' invoices for material purchases, received in duplicate in the mail room, are sent to the Purchasing Department and directed to the employee who placed the related order. The employee then compares the invoice with the copy of the purchase order on file in the Purchasing Department for price and terms, and she compares the invoice quantity received as reported by the Shipping and Receiving Department on its copy of the purchase order. The Purchasing Department employees also check discounts, footings, and extensions, after which they initial the invoice to indicate approval for payment. The invoice is then submitted to the voucher section of the Accounting Department, where it is coded for account distribution, assigned a voucher number, entered in the voucher register, and filed according to payment due date.

Required

Discuss the weaknesses, if any, in the internal control of Branden's purchasing and subsequent procedures. Suggest supplementary or revised procedures for remedying each weakness with regard to (a) requisition of materials and (b) receipt and storage of materials.   (CPA Examination)

12.13 For each of the six cases listed in Table 12.8, compute system reliability. Note that in case 1 all parameters have a value of 0.90, whereas in cases 2 through 6 one of the parameters drops from 0.90 to 0.80. For which parameter is the drop from 0.90 to 0.80 most critical in terms of the relative effect on R?

12.14 During a recent review ABC Corporation discovered that it has a serious internal control problem. It is estimated that the exposure associated with this problem is $1 million and that the risk is presently 5%. Two internal control procedures have been proposed to deal with this problem. Procedure A would cost $25,000 and would reduce risk to 2%. Procedure B would cost $30,000 and would reduce risk to 1%. If both procedures were implemented, risk would be reduced to a tenth of 1%.

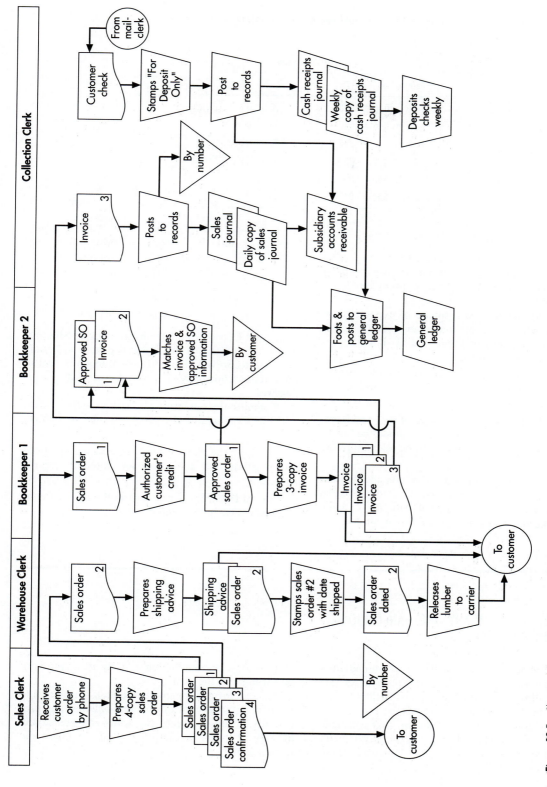

Figure 12.5 Shipping, billing, and collection processes for Smallco Lumber

Table 12.8
Six cases for computing reliability

Case	PROBABILITIES					
	P	D	N	C	F	R
1	0.90	0.90	0.90	0.90	0.90	
2	0.80	0.90	0.90	0.90	0.90	
3	0.90	0.80	0.90	0.90	0.90	
4	0.90	0.90	0.80	0.90	0.90	
5	0.90	0.90	0.90	0.80	0.90	
6	0.90	0.90	0.90	0.90	0.80	

Required

a. What is the estimated expected loss associated with ABC Corporation's internal control problem before any new internal control procedures are implemented?

b. Compute the revised estimate of expected loss (1) if procedure A were implemented, (2) if procedure B were implemented, and (3) if both procedures were implemented.

c. Compare the estimated costs and benefits of procedure A, procedure B, and both procedures combined.

d. Considering only the estimates of cost and benefit, which procedure or procedures should be implemented? What other factors might be relevant to the decision?

12.15 The Gibson Corporation is considering improving its existing internal control system. System reliability parameters associated with the existing system and the proposed system are as shown.

Parameter	Existing	Proposed
P	0.80	0.80
D	0.95	0.95
N	0.80	0.90
C	0.90	0.90
F	0.90	0.90

Gibson Corporation has an exposure of $100,000 due to the threat that this internal control system is designed to prevent. The proposed improvement in the internal control system would cost $300.

Required

a. Compute the reliability and risk associated with both the existing and the proposed internal control system.

b. Compute the expected loss associated with both the existing and the proposed internal control system.

c. Should the proposed change in the internal control system be implemented?

CASE 12.1 ANYCOMPANY, INC.: AN ONGOING COMPREHENSIVE CASE

One of the best ways to learn is to immediately apply what you have studied. The purpose of this case is to allow you to do that. You will select a local company that you can work with. At the end of most chapters you will find an assignment that will have you apply what you have learned using the company you have selected as a reference. This case, then,

may become an ongoing case study that you work on throughout the term.

Select a local company, and obtain permission to study its internal control systems, policies, and procedures. Then complete the following steps, and prepare a report describing your findings and conclusions.

1.   Obtain copies of organization charts, job descriptions, and related documentation on how authority and responsibility have been assigned within the organization. Evaluate whether lines of authority and responsibility seem to be clearly defined.

2.   Determine whether the company has an internal audit function. If so, visit with an internal audit supervisor or manager and learn (a) to whom in the organization the head of internal auditing reports and (b) what kinds of jobs the internal auditing function generally performs.

3.   If the company is a corporation whose equity securities are publicly traded, determine whether it has taken steps to document its compliance with the internal control provisions of the Foreign Corrupt Practices Act of 1977. If possible, examine and evaluate this documentation.

4.   If the company is a corporation whose equity securities are publicly traded, determine whether there is an audit committee of the board of directors. If so, obtain a list of the members of the audit committee and a copy of the committee's charter or bylaws.

5.   Interview someone in the personnel department who is involved in hiring employees for positions in accounting and data processing. Find out the following information.

a.   What sort of background checks are performed before these employees are hired

b.   Whether fidelity bond coverage is normally obtained for these employees

c.   Whether the company requires rotation of duties and enforced vacations for these employees

6.   Select any one of the five accounting data processing cycles described in this chapter (e.g., the revenue cycle, the procurement cycle, etc.), and examine your company's internal control procedures within that accounting cycle.

a.   Identify the persons responsible for transaction authorization, record keeping, and asset custody functions.

b.   Learn how transaction documents and/or records are used to facilitate internal control.

c.   Follow the audit trail by tracing one accounting transaction from its original source document through its entry in journals, ledgers, files, and so on, and ultimately the general ledger accounts.

d.   Identify some policies and procedures used to safeguard assets and records.

e.   Identify several internal check procedures.

CASE 12.2 THE GREATER PROVIDENCE DEPOSIT & TRUST EMBEZZLEMENT

On a Saturday afternoon in the spring of 1988 Nino Moscardi received an anonymous note in his mail. Moscardi, President of Greater Providence Deposit & Trust, was shocked to read the note's allegations: that an employee of the bank was putting through bogus loans. On the following Monday he directed the bank's internal auditors to investigate certain transactions detailed in the note. The investigation led to James Guisti, manager of a North Providence branch office and a trusted 14-year employee who had once worked as one of the bank's auditors. Guisti was later charged with embezzling $1.83 mil-

lion from the bank through 67 phony loans taken out over a 3-year period.

Court documents revealed numerous details of Guisti's embezzlement scheme. For example, the first bogus loan was written in April 1985 for $10,000. The loans were 90-day notes requiring no collateral and ranged in amount from $10,000 to $63,500. Guisti originated all of the loans; and when each loan matured, he would take out a new loan, or rewrite the old loan, to pay the principal and interest due. Some loans had been rewritten five or six times.

The 67 loans were taken out in various names, including his wife's maiden name, the name of his father, and the names of two of his friends. All of these persons denied that they had received any stolen funds or knew anything about the embezzlement scheme. In addition, one loan was in the name of James Vanesse, who police said did not exist. The Social Security number on Vanesse's loan application was issued to a female, and the phone number belonged to a North Providence auto dealer.

Court records also disclosed the details of police interviews with bank employees to determine how the loan money was dispensed. According to Lucy Fraioli, a customer service representative who co-signed checks to the five names to which Guisti had originated loans, Guisti was her supervisor and she thought nothing was wrong with the checks, though she didn't know any of the five people. Marcia Perfetto, Head Teller at the branch, told police that she had cashed checks for Guisti made out to four of the five persons. Asked if she gave the money to Guisti when he gave her the checks to cash, she answered, "Not all of the time," though she could not recall ever giving the money directly to any of the four, whom she said she didn't know.

According to news reports, Guisti was authorized to make consumer loans up to a certain dollar limit without loan committee approvals, which is a standard industry practice. Guisti's lending limit was $10,000 until January 1987, when it was increased to $15,000. In February 1988 it was increased again to $25,000. However, some of the loans, including the one for $63,500, far exceeded his lending limit. In addition, all loan applications should have been accompanied by a report on the applicant's credit history, purchased from an independent credit rating firm. The loan taken out in a fictitious name would not have had a credit report and should have been flagged by a loan review clerk at the bank's headquarters.

News reports raised several questions about why the fraud was not detected earlier. State regulators had examined the bank's books in September 1986. The bank's own internal auditors also failed to detect the fraud. However, in checking for bad loans, bank auditors do not examine all loans and generally focus on loans much larger than the ones in question. In addition, Greater Providence had recently dropped its computer services arrangement with a local bank in favor of an out-of-state bank, and this changeover may have reduced the effectiveness of

the bank's control procedures. Finally, the bank's loan review clerks were frequently rotated, making follow-up of questionable loans more difficult.

Court records indicate that Guisti was a frequent gambler and used the proceeds of the embezzlement to pay gambling debts. The bank's losses totaled $624,000, and its bonding company, Hartford Accident and Indemnity Company, covered the loss. The loss was less than the $1.83 million in bogus loans because Guisti used some of the borrowed money to pay back some loans as they came due.

According to financial reports made available by Greater Providence officials, the bank has assets of $220 million and outstanding loans of $184 million as of the end of 1987, and it earned a record $1.6 million in earnings for 1987. It has eight branches in the Providence area.

The bank has experienced other adverse publicity in recent years. In 1985 it was fined $50,000 after pleading guilty of failure to report a series of cash transactions exceeding $10,000, which is a felony. In 1986 the bank was taken private by its current owners, but only after a lengthy public battle with State Attorney General Arlene Violet. The state charged that the bank had inflated its assets and overestimated its capital surplus to make its balance sheet look stronger. The bank denied this charge.[27]

1.   Discuss how Greater Providence Deposit & Trust might improve its control procedures over the disbursement of loan funds in order to minimize the risk of this type of fraud. In what way, if any, does this case indicate a lack of proper segregation of duties?

2.   Discuss how Greater Providence might improve its loan review procedures at bank headquarters in order to minimize the risk of this type of fraud. Was it a good idea to rotate the assignments of loan review clerks? Why or why not?

3.   Discuss whether Greater Providence's auditors should have been able to detect this fraud.

4.   Are their any indications that the control environment at Greater Providence may have been deficient? If so, could this have contributed in any way to this embezzlement? How?

[27] Adapted from John Kostrezewa, "Charge: Embezzlement," *Providence Journal-Bulletin* (July 31, 1988): F-1.

CHAPTER Internal Control in Computer-Based Information Systems

LEARNING OBJECTIVES

After studying this chapter, you should be able to:

- Discuss key issues relating to the organization of the information systems function in business organizations.
- Identify and explain several of the more important organizational controls, management controls, and other general controls within a computer-based information system.
- Identify and explain several control procedures and techniques that should be incorporated into data processing applications of computer-based information systems.

INTEGRATIVE CASE: SEATTLE PAPER PRODUCTS

During his fifth month on the internal audit staff at Northwest Industries, Jason Scott is assigned to an audit of Seattle Paper Products, a Northwest subsidiary. Seattle Paper earns annual revenues of $50 million by producing and distributing paper products throughout the Pacific Northwest. Jason's first task is to do a transaction review of purchases, accounts payable, and cash disbursements. His supervisor provides Jason with a computer printout containing 50 randomly selected payables transactions. Jason's assignment is to track down all supporting documents and verify that all the transactions have been properly authorized and correctly processed.

Jason finds that Seattle Paper's data processing system is efficiently organized and well documented. Within a short time he has located vendor invoices and disbursement vouchers for all 50 transactions, and he finds purchase orders and receiving reports for 45 of them. By comparing details on these documents with data listed on the printout, Jason is able to satisfy himself that these 45 transactions are valid and accurate. He reports this to his supervisor and also asks her about the five transactions that lack purchase order and receiving report documents.

Jason's supervisor points out that these five transactions involve the purchase of services, for which there is generally no receiving report. Following past audits, she had recommended that purchase orders be required for all such transactions, but Seattle Paper's management considers this inefficient and unnecessary. So these transactions are processed solely on the basis of vendor invoices that have been approved for payment by authorized managerial personnel. Jason's supervisor points out how each of these invoices had been initialed to approve the disbursement.

However, to their surprise, one of the invoices contains no authorization signature. It is an invoice from Pacific Electric Services for maintenance and repair work, in the amount of $450. Jason remembers that he had seen a few other invoices from this firm in the file. After checking the file, he locates five other invoices from Pacific Electric, all for maintenance and repair services in amounts ranging from $300 to $500. All of these invoices bear the initials "JLC." Some checking reveals that JLC is Jack Carlton, the General Supervisor of the plant.

Jason carries the set of six invoices down to the plant floor to find Carlton. He expects Carlton to verify that all of the invoices are valid and that he simply forgot to initial one of them. However, much to his surprise, Carlton denies having initialed any of the invoices and claims that he has never heard of Pacific Electric Services. Together, they check the phone book and find that no such firm is listed.

While returning to his office, Jason ponders his dilemma. This is the second time during his tenure on the job that he has found something unusual and unexpected. "Why me?" he wonders. After brooding over his bad luck, he begins to think about the following questions:

1. Is Jack Carlton telling the truth?

2. If Carlton is telling the truth, where did the Pacific Electric Services invoices come from?

3. If Pacific Electric Services is a fictitious company, how could Seattle Paper's control systems allow its invoices to be processed and approved for payment? ■

INTRODUCTION

Chapter 12 discussed general concepts of internal control and illustrated their application to typical accounting data processing operations. This chapter focuses in greater detail on the topic of internal control, looking more specifically at the application of internal control concepts in the context of computer-based information systems. The importance of this topic is underscored by the following conclusion from a major research project on the current state of internal control in U.S. corporations.

> As organizations have become dependent on information systems, ensuring the appropriate level of control over these systems has become more important and, in many cases, critical. An airline could not function without adequate control over reservations systems; a bank would be exposed to inordinate risks if it did not implement appropriate controls over demand deposit systems. . . . Inadequate controls in medical and air traffic control systems could result in loss of life. Thus, the ability to achieve adequate control over the information resources of an organization should be a top management priority.[1]

In short, the widespread use of computer-based information systems in modern organizations to support critical operating functions as well as to process accounting information has greatly increased the importance of sound internal control systems.

Although the general objectives of internal control remain the same regardless of the method of data processing, the use of computer-based accounting information systems introduces some special control problems that require different internal control policies and procedures. For example, while computer processing reduces the potential for clerical error, it may increase the risks of unauthorized access to or modification of data files. In addition, the concept of segregating the authorization, recording, and asset custody functions must be applied differently within a computer-based accounting information system, since computer programs may be responsible for two, or possibly all three, of these functions. Fortunately, computers also provide opportunities for an organization to enhance its internal controls. This chapter examines internal control policies, procedures, and techniques that specifically address the control requirements of computer-based information systems. The reader should note, however, how the various controls examined in this chapter are based on the general control concepts covered in Chapter 12, including proper assignment of authority and responsibility, performance monitoring, segregation of duties, and independent checks on performance.

Computer controls are often classified as either general controls or application controls. **General controls** are designed to ensure that an organization's control environment is stable and well managed in order to enhance the effectiveness of application controls. **Application controls** are used to prevent, detect, and correct errors and irregularities in transactions as they flow through the input, processing, and output stages of processing.[2] Among the most critical general controls are those relat-

---

[1] Institute of Internal Auditors Research Foundation, *Systems Auditability and Control Report,* Module 1: Executive Summary (Altamonte Springs, Fla.: Institute of Internal Auditors Research Foundation, 1991), 1–1.

[2] Institute of Internal Auditors Research Foundation, *Systems Auditability and Control Report,* Module 2: Audit and Control Environment (Altamonte Springs, Fla.: Institute of Internal Auditors Research Foundation, 1991), 2–13.

ing to the plan of organization for data processing activities and segregation of duties within the data processing function; this topic is discussed in the first section of this chapter. General controls designed to provide effective management control over computer personnel, computer operations activities, computer resource utilization, and the systems development process are explained in the second section of the chapter. A variety of additional general control standards and policies are described in the third section. This broad coverage of general controls provides a necessary foundation for the study of application control procedures and techniques, which are explained in the final section of the chapter.

ORGANIZATION OF THE INFORMATION SYSTEMS FUNCTION

The information systems function may be organized in a variety of ways, depending on specific needs and circumstances. Furthermore, the MIS organization structure is subject to frequent changes due to the volatile nature of information technology and its commercial application. Nonetheless, there are some aspects of MIS organization that have remained relatively stable over time. For example, in most companies the two largest components of the MIS organization are the computer operations function, which deals with the day-to-day processing of data on the computer system, and the systems development function, which develops and maintains computer applications software.

This section describes one approach to the assignment of responsibilities within a typical MIS organization structure. The section is divided into two parts. The first describes the roles and responsibilities of the various departments or individuals within the information systems organization structure. The second focuses on the internal control considerations relevant to the allocation of those responsibilities.

Information Systems Responsibilities

Figure 13.1 is an organization chart illustrating a common pattern of distribution of MIS functions within a typical large company. This chart focuses on the upper levels of the MIS organization structure. Later in this section we examine the lower levels of the MIS organization structure, specifically in the areas of systems development and computer operations.

The top executive of the information systems function is often referred to as the Chief Information Officer, or CIO. In some companies the CIO reports to the Vice-President of Finance or the Vice-President of Administration. In other cases the CIO has equal status with other top-level executives in the organization and reports to the company President. In these latter cases the CIO participates in setting objectives for the organization, in long-range planning to meet objectives, in establishing broad policies for the organization, and in making decisions at the top-management level. One of the primary contributions of the CIO to these activities is to explain how information technology can contribute to the achievement of plans and objectives and the execution of

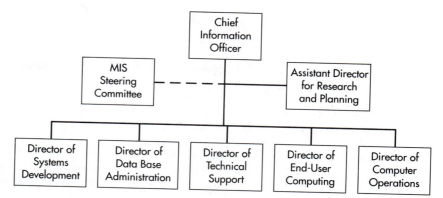

Figure 13.1
Organization of the information
systems function

policies and decisions. A top-management position also allows the CIO to encourage profitable use of information technology in all functional areas of the organization.

The CIO also has the responsibility of managing the systems function. Managerial responsibilities include supervising the development of profitable new applications and the efficient processing of existing applications. The CIO is accountable for the costs associated with the equipment and personnel required for the system and is responsible for maintaining a modern, up-to-date facility that utilizes the best available technology. Such responsibilities require a good combination of administrative skills and technical competence.

The CIO is assisted in carrying out these responsibilities by an executive-level information systems steering committee, whose role is discussed in Chapter 8, and by one or more administrative staff personnel. A key staff person here is the Assistant Director for Research and Planning, who is responsible for monitoring current developments in information technology, forecasting technological developments, investigating ways of applying these new technologies within the organization, preparing the organization's long-range systems plans and budgets, and serving as a liaison to the organization's strategic long-range planning activity. In a large information processing facility other staff officers at this level might include a Quality Control Manager, a Security Officer, a Personnel Administrator, and/or a Documentation Standards Officer.

The Director of Data Base Administration, often referred to as the Data Base Administrator, is responsible for the design and control of the organization's data bases. The data base administration function establishes the appropriate content and format of data records, the structure of data relationships, and the appropriate data names and key fields. This function also controls and monitors data base use through the assignment of user passwords and the collection of statistics on utilization of data and programs. The Data Base Administrator also is concerned with efficient use of physical data storage equipment. Data base administration personnel must maintain close contact with system users, providing documentation and other aids to the effective use of data base systems.

The Director of Technical Support is responsible for the effective functioning of the operating system, telecommunications and network control software, security software, utility routines, compilers, data base management systems, and other systems software. The technical support group also assists the Data Base Administrator and application programmers on matters relating to the systems software. Another technical support responsibility is the selection and implementation of enhancements to computer equipment and systems software to improve the efficiency of operation of the computer system.

The Director of End-User Computing provides support for end-user applications of information technology. Support includes assisting end users in the acquisition, implementation, utilization, and maintenance of personal computers and related software packages. It also involves training end users to effectively utilize decision support systems, query languages, and other user-oriented computer resources. As computer resources continue to become more user friendly, the end-user support function is taking on an increasingly important role within all well-managed systems departments.

The remaining two elements of the information systems organization structure, systems development and computer operations, are described in greater detail in the following sections.

Systems Development. The organization structure of a typical Systems Development Department is illustrated in Fig. 13.2. The primary role of the systems development function is to design and implement computer applications to support the organization's key operating activ-

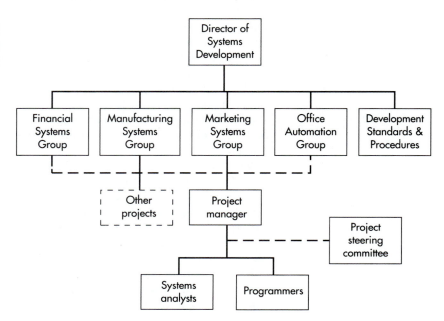

Figure 13.2
Organization of the systems development function

ities. Therefore systems development personnel must work closely with managers and system users in marketing, manufacturing, accounting, and other operating departments.

The Director of Systems Development manages the processes of designing and developing new information systems applications and maintaining and improving existing programs and data bases. The Director is also responsible for planning and controlling the implementation of new systems applications and is accountable for the costs and progress of systems development efforts. Reporting to the Director are various systems development groups, each devoted to serving the needs of a particular user department, including accounting and finance, manufacturing, marketing, office automation, and so forth. Each group includes a group manager and several analysts, programmers, and other systems personnel specializing in the development and maintenance of computer systems within their designated user function. Also reporting to the Director of Systems Development is a development standards and procedures group responsible for establishing and enforcing organizationwide standards for systems design, programming, and system documentation.

At the outset of each major systems development project a project manager is assigned to direct the systems analysis, design, programming, and implementation efforts. Each project manager supervises a team of systems analysts and programmers drawn from the related systems development group. This team carries out the design and implementation work. Some of these projects will involve performing program maintenance on existing applications. Each project manager is responsible to the Director of Systems Development for planning, administering, and controlling all phases of the development effort for a specific project. A project steering committee consisting of users, management representatives, and senior systems personnel should be appointed to provide guidance to the project manager during this process. As indicated on the chart, there will generally be more than one systems development project under way in an organization at any given time.

Systems analysts are primarily responsible for the design of computer applications to satisfy user needs in an organization. They identify the hardware, software, and other resources necessary to develop the required system, and they specify how these various resources will be employed to meet user requirements. The systems analyst must have both experience in systems design and familiarity with the operations of the organization, for this person must bridge the gap between the users and the technology of the computer system.

The programming function involves converting the designs of the analyst into a set of computer instructions. Programmers must have a good understanding of user needs and requirements as well as sound knowledge of programming languages and methods. As they gain experience and develop greater familiarity with the organization's operations, programmers often advance to systems analysis positions.

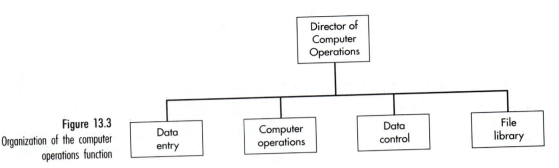

Figure 13.3
Organization of the computer
operations function

Computer Operations.   Figure 13.3 illustrates the organization structure of a typical computer operations function. This function is managed by a Director who is responsible to the CIO for the day-to-day performance of data processing operations. Once new systems designs have been developed and implemented, their successful execution becomes the responsibility of this department. As shown in Fig. 13.3, a common division of responsibilities within this department involves separation of the functions of (1) data entry, (2) computer operations, (3) data control, and (4) file custodianship.

The data entry function involves the preparation and verification of source data for computer processing. Data input may be performed using on-line terminals, data communications devices, optical character recognition (OCR) equipment, or some combination of these. A common arrangement is for user departments to route batches of source documents to the data entry department, where data entry personnel use keyboards to convert the source document data into machine-readable form. Because manual keying is costly, time-consuming, and error-prone, it is steadily being replaced by methods that automatically capture computer source data in machine-readable form, such as use of OCR or point-of-sale (POS) terminals and electronic data interchange (EDI) between companies.

The computer operations group is responsible for running the computer and its related input, output, and storage devices. Included in this function are such activities as mounting tapes and disk packs, loading and unloading forms on printers, monitoring and responding to console messages, responding to machine or program failures, and observing prescribed control procedures. In a multiprogramming environment in which several programs are running simultaneously the computer operator's job is dynamic and exacting.

The data control group maintains a record of all computer work in process, monitors the flow of work within and through the computer operations department, and distributes systems output when processing is complete. The data control group also checks that all batches of source data have been properly approved by user department personnel, verifies the accuracy of input and output against preestablished control totals, maintains a log of input data errors identified during computer processing, and monitors and maintains a record of the correction and resubmission of erroneous input data.

The file librarian is responsible for maintaining a separate storage area—the file library—for control of files and programs stored on magnetic tapes, disks, or diskettes. The file librarian should maintain an inventory of all files and programs in the library and should keep a record of files and program copies checked out for use by other systems personnel.

In many computer installations there are additional functional specialists not mentioned here, such as data communications specialists, operations research personnel, scheduling personnel, and training specialists. On the other hand, in a small installation many of the functions shown in Figs. 13.1, 13.2, and 13.3 might be combined. However, the basic separation of the systems development function and the computer operations function is virtually universal. In a typical data processing installation around a fourth of all systems personnel will be computer equipment operators, another fourth will be programmers, and the remainder will be split among data entry, systems analysis, technical support, end-user support, and other functions.

Segregation of Duties Within the Systems Function

In highly integrated computer-based accounting information systems, procedures that might otherwise be performed by separate individuals may be combined within the computer processing function. Therefore any person who has unrestricted access to the computer could have the opportunity to both perpetrate and conceal fraud. To compensate for this potential control weakness, an organization must implement various control procedures. One of the most important of these compensating controls is effective segregation of duties within the information systems function. Authority and responsibility must be clearly divided among the following functions:

1. Application systems analysis and programming
2. Computer operations
3. Systems programming
4. Transaction authorization
5. File library maintenance
6. Data control

The most important separation of duties within the information systems department is that between application systems analysis and programming, on the one hand, and computer operations, on the other. A programmer or systems analyst who is also permitted access to the computer could easily make unauthorized changes in application programs. Alternatively, a computer operator who has unrestricted access to program copies and detailed documentation could implement unauthorized program changes. Thus the systems analysis and programming function and the computer operations function are incompatible in a data processing environment. Organizational independence requires that programmers and analysts not have access to the computer room, and that operators have access to programs and documentation only when authorized and supervised.

To further separate the analysis and programming function from other functions, an organization should require formal authorization for any program changes. A written description of such changes and the reasons for them should be submitted to a data processing manager, chief analyst, or some other person in a position of authority, whose authorization should be required prior to the testing of such changes and whose approval of test results should be required prior to final implementation of program changes. Complete documentation of all program changes should be retained.

The systems programming function is very vulnerable from a control standpoint. With detailed knowledge of the operating system and other systems software, a systems programmer may have the opportunity to make unauthorized changes in application programs or data files. To minimize this risk, organizations must not give systems programmers access to application programs and their documentation or to live files and data bases. In addition, systems programmers should not be permitted to modify systems software without appropriate authorization, and all authorized modifications to systems software should be thoroughly tested prior to their acceptance.

The computer operations function is also particularly vulnerable from a control standpoint and thus requires tight control. Effective supervision of the operations activity is essential. Another important control policy is the rotation of operations personnel among jobs and shifts in order to avoid having any single operator always process the same job. Still another useful control procedure is to require that a minimum of two qualified computer operators be on duty in the computer room during all processing. In addition, the system should maintain a log of all processing activity during each operator's work shift, including a record of any manual intervention by the operator during regular processing, and a printout of this log should be reviewed periodically for any evidence of irregularities.

The existence of a separate file library function contributes to effective internal control by restricting access to data and program files. Access to all files should be limited to authorized personnel at authorized times, as determined by the data processing schedule or by special management authorization (as in the case of formally approved program changes). The file librarian also should maintain records of all use of data and program files, and these records should be reviewed regularly for evidence of unauthorized access.

For organizations large enough to be able to afford a greater degree of specialization, a separate data control function provides an additional measure of organizational independence. The presence of data control personnel inhibits unauthorized access to the computer facility, provides an additional element of supervision of computer operations personnel, and contributes to more efficient data processing operations.

The function of transaction authorization properly resides outside the systems department. User departments responsible for submitting computer input should submit a signed authorization form along with each batch of input. The signature verifies that the input has been properly prepared and reviewed and that appropriate control totals have been compiled. Data control personnel should verify the presence of appropriate authorization signatures and control totals prior to submitting user-prepared input for processing.

Proper assignment of authority and responsibility within the MIS organization is essential for effective internal control. However, several other control policies and procedures are also critical. Among these are policies and procedures to provide effective management control of the information systems function. This is the subject of the next section.

MANAGEMENT CONTROL OF THE INFORMATION SYSTEMS FUNCTION

In 1986 the Oklahoma State Insurance Fund terminated a contract with Policy Management Systems to develop a software system to issue policies and to process and track claims and premiums, after the project fell several months behind schedule and went $1 million over budget.[3] In 1991 the city of Seattle put into operation the Seattle Financial Management System, which cost $16.3 million, or $4 million above the original budget.[4] Later in 1991 Westpac Banking Corporation of Sydney, Australia, terminated a large-scale systems integration project after spending over $150 million (see Focus 13.1). These are but a few examples of poorly managed computer projects that have been endemic in the computer industry since it began in the 1950s. In each of these cases large sums of money were wasted owing to a failure to apply certain basic principles of management control.

To minimize the risk of management control failures, an organization should apply the basic principles of responsibility accounting to the information systems function through such means as documenting personnel activities and reporting on the performance of systems staff personnel and managers. The effective application of these principles greatly reduces the possibility of major cost overruns and spectacular project failures and substantially improves the efficiency and effectiveness of the information systems function.

Two key elements of management control of the systems function have been discussed in prior chapters. One is the long-range systems

---

[3] Mark Mehler, "Reining in Runaway Systems," *Information Week* (December 16, 1991): 20–27.

[4] Dick Lilly, "Costs Cited in Proposal to Eliminate 2 City Offices," *Seattle Times* (August 22, 1991): F–1.

13.1 FOCUS

Harnessing Runaway Systems

In 1988, Westpac Banking Corporation of Sydney, Australia, instigated a five-year systems development project that was designed to redefine the role of information technology for the huge bank. The project, designated Core System 90 (CS90), was budgeted for a cost of $85 million. The objective was to decentralize Westpac's information systems by equipping branch managers with CASE (computer-aided software engineering) tools and expert systems, to be used to generate new financial products. This would enable Westpac to respond more rapidly to customer needs and at the same time to downsize its internal MIS department.

Over three years after it began the project, in November of 1991, Westpac took stock of

CS90 and concluded that it was out of control. Almost $150 million had been spent on the project, but no usable results had been attained. In addition, bank officials determined that the scheduled 1993 completion date could not be realized. Facing serious problems with its loan portfolio and asset management programs, Westpac decided that it could not afford to risk several more million dollars on CS90. So, the bank fired IBM, the systems integrator* and primary software developer, and brought in Andersen Consulting to review the project and develop recommendations for salvaging it.

Westpac's CS90 boondoggle is merely one example of what has become an all-too-frequent story: a computer project that is

over budget and behind schedule, often due to a systems integrator that is unable to deliver on lofty promises. Industry experts refer to such projects as *runaways*. Since 1988, KPMG Peat Marwick has taken over about 50 runaway computer projects, and it estimates that, in about two-thirds of these cases, the problems arose from mismanagement by a systems integrator. Another study completed in 1990 reported that 40% of *Fortune* 500 companies have experienced runaways or near runaways on projects headed by a systems integrator.

Computer systems built by a third party are subject to the same cost overruns and missed deadlines as systems developed internally. Therefore, it makes sense to use the same basic rules

---

plan that, like all plans, provides a framework for management control and a standard against which performance may be measured (see Chapter 8). The other is the project development plan for each major systems project, often accompanied by a Gantt chart or a PERT schedule, which provides a basis for control of the systems development effort (see Chapter 10).

This section describes four additional elements of management control over the systems function. First is the measurement and evaluation of the performance of programmers and systems analysts. Second is the control of systems projects under development by means of periodic progress reviews and postimplementation follow-up. Third is the measurement and evaluation of the performance of the computer operations activity and its personnel. Fourth is the use of a system of of project management, including close monitoring of the progress of the system as it is being developed. Unfortunately, many companies are not doing this. Instead, they rely on the integrator's assurance that the project will be completed on time. Too often, the integrator falls behind schedule, but doesn't tell the client, figuring that the project can still be completed on time if a big push is made at the last minute. In such cases, the CIO and other IS executives are as much at fault as the systems integrator, according to experts in salvaging runaway systems.

These experts suggest that a systems integration project should be monitored by a sponsors committee, established by the CIO and chaired by the project's internal champion. Department managers for all units that will use the system should be on this committee. The role of this committee should be to establish formal procedures for measuring and reporting the status of the project. The best approach is to break

the project down into manageable tasks, assign responsibility for each task, and then meet on a regular basis (at least monthly) to review progress and assess quality.

Equally important are steps that should be taken at the outset of the project. Before third parties are called in to bid on a project, clear specifications must be developed, including exact descriptions and definitions of the system, explicit deadlines, and precise acceptance criteria at each stage of the project. While this may seem expensive, it usually saves money in the long run. For example, Suffolk County, New York, recently spent 12 months and $500,000 preparing detailed specifications for a new $16 million criminal justice information system before accepting bids. The county then hired Unisys Corporation and Grumman Data Systems to develop the system. County officials believe that their diligent upfront efforts helped ensure the success of their new system and saved the county $3

million in hardware costs.

Some systems integrators may object to detailed specifications and rigorous project control methods. For example, after reviewing Suffolk County's specifications, only six integrators made a bid on the project, out of 22 that had originally expressed interest. This should be viewed as a blessing, rather than a problem. Those integrators who disdain a company's attempts to rigorously control the cost and quality of its systems projects are most likely the same ones responsible for most of the recent profusion of runaway systems.

* A systems integrator is a vendor that takes the responsibility for managing a cooperative systems development effort involving its own development personnel, those of the buyer, and possibly the systems development personnel of one or more other vendors, using common standards as much as possible.

Source: Adapted from Mark Mehler, ''Reining in Runaway Systems,'' *InformationWeek* (December 16, 1991): 20–27.

---

internal pricing of computer services as a basis for allocating organizational resources to the information systems function.

Programmer/Analyst Performance Evaluation

A key element of the performance evaluation of systems personnel is the collection of information on the specific activities in which those personnel have been involved. A time-reporting system may be used for this purpose, whereby analysts and programmers are required to account daily for how their time was spent. Employees report the number of hours worked on specific projects and programs as well as the type of work performed (coding, testing, documentation, etc.). This information provides input not only for employee performance evaluation but also for project cost accumulation and reporting.

Because the analysis and programming effort involved in large systems development projects may span a long period of time, it is unwise to wait until the project is completed to evaluate the performance of the analysts and programmers involved. Instead, each project should be broken down into a series of small parts, or modules, each of which can be assigned to a single individual. For each module certain objectives should be established, such as test specifications for a section of program code or documentation specifications for a portion of the systems design. Estimates incorporated in the project plan provide standards of quality, time, and cost against which a person's performance on the job may be evaluated. The evaluation itself is performed immediately upon completion of each module.

It is possible to develop rough measures of programming accomplishments for comparative purposes. The number of instructions that a completed program module contains may be divided by the number of hours spent by the programmers in preparing the module, to provide a measure of "instructions per hour." This measure may then be used to compare the relative efficiencies of all programmers within the organization. Further provisions have to be made to take into account factors such as the differences in size and complexity of programs and the variations in experience levels of programmers. Nonetheless, this approach in its simplest form does at least furnish some objective information with which to control programming activities, and it also provides a basis for estimating the time and cost requirements of future development projects.[5]

If a reasonably standard measure of instructions per hour can be developed, programmer hours can be budgeted. Programmer performance reports can then compare estimates with actual performance and determine variances. An example of such a performance report is shown in Fig. 13.4. This report indicates that the programmer completed 660 instructions in 40 hours, or 16.5 instructions per hour. If the average for all programmers is 15 instructions per hour, then this programmer's performance is well above average. On the other hand, if this person is an experienced programmer and these programs are relatively simple, then a higher-than-average level of performance might have been expected.

Measures of the performance of systems analysts cannot be quite as precise as those used to evaluate programmer performance. Time and cost standards are difficult to develop in the absence of a unit of work such as number of instructions. Management can evaluate the quality of documentation prepared, however, and over a period of time can form a reasonably accurate subjective impression of how efficiently an analyst performs assigned tasks. Since effective systems analysis re-

---

[5] For further discussion of programmer performance evaluation, see Trevor D. Crossman, "Taking the Measure of Programmer Productivity," *Datamation* (May 1979): 144–147.

PROGRAMMER PERFORMANCE ANALYSIS

Name: Steven Brophy

Week Ended: 06/10/94

Project Number	Program Number	Description	Language	Number of Instructions Completed	PROGRAMMING HOURS		
					Actual	Estimated	Variance
2055	012	Order entry	COBOL	66	4.0	4.4	−0.4
2055	018	Order edit	COBOL	156	9.0	10.4	−1.4
2055	025	Customer file update	COBOL	129	7.5	8.6	−1.1
2055	026	Inventory file update	COBOL	150	9.5	10.0	−0.5
2055	029	General ledger update	COBOL	75	4.0	5.0	−1.0
2055	033	Print invoices	COBOL	54	4.0	3.6	+0.4
2055	035	Print shipping orders	COBOL	30	2.0	2.0	0.0
			Totals	660	40.0	44.0	−4.0

Figure 13.4
Programmer performance report

quires interaction with system users on the one hand and with programmers on the other, skill in interpersonal relations is very important. Therefore feedback from system users and programmers may also be useful to management in evaluating the performance of systems analysts.

Systems Project Controls   In addition to evaluating the performance of individual programmers and systems analysts, management must also ensure that the systems development *process* is subject to strict management control. One key element of this control is assigning responsibility for the success of each project to a project manager and a project team. Another is following a project development plan that divides the project into phases, with time and cost estimates for each phase. The plan should specify **project milestones**, or significant points in the developmental effort at which a formal review of progress will be made. An important element of such progress reviews is comparing actual completion times for each project phase with estimated completion times. Data on the actual completion times can be accumulated from the daily time sheets filled out by programmers and analysts. Figure 13.5 shows one possible format for such a progress report.

PROJECT PROGRESS REPORT

Project name: Customer Order Processing   Week Ended: 06/24/94

Project No.:   2055   Group Leader: John Kimbrough

Phase	PROGRAM/MODULE DESCRIPTION						
	Order Entry	Order Edit	Customer File Update	Inventory File Update	General Ledger Update	Print Invoices	Print Shipping Orders
Actual hours							
Requirements	16.0	24.0	24.0	24.0	16.0	12.0	12.0
User interface	24.0	36.0	48.0	40.0	16.0	8.0	8.0
Data design	24.0	36.0	48.0	40.0	12.0	12.0	4.0
Process design	24.0	40.0	40.0	32.0	16.0	0.0	0.0
Program specs	40.0	68.0	48.0	48.0	24.0	0.0	0.0
Program coding	40.0	56.0	32.0	48.0	8.0	0.0	0.0
Unit test	16.0	12.0	8.0	16.0	0.0	0.0	0.0
Documentation	8.0	8.0	8.0	8.0	8.0	0.0	0.0
Total hours							
Completed	192.0	280.0	256.0	256.0	100.0	32.0	24.0
Budgeted	240.0	400.0	400.0	320.0	160.0	128.0	120.0
Remaining	64.0	120.0	128.0	80.0	72.0	96.0	96.0
% completed	75.0	70.0	66.7	76.2	58.1	25.0	20.0
Variance	+16.0	0.0	−16.0	+16.0	+12.0	0.0	0.0

Figure 13.5
Systems project progress report

As an example, consider Westpac Banking's CS90 project. As described in Focus 13.1, this project was intended to be completed in five years, but it took three years (and $150 million) for Westpac to realize that the project was hopelessly behind schedule. Suppose, for the sake of simplicity, that this project had been broken down into 250 one-week modules, with responsibility for each module assigned to a specific group leader. Suppose that each module had an estimated completion time, and that weekly progress reviews had been scheduled to compare actual progress with estimated completion dates. Had these control procedures been followed, it seems likely that Westpac would have realized after only a few weeks that CS90's estimated completion time was unrealistic, and potentially it could have saved at least $100 million.

In addition to including a time and cost analysis, a project progress review should consider a number of other factors, such as the adherence of the project team to quality standards for documentation, program testing, and system auditability. Also, estimates of remaining project completion times, costs, and benefits should be reevaluated on the basis of the additional experience gained since the previous progress review. If this reassessment reveals a significant change in expectations, the entire project timetable should be revised. As Westpac's CS90 experience makes clear, there are times when this reassessment will show that it is necessary to discontinue a project.

Another important aspect of project control is the follow-up review subsequent to implementation of a new computer application. Each newly implemented computer application should be reviewed periodically to evaluate whether it is generating economic benefits that are consistent with the original project proposal and development plan. If there are any significant unfavorable variances, the persons responsible for the original estimates should be asked to find out why the variances are occurring and to initiate efforts to correct the situation, if possible. These follow-up reviews not only help control project development activities but also encourage more accurate and objective initial estimates of project costs and benefits.

Control of Computer Operations

As one of the largest components of the data processing organization, the computer operations function has a distinct need for effective management control. One key element of computer operations control is the data processing schedule. The schedule is prepared at the beginning of each shift by a supervisor or scheduling clerk. It should assign each incoming job to an appropriate time period to maximize the productive utilization of all available equipment. The schedule should also provide time for necessary preventive maintenance and should allow some slack time for system breakdowns that may require corrective action and for occasional reruns of incorrectly processed work.

Evaluation of the performance of each machine operator should be based on a comparison of actual processing time with scheduled processing time for all jobs run by that operator during a particular period, such as a week or month. Of course, actual processing time must be adjusted for losses of productive time due to system breakdowns or other factors not under the control of the operator. Furthermore, to provide an equitable standard, the scheduled processing time must be adjusted whenever the actual volume of processing is substantially above or below the average processing volume.

The performance of data entry personnel may be evaluated in two ways. One is by measuring their output in terms of keystrokes per hour or some similar measure and then comparing each individual operator's rate with an average or standard. A second is to measure the error rate of all data entry work in terms of the percentage of data entry errors identified by computer edit routines carried out during subsequent processing steps. Obviously, these two approaches complement each other, because one is basically a measure of efficiency and the other is a measure of quality.

Also useful for computer operations control are measures of system performance, including throughput (output per unit of time), utilization (fraction of time that the system is being productively used), and response time. Operating system software may be used to collect and report data on such measures. Whenever these performance statistics deviate from past trends or established standards, management should investigate the deviations to identify their cause. Some system performance deviations may be attributable to random events that are beyond the control of computer operators, while others may signal operating problems that require prompt corrective action.

In addition, system performance data collected by the operating system may be used to prepare various management reports and analyses. For example, data on computer resources used in testing a new system under development can be used to determine the cost of such testing and charge it to the specific project. Also, system utilization data can be aggregated to provide a breakdown of total available computer time for each week or month into categories such as productive time, idle time, reruns, and machine maintenance and downtime. Reports of this type are extremely useful to systems management in evaluating the efficiency of the computer operations activity, scheduling future processing operations, estimating operating costs for new projects, and establishing management policies for the operations function.

To summarize, the basic principles of responsibility accounting, which are employed throughout any well-managed organization to measure and evaluate performance, can and should be applied to the information systems function. This requires the use of procedures for collecting data on the productivity of programmers and systems analysts, on the progress of systems projects, and on the efficiency of the computer operations function. The data must be compiled into meaningful performance measures and periodically reported to management. Finally, management must regularly review these performance data and take whatever action is necessary in response to any apparent problems.

Internal Pricing of Computer Services[6]

No discussion of management control of the information systems function is complete without giving consideration to how the computer center is funded. Two approaches are possible. First, computer managers might compete for funds with other managers in the organization by submitting budget requests that specify what resources are required and for what purposes. This approach is generally not satisfactory, because it pits computer managers against other users of organizational resources (production, research and development, marketing, etc.) whose requirements are more directly related to the organization's

---

[6] This section is adapted, with permission, from Barry E. Cushing, "Pricing Internal Computer Services: The Basic Issues," *Management Accounting* (April 1976): 47–50.

objectives. This often leads to underfunding of the computer center, impairing its ability to provide important services to other organizational units.

Since the need for computer resources within an organization is derived from the demand for data processing and information services by other organizational units, a more rational approach to funding the computer center is to charge each organizational unit for its use of computer services. A system of charging user departments for computer services is analogous to a system of transfer pricing of products exchanged between two divisions of the same company. Such a system should produce more effective management and utilization of information systems resources. In this section the objectives of a pricing system for computer services are explained, and several different approaches and techniques used in such systems are described and compared.

A pricing system for computer services has several objectives:

1. To allocate computer resources equitably to the most worthwhile uses while discouraging frivolous uses
2. To motivate computer management and personnel to provide efficient, high-quality service to users
3. To establish an objective basis for evaluating the performance of computer management
4. To encourage user interest and participation in the development and implementation of information systems

The relative importance attached to each of these objectives will vary depending on the specific needs and characteristics of the organization.

In the determination of the amount to charge for computer services an allocation base is multiplied by a rate. The allocation base refers to the measure of work performed by the computer system, while the rate is the price charged per unit of work. Three different types of allocation bases are used: a single-factor base, a unit-pricing base, and a multiple-factor base. Under a single-factor base a single measure of time use is multiplied by a single rate to derive the charge. The single factor is usually either the total elapsed time for the system to complete the job, called wall clock time (WCT), or the total units of central processing unit time consumed in executing the job, called CPU time. The single-factor base is simple and easy for users to understand. It is also inexpensive and easily implemented, since relatively minor changes in the operating system software enable the charge to be computed and reported as each job is processed.

Unfortunately, single-factor allocation bases can provide distorted computer charges in a multiprogramming environment. WCT becomes very inconsistent, varying in accordance with the particular mix of jobs being processed. For example, a job that takes 15 minutes to complete when it is the only job being run may take 30 minutes when several other jobs are also being run. Both WCT and CPU time also tend to be inequitable in the sense that charges are not related to the resources used. If a job using five input/output devices consumes the same WCT or CPU time as a job using only two input/output devices, the same amount will be charged for the two jobs despite their differences in resource utilization. Once again, this disadvantage relates primarily to the multiprogramming environment, in which system components not required for one job may be used by any other job being executed at the same time.

Under **unit pricing** a single unit measure of work performed by the system is developed. This measure reflects all the system components available to the user during execution of the job. For example, the unit measure might be defined as the total amount of work the system can perform in one minute. For a given job this measure is derived by counting the various operations performed by the system during execution, such as reading a disk record or printing a line, and then applying a weighting factor to each count and summing the results. This unit measure is then multiplied by a single rate to compute the charge. The unit-pricing approach produces a reasonably stable charge for a given equipment configuration and is reasonably equitable. Furthermore, each user's bill for services is uncomplicated, showing the total units consumed, the rate, and the total charge. However, it can be difficult to determine the appropriate unit measure, and the concepts and techniques underlying the computation of the unit measure may not be easily understood by users.

Under a **multiple-factor base** a separate rate is charged for each of the system components used during the execution of a job. These components may include CPU time, CPU storage, lines printed, tape accesses, and disk accesses. Each measure is multiplied by a separate rate, and the resulting individual component charges are summed to arrive at a total job charge. This is probably the most equitable pricing method for the user. In addition, the information generated by this method may be used by the computer staff to evaluate and improve the efficiency of scheduling of computer operations. However, the multiple-factor allocation base may be difficult and costly to develop and implement, and its complexity may make it confusing to users.

With respect to the determination of rates charged for data processing services, three common methods are full costing, market pricing, or flexible pricing. Under **full costing** (also called average cost pricing) rates charged for computer services are computed on the basis of the actual total costs of the data processing operation. For example, where the single factor of CPU time is used as the allocation base, total cost is divided by total CPU time to derive a rate per hour. A full-cost rate is intended to generate revenues just sufficient to cover the costs of the computer center; in other words, the computer facility is treated as a cost center. The rates are generally recomputed at short intervals, such as at the end of each month. Full costing is a simple method and is generally equitable, although it sometimes produces unstable computer charges over time, particularly when there are substantial fluctuations in total computer system usage.

Market pricing involves the use of rates that are equal to the prices charged for equivalent services by commercial vendors. The use of market prices should provide an excess of revenues over costs and is therefore consistent with the profit center concept. The market-pricing method generally provides more stable computer charges than full costing. Furthermore, treating the computer facility as a profit center helps motivate computer center management to hold costs down and also to provide quality services that will maximize the satisfaction of user needs. The computer center manager becomes market-oriented and seeks to develop and provide new services that take advantage of the best available technology for the benefit of users and the total organization. The profit center approach also provides a better basis for economic evaluation of the computer facility by top management. Comparison of the return on investment of the computer facility with that of other divisions of the company gives some indication of whether the investment in computer resources is justified. If users are willing to pay the rates charged and to use most or all the available capacity, a large profit should be generated, signaling the need, as well as providing justification, for additional investment in computer facilities. The primary disadvantage of the market-pricing method is that satisfactory market prices may not be readily available, which may necessitate costly and time-consuming negotiations between users and data processing management to reach agreement on the rates to be charged.

Flexible pricing involves adjusting prices to stabilize the demand for computer services. High rates are charged for services rendered during periods of peak demand and for jobs requiring fast turnaround. Higher rates may also be charged for heavily used system components in order to prevent those components from becoming bottlenecks. When system capacity is substantially increased (as it may be by the acquisition of a new computer), lower rates may be charged for a brief period in order to encourage users to consume the available capacity. Thus under a flexible-pricing scheme those users whose needs are critical enough to justify fast turnaround and service during peak periods will presumably be willing to pay higher rates, and those users whose needs are less critical will be encouraged to accept slower turnaround and processing during slack periods. Flexible pricing thus seeks to establish a stable and acceptable equilibrium between the supply and demand for computer services. Note that under flexible pricing rates do not necessarily bear any relation to cost. Rates may be established to recover total costs or to recover costs plus a profit. Thus flexible pricing may be used in conjunction with either the cost center or the profit center approach. The primary disadvantage of flexible pricing is that it can be costly to administer, since prices may have to be changed frequently to accommodate changes in user behavior.

When an internal-pricing system is utilized, computer users make most of the decisions about which systems applications will be developed and implemented. An important exception to this involves large and expensive computer applications that have strategic implications for the organization. Decisions on such projects are generally the responsibility of the MIS steering committee, which establishes priorities among proposed large-scale systems projects as part of the organization's long-range information systems plan (see Chapter 8).

An effective system of internal pricing for computer services should encourage the acquisition of computer resources only when their benefits (as measured by the prices that users are willing to pay) exceed their costs. Internal-pricing systems also encourage user managers to involve themselves more deeply in decisions on the use of computer resources, and such involvement enhances the likelihood of successful computer applications. Moreover, an internal-pricing system motivates computer center management to minimize costs and maximize quality of services. Finally, these systems provide a better basis for evaluating computer center management. Computer manufacturers and software vendors now provide various software packages and algorithms for job costing in multiprogrammed systems. For these reasons internal pricing of computer services is now recognized as an important cornerstone of sound computer management.

OTHER GENERAL CONTROLS

The most fundamental general controls are those relating to the distribution of authority and responsibility within the MIS organization and the application of responsibility accounting principles to provide effective management control over all MIS activities. They have been described in the previous two sections. This section explains a variety of additional general controls that do not readily fit within these two broad categories. They include controlling physical access to the computer site, protecting stored data, utilizing a system of logical access controls, providing controls over data transmission, protecting personal computers, enforcing documentation standards, taking steps to minimize system downtime, and planning for disaster recovery. Application controls are covered in the following section.

Controlling Site Access

An organization's investment in computer hardware and software often amounts to hundreds of thousands or millions of dollars. It follows that the computer site should receive adequate physical protection. Access to the computer system should be restricted at all times to authorized personnel. This is generally done by arranging the layout of the computer site so that there are only one or two access points. To be allowed to pass through an access point, employees must present some kind of personal identification confirming that they have the proper authorization, and they must sign a log as they enter and leave the site. One common form of personal identification is the security badge, the simplest example of which is the laminated photo ID card. Modern security badges incorporate magnetic, electric, or optical codes that can be read only by special badge readers. More advanced personal identification techniques include the use of voice patterns, fingerprints, and retina scanners. When badge readers or other advanced methods are used, each employee's entry and exit may be automatically recorded in a log maintained on the computer.

Access to computer equipment must also be controlled at times when the system is not being used, such as evenings, weekends, and holidays. Entrances to computer facilities should be securely locked, and security guards should monitor these entrances carefully. Closed-circuit television systems may be used to continuously monitor points of access to the computer site. A security alarm system is also useful in detecting unauthorized access during off-hours. In addition, many computers can be switched off and on using a lock and key similar to those of an automobile ignition. In such cases steps should be taken to protect equipment keys from unauthorized access.

In addition to controlling physical access, management must restrict logical access to the software and data resources stored within the computer system. Logical access control procedures are described in detail in a subsequent part of this chapter.

Protecting Stored Data   Good internal control in a computer installation requires that provisions be made to protect data and program files from unauthorized disclosure or from destruction caused by human error, equipment malfunction, or natural disaster. Data protection controls fall into two categories. First are control procedures designed to *prevent* loss of data. Second are control procedures that enable users to *recover* data that have been lost.

A properly supervised file library (as described earlier in this chapter) is one essential means of preventing loss of data. The file storage area, as well as the computer room itself, should be protected against fire, dust, excesses of heat or humidity, and other conditions that could harm stored data.

File labels, both internal and external, are a useful means of protecting data files from inadvertent misuse. An **external label** is merely a gummed paper label attached to a tape reel or disk pack, upon which may be written the file identification, date processed, and other information. **Internal labels** are written in machine-readable form on the data recording media and are of three different types. A **volume label** identifies the contents of each separate data recording medium, such as a tape reel, diskette, or disk pack. Each volume may contain one or more files. A **header label** appears at the beginning of each file and contains the file name, expiration date, and other file identification information. The header label is read by the computer prior to processing the file and is checked against the program to ensure that the file is the correct one for the program. A **trailer label** appears at the end of each file and serves as an indicator that the end of the file has been reached. The trailer label often contains file control totals, which are checked against those accumulated during processing.

Tape rings and disk write protection mechanisms protect against users' accidentally writing over or erasing data files. A **tape file protection ring** is a removable plastic ring that, when inserted on a reel of magnetic tape, permits the system to write data onto the tape. When the ring is removed, the tape may not be written onto, and the data or program files on the reel are protected. Thus the tape ring should be removed whenever an application requires that data only be read from the tape and not written onto the tape. Many removable disks employ devices such as on/off switches or removable strips of plastic to perform a write protection function for disk files. Unfortunately, the effectiveness of all of these write protection mechanisms is limited by the fact that they can easily be circumvented. Operating policies for the computer facility should mandate that these file protection mechanisms be used in an appropriate manner.

Write protection features may also be incorporated into file management software. Before a file is used, it must first be opened. The syntax of the OPEN command should allow the programmer or user to specify whether the use is "read-only" or both "read and write." For applications that do not involve writing data onto the file, such as inquiry processing or report generation, read-only usage should be specified.

When a data base management system is used to maintain and process accounting data, additional data protection is provided by the presence of a data base administrator, the use of a data dictionary, and concurrent update controls. The data base administrator establishes and enforces standard procedures for accessing and updating the data base. The data dictionary ensures consistency in the way data items are defined and used. **Concurrent update controls** protect individual records from potential errors that could occur if two users attempted to update the same record simultaneously; this is accomplished by "locking out" one user until the system has finished processing the update entered by the other user.[7]

Highly confidential data can be protected against unauthorized disclosure by means of a paper shredder and data encryption. A shredder may be used to destroy confidential papers and printouts, such as customer listings, research data, and payroll registers, once they are no longer needed. **Data encryption**, sometimes referred to as **cryptography**, involves converting data into a scrambled format for storage purposes or prior to data transmission. The data are then converted back into meaningful form for authorized use. Data encryption is particularly important when confidential data are being transmitted to or from remote locations, because data transmission lines can be electronically monitored without the user's knowledge.

Computer viruses and unauthorized system access are two additional threats to the security of stored data. Methods of protecting

---

[7] For further discussion of control considerations in a data base environment, see Fred R. McFadden and Jeffrey A. Hoffer, *Database Management,* 3rd ed. (Redwood City, Calif.: Benjamin/Cummings, 1991), Chapter 9.

stored data from computer viruses and recovering from a virus infection are explained in Chapter 14. Logical access controls are described later in this chapter.

While preventing data loss is obviously preferred to recovering from it, no set of preventive controls is foolproof. Therefore procedures should also exist for recovering data files, should the files be lost or destroyed. The first line of defense is the preparation of duplicate copies of programs and of current data files. One common procedure is to use magnetic disk storage for regular copies of all files and magnetic tape to store backup copies. To protect duplicate copies from such disasters as fire or flood, companies should store them in a secure site that is located some distance away from the main computer site. Backup files may be either physically transported to the alternate site or transmitted electronically using a service called **electronic vaulting**, which permits prompt on-line access to backup data when necessary.

For files that are updated using batch processing, a data protection procedure known as the **grandfather-father-son concept** is often used. Under this plan, when a master file (the father) is updated with a set of transactions to generate a new master file (the son), a copy of the previous master file (the grandfather) is retained, along with a copy of the transactions that were processed against the grandfather to produce the father. Then if both the father and the son files are damaged or destroyed during the update process, it will be possible to reconstruct the father file using both the grandfather file and the copy of the prior transaction file. Once the father-son update has been successfully completed, the grandfather file is no longer needed and may be reused for other data.

For files that are updated on-line, a similar procedure may be employed to ensure that the master file can be reconstructed if necessary. On a periodic basis a duplicate copy of the master file is prepared and stored in a secure location. All subsequent update transactions are recorded in a transaction log. Then if anything happens to the current version of the master file, it may be reconstructed using the prior copy and the transaction log.

In an on-line system if there is a disk failure or other hardware or software malfunction during processing, it could be necessary to restart the system by reprocessing an entire day's worth of transactions. Since system failures cannot be prevented, more efficient recovery procedures are necessary. One such procedure is to take **checkpoints** at periodic intervals during processing. When a checkpoint is taken, the system temporarily does not accept new transactions, completes update procedures for all partially processed transactions, and then generates an exact copy of all data values and other information needed to restart the system. The checkpoint is recorded on a separate disk or tape file. This may be done several times per hour. If a hardware failure occurs at any time, the system can be restarted by reading in the last checkpoint and then reprocessing only those transactions that have occurred subsequent to that checkpoint.

A complementary recovery procedure for data files is called **rollback**, which is used to reverse the effects of a transaction that has been partially processed when a hardware failure occurs. For example, suppose that a customer order is being processed, and the system has recorded a reduction in the inventory file to reflect the items sold. However, before the system can post the sale amount to the customer's account, a hardware failure occurs. When steps are taken to recover from this problem, it may not be possible to tell how far the system went in processing this transaction. Under rollback a preupdate copy of both the inventory and customer records would have been created prior to processing the transaction. Recovery would then proceed by restoring, or "rolling back," each of these records to the values logged on the preupdate copy. The transaction would then be reprocessed from the beginning.

In extreme cases conventional data recovery procedures may not be successful, and a damaged disk may be all that is left of the user's files. In such cases data recovery engineers using special equipment and software may be able to recover part or all of the lost data.[8]

Logical Access Controls

Modern data processing systems are typically accessed through a network of on-line terminals, many of which are located at a distance from the central computer site. System access controls thus must include not only restrictions on physical access to the computer site but also controls over access to system resources and data from on-line terminals. These restrictions are referred to as **logical access controls**. Logical access controls are implemented through an access control program that controls the interaction between terminal users and the system, limiting system access to users who have proper authorization and restricting the functions that each user can perform on the system according to the specific authority that has been granted to each user.

Here is an example of the problems that can arise if logical access controls are deficient. In September 1990 a repairman was working late to repair a printing press at Webco Press in Lapeer, Michigan. Webco's owner had trusted the repairman to complete this assignment without supervision by Webco personnel. According to Michigan State Police, the repairman gained access to Webco's mainframe computer and made a printout of the company's customer list, complete with prices. The repairman later attempted to sell the customer list to a Webco competitor for $5000 but was apprehended.[9] This example underscores several important points. First, it is important to restrict both physical and logical access to computer facilities. Second, un-

---

[8] Professional data recovery services are described in Michael Rogers, "A Data Survival Guide," *Disaster Recovery Journal* (April/May/June 1992): 14–16.

[9] "Computer Service Firm Faces Forfeiture for Theft," *Crains Detroit Business* (June 22, 1992): section 1, p. 8.

authorized logical access may be initiated not only from remote terminals but also from the central computer site. Third, it is not only unseen hackers who pose a threat of unauthorized system access but also employees and service personnel who may be well known and trusted by company management.

The most essential and universally used form of logical access control is a system of user identification and authentication. When signing on to the system, the user must first respond to a system request for identification and will enter an employee number, name, or account number. Then the system will ask the user to authenticate his or her identity by entering a **password**, which is a code word or series of characters that uniquely identifies the user and is known only to the user and the system. The system compares the password entered by the user to the system record of the password associated with the user identification number previously entered. If these match, the system assumes that this is a bona fide user who has authority to access and use the system.

With any access control system there is a risk that an unauthorized person will gain access to the system by repeatedly entering identification numbers until a valid user number is discovered and/or by correctly guessing a user's password. The risk of this type of unauthorized system access can be all but eliminated by a well-designed logical access control system that includes the following features. First, the system should shut off service to the terminal of any user who is unable to provide a valid identification number or password within three attempts. Second, passwords should be randomly assigned by the system rather than selected by users, because users often choose a word or name that may be easily guessed. Third, if a user who has supplied a valid identification number is unable to supply a valid password within three or four attempts, the identification number itself should be invalidated. Fourth, in highly sensitive systems repeated attempts to access the system utilizing invalid identification numbers or passwords should cause security personnel to immediately investigate the terminal from which the attempts originated. Finally, the access control process should be performed by a device (i.e., a microcomputer) that is external to the mainframe computer so that no one can obtain access of any kind to the mainframe without first supplying a valid user number and password.

Because many unauthorized access attempts originate from unknown terminals, it is advisable to assign an electronic identification number to each authorized terminal. The system is then programmed to check whether it is being accessed from an authorized terminal and to accept transactions and commands only from terminals having authorized identification numbers. Also, an on-line system that needs to be operational only during business hours (such as a banking system) may be deactivated by a supervisor who signs off from a terminal at the end of each day. Then the system should accept no more transactions until the supervisor activates it by signing on at the beginning of the next day.

Once an authorized code number and password have been accepted by the system and the user is allowed to proceed, the system should apply a compatibility test to all transactions or inquiries entered by the user. This checks whether the user having the designated identification number and password is authorized to initiate the type of transaction or inquiry being entered. For example, factory employees would not be authorized to make entries involving accounts payable, and purchasing agents would not be allowed to enter sales orders. This procedure is necessary to prevent both unintentional errors and deliberate attempts to manipulate the system.

To perform compatibility tests, the system must maintain an internal access control matrix consisting of a list of all authorized user identification numbers and passwords, a list of all files and programs maintained on the system, and a record of the type of access each user is entitled to have to each type of file and program. *Type of access* refers to what the user is authorized to do with the file or program. Examples of possible types of access include no access permitted, access to summary information only, read and display individual records, and various combinations of types of changes, including modifying field values within a record, adding a new record, deleting an existing record, or redefining the record structure. An example of an access control matrix appears in Fig. 13.6. According to the access codes assigned to the various users in Fig. 13.6, user 12345-ABC is permitted only to read and

Figure 13.6
Access control matrix

USER IDENTIFICATION		FILES			PROGRAMS			
Code Number	Password	A	B	C	1	2	3	4
12345	ABC	0	0	1	0	0	0	0
12346	DEF	0	2	0	0	0	0	0
12354	KLM	1	1	1	0	0	0	0
12359	NOP	3	0	0	0	0	0	0
12389	RST	0	1	0	0	3	0	0
12567	XYZ	1	1	1	1	1	1	1

Codes for type of access:
 0 = No access permitted
 1 = Read and display only
 2 = Read, display, and update
 3 = Read, display, update, create, and delete

display file C and is permitted no access of any kind to any other file or program. User 12359-NOP may perform any operations on file A but may access no other file or program. User 12389-RST, apparently a programmer, is authorized to make any type of change in program 2 and also to read and display records in file B. User 12567-XYZ, probably a supervisor, is authorized to read and display the contents of all files and programs.

A system of logical access controls based on user identification numbers and passwords is effective only as long as each user's code number and password remain confidential. For this reason the system should be programmed never to display or print a user identification number or password, and users should be cautioned not to disclose theirs to other persons. In addition, all passwords should be modified frequently to reduce the likelihood that a current password will become known to someone other than its authorized user. One other procedure useful to the maintenance of system security is for the system to record all attempts to access it from an unauthorized terminal or use an unauthorized user identification number or password. Periodic review of this record by a security officer should disclose attempts by unauthorized persons to access the system.

| Data Transmission Controls | The use of distributed data processing by modern business organizations is now routine. This means that large volumes of business data are regularly transmitted over long-distance telecommunications facilities. On-site data transmission using local area networks is almost as common. The routine use of such data transmission facilities exposes an organization to several threats, including unauthorized access to the system, electronic eavesdropping, hardware or software malfunctions leading to system failure, and errors in data transmission. |

To minimize the risk of unauthorized system access, an organization should restrict physical access to remote terminals and other data communications equipment by using the site access control policies described earlier in this section. In addition, logical access to system files and programs should be restricted using logical access control techniques discussed in the previous section. The risk of unauthorized access to data through electronic eavesdropping is minimized by the use of data encryption, also described earlier.

To reduce the risk of system failures, the organization should design the network so that there is sufficient capacity to handle periods of peak processing volume, and redundant components should be employed so that the system can switch to a backup unit in the event of component failure. Redundant components may include multiplexors, front-end processors, modems, and related equipment. In addition, multiple communications paths should be made available between critical network nodes. Manual backup procedures should be established in the event that system failure is not avoided. Checkpoint and rollback procedures, as described earlier in the chapter, should be employed to facilitate recovery from system failures.

The risk of errors in data transmission is minimized through routing verification procedures, the transmission of redundant bits, and message acknowledgment procedures. Routing verification procedures, which help ensure that no messages are routed to the wrong system address, work as follows: Any transaction or message transmitted over a network should have a header label identifying its destination. Before the message is sent, the system should verify that the message destination is valid and is authorized to receive data. Then when the message is received, the system should verify that the identity of the receiving node is consistent with the message's destination code.

One form of data redundancy used to check the accuracy of data transfer within a computer system is the parity bit. As pointed out in Chapter 4, computers use a combination of bits to represent a single character. For example, the digit 5 might be represented by 0101, while 7 is represented as 0111. However, when these data are being transmitted from one computer device to another, there is a risk that a bit may be lost or received incorrectly, which obviously would cause an error in the corresponding character. So that such errors are detected, a redundant bit, called the **parity bit**, is added to every character, and its value is set at either 0 or 1 in such a way that the total number of bits with value 1 in every character is an even number. So the digit 5 is represented as 0101 0, which has two bits with value 1, while the digit 7 is 0111 1, which has four 1 bits.[10] **Parity checking** is performed by any device that reads or receives a set of characters, and it works by summing the number of 1 bits in each character to verify that it is an even number. If not, the corresponding character must contain an error.

Two-dimensional parity checking is an extension of parity checking that is commonly used for data transmission over telecommunications facilities. Under this technique a set of, say, 10 characters is transmitted in a block, which consists of a 4 × 10 matrix of zeros and ones (not including parity bits). However, in addition to the *column* of parity bits associated with each character, there is also a *row* of parity bits associated with the entire data block. Parity checking can then be done both vertically and horizontally. This form of control is important in telecommunications, because noise bursts frequently cause two or more adjacent bits to be lost or picked up. A one-dimensional parity check will not detect all such errors.

One common message acknowledgment technique is the **echo check**. Under this technique the system component that is transmitting the message calculates a summary statistic based on the message data. For example, the sending unit counts the number of bits in the message. Then the receiving unit performs the same calculation and signals the result to the sending unit. If the two counts agree, the data transmission is presumed to be accurate.

---

[10] This describes an even-parity system; some systems use odd parity, where the total number of 1 bits must always be an odd number.

Message acknowledgment techniques are also useful in preventing the loss of part or all of a message. For example, if messages are given a trailer label, the receiving unit can check each message for the presence of the trailer label to verify that the entire message was received. In addition, if a large message or a set of transactions is being transmitted in a batch, each transaction or message segment can be numbered sequentially, and the receiving unit can check whether all parts of the message were received and were in the correct sequence. In either case the receiving unit will signal the sending unit that a correct message was received.

Whenever a data transmission error is detected by parity checking or message acknowledgment techniques, the receiving unit will signal the error to the sending unit, and the data will be retransmitted. Generally, the system will do this automatically, and the user may not even be aware that it has occurred. Occasionally, the system may not be able to accomplish automatic retransmission and will request the user at the sending end to manually retransmit the data.

Data transmission controls take on added importance in organizations that utilize electronic data interchange (EDI) or electronic funds transfer (EFT). Because these systems use data transmission links between organizations, they increase the risk of unauthorized access to proprietary data. EFT systems are also vulnerable to fraudulent funds transfers. In these environments sound internal control is achieved through more rigorous application of standard control policies and procedures. For example, strict logical access control procedures are essential, with passwords and dial-in phone numbers changed on a regular basis. Electronic identification should be required for all authorized network terminals. Details of all transactions should be recorded in a log that is periodically reviewed for evidence of invalid transactions. Encryption should be used to secure stored data as well as data being transmitted. Physical access to network facilities should be strictly controlled. Finally, no organization should be allowed to participate in these networks unless it can demonstrate that its relevant systems employ satisfactory control procedures.[11]

Protecting Personal Computers

For several reasons personal computers tend to be more vulnerable to security risks than mainframe computers. First, personal computers are everywhere in modern organizations, which means that it is much more difficult to restrict physical access to them. Second, personal computer users tend to be less conscious of the importance of security and control. Third, there are many more people who are familiar with the operation of personal computers and are proficient at using them,

---

[11] For more on security and control in EDI and EFT networks, see Ronald A. Gove, "EDI Security," *EDPACS* (December 1990): 1–8; and Eric Guldentops, "Security and Control in Electronic Funds Transfer: The SWIFT Case," *EDPACS* (April 1991): 1–11.

either legitimately or illegitimately. Fourth, adequate segregation of duties is often not possible in a personal computer environment, because the computers may be physically located within user departments, and user department personnel may be responsible for both programming and operating them.

Many of the same control policies and procedures that are applicable in a mainframe environment should also be used with personal computers. The problem is to get users to follow these policies and procedures. This means that end-user training is an important aspect of personal computer control. Such training should stress the need to locate personal computers in a secure area, to restrict physical access to the area, to restrict computer access using the locks and keys on the machine, and to restrict logical access to the computer and its files using passwords and related access controls. Users should also be encouraged to back up all important data and program files and to store backup files in a locked storage area. In addition, users who develop their own personal computer application programs should be taught how to test these programs before using them and how to prepare satisfactory documentation for them. Finally, users should be educated about the risks of computer viruses and the steps that should be taken to minimize these risks (see Chapter 14 for further discussion of this issue).

In many organizations the use of personal computers on a standalone basis is becoming less common. Instead, personal computers are electronically linked using local area networks and/or mainframe-microcomputer networks. One important advantage of incorporating personal computers into a network is that improved security and control procedures can be enforced through the central network controller. In particular, the use of password access controls can be required, personal computer utilization can be centrally monitored, virus protection procedures can be carried out as a matter of routine, and file backup procedures can be performed automatically.

The development of an internal control strategy for personal computers begins by taking an inventory of all personal computers used throughout the organization and identifying the various applications for which each computer is used. Then each personal computer should be classified according to the types of risks and exposures associated with its applications. For example, a personal computer system used to maintain accounts payable records and prepare cash disbursements is subject to much greater risk and exposure than one used for word processing in a secretarial pool. Next, a security program should be tailored to each personal computer system according to the degree of risk and exposure and the nature of the system applications. Perhaps the most sensitive personal computer applications are accounting systems under the control of one individual, so that there is inadequate segregation of duties. In such cases sound personnel practices must be followed, including background checks prior to hiring, fidelity bond coverage, enforced vacations, and periodic rotation of duties.[12]

Documentation Standards

Good documentation is an important aid to the efficient operation and control of a computer-based information system. Without adequate documentation, systems personnel may not be aware of important data processing policies and procedures, users may find it difficult to operate the system, and persons responsible for modifying or auditing the system may have difficulty determining how it works. Data processing management must establish and enforce standards that specify what documentation is required for projects under development and for fully implemented systems. An important part of the progress reviews of systems projects is the management review of the adequacy of documentation.

Documentation may be classified into three basic categories: administrative documentation, systems documentation, and operating documentation. **Administrative documentation** provides a description of overall standards and procedures for the data processing facility, including policies relating to justification and authorization of new systems or systems changes; standards for systems analysis, design, and programming; and procedures for file handling and file library activities. **Systems documentation** includes a complete description of all aspects of each system application, including narrative material, flowcharts, and program listings. **Operating documentation** includes all information needed by a computer operator to run a program, including the equipment configuration used, program and data files to be loaded, procedures required to set up and execute the job, descriptions of conditions that may interrupt program execution, and corrective actions required in response to program interruptions.

The purposes served by well-planned and enforced documentation standards within an organization are many. Among the benefits resulting from good documentation are facilitation of communication among system users, analysts, and programmers during systems development; facilitation of regular progress reviews of systems development work; provision of a reference and training tool for system users, machine operators, and newly hired employees within the systems function; and simplification of the program maintenance function.

Good documentation is particularly important in view of the job turnover that is common among systems analysts and programmers. If a programmer leaves an organization in the middle of a major project,

---

[12] For more on personal computer control policies and strategies, see Tina Doedjak, "Controlling and Auditing Microcomputer Data Security," *EDPACS* (April 1992): 4–9; and Institute of Internal Auditors Research Foundation, *Systems Auditability and Control Report*, Module 7: End-User and Departmental Computing (Altamonte Springs, Fla.: Institute of Internal Auditors Research Foundation, 1991), Chapters 3–4.

much time may be wasted by colleagues attempting to continue the work if the programmer has not maintained up-to-date documentation. If a programmer responsible for developing some of the existing applications in a system leaves without having provided adequate documentation, maintaining and updating those applications may be extremely difficult, perhaps almost as difficult as developing completely new programs. These potential problems underscore the necessity of requiring analysts and programmers to adhere to documentation standards in their work.

Minimizing System Downtime

In modern organizations computer systems are often an integral part of critical operating activities. If hardware or software malfunctions cause the computer system to fail, the organization's primary operating activities could come to a halt, and significant financial losses could be incurred. This underscores the importance of minimizing the risk of system failure.

Two methods of minimizing system downtime are preventive maintenance and uninterruptible power systems. **Preventive maintenance** involves regular testing of all system components and replacement of those found to be in a weak condition. This greatly reduces the likelihood of a system failure during regular operations. An **uninterruptible power system** consists of an auxiliary power supply that operates as a buffer between the power input from the electric company and the power used by the computer. Such systems smooth out the flow of power to the computer, eliminating loss of data due to momentary surges or dips in power flow. In the event of complete power failure uninterruptible power systems provide a backup power supply to keep the computer operating without interruption until regular power is restored.[13]

When minor hardware or software failures occur, a well-designed system should be able to continue functioning, though at a lower performance level. The capability of a system to continue performing its functions in the presence of the failure of system components is known as **fault tolerance**. Within individual hardware devices, fault tolerance is provided by the use of redundant components that can take over in the event of failure. The same principle can be extended to systems that consist of several components. For example, in a real-time system in which a constant level of service is essential, system components such as terminals, multiplexors, data transmission lines, disk drives, or even CPUs may be duplicated so that the system can switch to the backup component if necessary.

Disaster Recovery Planning

In addition to being aware of the risks associated with temporary system failures, every organization should be prepared to respond to a

---

[13] The cost and benefits of uninterruptible power are discussed in greater depth in Neil D. Kelley, "The Economics of Uninterruptible Power," *Infosystems* (September 1980): 55–64.

major disaster. Such potential disasters as fire, flood, earthquake, hurricane, tornado, and acts of sabotage and vandalism can shut down a computer facility for days or weeks. Many modern organizations cannot survive a loss of computer capability for a period of this length. Therefore it is essential for an organization to have a **disaster recovery plan** that prepares it to recover its data processing capacity as smoothly and quickly as possible in response to any emergency that would otherwise disable its computer systems for an extended period of time. Sound disaster recovery plans have enabled many organizations to recover from unexpected catastrophes that might have been devastating, if not fatal (see Focus 13.2).[14]

A sound disaster recovery plan should contain several elements. It should establish priorities for the recovery process, identifying those applications most critical to keeping the organization running. It should identify all hardware and software requirements necessary to sustain these critical applications. It should include an inventory of all data and program files required, and, of course, duplicate copies of these files should be stored at a secure location at some distance from the primary computer site. The plan should assign responsibility for particular disaster recovery activities to specific individuals and teams, including the responsibility for arranging for and administering new facilities, operating the computer and related equipment, installing systems software, establishing data communications facilities, installing applications software, recovering vital records, arranging for the availability of forms and supplies, and arranging for damage assessment and salvage at the original computer site. The plan should specify the sequence and timing of activities that each recovery team should perform. Of course, the disaster recovery plan itself should be fully documented, with copies stored securely at multiple locations.

One of the most critical aspects of a disaster recovery plan concerns the arrangements made for backup computer facilities. This can be done in several ways. One option is to establish a reciprocal agreement with another organization that has compatible facilities, whereby each party agrees to allow the other to use its data processing facilities on a temporary basis in the event of an emergency. Another option available to a multilocation organization is to distribute its data processing capacity in such a way that should one computer facility be destroyed, other facilities have sufficient capacity to take over the necessary work load. Another approach is to establish a contract with a vendor or a service bureau that permits use of its facilities in a crisis situation. Some external vendors provide contingent sites, referred to as hot or cold sites, for emergency use. A **hot site** is a completely operational data

---

[14] Several case histories are described in Richard H. Baker, *Computer Security Handbook*, 2nd ed. (Blue Ridge Summit, Pa.: TAB Books, 1991), Chapter 12.

13.2 FOCUS

A Model for Disaster Recovery Planning

The value of a disaster recovery plan is underscored by numerous case histories. Perhaps the best-known is the story of the worst bank fire in history and of how the bank recovered from that fire by following a plan that has since become a disaster recovery planning model.

On Thanksgiving Day in 1982 a huge fire swept through the offices of Northwest National Bank of Minneapolis, destroying bank transaction records and data processing facilities. It was described as one of the worst fires in the city's history. Yet by the following Monday bank employees were back on the job in new quarters—handling deposits, withdrawals, investments, loans, and other routine bank transactions. The fire could have threatened the bank's viability as a going concern, but it did not, thanks to a detailed disaster recovery plan. Because a record of nearly every bank transaction was stored elsewhere in computers or on microfilm, the bank lost few important records, if any. The day after the fire computers at a local service bureau were hard at work making new copies of records destroyed in the fire. The recovery plan provided bank executives with a detailed blueprint for lining up new office space, replacing com-

processing facility, configured to meet the user's requirements, that can be made available to a disaster-stricken organization on short notice. A cold site is a location, also available on short notice, that provides everything necessary to quickly install computer equipment, including environmental controls, sufficient electrical power, raised flooring, and so forth. An organization using a cold site must also contract with its computer vendor to ensure prompt delivery of equipment and software in the event of an emergency.

Four other aspects of disaster recovery planning deserve mention. First, the plan is not complete until it has been satisfactorily tested by simulating interruption of regular data processing operations and having each disaster recovery team carry out its prescribed recovery activities. Second, the plan must be continuously reviewed and revised to ensure that it reflects the organization's current computer applications, equipment configuration, and personnel assignments. Third, the disaster recovery plan for data processing should be part of an overall business interruption plan for the organization, and so it is important to make sure that these two plans are properly integrated. Fourth, disas-

puter equipment and supplies, procuring new office equipment, and making other arrangements essential to the continuation of Northwest's banking operations.

A more recent example occurred on October 2, 1991, as an early morning fire struck the Bank of the Sierra in Porterville, California, destroying its corporate offices and melting its mainframe computer. Though the facility was seemingly well protected by a sprinkler system and a halon gas fire-extinguishing system, this fire burned through the building's roof, which collapsed, crushing the sprinkler system and releasing the halon gas into the air. The bank's central data bases and related records, including all

personal and mortgage loan records, credit card records, and unprocessed checks, were lost.

Using a 150-page disaster recovery plan grounded in Northwest National Bank's experience, Bank of the Sierra officials quickly identified key people, critical tasks, and required equipment, and it began an overnight effort to restore bank services. By 10:00 A.M. the following morning, nine hours after the fire started, backup files were on-line and tellers were conducting business at branch windows as if nothing had happened. For processing of the bank's 25,000 to 40,000 daily transactions a data processing hot site in nearby San Ramon was utilized. Updated files were

downloaded from the hot site to a mainframe computer provided by a Denver company, from which printouts were flown back to Porterville daily. Within six days after the fire the bank had cleaned up its transaction processing backlog, and its customer accounts were current.

Sources: Lawrence Ingrassia, "Planning, Luck Help Big Bank Overcome Fire," *Wall Street Journal* (December 3, 1982): 25, 43; and Mark Phillips, "Planning Speeds Bank's Recovery from Fire," *Disaster Recovery Journal* (January/February/March 1992): 56–58.

---

ter planning should include insurance coverage to defer costs of equipment replacement, recovery activities, and business interruption.[15]

This completes our discussion of general controls in computer-based information systems. Key aspects of the general controls that we have discussed are summarized in Table 13.1.

APPLICATION CONTROLS

Application controls are employed to regulate the accuracy and integrity of data that are processed in specific computer applications. Application controls are concerned with the data inputs, files, programs, and outputs associated with a specific computer application, rather than with the computer system in general. Their primary objective is to maintain the accuracy of the system's outputs, data files, and transaction records. Application controls include batch totals, source data controls of various kinds, programmed input validation routines, on-

[15] For further discussion of disaster recovery planning, see Institute of Internal Auditors Research Foundation, *Systems Auditability and Control Report*, Module 10: Contingency Planning (Altamonte Springs, Fla.: Institute of Internal Auditors Research Foundation, 1991).

Category of Controls	Threats/Risks	Description and Examples
Organizational controls	Lack of understanding of assignments and responsibilities among systems personnel	Clear assignment of authority and responsibility for carrying out MIS functions, from Chief Information Officer (CIO) at the top through specific systems development, operations, and support functions.
Segregation of duties	Leaving one individual in a position to both perpetrate and conceal computer fraud	Separation of the applications programming function from the computer operations function, and, where possible, both of these from the systems programming, transaction authorization, file library, and data control functions.
Programmer/analyst performance evaluation	Poorly motivated and ineffective systems analysts and programmers	Standards for programming and systems analysis performance that include performance measures; regular collection and reporting of performance data to appropriate managerial personnel.
Systems project controls	Systems development projects that consume excessive resources	A timetable for each systems development project that includes milestones for formal progress review; a policy of terminating projects that are not progressing toward a satisfactory conclusion.
Computer operations controls	Ineffective execution of computer operations activities	Adherence to a schedule for data processing work; standards and measures by which to assess the performance of computer operations personnel.
Controlling site access	Damage to computer equipment and files; unauthorized access to confidential data	Limited points of physical access to the computer site; employees required to show personal identification before passing through each access point; security guards and alarms; access control procedures using passwords.
Protecting stored data	Unauthorized disclosure or destruction of stored computer data	File library; file labels; write protection mechanisms; concurrent update controls; data encryption; virus protection; file backup and recovery procedures; checkpoint and rollback procedures.

Table 13.1
Summary of key general control policies

line data entry controls, file maintenance controls, output controls, and controls over the errors and exceptions detected by other controls.

At Seattle Paper Products Jason Scott discovered that several fictitious invoices may have been processed by the accounts payable and cash disbursements system. If that is indeed what happened, it represents a failure in the application controls associated with that system. However, inadequate general controls also may have contributed to this control breakdown. For example, inadequate segregation of duties, poor supervision, insufficient restrictions on site access, or other general control deficiencies may be present; and any of these could have weakened the effectiveness of the company's application controls. The point is that general controls and application controls are both important and necessary, because application controls will be much more effective in the presence of strong general controls.

Category of Controls	Threats/Risks	Description and Examples
Logical access controls	Unauthorized access to systems software, application programs, data files, and other system resources	User authentication by means of passwords; protect confidentiality of passwords; change passwords frequently; compatibility test of all user requests using access control matrix; electronic identification of terminals; record and follow up attempted system access by unauthorized users.
Data transmission controls	Unauthorized access to data being transmitted or to the system itself; system failures; errors in data transmission	Site access controls for data communications equipment; data encryption; access control procedures using passwords; redundant equipment components; checkpoint and rollback procedures; routing verification procedures; message acknowledgment procedures; parity checking.
Protecting personal computers	Damage to computer equipment and files; unauthorized access to confidential data; users who are not security-conscious	End-user training; site access controls; on-line access control procedures using passwords; backup procedures for data and program files; virus protection; application of sound personnel practices in areas of greatest risk and exposure.
Documentation standards	Ineffective design, operation, review, audit, and modification of applications systems	Development and enforcement of standards relating to administrative documentation covering overall data processing standards and procedures; both systems documentation and operating documentation for all computer applications.
Minimizing system downtime	Temporary system failure leading to interruption of critical business operations	Regular preventive maintenance on key system components; uninterruptible power system; fault-tolerant systems design incorporating duplicate system components.
Disaster recovery planning	Prolonged interruption of data processing and business operations due to fire, natural disaster, sabotage, or vandalism	Disaster recovery planning that identifies critical system applications and related hardware, software, and data files; specifies all necessary disaster recovery activities and assigns responsibility for them; arranges the availability of backup facilities in the event of emergency.

Table 13.1
Continued

If application controls are weak, output data are likely to contain errors. Erroneous data can lead to poor management decision making and can negatively affect a company's relationships with customers, suppliers, and other external parties. For example, TRW Information Services, a large credit reporting bureau, was sued in 1991 by several states for reporting inaccurate credit information and violating consumer privacy. These lawsuits were reportedly triggered by thousands of consumer complaints about negative but inaccurate information contained in their credit reports.[16]

Batch Totals Batch totals, described in Chapter 12, are easily implemented in a computerized data processing environment, since the computer can be

---

[16] Mitch Betts, "State File Suit Against TRW," *Computerworld* (July 15, 1991): 4.

programmed to calculate and check the totals. In a batch processing application, source documents are generally assembled in groups of 50 or so prior to processing. Batch totals are then manually computed from the source documents before the source data are entered into the system. In an on-line system, batch totals are sometimes computed for all transactions entered within a particular time frame, such as one hour. In any case, the original batch totals are subsequently compared with machine-generated totals after each ensuing processing step. It is important that these batch total checks be performed by an employee who was not involved in preparing the original batch totals.

Four types of batch totals commonly used in computer systems are financial totals, hash totals, record counts, and line counts. A **financial total** is simply the sum of a dollar field in a set of records, such as total sales or total cash receipts. A **hash total** is a sum generated from a field that would usually not be added, such as the sum of all customer account numbers or employee identification numbers. A **record count** is a total of the number of documents entered into a process, while a **line count** is a total of the number of lines of data entered, such as the number of line items on a sales order or a purchase order.

A special form of batch total is used in the **cross-footing balance test**. This test can be performed only on a set of data that can be added horizontally (across several columns) as well as vertically (down each column). When the amounts in the column that contains the horizontal sums of all the other columns are added (vertically), the resulting total should equal the horizontal sum of all the other column totals. For example, the sum of the gross pay column in a payroll application should equal the sum of the net pay column plus those of all deduction columns.

When batch totals are checked, a discrepancy may indicate that one or more records have been lost, that unauthorized records have been added to the batch, or that errors have occurred in data transcription or data processing. The cause of any discrepancy should be identified, and any related errors corrected, before the transactions are processed further. Finding the cause of a discrepancy may require checking each record against its original source document. If batch sizes are limited to around 50 records, less time is required to track down the cause of any individual discrepancy in batch totals.

It occurred to Jason Scott that batch total checks should have detected the insertion of fictitious invoices into Seattle Paper's accounts payable system. So he investigated how batch totals were employed within that system. He discovered that vendor invoices were approved for payment by an accounts payable clerk, who would assemble the invoices and related supporting documents into batches of 40 to 50 items. The accounts payable clerk would compute a record count and financial total for each batch, and then enter them on a batch control sheet. The batches, with their corresponding batch control sheets, were then taken to a data entry department. Data entry personnel would key the batch control record into the system, followed by transaction data for each record in the batch. The batch totals were checked and reconciled at the conclusion of the data entry process and at each subsequent stage of processing. The source documents were stored alphabetically in a manual file, and the batch control sheets were discarded.

Upon reflection, Jason realized that there were at least two flaws in this system. First, the batch totals were originally compiled by the same person who approved invoices for payment. If that person were to commit fraud by submitting a fictitious invoice, he or she would be able to include the fictitious invoice data in the batch totals. Second, the batch control sheet was discarded by the data entry clerk at the conclusion of the data entry process. Thus the data entry clerk would also be able to commit fraud by submitting a fictitious invoice and altering the batch totals accordingly, since this could only be detected by reference to the discarded batch control sheet. Jason concluded that while Seattle Paper's batch control procedures appeared to be strong on the surface, in reality they were not at all effective, at least not in minimizing the risk of fraud.

Source Data Controls

Source data controls regulate the accuracy, validity, and completeness of computer input data as it is submitted to the data entry process and entered into the system. Various activities of the data control group (described earlier in this chapter) contribute significantly to source data control. When source data are received for processing, data control personnel check for necessary user authorizations and then use a control log to record the name and source of the transactions, the record count, control totals, and other relevant information concerning the input. Data control personnel also monitor the progress of source data through the data preparation process, expedite the process when necessary to meet the processing schedule, recheck record counts and other control totals after the data entry process is completed, and initiate any necessary corrections to the data prior to submitting them for further processing.

If data entry is performed using a key-operated device, the accuracy of the process may be checked using **key verification**. After one employee keys in data from a set of source documents, another employee repeats the keying process using the same source documents, and the computer compares the two sets of keystrokes. Discrepancies are highlighted so that any related keying errors can be corrected without delay. Key verification is a relatively expensive form of source data control, and so it is generally only used for the most critical kinds of input data. An inexpensive (but less effective) alternative to key verification is the visual inspection of printed input listings prior to processing.

Another source data control is **check digit verification**, the use of which requires that all authorized identification numbers contain a redundant digit, called the check digit or **self-checking digit**. This digit is a mathematical function of the other digits in the number. For example, in a five-digit number the last digit could be generated by subtracting the sum of the first four digits from the next highest number ending in zero. The number 90614 would pass this check, since $9 + 0 + 6 + 1 = 16$, and $20 - 16 = 4$. However, the number 41365 would fail, since $4 + 1 + 3 + 6 = 14$, and $20 - 14 \neq 5$. The data entry device is programmed to perform the check digit test each time an identification number (such as an account number or employee number) is entered. If an error occurs in the keying of an identification number, check digit verification will probably (but not certainly) detect it and signal the operator. As a result, most such errors may be corrected prior to submitting the input for computer processing.

When sequentially prenumbered forms are employed, the data entry system should include a subroutine that examines the form numbers and reports any exceptions. First, the system can identify and report any missing form numbers in a sequence of forms that have been processed. Second, the system can identify any duplicate form numbers submitted for processing. In either case any exceptions should be investigated, and any errors should be corrected before the data are processed further.

The use of turnaround documents enhances source data accuracy. Often, it also substantially reduces the total volume of data preparation work. As described in Chapter 2, a turnaround document is a document that is prepared as output of a data processing operation, used as a record of an external process, and returned to the system as a machine-readable input record of the external process. Because turnaround documents are prepared by the computer, they are much more accurate than input records prepared by manual keying.

While examining Seattle Paper's batch control procedures, Jason Scott also became aware of some deficiencies in the company's source data controls. For example, sequential prenumbering of forms was not used because supplier invoice numbers were not subject to the company's control. However, sequentially prenumbered vouchers could have been used, with a separate voucher attached to each vendor invoice and its supporting documents. In addition, supplier numbers were not controlled using self-checking digits; in fact, there was no formal process of approving a supplier to be added to the supplier (accounts payable) file. In effect, if a supplier's invoice was approved for payment, that supplier became an approved creditor of the company. Jason would note in his report that the proper use of either sequentially prenumbered vouchers or check digit verification of supplier numbers could have prevented Seattle Paper from paying fictitious invoices.

Input Validation Routines

Input validation routines are programs or subroutines that check the validity and accuracy of input data after they have been entered and recorded

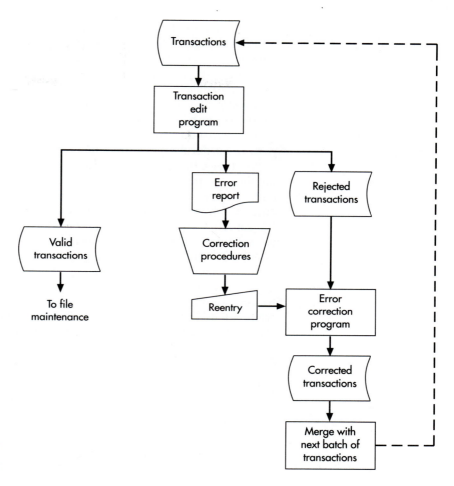

Figure 13.7
Edit program

on a machine-readable file. These programs are also called **edit programs**, and the specific types of accuracy checks they perform are called **edit checks**. Input validation is often performed by a separate program prior to regular processing (see Fig. 13.7). However, some edit checks may be performed during the source data entry process. In addition, many file update programs contain input validation routines that check the accuracy of transaction data by comparing them with corresponding master file data. Errors identified by edit programs should be corrected without delay, and the corrected data should be either resubmitted with the next batch of transactions (as shown in Fig. 13.7) or merged back into the same batch from which they came. In either case the corrected transaction records should again be edited by the same input validation routine.

There are several different types of edit checks used in input valida-tion routines. A **sequence check** tests whether a batch of input data is in the proper numerical or alphabetical sequence. A **field check** examines whether the characters in a field are of the class the field is supposed to contain. For example, a field check on a numeric field would indicate an error if the field contained blanks or alphabetic characters. A **sign check** is a check to ensure that the data in a field have the appropriate arithmetic sign. For example, data in a field such as inventory balance should never have a negative sign. In addition, check digit verification may be performed in an input validation routine in the same way as it is performed during the source data entry process.

Another edit check is the **validity check**, which compares identification numbers or transaction codes with ones already known to be authorized. For example, if a sale to customer account number 65432 is entered into the system, the computer must locate a customer master file record having that same account number. If no such master file record exists, then 65432 must be an invalid customer account number, and the transaction should be flagged as invalid by the edit program. As another example, suppose that the customer accounting system processes only three types of transactions, each identified by a unique transaction code. For sales transactions a code of S might be used, while a P code might be used for customer payments and a C code for other credit transactions. Then the computer should check the transaction code field in every input record and reject any records where this field does not contain either an S, a P, or a C.

Still another common form of edit check is the **limit check**, which is a test to ensure that a numerical amount in a record does not exceed some predetermined limit. For example, the hours-worked field in a payroll processing run may be checked to make sure that no input record's hours-worked field contains more than 60 for a single week. A variation of the limit check is the **range check**, in which both upper and lower limits on the value are specified. Range checks are commonly used on transaction date fields, since a transaction date should generally be within a few days of, but never in excess of, the current date.

A **reasonableness test** is a check on the logical correctness of the relationship between the value of a data item on an input record and the value of a related data item on the corresponding master file record. For example, a salary increase of $1000 per month would be reasonable for an executive whose current salary was $15,000 per month but not for a data entry clerk making $1500 per month. Similarly, the quantity of inventory items received might be tested for reasonableness by checking whether it exceeded twice the value of the order quantity of the item.

One other form of edit check is the **redundant data check**. This check requires that two identifiers be included in each transaction record that is entered into the system to update a master file record. Cross-checking is then used to confirm that the correct master file record has been obtained. For example, suppose that both the customer account number and the first five letters of the customer's name are included in a sales transaction record. On the basis of the account number the system will retrieve the corresponding customer master record from the file, and this master record will also include the customer's name. Using the redundant data check, the system compares the first five letters from the transaction record with the corresponding portion of the name field in the master file record and flags any exceptions. This check prevents the posting of transactions to the wrong master file records.

On-Line Data Entry Controls

On-line data entry controls are controls over the accuracy and integrity of transaction data entered into the system from on-line terminals. Some controls in this category are special types of edit checks that are unique to on-line systems. In addition, many of the edit checks described in the previous section are useful in on-line systems. These include field checks, validity checks, limit checks, reasonableness tests, and the redundant data check. It is also essential that all personnel who are authorized to enter transaction data from on-line terminals be assigned user identification numbers and passwords that enable them to access the system, but their access authority should be strictly limited to the data entry process. To enforce this restriction, the system must perform a compatibility test on every transaction or request entered by a data entry operator.

If the personnel assigned to enter data are generally inexperienced in the use of systems or terminals, then the system may be programmed to control the data entry process using a technique known as prompting. Under this approach the system displays a request to the user for each required item of input data and then waits for an acceptable response before requesting the next required item. In some cases the prompt may consist of a limited number of choices (for example, single or married) from which the user must select the one that applies. An alternative to prompting is preformatting, in which the system displays a document format with highlighted blank spaces for the data items that the user must fill in. If preformatting or other free-form methods of data entry are used, the system should also perform a completeness test on each input record, to check whether all the data items required for a particular transaction have in fact been entered by the terminal operator.

Depending on the type of transaction being entered, the system should be able to enter some of the transaction data into the input record automatically, which saves keying time and reduces the risk of error. For example, the system can enter the current date and time, the operator's identification number, and perhaps a batch number into the record. If the application involves the creation of documents that are sequentially prenumbered, such as purchase orders or sales invoices, the system can automatically determine the next available document number and enter it into the transaction record. If the application involves the creation of new accounts or other records where check digit verification is used to control the identification number, the system can generate new identification numbers that satisfy the check digit algorithm and do not duplicate existing numbers, and enter these into the input record.

As edit checks are performed on input data entered on-line, any errors or possible errors that are detected should cause an error message to be displayed to the terminal operator. Because terminal operators may be inexperienced system users, the error message should be as clear as possible with respect to which item is in error, what the error is, and what the operator should do. The system should then recheck the operator's response to the error message prior to accepting any further transaction input.

After all data for a transaction have been entered by a terminal operator, another technique for checking data accuracy is to have the system read the data entered, retrieve some related data from the data base, and display this data on the operator's terminal for comparison with other data available to the operator. This process is called closed-loop verification. For example, if one of the data items being entered is an item number or account number, the system could retrieve the item description or account name and display this on the operator's terminal. The operator would then check the source document for the related data and confirm whether the description or name displayed on the terminal corresponds to what is shown on the source document. This form of closed-loop verification may be used instead of the redundant data check to protect against entry of a valid but incorrect identification number.

For on-line data entry systems in which large numbers of transactions are entered, the system should create a detailed record of every transaction, called a transaction log. In addition to including the transaction data, each record on the log should contain the date and time of entry, the terminal and operator identification, and an internal sequence number indicating the sequence in which the transaction was entered. If the current version of an on-line file is damaged, the transaction log can be used to help reconstruct the file. If a system malfunction occurs that temporarily shuts down the system, the internal sequence number of the last transaction successfully processed by the system can be displayed on the operator's terminal once service is restored. This procedure ensures that no transactions are lost or inadvertently entered twice as a result of a system malfunction.

File Maintenance Controls

While source data controls, input validation routines, and on-line data entry controls all help to ensure the accuracy of transaction input data, file maintenance controls are designed to help preserve the accuracy and completeness of data stored in master files. File maintenance controls include checks on data currency, exception reporting, reconciliation with external data, file security procedures, and file conversion controls.

Data stored on master files often become out of date. Suppliers or customers may move or go out of business, employees may retire or be terminated, and so forth. These conditions need to be identified and investigated so that appropriate action (such as removing an employee record from the master file, or updating a customer address) can be taken. To help identify such conditions, every master file record should contain a field for "date of last transaction," which is updated to the current date whenever a transaction is processed against it. Periodically, the entire master file should be scanned to identify any master file records for which this date is more than one year old. These records should be displayed or listed on a report for appropriate follow-up.

While searching the master file for noncurrent records, the system can also check for other unusual conditions and list them on an exception report. Virtually all of the edit checks described earlier in this chapter can be employed in this procedure. Two that should always be employed are the sign check and the completeness test. The sign check will detect such conditions as a negative inventory balance or a negative customer account balance. The completeness test will detect any cases of data that may have been lost while the file was being copied or updated. Of course, any potential errors listed on the exception report should be investigated and corrected.

In many cases it is possible to reconcile selected master file totals with comparable data maintained outside the system. For example, the personnel department could maintain a count of the number of employees. Then every time that the payroll file is processed, the computer can count and report the number of employee records on the file, and this sum can be compared with the one maintained by the personnel department. Similarly, the purchasing department could maintain a count of the number of approved suppliers, and the credit department could maintain a count of the number of customers approved to purchase merchandise on credit. This procedure should detect attempts to add fictitious employees, customers, or suppliers to the corresponding master file—as happened, for example, in the case of Seattle Paper Products.

A general ledger accounting system affords numerous opportunities to use the reconciliation technique. For example, within the general ledger file there is an accounts receivable control account that contains the current balance. This control account balance should always be equal to the sum of the balances of all customer accounts in the accounts receivable master file. The same thing should be true of the inventory control account, the capital assets control account, and the accounts payable control account. These general ledger control account balances should be reconciled to the corresponding master file totals on a regular basis.

Selected master file totals, including a record count, hash totals, and financial totals of critical fields such as customer account balance, are generally computed every time the file is processed, and they are recorded in a trailer label record at the end of the file. The trailer label record represents a useful point of reference in performing reconciliation procedures.

File security procedures include many of the techniques described in the earlier section on protecting stored data. They bear repeating here because they are crucial to protecting the master and transaction files that are a central part of most accounting applications. When not in use, these files should be stored in a file library under the supervision of a librarian, who should require that each file be logged out or logged in whenever it is removed or returned. These files should also contain internal and external labels, which should be checked before each file is used. Write protection mechanisms should be employed when processing files that are to be read but not updated. Backup copies of these files should be generated at the conclusion of each file update process and should be stored at a secure off-site location.

Whenever a data processing system undergoes significant modifications or is replaced by a new system, the old master files must be converted into the formats and data structures of the new system. This file conversion process is often done using computer programs that have been specially written for this purpose. It is important to institute sound controls over the file conversion process to ensure that it does not engender errors in the new master file data. First, the file conversion programs should be adequately tested to ensure that they function as expected. Second, edit checks and batch control totals should be used to check all significant fields. Third, the old and new systems should be run in parallel through at least one operating cycle, and the results of the two updates should be compared to identify any discrepancies that may be caused by errors on the new master files. Finally, the file conversion process should be carefully supervised and also reviewed by internal audit personnel.

Output Controls

Controls over reports, checks, documents, and other printed computer outputs represent another important category of application controls. Output controls are performed by data control personnel and by the users of the output. Data control personnel should review all output for reasonableness and proper format and should reconcile output control totals with corresponding input control totals. Data control personnel are also responsible for distributing computer output to the appropriate user departments. Special care should be taken in handling checks and other sensitive documents and reports. Users are responsible for carefully reviewing the completeness and accuracy of all computer output that they receive.

Control of Errors and Exceptions

Output controls include procedures for investigating and correcting errors identified by edit programs, batch total checks, source data controls, and other application controls. These procedures are usually the responsibility of the data control department. Prescribed procedures for correction and reentry of erroneous data must be carried out accurately. Corrected input should again be submitted to validation routines, because the error rate on error corrections is higher than that on any other type of transaction. Exceptions encountered during processing, such as transaction amounts or file balances that exceed prescribed limits, should be investigated to reveal their cause. User department personnel should be notified of those errors caused by incorrect input submitted by them.

A useful technique for controlling data processing errors and exceptions is maintenance of an error log. For every error an entry is made in the log noting the type of record, the transaction identification number, the processing date, the specific field in error, and the error type. As errors are corrected and the corresponding data successfully resubmitted to the system, the status of the error record in the log is changed from "open" to "closed," and a notation of the resubmission date and the cause of the error is entered. The error log may be maintained manually by data control personnel, or it may be maintained by the computer. Periodically, the error log may be used to prepare management reports summarizing the number of errors by record type, by error type, and by cause. Also, reports listing all outstanding errors should be regularly provided to operations supervisors to enable them to follow up on uncorrected errors and make sure that all errors are corrected as quickly as possible.

This concludes our description of application control procedures used in computer-based information systems. Table 13.2 summarizes many of the principal features of these application controls.

Application Controls: An Example

As an illustration of the use of many of the application controls described in this section, let us consider the processing of a batch of credit sales transactions. At a minimum the required transaction data will include the sales order number, the customer's account number, the inventory item number, the quantity sold, the sale price, and the delivery date. If the customer purchases more than one type of product, then the inventory item number, quantity sold, and price fields will occur more than once in each sales transaction record. The processing of these transactions will include the following steps:

1. Preparing batch totals
2. Keying the source data into the system
3. Editing the transaction file
4. Accessing each inventory master record to subtract the quantity sold from the quantity on hand
5. Accessing each customer master file record to add the total sale amount to the customer's account balance
6. Preparing and distributing shipping and/or billing documents

Category of Controls	Threats/Risks	Description and Examples
Batch totals	Lost input records; bogus input records; errors in data entry or data processing	Totals should be manually prepared prior to processing and checked after each subsequent stage of processing; examples include financial totals, hash totals, record counts, line counts, and the cross-footing balance test.
Source data controls	Invalid, incomplete, or inaccurate source data input	Examples include key verification; check-digit verification; sequentially prenumbered forms; turnaround documents; review of source data input for appropriate authorization; control log; and monitoring and expediting data entry process by data control personnel.
Input validation routines	Invalid or inaccurate data in computer-processed transaction files	Transaction files are processed by edit programs that perform edit checks on key data fields, including sequence checks, field checks, sign checks, validity checks, limit checks, range checks, reasonableness tests, and redundant data checks.
On-line data entry controls	Invalid or inaccurate transaction input entered through on-line terminals	Examples include edit checks; prompting operators during the data entry process; preformatting; completeness test; automatic system data entry; closed-loop verification; and a transaction log maintained by the system.
File maintenance controls	Inaccurate or incomplete data in computer-processed master files	Examples include checks on currency of master file data; reporting exceptions identified by edit checks; reconciliation of master file totals with externally maintained totals; storage of files in secure file library; use of file labels and write protection mechanisms; backup file copies stored in secure off-site location; and file conversion controls.
Output controls	Inaccurate or incomplete computer output	Data control personnel should perform visual review of computer output, reconciliation of batch totals, and proper distribution of output; users should also review computer output for completeness and accuracy.
Control of errors and exceptions	Failure to properly correct inaccurate computer input or master file data	Data control personnel should maintain an error log listing all errors identified by batch controls, edit checks, etc., and should promptly investigate and correct all such errors; corrected data should be resubmitted to error-checking procedures; causes of errors should be identified and reported to users or other persons responsible for the errors.

Table 13.2
Summary of key application
control procedures

Figure 13.8 illustrates this process using a systems flowchart and also identifies the application controls that should be employed at each stage in the process.

At the beginning of the process the persons who assemble batches of sales order documents to be submitted for data processing should prepare, with the help of a calculator, the following batch totals:

1. A record count of the number of customer transactions
2. A line count of the number of inventory transactions
3. Hash totals of the quantity sold and price fields
4. A financial total of dollar sales (price × quantity)

These batch totals should be recorded on batch control forms appended to each batch of sales documents. The batches are then delivered to the data control section of the data processing department. Data control personnel should check each batch for proper authorization, record the receipt of the input in a control log, and convey the documents to the data entry department.

As the transaction data are keyed into the system to be written onto a transaction file disk, check digit verification should be used to verify the customer account number and the inventory item number. Field checks can also be performed to verify the presence of numeric characters in the quantity, date, and price fields. Because sales orders should be sequentially prenumbered, the system should also verify that every sales order number is accounted for. If it is deemed cost-effective, key verification could be employed to check the accuracy of the data entry process. Finally, the system should accumulate all relevant batch totals and print them on a control report to be compared with the original batch control sheets.

Errors detected during source data entry are generally of two types. Operator errors arise because an operator reads a source document incorrectly or accidently strikes the wrong key. These errors are generally benign and can be corrected at once by the operator. The second type of error entails source data that are incorrect, such as an unauthorized sales transaction, an invalid account number, or a missing sales order document. This type of error is more problematic and should be investigated and corrected before the sales transaction data are processed further.

Next, the sales transaction file is sorted into numerical sequence by customer account number, and an edit program (see Fig. 13.7) is used to edit the data in each record for possible errors. This program should perform the following edit checks:

1. A sequence check on the customer account number field
2. Limit checks on the quantity and price fields
3. A range check on the requested delivery date
4. A completeness test to verify that all fields in the input record contain data

Any transactions rejected by these edit checks should be listed on a control report. In addition, this program should accumulate batch totals and print them on the control report. Data control personnel are then responsible for reconciling the batch totals, for investigating and correcting any errors, and for resubmitting the corrected transactions.

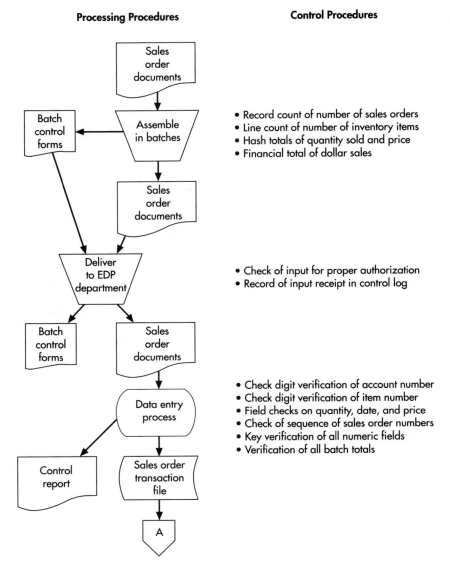

Figure 13.8
Flowchart of sales order processing
and related control procedures

The next step is file updating, which is done by processing the sales transaction file against the customer (accounts receivable) and inventory master files. At this point care must be taken to ensure that the right copies of these master files are retrieved from the file library and loaded on the system. The disk packs or tape reels containing the accounts receivable and inventory master files should have external labels containing the file name and date processed, and the operator should check these labels carefully prior to loading the files. Both files should also have an internal header label containing this information,

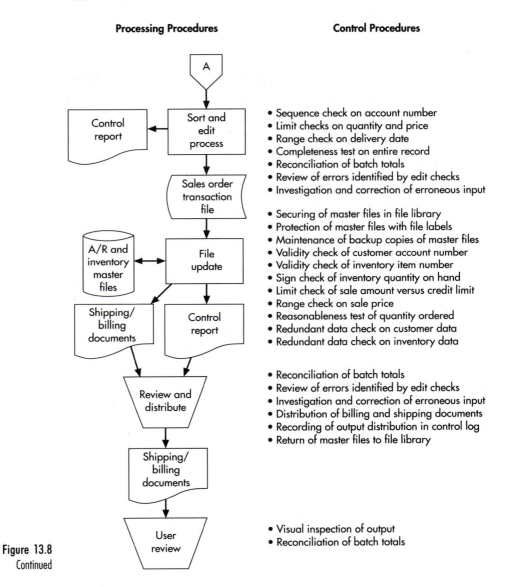

Processing Procedures

Control Procedures

Sort and edit process

Control report

- Sequence check on account number
- Limit checks on quantity and price
- Range check on delivery date
- Completeness test on entire record
- Reconciliation of batch totals
- Review of errors identified by edit checks
- Investigation and correction of erroneous input

Sales order transaction file

File update

A/R and inventory master files

- Securing of master files in file library
- Protection of master files with file labels
- Maintenance of backup copies of master files
- Validity check of customer account number
- Validity check of inventory item number
- Sign check of inventory quantity on hand
- Limit check of sale amount versus credit limit
- Range check on sale price
- Reasonableness test of quantity ordered
- Redundant data check on customer data
- Redundant data check on inventory data

Shipping/ billing documents

Control report

Review and distribute

- Reconciliation of batch totals
- Review of errors identified by edit checks
- Investigation and correction of erroneous input
- Distribution of billing and shipping documents
- Recording of output distribution in control log
- Return of master files to file library

Shipping/ billing documents

User review

- Visual inspection of output
- Reconciliation of batch totals

Figure 13.8
Continued

and the file-update program should be programmed to check these header labels prior to accepting any transactions for processing against the files. Each master file should also include a trailer label containing a record count and one or more other file totals, and these should be checked and updated during the file-updating run. Backup copies of the transaction file and both master files should be generated and conveyed to a secure off-site location for storage.

Because the file update program accesses the customer and inventory master file records, it can perform additional input validation tests by comparing data on each transaction record with data on the corresponding master file record. These tests include the following:

- Validity checks on the customer account numbers and inventory item numbers
- Sign checks on inventory balances on hand after subtracting sales quantities
- Limit checks on the total amount sold to each customer relative to that customer's available credit limit
- Range checks on the sale price of each item sold relative to the permissible range of prices for that item
- Reasonableness tests on the quantity sold of each item relative to normal sales quantities for that item

In addition, so that valid but incorrect account numbers or inventory item numbers are not entered, redundant data such as the customer name and item description should be included in each transaction record and cross-checked against the corresponding values in the respective master files. This procedure prevents the posting of the credit sale to the wrong customer accounts receivable record or the posting of an inventory reduction to the wrong inventory master record.

Outputs of the file update processing run will include billing and/or shipping documents and a control report. The control report will contain batch totals accumulated during the file update run and a listing of any transactions rejected by the input validation routines within the file update program. Data control personnel should reconcile the batch totals with those prepared prior to the file update run and should investigate any rejected transactions or discrepancies in batch totals and correct any related errors. Data control personnel are also responsible for distributing all copies of the billing and shipping documents to appropriate personnel in the billing and shipping departments, for recording the completion of the job and the distribution of the output in their control log, and for returning the updated master files to the file library.

When system users in the shipping and billing departments receive the shipping and billing documents from data processing, they should also perform a limited review. The output documents should be visually inspected for misaligned or incomplete data or other obvious deficiencies. In addition, the final batch control report should be reconciled to the batch control form prepared when the documents were originally submitted.

A commonly used alternative to batch processing of sales transactions is to enter them directly into the system using on-line processing. Let us briefly consider how the internal control procedures would differ if on-line processing were used. The most obvious difference is that most of the data entry controls are focused on the interaction between the terminal user and the system. First, when the user accesses the system, logical access controls should verify the identity of the terminal and confirm the validity of the user identification number and password entered. Of course, personnel authorized to enter sales transactions should be provided with user identification numbers and passwords that do not permit them to enter any other types of transactions or commands. For enforcement of this restriction a compatibility test should be performed on any request or command entered by these personnel.

To assist authorized personnel in entering sales transaction data, the system may be programmed to prompt for the customer account number, item number, and other required input. After each prompt the system will wait for a valid response from the terminal operator before displaying the next prompt. Alternatively, the system can display a sales order document format with highlighted blank spaces where data must be entered and wait for the operator to enter all the required data. Regardless of whether prompting or preformatting is used, the system should perform validity checks, field checks, limit checks, range checks, sign checks, check digit verification, reasonableness tests, and completeness tests as the data are entered. These tests are performed on the same fields as in the batch processing system. A significant advantage of an on-line data entry system is that when errors are detected by these edit checks, the system can immediately signal the errors to the terminal operator, who can then initiate a real-time correction and reentry of the data in question.

So that entry of valid but incorrect account numbers or item numbers is prevented, redundant data can be entered and cross-checked, as in the batch processing system. Alternatively, a form of closed-loop verification can be used, in which the terminal operator enters only the customer account number and inventory item numbers, and the system retrieves the corresponding customer name and item descriptions from the master files and displays them on the terminal. The terminal operator should visually examine the customer name and item descriptions displayed. If these match the corresponding values printed on the sales order document, the operator signals the system to proceed with the transaction. Whenever one or more values do not match, an operator keying error is likely, and the operator should recheck the account number and/or item numbers and reenter corrected values.

It should be clear from this example that the design of a system of application controls requires ingenuity and care. Each significant transaction data field should be checked by at least one method. However, cost-benefit relationships must also be considered in designing application control systems. Generally, tests performed by the computer, such as edit checks, are less costly and more effective than tests performed by people, such as key verification and visual inspection. Also, the earlier in the process that a data entry error is caught, the easier it is to correct it.

CASE CONCLUSION:
CORRECTING
COMPUTER CONTROL
PROBLEMS AT
SEATTLE PAPER
PRODUCTS

After further investigation Jason Scott and his supervisor have not been able to identify the source of the fictitious invoices processed through the cash disbursements system at Seattle Paper Products. They decide that they must request police assistance in identifying the person or persons having a bank account in the name of Pacific Electric Services, in the hope that this will lead to an employee in Seattle Paper's accounts payable or data entry function.

With police assistance they ascertain that the bank account of Pacific Electric Services is in the name of Patricia Simpson, who is employed as a data entry clerk at Seattle Paper. Under questioning by police fraud investigators, Patricia admits to an embezzlement scheme in which she created fictitious invoices, inserted them into batches of invoices submitted to her for data entry, modified the batch control totals accordingly, and destroyed the original batch control sheet containing the correct batch totals. According to Patricia, the scheme had been initiated only three months previously, and no one else at Seattle Paper was involved. She also claims that all of the fictitious invoices were in the name of Pacific Electric Services.

Jason is assigned to examine Seattle Paper's cash disbursement records in order to corroborate Patricia's story. He writes a small program that will read a cash disbursements transaction file and identify any disbursements to Pacific Electric Services. He then undertakes the daunting task of retrieving several hundred tape files containing cash disbursement transactions over the past two years from Seattle Paper's archives. After a few days he has identified 40 fraudulent transactions totaling over $20,000. Contrary to Patricia's account, the earliest of these transactions occurred 18 months ago, though there is a 2-month gap, ending 3 months ago, that contains no fraudulent transactions.

Since Patricia had not been truthful about the duration of her scheme, Jason wonders whether she might also have used other fictitious company names. By this time, however, she is providing no further assistance to the investigation on the advice of her lawyer. So Jason writes another computer program to scan the cash disbursement records and retrieve the supplier account number, name, address, and authorization code for every vendor invoice processed with no supporting purchase order or receiving report. This check eventually yields a file containing 175 supplier records, payment authorization for which have been granted by 23 different employees at Seattle Paper. Jason has this file sorted by authorization code and prepares 23 printouts containing data on the suppliers engaged by each of these employees. Each printout is sent to the corresponding employee, with a request that the employee verify the authenticity of every supplier on his or her list. After receiving back all of these printouts and following up to verify the legitimacy of two suppliers that no one could recall dealing with, Jason concludes that the embezzlement scheme was indeed confined to Pacific Electric Services.

Before this investigation is concluded, Seattle Paper implements several changes in its accounts payable and cash disbursements system in response to recommendations prepared by Jason and his supervisor. First, there must be an approved purchase order for every disbursement, including those for services only. Second, disbursements can only be made to approved suppliers, and every supplier must be approved by a purchasing agent who is not involved in the cash disbursements process. Approved suppliers are assigned a supplier account number that contains a check digit, and this account number must be included in every cash disbursement record. In addition, the purchasing department now maintains a count of the number of approved suppliers, and this is regularly compared with a computer-generated count of the number of supplier records on the accounts payable file. Third, when payment of vendor invoices is approved, a voucher record is prepared to document the approval, and the voucher accompanies the vendor invoice and supporting documents through all subsequent processing steps. These vouchers are sequentially prenumbered, and all outstanding voucher numbers are accounted for on a regular basis. Fourth, batch totals for the daily batch of cash disbursement transactions are prepared by an employee other than the person who approves the payments, and the accounts payable department retains a copy of the batch control sheet for comparison to the final batch control report generated by the cash disbursement system.

As he learns about the changes that Seattle Paper has made to improve its internal control system, Jason reflects on how the company's management had previously rejected similar changes suggested by Northwest's internal audit staff, including those made by his supervisor a year ago. Jason realizes that he has learned an important truth about internal control: There are many companies and many managers who do not realize the importance of internal control until they have been burned. ■

SUMMARY

The pervasive use of computers in modern organizations—not only to process accounting data but also to control critical operating functions—has caused widespread concern about the quality of the internal controls associated with computer-based information systems. Although computerization of information processing does not change overall control objectives and policies, it does require a focus on general control procedures that provide a sound control environment for computer processing and on application control procedures that control the accuracy and integrity of the input, output, and file data that are processed through various computer system applications.

Among the important general controls in a computer-based information system are organizational controls, including the separation of incompatible functions; performance evaluation standards for computer personnel; project scheduling and monitoring procedures; computer operations controls; internal-pricing systems to charge users for computer services; restrictions on access to computer sites; procedures to protect stored data; logical access controls involving user identification and authentication by means of passwords; data transmission control procedures; methods of protecting personal computer equipment and applications; documentation standards; techniques for minimizing system downtime; and disaster recovery planning.

Application controls are designed to prevent, detect, and correct errors and irregularities in transaction data as they flow through the input, processing, and output stages of a computer system application. Important application controls include batching and batch total checks, source data controls, programmed input validation routines, on-line data entry controls, file maintenance controls, output controls, and controls over errors and exceptions detected by other application controls.

The design of an efficient and effective internal control system is a complex task, and extensive computerization increases the degree of complexity. However, the general principles of cost-benefit analysis, explained in Chapter 12, provide a useful framework. First, the threats or hazards associated with possible deficiencies in internal control should be identified. Next, the exposure, or potential dollar loss, connected with each control threat should be estimated. Then the risk or likelihood of each threat should be assessed. This permits calculation of the expected loss (risk $\times$ exposure) associated with each threat. Finally, the expected loss should be compared with the cost of implementing internal control procedures that would minimize the risk. Internal control procedures should be implemented whenever their benefit (reduction in expected loss) exceeds their cost.

KEY TERMS   Define the following terms

general controls	full costing	data encryption
application controls	market pricing	cryptography
Chief Information Officer (CIO)	flexible pricing	electronic vaulting
project milestones	external label	grandfather-father-son concept
allocation base	internal labels	checkpoints
single-factor base	volume label	rollback
wall clock time (WCT)	header label	logical access controls
CPU time	trailer label	password
unit pricing	tape file protection ring	compatibility test
multiple-factor base	concurrent update controls	access control matrix

parity bit	financial total	field check
parity checking	hash total	sign check
echo check	record count	validity check
administrative documentation	line count	limit check
systems documentation	cross-footing balance test	range check
operating documentation	key verification	reasonableness test
preventive maintenance	check digit verification	redundant data check
uninterruptible power system	self-checking digit	prompting
fault tolerance	input validation routines	preformatting
disaster recovery plan	edit programs	completeness test
hot site	edit checks	closed-loop verification
cold site	sequence check	transaction log

Discussion questions

13.1 Many persons believe that programming is basically a creative activity and should therefore not be subject to cost controls and other managerial regulation. Discuss this point of view.

13.2 A computer implementation project is often performed in a state of crisis, with the implementation group working feverishly to keep pace with the implementation schedule. In this atmosphere corners are often cut with respect to documentation and application controls. What arguments do you feel would be effective to prevent such shortcuts, even though doing so could delay implementation?

13.3 Theoretically, a control procedure should be adopted if its benefit value exceeds its cost. Explain how the benefit value and cost of the following controls can be estimated.

a. Separation of functions

b. Data protection procedures

c. Logical access controls

d. Input validation routines

13.4 In 1990 Prudential-Bache Securities in New York entered into a contract to enable it back up all of its data (over 500,000 securities transactions per day) by transmitting it on a real-time basis to an electronic vaulting service provided by Comdisco Computing Service Corporation in New Jersey. The service includes use of a high-speed data transmis-

sion line and an automated tape library. Comdisco also agreed to make a hot site available to Prudential-Bache in the event that a disaster shuts down their central data center. The hot site has a direct link to the vaulting system, ensuring that all but the last 15 minutes of trading data would be recovered.

Though terms of the contract were not disclosed, this arrangement is certainly a very expensive proposition for Prudential-Bache. Discuss how this contract could have been justified on a cost-benefit basis. In addition, discuss the steps that Prudential-Bache should take to prevent unauthorized access to its backup data.

13.5 Discuss how reliability analysis (see Chapter 12) could be applied to the design and evaluation of internal controls in a computer-based information system. For which types of internal controls would it probably be most useful? Why?

13.6 For control purposes the function of transaction authorization should be performed by responsible persons outside the systems department. However, computers are increasingly being programmed to initiate transactions, such as by issuing a purchase order when an inventory balance is low. Discuss whether such automatic transaction generation represents a violation of good internal control principles.

PROBLEMS

13.1 Your company has procured a number of microcomputers for use in various locations and applications. One has been installed in the stores department, which has the responsibility for disbursing stock items and for maintaining stores records. In your audit you find, among other things, that a competent employee, trained in computer applications, receives the requisitions for stores, reviews them for completeness and for the propriety of approvals, disburses the stock, maintains the records, operates the computer, and authorizes adjustments to the total amounts of stock accumulated by the computer.

When you discuss the applicable controls with the department manager, you are told that the microcomputer is assigned exclusively to that department and that it therefore does not require the same types of controls applicable to the large computer systems.

Required
Comment on the manager's contentions, discussing briefly five types of control that would apply to this microcomputer application.
(CIA Examination, adapted)

13.2 You are general manager of a manufacturing company in Woodbridge, Virginia. During the past six months your company has been consistently losing competitive bids to a nearby company whose bids always seem to be slightly lower. Thinking that this could not have happened by chance, you hire a private detective to investigate what is happening. After some checking the private detective reports that an employee of your company who has access to your computer is stealing your bid data and selling it to the competitor for $25,000 per bid.

Required
Identify the likely deficiencies in internal control over your company's computer systems that could have allowed this to occur.

13.3 Prepare a segment of a computer program flowchart showing a check of a file header label as the file is loaded to be processed by a program.

13.4 Shown in Table 13.3 are data relating to the evaluation of job performance by four programmers employed in the state's Welfare Department.
Required
a. Which programmer's performance is best? Explain.

b. Which programmer's performance is worst? Explain.

c. Can you rank the other two programmers in terms of performance? Why or why not?

13.5 The Foster Corporation recently fired its Director of Information Systems after experiencing several years of budget overruns in systems development and computer operations. As an internal auditor with computer management experience, you have been appointed as interim director and charged with investigating the problems the department has experienced.

A significant obstacle to your investigation has been a lack of written information about the activities of the department or the policies under which it was managed. The previous director apparently managed in an informal manner, communicating assignments, standards, and performance evaluations to his employees verbally. This style of management was apparently popular with some employees but

Table 13.3
Job performance data

Performance Factor	PROGRAMMER			
	Adams	Baker	Cline	Davis
Instructions per hour	12	15	12	15
Program complexity	Low	Medium	Medium	Low
Years of experience	6	1	2	4

unpopular with many others, some of whom have left the company.

The major systems project under development is a management information system. Objectives for this project are loosely defined, although a good deal of analysis, design, and programming has been completed. The project director estimates that this project is roughly half-finished.

The computer operations department runs jobs on an as-received basis. The operations supervisor suggests that a newer, faster, and more reliable system is needed to satisfy demand during peak periods and to cope with expected growth in processing requirements.

Required

Identify and briefly describe several elements of control that appear to be lacking in this situation and that you feel should be implemented in the Information Systems Department.

13.6 The Dooley Company operates its Information Center as a cost center. Each year a budget for the center is developed by the company's Controller and the Manager of the Information Center. The Manager's performance is evaluated by comparing actual costs incurred with budgeted costs.

The Manager of the Information Center is responsible for accepting or rejecting proposals from user departments for new computer applications. User departments are not charged for either programming work or data processing service. Some of the main problems relating to the operation of the center have been as follows:

- The Manager has complained that budget allowances are not sufficient to pay for necessary new computer equipment and personnel.
- The Manager of the Information Center and department heads frequently disagree on whether proposed new computer applications should be undertaken.
- The accounting, production, and marketing departments have frequently argued over whose systems applications should have priority in development and scheduling.

Required

a. Identify the policy or policies that are the probable cause of each of the problems cited.

b. Describe an alternative system of management control that might be appropriate for the Information Center. Explain how this approach would be implemented and how it might contribute to solution of the problems.

13.7 The Hunter Company uses a system of full costing in charging its operating departments for computing services. Operating and cost data for a recent month follow.

Resource	Total Cost	Units Used
Central processor	$180,000	500 hours
Main memory	56,000	280,000 units
Disk/tape I/O	115,000	230,000 units
Printer output	60,000	60,000 pages
Total costs	$411,000	

Data on resources used by two jobs recently run on the computer system are given next.

Resource	Accounting Job	Engineering Job
Central processor	1 hour	2 hours
Main memory	500 units	2,000 units
Disk/tape I/O	500 units	100 units
Printer output	500 pages	40 pages

Required

a. If the single-factor base of CPU hours is used to price computer services, what will be the rate charged? How much will be charged to each of the two jobs described?

b. If a four-factor base is used, what will be the rates for each of the four factors? Under this scheme, how much will be charged to each of the two jobs?

c. Which of these two alternative pricing systems do you think is better? Discuss.

13.8 You are the data security administrator for a small computer installation. This system uses two programs—a payroll processing system and an inventory processing system—and maintains three files—a payroll master file, an inventory master file, and a master transaction log. You are to establish an access control matrix that permits the following system users to have the levels of access noted with respect to these systems and files.

Salesperson	Read and display records in the inventory master file
Inventory control analyst	Read, display, update, create, and delete records in the inventory master file
Payroll analyst	Read, display, and update records in the payroll master file
Personnel manager	Read, display, update, create, and delete records in the payroll master file
Payroll programmer	Perform any and all operations on the payroll system, plus read and display payroll master file records and transaction log records

Inventory programmer	Perform any and all operations on the inventory system, plus read and display inventory master file records and transaction log records
Data processing manager	Read and display any and all programs and files
Yourself	Perform any and all operations on any and all programs and files

You will assign each user a six-character user code and select access authority codes for each user based on the following access authority coding system.

0 = no access permitted
1 = read and display only
2 = read, display, and update
3 = read, display, update, create, and delete

Required

Prepare the access control matrix.

13.9 What control or controls would you recommend using in a computer system to prevent the following situations from occurring?

a. The "time worked" field for salaried employees is supposed to contain a 01 for one week. For one employee this field contained the number 40, and a check for $6872.51 was accidentally prepared and mailed to this employee.

b. A programmer obtained the master payroll file tape, mounted it on a tape drive, and changed his own monthly salary from $1400 to $2000 through the computer console.

c. The master accounts receivable file on disk was inadvertently destroyed and could not be reconstructed after being substituted for the accounts payable file in a processing run.

d. A company lost almost all its vital business data in a fire that destroyed the room in which it stored its magnetic tape files.

e. A programmer quit the firm in the middle of a programming assignment. Because no other programmers could make sense of the work already completed, the project was started over from scratch.

f. During payroll processing an error correction entry performed by the console operator resulted in the unintentional recording of data on the payroll master tape file, which destroyed several records on that file.

g. During keying of customer payment records, the digit 0 in a payment of $102.34 was mistakenly typed as the letter O. As a result, the transaction was not correctly processed, and the customer received an incorrect statement of account.

h. After the inventory master file maintained on magnetic tape was updated, the old master tape was removed for use in other applications. The updated master was then accidentally mislabeled, and its contents were subsequently erased. Considerable difficulty was encountered in reconstructing the master inventory file.

i. A bank programmer obtained the disk pack containing the program that calculates interest on customer accounts. She loaded the disk on a disk drive and then used the computer console to modify the program by adding a subroutine that she had written. The subroutine added to the programmer's own account the fractions of a cent of each customer's interest, which would otherwise be rounded off.

13.10 What control or controls would you recommend in an on-line computer system to prevent the following situations from occurring?

a. Unauthorized access to the system was gained by a teenager who programmed a microcomputer to enter repeated user numbers until a correct one was found.

b. An employee gained unauthorized access to the system by observing her supervisor's user number and then correctly guessing the password after 12 attempts.

c. A salesperson keying in a customer order from a remote terminal entered an incorrect stock number. As a result, an order for 50 typewriters was placed for a customer who wanted to order 50 typewriter ribbons.

d. A salesperson provided with a terminal with which to enter customer orders used it to increase his own monthly salary by $500.

e. A salesperson keying in a customer order from a remote terminal inadvertently omitted the delivery address from the order.

f. A company's research and development center utilized remote terminals tied into its computer center 100 miles away. Through a wiretap the company's largest competitor was able to steal secret plans for a major product innovation.

g. Because of a failure in a $400 multiplexor serving terminals at eight drive-in windows, a bank was forced to shut down the windows for two hours during a busy Friday afternoon.

h. A 20-minute power failure that shut down a firm's computer system resulted in loss of data for several transactions that were being entered into the system from remote terminals.

13.11 The headquarters of Gleicken Corporation, a private company with $3.5 million in annual sales, is located in California. Gleicken provides, for its 150 clients, an on-line legal software service that includes data storage and administrative activities for law offices. The company has grown rapidly since its inception three years ago, and its data processing department has mushroomed to accommodate this growth. Because Gleicken's President and sales personnel spend a great deal of time out of the office soliciting new clients, the planning of the EDP facilities has been left to the data processing professionals.

Gleicken recently moved its headquarters facility into a remodeled warehouse on the outskirts of the city. While remodeling the warehouse, the architects retained much of the original structure, including the wooden-shingled exterior and exposed wooden beams throughout the interior. The minicomputer distributive processing hardware is situated in a large open area with high ceilings and skylights. This openness makes the data processing area accessible to the rest of the staff and encourages a team approach to problem solving. Before Gleicken began to occupy the new facility, city inspectors declared the building safe (i.e., adequate fire extinguishers, sufficient exits, etc.).

In an effort to provide further protection for its large data base of client information, Gleicken has instituted a tape backup procedure that is on a time delay mechanism and automatically backs up the data base weekly, every Sunday evening, avoiding interruption in the daily operations and procedures. All the tapes are then labeled and carefully stored on shelves reserved for this purpose in the data processing department. The departmental operator's manual has instructions on how to use these tapes to restore the data base should the need arise. In the event of an emergency there is a home phone list of the individuals in the data processing department. Gleicken has recently increased its liability insurance for data loss from $50,000 to the current $100,000.

This past Saturday the Gleicken headquarters building was completely ruined by fire, and the company must now inform its clients that all their information has been destroyed.

Required

a. Describe the computer security weaknesses present at Gleicken Corporation that made it possible for a disastrous data loss to occur.

b. List the components that should have been included in the disaster recovery plan at Gleicken Corporation in order to ensure computer recovery within 72 hours.

c. What factors, other than those included in the plan itself, should a company consider when formulating a disaster recovery plan?
(CMA Examination)

13.12 Check digit verification schemes apply a series of mathematical operations to the first $n - 1$ digits of an $n -$ digit number to determine the correct value of the nth digit. Assume that check digit verification is to be applied to a five-digit number. One check digit scheme, called the "simple sum" method, determines the sum of the first four digits and subtracts that sum from the next highest multiple of 10 to obtain the check digit. Another scheme, called the "2-1-2" method, computes a weighted sum of the first four digits, with the first and third digits from the right (excluding the check digit) weighted by a factor of 2 and the second and fourth digits from the right weighted by a factor of 1. This sum is then subtracted from the next highest multiple of 10 to obtain the check digit. Thus the weighted sum for the number 2345 would be $2(1) + 3(2) + 4(1) + 5(2) = 22$, and the check digit would be $30 - 22 = 8$.

The following list gives two columns of five-digit numbers. All six of the numbers in the left-hand column are valid according to both check digit methods described above. (You might want to verify this.) The numbers in the right-hand column are erroneous versions of their column counterparts. The first two contain single transcription errors, in which one digit has been copied incorrectly. The second two contain transposition errors, in which two digits have been transposed. The final two are completely garbled.

14267	14567
23573	28573
32582	35282
43274	43724
50609	36609
92487	65937

Required

a. Determine which of the numbers in the right-hand column would fail check digit verification under (1) the simple sum method and (2) the 2-1-2 method.

b. Extrapolating from the results of part a, can you form any general conclusions about the relative effectiveness of the two check digit methods with respect to the different types of errors?

13.13 The Moose Wings Cooperative Flight Club owns a number of airplanes and gliders. It serves less than 2000 members, who are numbered sequentially from the founder, Tom Eagle (0001), to the newest member, Jacques Noveau (1368). Members rent the flying machines by the hour, and all planes must be returned on the same day. The club uses a CRT terminal on its premises and a dial-up line to send the billing data to a computer utility. The utility bills all members for the cost of flights taken on a monthly basis.

For each flight taken the record shown next is keyed in. A space is left between each data item.

Member number	0001–1368	4 digits
Date of flight start	Day: month: year	6 digits
Plane used	G, C, P, or L*	1 character
Time of take off	Hour minute	4 digits
Time of landing	Hour minute	4 digits

G = glider; C = Cessna; P = Piper Cub; L = Lear.

The following six records were among those entered for the flights taken on November 1, 1991.

1234	311191	G	0625	0846
4111	011191	C	0849	1023
1210	011191	P	0342	0542
0023	011191	X	0159	1243
012A	011191	P	1229	1532
0999	011191	L	1551	1387

Required

a. For each of the five data fields, suggest editing controls that could be included in the program to detect possible errors.

b. Identify and describe any errors in the records. (SMAC Examination)

13.14 Talbert Corporation hired an independent computer programmer to develop a simplified payroll application for its newly purchased computer. The programmer developed an on-line data entry system that minimized the level of knowledge required by the operator. It was based upon typing answers to input cues that appeared on the terminal's viewing screen. Examples of the cues follow.

a. Access routine:
  1. Operator access number to payroll file?
  2. Are there new employees?

b. New employees routine:
  1. Employee name?
  2. Employee number?
  3. Social Security number?

4. Rate per hour?
5. Single or married?
6. Number of dependents?
7. Account distribution?

c. Current payroll routine:
  1. Employee number?
  2. Regular hours worked?
  3. Overtime hours worked?
  4. Total employees this payroll period?

The independent auditor is attempting to verify that certain input validation (edit) checks exist to ensure that errors resulting from omissions, invalid entries, or other inaccuracies will be detected during the typing of answers to the input cues.

Required
Identify the various types of input validation (edit) checks the independent auditor would expect to find in the EDP system. Describe the assurances provided by each identified validation check. Do not discuss the review and evaluation of these controls. (CPA Examination)

13.15 Babbington-Bowles is an advertising agency that employs 625 salespersons who travel and entertain extensively. Salespersons are paid both salary and commissions and receive a check at the end of each month. The nature of their job is such that expenses of several hundred dollars a day might be incurred. In the past these expenses were included in the monthly paycheck. Salespersons were required to submit their expense reports, with supporting receipts, by the twentieth of each month. These reports would be reviewed suitably and then sent to data entry in a batch. Suitable controls were incorporated on each batch during input, processing, and output. This system worked well from a company viewpoint, and the internal auditor was convinced that while minor padding of expense accounts might occur, no major losses had been encountered.

With rising interest rates the salespersons were unhappy. They pointed out that they were often forced to carry several thousand dollars for a month. If they were out of town around the twentieth, they might not be reimbursed for their expenses for two months. They requested that Babbington-Bowles provide a service whereby a salesperson or his or her representative could submit receipts and expense reports to the Accounting Department and receive a check almost immediately.

The Data Processing Manager said that this procedure could be done. A CRT terminal would be set up in the accounting office, along with a small printer. The salesperson's name would be entered along with the required expense amount broken down into the standard categories. A program would process these data to the proper accounts and, if everything checked out suitably, print the check on presigned check blank stock in the printer.

Required

Identify five important controls, and explain why they might be incorporated in the system. These controls may be physical, they may relate to jobs and responsibilities, or they may be part of the program.   (SMAC Examination)

CASE 13.1: ANYCOMPANY, INC.: AN ONGOING COMPREHENSIVE CASE

One of the best ways to learn is to immediately apply what you have studied. The purpose of this case is to allow you to do that. You will select a local company that you can work with. At the end of most chapters you will find an assignment that will have you apply what you have learned using the company you have selected as a reference. This case, then, may become an ongoing case study that you work on throughout the term.

Select a local company, and obtain permission to study the internal control policies and procedures that it utilizes for computer-based information systems. Then complete the following steps, and prepare a report describing your findings and conclusions.

1.   Obtain copies of organization charts, job descriptions, and related documentation on how authority and responsibility have been assigned within the information systems function. Evaluate whether lines of authority and responsibility seem to be clearly defined and whether incompatible duties have been appropriately segregated.

2.   Determine how the company evaluates the progress of systems development projects during the design and implementation stages.

3.   Determine how the company evaluates the performance of systems analysts, programmers, and computer operations personnel.

4.   Observe how the company controls physical access to its mainframe computer site, as well as to its microcomputers and on-line terminals. Evaluate whether the company's site access controls seem to be effective.

5.   Determine the procedures used by the company to protect its stored program and data files from loss or destruction, including procedures for recovery of any program or data files that may be lost. Evaluate whether these procedures appear to be sound.

6.   Learn about the company's policies and procedures relating to the use of passwords to control logical access to its system resources. Evaluate these policies and procedures.

7.   Examine copies of the company's administrative documentation, systems documentation, and operating documentation. Evaluate the quality and completeness of this material.

8.   Determine the techniques used by the company to minimize the risk of system downtime.

9.   Ask whether the company has a written disaster recovery plan for its computer facilities. If so, examine a copy of the plan, and assess its strengths and weaknesses.

10.   Select a specific computerized accounting application, such as accounts receivable, accounts payable, or general ledger. Identify several application controls used in this system, including batch totals, source data controls, edit checks, file maintenance controls, and output controls. Examine copies of a batch control report, an edit report, and a data control log. Identify the strengths and weaknesses of the application controls used in this system.

CASE 13.2 THE STATE DEPARTMENT OF TAXATION

The Department of Taxation of one state is developing a new computer system for processing state income tax returns of individuals and corporations. The new system features direct data input and inquiry capabilities. Identification of taxpayers is provided by using the Social Security number for individuals and federal identification number for corporations. The new system should be fully implemented in time for the next tax season.

The new system will serve three primary purposes.

1. Data will be input into the system directly from tax returns through CRT terminals located at the central headquarters of the Department of Taxation.

2. The returns will be processed using the main computer facilities at central headquarters. The processing includes four steps.

    a. Verification of mathematical accuracy

    b. Auditing the reasonableness of deductions, tax due, and so on, through the use of edit routines, which also include a comparison of the current year's data with prior years' data

    c. Identification of returns that should be considered for audit by revenue agents of the department

    d. Issuing refund checks to taxpayers

3. Inquiry service will be provided to taxpayers upon request through the assistance of Tax Department personnel at five regional offices. A total of 50 CRT terminals will be placed at the regional offices. A taxpayer will be allowed to determine the status of his or her return or get information from the last three years' returns by calling or visiting one of the department's regional offices.

The State Commissioner of Taxation is concerned about data security during input and processing over and above protection against natural hazards such as fire and floods. This includes protection against the loss or damage of data during data input or processing or the improper input or processing of data. In addition, the Tax Commissioner and the State Attorney General have discussed the general problem of data confidentiality which may arise from the nature and operation of the new system. Both individuals want to have all potential problems identified before the system is fully developed and implemented so that the proper controls can be incorporated into the new system.

Required

1. Describe the potential confidentiality problems that could arise in each of the following three areas of processing, and recommend the corrective action(s) to solve the problem.

    a. Data input

    b. Processing of returns

    c. Data inquiry

2. The State Tax Commission wants to incorporate controls to provide data security against the loss, damage, or improper input or use of data during data input and processing. Identify the potential problems (outside of natural hazards such as fire or floods) for which the Department of Taxation should develop controls, and recommend the possible controls for each problem identified.

(CMA Examination)

14

CHAPTER

Computer Fraud

LEARNING OBJECTIVES

After studying this chapter, you should be able to:

- Explain the threats to computer security that information systems face.
- Explain what fraud is, including the difference between management and employee fraud and the process that constitutes a fraud.
- Explain the approaches and techniques that are used to commit computer fraud.
- Describe the pressures, opportunities, and rationalizations that interact and cause and allow people to commit a fraud.
- Describe the steps that can be undertaken to deter and detect computer fraud.

INTEGRATIVE CASE: NORTHWEST INDUSTRIES

It was late at night on the last Sunday of March when Jason Scott, an internal auditor for Northwest Industries, finished his tax return. Before he sealed the envelope and placed it in his briefcase to mail the next morning, he decided to review the return for a final time. Jason quickly went through all of the documents he used to prepare his return and compared them with the numbers he had written on the return. Everything seemed to be in order except for his withholding amount. For some reason the amount of federal income tax withholdings for the year shown on his final paycheck was $5 higher than what was shown on his W-2 form. He decided to use the amount on his W-2 form and made a note to check with payroll the next day to find out what happened to the other $5. The next day was a typical Monday at Northwest Industries and Jason was swamped. When he reviewed his "To Do" list, he decided to dismiss the $5 difference because it was so immaterial.

At lunch on April 16 several people were joking about their last-minute attempts to complete their returns. In the course of the conversation one of them grumbled about the company taking out $5 more from his check than he was given credit for. No one followed up on the comment and it was not until after lunch that the coincidence hit Jason: Another person had a discrepancy in his W-2 that was the same amount as his. He decided to investigate. It took several phone calls to get the appropriate permission and clearances, but by the end of the following day he was worried. Many of the 1500 company employees had a $5 discrepancy between their reported withholdings and the actual amount withheld. And interestingly enough, the W-2 of Don Hawkins, who was one of the main programmers in charge of the payroll system, showed that several thousand dollars more in witholdings had been reported to the IRS than had been withheld from his paycheck.

It certainly looked to Jason like he had a serious problem on his hands. He knew he was going to have to report this to management as soon as possible. He also knew they were going to ask a lot of questions, and he decided to try and anticipate their questions so that he could be prepared. These are some of the questions he thought management might ask.

1. Is this a fraud? If so, what constitutes a fraud?
2. If this is a fraud, how was it perpetrated? What motivated Don to commit it?
3. If this is a fraud, why didn't the company catch it earlier? Was there a breakdown in controls?
4. What can the company do to detect fraud? To prevent fraud?
5. Just how vulnerable are computer systems to fraud, and are there other security threats that we should be concerned about? ■

INTRODUCTION

As a result of the technological advancements that were described in Chapters 4–7, our society has become increasingly dependent upon computerized information systems. These systems have grown more complex in order to meet our ever-increasing needs for information. As the complexity of these systems and our dependence on them increase, companies face the growing risk of the security of their systems being compromised. As a result, the security and integrity of computer systems has become an extremely important issue. Computer security includes all of the policies, procedures, tools, and other means for safeguarding information systems from unauthorized access or alteration and from intentional or unintentional damage or theft. Computer security policies and procedures are described in Chapter 13.

If a system is damaged or fails, the company suffers economic losses. For example:

- Between 1980 and 1988, bugs in a new tax accounting system caused the state of California to fail to collect $635 million in business taxes.

- At the Bank of New York a field used to count the number of transactions was too small to handle the volume on a busy day in November 1985. The error shut the system down and left the bank $23 million dollars short when it tried to close its books. It had to borrow the money overnight at a significant cost.

- A data entry clerk at Giant Food, Inc., mistakenly keyed in a quarterly dividend of $2.50 instead of $0.25. As a result, over $10 million dollars in excess dividends were paid out that quarter.

As shown in Fig. 14.1, today's information systems face threats from several different sources. They include natural and political disasters, software errors and hardware malfunctions, unintentional errors and accidents, and intentional acts of fraud or abuse, typically referred to as computer crimes. Computer crimes can be acts of sabotage, where the intent is to destroy a system or some of its components. Or they can be acts of computer fraud, where the intent is to steal something of value such as money, data, or computer time or services. Chapters 12 and 13 dealt with the controls that help protect systems against many of these threats. This chapter focuses on computer fraud.

This chapter has four main sections. The first defines fraud and distinguishes between management and employee fraud. It also discusses the fraud process, which includes the actual theft, converting the stolen item into cash, and concealment of the fraud. The second section defines computer fraud and discusses why it is becoming so

Figure 14.1
Threats to information systems

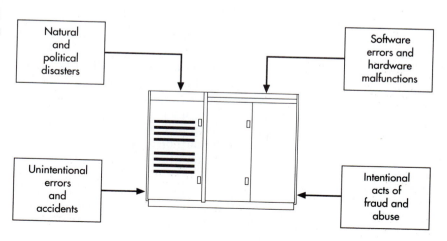

prevalent. It also describes the various approaches to fraud and the specific techniques used to commit fraud.

The third section discusses the profile of fraud perpetrators and why fraud occurs. The pressures, opportunities, and rationalizations underlying the crime are also discussed. The final section describes several methods companies can use to deter computer fraud. More specifically, it discusses how to make fraud less likely to occur, how to increase the difficulty of committing a fraud, and how to reduce the losses to computer fraud. It also explains how to increase the likelihood of detecting fraud and how to increase the penalty for committing a computer fraud.

WHAT IS FRAUD?

In order to better understand computer fraud, we must first define the act of fraud in general. **Fraud** can be defined as any and all means that a person uses to gain an unfair advantage over another person. Fraudulent acts include lies, suppressions of the truth, tricks, and cunning. Fraud perpetrators are often referred to as **white-collar criminals**, to distinguish them from criminals who commit violent crimes. White-collar crimes often involve a violation of a trust or a confidence.

One of the most famous white-collar criminals was Charles Bianchi, who used the alias of Charles Ponzi. In 1920 Ponzi told potential investors that his company was able to purchase postal reply coupons in Europe for 1¢ each and exchange them in the United States for 10¢ worth of postage stamps. These stamps could then be converted into cash. However, he did not have the financial resources to buy all of the postal reply coupons he could find, so he was willing to let others invest with him. In exchange for the use of their money he promised to pay the investors a 50% return on their money every 45 days. However, Ponzi never invested more than a few dollars in postal reply coupons. Instead, he took the money of later investors and used it to pay off earlier investors. As he began to pay off his first investors, the word got around and hundreds of investors flocked to him seeking the high returns he promised. In eight months Ponzi cheated his investors out of $15 million. Ponzi's only expense was the 50% he promised to pay his investors. He spent the rest. Ponzi's scheme required an ever-increasing amount of invested money to keep it from collapsing. However, the scheme never grew big enough to collapse. A Boston newspaperman investigated Ponzi's scheme and found that Europe had a total of less than $1 million in postal reply coupons. Ponzi was arrested, given federal and state jail sentences, and was later deported. Although Ponzi died a pauper in Brazil, he has had many imitators over the years, and this type of fraud has come to be known as a Ponzi scheme.

The economic losses to fraud each year are staggering. The Justice Department has estimated that white-collar crimes cost the United States $200 billion a year. In comparison, violent crimes cost us $11 billion each year.

Fraud perpetrators share a number of common characteristics. Most perpetrators spend all of their ill-gotten gains rather than invest or save them. Once they begin the fraud, it is very hard for them to stop. Sometimes they come to rely on the extra income, but sometimes their scheme is self-perpetuating and they cannot quit without being caught. If the perpetrators are not caught shortly after they begin, they typically become more confident of their scheme. This confidence and a desire for more money can cause them to increase the amount they take. As time passes many perpetrators grow careless, overconfident, or greedy. Those that do usually make a mistake that leads to their apprehension.

Internal Versus External Frauds

A fraud can be committed by someone within the organization or by an external party. Most organizations have safeguards over corporate assets that make it relatively difficult for an outsider to steal company assets. More often, the theft comes from an insider who has a knowledge and understanding of the company's policies and procedures for safeguarding assets. With that knowledge the person is able to violate a trust, evade the control procedures, and commit and conceal the crime. The National Center for Computer Crime Data studied 75 cases of fraud that were prosecuted over an eight-year period. They found that 80% of the frauds studied were the work of insiders. In their study the frauds were carried out most frequently by programmers, data input clerks, and bank tellers.

Internal fraud is often categorized as employee fraud, fraudulent financial reporting, or management fraud. **Employee fraud**, such as that found by Jason Scott, is committed by a person or group of persons for personal financial gain. An example is a company employee who uses a computer to illegally access payroll records and increase his monthly salary. The National Commission on Fraudulent Financial Reporting (also known as the Treadway Commission) defines **fraudulent financial reporting** as intentional or reckless conduct, whether by act or omission, that results in materially misleading financial statements. **Management fraud** is the intentional reporting of misleading financial information, the theft of company assets by top management, or both.

Management fraud is a very serious issue and of great concern to independent auditors. This was borne out by the Treadway Commission's study of over 450 lawsuits against auditors between 1960 and 1985. They found fraud to be a factor in approximately 50% of the cases. Management fraud is usually committed by those high enough in an organization to override internal controls. Examples of management fraud include falsifying the financial statements in order to deceive investors and creditors, to cause the company's stock price to rise, to meet cash flow needs, or to hide company losses and problems. The perpetrators receive indirect benefits: They keep their jobs, the price of their stock rises, and they receive pay raises they do not deserve. They are also perceived as very good managers, which means that they are highly respected and are able to wield considerable power.

When the Treadway Commission issued its recommendations, it suggested four things that could be done to reduce the possibility of fraudulent financial reporting.

1. Establish an organizational environment and tone that contributes to the integrity of the financial reporting process.

2. Identify and understand the factors that can lead to fraudulent financial reporting.

3. Assess the risk of fraudulent financial reporting within the company.

4. Design and implement internal controls that provide reasonable assurance that fraudulent financial reporting will be prevented.

Another way to reduce the incidence of employee and management fraud is to better understand the fraud process.

Theft, Conversion, and Concealment: The Fraud Process

Most employee frauds involve three steps. First is the theft of something of value, such as cash, inventory, tools, supplies, equipment, or data. Second is the conversion of the assets into some form usable by the perpetrator if the theft is of an asset other than cash. For example, stolen inventory and equipment must be sold or otherwise converted into cash. Third is the concealment of the crime in order to avoid detection and to continue the fraud.

Most employee fraud involves the theft of assets. Most fraudulent financial reporting involves the overstatement of assets or revenues. Few employees or companies are motivated to steal or overstate liabilities. Likewise, there are not very many frauds that involve the theft or direct overstatement of equities. When assets are stolen or overstated, the only way to balance the basic accounting equation is to inflate other assets or to decrease liabilities or equity. In other words, the concealment step requires perpetrators to find some way to keep the accounting equation in balance so that their theft or misrepresentation is not discovered.

Concealing the fraud often takes more effort and time to accomplish and leaves behind more evidence than the actual theft does. For example, taking cash requires only a few seconds, but altering records to hide the theft can be more challenging and time-consuming. The most common and often the most effective way to hide an employee theft is to charge the stolen item to an expense account. For example, suppose that an employee was able to steal $10,000 and charge it to miscellaneous expense. Assets would be reduced by $10,000 but so would equity, since expense accounts decrease net income as they are closed out, which in turn makes retained earnings lower than they would have been. Alternatively, suppose that a payroll clerk was able to add a fictitious name to the employee payroll records, intercept the paycheck, and cash it. The company would be missing funds, but the books would be in balance because there was a debit to a wages expense and a credit to cash. In both cases the perpetrator's exposure is limited to a year or less, because the expense accounts are zeroed out at the end of the year. On the other hand, if perpetrators hide the theft by affecting another balance sheet account, they will have to continue to hide it. Hence one of the most popular ways to cover up a fraud is to hide the theft in an income statement account.

Another common method of hiding a decrease in assets is called lapping. In a lapping scheme the perpetrator steals cash received from customer A to pay its accounts receivable. Funds received at a later date from customer B are used to pay off customer A's balance. Funds from customer C are used to pay off B, and so forth. Since the time between the theft of cash and the subsequent recording of a payment is usually short, the theft can be effectively hidden. However, the cover-up must continue indefinitely unless the money is replaced, since the theft will be uncovered if the scheme is stopped.

One method of inflating assets to hide the theft of assets is called kiting. In a kiting scheme the perpetrator covers up a theft of cash by creating cash through the transfer of money between banks. For example, the perpetrator creates cash by depositing a check from bank A in bank B. However, there are insufficient funds in bank A to cover the check to bank B. The perpetrator then withdraws the money from bank B and spends it. To avoid detection, the perpetrator must deposit a check to his account in bank A before his check to bank B clears. This check comes from bank C, which also has insufficient funds to cover the check written on the account. Therefore, funds must be deposited to bank C before its check to bank A clears. The check to bank C comes from bank A, B, or D, which also have insufficient funds. The scheme continues, with checks written and deposits made as needed to keep checks from bouncing.

In this section we have discussed fraud in general. We now turn our attention to computer fraud.

COMPUTER FRAUD

Of special interest to the study of information systems is computer fraud, which is also referred to as computer crime. The U.S. Department of Justice defines computer crime as any illegal act for which knowledge of computer technology is essential for its perpetration, investigation, or prosecution. More specifically, computer crime includes the following:

- The unauthorized use, access, modification, copying, and destruction of software or data
- The theft of money by altering computer records or the theft of computer time
- The theft or destruction of computer hardware
- The use or the conspiracy to use computer resources to commit a felony
- The *intent* to illegally obtain information or tangible property through the use of computers

It is important to realize that computers do not commit frauds or crimes; people do. A computer is only a tool that a person uses to perpetrate a fraud. However, it is a very powerful tool. Using a computer, perpetrators are able to do much more damage, in much less time, and with much less effort. For instance, they are able to steal millions of dollars in less than a second. They are able to commit the fraud and leave little or no evidence. Therefore, computer fraud is often much more difficult to detect than other types of fraud.

The Growing Problem of Computer Fraud

Just how serious a problem is computer fraud? It is quite serious, judging from the estimates. Organizations that track computer fraud and computer fraud experts estimate that computer crime nets its perpetrators $300 million to $9 billion per year, with an average of $50,000 to over $1 million per incident.

However, the truth is that no one really knows how much is lost to computer fraud each year, for several reasons. First, not everyone agrees on what constitutes computer fraud. For example, for some people the definition is restricted to a crime that takes place inside or is directed at a computer. For others it is any crime where the perpetrator uses the computer as a tool in the crime. Many people do not think that making a copy of the software they use at work for home use is computer fraud. Others, including the publishers of the software, think that it is a crime. Similarly, some people do not think it is a crime to browse through the data on someone else's computer if there is no intent to do harm. Others think this is a computer crime.

Another reason that it is difficult to estimate the extent of fraud is that many computer frauds go undetected. The FBI estimates that only 1% of all computer crime is detected; other estimates are between 5% and 25%. Again, the truth is that no one really knows.

Further complicating matters is that an estimated 80%–90% of the frauds that are uncovered are not reported. Only the banking industry is required by law to report all frauds that take place. The most frequent reason for not reporting computer fraud is a fear that adverse publicity would cost the company more than the fraud itself. The result is that all fraud estimates are based on the supposedly limited sample of frauds that are detected.

What is known, however, is that computer fraud is growing. In fact, as early as 1979 *Time* magazine labeled computer fraud a "growth industry." One reason for the growth is that each year more and more computers of all sizes are accessible to more and more people. In addition, more people are becoming more computer-literate. Thus the knowledge needed to use computers to commit crime is much more common than it used to be. Another reason for the growth of fraud is the ability to access remote computers through both public and private data networks. Still another reason is that many businesspeople have the attitude that "it won't happen to us" and therefore do not take adequate precautions against fraud.

A number of organizations have studied computer fraud. The National Center for Computer Crime Data, for example, concluded that the costs of computer crime in 1988 exceeded $555 million and resulted in 15 years of company downtime. It required 930 man-years to detect and recover from this fraud and abuse. The center concluded that the average computer fraud loss is $109,000, 26 computer-hours, and 365 man-hours. According to an Ernst and Whinney study, between 50% and 90% of companies have lost money to a computer fraud. An American Bar Association study found that half of business and governmental institutions had a fraud in the year of the study. The Bank Administration Institute has calculated that U.S. banks lose over $1 billion a year because of information system abuse.

There is no way of knowing exactly how much money is lost to computer fraud each year. However, it is realistic to say that if the salaries of the hundreds of people who spend time fighting it are included, computer fraud and abuse costs society over $1 billion a year.

Approaches to Computer Fraud

Various studies have examined cases of fraud to determine the types of assets stolen and the approaches used by the perpetrators. The results of two such studies are shown in Fig. 14.2. As these estimates show, there are many different types of fraud and many different ways in which the computer can either be used as a tool to commit fraud or be the object of fraud. One approach to analyzing computer fraud is the data processing model presented in Chapter 2. Each of the five components in the model (input, processor, computer instructions, stored data, and output) can be the means of committing a fraud.

Figure 14.2
Computer crime

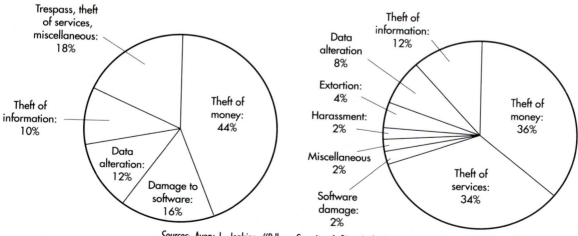

Major Types of Computer Crime: Results of Two Studies

Sources: Avery L. Jenkins, "Rdbms Security: A Dirty Little Secret," *Digital Review* (February 11, 1991): 23.
Michael Alexander, "Computer Crime: Ugly Secret for Business," *Computerworld* (March 12, 1990): 104.

Input.   One very popular way to commit a fraud is to alter computer input. This approach to computer fraud is the most common because it is the simplest. It requires little, if any, computer skills. Instead, perpetrators need only understand how the system operates so that they can cover their tracks.

One case of input fraud was committed by a young man named Paul Sjiem-Fat. He used desktop publishing technology to perpetrate one of the first cases of computer forgery. Sjiem-Fat created bogus cashier's checks from banks such as Chase Manhattan. He then used the checks to buy computer equipment, which he subsequently sold in the Caribbean. He was caught after he defrauded Bank of Boston of $20,000. When the bank checked his credit card application, it found that he had lied about being an employee of the Dutch consulate. The bank called in the Secret Service, who raided his apartment and found 9 bogus checks totaling almost $150,000. Sjiem-Fat was prosecuted and sent to prison in September 1989.

Another perpetrator opened up a bank account at a bank in New York and then had a printer prepare blank deposit slips that looked just like the ones available in bank lobbies. They *were* alike, except that his account number was encoded on the slips. Early one morning he replaced all the blank deposit slips in the bank lobby with his special deposit slips. For three days everyone who made a deposit using one of those slips unknowingly made a deposit into the perpetrator's account instead of his or her own. At the end of the three days he wrote a series of checks to withdraw all of the money from the account and disappeared. The perpetrator used an alias, his identity was never uncovered, and he was never found.

One perpetrator used a desktop publishing package to set up a dummy company whose only business was to send out fraudulent bills. The company kept the dollar amount low enough so that most companies would not require purchase orders or approvals. They mailed the bills to companies all over the country, billing them for products they never purchased. An amazing percentage of the companies paid the bills without question. Frauds of this nature, where the perpetrator causes a company to pay too much for something it has ordered or to pay for something it never ordered or received, are called disbursement frauds.

To steal inventory, a perpetrator can enter data into the system to show that stolen inventory has been scrapped. For example, at a railroad company on the East Coast several employees entered data into their employer's system to show that over 200 railroad cars were scrapped or destroyed. They then repainted and sold them.

To commit payroll frauds, perpetrators enter data to increase their salary to create a fictitious employee, or to keep an employee who has been terminated on the records. Under the latter two approaches the perpetrator intercepts and cashes the check.

In a cash receipts fraud the perpetrator hides the theft of the cash by falsifying system input. For example, an employee at the Arizona Veteran's Memorial Coliseum sold customers full-price tickets, entered the sale as a half-price ticket, and pocketed the difference.

Processor. A second way computer fraud can be committed is by operating a system in an unauthorized way. This includes the theft of computer time and services as well as the use of a system for unauthorized purposes. For example, some employees use the company computer to keep personal records or records for an outside business, a church, or a charitable organization. If the company considers these uses to be improper, it should clearly state as much so that the employees can be aware of the impropriety.

Computer Instructions. Computer fraud can also be accomplished by affecting the software that processes company data. This may involve modifying the software, making illegal copies of the software, or using the software in an unauthorized manner. It might also involve developing a software program or module to carry on unauthorized activity. This approach to computer fraud is one of the least common because it requires specialized knowledge about computer programming. As a result, few people are capable of committing this kind of fraud.

Data. A fourth way computer fraud can be perpetrated is by altering or damaging a company's data files or by copying, using, or searching them without authorization. This approach takes less skill than modifying software but more skill than modifying input. Accordingly, it falls in between the other two in terms of likelihood of occurrence and exposure to threats.

There have been numerous instances of data files being scrambled, altered, or destroyed by disgruntled employees. In one instance the employee took off all the external labels from hundreds of tape files. In another case an employee used a powerful magnet to scramble all the data on magnetic tape files.

Company data can also be stolen. In one case the office manager of a Wall Street law firm found information about prospective mergers and acquisitions in the firm's word processing files. He sold the information to friends and relatives, who used this insider information to make several million dollars by trading securities. In Europe a disgruntled employee removed all of a company's data files from the computer room. He then drove to the off-site storage location and removed the company's backup files. He demanded half a million dollars in return for the files, but he was arrested while trying to exchange the tapes for the money.

Output. A fifth way computer fraud can be carried out is by stealing or misusing system output. System output is usually displayed on monitors or printed on paper. Anything on a monitor can be read by others who are near the screen. Many people share printers, and unless properly safeguarded, this output is subject to prying or curious eyes and unauthorized copying.

Few people are aware of how easy it is to monitor system output. A study by a Dutch engineer has shown that many computers emit a televisionlike signal that can be picked up, restructured with the help of some very inexpensive electronic gear, and displayed on a standard TV screen. Under ideal conditions these signals can be picked up from terminals as far as 2 miles away. During one experiment the engineer was able to set up his equipment in the basement of an apartment building and read the screen on a terminal on the eighth floor of the building.

Computer Fraud Techniques

Fraud perpetrators have developed a number of ways to commit computer crimes. This section discusses many of these techniques.

A **Trojan horse** is a set of unauthorized computer instructions in an authorized and otherwise properly functioning program. It performs some illegal act at a preappointed time or under a predetermined set of conditions. An example is one of the first-known computer frauds, committed in 1966 by a computer programmer for a bank in Minneapolis. The programmer instructed the computer to ignore an overdraft on his account when it occurred. He was caught when the computer broke down and the bank had to operate manually.

The **round-down technique** is another of the earliest approaches to computer fraud. This technique is used most frequently in financial institutions that pay interest. In the typical scenario the programmer instructs the computer to round down all interest calculations to two decimal places. The fraction of a cent that is rounded down on each calculation is put into the programmer's account or one that he or she controls. No one is the wiser since all the books balance. Over time these fractions of a cent can add up to a significant amount, especially when interest is calculated daily.

With the **salami technique** tiny slices of money are stolen. The disgruntled chief accountant for a produce-growing company in California used the salami technique to get even with his employer. He used the company's computer system to falsify and systematically increase all the company's production costs by a fraction of a percent. These tiny increments were put into the accounts of dummy customers and then pocketed by the accountant. Every few months the percentage was raised another fraction of a percent. Since all expenses were rising together, there was no one account or expense that would bring attention to him. He was caught when an alert bank teller did not recognize the name of the company on the check he was trying to cash and called his employer to inquire about it.

A **trap door** is a set of computer instructions that allows a user to bypass the system's normal controls. Trap doors are placed in programs by system developers to allow them to modify a program during systems development. They are normally removed before the system is put into operation. When they are used for unauthorized purposes, they can cause a great deal of damage.

A software utility, called Superzap, was developed by IBM to handle emergencies, such as restoring a system that has crashed. **Superzapping** is the unauthorized use of special system programs such as Superzap to bypass regular system controls and perform illegal acts.

Software piracy is the unauthorized copying of software. It is estimated that for every legal copy of software there are between one and five illegal copies. The software industry estimates its economic losses at between $2 and $4 billion a year. Piracy is such a serious problem that the Software Publishers Association (which represents over 500 software publishers) has begun to file lawsuits against companies. One lawsuit claimed that the University of Oregon's Continuing Education Center violated copyright law by making illegal and unauthorized copies of programs and training manuals. The university settled the case in 1991 by agreeing (1) to a $130,000 fine, (2) to launch a campaign to educate its faculty, staff, and students on the lawful use of software, and (3) to host a national conference on copyright law and software use.

Data diddling is changing data before it enters, as it enters, or after it has already been entered into the system. The change can be made to delete data, to alter data, or to add data to the system. For example, in Denver a clerk for a brokerage altered a transaction to record 1700 shares of Loren Industries worth about $2500 as shares in Long Island Lighting worth more than $25,000.

Data leakage refers to the unauthorized copying of company data, often without leaving any indication that it was copied. The Encyclopedia Britannica company claimed losses in the millions of dollars when several of its employees made a copy of its customer list and began selling it to other companies.

In **piggybacking** the perpetrator taps into a telecommunications line and latches on to a legitimate user who is logging into a system. The legitimate user unknowingly carries the perpetrator with him into the system. In **masquerading** or **impersonation** the perpetrator gains access to the system by pretending to be an authorized user. This approach requires that the perpetrator know the legitimate user's identification numbers and passwords. Once inside the system, the perpetrator enjoys the same privileges as the legitimate user being impersonated.

A **logic time bomb** is a program that lies idle until some specified circumstance or a particular time triggers it. Once triggered, the bomb sabotages the system by destroying programs or data or both. Most bombs are written by disgruntled programmers who want to get even with the company. In one case Donald Burleson allegedly broke into his former employer's system two days after he was fired in September 1985. As a former security officer at USPA & IRA Company, he knew everyone's passwords. Using these passwords and his knowledge of computer programming and system controls, he broke into the company's system and erased 168,000 records of sales commissions. As a result, company paychecks were held up for a month. The program, which was attached to a legitimate program, was designed to go off at certain times and erase more records every month. The bomb was discovered before it could go off by a fellow programmer who was testing a new bonus system for employees. The company had to shut down its computers for two days to find the bomb and diffuse it.

Hacking is the unauthorized access to and use of computer systems, usually by means of a personal computer and a telecommunication network. Many hackers do not intend to cause any damage. They are usually motivated by the challenge of breaking and entering and are just browsing or looking for things to copy and keep. There have been numerous cases of students tapping into their school's computers and changing their grades. In addition, hackers have broken into the computers of governmental agencies such as the U.S. Department of Defense, NASA, and the Los Alamos National Laboratory.

Hackers have also broken into the computers of numerous companies. One 17-year-old hacker, nicknamed "Shadow Hawk," was convicted of electronically penetrating the Bell Laboratories national network in 1987, destroying files valued at $174,000 and copying 52 proprietary software programs worth $1.2 million. He was also accused of publishing confidential information on underground bulletin boards. The published information included telephone numbers, passwords, and instructions on how to breach AT&T's computer security system. He was sentenced to nine months in prison and given a $10,000 fine. Like Shadow Hawk, many hackers are fairly young, some as young as 12 and 13.

Scavenging is the unauthorized access to confidential information by searching corporate records. Scavenging methods range from searching trash cans for printouts or carbon copies of confidential information to scanning the contents of computer memory. In one of the most famous cases Jerry Schneider noticed a trash can full of papers on his way home from a Los Angeles area high school. Rummaging through them, he discovered they contained operating guides for Pacific Telephone and Telegraph's computers. Over time his scavenging activities resulted in a technical library that later allowed him to steal a million dollars worth of electronic equipment.

Eavesdropping allows computer users to observe transmissions intended for someone else. One way unauthorized individuals can intercept signals is by setting up a **wiretap**. The equipment needed to set up a wiretap of an unprotected communications line is readily available at local electronics stores. One alleged fraud attempt that involved wiretapping was set up by Mark Koenig, a 28-year-old consultant to GTE, and four associates. Federal agents say they pulled personal identification numbers and other critical information of Bank of America customers from GTE telephone lines. They used this data to make 5500 fake ATM cards. They allegedly intended to use the cards one weekend in February 1989 to withdraw money from banks all over the country. However, authorities were tipped off and they were apprehended before they were able to use the cards. They could have misappropriated up to $14 million over a single weekend.

One of the most serious problems facing systems today is a computer virus. Computer viruses are written by people and are intended to damage the systems of others, to spread a particular message, or as pranks. A **computer virus** is a segment of executable code that attaches itself to an application program or some other executable system component. Viruses are contagious and are easily spread from one system to another. A virus creates copies of itself and inserts them into other programs or data files. For a virus to spread rapidly, it needs to be introduced into a network with a large number of computers. In a relatively short period of time the virus can spread to thousands of systems. When the virus is confined to a single machine or to a small LAN, it will soon run out computers to infect. A virus also spreads when users share programs or diskettes or when they access and use programs from external sources such as bulletin boards and suppliers of free software.

Many viruses lie dormant for extended periods of time without doing any specific damage except propagating themselves. When the hidden program, which leaves no external signs of infection, is triggered, it makes unauthorized alterations to the way a system operates and causes widespread damage. For example, a virus may destroy or alter data or programs. It can take control of the computer, destroy the hard disk's file allocation table, or keep users from booting the system or accessing data on a hard disk. They can intercept and change transmissions, print disruptive images or messages on the screen, or cause the screen image to disappear. As the virus spreads, it takes up space, clogs communications, and hinders system performance.

Many computer viruses have long lives because they can create copies of themselves faster than they can be destroyed. A number of viruses, such as Stone and Jerusalem-B, have spread so far that they have become epidemics. According to a survey conducted by Dataquest, 63% of the 600,000 microcomputer users surveyed had experienced a virus, and 38% of those affected had lost data.

A **worm** is like a virus, except that it is a program rather than a code segment hidden in a host program. A worm also copies itself and actively transmits itself directly to other systems. It usually does not live very long, but it is quite destructive while it is alive. One of the more destructive worms, written by Robert T. Morris, affected 6000 computers in a very short time. This worm and how it worked is explained in Case 14.1.

WHY FRAUD OCCURS

Having described what fraud is and discussed some of the ways it is perpetrated, we now turn to an explanation of why fraud occurs. But if we are to understand why it occurs, we need to have a profile of fraud perpetrators.

Researchers have compared the psychological and demographic characteristics of three groups of people: white-collar criminals, violent criminals, and the general public. Significant differences were found between violent and white-collar criminals. However, they found few differences between white-collar criminals and the general public. White-collar criminals tend to mirror the general public in terms of education, age, religion, marriage, length of employment, and psychological makeup. In other words, there are few characteristics that can be used to distinguish white-collar criminals from the general public.

Most white-collar criminals are talented, intelligent, and well educated. Some are disgruntled and unhappy with their job and are seeking to get even with their employer. Others are regarded as ideal employees. They are dedicated, they work long hours, and they often do not take vacations. They usually occupy a position of trust. They consider themselves to be honest, upstanding citizens. The fraud they perpetrate is usually their first criminal offense.

Computer fraud perpetrators are classified as white-collar criminals. However, there are a few differences between computer fraud perpetrators and other white-collar criminals. Perpetrators of computer fraud, as would be expected, often have more technical and computer knowledge, experience, and skills. In fact, they are sometimes described as being able to do anything with computers. On average, computer criminals are younger than other white-collar criminals. Computer criminals are motivated by the challenge of "beating the computer system." They often view their actions as a game rather than as something dishonest.

A study performed by the National Center for Computer Crime Data shows that computer crime is an equal opportunity employer: 32% of the people arrested for computer crime were women, 43% were minorities, and 67% were between 21 and 35. Not surprisingly, most are company employees. Former and current employees are much more likely to perpetrate a computer fraud than are nonemployees. Employees are much more likely to evade detection when they commit a fraud because they better understand the company's system, its weaknesses, and the way they can cover their tracks.

One study of 259 cases of computer fraud found that 69% were committed by people in six different occupations: 18% by application programmers, 14% by clerical users, 14% by nonclerical and nonmanagerial users, 12% by students, and 11% by managers. No other occupation had committed more than 10% of the frauds. But just what is it that motivates these people to perpetrate a computer fraud?

Most white-collar criminals, including computer fraud perpetrators, have no previous criminal record. Prior to their committing fraud they were honest and upright citizens who were valued and respected members of their communities. Why, then, would they risk everything by committing a fraud? Fraud research shows that three conditions are necessary for fraud to occur: a pressure or motive, an opportunity, and a rationalization. Each of these three conditions is described in detail in this section.

Pressures   A pressure is a person's motivation for committing the fraud. This pressure can be financial, such as living beyond one's means or having bad investments or other financial losses, heavy debts, or unusually high bills. An illustration of how financial losses can create enormous pressures is the case of Raymond Keller, the owner of a grain elevator in Stockport, Iowa. Raymond was a local boy who worked his way up from driving a coal truck to owning a local grain company. He made money in the early 1970s by trading on commodities, and he built a lavish house overlooking the Des Moines River, complete with swimming pool, sauna, and three-car garage. No one knows why his financial situation declined sometime in 1979. Some say he lost a lot of money speculating on the commodities markets; others say it was a grain embargo that virtually halted the buying and selling of grain. Whatever the reason, Raymond had a severe cash shortage and went deeply into debt. He asked some farmers to wait for their money, and he gave others bad checks. Finally, the seven banks to which he owed over $3 million began to call in their loans. So Raymond began to embezzle the grain to cover his losses. But one day, a state auditor showed up at his door unexpectedly. Rather than face the consequences that he must have known would follow, Raymond chose to end it all by taking his life.

Pressures can also be work-related. Some employees turn to fraud because of strong feelings of resentment or of being treated unfairly. They may feel that their pay is too low, that their contributions to the company are not appreciated sufficiently, or that the company is taking advantage of them. Or they may fear the loss of their job and commit a fraud to make themselves or their company look better, hoping that it will preserve their job. In one case an accountant in California was passed over for a raise and decided to take matters into his own hands. He calculated that the average raise had been 10%, so he increased his salary by that amount. When he was finally apprehended, he defended his actions as being honest. He could not understand why he had been arrested; he was only taking what was rightfully his. When asked how he would have felt if he had increased his salary by 11%, he responded that that would have been stealing 1%.

Other motivations that lead to fraudulent actions include family or peer pressure, emotional instability, and the challenge of "beating the system." The challenge factor is especially prevalent in computer fraud. Many of the hackers who do so much damage to systems want to show that they can subvert the controls and break into a system. In one case a company advertised a new system as being so secure that outsiders would not be able to break into it. Within 24 hours of the system's being implemented a team of individuals had broken into the system and left a message that the impenetrable system had just been compromised.

A few of the pressures that may lead some people to fraudulent acts are summarized in Table 14.1.

Opportunities

An **opportunity** is the condition or situation that allows a person to commit and conceal a dishonest act. The most prevalent opportunity is a company's failure to enforce an adequate system of internal controls. Other common opportunities stem from a lack of adequate internal controls. For example, a company might lack proper procedures for authorizations, clear lines of authority, or independent checks on performance. Likewise, there may not be a separation of duties between the authorization, custodial, and record-keeping functions.

One control feature that is often lacking is a background check on all potential employees. A background check would have saved one company the embarrassment of hiring the "phantom controller." One night the company president stopped by the company's offices, saw a light on in the controller's office, and went over to see why he was working so late. He was surprised to find a complete stranger in the controller's office. After an investigation the company found out that the controller was not an accountant and had been fired from three of his previous five jobs in the last eight years. Because he could not do the accounting work, he had hired someone to come in at night to do it for him. In addition, the controller had defrauded the company of several million dollars.

There are a number of other situations that make it easy for someone to commit a fraud, such as too much trust in key employees, incompetent supervisory personnel, inattention to details, inadequate staffing, a lack of training, and no clear definition of what is ethical and what is not. Also, many frauds arise when employees build mutually beneficial

Table 14.1
Pressures that can lead to fraud

Financial	Work-Related	Other
Living beyond means	Pay is too low	Challenge
Too much debt	Nonrecognition of	Family/peer pressure
"Inadequate" income	performance	Emotional instability
Poor credit ratings	Job dissatisfaction	
Financial losses	Fear of losing job	
Bad investments		
Health care expenditures		
Large gambling debts		
Need to support a drug or		
alcohol addiction		

Table 14.2
Perceived opportunities

Internal Control Factors	Other Factors
Failure to enforce internal controls	Too much trust in key employees
Lack of proper procedures for authorizations	Close association with suppliers/customers
No separation of transaction authorization from custody	Incompetent personnel
	Operating on a crisis basis
No independent checks on performance	Failure to discipline violators
No separation of accounting duties	Confusion about ethics
Lack of clear lines of authority	Lack of explicit conflict-of-interest statements
Lack of frequent reviews	Inadequate physical security
Inadequate documentation	Inadequate staffing
No background checks	Poor management philosophy
	Lack of employee loyalty
	Inadequate training
	Apathy
	Inattention to details

personal relationships with customers or suppliers. Others are possible because a crisis arises and the company disregards the normal control procedures. For instance, one *Fortune* 500 company was hit with three multimillion dollar frauds in the same year. All three took place when the company was trying to resolve a series of crises and neglected to follow the standard internal control procedures.

The list of opportunities that make fraud easy to commit and conceal is almost endless. Table 14.2 notes some of the more frequently mentioned opportunities in fraud research studies.

Rationalizations
Most fraud perpetrators consider themselves to be honest and upright citizens, even though they broke the law. Thus they had to have some internal mechanism that allowed them to rationalize their actions as not actually being dishonest. They had to have an excuse or a **rationalization** that made their actions more important than honesty and integrity.

Perhaps the most frequently used rationalization is that the perpetrator is just borrowing the money. He just needs a little money to tide him over a rough spot for a time. Therefore, he is not really being dishonest, since he has every intention of paying it back.

Some perpetrators rationalize that they are not hurting a real person. It is just a faceless and nameless computer system that will be hurt or a large, impersonal company that won't miss the money. For example, in one instance a perpetrator took pains to steal no more than $20,000, which was the maximum that the insurance company would reimburse the company for losses.

The list of rationalizations people use is lengthy. Here are some that are frequently used.

- You would understand if you knew how badly I needed it.
- What I did was not that serious.
- It was for a good cause. (This is the Robin Hood syndrome, robbing from the rich to give to the poor.)
- I occupy a very important position of trust. I am above the rules.
- Everyone else is doing it, so it can't be that wrong.
- No one will ever know.
- They owe it to me, and I am taking no more than is rightfully mine.

DETERRING COMPUTER FRAUD

Because fraud is such a serious problem, organizations must do all they can to protect their information systems. There are a number of things that can be done to significantly decrease the potential for fraud and limit the losses from fraud. For example, a company can create a climate that makes fraud less likely, increase the difficulty of committing a fraud, reduce the amount it loses when a fraud occurs, increase the likelihood of detecting fraud, and prosecute fraud perpetrators and increase the penalty for committing fraud. This section discusses these approaches and some of the controls for deterring fraud. A more complete discussion of all system controls is provided in Chapters 12 and 13.

Make Fraud Less Likely to Occur

Some computer consultants claim that the most common and effective method of obtaining adequate system security is to rely on the integrity of company employees. At the same time, research shows that most fraud is committed by current and former employees. In fact, in some studies up to 80% of computer frauds were insider jobs. Thus employees are both the greatest control strength and the greatest control weakness. Therefore any steps that an organization can take to increase employee integrity and to reduce the likelihood of employees' committing a fraud can reap big dividends. The sections that follow describe things companies can do to make fraud less likely.

Hiring and Firing Practices.   One of the most important things that management can do is to hire and retain honest people. The personnel policies and practices required to achieve this were discussed in Chapter 12.

In like manner, a company should be very careful when it must dismiss employees. Employees who are dismissed should immediately be removed from all sensitive jobs and be denied access to the computer system. This step reduces the chance that an employee who is seeking revenge against the company can sabotage the information system.

Managing Disgruntled Employees.   Many employees who commit fraud are disgruntled. Some are seeking revenge or "justice" for some wrong that they perceive has been done to them. Hence companies should have procedures for identifying these individuals and either helping them resolve their feelings or removing them from jobs that allow them access to the system. One way to avoid disgruntled employees and to keep morale high is to provide grievance channels and employee counseling. Employees need someone outside the normal chain of command that they can talk to about their grievances and their personal problems. Having someone who will listen to them and help them to resolve their problems can significantly decrease the number of dissatisfied employees.

Employee Training. Fraud is much less likely to occur in an environment where all company employees believe that security is everyone's business. An ideal corporate culture for fraud deterrence is one where all employees are proud of their company and its progress and, as a result, are protective of its assets. They all believe that they have a responsibility to report cases of fraud or abuse because it hurts the company and themselves as employees of the company. This type of corporate culture does not just happen; it has to be created. It has to be taught and then practiced. To develop this type of culture, a company should educate and train employees in the following areas.

- *Security measures:* Employees should be well schooled in all types of security measures and should be taught to take security measures very seriously. Security measures should be monitored and enforced as a way of reinforcing this training.

- *Fraud awareness:* Employees should be made aware of fraud, its prevalence, and its dangers. They should be taught why people commit fraud and how to deter and detect it.

- *Ethical considerations:* Employees should be told that the company expects ethical behavior. Many things in business fall into a gray area between definitely right or definitely wrong. This problem is especially prevalent among professionals in the computer industry. For example, many professionals see nothing wrong with utilizing corporate computer resources for personal use. Likewise, many see nothing wrong with gaining unauthorized access to other companies' data bases and browsing through them. One programmer, when arrested for unauthorized browsing, was shocked to find out that he was going to be prosecuted for it. He felt that he had done nothing wrong; he believed it was normal industry practice to do what he had done. So that employees know what is ethical and what isn't, acceptable and unacceptable practices should be defined.

- *Punishment for unethical behavior:* Employees should be informed of the consequences of unethical behavior (reprimands, dismissal, prosecution, etc.). This information should be disseminated not as a threat but as the consequence of choosing to act unethically. For example, employees should be informed that it is a federal crime to use a computer to steal or commit fraud and that anyone so doing faces immediate dismissal. Likewise, the company should display notices of program and data ownership and inform employees of the penalties of misuse.

As simple as it sounds, educating people in security issues, fraud awareness, ethical considerations, and the consequences of choosing to act unethically can make a tremendous difference. This education process can be accomplished by conducting informal discussions and formal meetings, issuing periodic departmental memos, distributing written guidelines and codes of professional ethics, circulating reports of securities violations and the consequences of the violations, and having a variety of security and fraud training programs.

Increase the Difficulty of Committing a Fraud

One way to deter fraud is to hire skilled, honest people and to train them to help protect the system. Another way is to design a system with sufficient controls to make the perpetration of fraud difficult to accomplish. The purpose of these controls is to help ensure the accuracy, integrity, and safety of all information systems resources. This section discusses how companies should go about developing a strong system of internal controls; then it discusses some of the more important controls for preventing fraud.

Develop a Strong System of Internal Controls. The overall responsibility for a secure and adequately controlled system lies with top management. Managers typically delegate the design of adequate control systems to systems analysts and designers and to end users. The corporate information security officer and the operations staff of the organization are typically responsible for ensuring that control procedures are followed.

One way to design an effective system of internal controls is to follow the risk assessment strategy shown in Fig. 14.3. The analysis of the costs, benefits, and reliability of internal control systems is discussed in Chapter 12.

To develop a set of controls, designers must first decide what objectives they want the controls to achieve. They then select the most efficient and cost-effective control to achieve the objectives. These controls are much more effective if they are placed in the system as it is built, rather than as afterthoughts. Finally, management must put in place a set of procedures to see that the controls are complied with and are enforced.

Some of the more important controls a company can use are briefly discussed next.

Segregation of Duties. As discussed in Chapter 12, there must be an adequate separation of duties to prevent individuals from stealing assets and covering up their tracks.

Enforced Vacations and Rotation of Duties. Many fraud schemes require the ongoing attention of the perpetrator. For example, the lapping technique requires that subsequent payments be applied to earlier payments that were stolen. If mandatory vacations are coupled with a

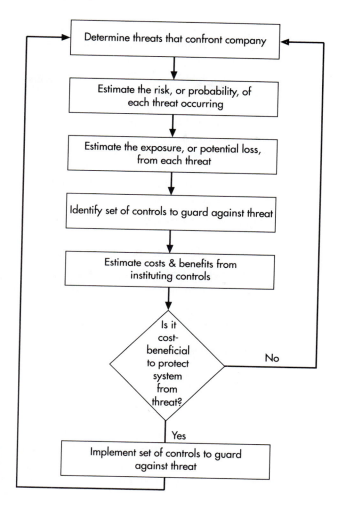

Figure 14.3
Risk assessment approach to designing internal controls

temporary rotation of duties, as explained in Chapter 12, these ongoing fraud schemes fall apart. As an example, consider the case of Roswell Steffen. When federal investigators raided an illegal gambling establishment, they found that a man who was making $11,000 dollars a year was betting up to $30,000 a day on the racetrack. Working together with his employer, Union Dime Savings Bank, the investigators discovered that he had embezzled and gambled away $1.5 million dollars over a three- or four-year period. Steffen, a compulsive gambler, started out by borrowing $5000 to place a bet on a "sure thing" that did not pan out. He said that he had been trying to replace that $5000 ever since. After he was caught, he was asked how the fraud could have been prevented. He said that if the bank had coupled a two-week vacation period with several weeks of rotation to another job function, the embezzlement would have been almost impossible to cover up.

Restrict Access. Computer fraud can be reduced significantly if access to computer equipment and data files is restricted. As explained in Chapter 13, both the physical access and the logical access to the computer equipment needs to be restricted.

One potential problem with access restriction is that companies can forget to update the data for restricting access. Companies usually do not have a problem remembering to add people to the file, but they do forget to delete them. For example, a company could forget to cancel the passwords of people who leave the company, allowing them to access the system after they have left. Therefore companies must make sure that all data used in restricting access is updated immediately when someone leaves.

Encrypt Data and Programs. Another way to protect data is to translate it into a secret code, thereby making it meaningless to others. This process, called data encryption, is explained in Chapter 13.

Protect Telephone Lines. Computer hackers use telephone lines to transmit viruses and to access, steal, and destroy data. They also steal telephone services. Recent technology allows companies to attach an electronic lock and key to their telephone lines. When one such device was tested, the researchers concluded that it would take a hacker 188 days working nonstop to break the more than 1 trillion combinations. Few hackers would make the attempt; and if they did, they would most likely be detected before they were successful.

Protect the System from Viruses. In 1992 there were over one hundred fifty thousand documented virus attacks on personal computers. The figure is actually much higher because most people do not like to advertise the problems they have with viruses. It has been estimated that 90% of the people who suffer a virus attack are reinfected within 30 days. These statistics point out the need to protect systems from viruses. Fortunately, there are some very good virus protection programs available, and some of them are free of charge. A few virus protection programs are designed to remain in computer memory and monitor system activity to search for an indication that a virus is trying to infiltrate the system. The intrusion is usually detected when there is an unauthorized attempt to access an executable program. When an attempt to infect a system is detected, the software freezes the system and flashes a message to the user. The user can then instruct the prevention program to remove the virus.

There are also virus detection programs that detect an infection soon after it starts. They are more reliable than virus protection programs. Finally, there are virus identification programs that scan all executable programs to find and remove all known viruses from the system. These programs work by scanning the system for specific characteristics of known virus strains. One problem with this approach is that it cannot detect a virus until it has been discovered.

A system can also be protected from viruses by following the guidelines listed in Focus 14.1.

Proper Control of Sensitive Data.   In the example given earlier to illustrate scavenging, a young man used sensitive data found in trash cans to defraud a telephone company of over $1 million. In another example an encyclopedia company lost several million dollars because sensitive files were copied and sold. These examples illustrate the need for a company to protect sensitive data.

Paper documents to be discarded should be shredded. Controls can be placed over data files to prevent or discourage their being copied. Employees should be informed of the consequences of using illegal copies of software, and the company should institute controls to see that illegal copies are not in use. Sensitive and confidential information should be locked up at night and not left out on desks. Local area networks can use dedicated servers that allow data to be downloaded but never uploaded. In that way the server can never be infected by a computer in the network. Closed-circuit televisions can be used to monitor areas where sensitive data or easily stolen assets are handled.

Some organizations with particularly sensitive data are installing diskless PCs or workstations. All data is stored centrally in a network and users download the data they need to work on each day. At the end of the day all data that is to be kept must be stored in the network, thereby controlling the problem of unguarded information created and stored in desktop computers. Since users can only delete or destroy the data on their screens, the company's data is more secure; the system is virtually immune to disasters a user might intentionally or unintentionally cause. In addition, without disks, users cannot introduce viruses into the system by reading a contaminated diskette. Nor does the company lose valuable data, because employees cannot copy company data on diskettes and remove them from company premises.

Reduce Fraud Losses

No matter how well a company tries to deter or prevent fraud, the chances are that it will occur sooner or later. Therefore the best strategy is to do everything possible to prevent it and then prepare for it, so that when it does occur, losses are minimized. One simple way to minimize losses is to have adequate insurance. Another is to keep a current backup copy of all program and data files in a secure off-site location. A third approach is to develop a contingency plan for fraud occurrences and other disasters that might occur.

Software was recently introduced to monitor system activity and help companies recover from frauds and malicious actions. One such software utility helped a company recover from a rampage that a disgruntled employee went on after he received a negative performance evaluation. The perpetrator ripped cards and cables out of PCs, changed the inventory control files, and edited the password file to stop people from logging onto the local area network. The company

14.1 FOCUS

Keeping Your Microcomputers Virus-Free

While there is no technological reason why a virus cannot attack a mainframe or a minicomputer (some have), the virus has traditionally targeted the microcomputer and micro-based networks, especially local area networks (LANs). Why? Because they are so much more accessible and because there are so many more of them. Here are some practical suggestions for protecting microcomputers.

- Vaccinate machines with software that prevents virus execution. Vaccination programs are different from virus detectors, which uncover viruses. A vaccination can keep a virus out, but it may not alert you to its presence; a virus detector will tell you if a virus is there.

- Don't put your diskettes in strange machines; your diskette may become infected. Don't let others put their diskettes in your disk drives; your machine may become infected. Scan strange diskettes with antiviral software before any data or programs are copied to your machine.

- Use write-protect tabs that prohibit writing to diskettes; a virus cannot spread to a write-protected diskette.

- Obtain software and diskettes only from known and trusted sources. While the likelihood of contracting a virus in this manner is small, even this software may be infected.

- Be wary of software or dis-

---

had programmed the utility package to protect the system against such actions. Therefore shortly after the incident the software identified the corrupted files and flashed an alert to company headquarters. The damage was undone by issuing simple commands to the utility software, which restored the corrupted file to its original status.

Increase the Likelihood of Detecting Fraud

There are thousands of fraud cases uncovered every year. Those frauds often have been going on for some time before they are discovered. Thus many companies are now being defrauded and do not know it. So companies should do everything they can to try and detect fraud as soon as possible. This section discusses some of the ways they can do that.

Conduct Frequent Audits.   One way to increase the likelihood of detecting fraud is for external and internal auditors to conduct periodic audits. Auditors should also periodically test system controls. In addition to doing their normal tests, auditors can periodically "browse" through the company's data files looking for suspicious activities. However, care must be exercised to make sure that employees' privacy rights are not violated. Informing employees that auditors will conduct a **random surveillance** not only helps resolve the privacy issue but also has a signifi-

kettes from unknown sources. They may be virus bait, especially if they offer prices or functionality that sound too good to be true.

- Deal with software retailers you trust. Some dealers rewrap and sell used software as if it were new.

- Some software suppliers use electronic techniques designed to make tampering evident. Ask whether the software you are purchasing has such protection.

- Write-protect new software diskettes before installing them. This will prevent infection and provide you with backup.

- Check new software on an isolated machine with virus

detection software.

- If you can, use the B: drive for data entry. Because of microprocessor design conventions, it is marginally more difficult for a virus to execute from the B: drive.

- Contrary to popular belief, importing software through LANs and modems is safer; most infection originates from diskettes.

- When you restart, use the "power-off-power-on" to clear and reset the system. It is possible for a virus to survive a warm start-up using Ctrl-Alt-Del or Reset keys.

- It's safer to start up or "boot" the machine from a write-protected diskette than from a hard disk. This type of

start-up will resist viruses that obtain control via the "boot sector" of the hard disk.

- Back up your data. Data files should be backed up separately from programs; this resists the contamination of backup data. Keep write-protected copies of the original disks and restore from them.

- Restrict the use of public bulletin boards. All software acquired from outside sources should be certified as virus-free before loading it into the system.

Source: Information Protection Review 2 (1) Deloitte & Touche: 6.

cant deterrent effect on computer crime. One large financial institution that implemented this strategy uncovered a number of abuses, including some that resulted in the termination of one employee and the reprimand of another. Auditing computer systems is addressed in depth in Chapter 15.

Use a Computer Security Officer. Unfortunately, most frauds are not detected by either the internal or the external auditors. In a study published in the *Sloan Management Review*, only 4.5% of the 259 cases of abuse studied were uncovered by the auditors. Normal system controls uncovered 45%, 32% were discovered by accident, and 8% were found by computer security officers. The authors also found that having active security officers had a significant deterrent effect on computer frauds. Therefore one way to not only detect fraud but also deter it is to have a computer security officer who is responsible for fraud deterrence and detection. The security officer can head a data and system security organization that is responsible for monitoring the system and disseminating information about improper uses of the system and their consequences.

Set up a Fraud Hot Line. Researchers at Brigham Young University studied 212 frauds and found that 33% were uncovered by anonymous tips. Therefore fraud consultants say that the single most effective thing a large company can do to uncover fraud is to set up a **fraud hot line**.

People witnessing fraudulent behavior in others are often torn between two conflicting feelings. On the one hand, they feel an obligation to their company to protect its assets and to turn the person in for the good of everyone concerned. On the other hand, they have been taught all their lives not to inform on others. In fact, the whistle-blower is often ostracized and suffers more than the perpetrator. When employees are able to report someone anonymously, it is easier for them to resolve this conflict.

Hot lines have been very effective. The insurance industry set up a hot line so that people could report dishonest practices in an attempt to control an estimated $17 billion a year in fraudulent claims. In the first month they received in excess of 2250 calls. Between 10% and 15% of the calls resulted in investigative action. The downside of hot lines is that many of the calls are not worthy of investigation. Some are made seeking revenge, others have vague reports of wrongdoing, and others have no merit at all.

Use Computer Consultants.   Many companies hire computer consultants to try and find weaknesses in their computer systems. These consultants, often referred to as tiger teams, attempt to breach the security of a system. Each means of breaching the system that is uncovered is closely evaluated, and protective measures are put in place to protect against further occurrences.

Some companies do not like this approach, however, because of the risk in having people break into the system and the message that it sends to employees. In essence, they do not want their weaknesses exposed, nor do they want to give their employees any ideas.

Monitor System Activities.   Systems software should keep a log of who accessed what data from which terminal and when they accessed it. These logs are very useful in monitoring system activity and tracing problems to their source.

Prosecute and Incarcerate Fraud Perpetrators

Most fraud cases go unreported and unprosecuted, for a number of reasons. One reason is that many cases of computer fraud are as yet undetected. A second reason is that companies are reluctant to report computer crimes when they are detected because a highly visible computer fraud is a public relations disaster: The company loses a lot of business due to the adverse publicity. It also reveals the vulnerability of its system, possibly attracting more acts of fraud. In one study less than 10% of the computer abuses were reported to law enforcement officials. One result of not reporting fraud is that a false sense of security is created; people think systems are more secure than they really are.

A third reason fraud is unreported is that law enforcement officials and the courts are so busy with violent crimes that they have little time for fraud cases where there is no bodily harm. Also, because the definition of computer fraud is so vague, no one knows how much it really costs; and so there is little motivation to investigate computer fraud cases. A fourth reason is that fraud is difficult, costly, and time-consuming to investigate and even harder to prove. It is hard to successfully prosecute computer fraud cases and to get convictions. A fifth reason is that most law enforcement people, lawyers, and judges lack the skills necessary to investigate, prosecute, and evaluate computer crimes.

When fraud cases are prosecuted and a conviction is obtained, the sentences received are often very light. For example, Judge John Lord, when sentencing convicted white-collar criminals in the early 1960s, stated that all the perpetrators were God-fearing men, highly civic minded, who had spent their lifetimes in sincere and honest dedication and service to their families, their churches, their country, and their communities. He said he could never send them to jail. Columnist Jack Anderson noted in 1974 that the average sentence for a fraud perpetrator was one year in jail for every $10 million stolen.

One of the most famous cases of a light sentence involved C. Arnoldt Smith, former owner of the San Diego Padres baseball team who was named Mr. San Diego of the Century. Smith was very involved in the community and made large political contributions. When investigations showed that he had stolen $200 million from his bank, he pleaded nolo contendere. He was given a sentence of 4 years probation and a fine of $30,000. The fine was to be paid at the rate of $100 a month for the following 25 years, with no interest. Mr. Smith was 71 at the time.

One very important way to deter fraud is to prosecute perpetrators frequently and vigorously. Law enforcement people need better laws with which to prosecute the perpetrators and more training in order to understand and detect computer fraud. Also needed are more lawyers and judges who understand computer crimes and who are able to prosecute and sit in judgment on computer crimes.

Until 1986 law enforcement officials did not have a law that dealt specifically with computer crimes. As a result, they had to apply laws written for other purposes in their prosecution attempts. This problem was partially resolved in the United States when Congress passed the Computer Fraud and Abuse Act of 1986. The law covers computers used by the federal government, financial institutions, and certain medical organizations. It also covers computers used in interstate or foreign commerce. The law makes it illegal to knowingly gain access to computers with intent to defraud. Trafficking in computer access passwords is also prohibited. The crime is a felony if more than $1000 worth of software is damaged or if money, goods, or services are stolen. The penalties are severe: 1–5 years for the first offense, 10 for the second, and 20 for three or more. The range of possible fines is up to $250,000 or twice the value of the stolen data. While the law is an improvement, there are many who say it is vague, unclear, loose, and an easy target for defense attorneys. The laws are supplemented by computer fraud statues in all 50 states.

The desire to better detect and prevent fraud and to do a better job of prosecuting fraud perpetrators has given rise to a new profession. **Forensic accountants** are people who specialize in fraud auditing and investigation. In the past few years it has been the fastest-growing area in accounting. Many forensic accountants have degrees in accounting and have received specialized training with the FBI, the IRS, or other law enforcement agencies. A new professional designation has also been created. The National Association of Certified Fraud Examiners in Austin, Texas, has developed a Certified Fraud Examiner certification program. To become a CFE, candidates must pass a two-day exam. Today there are approximately eight thousand CFEs scattered all over the world.

CASE CONCLUSION: THE DIFFERENCES IN WITHHOLDINGS AT NORTHWEST INDUSTRIES

Jason Scott believed that Don Hawkins had committed a fraud, but he needed more details about how the fraud was committed before he could support his conclusion. So in preparation for his meeting with management, he expanded the scope of his investigation.

A week later Jason presented his findings to the President of Northwest. To introduce the problem and to make it hit a little closer to home, Jason showed the President a copy of the withholding report filed with the IRS and pointed out the President's withholdings. Then he showed him a printout of withholdings from the payroll records and pointed out the $5 difference in withholdings. Next, he pointed out that Don Hawkins had a several-thousand-dollar difference in his withholdings. This immediately got the President's attention, and Jason proceeded to tell him how he believed a fraud had been perpetrated.

During the latter part of the prior year the payroll system had undergone some minor modifications. Don had been in charge of the project. Owing to some problems with several other projects, the payroll project had been completed without the usual review by other systems personnel. So Jason requested a member of his staff, who was a former programmer, to review the code changes. She found a few lines of code in the program for generating the withholdings report for the IRS that subtracted $5 from selected employee's withholdings and added it to Don's withholdings. Apparently, Don got his hands on the money when the IRS sent him a huge refund check.

It looked as if Don had intended to use the scheme every year, since he had not removed the incriminating code. He must have also been fairly confident of his scheme, since he had not tried to modify the copy of the withholdings report maintained by the company. Somehow he had known that there was no reconciliation of withholdings from the payroll records and the withholdings from the IRS report. It was a fairly simple plan, and it possibly would have gone undetected for years if Jason had not chanced to overhear someone in the cafeteria talk about a $5 difference.

Jason had quietly investigated Don. He found out that Don had a reputation of being hard to work with. So he had been passed over last year for a managerial position in the Programming Department, and he had been unhappy ever since. He had made numerous comments to co-workers about favoritism and being treated unfairly. He had even mentioned getting even with the company somehow. Don had also recently bought a brand new and fairly expensive sports car. No one knew where he got the money, but he had mentioned to a co-worker that he had made a sizable down payment when he bought the car the third week in April.

When the President asked the inevitable question of how the company could prevent this type of thing from happening again, Jason suggested several things. First, a review of the company's internal controls should be conducted to see what measures could be taken to prevent fraud from occurring. One control, reviewing program changes, that could have prevented this type of thing from happening already existed but had just not been followed. Jason suggested a stricter enforcement of the existing controls. Second, controls should be put into place to detect this type of fraud. He suggested a reconciliation of the withholdings shown on the report to the IRS and the withholdings shown on the payroll records. Third, employees should be trained in fraud awareness, security measures, and ethical issues.

Jason also urged the President to prosecute the case. The President was reluctant to do so because of all the adverse publicity and the problems it would cause for Don's wife and children. Jason's supervisor tactfully suggested that if Don was not prosecuted and others found out that he wasn't, it would send the wrong message to the rest of the company's employees. The President finally conceded to prosecute if the company could prove that Don was guilty. The President agreed to hire a forensic accountant who specialized in fraud to build a case against Don and to try and get him to confess. ■

SUMMARY

As the complexity of information systems technology increases, the security risks that information systems face increase. Computer systems today face four types of threats: natural and political disasters, software errors and hardware malfunctions, unintentional errors and accidents, and intentional acts of fraud and abuse.

This chapter discussed fraud, which is the intentional theft or misuse of company assets, often accomplished by the violation of a trust or confidence. Fraud can be perpetrated by insiders, such as employees for their own benefit or management on behalf of the company, and by those outside the company. The fraud process consists of three parts: theft, conversion, and concealment.

Computer fraud is a growing problem in today's world because there are so many more computers and so many more people trained in computers. People can commit computer fraud by manipulating computer input, by modifying computer software, by changing company data, by misusing computer resources, and by stealing or misusing computer output. The chapter explained the many different techniques perpetrators have developed to commit computer crimes.

It is difficult to develop an accurate profile of a typical fraud perpetrator. Many, however, are motivated by the challenge of beating the system and are younger than other criminals.

Fraud usually occurs when three conditions are present. First, there is usually some pressure or overriding motivation that causes a person to turn to fraud. Second, there is an opportunity to commit the fraud and conceal it. Third, the perpetrator is able to rationalize or justify his or her actions.

The chapter discussed five approaches for deterring and preventing fraud. First, companies can make fraud less likely through hiring practices and training. Second, companies must increase the difficulty of committing a fraud by implementing internal controls and restricting access to the system. Third, companies can reduce fraud losses by having adequate insurance, keeping backup copies of systems data, and using special software for monitoring the system. Fourth, companies can increase the likelihood of detecting fraud by implementing frequent audits, setting up fraud hot lines, and using fraud consultants and computer security officers. Fifth, companies must prosecute perpetrators and seek stiffer penalties for those convicted.

KEY TERMS   Define the following terms.

computer security	round-down technique	hacking
sabotage	salami technique	scavenging
fraud	trap door	eavesdropping
white-collar criminals	superzapping	wiretap
employee fraud	software piracy	computer virus
management fraud	data diddling	worm
fraudulent financial reporting	data leakage	pressure
lapping	piggybacking	opportunity
kiting	masquerading	rationalization
computer fraud	impersonation	random surveillance
computer crime	logic time bomb	computer security officer
Trojan horse		fraud hot line
		forensic accountants

Discussion questions

14.1 Evaluate the following statement: "Some computer consultants claim that the most common and effective method of obtaining adequate system security is to rely on the integrity of company employees." Do you agree with this statement? Explain. Why does this statement seem ironic? What can employers do to ensure the integrity of their employees?

14.2 You are the president of a multinational company. You recently discovered that a senior executive confessed to embezzling nearly $100,000 in funds using a kiting scheme. Explain what kiting is and what your internal audit staff could do to prevent it in the future. How would you respond to your employee's confession? What issues must you consider before pressing formal charges?

14.3 One December morning the computers at U.S. Leasing Company began acting sluggish. Computer operators were relieved when a software troubleshooter from Digital Equipment called several hours later. They were more than happy to let him help correct the problem they were having with the Digital software. The troubleshooter asked for a phone number for the computers as well as a log-on number and passwords—a common procedure employed by Digital in handling software problems.

The next morning the computers were worse. A call to Digital confirmed U.S. Leasing's suspicion: Someone had impersonated a Digital repairman to gain unauthorized access to the system and destroy the entire computer data base. U.S. Leasing was also concerned that the intruder had devised a program that would let him get back into the system even after all the passwords were changed.

What techniques could the imposter have employed to breach U.S. Leasing's internal security? What could U.S. Leasing do to avoid future incidents?

14.4 Addressing the need for tighter data controls and lower support costs, Manufacturers Hanover has adopted a new diskless PC, little more then a mutilated personal computer described as the "gutless wonder." The concept behind the diskless PC is simple: a LAN server-based file system of high-powered diskless workstations is assembled throughout an organization and connected with a central repository or mainframe. The network improves control by limiting user access to company data previously stored on desktop hard disks. Since the user can only destroy or delete information currently on the screen, a company's financial data is protected from user-instigated catastrophes.

The diskless computer also saves money in user support costs. According to Vice-President Arthur Block, "Two-thirds of the cost of desktop computing is training and support." The new system reduces support costs by distributing applications and upgrades automatically, as well by offering on-line help.[1]

What threats in the information processing and storage system does the diskless PC minimize? Do the security advantages of the new system outweigh potential limitations?

14.5 Biometric security systems, once the product of future-oriented science fiction novels, are becoming a cost-effective solution to the troubling problem of computer security. Biometric security devices measure physical traits in each of us that make us unique. Such traits include speech patterns, eye and finger physiology, written signature dynamics, and other common physical traits. In selecting which trait should be measured, systems analysts must weigh the costs of such systems against the level of security desired. Current devices begin at $1000 for a fingerprint reader and can go as high as $20,000 for a voice verification system.

The ideal system must be reliable and yet flexible in handling minor changes in physical characteristics. Often a lack of flexibility can create a problem for a person who cuts her finger or wakes up with a hoarse voice. The system also requires that the user be physically present to gain access to the system.

Hertz and Security Pacific Bank are two major companies seeking to use the new technology. For both companies the security devices will aid in ensuring that only authorized individuals have access to computer systems and the related operations.[2]

---

[1] *Source:* Patricia Keefe, "Doing Away with Hard Disks," *Computerworld* (March 12, 1990): 39.

[2] *Source:* Michael Alexander, "Biometric System Use Widening," *Computerworld* (January 8, 1990): 16.

Why are biometric security devices increasing in popularity? What advantages do these security systems have over traditional security measures (e.g., passwords, locked doors, etc.)? What drawbacks do these security devices have?

14.6 On October 16, 1989, the inventory control system for Revlon Inc., the cosmetics giant, went down for three days. Revlon was shocked a few days later to discover the downtime was directly caused by Logisticon, a software manufacturer who had provided Revlon with the inventory system software.

In February 1989 Revlon signed an agreement to have Logisticon install a real-time invoice and inventory processing system. Prior to completing phase I of the project, Revlon discovered a series of programming bugs. Revlon proceeded to withhold any additional payment on the contract to Logisticon. Logisticon contended that the software was fine and that the computer hardware was faulty.

When Revlon continued to refuse payment, Logisticon then sought repossession the only way it knew how: by making the system unusable for Revlon by a disabling phone call through a telephone dial-in feature of the new inventory system.

After a three-day standoff Logisticon reactivated Revlon's inventory system software. On October 22, 1989, Revlon filed suit in California Superior Court charging Logisticon with trespassing, breach of contract, and misappropriation of trade secrets (use of Revlon passwords). Logisticon filed a countersuit for contract breach. Revlon and Logisticon later settled out of court.[3]

Do the acts of Logisticon represent an act of sabotage or repossession? Why? Is this a computer crime? Explain.

14.7 Improved computer security measures create their own set of additional problems: user antagonism, sluggish response, and hampered performance. Many professionals feel that the most effective way to promote computer security is to educate users about good moral conduct.

According to Richard Stallman (President of the Free Software Foundation, MIT programmer, and computer activist), "Software licensing is antisocial because it keeps information away from your neighbors and it prohibits the growth of the technology."

He also said that high school and college students should have access to computers without security to teach "constructive, civilized" behavior. "It's human nature to solve puzzles, which is what a protected system is to some. A lot of people believe one way to get rid of hacking might be to eliminate computer security. With no reason to figure something out, there's no temptation to break in."[4]

Do you agree with Stallman's statements? Do you agree that software licensing is antisocial? Is ethical teaching the solution to computer security problems? Would the removal of computer security measures reduce the incidence of computer crime?

14.8 Discuss the following statement by Roswell Steffen, a convicted embezzler: "For every foolproof system, there is a method for beating it." Would you say there is such a thing as a secure computer system? Explain. If internal controls are less then 100% effective, why should internal controls be employed at all?

14.9 *Time* magazine describes computer fraud as a "growth industry." Why does the incidence of computer fraud continue to grow at such an alarming rate? Who ultimately pays for the deeds of most computer criminals?

14.10 Computer criminals use many different techniques to exploit computer systems for their own purposes. List and briefly explain the techniques computer criminals employ and the related purpose for each technique. Which techniques are used most frequently? Which techniques do you think are most damaging to a system?

14.11 What motives do people have for hacking? Why has hacking become so popular in recent years? Would you regard hacking as a crime? Explain your position.

---

[3] Adapted from Fred Davis, "Could the Repo Man Grab Your Invaluable Software?" *PC Week* (November 12, 1990): 266.

[4] Adapted from Jeff Goldberg, "Computerized Breaking and Entering," *OMNI* (September 1990): 18.

PROBLEMS

14.1 An experienced senior auditor was assigned to investigate a possible fraudulent situation characterized by extremely high, unexplained merchandise shortages at one location of the company's department store chain. During the course of the investigation the auditor determined the following.

1. Unknown to the chain store's general manager the supervisor of the receiving department was also the owner and operator of a small boutique. The boutique carried many of the same labels as the chain store.
2. The receiving supervisor signed receiving reports showing that the total quantity shipped by a vendor had been received. From 5% to 10% of each shipment was diverted to the boutique.
3. The chain's buyers were unaware of the short shipments because the receiving supervisor would enter the correct quantity on the move ticket accompanying the merchandise to the sales areas.
4. The chain's accounts payable department paid vendors for the total quantity shown on the receiving report.
5. On the supervisor's instructions no one compared quantities on the move tickets with those on the receiving report.

Required

Classify each of the five situations listed above as one of the following and justify your answer.

- A fraudulent act
- An indicator of fraud
- Unrelated to the investigation

(CIA Examination, adapted)

14.2 A small but growing firm has recently hired you to investigate a potential fraud. The company heard through its hot line that the purchases journal clerk periodically enters fictitious acquisitions. The nonexistent vendor's address is given as a post office box, which is rented by the clerk. The clerk forwards notification of the fictitious purchases for recording in the accounts payable ledger. Payment is ultimately mailed to the post office box. The purchases journal clerk deposits the check in an account established in the name of the nonexistent vendor.

Required

a. Define the following.

1. Fraud
2. Deterrence of fraud
3. Detection of fraud
4. Investigation of fraud
5. Reporting of fraud

b. List four red-flag indicators (personal as opposed to organizational) that might point to the existence of fraud.

c. List two procedures you could follow to uncover the fraudulent behavior of the purchases journal clerk in this situation.

(CIA Examination, adapted)

14.3 It is estimated that several hundred million dollars are lost annually through computer crime. The first conviction of a computer hacker under the Computer Fraud and Abuse Act of 1986 occurred in 1988. There have been other cases of computer break-ins reported in the news, as well as stories of viruses spreading throughout vital networks. While these cases make the headlines, most experts maintain that the number of computer crimes publicly revealed represent only the tip of the iceberg. Companies have been victims of crimes but have not acknowledged them in order to avoid adverse publicity and not advertise their vulnerability.

Although the threat to security is seen as external, through outside penetration, the more dangerous threats come from insiders. Management must recognize these problems and commit the company to the development and enforcement of security programs to deal with the many types of fraud that computer systems are susceptible to on a daily basis. Types of computer systems fraud include (1) input manipulation, (2) program alteration, (3) file alteration, (4) data theft, (5) sabotage, and (6) theft of computer time.

Required

For the six types of fraud identified, explain how each is committed. Also, identify a different method of protection for each type of fraud, describing how the protection method operates. The same protection method should not be used for more than one type of fraud—that is, six different methods must be identified and described. Use the following format.

Type of Fraud	Explanation	Identification and Description of Protection Methods
1.		
2.		
3.		
4.		
5.		
6.		

(CMA Examination, adapted)

14.4 The studies conducted by the National Commission on Fraudulent Financial Reporting (the Treadway Commission) revealed that fraudulent financial reporting usually occurs as the result of certain environmental, institutional, or individual influences and opportune situations. These influences and opportunities, present to some degree in all companies, add pressures and motivate individuals and companies to engage in fraudulent financial reporting. The effective prevention and detection of fraudulent financial reporting requires an understanding of these influences and opportunities while evaluating the risk of fraudulent financial reporting that these factors can create in a company. The risk factors to be assessed include not only internal ethical and control factors but also external environmental conditions.

Required

a. Identify two situational pressures in a public company that would increase the likelihood of fraud.

b. Identify three corporate circumstances (opportune situations) when fraud is easier to commit and when detection is less likely.

c. For the purpose of assessing the risk of fraudulent financial reporting, identify the external environmental factors that should be considered in the following areas.

1. The company's industry
2. The company's business environment
3. The company's legal and regulatory environment

d. According to the Treadway Commission, what can top management do to reduce the possibility of fraudulent financial reporting?

(CMA Examination, adapted)

14.5 Lexsteel Corporation is a leading manufacturer of steel furniture. While the company has manufacturing plants and distribution facilities throughout the United States, the purchasing, accounting, and treasury functions are centralized at corporate headquarters.

While discussing the management letter with the external auditors, Ray Landsdown, Controller of Lexsteel, became aware of potential problems with the accounts payable system. The auditors had to perform additional audit procedures in order to attest to the validity of accounts payable and cutoff procedures. The auditors have recommended that a detailed systems study be made of the current procedures. Such a study would not only assess the exposure of the company to potential embezzlement and fraud but also identify ways to improve management controls.

Landsdown has assigned the study task to Dolores Smith, a relatively new accountant in the department. Because Smith could not find adequate documentation of the accounts payable procedures, she interviewed those employees involved and constructed a flowchart of the current system. This flowchart is shown in Fig. 14.4, and descriptions of the current procedures follow.

Computer Resources Available.   The host computer mainframe is located at corporate headquarters with interactive, remote job entry terminals at each branch location. In general, data entry occurs at the source and is transmitted to an integrated data base maintained on the host computer. Data transmission is made between the branch offices and the host computer over leased telephone lines. The software allows flexibility for managing user access and editing data input.

Procedures for Purchasing Raw Materials.   Production orders and appropriate bills of material are generated by the host computer at corporate headquarters.

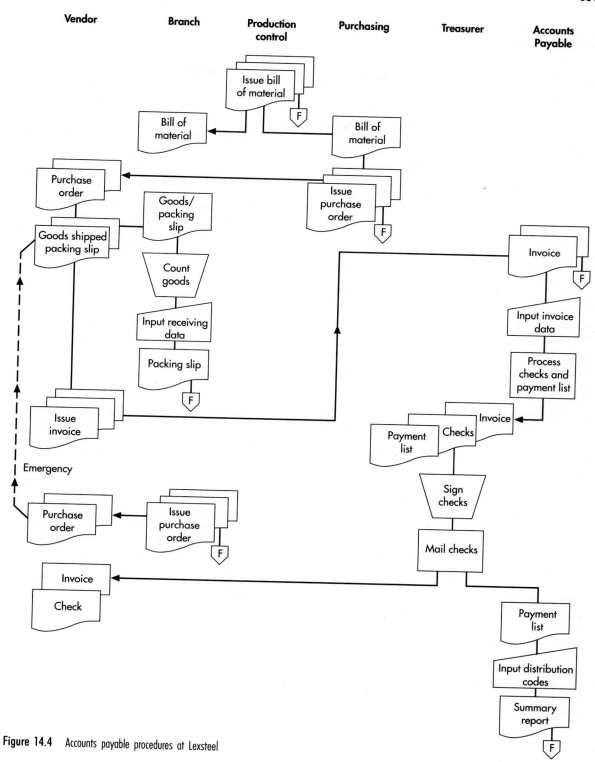

Figure 14.4 Accounts payable procedures at Lexsteel

From these bills of material purchase orders for raw materials are generated by the centralized purchasing function and mailed directly to the vendors. Each purchase order instructs the vendor to ship the materials directly to the appropriate manufacturing plant. The manufacturing plants, assuming that the necessary purchase orders have been issued, proceed with the production orders received from corporate headquarters.

When goods are received, the manufacturing plant examines and verifies the count to the packing slip and transmits the receiving data to accounts payable at corporate headquarters. In the event that raw material deliveries fall behind production, each branch manager is given the authority to order materials and issue emergency purchase orders directly to the vendors. Data about the emergency orders and verification of materials receipt are transmitted via computer to accounts payable at corporate headquarters. Since the company employs a computerized perpetual inventory system, physical counts of raw materials are deemed not to be cost-effective and are not performed.

Accounts Payable Procedures. Vendor invoices are mailed directly to corporate headquarters and entered by accounts payable personnel when received; this often occurs before the receiving data are transmitted from the branch offices. The final day of the invoice term for payment is entered as the payment due date. This due date must often be calculated by the data entry person using information listed on the invoice.

Once a week invoices due the following week are printed in chronological entry order on a payment listing, and the corresponding checks are drawn. The checks and the payment listing are sent to the Treasurer's Office for signature and mailing to the payee. The check number is printed by the computer, displayed on the check and the payment listing, and validated as the checks are signed. After the checks are mailed, the payment listing is returned to accounts payable for filing. When there is insufficient cash to pay all the invoices, certain checks and the payment listing are retained by the Treasurer until all checks can be paid. When the remaining checks are mailed, the listing is then returned to accounts payable. Often weekly check mailings include a few checks from the previous week, but rarely are there more than two weekly listings involved.

When accounts payable receives the payment listing back from the Treasurer's Office, the expenses are distributed, coded, and posted to the appropriate plant/cost center accounts. Weekly summary performance reports are processed by accounts payable for each cost center and branch location reflecting all data entry to that point.

Required

a. Identify and discuss three areas where Lexsteel Corporation may be exposed to fraud or embezzlement due to weaknesses in the procedures described, and recommend improvements to correct these weaknesses.

b. Describe three areas where management information could be distorted owing to weaknesses in the procedures described, and recommend improvements to correct these weaknesses.

c. Identify three strengths in the procedures described, and explain why they are strengths.
(CMA Examination, adapted)

14.6 The impact of employee and management fraud is staggering both in terms of dollar costs and effect on the victims. Presented here are three independent cases of employee wrongdoing. For each of the three situations, describe the recommendations that the internal auditors should make to prevent similar problems in the future.

a. A retail store that was part of a national chain experienced an abnormal inventory shrinkage in its audiovisual department. The internal auditors, noting this shrinkage, included an in-depth evaluation of the department in the scope of their audit of the store. During their review the auditors were "tipped" by an employee that a particular customer bought a large number of small electronic components and that the customer always went to a certain cashier's checkout line. The auditors' work revealed that the cashier and the customer had colluded to steal a number of electronic components. The cashier did not record the sale of several of the items that the customer took from the store.

b. Internal auditors discovered a payroll fraud in a large hospital when they observed the distribution of paychecks on a surprise visit. The supervisors of each department distributed paychecks to employees and were supposed to return unclaimed checks to the payroll department. When the auditors took control of, and followed up on, an unclaimed paycheck for an employee in the food service department, they discovered that the employee had quit four months previously. The employee and the supervisor had had an argument, and the employee had simply left and never returned. The supervisor had continued to turn in a time card for the employee and, when the paychecks came for distribution, had taken the unclaimed checks and cashed them.

c. While performing an audit of cash disbursements in a manufacturing firm, internal auditors discovered a fraud committed by an accounts payable clerk. The clerk had made copies of supporting documents and used the copies to support duplicate payments to a vendor of materials used in the manufacturing process. The clerk, who had opened a bank account in a name similar to that of the vendor, took the duplicate checks and deposited them in the bank account.

(CMA Examination, adapted)

14.7 Ward Corporation is a manufacturer of cleaning products with three wholly owned subsidiaries that are operated as separate divisions. Ward's corporate headquarters are located in an industrial park in a Chicago suburb. The Industrial Products Division is located in the same industrial park but in its own building. The other two divisions are located in Milwaukee and Indianapolis.

The corporation's operating and financial records are maintained on a mainframe computer at corporate headquarters. Each division has a small accounting department that submits operating and financial data to corporate headquarters on a regular basis.

The Profit Planning Department at corporate headquarters is responsible for preparing special analyses and reports for Ward. To facilitate its work, the Profit Planning Department has linked a microcomputer to the mainframe to download data. The special analyses are prepared using these data and a purchased spreadsheet software package.

Beth Simons recently joined the Industrial Products Division as an accounting analyst. Simons is proficient in the use of microcomputers and spreadsheet software. She has been given an assignment to work with Doug Laird, Marketing Manager of the Industrial Products Division, to develop analyses and reports. One week into the assignment she suggested that the microcomputers used in the Marketing Department for word processing could be valuable analytical tools if spreadsheet software were acquired. Laird knows little about computers,

but he has received some of the special analyses prepared by the Profit Planning Department at corporate headquarters. Laird wants Simons to try her idea, but has suggested that she first borrow the software from the Profit Planning Department.

Simons approached Tom Field, Manager of Profit Planning, regarding the use of the software package. Field was very sympathetic to Simons's request, but the software is used extensively in his department. Therefore he did not want to loan the original system disk. Furthermore, the software was copy-protected. However, Field did have a utility program that allowed him to make backup copies of most copy-protected software. Since there was no backup of the spreadsheet software, Field decided to make a copy and give it to Simons for her use. Simons indicated that she planned to use the software during regular business hours.

Upon giving the copy to Simons, Field said, "This is my only copy, but you may borrow it for your use only. Don't give it to anyone else. Once you have tried the software for your assignment, you must return this copy to me. Industrial Product's Accounting or Marketing Department will have to purchase its own copy."

Field did not give Simons a copy of the licensing agreement that accompanied the original software package. The license agreement that follows was affixed to the original sealed disk package. While Simons was not aware of the specific provisions of the licensing agreement that pertained to the borrowed software, she knew that licensing agreements accompanied computer software packages.

Software License Agreement

IMPORTANT: Please read this agreement before opening the envelope.

Opening the disk envelope indicates the user's acceptance of the agreement to abide by these terms.

1. The software may be used on any compatible hardware that the purchaser owns or uses.
2. Backup copies of the software can be made provided that these copies are for exclusive use of the purchaser and only one copy of the software is in use at any one time.
3. No alterations to the software or the documentation are permitted.
4. The software may not be distributed to others on a permanent or temporary basis.
5. This license and the software may be transferred to another party provided that all copies of the software and documentation are transferred and the original party ceases to use the software after the transfer.

Required

a. Consider the stipulations enumerated in the license agreement for the spreadsheet software.

1. Did Field violate the agreement when he made a copy of the software disk using the utility program?

2. Did Field violate the agreement when he gave Simons the copy of the software disk he had made?

b. Without prejudice to your answer in part a, assume that Field did violate the license agreement when he copied the software disk and gave it to Simons. Identify the alternatives that Field could have employed to determine the applicability of the spreadsheet software to the application of the Marketing Department of the Industrial Products Division without violating the license agreement.

(CMA Examination, adapted)

14.8 An organization's policy requires a "sealed bid" to sell motor vehicles that could no longer be used efficiently. In reviewing the sale of some vehicles that had been declared obsolete, the auditor found that management had not always complied with the stated policy. Records indicated that several vehicles on which major repairs had recently been performed had been sold at "negotiated prices." The auditor was assured by management that by accomplishing some limited repairs and negotiating with knowledgeable buyers, better prices had been obtained for the salvaged vehicles than could have been obtained using the required sealed-bid procedures. The auditor suspected that there might be more involved than management indicated. Further investigation by the auditor revealed that the vehicles had been sold to employees at "negotiated prices" that were below market value. The auditor's work eventually resulted in three managers and five other employees pleading guilty to criminal charges and making restitution to the organization.

Required

a. From the information given, outline the symptoms or indications of possible fraud that should have aroused the auditor's suspicion.

b. Suggest audit procedures that the auditor might have employed to establish the fact that fraud had in fact occurred.

(CIA Examination, adapted)

14.9 On March 6, 1992, the computer world braced for a shock. News began circulating months before about a computer virus named Michelangelo that was set to "ignite" on the birthday of the famous Italian artist. The virus itself was carried between IBM compatible computers on floppy disks. When a software package containing the virus was introduced to the computer system, the virus would attach to the computer's operating system boot sector. On the magical date the virus would release itself, freezing the system's boot function and destroying data.

When March 6 arrived, the virus did minimal damage. Preventive techniques limited the damage to isolated personal and business computers. Though the excitement surrounding the virus was largely illusory, Michelangelo helped the computer-using public realize their own system's vulnerability to outside attack.

Required

a. What is a computer virus? Why is no one completely safe from a computer virus?

b. Why do viruses represent a serious threat to information systems? What damage can a virus do to a computer system?

c. Why is a virus often classified as a Trojan horse?

d. What steps can individuals and companies take to prevent the spread or propagation of a computer virus?

14.10 The auditor of a bank is called to a meeting with a senior operations manager because of a customer's report that an auto loan payment was not credited. According to the customer, the payment was made at a teller's window using a check drawn on an account in that bank. The payment was made on its due date, May 5. On May 10 the customer decided to sell the car and called the bank for a payoff on the loan. The payment had not been credited to the loan. The customer came to the bank on May 12 to inquire about the payment and met with the manager. The manager found that the payment had been credited the night before the meeting (as of May 11); the customer was satisfied since no late charge would be assessed until May 15. The manager asked if the auditor was comfortable with this situation.

The auditor located the customer's paid check in the deposit department and found that it had cleared as of May 5. The auditor traced the item back through the computer entry records and found that the check had been processed by the teller as a cashed check. The auditor traced the payment through the entry records of May 11 and found that the payment had been made with cash instead of a check. What type of defalcation (embezzlement) scheme does this appear to be, and how does that scheme operate?

(CIA Examination, adapted)

14.11 It was a typical quiet Wednesday on the UCLA campus when everything began going wrong in the student computer lab. The computer lab was filled to capacity as the end of the semester neared. Nearly 70 students were logged into the UCLA computer network, run by Netware software, when the system came to a halt. Students tried running software without success, and many students couldn't even log in without getting a frustrating ABORT-RETRY message from the Netware operating system.

Initially, system directors expected a cable break or an operating system failure. Diagnostics were run, revealing nothing. After several frustrating hours a staff member began running the SCAN virus detection program and uncovered a Jerusalem virus

on the lab's main server. The virus was eventually traced to floppy disks used by unsuspecting UCLA students. When staff workers used the infected computers to gain supervisor access to the operating system, the virus spread.

The virus cost UCLA about 25 person-hours and disrupted the lives of frantic students preparing for finals. Later that evening the system was brought back on-line after infected files were replaced with backup copies.[5]

Required

a. What conditions made the UCLA system a potential "breeding ground" for the Jerusalem virus?

b. What symptoms indicated that a virus was present?

c. What advice would you give the Director of Computing at UCLA to prevent the same incident from reoccurring?

CASE 14.1 ROBERT T. MORRIS: A WORM RUN AMOK

Scientists at Berkeley's famous Experimental Computing Facility were quick to notice an intruder named *daemon* trying to log into their computer facility on November 2, 1988. It soon became apparent that other unknown users were also trying to log into the system. In fact, the break-in attempts increased in frequency until they could no longer be monitored. At this point they realized that it was a program that was trying to access the system. Within minutes the program invaded computer processing space and brought Berkeley's mammoth machines to a halt.

Within a half hour it was clear that the program had not limited itself to the Berkeley system. In fact, the program was invading the *entire* national information network known as Internet. Within hours computer experts discovered the existence of a powerful "worm" in Internet. A worm is a rogue computer program that travels through the system carrying out its independent and often destructive program commands. To defeat the worm, scientists had to dissect the worm's programming code to understand what it did. With that understanding the

scientists were able to develop a way to destroy the worm.

While scientists attempted to stop the worm, law enforcement officials and the press were beginning their own investigations of the unauthorized entry. Information on a possible suspect was scarce until an unidentified phone caller tipped a *New York Times* writer by inadvertently referring to the criminal programmer as RTM.

Robert Tappan Morris loved challenges. His father was a gifted scientist who worked with Bell Labs and the National Security Agency (NSA). His mother was a noted environmentalist and community leader in their home state of New Jersey. At an early age Robert developed a passion for computer security issues from work he did with his father at Bell Labs. Robert's most successful projects centered around improving the Bell systems Internet operations and its operating system, UNIX.

---

[5] *Source:* Barry Gerber, "Sometimes 'Abort, Retry' Means 'Network Virus,'" *PC Week* (April 2, 1990): 57.

Robert entered Harvard in the fall of 1983 and received extensive recognition for his work in problem solving using the school's main computer facility linked to the Internet system. By the age of 20 Robert's skills in UNIX security issues were so extensive that his father had him address a computer security conference at the NSA. The next day he delivered the same address to the Naval Research Laboratory. This national recognition may have caused Robert to feel that he could do no wrong in exploiting computer systems.

Robert was attending graduate school in 1988 at Cornell University in New York. About this time the first computer viruses were receiving national media attention. This sparked Robert's interest in seeing if he could develop an undetectable worm that would invade the Internet system. His challenge and goal: to reach as many computers as possible.

With Robert's background in UNIX security issues and his unlimited access to the Cornell computer, the development of a worm was easy. After weeks of reviewing UNIX source code, Robert discovered three programming flaws in the UNIX operating system. These flaws allowed him unauthorized access to any computer in the Internet system. Using the flaws, Robert developed a worm capable of entering a given system without any authorization. The system was entered through a bug in the Sendmail subprogram. Using the Sendmail feature, the worm was designed to replicate and enter related systems entirely undetected.

On November 2, 1988, Robert put the finishing touches on the worm. At 8:30 P.M. he logged on illegally to the artificial intelligence lab computer at MIT from his system at Cornell and released his creation. With that done, he went to dinner. After dinner Robert attempted to log on, but the computer didn't respond. Robert immediately knew something was wrong and attempted to remedy the problem with no success. Within a few moments the significance of the problem was clear. Robert had made a fatal error in his programming that allowed the worm to replicate out of control throughout Internet.

Cleaning out the Internet system and recreating the files destroyed by the worm took several months. On final tally the worm had infected more than six thousand computers, and the estimated costs to resolve the problem ranged from $150,000 to almost $200 million. Robert was arrested and charged with a felony

violation of the 1986 Counterfeit Access Device and Computer Fraud and Abuse Act, which prohibits unauthorized computer access. The 1986 act was largely untested in the courts and contained a controversial provision that allowed a criminal conviction without proof of criminal intent. The case was brought to a jury trial.[6]

The RTM case plays a significant role in the development of computer fraud law. As a juror involved in the RTM case, you've listened to the case background and other relevant issues during the trial. From your analysis, answer the following questions.

1. What motivated Robert to create the worm program? What rationale did he use to justify his actions?

2. What program feature in the UNIX operating system allowed Robert to send his worm through the Internet system undetected? What could have been done to prevent such a opportunity?

3. In your opinion, did Robert commit a crime? Explain.

4. What sentence would you give Robert for his crimes? Explain your position.

5. Evaluate the reasonableness of the following three independent opinions concerning the improvement of computer fraud laws.

   a. In an age of rapid changes in technology computer laws become antiquated as rapidly as the systems the laws were designed to protect. Computer laws should be designed to evolve with changes in technology.

   b. Computer laws should focus on current and potential future behavior that repudiates current public policy. The law should attempt to distinguish specific forms of fraudulent behavior involving computers.

   c. Computer laws should specifically punish users for the use of a computer in committing a felony crime. (Similar statutes exist governing the use of a gun in an assault.)

Of the three opinions, which do you feel is most practical? With which opinion do you concur?

---

[6] *Source:* Katie Hafner and John Markoff, *Cyberpunk* (New York: Simon and Schuster, 1991; and Jeff Goldberg, "Computerized Breaking and Entering," *OMNI* (September 1990): 18.

CASE 14.2 KEVIN MITNICK: THE DARK-SIDE HACKER

No one is entirely certain when Kevin Mitnick's "professional" hacking career began. Beginning in his midteens, Kevin was a part of the "phone phreak" subculture in California. By their own definition, phone phreaks were telephone hobbyists more expert at understanding the workings of the Bell system than most Bell employees. Using their knowledge of the phone system and computers, phreaks would often arrange free phone service, free long-distance calling, and free airline tickets for desiring friends.

In spite of his unique talents Kevin never sought pay for his efforts. His reward came in defeating the computer system and gaining power and control over others in the process. The phone phreak logo said it all: If it could be done, it was legal. As a phreak and as a programmer, Kevin often used his talents to injure those who would stop his work, including judges and past employers. When Kevin's telecommunications hobby culminated in one of the boldest acts of commuter piracy, no one was the least bit surprised.

As the manager of research and development for the University of California's (USC) computer services, Mark Brown was all too familiar with the threat of unauthorized break-ins. Most of the hackers were harmless, many just wanting to take a look around. One day Mark began a low-key investigation of some intruders and discovered that they were accessing the USC system through a modification in the Gatekeeper subprogram of the computer's VMS operating system.

A few days later Mark's amusement turned to concern as he noted that storage space was disappearing from the computer system at an alarming rate. After a more thorough investigation Mark discovered that the intruders were storing vast amounts of information in bogus system index files. When Mark opened the files, he was alarmed to find a source code copy of the newest version of the Digital VMS operating system.

Source code represents the lifeblood of software development. Computer programs are written in a user-friendly source code language such as FORTRAN or C and then converted into unreadable binary code for distribution. Such a process allowed software developers to protect the integrity of their programs from alterations and modifications from outside sources. Digital's source code had clearly been compromised.

Mark immediately called Digital Equipment to inform them of his discovery. He was surprised by the guarded reception he received from Digital representatives. Digital asked Mark to continue monitoring the intruders and keep careful logs of all that he saw.

Kevin and his friend Lenny DiCicco had years of experience with computers, networks, and VMS operating systems. They used that knowledge, the computer at Voluntary Plan Administrators (VPA), Lenny's workplace, and a list of stolen MCI long-distance accounts to exploit Digital's Easynet network. They gained access through an operating system bug in Easynet and sent a copy of the VMS operating system to the USC computer. With help from a friend the data was retrieved from the USC computer and stored on magnetic disk. From their viewpoint their actions were harmless. It wasn't really stealing because they never tried marketing the software.

However, Kevin was not satisfied with a copy of the VMS source code. He also wanted a copy of the source code for Doom, a lucrative game developed by Digital. This time Lenny hesitated. When Lenny refused to help any further, Kevin became angry and caused problems for Lenny at work. When Lenny's boss called him into his office to discuss the problem, Lenny came unglued. Lenny's boss, Ralph Hurley, was stunned when Lenny confessed to using VPA's computer to exploit Digital Equipment. Ralph convinced Lenny to call Digital and relate a similar confession to a Digital security team.

A Digital security expert, accompanied by an FBI agent, arrived the following morning to verify Lenny's claims and to compare them with the statements made by Mark Brown from USC. With Lenny's help the police spent the evening monitoring Kevin as he logged onto Digital's Easynet system with the VPA computer system.

Kevin kept much of his pirated software in a duffel bag in his car. Hoping to catch Kevin with stolen software and data, the FBI had Lenny ask he could make copies of some of Kevin's pirated software. When Kevin went to the car and retrieved the duffel bag, the police made the arrest.

Kevin was charged with four felony counts, including unauthorized computer entry, theft of data, and software piracy. Hoping to avoid additional publicity, Digital sought a plea-bargain arrangement. Although the judge initially rejected the plea bargain, a plea arrangement was eventually made and Kevin was sentenced to one year in prison and six months in a rehabilitation program working to overcome his obsession with computer piracy. For his role in the crime Lenny received five years probation after pleading guilty to one felony count.[7]

As the security expert at Digital Equipment, you've been asked to review the allegations against Kevin Mitnick and Lenny DiCicco and discuss with Digital's top management its concerns surrounding the hackers' unauthorized break-in to the Easynet network.

1. What exactly is source code? What role does source code play in software design and maintenance? What is the danger of having source code exposed to unauthorized users?

2. In what ways do Kevin and Lenny represent typical white-collar computer criminals? How are they different?

3. What was the motive of the hackers in entering Digital's Easynet network without authorization? What rationale did Kevin and Lenny use to justify their invasion of the Easynet network?

4. How were the hackers so readily able to gain access to the USC computers as well as Digital's Easynet? What steps should Digital take to minimize the impact of computer crime on its operations in the future?

5. Discuss whether or not Digital Equipment should press charges against Kevin and Lenny for their piracy of Digital's VMS operating system source code.

    a. What charges should be brought against the hackers?

    b. What impact could publicity have upon Digital Equipment?

6. Several eavesdropping devices, including wiretaps and hidden microphones, were employed by law enforcement officials in making Kevin's arrest.

    a. What advantages do eavesdropping devices provide law enforcement?

    b. What problems arise when police officers employ such equipment?

    c. When, if ever, should eavesdropping techniques be employed by law enforcement?

    d. Were the officers justified in monitoring Kevin's activities?

CASE 14.3 DAVID L. MILLER: PORTRAIT OF A WHITE-COLLAR CRIMINAL

There is an old saying in crime-fighting circles: Crime doesn't pay. However, for David Miller crime has paid rich dividends. It paid for two Mercedes-Benz sedans, a $280,000 suburban house, a condominium at Myrtle Beach, South Carolina, $500 suits, and $75 tailored, monogrammed shirts. It also paid for diamond, sapphire, ruby, and emerald rings for his wife and a new car for his father-in-law.

Though he has confessed to embezzling funds from six different employers over a 20-year period, he has never been prosecuted and has never been incarcerated. In large part Miller's freedom is the result of the fear that companies have about turning in employees who defraud them.

Miller's first employer was also his first victim. In 1965, after ten months of selling insurance in Wheeling, West Virginia, he was fired for stealing about $200. After an assortment of odd jobs he moved to Ohio and worked as an accountant for a local baker. Miller was caught embezzling funds and paid back the $1000 he had stolen. Again, he was not

[7] Source: Katie Hafner and John Markoff, Cyberpunk (New York: Simon and Schuster, 1991).

reported to the authorities and was quietly dismissed.

Miller returned to Wheeling and went to work for Wheeling Bronze, Inc., a bronze-castings maker. In December 1971 the President of Wheeling Bronze discovered that several returned checks were missing and that there was a $30,000 cash shortfall. After an extensive search workers uncovered a number of canceled checks with forged signatures in an outdoor sandpile. Miller was questioned and confessed to the scheme. Miller was given the choice of paying back the stolen amount or going to jail. Miller's parents took out a mortgage on their home and used the money to pay back the stolen money. No charges were ever filed and Miller was dismissed.

Several months later Miller found a job in Pennsylvania working for Robinson Pipe Cleaning. When Miller was caught embezzling funds, he again avoided prosecution by promising to repay the $20,000 he had stolen.

In 1974 Crest Industries hired Miller as an accountant. Miller proved to be the ideal employee and was quickly promoted to the position of Office Manager. He was very dedicated, worked long hours, and did outstanding work. Soon after his promotion he purchased a new home, a new car, and a new wardrobe.

In 1976 Miller's world unraveled again when Crest's auditors discovered that $31,000 was missing. Once again there was a tearful confession and a promise to repay all money stolen. Miller confessed that he'd written several checks to himself and had then recorded payments to vendors on the carbon copies of the checks. To cover his tracks he intercepted and altered the company's monthly bank statements. He had used the money he had stolen to finance his life-style and to repay Wheeling Bronze and Robinson Pipe Cleaning.

Miller claimed in his confession that he had never before embezzled funds. He showed a great deal of remorse, so much so that Crest even hired a lawyer for him. He gave Crest a lien on his house, and he was quietly dismissed. Because the President of Crest did not want the publicity to harm Miller's wife and three children, Crest never pressed charges against Miller.

Miller next took a job as an accountant in Steubenville, Ohio, with Rustcraft Broadcasting Company, a chain of radio and TV stations. Rustcraft was acquired in 1979 by Associated Communications, and Miller moved to Pittsburgh to become Associated's new controller.

Miller immediately began dipping into Associated's accounts. Over a six-year period he embezzled approximately $1.36 million, $445,000 of that in 1984 when Miller was promoted to CFO. Miller used various methods to embezzle the money. One approach to circumvent the need for two signatures on every check was to ask another executive who was leaving on vacation to sign several checks "just in case" the company needed additional cash while he was gone. Miller used most of these checks to siphon funds off to his personal account. To cover the theft, Miller retrieved the canceled check from the bank reconciliation and destroyed it. The amount stolen was then charged to an expense account of one of the units to balance the company's books.

While working at Associated, Miller was able to lead a very comfortable life-style. He bought a new house and several expensive cars. He bought vacation property and a very expensive wardrobe, and he was very generous with tips and gifts. The life-style could not have been supported by his $130,000 salary, yet no one at Associated ever questioned the source of his conspicuous consumption.

Miller's life-style came crashing down in December 1984 while he was on vacation. A bank officer called to inquire about a check written to Mr. Miller. An investigation ensued and Miller confessed to embezzling funds. As part of the 1985 out-of-court settlement with Miller, Associated Communications received most of Miller's personal property.

Miller can't explain why he was never prosecuted. He always insisted that he was going to pay the company back. Such statements would usually satisfy his employers and get him off the hook. He believes that these agreements actually contributed to his subsequent thefts. For example, one rationale for starting to steal at a new employer was to pay back former employers.

After leaving Associated, Miller was hired by a former associate at Associated. Miller underwent therapy and believed he had his problem with compulsive embezzlement resolved.

When interviewed about his past activities, Miller said that he felt his problem with theft was an illness, just like alcoholism or compulsive gambling. The illness was driven by a subconscious need to be admired and liked by others. He thought that by spending all of that money, others would like him. Ironically, he was universally well liked and admired at each job, and it had nothing to do with money. In fact, one associate at Associated was so surprised at the news of the thefts that he said that it was like finding out that your brother was an ax murderer. In the interview Miller also claimed that he is not a bad person. He says he never intended to hurt anyone, but once he got started, he just could not stop.[8]

Estimates concerning the extent of white-collar crime are staggering. In spite of the efforts of law enforcement most white-collar criminals go unpunished. As a forensic accountant, you've been asked to address a conference of top business leaders concerning the David Miller case and the prevention of fraud.

1.   How does Miller fit the profile of the average fraud perpetrator? How does he differ? How did these characteristics make him difficult to detect?

2.   Discuss the threefold fraud process (theft, conversion, concealment) Miller followed in embezzling

funds from Associated Communications. What specific technique did Miller use to conceal the fraud?

3.   What pressures motivated Miller to embezzle? What opportunities allowed him to steal and cover up his theft? How do you think Miller rationalized his actions?

4.   Miller had a framed T-shirt in his office that said, "He who dies with the most toys wins." What does this tell you about Miller? What life-style red flags could have tipped off the company to the possibility of fraud?

5.   Identify several reasons why companies hesitate in prosecuting white-collar criminals. What are the problems with such rationalizations? What could law enforcement officials do to encourage more rigorous prosecution of white-collar criminals?

6.   Identify the primary thing each of the victimized companies could have done to prevent Miller's embezzlement. What other controls could help in preventing future fraud?

---

[8] *Source:* Bryan Burrough, "David L. Miller Stole from His Employer and Isn't in Prison," *Wall Street Journal* (September 19, 1986): 1.

CHAPTER

Auditing of Computer-Based Information Systems

LEARNING OBJECTIVES

After studying this chapter, you should be able to:

- Describe the scope and objectives of audit work, and identify the major steps in the audit process.
- Identify the objectives of information systems audits, and describe a four-step approach to carrying out information systems audits to meet these objectives.
- Design a plan for the study and evaluation of internal control in a computer-based information system, and explain several techniques that may be useful in carrying out your plan.
- Describe computer audit software, and explain how it is used in the audit of computer-based information systems.
- Describe the nature and scope of operational audits.

INTEGRATIVE CASE: SEATTLE PAPER PRODUCTS

During his twelfth month at Northwest Industries, Jason Scott spends a week at the training center of one of the large Big 6 public accounting firms. There he is trained to use the CPA firm's computer audit software, which Northwest's internal audit staff is also licensed to use in their audit work. Jason had enjoyed his university computer classes, so he finds this training to be interesting and educational, although it is also hard work.

Shortly after completing this training program, Jason is assigned to a project at Seattle Paper Products, the site of his discovery of source data entry fraud only a few months earlier (see Chapter 13). Seattle

Paper is in the final stages of modifying its Sales Department payroll system to implement a change in the method of calculating sales commissions. Under the old system sales commissions were a fixed percentage of dollar sales. The new system is considerably more complex, with commission rates varying for different classes of products and increasing at higher levels of dollar sales.

Jason's assignment is to test the new system by using the computer audit software. He is told to write his own program to calculate sales commissions and to compare his results with those generated by the new system. His supervisor refers to this as a "parallel simulation test." Jason obtains the necessary payroll system documentation, including record formats for the payroll and sales transaction files, plus the details on the new sales commission policy. After asking some questions to clarify his understanding of the new policy, he begins to prepare his program. After a few days his program is ready to be run.

The systems development team has completed a test run on the new system using actual sales transaction data from the last payroll period. Jason obtains the same input file and runs it on his program. This produces a printout listing the amount of sales commission for each of the company's salespersons, plus summary totals. Jason undertakes a comparison of this printout to a comparable report generated from the systems development team's test.

To his surprise, Jason discovers that the two printouts do not match. The commission total on his printout is about $5000 less than on the test report. Individual differences exist for about half of the company's salespeople. Jason is sure that there must be an error in his program. He double-checks his program code but can't locate any errors. He selects one salesperson for whom there is a large discrepancy and recalculates the commission by hand. The result agrees with his program. He again reviews the new commission policy with the Sales Manager, line by line, to make sure that he has an accurate understanding of it. He concludes that he understands the new policy completely.

Jason is becoming convinced that his program is correct and that there must be an error in the system development team's program. But if that is true, Jason wonders, then:

1. How could a programming error of this significance be overlooked by a team of experienced programmers who have thoroughly reviewed and tested the new system?

2. Is this an inadvertent error, or could it be another attempted fraud?

3. What can be done to find the error in the system development team's program? ■

INTRODUCTION

To conclude our coverage of the control and audit of accounting information systems in Part 4, this chapter focuses on the concepts and techniques used in auditing computer-based information systems. As discussed in Chapter 12, the internal audit function is an important element of an organization's control environment, providing an independent appraisal of management performance as well as a review of the effectiveness of information systems and related internal controls. The rapid growth of the internal auditing profession in recent years reflects a growing recognition of the importance of the internal auditor on the management team.

Of course, there are a number of other categories of auditors in addition to internal auditors. For example, the General Accounting Office of the United States Congress and various legislative audit agencies of state governments employ auditors to evaluate management performance and compliance with legislative intent in government departments and bureaus. The Defense Contract Audit Agency of the Department of Defense employs auditors to review the financial records of companies having defense contracts with the government. Public accountants, or "external auditors," provide an independent review of the financial statements of publicly held corporations.

While these other types of auditors are important, this chapter is written primarily from the perspective of the internal auditor. This is consistent with the overall perspective of this book, which is to explain how business managers can design and implement accounting information systems that will be most effective in contributing to the organization's goals. Internal auditors are directly responsible for assisting management in this effort. In contrast, other types of auditors are primarily responsible to some entity or group that is external to the organization. For example, public accountants are responsible to corporate shareholders and investors for the fairness of corporate financial statements and are only indirectly concerned with the effectiveness of corporate accounting information systems. Despite this distinction, many of the internal audit concepts and techniques discussed in this chapter are applicable to other types of auditing.

This chapter is divided into four major sections. The first section provides a brief overview of the nature of auditing, the scope and objectives of internal audit work, and the steps in the auditing process. The second section describes a methodology and a set of techniques for evaluating internal controls in a computer-based information system. The third section discusses techniques for evaluating the reliability and integrity of financial and operating information maintained on the computer. The fourth section briefly reviews the process of evaluating management and operating performance in a computer-based information systems environment.

THE NATURE OF AUDITING

The American Accounting Association has formulated the following general definition of auditing.

Auditing is a systematic process of objectively obtaining and evaluating evidence regarding assertions about economic actions and events to ascertain the degree of correspondence between those assertions and established criteria and communicating the results to interested users.[1]

Certain aspects of this definition are of particular interest. For example, note that the auditor *objectively* obtains and evaluates evidence. Objectivity is critical to the credibility and usefulness of the auditor's findings, which is why the audit function should be organizationally independent of those functions it is assigned to review. Also, auditing is described as a *systematic process*, which suggests a step-by-step approach characterized by careful planning and judicious selection and execution of appropriate techniques. A later section of this chapter reviews the steps in the auditing process. Furthermore, note that auditing involves the collection, review, and documentation of audit *evidence*. Finally, in developing recommendations, the auditor uses *established criteria* as a basis for evaluation. In audits of computer-based information systems these established criteria are the principles of management and control of information systems described in earlier chapters of this book, especially Chapters 12 and 13.

While the general concepts and principles of auditing have changed little in recent years, auditing methods and techniques have changed substantially. The reason is that computer-based systems have become the dominant form of information technology for accounting systems. In modern computer-based information systems many paper documents and records that once provided a visible audit trail have been eliminated. These modern systems maintain records on machine-readable media, such as magnetic tape or disk. Record contents may be printed out infrequently or at irregular intervals. A history of the activity relating to individual records may not be maintained. With on-line processing even a printed record of input may not be produced. As a result, the methods employed to collect and evaluate audit evidence have changed significantly and continue to change.

Years ago, auditors tried to perform their audits of computerized information systems with the printed records and output provided by the system, ignoring the computer and its programs. This approach was referred to as auditing "around" the computer. The assumption underlying this approach was that if the sample of system output was correctly obtained from system input, then the processing itself must be reliable. This approach was reasonable 20 or 30 years ago, when auditors' knowledge of electronic data processing was limited. Since then, however, both the increasing difficulty of applying this approach to a disappearing audit trail and the development of better methods of auditing computer-based information systems have discredited auditing around the computer.

---

[1] Committee on Basic Auditing Concepts, *A Statement of Basic Auditing Concepts* (Sarasota, Fla.: American Accounting Association, 1973), 2.

The alternative to auditing around is referred to as auditing "through" the computer. This approach uses the computer itself to check the adequacy of system controls and the accuracy of system output. Most of the auditing techniques discussed in this chapter involve auditing through the computer.

Given the importance of internal control and the tendency for visible audit trails to be eliminated in computerized information systems, the internal auditor should have the opportunity to participate in the design phase of new systems development. In that way the auditor can review proposed systems designs and suggest the incorporation of necessary internal controls and audit trails while there is still time to implement such suggestions economically. This process will not only minimize the need for expensive modifications of systems after implementation but also reduce the testing required during the regular audit process.

In the remainder of this section we describe the scope and objectives of internal audit work and provide an overview of the steps in the auditing process.

Scope and Objectives of Audit Work

Internal Auditing Standards. According to the *Standards for the Professional Practice of Internal Auditing* promulgated by the Institute of Internal Auditors in 1978,

> the scope of the internal audit encompasses the examination and evaluation of the adequacy and effectiveness of the organization's system of internal control and the quality of performance in carrying out assigned responsibilities.[2]

The institute delineates five specific standards dealing with the following aspects of the scope of audit work.

1. Reliability and integrity of information
2. Compliance with policies, plans, procedures, laws, and regulations
3. Safeguarding of assets
4. Economical and efficient use of resources
5. Accomplishment of established objectives and goals for operations or programs

This section describes each of these five standards and discusses their implications with respect to computer-based information systems.

The first internal audit scope standard states that

> internal audits should review the reliability and integrity of financial and operating information and the means used to identify, measure, classify, and report such information.[3]

---

[2] Institute of Internal Auditors, *Standards for the Professional Practice of Internal Auditing* (Altamonte Springs, Fla.: Institute of Internal Auditors, 1978), 3.

[3] *Ibid.*, 3.

In modern organizations much of the information referred to in this standard is maintained on a computer system. Therefore the auditor must have a clear understanding of how this information is processed on the computer in order to meet this standard. Furthermore, the auditor will have to rely on the computer in order to access the information to be reviewed. To best fulfill the requirements of this standard, the auditor should use the computer itself as a primary tool for carrying out many of the necessary auditing procedures.

The second standard states that

internal auditors should review the systems established to ensure compliance with those policies, plans, procedures, laws, and regulations which could have a significant impact on operations and reports and should determine whether the organization is in compliance.[4]

There are numerous examples of policies, plans, procedures, laws, and regulations relating to computer-based information processing. These include policies on hiring, assigning, evaluating, and promoting EDP personnel; three- or five-year plans for the information processing facility; operating procedures for data processing equipment; and laws and regulations dealing with corporate financial reporting, information privacy, and internal controls. Ensuring compliance with matters such as these requires an in-depth review of the information processing facility itself.

The third scope standard states that

internal auditors should review the means of safeguarding assets and, as appropriate, verify the existence of such assets.[5]

In today's environment a review of the means of safeguarding assets is to a great extent a review of computer processing of asset information. In addition, to verify the existence of recorded assets, the auditor must use the computer to obtain a listing of the assets to be verified, because today's organizations generally use computers to account for and control such assets as inventories, plant and equipment, and receivables. Furthermore, many organizations use their computers to prepare checks.

The fourth standard is that

internal auditors should appraise the economy and efficiency with which resources are employed.[6]

This standard is applicable to all operations, departments, and managers within the organization, including the systems department. Information processing resources include both data processing equipment and personnel such as systems analysts, programmers, and equipment

---

4 *Ibid.*, 4.
5 *Ibid.*, 4.
6 *Ibid.*, 4.

operators. Chapters 8–14 of this book discuss a number of principles underlying the effective and efficient use of these resources. It is the proper application of these principles that the auditor must review in order to comply with this standard.

According to the fifth standard,

> *internal auditors should review operations or programs to ascertain whether results are consistent with established objectives and whether the operations or programs are being carried out as planned.*[7]

This standard is applicable to all parts of an organization. In the systems management area it applies to such operations and programs as feasibility studies for new systems, long-range information systems plans, and system project development activities.

Types of Internal Auditing Work. Internal auditing work consists of three major types of audits, referred to as information systems audits, financial audits, and operational audits.[8] The **information systems (IS) audit** involves a review of general and application controls associated with an organization's computer-based information systems. The scope of the IS audit roughly corresponds to the second and third standards delineated previously. Specifically, IS audits assess the information system's compliance with internal control policies and procedures and its effectiveness in safeguarding assets.

The second type of audit is the **financial audit**, which examines the reliability and integrity of accounting records and therefore correlates with the first of the five scope standards. Note that the first standard refers to both "financial and operating information," so it would perhaps make better sense to use the term *information audit*. Because of the traditional emphasis of internal auditors on financial information, however, the term *financial audit* has become generally accepted, even though the scope of such audits is expanding to encompass nonfinancial information.

The third type of audit is the **operational audit**, often referred to as the **management audit**, which involves a review of the operating performance of specific activities within an organization in comparison to organizational goals and/or other specific criteria. The scope of the operational audit corresponds to the fourth and fifth scope standards. In particular, operational audits are concerned with the economical and efficient use of resources within the organization and the accomplishment of established objectives and goals.

These three types of internal audit work are examined in this chapter. A fourth category of lesser importance is referred to as the **compliance audit**. The purpose of a compliance audit is to assess an organization's

---

[7] *Ibid.*, 4.

[8] Institute of Internal Auditors Research Foundation, *Systems Auditability and Control Report, Module 2: Audit and Control Environment* (Altamonte Springs, Fla.: Institute of Internal Auditors Research Foundation, 1991), 29.

compliance with laws, contract provisions, government regulations, and other obligations to external parties. This type of audit is a subset of the work referred to in the second scope standard. Compliance audits are not discussed further in this chapter.

An Overview of the Auditing Process

Whether performed by internal, external, or governmental auditors and whether focused on information systems internal controls, financial information, or operating performance, all audits follow a very similar sequence of activities. Generally, the auditing process may be divided into the following four stages:

1. Planning
2. Evidence collection
3. Evidence evaluation
4. Communication of results

Figure 15.1 presents an overview of the auditing process, specifying many of the procedures typically performed within each of these stages. This section discusses the auditing stages and activities in greater detail.

Audit Planning.   The purpose of audit planning is to determine why, how, and when the audit will be performed and who will perform it. The first step in audit planning is to establish the scope and objectives of the audit. These depend on whom the audit is for and what type of audit is desired. For example, the independent audit of financial statements of publicly held corporations is done for the corporate stockholders, and its purpose is to evaluate the fairness of presentation of corporate financial statements. In contrast, the scope and objectives of internal audits vary widely. For example, an internal audit may examine an entire division or subsidiary company, or a specific department or computer application; and it may focus on information systems internal controls, financial information, operating performance, or some combination of these. The scope and objectives of each internal audit engagement are established based on perceived organizational needs and opportunities for improvement.

Once the scope and objectives of the audit have been defined, an audit team is established consisting of personnel who possess the experience and expertise required to complete the audit work. Then members of the audit team must develop a general familiarity with the operations of the operating unit they will audit. Discussions with supervisory and operating personnel are useful for this purpose. Summary documentation and operating information should also be examined. A review of the findings and conclusions from any prior audits is also useful.

An important step in audit planning is to identify significant risk factors associated with the operating unit that is being audited. First, the auditor should consider inherent risk factors. For example, a system that processes large volumes of transactions involving large dollar

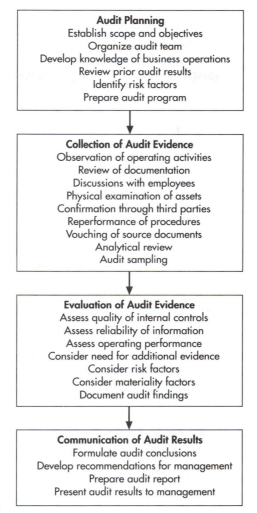

Audit Planning
Establish scope and objectives
Organize audit team
Develop knowledge of business operations
Review prior audit results
Identify risk factors
Prepare audit program

Collection of Audit Evidence
Observation of operating activities
Review of documentation
Discussions with employees
Physical examination of assets
Confirmation through third parties
Reperformance of procedures
Vouching of source documents
Analytical review
Audit sampling

Evaluation of Audit Evidence
Assess quality of internal controls
Assess reliability of information
Assess operating performance
Consider need for additional evidence
Consider risk factors
Consider materiality factors
Document audit findings

Communication of Audit Results
Formulate audit conclusions
Develop recommendations for management
Prepare audit report
Present audit results to management

Figure 15.1
Overview of the auditing process

amounts has a high level of inherent risk. A system that employs on-line processing, networks, data base software, telecommunications, and other forms of advanced technology has more inherent risk than a traditional batch processing system. Next, the auditor should assess control risk by undertaking a preliminary review of the control environment. The auditor should also consider any control weaknesses identified in prior audits and evaluate how they have been rectified. The purpose of these risk assessment procedures is to assist the auditor in allocating audit effort. Specifically, greater audit effort should be focused on those aspects of the audit engagement where risk factors are greatest.

To conclude the planning stage, the auditor prepares a preliminary audit program that delineates the nature, extent, and timing of specific audit tests and procedures that will achieve the desired audit objectives and minimize the related audit risks. In conjunction with this step a preliminary time budget for the audit is prepared, and audit staff members are assigned to perform specific portions of the audit work. This audit program is "preliminary" in the sense that it may be revised during the audit if necessary in view of the audit findings.

Collection of Audit Evidence. The bulk of the audit effort is expended in the process of collecting audit evidence. Audit evidence is gathered using a number of different kinds of tests and procedures. Some of the most commonly used methods of collecting audit evidence are briefly reviewed here. First, auditors may *observe* the activities of employees within the operating unit being audited—for example, by watching how employees enter the computer site or how data control personnel handle data processing work as it is received. Second, auditors might perform a *review of documentation* to develop a detailed understanding about how a particular information system or internal control system is supposed to function. Third, auditors may have *discussions* with employees about their jobs and how they carry out certain procedures; these discussions are often facilitated by standardized questionnaires or interview checklists. Fourth, auditors may *physically examine* the quantity and/or condition of tangible assets such as equipment, inventory, or cash. Fifth, auditors may *confirm* the accuracy of certain information by communicating with independent third parties—for example, by asking customers to confirm their account balances. Sixth, auditors may *reperform* selected calculations in order to verify quantitative information on records and reports; for example, the auditor could recompute a batch total or recalculate the annual depreciation charge. Seventh, auditors may *vouch* for the validity of a transaction by examining all supporting documents, such as the purchase order, receiving report, and vendor invoice supporting an accounts payable transaction. Eighth, auditors may perform an *analytical review* of relationships and trends among financial and operating information in order to detect items that should be further investigated. As an example of the value of analytical review, consider the auditor for a chain of dress shops who discovered that the ratio of accounts receivable to sales for one shop was far too high. This triggered an investigation that revealed that funds had been diverted from collections to personal use by the dress shop manager.[9]

A given audit will consist of a mix of these and other audit tests and procedures. The specific procedures utilized will depend on the audit objectives. For example, an audit designed to evaluate information systems internal controls would probably make greater use of observation, review of documentation, discussions with employees, and reperformance of control procedures; while an audit of the veracity of

---

[9] E. Theodore Keys, Jr., "Round Table," *Internal Auditor* (August 1990): 77.

reported financial information would make greater use of physical examination, confirmation, vouching, analytical review, and reperformance of account balance calculations. It is also appropriate to point out that many audit tests and procedures cannot feasibly be performed on the entire set of activities, records, assets, or documents under review and so must be performed on a sample basis.

Evaluation of Audit Evidence.   Once all the audit evidence has been gathered, the auditor must evaluate the entire body of evidence in relation to the audit objective and then decide whether (1) the evidence supports a favorable conclusion with respect to the operations, controls, or information being audited; (2) the evidence supports an unfavorable or negative conclusion; or (3) the available evidence is inconclusive and more evidence is required, in which case the auditor will plan and execute additional procedures until satisfied that sufficient evidence has been obtained to reach a definitive conclusion.

In making the evaluation decision, the auditor utilizes the concepts of **materiality** and **reasonable assurance**. That is, the auditor seeks reasonable assurance that there is not a material error or deficiency in the information or process being audited. The concept of reasonable assurance implies that the auditor does not seek complete assurance, because to do so would be prohibitively expensive; the auditor is willing to accept some degree of risk that the audit conclusion will be incorrect. Risk assessment is important here, because when inherent risk or control risk is high, the auditor faces greater uncertainty and must obtain greater assurance from the audit procedures in order to offset this greater uncertainty. The concept of materiality recognizes that some errors or deficiencies are bound to exist in any system, and therefore the auditor should focus on detecting and reporting only those errors and deficiencies that could possibly have a significant impact on management's interpretation of the audit findings. Determining what is and what is not material in a given set of circumstances is primarily a matter of judgment. It should be noted that consideration of materiality and reasonable assurance is important both at the audit planning stage, when the auditor is deciding how much audit work is necessary, and at the evidence evaluation stage.

As the audit proceeds, the auditor should carefully document his or her findings and conclusions in a set of audit working papers. Documentation should occur at all stages of the audit, but it is especially critical at the evaluation stage when final conclusions must be reached and supported.

Communication of Audit Results.   Once the audit evidence has been evaluated and the audit findings documented, the auditor formulates a final set of conclusions and recommendations to be communicated to management. The vehicle for this communication usually consists of a written report summarizing the audit findings and recommendations, with references to supporting evidence in the related working papers.

This report is provided to management, the audit committee, the board of directors, or other appropriate parties. In some cases an oral presentation may accompany the written report. At some point following the communication of audit results the auditor may perform a follow-up study to ascertain whether his or her recommendations have been implemented.

This completes our brief overview of the nature of auditing, the different types of audit work, and the steps in the auditing process. For those who seek a more in-depth treatment of the subject, we suggest reading one of the numerous textbooks available.[10] We have attempted to provide only the background information necessary for readers to understand the objectives of auditors and the methods they employ when performing an information systems audit, a financial audit, or an operational audit. These three types of audits are examined in greater detail in the following sections.

INFORMATION SYSTEMS AUDITS

The purpose of an information systems (IS) audit is to review and evaluate the internal controls that are in place to protect the security and reliability of the information system and its operations and applications. There are a variety of techniques employed in IS audits, and most presentations on this topic simply list and describe these techniques. We believe that it is more useful to focus on the *objectives* of performing an IS audit and the *process* of designing and carrying out auditing procedures to meet these objectives. We introduce and explain specific techniques only in relation to the objectives they help meet and the stage in the process where they are most useful. In this way our readers should learn not only the techniques of IS auditing but also when and why each technique is most useful.

In performing a complete IS audit, the auditor should attempt to accomplish each of the six objectives listed next. In many cases a complete audit will not be called for, and the auditor may wish to achieve only one, or a limited number, of these objectives. The objectives are as follows:

1. To ascertain that security provisions are in place to protect computer equipment, programs, and data files from unauthorized access, modification, or destruction

2. To ascertain that the design and implementation of application programs is performed in accordance with management's general and specific authorization

3. To ascertain that any and all modifications in application programs have the authorization and approval of management

---

[10] For example, see Alvin A. Arens and James K. Loebbecke, *Auditing: An Integrated Approach,* 5th ed. (Englewood Cliffs, N.J.: Prentice-Hall, 1991); or Jack C. Robertson, *Auditing,* 7th ed. (Homewood, Ill.: Irwin, 1993).

4. To ascertain that provisions exist to ensure the accuracy and integrity of computer processing of transactions, files, reports, and other computer records

5. To ascertain that application program source data that are inaccurate or not properly authorized are identified and dealt with in accordance with prescribed managerial policies

6. To ascertain that provisions exist to preserve the accuracy, completeness and confidentiality of computer data files

A diagram showing the relationship of these objectives to the various components of a computer-based information processing system appears in Fig. 15.2. This section discusses each of these objectives in turn, describing an audit plan to accomplish each objective and explaining the auditing techniques and procedures used to carry out the audit plan.

Figure 15.2
Information systems components and related IS audit objectives

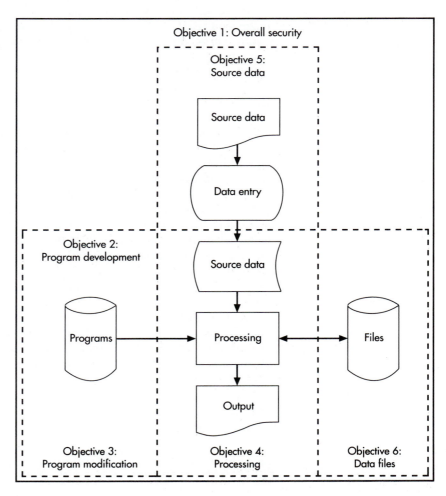

The following four-step approach to internal control evaluation provides a logical framework for carrying out an IS audit to realize these objectives.[11]

1. Consider the types of errors and irregularities that could occur.

2. Determine the accounting control procedures that should prevent or detect such errors and irregularities.

3. Determine whether the necessary procedures are prescribed and are being followed satisfactorily.

4. Evaluate any weaknesses, i.e., types of potential errors and irregularities not covered by existing control procedures—to determine their effect on (a) the nature, timing, or extent of auditing procedures to be applied and (b) suggestions to be made to the client.

This framework is consistent with what is sometimes called a "risk-based" audit approach, in the sense that it begins by delineating the threats or risks facing the information system (step 1). Then the auditor must identify the control procedures that should be in place to minimize each risk (step 2) and plan the audit to review and evaluate those control procedures (step 3). Note that step 3 has two parts. The examination of "whether the necessary procedures are prescribed" is called the **system review**, and the determination of whether these procedures "are being followed satisfactorily" is made via **tests of controls**. Generally, the system review will consist of such audit procedures as reviewing system documentation and interviewing appropriate personnel. Audit procedures most commonly associated with tests of controls include observing system operations; inspecting documents, records, and reports; checking samples of system inputs and outputs; and tracing transactions through the system.

A key element of the risk-based audit approach is the evaluation of control weaknesses (step 4). Suppose that the review and evaluation process reveals that there is a standard control procedure that is not being used. Is this a problem? If the auditor is simply filling out an internal control checklist or questionnaire, it will be difficult to assess the impact of a particular control deficiency. However, under the risk-based approach the focus is not on the control procedures directly but, rather, on the control risks and whether the control system as a whole adequately addresses those risks. So if a control deficiency is identified, the auditor asks whether there are **compensating controls**, other control procedures that are in place that should compensate for the deficiency by minimizing the related risks. If there is a control weakness with respect to a particular type of error or irregularity, the auditor should consider whether compensating controls exist that will minimize the

---

[11] This four-step approach was advocated by the AICPA in its *Statement on Auditing Standards (SAS) No. 1,* AU Sec. 320.65 (New York: American Institute of Certified Public Accountants, 1973). Although this section of the auditing standards was superseded by SAS No. 55, issued in 1988, this four-step approach still provides an excellent method of reviewing and evaluating internal controls in a logical manner.

risk or reduce the exposure relating to that type of error or irregularity. It is not uncommon for controls to overlap with respect to certain types of errors and irregularities, because the concept of redundancy is central to many kinds of control systems. So control weaknesses in one area may be acceptable if they are compensated for by control strengths in other areas.

Once the system review and tests of controls have been completed with respect to each objective, and once the adequacy of compensating controls has been considered, the auditor should have a clear understanding of the kinds of errors and irregularities that could occur and of the related risks and exposures. This understanding provides a sound basis for developing recommendations to management on how the IS control system should be improved.

Objective 1: Security

For the four-step approach described previously a framework for the audit of security policies and practices in a computer facility is listed in Table 15.1. The focus here is on controls over physical access to computer equipment, logical access to computer programs and data files, and contingency plans for system failures or severe disasters. The potential errors and irregularities include accidental or intentional damage to computer equipment and files; unauthorized access to programs, data files, and other system resources; theft or unauthorized modification of programs or data files; unauthorized disclosure of confidential data; and interruption of critical business activities.

Numerous control procedures should be in place to prevent these security problems. As described in Chapter 13, controls include restrictions on physical access to computer equipment, including not only the mainframe and its peripheral equipment but also personal computers and data communications equipment; logical access controls utilizing passwords for user authentication; encryption of data during storage and transmission; virus protection procedures; file backup and recovery procedures; fault-tolerant systems design including the use of preventive maintenance, uninterruptible power supplies, and duplicate system components; and a disaster recovery plan that has been soundly conceived and thoroughly tested.

During the system review phase of the security evaluation the auditor should inspect computer sites to become familiar with the physical layout and access points. The auditor should interview information systems personnel responsible for computer security and review related administrative documentation to learn about the security policies and procedures that have been established to restrict both physical and logical access to the system. Documentation relating to file backup and recovery policies and procedures should also be reviewed. The auditor should review logs that identify the timing and duration of system access by authorized personnel. Through discussions with IS personnel or review of system documentation the auditor should determine the extent of use of fault-tolerant systems design techniques. Finally, the auditor should carefully examine copies of the disaster recovery

Types of Errors and Irregularities	
• Accidental or intentional damage to computer equipment and files • Unauthorized access to programs, data files, and other system resources	• Theft or unauthorized modification of programs and data files • Unauthorized disclosure of confidential data • Interruption of critical business activities

Control Procedures	
• Restrictions on physical access to computer equipment • Logical access controls based on password protection • Encryption of data during storage and transmission • Virus protection procedures	• File backup and recovery procedures • Fault-tolerant systems design • Disaster recovery planning

Audit Procedures: System Review	
• Inspect computer sites • Interview IS personnel about security procedures • Review written documentation about physical access policies and procedures • Review logical access policies and procedures	• Examine system access logs • Review file backup and recovery policies and procedures • Review procedures employed to minimize system downtime • Examine disaster recovery plan • Examine casualty insurance policies

Audit Procedures: Tests of Controls	
• Observe computer site access procedures • Review records of password assignment and modification • Investigate how cases of attempted unauthorized access were dealt with • Verify the extent of use of data encryption • Verify the effective use of virus protection procedures	• Verify the use of preventive maintenance and uninterruptible power • Observe the preparation and off-site storage of backup files • Verify amounts and limitations on insurance coverage • Examine results of test simulations of disaster recovery plan

Compensating Controls	
• Sound personnel policies • Effective user controls	• Segregation of incompatible duties

Table 15.1
Framework for audit of computer security

plan and of insurance policies providing coverage for losses attributable to fire, sabotage, and natural disasters.

The auditor should begin testing security controls by observing access points to the computer center to verify that access is controlled according to prescribed policies. Such observation should encompass evening and overnight shifts if significant application programs are processed at those times. To test logical access controls, the auditor should study a sample of password assignment requests for evidence of compliance with prescribed procedures. The auditor should verify that passwords are never displayed or printed and are changed on a frequent basis. The auditor should examine a sample of assigned passwords and their associated access authority to determine whether the password holders have access authority incompatible with their other responsibilities. Logs of attempts by unauthorized users to access the system should be examined for evidence that such attempts are identified and recorded, reviewed by security personnel on a regular basis, and adequately investigated and resolved.

One method that may be used to test the effectiveness of logical access controls is for the auditor to attempt to gain access to the system in an unauthorized manner. For example, during a 1989 security audit of a U.S. federal government agency, auditors from the agency's inspector general offices used the agency's own terminals to gain unauthorized access to its central computer system, disable its security-checking procedures, and convert the terminals into the functional equivalent of a master operator's console. The auditors attributed this security breakdown to poor administrative controls and lack of adequate security software and offered several recommendations on how access security should be improved.[12]

If data encryption is employed, the auditor's tests should include verification that data are encrypted according to the policies established by management. The auditor should verify that effective virus protection programs have been installed in all computers. The auditor should inspect duplicate system components and uninterruptible power supplies and verify that they are operational. The auditor should examine computer maintenance records to confirm that preventive maintenance procedures are regularly followed. The auditor should observe the preparation of backup file copies and verify that they are promptly removed and stored in a secure off-site location.

The auditor should also confirm that the organization's disaster recovery plan contains a current inventory of all hardware and software, identifies the computer applications that are most critical to the continuity of business operations, includes formal agreements for the use of a disaster recovery site with a suitable system configuration, assigns specific responsibilities for disaster recovery activities, includes a schedule of required emergency actions, and is regularly updated as conditions change. The auditor should also verify that the disaster recovery plan has undergone a rigorous test and that any deficiencies in the plan revealed by the test have been satisfactorily corrected.[13] Finally, the auditor should evaluate the adequacy of the organization's insurance coverages with respect to disasters that disable or destroy its computer systems.

If the auditor concludes that computer security controls are seriously deficient, the organization faces substantial risks to its computer facilities and data and possibly to its future viability. There are no other

---

[12] Kevin Power, "Security Guidance Is Urged for Government Computer Centers," *Government Computer News* (February 6, 1989): 89–90.

[13] For an excellent discussion on auditing the disaster recovery plan, see Bruce J. Lamond, "An Auditing Approach to Disaster Recovery," *Internal Auditor* (October 1990): 38–48.

controls that can fully compensate for this. Sound personnel policies and effective segregation of incompatible duties can partially, but not completely, ameliorate the effects of poor computer security. Good user controls will also help, if user personnel are essentially able to recognize anything unusual in the output they receive from the computer. However, it is unlikely that even the combination of these controls can continue to compensate indefinitely for poor computer security. Hence an auditor who concludes that the organization's computer security is weak should strongly recommend that steps be taken to correct the weaknesses.

Objective 2: Program Development

The focus of the second objective is on the program development process, particularly as it relates to accounting application programs. A framework for the review and evaluation of program development control procedures is given in Table 15.2. Essentially, two things could go wrong in this process. First, errors could be inadvertently introduced into the programs through misunderstanding of system specifi-

Table 15.2
Framework for audit of program development

Types of Errors and Irregularities	
• Inadvertent programming errors	• Unauthorized program code
Control Procedures	
• Management approval of programming specifications	• User acceptance testing
• User approval of programming specifications	• Complete systems documentation, including approvals
• Thorough testing of new programs	
Audit Procedures: System Review	
• Independent and concurrent review of systems development process	• Review program testing and test approval procedures
• Review systems development policies and procedures	• Discuss systems development procedures with:
• Review systems authorization and approval procedures	Management
• Review programming evaluation standards	System users
• Review program documentation standards	IS personnel
	• Review final applications systems documentation
Audit Procedures: Tests of Controls	
• Interview users about involvement in systems design and implementation	• Verify user sign-off at milestone points in the development process
• Review minutes of development team meetings for evidence of involvement	• Review test specifications, test data, and results of systems tests
Compensating Controls	
• Strong processing controls	• Independent processing of test data by auditor

cations or careless programming. Second, unauthorized instructions could be deliberately inserted into the programs by persons whose motives are contrary to those of management.

The control procedures that should prevent these problems involve the quality and integrity of the process of systems analysis, design, and implementation. Generally, specifications for application programs should have the authorization and approval of management and, in particular, the approval of those functional departments and system users whose operations are affected by the new system. New systems should be thoroughly tested, and test results should be approved. Finally, the system itself and all related authorizations and approvals should be well documented.

The auditor who participates in the systems design process is in a position to influence the project manager to follow these preferred practices. However, the auditor's role should be limited to an independent review of, rather than participation in, systems development activities. This limitation is important because there is a danger that the auditor will lose the objectivity necessary to perform an independent evaluation function. For maximum effectiveness this independent review by the auditor should take place *during* the systems development process.

During the system review stage of the examination the auditor should obtain copies of written policies and procedures pertaining to systems development. He or she should then review those standards that relate to the authorization and approval of new systems, the involvement of user departments and other appropriate personnel in the systems design process, the review and evaluation of programmer output, the documentation and testing of new systems, and the review and approval of test results. The auditor should discuss these prescribed policies and procedures with management, system users, and IS personnel to determine their understanding of how such policies and procedures are intended to be applied. Finally, the auditor should review in some detail the application systems documentation.

The auditor's tests of controls with respect to systems development policies should include interviews with managers and system users to ascertain the extent of their involvement in the design and implementation of specific application systems. In addition, evidence of such involvement, in the form of participation in systems development groups and signed approvals at various stages of the development process, should be sought. Obtaining the former involves reviewing minutes of meetings of systems teams. Procuring the latter requires checking system specifications, preliminary systems design documentation, test data specifications, test results, and records of final conversion for signatures evidencing the necessary authorizations and approvals.

One of the most important controls over new system development is the processing of test data. The auditor should review thoroughly all available client documentation relating to the testing process and should ascertain that all program routines affecting accounting data were tested. The auditor should examine the test specifications, review the test data, and evaluate the test results. When unexpected test results were obtained, the auditor should ascertain how the problem was resolved.

The review and evaluation of internal controls relating to information systems development should be performed for each significant application program. Once this review has been completed for a particular application, it need not be done again in future years. Therefore the auditor should regularly perform such reviews only for newly developed application programs. For ongoing applications the auditor's concern shifts to controls over program changes, the focus of the third of our six objectives.

An inadequacy in systems development controls for a particular application program may be compensated for by the presence of strong processing controls (see objective 4). If compensatory processing controls are to be relied on, however, the auditor should obtain persuasive evidence of compliance with these controls through such techniques as independent processing of test data. If it is not possible to obtain evidence of effective compensating controls, the auditor may have to conclude that a material weakness in internal control exists such that the risk of significant errors or irregularities in application programs is unacceptably high.

Objective 3:
Program Modification

Table 15.3 presents a framework for the audit of controls over program changes. Essentially, the same things can go wrong with respect to program changes as with respect to new program development. First, errors can be inadvertently introduced into programs undergoing an authorized change either because of a misunderstanding of change specifications or because of careless programming. Second, unauthorized instructions can be deliberately inserted into existing programs. For example, one programmer assigned to modify his company's payroll system inserted a command to erase all company files if a termination notice was ever entered into his own payroll record. Later the programmer was fired and the termination notice duly entered into the system, which immediately crashed.

The auditor's concerns about programming errors and unauthorized program code pertain mainly to application programs. However, these problems could potentially affect systems software, such as data base systems, operating systems, and utility programs. Accordingly, the suggested internal controls and audit procedures discussed in this section apply to all types of programs maintained by the information systems department.

Internal controls should exist to ensure the authorization, documentation, review, testing, and approval of all program changes. User personnel should participate in the authorization, testing, and final approval processes. When a program change is submitted for approval, it should include a list of all components of the program that are to be

Types of Errors and Irregularities	
■ Inadvertent programming errors	■ Unauthorized program code

Control Procedures	
■ Management authorization and approval of program modifications ■ Listing of program components that are to be modified ■ User approval of program change specifications ■ Thorough testing of program changes, including user acceptance test ■ Prepare complete program change documentation, including approvals	■ Maintain separate development, test, and production versions of program ■ Changes implemented by personnel independent of users and programmers ■ Logical access controls

Audit Procedures: System Review	

■ Review program modification policies, standards, and procedures
■ Review documentation standards for program modification
■ Review program modification testing and test approval procedures
■ Discuss program modification policies and procedures with:
    Management
    System users
    IS personnel
	■ Review final documentation for some typical program modifications
	■ Review test specifications, test data, and results of systems tests
	■ Review logical access control policies and procedures

Audit Procedures: Tests of Controls	

■ Verify user and IS management approval for program changes
■ Verify that program components to be modified are identified and listed
■ Verify that program change test procedures comply with standards
■ Verify that program change documentation complies with standards
■ Verify that logical access controls are in effect for program changes
	■ Observe a program change being implemented and verify that:
	    Separate development, test, and production versions are maintained
	    Changes are not implemented by either user or programming personnel
	■ To test for unauthorized or erroneous program changes, use:
	    Source code comparison program
	    Reprocessing
	    Parallel simulation

Compensating Controls	
■ Independent audit tests for unauthorized or erroneous program changes	■ Strong processing controls

Table 15.3

Framework for audit of program modification procedures

modified. During the program change process, separate versions of the program should be maintained for development and testing purposes, and these versions should be kept isolated from the current production version of the program. After the amended program has received final approval, the change is implemented by replacing the production version of the program with the development version; it is important that this implementation process be carried out by personnel who are organizationally independent of both the user and programming functions. Finally, logical access controls must be in place to prevent deliberate and unauthorized program modification.

The auditor's system review of program change procedures should include the examination of written policies and standards, including standards relating to the documentation, testing, and approval of program changes. The auditor should hold discussions with IS and user personnel concerning how these policies and standards are supposed to be applied. The auditor should also review a complete set of final documentation materials for a limited number of recent program changes, including details on the program change testing procedures and test results. Finally, the auditor should review procedures relating to the use of logical access controls to restrict access to the development and test versions of amended programs.

An important part of the auditor's tests of program change controls is the examination of change documentation to verify that (1) user and IS management approval procedures are observed, (2) program components to be modified are identified and listed, (3) program change documentation is complete and in compliance with standards, and (4) program change test procedures have been carried out effectively. In addition, the auditor should observe the implementation of a typical program change in order to verify that separate development and test versions of the program are maintained independent of the current production version, and that approved program changes are implemented by personnel who are independent of the user and programming functions. The auditor should review the access control table for the development and test versions of programs undergoing modification to verify that access to these program versions is restricted to only those individuals who have been assigned to carry out the program modification process.

A powerful tool to test for the presence of unauthorized program changes is a source code comparison program, which performs a detailed comparison of two sets of program source code and identifies all differences. To use this tool, the auditor must prepare and maintain a copy of each source program that is to be tested. Ideally, this copy will be made by the auditor at the time the source program is implemented so that the auditor can have confidence in its integrity. At any subsequent time the auditor may use the source code comparison program to compare the installation's current version of the program with the original source code. If no changes have been authorized, these two versions should be identical, so any differences identified here are cause for concern and must be investigated. The auditor can also use a source code comparison program to verify that an application program has been modified strictly in accordance with specifications. In this case the comparison process will identify differences, and the auditor must review each difference to verify that it represents an authorized change. To perform this review, the auditor must refer to the program change specifications to ascertain which segments of the program were approved for modification.

Two additional techniques that use the computer to detect unauthorized program changes are reprocessing and parallel simulation. To use the **reprocessing** technique, the auditor must verify the integrity of a copy of the application program and then save that copy for future use. At subsequent intervals, on a surprise basis, the auditor uses the previously verified version of the program to reprocess data that have been processed by the current version, and the outputs of the two runs are compared. Any discrepancies in the two sets of output are then investigated to ascertain their cause.

Parallel simulation is similar to reprocessing, except that instead of using a previously verified copy of the application program, the auditor writes his or her own version of the program or of those parts of the program that are of audit interest. The auditor's version of the program is then used to reprocess the data, and the output is compared with the output from the current version of the program. This technique may be used to provide an independent test of a program during the implementation process, as, for example, in the test of Seattle Paper's new sales department payroll system performed by Jason Scott. The Seattle Paper case is also a good example of how parallel simulation may be used to test only a portion of a program instead of the entire program.

The auditor's review of program change controls should encompass each significant application program and should be repeated periodically. In fact, whenever the organization is implementing a major change in an application program, the auditor should be called in to observe the testing and implementation, to review related authorizations and documents, and, if necessary, to perform independent tests. If this is not done and the auditor's subsequent examination reveals inadequacies in the program change controls, it may not be possible to rely on the accuracy of program outputs subsequent to the change. In addition, the auditor should always perform some program tests on a surprise basis as a precaution against unauthorized program changes that may be inserted after the auditor's examination is completed and then removed prior to the next scheduled audit.

If the auditor concludes that internal controls over program changes are deficient, a compensating control is the auditor's own performance of independent tests using source code comparison, reprocessing, or parallel simulation. In addition, the presence of excellent processing controls, also independently tested by the auditor, may partially compensate for such deficiencies. However, if these deficiencies are caused by inadequate restrictions on access to program files, the auditor should strongly recommend that steps be taken to strengthen the organization's logical access controls.

Objective 4: Processing   The focus of the fourth objective is on computer processing of transactions, master files, and related computer records for purposes of updating files and data bases and generating reports. A framework for the audit of computer processing controls is given in Table 15.4. During computer processing several things could go wrong. The system might fail to detect incorrect, incomplete, or unauthorized transaction data. Attempts to correct erroneous input flagged by data editing procedures could fail or could introduce additional errors. File update procedures could introduce errors into master file or data base records due to improper operating procedures, system malfunctions, or program errors of either a deliberate or an unintentional nature. Computer output could be distributed improperly or be accessed by unauthorized persons. The fourth objective is to ascertain that processing controls exist to prevent or to detect and correct these kinds of problems.

The processing controls that should be present in a well-managed data processing facility include data edit routines in application programs, file labeling, reconciliation of batch totals, effective error correction procedures, understandable operating documentation and run manuals, competent supervision of computer operations, effective handling of input and output by data control personnel, file change listings and summaries prepared for user department review, and the maintenance of proper levels of temperature, humidity, and other environmental conditions in the computer facility.

The auditor's system review of processing controls should begin with a review of documentation. Administrative documentation should be studied to obtain an understanding of the organization's standards relating to the use of batch totals and file labels, correction of errors flagged by data entry, maintenance of suitable environmental conditions in the computer facility, and distribution of computer output. The systems documentation for selected accounting applications should be reviewed to ascertain the nature of the data editing procedures and other processing controls employed. Samples of operating documentation for application programs should also be reviewed and evaluated for completeness and clarity. In addition, the auditor should review copies of error listings generated by data edit routines and of batch total reports and file change listings generated by file update processes. The auditor should also observe the computer operations and data control functions while application programs are being processed to develop an understanding of the way in which data processing work flows through the computer center. Finally, the auditor should interview computer operators, data control personnel, operations supervisors, IS management, and other appropriate personnel to determine how the processing controls are supposed to be applied.

As part of the testing of processing controls, the auditor should evaluate the adequacy of controls prescribed by run manuals and other operating documentation and then observe computer operations for evidence that these prescribed controls are actually being followed. Specific processes that the auditor should observe are the logging of input and work in progress by data control personnel, the reconciliation of batch control totals, the checking of file labels and other file-

Types of Errors and Irregularities	
• Failure to detect incorrect, incomplete, or unauthorized input data • Failure to properly correct errors flagged by data editing procedures	• Introduction of errors into master files during file updating • Improper distribution or disclosure of computer output
Control Procedures	
• Computer data editing routines • Proper use of internal and external file labels • Reconciliation of batch totals • Effective error correction procedures • Understandable operating documentation and run manuals • Competent supervision of computer operations	• Effective handling of data input and output by data control personnel • File change listings and summaries prepared for user department review • Maintenance of proper environmental conditions in computer facility
Audit Procedures: System Review	
• Review administrative documentation for processing control standards • Review systems documentation for data editing and other processing controls • Review operating documentation for completeness and clarity	• Review copies of error listings, batch total reports, and file change lists • Observe computer operations and data control functions • Discuss processing controls with operators and IS supervisory personnel
Audit Procedures: Tests of Controls	

• Evaluate adequacy of processing control standards and procedures
• Evaluate adequacy and completeness of data editing controls
• Verify adherence to processing control procedures by observing
    Computer operations
    Data control function
• Verify that selected application system output is properly distributed
• Verify adherence to prescribed environmental controls
• Reconcile a sample of batch totals, and follow up on discrepancies
• Trace disposition of a sample of errors flagged by data edit routines
	• Verify processing accuracy for a sample of sensitive transactions
	• Verify processing accuracy for selected computer-generated transactions
	• Search for erroneous or unauthorized code via analysis of program logic
	• Check accuracy and completeness of processing controls using test data
	• Monitor on-line processing systems using concurrent audit techniques

Compensating Controls	
• Strong user controls	• Effective source data controls

Table 15.4
Framework for audit
of computer processing controls

handling procedures, the distribution of computer output, and adherence to prescribed environmental controls. The auditor should perform an independent test of the reconciliation of a sample of batch control totals with corresponding input totals and follow up on any discrepancies. The auditor should also verify that outputs generated by accounting application programs have been properly distributed to authorized recipients.

The auditor should evaluate the adequacy of data edit routines incorporated into application programs and then review the output of such programs for evidence that the edit tests were applied. Procedures for follow-up and correction of edit errors should be observed and evaluated. The auditor should also trace the disposition of a sample of errors flagged by data edit programs to verify that these have been properly dealt with. Additional assurance as to the adequacy of data editing may be obtained by using computer audit software to independently edit selected accounting files, as explained in a later section of this chapter. The use of test data is another method of testing the data edit provisions that have been incorporated into application programs. By presenting test transactions to computer operators as if they were live data, the auditor can test the operating procedures for dealing with unusual or erroneous transactions.

There are certain types of accounting transactions that are subject to greater control risk and exposure than more routine transactions. Among these are changes in customer credit ratings, product prices, approved suppliers, and employee pay rates. Also in this category are transactions generated automatically by the computer system as a byproduct of routine processing—for example, a purchase order generated when an inventory balance falls below a critical reorder level. The auditor should obtain evidence that output listings of these kinds of transactions are regularly prepared and reviewed by appropriate user department personnel. The auditor may also wish to select a sample of these transactions and verify their authenticity by comparing them with user department records or by confirming them with independent third parties.

Generally, it will be necessary for the auditor to reevaluate the processing controls periodically in order to justify continuing confidence in them. If the auditor concludes that the organization's processing controls with respect to some or all application programs are not satisfactory, he or she may nonetheless decide that internal controls in the related user departments (user controls) and source data controls are strong enough to compensate for such deficiencies. If these alternative controls are not sufficient to compensate for the deficiencies in processing controls, however, the auditor must conclude that a material weakness exists in the organization's internal control system and should strongly recommend that steps be taken to eliminate the control deficiencies.

Several specialized techniques allow the auditor to use the computer to test data edit routines and other processing controls in application systems. They include (1) analysis of program logic, (2) processing of test data, (3) on-line testing, and (4) using concurrent audit techniques. The nature and application of each of these techniques are explained in the following paragraphs.

Analysis of Program Logic. If the auditor suspects or uncovers evidence indicating that a particular application program may contain unauthorized code or serious errors, then a detailed analysis of some or all of the program logic may be necessary. This is a time-consuming procedure that requires the auditor to be proficient in the programming language. Therefore it should be used only when no alternative method is available to accomplish the auditor's objective. To perform such an analysis, the auditor would normally refer to systems flowcharts, program flowcharts, and other program documentation in addition to a listing of the program source code. There are various software packages the auditor may use to assist in this analysis, including **automated flowcharting programs**, which interpret the program source code and generate a program flowchart corresponding to it; **automated decision table programs**, which generate a decision table representing the program logic; and **scanning routines**, which search a program for occurrences of a specified variable name or other combinations of characters.

The auditor's analysis of program logic is enhanced by information about how the program actually functions when it is processed. Two software techniques that provide such information are mapping programs and program tracing. **Mapping programs** can be activated during regular processing of application programs to identify those portions of the application program that are not executed. Mapping programs help the auditor to identify unauthorized program code that is not executed unless it is triggered by some event. An example described earlier is the command inserted by an unscrupulous programmer to erase all company files if and when a termination notice was entered into his payroll record.

Program tracing is a technique that enables the auditor to obtain a detailed knowledge of the logic of an application program as well as test the program's compliance with its control specifications. To use this technique, the auditor processes the application program either with regular or test transactions but activates a trace routine built into the systems software. This routine causes the computer to print out in sequential order a list of all the application program steps (line numbers or paragraph names) executed during the program run. This list is intermingled with the regular program output so that the auditor can observe the precise sequence of events occurring during program execution. The auditor then reviews a copy of the source program in conjunction with the trace output to confirm expectations of the way the program works. Program tracing enables the auditor to detect the presence of unauthorized program instructions, incorrect logic paths, or unexecuted sections of application programs. Such conditions should be investigated further to ascertain their cause and effect.

Processing of Test Data. Processing test data involves the introduction of hypothetical transactions into an information system application to check the completeness and accuracy of the system's processing and control procedures. Previous chapters have referred to this technique as an important means of testing new computer programs before they become operational. It used to be referred to as the "test deck" approach, because punched cards were once the primary medium for introducing the test transactions.

Figure 15.3 is a systems flowchart depicting the processing of test data to test a batch processing application. As the first step in this process, the auditor reviews the system documentation to develop a clear understanding of the nature and function of the program being tested and to determine the content of input transaction records. The auditor should identify edit routines, other processing controls, and alternative logic paths within the application program and then prepare a set of hypothetical transactions containing both valid and invalid data that will test all portions of the program having audit significance. Examples of the kinds of invalid data that might be included are records with missing data, fields containing unreasonably large amounts, unusual relationships among data in two or more fields, invalid account numbers or processing codes, nonnumeric data in numeric fields, records out of sequence, and erroneous batch totals. Some transactions should contain multiple errors. All the alternative logic paths should be checked for proper functioning by one or more of the test transactions.

To facilitate the preparation of test transactions, the auditor may obtain a listing of actual transactions as well as test transactions used by the programmer. The programmer's test data may be useful for reference purposes, but the auditor should perform an independent test using independently prepared test data. If available, the auditor may use a **test data generator** program to automatically prepare a set of test data based on specifications describing the logical characteristics of the program to be tested.

Once the hypothetical transactions have been prepared, the auditor should review a listing of the current version of the master file or files maintained by the application program and manually determine what the expected results of processing the test transactions should be. The test data are then introduced into the system, either as source documents (as shown in Fig. 15.3) or in machine-readable form at a subsequent processing step. Alternatively, the auditor may process the test data independently of the organization's data processing personnel.

After the test data have been processed, the actual system output—including error reports or logs, batch control reports, documents, management reports, and a printout of the updated master file records—is compared with the predetermined correct output. Any discrepancies indicate potential deficiencies in processing controls and should be thoroughly investigated to determine their cause.

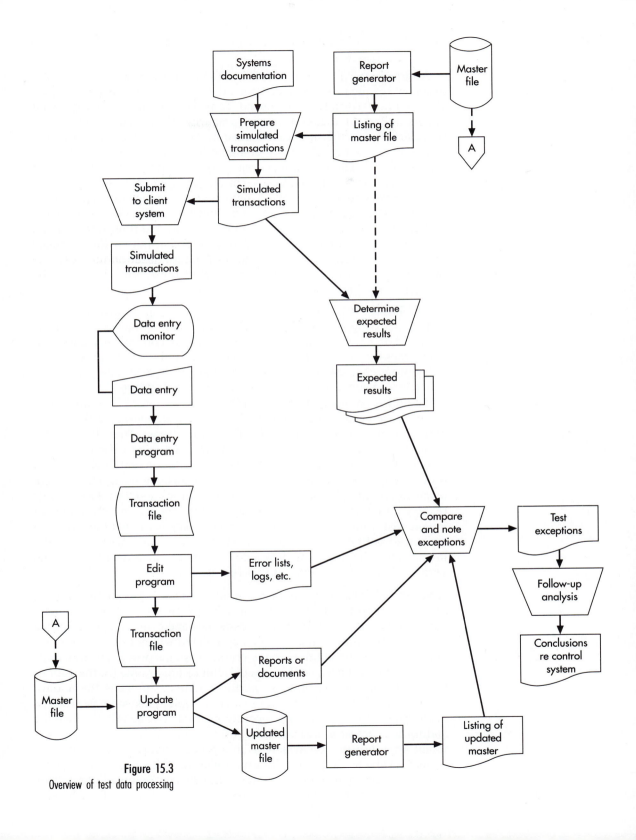

Figure 15.3
Overview of test data processing

Although the processing of test transactions is a very effective means of testing processing controls, it does have some disadvantages. The auditor typically must spend considerable time developing an understanding of the system and preparing an adequate set of test transactions. Furthermore, care must be taken to ensure that the test transactions do not affect the company's actual master file records. The auditor might use procedures to reverse the effects of the test transactions or perhaps make a separate run in which test transactions are processed against a copy of the master file rather than against the real file. The use of a separate run, however, removes some of the authenticity that is obtained from processing the test transactions along with the regular transactions. A further problem is that these special procedures may reveal the existence and nature of the auditor's test to the employees of the computer facility. Thus these procedures may be less effective than a concealed test would be.

On-Line Testing.   Conventional test data processing, as just described, tests processing controls in a batch processing application. Because on-line data entry and on-line processing are becoming very common, it is necessary to test the processing controls built into on-line data entry programs, using a method analogous to the test data processing procedure. Such a method is referred to as **on-line testing**.

To utilize on-line testing, the auditor must review system documentation to determine the content of input transaction records and the nature of data editing and validation procedures. Then the auditor prepares a set of hypothetical transactions containing various kinds of errors. These steps are the same as those in conventional test data processing. Next, the auditor enters these transactions into the system using an on-line data entry terminal and observes and logs the system's response to each transaction. If the system accepts any erroneous or invalid test transactions, the auditor must first ensure that the effects of such transactions are removed from the files, and then he or she investigates the apparent deficiency in the application program and verifies that steps are taken to correct it.

Concurrent Audit Techniques.   In many on-line processing systems, millions of dollars worth of transactions may be processed without leaving a satisfactory audit trail. In such cases review and evaluation of evidence obtained after processing has been completed will not be sufficient for audit purposes. In addition, many on-line systems process transactions on a continuous basis, so that it is difficult or impossible for the auditor to stop the system in order to perform audit tests. Thus the auditor needs to be able to collect audit evidence while the system is processing live data during its regular operating hours. To accomplish this, the auditor uses **concurrent audit techniques**, software routines that continuously monitor an information system as it is processing live data in order to collect, evaluate, and report information about the system's reliability.

Concurrent audit techniques have three main features. First, they involve the use of **embedded audit modules**, special software routines located within application programs and designed to perform audit functions. Second, they often use special files to store the audit evidence that they collect so that the auditor can review this information at a later time. Third, they must include a system of reporting test results to the auditor. Concurrent audit techniques may be used either to test the internal controls in a system or to identify questionable transactions for further audit review.

One concurrent audit technique used to test the processing procedures and controls built into an application system is called the **integrated test facility (ITF)**, or minicompany test. An extension of the concept of test data processing, this technique involves introducing a small set of records representing a fictitious entity into the master files of the system under review. The fictitious entity might be a dummy division, department, or branch office; a set of dummy customer or supplier accounts; or some combination of these. Test transactions are then processed to update these dummy records without affecting the real records. Furthermore, the test transactions may be processed along with the real transactions, and the employees of the computer facility need not be aware that the testing is being done. The system must include a routine that distinguishes ITF records from real records and collects information on the effects of the test transactions to be reported to the auditor. The auditor compares this output with expected results previously calculated independently of the application system to verify that the system and its controls are operating correctly.

The ITF technique eliminates two of the primary disadvantages of conventional test data processing. First, there is no need to reverse the effects of test transactions on the actual master file records. Second, the existence of the test is easily concealed from the employees who operate the system. In addition, though it can be used to test a batch processing application, ITF is well suited to testing on-line processing systems because test transactions can be submitted on a frequent basis, processed along with real transactions by the live version of the application program, and traced through all stages of the processing cycle, all without any disruption of regular processing operations. Care must be taken in designing the ITF, however, to ensure that real transactions are not initiated unnecessarily and that the dummy records are not aggregated with regular records during the reporting process.

Many on-line processing systems are large and complex and may retrieve or update data in several system files during the processing of a single transaction. It is far too time-consuming for the auditor to analyze these programs by reviewing the program code or using a trace routine. Instead, the auditor can examine how a transaction is processed at each major stage in the program by using the **snapshot technique**. This technique uses audit modules embedded at various processing points in the program to record the content of both the transaction record and the related master file record, both before and after each processing step is executed. Snapshots are taken only of selected transactions that are identified to the system by **tagging** them, or marking them with a special code that triggers the snapshot process. The snapshot data are recorded in a special file and reported to the auditor. The auditor subsequently reviews this output to verify that all processing steps have been properly executed.

A third concurrent audit technique is called **SCARF**, an acronym for "system control audit review file." This involves embedding audit modules into applications software to continuously monitor all transaction activity and collect data on transactions having special audit significance. These data are recorded on a SCARF file, sometimes called an **audit log**. Among the kinds of transactions that might be so recorded are those exceeding a specified dollar limit, those involving inactive accounts, those involving deviations from company policy, or those involving write-downs of asset values. On a periodic basis the auditor receives a printout of the SCARF file, examines the information to identify any questionable transactions, and, if necessary, performs a follow-up investigation.

A fourth concurrent audit technique involves the use of **audit hooks**. These are routines embedded within application programs to flag certain kinds of transactions that might be indicative of fraud. For example, internal auditors at State Farm Life Insurance Company determined that their policyholder information system was vulnerable

15.1 FOCUS

Using Audit Hooks at State Farm Life

At State Farm Life Insurance Company the computer system consists of a host computer located in Bloomington, Illinois, and 26 minicomputers located in the regional offices. The system is an on-line, real-time system. More than fifteen hundred CRT input devices located in the regional offices are used to update the 3.9 million individual policyholder master records that

reside in the host computer in Bloomington. During 1989 the system handled more than 29.6 million transactions submitted by the regional offices.

Since the system is an on-line, real-time system, all master record updating and transaction processing take place almost instantly. Paper audit trails have virtually vanished. Documents in support of changes to the policyholder master record have

been all but eliminated or are only held a short time before disposition. Sitting in the 3.9 million asset records are policyholder funds valued at more than $6.7 billion. Anyone with access and a working knowledge of the system could potentially commit fraud.

The challenge facing State Farm Life's internal audit staff

to a fraud perpetrated by first changing a policyholder's name or address and then withdrawing funds from the policy. They devised a system of audit hooks that involved tagging any policyholder record against which a name or address change is processed. Then any time a fund withdrawal is processed, the system checks whether the policyholder master record is tagged. If so, the internal audit department is notified and investigates the transaction for potential fraud.[14] When audit hooks are employed, the auditor is often informed of questionable transactions as soon as they occur by means of a message displayed on the auditor's terminal; this technique is called **real-time notification**. For additional information on State Farm Life's use of audit hooks, including the story of how one fraud was detected by an audit hook, refer to Focus 15.1.

The final concurrent audit technique described here is **continuous and intermittent simulation (CIS)**. Under this approach an audit module is embedded into the data base management system (DBMS) rather than the application program. When an application system transaction is conveyed to the DBMS, it invokes the CIS module, which examines the

---

[14] Linda Marie Leinicke, W. Max Rexroad, and Jon D. Ward, "Computer Fraud Auditing: It Works," *Internal Auditor* (August 1990): 26–33.

---

was to identify the key life insurance transactions where the potential for fraud existed. From their knowledge of the system the internal auditors began by simply brainstorming with one another to identify possible ways to defraud the system. Various employee users of the system were interviewed for their ideas, and they provided the internal audit staff with extremely valuable insights.

The internal auditors currently have 33 embedded audit hooks monitoring 42 different transactions. One of these hooks is designed to monitor unusual transactions in transfer accounts, which are clearing accounts for temporarily holding funds that are to be credited to multiple accounts.

The audit hooks have been very successful. For instance, one employee obtained cash by processing a fraudulent loan for $250 on her brother's life insurance policy, forging her brother's endorsement on the check, and cashing it at a liquor store. To cover up this fraud, the employee needed to repay the $250 loan before the annual status report was sent to her brother. She did so by using a series of fictitious transactions involving a transfer account. However, this fraud was uncovered almost immediately when the transfer account audit hook, in response to the first of these fictitious transactions, generated a computer output notification (CON) to be sent to the auditor. Within one month after the CON was received, the case had been investigated and the employee terminated. This is but one of a number of frauds that have been discovered by the audit hooks in very early stages.

Source: Linda Marie Leinicke, W. Max Rexroad, and Jon D. Ward, "Computer Fraud Auditing: It Works," *Internal Auditor* (August 1990): 26–33.

transaction data (using criteria similar to those of SCARF) to determine whether or not to analyze the transaction further. If not, the CIS module will simply allow the DBMS to finish processing the transaction. Otherwise, the CIS module will independently replicate the steps required for the DBMS to process the transaction (in a manner similar to parallel simulation), record the results, and then compare its results with those obtained by the DBMS. If there are any discrepancies, the details are written onto an audit log for subsequent investigation by the auditor. In the event of serious discrepancies the CIS may prevent the DBMS from executing the update process.

In summary, concurrent audit techniques rely on special audit modules embedded into application systems or related software to monitor live processing activity, perform audit tests, identify unusual transactions that require audit attention, and report to the auditor on a timely basis. The use of concurrent audit techniques can be difficult and time-consuming for the auditor, but it will be less so if the auditor is able to incorporate the audit modules into the application programs when they are initially developed and implemented. Concurrent audit techniques are very effective because they allow the auditor to test an organization's processing controls on a continuous basis. They are especially useful in complex on-line processing systems where the audit trail is so limited that conventional audit techniques are likely to be ineffective.

Objective 5: Source Data

The focal point of objective 5 is the accuracy and integrity of the data input to application programs. A framework for the audit of source data controls is given in Table 15.5. Potential errors or irregularities in source data entry include the introduction of inaccurate or unauthorized source data into the system and the processing of these data to update system files and generate erroneous output.

Internal controls should exist to prevent, detect, and correct inaccurate or unauthorized source data. Among the most important of such controls is the assignment of responsibility for monitoring source data accuracy and integrity to an independent data control function. Specific control techniques include user authorization of source data; reconciliation of batch control totals; logging of the receipt, movement, and disposition of data input; check digit verification; key verification of important data items; the use of turnaround documents where feasible; the use of edit programs to check source data accuracy prior to processing; the preparation of reports listing file change transactions for user review and verification; and effective procedures for correcting and resubmitting any erroneous transactions detected by these controls.

In on-line processing systems the source data entry and processing functions are effectively merged into one operation. Therefore source data controls such as proper authorization and editing of data input are integrated with processing controls. A program for the auditor's review and testing of these control procedures was described in the previous section.

Types of Errors and Irregularities	
■ Inaccurate source data	■ Unauthorized source data

Control Procedures	
■ Effective handling of source data input by data control personnel ■ User authorization of source data input ■ Preparation and reconciliation of batch control totals ■ Logging of the receipt, movement, and disposition of source data input ■ Check digit verification ■ Key verification	■ Use of turnaround documents ■ Computer data editing routines ■ File change listings and summaries prepared for user department review ■ Effective procedures for correcting and resubmitting erroneous data

Audit Procedures: System Review	

■ Review documentation about responsibilities of data control function
■ Review administrative documentation for source data control standards
■ Review methods of authorization and examine authorization signatures
■ Review accounting systems documentation to identify
    Source data content and processing steps
    Specific source data controls used
	■ Document accounting source data controls using input control matrix
	■ Discuss source data control procedures with:
	    Data control personnel
	    IS management
	    System users

Audit Procedures: Tests of Controls	
■ Observe and evaluate data control department operations ■ Verify proper maintenance and use of data control log ■ Reconcile a sample of batch totals, and follow up on discrepancies ■ Examine samples of accounting source data for proper authorization	■ Observe the performance of specific data control procedures ■ Trace disposition of a sample of errors flagged by data edit routines ■ Evaluate how items recorded in the error log are dealt with

Compensating Controls	
■ Strong user controls	■ Strong processing controls

Table 15.5

Framework for audit of source data controls

As part of the system review, the auditor should examine organization charts and job descriptions to ascertain whether a data control function exists and whether it is organizationally independent of user departments and the computer operations function. Administrative documentation describing the general standards governing control of source data should be reviewed. The auditor should ascertain how user authorization of source data input is supposed to be documented and obtain copies of the signatures or other forms of authorization required for each significant type of input transaction. The auditor should also

Record Name: Employer Weekly Time Report — Input Controls	Employee number	Last name	Department number	Transaction code	Week ending (date)	Regular hours	Overtime hours	Comments
Batch totals					✓	✓		
Hash totals	✓							
Record counts								Yes
Cross-footing balance								No
Key verification	✓				✓	✓		
Visual inspection								All fields
Check digit verification	✓							
Prenumbered forms								No
Turnaround document								No
Edit program								Yes
Sequence check	✓							
Field check	✓		✓			✓	✓	
Sign check								
Validity check	✓		✓	✓	✓			
Limit check						✓	✓	
Reasonableness test						✓	✓	
Redundant data check	✓	✓	✓					
Completeness test				✓	✓	✓	✓	
Overflow procedure								
Other:								

Figure 15.4
Input controls matrix

examine the documentation of significant accounting applications to determine the flow of accounting data to and from the MIS function and to understand the specific source data control procedures applied to such data. One tool the auditor may use to document the results of a review of source data controls for a particular application is an **input controls matrix** (see Fig. 15.4), which shows the control procedures applied to each field of an input record. Finally, the auditor should interview system users, IS management, and data control personnel to find out how the prescribed source data control procedures are intended to be applied.

A small-business data processing operation or a microcomputer installation located in a department or small division of a larger company is unlikely to have an independent data control function, simply because it is not economically feasible. To compensate for this deficiency, other control procedures must be that much stronger. They include user department controls over data preparation, batch control totals, edit programs, restrictions on physical and logical access to the system, and error-handling procedures. These procedures should be the focus of the auditor's system review and tests of controls whenever there is no independent data control function.

The auditor's tests of source data controls should include observation of the operations of the data control function to verify its independence from other functions within the MIS department as well as from user departments and to evaluate its effectiveness in performing source data control procedures. In particular, proper maintenance and utilization of a data control log should be observed, and the auditor should evaluate whether access to the data control log is adequately controlled. To verify that batch control totals are being properly applied, the auditor should trace a sample of control totals through the input process. Control totals provided by user departments should be compared with those recorded in the data control log and with those generated by the computer during the processing of data edit programs. Any exceptions to proper reconciliation of control totals should be investigated.

Using the list of authorized source data approval signatures obtained during system review, the auditor should examine samples of accounting source data for evidence that proper authorizations were present and were checked by data control personnel prior to acceptance of the data for computer processing. Any significant exceptions to proper source data authorization should be investigated by the auditor. Furthermore, the auditor should observe the performance of specific source data control procedures, such as checking for authorizations, logging of input and errors, key verification, reconciliation of batch totals, the use of turnaround documents, and the processing of edit programs. The auditor should also select a sample of errors flagged by data edit programs and verify that they have been properly investigated, corrected, and resubmitted for processing by data control personnel.

If erroneous transactions detected by source data controls are recorded in an error log by data control personnel, the auditor should examine the error log to determine that the disposition of errors was properly noted and that errors were not allowed to go unresolved for an excessive period of time. The auditor may wish to check the recording, investigation, and correction of a sample of errors. Any errors recorded in the log that have not been resolved within a reasonable time period should be investigated by the auditor.

Even though prescribed source data controls may not change from year to year, the strictness with which they are applied may change. Therefore, the auditor should perform tests of them on a regular basis. If the auditor concludes that source data controls are not adequate with respect to a particular application system, other controls that may compensate are user department controls and computer processing controls. If these other controls are not strong enough to compensate for the inadequacies in source data controls, the auditor should strongly recommend that steps be taken to correct the source data control deficiencies.

Objective 6: Data Files

Objective 6 is concerned with the accuracy, integrity, and security of data stored in machine-readable files. Table 15.6 provides a framework for the audit of data file controls. In the absence of good controls stored data could be modified in an unauthorized manner, inadvertently or intentionally destroyed, or made available to persons outside the organization against the wishes of management.

Internal controls should exist to restrict physical access to data stored on disk and tape files through the operation of a secure file library. Logical access to data files stored on-line should be controlled through the use of password access control techniques. File-handling procedures that should be employed include internal and external file labels and write protection mechanisms. In a data base environment concurrent update controls should be employed to prevent errors that might arise when two users attempt to update the same record simultaneously. Other important control procedures include the use of data encryption to protect highly confidential data from unauthorized disclosure, the use of virus protection software to prevent damage to files from computer viruses, the preparation and off-site storage of backup copies of all data files, provisions for reconstruction of lost data or files, system recovery procedures involving checkpoint and rollback techniques to recover from system failures caused by hardware or software malfunctions, special controls over master file conversions during system changeovers, and the maintenance of file control totals by persons independent of the MIS function. Finally, a sound disaster recovery plan should be prepared, tested, and maintained on a current basis.

As part of the system review, the auditor should examine administrative documentation to ascertain the responsibilities of the file librarian function and the procedures that are prescribed relating to logging of files as they are removed and returned to the file library. The auditor should review policies relating to the assignment and modification of passwords and the validation of user requests for access to on-line data. Operating documentation should be reviewed to determine prescribed operating standards relating to the use of file labels, write protection mechanisms, virus protection software, and system recovery procedures. Systems documentation should be reviewed to ascertain prescribed procedures for control of concurrent update, the use of data encryption, and the reconciliation of master file totals with independently maintained control totals. The auditor should also examine the disaster recovery plan, paying particular attention to provisions relating to the protection and recovery of data files. Finally, the auditor should hold discussions with IS management, file librarians, and other operating personnel to develop an understanding of the way in which these controls are supposed to be applied.

Types of Errors and Irregularities	
■ Destruction of stored data due to: 　Inadvertent errors 　Hardware or software malfunctions 　Intentional acts of sabotage or vandalism	■ Unauthorized modification of stored data ■ Unauthorized disclosure of stored data

Control Procedures	
■ Secure file library and restrictions on physical access to data files ■ Logical access controls using passwords and access control matrix ■ Proper use of file labels and write protection mechanisms ■ Concurrent update controls ■ Use of data encryption for highly confidential data ■ Use of virus protection software	■ Maintenance of backup copies of all data files in an off-site location ■ Use of checkpoint and rollback to facilitate system recovery ■ File conversion controls ■ Reconciliation of master file data with independent control totals ■ Disaster recovery planning

Audit Procedures: System Review	
■ Review documentation for functions of file library function ■ Review logical access policies and procedures ■ Review operating documentation to determine prescribed standards for 　Use of file labels and write protection mechanisms 　Use of virus protection software 　Use of backup data storage 　System recovery, including checkpoint and rollback procedures	■ Review systems documentation to examine prescribed procedures for: 　Use of concurrent update controls and data encryption 　Control of file conversions 　Reconciling master file totals with independent control totals ■ Examine disaster recovery plan ■ Discuss data file control procedures with IS managers and operators

Audit Procedures: Tests of Controls	
■ Observe and evaluate file library operations ■ Review records of password assignment and modification ■ Observe and evaluate file-handling procedures by operations personnel ■ Observe the preparation and off-site storage of backup files ■ Verify the effective use of virus protection procedures	■ Verify the use of concurrent update controls and data encryption ■ Verify completeness, currency, and testing of disaster recovery plan ■ Reconcile master file totals with separately maintained control totals ■ Observe the procedures used to control file conversions

Compensating Controls	
■ Strong user controls ■ Effective computer security controls	■ Strong processing controls

Table 15.6
Framework for audit of data file controls

The auditor's tests of data controls should include observation of the file librarian's activities to ascertain that other systems personnel are not permitted unrestricted access to data files, that a use record is maintained for such data files, and that the file librarian is not permitted to operate computer equipment. The auditor should examine a sample of assigned passwords and their associated access authority to verify that the password holders do not have access authority that is incompatible with their other responsibilities. The auditor should observe file-handling procedures performed by computer operators to verify that file labels are properly checked, that write protection mechanisms are properly used, and that backup copies of data files are prepared and promptly removed to a secure off-site location. The auditor should verify that virus protection procedures, concurrent update controls, data encryption, and system recovery procedures are employed according to prescribed standards. In addition, the auditor should confirm that the disaster recovery plan is complete and up to date, and verify that it is effectively tested on a regular basis.

If file control totals are regularly checked against corresponding user totals maintained outside the MIS function, the auditor should check a number of these comparisons for accuracy. Simultaneously, the auditor should foot the data file, using computer audit software, to check the accuracy of the file totals maintained by the MIS function.

Whenever the implementation of a new information system requires that data files be converted from one storage medium or format to another, the auditor should verify that this file conversion process is properly controlled. The auditor should evaluate the prescribed file conversion controls and test the conversion of files by comparing selected records from the new file with their counterparts from the old. The auditor may wish to independently perform a series of edit checks on the new file using a computer audit software package. Ideally, IS personnel will inform the auditor when important conversions of files are scheduled so that the auditor may be present to observe the process and accompanying control procedures.

If the auditor concludes that data file controls are seriously deficient, especially with respect to physical or logical access or to backup and recovery procedures, then strong recommendations should be made that these deficiencies be rectified. Deficiencies in other areas of data file control leave the organization vulnerable to the effects of inadvertent errors, which are generally not as severe. In such cases strong user controls, effective data security procedures, and strong controls over processing may be sufficient to compensate for weaknesses in data file controls.

In conclusion, auditing by objectives gives focus to the auditor's study and evaluation of internal controls in computer-based information systems. The auditing-by-objectives approach may be implemented by means of an audit procedures checklist organized around the six objectives. Such a checklist should direct the auditor to reach a separate conclusion regarding the extent of achievement of each objective and suggest appropriate compensating controls when a particular objective is not fully achieved. When distinct application programs are being reviewed, separate versions of the checklist should be completed for each significant application. This approach represents a comprehensive, systematic, and effective means of evaluating internal controls in a computer-based information system.

One other point should be emphasized based on our review of auditing techniques in this section. Techniques such as the integrated test facility, the snapshot technique, SCARF, audit hooks, and real-time notification, all should be incorporated into a system during the design process, rather than as an afterthought once the system has been implemented. Similarly, many of the application control techniques the auditor expects to find in a system are easier to design into the system in the first place than to attach later on. These points underscore the importance of having auditors review application systems designs while there is still time to adopt their suggestions for incorporating control techniques and audit features into these systems.

This completes our description of the auditor's objectives and procedures relating to the first of three major types of audits, the information systems audit. Next, we consider the financial audit, with emphasis given to the way in which the computer is employed to retrieve information that is useful in the financial auditing process.

FINANCIAL AUDITS AND COMPUTER AUDIT SOFTWARE

As explained earlier in this chapter, the first of the five standards dealing with the scope of internal audit work is that

internal auditors should review the reliability and integrity of financial and operating information and the means used to identify, measure, classify, and report such information.[15]

The general methodology for this type of audit work is discussed extensively in numerous standard textbooks on auditing[16] and so is not elaborated upon here. Accordingly, this section deals with specific auditing procedures and techniques directed at auditing financial and operating information maintained in a computer-based information system.

In those situations in which the computer plays a significant role in processing, storing, and reporting the information subject to audit, the auditor should generally audit through the computer if possible. This means that the auditor should use the computer to the maximum extent feasible in (1) gathering evidence about the reliability of internal controls in the systems that produced the information (using the methodology explained in the previous section), which will influence the auditor's preliminary judgments concerning the accuracy of the system outputs, and (2) performing a variety of auditing operations on the computer files used to store the information. These latter operations are performed using computer programs written especially for auditors, called **generalized audit software (GAS)** or simply **computer audit software.**

---

[15] Institute of Internal Auditors, *Standards for the Professional Practice of Internal Auditing,* 3.

[16] For example, see Alvin A. Arens and James K. Loebbecke, *Auditing: An Integrated Approach,* 5th ed. (Englewood Cliffs, N.J.: Prentice-Hall, 1991); or Jack C. Robertson, *Auditing,* 7th ed. (Homewood, Ill.: Irwin, 1993).

15.2 FOCUS

Battling Federal Budget Deficits with Audit Software

As the United States government attempts to reduce its massive federal budget deficits, it is finding that computer audit software is a valuable tool. Audit software is being used to identify fraudulent Medicare claims, pinpoint excessive charges by defense contractors, and in numerous other ways.

For example, by cross-checking figures with the Internal Revenue Service, a computer audit by the General Accounting Office discovered that thousands of veterans lied about their income to qualify for pension benefits. The results of the GAO audit, released in December 1991, revealed that 116,000 veterans receiving pensions on the basis of need failed to disclose $338 million in 1989 income from savings accounts, stock divi-

Several programs of this type are available from software vendors as well as from the larger public accounting firms. Computer audit software is ideally suited to examining large data files in order to identify specific records that should be subjected to further audit scrutiny (see Focus 15.2). This section describes the nature of computer audit software and explains how it may be applied in the auditing process.

The systems flowchart in Fig. 15.5 provides an overview of the processing steps required to utilize computer audit software. The auditor must first establish the audit objectives of the application, obtain knowledge of the format and content of the files to be audited, design the format of the desired audit reports, and determine the operations necessary to accomplish the objectives and produce the reports. All these details concerning the application are then encoded by the auditor on a set of preformatted specification sheets. The data on the specification sheets are keyed into the system under the control of a GAS data entry program. This program creates a set of specification records, which are then processed as input to the GAS. This processing generally results in a computer program, or set of programs, either in machine language or in a higher-level language such as COBOL. (In the latter case the higher-level-language program must then be compiled before being processed.) In essence, the GAS is a computer program that generates other computer programs based on the auditor's specifications, and it is these other computer programs that perform the audit functions.

In the next step the source files containing the information subject to audit are processed as input to the audit program generated by the

dends, or rents.

The Veterans Administration said it will request explanations from 60,000 veterans about the discrepancies in their income. The other 56,000 veterans will be questioned after more figures arrive from the Social Security Administration.

"One individual had not reported over $300,000 in unearned income received in 1989," the GAO said in its report to Congress. The report said 13,600 veterans underreported their income by at least $4000 in 1989.

Another 5500 did not report $10,000 or more to the VA when applying for the pensions.

Before the computer check was instituted, the VA relied on the vets for accurate income reports. Once the VA notified beneficiaries that their income would be verified with the IRS and the Social Security Administration, the pension rolls dropped by more then 13,000, at a savings of $9 million a month, the GAO reported.

The VA plans to use the same system for checking income levels of those applying for medical care. If their income is found to be above a certain level, patients will be required to make some copayments.

Source: "Audit: Vets Cheating on Pensions," Chicago Tribune (December 26, 1991): C-12.

GAS. Usually, there are a series of such computer runs, each designed to perform selected auditing operations as necessary to produce one of the specified audit reports. A list of the functions performed by computer audit software, together with an explanation and one or more audit examples of each function, is given in Table 15.7. Frequently, the major objective of the initial GAS computer run is to extract specific information of interest to the auditor from the source file or files and reformat it into an audit work file. Additional audit reports and analyses are then generated by a subsequent series of computer runs that use the audit work file as input.

For an example of the value of audit software and the various functions it can perform, consider the following case. In a small New England town a new city tax collector was elected, defeating the incumbent. As was customary, the new tax collector requested an audit of the city's tax collection records. Using computer audit software, the auditor accessed the tax collection records of the four prior years, sorted them by collection date, summed the amount of taxes collected by month, and prepared a summary report of monthly tax collections over the four-year period. This analysis revealed that tax collections during the previous January and July, normally the two busiest months, had declined by 58% and 72%, respectively. Auditors then used the audit software to compare the tax collection records, one by one, with the city's property records, which contained data on whether the property tax payments were current. This comparison identified several discrepancies, including one case where the former tax collector used another taxpayer's payment to cover her own delin-

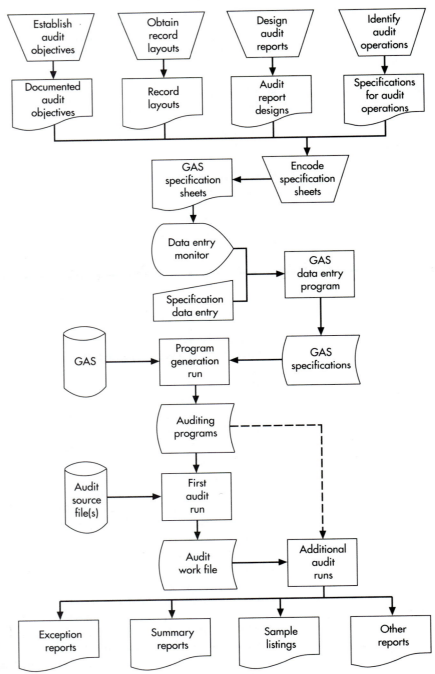

Figure 15.5
Overview of GAS processing

Function	Explanation	Examples
Reformatting	Read data in different formats and data structures, and convert to a common format and structure	Read inventory records from purchasing data base and convert to an inventory file usable by the GAS program
File manipulation	Sort records into sequential order; merge files sequenced on the same sort key	Sort inventory records by location; merge customer transaction files with receivables master file
Calculation	Perform the four basic arithmetic operations: add, subtract, multiply, and divide	Foot client accounts receivable file; recalculate client inventory valuation; recalculate client depreciation; sum employee payroll by department
Data selection	Review of data files to retrieve records meeting specified criteria	Identify customer accoaunts having a balance exceeding the credit limit; select all purchase transactions in excess of a specified dollar amount
Data analysis	Examine records for errors or missing values; compare fields in related records for inconsistencies	Perform data editing of client files; compare personnel and payroll files to verify consistency
File processing	Provide programming capability for file creation, updating, and downloading to a personal computer	Use parallel simulation to verify that client gross pay calculations are correct; download sample of client inventory records to personal computer for further analysis to support inventory test counts
Statistics	Stratification of file records by item valuation; selection of statistical samples; analysis of statistical sampling results	Stratify customer accounts by size of account balance and select a stratified sample of accounts for audit confirmation
Report generation	Format and print reports and documents	Prepare analysis of financial statement ratios and trends; prepare accounts receivable aging schedule; prepare audit confirmations

Table 15.7
General functions of computer audit software

quent tax bills. As a result, the former tax collector was arrested and charged with embezzlement, and the auditor's investigation was expanded.

The primary purpose of GAS is to assist the auditor in reviewing and retrieving information stored on computer files. Note, however, that the use of GAS is normally one of the first steps in the financial audit. Once the auditor receives the reports prepared by the GAS application, most of the audit work still remains to be done. Items listed on exception reports must be investigated, file totals and subtotals must be verified against other sources of information such as the general ledger, and items selected for audit samples must be examined and evaluated. Thus, although the advantages to the auditor of using GAS (summarized in Table 15.8) are numerous and compelling, a computer program cannot replace the auditor's judgment or free the auditor from significant participation in all phases of the audit.

Advantage	Explanation
Access	Audit software provides improved access to data stored in machine-readable form.
Scope	Audit software enables the auditor to examine more records than can otherwise be examined.
Cost	Audit software reduces the cost of auditing in large organizations that are extensively computerized.
Independence	Audit software is used under the auditor's control, thereby lessening the auditor's dependence on EDP personnel.
Simplicity	Audit software is easy to learn about and to use, and it requires only minimal knowledge of computer technology.
Generality	Audit software performs a variety of auditing tasks and can function in a variety of auditing environments.
Understanding	A by-product of using audit software is that the auditor gains a better understanding of the information system.

Table 15.8
Summary of audit
software advantages

An Example of an Audit Software Application

This section explains in greater detail the functions that can be performed with computer audit software, using as an example an audit carried out by Jason Scott at Northwest Builders Supply (NBS), a large retailer of lumber and building materials located in Tacoma, Washington, and a subsidiary company of Northwest Industries. Jason was assigned to audit accounts receivable information produced by NBS's computerized customer accounting system. This system maintains an accounts receivable master file and transaction detail files for sales on account, cash collections, and credit memos. Copies of record layouts for these files were obtained by Jason and are reproduced in Fig. 15.6.

Jason's supervisor delineated the following objectives for the GAS application:

1. Recalculate the current balance of every customer master record from the previous balance and the intervening transactions and identify all accounts having an incorrect current balance.

2. Sum the current balance, credit sales, cash collections, and credit memo amounts for verification of their totals against other independently maintained information.

3. Perform edit checks on selected fields in each file to confirm the reliability of data editing performed within NBS's data entry function.

4. Check the transaction files for any records that do not match with a master record.

5. Prepare an aging schedule of the receivables and an analysis of accounts having current balances in excess of their credit limit in order to evaluate the sufficiency of NBS's allowance for uncollectible accounts and to assess the performance of NBS's credit department.

6. Select a sample of accounts for confirmation in order to verify the existence and accuracy of the receivables recorded on NBS's customer master file.

Record Name: Accounts Receivable Master

Field Name	Account number	Name	Address				Credit code	Credit limit	Previous balance	Current balance
			Street	City	State	Zip				
Position	1 – 6	7 – 31	32 – 56	57 – 74	75 – 76	77 – 81	82 – 83	84 – 91	92 – 99	100 – 107

Record Name: Sales Detail

Field Name	Account number	Transaction code	Transaction date	Invoice number	Amount	
Position	1 – 6	7	8 – 13	14 – 18	19 – 26	

Record Name: Cash Collections Detail

Field Name	Account number	Transaction code	Transaction date	Reference number	Amount	
Position	1 – 6	7	8 – 13	14 – 18	19 – 26	

Record Name: Credit Memo Detail

Field Name	Account number	Transaction code	Transaction date	Credit memo number	Amount	
Position	1 – 6	7	8 – 13	14 – 18	19 – 26	

Figure 15.6
Record layouts for accounts receivable system

7. Analyze cash collections and credit memos subsequent to the test date for those customers who do not respond to confirmation requests.

The following paragraphs describe the way Jason accomplished these objectives using computer audit software. Note that each of the general audit software functions delineated in Table 15.7 is utilized one or more times in the course of this application.

A systems flowchart showing the sequence of computer operations designed by Jason to achieve the first six objectives appears in Fig. 15.7. Input to RUN 1 consisted of all four of the source files. This run sorted each of these files into sequence by account number and merged the four files into a combined master and transaction file. As the transaction records were merged with the master file, two transaction detail records for which there was not a master record having the same account number were identified. Details relating to these transaction records were listed on the unmatched transaction report. After a follow-up investigation Jason concluded that keying errors had caused invalid account numbers to be entered into these transaction records. Corrections were promptly recorded in NBS's records and in Jason's merged file.

RUN 2 created an audit work file by extracting from the combined master and transaction file only those data that were needed to perform

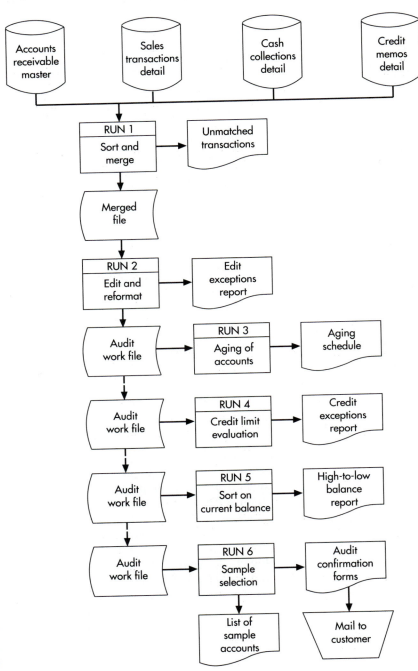

Figure 15.7
Application of computer audit software to accounts receivable

the subsequent audit operations. Jason elected to include the following items in the audit work file: (1) account number, (2) name, (3) address, (4) credit limit, (5) current balance, (6) last invoice (sale) date, (7) last invoice amount, (8) last credit (payment or credit memo) date, and (9) last credit amount. An audit record containing these data was created for each customer account record, and these audit records were written in sequential order onto a separate audit work file.

The second run also performed a variety of edits and other tests on the information recorded on the merged master and transaction file, and it printed an exception report containing the results of these tests. For each set of customer records all sales on account were added to the previous balance, and all cash collections and credit memo amounts were subtracted; whenever the result was not equal to the customer's current balance amount, the GAS was directed to print all data pertaining to the account on an exception report. A series of edit checks were also performed on selected data fields, with all erroneous records listed on the exception report. Among the edit checks performed in this case were validity checks on the transaction codes and dates, a completeness test of each type of record, a sign test of the current balance, field checks of all numeric fields, and a sequence check of each file based on account number. These various tests identified a few minor errors in the records. After further investigation Jason concluded that these errors had a negligible effect on NBS's accounts, that they were probably caused by inadvertent mistakes in data entry, and that they did not have serious implications with respect to the overall reliability of NBS's accounts receivable information.

Additional operations performed during this second pass included footing the amount fields for cash collections, sales on account, credit memos, and account balances and printing the summary totals at the bottom of the edit exceptions report. Jason then compared these totals with corresponding totals from NBS's sales and cash receipts journals and general ledger accounts for credit sales, sales returns and allowances, and accounts receivable. Had he not been able to reconcile these totals, Jason would have been concerned that a serious deficiency might exist in the quality of the information maintained by NBS's system. Fortunately, however, these totals did agree.

In RUN 3 the audit work file was processed to generate an aging schedule for the receivables. Northwest's audit software contains built-in logic specifically designed to perform aging operations. Immediately following this step, RUN 4 was executed, during which the current balance for each customer was compared with the credit limit, and several accounts having balances in excess of the credit limit were printed on a report. During this fourth run the total of all such balances and the total excess of such balances over the corresponding credit limit were accumulated and then printed at the bottom of the report. Jason provided both the aging schedule and the credit exceptions report to his supervisor, who used them to prepare an appraisal of the

adequacy of the allowance for uncollectible accounts and an evaluation of the credit department's effectiveness in administering credit
policies.

In RUN 5 the records on the audit work file were re-sorted into
sequence from high to low current balance. On the basis of its current
balance, each account was classified in a dollar range, starting with
balances over $20,000, then $19,501 to $20,000, $19,001 to $19,500, and
so on, down to $0 to $500. A summary report was printed listing the
number of accounts and the cumulative dollar amount for each range.
Jason used this report to design a plan for selecting a sample of
customers to whom account confirmations would be mailed. Specifically, he chose to select all customer accounts with balances above
$15,000, 10% of the accounts between $15,000 and $5001, 2% of the
accounts between $5000 and $1001, and 1% of the accounts of $1000 or
less. This type of sampling plan, called **stratified sampling**, enables auditors
to include in their samples a relatively high percentage of the total
number of dollars in the population, even though the sample may
include a very low percentage of the total number of accounts. The
high-to-low-balance summary report helps the auditor decide how
many sample strata (or ranges) to use and what strata boundaries to
establish.

Once the sampling plan was established, the re-sorted audit work
file was input to RUN 6, which randomly selected the specific accounts
to be included within each of the three smaller sample ranges. A list of
these accounts was printed. Northwest's audit software program has a
built-in formatting capability for audit confirmations, so this run resulted in the printing of these confirmations for the accounts in the
sample. Jason then made sure that the confirmation forms were properly mailed to the sample customers.

Generally, some customers do not respond to confirmation requests. Jason planned to obtain evidence concerning the validity of
those accounts by examining subsequent collections from those customers. He intended to wait four weeks after sending out the confirmations and then, using the audit software package, write a program to
scan the cash collections and credit memo files and identify and print
records of all cash collections and credit memos for those customers in
the sample who had not responded to the confirmation request.

Once Jason obtained and examined confirmation responses and
other related evidence, he would use the audit software to evaluate the
results of the sample. Northwest's audit software program is capable of
statistically evaluating sample results by computing means, variances,
confidence intervals, and sampling risks.

In summary, this example demonstrates the capabilities of GAS as
well as its advantages. In particular, the use of GAS allowed Jason to
quickly and inexpensively review NBS's accounts receivable information, identify questionable records that should be investigated further,
prepare several summary reports, select a sample of accounts for
confirmation and automatically print the confirmation forms, and sub-

sequently perform a statistical evaluation of the sample results. Note that Jason was able to perform these functions independently of NBS's IS personnel. The results Jason obtained from using the GAS, however, represented only the first step in the audit. Once these results were obtained, Jason still needed to investigate exceptions, audit sample items, independently verify file totals, evaluate the significance of summary reports, and perform numerous other auditing procedures.

OPERATIONAL AUDITS OF COMPUTER-BASED INFORMATION SYSTEMS

The steps involved in an operational audit of a computer-based information system, and many of the techniques and procedures used, are very similar to those used in information systems audits or financial audits. The basic differences involve the scope and objectives of the audit. Whereas the scope of the information systems audit is confined to internal controls and the scope of the financial audit is confined to the output of information systems, the scope of the operational audit is much broader, encompassing all aspects of the management of the information systems activity. Furthermore, the objectives of operational audits involve evaluating such factors as effectiveness, efficiency, and the accomplishment of organizational objectives. This section briefly reviews some of the most significant aspects of the management of computer-based information systems in order to provide a framework for understanding the scope of operational audits of such systems. The section concludes with a brief discussion of the application of standard auditing procedures and techniques to the performance of operational audits.

The principles of good systems management provide a standard against which the attributes of an actual system can be measured. Many of these principles were described at length in portions of the previous seven chapters. Accordingly, the following outline of six basic categories of systems management principles is intended merely as a review.

1. *Organizational arrangements:* Organizational arrangements include such matters as the role and responsibilities of the MIS director, the existence and effective functioning of an MIS steering committee, and the proper distribution of functions within the systems department.

2. *Systems planning:* Systems planning encompasses the prioritization of potential systems development projects, the preparation of systems development plans, the projection of future hardware and personnel requirements, and the preparation of an overall long-range financial plan for the systems development activity that is integrated with the organization's long-range planning process.

3. *Personnel policies:* Personnel policies are standards for hiring, training, and assigning IS personnel; establishing job descriptions and performance standards; evaluating employees' performance; and effectively involving appropriate management personnel in activ-

ities such as systems planning, project selection, and development of new systems.

4. *Management of systems development projects:* Good management of systems development projects involves using feasibility studies and other systematic methods in selecting projects and vendors; preparing systems development schedules and budgets; establishing project milestones; carrying out project progress reviews at regular intervals; and adhering to good documentation standards.

5. *Financial controls:* Financial controls encompass the application of responsibility accounting and reporting standards to systems departments and projects, including the use of financial budgets and performance reports and of a system of charging computer users for the cost or value of the computer services they consume.

6. *Computer operations:* Computer operations management involves establishing a data processing schedule, maintaining activity logs, providing good operating documentation such as run manuals, monitoring the performance of computer hardware and software, adhering to a regular equipment maintenance schedule, and maintaining proper control over physical access to computer equipment, files, documentation, and other resources.

The process of performing an operational audit parallels the process of performing an information systems audit or a financial audit. The first step is audit planning, during which the scope and objectives of the audit are established, a preliminary review of the system is performed, and a tentative audit program is prepared. Evidence collection includes reviewing operating policies and documentation; asking management and operating personnel about procedures, perhaps by using questionnaires or checklists; observing operating functions and activities; examining financial and operating plans and reports; testing the accuracy of operating information; and testing controls with respect to prescribed policies and procedures.

At the evidence evaluation stage the auditor is basically measuring the actual system against an ideal system that would follow all the best principles of systems management. One important consideration here is that the *results* of management policies and practices are more significant than the policies and practices themselves. That is, if excellent results are being achieved through policies and practices that are theoretically deficient, then the auditor must carefully consider whether recommended improvements would substantially improve results. In any event, the auditor should thoroughly document the findings and conclusions and communicate the audit results to management in an effective manner.

Being a good operational auditor probably requires some degree of management experience. Persons with excellent backgrounds in auditing but without management experience often lack the perspective necessary to understand the management process. Thus the ideal operational auditor is probably a person with training and experience as an auditor but also with a few years' experience in a managerial position.

CASE CONCLUSION: RESOLVING AUDIT ISSUES AT SEATTLE PAPER PRODUCTS

While Jason Scott is puzzling over how his parallel simulation program could have generated sales commission figures different from those of the program prepared by Seattle Paper's systems development team, he begins to notice that all of the differences occur in cases where the sales commission is higher than average. He realizes that this could mean that there is a systematic error either in the development version of the program or in his version. After once again verifying that his program code is correctly formulated to compute larger commission accounts, he asks to review a copy of the development program code. He is given the proper access code and calls up a copy of the program on his terminal.

The full program code is very lengthy, but Jason remembers that his training instructor had told him about a technique called "scanning," which will allow him to search a block of text for a specified set of characters. Under the new commission policy the commission rate is supposed to change when total sales for the period exceed $40,000, so Jason decides to search the code for occurrences of "40000." First, he copies the program code into a text editor, and then he executes the search. This quickly directs him to the portion of the program code where the commission rate structure resides. To his astonishment, he discovers that the program uses a commission rate of 0.085 for sales in excess of $40,000, while the policy specifies that the commission rate should be 0.075. Some quick and dirty calculations confirm that this is the source of the differences between the two program outputs.

Jason reports his findings to his supervisor. After listening to Jason's story, she calls in the audit manager for the job to hear the report. Shortly thereafter, a meeting is arranged between the audit manager and the head of the systems development team. This meeting turns out to be quite embarrassing for the systems team head and her staff, but the coding error is acknowledged and corrected.

The audit manager calls on Jason to congratulate him for doing a good job. The manager tells Jason that had the programming error gone undetected, Seattle Paper would have paid out over $100,000 per year in excess sales commissions. While Jason is grateful to receive the manager's praise, he also takes the opportunity to question the programming practices employed by the development team. First, he points out that the commission rate table had been embedded in the program code, when good programming practice would require that it be stored in a separate table to be called by the program when needed. Second, he suggests that the incident calls into question the quality of Seattle Paper's program development and testing practices, and he asks whether a more extensive operational audit of those practices might be appropriate. The audit manager agrees that this might be worth looking into, and he promises that he will raise the issue at his next meeting with Northwest's Director of Internal Auditing. ■

SUMMARY

An audit is a systematic and objective process that involves planning audit procedures, collecting and evaluating evidence, and communicating results and conclusions. Audits of computer-based information systems evaluate the effectiveness of these systems in meeting standards for the reliability and integrity of information; compliance with policies, plans, procedures, laws, and regulations; safeguarding of assets; economical and efficient use of resources; and accomplishment of established objectives and goals for operations or programs.

Three major categories of audits of computer-based information systems are information systems audits, financial audits, and operational audits. Information systems audits are designed to evaluate the quality of control policies and procedures relating to computer security, computer program development, program changes, computer processing, source data entry, and computer data storage. Financial audits focus on the reliability and integrity of financial and operating information and make extensive use of computer audit software. Operational audits involve evaluation of the effectiveness and efficiency of information systems management in accomplishing the objectives of the organization.

KEY TERMS

Define the following terms

auditing	automated flowcharting programs	snapshot technique
information systems (IS) audit		tagging
financial audit	automated decision table programs	SCARF
operational audit		audit log
management audit	scanning routines	audit hooks
compliance audit	mapping programs	real-time notification
materiality	program tracing	continuous and intermittent simulation (CIS)
reasonable assurance	test data generator	
system review	on-line testing	input controls matrix
tests of control	concurrent audit techniques	generalized audit software (GAS)
compensating controls	embedded audit modules	
reprocessing	integrated test facility	computer audit software
parallel simulation	minicompany test	stratified sampling

DISCUSSION QUESTIONS

15.1 To effectively audit a computer-based information system, an auditor should have some knowledge of computers and their accounting applications. However, it may not be feasible for every auditor to be a "computer expert." Discuss the extent to which auditors should possess computer expertise in order to be effective auditors.

15.2 Should internal auditors be members of systems development teams that design and implement computer-based accounting information systems? Why or why not?

15.3 Berwick Industries is a fast-growing corporation that manufactures industrial containers. The company has a very sophisticated information system utilizing advanced technology. Berwick's executives have decided to pursue listing the company's securities on a national stock exchange, but they have been advised that their listing application would be stronger if they were to create an internal audit department.

At present, Berwick has no employees with audit experience. To staff its new internal audit function, Berwick could (a) train some of its computer specialists in auditing, (b) hire experienced auditors and train them to understand Berwick's information system, (c) use a combination of the first two approaches, or (d) use some other approach. Which approach would you support, and why?

15.4 In 1985 the Assistant Finance Director for the city of Tustin, California, was fired after city officials discovered that she had used her access to city computers to cancel her daughter's $300 water bill. An investigation revealed that she had embezzled about $165,000 from the city in this manner over a four-year period, and that she was able to conceal the embezzlement for so long because the amount embezzled always fell within a 2% error factor used by the city's internal auditors.[17] Should Tustin's internal auditors have discovered this fraud earlier? Discuss.

PROBLEMS

15.1 You are the director of Internal Auditing at a university. Recently, you met with the Manager of Administrative Data Processing and expressed the desire to establish a more effective interface between the two departments.

Subsequently, the Manager of Data Processing requested your views and help on a new computerized accounts payable system being developed. The Manager recommended that Internal Auditing assume line responsibility for auditing suppliers' invoices prior to payment. The Manager also requested that Internal Auditing make suggestions during development of the system, assist in its installation, and approve the completed system after making a final review.

Required

State how you would respond to the Administrative Data Processing Manager, giving the reason why you would accept or reject each of the following.

a. The recommendation that your department be responsible for the preaudit of suppliers' invoices.

b. The request that you make suggestions during development of the system.

c. The request that you assist in the installation of the system and approve the system after making a final review.

(CIA Examination)

---

[17] Jerry Hicks, "Ex-Tustin Official Given Year in Jail for Embezzling $165,000," *Los Angeles Times* (April 23, 1987): part 2, p. 3.

15.2 As an internal auditor for the Quick Manufacturing Company, you are participating in the audit of the company's computer-based information system. The company uses the computer in most of its accounting applications. You have been reviewing the internal controls associated with these computer systems. You have studied the company's extensive documentation of its systems, and you have interviewed the MIS Manager, Operations Supervisor, and other employees in order to complete your standardized computer internal control questionnaire.

You report to your supervisor that the company has designed an excellent and comprehensive set of internal controls into its computer systems. The supervisor thanks you for your efforts and asks you to prepare a summary report of your findings for inclusion in a final overall report on accounting internal controls.

Required

Have you forgotten an important audit step? Explain. List five examples of specific audit procedures that you might recommend be performed before you reach a final conclusion.

15.3 As an internal auditor, you have been assigned to evaluate the controls and operation of a computer payroll system. The audit technique you will be using is a test of the computer systems and/or programs by submitting independently created test transactions with regular data in a normal production run.

Required

a. List four advantages of this technique.

b. List two disadvantages of this technique. (CIA Examination, adapted)

15.4 You are involved in the internal audit of accounts receivable, which represent a significant portion of the assets of a large retail corporation. Your audit plan requires the use of the computer, but you encounter the following reactions.

a. The Computer Operations Manager says that all time on the computer is scheduled for the foreseeable future and that it is not feasible to perform the work for the auditor.

b. The Computer Scheduling Manager suggests that your computer program be cataloged into the computer program library (on disk storage) to be run when computer time becomes available.

c. You are refused admission to the computer room.

d. The Systems Manager tells you that it will take too much time to adapt the computer audit program to the EDP operating system and that the computer installation programmers would write the programs needed for the audit.

Required

For each of the four situations described, state the action the auditor should take to proceed with the accounts receivable audit. (CIA Examination)

15.5 You are a manager for the regional CPA firm of Dewey, Cheatem, and Howe. You are reviewing working papers prepared by staff accountants working under your supervision on an audit of the State Welfare Agency. You find that the test data concept was used to test a computer program used by the agency to maintain accounting records. Specifically, your staff obtained a duplicate copy of the program and of the welfare accounting data file from the Manager of Computer Operations, and borrowed the test transaction data file used by the Welfare Agency's programmers when the program was written. These were processed on DC&H's home office computer. A copy of the edit summary report listing no errors was included in the working papers, along with a notation by the audit senior that the test indicates good application controls.

You note that the quality of the audit conclusions obtained from this test is flawed in several respects, and you decide to ask your subordinates to perform the test over again.

Required

Identify three problems (or potential problems) with the way this test was performed. For each of the problems that you identify, suggest one or more procedures that might be performed during the revised test in order to avoid flaws in the audit conclusions obtained from it.

15.6 You are auditing the financial statements of Aardvark Wholesalers, Inc. (AW), a wholesaler having operations in 12 western states and total revenues of about $125 million. AW uses a computer system in several of its major accounting applications. Accordingly, you are carrying out an information systems audit to evaluate internal controls in AW's computer system.

You have obtained a manual containing job descriptions for key personnel in AW's Information Systems Division. Excerpts from these follow.

■ *Director of Information Systems:* Reports to Administrative Vice-President. Responsible for defining the mission of the Information Systems Division in the organization and for planning, staffing, and managing a department that optimally executes this mission.

■ *Manager of Systems and Programming:* Reports to Director of Information Systems. Responsible for managing a staff of systems analysts and programmers whose mission is to design, program, test, implement, and maintain cost-effective data processing systems. Also responsible for establishing and monitoring documentation standards.

■ *Manager of Operations:* Reports to Director of Information Systems. Responsible for cost-effective management of computer center operations, for enforcement of processing standards, and for systems programming, including implementation of vendor upgrades of operating systems.

■ *Data Entry Shift Supervisor:* Reports to Manager of Operations. Responsible for supervision of data entry operators and monitoring of data preparation standards.

■ *Operations Shift Supervisor:* Reports to Manager of Operations. Responsible for supervision of computer operations staff and monitoring of processing standards.

■ *Data Control Clerk:* Reports to Manager of Operations. Responsible for logging and distributing computer input and output, monitoring source data control procedures, and custody of program and data files.

Required

a. Prepare an organization chart for AW's Information Systems Division.

b. Comment on the adequacy (from an internal control standpoint) of this organization structure.

1. What, if anything, is good about it?
2. What, if anything, is bad about it?
3. What additional information, if any, would you require before you could make a final judgment on the adequacy of AW's separation of functions in the Information Systems Division?

15.7 Robinson's Plastic Pipe Corporation uses a computerized inventory data processing system. The basic input record to this system has the format shown in Table 15.9. You are performing an audit of source data controls for this system, and you have decided to use an input controls matrix for this purpose.

Required

Prepare an input controls matrix using the same format and listing the same input controls as the one in Fig. 15.4, but replace the field names shown in Fig. 15.4 with those of the inventory transaction file shown in Table 15.9. Place checks in the cells of the matrix that represent input controls you might expect to find for each field.

15.8 As an internal auditor for the State Auditor's Office, you have been assigned to review the implementation of a new computer system in the State Welfare Agency. The agency is installing an on-line computer system to maintain the state's data base of welfare recipients. Under the old system, when state residents apply for welfare assistance, they complete a form giving their name, address, and other personal data, plus details about their income, assets, dependents, and other data needed to establish their eligibility. The data on these forms are then checked by welfare examiners to verify their authenticity. The welfare examiners then certify the

Table 15.9 Parts inventory transaction file

Field Name	Field Type	Positions
Item number	Numeric	1–6
Description	Alphanumeric	7–31
Transaction date	Date	32–37
Transaction type	Alphanumeric	38
Document number	Alphanumeric	39–46
Quantity	Numeric	47–51
Unit cost	Monetary	52–58

applicant's eligibility for assistance and determine the form and amount of aid.

Under the new system welfare applicants will provide their case data to clerks, who will simultaneously enter the data into the system using on-line terminals. Each applicant record will be assigned a "pending" status until a welfare examiner can verify the authenticity of the critical data used in determining eligibility for assistance. When this verification process has been completed, the welfare examiner will enter a change in the status code from "pending" to "approved," and the system will then execute a program to calculate the appropriate amount of aid.

Periodically, the circumstances (income, assets, dependents, etc.) of welfare recipients change and it will be necessary to update the data base to reflect these changes. Welfare examiners will enter these change transactions into the system as soon as their accuracy has been verified. The system will then immediately recalculate the recipient's welfare benefit. At the end of each month the data base will be processed to generate checks to be mailed to all eligible welfare recipients.

Welfare assistance in your state amounts to several hundred million dollars annually. You are concerned about the possibilities of fraud and abuse of this system.

Required

a. Describe how you could employ concurrent audit techniques within this system to reduce the risks of fraud and abuse.

b. Describe how computer audit software could be employed to review the work of welfare examiners in verifying applicant eligibility data. For this purpose you may assume that the State Auditor's Office has access to computerized data bases maintained by other state and local government agencies.

15.9 You are an internal auditor for the Military Industrial Company. You are presently preparing test transactions for the company's weekly payroll processing program. Each input record to this program contains the following data items.

Spaces	Data Item
1-9	Social Security number
10	Pay code (1 = hourly; 2 = salaried)
11-16	Wage rate or salary
17-19	Hours worked, in tenths
20-21	Number of exemptions claimed
22-29	Year-to-date gross pay, including cents
30-80	Employee name and address

The program performs the following edit checks on each input record.

■ Field checks to identify any records that do not have numeric characters in the fields for wage rate/salary, hours, exemptions, and year-to-date gross pay
■ A validity check of the pay code
■ A limit check to identify any hourly employee records with a wage rate higher than $20.00
■ A limit check to identify any hourly employee records with hours worked greater than 70.0
■ A limit check to identify any salaried employee records with a weekly salary greater than $2000.00 or less than $100.00

Those records that do not pass all of these edit checks are listed on an error report. For those records that do pass all of these edit checks, the program performs a series of calculations. First, the employee's gross pay is determined. Gross pay for a salaried employee is equal to the salary amount contained within spaces 11-16 of the input record. Gross pay for an hourly employee is equal to the wage rate times the number of hours up to 40, plus 1.5 times the wage rate times the number of hours in excess of 40.

The program computes federal withholding tax for each employee by multiplying gross pay times a tax rate determined from Table 15.10. The program next computes state withholding tax for each em-

Table 15.10
Computation of federal
withholding tax

Number of Exemptions	Gross Pay Range			
	$0–$99.99	$100–$249.99	$250–$499.99	Over $500
0–1	0.06	0.12	0.18	0.24
2–3	0.04	0.10	0.16	0.22
4–5	0.02	0.08	0.14	0.20
Over 5	0.00	0.06	0.12	0.18

Table 15.11 Computation of state withholding tax

Number of Exemptions	GROSS PAY RANGE	
	$0–$249.99	Over $500
0–3	0.03	0.05
Over 3	0.01	0.03

ployee by multiplying gross pay times a tax rate determined from Table 15.11. The program then computes FICA tax withholdings by multiplying gross pay by 6%, except that no FICA taxes are withheld once year-to-date gross pay exceeds $25,000.

The program next computes the employee's pension contribution, which is 3% of gross pay for hourly employees and 4% of gross pay for salaried employees. Finally, the program computes the employee's net pay, which is gross pay minus tax withholdings and pension contribution. Once all these calculations have been completed for one employee record, the program prints that employee's paycheck and summary earnings statement and then proceeds to the next employee input record to perform edit checks and payroll calculations, continuing this cycle until all input records have been processed.

For the moment you are concerned only with preparing a set of test transactions containing one of each possible type of error and another set of test transactions that will test each of the computational alternatives one at a time. Transactions to test for multiple errors in one record, or to test for multiple combinations of logic paths, are to be developed later.

The test transactions you prepare need not include a Social Security number or an employee name and address (your assistant will add those after reviewing a file printout). Accordingly, each of your test transactions will consist of a series of 20 characters representing data in spaces 10–29 of an input record. For example, for an hourly employee who has a wage rate of $9.50, worked 40.5 hours, claims two exemptions, and has a year-to-date gross pay of exactly $12,000, the test transaction would be 10009504050201200000.

Required

a. Prepare a set of test transactions, each of which contains one of the possible kinds of errors tested for by the edit checks. Determine the expected results of processing for each of these test transactions.

b. Prepare a set of test transactions, each of which tests one of the ways in which gross pay may be determined. Determine the expected gross pay for each of these transactions.

c. Prepare a set of test transactions, each of which tests one of the ways in which federal withholding tax may be computed. Determine the expected value of federal withholding tax for each of these test transactions.

d. Prepare a set of test transactions, each of which tests one of the ways in which state withholding tax may be computed. Determine the expected value of state withholding tax for each of these test transactions.

e. Prepare a set of test transactions, each of which tests one of the ways in which FICA withholding tax may be computed. Determine the expected value of FICA withholding tax for each of these test transactions.

f. Prepare a set of test transactions, each of which tests one of the ways in which the pension contribution may be computed. Determine the expected value of the pension contribution for each of these test transactions.

15.10 The Internal Audit Department of Sachem Manufacturing Company is considering the purchase of computer software that will aid the auditing process. Sachem's financial and manufacturing control systems are completely automated on a large mainframe computer. Melinda Robinson, the Director of Internal Audit, believes that Sachem should acquire computer audit software to assist in the financial and procedural audits that her department conducts. The types of software packages that Robinson is considering are described next.

■ A generalized audit software package that assists in basic audit work such as the retrieval of live data from large computer files. The department would review this information using conventional audit investigation techniques. More specifically, the department could perform criteria selection, sampling, basic computations for quantitative analysis, record handling, graphical analysis, and the printing of output (i.e., confirmations).

■ An integrated test facility (ITF) package that uses, monitors, and controls "dummy" test data through existing programs and checks the existing programs and checks the existence and adequacy of program data entry controls and processing controls.

- A control flowcharting package that provides a graphical presentation of the data flow of information through a system, pinpointing control strengths and weaknesses.
- A program (parallel) simulation and modeling package that uses actual data to conduct the same systemized process by using a different computer logic program developed by the auditor. The package can also be used to seek answers to difficult audit problems (involving many comparisons) within statistically acceptable confidence limits.

Required

a. Without regard to any specific computer audit software, identify the general advantages to the internal auditor of using computer audit software to assist with audits.

b. Describe the audit purpose facilitated and the procedural steps to be followed by the internal auditor in using the following.

1. Generalized audit software package
2. Integrated test facility package
3. Control flowcharting package
4. Program (parallel) simulation and modeling package

(CMA Examination)

15.11 The Thermo-Bond Manufacturing Company maintains its fixed asset records on its computer. The fixed asset master file includes data items listed in Table 15.12.

Required

Refer to Table 15.7 describing the general functions of computer audit software. Then explain several ways in which computer audit software could be used by an auditor in performing a financial audit of Thermo-Bond's fixed asset account.

15.12 An auditor is conducting an examination of the financial statements of a wholesale cosmetics distributor with an inventory consisting of thousands of individual items. The distributor keeps its inventory in its own distribution center and in two public warehouses. An inventory computer file is maintained on a computer disk, and at the end of each business day the file is updated. Each record of the inventory file contains the following data.

Item number	Cost per item
Location of item	Date of last purchase
Description of item	Date of last sale
Quantity on hand	Quantity sold during year

Table 15.12   Fixed asset master file

Item Number	Location	Description
1	1–6	Asset number
2	7–30	Description
3	31	Type code
4	32–34	Location code
5	35–40	Date of acquisition
6	41–50	Original cost
7	51–56	Date of retirement*
8	57	Depreciation method code
9	58–61	Depreciation rate
10	62–63	Useful life (years)
11	64–73	Accumulated depreciation at beginning of year
12	74–83	Year-to-date depreciation

* For assets still in service the retirement date is assigned the value 99/99/99.

The auditor will have available a computer tape of the data on the inventory file as of the date of the distributor's physical count of the inventory and a general-purpose computer audit software package. The auditor is planning to perform the following audit procedures.

1. Observe the distributor's physical count of inventories as of a given date, and test a sample of the distributor's inventory counts for accuracy.
2. Compare the auditor's test counts with the inventory records.
3. Compare physical count data with the inventory records.
4. Test the mathematical accuracy of the distributor's final inventory valuation.
5. Test the pricing of the inventory by obtaining a list of costs per item from buyers, vendors, or other sources.
6. Examine inventory purchase and sale transactions on or near the year-end date to verify that all such transactions were recorded in the proper accounting period.
7. Ascertain the propriety of items of inventory located in public warehouses.
8. Analyze inventory for evidence of possible obsolescence.

9. Analyze inventory for evidence of possible overstocking or slow-moving items.

10. Test the accuracy of individual data items listed in the distributor's inventory master file.

Required

Describe how the use of the general-purpose soft-ware package and the tape of the inventory file data might be helpful to the auditor in performing each of these auditing procedures. (CPA Examination, adapted)

CASE 15.1: ANYCOMPANY, INC.—AN ONGOING COMPREHENSIVE CASE

One of the best ways to learn is to immediately apply what you have studied. The purpose of this case is to allow you to do that. You will select a local company that you can work with. At the end of most chapters you will find an assignment that will have you apply what you have learned using the company you have selected as a reference. This case, then, may become an ongoing case study that you work on throughout the term.

Select a local company that has an Internal Auditing Department, and obtain permission to study its internal auditing policies and procedures. Then complete the following steps, and prepare a report describing your findings and conclusions.

1. Determine to whom in the organization the head of Internal Auditing reports. Does this reporting arrangement provide the internal audit function with sufficient independence?

2. Does the internal audit function perform information systems audits, financial audits, and operational audits? Does it perform other kinds of audits? About what percentage of its total audit work falls into each of these categories?

3. Are the company's internal auditing jobs scheduled on a regular basis, a random basis, or some mix of these? Comment on the internal audit scheduling practices.

4. Determine how the internal auditors perform information systems audits. If possible, obtain copies of audit programs, checklists, and/or question-naires used in performing information systems audits. Comment on the company's approach to information systems auditing.

5. In performing information systems audits, do the internal auditors use methods of auditing *through* the computer, such as reprocessing, parallel simulation, program tracing, test data processing, on-line testing, and concurrent audit techniques? Describe how the internal auditors use these methods.

6. In carrying out financial audits, does the internal audit function employ computer audit software? If so, obtain a copy of the audit software documentation, and describe the functions that the audit software can perform. If possible, observe how the audit software is used in carrying out a financial audit, and examine copies of the output.

7. Determine how the internal auditors perform operational audits. If possible, obtain copies of operational audit programs, checklists, and/or questionnaires. Comment on the company's approach to operational auditing.

8. Ask the internal auditors if they will tell you about some specific audit jobs where they discovered something unusual and/or were able to recommend improvements in controls or operating procedures that saved the company substantial amounts of money.

CASE 15.2: PRESTON MANUFACTURING COMPANY

You are performing a financial audit of the general ledger accounts of the Preston Manufacturing Company. At the beginning of the current fiscal year the company converted its general ledger accounting from a manual to a computer-based system. The new system uses two computer files, whose contents are specified below.

GENERAL JOURNAL		
Field Name	Field Type	Size
Account number	Numeric	6
Amount	Monetary	9.2
Debit/credit code	Alphanumeric	1
Date (MM/DD/YY)	Date	6
Reference document type	Alphanumeric	4
Reference document number	Numeric	6

GENERAL LEDGER CONTROL		
Field Name	Field Type	Size
Account number	Numeric	6
Account name	Alphanumeric	20
Beginning balance/year	Monetary	9.2
Beg-bal-debit/credit code	Alphanumeric	1
Current balance	Monetary	9.2
Cur-bal-debit/credit code	Alphanumeric	1

Each day as detailed transactions are processed by Preston's other computerized accounting systems, summary journal entries are accumulated; at the end of the day they are added to the general ledger file. At the end of each week and also at the end of each month the general journal file is processed against the general ledger control file to compute a new current balance for each account and to print a trial balance.

In performing the financial audit, you have the following things available to you.

- Your firm's generalized computer audit software package, which can perform the general functions listed in Table 15.7
- A complete copy of the general journal file for the entire year
- A copy of the general ledger file as of the fiscal year end (i.e., current balance = year-end balance)
- A printout of Preston's year-end trial balance listing the account number, account name, and balance of each account on the general ledger control file

You are to design a series of procedures utilizing the audit software package to analyze the data in these files and prepare various reports that will be useful in carrying out your financial audit. Your application design should include the following.

1. A description of the data content of each output report, preferably in the form of a tabular layout chart of the report format

2. A description of the auditing objectives of each report and how the report would be used in subsequent auditing procedures to achieve those objectives

3. A detailed system flowchart showing each of the processing steps in the computer audit software application

PART V

CHAPTER

The Revenue Cycle: Sales and Accounts Receivable

LEARNING OBJECTIVES

After studying this chapter, you should be able to:

■ Describe the key activities and data processing operations included in the revenue cycle.

■ Describe the decision responsibilities and information requirements of marketing management.

■ Give several examples of the information provided to marketing management by the accounting information system.

■ Flowchart data and information flows in typical sales order processing systems.

■ Evaluate and recommend control policies and procedures for a sales order processing system.

INTEGRATIVE CASE: ELECTRONICS INCORPORATED

Paul Watson is Vice-President of Marketing at Electronics Incorporated (EI), a manufacturer of a variety of inexpensive consumer electronic products, including calculators, digital clocks, radios, pagers, toys, games, and small kitchen appliances. EI operates two manufacturing plants located in the Midwest, and it distributes its products through a network of five warehouses located throughout the country. EI's primary customers are discount retail stores, but the company has recently begun selling in bulk to mail-order firms who advertise their products through catalogs and magazines.

Due to a recent economic recession, the volume of orders received by EI has declined. In addition, a large retailer that had been one of the company's best customers recently went bankrupt, and Paul is not sure whether they will be able to collect the large balance due from this customer. He is also worried about the uncertain prospects facing some other retail customers. In response to these problems, Watson has suggested to EI's president that the company try to obtain a larger volume of mail order business, which he believes could be more lucrative and less volatile than the retail trade. However, the president was skeptical of this recommendation.

As he ponders a disappointing sales report recently generated by EI's computer-based information system, Paul thinks about how this system could provide him with information that would be useful in addressing the company's current problems. In particular, he wonders whether the information system could answer questions like these:

1. Which products and markets have higher profit margins?
2. What is the effect of EI's liberal return policies on profit margins?
3. Should credit policies be tightened for customers facing financial difficulties? If so, then for which customers?
4. Should prices be raised on some of EI's products?
5. How could the information system assist EI in providing better service to its customers?

What would you suggest to Paul about how EI's information system could be used to address these issues? ■

INTRODUCTION

The revenue cycle is a recurring set of business activities and related data processing operations associated with providing products and services to customers in exchange for revenue. The business activities include soliciting customer orders, executing sales transactions, and delivering products and services. These business activities comprise the marketing function within a typical business organization. The related data processing operations include processing customer sales orders, billing customers, updating product inventory records, and maintaining customer account records. These are examples of the kinds of data processing operations performed in accounting cycles, as described in Chapter 2, and are generally carried out by the accounting information system.

Electronics Incorporated, like all business organizations, must provide products or services for which there is a market demand. This market demand must produce a stream of revenue sufficient to cover the firm's costs and expenses, replace its assets, and provide its capital suppliers with a return on their investment. The accounting information system plays an important role here in processing sales and related customer transactions and providing marketing executives and sales personnel with the information they need to manage the marketing function effectively. As you read this chapter, several ways that EI could use its computer-based information system to support its marketing activities should become apparent to you.

A close relationship must exist between the accounting and marketing functions in any business organization. This chapter examines that relationship, starting with a description of the decision responsibilities and information requirements of marketing managers. This reveals the kinds of information that marketing managers need from their information systems. The next section of the chapter explains the basic functions and procedures that are performed within the revenue cycle of a typical business organization. The rest of the chapter describes and illustrates the sales order processing system, which is the part of the accounting information system that carries out the basic revenue cycle functions and procedures, and generates information to meet the information needs of marketing managers.

Part V describes how accounting data are processed in business information systems. As explained in Chapter 1, a typical business has a number of related cycles of activity, such as the five business cycles of a manufacturing company illustrated in Fig. 1.6. Corresponding to each business cycle are one or more accounting cycles, in which accounting transaction data are collected and processed to generate information that is useful in the management of the related business cycle. Each of the five chapters in Part V covers one of these five primary business cycles and its related accounting cycle or cycles. The revenue cycle is covered in Chapter 16, the procurement cycle in Chapter 17, the production cycle in Chapter 18, the personnel/payroll cycle in Chapter 19, and the financial management cycle in Chapter 20.

Although the various business and accounting cycles are described in separate chapters, this treatment is basically a matter of convenience of presentation. In reality, the underlying business and accounting activities in these areas are very much interdependent in terms of both operations and information. These interrelationships are partly, though not completely, reflected in Fig. 1.6. As we proceed through Part V, the nature of these interrelationships among the business and accounting activities within these cycles should become more apparent to you.

To further illustrate the relationship between business functions and their related business and accounting cycles, consider Fig. 16.1. At the top of the diagram is an abbreviated organization chart encompassing five of the primary business functions in a typical manufacturing company. In the middle of the diagram, each of the five major business cycles is listed and linked to its corresponding business function. At the bottom, the accounting cycles associated with each business cycle are identified. This diagram emphasizes the important role of accounting information systems in controlling and managing business operations. Specifically, the information generated within each accounting cycle is of crucial importance in the related business cycle, and is essential in managing the operations of the related business function.

The chapters in Part V also illustrate and integrate the application of many of the concepts, tools, technologies and techniques, covered in the previous parts of this book. In particular, the concept of informa-

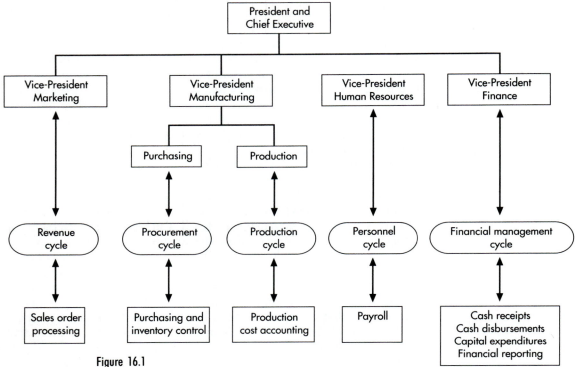

Figure 16.1
Business functions, business cycles, and accounting cycles

tion requirements analysis, the tools of flowcharting and data base diagraming, the technology of computer-based information systems, and the techniques of internal control are stressed.

THE MARKETING MANAGEMENT FUNCTION

To apply the concept of information requirements analysis, the chapters in Part V begin by presenting sample organization charts within each of the major functional areas of business firms. These charts provide a framework for describing decision-making responsibilities and information requirements within each functional area. Figure 16.2 is an example of a typical marketing organization structure. Each of the executive positions shown in the chart is examined in this section.

The Top Marketing Executive

The Marketing Vice-President is responsible for the effective planning, coordination, and control of the marketing effort, and participates in companywide planning and resource allocation. This executive also plays a major role in establishing pricing policies, including the determination of discount policies, credit terms, return policies, and warranty policies. He or she also participates in making decisions on various matters that are the responsibility of marketing staff executives, such as new product introduction and the planning of major advertising and promotion campaigns. Finally, the Marketing Vice-President must review and evaluate the performance of subordinate marketing executives.

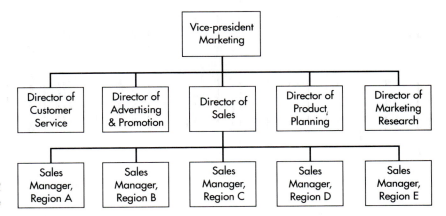

Figure 16.2
Marketing organization structure

The Marketing Vice-President in a business organization may be looked upon as a strategist seeking an optimal allocation of scarce resources to achieve the maximum advantage for the firm in the environment of the marketplace. The most important of these scarce resources are people (sales personnel and staff specialists) and funds. The Marketing Vice-President must allocate these resources among such activities as selling effort, advertising and promotional campaigns, and marketing research studies. Environmental forces include customers, competitors, the economy, and government.

The Marketing Vice-President relies on extensive information obtained from various sources. The planning function requires environmental information on such matters as economic trends, competitors' plans, and customers' attitudes, as well as internally generated information such as sales forecasts and market research studies. The pricing decision requires all of the preceding kinds of information plus internal information on the cost of products and the cost of credit, return, and warranty policies. Performance evaluation decisions are based on the results of marketing activities, including information on profitability, unit and dollar sales volume, and trends in market share. Much of this information is generated as a by-product of the processing of sales transactions within the revenue cycle.

Director of Sales
The Director of Sales is responsible for the effectiveness of the firm's selling effort and works with the Marketing Vice-President to establish standards and quotas for the sales force. If the firm's products are consumer goods sold through wholesale and retail outlets, the Director of Sales will be involved in the selection of the most effective distribution channels. The regional sales managers who report to the Director of Sales have similar responsibilities on a smaller scale. The Director of Sales must review, evaluate, and control the performance of the regional sales managers, who, in turn, must review, evaluate, and control the performance of their respective sales forces.

Sales forecasts provide the Director of Sales and the regional sales managers with an information base for planning the sales effort. Similarly, reports of actual sales, or **sales analyses**, provide an information base for control. Sales analysis reports may classify sales in several ways. For the Regional Sales Manager, classification by salesperson is most meaningful as a tool for evaluating salespeople. For the Director of Sales, a sales analysis by regions and perhaps by territories within regions is useful. For individual salespeople, sales analysis by customer is very useful. All of this information should be available on a routine basis from the data collected and processed within the revenue cycle.

Whereas a sales analysis reports only sales volume, a **profitability analysis** breaks down the marginal contribution to profit made by each territory, customer, distribution channel, or other unit. For example, Electronics Incorporated could use profitability analysis information to assess the relative profitability of its retail and mail-order distribution channels. Profitability is a function of both sales volume and profit margin; in turn, profit margin is a function of sales revenues, variable product costs, and incremental selling costs. For planning and control purposes profitability analyses are even more useful to sales managers and selling personnel than are sales analyses, because they indicate directly the marginal contribution to profit of each individual selling activity. However, profitability information is more difficult for an information system to generate because it requires incremental cost data in addition to sales volume and revenue data.[1]

Also useful in managing the selling effort are analyses of the activities of individual salespeople, including customers called upon, time spent with each, literature distributed, and demonstrations presented. Individual salespersons require certain operational information for use in executing sales transactions, such as information on the availability and location of inventories, the delivery arrangements for each customer, and the credit standing of each customer. Providing current information on inventories and customers, based on data processed within the revenue cycle, is an important function of the accounting information system. In addition, information on the incremental cost of various selling activities is useful to salespeople and sales managers for purposes of cost control. Important in this respect are analyses of the incremental costs of calling on a particular class of customer, of utilizing a particular mode of delivery of the product, or of servicing customers within a particular territory.

Director of Advertising and Promotion

The Director of Advertising and Promotion is responsible for planning and control of promotional activities. Together with his or her staff, the Director plans advertising campaigns and other promotional strategies, such as dealer incentives, contests, and trade show displays, and then

---

[1] Examples of sales analysis and profitability analysis reports are presented later in this chapter, in the section on reporting. See Tables 16.1 and 16.2.

must coordinate the execution of these strategies and evaluate their effectiveness as a basis for subsequent planning. The Director must allocate a limited promotional budget among various product lines, territories, and so forth, to obtain maximum results.

Various types of information are needed by the Director of Advertising and Promotion. Sales and profitability analysis information that provides breakdowns by territory, product line, and perhaps customer is relevant to the planning and control of advertising and promotion. Information on customer attitudes and plans is also useful for planning. Information on the cost of individual advertising and promotional campaigns is necessary for control purposes. Information that specifically relates sales and profit performance to advertising and promotional efforts is especially useful for planning and control. Much of this information is made available through the accounting information system.

Director of Product Planning

The Director of Product Planning is responsible for planning the characteristics of the product line. The Director must make decisions related to styling and packaging as well as to the planning and introduction of new products. Another function of the Director is to review the performance of existing products—their sales, profitability, and potential—and decide or recommend whether any products should be removed from the product line.

Sales analyses and profitability analyses by product line provide information that is vital to the product planning function. Information on incremental product costs and revenues is very useful in making decisions on styling, packaging, and the deletion of products from the line. For example, a company such as Electronics Incorporated, which has many product lines, must have information on the relative product profitability in order to best allocate its marketing resources among its product lines. Information on customer attitudes is also important to decisions on styling and new-product introduction. Projected cost and revenue information is essential for making recommendations on new-product introduction.

Director of Customer Service

The Director of Customer Service is responsible for policies and decisions relating to the servicing of customer needs, both prior and subsequent to the sale of the product. Prior to the sale potential customers need information about product prices and availability and delivery timetables. For example, the primary customers of Electronics Incorporated are the discount retailers, for whom cost minimization is an important objective. By having quick access to information on product prices, these retailers would be able to shop for the best bargains for their customers. By having access to information on product availability and delivery timetables, these retailers would be able to maintain smaller inventories, thus reducing their overhead costs. As this example suggests, attention to customer service prior to the sale has enabled many companies to obtain significant competitive advantages. Note that the key to providing such service is the quality of the information available to customers, and that most of this information is provided by the accounting information system.

Subsequent to the sale customers may need information about product features and functions, warranties, maintenance and repairs, and enhancements. Such information is often provided by a customer service staff administered by the Director of Customer Service. These staff personnel respond to customer inquiries and complaints and are responsible for evaluating the adequacy of products, services, distribution channels, retail facilities, and so on, in meeting customer needs. In companies that market expensive technical products such as computers and other electronic equipment, the Director of Customer Service may administer a staff of maintenance personnel responsible for servicing and repairing the product.

The basic objective of the customer service function is to ensure that customers achieve the highest feasible level of satisfaction of needs or desires from the company's products and services. For purposes of evaluating the effectiveness of customer service activities, marketing executives should regularly obtain information from customers about their level of satisfaction with existing products and services and their needs for additional products and services. Information on the incremental cost of customer service activities is also useful for control purposes.

Director of Marketing Research

The Director of Marketing Research is responsible for planning and administering the data gathering and analysis activities of the marketing research staff. This staff carries out special studies of consumer behavior and other subjects of interest to marketing executives. The Director must allocate scarce resources among alternative projects and interpret the results of such projects for other marketing executives and top management. Marketing research studies are often a primary basis for planning in such areas as new-product introduction, advertising, and pricing. For the most part the marketing research staff members are not users but producers of information, which they generate from data collected by means of scanning the environment.

Summary

It should now be clear that marketing executives require a variety of information from a number of different sources. The accounting information system is one important source. Accounting information generated as a by-product of processing sales order transactions within the revenue cycle is very useful to marketing executives; it represents the largest source of marketing information in terms of volume of information provided. The cost accounting system also provides information on the costs of products and services, the costs of advertising and promotion efforts, and other costs of concern to marketing executives.

A well-managed marketing activity cannot rely solely on financial information, however, and must therefore exploit other information sources inside and outside the organization. Examples include sales forecasts prepared within the Sales Department, call reports in which salespeople summarize information obtained from calling on customers; market research studies prepared by the Marketing Research Department; information on customer satisfaction gathered by the customer service staff; market and industry analyses prepared by the economics staff; product engineering specifications prepared by the Engineering Department; summaries of technological developments provided by research and development personnel; and information on customers, competitors, and economic trends obtained from sources external to the organization.

Although these other sources of marketing information are all important, the remainder of this chapter focuses on the accounting information system. In particular, the next section describes in detail the basic functions and procedures that are performed within the revenue cycle in the processing of sales transactions. This subset of the accounting information system plays an important role in producing accounting information that is useful in the effective management of marketing operations.

BASIC REVENUE CYCLE FUNCTIONS AND PROCEDURES

This section reviews at a very general level the basic functions and procedures that are performed in the revenue cycle of typical business organizations. These functions, identified in Fig. 16.3, include receiving orders from customers and preparing sales order records, checking the creditworthiness of prospective customers, checking product availability and retrieving products from inventory, arranging for delivery of products to customers, billing customers for products and services provided, maintaining records of amounts due from customers, and posting summary accounting transactions to the general ledger. This section describes each of these functions in more detail in the context of a typical manufacturing company. Variations on these basic procedures for companies in different industries—including retailing, public utilities, services, transportation, and construction—are described at the conclusion of this section.

Sales Order Preparation

The revenue cycle begins with the receipt of sales orders from customers. Customer orders may be received (1) by telephone, (2) in the mail, in the form of a customer purchase order document, (3) electronically, through telecommunications links with customers, or (4) from salespeople as a result of direct contact with customers. In some organizations the receipt of a customer order results in the preparation of a sales order document listing the customer, the items ordered, and delivery instructions. In other organizations a sales order record is created by entering these data directly into the computer. Once an order is received, many firms then transmit some form of acknowledgment to the customer, either electronically or in the form of a duplicate copy of the customer's purchase order.

When orders are received for products that must be custom-produced to customer specifications, it is usually necessary to prepare a price quotation indicating how much the customer will be charged for the work. Such orders are held pending preparation of a price quotation by engineering and/or cost accounting personnel. After the quotation has been prepared and transmitted, the customer must approve the price before the order is processed further.

Credit Check

Credit sales transactions should be approved by authorized personnel before they are processed. For long-time customers having well-established payment histories it is usually not necessary to run a formal credit check; order takers may be authorized to approve orders from such "customers in good standing." However, in difficult economic times, such as those facing the customers of Electronics Incorporated, it may become necessary to perform a formal credit check on all sales orders. A common approach is to establish a **credit limit** (maximum allowable account balance) for each customer based on that customer's credit history and ability to pay. Then order takers may approve sales orders if the credit available (credit limit minus outstanding account balance) exceeds the amount of the sales order transaction. For those customers who are new and seeking to establish credit or are overdue in paying their existing accounts, sales order records should be routed to a credit department or other location for formal approval.

Checking Inventory Availability

Once a sales order has been approved, it is necessary to determine whether the products ordered are available in inventory. This is usually done by checking the "quantity available" field in the inventory record, which represents the quantity on hand minus the total quantity reserved for orders that have been received and approved but not yet shipped. For items that are available, authorization for shipment to the customer is granted, and the "quantity available" field in the inventory record is reduced accordingly.

Some companies, notably American Airlines, Bergen Brunswig, GESCO, Westinghouse Electric Supply Company, and American Hospital Supply, allow their customers to access their inventory control systems, check the availability of inventories, and initiate orders. For example, consider American Hospital Supply (AHS), which supplies products to doctors, hospitals, and medical laboratories. Several years ago AHS provided many of its customers with terminals linked directly to its computerized order entry and inventory control system. Using these terminals, AHS customers can check inventory prices and availability and place orders. This system provided AHS with a significant competitive advantage because it simplified customer ordering, cut order processing costs, and permitted faster servicing of customer orders. A company such as Electronics Incorporated might be able to achieve similar advantages from developing a system of this kind.

Items that are ordered but are not available in inventory are listed as **back orders**, which means that they will be shipped as soon as the stock is replenished. For items on back order a notation to that effect is made

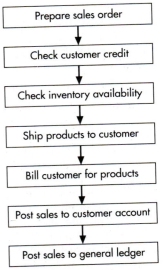

Figure 16.3

Basic revenue cycle processing functions and procedures

Prepare sales order

Check customer credit

Check inventory availability

Ship products to customer

Bill customer for products

Post sales to customer account

Post sales to general ledger

(1) on the sales order record, so that the billing process will result in the customer being billed only for goods actually shipped, and (2) in the finished goods record, so that when the stock is replenished, the shipment and billing processes may be restarted automatically.

Shipping   Once the availability of goods ordered has been confirmed, a **shipping order** record is prepared detailing the items and quantities to be shipped, the shipment date, destination, and mode of shipment. This record provides authorization for the items to be retrieved from available stock in the finished goods storeroom and moved to the Shipping Department, where they are prepared for shipment. At this time the "quantity on hand" field in the inventory record is reduced. In the Shipping Department the goods are packaged, and arrangements are made to ship them to the customer. A list of the goods shipped, called a **packing slip**, is enclosed with the shipment to inform the customer of the items and quantities included in the shipment. The packing slip is often simply a copy of a shipping order document or a sales order document that notes quantities ordered, shipped, and back ordered.

If a commercial carrier is used to transport the shipment, shipping personnel will prepare a **bill of lading** using standard forms provided by the carrier. This document identifies the carrier, describes the shipment, indicates the source of the shipment, provides instructions on how and where the shipment is to be delivered, and indicates who (customer or vendor) is to pay the carrier for the shipment. The bill of lading is recognized as a legal contract that defines responsibility for goods in transit. Multiple copies of the bill of lading accompany the shipment, with one copy serving as the freight bill, while other copies are distributed to the customer, vendor, and carrier.

Billing   The shipping order record is the key input to the billing process. This record may be transmitted electronically or by using a copy of a shipping order document. Some firms use a copy of the sales order document upon which shipping quantities are noted. From this record of items shipped the billing process generates a **sales invoice** document, which is sent to the customer as a bill. For all items ordered the invoice indicates the order quantities, back-order quantities, quantities shipped, unit prices, and **extensions** (price times quantity calculations). An example of a sales invoice is illustrated in Fig. 16.4. To expedite the billing process, some companies transmit sales invoices to their customers electronically using electronic data interchange (EDI).

The sales invoice is the principal record in the revenue cycle. In addition to serving as a request for customer payment, the sales invoice record is used by accounts receivable personnel to support the debit to the customer's account for the amount billed. Often, customers return a copy of the sales invoice with their remittance. It may also be used by sales order personnel to confirm shipment and billing status for outstanding sales orders, and by inventory personnel to support a credit to the inventory account for the cost of the inventory items sold.

ELECTRONICS INCORPORATED			No. 10098

ELECTRONICS INCORPORATED
3001 Dryden Rd.   Dayton, OH 45439
Phone (513) 836-0100

SALES INVOICE

No. 10098

Customer Order No.	Customer Account No.	Order Date	Salesperson No.
45236	2493106	7/15/94	24-7613

Sold to:
   Discount Electronics
   1356 South Logan
   Lansing, Michigan 48421

Bill to:
   Same

Shipper:	Date Shipped:	Invoice Date:	Terms of Sale:
Ohio Trucking Co.	7/22/94	7/22/94	2/10, net 30

Item Code	Description	Quantity Ordered	Back Ordered	Quantity Shipped	Unit Price	Item Total
10562	Calculator model 15A	100		100	$4.95	$495.00
10651	Calculator model 21A	50	20	30	7.95	238.50
28214	Digital Clock model 200	50		50	5.95	297.50
38526	Clock radio model 555	80	20	50	8.95	447.50

Freight charges	$ 25.50
Invoice Total	$1504.00

Figure 16.4
Sales invoice

Sales invoice records may be transmitted to these various locations electronically or through separate copies of a sales invoice document.

Data from the sales invoice are one of the primary inputs to the marketing data base, which is the major repository of information useful to marketing management. Therefore many of the data recorded on the sales invoice are coded to facilitate subsequent processing. For example, the customer account number, item code, and salesperson number provide a basis for updating customer records, inventory records, and salesperson commission records, and for generating sales and profitability analyses by customer, by product, and by salesperson. In addition, the invoice itself is numbered to provide a basis for future reference and audit.

An important output of the billing process (and of many other processes that are part of accounting cycles) is a summary journal entry that reflects the accounting impact of the transactions processed. In the case of billing the summary journal entry debits accounts receivable and credits sales revenue for the total amount billed to all custom-

JOURNAL VOUCHER

Date: 7/15/94   Voucher No.: 37067

Prepared by:	Approved by:	Posted by:
J. Mitchell	J. Hoover	N. Richards

Account Numbers	Account Titles	Debit Amounts	Credit Amounts
72-120	Accounts Receivable	$84,635.91	
40-500	Sales Revenue		$84,635.91

EXPLANATION

To record total daily billings.

Figure 16.5
Journal voucher

ers during a particular period of time, typically one day. Summary journal entries such as this are often documented in a journal voucher (see Fig. 16.5). The journal voucher record becomes input to the general ledger process, in which the journal entry is posted to the general ledger.

Accounts Receivable   Simultaneously with or immediately following the billing process the amounts billed to each customer are posted to the individual customer account records within the accounts receivable subsidiary ledger (or accounts receivable master file). This is done by adding the gross amount of each invoice to the "balance due" field in the corresponding customer's account.[2] For customers that have a credit limit the update process will include subtracting the gross invoice amount from the balance of the "credit available" field.

---

[2] For an example of this process refer to Fig. 2.7 in Chapter 2 and the related discussion.

With respect to updating accounts receivable records for customer payments, there are two alternative methods of maintaining the accounts receivable balance. Most manufacturing companies use the **open-invoice method**, under which the customer balance is treated as the sum of all outstanding invoices. Customers are billed by the invoice and are expected to pay by the invoice. When customer payments are received, each is matched against a specific invoice or invoices. This requires that a record of each outstanding invoice be maintained in each customer's accounts receivable record. In contrast, retail companies generally use the **balance-forward method**, under which customers receive a monthly bill listing the previous balance; all charges, payments, and other credits during the most recent month; and the current balance. Customer payments are not matched with specific charges but are instead subtracted from the total outstanding balance due to obtain a new balance due.

Special procedures must be established for handling bad debt write-offs and sales returns and allowances, both of which cause the balance of the customer's account receivable to be reduced. Bad debt write-offs should only be implemented after repeated attempts to collect the customer's balance have failed. A typical procedure is for the credit manager to prepare a formal memorandum authorizing the write-off, after which the balance of the customer's account is reduced to zero.

Sales returns and allowances should also be approved by a person in a position of responsibility, such as the Credit Manager. The basis for approval should be a letter from the customer explaining the reason for the adjustment. Issuance of a credit memo (see Fig. 10.4) formally recognizing the adjustment should, in the case of sales returns, also require a receiving report as verification of the return of goods. The credit memo record is used to support the posting of a credit to the customer's account.

General Ledger   After customers have been billed and the customer accounts have been updated, the final step in the revenue cycle (as in all other accounting cycles) is the posting of summary accounting journal entries to the control accounts in the general ledger. The journal voucher is the input record that initiates this process. The primary accounting journal entry representing sales order processing is exemplified in the journal voucher shown in Fig. 16.5:

Accounts Receivable (debit)	$84,635.91	
Sales Revenue (credit)		$84,635.91

The debit portion of this entry represents the sum of all charges posted to individual customer accounts during the accounts receivable process. In the general ledger posting process these summary amounts are posted to the corresponding general ledger control accounts.[3]

---

[3] For an example of a typical list of general ledger accounts, refer to Tables 2.6 and 2.7 in Chapter 2.

Some general ledger control accounts represent the sum of individual account balances within a subsidiary ledger. Here, this is true of the accounts receivable control account, which should be equal to the sum of all customer account balances within the accounts receivable master file. On a regular basis this equality should be verified. For example, at the end of each day the sum of all customer account balances could be computed and compared with the current balance of the accounts receivable control account within the general ledger.

The processing of sales orders results in a reduction of finished goods inventories. As the goods are shipped, firms that maintain inventory records on a perpetual basis must record a reduction in their inventory account for the goods sold. This results in the following journal entry:

Cost of Goods Sold	$27,502.50	
Finished Goods Inventory		$27,502.50

In contrast, firms that keep inventory records on a periodic basis do not attempt to maintain their inventory account on a current basis. Instead, these firms take an inventory count at the end of each year, at which time they make an adjusting entry to record cost of goods sold as the cost of beginning inventory plus inventory purchases minus the cost of ending inventory.

When a customer returns merchandise or asks for an adjustment in price because of damaged merchandise, the issuance of a credit memo results in the following journal entry:

Sales Returns and Allowances	$101.20	
Accounts Receivable		$101.20

Finally, the write-off of a customer account as uncollectible results in a journal entry such as the following:[4]

Bad Debts Expense	$576.98	
Accounts Receivable		$576.98

Both of these transactions must be posted to the individual customer accounts in the accounts receivable ledger as well as to the appropriate control accounts in the general ledger.

These journal entries represent the most important accounting transactions that are initiated as a result of sales order processing. Transactions involving the collection of customer accounts receivable are discussed in Chapter 20.

---

[4] The example shown represents the direct write-off method. Another common approach is the allowance method. Details of these alternative accounting methods are beyond the scope of this book, but they may be found in any standard accounting textbook.

Industry Variations   The functions and procedures performed within the revenue cycle of a manufacturing company, as described above, are more complex than in most other kinds of companies. For this reason we will use manufacturing as a sort of benchmark case for describing the revenue cycle and other accounting cycles throughout Part 5. However, for a complete understanding of the revenue cycle and its variations, one must be aware of some of the key differences that exist among various kinds of companies. Accordingly, this section briefly reviews some of the unique characteristics of revenue cycle functions and procedures within retail companies, public utilities, service companies, transportation companies, and construction companies.

Retailing.   The revenue cycle in a retail company is different in several respects from the revenue cycle of a manufacturing company. First, a significant proportion of retail sales are for cash, rather than on account. Second, retailers place their inventories on display to be retrieved by their customers. Third, retail customers usually take their purchases home after buying them. The net effect of these differences is to simplify the processing of sales transactions. Sales order, shipping order, and bill of lading records and documents generally are not prepared. An invoice is prepared to record the sale and must indicate whether the sale is for cash or on account. The customer's credit must be checked only for sales on account. Inventory availability is checked only on customer request, if an item the customer wants is not on display. Merchandise is usually not shipped to customers, except in the case of bulky items such as furniture and large appliances.

Cash sales need not be posted to customer accounts. Sales on account are charged to the customer's account but are not billed separately to customers. Instead, under the balance-forward method a monthly statement is mailed the customer, who may remit the entire balance due or a percentage thereof, according to the retailer's credit program. In order to even out the volume of customer statements sent out during a month, many retail companies mail a fraction of their customer statements each day, so that all customers will have been mailed a statement at some time during each month; this practice is called cycle billing. The sales invoice and the monthly customer statement are thus the primary accounting records within the revenue cycle of a retail company.

Retailers require special procedures for handling cash sales. Most important is the use of a cash register, which records all sales on an internal record, such as a cash register tape. At the end of each cashier's shift the amount of cash in the register is reconciled to the internal record. All cash receipts should then be deposited intact in the company's bank account. Since currency is vulnerable to theft, these procedures are preventive in nature. Cash sales result in a journal entry debiting cash and crediting sales revenue.

Public Utilities. Utilities include organizations that provide electricity, natural gas, water, telephone services, and similar public services. These services are often provided by government agencies or by private companies regulated by government agencies. In a public utility the revenue cycle begins with the monitoring of customer use of the service. Long-distance telephone companies utilize computer systems to record use as calls are placed. Electric, gas, and water companies generally use a meter to monitor use. This requires that the meter be read on a periodic basis, often by an employee who visits each customer location and records the current meter reading in a log. From these readings a monthly statement is prepared and mailed to each customer, generally on a cycle billing basis.

Services. This category includes a wide variety of companies, including professional services (such as accounting, legal counsel, stockbrokerage, and medical care) and companies that provide repairs and maintenance, advertising, entertainment, and other miscellaneous services. Here the revenue cycle begins when the company and customer agree on the services to be performed. This agreement is sometimes documented in a contract, a letter of agreement, or a **service order** authorizing the performance of specified services, such as repairs. If the services to be performed are extensive and costly, a check of the customer's credit may be performed. Specific service personnel must be assigned and scheduled to work on each customer job according to the needs of each job; this is analogous to checking inventory availability in a manufacturing or retail company.

The key feature of a data processing system for the revenue cycle of a service company is the method of documenting work performed for each customer. This could be done on the service order record or on employee time sheets that also serve as input to the payroll process. In some cases charges for materials such as parts or supplies are also included. At the completion of the job, or at monthly intervals, all charges are accumulated by customer, and bills are prepared and sent to all customers. At this time these charges are also posted to customer accounts within the accounts receivable subsidiary ledger, and the total of all charges billed is posted to the accounts receivable and service revenue control accounts in the general ledger.

A variation on this pattern involves what might be called "passive" services, such as insurance, mortgage and installment loans, leases of real estate or equipment, and membership dues. These typically require payment of a fixed amount on a regular basis, such as monthly or annually. A key feature of data processing systems here is that there is no specific input, such as a shipping order or service order, to initiate the billing process. Therefore the system must be programmed to generate customer bills at the appropriate time. In some cases, when payments are due monthly, the customer is sent a book of 12 payment coupons at the beginning of each year, in lieu of a monthly bill. Charges to accounts receivable and revenue accounts must be accrued as the customer payments come due.

Transportation.   Transportation companies fall into two categories: those that transport freight, and those that transport passengers. Freight haulers receive orders by phone or through sales personnel, at which time a shipping order record is prepared to document the nature of the cargo to be shipped, the customer name and address, the pickup and delivery locations, the shipment dates, and an estimated charge. The shipment is then scheduled by a dispatcher, who arranges for a specific vehicle and crew to pick up and transport the cargo. At the time of pickup a bill of lading is prepared detailing the contents of the shipment and specifying the shipment terms and cost. In some cases a copy of the bill of lading serves as a bill; otherwise, a separate bill is prepared and sent to the customer after the shipment is delivered. Charges to accounts receivable and revenue accounts are also recorded at this time. Freight companies generally use the open-invoice method of maintaining customer accounts.

Passenger carriers receive orders by phone or through travel agents. When orders are booked, a ticket is issued identifying the passenger, the travel date, the point of origin and destination, and the amount charged. Tickets are generally paid for in advance, so extensive billing and accounts receivable functions are not required. Instead of accounts receivable, prepaid service revenue accounts (e.g., liability accounts) are maintained for ticketed passengers, and service revenue is not recognized until after the passengers have completed their travel.

Construction.   Most construction companies obtain business by submitting bids on pending construction projects, based on customer specifications detailing the scope of the job, the required quality of materials and workmanship, and the timetable of the job. The preparation of accurate bids is crucial, since bids that are too high will not secure work, while bids that are too low will lead to unprofitable work. Thus construction companies must have effective systems of estimating the costs of prospective jobs for purposes of preparing bids.

After a construction contractor receives a job, a contract is prepared detailing the work to be done, the construction timetable, the contract cost, and the method of payment. The key feature of revenue cycle data processing systems in this industry is the accumulation of material, labor, overhead, and subcontract costs for each job in progress as the work proceeds. Most large construction contracts call for progress payments to be made at regular intervals, usually monthly, based on the portion of work completed. Thus at the appropriate interval a progress billing is rendered to the customer and an account receivable is recorded.

THE SALES ORDER PROCESSING SYSTEM

The sales order processing system is the primary data processing component of the revenue cycle. A sales order processing system must execute the basic revenue cycle functions and procedures discussed in the previous section. This section describes and illustrates the use of computer-based systems to process sales orders transactions, with emphasis on methods of data capture, data processing, data base updating, and reporting information to marketing management. Internal control objectives and procedures associated with sales order processing are also explained.

Data Capture

The first step in computerized sales order processing is to enter sales order data into the system. The necessary data are identified in the sales order transaction record structure diagramed in Fig. 16.6. Note that the record structure incorporates a single order record containing customer and order data, and this is linked to one or more order item records, each indicating the item number and quantity of each product ordered. In this section we describe a variety of ways in which these data are captured in machine-readable form for entry into the sales order processing system.

Under the traditional approach to sales order data entry, illustrated in Fig. 16.7, sales personnel or order takers record sales order data on a preprinted form. These sales order documents are then assembled in batches, and batch control totals are computed. Batch totals include a record count and perhaps hash totals of customer numbers and order quantities. The documents are then transmitted to a data entry department to be keyed into the computer system by data entry clerks using on-line terminals. While data such as customer account number, salesperson number, product item numbers, order quantities, and requested delivery date are keyed in, the system automatically enters the order date and a sales order number and retrieves the customer's name and the item description from on-line customer and inventory files. This technique reduces the number of keystrokes necessary to create the

Figure 16.6
Sales order transaction
record structure

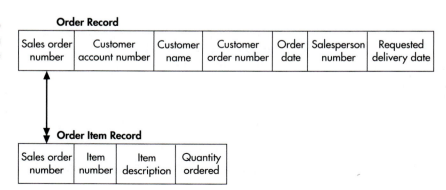

Order Record

Sales order number	Customer account number	Customer name	Customer order number	Order date	Salesperson number	Requested delivery date

Order Item Record

Sales order number	Item number	Item description	Quantity ordered

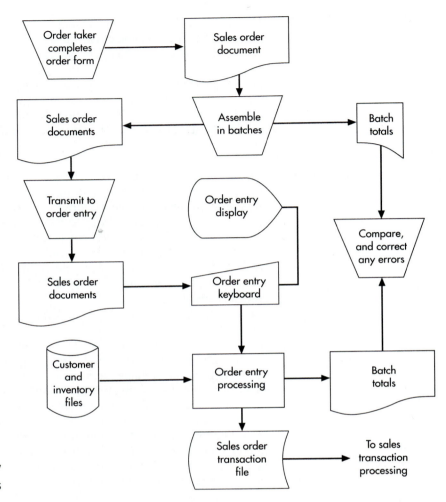

Figure 16.7
Sales order data entry process

sales order transaction record. As they are entered, sales order transactions are recorded on a temporary disk file. After all transactions have been entered, the computer calculates batch totals, writes the batch totals on a control record in the transaction file, and prints a batch total report. The batch totals are compared with the ones computed prior to data entry, and any discrepancies are investigated. After any errors are corrected, the sales order transaction file is cleared for the next stage of processing.

While the traditional approach is still commonly used, it has a number of flaws. First, it slows the processing of customer orders, which may be a problem for a company in a highly competitive market. Second, it involves manual keying, which is an expensive form of data capture. And third, it is error-prone, both because it is done manually and because the customer is not present to provide confirmation of the accuracy of the data entered into the system. For these reasons the traditional approach is rapidly becoming much less common.

The alternative to the traditional approach is to capture sales order data in machine-readable form at the point of receipt of the order. There are many different ways to do this. One approach is for order takers to use on-line terminals to enter order data while they are in direct contact with the customer. The order taker may be an order entry clerk who receives customer orders by phone or a salesperson with a portable terminal who is in personal contact with the customer. This approach speeds the processing of customer orders, saves paperwork by eliminating the need for a separate order document, and enables the order taker to both confirm the availability of inventory to the customer and verify the accuracy of the data entered with the customer.

Sales data also may be recorded in machine-readable form using optical character recognition (OCR). Perhaps the most common example involves the use of preprinted order documents by mail-order firms, which request that the customer mark a product selection and/or a quantity ordered in a specified location on the document so that these data may be interpreted by OCR equipment. Once these data have been read by the OCR reader, they are recorded on a temporary disk file for subsequent processing.

Many retail stores use point-of-sale (POS) recorders (on-line cash registers) to capture sales data in machine-readable form. As a by-product of the keying in of a sales transaction on the cash register keyboard, POS equipment records the product class and dollar amount of each sale on a computer file. POS devices often utilize optical scanners, which record the item number by reading the universal product code from the product's package or tag. The item price is then retrieved from an on-line file. In retail organizations that accept credit cards POS devices often incorporate a magnetic reader that reads the account number and other customer data from a magnetic strip on the customer's credit card.

Still another way of capturing sales transaction data is through direct data entry by customers. For example, several large airlines permit travel agents to access their reservation files directly in order to make flight reservations for their clients. Some companies have established systems that permit customers to order products by using a push-button telephone to enter their account number, product stock numbers, and order quantities. A few industrial firms, including General Motors, Westinghouse, and Cummins Engine, have established electronic data interchange systems that provide a direct link between their computer system and those of their suppliers. These companies use their systems to monitor their own inventory requirements, check supplier inventories and prices when reordering is necessary, and automatically initiate orders.[5] In all of these cases the selling company

[5] For more on sales order data capture using EDI, see Willie Schatz, "EDI: Putting the Muscle in Commerce & Industry," *Datamation* (March 15, 1988): 56–64; Frederick A. Henderson, "EBDI: A Radical Approach to Paper Work," *Corporate Accounting* (Winter 1988): 40–45; and Jack M. Cathey, "Electronic Data Interchange: What a Controller Should Know," *Management Accounting* (November 1991): 47–51.

captures customer order data automatically in machine-readable form. As more and more companies become fully automated, these methods of initiating sales orders will become more common.

Preliminary Data Processing Procedures

Once transaction data are captured in machine-readable form, it is often necessary to perform some additional procedures on the data before the transactions are processed to update the master files or data base. The nature of these preliminary data processing procedures depends on whether the data processing system employs batch processing or on-line processing, both of which are commonly used in sales order processing systems.[6] In a batch processing environment these procedures include merging separate batches of transactions, sorting the combined batch of transactions into sequential order for subsequent processing, checking the validity and accuracy of the transaction data using an edit program, checking batch totals, investigating and correcting any errors, and preparing transaction listings. However, when on-line processing is employed, procedures such as merging and sorting batches of transactions are not necessary because the transactions are generally processed one at a time, while the rest of these procedures are generally integrated with on-line data entry or data base update. Accordingly, this section describes preliminary data processing procedures strictly in the context of a batch processing system.

Transaction batches may be established in one of several ways. For example, if sales orders are transmitted daily to a central location from each of several branch sales offices, then each day's sales orders from each location might constitute a batch. On the other hand, if all orders are received at a central location, then a batch might consist of all orders received in the morning or afternoon, or every set of 50 orders received in sequence. At the data entry stage of processing small batch sizes are maintained in order to facilitate the identification of errors identified through the checking of batch control totals. However, subsequent batch processing steps are performed more efficiently in large batches. This requires that transactions in separate batches be merged into one large batch and that new batch control totals be computed for the combined batch and reconciled to the initial totals. In addition, since batch processing is often done sequentially, the transaction records must be sorted into sequential order according to the primary key of the master file (in this case, customer account number).

After the sales order transaction files have been merged and sorted, the combined file is processed against an edit program, as shown in Fig. 16.8. This program is designed to identify common errors in sales input data. Here are some examples of edit checks that might be performed:

---

[6] To briefly review these concepts as explained in Chapter 2, batch processing involves accumulating and processing transactions in groups (batches) at regular intervals, whereas on-line processing involves processing each transaction on the system as it occurs, from its point of origin.

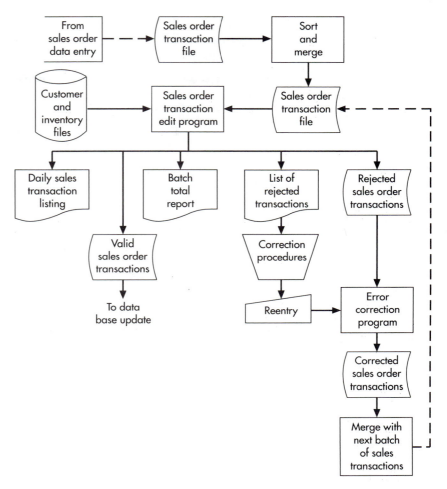

Figure 16.8
Editing of batched sales order transactions

1. Checking the validity of the customer account number and inventory stock numbers on each transaction by verifying that these numbers match those on master file records in the data base

2. Performing redundant data checks of (a) customer account number and customer name and (b) product item number and item description in order to detect cases where a valid but incorrect account number or item number was keyed in

3. Performing a check digit verification of sales order numbers and salesperson numbers

4. Performing field checks for numeric data in all other numeric fields

5. Checking the reasonableness of quantities ordered relative to a usual range of order quantities indicated in the corresponding inventory item record

6. Performing range checks on the order date and delivery date

7. Performing a completeness test to verify that each record contains all required data items

The edit program produces a listing and a file of all valid sales order transactions; these may then be processed against the appropriate master files. It also produces a listing and a file of any transactions rejected by the edit program. These rejected transactions should be examined promptly, and corrected if necessary, so that they may be processed without undue delay. Finally, the edit program produces a batch control report with separate control totals for valid and rejected transactions. This report must be reconciled with the original batch control record before the transactions are processed further.

Data Base Update

After sales order transaction data have been captured in machine-readable form and validated by edit programs, the next step in the sales order processing system is to update the data base. In particular, the customer and inventory records in the marketing data base must be updated to reflect the effects of sales and other revenue cycle transactions. This section describes the content and structure of these key elements of the marketing data base, and then it explains the procedures involved in updating this data base for sales order transactions. Both batch processing and on-line processing procedures are explained.

The Marketing Data Base.   The marketing data base contains data on customers and product inventories that are useful both for accounting purposes and for purposes of marketing management. A simplified example of the data content and organization of a marketing data base appears in Fig. 16.9. This data base essentially consists of three records: a customer record, a finished goods inventory record, and a sales invoice record. The sales invoice record also includes a line item record, which contains details of the items shipped to the customer. Note that these records represent only the core elements of the marketing data base. A "real" marketing data base would include numerous other transaction records, such as the sales order transaction records, records of salesperson's calls on customers, shipping order records, records of customer payments on account, credit memo records for sales returns and allowances, and records of inventory replenishment through purchase or manufacture of products. To simplify the discussion, we will focus only on the core elements of the marketing data base shown in Fig. 16.9. This data base could be used for either batch or on-line processing.

Each customer record in the data base contains a single value for each of the data fields listed within the customer record. In addition, customer records are associated with invoice records in a one-to-many relationship; that is, one customer may be linked to several invoices, but each invoice relates to only one customer. This is reflected in the diagram by the direction of the arrows connecting these two records.

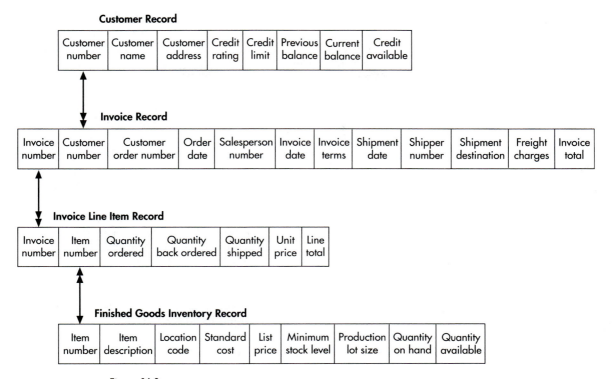

Figure 16.9
Key elements of the marketing data base

Note also that this link is implemented through the presence of a common field (customer number) within both the customer and invoice records.

Each invoice record within the data base is associated with one or more invoice line item records. Together, these records represent the content of a sales invoice document, such as the one illustrated in Fig. 16.4. Within the invoice document line, items appear as a repeating group. Within a data base such repeating groups are represented by separate records linked to their parent record through a one-to-many relationship. As indicated, the link is implemented through the presence of the invoice number within both the invoice and line item records.

Each finished goods inventory record in the marketing data base contains a single value for each of the data fields listed under finished goods inventory in Fig. 16.9. Furthermore, each finished goods inventory record is associated with one or more invoice line item records, since finished goods items may be sold to many customers and appear on many invoices, while each invoice line item identifies only one type of finished goods item. Item number is the common field within these two records and thus provides the link between them within the data base. The data stored in the finished goods inventory record provide important reference information for production planning, warehouse and stockroom operations, and selling operations.

As the organization grows and adds new customers and products, new customer records and finished goods inventory records will be added to the data base. Sales orders, invoices, and other transaction records will add to the size of the data base at an even faster rate. Therefore rules should be established concerning the period of time that any transaction record should remain part of the data base. For example, sales invoice records might remain in the current data base for 12 months, after which they would be removed and stored off-line in an archive file.

In a simple data processing system the marketing data base is in the form of a series of separately maintained files. For example, there might be separate files for customer data, finished goods data, sales data, sales call reports, and so on. Updating each of these files for input transactions frequently requires a separate set of procedures, each performed in a batch processing mode at a regularly scheduled time. In addition, it is often true that each file must be separately processed to generate output reports, and each report can reflect only the information contained on the specific file from which it was generated. Furthermore, such systems generally prepare output reports only at predetermined intervals (such as weekly or monthly), and these reports usually conform to a predetermined fixed format.

In contrast, if the marketing data base is maintained using a data base management system of the kind described in Chapter 7, it is possible to combine many of the separate file maintenance procedures referred to previously into an integrated data base updating process. Furthermore, if on-line processing is also employed, this updating process may be performed continuously, which speeds customer service and ensures that the marketing data base is always current. For example, once a customer sales order has been approved and a sales order record entered into the system, the system can retrieve customer name and address data from the customer record and inventory quantity and price data from the inventory record and add these to the data in the sales order record to create both a shipping order record and a sales invoice record. These records are then added to the data base, while copies of the corresponding documents are printed and distributed. At the same time the "quantity on hand" fields in the inventory records are reduced for the quantities to be shipped, and the "account balance" field in the customer record is increased for the amount billed. In addition, the data base management system enables users to generate reports at any time in any format they wish to specify, and the content of such reports is not limited to the information in one particular file but, rather, may include any of the data items contained in the marketing data base. In short, the use of an integrated data base system in sales order processing provides some important benefits for marketing operations and marketing management.

Batch Processing.   Batch processing remains a very common method of processing sales order transactions to update the marketing data base. Figure 16.10 is a systems flowchart illustrating this process. Input to

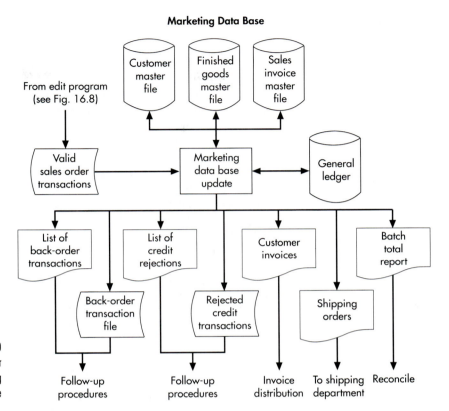

Figure 16.10
Batch processing of sales order
transactions to update the marketing
data base

this process consists of a batch of sales order transactions that have
successfully passed all input validation procedures in the edit program
(Fig. 16.8). Each order transaction is read into the system and processed individually. After each transaction record is read, the system
retrieves the corresponding customer and inventory records. The inventory record for each item ordered is checked to ascertain whether
the quantity ordered is available in stock. If so, the "quantity available" field is reduced by the quantity ordered to reserve the items. If
not, then a back-order record is appended to the inventory file, and
details about the order are printed on a back-order report and written
on a back-order transaction file. On the basis of this report follow-up
procedures are then undertaken, including communicating with the
customer and arranging to replenish the out-of-stock items. When the
stock is replenished and the inventory file updated, the back-order
record is removed from the back-order file and reentered into the
current sales order transaction file.

If the items ordered are in stock, the next step is to price the order
by multiplying quantities available to be shipped by unit prices (from
the inventory record), summing over all items ordered, and adding
shipping charges, sales taxes, and/or other additional charges to obtain
the total invoice amount. The system compares this with the custom-

er's available credit (credit limit minus outstanding account balance) and also checks whether the customer is substantially past due in paying previous billings. Orders that fail this credit-checking process are written on a "rejected credit" transactions file and printed on a "credit rejections" report. This report is provided to the Credit Manager, who must decide whether to increase the customer's credit limit and accept the order or to reject the order. Order transactions that receive this separate authorization from the Credit Manager must be removed from the "rejected credit" transactions file and reentered into the current sales order transaction file.

In the credit-checking process, the data assembled in pricing the order essentially comprise the invoice record. If the order passes the credit check, this record is assigned an invoice number and added to the sales invoice file in the marketing data base (see Fig. 16.9). Next, the customer's name, billing address, and shipping address, as well as inventory item descriptions, are retrieved from the data base, and copies of the complete sales invoice document are printed for distribution. If the company is linked to the customer through an EDI network, the invoice record may be transmitted electronically to the customer's computer system rather than mailed. In addition to the invoice, a shipping order record is also created at this time, assigned a shipping order number, and written onto the data base. The system prints one or more copies of the shipping order for distribution to the shipping department to authorize the assembly, packaging, and shipment of the order to the customer.

Once the shipping order and invoice records have been created and added to the data base, the inventory and customer files are updated for the sales transaction. Inventory-on-hand quantities are reduced by the number of units shipped. The customer's account balance is increased by the invoice total, and the customer's credit available is reduced by the same amount.

At the conclusion of the update program, the sum of all amounts billed to all customers is accumulated as the basis for the summary journal entry debiting accounts receivable and crediting sales. One of the final steps in the update program is to access the general ledger file, read these two control account records, and post this summary journal entry by adding the total amount billed to the balance of each of these control accounts.

A summary report containing batch control totals, the composite journal entry, and other summary information relating to the run is also printed at the conclusion of processing. The batch control totals must be reconciled with the batch total report produced by the previous (edit) program (see Fig. 16.8). The most critical batch total here is the total of all amounts billed to customers, which should be reconciled to the total of all debits to customer accounts as well as to the total debit to the accounts receivable control account in the general ledger.

Other revenue cycle transactions—such as approval of credit for new customers, modification of credit limits for existing customers, sales returns and allowances, and corrections or adjustments of master file records—should be approved by authorized personnel before being processed. Because the volume of such transactions is likely to be small, it is generally more efficient to enter them directly into the system from an on-line terminal as they occur. For control purposes the system should be programmed to accept such transactions only from an authorized user, as indicated by the user's password. Additional control is provided by having the system prepare a report of such transactions for distribution to appropriate supervisory personnel.

On-line Processing.   On-line processing of sales order transactions is becoming increasingly common as an alternative to batch processing. Figure 16.11 presents a systems flowchart illustrating an on-line sales

Figure 16.11
On-line sales order processing system

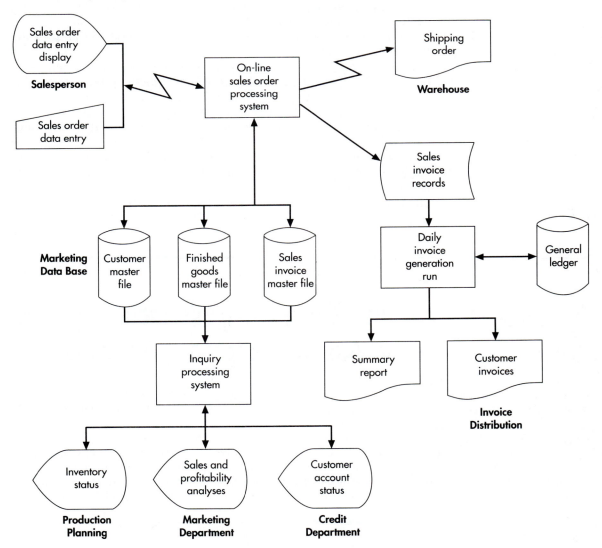

order processing system. The illustration shows a salesperson gaining access to the on-line system from the field, using either a portable terminal or a terminal located at a regional sales office. Alternatively, orders could be entered by order clerks or directly by customers. When a customer order is entered, the system verifies the accuracy of the data entered and then accesses the inventory records to check the availability of the inventory items requested by the customer. Next, the system accesses the customer record to check the customer's credit. If inventories are available and the credit status is satisfactory, the order is accepted and immediately confirmed to the salesperson and the customer. Upon final confirmation of the order all appropriate records in the marketing data base are immediately updated for the transaction. Simultaneously, a shipping order is transmitted to an on-line printer or display terminal located in the warehouse closest to the customer, and the order is packaged and shipped without delay.

Copies of the customer invoice may also be printed out as soon as the order is confirmed. Alternatively, as shown in Fig. 16.11, the invoice records may be written onto a temporary disk file and then printed out in a batch once a day or at some other regular interval. At the conclusion of this run a summary journal entry would be posted to the general ledger, and a summary report would be printed.

An important advantage of an on-line system is that the marketing data base is always up to date. As illustrated in Fig. 16.11, clerical and managerial personnel throughout the organization can then use the inquiry processing system to retrieve current information useful in carrying out their responsibilities. For example, at any time production planning personnel may determine which inventory items are in short

16.1 FOCUS   Atlas Door: Using Information Systems to Achieve Competitive Advantage

To understand the meaning of information systems "productivity" and "strategic advantage," consider a 10-year old company, Atlas Door. It has outperformed its industry by growing three times faster and earning five times more than average. It has no debt. How did Atlas achieve its superior performance?

Atlas's strategic advantage is quick delivery. Most competitors need four months to deliver a custom or out-of-stock industrial door. Atlas has organized its order entry, engineering, scheduling, and shipping information systems for much faster response.

Traditionally, customers had to wait over a week just for a firm quote. For special orders lead time could be much longer.

supply and need to be replenished, marketing managers may analyze recent sales trends to evaluate the effectiveness of marketing strategies and sales personnel, and credit department personnel may examine information on customer accounts to assess the effectiveness of credit policies.

On-line systems also provide the advantages of efficiency and timeliness in processing sales transactions. In a batch processing system data capture, data editing, and file maintenance are three separate steps. Therefore there is bound to be some delay between the receipt of an order and the shipment of the order to the customer. In an on-line system these three steps are combined into one step, which is more efficient and also enables the shipment of a customer order to be initiated as soon as the order is received. For this reason, in industries in which prompt customer service and delivery are important, companies that employ an on-line sales order processing system may have a crucial competitive advantage (see Focus 16.1).

From a control standpoint the data entry process is critical in an on-line system, because any errors not detected at the data entry point will result in erroneous transactions, documents, and files. Therefore an important part of any on-line system is a set of input validation routines built into the user interface.

One essential control feature in an on-line sales order processing system is the assignment of a unique user code number and password to each salesperson or other authorized user. The user number and password should be known only by the user to whom they are assigned. When the user first accesses the system, he or she must enter

Using an order entry terminal tied directly into engineering, pricing, scheduling, and shipping systems, Atlas salespeople can price and confirm delivery times for 95% of orders while a customer is still on the phone. Special orders have the fastest turnaround in the industry. Design and production information about prior orders is stored in computers, facilitating quicker estimating and engineering for new orders.

Atlas created added value for its customers with its information system by developing a method of dispatching multicomponent orders only after its computer verifies that all the correct parts are together. For this service Atlas can charge a premium price. The cost to Atlas is only a fraction of the savings realized by a customer whose installation can proceed without expensive delays.

Atlas Door provides an outstanding example of information systems productivity and strategic advantage. It has achieved superior revenue growth and profitability by using information systems to control its business and create its primary strategic advantage over competition.

Source: From Paul Strassmann, "Productivity and Strategic Advantage Through Information Systems," *FORTUNE* (December 5, 1988): 198. Reprinted with permission from a paid Advertising Section in the December 5, 1988 issue of *FORTUNE* magazine.

the user number and password. The system checks their validity before accepting any further data or instructions from the user. Each user number and password should be associated with an authorization level that defines the types of transactions the user is authorized to initiate and identifies the files to which he or she is allowed access. A salesperson or order entry clerk should be authorized only to initiate sales orders or to inquire into the marketing data base.

On-line data entry is also controlled by using simplified data entry procedures. For example, the system might display a sales order document format for the user to fill in, or it might display a series of requests for necessary data items. The system thereby guides the user through the data entry process and does not accept an order until all the required data have been entered.

The on-line system should be designed to perform various edit checks on sales order data as they are entered. These include validity checks, field checks, limit checks, range checks, reasonableness tests, and redundant data checks. The application of each of these edit checks to particular data items is much the same as under batch processing, described in earlier parts of this section. A major advantage of the on-line system is that if errors are detected, the system can display a request to the user to check the data or reenter it. As a result, few, if any, errors should get into the system in the first place, thus reducing or eliminating the need for a series of formal error detection and correction procedures at each subsequent stage of processing.

Another control procedure that is well suited for on-line processing systems is closed-loop verification. For example, after the user enters the customer account number, the system might retrieve and display the customer's name and address and then wait for the user to confirm that they are correct. If an incorrect account number is entered, this procedure enables the user to easily detect and correct the error. A similar procedure may be used with salesperson number and name and with inventory item numbers and item descriptions. Also, after all data have been entered and have passed the separate edit routines, the entire order record may be displayed for the user to verify and confirm.

To Paul Watson at Electronics Incorporated, an on-line order entry system had always been considered a luxury that the company could not afford, because its strategy had always been to minimize overhead costs and pass the savings along to customers. However, in response to the company's recent problems, Paul has begun to reconsider this position. He believes that an on-line system could substantially improve EI's level of customer service and thus improve its position in the highly competitive electronics market. He is also coming to believe that an on-line system could effect some cost savings that would partially or completely outweigh its costs. By streamlining the order entry process, it would eliminate some clerical positions. By detecting erroneous input data before order transactions are entered into the system, it could minimize expensive reprocessing procedures. By checking customer credit before orders are approved and shipped, it could reduce EI's bad debt losses. And finally, by tracking inventories on a continuous basis, it could enable EI to reduce its expensive investment in product inventories without degrading inventory availability. After giving much thought to these matters, Paul has asked EI's Director of Information Systems to initiate a feasibility study of an on-line sales order processing system.

Control Objectives and Procedures

Within each accounting cycle, internal control procedures should be designed to ensure that specific objectives are met. Therefore, in examining internal controls within any accounting cycle, one should begin by delineating the control objectives and then identify the set of control procedures that will achieve each objective. This approach is followed here and in all of the remaining chapters on accounting applications in Part V.

Internal control procedures within the revenue cycle should be designed to ensure that the following objectives are met.

1. All revenue cycle transactions are properly authorized on the basis of established criteria.
2. Finished goods inventories are properly safeguarded while in stock and during the shipment process.
3. All valid revenue cycle transactions are accurately recorded and executed.
4. Accurate records of customer accounts and finished goods inventories are maintained.

Numerous internal control procedures have been described in earlier sections of this chapter. Our goal here is to associate these procedures with the four internal control objectives just listed and to identify any other control procedures necessary to achieve each objective.

Four important authorization procedures are described earlier in the chapter. First, all credit sales transactions should be approved by the Credit Manager or other authorized person. Second, authorization for the transfer of finished goods from a storeroom or warehouse to the Shipping Department should be documented by means of a shipping order, which is issued after the sale has been approved. Third, the Credit Manager should prepare a formal memorandum authorizing bad debt write-off transactions. Fourth, someone such as the Credit Manager should authorize sales return and allowance transactions, and then only upon receipt of appropriate documentation, including a formal request from the customer and a receiving report for returned items.

Within a computer-based system many transactions, particularly those of a recurring nature such as credit approvals and shipments, are approved by the system based on criteria incorporated into the order processing program. These criteria must be established by responsible managers before they are programmed into the system. Furthermore, the system should provide these managers with regular reports listing or summarizing recent computer-approved transactions so that managers can look for any sign of unusual activity. Finally, transactions of a less regular nature, such as bad debt write-offs, sales returns and allowances, or increases in credit limits, should require supervisory approval.

The safeguarding of finished goods inventories is expedited by having a separate stores department or warehouse staffed by personnel responsible for maintaining the inventory stocks. If accurate and current perpetual inventory records are maintained on the computer, the custodial and recording functions are effectively separated, and safeguarding of inventories is enhanced even further. Storeroom personnel are responsible for protecting inventories from damage or theft and for retrieving them efficiently when shipping orders are received. Counts of actual quantities on hand should be taken periodically and compared with the inventory records, and storeroom personnel should expect to be held accountable for any shortages.

Safeguarding of inventories is also enhanced by documenting all movement of inventories between operating departments. Specifically, when goods enter or leave the inventory storeroom, documentary evidence of the transfer of responsibility should be prepared. For example, to acknowledge the transfer of responsibility for goods from the storeroom to the Shipping Department, a shipping employee should count all items to verify that the quantities match those on the shipping order and then sign a copy of the shipping order to acknowledge receipt of the specific items and quantities listed. Such a procedure permits any shortage of inventories to be traced to the person responsible. In turn, this accountability encourages employees to prepare accurate transaction records.

Accurate recording of amounts billed is a primary concern within the revenue cycle. This objective is accomplished through the use of batch totals, edit programs, and input validation routines, as described in some detail in previous sections. Any discrepancies identified using these procedures should be investigated in order to correct any errors as quickly as possible, determine the causes of the errors, and take any steps necessary to remedy these causes and prevent future errors.

So that accurate records of customer accounts and of finished goods inventories are preserved, the focal point is maintenance of the security and integrity of the marketing data base. Although this objective is certainly facilitated by the use of batch totals, edit checks, and other procedures associated with the third objective, a variety of data security controls must also be employed. For example, internal and external file labels should be properly used to ensure that the data base is not inadvertently erased or processed by the wrong program. Backup copies of the data base should be prepared on a regular and frequent basis, and a log should be kept of all transactions entered since the last backup file was created. In this way, if anything happens to the data base, a current copy can be restored by processing the transaction log against the last backup copy. All backup files should be stored in a secure off-site location. Finally, user numbers and passwords to limit access to authorized personnel are another important means of protecting the integrity of the marketing data base.

The accuracy of the marketing data base is also enhanced by regular reconciliation of key amounts with other amounts in the data base and with external data. For example, every time customer records are processed, the sum of the "balance due" fields in all customer accounts should be reconciled to the total balance of the accounts receivable control account in the general ledger. In accounting terms this is called reconciling the accounts receivable subsidiary ledger to its corresponding general ledger control account. A similar reconciliation procedure should be performed on the perpetual inventory records. In addition, the regular reconciliation of inventory records of quantities on hand to physical inventory counts helps to maintain the accuracy of the finished goods inventory records.

Maintaining appropriate segregation of duties by keeping the recording, custodial, and authorization functions separate within the revenue cycle also helps to safeguard inventories and to ensure the accuracy of sales transaction and customer and inventory master file records. The recording functions are primarily performed by the computer and by personnel responsible for entering sales order records into the computer. Maintaining custody of inventories is the responsibility of personnel in the finished goods storeroom and shipping department. Authorization functions are performed by order-taking personnel, by the Credit Manager, and in some cases by the computer.

When the computer performs both recording and authorization functions, additional safeguards are necessary. Compatibility tests based on user passwords can ensure that no single user is able to perform both recording and authorization functions with respect to a particular type of transaction. Compatibility tests can also ensure that persons responsible for modifying sales order processing software cannot also enter sales transaction data or that persons responsible for entering sales transaction data cannot also modify sales order processing software. It is also important to control physical access to the computer facility.

Reporting   Sales order data entry, data processing, data base update, and internal control are all of critical importance to ensure that revenue cycle activities are carried out effectively. However, from a management perspective the reports generated as a by-product of sales order processing are of prime importance. This section describes several examples of such reports.

In any computer-based information system, some reports are issued on a regularly scheduled basis, such as daily or weekly, and others are issued on demand, as requested by a decision maker. Scheduled reports are usually prepared on a mainframe printer. Demand reports, which are usually requested from an on-line terminal or personal computer, are often prepared on a remote printer located in or near the decision maker's office. Demand reports fulfill a specific information need of the user. They may be created by using query languages to retrieve specific information from the data base, by using decision support system (DSS) software that employs sophisticated analytical models to analyze information on the data base, by using personal computer software to analyze a portion of the data base that has been downloaded, or by using expert systems software to evaluate complex decisions on the basis of a large number of factors. Examples of the use of all of these methods to create a report with a marketing information system are described in this section.

A sales analysis report that is prepared weekly or monthly is an example of a scheduled report. Such reports generally present total dollar and/or unit sales information, broken down by regions, territories within regions, salespeople, customers, customer classes, products, product classes, distribution channels, or some combination of these. Sales during the most recent period (week or month) and cumulative sales for the year to date are generally presented. As a standard for evaluation of current sales performance, current sales figures are compared with sales during the equivalent period of the prior year and/or to a sales forecast or quota, and performance variances or percentage changes are highlighted. An example of a report analyzing sales by territory and by salesperson within territory is presented in Table 16.1. Note that to enable the system to generate this type of report, monthly quotas and the prior year's monthly sales totals must be stored in the data base, either as additional records or as part of the salesperson record. Sales analysis reports of this kind provide useful information for performance evaluation purposes and are also

Table 16.1
Sales analysis by salesperson and territory

Period Ending: October 31, 1993						Territory: East Texas
Salesperson	Period	Actual Sales	Prior Year Sales	Percent Change	Sales Quota	Percent Variance from Quota
Benjamin, H. L.	This month	$ 50,000	$ 40,000	+25	$ 48,000	+4
	Year to date	120,000	115,000	+4	125,000	−4
Carlton, J. C.	This month	40,000	38,000	+5	45,000	−11
	Year to date	105,000	110,000	−5	130,000	−19
.	.	.	.	.	.	.
.	.	.	.	.	.	.
.	.	.	.	.	.	.
.	.	.	.	.	.	.
.	.	.	.	.	.	.
Territory totals	This month	$300,000	285,500	+5	$350,000	−14
	Year to date	850,000	840,000	+1	950,000	−11

relevant to such activities as planning advertising and promotion campaigns, allocating sales effort, establishing product prices, and adding or deleting product lines.

The preparation of sales analysis reports broken down by different analysis categories is facilitated if there are several key fields in the sales transaction file. These keys must contain subcodes that indicate important categories within each type of record. Salesperson number, inventory item number, and customer number are the primary key fields within the sales transaction record. Subcodes for territory, region, customer class, and product class should be incorporated within these key fields. This will allow the system to generate several different sales analysis reports without sorting the file. For example, after generating a sales analysis report by salesperson and territory utilizing the salesperson number key and territory subcode, the system can immediately generate a sales analysis by product and product class utilizing the inventory item number key and product class subcode.

Other examples of scheduled reports produced by a marketing information system include monthly customer statements; an inventory **stock status report** listing quantities on hand and other critical data values for each inventory item, which serves as a planning and reference tool for marketing and production operations; and an inventory reorder report listing items back-ordered, out of stock, or below the prescribed minimum stock levels, which should trigger production, purchasing, or other actions necessary to replenish the stock levels.

Inquiry processing is generally used to retrieve limited amounts of information from the data base to satisfy a specific decision-making need. A few examples were briefly described earlier (see Fig. 16.11 and the related discussion). Two additional examples will be discussed here. First, consider marketing executives at a company like Nabisco or Procter & Gamble who must select a test market for a new consumer product. These executives could employ an inquiry processing system to retrieve sales information on similar products for each of the past 24 months and/or sales information on each of several territories that are potential test markets. Although this information might already be available on previously generated sales analysis reports, it would probably be scattered throughout several different reports and not organized in the most useful manner. The inquiry processing system allows these decision makers to retrieve selected information relevant to this particular task in the format that is most useful for carrying out that task.

As another example, suppose that a company is opening a new regional sales office in Quebec and wants to select a regional sales manager. Candidates for the new position need to be effective in selling those product lines that are to be featured in the new region and must speak both French and English. An inquiry processing system could be used to access the personnel files and retrieve a list of all sales managers and salespersons meeting the second criterion. Then the system could be used to retrieve information about the sales performance of these candidates with respect to specific products. This example shows how inquiry processing can be useful when information is needed from two different data bases.

DSS software enables decision makers to employ statistical or quantitative decision models in analyzing data retrieved from the data base. An example in marketing is the use of regression analysis to evaluate the effectiveness of various advertising appeals for a particular product. Suppose that Coca-Cola tested five different advertising approaches by using each for three-months in one of five different sales regions. To evaluate the relative effectiveness of the different approaches, the DSS software would first retrieve sales analysis data by region for the three-month period. Then a regression analysis model would be used to identify the mathematical relationship between changes in sales (from some baseline level prior to the test) and each advertising method tested, after adjusting for trends in regional sales of other products or for other potential confounding factors.

Downloading is employed to read selected portions of one or more mainframe data bases into a personal computer for further analysis. For example, Paul Watson at Electronics Incorporated requested a report analyzing the relative profitability of EI's various product lines but was told by MIS personnel that preparing such a report would take several weeks, because sales revenue data are stored on the marketing data base while variable product cost data are stored on the production data base. After he complained about this problem to his assistant, Susan Chalmers, she insisted that she could construct the report in a few hours by using her personal computer to retrieve the necessary data from EI's mainframe data bases. First, she accessed product cost accounting records within the production data base to retrieve variable cost data for each product and loaded these data into her spreadsheet program. Then she accessed sales transaction records within the marketing data base to retrieve unit and dollar sales information for each product for the most recent month and for the year to date. She then used the spreadsheet software to compute the per-unit contribution margin of each product, to multiply these values by actual units sold to obtain an analysis of total contribution margins by product, and then to sum these values over all products within each product line. The resulting spreadsheet, shown in Table 16.2, surprised Paul in three ways. First, it appeared on his desk by 5:00 P.M. on the day of his conversation with Susan. Second, he was told that Susan had stored the data base access paths and spreadsheet template on her personal computer so that an equivalent report could be generated automatically on demand at any time in the future. And third, he learned from the report that EI's toys and games product line was its most profitable, despite ranking near the bottom in total sales revenue.

Expert systems software can assist marketing personnel in complex decision processes that utilize large amounts of data. For example, at

ELECTRONICS INTERNATIONAL PRODUCT PROFITABILITY ANALYSIS

	A	B	C	D	E	F	G
1							
2			For the Month of January 1993				
3							
4			Unit	Total	Variable	Contribution	Margin
5	Product Class		Volume	Revenue	Cost	Margin	Percent
6	Calculators		164500	$ 259,750	$ 184,500	$ 75,250	28.97
7	Digital clocks		109750	$ 318,500	$ 220,500	$ 98,000	30.76
8	Radios		128750	$ 335,400	$ 230,200	$105,200	31.36
9	Small appliances		142200	$ 382,900	$ 251,500	$131,400	34.31
10	Pagers		56800	$ 246,700	$ 144,800	$101,900	41.3
11	Toys and games		124500	$ 253,200	$ 121,400	$131,800	52.05
12	Totals		726500	$1,796,450	$1,152,900	$643,550	35.82

Table 16.2
Product profitability analysis
prepared by spreadsheet.

Digital Equipment Corporation (DEC), a major computer manufacturer, sales are obtained by responding to customer requests for competitive bids on prospective computer installations. To prepare these bids, DEC salespeople must collect and analyze large volumes of data about customer requirements and facilities. Delays in providing a bid can result in lost business opportunities, but bids that are developed too quickly can be highly inaccurate. To address this problem, DEC uses an expert system to assist in preparing its bids. Sales personnel enter customer requirements, including data processing volume, software needs, and such details as room dimensions. The expert system recommends the proper equipment configuration, prices all of the system components, and prints a detailed list of preparations required to implement the system at the customer's site.[7]

As another example of an application of an expert system, consider the decision of whether to approve or deny credit applications from prospective customers of a bank, automobile dealer, or department store. This decision is based on a number of facts about the applicant obtained from the application document and from reports obtained

---

[7] Paul Strassmann, ''Productivity and Strategic Advantage Through Information Systems,'' *FORTUNE* (December 5, 1988): 208. See also John J. Sviokla, ''An Examination of the Impact of Expert Systems on the Firm: The Case of XCON,'' *MIS Quarterly* (June 1990): 127–140.

from credit bureaus. These facts are weighted according to complex decision rules employed by expert credit personnel. Expert systems software can capture those decision rules within a computer program, and this program can then be employed to expedite the review of credit applications. After evaluating each applicant, the system would prepare a report summarizing the most important factors in the decision, and this report could then be reviewed by the Credit Manager responsible for making the final decision.

Another example of an expert system used in sales management is a personal computer software package called SELL! SELL! SELL!, which is used in motivating and training sales personnel. This system contains rules of good selling strategy and a data base of past sales data indicating which types of sales strategies have been effective for particular types of customers. Salespeople use the system to learn basic selling skills and to assess their own selling strengths and weaknesses. As a salesperson enters information about customers and markets into the system, it questions and responds to the information provided by giving advice on selling approaches to be used for particular customers. The system also assists the salesperson in developing sales reports, customer logs, prospect lists, and other useful sales information.[8]

These examples illustrate how the power of the computer can substantially improve the quality of the information available to marketing managers. Scheduled reports can regularly provide large volumes of information for reference purposes and also summarize this information according to various decision-relevant categories. Demand reports can provide selected information relevant to a specific purpose, as well as analyses of the information. A well-designed marketing information system employs all of these tools to enhance the effectiveness of marketing executives.

CASE CONCLUSION: IMPROVING MARKETING INFORMATION SYSTEMS AT ELECTRONICS INCORPORATED

Paul Watson has obtained several ideas about how the information system at Electronics Incorporated could improve the effectiveness of EI's marketing programs, but he is still not satisfied. The profitability analysis prepared by Susan Chalmers was useful but did not include incremental selling costs, including the cost of product returns, and did not provide a breakdown of retail versus mail-order sales. He also needs information to help him decide whether prices should be raised to improve profit margins or lowered to prevent further declines in sales. He is still unsure of the most effective way to monitor the creditworthiness of key customers. Finally, he must act on a recom-

[8] For more information on SELL! SELL! SELL!, see Margery Steinberg and Richard E. Plank, "Expert Systems: The Integrative Sales Management Tool of the Future," *Journal of the Academy of Marketing Science* (Summer 1987): 55–62.

mendation from the Director of Information Systems to spend $1 million to implement a new on-line sales order processing system over a 12-month period.

After much analysis and consultation with EI's President and other top executives, a decision was made to implement the new on-line system. However, Paul could not wait 12 months to address his other pressing problems. First, he instructed the Director of MIS to modify EI's method of coding sales transactions so that retail sales could be differentiated from mail-order sales. This refinement was implemented in less than a month. He also asked the MIS Director to work with EI's Controller to develop a system that would code all marketing costs, including product return costs, so that they could be allocated to specific product lines. The development and implementation of this system took about 4 months, after which Susan Chalmers was asked to generate revised profitability analyses reflecting the new information. These analyses confirmed that the mail-order business was highly profitable, leading Paul to assign three additional salespeople to further develop this market. These analyses also indicated that selling costs, especially product return costs, were driving retail profit margins on some products to near zero.

Paul also directed Susan to develop a spreadsheet-based decision support system that could help him determine product prices. Using the more precise product cost information, Susan developed a what-if simulation program that estimates changes in product demand and incremental profits in response to hypothetical increases or decreases in prices. To develop more precise estimates of the sensitivity of demand to price changes, Susan downloaded five years of sales data to her personal computer for each product and used her graphics software package to plot unit sales data against selling prices over the five-year period. After experimenting with the final version of this decision support system, Paul recommended that retail prices be raised on several of EI's products. This action restored EI's retail profit margins to more reasonable levels without significantly reducing unit sales volume.

To address EI's credit evaluation problem, Paul subscribed to the Dow Jones information service, which provides current business and financial news and other information through an on-line data link. A system was developed to retrieve any information available from this service on EI's customers, especially the large retailers. The system was programmed to flag any customer whose corporate common stock price declined by more than 5% over a period of one week or less, on the theory that stock price movements are the best early-warning indicator of potential business problems. Within 30 days after this system was implemented, Paul suspended credit sales to a retail chain whose stock price had declined by 15%. Six months later this chain closed its stores and filed for bankruptcy. Paul estimated that EI saved over $400,000 on this decision, or more than 400 times the cost of the information service. By relying more on this system, EI has expedited its regular credit review process, and sales personnel report that their relationships with several retail customers have improved as a result.

After a costly development effort that required over 15 months, EI implemented its new on-line sales order processing system early in October, just in time for the rush of Christmas sales orders. The system is organized around a fully integrated marketing data base that includes data on customers, products and product costs, inventories, sales personnel and their activities, shipping schedules, and all sales and related transactions. Data links established within this data base enable the system to routinely generate, on a monthly basis, the profitability analyses reports originally designed by Susan using the spreadsheet program on her personal computer.

Each field salesperson has been provided with an on-line terminal and has received over 20 hours of training in how to use the new system to retrieve information on customers, products, and inventories and to enter sales orders and other input data. As transactions are entered into the system, all affected files and data bases, including the general ledger, are immediately updated, so that the information available to sales personnel through the data base is always current. Sales personnel have been enthusiastically demonstrating the virtues of this new system to their customers by showing them how inventory availability can be instantly confirmed and by promising delivery of all orders to specified customer locations within 24 hours of order placement. October will generate the largest monthly volume of orders in EI's history, and Paul will conclude that the company's $1.5-million investment in the new system will be fully recouped by the end of the Christmas season. ■

Summary

Revenue cycle activities include soliciting customer orders, executing sales transactions, and delivering products and services to customers. These activities are managed by a staff of marketing executives whose responsibilities include supervising the sales force, selecting advertising and promotion strategies, participating in product planning, establishing customer service policies and procedures, and carrying out marketing research studies.

One of the primary data processing operations supporting these activities is the processing of customer sales orders. The sales order processing system must be designed to capture customer order data in machine-readable form both quickly and efficiently. These data are then processed against a marketing data base that includes information on customers, product inventories, and past sales. Sales order processing may be accomplished using either batch processing or on-line processing. The system must incorporate internal controls that ensure proper authorization of all transactions, provide for the safeguarding of finished goods inventories, and secure the accuracy of all transaction and master file data. A well-designed computer-based sales order processing system enables sales transactions to be processed in a timely and efficient manner, which is essential for serving customers in highly competitive markets. Such a system may also be used to generate a variety of scheduled and demand reports that will enhance the effectiveness of marketing managers.

KEY TERMS

Define the following terms.

revenue cycle	shipping order	open-invoice method
sales analysis	packing slip	balance-forward method
profitability analysis	bill of lading	cycle billing
sales order	sales invoice	service order
credit limit	extensions	stock status report
back orders	journal voucher	downloading

DISCUSSION QUESTIONS

16.1 Some companies have created the position of Product Line Manager within the Marketing Department. There may be several product line managers, each responsible for a related group of products. Discuss the effects of this type of organization on responsibilities and information requirements within the Marketing Department.

16.2 This chapter emphasized the marketing information requirements of a manufacturing firm with a large sales force. Compare the organization structure, information requirements, and data sources of this type of organization with those of the following.

a. A large insurance company
b. A firm that does all selling by direct mail
c. A large motel chain
d. A hospital

16.3 Sam's Manufacturing Company produces barbecue grills that are sold in department stores. In processing its customer orders, the company prepares a sales order document when orders are received and then prepares a separate sales invoice document when the customer is billed. Sam's has just acquired a computer, and you have been asked to redesign the sales order processing system. One design choice that you must make is whether to (1) continue to use separate sales order and invoice

documents or (2) eliminate the sales order document and redesign the invoice so that it can serve the dual function of an order document and a billing document. Discuss the relative advantages and disadvantages of these two alternatives.

16.4 Woody's Lumberyard has decided to implement a credit policy that will enable customers with approved credit to purchase lumber and other merchandise on account. Customer account records will be maintained on a computer. In designing the system, you must decide whether to (1) bill customers for each purchase by mailing a copy of the invoice or (2) bill customers monthly by preparing and mailing a statement that details customer purchases and payments since the previous statement and computes a balance due. Discuss the relative advantages of these two alternatives.

16.5 At the ABC Company the Marketing Department maintains a computerized customer file that contains information on each customer, including the products in which the customer is interested, recent requests for information, recent contacts with sales personnel, recent order and delivery activity, reports on the customer's satisfaction with products purchased, and customer service requirements. The Accounting Department maintains a separate computerized customer file that contains accounting information on recent transactions with the customer and maintains each customer's accounts receivable balance.

The ABC Company has recently acquired a data base management system. The Systems Department has proposed that the customer files maintained by the Marketing and Accounting Departments be combined into an integrated customer data base. Personnel in both the Marketing and the Accounting Department have expressed reservations about this proposal. Discuss the advantages of the proposal.

Problems

16.1 Kids Choice Corporation is a manufacturer and distributor of children's toys. Over the past three years the company's sales volume has declined as several important distributors have dropped the Kids Choice product line. In response the company's top management has just ordered every department within the company to reevaluate its operations, identify possible problems that may be contributing to the company's loss of business, and prepare recommendations for improvement.

You have been asked to evaluate the way in which Kids Choice processes customer orders. At present customers are sent catalogs, price lists, and order forms each quarter, and they mail completed order forms to a central data processing facility. There the orders are keyed into a computer system and processed in batches through several stages, including edit checks, credit review, inventory availability checks, and back ordering. For approved orders a shipping document is routed to a Kids Choice distribution center located close to the customer, where items are selected from inventory, packaged, and shipped to the customer. The process takes between two and three weeks.

Required

Could Kids Choice Corporation's sales order processing system have anything to do with the decline in its competitive fortunes? Describe several ways this system might be improved.

16.2 What internal controls in a sales order processing system would provide the best protection against the following errors or manipulations?

a. Theft of goods by Shipping Department personnel, who claim that subsequent shortages are due to errors made by personnel in the finished goods storeroom

b. An error in the amount of a sale posted from an invoice to the accounts receivable master file

c. The posting of the amount of a sale to the wrong customer account, because a customer account number was incorrectly keyed into the system

d. Sale to a customer who is four months behind in making payments on his account

e. A computer error during sales order processing that resulted in the loss of data in several customer records in a disk file

f. Authorization of a credit memo for a sales return when the goods were never actually returned

g. Writing off good customer accounts receivable as uncollectible in order to conceal theft of subsequent collections

h. Billing a customer for the quantity of materials ordered when the quantity shipped was actually less than the quantity ordered owing to an out-of-stock condition

16.3 Your company has just acquired a data base management system, and one of its first applications will be to marketing data. A sales invoice form identical to that in Fig. 16.4 is used. You are to diagram the data structure reflected in the invoice as a first step in the application design. Use a format similar to that in Fig. 16.9. Note that the data base will contain only the variable data on the invoice, not the constant data.

16.4 When a shipment is made, the Shipping Department prepares a shipping order form in three copies. The first copy is sent out with the goods to the customer as a packing slip. The second copy is forwarded to the Billing Department. The third copy is sent to the accountant. When the Billing Department receives the second copy of the shipping order, it uses the information to prepare a two-part sales invoice. The second copy of the shipping order is then filed in the Billing Department. The first copy of the sales invoice is sent to the customer. The second copy of the sales invoice is forwarded to the accountant. Periodically, the accountant matches the copy of the shipping order with the copy of the sales invoice and files them alphabetically by customer name. Before doing so, however, the accountant uses the copy of the sales invoice to post the sales entry in the subsidiary accounts receivable ledger.

Required

a. For use in appraising internal control, prepare a flowchart covering the flow of documents reflected in this situation.

b. List those deficiencies and/or omissions revealed by the flowchart that would lead you to question the internal control.

c. The efficiency of this manual system could be improved if some functions were computerized. Draw a systems flowchart indicating how the existing functions of the Billing Department and accountant could be computerized.

(CIA Examination, adapted)

16.5 As a systems analyst for the Dolphin Motor Company, you have been asked to design a computer report that will analyze product sales by dealers. The company sells three major lines of cars—the Dolphin, the Eagle, and the Flyer—and all dealers carry all three lines. Assume that space constraints limit the report to a maximum of eight columns of data across the width of a page. Of course, there are no constraints regarding how many lines of data may be used for each dealer.

In designing the report, you may make any reasonable assumptions about the availability of data. Make sure that you take into account the need for effective presentation of information, the need for standards of comparison, and the principle of management by exception.

16.6 The Quality Building Supplies Company operates six wholesale outlets that sell lumber, roofing materials, electrical supplies, plumbing supplies, and other building materials to building contractors in a large metropolitan area. The company is studying the feasibility of introducing a guaranteed same-day delivery plan, under which it would guarantee delivery by 6 P.M. of all orders received from approved customers prior to noon of the same day. For orders received in the afternoon, delivery would be guaranteed prior to noon on the following day. The company believes that this system would give it a substantial competitive advantage relative to other regional building wholesalers, because it would enable contractors to maintain smaller inventories and yet be assured of having building supplies when needed.

You have been asked to assist in designing a computerized order entry and dispatching (delivery-scheduling) system. Assume that orders will be received over the phone by order clerks in the company's centrally located administrative offices. Approved customers are those whose credit has been approved and whose accounts are no more than 15 days past due. Customers are to be billed separately for each order.

Required

a. In addition to credit status, what other criteria might Quality Building Supplies use in approving customers for this special service?

b. Identify the master files that should be maintained in this system, and list the data content of each.

c. Identify the input transactions that this system must process and the output documents that the system must produce. Focus on the order processing system; that is, assume that inventory replenishment and collections on customer accounts will be handled by other systems that are already in place.

d. List the components of the hardware configuration needed to perform the required data processing operations.

e. Prepare a systems flowchart of your proposed order entry and dispatching system.

16.7 Company A is a small manufacturer of farm equipment and related parts. Its finished products can be shipped as a complete unit or in subassemblies that the end user would put together.

Orders are received by the company either by mail or by telephone from its various distributors or the company's sales personnel. These orders are processed, and a three-part shipping document is produced showing the complete units and/or parts. This document is then filed by territory. Periodic checks are made against this file, and orders destined to be sent to certain territories are pulled and given to the Credit Department for approval. If the order is not approved, it is returned to the salesperson. On approval of the order the three-part shipping document is sent to the Shipping Department, where individual items are pulled out of stock and loaded on a truck. The goods being shipped are accompanied by one copy of the shipping document; the other two are retained by the company. One copy is filed, and the remaining copy is sent to the Invoicing Department, where a check is made for any back-ordered items. Extensions are made on this copy of the shipping document, and a four-part invoice is produced. Invoice totals are posted to the customer's accounts receivable file. The copy of the shipping document is then sent to the Inventory Department to update its records. Two copies of the invoice are sent to the customer. The third is filed by customer, and the fourth is filed by salesperson.

Upon receipt of monies owing to the company, a credit is posted against the customer's accounts receivable file, and the salesperson's copy of the invoice is marked as paid. The salesperson's paid invoices for a certain period will produce a commission report for input to the payroll.

Credits are issued to customers for damaged stock. These credits are again posted against the accounts receivable file and filed by customer and salesperson.

Required

a. Draw the document flowchart for the existing manual system.

b. Assume you have acquired a minicomputer with on-line disk storage, CRT input, printer, and disk backup.

    1. Prepare a system flowchart showing how you would modify part a to computerize the system.

    2. Specify the information contained in each file required.

(SMAC Examination, adapted)

16.8 The Rocket Recording Company produces and distributes music on records, tapes, and compact discs (CDs). It has 10 regional sales offices located around the United States, and its corporate headquarters is located in New York City. At its computer center at headquarters the company maintains a marketing data base whose content and format are similar to that shown in Fig. 16.9.

Regional sales managers have requested more current information on salesperson performance, including sales breakdowns by distributor (customer), medium (record, tape, or CD), and release, for the most recent day, week, month, or other period of time specified by the manager. Note that a release is the music industry's equivalent of a product, and some of its key attributes include the release number, release date, artist, and title.

To satisfy this request, the company has installed personal computers at each regional sales office. You have been asked to design a system that will download the required information from the corporate data base to the regional PCs and then prepare the requested reports.

Required

a. Identify the data items that must be retrieved from the marketing data base and/or related data bases in order to prepare the necessary reports.

b. What security factors, if any, need to be taken into consideration in designing this system?

c. Assuming the availability of the data items you identified in part a, design a format for the salesperson performance report.

16.9 The sales manager of a furniture manufacturer uses a Customer Listing by Salesperson program to generate the report shown in Fig. 16.12. Assume that a customer is serviced only by one salesperson, but one salesperson may handle many accounts.

Required

a. In order for a computer program to generate the report, what file(s) would the program access?

b. Provide a record layout for the file(s). The record layout should indicate the field name, description, and size and type for each field in the record.

c. Assuming that a sort program is not necessary and that the customer numbers are assigned at random, identify the record key (access key) of the file containing the customer's name that would be accessed in order to generate the report. Explain your choice of record key (access key).

(SMAC Examination, adapted)

16.10 The Home Distribution Company is a wholesaler of hardware to the construction industry. The company has decided to replace its current order entry system operating under a batch system with an on-line computer system. The company has hired a software house to design and program this system. As a part of their system's design, the software house has provided the on-line, real-time systems flowchart shown in Fig. 16.13.

Required

a. Evaluate the systems flowchart provided. Your evaluation should identify two system weaknesses and recommend a process to strengthen each weak-

20-Jan-84	Customer Listing by Salesperson				Page 4

Salesperson: #23 John Doe

Customer		Sales		Commission	
		YTD	MTD	YTD	MTD
.		.	.	.	.
.		.	.	.	.
.		.	.	.	.
12467	Baby Bear Furniture Company	50,261	5,300	2,513	265
12475	Home Distribution Company				
.		102,567	10,425	2,051	208
.					
.					
99999	X -------- 30 -------- X	999,999	999,999	9,999	9,999
.	.	.	.	.	.
.	.	.	.	.	.

Figure 16.12
Furniture manufacturer: Customer
listing by salesperson

ness. Outline the required input and output generated by each recommended process. Assume that the systems flowchart represents the entire order entry system of Home Distribution Company. Your response should be in the format shown.

	Recommended Improvements		
System Weakness	Additional Processing Required	Required Input	Output Generated

b. What are the limitations of systems flowcharting for use by the systems analyst in his or her analysis of a system?

c. Differentiate between batch processing and on-line processing. Include both the advantages and disadvantages of each method in your discussion. (SMAC Examination)

16.11 Value Clothing is a large distributor of all types of clothing acquired from buy-outs, over-stocks, and factory seconds. All sales are on account with terms of net 30 days from date of monthly statement. The numbers of delinquent accounts and uncollectible accounts have increased significantly during the last 12 months. Management has determined that the information generated from

the present accounts receivable system is inadequate and untimely. In addition, customers frequently complain of errors in their accounts.

The current accounts receivable system has not been changed since Value Clothing started its operations. A new computer was acquired 18 months ago, but no attempt has been made to revise the accounts receivable application because other applications were considered more important. The work schedule in the Systems Department has slackened slightly, enabling the staff to design a new accounts receivable system. Top management has requested that the new system satisfy the following objectives.

1. Produce current and timely reports regarding customers that would provide useful information for the following purposes:

a. To aid in controlling bad debts
b. To notify the Sales Department of customer accounts that are delinquent (accounts that should lose charge privileges)
c. To notify the Sales Department of customers whose accounts are considered uncollectible (accounts that should be closed and written off).

2. Produce timely notices to customers regarding the following:

a. Amounts owed to Value Clothing

Entry Process

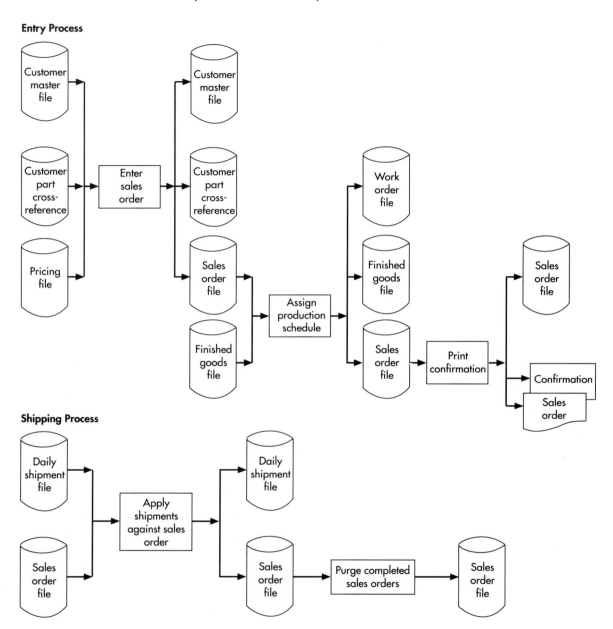

Shipping Process

Figure 16.13
Home Distribution Company: Order
entry system flowchart

b. A change of status of their accounts (loss of charge privileges, account closed)

3. Incorporate the necessary procedures and controls to minimize the chance for errors in customers' accounts

Input data for the system would be taken from four source documents: credit applications, sales invoices, cash payment remittances, and credit memoranda. The accounts receivable master file will be maintained on a machine-readable file by customer account number. The preliminary design of the new accounts receivable system has been completed by the Systems Department. A brief description of the proposed reports and other output generated by the system follows.

1. *Accounts receivable register:* A daily alphabetical listing of all customers' accounts that shows balance as of the last statement, activity since the last statement, and account balance.

2. *Customer statements:* Monthly statements for each customer showing activity since the last statement and account balance; the top portion of the statement is returned with the payment and serves as the cash payment remittance.

3. *Aging schedule—all customers:* A monthly schedule of all customers with outstanding balances displaying the total amount owed, with the total classified into age groups: 0–30 days, 30–60 days, 60–90 days, over 90 days; the schedule includes totals and percentages for each age category.

4. *Aging schedule—past-due customers:* A schedule prepared monthly that includes only those customers whose accounts are past due—that is, over 30 days outstanding—classified by age. The Credit Manager uses this schedule to decide which customers will receive delinquent notices, will receive temporary suspension of charge privileges, or will have their accounts closed.

5. *Activity reports:* Monthly reports that show the following:

a. Customers who have not purchased any merchandise for 90 days

b. Customers whose account balance exceeds their credit limit

c. Customers whose accounts are delinquent but have current sales on account

6. *Delinquency and write-off register:* A monthly alphabetical listing of customers' accounts that are (a) delinquent or (b) closed. These listings show name, account number, and balance. Related notices are prepared and sent to these customers.

7. *Summary journal entries:* Entries prepared monthly to record write-offs to the accounts receivable file.

Required

a. Identify the data that should be captured and stored in the computer records for each customer.

b. Review the proposed reports to be generated by the new accounts receivable system.

1. Discuss whether the proposed reports should be adequate to satisfy the objectives enumerated.

2. Recommend changes, if any, that should be made in the proposed reporting structure generated by the new accounts receivable system.   (CMA Examination)

16.12 O'Brien Corporation is a medium-sized, privately owned industrial instrument manufacturer supplying precision equipment manufacturers in the Midwest. The corporation is 10 years old and operates a centralized accounting and information system. The administrative offices are located in a downtown building, while the production, shipping, and receiving departments are housed in a renovated warehouse a few blocks away. The shipping and receiving areas share one end of the warehouse.

O'Brien Corporation has grown rapidly. Sales have increased by 25% each year for the last three years, and the company is now shipping approximately $80,000 of its products each week. James Fox, O'Brien's Controller, purchased and installed a computer last year to process the payroll and inventory. Fox plans to fully integrate the accounting information system within the next five years.

The Marketing Department consists of four salespersons. Upon obtaining an order, usually over the telephone, a salesperson manually prepares a prenumbered, two-part sales order. One copy of the order is filed by date and the second copy is sent to the Shipping Department. All sales are on credit, FOB destination. Because of the recent increase in sales the four salespersons have not had time to check credit histories. As a result, 15% of credit sales are either late collections or uncollectible.

The Shipping Department receives the sales orders and packages the goods from the warehouse, noting any items that are out of stock. The terminal in the Shipping Department is used to update the perpetual inventory records of each item as it is removed from the shelf. The packages are placed near the loading dock door in alphabetical order by customer name. The sales order is signed by a shipping clerk indicating that the order is filled and ready to send. The sales order is forwarded to the Billing Department, where a two-part sales invoice is prepared. The sales invoice is only prepared upon receipt of the sales order from the Shipping Department, so that the customer is billed just for the items that were sent, not for back orders. Billing sends the customer's copy of the invoice back to Shipping. The customer's copy of the invoice serves as a billing copy, and Shipping inserts it into a special envelope on the package in order to save postage. The carrier of the customer's choice is then contacted to pick up the goods. In the past, goods were shipped within two working days of the receipt of the customer's order; however, shipping dates now average six working days after receipt of the order. One reason is that there are two new shipping clerks who are still undergoing training. Because the two shipping clerks have fallen behind, the two clerks in the Receiving Department, who are experienced, have been assisting the shipping clerks.

The Receiving Department is located adjacent to the shipping dock, and merchandise is received daily by many different carriers. The clerks share the computer terminal with the Shipping Department. The date, vendor, and number of items received are entered upon receipt in order to keep the perpetual inventory records current.

Hard copy of the changes in inventory (additions and shipments) is printed once a month. The Receiving Supervisor makes sure that the additions are reasonable and forwards the printout to the Shipping Supervisor, who is responsible for checking the reasonableness of the deductions from inventory (shipments). The inventory printout is stored in the Shipping Department by date. A complete inventory list is only printed once a year when the physical inventory is taken.

The diagram in Fig. 16.14 presents the document flows employed by O'Brien Corporation.

Required

a. Identify each weakness in O'Brien Corporation's marketing, shipping, billing, and receiving information system, and describe the potential problems caused by each weakness. Recommend controls or changes in the system to correct each weakness. Use the following format in preparing your answer.

Weaknesses and Potential Problem(s)	Recommendation(s) To Correct Weaknesses

b. Discuss how O'Brien Corporation could use its new computer system to improve control and efficiency in processing sales orders.
(CMA Examination, adapted)

16.13 Ajax Inc., an audit client, recently installed a new EDP system to process more efficiently the shipping, billing, and accounts receivable records. During interim work an assistant completed the review of the accounting system and the internal accounting controls. The assistant determined the following information concerning the new EDP system and the processing and control of shipping notices and customer invoices.

Each major computerized function—shipping, billing, accounts receivable, and so forth—is permanently assigned to a specific computer operator, who is responsible for making program changes, running the program, and reconciling the computer log. Responsibility for the custody and control over the magnetic tapes and system documentation is randomly rotated among the computer operators on a monthly basis to prevent any one person from having access to the tapes and documentation at all times. Each computer programmer and computer operator has access to the computer room via a magnetic card and a digital code that is different for each card. The systems analyst and the supervisor of the computer operators do not have access to the computer room.

The EDP system documentation consists of the following items: program listing, error listing, logs, and record layout. For efficiency, batch totals and processing controls are omitted from the system.

Ajax ships its products directly from two warehouses, which forward shipping notices to general accounting. There the billing clerk enters the price of the item and accounts for the numerical sequence of the shipping notices. The billing clerk also prepares daily adding machine tapes of the units shipped and the sales amounts. Shipping notices and adding machine tapes are forwarded to the Computer Department for processing. The computer output consists of the following items.

■ A three-copy invoice that is forwarded to the billing clerk

■ A daily sales register showing the totals of units

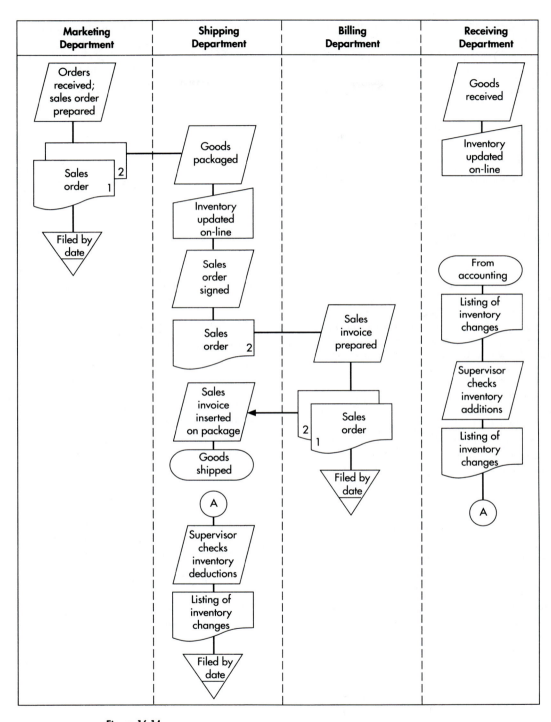

Figure 16.14
O'Brien Corporation: Order processing
document flows

shipped and sales amounts, which the computer operator compares to the adding machine tapes

The billing clerk mails two copies of each invoice to the customer and retains the third copy in an open-invoice file that serves as a detailed accounts receivable record.

Required

Describe one specific recommendation for correcting each weakness in internal accounting controls in the new EDP system and for correcting each weakness or inefficiency in the procedures for processing and controlling shipping notices and customer invoices.   (CPA Examination)

Case 16.1: ANYCOMPANY, INC.—AN ONGOING COMPREHENSIVE CASE

One of the best ways to learn is to immediately apply what you have studied. The purpose of this case is to allow you to do that. You will select a local company that you can work with. At the end of most chapters you will find an assignment that will have you apply what you have learned using the company you have selected as a reference. This case, then, may become an ongoing case study that you work on throughout the term.

Select a local company and obtain permission to study their sales order processing system. Then answer the following questions.

1.   Who are the individuals responsible for sales order preparation, credit checks, safeguarding of physical inventories, shipping, billing, and accounts receivable? Prepare a partial organization chart and identify these individuals on this chart.

2.   What documents are used in the system? Obtain a sample copy of each document, if you can.

3.   What master files are maintained in the system? What is the data content of each master file? Prepare (or obtain copies of) record layouts for each file.

4.   For each master file, explain how it is updated. Identify each of the different types of transactions that cause the file to be updated. What is the data content of each transaction record? Describe how these transaction data are captured in machine-read-able form for entry into the company's computer system. Prepare (or obtain copies of) record layouts for each transaction record.

5.   If the company uses a data base management system, prepare (or obtain a copy of) a schema diagram identifying the linkages among the various master files within the system.

6.   Prepare (or obtain copies of) system flowcharts for each major master file update process. For each process, indicate whether the company uses batch processing, on-line processing, or a combination.

7.   Describe internal control procedures employed by the company in this system. Do you feel that the company's internal controls are satisfactory?

8.   Identify and obtain sample copies of reports that are prepared by the system. For each report, identify the file or files from which the information originates. Indicate the frequency with which each report is prepared and whether it is prepared on the mainframe computer or a personal computer. Identify who receives each report and how it is used. Evaluate the content and format of each report.

9.   Describe how accounting transaction information that originates in this system is transmitted to the company's general ledger system.

CASE 16.2: ELITE PUBLISHING COMPANY

Elite Publishing Company has established a subsidiary, Business Book Club, Inc. (BBC), that will operate as described here. BBC's editors will select from among recently published books in the business area those it feels will be of most interest to businesspeople. These books will be purchased in large lots at approximately 40% of list price. BBC plans to sell these books to its club members at approximately 75% of list price.

Solicitation of new customers will be done through advertising by direct mail and in selected publications. Such advertisements will offer an introductory membership bonus whereby persons can enroll by purchasing one book and receiving four free books. Each month club members will be sent a list of new selections and a book order form, but they are not obligated to buy any books. After purchasing four books, a member will be sent a special order form and a list of selections from which he or she may choose a free book.

You have been called upon to design a computerized billing and book inventory system for BBC. Assume that you have asked various managers about their information needs and found out that the Advertising Manager wants to know which advertising media are most effective, the Credit Manager wants to know which accounts are more than 90 days past due, and the editors want to know which books are best-sellers for the club.

1. Identify the master files you feel should be maintained in this system, and list the data content of each.

2. Identify the input transactions that this system must process and the output documents and reports that the system must be designed to produce.

3. Assume that member orders will be received on OCR-readable documents, and that new-member enrollment forms and all other inputs will be keyed into the system using on-line terminals. All transactions will be recorded on temporary disk files and processed in batches. Master files will also be stored on disk. Prepare systems flowcharts of all computer runs necessary to process the inputs, maintain the master files, and generate the outputs for your system.

CHAPTER 17

The Procurement Cycle: Purchases, Inventories, and Accounts Payable

LEARNING OBJECTIVES

After studying this chapter, you should be able to:

- Describe the key activities and data processing operations included in the procurement cycle.
- Describe the decision responsibilities and information requirements of the purchasing and inventory management function.
- Give several examples of the information provided by the accounting information system to support the purchasing and inventory management function.
- Flowchart data and information flows in typical purchasing and inventory data processing systems.
- Evaluate and recommend control policies and procedures for a purchasing and inventory data processing system.

INTEGRATIVE CASE: ELECTRONICS INCORPORATED

Tom Morris is Vice-President for Production at Electronics Incorporated (EI), a manufacturer of a variety of inexpensive consumer electronic products sold primarily in discount retail stores (see Chapter 16). In recent years the company's sales volume has leveled off after a period of strong growth. Surveys have indicated that product pricing and quality have become significant concerns among customers.

Tom has just reviewed EI's financial results for the second quarter. These results were very disappointing, due primarily to production cost overruns at both the Dayton and Wichita plants. At the Wichita plant several production runs were delayed owing to lack of availability of components that, according to inventory records, should have been in stock. At the Dayton plant there were numerous instances where key suppliers either did not deliver components on a timely basis or delivered substandard components. The net effect of these problems was that the company's gross margin declined by 15%.

Tom recently attended a seminar on advanced manufacturing methods. He remembers how the instructors stressed the need for current and accurate information to support all of the modern manufacturing methods now in vogue. The seminar has convinced Tom that EI's recent problems are probably due to weaknesses in the company's purchasing and inventory information system. As he thinks about the best way to proceed, the following questions arise in his mind:

1. What must be done to ensure that EI's inventory records are maintained on a current and accurate basis?
2. How can EI reduce its substantial investment in materials inventories?
3. What can be done to assist EI's purchasing agents in selecting suppliers that offer the best value with respect to materials cost, quality, and delivery reliability?
4. How can EI do a better job of monitoring and following up on supplier performance? ■

What would you suggest to Tom about how EI's information system might be utilized to address these issues?

INTRODUCTION

The procurement cycle is a recurring set of business activities and related data processing operations associated with the purchase of raw materials, merchandise, supplies, and services. The business activities include determining the amount and timing of purchases; selecting vendors; arranging for the delivery, receipt, and storage of inventories; and arranging for the rendering of services. These business activities are a major part of the production planning and control function within a typical manufacturing company. The related data processing operations include requisitioning goods and services, preparing purchase orders, documenting receipt of inventories and services, maintaining records of inventories on hand and on order, and maintaining records of accounts payable and vendor performance. The information provided by these data processing operations is crucial to the successful performance of the related business activities.

As the Electronics Incorporated case suggests, deficiencies in purchasing and inventory information systems can often cause severe business problems that threaten a company's profitability. In particular, the availability of current and accurate information on inventories, vendors, and the status of outstanding purchase orders is crucial for effective purchasing and inventory management. As you read this chapter, think about how improvements in EI's information systems might help to resolve its problems.

In manufacturing firms the procurement cycle is closely related to the production cycle. In a similar vein, the purchasing function in a manufacturing company is an integral part of the production management organization. For example, at EI and most other manufacturing companies the Purchasing Department is responsible to the Production Vice-President (refer back to Fig. 16.1). Other departments involved in procurement operations in a typical manufacturing organization include a Receiving Department, responsible for accepting and processing materials received from suppliers, and an Inventory Stores Department, responsible for safeguarding materials inventories while they are in stock. Several related functions and departments are also involved in the production cycle of a typical manufacturing company. The information requirements and data processing procedures associated with the production cycle are described more fully in Chapter 18. To examine the organizational relationships between the purchasing and production functions in a typical manufacturing company, you may wish to refer ahead to Fig. 18.1.

This chapter describes the procurement cycle functions of purchasing and inventory management and the data processing operations that support these business functions. A related data processing operation, cash disbursements in payment of vendor accounts payable, is covered in Chapter 20. This chapter focuses on the central role played by the accounting information system both in carrying out data processing operations within the procurement cycle and in providing information to support the purchasing and inventory management functions. The chapter begins by describing the decision responsibilities and related information requirements of managers within the purchasing function. This establishes the kinds of information that must be produced by information systems designed to support purchasing operations. The next section of the chapter describes in general terms the basic functions and procedures that must be performed within the procurement cycle of a typical business organization. These procedures generate the raw data that is the source of information used in purchasing and inventory management. The remainder of the chapter explains and illustrates the purchasing and inventory data processing system, which is the segment of the accounting information system that executes the basic procurement cycle functions and procedures and so plays a key role in meeting the information requirements of the purchasing function.

THE PURCHASING AND INVENTORY MANAGEMENT FUNCTION

Purchasing is the primary management function in the purchasing and inventory management system. In most larger business organizations the purchasing function is the responsibility of purchasing agents within a Purchasing Department. The basic decisions involved in the purchasing function include what to purchase, when to purchase, how much to purchase, and from whom to purchase. The importance of these decisions is underscored by the problems that arose at Electronics Incorporated: The Wichita plant's inventory shortages stem from failures in determining what should be purchased and when, while the Dayton plant's difficulties with suppliers reveal a lack of attention to the selection of reliable suppliers.

Deciding what, when, and how much to purchase is the inventory control function. There are two basic approaches. Under the traditional approach inventories are maintained to provide a buffer against the uncertainties associated with inventory use and supplier delivery times. That is, if inventory use is greater than expected, and/or if suppliers are slower than expected in delivering items ordered, there should be sufficient inventory on hand so that production can continue without interruption. Under this approach the timing of purchases is based on a **reorder point**, which is a minimum balance on hand for each inventory item such that, when the actual balance on hand falls below this level, an order is triggered to replenish the stock. Ideally, inventory control personnel will determine, for each inventory item, the reorder point and order quantity that minimize the sum of the costs of ordering the item, carrying the item in inventory, and being out of stock. This optimal order size is referred to as the **economic order quantity**. Mathematical-modeling techniques are often used to determine the economic order quantity and optimal reorder point. Application of a mathematical model requires quantitative estimates of the three cost factors listed earlier and of vendor lead times; also, the future requirements for the inventory item must be known or estimated.[1]

The information required to estimate future requirements for an item and vendor lead time can be generated by formal information systems within an organization. Vendor lead time can be estimated if formal records of past dealings with vendors are maintained. In a retail organization future demand can be estimated by applying forecasting techniques to historical records of past sales. In a manufacturing organization future requirements can be accurately estimated if production planning is effectively integrated with sales forecasting. For example, Electronics Incorporated should forecast the number of calculators, digital clocks, radios, pagers, and so forth, that it expects to sell each quarter. Then from engineering specifications of the kind and quantity of components required for each of these products, inventory control personnel can project the total quantity of each component that must be ordered in order to produce sufficient quantities of each product to meet the forecasted demand for the quarter. Similarly, by examining records of past transactions with specific vendors, EI should estimate how long each vendor will take to deliver the required items so that it can place its orders far enough in advance to ensure delivery of the items before they are required in the production process.

---

[1] For more on mathematical modeling in inventory control, see Frederick S. Hillier and Gerald J. Lieberman, *Introduction to Operations Research,* 5th ed. (New York: McGraw-Hill, 1990), Chapter 18.

The three types of inventory costs are more difficult to estimate. Carrying costs include all costs that vary with the quantity of parts and materials in inventory. The most significant element of carrying costs is the opportunity cost of the funds tied up in inventory. Stated another way, this cost represents the revenue lost because funds are invested in inventory rather than in revenue-generating activities. Other elements of inventory carrying costs include the incremental costs of spoilage, breakage, pilferage, obsolescence, insurance, taxes, and space utilization. Ordering cost refers only to those costs that vary with the number of orders placed and generally involves the costs of processing the order and the fixed costs of shipping. Finally, stockout cost, which involves lost goodwill or inefficiencies in operations, is practically impossible to measure precisely, so rough estimates must often be employed.

Mathematical-modeling techniques generally are applied only to the high-cost and high-use items of inventory, such as the electronic components, displays, and casings used by EI in its most popular products. For low-cost and low-use items, carrying and ordering costs are so insignificant that reorder point and order quantity can be set with the sole objective of eliminating stockouts. This would be true of inexpensive screws, springs, and so forth, used in assembling EI's products or of components used only in specialized products for which sales volume is low.

Once the order quantity and reorder point of an item have been determined, they are stored along with other data pertaining to the item in the inventory master file. The data processing system then monitors inventory balances on a continuous basis and routinely initiates orders for any items for which the on-hand balance falls below the reorder point.

The alternative to the traditional approach to inventory control in a manufacturing company is called **materials requirements planning** (MRP). The fundamental difference between MRP and the traditional approach is that MRP attempts to plan inventory use in order to minimize or eliminate the uncertainty about when inventory items will be required. This strategy reduces the amount of inventory required as a buffer against uncertainty. Under MRP a Production Planning Department prepares a detailed schedule of the quantities of each product to be manufactured during, for example, the next three months. From this schedule and the engineering specifications for each product, planners then determine exactly what quantities of raw materials, parts, and supplies will be required and at what points in time. The Purchasing Department can then purchase exactly those items that are needed and request their delivery when they are needed. Note that under MRP inventory requirements are *scheduled*, while under the traditional approach they are merely *estimated*. As a result, there is less need to hedge against uncertain production requirements, so that smaller levels of parts and materials inventories are required. However, while MRP reduces materials inventory levels, it also places much greater demands on the information system to maintain accurate and current inventory records.[2]

An extension of MRP is the just-in-time (JIT) system of inventory and production management. JIT systems attempt to eliminate the other source of uncertainty in inventory ordering: vendor lead time. The ultimate goal is to minimize, if not virtually eliminate, manufacturing inventories by scheduling all inventory deliveries at the precise times and locations needed. A factory utilizing a JIT system establishes multiple receiving docks, each assigned to accept deliveries of materials needed at work centers located nearby—which contrasts with the traditional approach of having a single receiving facility located adjacent to a centralized Factory Stores Department. JIT calls for frequent deliveries of small lots of materials to the specific locations that require them, rather than infrequent bulk deliveries to a central receiving and storage facility.

In terms of the three categories of inventory costs mentioned earlier JIT systems are designed to minimize or eliminate inventory carrying costs and stockout costs. This leaves only ordering costs. In essence, manufacturing organizations using JIT are spending virtually all of their inventory control resources to operate a complex and sophisticated inventory ordering system. At the heart of this system is an information system that can effectively coordinate and monitor purchasing, delivery, and production activities on a real-time basis. In recent years many prominent U.S. manufacturing companies have embraced JIT systems, including Xerox, Ford, Motorola, McDonnell Douglas, NCR, Intel, and Delco Electronics.

The other significant management decision made by the purchasing function is the selection of vendors for inventory items. A retail organization has buyers who specialize in related lines of merchandise. Once the decision is made to carry a particular type of merchandise in the store, the buyer is responsible for selecting a supplier. Factors relevant to the decision include price, reliability, product styling, brand image, and quality. Information on prices and styles is provided by representatives of the various suppliers. Information on brand image and quality should be part of the buyer's knowledge about the lines of merchandise in which he or she specializes. Information on reliability—the supplier's history of meeting quantity specifications and delivering goods promptly—should be maintained as part of a vendor history file within the information system.

In a manufacturing organization the Purchasing Department selects vendors for raw materials. When the Engineering Department provides

---

[2] For further discussion of MRP, see Thomas E. Vollmann, William L. Berry, and D. Clay Whybark, *Manufacturing Planning and Control Systems*, 3rd ed. (Homewood, Ill.: Irwin, 1992), Chapter 2; and Joseph R. Biggs and Ellen J. Long, "Gaining the Competitive Edge with MRP/MRP II," *Management Accounting* (May 1988): 27–32.

the specifications for a new part to the Purchasing Department, a purchasing agent prepares requests for price quotations, which are sent to potential suppliers. Once the vendors' price quotations have been returned, the purchasing agent selects a vendor for the item. This decision is based not only on price but also on reliability, quality, and perhaps whether a given supplier is also a significant customer. The information system should maintain records of dealings with vendors in order to provide information about reliability and product quality. The quality of a vendor's products can be measured in terms of how frequently products received from the vendor fail to pass inspection or testing performed upon receipt of the items in a Receiving Department. Note that if information of this kind were readily available to purchasing agents at Electronics Incorporated and were used routinely in selecting vendors, the problems experienced with suppliers at EI's Dayton plant could have been avoided.

Under a JIT system the two critical factors in selecting vendors are the quality of their products and their dependability in delivering the exact materials needed to the proper locations at the specified times. A late delivery or a delivery of defective parts and materials will wreak havoc with a finely tuned JIT production schedule and so cannot be tolerated. As a result, a key component of most JIT systems is the certification of suppliers. Only a small number of carefully chosen supplier companies are certified, based on their commitment to reliability and quality control. For example, since 1980 Ford has reduced the number of suppliers of its production parts by over one-third and plans to further reduce the number from 1700 to 1100 by 1995. Since 1980, the supplier base has been reduced from 5000 to 300 at Xerox and from 4200 in 1985 to 1155 in 1991 for Motorola's communications group. One consequence of this method is that JIT engenders a very close relationship between a manufacturing company and its suppliers; the manufacturer may even assist its suppliers in product design, production scheduling, and quality control.[3] Furthermore, in recent years many JIT manufacturers have required their vendors to maintain an electronic data interchange (EDI) link between the manufacturer and vendor information systems.

Once a vendor has been selected for a product, the identity of the vendor becomes a part of the inventory master record for that product. Vendor selection thus does not have to be performed each time the product is ordered. The identity of possible alternative vendors may also be included in the file in case the primary vendor is temporarily out of stock. Periodically, decisions may be made to change primary

---

[3] An excellent general discussion of JIT is provided by Arjan T. Sadhwani, M. H. Sarhan, and Dayal Kiringoda, "Just-In-Time: An Inventory System Whose Time Has Come," *Management Accounting* (December 1985): 36–44. The use of vendor evaluation procedures to support JIT is discussed in Michael A. Robinson and John E. Timmerman, "How Vendor Analysis Supports JIT Manufacturing," *Management Accounting* (December 1987): 20–24.

vendors for some products if a primary vendor does not provide satisfactory service, raises prices substantially, or goes out of business.

In summary, the primary purchasing and inventory management functions involve determining what to purchase, when to purchase, how much to purchase, and from whom to purchase. These decisions are generally made by purchasing agents supported by information provided by a purchasing and inventory data processing system. This system processes all purchasing and inventory transactions and provides information on inventory requirements, costs, and quantities on hand and on order, and on vendor prices, product quality, and delivery performance.

The next section describes in detail the basic functions and procedures performed within the procurement cycle in the processing of purchasing and inventory transactions. This subset of the accounting information system plays an important role in producing accounting information that is useful for effective purchasing and inventory management.

BASIC PROCUREMENT CYCLE FUNCTIONS AND PROCEDURES

This section reviews at a very general level the basic functions and procedures that are performed in the procurement cycle of typical business organizations. These functions, identified in Fig. 17.1, include requisitioning goods and services, preparing purchase orders, documenting receipt of goods and services, maintaining records of raw materials or merchandise inventories on hand and on order, processing vendor invoices, maintaining records of accounts payable and vendor performance, and posting summary accounting transactions to the general ledger. This section describes each of these functions in detail in the context of a typical manufacturing company. Variations on these basic procedures for companies in different industries, including retailing, insurance, construction, and services, are described at the conclusion of this section.

Requisitioning

The first step in the purchasing process is recognition and documentation of a need within the organization for the purchase of goods or services. This leads to the preparation and approval of a **purchase requisition**, which is an internal document[4] requesting that specified goods or services be purchased. A sample purchase requisition is illustrated in Fig. 17.2. Within a manufacturing company those authorized to requisition raw materials and supplies may include production planning personnel, factory supervisors, and inventory control personnel. Ser-

---

[4] The phrase *internal document* refers to a document that is intended to be used only within an organization, rather than as a record of an exchange transaction with an outside party.

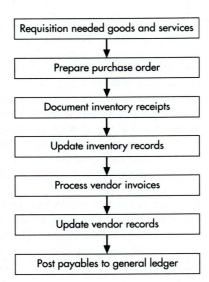

Figure 17.1
Basic purchasing and inventory data
processing functions

Figure 17.2
Sample purchase requisition

ELECTRONICS INCORPORATED			No. 89010
PURCHASE REQUISITION			

Date Prepared: 11/05/93	Prepared by: Richard Kirkland RK		Suggested Vendor: Wholesale Office Supply

Deliver to: Copy Center		Attn. R. Kirkland	Date Needed: 11/12/93

Stock No.	Quantity	Description	Price/Unit
3R2047	15 boxes	Xerox 4200 DP paper, 20 wt., 10 ream box	$33.99
80170	5 boxes	Moore 2600 continuous form, 20 lb	$31.99
817052-51	20 boxes	Dysan 100 MF2DD diskettes, box of 10	$6.49
1040475	10	IBM 4207 Proprinter ribbon, black	$8.99

Approved by: M. Thomson	Department: Admin. Services	Date: 11/05/93	Account No. 91-850

vices, such as advertising, insurance, consulting, travel, maintenance, and legal services, are requisitioned by supervisory personnel. Generally only certain personnel within an organization, such as those with authority over an operating budget, are authorized to prepare or approve a purchase requisition.

The purchase requisition serves two important functions: It documents the authorization to purchase goods and services, and it informs those responsible for the purchasing function that formal buying procedures should be initiated. The requisition identifies the requisitioner; specifies the delivery location, date needed, and item numbers, quantities, descriptions, and unit prices of each item requested; and may suggest a vendor. The person approving the requisition indicates the department number and account number to which the purchase cost is to be charged. As soon as the requisition is prepared, it should be transmitted to the Purchasing Department, either electronically or through a copy of a requisition document, so that the purchasing process can proceed on a timely basis.

Purchase Order Preparation

On the basis of the information provided by the purchase requisition, a purchase order is prepared. A purchase order is a document used to formally request a vendor to sell and deliver specified products or services at a designated price. An example of a purchase order is shown in Fig. 17.3. Purchase orders may be prepared by purchasing agents within a Purchasing Department or may be generated by a computer system based on the requisition and on data in inventory and vendor files. The order may be placed with a primary vendor identified in the inventory master file, with a vendor suggested on the requisition, or with some other vendor who may temporarily offer better prices or availability. The quantity requisitioned may be modified so that the order quantity is sufficient to obtain quantity discounts or is consistent with the number of units contained in a standard shipping package. Once the purchase order is prepared, it is immediately transmitted to the vendor, either electronically by using an EDI network or by sending two copies of the document through the mail. It is common for vendors to acknowledge receipt of purchase orders by returning one copy of the purchase order to the buyer or by transmitting an electronic acknowledgment message.

The purchase order is the primary record in the procurement cycle. In addition to serving as a request for vendors to deliver products or services, it is used to inform receiving personnel that deliveries from a particular vendor are expected, to inform inventory control personnel that particular inventory items and quantities are on order, and to inform accounting personnel that a financial commitment has been made to pay for the items ordered. Purchase order records may be transmitted to these various personnel electronically or through separate copies of a purchase order document.

Between the time that the purchase order is issued and the time that the last items ordered are delivered, the purchase order record is

ELECTRONICS INCORPORATED

3001 Dryden Rd. Dayton, OH 45439
Phone (513) 836-0100

No. 12153

PURCHASE ORDER

To: Wholesale Office Supply
     3344 Main Street
     Dayton, OH 45439

Show the above order
number on all invoices
and shipping papers.

Vendor Number: 451967	Order Date: 11/10/93	Requisition No.: 89010	Buyer: Dave Watson	Terms: 2/10, n/30
F.O.B. Destination	Ship via: Your truck	Deliver on: At once	Remarks:	

Item	Stock Number	Quantity	Description	Unit Price
1	3R2047	15 boxes	Xerox 4200 DP paper, 20 wt., 10 ream box	$33.99
2	80170	5 boxes	Moore 2600 continuous form, 20 lb	$31.99
3	817052-51	20 boxes	Dysan 100 MF2DD diskettes, box of 10	$6.49
4	1040475	10	IBM 4207 Proprinter ribbon, black	$8.99

Buyer: *George Deverick*

Figure 17.3
Sample purchase order

maintained in an "open" status. While the purchase order itself is basically a transaction record, the open purchase order is treated like a master record; that is, it is updated to reflect specific events that affect the status of the order. When the vendor's acknowledgment is received, this is noted in the open purchase order. The open purchase order record is also updated to reflect inventory receipts, returns, adjustments, and any other transactions associated with the order. Purchasing personnel are responsible for entering these transactions into the system. Once the order has been completely filled, the purchase order record can be removed from "open" status.

Many companies maintain special purchasing arrangements with their most important vendors. Under one approach the buying firm places blanket orders with particular suppliers. A **blanket order** represents a commitment by the buying firm to buy all quantities of specified items from a particular supplier for a designated time period, often one year. Sometimes the blanket order will not indicate specific quantities to be ordered but will only provide estimates. However, a more definitive relationship between buyer and vendor can be maintained if the buyer commits to a specific schedule of requirements, including quantities and delivery dates. For example, the Steelcase Company maintains an arrangement with Cannon Mills to purchase fabrics for upholstered furniture in large volumes. Steelcase provides detailed weekly reports to Cannon listing quantities required of specific products for several weeks into the future and designates orders for the most imminent weeks as definite.[5] Such an arrangement reduces the buyer's uncertainty about reliable sources of raw materials and provides the vendor with a better basis for planning its capacity and operations. For buyers to be able to make such commitments, they must employ advanced purchasing information systems that incorporate MRP or JIT.

Documentation of Inventory Receipts

Goods shipped by a vendor are generally delivered to a Receiving Department. Personnel in this department must first verify that the goods received were in fact ordered by checking the purchase order record. Then a **receiving report** is prepared to record details about the shipment, including the date received, shipper, vendor, purchase order number, and for each item received, the item number, description, unit of measure, and a count of the quantity received (see Fig. 17.4). To encourage an accurate count of items received, receiving personnel should not have access to data on quantities ordered.

Inspectors in the Receiving Department examine the shipment for damage or poor quality and indicate whether the goods are accepted or rejected in the ''remarks'' section of the receiving report. Both the receiver and the inspector enter their names on the receiving report. Then a copy of the receiving report accompanies the goods to a Stores Department or warehouse, where custodial personnel verify the count of items received and sign the document to accept responsibility for receipt of the goods. This documentation of the transfer of responsibility for the goods within the organization is a crucial internal control step, because it helps ensure that all goods received are properly conveyed to a secure location. After the receiving report has been signed by Stores Department personnel to acknowledge receipt of the goods, it is then used to support the recognition of an account payable to the vendor.

As inventory receipts are documented, the ''on-order'' records in the open purchase order file should be promptly updated to reflect the quantity and condition of the goods received. Purchasing Department personnel are responsible for monitoring the status of all open purchase orders and must follow up promptly on any orders for which no acknowledgment has been received or for which delivery is overdue. In the event that goods received are damaged or do not pass quality inspection, Purchasing Department personnel must correspond with

---

[5] Vollmann *et al.*, *Manufacturing Planning,* 191–193.

ELECTRONICS INCORPORATED		No. 60405
RECEIVING REPORT		

Vendor: *Wholesale Office Supply*	Date Received: *11/12/93*
Shipped via: *Vendor truck*	Purchase Order No. *12153*

Stock Number	Quantity	Description
817052-51	20	Dysan 100 MF2DD diskette boxes
1040475	10	IBM 4207 Proprinter ribbon
80170	5	Moore 2600 continuous form paper
3R2047	15	Xerox 4200DP paper, 10 ream boxes

Remarks: *Two boxes Moore 2600 paper received water damage.*

Received by: *Les Hale*	Inspected by: *GW*	Delivered to: *RK*

Figure 17.4
Sample receiving report

the vendor to arrange for return of the goods and/or for an adjustment of the amount billed.

To document the receipt of services, such as advertising or consulting, many companies utilize a copy of the vendor's invoice that has been approved for payment by authorized supervisory personnel and that indicates the account to which the expenditure is to be charged. This takes the place of a formal receiving report. To control expenditures for services, each supervisor is granted a budget that provides authority to spend a certain amount on services during the year. Actual expenditures are charged against budgeted amounts by the accounting system, and special approval is required for any expenditures that exceed the budgeted amount.

Inventory Accounting

If a perpetual inventory accounting system is maintained, then records must be kept for each inventory item of the amounts on order and on hand. When the purchase order is created, a record of the quantities ordered is added to the "on-order" field in the inventory record, with a cross-reference to the purchase order number. When items are received, the quantities received are subtracted from the "on-order" field and added to the "on-hand" field, with a cross-reference to the related receiving report number. The unit cost of items received is also recorded. The records of inventory quantities and costs must also be updated when inventory items are returned, scrapped, sold, or used in the production process.

On a regular basis, counts of actual inventory quantities on hand should be reconciled with on-hand quantities recorded in inventory master records and appropriate adjustments made to the records to correct any discrepancies. Reconciliations may be done on a periodic basis, with high-cost and high-use items being reconciled more frequently than low-cost, low-use items. In addition, a reconciliation should be performed whenever it becomes obvious that there is a discrepancy—for example, when the inventory record shows a negative balance or when no parts are available even though the record shows a positive balance. These reconciliations should be performed by personnel who are independent of both the inventory record keeping function and the inventory stores or warehousing function.

Processing of Vendor Invoices

Vendor invoices requesting payment for goods delivered are generally transmitted to the Accounts Payable Department, either electronically using an EDI network or through the mail. Before each invoice is approved for payment, accounts payable personnel check it against the corresponding receiving report and purchase order records. The purchase order record is checked to ensure that the goods were ordered and that the quantities received and prices charged are consistent with the order. The receiving report is checked to ensure that the quantities received are equal to the quantities invoiced. The accuracy of the extensions on the vendor's invoice must also be verified.

Once the invoice has been approved for payment, a disbursement voucher is prepared that authorizes the cash disbursement in payment of the invoice. The disbursement voucher also indicates any deductions for purchase discounts or returns and specifies the general ledger accounts to which the net disbursement is to be charged. Cash disbursement procedures are discussed further in Chapter 20 (see Fig. 20.3).

Ford Motor Company has developed a highly streamlined approach to vendor payments which it calls "invoiceless processing." It tells its vendors not to send invoices. Instead, purchase orders are maintained in an on-line data base, and prices specified on the purchase order are considered final. Receiving personnel check deliveries to verify that they correspond to an outstanding purchase order and then enter quantities received into the system. Rather than having accounts payable personnel match 14 data items between the purchase order, receiving report and vendor invoice, the new system automatically matches only three data items (supplier code, part number, and unit of measure) between the purchase order and receiving report and then prints a check for accounts payable personnel to send to the vendor. This system enabled Ford to achieve a 75% reduction in its staff of 500 accounts payable clerks in its North American operations.[6]

Generally, a large batch of vendor invoices will be processed together. At the conclusion of this process a summary journal entry is prepared for the entire batch of vendor invoices approved for payment. This summary journal entry is often documented in a journal voucher record. The journal voucher supports the posting of the summary journal entry to the general ledger.

Updating of Vendor Records

The authorization of a disbursement in payment of a vendor invoice creates an account payable to the vendor. Therefore the vendor's account payable record must be updated by appending a record of the vendor invoice to it and by adding the total invoice amount to the outstanding amount payable. It is important that the due date of each invoice be noted in the accounts payable record, because many vendors offer discounts if their invoices are paid on a timely basis.

Occasionally, vendors will deliver goods that are unsatisfactory to the buying company, which will either return the goods for full credit or negotiate an allowance in the amount to be paid. The buying company must then adjust its accounts payable records for these purchase returns and allowances. Authorization for such adjustments originates in the Purchasing Department, which is responsible for arranging to receive the appropriate credit from the vendor. Once this is done and the necessary documentation prepared and transmitted, the amount of credit is subtracted from the total amount payable in the vendor's account.

In addition to accounting data, vendor records must be updated to reflect several other aspects of every transaction with each vendor. Were the correct quantities delivered? Were they delivered on a timely basis? Were the goods in satisfactory condition? Did the vendor invoice specify correct quantities, prices, and so on? Were any problems rectified in a timely manner? Data on these aspects of vendor transactions are relevant to the evaluation of vendor performance and the selection of future vendors, and they should be recorded and maintained in a vendor history file. This is one way in which Electronics Incorporated should address its problems with vendors by improving its purchasing information systems.

General Ledger

The final step in the procurement cycle is the posting of summary accounting journal entries to the general ledger. The journal voucher, prepared when the invoices are approved for payment, is the input record that initiates this process. The basic accounting journal entries

---

[6] Michael Hammer, ''Reengineering Work: Don't Automate, Obliterate,'' *Harvard Business Review* (July/August 1990): 105–106.

that summarize the purchasing process vary depending on whether the firm uses a perpetual or a periodic inventory accounting system. In a perpetual system the inventory accounts are kept continuously up to date by recording all inventory purchases and sales as they occur. Thus the entry used to record inventory purchases on account under a perpetual inventory system is as follows:

Inventory	$ 21,956.50	
Accounts Payable		$ 21,956.50

Note that this entry is a composite of many individual inventory purchases that are processed together in a batch. Purchase returns and allowances are recorded by reversing this entry for the amount of the credit. If inventory counts reveal that the actual quantity on hand is less than the quantity recorded on the books, the inventory account is written down, and the debit is charged to an "inventory shrinkage" account.

A periodic inventory system keeps track of inventory purchases but does not account directly for inventory sales or use. As a result, the inventory accounts are not maintained in a continuously current status. Instead, inventory is physically counted and priced at the end of each year, and this information is used to estimate the cost of inventory sold or used in the production process during the year. Under this system the following journal entry is made to record inventory purchases on account.

Purchases	$ 21,956.50	
Accounts Payable		$ 21,956.50

Purchase returns and allowances are then recorded in a special contra-account as follows:

Accounts Payable	$ 978.25	
Purchase Returns and Allowances		$ 978.25

When a complete physical inventory is taken at year-end, an adjusting journal entry is made as follows:

Inventory (Ending)	$ 75,266.43	
Cost of Goods Sold	$459,234.98	
Purchases		$466,535.36
Inventory (Beginning)		$ 67,966.05

This entry closes the purchases account, adjusts the ending inventory balance to the level indicated by the physical count, and records cost of goods sold for the period as the total of purchases for the period plus the net reduction (or minus the net increase) in the inventory account.

Industry Variations   The functions and procedures performed within the procurement cycle of a manufacturing company, as just described, are more complex than they are in most other kinds of companies. For this reason we will use manufacturing as a sort of benchmark case for describing the procurement cycle and other accounting cycles throughout Part 5. However, for complete understanding of the procurement cycle and its variations, one must be aware of some of the key differences that exist among various kinds of companies. Accordingly, this section briefly reviews some of the unique characteristics of procurement cycle functions and procedures associated with retail companies, construction companies, and claims processing in insurance companies. In addition, we point out here that "procurement" in service companies is analogous to the acquisition of human resources, which is covered in Chapter 19.

Retailing.   There are several differences between retail and manufacturing companies that affect their respective procurement cycles. The fundamental difference is that demand for materials inventories in manufacturing companies is more predictable, based on planned production. In contrast, retailers purchase goods for resale to consumers and thus face product demands that are much less predictable. For retailers the decision of what to buy is very critical to their success. Sales forecasting is an important input to the procurement process. Retailers must also maintain larger safety stocks to allow for the uncertainty of consumer demand and must continually monitor sales activity and inventory levels and adjust their buying plans accordingly.

Larger retail organizations employ individuals called "buyers," each of whom is responsible for purchasing and inventory control for a specific category of merchandise. On the basis of sales forecasts, a budget is established for each category of merchandise. After reviewing the sales forecasts and the existing levels of inventory, the buyer selects the merchandise to be ordered from each vendor and prepares purchase orders. Each buyer's budget is regulated by an **open-to-buy (OTB) control system.** OTB represents the amount of the budget that is still available for purchases of merchandise in a particular category for a specified period of time, such as a month. OTB is computed by taking the initial purchasing budget, subtracting the retail value of purchases already received or on order, and adding any merchandise returns. OTB provides a budgeted monetary limit on what each buyer may spend, but it may be adjusted upward or downward within a buying period on the basis of actual sales and sales forecast revisions.

Continuous monitoring of sales and inventory levels is important to the success of retail organizations and requires an effective information system. When actual sales deplete the inventory of a particular item to its reorder point, an additional purchase order will be issued to replenish the stock. The order quantity is determined at the time of the order from recent data on actual sales and from the most recent sales forecast. Once the order is placed, the processing of inventory receipts and vendor invoices and the maintenance of inventory and vendor data files proceed in much the same way as in a manufacturing company.[7]

Construction. Procurement by a construction company takes place almost entirely through subcontractors. The construction company, serving as a general contractor, divides each construction project into separate tasks (masonry, plumbing, electrical, flooring, etc.). The general contractor may perform some of these tasks but is primarily responsible for selecting subcontractors to perform each task, scheduling their work, monitoring their progress, and verifying the quality of their finished work.

The critical procurement decision for a general contractor is the selection of subcontractors. Typically, several subcontractors are invited to submit bids for each job. While the amount bid is certainly one important factor in the selection decision, the general contractor must also consider the reliability and quality of each subcontractor's work. The subcontract specifies what work will be done, when it will be done, what materials will be used, and what amount will be paid for the work; essentially, it serves the same function as the purchase order in a retail or manufacturing company. Inventory control is a less critical issue, because material requirements are quite predictable based on the construction schedule, and each subcontractor is responsible for purchasing the materials needed for its portion of the project. Generally, the only inventories consist of materials delivered to the construction site shortly before they are needed for construction work in process.

The general contractor is also responsible for administering the funds used to finance the construction project and for paying subcontractors once their specific tasks are completed satisfactorily. Usually, there is a client who is paying for the construction project, either directly or by using borrowed funds. As expenses are incurred for materials, labor, and payments to subcontractors, they are charged to a construction work in progress account. Once each month the general contractor requests reimbursement for all outstanding charges not yet reimbursed, plus a portion of overhead and profit based on the percentage of the work completed.

Claims Processing in Insurance Companies. Insurance companies receive revenues in the form of premiums from policyholders who desire financial protection for themselves and their families against the risks of accidental death, poor health, and unexpected loss of property. In exchange, they reimburse policyholders for proven losses covered under their policies. In essence, the processing of policyholder claims is the primary procurement function within an insurance company. How-

---

[7] For more on retail merchandise planning and buying systems, see Institute of Internal Auditors Research Foundation, *Systems Auditability and Control Report, Module 6: Business Systems* (Altamonte Springs, Fla.: Institute of Internal Auditors Research Foundation, 1991), Chapter 8.

ever, the insurance claims processing cycle is very different from the typical procurement cycle.

One major difference is that claims processing is initiated by the policyholder rather than by the insurance company itself. When the policyholder notifies the insurance company of a claim, a record specifying details of the claim is created and entered into a claim file. The next step is to verify that the claimant is covered for the claimed loss. Then the claim itself is validated and the amount of benefit payable is determined. In the case of life insurance this amount is stated in the policy. In the case of health insurance the amount is determined from documents provided by the claimant or a health care provider. In the case of property and casualty insurance the amount is often determined by an examiner or adjuster who ascertains the amount of the claimant's loss by reviewing the property damage and obtaining estimates of repair or replacement costs. The examiner then prepares a report summarizing his or her findings and decision on the resolution of the claim. After this report is reviewed and approved by a senior examiner or supervisor, the claim is authorized for payment.

THE PURCHASING AND INVENTORY DATA PROCESSING SYSTEM

The purchasing and inventory data processing system is the primary data processing component of the procurement cycle. This system must execute the basic procurement cycle functions and procedures described in the previous section. This section describes and illustrates the use of computer-based systems to process purchase order and inventory transactions, with emphasis on methods of data capture, data processing, data base updating, and reporting. Internal control objectives and procedures associated with purchase order and inventory data processing are also explained.

Data Capture

For the computer to be used within the procurement cycle, data on three key input records must be captured in machine-readable form. These records are the purchase requisition (see Fig. 17.2), the inventory receiving report (Fig. 17.4), and the vendor invoice (Fig. 16.4). In each case there are a number of options.

In the case of purchase requisitions a common approach is for requisition documents to be prepared, approved, and then sent to a Data Entry Department to be keyed into the system in batches by a clerk at an on-line terminal (see Fig. 17.5). Batch totals are prepared by the requisitioning department and then checked at the conclusion of the data entry process. A variation of this approach is for certain personnel in production planning, inventory control, or related operating departments to be authorized to create and enter requisition records from on-line terminals located in their offices. In either case data items to be keyed in include inventory item number, quantity requested, quoted or catalog price, requested delivery date and location, identity of the persons who prepared and approved the requisition, and the account number or numbers to be charged with the cost of

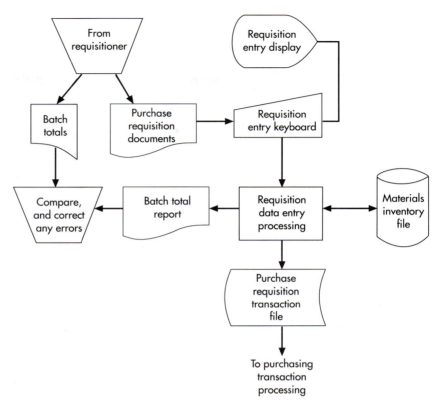

Figure 17.5
Purchase requisition
data entry process

the purchase. Data items such as a requisition number, date entered, and vendor code number can be automatically added to the requisition record by the system. Once a complete requisition record has been entered, it may either be processed immediately to generate a purchase order or be written onto a temporary disk file to be processed later as part of a batch of requisitions.

An alternative approach, commonly employed by companies in which production planning and inventory control are fully automated, is for the system to automatically create requisition records as a by-product of automated inventory control. In a simple inventory control system a requisition for a preset order quantity is generated when the inventory quantity on hand falls below a predetermined reorder point. In a more advanced system, such as MRP or JIT, when production plans are created in response to sales orders or anticipated demand, the specific raw materials required to accomplish the projected production operations are identified, and requisition records are created and assigned a requested delivery date consistent with the plan. Once created, each requisition record is subject to review and approval by a buyer in the Purchasing Department.

As shipments are received and accepted in the Receiving Department, data on items and quantities received, vendor and purchase order identification, and the identity of the receiver and inspector must be captured in machine-readable form. As with purchase requisitions, one common approach is for receiving personnel to manually prepare receiving report documents, which are then physically transmitted to the Data Entry Department to be keyed into the system using an on-line terminal; this procedure is very similar to that illustrated for purchase requisitions in Fig. 17.5. The problem with this approach is that the updating of inventory records may be subject to a delay of several hours or days, during which production planning personnel may be unaware of the receipt of inventory items that are needed in the production process.

An alternative approach is to locate on-line terminals within the Receiving Department so that receiving personnel can enter inventory receipts data directly into the system as shipments are received. Under this approach the receiver obtains the purchase order number from the shipping document or packing slip and enters it into the system. The system then accesses the purchase order record and retrieves vendor and shipper information, item numbers, and item descriptions for display on the receiving terminal. The receiver confirms this information and then enters the item counts, the condition of each item, and the identity of the inspector. To complete the receiving record, the system automatically adds the receipt date and the receiver's identity.

In factories using JIT and other advanced manufacturing methods bar code scanning is becoming an increasingly common way of automating the receiving process. This method requires that vendors attach a special label to each package shipped. The label contains the item number and quantity per package, recorded in a bar code similar to the universal product code commonly used in grocery and retail applications (see Fig. 4.9). Receiving personnel then use either stationary or hand-held scanners (such as a light pen) to read the bar code on each package received (see Fig. 17.6). The speed and accuracy of data collection provided by bar code scanning makes it feasible to schedule the delivery of materials just prior to their use in the production process, as in a JIT system.[8]

Another method of automating the capture of inventory receipts data involves the use of a "smart card," as pioneered in the grocery industry. The smart card is the size of a credit card and contains a computer chip with memory and logic capability. When shipping an order, the vendor loads the smart card with all relevant order data. Upon receipt of the order, the customer uses the smart card to create a receiving record, checks the goods actually received against this record, and then loads the smart card with an acknowledgment of receipt, including an electronic signature. The receiving record is auto-

---

[8] For more on the use of bar code scanning in inventory control, see Thomas Tyson and Arjan T. Sadhwani, "Does Your Firm Need Bar Coding?" *Management Accounting* (April 1990): 45–48; and Susan Avery, "Bar Coding: How Did We Ever Get Along Without It?" *Purchasing* (April 5, 1990): 82–89.

Figure 17.6
Use of bar code scanning in the receiving function

matically captured by the customer's information system, while the delivery confirmation record may be transmitted to the vendor's information system through an EDI link.[9]

Data on vendor invoice documents are often keyed into the system by data entry clerks. Although these clerks could key in all of the data on each invoice, a much more efficient approach is to have them simply enter the purchase order number. Based on this, the system can access the purchase order and receiving report records and then display most of the information that should be on the invoice. The data entry clerk merely checks this information against the invoice document and enters any necessary changes.

EDI may also be used to capture vendor invoice data in machine-readable form. As invoices are prepared on vendor company computers, copies are transmitted via telecommunications links to on-line files in buying company computers or to an EDI mail file maintained by a third-party provider of EDI services. Buying company personnel then periodically access these files to retrieve the most recent batch of invoices transmitted, verify the accuracy of these invoices by comparing them with corresponding purchase order and receiving report records retrieved from the purchasing data base, and accept the invoice records for entry into the buying company's accounts payable file.[10] A good example of the advantages of the use of EDI in purchasing is provided by Caterpillar Inc. (see Focus 17.1).

[9] The Globecon Group, Ltd., *Electronic Data Interchange and Corporate Trade Payments* (Morristown, N.J.: Financial Executives Research Foundation, 1988), 50–51.

[10] For more information on EDI, see Willie Schatz, "EDI: Putting the Muscle in Commerce and Industry," *Datamation* (March 15, 1988): 56–64; The Globecon Group, Ltd., *Electronic Data Interchange and Corporate Trade Payments* (Morristown, N.J.: Financial Executives Research Foundation, 1988); and Joseph R. Carter and Lawrence D. Frendendall, "The Dollars and Sense of Electronic Data Interchange," *Production and Inventory Management Journal* (Second Quarter 1990): 22–26.

17.1 FOCUS

Caterpillar Embraces EDI

Caterpillar Incorporated, head-quartered in Peoria, Illinois, is the world's largest heavy-equipment manufacturer. Caterpillar began implementing its EDI system in the 1980s, at at time when fewer than 1% of American manufacturing companies were using EDI. The company's initial ob-jective was to enhance the efficiency of its purchasing function in order to improve its competitiveness.

By 1991, it was acknowledged that Caterpillar has one of the most established and successful large-scale EDI installations in manufacturing. The EDI system processes over 80% of Caterpillar's total purchase orders, and over 90% of its blanket orders, and links the company with hundreds of vendors in North America, Europe, and the Far East. In addition to purchasing documents, the system processes the related financial documents

Preliminary Data Processing Procedures

Requisitions, inventory receipts, and vendor invoices may be processed in batch mode, using sort, merge, and edit procedures very similar to those employed in preliminary processing of batches of sales order transactions (see Fig. 16.8). Transactions of each class are accumulated on temporary disk files, periodically merged into large batches, and sorted into sequential order by vendor number. These batches are then processed by editing programs that perform validity checks on inventory item numbers, vendor code numbers, and account numbers; range checks on delivery dates; field checks on all numeric data fields; reasonableness tests on quantities requisitioned or received and on prices quoted or billed; sign checks on inventory on-hand balances; and completeness tests on all records. Batch totals are prepared and checked at each stage of processing, and any errors detected are investigated and corrected prior to further processing.

Although batch processing of purchasing transactions is feasible and is used in some businesses, the nature of purchasing transactions is such that a mix of batch and on-line processing is generally employed. For example, consider a batch of purchase requisition records that have been created and stored on a temporary disk file, as shown in Fig. 17.5. Before these records are processed to generate a purchase order, each one must be reviewed and approved by a buyer in the Purchasing Department. In a computerized purchasing system it is common for buyers to perform this function using an on-line terminal (see Fig. 17.7). The system displays each requisition record on the buyer's terminal, giving priority to those requisition records that have the earliest required delivery date, and accesses the related vendor and

and performs material control functions.

Caterpillar's EDI software runs on IBM PC and PC-compatible microcomputers. This makes it easier for the company's smaller suppliers, as well as its international suppliers, to afford EDI capability. The software is menu-driven, user-friendly, and offers a broad range of transaction formats. The menus guide users step by step through each stage of the process. The software also provides an interface with the user's other applications. These fea-tures helped persuade many of Caterpillar's suppliers to make the move to EDI.

Caterpillar's EDI system provides several advantages, including quick turnaround for JIT capability, better inventory management, improved data accuracy, a reduced paperwork burden, and increased office productivity. By eliminating postal delays, EDI reduces the order entry and acknowledgment cycle from several days to a few hours. Improving the timeliness of data processing tends to enhance inventory control.

Computer-to-computer data transmission precludes data transcription errors and eliminates lost or misplaced documents. Finally, the electronic capture of data supplants the functions of opening the mail, sorting and filing paper documents, and re-keying basic transaction data.

Source: Adapted from Kate Evans-Correia, "Caterpillar Digs into EDI Purchasing," *Purchasing* (August 15, 1991): 91–95.

Figure 17.7
Preliminary processing of purchase requisition transactions

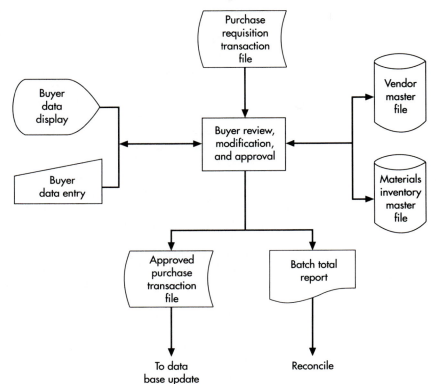

inventory records. The buyer activates an edit subroutine that checks the accuracy and reasonableness of inventory item numbers, quantities requested, prices, and requested delivery dates on each requisition record, and verifies that requisitioned items are not already on hand or on order. Fields that contain likely data errors are highlighted for review and possible correction by the buyer. The advantage of this approach is that the buyer can immediately correct any erroneous transactions so that they can be processed without delay. In contrast, in the pure batch processing system illustrated in Fig. 16.8, erroneous transactions are rejected from the batch and subjected to potentially time-consuming manual investigation and correction procedures.

Once the accuracy of the purchase requisition record has been confirmed, the buyer may consider modifying order quantities to obtain quantity discounts or to be consistent with a standard package size. The buyer must also decide whether to purchase the item from the primary vendor listed in the inventory master file or to select another vendor who may temporarily offer better prices or material availability. Once each requisition record has been reviewed and (if necessary) modified, the buyer enters his or her buyer approval code, which authorizes the generation of a purchase order. Each approved purchase requisition record is then written on a batch file for subsequent processing to generate purchase orders and update the purchasing data base. A batch total report may also be prepared and reconciled to previous batch totals and to a control total of pending purchase requisition transactions.

A similar review process may be employed to control the on-line entry of inventory receipt records by receiving personnel. As noted earlier, once the receiver enters the purchase order number, the system can retrieve and display vendor and shipper information, item numbers, and item descriptions. The receiver can then verify this information by checking the packing slip and shipping document and enter a count of each item received. The count may be obtained manually or through the use of a bar code scanner. The system compares the count with the quantity ordered and displays any discrepancy on the receiver's terminal for further review and possible modification. To complete the receiving record, the receiver enters receiving inspection results, including a description of the condition of any items rejected by the inspector. Once a completed receiving record has been entered into the system, it may be processed immediately to update all related records in the purchasing data base.

Finally, consider the on-line entry of vendor invoice data. As noted earlier, if the purchase order number is keyed in, much of the content of a vendor invoice may be retrieved from the purchasing data base. Alternatively, the invoice may be received electronically through EDI. In either case the invoice record must be displayed on an on-line terminal for review and verification by an accounts payable clerk. After examining the record for obvious errors, the clerk activates a subroutine that retrieves the corresponding purchase order and receiving report records, compares the order quantities with the quantities received, compares the item prices on the purchase order with the prices billed, checks the invoice terms against the purchase order, and compares the quantities received with the quantities billed. If these steps identify any discrepancies, the invoice record is assigned a status of "pending," and an error report is printed to provide a basis for seeking, identifying, and correcting any errors. For valid invoices the accounts payable clerk determines a payment due date, based on the invoice date and payment terms. The invoice record is then assigned an "approved for payment" status and added to the accounts payable master file, where it is indexed by payment due date.

For each of these transactions it is important that a unique user code number and password be assigned to each authorized user. Each user's code number authorizes that user to enter only certain types of transactions. For example, only authorized buyers may enter requisition approvals, and only authorized accounts payable personnel may approve vendor invoices for payment. As each transaction is entered, the system is programmed to perform a compatibility test, checking the access control matrix to determine whether the user is allowed to perform that type of transaction (see Chapter 13).

There are at least three other useful control features of the on-line data entry mode. First, simplified data entry procedures, such as prompting or preformatting (see Chapter 13), facilitate the data entry process and ensure the completeness of each transaction record. Second, the accuracy of key fields, such as inventory item number or vendor number, can be checked through closed-loop verification, in which the system displays the corresponding item description or vendor name for user verification. Third, any data entry errors not prevented by these procedures can usually be detected by edit checks, flagged on the user's terminal, and corrected on the spot, before any data base records are affected.

Data Base Update   After purchase transaction data have been captured in machine-readable form and validated by edit programs or reviewed by authorized personnel, the next step is to update the purchasing data base to reflect these transactions. This involves modifying all appropriate fields within the various records that are part of the data base to reflect the effects of requisitions, purchase orders, vendor invoices, and related procurement cycle transactions. This section describes the basic content and structure of the purchasing data base and then explains the procedures involved in updating this data base for these various transactions. Both batch processing and on-line processing procedures are explained.

The Purchasing Data Base.   The purchasing data base contains data on materials inventories, vendors, open purchase orders, and other current purchasing transactions. These data are useful both for accounting purposes and for purposes of purchasing and inventory management. A simplified example of the data content and organization of a purchasing data base appears in Fig. 17.8. This sample data base consists of

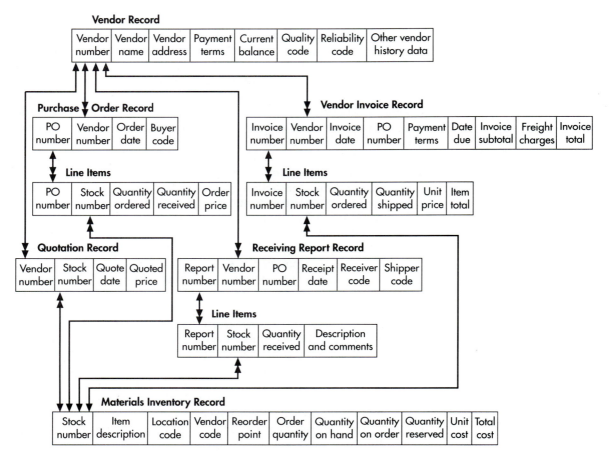

Figure 17.8
Key elements of the
purchasing data base

two master records (vendor and materials inventory), each of which is linked to four transaction records (price quotation, purchase order, receiving report, and vendor invoice). Each of the latter three records includes line items detailing inventory items ordered, received, and invoiced, respectively. Note that these records represent only the core elements of the purchasing data base. In a real application, other transaction records would be included, such as purchase requisitions, purchase returns and allowances, disbursement vouchers, cash disbursements, and materials requisitions (which authorize the transfer of materials from inventory stores). In addition, a separate vendor history file would contain summary data on past vendor performance with respect to product quality and timeliness of deliveries. However, to simplify our discussion, we will focus only on the core elements of the purchasing data base that are shown in Fig. 17.8. This data base could be used for either batch or on-line processing.

Each vendor record in the purchasing and inventory data base contains a single value for each of the data fields listed within the vendor record in Fig. 17.8, with the vendor number serving as the primary key. In addition, each vendor record is associated, in one-to-many relationships, with price quotation records, purchase order records, receiving report records, and vendor invoice records. In each case the "vendor number" field is common to both records and establishes the link. These links reflect the fact that at any given time a vendor may have submitted price quotations for one or more inventory items, may have received one or more purchase orders, may have made one or more shipments (resulting in receiving reports), and may have submitted one or more invoices to the buying company. Within each vendor record, the "payment terms" field indicates the arrangements established with the vendor regarding invoice payment discount and due date, while the quality and reliability codes provide summary indicators of the vendor's past performance. The "current balance" field is the sum of the invoice total for all unpaid invoices; thus the vendor file also doubles as an accounts payable subsidiary ledger.

Each materials inventory record in the data base contains a single value for each of the data fields listed within the materials inventory record, with stock number serving as the primary key. In addition, each materials inventory record is associated, in one-to-many relationships, with price quotation records, purchase order line item records, receiving report line item records, and vendor invoice line item records. Each line item record contains details about the material items involved in the corresponding transaction. In each case the "stock number" field is common to both records and establishes the link. These links reflect the fact that at any given time for a particular item of materials inventory one or more price quotations may have been submitted by different vendors, one or more purchase orders for the item may be outstanding, one or more shipments of the item may have been received, and one or more invoices for the item may be outstanding. The data fields within each materials inventory record contain details about the inventory item, including quantity and cost data, a location code indicating where the item is stored, and a vendor code identifying the primary vendor from whom the item is purchased. Quantity fields include amounts on hand, on order, and reserved for planned production. The presence of a "total cost" field suggests that a perpetual inventory system is employed for materials inventories; so the materials inventory file doubles as a raw materials inventory subsidiary ledger.

In addition to having the links just mentioned, the data base should also contain links between each purchase order and its related purchase requisition records, receiving report records, and vendor invoices records. While these links are not shown explicitly in Fig. 17.8, they exist implicitly in that the purchase order number is included within the receiving report and vendor invoice records.

As the organization grows and adds new vendors and inventory items, new vendor records and materials inventory records will be added to the data base. New purchase orders, vendor invoices, and other transactions will add to the size of the data base at an even faster rate. Therefore rules must be established concerning the period of time that transaction records should remain part of the data base. Generally, purchase requisition records, purchase order records, and receiving report records will remain in the data base until the purchase order is completely filled, while vendor invoice records will remain in the data base until they are paid. Each price quotation record will remain in the data base until its expiration date or until it is superseded by a more current quotation. After these transaction records are removed from the on-line data base, they should be stored in an off-line archive file for an additional period of time.

In the relatively simple data processing system employed at Electronics Incorporated, there is no integrated purchasing data base. Instead, purchasing data are maintained in a series of separate files. There is a vendor file, a separate accounts payable file, a materials inventory file, an open purchase order file, and so on. Updating each of these files for purchasing transactions requires a separate set of procedures, each performed in a batch processing mode at daily or weekly intervals. As a result, the information available from EI's purchasing information system is not always current. In addition, output reports are generally prepared weekly, and each report conforms to a predetermined fixed format and reflects only the information contained in the specific file from which it is generated. Therefore EI's purchasing and inventory control personnel often have difficulty obtaining the information they need to deal with special problems and opportunities.

From a presentation he attended while at a recent seminar, Tom Morris believes that EI should consider acquiring a data base management system (see Chapter 7) to be used to implement an integrated purchasing data base system. Then EI could combine many of its separate purchasing transaction updating procedures into a set of integrated processes. For example, the approval of a purchase requisition could lead to the automatic generation of a purchase order record and the simultaneous updating of the "quantity on order" field in the related inventory record. The entry of a receiving report record into the system could initiate the simultaneous updating of the "on-order" fields in the related open purchase order line item records, the "on-hand" and "on-order" fields in the affected materials inventory master records, and various vendor performance fields in the vendor file; and this entry could also lead to the creation of a preliminary version of a vendor invoice record. These procedures could be performed as frequently as necessary, perhaps even as the transactions arise, thus ensuring that data in EI's inventory and vendors files would be as current as possible. This system should enable EI to avoid scheduling production runs when critical inventory components are not available. In addition, the data base management system would enable EI's purchasing and inventory control personnel to generate reports at any time and in any format they specified. The content of the reports would not be limited to the information in one particular file but, rather, could include any of the data items contained in the purchasing data base.

Thus EI's purchasing agents could monitor and evaluate vendor performance more effectively. In short, the implementation of an integrated purchasing data base system could have substantial advantages for EI's purchasing function.

Batch Processing. Batch processing remains a very common method of processing purchasing transactions to update the purchasing data base. Among the types of transactions to be processed are vendor price quotations, purchase requisitions, inventory receipts, vendor invoices approved for payment, purchase returns and allowances, and raw materials inventory use (in a manufacturing company) or merchandise inventory sales (in a wholesale or retail company). Batches of these transactions are generally accumulated on a temporary disk file over a period of time, such as a day, to be processed at a regularly scheduled time. Rather than attempt to describe and illustrate batch processing of all these various kinds of transactions, we focus here on two of them: purchase requisition transactions and inventory receipt transactions.

Figure 17.9 is a systems flowchart depicting batch processing of purchase requisition transactions. Input to this process consists of a batch of requisition transactions that have been reviewed, modified

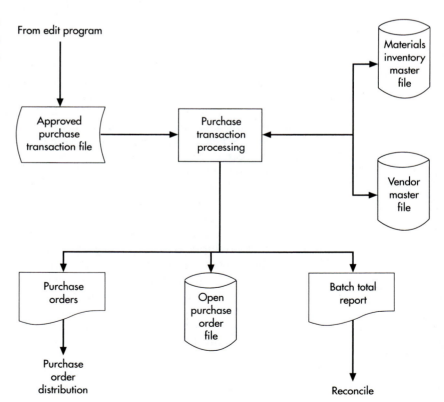

Figure 17.9
Batch processing of purchase
requisition transactions

where necessary, approved by a buyer (see Fig. 17.7), and sorted into sequential order by vendor number. As each requisition record is read, the system keys on the inventory stock number and reads the corresponding materials inventory record. The "on-order" field in the inventory record is modified to reflect the quantity ordered, and the updated inventory record is written back onto the materials inventory master file. These steps are repeated for all inventory items that are to be ordered from a specific vendor. Then by keying on the vendor number, the system accesses the vendor record to retrieve the vendor's name and address and creates a complete purchase order record. This record is dated with the current date and assigned the next available purchase order number in sequence. Next, the purchase order document is printed, and the purchase order record is added to the open purchase order master file. The system then proceeds to the next set of requisition records associated with a particular vendor and cycles through these same steps. At the conclusion of processing, a batch total report is printed and reconciled to batch totals prepared at earlier stages of processing. Copies of the printed purchase order documents are distributed to the vendors and to various departments within the buying company.

Inventory receipt transactions usually originate in a Receiving Department as employees prepare receiving report documents listing details about inventory shipments received. If batch processing is employed, these documents are accumulated in batches and keyed into the system once each day, using a data entry process very similar to that illustrated for purchase requisitions in Fig. 17.5. The data structure of each receiving report record is shown in Fig. 17.8. After they are entered into the system, these transactions are written onto a receiving report transactions file, which is then processed through an edit program to verify the accuracy and completeness of the inventory receipt data and sorted into sequential order by purchase order number. When these steps are completed and any errors in the data are corrected, the receiving report transactions file is processed to update the purchasing data base, as depicted in the systems flowchart in Fig. 17.10.

This system operates by reading both an open purchase order record from the data base and a receiving report transaction record from the input file, proceeding in sequential order by purchase order number. It then attempts to match these records on the purchase order number. If they do not match, the purchase order is checked to determine whether there are any items on order for which delivery is past due. If so, details about the order are printed on an overdue-deliveries report. The system then reads the next purchase order record in sequence.

When a match is found, the system updates the "quantity received" field in the purchase order record for each item received. Then the system keys on the vendor number and reads the corresponding vendor record from the purchasing data base. From the receiving report data the system updates the performance history data in the vendor

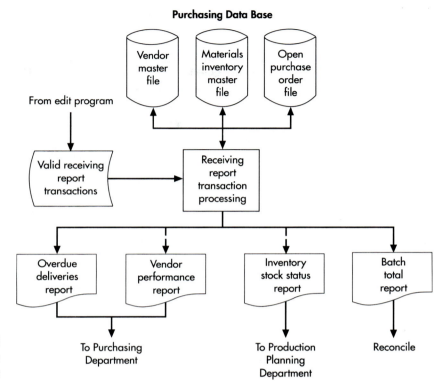

Figure 17.10
Batch processing of inventory
receipt transactions

master file to reflect the vendor's performance with respect to the timeliness of delivery, the quality of the materials received, and other dimensions of vendor performance. The updated vendor and purchase order records are then written back onto the data base.

Next, for each line item within the receiving report record, the system keys on the inventory stock number and reads the corresponding materials inventory record from the purchasing data base. The quantity received, as noted in the receiving report record, is then subtracted from the quantity on order and added to the quantity on hand in the materials inventory record. The updated materials inventory record is then written back onto the purchasing data base. This step is repeated for every item received on the receiving report record. When all items received on a receiving record have been processed, the system proceeds to the next receiving report and commences the steps described in the previous two paragraphs.

At the conclusion of processing, a batch total report is printed. This report contains record counts of the number of receiving report records and inventory line item records processed and hash totals of such fields as vendor number and quantity received. These are reconciled to batch total reports prepared at the data entry and editing stages of processing. Any discrepancies in reconciling these batch totals are investigated, and steps are taken to correct any errors that are detected.

One or more reports are also prepared as a by-product of this updating process. The overdue-deliveries report is prepared daily and distributed promptly to the Purchasing Department so that purchasing agents can immediately follow up on any critical inventory items for which delivery was unexpectedly delayed. Vendor performance reports are prepared and distributed to the Purchasing Department to assist in the vendor selection process. A materials inventory stock status report is prepared to provide reference information for the Production Planning Department. The latter two reports are prepared on a less regular basis, perhaps weekly or monthly, as indicated by the dashed lines in the flowchart. Each of these reports is discussed more fully later in the chapter.

Another important batch operation, not shown in the flowchart, is the processing of vendor invoices that have been approved for payment. In this operation each vendor invoice record is added to the purchasing data base (see Fig. 17.8), and the current balance in the corresponding vendor record is increased by the net amount of the invoice. As a by-product of this process, a summary journal entry is prepared debiting materials inventory[11] and crediting accounts payable, and this entry is posted to the general ledger file.

Other procurement cycle transactions for which processing volume is lower—such as price quotations, purchase returns and allowances, and corrections or modifications of specific fields within the purchasing data base—would generally be entered directly into the system from an on-line terminal as they occur. For control purposes the system should be programmed to accept such transactions only from an authorized user, as indicated by the user's password. Additional control is provided by having the system prepare reports on such transactions for distribution to appropriate supervisory personnel.

On-Line Processing.   On-line processing of purchasing transactions is becoming an increasingly popular alternative to batch processing. A systems flowchart of an on-line purchasing and inventory data processing system appears in Fig. 17.11. In this system several different categories of users have on-line access to the system, and each is authorized to enter specific types of transactions. Categories of users include inventory control personnel (and/or others with authority to enter purchase requisitions), buyers in the Purchasing Department, receiving personnel, and accounts payable personnel. As transactions are entered, the system interacts with the user to facilitate entry of the necessary data and to verify their accuracy, as explained previously in the discussion of preliminary data processing. Once a complete transaction record has been entered and validated, all of the affected records in the data base are immediately updated for the transaction.

---

[11] If fixed assets and services are also purchased, then this journal entry would also include debits to the fixed assets account and to various expense accounts.

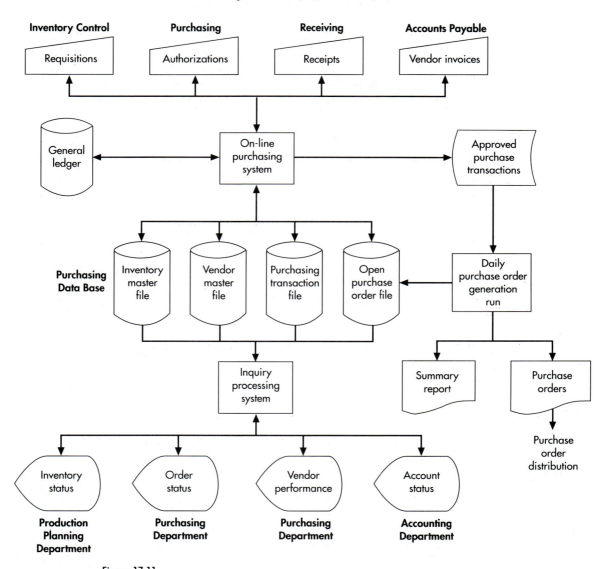

Inventory Control   Purchasing   Receiving   Accounts Payable

Requisitions   Authorizations   Receipts   Vendor invoices

General ledger

On-line purchasing system

Approved purchase transactions

Purchasing Data Base

Inventory master file   Vendor master file   Purchasing transaction file   Open purchase order file

Daily purchase order generation run

Inquiry processing system

Summary report   Purchase orders

Inventory status   Order status   Vendor performance   Account status

Production Planning Department   **Purchasing Department**   **Purchasing Department**   **Accounting Department**

Purchase order distribution

Figure 17.11
On-line purchasing and inventory information system

The specific types of transactions and the effect that each has on the data base are much the same as under batch processing, as described in the previous section. Briefly, purchase requisition transactions are edited for data errors, checked to verify that the items requisitioned are not already on hand or on order, and then added to a file of pending requisitions. Buyer approvals of requisitions result in the addition of new purchase order records to the purchasing data base and the generation of purchase order documents. Inventory receipt transactions are processed to update the corresponding open purchase order record and inventory records of quantities on hand and on order. Vendor invoice records are checked against their corresponding purchase order and receiving report records and then are processed to update the "balance-due'' field in the corresponding vendor (accounts payable) record. The approval of vendor invoices for payment also generates accounting journal entries to be posted to the general ledger.

As purchase requisition approvals and vendor selections are entered into this system by buyers in the Purchasing Department, the system assembles a purchase order record by retrieving vendor data from the vendor master file and inventory data from the materials inventory master file. In an on-line purchasing system these purchase orders could be printed immediately as requisition approvals are entered. However, a more typical approach is for the approved purchase transaction records to be written onto a temporary disk file, as shown in Fig. 17.11. Then at regular intervals, such as the end of each day, all items to be ordered from the same vendor are consolidated into a single purchase order record. Each of these records is assigned a purchase order number and added to the open purchase order file. The system then prints the required number of copies of each purchase order document, together with a short report containing batch totals and other summary information.

An on-line purchasing and inventory data processing system is essential to the use of such advanced techniques as MRP or JIT in purchasing and production management. The on-line availability of continuously up-to-date information on inventories, vendors, and outstanding orders, as illustrated in the bottom portion of Fig. 17.11, offers several advantages. Specifically, given continuously current information on raw materials inventory on hand and scheduled for delivery, production planning personnel can very carefully plan production to make the most efficient use of productive capacity. In turn, inventory quantities can be substantially reduced, because there is less need for inventory to serve as a hedge against the uncertainties of production planning and scheduling. The Purchasing Department can continuously monitor the status of pending requisitions and outstanding orders and take prompt corrective action whenever there is an unplanned delay. The Purchasing Department also has immediate access to complete information on vendor performance, which should enable buyers to select the best vendor for each item to be purchased. Finally, accounts payable personnel can continuously monitor the status of vendor accounts to ensure that amounts due are correct, that adjustments are posted promptly, and that discounts are earned through timely payment of invoices.

Wholesale and retail establishments that have large sales volumes often employ on-line purchasing and inventory management systems. In high-volume retail stores, such as groceries and department stores, a key element of such a system is point-of-sale (POS) terminals equipped with scanners that record reductions in perpetual inventory balances as merchandise is sold. These systems are programmed to continuously monitor inventory balances and to initiate the reordering of an item when the balance falls below a specified reorder point.

From a control standpoint the data entry process is the most critical point of vulnerability in an on-line purchasing and inventory information system. The most important controls that should be in place have been explained in detail in previous chapters and are mentioned only briefly here. They include user access controls that employ passwords and compatibility tests, prompting or preformatting to simplify the data entry process, edit checks on critical transaction input data, and closed-loop verification.

To Tom Morris at Electronics Incorporated an on-line purchasing and inventory information system had always seemed to be too sophisticated and too expensive for a company of moderate size like EI. However, in response to the company's recent problems Tom has begun to reconsider this position. He now realizes that on-line access to current and accurate information on inventory status, purchase order status, and vendor performance can have tremendous advantages. He is also coming to believe that an on-line system could effect some cost savings that would partially or completely outweigh its costs. By streamlining the data entry process, it would eliminate some clerical positions. By detecting erroneous input data before purchasing transactions are entered into the system, it could minimize expensive reprocessing procedures. By tracking inventory balances on a continuous basis and automatically initiating purchase orders when stocks are low, it could minimize costly and disruptive inventory stockouts. By tracking order status on a continuous basis, it could notify purchasing agents promptly of any overdue vendor shipments and help EI minimize the incremental costs associated with late deliveries. And finally, by providing purchasing agents with current and accurate information on vendor performance, it could enable EI to select those vendors that offer the best value with respect to materials cost and quality and delivery reliability. After giving much thought to these matters, Tom has asked EI's Director of Information Systems to initiate a feasibility study of an on-line purchasing and inventory information system.

Control Objectives and Procedures

Within each accounting cycle, internal control procedures should be designed to ensure that specific objectives are met. Therefore when one examines internal controls within the procurement cycle, it is useful to begin by delineating internal control objectives for the procurement function and then identifying the set of control procedures that will achieve each objective. This approach is followed here.

Internal control procedures within the procurement cycle must be designed to ensure that the following objectives are met.

1. All purchase transactions are properly authorized on the basis of established criteria.
2. Materials inventories are properly safeguarded during the process of receipt and transfer to inventory stores.

3. All valid purchase transactions are accurately recorded and processed.
4. Accurate records of material inventories and vendor accounts payable are maintained.

Numerous internal control procedures have been described in earlier sections of this chapter. Our goal here is to associate these procedures with the four internal control objectives just listed and to identify any other control procedures necessary to achieve each objective.

Proper authorization of purchase transactions is especially critical because of the significant control risks associated with purchases. Among these risks are ordering goods or services that are not needed, ordering at unnecessarily high prices, and ordering from unauthorized vendors, including vendors who offer kickbacks to purchasing agents or vendor companies in which purchasing agents have a financial interest. Another significant control risk is represented by a problem encountered at EI: ordering from vendors who are unreliable with respect to material quality or timeliness of delivery.

The requirement that a purchase requisition must be prepared and approved prior to the issuance of a purchase order helps minimize the first of these control risks. Budgetary control over purchases is also exercised by charging each purchase to an account that is the responsibility of the person submitting the requisition. Actual costs incurred should then be compared periodically with budgeted costs. Another means of minimizing the risk of unauthorized purchases is to use sequentially prenumbered purchase order forms, limit access to blank purchase orders, and periodically verify that all purchase order forms can be accounted for.

Formal vendor selection procedures protect an organization against the other three control risks. Criteria for vendor selection must include low prices (as documented by price quotations or catalogs), high reliability with respect to quality of materials and timeliness of deliveries, and high integrity. Data on vendor performance with respect to these criteria should be maintained by the purchasing information system, and these data should be reviewed as part of the vendor selection process. Special approval procedures should be required before any orders are placed with vendors not on the approved supplier list.

It is also important that personal integrity be a primary consideration in the selection and evaluation of Purchasing Department personnel. Purchasing agents must not be allowed to accept gifts or kickbacks from suppliers. All purchasing employees should be required to make known any significant financial interest they may have in supplier companies. The performance of purchasing agents in selecting appropriate vendors should be periodically reviewed. Budgetary control could be exercised here by charging the Purchasing Department with purchase price variances (the cost of purchasing items at above standard prices) and with losses attributable to ordering from unauthorized or unreliable vendors.

Receiving Department personnel are responsible for authorizing the acceptance of materials or merchandise inventories shipped to the organization, as well as for furnishing an accurate description and count of the goods received. Criteria used by receiving personnel in accepting shipments should be established by management. Depending on the nature of the goods received, formal inspections by technically qualified inspectors may be performed as part of the receiving and acceptance process.

A computer-based purchasing system may be programmed to automatically perform certain functions, such as purchase order generation and vendor selection. However, there will always be certain criteria that must be met before the system is authorized to carry out these functions. For example, the system should not initiate orders for inventory items having a balance on hand that is sufficient to meet planned or projected requirements. Similarly, the system should not place orders with vendors who are not on the company's approved vendor list. These and other criteria must be established by responsible managers and then programmed into the system. In addition, the system should prepare regular reports listing or summarizing recent computer-generated transactions, and each such report should be reviewed by the appropriate manager for any sign of unusual activity.

Finally, transactions of a less routine nature—such as certification of new vendors, purchase returns and allowances, or adjustments in vendor account balances—should require special authorization procedures involving the approval of supervisory personnel.

The safeguarding of materials inventories is facilitated by assigning responsibility for securing the inventory stocks to a stores-keeping or warehousing function. The maintenance of independent and accurate records of inventory quantities on hand, against which counts of actual quantities on hand are regularly compared, is also of critical importance. In addition, documentary evidence of all transfers of responsibility for inventories should be meticulously maintained. This includes transfers from (1) the shipper to the Receiving Department, (2) the Receiving Department to the inspector or an Inspecting Department, (3) the Receiving or Inspecting Department to the inventory storeroom, and (4) the storeroom to the using department. If accurate and complete records of such transfers are maintained, it will always be possible to identify who is responsible for any shortages that are subsequently discovered. In turn, this fact will encourage all personnel involved in inventory transfers to take special care in recording these transfers accurately. If these simple control procedures had been followed at EI's Wichita plant, the costly production delays attributed to inventory shortages could probably have been avoided.

Accurate recording and processing of purchase transactions is enhanced by the following control procedures, many of which have already been mentioned.

1. Review and approval of purchase requisitions by supervisory personnel before they are acted upon by purchasing agents

2. Use of preformatting or prompting to simplify the entry of purchasing and inventory transaction data into the computer

3. Counting and inspection of goods by Receiving Department personnel as they are received

4. Counting of goods transferred from the Receiving Department by storeroom personnel

5. Use of bar code scanning for data capture by receiving and stores personnel

6. Use of interactive data entry procedures to capture some transaction data automatically from the data base and to carry out input validation routines that check the accuracy of data entered by computer terminal operators

7. Comparison of receiving reports and purchase orders to check for discrepancies between quantities received and quantities ordered, or between requested and actual delivery dates

8. Use of formal procedures for approval of vendor invoices for payment, including checking for arithmetic errors in extensions or invoice totals and checking for discrepancies in quantities, prices, or terms between the invoices and the purchase orders or receiving reports

So that accurate inventory and vendor accounts payable records are preserved, it is essential that the security and integrity of the purchasing data base be protected. A variety of data security controls are employed for this purpose, including internal and external file labels, proper file backup procedures, off-site storage of backup files, and control of access through the proper use of user numbers and passwords. This objective also requires that key amounts in the purchasing data base be regularly reconciled and adjusted, based on other values in the same or related data bases, or on external data such as physical counts of inventory.

In modern purchasing and production systems that employ MRP, JIT, or other advanced techniques based on a tightly controlled schedule, it is essential that the inventory balances maintained by the information system be as accurate as possible. In general, the annual physical inventory count that is performed for accounting purposes will *not* be sufficient. Instead, a technique called cycle counting is usually employed. This involves counting the quantity on hand of each inventory item on a regular basis (e.g., monthly) according to a schedule that calls for a certain portion of all inventory items to be counted each day. The count frequency for each item is often based on ABC analysis, under which the most critical items (A items) are counted most frequently, while the least critical items (C items) are counted least frequently. Inventory records are corrected for any discrepancies identified from the count, and an attempt is made to identify and correct the cause of each discrepancy. Cycle counting requires additional staff, but the benefit of avoiding schedule disruptions more than outweighs the additional cost. Cycle counting often produces inventory records so accurate that the need for (and expense of) an annual physical inventory is eliminated.

Maintaining appropriate segregation of duties—by keeping the recording, custodial, and authorization functions separate within the procurement cycle—also helps to safeguard materials inventories and to ensure the accuracy of purchasing transaction and vendor and inventory master file records. The recording functions are primarily performed by the computer and by personnel responsible for entering purchase requisition, inventory receipt, and vendor invoice transactions into the computer. Maintaining custody of inventories is the responsibility of personnel in a storeroom or warehouse. Authorization functions are performed by supervisory personnel responsible for approving purchase requisitions, by purchasing agents responsible for vendor selection, by inspectors within the Receiving Department who appraise the quality of goods received from vendors, by accounting personnel who approve vendor invoices for payment, and often by the computer.

When the computer performs both recording and authorization functions, additional safeguards are necessary. Compatibility tests based on user passwords can ensure that no single user is able to perform both recording and authorization functions with respect to a particular type of transaction. Compatibility tests can also ensure that persons responsible for modifying purchasing and inventory data processing software cannot also enter purchasing transaction data, and vice versa. It is also important to control physical access to the computer equipment by installing locks on all doors to the facility and issuing keys only to authorized personnel.

Reporting   Purchasing transaction data entry, data processing, data base update, and internal control are all of critical importance to ensure that procurement cycle activities are carried out effectively. However, from a management perspective the reports generated as a by-product of purchasing transaction processing are of prime importance. Scheduled reports, demand reports, and triggered reports all facilitate purchasing and inventory management activities. Some examples of these reports are identified in Figs. 17.10 and 17.11. The content and use of these and other purchasing and inventory management reports are described in this section.

Stock status reports were mentioned in Chapter 16 in connection with the management of finished goods inventories. The materials inventory stock status report, prepared on a regularly scheduled basis (as in Fig. 17.10) or on demand, is used to facilitate the management of materials inventories. For each inventory item this report gives details on quantity on hand, location code, standard cost, quantity on order, scheduled delivery date, and purchase order number. Stock status information should be provided to inventory stores-keeping personnel, who need details on inventory availability and location, and to production planning personnel, who need to assess inventory availability as part of the production planning and scheduling process.

When an on-line purchasing and inventory data processing system is employed, the need for regular preparation of a printed stock status report is diminished. Current stock status information should always be available on demand through an inquiry processing system that accesses the inventory master file, as illustrated in Fig. 17.11. On-line terminals can be used by inventory stores personnel, production planners, and others who need access to current inventory status information. The system retrieves and displays only the specific stock status information requested for a particular purpose.

The **cash flow commitments report**, illustrated in Table 17.1, summarizes projected cash outflows associated with commitments in the form of vendor invoices approved for payment and open purchase orders. This report is generally prepared at regular intervals, such as weekly or monthly. The report generation program first examines all vendor invoices approved for payment, sums the payment amounts by scheduled date of payment, and lists these amounts by date in one column of the report. Then it examines each open purchase order; projects a total payment amount and payment date based on the quantities ordered, item prices, scheduled delivery dates, and anticipated payment terms; and lists these projected payment amounts in another column. These two projected payment amounts are summed for each date in a third column, and the projected cumulative total payout is computed and listed in a fourth column. The final report forecasts cash outflows for each business day over the next few weeks or months, and it is very useful to the controller or treasurer in planning short-term cash flows.

Projected cash flow data from a variety of sources can be downloaded to a personal computer for use in budgeting cash flows. As a supplement to the cash flow commitments data obtained from approved vendor invoices and open purchase orders, data on anticipated cash outflows to meet payroll may be generated by examining payroll records and hourly employee work schedules. Projected revenues may be obtained by analyzing approved sales orders. Combining all of these data will yield a companywide, short-term cash operating budget. Once the programs and procedures for computing this budget are in place, this analysis may be done weekly or even on a demand basis. This reporting procedure is very useful in monitoring the financial health of a company on a continuous basis. It also permits financial executives to anticipate short-term cash requirements so that a line of credit can be arranged, if necessary, and to foresee any cash surpluses that will necessitate temporary investment of excess funds.

An **open-requisitions report** is simply a listing of purchase requisitions for which purchase orders have not yet been written. This report is prepared daily and given to the Purchasing Department, to be used by buyers in the processes of requisition approval and purchase order preparation. The report should highlight those requisitions for which

BLACKWELL INDUSTRIES CASH FLOW COMMITMENTS SCHEDULE FOR THE MONTH OF AUGUST 1993				
Date	Vendor Invoices	Purchase Orders	Daily Total	Cumulative Total
08/03/93	$25,713.39		$25,713.39	$ 25,713.39
08/04/93	25,958.45		25,958.45	51,671.84
08/05/93	29,424.07		29,424.07	81,095.91
08/06/93	25,721.34		25,721.34	106,817.25
08/07/93	19,681.02		19,681.02	126,498.27
08/10/93	17,851.80		17,851.80	144,350.07
08/11/93	22,628.21		22,628.21	166,978.28
08/12/93	14,847.70		14,847.70	181,825.98
08/13/93	21,558.70		21,558.70	203,384.68
08/14/93	15,771.19	$10,035.70	25,806.89	229,191.57
08/17/93	11,620.24	12,292.75	23,912.99	253,104.56
08/18/93	12,561.83	14,565.10	27,126.93	280,231.49
08/19/93	13,967.76	12,374.55	26,342.31	306,573.80
08/20/93	14,571.26	10,233.61	24,804.87	331,378.67
08/21/93	10,254.06	12,366.95	22,621.01	353,999.68
08/24/93	12,266.69	11,407.02	23,673.71	377,673.39
08/25/93	13,088.30	10,802.22	23,890.52	401,563.91
08/26/93	10,702.33	11,467.34	22,169.67	423.733.58
08/27/93	11,990.40	12,711.67	24,702.07	448,435.65
08/28/93	10,707.45	10,969.48	21,676.93	470,112.58
08/31/93	8,482.93	17,695.82	26,178.75	496,291.33

Table 17.1
Cash flow commitments report

the requested delivery date is imminent so that they may be given priority in the approval process.

The **vendor performance report** is a summary of past dealings with each vendor, highlighting those factors that are of particular interest to buyers in the vendor selection process. Data include the volume of past business, compliance with requested delivery dates, discrepancies between quantities ordered and quantities received, discrepancies between prices quoted and prices billed, and the number of defective items received. A reference copy of this report might be printed on a regular basis, such as once a month. With on-line processing current information on the performance of selected vendors is also available to buyers on demand through an inquiry processing system.

Among the recommendations received by Tom Morris at Electronics Incorporated was a suggestion from Bill Freedman, a purchasing supervisor, that vendor performance reports be generated to assist purchasing agents in vendor selection. Tom arranged for Bill to work with Anne Williams, a senior systems analyst, to design a prototype report. Within three days Tom received the sample report shown in Table 17.2. This report is designed to be displayed on a purchasing agent's terminal and/or printed on request. It summarizes all purchase transactions for a specified inventory item from a specified vendor over the most recent three-month period. Any deviations from expectations are highlighted with triple asterisks. These deviations include prices higher than expected, delivery delays, incorrect shipment quantities, and returns of defective merchandise, all of which are represented in Table 17.2.

Information on vendor performance might also be downloaded to a purchasing agent's personal computer to support decision making within the purchasing function. For example, suppose that Carrier Corporation must select a new vendor to provide fans for a high-

Table 17.2
Vendor performance report

ELECTRONICS INCORPORATED
VENDOR PERFORMANCE REPORT
AS OF 12/31/93

Vendor #	Vendor Name	Telephone	Salesperson Name
729301	Ajax Semiconductor	406-585-2698	Murray Logan

Item Number	Item Description	Standard Unit Cost	
S14853	Semiconductor	$2.08	

Purchase Order #	Order Status	Order Date	Unit Price	Delivery Date	Receipt Date	Quantity			
						Ordered	Received	Accepted	Returned
54391	Closed	10/14/93	$2.08	10/21/93	10/21/93	2000	2000	2000	0
54872	Closed	11/04/93	2.08	11/11/93	11/11/93	2000	2000	1500***	500***
55104	Closed	11/18/93	2.18***	11/25/93	11/29/93***	2000	3000***	3000***	0
55539	Closed	12/09/93	2.18***	12/16/93	12/16/93	1000	1000	1000	0
55682	Open	12/30/93	2.08	01/06/94		2000			

*** Deviations.

performance air conditioner. First, the purchasing agent responsible for vendor selection would access the purchasing data base from a PC. Price quotations for the component would be retrieved from the inventory master file. Each quotation record contains a vendor code number, enabling the buyer to identify the potential vendors. Then performance data on these specific vendors would be downloaded from the vendor master file to the PC. For each vendor the buyer would enter any additional information that is not available in the purchasing data base, such as a subjective assessment of quality or vendor support or an indication that the vendor is also a significant customer. Next, each of the vendor selection factors would be assigned a weight reflecting its relative importance, and each vendor would be rated on each factor. Finally, a spreadsheet program on the PC would calculate a weighted rating for each vendor, using a point-scoring method such as the one described in Chapter 11 (see Table 11.6). The vendor with the highest overall rating would generally be selected to supply the component.[12]

A more sophisticated example of a vendor performance evaluation system was recently implemented by Rockwell Incorporated, a large defense contractor. This system attempts to standardize vendor ratings by measuring the cost to Rockwell of vendor failures. Rockwell has identified specific vendor-related "events" that cause it to incur unnecessary costs. These events include goods rejected by receiving inspection, goods reworked by Rockwell, goods returned to the vendor, incorrect paperwork, goods received too early, goods received too late, and receipt of excess quantities. For each of these events Rockwell estimates the nonproductive costs that it incurs based on a standard number of man-hours per event and its average hourly manufacturing cost. For each vendor a performance index is calculated based on the total cost of all purchases within the preceding twelve months. The index is equal to total cost plus nonproductive costs divided by total cost; thus a vendor that causes no nonproductive costs will have an index of one. On a quarterly basis each vendor is provided with a summary report indicating how its index was determined and how it ranks compared with other vendors in the same commodity category. Rockwell uses the index as a multiplier on bids received from vendors, on the theory that this provides a truer estimate of the cost of purchasing from each vendor. In addition, Rockwell will discontinue soliciting bids from vendors that cannot maintain a satisfactory performance index.[13]

---

[12] An example of this method of rating vendor performance is described in Michael A. Robinson and John E. Timmerman, "How Vendor Analysis Supports JIT Manufacturing," *Management Accounting* (December 1987): 20–24.

[13] Tom Stundza, "Can Supplier Ratings Be Standardized?" *Purchasing* (November 8, 1990): 60–64.

In addition to using cash flow commitments reports, vendor performance reports, and other standard reports produced either on demand or according to a regular schedule, an effective purchasing information system should employ decision support systems to provide information and analysis for more complex decision problems. For example, the development of a prototype expert system to provide decision support for military procurement is described by Dillard et al.[14] This system is designed to assist procurement specialists in determining the "fairness and reasonableness" of a contractor's proposed price. It provides assistance in verifying user technical specifications and delivery requirements, identifying prospective vendors, evaluating prior vendor performance, and estimating an objective price. The objective price provides a benchmark for determining whether the item should be procured through competitive pricing, published catalog prices, prior price quotations, or cost-plus contracting. The system also assists the procurement specialist in evaluating vendor prices and negotiating a final contract.

Another type of report often employed in the purchasing function is called a **triggered report**, a report generated only in response to a specific condition that calls for some sort of action. One example of a triggered purchasing report is the **overdue-deliveries report**, which is generated as follows: Each day the purchasing information system compares the due dates of all pending deliveries with the current date. If this procedure identifies any deliveries not yet received as of the day following the scheduled delivery date, a report is triggered listing all pertinent information concerning the order, the vendor, and the inventory item or items and highlighting the overdue-delivery status. One copy of this report is sent to the Purchasing Department, where a buyer contacts the vendor to ascertain the problem. Another copy is sent to the Production Planning department to alert production planners to a possible need to reschedule production operations.

Another example of a triggered report is a list of invoices due pending approval. At the beginning of each day the system scans the vendor invoice file to determine whether any invoices due for payment on that day have not yet been approved for payment. Relevant information concerning such invoices is listed on a report that is provided to accounts payable personnel so that the payment approval process may be expedited. Effective use of this report helps minimize losses due to failure to take purchase discounts.

These examples illustrate how the power of the computer can substantially improve the quality of the information available to those re-

---

[14] Jesse F. Dillard, Kamesh Ramakrishna, and B. Chandrasekaran, "Knowledge-Based Decision Support Systems for Military Procurement," in Barry G. Silverman, ed., *Expert Systems for Business* (Reading, Mass.: Addison-Wesley, 1987), 120–139.

sponsible for purchasing and inventory management. Scheduled reports can regularly provide large volumes of information for reference purposes and also highlight and summarize this information according to various decision-relevant criteria. Demand reports can provide specific information relevant to a particular purpose. Triggered reports can highlight information about specific conditions or transactions that require immediate attention. A well-designed information system utilizes all of these tools to enhance the effectiveness of the purchasing and inventory management functions.

CASE CONCLUSION: IMPROVING PROCUREMENT CYCLE INFORMATION SYSTEMS AT ELECTRONICS INCORPORATED

Tom Morris received several recommendations on how to improve the information system at Electronics Incorporated to better support EI's purchasing and inventory management activities. Virtually all of these recommendations called for the development of an on-line purchasing and inventory control system based on materials requirements planning (MRP). This system would provide more accurate and current information on inventory status and vendor performance and would be the first step in the eventual implementation of a just-in-time (JIT) inventory management system. While he was convinced that this new system was needed and was willing to absorb the estimated $1 million required to develop and implement the system, Tom was discouraged by Anne Williams's forecast that over 10 months would be required for the system to become fully operational. He believed that EI's inventory management problems needed to be addressed immediately in order to avoid more serious and costly production delays. He was also concerned that the information available for vendor evaluation, as reflected in the vendor performance report shown in Table 17.2, was not adequate to foster optimal vendor selection decisions.

After further consultation between Tom and Anne a phased implementation plan was developed for the new system. The first phase was to develop an on-line data entry system for inventory receipts, which included writing a software interface, installing on-line terminals in the Receiving Department, training receiving personnel to enter receiving report data into the system, and developing new reporting formats for inventory stock status reports. Following a concentrated development effort this system became operational within four months. In the month following its implementation production planners made heavy use of the new system, and production delays declined by over 40%.

The second phase of the implementation process, which actually began before the first phase was completed, was to modify the data structure of the open purchase order file to include actual prices charged by vendors, actual delivery dates for each item ordered, and data on the condition of items received, including the number of defective items. A subroutine was also written to monitor all open purchase orders on a daily basis and report any orders for which delivery was past due. In addition, a system was developed to allow purchasing agents to download the purchase order data and other vendor performance data to their PCs and load it into a spreadsheet program. A point-scoring system was created to analyze these data and compute vendor performance ratings based on weighting factors set by the purchasing agent using the system. A prototype version of the vendor-rating system was implemented within three months, and a complete version became operational after six months. Most purchasing agents were very enthusiastic about this system and quickly became regular users. While average inventory purchase prices increased slightly in the months after this system was implemented, vendor performance improved steadily in each of the next six months. Within one year EI had reduced its supplier base by over 30%, late deliveries had declined by 80%, and shipments of defective items fell by 60%.

While these phases of implementation of the new system were an unqualified success, the third phase, full implementation of MRP, proceeded slowly. Eighteen months after the project began, the new system was still not fully operational. Production planning personnel were slow to adapt to the idea of projecting production quantities six months in advance, arguing that accurate sales forecasts were difficult to obtain. In addition, while inventory receipts input data were over 98% accurate, the perpetual inventory records still contained many errors left over from the previous system. These errors eventually had to be corrected on the basis of a complete count of inventory quantities on hand. Finally, further improvement in vendor delivery and quality performance was necessary for the MRP system to work effectively. As EI began a new year, Tom was pleased by the success of the first two phases of the new system, but he was concerned about the uncertain outcome of phase 3. He had learned that effective information systems were crucial to EI's success but that the difficulties involved in developing these systems could not be overestimated. ■

SUMMARY

Procurement cycle activities include determining the amount and timing of purchases; selecting vendors; arranging for the receipt, delivery, and storage of inventories; and arranging for the rendering of services. Related data processing activities include requisitioning goods and services, preparing purchase orders, documenting receipt of inventories and services, maintaining records of inventories on hand and on order, and maintaining records of accounts payable and vendor performance. The accounting information system plays an important role in carrying out these data processing activities and in generating information useful in managing the related procurement cycle activities.

Purchasing and inventory data processing may be accomplished using either batch processing or on-line processing. In either case the focal point of the system is a purchasing data base that includes data on inventories, vendors, open purchase orders, and unpaid vendor invoices. The system must incorporate internal controls that ensure proper authorization of all transactions, provide for the safeguarding of materials inventories, and ensure the accuracy of all transaction and master file data. A well-designed computer-based system enables purchasing and inventory transactions to be processed in a timely and efficient manner, which is necessary to achieve satisfactory levels of production efficiency and quality. Such a system is also used to generate a variety of scheduled, demand, and triggered reports that facilitate the management of the procurement process. In addition, on-line computer-based systems support the use of advanced purchasing and production management methods, such as materials requirements planning (MRP) and just-in-time (JIT) inventory management.

KEY TERMS

Define the following terms.

procurement cycle	purchase requisition	cycle counting
reorder point	purchase order	cash flow commitments report
economic order quantity	blanket order	open-requisitions report
materials requirements	receiving report	vendor performance report
planning	disbursement voucher	triggered report
just-in-time (JIT) system	open-to-buy (OTB) control system	overdue-deliveries report

DISCUSSION QUESTIONS

17.1 The procurement operations and systems described in this chapter relate to a single plant or store. Discuss the differences between the information systems described in this chapter and those needed for a multiplant or multistore company in which the purchasing function is centralized.

17.2 The Consumer Manufacturing Company manufactures home appliances, including refrigerators, stoves, washing machines, and dryers. To support its purchasing operations, the company presently employs a computer-based batch processing system similar to that illustrated in Figs. 17.5, 17.7, 17.9,

and 17.10. The company is studying the feasibility of implementing a JIT inventory management system. Discuss the changes that would need to be made to the company's data processing system in order for a JIT system to be feasible.

17.3 Two approaches to reporting on vendor performance discussed in this chapter are (a) ratings based on point scoring on key performance factors, each weighted according to its relative importance, and (b) ratings based on a performance index that incorporates the costs caused by vendor failures. Discuss the relative merits of these two approaches.

PROBLEMS

17.1 Kids Choice Corporation is a manufacturer and distributor of children's toys. Within the past three years the company's sales volume has declined as several important distributors have dropped the Kids Choice product line. Some of these distributors have complained about product quality and delays in shipments. In response the company's top management has just ordered every department within the company to reevaluate its operations, identify possible problems that may be contributing to the company's loss of business, and prepare recommendations for improvement.

You have been asked to evaluate Kids Choice purchasing and materials inventory control system. You have determined that when a production run for a particular toy is scheduled, production planning personnel prepare a batch of purchase requisitions for the necessary materials, specifying quantities, vendors, and requested delivery dates. The data on these requisitions are keyed into a computerized purchasing system by data entry clerks. The system generates purchase orders, which are mailed to the appropriate vendors. When shipments are received and inspected, receiving personnel access the purchase order record on terminals located at the receiving dock and key in data on quantities received, accepted, and rejected by inspectors. Once all material inventory quantities for a particular production order have been received, the order is released to the plant and the production run commences.

Required
Could Kids Choice Corporation's purchasing and materials inventory control system have anything to do with the decline in its competitive fortunes? Describe several ways in which this system might be improved.

17.2 Which internal controls in a purchasing and inventory data processing system would provide the best protection against the following situations?

a. A purchasing agent ordered unnecessary goods from a company of which he is one of the officers.

b. Inventory was stolen by stores personnel, who claim to have never received the goods from the Receiving Department.

c. A vendor invoiced the company for a greater quantity of goods than was received.

d. A vendor delivered unordered goods and sent an invoice requesting payment for them.

e. The inventory update program posted an inventory receipt to the wrong inventory master record owing to an incorrect item number.

f. Several inventory transaction records were lost and not processed due to a software error in the file update program.

g. The only copy of the inventory master file was erased owing to inadvertent use of the disk as an output file in another program.

h. The unit cost of an inventory item received was incorrectly keyed in and posted as $20.00; the correct unit cost was $2.00.

i. A vendor overcharged for goods purchased.

j. A vendor sent two copies of an invoice. The copies became separated, and eventually two checks in payment of the two copies of the same invoice were prepared and mailed.

k. An inventory issue transaction was processed in which the quantity issued was erroneous, with the result that the on-hand balance in the inventory record fell below zero.

l. Owing to several miscellaneous errors occurring over a period of several years, a large discrepancy emerged between the quantity on hand of an important subassembly and the balance on hand according to the inventory master.

17.3 In 1984 XY Company purchased over $10 million of office equipment under its "special" ordering system, with individual orders ranging from $5000 to $30,000. "Special" orders entail low-volume items that have been included in an authorized user's budget. Department heads include in their annual budget requests for the types of equipment and their estimated cost. The budget, which limits the types and dollar amounts of office equipment a department head can requisition, is approved at the beginning of the year by the Board of Directors. Department heads prepare a purchase requisition form for equipment and forward the requisition to the Purchasing Department. XY's "special" ordering system functions as follows.

- *Purchasing:* Upon receiving a purchase requisition, one of five buyers verifies that the person requesting the equipment is a department head. The buyer then selects the appropriate vendor by searching the various vendor catalogs on file. The buyer then phones the vendor, requesting a price quotation, and gives the vendor a verbal order. A prenumbered purchase order is then processed, with the original sent to the vendor, a copy to the department head, a copy to receiving, and a copy to accounts payable, and one copy is filed in the open-requisition file. When the buyer is orally informed by the Receiving Department that the item has been received, the buyer transfers the purchase order from the unfilled file to the filled file. Once a month the buyer reviews the unfilled file to follow up and expedite open orders.

- *Receiving:* The Receiving Department receives a copy of the purchase order. When equipment is received the receiving clerk stamps the purchase order with the date received, and, if applicable, in red pen prints any differences between quantity on the purchase order and quantity received. The receiving clerk forwards the stamped purchase order and equipment to the requisitioning department head and orally notifies the Purchasing Department.

- *Accounts payable:* Upon receipt of a purchase order the accounts payable clerk files the purchase order in the open purchase order file. When a vendor invoice is received, the invoice is matched with the applicable purchase order, and a payable is set up by debiting the equipment account of the department requesting the items. Unpaid invoices are filed by due date, and at due date a check is prepared. The invoice and purchase order are filed by purchase order number in a paid invoice file, and then the check is forwarded to the Treasurer for signature.

- *Treasurer:* Checks received daily from the Accounts Payable Department are sorted into two groups: those over $10,000 and those $10,000 and less. Checks for $10,000 and less are machine-signed. The cashier maintains the key and signature plate to the check-signing machine and maintains a record of use of the check-signing machine. All checks over $10,000 are signed by the Treasurer or the Controller.

Required

Describe the internal accounting control weaknesses relating to purchases and payments of "special" orders of XY Company for each of the following functions:

a. Purchasing
b. Receiving
c. Accounts payable

(CPA Examination)

17.4 Lecimore Company has a centralized Purchasing Department managed by Joan Jones. Jones has established policies and procedures to guide the clerical staff and purchasing agents in the day-to-day operation of the department. She is satisfied that these policies and procedures are in conformity with company objectives and believes there are no major problems in the regular operations of the Purchasing Department.

Lecimore's Internal Audit Department was assigned to perform an operational audit of the purchasing function. Its first task was to review the specific policies and procedures established by Jones. The policies and procedures follow.

- All significant purchases are made on a competitive-bid basis. The probability of timely delivery, reliability of vendor, and so forth, are taken into consideration on a subjective basis.

- Detailed specifications of the minimum acceptable quality for all goods purchased are provided to vendors.

- Vendor's adherence to the quality specifications is the responsibility of the Materials Manager of the Inventory Control Department and not the Purchasing Department. The Materials Manager inspects the goods as they arrive to be sure the quality meets the minimum standards and then sees that the goods are transferred from the receiving dock to the storeroom.

- All purchase requests are prepared by the Materials Manager and are based upon the production schedule for a four-month period.

The internal audit staff then observed the operations of the purchasing function and gathered the following findings.

- One vendor provides 90% of the critical raw material. This vendor has a good delivery record and is very reliable. Furthermore, this vendor has been the low bidder over the past few years.

- As production plans change, rush and expedite

orders are made by production directly to the Purchasing Department. Materials ordered for canceled production runs are stored for future use. The costs of these special requests are borne by the Purchasing Department. Jones considers the additional costs associated with these special requests as "costs of being a good member of the corporate team."

■ Materials to accomplish engineering changes are ordered by the Purchasing Department as soon as the changes are made by the Engineering Department. Jones is very proud of the quick response by the purchasing staff to product changes. Materials on hand are not reviewed before any orders are placed.

■ Partial shipments and advance shipments (i.e., those received before the requested date of delivery) are accepted by the Materials Manager, who notifies the Purchasing Department of the receipt. The Purchasing Department is responsible for follow-up on partial shipments. No action is taken to discourage advance shipments.

Required

Based upon the Purchasing Department's policies and procedures and the findings of Lecimore's internal audit staff:

a. Identify weaknesses and/or inefficiencies in Lecimore Company's purchasing function.

b. Make recommendations for the weaknesses or inefficiencies that you identify.

Use the following format in preparing your response.   (CMA Examination)

Weaknesses/Inefficiencies	Recommendations

17.5 You have been engaged by the management of Alden, Inc., to review its internal control over the purchase, receipt, storage, and issue of raw materials. You have prepared the following comments that describe Alden's procedures.

■ Raw materials, which consist mainly of high-cost electronic components, are kept in a locked storeroom. Storeroom personnel include a supervisor and four clerks. All are well trained, competent, and adequately bonded. Raw materials are removed from the storeroom only upon written or oral authorization of one of the production foremen.

■ There are no perpetual inventory records; hence the storeroom clerks do not keep records of goods received or issued. To compensate for the lack of perpetual records, a physical inventory count is taken monthly by the storeroom clerks, who are well supervised. Appropriate procedures are followed in making the inventory count.

■ After the physical count, the storeroom supervisor matches quantities counted against a predetermined reorder level. If the count for a given part is below the reorder level, the supervisor enters the part number on a materials requisition list and sends this list to the accounts payable clerk. The accounts payable clerk prepares a purchase order for a predetermined reorder quantity for each part and mails the purchase order to the vendor from whom the part was last purchased.

■ When ordered materials arrive at Alden, they are received by the storeroom clerks. The clerks count the merchandise and check to see that the counts agree with the shipper's bill of lading. All vendors' bills of lading are initialed, dated, and filed in the storeroom to serve as receiving reports.

Required

Describe the weaknesses in internal control, and recommend improvements of Alden's procedures for the purchase, receipt, storage, and issue of raw materials. Organize your answer sheet in the following format.   (CPA Examination)

Weaknesses	Recommended Improvement

17.6 Goodstone Aerospace Corporation is trying to select a vendor for an expensive component in a guided missile that it is developing for the U.S. Air Force. It has received bids for 1000 units of the component from two of its best vendors. Vendor A's bid was $950 per unit, while Vendor B bid $935 per unit.

Goodstone evaluates the performance of its vendors using a cost index method and has designed its purchasing information system to keep track of the costs associated with defects in vendor shipments. Within the past 12 months Goodstone has purchased a total of $10 million in materials from Vendor A and $12 million from Vendor B. Though defects in the performance of these vendors are infrequent, problems with Vendor A's shipments cost Goodstone an estimated $300,000 in nonproductive costs during the past 12 months, while nonproductive costs associated with Vendor B's shipments totaled $480,000.

Required

a. Compute a cost performance index for each vendor.

b. Using the index, compute adjusted bids on the component for each vendor. Which vendor should get the contract?

c. Identify the data items that must be stored in Goodstone's purchasing data base in order to produce the information necessary for this analysis. In what file or files would these data items be stored?

17.7 Your company has just acquired a data base management system, and one of its first applications will be to purchasing data. A purchase order identical to that in Fig. 17.3 is used. You are to diagram the data structure of the purchase order as a first step in the application design. Use a format similar to that in Fig. 17.8. Note that the data base will contain only the variable data on the purchase order, not the constant data.

17.8 The management at Megafilters Inc. has been discussing the possible implementation of a JIT production system at its Illinois plant, where oil filters and air filters for heavy construction equipment and large, off-the-road vehicles are manufactured. The Metal Stamping Department at the Illinois plant has already instituted a JIT system for controlling raw materials inventory, but the remainder of the plant is still discussing how to proceed with the implementation of this concept. Some of the other department managers have grown increasingly cautious about the JIT process after hearing about the problems that have arisen in the Metal Stamping Department.

Robert Goertz, Manager of the Illinois plant, is a strong proponent of the JIT production system and recently made the following statement at a meeting of all department managers: "Just-in-time is often referred to as a management philosophy of doing business rather than a technique for improving efficiency on the plant floor. We will all have to make many changes in the way we think about our employees, our suppliers, and our customers if we are going to be successful in using just-in-time procedures. Rather than dwelling on some of the negative things you have heard from the Metal Stamping Department, I want each of you to prepare a list of things we can do to make a smooth transition to the just-in-time philosophy of management for the rest of the plant."

Required

a. The JIT management philosophy emphasizes objectives for the general improvement of a production system. Describe several important objectives of this philosophy.

b. Discuss several actions that Megafilters Inc. can take to ease the transition to a JIT production system at the Illinois plant.

c. In order for the JIT production system to be successful, Megafilters Inc. must establish appropriate relationships with its vendors, employees, and customers. Describe each of these three relationships.

(CMA Examination)

17.9 Lynn Duncan, controller of Lankar Company, has decided that the company needs to redesign its purchase order form and design a separate document to record the receipt of goods. Currently, a copy of Lankar's purchase order is serving as a receiving report, and the receiving clerk records the quantities received on the copy of the appropriate purchase order. Duncan has decided to implement these changes because there have been a number of inconsistencies and errors in ordering materials for inventory and in recording the receipt of goods. She believes these mistakes have resulted from the poor design of the current purchase order and the use of a copy of the purchase order as a receiving report. In addition to improving reporting, the introduction of these new forms will provide Duncan with an excellent opportunity to reinforce the need for accuracy and thoroughness among the employees in the Purchasing Department.

Shown in Fig. 17.12 is the revised purchase order; there will be multiple copies of the form, with the original and one copy being mailed to the vendor. The form will be letter size for ease in filing. The clerical staff in the Purchasing Department will complete the form from the information provided on the purchase requisition, and the form will be signed by the Purchasing Manager before being mailed to the vendor.

Shown in Fig. 17.13 is a condensed version of a draft of the new receiving report. This form will be approximately 5 inches wide and 8 inches long and will be prenumbered. There will be multiple copies so that all of the relevant departments will receive a copy. The new receiving report will be filled out in the Receiving Department by the receiving clerks.

Required

a. Duncan believes the inconsistencies and errors experienced by Lankar Company were due in part to the use of a copy of the purchase order as a

```
┌─────────────────────────────────────────────────────────────────┐
│                  Lankar Company Purchase Order                    │
│                      One Fordwick Place                           │
│                     Arion, Indiana  36999                         │
│                                                                   │
│   To:                                  Ship to:                   │
│                                                                   │
│                                                                   │
│                                                                   │
│                                                                   │
│                                                                   │
│                                                                   │
│                                                                   │
│                                                                   │
├─────────────────────────────────────────────────────────────────┤
│   Delivery Date:                       P.O. Date                  │
├─────────────────────────────────────────────────────────────────┤
│   Shipping Instructions:                                          │
├───────┬──────────┬────────┬────────┬──────────────────┬──────────┤
│ Item  │          │ Lankar │ Vendor │                  │  Unit    │
│ No.   │ Quantity │ Part # │ Part # │   Description    │  Cost    │
├───────┼──────────┼────────┼────────┼──────────────────┼──────────┤
│       │          │        │        │                  │          │
├───────┼──────────┼────────┼────────┼──────────────────┼──────────┤
│       │          │        │        │                  │          │
├───────┼──────────┼────────┼────────┼──────────────────┼──────────┤
│       │          │        │        │                  │          │
├───────┴──────────┴────────┴────────┴──────────────────┴──────────┤
│   Special Instructions:                                           │
│                                                                   │
│                                                                   │
│                              ─────────────────────────────        │
│                                   Purchasing Manager              │
└─────────────────────────────────────────────────────────────────┘
```

Figure 17.12
Lankar's revised purchase order

receiving report. Discuss several problems that can occur when a copy of a purchase order is used as a receiving report.

b. Review the new forms that Duncan has designed for Lankar Company, and explain what should be added and/or deleted to improve the following:

1. The purchase order
2. The receiving report

c. With regard to providing good internal control and ensuring efficient document flow at Lankar Company,

1. Identify the departments of Lankar Company that should receive a copy of the purchase order.
2. Explain why each of the identified depart-

ments needs a copy of the purchase order. Use the following format for your answer.

Department	Specified Use

d. Despite its apparent simplicity a Receiving Department performs several vital control functions. Describe four of these functions.
(CMA Examination, adapted)

17.10 Bargins Unlimited, a retail firm located in Regina, Saskatchewan, purchases merchandise for resale. A wide variety of items are acquired from approximately 500 suppliers. The firm employs an on-line, real-time purchasing system, with terminals

```
                                              No.  NNNNNN
                        Lankar Company
                        One Fordwick Place
                        Arion, Indiana  36999

    Received From:      _____
    (Name/Address)      _____
                        _____
                        _____
```

Quantity	Description	Unit Price	Amount
		Subtotal	
		Frt. Charges	
		Total	
Remarks/Conditons:		Department Delivered to:	

BE SURE TO MAKE THIS RECORD
ACCURATE AND COMPLETE

Figure 17.13
Draft of Lankar's new receiving report

located in the Purchasing and Receiving departments (among other areas) to handle its purchasing/receiving procedures.

Purchase orders are prepared by buyers, who select suitable suppliers from which to order needed merchandise specified on requisition sheets. These requisition sheets are prepared by the Inventory Control Department. The buyers place orders by first making on-line inquiries using their terminals and obtaining displays of suppliers' records. Next, the buyer enters the necessary data relating to each purchase, including the following: vendor number, product number, quantity required, estimated unit cost, date required, payment terms, the shipping method, shipper, warehouse code to which the merchandise is to be shipped, and buyer's number.

The system then generates a printed purchase order that contains the information just described plus a computer-generated purchase order number, order date, vendor name and address, description of the items ordered, unit of measurement, and shipping address. On confirmation of the order being accepted by the supplier, the system automatically updates the pertinent records in the inventory master file.

When ordered merchandise arrives at the receiving dock, it is counted by a receiving clerk, who records the following on a receiving report: receiving date, vendor number, related purchase order numbers, product number, and quantities received. Furthermore, the receiver records the condition of the goods received and then initials the receiving report. After completing the form, the receiver enters this information into the computer system. Upon acceptance of the entry the computer system then posts the receipt of the quantities to the perpetual inventory master file and the open purchase order master file. It then generates a prenumbered printed copy of the receiver's report. The receiver's report contains the information entered from the receiving report.

Required

Prepare record layouts for the following files.

a. Open purchase order file

b. Vendor master file

c. Inventory master file

d. Receiving report file

(SMAC Examination)

17.11 Kitchenware Inc. manufactures cookware and kitchen utensils. Its controller is presently evaluating a proposal to acquire bar coding equipment. The net cost of acquiring and implementing the equipment would be $24,000. Estimated monthly cost savings, in terms of labor hours and average hourly rates, are as follows:

Receiving and inspection	35 hours @ $20
Data entry	20 hours @ $15
Factory	40 hours @ $25

Required

a. Does the acquisition of bar coding equipment appear to be a good investment from a purely financial standpoint? Support your answer with calculations.

b. What factors other than the financial effects should Kitchenware's controller consider in making this decision?

17.12 The Doyle Company processes its inventory transactions by computer. Data on inventory receipts, issues, and other file update transactions are keyed directly from batches of source documents onto a temporary magnetic disk file. The transaction file is then sorted and processed to update an inventory master file, maintained on disk. Outputs of this process include (1) a listing of inventory items to be reordered, which is written onto a temporary disk file and subsequently processed to print this information in a report, (2) a printed stock status report, and (3) a summary printout listing error transactions and run totals.

Required

a. Prepare a systems flowchart of all operations described.

b. Describe a comprehensive set of control policies and procedures for this computerized inventory processing system. Identify the control objectives, and relate each control policy or procedure to a specific control objective. Explain the functioning of each control policy or procedure within the specific context of this inventory data processing application.

17.13 Culp Electronics Company processes inventory receipts as they arrive at the receiving dock by means of on-line data terminals located in the Receiving Department. All of the six Receiving Department employees have been taught to operate the terminals. Each inventory receipt entered into the system is processed to update the appropriate records in both an inventory master file and a file of open purchase orders.

Required

a. What items of data should be entered into the system each time an operator uses the terminal to report the receipt of a shipment?

b. Describe several means by which the system could be programmed to check the accuracy and validity of the input data entered from the Receiving Department. Relate your answer specifically to the data items mentioned in part a.

17.14 Lawn Care Company is a large assembler of electric and gasoline-powered lawn and garden equipment. The company needs a computerized system to record its purchases of raw material, to process accounts payable, and to maintain inventory control. The on-line system should store, provide, and access information such as the following:

■ For each item purchased, the purchase order number, the part number purchased, the vendor number for the company from whom the item is to be obtained, the quantity ordered, the total quantity received, the unit price, the anticipated delivery date(s), and the date of purchase order

■ Vendor's name, number, and address, normal terms, and the balance due

■ Vendor's invoice number, invoice date, invoice amount, amount of payments applied against invoice, account distribution(s), the amount for each account distribution, the invoice due date, terms, and the discount amount

■ Part number, type of inventory (raw material or finished goods), quantity on hand, quantity on order, units of measurement, unit price

■ A daily report of all goods ordered and a daily log of all goods received

Required

a. Identify three files required in the purchasing system of the Lawn Care Company, and give the field contents for each file.

b. To ensure that each record on a file is unique, indicate the record key (access key) for each file identified in your answer to part a.

c. Lawn Care Company wants a list of all vendors, with their names and addresses, to whom a purchase order has been issued for $2000 or more of part number 4Z5tr12, a mower handle. This list should include the purchase order number.

1. What files would require accessing in order to generate this required report?

2. Assuming that the report is to be in vendor number order and a sort program cannot be executed, what secondary record key would be necessary? Explain.

3. Describe the processing a computer would follow in order to generate this report from the data files. Express your answer in either a narrative or flowchart format.

d. Differentiate between an index file and a sequential file. Explain the advantages and disadvantages of both types of file organizations.

e. From your response to part a, choose one file and indicate how it should be accessed. Support your answer.

(SMAC Examination)

17.15 Electrophonics Ltd. assembles electronic equipment of a specialized nature from parts purchased from a number of different vendors. Three product lines (burglar alarms, automatic telephone-answering systems, and telephone amplifiers) are handled by three separate product departments, which make use of a single, small Purchasing Department responsible for purchase orders, inventory control, and cash disbursements to vendors. All purchases of components are made on credit. The Purchasing Department consists of a manager who investigates and selects the vendors, a data entry clerk, and a stock control clerk who receives and issues inventory items.

The Purchasing Department has ordered a minicomputer to be dedicated to this function. All files will be stored on magnetic disk. The computer will support two main systems. The first is responsible for processing purchase orders, receiving invoices from vendors, and generating payment authorizations. The second is responsible for registering the receipt of items to inventory and the issue of items from inventory and for producing lists of approved vendors and products and current inventory levels. Because of the volatile nature of the business, reorder decisions are made by the three product line departments. In this problem we are solely concerned with the first system. The following narrative describes the proposed operation of this system.

Purchase requisition forms (PRF) will be received from each of the three product line departments. Once each day the batch of requisitions will be keyed into the computer. A program called Purchase Requisition Log (PRLP) will check that each field on the purchase order is complete and of the right data type and will enter the details on a file for unsorted purchase requisitions (UPRF). Once all orders are entered, a program called Purchase Requisition Sort (PRSP) will sort all requisitions by vendor number, creating a file for sorted purchase requisitions (SPRF). The completion of this program will trigger a third, called Purchase Order Generate (POGP), which will access data from a vendor file (VF) and print actual purchase orders (APO) for transmittal to the vendor. Each purchase order will contain all items to be ordered from the vendor in question and will be assigned a purchase order number. This program will also add the new purchase orders to a file of "pending purchase orders" (PPOF), creating an updated file of pending purchase orders (UPPOF).

Toward the end of each day all invoices received that day from vendors (VI) will be keyed in. A program called Vendor Invoice Log (VILP) will check that the invoice contains a purchase order number and will create an unsorted file for new vendor invoices (UVIF).

Finally, a program called Match Orders to Invoices (MOIP) will process the items in the unsorted vendor invoice file (UVIF) against the current inventory status file (CISF) (which contains details of receipts to inventory) and the pending purchase orders file. This program will use the updated pending purchase orders file (UPPOF) to create the new pending purchase order file (PPOF) by removing orders that have arrived and will print checks for vendor payments (VP), including vendor name, amount, and purchase order number. It will also print address labels (AL) containing vendor name and address.

Required

a. Using standard symbols, draw a systems flowchart for the operations described in the narrative.

Place the letter abbreviations used in the narrative in each box.

b. As described, the system is incomplete. Excluding possible controls or additional reports that might be useful to management, identify three additional output files or reports that are essential for the operation of the system as described, and state which program would produce them.

c. Apart from the simple edit checks in the Purchase Requisition Log program and the Vendor Invoice Log program, no controls are built into the system. Identify and describe three desirable manual or computer controls.
(SMAC Examination)

CASE 17.1: ANYCOMPANY, INC.—AN ONGOING COMPREHENSIVE CASE

One of the best ways to learn is to immediately apply what you have studied. The purpose of this case is to allow you to do that. You will select a local company that you can work with. At the end of most chapters you will find an assignment that will have you apply what you have learned using the company you have selected as a reference. This case, then, may become an ongoing case study that you work on throughout the term.

Select a local company and obtain permission to study its purchasing and inventory control information system. Answer the following questions about its system.

1. Who are the individuals responsible for requisitioning, vendor selection, purchase order preparation, documentation of inventory receipts, safeguarding of physical inventories, and processing vendor invoices? Prepare a partial organization chart, and identify where these individuals are located on this chart.

2. What documents are used in the system? Obtain a sample copy of each document.

3. What master files are maintained in the system? What is the data content of each master file? Prepare (or obtain copies of) record layouts for each master file.

4. For each master file, explain how it is updated. Identify each of the different types of transactions that cause the file to be updated. What is the data content of each transaction record? Describe how these transaction data are captured in machine-readable form for entry into the company's computer system. Prepare (or obtain copies of) record layouts for each transaction record.

5. If the company uses a data base management system, prepare (or obtain a copy of) a schema diagram identifying the linkages among the various master files within the system.

6. Prepare (or obtain copies of) system flowcharts for each of the major master file update processes. For each process, indicate whether the company uses batch processing, on-line processing, or a combination of these.

7. Describe internal control procedures employed by the company in this system. Do you feel that the company's internal controls are satisfactory?

8. Identify and obtain sample copies of reports that are prepared by the system. For each report, identify the file or files from which the information originates. Indicate the frequency with which each report is prepared and whether it is prepared on the mainframe computer or a personal computer. Identify who receives each report and how it is used. Evaluate the content and format of each report.

9. Describe how accounting transaction information that originates in this system is transmitted to the company's general ledger system.

Case 17.2: BLACKWELL INDUSTRIES

You are a systems analyst for Blackwell Industries, a manufacturer of sporting goods. Blackwell utilizes a large state-of-the-art computer facility for its business data processing. Recently, the company has begun to redesign several of its data processing systems in order to achieve greater integration of its many system applications.

You have been assigned to design an integrated system for processing purchase transactions. The system will utilize a materials inventory master file, an open purchase order master file, and a vendor history file, all stored on magnetic disk files. System inputs will be materials inventory receipt and issue transactions, keyed in as they occur from on-line terminals in the receiving or stores departments. System outputs will be batches of purchase orders and periodically generated reports of overdue deliveries, vendor performance, and cash flow commitments. These system outputs will be generated by programs that are separate from the main update program.

The main update program will begin by reading the transaction record and checking whether it is a receipt or issue transaction. Then it will read and update the inventory master record and write the updated inventory record back to the disk. For an issue transaction, if the balance of the item falls below its reorder point, a reorder record will be written to a temporary reorder file on a separate disk. This file will be processed at the end of each day to prepare purchase orders. For an inventory receipt transaction, the main update program will read and update the corresponding open purchase order record. If a receipt completes the purchase order, the purchase order record will be deleted from the file, and the vendor's history record will be read and updated for performance data obtained from the completed purchase order. After a master file record is updated by the computer, it must then be written back onto the disk.

The purchase order preparation program will operate on the temporary reorder file after that file has been sequenced by vendor code number. After reading a reorder record, it will key on the vendor number in that record and then read the vendor history file to obtain the vendor's name and address for the purchase order. Next, it will read all other reorder records for the same vendor and add them to the purchase order record. Then it will generate the completed purchase order, add it to the open purchase order file, print the purchase order document, and proceed to process the next reorder record.

At the end of each day the open purchase order file will be processed to identify purchase orders for which delivery is past due, and an overdue-deliveries report will be generated. At the end of each month the vendor history and open purchase order files will be processed to generate vendor performance reports and a cash flow commitments report.

1. Prepare a systems flowchart of the main update program.

2. Prepare a systems flowchart of the purchase order preparation program.

3. Prepare systems flowcharts of the programs that generate (a) the overdue-deliveries report and (b) the vendor performance reports and the cash flow commitments report.

4. Prepare a program flowchart of the main update program that shows the primary input, output, processing, and logical operations, but not in complete detail; closely related operations may be combined in one flowchart symbol. (*Note:* This type of summary program flowchart is sometimes called a macroflowchart.)

5. Prepare a macroflowchart of the purchase order preparation program.

6. Identify a set of internal control objectives for this system. For each internal control objective, describe some specific internal control procedures that should be implemented in this system in order to achieve the objective.

CHAPTER 18

The Production Cycle

LEARNING OBJECTIVES

After studying this chapter, you should be able to:

- Describe the key activities and data processing operations included in the production cycle.
- Describe the decision responsibilities and information requirements of the production management function.
- Give several examples of the information provided by the accounting information system to support the production management function.
- Flowchart data and information flows for typical production data processing systems.
- Evaluate and recommend control policies and procedures for a production data processing system.

INTEGRATIVE CASE: ELECTRONICS INCORPORATED

Tom Morris, Vice-President for Production at Electronics Incorporated (EI), is becoming discouraged. Several months ago EI's top management made a strategic decision to move the company away from its traditional position as a low-cost producer of consumer electronic products (see Chapters 16 and 17). Instead, while EI would serve the same product markets, it would offer a much wider variety of sizes, styles, and features within each of its product lines, and it would position itself as a producer of good-quality products sold at moderate prices.

While Tom believes that this decision will enhance EI's prospects for success in the long run, he is very concerned about the difficulties it has caused for the management of production operations in the short run. Under the old strategy there were only 25 distinct products, and EI's plants were often geared to produce the same product for several consecutive days. Now there are over 200 products, and both the Dayton and Wichita plants have experienced great difficulty in scheduling production operations effectively and in adhering to established timetables once a production job falls behind schedule. In addition, production quality problems have actually increased as factory supervisors continue to stress high volume and minimum cost while downplaying the desired emphasis on product quality. Moreover, manufacturing overhead costs at both plants are growing at astounding rates. The old cost accounting system is under serious strain, and marketing executives have complained that product cost figures produced by this system seem to be distorted and not very useful in setting product prices. Finally, EI's production planners have not been able to obtain reliable forecasts of product demand, resulting in overproduction of some products and shortages of others.

Tom would like to sell EI's executive team on the need to invest several million dollars to implement flexible manufacturing system (FMS) technology in order to support the company's new strategic direction. However, unless he can make headway in resolving the recent glut of problems, he fears that he will not be able to make a credible case for the necessary investment and that his own job may be in jeopardy. In desperation, he has arranged a meeting with Grace Healy, EI's Chief Information Officer (CIO), to discuss how the company's information systems can be improved to resolve several critical issues, including:

1. How can production schedules be made more reliable?
2. How can production quality be controlled more effectively?
3. How can manufacturing overhead costs be monitored more closely?
4. How can product costs be determined more accurately?
5. How can product demand be forecast with greater precision?

What would you suggest to Tom Morris about how to improve EI's information systems in order to resolve these issues? ∎

INTRODUCTION

The **production cycle** is a recurring set of business activities and related data processing operations associated with manufacturing a product. The business activities include planning the production process by determining what is to be produced, how it is to be produced, and when it is to be produced; controlling the operations necessary to convert raw material into a finished product; and monitoring the efficiency and quality of these operations. These activities make up the production management function. The related data processing operations include preparing production orders, requisitioning raw materials for the production process, recording production activity, maintaining records of the status of all production work in process, and reporting to management on the status of production activities and the results of production operations. The information provided by these data processing operations is crucial to the effective completion of the related business activities.

As the Electronics Incorporated case suggests, weaknesses in a company's production information systems can often cause severe operating problems that threaten its ability to achieve its strategic objectives. In particular, the availability of current and accurate information on customer demand, product costs, manufacturing quality, and the status of production work in process is crucial to effective management of production operations. As you read this chapter, try to identify some improvements in EI's information systems that could help to resolve its problems.

In a manufacturing company the production management function is closely related to the purchasing and inventory management function described in Chapter 17. Purchasing involves procuring raw material to be used in the manufacturing process, while production involves converting that raw material into a finished product. Furthermore, as pointed out in Chapter 17, in order to determine what needs to be purchased, one must develop production plans. These and other relationships between the purchasing and production functions should become clearer as we proceed through this chapter.

This chapter describes the production cycle functions of production planning and scheduling and operations control and the data processing operations that support these business functions. It emphasizes the important role played by the accounting information system both in carrying out these data processing operations and in providing information to support the production management function. The chapter begins by explaining the decision responsibilities and related information requirements of production managers in order to identify the kinds of information that must be provided by data processing systems that support production operations. The next section of the chapter describes in general terms the basic functions and procedures that must be performed within the production cycle of a typical manufacturing company. These procedures generate the raw data that are the source of information used in production management. The remainder of the chapter describes the production data processing system and explains how it supports the basic production cycle functions and procedures and generates information to meet the requirements of production managers.

THE PRODUCTION MANAGEMENT FUNCTION

For an understanding of the decision-making responsibilities and related information requirements of production managers, it is useful to begin by examining the organization structure of the production function. To provide a basis for our discussion, Fig. 18.1 provides a simple example of the organization of the production function within a typical manufacturing company. This section describes the major decisions that are the responsibility of each management function shown in the organization chart and discusses the nature and sources of information used in addressing these decisions.

The Top Production Executive

The Vice-President for Production is responsible to the company President for the effective planning, coordination, and control of manufacturing operations. This executive is a central participant in the company's overall strategic planning and brings the manufacturing perspective to these strategic deliberations. The Production Vice-President also participates in establishing product prices, based on product cost information provided by the company's cost accounting system, and plays an important role in decisions relating to the identification of new-product opportunities, the design and development of new products, and the introduction of new products into the marketplace. Information on market demand and projected product costs is important to these new product decisions.

Another important decision in which the Production Vice-President is a key participant involves facilities planning. In the long run this planning entails deciding how many manufacturing plants the company needs, and in what locations, in order to produce a sufficient volume of products to serve the company's markets effectively. It also involves

Figure 18.1
Production organization structure

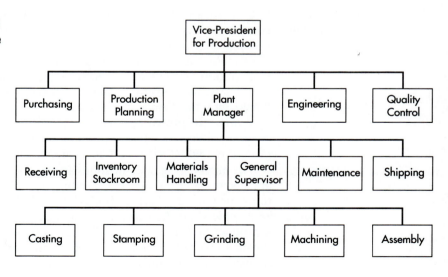

selecting the best mix of manufacturing technology to fulfill the company's production requirements. In the short run it involves estimating the labor hours and machine hours that are required to execute the company's production plans, and acquiring the necessary resources to fulfill these requirements. To make sound facilities planning decisions, the Production Vice-President needs information on economic conditions, current and projected market demand for the company's products, the characteristics of potential plant locations, and the features of available manufacturing technology; this information is obtained primarily from sources external to the company. In addition, detailed information on the capacity of the company's existing manufacturing facilities is also essential to facilities planning decisions; this information is provided by the company's production information system.

The Vice-President for Production must also establish performance standards for production operations and then evaluate actual performance to determine how well it meets the performance standards. Three categories of manufacturing performance standards that are important are time standards, cost standards, and quality standards. Time standards are based on engineering estimates of the time required to perform specific manufacturing operations. Cost standards are based on estimates, prepared by cost accountants and engineers, of the cost of performing specific manufacturing tasks efficiently. Quality standards are based on the judgments of engineers and quality control personnel regarding the maximum allowable rate of defects in manufacturing operations. The production information system plays a central role in collecting data on actual manufacturing performance along each of these three dimensions and in processing this data to generate information useful for performance evaluation.

The Engineering Function

The engineering function involves establishing, for each product or component that the firm manufactures, the standard quantity of each raw material or part required, the precise labor operations required, the standard amount of time each operation should consume, and the workstation or machine at which each operation should be performed. These specifications are developed for a product when it is first introduced into the firm's product line and may be revised periodically thereafter. In preparing these specifications, engineers must balance several criteria, including product quality, durability, functionality, ease of manufacturing, and cost minimization.

The engineering specifications for a product or product component are documented in two key production records. Materials specifications for a product are embodied in a bill of materials, illustrated in Fig. 18.2, which lists the part number and description of each component of a product and indicates the quantity of each part that is used in the finished product. Labor operations, with their corresponding machine requirements, are indicated on an operations list or routing sheet, illustrated in Fig. 18.3. The operations list indicates how a product or component is routed through the factory, what is done to it at each step in the

ELECTRONICS INCORPORATED

BILL OF MATERIALS

Assembly No. 2742816	Assembly Name: Miniature calculator	Approved by: FDK	Date: 01/13/94	Page: 1 of 1

Part No.	Description	Quantity per Assembly
7054396	Calculator unit	1
4069136	Lower casing	1
1954207	Screw	8
3099218	Battery	1
4069245	Upper casing	1
1954209	Screw	6

Figure 18.2
Bill of materials

manufacturing process, and how much time is required to set up the machines for each step and to complete each step for a standard lot size. Both of these records are prepared and kept current by engineering personnel for every item produced, and they are important elements of the production data base.

Modern engineers generally use computer technology in product development. In **computer-aided design (CAD)** a computer system featuring high-resolution graphics terminals and graphics software assists engineers in the design and alteration of manufactured products. Such a system enables product designers to create an image of a product design, rotate it on the screen for viewing from various perspectives, scale it up or down, create product specifications for a completed design, store them in memory, and prepare engineering drawings. Advanced CAD software can also assist in design evaluation by simulating product testing, by generating performance information, and by preparing cost estimates for proposed designs. The advantages of CAD are that it speeds product design and evaluation and facilitates the alteration of existing product designs.

BLACKWELL INDUSTRIES

OPERATIONS LIST NO. 7228

Part No. SP4430	Part Description Cabinet side panel	Used in Product FC2530 file cabinet	Raw Material S2480 sheet steel

Department No.	Machine No.	Operation No.	Operation Description	Setup Hours	Run Hours per 1000
MH25	FL105	M101	Transfer from stock	—	—
ML15	ML254	3394	Cut to shape	1	25
ML15	ML581	8352	Corner cut	2	40
S28	ST164	4921	Turn and shape	2	50
F54	F824	6628	Finish	1	20
P89	P204	9743	Paint	0.5	20
QC94	—	9925	Inspect	—	5
MH25	FL105	M102	Transfer to stores	—	—

Figure 18.3
Operations list

The engineering function is also responsible for designing the production process for each product and for implementing factory automation whenever it is cost-effective to do so. Among the more common forms of factory automation are numerical control, robotics, computer-aided manufacturing, and flexible manufacturing systems. **Numerical control** is the use of a computer system to automatically control the operation of a machine tool in the performance of standardized production operations. Numerical control yields substantially more precise and consistent machine operations than does manual control.

The manufacture of a product generally requires that a series of machine operations be performed on a set of materials (refer to Fig. 18.3). **Computer-aided manufacturing (CAM)** involves using the computer to prepare an integrated set of numerical control specifications for this series of machine operations and to track the status of the production work in process as it moves through the factory. When CAD systems are employed in product design, it is logical to utilize the product specifications prepared through CAD to automatically generate manufacturing specifications for machine operations under CAM; systems that integrate these two processes are referred to as **CAD/CAM systems**.

In **robotics**, programmable machines (robots) are used to manipulate tools, parts, or materials to perform a variety of specific production tasks. Among the more common production tasks performed by robots are parts handling, simple assembly, machining, spray painting, and welding. Robots are especially appropriate for moving heavy materials, for monotonous and repetitive tasks, and for hazardous work. Advantages include their ability to work around the clock, the quality and consistency of their work, and their dependability.

A **flexible manufacturing system (FMS)** utilizes a computer to automate the production of a family of products and components that require similar materials and machine operations. The key feature of an FMS is flexibility: It can produce several related products on the same machines or produce the same product on different machines, and it is also set up to allow rapid modification of machine specifications so that new products or new variations of existing products can be easily accommodated. An FMS employs the computer to integrate numerical control, automated materials handling using robotics, scheduling of machine operations, and monitoring the status of work in progress. An effectively operating FMS improves plant and equipment capacity utilization, reduces retooling and setup costs, improves product quality, reduces direct labor costs, reduces work-in-process inventories, and permits rapid adjustment of production in response to shifts in customer demand. Among the manufacturing companies that are leading users of FMS technology are Allen-Bradley, Hughes Aircraft, General Electric, Ingersoll Milling Machine Company, and Chrysler Corporation.[1] Casio Computer Company operates a flexible manufacturing and assembly line that utilizes 70 robots to manufacture 16 different models of calculators, and can convert this system from producing one model to another in less than one minute.[2]

To perform their various tasks effectively, engineers require information from a variety of sources. Some of this information is obtained from sources external to the company, including information on customer requirements and on the features of contemporary manufacturing technology. However, much useful engineering information is maintained in the production data base, including information on material and labor specifications for existing products, on the capacity of existing factory resources, on sources of material for products that are being designed, and on the costs of materials, labor, and manufacturing overhead required for production operations.

---

[1] R. Anthony Inman, "Flexible Manufacturing Systems: Issues and Implementation," *Industrial Management* (July/August 1991): 7–11.

[2] John E. Ettlie and Stacy A. Reifeis, "Integrating Design and Manufacturing to Deploy Advanced Manufacturing Technology," *Interfaces* (November/December 1987): 63–74.

Production Planning

The production planning function involves determining what is to be produced and when it will be produced. Deciding what should be produced during a given time period involves specifying the planned quantities of each product to be manufactured, including a suitable mix of styles, sizes, colors, and other features. For those firms that manufacture goods to fill customer orders, this aspect of production planning may be quite simple, especially if there is a large **backlog** of orders that have been received but not filled. In firms that manufacture goods for inventory to meet uncertain customer demand, production planning is more complex. Here planners must utilize information on current inventory levels and on product sales forecasts prepared by sales managers. As illustrated by the Electronics Incorporated case, an inadequate system of forecasting product sales can be costly when it leads production planners to plan insufficient production of some products and excessive production of others.

Establishing the timetable by which specific factory resources will be used to manufacture specific products is referred to as production scheduling. From the production planner the scheduler determines what quantities of each product are to be produced. From the engineer the scheduler obtains information about the resources required to manufacture each product, including materials (reflected in the bill of materials) and labor and equipment (reflected in the operations list). Total resource requirements are then established by multiplying the quantity of each product to be produced by the per-unit requirements specified in the bill of materials and operations list. The scheduler determines the availability of these resources by checking materials stock status reports, personnel reports, machine availability and capacity reports, and existing production schedules. Finally, the production scheduler must know the relative priorities of the various items to be produced. Some items will have high priority because they are out of stock, back-ordered, rush-ordered, or behind schedule for a promised delivery date. Such high-priority items must be given preference by the scheduler over lower-priority items.

Taking all of these factors into account, the scheduler prepares a production schedule that coordinates the work of all production employees and the use of all available machines and materials throughout the plant to achieve maximum production output with a minimum expenditure of time and resources. The resulting production schedule specifies, for each factory department, what jobs will be performed, at what times and at what machines, during the period covered by the schedule. Working out this scheduling is much easier said than done, because the complexities of production scheduling have made it impossible for experts to identify an optimal approach or technique.[3] For

---

[3] For a good discussion of contemporary methods of production scheduling, see Thomas E. Vollmann, William L. Berry, and D. Clay Whybark, *Manufacturing Planning and Control Systems,* 3rd ed. (Homewood, Ill.: Irwin, 1992), Chapters 6 and 13.

example, recall the difficulties in production scheduling Electronics Incorporated experienced after expanding its product line from 25 to over 200 items.

Advanced information technology is often used to integrate production planning and scheduling with other manufacturing applications. Three of the more commonly used approaches are manufacturing resource planning, just-in-time manufacturing, and computer-integrated manufacturing. These techniques are generally employed in conjunction with one or more of the methods of factory automation described earlier. In the remainder of this section each of these approaches is briefly described.

Manufacturing resource planning (labeled MRP-II to distinguish it from the original MRP, materials requirements planning) is a comprehensive computerized planning and control system for manufacturing operations. As described in Chapter 17, MRP utilizes the production plan and bill of materials to generate inventory requirements and purchasing schedules. MRP-II builds upon these applications by incorporating capacity planning for factory work centers, scheduling of production operations, and manufacturing cost accounting. An MRP-II system establishes a master production schedule (MPS) that plans factory operations over a planning horizon of up to 12 months. From the MPS and its links to MRP and related applications, the system forecasts future requirements for the three key manufacturing resources—materials, labor, and equipment—over the planning horizon. In some MRP-II systems, simulation may be used to examine how changes in market demand, product mix, or related factors will affect resource requirements. Effective MRP-II systems provide several advantages:

- More efficient use of manufacturing capacity
- Reduced inventory levels
- Less factory overtime
- Less need for continuous monitoring of production work in process
- Quicker and easier adjustment of work loads, inventory deliveries, and equipment schedules whenever production plans must be altered.[4]

Just-in-time (JIT) production is an approach to planning and control of production operations that strives to minimize or eliminate inventories of raw materials and work in process. It is generally applied in manu-

---

[4] For some examples of the use of MRP-II in practice, see Joseph G. Ormsby, Susan Y. Ormsby, and Carl R. Ruthstrom, "MRP-II Implementation: A Case Study," *Production and Inventory Management Journal* (Fourth Quarter 1990): 77–81; Charlotte S. Stephens, William N. Ledbetter, and James L. Eddy, "The Best of Both Worlds: A Mainframe- and Microcomputer-Based MRP-II System," *Production and Inventory Management Journal* (Third Quarter 1990): 35–40; and Joseph R. Biggs and Ellen J. Long, "Gaining the Competitive Edge with MRP/MRP II," *Management Accounting* (May 1988): 27–32.

facturing facilities having high-volume repetitive production methods, such as Toyota's automobile factories and Hewlett-Packard's computer manufacturing facilities. Rather than produce discrete batches of a variety of products, a JIT production facility strives to achieve a constant rate of production of a group of related products. Work-in-process inventory is held to a minimum by locating successive workstations close together and by arranging for each workstation to receive each job precisely when it is ready to process that job. Materials inventories are held to a minimum by using JIT purchasing (see Chapter 17) to arrange supplier deliveries precisely at the required time and location. Other key objectives of JIT production are as follows:

- To eliminate production defects by doing things right the first time

- To minimize or eliminate non–value-added activities such as materials handling and storage, paperwork, machine setups, inspections, and production downtime

- To minimize production cycle times (the time between the start of production and the completion of the product)

- To strive for continuous improvements in quality and productivity

- To maintain a high level of worker involvement

JIT production requires an information system that maintains highly accurate data on productive capacity, material requirements, purchasing delivery schedules, manufacturing timetables, and quality problems and their resolution. However, to the extent that JIT production virtually eliminates deviations from routine execution of a standard production schedule, the information system can place less emphasis on tight monitoring of production work in process and on detailed accounting for inventories, production costs, and cost variances.[5]

Computer-integrated manufacturing (CIM) provides for the integration of all the key applications of information technology in a manufacturing organization. These include engineering applications (CAD and CAM), factory automation (numerical control, robotics, and FMS), production planning (MRP, MRP-II, capacity planning, and production scheduling), quality control, marketing (product inventories, sales order entry, and sales forecasting), and accounting (cost accounting and budgeting). Among the successful pioneers in the implementation of CIM have

---

[5] For further discussion of JIT production and its effects on factory information systems, see Thomas E. Vollmann, William L. Berry and D. Clay Whybark, *Manufacturing Planning and Control Systems,* 3rd ed. (Homewood, Ill.: Irwin, 1992), Chapter 3; Ellen Harris, "The Impact of JIT Production on Product Costing Information Systems," *Production and Inventory Management Journal* (First Quarter 1990): 44–48; George Foster and Charles T. Horngren, "JIT: Cost Accounting and Cost Management Issues," *Management Accounting* (June 1987): 19–25; and James M. Patell, "Adapting a Cost Accounting System to Just-in-Time Manufacturing: The Hewlett-Packard Personal Office Computer Division," in William J. Bruns, Jr., and Robert S. Kaplan, eds., *Accounting and Management: Field Study Perspectives* (Boston: Harvard Business School Press, 1987), 229–267.

been General Motors, Allen-Bradley (see Focus 18.1), Deere, Weyerhaeuser, and Monsanto.[6] CIM obviously places great demands on the information system—first, to be fully integrated across functional areas, and second, to maintain complete, accurate, and current information on all operations and events that are relevant to the planning and control of manufacturing activities.

Other Production Management Functions

Refer to Fig. 18.1; the other key production management functions shown are purchasing, quality control, and the supervisory functions carried out by the Plant Manager (whose responsibilities include both production and service departments), General Supervisor (production departments only), and supervisors within each individual production and service department. The purchasing function is covered in Chapter 17 and is not discussed further here.

The quality control function involves establishing specifications for satisfactory completion of a manufacturing process and testing or inspecting completed items of production for defects in materials or workmanship to ensure that they meet or exceed the quality control standards. Tests and inspections are often performed on a sample basis, in which case an entire lot of completed items is not inspected unless a certain portion of the sample is found to be defective. All defective units are returned to the appropriate factory department for reworking. Costs of reworking are relevant to performance evaluations of department supervisors and the General Supervisor; therefore, the accounting system should be designed to charge these costs to the department in which the defective work occurred. It is particularly important to identify the cause of any quality control problem so that steps can be taken to modify the production process and ensure that the same problem does not recur.

Factory supervisory personnel are responsible for ensuring that employees within their respective departments adhere to time standards embodied in production schedules, quality standards embodied in quality control specifications, and cost standards embodied in standard cost measures and budgets. The departmental supervisors decide which employees to assign to particular jobs on the basis of each employee's experience, efficiency, and skills. Factory supervisors must also pay careful attention to the priorities attached to various production jobs; their success in meeting scheduling priorities is another important element of their performance. Supervisory effectiveness is reflected in materials use costs, production labor and overhead costs, scheduling delays, and the quality of production output. The performance of departmental supervisors is evaluated by the General

---

[6] For more on CIM, see Mohsen Attaran, "The Automated Factory: Justification and Implementation," *Business Horizons* (May/June 1989): 80–86; Willie Schatz, "Making CIM Work," *Datamation* (December 1, 1988): 18–21; and William J. Doll and Mark A. Vonderembse, "Forging a Partnership to Achieve Competitive Advantage: The CIM Challenge," *MIS Quarterly* (June 1987): 205–220.

18.1 FOCUS

CIM at Allen-Bradley

Allen-Bradley has been involved in numerous CIM projects throughout the world, but one of the most successful is the world contactor assembly facility in Milwaukee.

Some years ago, management saw that the merging international standards for motor controls would eventually threaten one of Allen-Bradley's core businesses. To remain competitive, the company not only needed a new product but also needed one that could be sold profitably anywhere in the world. Offshore sourcing was examined and quickly discarded. The engineer-

ing skills were already in place in Milwaukee—and they were unmatched anywhere in the world. The solution was a new product, and a new production line, developed by design and production engineers working as a team.

Other experts were assigned

Supervisor and Plant Manager through comparison of expected results with actual results. The production information system is responsible for collecting and maintaining the performance data on which these evaluations are based and for preparing and distributing the necessary performance reports on a timely basis.

Another important activity in the production process is **expediting**, which involves monitoring the status of production work in process, particularly of high-priority items. Expediting is often performed by employees within the production planning function, but in a large factory it may be the responsibility of a separate department. The expediter is frequently called on to report information on the current status of jobs in process in response to the requests of customers or production planners. The expediter is responsible for maintaining a smooth flow of production through the factory and may authorize deviations from the production schedule if necessary to accomplish this goal. The expediter must also report significant deviations from scheduled production to the Plant Manager, the General Supervisor, and the Production Planning Department.

In summary, the primary production management functions involve determining how production will be accomplished, what products will be produced, and when they will be produced; and monitoring production operations to ensure that actual production is completed on schedule and meets cost and quality standards. To support these functions, the production information system must maintain and report product engineering information (bill of materials, operations list, and quality control specifications), production plans and schedules, and information on the current status of inventories and production work in proto the project from Quality Assurance, MIS, Marketing and Purchasing. The objectives were to develop a world-class product and a production facility with the following goals:

- High volume of 600 per hour
- 125 product variations in lot sizes of one
- Products built to order in 24 hours
- Located within the existing plant
- Competitively insignificant labor costs

So Allen-Bradley built its World Contactor Facility as part of a strategic plan to capture a higher share of the world market for electronic contactors. The result? All of these objectives have been met. Today Allen-Bradley has a totally integrated CIM facility whose relative cost per unit is 60% that of machine-assisted labor. And this system has already demonstrated a flexibility to respond to market demands.

Instead of the original 125 product variations, it now offers 837 variations in lot sizes as small as one. And relative return on assets is five times what it would have been with traditional manufacturing. Today the CIM facility is producing consistently higher-quality contactors at a lower per-unit cost than anyone else in the world.

Source: from J. Tracy O'Rourke, "The Common Sense of CIM," *Industrial Management & Data Systems* **90** (7) (1990): 3–8. Reprinted with permission of MCB University Press Limited.

cess. In addition, the production information system must be linked to the marketing information system, which provides information on the products that should be manufactured to meet market demands. Finally, the production information system must be integrated with the accounting information system, which records all accounting transactions associated with the production process and maintains and reports information on actual and budgeted production costs. The next section of the chapter describes the basic data processing functions and procedures that are performed within the production cycle, with emphasis given to processing activities that are part of the accounting information system.

BASIC PRODUCTION CYCLE FUNCTIONS AND PROCEDURES

This section reviews at a very general level the basic data processing functions and procedures that are performed in the production cycle of a typical manufacturing organization. These functions, identified in Fig. 18.4, include preparation of production plans, scheduling of production, requisitioning of raw materials and parts to be used in the production process, documenting production operations, documenting the completion of production and the transfer of finished products from the factory to a warehouse or shipping area, accounting for production costs, and posting accounting journal entries to the general ledger to recognize the costs of production. This section describes each of these functions in detail.

Production Planning

Determination of the number of units of each product to be produced is based on a master production schedule (MPS); an example of an MPS

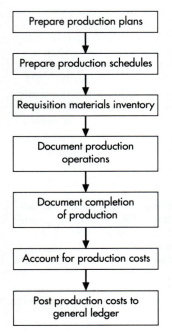

Figure 18.4

Basic production cycle data
processing functions and procedures

is shown in Fig. 18.5. Gross production requirements for each period are determined by adding the quantity committed to fill outstanding customer orders to the quantity needed to meet forecasted demand. The gross quantity available in any period is equal to the beginning quantity in stock plus the quantity scheduled to be produced in that period. The net quantity available is equal to the gross quantity available minus the gross requirements. From these relationships the scheduled production quantity in each period is established in order to ensure that sufficient quantities will be available to meet projected demand, allowing for a certain amount of safety stock to meet any unexpected increase in demand. The MPS is prepared for a planning horizon of anywhere from eight weeks up to one year. While planned production beyond four to eight weeks into the future may be easily modified if market demand changes, scheduled production quantities must be "frozen" (no changes allowed) for a period of two to four weeks following the current date in order to allow time for procurement of raw materials and other resources needed to complete the production process.

Once the production quantity of a product is frozen, production planners use the bill of materials to determine the quantities of all raw materials needed to manufacture the required quantity of the finished product. Then inventory records are checked to determine whether the needed materials are available in stock. For those items that are in stock a "hold" is placed on the necessary quantity in the inventory

Figure 18.5

Example of master
production schedule

MASTER PRODUCTION SCHEDULE								
Product Number ET-341			Oak End Table					
	Week Number							
	1	2	3	4	5	6	7	8
Quality in stock	500	200	500	100	450	150	500	200
Scheduled production	0	600	0	600	0	600	0	600
Gross available	500	800	500	700	450	750	500	800
Outstanding orders	150	100	100	0	0	0	0	0
Forecasted sales	150	200	300	250	300	250	300	250
Gross requirements	300	300	400	250	300	250	300	250
Net available	200	500	100	450	150	500	200	550

record in order to reserve the items for planned production. For those items not in stock the necessary purchasing procedures are initiated. These steps should ensure that all required raw materials are available when the production process commences.

Production planners must also verify that the necessary labor and equipment (as reflected in the product's operations list) are available for each scheduled production job. Available capacity is determined by taking existing total capacity and subtracting the labor and equipment requirements associated with all other scheduled production jobs. Temporary shortages may be dealt with by hiring additional employees and/or modifying existing production schedules. If deficiencies in factory capacity persist, it may be necessary to expand the factory and/or acquire additional equipment.

When the availability of all necessary resources is assured, a formal production order is issued. A **production order** is a record that documents the production planner's authorization to produce a specified quantity of a particular product. An example of a production order appears in Fig. 18.6. The production order provides basic information about the

Figure 18.6
Production order

BLACKWELL INDUSTRIES
PRODUCTION ORDER

Order No. 55912	Product No. Part No. SP4430	Product Description Cabinet side panel		Production Quantity 1000			
Approved by J. Carlton	Release Date 02/24/94	Issue Date 02/25/94	Completion Date 03/09/94	Deliver to Assembly Department			
Workstation No.	Operation No.	Scheduled Quantity	Operation Description	Start Date & Time		Finish Date & Time	
MH25	M101	250 S2480 sheets	Transfer from stock	2/28	7:00 A.M.	3/1	3:00 P.M.
ML15-12	3394	1000	Cut to shape	2/28	8:00 A.M.	3/2	5:00 P.M.
ML15-9	8352	1000	Corner cut	2/28	9:00 A.M.	3/4	5:00 P.M.
S28-17	4921	1000	Turn and shape	2/28	10:00 A.M.	3/8	11:30 A.M.
F54-5	6628	1000	Finish	2/28	1:00 P.M.	3/8	3:00 P.M.
P89-1	9743	1000	Paint	2/28	3:00 P.M.	3/8	5:00 P.M.
QC94	9925	200	Inspect	3/1	8:00 A.M.	3/8	5:00 P.M.
MH25	M102	1000	Transfer to assembly	3/1	11:00 A.M.	3/9	10:00 A.M.

product and the customer (if the item is being produced to fill a customer order); it also lists detailed information about the specific production tasks necessary to complete the production process. As it is issued, the production order record is added to the production data base, where it remains in an "open" status until the order is completed. As specific production tasks are performed, the open production order is updated to reflect the completed operations.

Open production order records are an important source of information on the status of production work in process. Factory employees refer to the production order to determine what tasks must be completed at their workstations. Cost accounting personnel use the production order to set up a cost accounting record for each production job in process. Production schedulers refer to the production order to determine which production tasks remain to be completed. The production order record may be made available to these various locations electronically or by transmitting a copy of a production order document. However, the obvious need for continuously current information on production order status induces a preference for maintaining and transmitting production order records electronically.

Production Scheduling

When a production order is issued, the items to be produced become part of the final assembly schedule. Whereas the MPS deals with anticipated production and can theoretically be changed at any time up to the issuance of the production order, the final assembly schedule provides a definitive specification of what will be produced and when. At any point in time, all open production orders are incorporated into the final assembly schedule. This schedule effectively reserves the production resources (materials, labor, and machine time) necessary to complete each outstanding order.

On a daily basis the status of all open production orders is checked to identify the operations that remain to be performed. From this information, daily production schedules for all factory production departments are prepared. The production schedule for each department lists all operations to be performed in the department each day, including the production order number, machine number, quantity, total time required, start and stop time, priority of the order, location from which the work in process is to arrive, and location to which it must be sent when completed. Each departmental production schedule must, of course, properly reflect the availability of machine time and labor resources within the department. At the beginning of each day, each department's production schedule is transmitted to the department supervisor as well as to the General Supervisor and the Plant Manager. These supervisory personnel use the departmental production schedules to help them manage the progress of production jobs under their span of control.

Unexpected events often occur in the factory environment. Machines may break down, employees may become sick, materials may be found to be defective, suppliers may not deliver required materials on time, and so on. Such events will usually require adjustments in the timing of specific production tasks. Often factory supervisors make these adjustments on an ad hoc basis. However, in a modern factory, data on such unexpected events is entered into the information system as the events occur, and the production schedule is adjusted on a real-time basis. This ensures that the factory's productive capacity will be used as efficiently as possible, even under adverse conditions.

Requisitioning of Materials

At the time a production order is issued, the Production Planning Department must authorize the transfer of the necessary quantity of raw materials from the inventory stockroom to the factory department in which production operations are to begin. The record that documents this authorization is called a **materials requisition** (see Fig. 18.7). It specifies the production order number, the issue date, the specific items and quantities issued, and the department to which the materials are to be routed. The items and quantities specified on the materials requisition are based on the product specifications from the bill of materials. For each order, production planners may issue one or more materials requisitions: one for each department at which materials enter the production process. In some cases all materials may be issued

Figure 18.7
Materials requisition

| | BLACKWELL INDUSTRIES | | | No. 14160 |
| | MATERIALS REQUISITION | | | |

Issue Date: 02/25/94	Production Order No: 55912		Department Issued to: ML15	
Part No.	Item Description	Quantity	Unit Cost	Total Cost
SP4430	Sheet steel, 4x10, 1/16"	250 sheets	$43.60	$10,900.00
Received by _____		Receipt Date _____		$10,900.00

to one department, whereas in other cases various portions of the materials may be issued to several different production departments as the work proceeds through the factory.

When the transfer of materials takes place, the materials requisition serves as a record of the transfer. An employee in the department that receives the materials should review the materials requisition and verify that the items and quantities being received are accurate. This employee should then enter his or her name or employee code into the materials requisition record. This is an important internal control procedure that establishes accountability for materials inventories within the factory.

As the inventory items are issued into the production process, the materials inventory records must be updated to reflect the use of the materials. The quantity of each item issued is subtracted from both the quantity on hand and the quantity committed for future production. In addition, the open production order record is updated to reflect the transfer of materials, and cost accounting records for the job are updated to reflect the cost of the materials issued.

Special procedures are necessary whenever actual materials use is greater than or less than the amount requisitioned. If a factory department supervisor determines that a larger quantity of materials is needed to complete a job, then the Production Planning Department must be informed of the items and quantities required. The Production Planning Department will then issue another materials requisition, which will be processed much like the original version. To provide control over materials issued in this manner, an organization must restrict authority to initiate requests for additional materials to supervisors, who will eventually be held accountable for any excess materials costs.

If a quantity of raw materials is left over after production within a department has been completed, the departmental supervisor must prepare a returned materials report. This report is taken, together with the materials themselves, to the raw materials stockroom. There the custodian signs the report to acknowledge receipt of the exact items and quantities listed on it. The report data are entered into the production data processing system to update the materials inventory records for the returned materials. In addition, the cost accounting records for the production job are credited for the cost of the unused inventory.

Production Operations   In the individual factory departments, scheduled production operations are completed by factory employees under the guidance of a department supervisor. When a factory employee completes an assigned operation, a **job time ticket** is prepared to document the work performed. The job time ticket, illustrated in Fig. 18.8, identifies the order number, operation number, department or workstation number, employee number, date, quantity completed, and other details about the operation. Each job time record is reviewed and approved by the

BLACKWELL INDUSTRIES

EMPLOYEE JOB TIME TICKET

Date	Dept. No.	Dept. Name
02/28/94	ML15	Milling

Order No.	Operation No.	Operation Description
55912	3394	Cut to shape

Employee No.	Employee Name	Hourly Rate
1713	Rod Johnson	$8.40

Start Time	Stop Time	Total Hours	Quantity Completed
8:00 A.M.	12:30 P.M.	4.5	47 sheets/188 panels

Approved by ___Theo. Nixon___
Department Supervisor

Figure 18.8
Job time ticket

department supervisor, whose name is then entered into the record to confirm the approval. The job time data are then entered into the production data processing system to update the open production order record for the completed operations. In addition, cost accounting records for the job are updated to reflect the labor costs incurred to complete the work.

A similar record, called a **move ticket**, is used to document the transfer of work in process from one workstation or department to another as individual production operations are completed. As for the materials requisition, the accuracy of the move ticket should always be verified by the employee receiving the work, and this employee should then enter his or her name into the move ticket record to establish accountability for the transfer. Job time records and move ticket records should be processed on a timely basis to update the production data base; this will ensure that records of the status of production work in process are as current as possible.

Completion of Finished Products

The final move ticket documents the transfer of the product to the finished goods stockroom. When this copy of the move ticket is entered into the production data processing system, the status of the corresponding production order is reviewed to verify that input records have been processed for all operations necessary to complete the order. When this is verified, the order status is changed from ''open'' to ''completed.'' The finished goods inventory records are then updated to increase the quantity on hand by the quantity completed. The final cost accounting procedures for the order are completed, and an accounting journal entry is prepared and posted to the accounting data base.

Cost Accounting

When a production order is issued, a cost accounting record is created for the job. This record is updated for all events and transactions that affect the cost of completing the production order. Production costs are generally classified into three categories: materials, labor, and overhead. The cost accounting records are updated for the cost of materials at the time that materials requisitions are issued detailing the quantity and cost of materials inventories dispensed to the job. As job time tickets are processed to document the factory labor applied to the job, the cost accounting records are updated for the cost of this labor. Manufacturing overhead costs are charged to individual factory departments and then allocated to production orders in process based on formulas that reflect how overhead costs are impacted by the production of specific types of products. Overhead allocation methods are discussed further in the next section. As these various transactions occur, the Cost Accounting Department prepares summary accounting journal entries, documented in journal voucher records, and enters them into the information system to update the general ledger.

One important output of the cost accounting process consists of weekly or monthly cost performance reports for each factory department. For this purpose actual materials, labor, and overhead costs are accumulated by factory department. The performance reports compare these actual costs with budgeted or standard costs that are determined on the basis of the amount of production work completed in each department. These reports provide feedback to departmental supervisors on the effectiveness of their supervisory performance and also are used by the General Supervisor, the Plant Manager, the Controller, and other manufacturing executives to evaluate the performance of production management.

General Ledger

The final step in production cycle data processing is the posting of summary accounting journal entries to the general ledger. These journal entries are initially recorded on journal voucher records prepared as part of the cost accounting function. The nature of these journal entries varies depending on whether job order costing or process costing is used. Under job order costing all manufacturing costs are charged to specific production jobs in process, and a single work-in-process control account is used to record the total amount charged to all jobs in process. For example, as materials requisitions are issued authorizing the use of materials in production, the following journal entry would be made.

Work-in-Process Inventory	$31,503.25	
Raw Materials Inventory		$31,503.25

At the conclusion of a factory payroll period, normally every one or two weeks, the following journal entry is made to recognize the cost of direct factory labor.

Work-in-Process Inventory	$12,160.10	
Accrued Payroll		$12,160.10

The third major category of production cost is manufacturing overhead. The subject of accounting for manufacturing overhead is quite complex. However, because it is such an important aspect of a manufacturing cost accounting system, it deserves further explanation. The complexity arises because manufacturing overhead costs, unlike materials and labor, cannot be traced directly to specific production orders in process. Instead, overhead costs are accumulated for a period of time, such as a month, and then allocated among the various jobs in process. This process begins as actual overhead costs are incurred, which leads to a series of journal entries such as the following:

Manufacturing Overhead	$25,768.85	
Accounts Payable		$ 8,112.25
Supplies Inventory		$ 1,203.15
Accrued Payroll		$ 7,033.45
Accumulated Depreciation		$ 9,420.00

This journal entry is a composite of several different entries that would be recorded at different times during an accounting period. The manufacturing overhead account is a control account, which means that there is a manufacturing overhead subsidiary ledger that contains individual overhead expense accounts. These accounts are classified by type of cost and by cost center. Cost centers are the various production and service departments within the factory. Among the different types of overhead costs are materials handling, supplies and small tools expense, depreciation of plant and equipment, power and other utilities, quality control and inspection, supervisory labor, overtime premium, materials spoilage, maintenance expense, property taxes, and insurance. The credit side of the previous journal entry records various liabilities and asset expirations that are typically associated with expense recognition.

At the end of the accounting period a two-stage process is employed to allocate total production costs to the items produced during the period. The first stage is the accumulation of costs by cost center.

Some costs can be traced directly to the specific cost center in which they are incurred. However, certain overhead costs must be allocated on some systematic basis. For example, depreciation expense for the plant might be allocated to factory departments based on their relative square footage.

The second stage is the allocation of costs from cost centers to products. Both direct materials and direct labor costs can be traced directly to specific production orders, based on materials requisitions and job time tickets. However, manufacturing overhead costs must be allocated on a systematic basis that reflects how each type of cost varies with the production of each type of product. For example, materials handling and materials spoilage costs might be allocated in proportion to the total cost of direct materials used in producing a product. Supervisory costs and overtime premium costs might be allocated in proportion to the direct labor hours applied to the product. Power costs and equipment depreciation costs might be allocated based on the total machine hours used on the product. After these allocations are determined, the following journal entry is prepared to summarize the application of manufacturing overhead to specific production orders in process.

Work-in-Process Inventory	$25,768.85	
Manufacturing Overhead		$25,768.85

Though not reflected in this example, the total manufacturing overhead applied is not always equal to the total incurred. The treatment of this matter is beyond the scope of this book.[7]

Though seemingly an arcane topic, product cost accounting is actually of great strategic importance in today's manufacturing environment. For example, recall that the cost accounting system at Electronics Incorporated is generating distorted product cost information that has not been very useful in establishing product prices. In recent years many manufacturing companies have experienced this same problem. This situation can be attributed to the traditional method of allocating virtually all manufacturing overhead costs to products in proportion to the direct labor hours used in the production process. This traditional approach has been made obsolete by two recent trends. First, factories are becoming increasingly automated, which means that direct labor costs are becoming a less significant proportion of total manufacturing costs, while manufacturing overhead costs are becoming relatively more significant. Second, modern factories are producing a larger variety of products, which makes the factory environment more complex and also tends to increase overhead costs. EI

---

[7] For a more extensive discussion of accounting for overhead costs, see Charles T. Horngren and George Foster, *Cost Accounting: A Managerial Emphasis*, 7th ed. (Englewood Cliffs, N.J.: Prentice-Hall, 1991), Chapters 4 and 8.

has experienced both of these trends but continues to allocate its manufacturing overhead costs on the basis of direct labor hours. According to recent evidence, unit production costs for some products have changed by several hundred percent following the introduction of a more precise cost accounting system.[8] This has profound implications for product pricing, which is a matter of great strategic importance for any business organization. Until EI can adjust its cost accounting system to better reflect its new manufacturing environment, the company will continue to have difficulty in establishing sound product prices.

Throughout this chapter and this section, the discussion of cost accounting systems has assumed the use of a job order costing system. The alternative method, called **process costing**, is generally used in petroleum refining, chemical manufacturing, and other situations where a uniform product is produced using a continuous manufacturing process. Under process costing, manufacturing costs are accumulated by departments, and there is a separate work-in-process account for each department. As work in process is transferred from one department to another, a journal entry is made to transfer the accumulated manufacturing costs from one department's work-in-process account to the other's. At the end of each accounting period an averaging method is used to allocate each department's total production cost to the units processed within that department during the period.[9]

At the conclusion of the production process, as completed items are transferred to a finished goods stockroom, the following accounting journal entry is recorded.

Finished Goods Inventory	$68,305.75	
Work-in-Process Inventory		$68,305.75

This entry reduces the work-in-process account by the accumulated cost of the items manufactured and transfers this cost to the finished goods inventory account.

Industry Variations

This chapter focuses on production information systems within one specific industry, namely, manufacturing. Accordingly, the opportunity for discussion of variations on these information systems in other industries may appear limited. However, companies in many other industries encounter operating problems and related data processing issues that are analogous to those of manufacturing companies. To use more general terminology, we might refer to these as logistical

---

[8] Robin Cooper and Robert S. Kaplan, "How Cost Accounting Systematically Distorts Product Costs," in William J. Bruns, Jr., and Robert S. Kaplan, eds, *Accounting and Management: Field Study Perspectives* (Boston: Harvard Business School Press, 1987), 204–228.

[9] For a more extensive description and comparison of job order and process costing, see Horngren and Foster, *Cost Accounting*, Chapters 4, 5, and 17.

problems and issues. This section identifies some of the important logistical problems and issues faced by companies in the transportation, construction, and service industries, and it briefly reviews how information systems are employed to address these problems and issues.

Transportation. Both freight and passenger transportation companies have similar logistical problems. These problems revolve around the use of productive resources (trucks, airplanes, etc.) to service customer transportation needs. Planning is important to anticipate customer requirements and to ensure that sufficient resources are available to satisfy specific customer demands. The availability of accurate information on existing capacity is also important. However, the focal point of the logistical information system in a transportation company is the transportation schedule. Perhaps the best-known examples are the flight schedules prepared by the major commercial airlines. These schedules indicate the equipment, labor, and other resources needed to provide transportation services, and specify when and where they are needed.

As transportation services are delivered, an information system captures data on revenue, cost, timeliness, customer satisfaction, and other performance dimensions for each trip, each route, and so on. The system processes these data to produce information that assists management in establishing sound prices, evaluating operating performance, assessing the profitability of alternative resource deployments, and making other management decisions.

Construction. In preparing bids to obtain construction contracts, a general contractor must undertake some planning to ensure the availability of sufficient resources (labor, materials, equipment, and subcontractors) to complete the work on a timely basis. Once the construction contract is obtained, the contractor prepares a list of the specific tasks that must be performed to complete the project. These tasks are then assigned to specific time periods to produce the construction schedule. This schedule is the heart of the construction company's information system, since it dictates when and where specific construction resources are required to complete all construction work in process.

As the construction project proceeds, an information system captures data on construction costs, the timeliness of completion of construction tasks, and other relevant operating data. The system processes these data to produce information that assists construction contractors in billing clients for work completed, evaluating operating performance, monitoring the progress of the project relative to the contract timetable, assessing the profitability of the project, and making other management decisions.

Services. In both professional and personal service organizations the primary resource is employee time. Planning is important to ensure that a sufficient number of employees are engaged to satisfy client demands. As specific customer requirements become known, one or more employees are assigned to serve each client. For example, Andersen Consulting might assign two staff consultants to develop a new cost accounting system for Nike, Inc., during the first six months of 1994. As these employee assignments are aggregated, the result is a matrix of employee-customer assignments that serves the same function as the schedule in a manufacturing, transportation, or construction company.

As service employees carry out their assignments, an information system collects data on time expended, adherence to work schedules, revenue generated, expenses incurred, quality of services delivered, and so on. The system processes these data to produce information that assists management in billing clients for work performed, evaluating the performance of employees, assessing the profitability of individual service assignments, and making other management decisions.

Note that there are several common threads running through our descriptions of the information systems needed to address the logistical problems of these various kinds of businesses. First, information is needed about anticipated consumer demand. Second, information is needed about available productive capacity. Third, the information system produces a schedule that specifies how the available capacity will be deployed to meet the anticipated demand, and this schedule regulates the company's operations. Finally, as work is performed, data are collected and processed to generate information that is used by management in setting prices and evaluating operating performance.

THE PRODUCTION INFORMATION SYSTEM

Within the production cycle there are two closely related data processing systems. One focuses on the collection and processing of operating data: factory capacity, production operations scheduled and completed, inventory quantities utilized, labor and machine hours expended, and so forth. The other focuses on collecting and processing cost accounting data to help management determine the cost of producing specific products. In many modern manufacturing companies these two data processing systems are fully integrated. Many other manufacturers are moving in this direction but have not yet achieved this level of integration. The combination of these two data processing systems is referred to in this chapter as the production information system. The production information system carries out the basic production cycle data processing functions and procedures described in the previous section of the chapter. This section describes and illustrates the use of computer-based systems to process operating and accounting transactions within a manufacturing environment. As in the previous two chapters, the material is presented in five subsections dealing with data capture, preliminary data processing procedures, data base updating, internal control objectives and procedures, and reporting of information to management.

Data Capture   In a computer-based production data processing system, data on two basic types of activities must be captured in machine-readable form. The first is the initiation of production orders. The second is the completion of production tasks, including each of the operations listed on each outstanding production order and the movement of (and transfer of responsibility for) production work in process from one factory workstation or responsibility center to another.

Production orders are initiated in one of two ways. First, if items are produced to fill customer orders, then production order records are generally created as a by-product of sales order processing. The customer order specifies the product stock number, description, quantity ordered, and a requested delivery date. As customer order data are entered into the system, an order processing module checks the availability of materials, machine time, labor, and other necessary resources, and then it schedules the job to meet the customer's requested delivery date as closely as possible. After the order is scheduled, it exists in the production information system as a planned order. Just before the production work is to begin, a production planner accesses the system from an on-line terminal to verify resource availability. When resource availability is confirmed, the production planner enters an **order release** record into the system to authorize the creation of a formal production order.

Alternatively, if items are produced for inventory, then planned orders are embodied in the MPS illustrated in Fig. 18.5. The MPS specifies product stock numbers, planned production quantities, and scheduled completion dates. At the beginning of each week, production planners use the system to verify the availability of manufacturing resources for all planned orders that are scheduled to begin that week. As resource availability is confirmed, order release records are entered into the system and formal production orders are generated.

The completion of production tasks is documented by creating detailed records of these activities as they take place within the factory. When each production operation is completed, a job time record is created containing the employee identification number, production order number, operation number, workstation or machine number, quantity completed, and start and stop time (see Fig. 18.8). In addition, as inventories are moved from one location in the factory to another, a move ticket record is created that contains the production order number, material description and quantity, and identification numbers of the employees and departments involved in the transfer.

One possible way of capturing data on the completion of production tasks is to have data entry clerks manually key in these data from job time ticket and move ticket source documents. However, because this approach uses paper source documents, it has at least two serious problems. First, because of the high volume of production activity, manual keying is very expensive. Second, effective management of factory operations requires that information on these operations be as current as possible, and manual keying of production transactions injects a significant delay into the process of updating the production data base. Both of these considerations support the need to automate the capture of data on factory operations.

One method of automating the capture of data on production activities is to use turnaround documents on which production order number, operation number, department number, and related data are recorded in machine-readable form by the computer when the production orders are prepared. As each operation is completed, the employee number, time worked, and quantity completed are manually entered into specific fields in such a way that these data can be read by a scanning device. Optical character readers (see Chapter 4) may be used for this purpose.

On-line data collection terminals located within each factory department are frequently used to capture data on production operations. One approach is to link these terminals to a factory data collection system controlled by a minicomputer. When production operations begin or conclude, factory employees key in job identification data using terminals located at or near their factory workstations. The system performs input validation checks on the data, computes the elapsed time for each completed job, and adds these data to the corresponding operations record in the production data base.

Specialized data collection devices are often used in conjunction with on-line terminals for factory data collection. One example is a badge reader that reads employee data from specially coded employee identification cards. Similar devices may be used to read machine identification cards or work order cards containing production order and job operations data.

One of the fastest-growing data collection methods in the factory environment is bar code scanning. An example of a preprinted bar-coded template used for recording data on standard factory operations is shown in Fig. 18.9. At the Pittsburgh plant of Ametek-Thermox Instruments, bar codes are used to collect receiving data, to count materials inventories, to track employee time and attendance data for payroll and shop floor control, and to monitor work-in-process accounting. Microcomputers with attached reading wands are located in the receiving area, stockroom, shop floor, and timekeeping area. These micros are networked with a host computer that directs the system. The reading wands are used to capture data from employee identification cards, work orders, and parts lists. When job start and stop codes are scanned, the system retrieves the start and stop times from its internal clock and determines the elapsed time for the job. The system verifies all input data in real-time, so error rates are extremely low. The system is designed to generate cost variance information by product code, product category, and even by individual employee.[10]

---

[10] This system is described in greater detail in Thomas Tyson and Arjan T. Sadhwani, "Bar Codes Speed Factory Floor Reporting," *Management Accounting* (April 1988): 41–46.

Figure 18.9
Bar-coded template for recording
factory operations data
(*Source:* Courtesy of
INTERMEC Corporation.)

**Preliminary Data
Processing Procedures**

This section discusses the steps involved in processing both production order release records and production activity records.

First, consider the processing of order release records, as illustrated in the flowchart in Fig. 18.10. This process begins as production planners enter order release data into the production information system from on-line terminals. Prior to order release the order should exist within the production information system as a planned order. To access the planned order, the planner enters the product number, order quantity, and schedule date. The system verifies that a planned order with these attributes exists in the system and displays the planned order data on the screen. The planner reviews the validity of the order

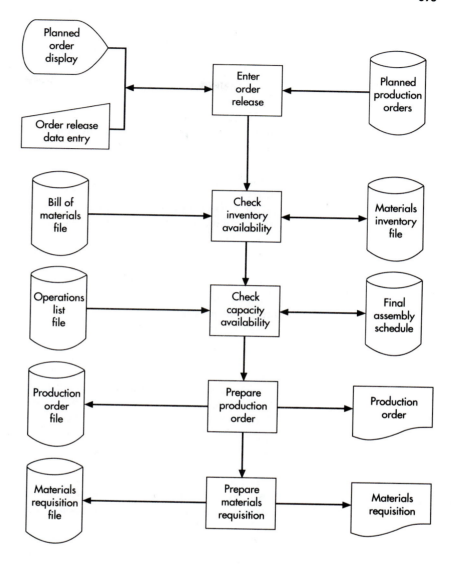

Figure 18.10
Processing of production order releases

data and then enters the order release by changing the order status from "planned" to "released for production." Before accepting the order release, the system must perform a compatibility test to verify that the planner has the authority to release the order into production.

Once the system accepts the order release, the next step is to verify resource availability. In an effective production information system resource availability will have been provided for at the time the planned order is created. However, delivery delays, machine break-downs, or other unforeseen events often disrupt the best of plans, so this reconfirmation step is important. The first step in this process is to check the availability of the quantity of raw material required to complete the planned production. The system reads the bill of materials file to determine which materials, in what quantities, are needed for production. Then the related materials inventory records are read to check the availability of the needed inventory items. In each affected materials inventory record, an entry is made to reserve the required quantities for this production order and subtract them from the quantities available. In the unlikely event that materials are not available in sufficient quantities, steps must be taken to initiate a purchase requisition (not shown), and the production order release is put on hold until the materials are available.

A similar process is followed to check the availability of factory capacity. First, the system reads the operations list file to ascertain the quantities of human and machine resources required to complete the production process. Next, the final assembly schedule is read to check the availability of the necessary machines and to schedule the work on those machines. If sufficient labor or machine resources are not available to schedule the job by the planned schedule date, the final assembly schedule may be modified in accordance with the priorities established for various jobs to be completed. At the conclusion of this process the final assembly schedule is updated to reflect all newly released production orders.

For those production order releases for which resource availability is confirmed, a formal production order is created. The operations required to manufacture the product, obtained from the operations list file, are added to the planned order record to create a final production order record. A production order number is assigned to this record, and the order release date and scheduled start and completion dates for each operation are added to the record. This record is then added to the production order file in the production data base. Also at this time, based on data from the bill of materials file, materials requisition records are created for each raw material item used in manufacturing the product, and these records are added to the production data base. All necessary copies of the production order document (see Fig. 18.6) and of related materials requisition documents (see Fig. 18.7) may be printed at this time, or printing may be delayed until the production operations are scheduled to commence.

Production activity records include job time records, move ticket records, and records of certain nonroutine transactions such as a returned materials report or a scrap ticket for inventory spoiled during the production process. To simplify our discussion, we focus here on job time records and move ticket records. These records may be processed in either an on-line or a batch processing mode. If batch processing is employed, these records are accumulated on a temporary disk file to be processed against the production data base at regular intervals during each production shift. A count of the number of records in each batch is obtained, and other appropriate batch totals are computed. File maintenance is facilitated by sorting each batch of records first by production order number and then by operation number within the production order.

For both batch and on-line processing a critical step is to perform edit checks on production activity records. First, validity checks should be performed on production order numbers, operation numbers, employee identification numbers, inventory stock numbers, and other primary key field values. Next, redundant data checks should be performed on these values by assessing whether (1) the operation number represents a valid operation for the production order, (2) the employee number and workstation number belong to the department in which the operation should be performed, and (3) the product number or part number is valid for that particular production order. Also, the system can check whether each reported operation was actually scheduled to be performed within the time frame for which it was reported. In addition, a sequence check should be performed on operation numbers within each production order to assure that, for example, operation five is not posted as completed before operations three and four have been recorded. Also, the quantity completed or transferred can be checked against the actual quantity in process. Field checks and range checks should be performed on the dates and times that are reported for starting and completing operations; alternatively, the actual dates and times can be captured automatically by the system as the operations are performed. Finally, a reasonableness test should be performed on the quantity completed and the actual time required in relation to the scheduled time.

If any production activity records do not pass these tests, immediate steps should be taken to identify and correct the errors so that the production data base can be as current and accurate as possible. If batch processing is employed, error transactions are listed on a report for subsequent review and correction, while all valid production activity transactions are listed on an activity report and written onto a temporary disk file to be processed against the production data base. Under on-line processing, error transactions cause a message to be displayed on the terminal of the employee who is entering the data so that the employee can recheck and correct the input data in real time. After all production activity data have been checked, and corrected if necessary, an on-line system processes these data immediately to update the production data base.

Data Base Update   After production activity transaction data have been captured in machine-readable form and validated by edit programs, the next step is to update the production data base to reflect these transactions. This involves modifying all appropriate fields within the various records that are part of the data base to reflect the effects of job time records, move ticket records, materials requisition issue records, and related production cycle transactions. This section describes the basic content and structure of the production data base and then explains the procedures involved in updating this data base for these production transactions. Both batch processing and on-line processing procedures are explained.

The Production Data Base. The production data base contains data on product structure (bill of materials and operations list), scheduled production activity, actual production activity, and the current status of production work in process. A simplified example of the data content and organization of a production data base appears in Fig. 18.11. In many real applications the purchasing data base (see Fig. 17.8) would be closely linked to, if not actually part of, the production data base. Note that the production data base contains both operating data (quantities, locations, dates, times, etc.) and accounting data (setup and run costs for operations, unit inventory costs, and total materials, labor, and overhead costs for each production order).

To best understand the production data base, it is helpful to first examine its overall structure. The data base shown in Fig. 18.11 has primarily a tree (hierarchical) structure, with the product inventory record at the root. Associated with each product inventory record, in

Figure 18.11
A sample production data base

Master Production Schedule Record

Product number	Week number	Beginning quantity	Scheduled production	Scheduled for delivery	Forecasted unit sales	Net quantity available

Product Inventory Record

Product number	Product description	Location code	Standard cost	List price	Minimum stock level	Production lot size	Quantity on hand	Quantity available

Production Order Record

Order number	Product number	Order quantity	Order status	Release date	Issue date	Scheduled date of completion	Materials total cost	Labor total cost	Overhead total cost

Production Order Detail

Order number	Operation number	Workstation number	Employee number	Quantity completed	Starting date and time		Completion date and time	
					Planned	Actual	Planned	Actual

Operations List Detail

Product number	Operation number	Operation description	Workstation number	Setup hours	Run hours per 1000	Setup cost per hour	Run cost per hour

Materials Requisition Record

Order number	Part number	Issue status	Issue date	Issue time	Workstation number issued to	Quantity issued	Unit cost

Bill of Materials Detail

Product number	Part number	Quantity per item

one-to-many relationships, are (1) master production schedule records, (2) two product structure records, the operations list detail and the bill of materials detail, that provide engineering specifications for the product, and (3) production order records that provide details about production work in process for each product. Associated with each production order record, in one-to-many relationships, are two activity records: the production order detail record, which lists details on scheduled and actual operations for each production order; and the materials requisition record, which lists details on raw materials items scheduled and actually issued for each production order. Note that production order detail records are created from the operations list for the product, so this link is also reflected in Fig. 18.11. Similarly, materials requisition records are derived from the bill of materials, so this link also appears in Fig. 18.11. Technically, the existence of these latter two links makes this a network data structure.

Product structure data are embodied in the production data base in the form of the operations list detail record, which specifies details about the operations performed in manufacturing the product, and the bill of materials detail record, which lists the quantities of various raw materials required to manufacture the product. Both of these records are associated with a specific product through one-to-many links to the product inventory record, reflecting the fact that multiple operations and multiple parts are generally required to produce one unit of a product. For each of these links the "product number" field is common to both records and establishes the relationship. Maintaining and updating these product structure records is the responsibility of engineering personnel.

Data on scheduled production activity are reflected in the production data base through the master production schedule record and through the data on scheduled production quantities, labor operations, and materials use that appear, respectively, in the production order record, the production order detail record, and the materials requisition record. For each product inventory record, there are several master production schedule records, one for each week in the time period covered by the schedule (see also Fig. 18.5). Each master production schedule record lists the projected beginning inventory quantity for the product for that week, the quantities scheduled for production and delivery during that week, and the forecasted unit sales quantity for that week. The master production schedule is updated weekly to reflect new customer orders and revised sales forecasts.

The portions of the production data base that deal with scheduled production operations are updated as new production orders and materials requisitions are issued. At this point these newly scheduled operations are added to the final assembly schedule. Note that the final assembly schedule does not exist as a separate file within the production data base shown in Fig. 18.11. Instead, it can be generated on demand from the production order detail records. Starting with the complete production order detail file, all records of finished operations are removed, leaving a file of scheduled operations. This file is sorted first by workstation number and then by planned starting date and time to produce the final assembly schedule.

Data on actual production activity are found in the production order record, the production order detail record, and the materials requisition record. The production order record indicates the order release date and the issue date for each production order; they are entered into the data base when the order release is processed and when the order is issued, respectively. The production order detail record indicates the quantity completed, the actual starting and completion date and time, and the employee and workstation numbers for each labor operation; these data are entered into the system as production operations are performed in the factory. The materials requisition record indicates the issue date and time, the quantity issued, the unit cost, and the workstation issued to, for each batch of materials used, and these data are entered into the system when the materials are issued into production. The production order number field is common to all three of these activity records and establishes the link between them.

Data on the current status of production work in process appear in the product inventory record, the production order record, the production order detail record, and the materials requisition record. For each product the product inventory record includes the quantity on hand and the quantity available, where the quantity available is equal to the quantity on hand plus the quantity currently being produced minus the quantity committed for outstanding customer orders. The production order record indicates the current order status (planned, released, issued, in process, or completed) and the accumulated total cost of materials issued, labor operations performed, and overhead allocated for each production order in process. The production order detail record indicates the quantity completed for each production operation. Finally, the materials requisition record indicates the issue status (pending or issued into production) for each batch of materials used in the production process.

In the relatively simple production data processing system employed at Electronics Incorporated, there is no integrated production data base. Instead, both plants maintain separate files for the master production schedule, the final assembly schedule, product inventories, production orders in process, and cost accounting records. Each of these files is updated separately. As a result, inconsistencies often arise between data in separate files. For example, the quantity available data in the master production schedule and in the product inventory record often conflict with each other and with the actual number of units being produced. This causes uncertainty and error in planning how many units of some products should be produced. Also, the final assembly schedule and the production order detail records often do not agree. This has caused errors in daily production schedules for factory departments at both plants, resulting in either idle capacity or unforeseen delays in completing orders. These scheduling problems occurred infrequently when EI was producing only 25 different products, but they arise on almost a daily basis now that the product line exceeds 200 products.

During her meeting with Tom Morris, one of Grace Healy's first recommendations was that EI's production data base be integrated along the lines of the sample data base shown in Fig. 18.11. In this way, when any production cycle transaction is processed on the system, all affected records would be updated for that transaction at the same time. This would eliminate the data inconsistencies that have recently afflicted EI's production information system and enable EI to improve the accuracy and reliability of its production scheduling. In addition, Grace suggested that links be established between the production data base and the purchasing data base to facilitate the ongoing attempt to implement material requirements planning (MRP). In Grace's judgment these steps are a necessary prelude to replacing EI's present batch processing system with an on-line production information system that would maintain the entire production data base on a continuously current basis. In turn, this would allow EI to implement FMS technology, MRP-II, and possibly other forms of advanced manufacturing technology. In short, implementation of an integrated production data base is an important first step in improving EI's production information system to meet its strategic objectives.

Batch Processing. This section describes the procedures involved in batch processing of production activity transactions to update the production data base. This process is illustrated in the systems flowchart in Fig. 18.12. To simplify the discussion, we focus on the three most common transactions: materials issues (documented by the materials requisition), labor operations (documented by the job time ticket), and movements of work-in-process inventory from one workstation to another (documented by the move ticket). As indicated in the flowchart, records of these transactions are accumulated in batches on a temporary disk file, to be processed at regular intervals, such as at the conclusion of each production shift. Before the update run, batch totals are accumulated and the records are sorted into sequential order by production order number. In addition, each transaction record is subjected to a variety of edit checks, as described in the section on preliminary data processing procedures. Any errors detected by these edit checks must be corrected before the update run.

A materials issue record indicates that requisitioned materials have been transferred from the inventory stockroom to the appropriate factory department and that an employee of the receiving department has signed a copy of the requisition acknowledging receipt of the materials. As each materials issue record is read, the system keys on

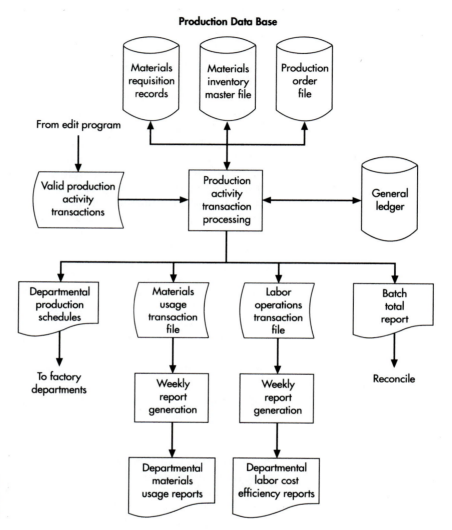

Figure 18.12
Batch processing of production
activity transactions

the production order number and part number and reads the materials requisition record, the materials inventory record,[11] and the production order record from the production data base. The materials requisition record is updated by changing the issue status from pending to issued and by recording the actual issue date and time and the quantity issued. In addition, the unit cost of the inventory items is retrieved

---

[11] To simplify our presentation, we did not include the materials inventory record in our diagram of the production data base, but it does appear in our purchasing data base diagram (Fig. 17.8). As mentioned earlier in the chapter, the purchasing data base is closely linked to, and often viewed as part of, the production data base, primarily because information on the availability of raw materials is important for production planning and because the materials inventory records must be updated to reflect materials used in production, as explained in this paragraph.

from the materials inventory record and entered into the requisition record. The materials inventory record is updated by subtracting the quantity issued from both the quantity on hand and the quantity reserved for this job. Finally, the quantity issued is multiplied by the unit cost, and the result is added to the accumulated total materials cost in the production order record.

A job time record indicates the order number, operation number, machine or workstation number, employee number, quantity completed, and the actual start and stop time for a labor operation. Generally, the date of the operation is the current date, which is entered into the record by the system at the time the record is created. As each job time record is read, the system keys on the production order number and operation number and reads the corresponding production order record and production order detail record from the production data base. The production order detail record is updated by recording the workstation number, employee number, quantity completed, and the actual start and stop time for the operation. In addition, the actual cost of the operation is determined by multiplying the elapsed operation time either by the employee's actual hourly wage rate, obtained by reading the employee record from the personnel data base, or a standard hourly wage rate obtained from the operations list detail record. The operation cost is added to the accumulated total labor cost in the production order record.

A move ticket record identifies the production order number, identification numbers of the employee and workstation receiving the inventory, quantity transferred, and date and time of the transfer. From the standpoint of the production data base shown in Fig. 18.11, a move ticket record may be viewed as a different type of production order detail record, where the operation is simply the movement of work-in-process inventory. Thus to update the production data base for a move ticket, the system merely records the move ticket data in the corresponding production order detail record. The final move ticket for each production order documents the transfer of finished products from the factory to the shipping department (if the units were produced to fill a customer order) or the finished goods stockroom (if the units were produced for inventory). At this point the status of the production order record is changed from "in process" to "completed." In addition, if the units were produced for inventory, it would be necessary to access the finished goods inventory file and update the quantity on hand by adding the number of units completed.

During this update process the system maintains a running total of all material and labor costs that have been charged to production orders and of the total cost of all production orders that have been completed. At the conclusion of the process, these running totals are the basis of summary journal entries: first, debiting work-in-process inventory and crediting raw materials inventory and accrued payroll for all material and labor costs incurred; and second, debiting finished goods inventory and crediting work-in-process inventory for all completed orders. To post these journal entries, the system reads these accounts from the general ledger, updates the account balances, and writes the updated accounts back to the general ledger. The summary journal entries, along with other batch totals accumulated during the run, are then printed on a summary batch total report. These batch totals should be reconciled with those prepared prior to the run.

As each production activity transaction is processed, the system determines the standard and actual labor hours for each operation and the standard and actual materials usage for each operation. These items are recorded on two separate temporary disk files. The data continue to accumulate on these files for a specific period of time, such as a week or month. At that time all records on these files are sorted by department number (which exists as a subcode within the workstation number). The files are then processed using a report generation program to prepare departmental summary reports on materials usage and labor efficiency. These reports compare actual and standard costs of materials and labor for each department, perhaps broken down further by workstation, operation, or employee. Variances that exceed a predetermined percentage may be highlighted. The reports are delivered to the respective factory department supervisors to assist them in evaluating their own performance and that of their subordinates.

After the production order detail records have been updated to reflect all completed production operations, all records of operations still to be performed are sorted by workstation number and then by scheduled starting date and time. The resulting file is then processed to prepare a production schedule for the next shift for each factory department. The scheduling routine takes into account the machine and labor capacity of each department and the relative priorities of outstanding production orders, and it balances these factors as necessary to generate an efficient production timetable. Printed copies of the departmental production schedules should be distributed promptly to the respective factory departments to guide the department supervisors in organizing production work within their departments.

One other important step not reflected in Fig. 18.12 is the allocation of manufacturing overhead costs to production orders in process. For each category of overhead cost this allocation is done by multiplying an overhead rate by a base factor that reflects how that type of cost varies with the production of finished products. For example, power costs might be allocated to products at the rate of $2.00 for every machine hour used in manufacturing the products. This means that the values of various base factors, such as machine hours, direct labor hours, and direct materials cost, must be accumulated for each production order in process and recorded in the production order record. In addition, overhead rates must be computed on a periodic basis, such as monthly or annually.

There are two ways to compute overhead rates. Under the first approach estimates are developed at the beginning of each year of the total number of units of each product to be manufactured, the total of each type of overhead cost, and the total of each of the overhead base factors. Then each overhead cost estimate is divided by the value of its associated base factor to derive an overhead rate for that cost category for the subsequent year. These estimates are called **predetermined overhead rates**. If predetermined rates are used, then overhead costs are applied to production orders as part of the processing of production activity transactions illustrated in Fig. 18.12. The amount of overhead applied to the production order for each transaction would be added to the accumulated total overhead cost in the production order record.

Under the second approach, a separate month-end process is employed to compute **actual overhead rates** for the month, and these rates are used to allocate the related overhead costs to all production orders that were processed during the month. A systems flowchart of this process appears in Fig. 18.13. As shown, the process utilizes the manufacturing overhead subsidiary ledger, in which all actual overhead costs for the month are recorded in separate accounts by cost category (indirect labor, depreciation, supplies, etc.). In addition, some of these overhead costs are further classified in the accounts by cost center (department or workstation), because they can be directly traced to a particular cost center; examples include equipment depreciation and the salaries of factory department supervisors. Other overhead costs, such as plant depreciation, factory power, and the plant manager's salary, cannot be directly traced to specific cost centers and so are

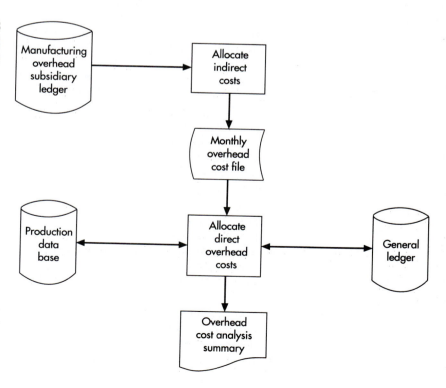

Figure 18.13
Allocation of manufacturing overhead using actual overhead rates

allocated to the cost centers on some systematic basis. This process of allocating indirect overhead costs to cost centers is the first step illustrated in Fig. 18.13. It produces a temporary file of all overhead costs classified by cost center.

In the second process shown in Fig. 18.13 actual overhead rates are computed for each cost center by reading the actual overhead costs from the overhead cost file and dividing each of these costs by its corresponding overhead base factor retrieved from the production data base. Next, the system reads each production order record from the production data base and computes the overhead amounts to be allocated from each cost center to that production order. These amounts are summed across all overhead cost centers to determine the total manufacturing overhead to be applied to the production order for the month. This sum is added to the accumulated total overhead cost in the production order record. After completing this process for each production order record, the system accesses the general ledger to post the summary journal entry debiting work-in-process inventory and crediting the manufacturing overhead control account. A report is also printed summarizing the results of the overhead allocation process.

On-line Processing.   Spurred by the increasing popularity of factory automation, on-line production information systems are rapidly displacing batch processing systems for production data processing. In higher-level automated factory systems such as CIM, production planning and scheduling, cost accounting, engineering, and related data processing functions are integrated with the systems that control factory machines and processes. The systems flowchart in Fig. 18.14 depicts a simplified example of an integrated on-line production information system of this type.

In this system several different types of users have on-line access to the system, and each is authorized to enter specific types of transactions. Engineering personnel enter data on product specifications, in the form of bills of materials and operations lists. Production planning personnel enter data necessary to maintain the master production schedule, including quantities scheduled for delivery to customers and forecasted sales quantities. Cost accounting personnel enter data on standard production costs and current manufacturing overhead rates. Data on factory production activities may be captured automatically as a by-product of the operations themselves, or they may be entered via on-line terminals, badge readers, or other on-line data collection devices in the individual factory departments.

As these various kinds of data are entered, the system interacts with the user to facilitate the data entry process and to check the accuracy and completeness of the data being entered. If potentially inaccurate input data are detected, the system requests that the user recheck these data and reenter them, if necessary. Once an input transaction has been accepted, the system proceeds to update the affected portions of the production data base. New or modified product engineering specifi-

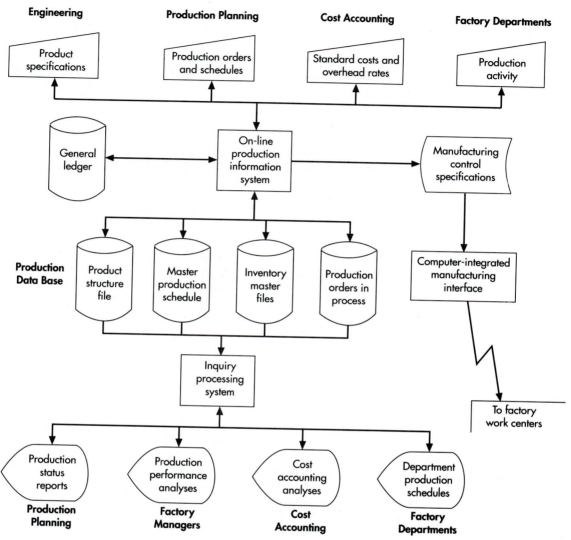

Figure 18.14
On-line production information system

cations update the product structure file. Data on standard resource quantities and costs for each product, developed and entered by cost accounting personnel, also become part of the product structure file. Scheduling transactions entered by production planning personnel are posted to the master production schedule. Production activity records are posted to the master files associated with production orders in process, including production order detail records, materials requisition records, and all affected inventory records. In addition, summary accounting journal entries reflecting all production activity are posted to work-in-process and related manufacturing cost accounts in the general ledger.

In a CIM environment the production information system also generates a set of manufacturing control specifications that are used to direct machine operations in the factory. These specifications include details about the nature, timing, volume, and location of specific manufacturing operations. A separate CIM control program transmits these specifications to factory work centers through a data communications network. Nodes in this network may include machine tools guided by numerical control or CAM programs, robots, a group of related machines in an FMS cell, and/or virtually all machines in the factory if a full-blown CIM operation is employed.

This system continuously monitors the master production schedule for each product. When it is time to initiate a production order for a particular product, the system automatically accesses the appropriate files in the production data base and assembles the necessary records. General data such as the product description and standard unit cost are obtained from the product inventory file. The production order quantity is obtained from the master production schedule. Data necessary to construct the production order detail records are obtained from the operations list file. Materials requisition records are assembled by referring to the bill of materials for the product. Once created, all these records are added to the production data base. The production order then exists within the system as a planned order until an order release transaction is entered by an authorized production planning employee.

Note that although it is possible for this system to print copies of production order and materials requisition documents, it is not essential. In a fully automated factory, all the functions otherwise performed by printed copies of these documents—such as authorizing production operations and materials use and providing reference information on production orders in process—are performed by the information system. When the data in these records are needed for reference purposes, copies of the appropriate documents can be displayed on request on any terminal linked to the system.

Because data on all production activities are entered into the on-line system as these activities occur, the production data base always contains current information on the status of all production orders, employees, machines, materials, schedules, costs, product specifications, and so on. This information is available to production personnel through an on-line inquiry processing system. Such a system facilitates the production management function in a number of ways. The status information helps production planning personnel respond to customer inquiries, expedite work in process, and plan and schedule future production. In addition, production managers and cost accountants can monitor the efficiency, cost, and quality of production work in process by generating, on demand, performance analyses for individual departments, machines, employees, or production orders. The content and format of these analyses may be either predesigned or specified by the user at the time of the inquiry.

Another major advantage of the on-line system involves production scheduling. In a manual or computer-based batch processing system, production schedules are prepared once for each production shift. Such fixed production schedules rarely hold for an entire production shift because of machine breakdowns, employee absences or illnesses, faulty materials, unforeseen work delays, the introduction of rush orders, and other unscheduled events that are common in a factory environment. Factory supervisors must do the best they can to adjust the official production schedule as conditions of this kind arise. An on-line system, however, may be designed to automatically adjust the production schedule in an optimal manner as unforeseen events occur. As shown in Fig. 18.14, on-line terminals located within each factory department may be used to display each department's current production schedule. This continuous optimization of production scheduling accomplishes several objectives, including maximizing factory throughput and machine utilization, minimizing the value of work-in-process inventories, and balancing production order completion times with the relative priorities of the orders.

The on-line production information system also facilitates the product design process. For example, suppose that a customer requests a product that is a slightly modified version of an existing product. A production engineer may use CAD/CAM software to simplify the process of preparing new-product specifications, creating new-product structure records, and possibly programming machine tools to carry out the necessary production operations. Clearly, such a system greatly enhances the ability of a manufacturing company to respond rapidly to changes in customer demand.

Finally, the on-line production information system enables managers to continuously monitor production operations to identify situations in need of immediate attention. For example, the system can check the status of rush orders at periodic intervals and report on any rush orders that are behind schedule. Production operations that have not yet commenced as of the scheduled starting time may be reported to the appropriate supervisor. Significant cost overruns for any operations can be reported as they occur. If materials utilization is in excess of planned amounts, immediate adjustments in purchase requisitions and purchase orders may be made. All of these capabilities greatly enhance the effectiveness of production management.

Note that Fig. 18.14 does not indicate the preparation of periodic departmental performance reports on material and labor costs, as Fig. 18.12 does. It does not do so because an effective on-line production information system changes the pattern of accounting and management control in a factory environment. By providing immediate feedback on the status of the production process, the system flags control problems as they occur and triggers prompt corrective action. Traditional control systems, based on daily, weekly, or monthly summaries of cost, schedule, or quality deviations, are outmoded in the modern factory environment, as the conditions they would report have long since been identified, reported, and corrected.

At Electronics Incorporated batch processing systems have been employed for several years at both manufacturing plants to support the production information system. So that the files are as current as possible, production activity transactions are processed twice during each factory shift. However, during his recent meeting with Grace Healy, Tom Morris became convinced that in order to successfully develop the FMS that the company needs to support its new strategic direction, EI must first implement an on-line production information system in which production activity transactions are captured in machine-readable form as they occur and immediately entered into the system to update the production data base. He felt that one major advantage of an on-line system is that it could detect most data entry errors as the data are entered, so that only correct data are accepted for processing by the system. In addition, an on-line system would enable production schedules to be adjusted on a real-time basis, thus alleviating many of the scheduling problems EI has experienced following the recent expansion of its product lines. Finally, an FMS requires continuously current information on inventories, order status, and work schedules and cannot easily coexist with a batch processing system. Recognizing that the on-line system could not be implemented until EI's production data base was fully integrated, Tom and Grace established a task force charged with designing the new system and preparing a timetable under which the implementation would commence after detailed specifications for the new data base were completed and approved.

Control Objectives and Procedures

Within each accounting cycle, internal control procedures should be designed to ensure that specific objectives are met. Therefore in examining internal controls within the production cycle, one should begin by delineating internal control objectives for the production function and then identify the set of control procedures that will achieve each objective. This approach is followed here.

Internal control procedures within the production cycle must be designed to ensure that the following objectives are met.

1. All production work is properly authorized on the basis of established criteria.
2. Work-in-process inventories are properly safeguarded during the production process.
3. All valid production activity is accurately recorded and processed.
4. Accurate records of the completion status and cost of production work in process are maintained.
5. All production work meets high standards of efficiency and quality.

Numerous internal control procedures have been described in earlier sections of this chapter. Our goal in this section is to associate

Control Objective	Related Control Procedures
Proper authorization of production work	Preparation of master production schedule (MPS) Preparation of production orders Order release Preparation of production schedules Preparation of materials requisitions
Safeguarding of work-in-process inventories	Effective supervision Physical security measures Work-in-process inventory counts and reconciliations to production data base records Documentation of all transfers of work-in-process inventory Separation of authorization, recording, and custodial functions
Accurate recording and processing of production transaction data	Counting all materials and work-in-process inventories transferred within the factory Supervisory review of job time records Automation of factory data capture Edit checks of production data entry Exception reports highlighting discrepancies between actual and expected production results
Accurate records of status of production work in process	Maintaining the security and integrity of the production data base using file labels, file backup procedures, off-site storage of backup files, effective access control procedures, and compatibility tests Work-in-process inventory counts and reconciliations to production data base records Separation of authorization, recording, and custodial functions
Efficiency and quality of production work	Regular comparison of actual and scheduled production Expediting of production work in process Departmental cost performance reports Quality control inspections Quality control performance reports

Table 18.1

Overview of production cycle control objectives and procedures.

these procedures with the five internal control objectives just listed and to identify any other control procedures necessary to achieve each objective. To support this presentation, we give an overview of the control procedures employed to achieve each objective in Table 18.1.

The authorization of production work is the responsibility of the Production Planning Department. As explained earlier, determination of the items and quantities to be produced is based on the MPS, which takes into account finished goods inventory quantities, outstanding customer orders, and forecasted sales. Drawing on the MPS, the production information system often generates planned production orders automatically. In such cases the integrity of the computer program that generates planned orders is of critical importance. Software development control procedures must be in place that provide for effective control over the design, implementation, and maintenance of production planning software.

Final authorization of the production order takes effect as a production planning employee initiates an order release transaction, generally using an on-line terminal. Access controls based on passwords and compatibility tests are essential here to ensure that authorized production planners are the only personnel permitted to enter order releases. In addition, so that the production planner does not release the wrong planned order into production, redundant data checks and/or closed-loop verification should be used to control this process. If a redundant data check is used, the production planner will access the desired planned order record by entering not only the product stock number but also the product description, quantity to be produced, and/or some other redundant data value. If the system cannot find a planned order record having all of these values, it is likely that one or more of the input data values is erroneous. In contrast, if closed-loop verification is used, the production planner accesses the desired planned order by entering the product stock number. The system then retrieves the planned order record; displays the product description, order quantity, and other relevant data on the user's terminal; and requests the user to verify the accuracy of these planned order data prior to releasing the order.

Production plans are documented in the form of production orders, materials requisitions, and production schedules. In turn, these documents authorize employees within the factory to carry out planned production tasks. Therefore the production information system should be designed to ensure that the employees assigned to perform particular production tasks have access to the related documents, either in printed form or in display form on easily accessible on-line terminals. Specifically, production orders should be available to factory employees as production operations are being performed; materials requisitions should be available to inventory stockroom personnel as materials are being issued into production; and departmental production schedules should be available to factory supervisors as they are assigning factory employees to specific production tasks.

Finally, transactions of a less routine nature—such as requisitioning of additional materials, returning excess materials to the inventory stockroom, or approving overtime work for factory employees— should require special authorization procedures involving the approval of supervisory personnel.

Control procedures designed to safeguard work-in-process inventories include effective supervision by factory department heads and stockroom supervisors. Also important are physical security measures such as burglar and fire alarms and plant protection personnel at factory gates. These measures help protect production work in process from damage or theft. Safeguarding of work-in-process inventories is further enhanced by a production information system that maintains accurate and current records of production orders in process. Physical counts of production quantities in process should be made periodically and compared with inventory records maintained in the production data base.

Safeguarding of production work in process is also strengthened by the proper use of documentary controls over the transfer of all work-in-process inventories within the factory. For all such transfers the recipient must sign a document (materials requisition or move ticket) acknowledging the receipt and verifying the accuracy of the quantity recorded. Once these documents are approved, records of the transfers should be promptly entered into the production information system. Alternatively, inventory movements may be recorded using automated data capture devices, such as bar code scanners. If these controls are properly applied, then any shortage of work in process that may arise can be traced to the department and supervisor who are responsible. In turn, this process encourages all factory employees to be conscientious in recording inventory movements.

Accurate recording and processing of data on production activity is crucial in the manufacturing environment, since inaccurate input data can diminish the effectiveness of production scheduling and reduce manufacturing productivity. This objective is accomplished through the following control procedures, many of which have already been mentioned:

1. Counting all materials and work-in-process inventories transferred within the factory, and requiring the recipient to sign the materials requisition or move ticket, acknowledging the accuracy of the count
2. Having supervisory personnel review and approve job time tickets prior to their entry into the production information system
3. Incorporating edit routines into production data entry programs
4. Automating factory data capture
5. Regularly preparing and reviewing exception reports that highlight discrepancies between actual and expected production results

The key to ensuring that accurate records of the completion status and cost of production work in process are maintained is to preserve the security and integrity of the production data base. Among the important control procedures here are data security controls such as internal and external file labels, proper file backup procedures, and off-site storage of backup files. Also of critical importance are access control procedures employing user code numbers and passwords to restrict access to the production data base to authorized personnel. In addition, once authorized users obtain access to the system, compatibility tests should be used to ensure that they perform only the specific operations they have authority to perform. Finally, periodic reconciliation of inventory records of work-in-process quantities to physical counts of production quantities in process also helps to preserve the accuracy of work-in-process inventory records.

Maintaining appropriate separation of functions by keeping the recording, custodial, and authorization functions separate within the production cycle also helps to safeguard work-in-process inventories and to ensure the accuracy of the input transactions and data bases associated with the production information system. The recording functions are primarily performed by the computer and by personnel responsible for entering production activity transactions into the computer. Maintaining custody of work-in-process inventories is essentially the responsibility of departmental supervisors within the factory. The authorization function, represented by the preparation of production orders and production schedules, is the responsibility of production planning personnel, though it is often carried out by the production information system. Effective separation of functions ensures that those who might have an incentive to falsify records of production work in process have no opportunity to do so.

Control of production efficiency is provided by comparisons of actual production with scheduled production and by departmental cost performance reports. Comparisons of actual and scheduled production by factory department supervisors and other production managers establishes a basis for daily control of operations. The expediting function, which closely monitors the progress of high-priority items through production and brings any delays to the attention of the appropriate managers, also contributes to the day-to-day control of production efficiency. Departmental cost performance reports measure production efficiency in financial terms, on a daily, weekly, or monthly basis. In an on-line production information system, production performance may be continuously monitored, which greatly enhances the attainment of high standards of efficiency and quality. In the long run, regular evaluations of the effectiveness and efficiency of factory departments contribute to production efficiency by encouraging supervisors and managers to improve their decisions, policies, and procedures.

One other important aspect of production control is quality control. Quality control inspections should be performed on production work in process at each stage in the manufacturing process. If the work passes inspection, the inspector records this by initialing the move ticket. Any work that does not pass inspection is sent back to the appropriate factory department for reworking, and an inspector's report indicating the rejection is entered into the production information system. The system must then adjust subsequent production schedules to incorporate the necessary rework operations. Periodically, summaries of work failing to pass inspection should be prepared and used by production management to identify any potential quality control problems within the factory.

Reporting

Production planning and scheduling, data capture, data base updating, and internal control are all of critical importance to ensure that production cycle activities are carried out effectively. However, from a management perspective the reports generated as a by-product of production transaction processing are also of critical importance. Scheduled reports, demand reports, and triggered reports all facilitate production management activities. A few examples of such reports are identified in Figs. 18.12, 18.13, and 18.14. This section describes the content and use of these and other production management reports.

Production cost accounting reports prepared on a daily, weekly, and/or monthly basis are a familiar example of scheduled reports. These reports compare actual costs with budgeted or standard costs for particular responsibility centers, such as a machine or workstation, department, or plant. Some reports focus exclusively on materials, labor, or overhead costs, whereas others combine all three of these cost categories. Significant variances of actual from budgeted or standard costs are highlighted. Figure 18.15 is an example of a daily labor cost efficiency report that compares actual and standard hours and costs by operation and by employee for a production department.

Reports prepared for a higher-level responsibility center, such as a plant, generally provide highly aggregated information, whereas reports for lower-level responsibility centers are more detailed. This hierarchical feature of performance reporting was described in Chapter 2. Figure 2.11 illustrates this point and provides some additional examples of performance reports employed within the production function.

While meeting financial standards and budgets is certainly a critical aspect of manufacturing performance, other important dimensions of manufacturing performance should not be overlooked. An effective production information system also provides management with scheduled reports on productivity, quality, and customer service. Productivity reports analyze numbers of units produced per hour or per day, ratios of output quantities to inputs employed, and measures of machine throughput, material yield, and inventory turnover. Quality re-

Figure 18.15
Labor cost efficiency report for a production department

DAILY LABOR COST EFFICIENCY REPORT										
Dept.: 473 Machining			Supervisor: Oscar Nagursky			Shift: Evening		Date: August 12, 1993		
Employee		Order No.	Operation		Standard Rate	Hours		% Efficiency	Total Cost	
No.	Name		No.	Description		Actual	Standard		Actual	Standard
4099	Jones, Hal	1406	352	Drill	$6.00	3.6	3.5	97	$21.60	$21.00
4099	Jones, Hal	1406	382	Burr	$6.00	4.4	4.0	91	26.40	24.00
4166	Bond, Jim	1381	425	Grind	$5.80	3.0	3.6	120	8.70	10.44
4166	Bond, Jim	1406	392	Bore	$5.80	5.0	5.5	110	14.50	15.95
	Dept. totals					128.0	125.4	98	$724.40	$712.40

ports focus on numbers of rejected supplier deliveries, manufacturing defect rates, rework costs, customer return rates, warranty costs, and related quality measures. Customer service reports focus on order processing time, on-time delivery performance, rush order performance, customer return rates, and market share. Reports such as these may be prepared for individual employees, machines, departments, or plants, and they may be prepared daily, weekly, or monthly. Such reports generally provide comparisons of actual results with a standard or with past trends as a basis for gauging the effectiveness of management's performance.[12]

At Electronics Incorporated Tom Morris at first, could not understand why factory supervisors seemed to be unwilling to stress quality improvement according to the company's new strategic emphasis. So he met with several key supervisory personnel to try to find out. They told him that the reports that were being used by their superiors to evaluate their performance stressed productivity, efficiency, and cost control but did not incorporate any measures of quality. Essentially, they had no incentives to stress quality improvement. This meeting made Tom realize that management can only control what it first measures and reports, and therefore the output of the production information system plays a critical role in the effectiveness of production management. Shortly thereafter, he met again with Grace Healy and with Ben Harper, EI's Director of Quality Assurance, to identify quality measures that could be collected from the factory floor, stored in EI's production data base, and incorporated into a new set of management reports. From preliminary guidelines developed during this meeting, Grace and Ben agreed to assign some of their best staff to develop and implement this new reporting system.

Reports that integrate two or more dimensions of manufacturing performance are often very useful to production managers. For example, several companies, including Xerox, ITT, and the Consumer Electronics Corporation division of North American Phillips (NAPCEC), have developed systems of reporting on quality costs. These systems typically utilize several categories of quality costs, including preventive costs (quality planning, design reviews, training, etc.), appraisal costs (inspection, testing, maintenance, etc.), costs of internal failures (design changes, manufacturing rework, material spoilage and scrap, etc.), and costs of external failures (customer returns, warranty costs, product liability costs, etc.). In the system employed by NAPCEC, the chart of accounts was expanded to add accounts for these and several other categories of quality costs. This system generates monthly reports comparing actual quality costs in each category with standard

---

[12] For more on the measurement of manufacturing performance, see Mark E. Beischel and K. Richard Smith, "Linking the Shop Floor to the Top Floor," *Management Accounting* (October 1991): 25–29; and Robert A. Howell, James D. Brown, Stephen R. Soucy, and Allen H. Seed, *Management Accounting in the New Manufacturing Environment* (Montvale, N.J.: National Association of Accountants, 1987), Chapter 4.

costs and with prior-year costs, and analyzing quality costs by product line. By providing detailed breakdowns of quality costs, these reports allow production managers to establish priorities and make effective trade-offs in addressing quality problems.[13]

Inquiry processing is frequently employed by production personnel to retrieve current status and performance information. For example, to respond to customer inquiries about the status of a production order, production personnel might retrieve and display an order status report on an on-line terminal. This report would list the production operations that have been completed, the operations currently in progress, and the scheduled dates and times of operations yet to be performed. Similar information on the current status of machines, materials, employees, and so forth, may also be retrieved on demand.

Inquiry processing systems are also used by production managers to retrieve and display information on cost, quality, or productivity performance. This information may be similar in content and format to that provided by scheduled reports, as described earlier. Two important advantages of inquiry processing are that performance reports may be generated on demand at any time, and that management may choose the responsibility unit and time interval most appropriate to the report's purpose.

Production planners often employ decision support systems to facilitate production planning and scheduling. For example, at its Sparrows Point plant, Bethlehem Steel uses a microcomputer-based spreadsheet simulation model to optimize product flows through its largest steel-making plant (see Focus 18.2). And IBM developed a spreadsheet program for manufacturing capacity planning. This program combines data from the MPS (production quantities of specific products for the current month) with data from the operations list (labor hours required to produce one unit of each product) to develop projections of total employee requirements for a plant over the time horizon of the MPS. Data on inventory levels and production costs are also incorporated into this program. Production managers can use this program to simulate the effects of various production plans on employee requirements, inventory levels, and manufacturing costs.[14]

Cost accountants often download cost information from the production data base to a personal computer to perform analyses of various kinds. For example, cost standards for materials use and labor time requirements for each production operation must be periodically reviewed and adjusted to reflect changes in operating conditions. To obtain the information necessary to perform such a review, a cost accountant might download materials use or labor time data for several

---

[13] For additional details, see Wayne J. Morse, Harold P. Roth, and Kay M. Poston, *Measuring, Planning, and Controlling Quality Costs* (Montvale, N.J.: National Association of Accountants, 1987).

[14] For more details, see Rajen Parekh, "Capacity/Inventory Planning Using a Spreadsheet," *Production and Inventory Management Journal* (First Quarter 1990): 1–3.

18.2 FOCUS

Production Planning and Cost Analysis at Bethlehem Steel

Bethlehem Steel Corporation operates five steel-making plants, including Sparrows Point, one of the largest steel plants in the United States. In each plant, products may pass through as many as 35 major production areas. In addition, a number of different production paths are possible for each product. Clearly, a large variety of production schemes can be used to meet specified product demands. Bethlehem now uses a microcomputer-based model to help determine the best production scheme and the profit contribution margin for each product.

Based on an optimization of product flows through a steel-making plant, the model uses the Lotus 1-2-3 software package on an IBM PC-XT microcomputer to assess the impact of changes in product demands, facility capacities, and costs. This model can quickly and easily answer questions such as these:

- How many turns (eight-hour shifts) per week would the plate mill run if this year's

recent periods to a personal computer file. These data could then be statistically analyzed to determine whether actual average costs are significantly different from standard values.

Downloading can also be used to facilitate the selection of the most appropriate allocation bases for various categories of manufacturing overhead. For example, Novin describes the use of Lotus 1-2-3 to perform regression analysis to determine which of several cost drivers best explains the variation in a particular category of overhead cost.[15] For each category of overhead cost, downloading is used to create a spreadsheet containing values of that cost for the most recent 12 months together with values of several potential base factors that might drive that cost. The overhead cost values are then regressed separately on each of the different base factors. The base factor that best explains variations in the overhead cost is chosen as the allocation base. In some cases multiple regression might be used to select two or more allocation bases for a particular overhead cost category. This process is then repeated for each category of overhead cost until a complete set of overhead allocation bases is established.

A variety of expert systems have been employed in manufacturing applications such as process planning, operations planning, inventory control, process control, factory scheduling, and process design. One

---

[15] Adel M. Novin, "Applying Overhead: How to Find the Right Bases and Rates," *Management Accounting* (March 1992): 40–43.

demand for steel plate products were 500,000 tons?

■ How would the final costs of products be affected if the price of natural gas increased by 20%?

In short, the model provides a fast and user-friendly approach for investigating a variety of scenarios more efficiently than would be possible on a mainframe computer.

The model consists of two modules, a production planning module and a cost module. In the production planning module, three primary operating parameters characterize each major production area. These parameters are yield (in percent), production rate (in tons per hour), and production time available (in hours per week). For given product demands, the module determines the level of production in each area that will maximize yield, subject to production time constraints.

The cost module then uses facility production and use rates from the production planning module as input. Additional inputs to the cost module, supplied by the user, include variable costs, non–volume-related costs, and selling prices. By combining these sets of inputs, the cost module determines the contribution margin for each product. Together, or individually, these two modules allow a user to quickly and easily perform a number of what-if calculations to determine the effects of changes in production or cost parameters.

Source: From Gordon L. Baker, William A. Clark, Jr., Jonathan J. Frund, and Richard E. Wendell, "Production Planning and Cost Analysis on a Microcomputer," *Interfaces* (July/August 1987): 53–60. Reprinted with permission of The Institute of Management Sciences.

of the best-known expert systems is the intelligent scheduling and information system (ISIS), a knowledge-based expert system for factory scheduling developed at Carnegie-Mellon University and first tested at Westinghouse Electric Corporation. Given details about production orders in process and about factory labor and machine capacity, ISIS establishes start and finish times and assigns appropriate resources for each required operation. The system attempts to minimize production costs subject to required completion dates and relative priorities assigned to the production orders. Production schedulers may specify their own preferences and decisions, using the system to advise them on schedule feasibility and consistency.[16]

On-line production information systems frequently employ triggered reports to assist production managers in monitoring factory operations and identifying situations in need of immediate attention. Examples of situations that might trigger a report include machine breakdowns, quality control problems, delays in the production of rush orders, and significant cost overruns. Such reports are generated as soon as these events become known to the system and are displayed on the on-line terminals of the appropriate supervisory personnel without delay.

---

[16] For more on ISIS and other expert systems used in manufacturing, see Yunus Kathawala, "Expert Systems: Implications for Operations Management," *Industrial Management & Data Systems* **90** (6) (1990): 12–16.

These examples illustrate how the power of the computer can substantially improve the quality and timeliness of the information available to production managers. Scheduled reports can regularly provide large volumes of information for reference purposes and also highlight and summarize this information according to various decision-relevant criteria. Demand reports can provide specific information relevant to a particular management purpose. Triggered reports can highlight information about specific events or conditions that require immediate management attention. A well-designed production information system utilizes all of these reporting techniques to enhance the effectiveness of the production management function.

CASE CONCLUSION: IMPROVING PRODUCTION CYCLE INFORMATION SYSTEMS AT ELECTRONICS INCORPORATED

In the 12 months following his initial meeting with Grace Healy, Tom Morris has initiated several information systems development projects to address EI's production management problems. Prototypes for the new quality reporting system were introduced 6 months ago, and EI's factory managers began to learn how to incorporate quality criteria into their evaluations of departmental supervisors. Following final implementation of this system 3 months ago, Tom began to observe a gradual decline in production quality problems at both manufacturing plants. He expects this trend to continue as manufacturing quality control becomes further ingrained in EI's management culture.

Another project arose from a meeting that Tom arranged with Jay Duncan, EI's Director of Cost Accounting, to discuss ways to improve the accuracy of EI's product cost information. Jay suggested that EI's product costing system might be outmoded due to the policy of allocating overhead based exclusively on direct labor hours, but he indicated that he did not have the time or expertise to fix this problem. Tom asked his assistant, Sam Boswell, to work on the problem under Jay's guidance. Sam downloaded several months of cost data from the production data base into a spreadsheet program on his personal computer. He then performed a series of regression analyses to identify the best overhead allocation bases for each major category of overhead cost and to determine the overhead rates associated with each base. Applying these new overhead allocation formulas, he computed revised product cost estimates for each product in EI's product line. The results were very surprising. With the revised product cost estimates as a benchmark the analysis showed that the existing cost accounting system overstated product costs for EI's higher-volume products by up to 15% and understated product costs for lower-volume products by up to 40%. Jay quickly agreed to implement the necessary changes in the cost accounting system. In the meantime Sam's revised product cost estimates were the basis of a complete review of EI's product prices. New prices were established for 80% of EI's products; after this change marketing executives reported that product prices were much more consistent with the prices charged by competitors.

Tom was also pleased that some of EI's other problems had dissipated over the past 12 months. After gaining more experience with the extended product lines, marketing executives were now able to provide much more accurate forecasts of product demand. Reports comparing forecasted and realized demand, prepared each month by EI's information system, provided feedback that was also helpful to marketing executives in preparing these forecasts. In addition, the growth in manufacturing overhead costs at both plants had suddenly leveled off. Tom now understood that higher overhead costs were a natural consequence of the increasing automation of manufacturing processes and of the additional complexity associated with an eightfold expansion of EI's product lines. While the new overhead allocation system would provide a better basis for monitoring and controlling manufacturing overhead costs, Tom was no longer concerned that overhead costs would escalate out of control.

To Tom the most critical project involved integration of the production data base and implementation of an on-line production information system. Specifications for the new data base had been approved seven months ago, and development of the new on-line system had begun shortly thereafter. Progress was slow owing to the poor quality of the data in EI's existing production data files. However, the process of cleaning up this data had partially alleviated EI's production scheduling problems. But projected costs to implement the new on-line system continued to mount, and the projected installation date kept being extended. In the meantime Tom met with several FMS suppliers, one of whom was particularly helpful in providing guidance in developing the new system so that it would properly interface with an FMS installation. While he was very anxious to begin installing the FMS, Tom could only wait for the final design of the on-line system to be completed and reflect on how crucial an effective information system had become to the achievement of EI's strategic goals. ∎

SUMMARY

Production cycle activities include determining what is to be produced, planning how and when it is to be produced, directing the operations necessary to convert raw materials into a finished product, and monitoring the efficiency and quality of these operations. Related data processing activities include preparing production orders and schedules, requisitioning raw materials for the production process, recording production activity, and maintaining records of the status of all production work in process. The focal point of these data processing activities is the maintenance of a production data base that includes information on production orders in process, planned orders, raw materials and finished goods inventories, and engineering specifications for all products. The accounting information system plays an important role by collecting and reporting information on production costs.

Production data processing may be accomplished using either batch processing or on-line processing. The production information system must be designed to capture data on planned production quantities and on production activity within the factory and to generate production schedules, production orders, and materials requisitions, all of which are important in directing and controlling factory operations. The system must incorporate internal controls that ensure proper authorization of all transactions, provide for the safeguarding of production work-in-process inventories, protect the accuracy of all transaction and master file data, and ensure that all production output meets high standards of efficiency and quality. The system is also used to generate a variety of scheduled, demand, and triggered reports that facilitate the production management process. In addition, on-line systems support the use of advanced production management methods, such as flexible manufacturing systems (FMS), manufacturing resource planning (MRP-II), just-in-time (JIT) production, and computer-integrated manufacturing (CIM). As the automation of factory operations becomes increasingly widespread, the use of on-line production information systems is becoming commonplace.

KEY TERMS

Define the following terms.

production cycle	flexible manufacturing systems (FMS)	production order
bill of materials		materials requisition
operations list	backlog	job time ticket
routing sheet	manufacturing resource planning (MRP-II)	move ticket
computer-aided design (CAD)		job order costing
numerical control	just-in-time (JIT) production	process costing
computer-aided manufacturing (CAM)	computer-integrated manufacturing (CIM)	order release
		predetermined overhead rates
CAD/CAM systems	expediting	actual overhead rates
robotics		

DISCUSSION QUESTIONS

18.1 The Consumer Manufacturing Company manufactures home appliances, including refrigerators, stoves, washing machines, and dryers. To support its production operations, the company presently uses a computer-based batch processing system similar to that illustrated in Fig. 18.12. The company is studying the feasibility of automating its factory operations by implementing MRP-II and then progressing to robotics and FMS technology. Discuss the modifications that would need to be made to the company's data processing system in order for these changes to be feasible.

18.2 Advanced factory automation technology generally incorporates an on-line production information system that integrates production and accounting data to provide continuous monitoring and control of production operations. Discuss the implications of these advanced technologies for traditional management accounting control concepts.

18.3 At the ABC Company the Production Department maintains a computerized work order file that contains information on each production order in process, including details about operations performed and scheduled and the current location and status of the job. The Accounting Department maintains a separate computerized work-in-process file that contains accounting information on materials, labor, and overhead costs charged to the job.

The ABC Company has recently acquired a data base management system. The Systems Department has proposed that the work order and work-in-process files maintained by the Production and Accounting departments be combined into an integrated production data base. Personnel in both the Production and the Accounting departments have expressed reservations about this proposal. Discuss the advantages and disadvantages of the proposal.

18.4 It has been reported that Japanese auto manufacturing plants have extensive information systems for measuring and reporting on production quality but very limited information systems for measuring and reporting on production costs. In contrast, information systems at U.S. auto manufacturing plants have exactly the opposite emphasis. Discuss the possible effects of these differences on the behavior of employees and managers and on the products manufactured at these plants.

Problems

18.1 Kids Choice Corporation is a manufacturer and distributor of children's toys. Within the past three years the company's sales volume has declined because several important distributors have dropped the Kids Choice product line. In response the company's top management has just ordered every department in the company to reevaluate its operations, identify possible problems that may be contributing to the company's loss of business, and prepare recommendations for improvement.

You have been asked to evaluate the production information system at Kids Choice. You have learned that production lot sizes are planned on the basis of actual product sales over the past 12 months. Once the production order and materials requisition documents are issued by the production planning department and transmitted to the factory, work commences on the order at the soonest available time. As operations are performed or materials moved in the factory, transaction data are recorded on cards, which are transmitted to the Accounting Department. At the end of each day the accumulated batch of transactions is keyed into the information system, edited, and processed to update the

work-in-process accounting records. When orders are completed, the finished goods are immediately transferred to the shipping area for packaging and shipment to Kids Choice distribution centers or (in some cases) directly to customers. The Accounting Department regularly prepares detailed reports comparing actual and standard manufacturing costs for individual orders and for each factory department.

Required

Could Kids Choice Corporation's production information system have anything to do with the decline in its competitive fortunes? Describe several ways in which this system might be improved.

18.2 What internal control policies and procedures in a production information system would provide the best protection against the following situations?

a. A production order was initiated for a product for which demand no longer exists.

b. Items of work-in-process inventory were stolen by a production employee.

c. The "rush order" tag on a partially completed production job became detached from the materials and lost, causing a costly delay in completing the job.

d. A production employee prepared a materials requisition, used the document to obtain $300 worth of parts from the parts storeroom, and stole the parts.

e. A supervisor's insistence that every worker in his department learn to use every machine in his department resulted in an increase in the proportion of work done by the department that failed to pass quality control tests.

f. A production worker entering job time data over a terminal mistakenly entered 3000 instead of 300 in the "quantity completed" field.

g. A production worker entering job time data over a terminal mistakenly posted the completion of operation number 562 to production order number 7569 instead of to number 7596.

h. A dishonest parts storeroom employee issued parts in quantities 10% lower than those indicated on several materials requisitions and stole the excess quantities.

i. Incorrect keying of the production order number from a materials requisition caused a materials issue to be posted to the wrong production order.

18.3 Your company has just acquired a data base management system that will first be applied to production data. A production order form identical to that in Fig. 18.6 is used. As a first step in the application design, you are to prepare a data base diagram representing the data structure reflected in the production order. Use a format similar to that in Fig. 18.11. Note that the data base will contain only the variable data on the production order, not the constant data.

18.4 Your company has just acquired a data base management system that will first be applied to production data. A job time ticket identical to that in Fig. 18.8 is used to record labor hours employed on specific production orders. As a first step in the application design, you are to prepare a data base diagram representing the data structure reflected in the job time ticket. Use a format similar to that in Fig. 18.11. Note that the data base will contain only the variable data on the job time ticket, not the constant data.

18.5 You are a cost accounting analyst for a large manufacturing firm. You have been assigned to review the accuracy of the labor time standards currently in place for all production operations

performed in the Assembly Department. Data on completed production operations are maintained in a production data base, whose content and format are similar to those shown in Fig. 18.11. To perform the review, you will download the necessary data from this data base to your personal computer for analysis.

Required

a. At a minimum, what data items must you retrieve from the data base to perform your review?

b. What, if any, data will you need from sources other than this data base to complete your review?

c. Briefly explain how you will conduct your review.

d. In addition to the minimum data requirements that you identified in response to part a, what other data items might also be retrieved and analyzed, and for what purposes?

18.6 You are a management consultant for a large public accounting firm. One of your firm's clients is the Willard Corporation, a medium-sized manufacturing firm. Willard's Controller has recently come to you for advice regarding the following problems.

■ The proportion of customer orders filled by the promised delivery date has declined from 90% to 50% within the past year.

■ Production costs have risen dramatically because of increased charges for overtime, rework, and idle time waiting for materials or machines.

■ The company has doubled the number of expediters employed from three to six with no noticeable lessening of the problems.

Required

What are some important questions you would ask the Controller in attempting to gain insight into these problems? Relate your questions specifically to the company's production information system and its approach to production management.

18.7 You are a cost accounting analyst for a large manufacturing firm. Your firm allocates all manufacturing overhead to production work in process in proportion to direct labor hours. However, in recent years the firm has automated many of its production processes, and the direct labor hours required for most products have declined substantially. Your supervisor believes that direct labor hours may no longer be an appropriate basis for overhead allocation and has asked you to perform some analyses using alternative bases, including direct materials costs and machine hours.

Data on completed production operations are maintained in a production data base, whose content and format are similar to those shown in Fig. 18.11. To perform the analysis, you will download the necessary data from this data base to your personal computer.

Required

a. At a minimum, what data items must you retrieve from the data base to perform your analysis?

b. What, if any, data will you need from sources other than this data base to complete your analysis?

c. Explain how you will conduct the analysis.

d. In addition to the minimum data requirements that you identified in response to part a, what other data items might also be retrieved and analyzed, and for what purposes?

18.8 The Caesar Manufacturing Company uses sheet metal and other uncut and unshaped raw materials in its production process. Accordingly, control of materials use and spoilage is a significant management problem. The company utilizes a standard cost system that specifies standard materials use for each operation performed in production. Each departmental supervisor is responsible for materials use variances arising from operations performed by the employees under his or her supervision on the machines in the department. The primary means of control available to supervisors are the assignment of employees to machines and supervision of employee work.

Required

Design a format for a daily materials use report for a factory department. Make any reasonable assumptions about the availability of data for inclusion in the report. Make sure that you take into account the need to relate the report to the supervisor's objectives and decision alternatives. The report should present the vital information effectively and use the principle of management by exception.

18.9 XYZ Company manufactures widgets. Shown in Table 18.2 are (a) an incomplete master production schedule for widgets for the next four weeks, (b) the bill of materials for widgets, and (c) the operations list for widgets.

Required

a. To complete the master production schedule, calculate the number of widgets that should be scheduled for production in each of the next four weeks.

b. From the bill of materials and your answer to part a, determine the number of units of parts A, B, C, and D that must be scheduled for delivery prior to the beginning of the production runs for widgets during each of the next four weeks. Also, compute

Table 18.2
Data for XYZ Company

a. Master Production Schedule

	Week 1	Week 2	Week 3	Week 4
Beginning quantity	100	200	100	200
Scheduled production				
Outstanding orders	200	100	100	0
Forecasted sales	200	400	300	400
Ending quantity	200	100	200	100

b. Bill of Materials

Part	Cost per Part	Quantity per Product
A	$10.00	1
B	4.00	2
C	3.00	4
D	1.00	8

c. Operations List

Operation No.	Machine	Set-up Hours	Machine Hours per 100
1	A	3	6
2	B	2	8
3	B	2	4

the total cost to purchase these parts for each of the four weeks.

c. From the operations list and your answer to part a, determine the number of hours required on machines A and B to complete the scheduled production of widgets during each of the next four weeks.

d. Assume that one hour of direct labor is required for every machine hour. Compute the total direct labor hours required to complete the scheduled production of widgets during each of the next four weeks. Also, assuming that the cost of one hour of direct labor averages $9.00, compute the total cost of direct labor that will be incurred to complete the scheduled production of widgets during each of the four weeks.

e. Assume that manufacturing overhead costs are applied to widgets at the rate of $7.00 per machine hour. Compute the total manufacturing overhead applied to widget production during each of the next four weeks.

18.10 Valpaige Company is an industrial machinery and equipment manufacturer with several production departments. The company employs automated and heavy equipment in its production departments. Consequently, Valpaige has a large Repair and Maintenance Department (R&M) for servicing this equipment.

The operating efficiency of the R&M Department has deteriorated over the past two years. Furthermore, repair and maintenance costs seem to be climbing more rapidly than other department costs. The Assistant Controller has reviewed the operations of the R&M Department and has concluded that the administrative procedures used since the early days of the department are outmoded, due in part to the growth of the company. The two major causes for the deterioration, in the opinion of the Assistant Controller, are an antiquated scheduling system for repair and maintenance work and the actual cost system to distribute the R&M Department's costs to the production departments. The actual costs of the R&M Department are allocated monthly to the production departments on the basis of the number of service calls made each month.

The Assistant Controller has proposed that a formal work order system be implemented for the R&M Department. The production departments would submit a service request to the R&M Depart-

ment for the repairs and/or maintenance to be completed, including a suggested time for having the work done. The Supervisor of the R&M Department would prepare a cost estimate on the service request for the work required (labor and materials) and indicate a suggested time for completing the work on the service request. The R&M Supervisor would return the request to the production department that initiated the request. Once the production department okayed the work by returning a copy of the service request, the R&M Supervisor would prepare a repair and maintenance work order and schedule the job. This work order provides the repair worker with the details of the work to be done and is used to record the actual repair/maintenance hours worked and the materials and supplies used.

Producing departments would be charged for actual labor hours worked at a predetermined standard rate for the type of work required. The parts and supplies would be charged to the production departments at cost.

The Assistant Controller believes that only two documents would be required in this new system: a *repair/maintenance service request* initiated by the production departments and the *repair/maintenance work order* initiated by the R&M Department.

Required

a. For the *repair/maintenance work order* document, answer the following:

1. Identify the data items that would be important to the R&M Department and the production departments, and that should be incorporated into the *work order*.

2. Indicate how many copies of the *work order* would be required, and explain how each copy would be distributed.

b. Prepare a document flow diagram to show how the *repair/maintenance service request* and the *repair/maintenance work order* should be coordinated and used among the departments of Valpaige Company to request and complete the repair and maintenance work, to provide the basis for charging the production departments for the cost of the completed work, and to evaluate the performance of the R&M Department. Provide explanations to the flow diagram as appropriate.
(CMA Examination)

18.11 The Miller Manufacturing Company maintains

an on-line production data base and updates it using an on-line factory data collection system. Upon completing a job, a factory employee enters (1) his or her employee number, (2) the machine number, (3) the production order number, (4) the operation number, and (5) the quantity completed. The system notes the time of each transaction, performs a variety of edit checks on the data input, and if the data are accepted, updates the appropriate records on the data base.

Required

Prepare a program flowchart of an input validation routine that checks the accuracy of each item of input data listed. Note that it will be helpful for the system to access some data within the data base as a means of checking some or all of the input items. However, your flowchart should not illustrate update procedures.

18.12 The Gibson Manufacturing Company utilizes an on-line production information system that has access to the following files stored on a disk unit.

- A production order file, keyed by order number, which keeps track of the operations performed and still to be performed, the quantities in process, and the accumulated materials, labor, and overhead costs for all outstanding production orders
- A finished goods inventory file, keyed by product stock number, which includes data on the quantity on hand and production cost of all finished products in stock
- An employee data file, keyed by employee number, which includes the employee's pay rate and all other essential payroll data.

One of the programs in this system processes data on completed operations. For each operation completed, factory employees enter the following data, using their on-line terminals: production order number, operation number, employee number, quantity completed, start time, and stop time. The program performs various edit checks and validity checks on data entered. If the input is valid, the program updates the production order record for completion of the operation and corresponding labor cost data. If the operation represents the completion of the entire production order, the program updates the finished goods inventory file for the completed stock, writes a completed production order cost summary report on a separate disk file for subsequent processing by another program, and removes the completed production order record from the production order file.

Required

Prepare a macroflowchart of the program described. Assume that checking whether the input data are valid is one macrostep. Show all necessary input and output steps and each major decision and processing step required to complete the necessary processing.

18.13 Processing of production orders in the Monahan Manufacturing Company is performed as follows: At the end of each week the Production Planning Department prepares a list of products and quantities to be produced during the next week. Using this list as a source, data entry personnel key production order release records onto a temporary disk file. Once data entry has been completed, a production order preparation program accesses the operations list (stored on a permanent disk file) for each product to be produced and creates a production order record. For each new production order, the program (1) prints three copies of a production order document, (2) writes the production order record onto a master file of open production orders stored on disk, and (3) prints an operations card for each operation to be performed.

The operations cards are used as turnaround documents. Each card is sent to the factory department where the operation will be performed. After completing an operation, factory employees mark the elapsed time, quantity completed, and other pertinent data on the card and submit it to the data processing center. There a scanner is used to read the operations data and write them onto a temporary disk file. At the end of each day, this file is processed to update the open production order master file. Once this update has been completed, the program generates departmental production schedules for the next day.

Required

a. Prepare a systems flowchart of all operations described.

b. Describe a comprehensive set of internal control policies and procedures for this production data processing system. Prepare a list of internal control objectives, and identify a set of control policies and procedures to attain each control objective. Relate your answer specifically to the data processing operations described.

CASE 18.1: ANY COMPANY, INC.—AN ONGOING COMPREHENSIVE CASE

One of the best ways to learn is to immediately apply what you have studied. The purpose of this case is to allow you to do that. You will select a local company that you can work with. At the end of most chapters you will find an assignment that will have you apply what you have learned using the company you have selected as a reference. This case, then, may become an ongoing case study that you work on throughout the term.

Select a local manufacturing company and obtain permission to study its production information system. Answer the following questions about its system.

1. Identify the people responsible for production planning and scheduling, requisitioning of materials, safeguarding of work-in-process inventories, quality control, and cost accounting. Prepare a partial organization chart, and show where these people are located on this chart.

2. What documents are used in the system? Obtain a sample copy of each document.

3. What master files are maintained in the system? What is the data content of each master file? Prepare (or obtain copies of) record layouts for each file.

4. For each master file, explain how it is updated. Identify each of the different types of transactions that cause the file to be updated. What is the data content of each transaction record? Describe how these transaction data are captured in machine-readable form for entry into the company's computer system. Prepare (or obtain copies of) record layouts for each transaction record.

5. If the company uses a data base management system, prepare (or obtain a copy of) a schema diagram identifying the linkages among the various master files within the system.

6. Prepare (or obtain copies of) system flowcharts for each of the major master file update processes. For each process, indicate whether the company uses batch processing, on-line processing, or a combination of these.

7. Describe internal control procedures employed by the company in this system. Do you feel that the company's internal controls are satisfactory?

8. Identify and obtain sample copies of reports that are prepared by the system. For each report, identify the file or files from which the information originates. Indicate the frequency with which each report is prepared and whether it is prepared on the mainframe computer or a personal computer. Identify who receives each report and how it is used. Evaluate the content and format of each report.

9. Describe how accounting transaction information that originates in this system is transmitted to the company's general ledger system.

CASE 18.2: THE POWERFLOW CORPORATION

The PowerFlow Corporation manufactures pumps, valves, flow meters, and related products for industrial and commercial use. PowerFlow does not manufacture its products for inventory but, rather, manufactures all products in response to customer orders. To ensure fast delivery to its customers, PowerFlow uses just-in-time principles in its purchasing and production processes and an on-line computer system for processing customer orders, purchasing transactions, and production data.

When PowerFlow receives an order from a customer, a series of data processing steps occur. In sequence, these steps are as described in the following paragraphs.

Run #1: Customer order data are entered into the computer system by sales representatives. Each order is classified as either (1) a standard order, for a product that is part of PowerFlow's regular product line, or (2) a custom order, for a product that must be custom-built based on customer specifications. Custom-built products are generally variations on PowerFlow's existing products. The system edits the order entry data and requests reentry of any erroneous data. Then it prices the order by accessing a product price list stored in an on-line disk file. For custom orders pricing is based on estimates derived using prices of similar products. Once the order is priced, the system accesses an on-line customer file to retrieve data on the customer's account and perform a credit check. For customer orders that pass the credit check, the customer file is updated for the estimated order total. For orders that fail the credit check, selected order data are displayed on a Credit Department terminal for follow-up by credit personnel. The complete customer order record is then written onto one of two temporary disk files, one for standard orders and one for custom orders. Each order record is given a priority number based on the customer's required delivery date and credit status and the volume of sales generated by that customer.

Run #2: Custom orders that have passed the credit check are read (in priority order) from the custom order file and processed by an engineering design system under the control of product design engineers linked to the system from on-line terminals. The system uses a CAD/CAM program to develop engineering specifications for each custom-built product. To assist in this process, the system retrieves bills of materials and operations lists for related products from the engineering data base, stored in an on-line disk file. When the design process is complete, the bill of materials and operations list for the new product are added to the engineering data base, and the product becomes part of PowerFlow's standard product line. In addition, manufacturing specifications for numerical control of factory machines are recorded on a temporary disk file, to be utilized as the product is going through the manufacturing process. Finally, product details are added to the custom order record, which is written back onto its temporary disk file.

Run #3: Custom order records are merged into the standard order file and assigned a priority number within the context of the merged file. For convenience, the merged file is subsequently referred to as the "customer order file."

Run #4: Records from the customer order file are processed (in priority order) by a purchase order generation system. This system utilizes material re-

quirements planning (MRP) and manufacturing resource planning (MRP-II) software to identify specific items and quantities of parts and materials required to manufacture the products ordered, to determine the factory resources (labor and machine hours) required, to schedule the production operations through the various factory workstations, and (based on this production schedule) to identify specific times and delivery locations for each batch of parts and materials ordered. To perform these operations, this system references the appropriate bill of materials and operations list records from the engineering data base, and also an on-line final assembly schedule file detailing how each factory machine and workstation is scheduled over the next several weeks. After each order is scheduled, the final assembly schedule file is updated accordingly. Purchase order records are written onto a temporary disk file. Finally, the system generates a planned work order (production order), which is written onto an on-line work order master file.

Run #5: The temporary purchase order file is processed together with an online vendor master file to select a vendor, add the vendor data to the purchase order record, and add the new purchase order to an online file of open purchase orders. Simultaneously, the orders are transmitted to vendors through an electronic data interchange (EDI) network.

Run #6: Planned work order records are read (in priority order) from the work order master file and processed by an order release processing system under the direction of a production planner linked to the system from an on-line terminal. The planner checks the projected availability of all required parts and materials by verifying that vendor acknowledgments have been received for all related purchase orders. The planner also double-checks the final assembly schedule to verify the availability of labor and machine resources for the job. After these verification steps have been completed, the planner enters an order release. The system changes the status of the work order and of all related operations in the final assembly schedule from "planned" to "released for production." Also at this time the system assigns a work order number to the record and prints three copies of a work order document.

Run #7: Prior to the beginning of each factory shift the system reads the final assembly schedule file and the file of outstanding work orders, sorts the records by factory workstation, prepares a work schedule for each workstation, and displays these schedules on on-line terminals located in the offices of each factory department supervisor.

Run #8: As work proceeds on each scheduled work order, production activity records are entered into the system from on-line terminals located throughout the factory. These records include records of receipts of parts and materials from suppliers, completion of production operations, and movement of work in process between factory workstations. These records are processed by an on-line production data processing system that (1) reads and updates the appropriate open purchase order records for all receipts of parts and materials, (2) reads and updates the appropriate work order records and related final assembly schedule records for all completed production operations, and (3) reads and updates the accounting data base (including accounts payable, work-in-process inventory, and general ledger) for the financial effects of all of these production activities. As the final assembly schedule is updated, the display consoles in each factory supervisor's office are also modified to reflect the operations completed.

Run #9: When the work order is completed, the finished products are moved to the shipping dock for packaging and shipment to customers. Records of these transactions are entered into the system from on-line terminals, along with all other production activity records. However, when this "completed order" record is received by the system, a separate shipping and billing process is initiated. The system generates a customer invoice record, appends this record to the master file of outstanding customer invoices, and transmits the invoice record to the customer over the EDI network. At the same time it reads the customer's master file record and updates the account balance for the invoice amount. It also generates a shipping order document, three copies of which are printed on a printer located at the shipping dock. Finally, the system reads and updates the accounting data base (work-in-process inventory and general ledger) for the financial effects of completion and shipment of the work order.

1. Prepare a systems flowchart of each of the computer runs described. To simplify your flowcharts, use only one file symbol to represent the "engineering data base" and the "accounting data base," instead of using separate symbols for each file within these data bases.

2. For each of these computer runs, prepare an outline listing (a) important internal control objectives associated with the run and (b) key internal control policies and procedures directed at achieving each objective.

3. Note that the system described approaches a paperless system, in which records that are traditionally printed in document form are either eliminated or recorded in the computer and displayed on on-line terminals only when necessary. To evaluate this system, make a list of all documents described in this and the previous two chapters. For each document, indicate whether it exists in this system (a) in paper form, (b) as a computer record only, or (c) not at all. For those in category (a), explain how this system might be modified to eliminate the paper version of the document. For those in category (c), explain why the functions of the document are no longer required in this system.

4. Deviations from the production schedule are always possible owing to delays in receiving ordered parts and materials, machine breakdowns, employee absenteeism, and so forth. How can PowerFlow's production information system contribute to (a) the prevention of these problems and (b) the organization's response to these problems if and when they do arise?

5. Runs #8 and #9 result in the preparation of accounting journal entries that are posted to the general ledger. Identify all of these accounting journal entries. What, if any, accounting journal entries would be generated as a by-product of the first seven runs?

6. In run #1 the customer file is updated for the estimated order total. Why is this done? Would this estimate ever be removed from the customer file, and if so, when?

CHAPTER

The Personnel/Payroll Cycle

LEARNING OBJECTIVES

After studying this chapter, you should be able to:

- Describe the key activities and data processing operations included in the personnel/payroll cycle.
- Describe the decision responsibilities and information requirements of the personnel management function.
- Give several examples of the information provided by the accounting information system to support the personnel management function.
- Flowchart data and information flows in typical personnel/payroll data processing systems.
- Evaluate and recommend control policies and procedures for a personnel/payroll data processing system.

**INTEGRATIVE CASE:
ELECTRONICS
INCORPORATED**

Lisa Jackson has just been hired as Vice-President for Human Resources at Electronics Incorporated. In selecting her over 50 other applicants for the position, EI's executive committee cited her enthusiasm, her experience as personnel director for a regional retail chain, and her ideas for implementing such programs as flexible benefits, incentive compensation, and skills inventory management.

However, during her first month at EI, Lisa began to assess the best way to implement these new programs. She discovered that her progress was likely to be obstructed by the current state of EI's personnel and payroll data processing systems. Presently, these two systems operate as separate batch processing systems, each maintaining its own data base on EI's mainframe computer. The payroll system, which is under the control of the Accounting Department, runs biweekly for hourly employees and monthly for employees paid a salary and/or commissions. The personnel system consists of several different files, most of which are updated once weekly, and generates a variety of reports on a weekly, monthly, or quarterly basis. These systems are afflicted with numerous problems, including inconsistencies between the two data bases, unwarranted delays in transaction processing, and excessive waste of staff time in responding to inquiries about employee status and job history.

Lisa has held several meetings with EI's Payroll Supervisor, Director of Personnel Administration, and other personnel managers in her attempts to determine how she might begin implementing her new personnel programs. In most cases she has been told that her proposals "won't work" because they are incompatible with EI's payroll and personnel data processing systems. She has concluded that these systems must be upgraded in some way, but her own data processing experience is limited and she is unsure how to proceed. To complicate matters, the Payroll Supervisor (who reports to EI's Controller) seems threatened by her proposals and has been unwilling to provide any support.

One month after accepting her new position, Lisa reviews her original goals. She concludes that there are five critical questions that must be resolved in order to achieve these goals. These questions are:

1. How can inconsistencies between the payroll and personnel data bases be eliminated?

2. How can timely transaction processing be ensured?

3. How can the amount of personnel staff time consumed in responding to inquiries be reduced?

4. How can the payroll system be modified so that EI's employees can receive flexible benefits and incentive compensation?

5. Can a skills inventory system be implemented to enhance EI's human resource management?

What would you suggest to Lisa Jackson about how EI's personnel and payroll data processing systems might be improved in order to resolve these questions? ■

INTRODUCTION

The **personnel/payroll cycle** is a recurring set of business activities and related data processing operations associated with maintaining an employee work force. The business activities include recruiting, hiring, training, assigning, compensating, evaluating, and discharging employees. These activities constitute the personnel (or human resource) management function. The related data processing operations include maintaining a data base on employee attributes, job history, payroll details, and job performance; processing a variety of transactions to update this data base; calculating employee compensation and benefits; preparing and distributing paychecks; allocating compensation costs to products, departments, projects, and other cost centers; and preparing a variety of reports to meet regulatory requirements and facilitate human resource management.

As the Electronics Incorporated case suggests, weaknesses in a company's personnel and payroll data processing systems can frustrate attempts to implement human resource management programs that are important to its strategic objectives. In particular, the availability of current and accurate employee information is crucial to effective human resource management. As you read this chapter, try to identify some improvements in EI's data processing systems that could help to resolve its problems.

In a manufacturing company the personnel/payroll function is closely related to the production cycle activities described in Chapter 18, because the manufacturing function usually employs more people than any other part of the organization. In addition, manufacturing labor costs must be allocated to production work in progress in order to properly determine product costs. Therefore much of the input data required for personnel and payroll data processing is collected through the manufacturing function. The close relationship between the production and personnel/payroll functions should become apparent as you study this chapter.

This chapter describes the personnel management function and the data processing operations that support personnel management. Particular emphasis is given to the payroll data processing system, which is one of the largest and most important components of the accounting information system in virtually all organizations. The role of the accounting information system in supporting the personnel management function is also stressed. The chapter begins by explaining the decision responsibilities and related information requirements of personnel managers in order to identify the kinds of information that must be provided by data processing systems that support personnel management. The next section describes in general terms the basic functions and procedures that must be performed within the personnel/payroll cycle. These procedures generate the raw data that is the source of information used in human resource management. The remainder of the chapter describes the personnel/payroll data processing system and explains how it supports the basic personnel/payroll cycle functions and procedures and generates information to meet the requirements of personnel managers.

THE PERSONNEL MANAGEMENT FUNCTION

For an understanding of the decision-making responsibilities and related information requirements of personnel managers it is useful to begin by examining the organization structure of the personnel function within a typical business entity. Figure 19.1 provides an example for discussion purposes. However, the personnel management function does not take place entirely within the personnel department. Every supervisor within an organization plays an important role in the management of the personnel under his or her supervision. In this sense the personnel management function is the most decentralized of all the management functions. The personnel department is responsible for those personnel management activities that are most conveniently performed on a centralized basis. This section reviews the personnel management responsibilities and related information requirements of the typical departmental supervisor, as well as of the top personnel executive and the various personnel staff functions identified in Fig. 19.1.

The Top Personnel Executive

The position of the top personnel executive in the organizational structure varies from company to company. In some companies he or she is a vice-president with status equal to that of the vice-presidents for production, marketing, and finance. In other companies the position is subordinate to the Vice-President for Production. In the latter case the primary focus of the personnel function involves production employees, and executives in other functional areas hold primary responsibility for personnel management within their respective areas.

Executives in today's business organizations have become increasingly aware of the vital importance of human resources. As a result, the top personnel executive often participates in top-management planning for corporate resource allocation, contributing a perspective on the human resource management implications of corporate plans for expansion or downsizing of operations. These implications are generally delineated in a human resource plan, which forecasts the organization's needs for personnel with various skills and levels of education and experience, analyzes the supply of human resources both within and outside the organization, and develops objectives and programs to ensure that the organization's human resource needs are met. In addition, the top personnel executive is responsible for developing recom-

Figure 19.1
Sample organization structure for the personnel management function

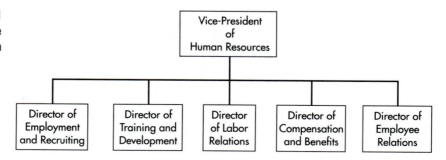

mendations to top management concerning companywide human resources policies. These policies cover such matters as hiring practices, training and development programs, job performance standards, labor relations, health and safety standards, wage and salary plans, and employee benefits.

The top personnel executive is also responsible for overseeing the various personnel staff functions. The staffing plan provides a basis for planning and controlling the activities of employment and recruiting as well as training and development of employee skills. Major decisions in the areas of labor relations, compensation and benefits, and employee relations require the approval of the top personnel executive. The development of a human resources management staff organization, the delegation of authority to carry out human resource management activities, and the monitoring of performance of those activities are further administrative functions of the top personnel executive.

The information needs of the top personnel executive are broad. On the one hand, there is the need for *quantitative* information, such as the number of employees in various skill and experience categories; trends in hours worked, efficiency, accident rates, turnover, and absenteeism; future staffing requirements; cost of alternative wage, salary, and benefits programs; and existing labor market conditions. Formal information systems are designed to fulfill many of these information requirements. On the other hand, the top personnel executive requires *qualitative* information about such factors as employee motivation, morale, abilities, performance, and interpersonal relationships. Factors of this sort are not as easily evaluated through formal information systems. Information of this type is one of the primary products of informal information channels within an organization.

The Personnel Staff Functions

The separation of personnel staff functions into the five departments illustrated in Fig. 19.1 is typical of the way in which human resource management responsibilities are functionally allocated in many large organizations. The primary responsibilities of each of these staff functions are briefly reviewed here.

The Director of Employment and Recruiting is responsible for such activities as developing job specifications identifying the knowledge, skills, and abilities required to perform each job within the organization; recruiting, interviewing, and testing potential employees; and maintaining files of job applicants. The Director also plays an important role in selecting, placing, and counseling new employees. Programs for recruitment, hiring, training, and advancement of members of minority and disadvantaged groups are an important aspect of this function. The information requirements of the Director of Employment are both internal and external. The primary internal information need concerns staffing requirements within the firm, with respect to both job specifications and number of employees required. The primary external information need concerns sources of staffing, such as employment agencies, training schools, and college placement offices.

An example of an information system used in human resource planning to determine personnel requirements is provided by Grumman Data Systems of Bethpage, New York. Most of Grumman's employees are assigned to contracts that involve the development of large-scale information systems for government and commercial clients. When a new contract is under consideration, the information system analyzes current human resource allocations to determine the extent to which the necessary skills are available within the organization. From this analysis the system prepares schedules indicating personnel requirements over the time horizon of the contract and calculating human resource costs. If the contract is obtained, the personnel requirements analysis is provided to the Employment and Recruiting Department so that it can hire the required number of employees within each job category.[1]

The Director of Training and Development is responsible for developing the skills and abilities of personnel at all levels of the organization. At the lowest level this involves training clerical personnel, machine operators, salespeople, and service personnel. At a higher level it entails training supervisors and professional staff personnel. At its highest level it concerns the development of executive skills and experience. Essential elements in the administration of training programs are organizing and planning the program; developing training materials; selecting trainees, instructors, and training sites; and evaluating the results. Administration of executive development programs includes determining desired executive capabilities, selecting candidates, choosing a program of development, and evaluating the results. The training and development function requires information about the knowledge and skills that employees need in order to perform their jobs effectively; this information is derived from the job specifications prepared by the employment and recruiting function.

A system established by AT&T's Corporate Human Resources Organization in Morristown, New Jersey, provides a good example of an information system that supports the development of executive skills. AT&T is a large organization that employs around 120,000 managers at various levels. To provide a framework for companywide career development and management succession, AT&T implemented the Leadership Continuity Program (LCP) in 1988. This program focuses on developing the leadership skills of 3000 high-potential managers through a series of challenging assignments selected to prepare them for increased responsibilities. To provide a means of tracking and monitoring the development of LCP participants, an information system called the LCP Tracking System (LTS) was created. This system is used to identify candidate pools for succession planning for key man-

---

[1] Margot Dugan, "Meeting a Competitive Challenge: Upgrading Computer Resources at Grumman Data Systems," *Industrial Management* (September/October 1990): 21–23.

agement positions, to identify reasons for management turnover by analyzing historical data on previous LCP managers, to identify managerial and professional skills and talents required companywide to respond to changing business requirements, and to produce a variety of standard and demand reports to serve the information requirements of human resource management. According to LCP manager Jerry Rocco, the LTS provides managers at both AT&T's headquarters and its business units and divisions with the ability to plan and carry out the development of leaders needed to manage a new and continually changing organization.[2]

If a significant percentage of a company's employees belong to a union, the Director of Labor Relations plays an important role in the organization. This individual's primary responsibility is to prepare for and conduct collective bargaining negotiations with union representatives. This job requires information about the costs and benefits of alternative wage and benefit plans and other contract provisions. Other responsibilities of the labor relations function include handling grievances and arbitration with respect to the union contract and maintaining compliance with federal and state labor legislation.

The Director of Compensation and Benefits is responsible for establishing a compensation system that will encourage prospective employees to seek and accept employment with the organization and that will motivate existing employees to stay with the organization and to perform their jobs at a high level of effectiveness. At the most basic level this function involves establishing wage and salary levels for each job grade or classification within the organization. Also important are employee benefits, including group life, health, and disability insurance; pension plans; and vacation and sick leave policies. Various forms of incentive compensation are also widely used, including merit pay and bonus plans, sales commissions, profit-sharing plans, and employee stockownership plans. In addition, executive compensation packages generally include such incentives as stock options and bonuses based on financial measures of company performance. The information requirements of the compensation and benefits function are both internal and external. Internal information is required about the relative value of various jobs within the organization. External information is required about wages, salaries, and benefits provided for comparable jobs by other organizations operating in the same labor markets and industries.

The Director of Employee Relations is responsible for a variety of programs designed to enhance the welfare and morale of employees. They include recreation programs, employee suggestion plans, health and safety programs, day-care programs for the children of employees, plant cafeterias, in-house publications, and employee credit unions.

---

[2] Jerry Rocco, "Computers Track High-Potential Managers," *HR Magazine* (August 1991): 66–68.

This function also encompasses the maintenance of an up-to-date employee data base containing personnel information on all employees within the organization. This data base includes detailed information about each employee's personal, educational, and employment background; job qualifications; job history with the organization; training programs completed; current and prior levels of compensation and benefits; and performance reviews and evaluations. The employee data base is the heart of the human resources information system (HRIS) and is the source of a variety of personnel reports useful to managers throughout the organization.

A state-of-the-art human resources information system is HR-Link, originally developed for the human resources department at Apple Canada in 1988. This system, written in a data base language, was designed to provide a powerful information retrieval tool that would be easy to use and modify. The original system included modules for applicant tracking, maintenance of basic employee records, compensation and benefits, employee development, position control, and employee time and attendance reporting. Additional modules planned for the future include human resources planning, career planning, succession planning, health and safety, and labor relations management. Apple was so impressed with this system that it eventually marketed the software as part of its own product line.[3]

The Departmental Supervisor

A very important group of users (and providers) of human resources information consists of supervisory personnel in charge of various departments and other units throughout an organization. Each departmental supervisor is directly responsible for the day-to-day planning, coordination, and control of that department's employees. The supervisor must organize the tasks to be performed, assign employees to jobs, coordinate their activities, motivate them, monitor their performance, evaluate their abilities, provide on-the-job training, enforce company policies, and prepare reports and other information on employee activities.

Much of the information required by departmental supervisors to perform their personnel management functions may be obtained simply from observation and experience. The formal information system provides useful supplementary information, however, such as statistics concerning the productivity (output per work hour) of each employee at each job within the department. Other useful information on individual employees includes levels of skill and training attained, performance ratings on various jobs, quality of work performed, and rates of absenteeism and tardiness. Qualitative assessments provided by other employees or supervisors concerning personality and character may also be useful.

---

[3] Kenneth Duff, "HR-Link: An HRIS from Apple Canada," *Personnel* (May 1990): 6–14.

Summary   It should be apparent that effective personnel management requires information from a variety of sources, both within and outside the organization. The primary internal source is the human resources information system maintained by the employee relations function. The accounting information system is another important internal source. Through its payroll processing function the accounting information system maintains and provides information on individual employees' wage or salary history, productivity, attendance, compensation, benefits, and so forth. Aggregate statistics—such as total numbers of employees by department, total hours worked, total labor cost, average wage rate, absenteeism rates, turnover rates, and average and total fringe benefit costs—and trends in these statistics can be generated as a by-product of payroll processing.

Numerous other sources of information inside and outside the organization are also important to personnel managers. Examples include job specifications and forecasts of staffing requirements by department provided by departmental managers; surveys of labor market conditions provided by the Economics Department or by external trade associations; information on the costs of current and proposed employee wage and benefit plans, often generated by decision support systems utilizing simulation methods; information on employee grievances and morale provided by employees themselves, by supervisors, or by labor unions; information on legal requirements and company compliance with equal employment opportunity (EEO) guidelines; and information about prospective employees provided by employment agencies, vocational and trade schools, and college placement offices.

Although effective human resource managers must be aware of all these sources of personnel information, the remainder of this chapter focuses primarily on the payroll processing system, since it is the segment of the accounting information system that directly serves the human resource management function. The next section of the chapter briefly describes the personnel cycle and then describes in greater detail the basic functions and procedures that are performed within the payroll cycle of a typical business organization.

BASIC PERSONNEL/ PAYROLL CYCLE FUNCTIONS AND PROCEDURES

What this chapter refers to as the "personnel/payroll cycle" is perhaps better thought of as two related cycles. The **personnel cycle** refers to the stages in the relationship between the employee and the organization, including recruitment, hiring, placement, training, compensation, performance evaluation, career development, and separation. The **payroll cycle** refers to the set of activities associated with calculating and dispensing employee compensation and thus might be viewed as a subset of the personnel cycle. These two cycles are closely related in the sense that they both utilize the same data base, the employee data base. However, these cycles differ in their duration and focus. In particular, the duration of the personnel cycle varies with the period of employment of the employee but is often many years in length, while the duration of the payroll cycle is both fixed and short. In addition, the focus of the personnel cycle, in terms of information requirements, is very broad, while the payroll cycle utilizes a very narrow and precise set of information.

This section begins by briefly reviewing the stages of the personnel cycle, with emphasis given to data processing and information requirements. Then the basic functions and procedures performed within the payroll cycle are examined at a very general level. These functions include (1) recording employee activity as the basis for calculating gross compensation and benefits, (2) preparing payrolls, which includes the calculation of gross and net pay and all payroll deductions, (3) calculating employer-paid benefits, (4) updating the employee data base, (5) disbursing employee pay, (6) accounting for the cost of employee compensation, and (7) posting summary accounting transactions to the general ledger.

The Personnel Cycle

The human resources department generally maintains a **position control file** listing all job positions within the organization, indicating their location (department and supervisor), the job description, the qualifications required, and the pay grade or base level of compensation. When a job opening arises, data in the position control file are used as the basis for advertising the position and recruiting someone to fill it. When prospective employees apply for the position, they complete an application form that provides information about their background and qualifications. These data are entered into an **applicant file.** Applicants whose qualifications meet the job requirements are interviewed and tested, and the results are recorded in the applicant file. The top candidates for the position are ranked, and the position is offered to each in turn until it is accepted. At this point data from the newly hired employee's application record are transmitted to his or her employee record.

Before starting on the job, the new employee goes through an orientation and training program. The orientation is designed to familiarize the employee with the company and its policies and benefits. As part of this program, the employee provides basic payroll data, such as Social Security number and number of payroll exemptions claimed, and selects levels of insurance coverage, retirement plan options, and other benefit programs. These data are added to the employee record. Data relating to the employee's completion of initial training programs are also entered into the employee record.

As employees perform their assigned jobs, data are collected about their time on the job, including attendance, sick leave, vacation leave, and the distribution of job time among projects, departments, and products. Data on employee output, productivity, or other performance measures may also be collected. As the employee is paid, payroll history data are generated providing details about gross pay, payroll deductions, and net pay for each payroll period. All of these data become part of the employee record.

On a periodic basis each employee will undergo a performance appraisal in which previous job performance is evaluated by supervisory personnel and recommendations are made for improvement. Employees will also receive additional training to improve their effectiveness and make them eligible for promotion to higher-level positions. Data on each employee's performance appraisal and training programs completed become part of the employee record. As employees are promoted or transferred to new positions within the organization, job history records are created giving details about positions formerly held. These job history records also become part of the employee record. As employees develop additional skills, qualifications, and abilities through their training and experience, details about these are encoded and added to the employee record.

By now it should be apparent that what we have referred to as the "employee record" is actually part of a large and complex employee data base. To summarize the discussion to this point, the employee data base includes the following data about each employee.

- Prior educational and employment background
- Current job grade, title, department, and supervisor
- Current level of compensation and benefits
- Training programs completed
- Time and attendance
- Output, productivity, and performance measures
- Special skills and abilities
- Payroll history
- Performance appraisals
- Job history within the organization

The employee data base, together with the position control file and the applicant files for each position, form the organization's human resources data base. The human resources data base stores large volumes of information on the organization's job positions, prospective employees, and the skills, experience, performance, and compensation of its current employees. This data base is a very useful source of information to support the management of human resources within the organization.

The employee data base is updated as data are collected and processed on each employee's job status, productivity and performance, education and training, and other employment activity. From the standpoint of payroll accounting, the processing of transactions relating to new employees, employee terminations, and changes in employee compensation and benefits is of critical importance. These transactions must be processed on a timely basis so that the employee data base is properly updated by the time that payroll processing occurs. In addition, care must be taken to ensure that all such transactions are properly authorized and accurately processed.

The end of the personnel cycle is reached when the employee's association with the organization is terminated. Termination may be the result of the employee's retiring, being discharged due to unsatisfactory performance or a reduction in work force, or resigning voluntarily to pursue other employment. Details about the employee's separation from the organization (reasons for discharge or voluntary turnover) should be collected and maintained as part of the employee's data base record. The organization should continue to maintain a record for each separated employee in the employee data base for some period of time following the employee's separation.

Recording Employee Activity

The basic data processing functions and procedures performed in the payroll cycle are illustrated in Fig. 19.2. The payroll process is very routine, always occurs at fixed intervals (e.g., weekly or monthly), involves carrying out a well-defined set of activities, and places a high premium on accuracy.

The first step in the payroll cycle is to record data on those aspects of each employee's job activity that form the basis for calculating employee pay. The most common example involves the collection of data on hours worked for employees who are paid an hourly wage, including factory workers, service personnel, and many others. Traditionally, this has been done using an **employee clock card**, like the one shown in Fig. 19.3. This card identifies the employee and the pay period and records the employee's arrival and departure time for each work shift; the latter data are recorded on the card automatically by a time clock into which the card is inserted by the employee. Alternatively, these data may be recorded electronically using employee badge readers or other automatic data collection devices.

It is also common to record data on the allocation of employee time among various jobs, tasks, departments, projects, contracts, and so on. For example, in a factory environment the job time ticket (see Fig. 18.8) is used to record the application of a factory employee's time to a specific production order in process. Job time data form the basis for manufacturing cost accounting, in which labor costs are allocated to production jobs and to departments or other cost centers.

Since the employee clock card and job time ticket are prepared independently of each other, it is common practice to compare and reconcile them prior to doing payroll calculations. This reconciliation step checks whether the total time spent at work by each employee is equal to the sum of the time spent on all jobs on which the employee worked during the day. This internal check helps to verify the accuracy of time-worked data before these data are used in payroll processing and cost accounting.

In previous chapters we have discussed variations in the way that particular transactions are processed in different industries. With respect to payroll processing variations do not occur across industries as much as they occur across employee types, generally within the same company. In particular, the primary variations involve the basis for

Figure 19.2
Basic payroll cycle data processing functions and procedures

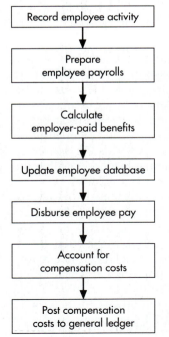

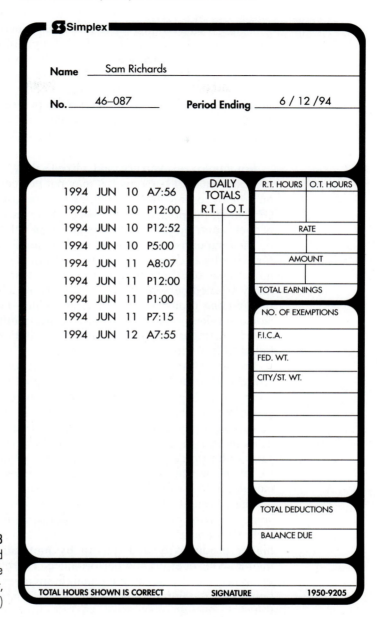

⊠ Simplex		

Name   Sam Richards

No.   46–087   **Period Ending**   6 / 12 /94

	DAILY TOTALS	R.T. HOURS	O.T. HOURS
1994 JUN 10 A7:56	R.T. | O.T.		
1994 JUN 10 P12:00			
1994 JUN 10 P12:52		RATE	
1994 JUN 10 P5:00			
1994 JUN 11 A8:07		AMOUNT	
1994 JUN 11 P12:00			
1994 JUN 11 P1:00		TOTAL EARNINGS	
1994 JUN 11 P7:15		NO. OF EXEMPTIONS	
1994 JUN 12 A7:55		F.I.C.A.	
		FED. WT.	
		CITY/ST. WT.	
		TOTAL DEDUCTIONS	
		BALANCE DUE	
TOTAL HOURS SHOWN IS CORRECT	**SIGNATURE**		1950-9205

Figure 19.3
Employee clock card
(*Source:* Courtesy of Simplex Time
Recorder Co., Gardner,
Massachusetts.)

calculation of employee pay. Some of the most common alternatives to the payment of a straight hourly wage include (1) an hourly wage plus a piece rate based on the number of units produced, (2) a straight salary, which may or may not include extra pay for overtime work, (3) a straight sales commission, generally based on the volume of sales made by the employee, (4) salary plus sales commission, and (5) salary plus incentive bonus based on individual, group, or company performance (e.g., profit sharing). Each of these variations is briefly discussed here.

Employees paid on a piece-rate basis generally earn an hourly wage for completing a standard number of units of production. In addition, for every unit completed in excess of the standard, the employee earns a fixed amount (the piece rate). From the standpoint of payroll processing, this process requires that data be collected both on the number of hours worked and on the number of units produced for each employee. In addition, job time data may be collected so that the employee's labor costs may be assigned to specific production orders, departments, contracts, and so forth.

For employees who are paid a fixed salary, including managerial and professional staff personnel, it may not be necessary to report any data on employee time and attendance for purposes of payroll processing. Of course, the presence of salaried employees on the job and the value of their contributions to the organization will be informally monitored by their supervisors. Some salaried personnel do receive overtime pay for working evening, weekends, and holidays, and this obviously requires that overtime hours be measured and recorded. In addition, many salaried personnel must report on the allocation of their total job time among projects, contracts, or clients. For employees of professional service organizations (such as accounting or law firms) this job time reporting is very important because it directly affects the amounts billed to firm clients for services rendered.

Employees involved in the sales function are often paid either a straight sales commission or a salary plus a sales commission. The commission is generally calculated as a percentage of the dollar sales generated by the salesperson. In addition, some sales personnel receive bonus payments for sales made in excess of a quota. Whenever sales incentives are paid, the payroll system must interface with the sales order processing or billing system so that the dollar sales volume for each salesperson is captured by the payroll system for use in calculating the sales commissions.

The payment of incentive bonuses to employees, in proportion to some measure of the employee's performance, is becoming increasingly common as U.S. companies respond to competitive pressures for higher productivity and quality by motivating employees to attain higher levels of effort and performance. There are many different types of bonus plans. One simple example involves paying all employees a bonus that is computed by formula and is contingent on some organizational performance measure, such as total output or net profit. For example, the formula might specify that the total bonus will be 10% of reported net income and that this total amount will be allocated among nonexecutive personnel in proportion to their total annual compensation. Two other popular incentive compensation schemes are group incentives and gainsharing. Group incentive plans involve the payment of bonuses to employees within a department or work team based on some measure of the group's performance. Gainsharing involves computing the benefits obtained from a program to reduce costs or improve productivity or quality and then sharing these benefits with employees through bonus payments. Finally, the compensation of top executives generally includes incentives, including stock options and performance bonuses based on financial measures such as net income or return on investment.

To develop and implement an incentive compensation system, an organization must have an information system that is capable of handling the additional data processing requirements. For example, when Lisa Jackson began to explore the possibility of initiating an incentive compensation plan for supervisory and production employees at Electronics Incorporated, she discovered that few measures of employee productivity and performance were routinely collected and maintained on EI's information systems. Furthermore, those measures that were available were maintained on EI's personnel information system, and the interface between this system and EI's payroll data processing system was, at best, primitive. In short, deficiencies in EI's information systems threatened the development of an important strategic initiative for the company.

However, under many incentive bonus plans the incentive compensation is not paid as part of the employee's regular (e.g., weekly or monthly) compensation. Instead, the bonuses are generally paid quarterly or annually, at the time when financial measures of performance become available. This means that the incentive compensation system need not be fully integrated with the payroll system. Instead, a separate system may be used to (quarterly or annually) collect the necessary performance data, compute the amount of each employee's bonus, and report these bonus amounts to the payroll processing function to be added to each employee's gross pay for the bonus period only.

Payroll Preparation

Payroll preparation may be viewed as a three-step process. First, each employee's gross pay must be computed. Second, each employee's payroll deductions and net pay are computed. Third, employee paychecks and earnings statements are prepared, along with a report listing each employee's payroll details for the pay period.

For employees paid an hourly wage, gross pay is computed by multiplying hours worked times the employee's wage rate and then adding any applicable premium for overtime or piecework. U.S. federal law requires that hourly employees who work more than 40 hours in a week must be paid an overtime wage of one and one-half times the employee's regular wage rate. In many cases companies also pay overtime wages, sometimes at double the regular rate, for work on Sundays or holidays. The premium for piecework is simply the number of units produced in excess of the standard multiplied by the piece rate.

For salaried employees gross pay is a fraction of the annual salary, where the fraction is based on the length of the payroll period (e.g., one-twelfth if paid monthly). Sales commissions are generally computed by multiplying the salesperson's total dollar sales for the payroll period by the commission rate. Sales bonuses may be a fixed amount or an incremental percentage of sales volume in excess of the sales quota for the payroll period. Other incentive bonus amounts are generally computed quarterly or annually, based on the stipulated bonus formula. In all of these cases, gross pay is simply equal to the salary amount plus any applicable commission or bonus.

After the employee's gross pay is determined, payroll deductions and net pay are computed. Payroll deductions fall into two broad categories: payroll tax withholdings and voluntary deductions. Payroll tax withholdings include federal, state, and local income tax and Social Security taxes levied on the employee but withheld from the employee's pay and remitted to the taxing authority by the employer. State and local income tax withholdings are often computed simply as a percentage of gross pay. Federal income tax withholdings are based on the employee's marital status and number of exemptions claimed and are determined by referencing the applicable withholding table from a set of tables furnished by the Internal Revenue Service (IRS). Social Security tax withholdings are computed as a percentage of the employee's gross pay up to the point where year-to-date gross pay reaches a predefined limit, after which no additional Social Security taxes are levied on the employee. Periodically, the employer must file a report with the IRS listing all federal income tax and Social Security tax withholdings and must remit the total amounts withheld to the government. Companies with small payrolls must file this report at least once each month, while companies with larger payrolls are required to file more frequently.

Voluntary deductions include contributions to a pension plan; premiums for group life, health, and disability insurance; union dues; and contributions to United Way or other charities, and various others. Pension contributions are often a standard percentage of the employee's gross pay, but additional amounts may be contributed at the employee's option. Insurance coverage is optional, and the premiums are based on the amount of coverage chosen by the employee. Union dues are determined by employees through their collective bargaining unit. For each such deduction category, the employer must periodically prepare a report of all withholdings and remit the total amount to the appropriate organization.

Once all payroll deductions have been computed, the employee's net pay is calculated by subtracting the total of all payroll deductions from gross pay. Then each employee's paycheck and earnings statement are prepared. The employee's earnings statement lists the amount of gross pay, deductions from gross pay, and net pay for the current payroll period. Year-to-date totals of gross pay, net pay, and some deduction items are also listed on each earnings statement. The paycheck is prepared for the amount of the employee's net pay.

To summarize the results of the payroll process, many companies also prepare a report called a **payroll register**, which lists each employee's gross pay, payroll deductions, and net pay in a multicolumn format. At the conclusion of the payroll process the accuracy of payroll calculations may be checked by cross-footing the payroll register to verify that total gross pay for all employees is equal to the sum of total net pay plus the total of all payroll deductions for the payroll period. After this is done, the column totals on the payroll register are the basis for preparing a summary journal entry debiting the payroll control account for the gross pay amount, crediting cash for the net pay amount, and crediting assorted liability accounts for the various payroll deductions.

Calculating Employer-Paid Benefits

Some payroll taxes and employee benefits are paid directly by the employer rather than by the employee through payroll withholdings. Payroll taxes levied on the employer include Social Security taxes and unemployment insurance taxes. Specifically, for every dollar of Social Security taxes paid by the employee, the employer must also contribute a dollar. In addition, federal and state laws require employers to contribute a specified percentage of each employee's gross, up to a maximum limit, to federal and state unemployment compensation insurance funds. The employer may also contribute some or all of the amounts paid for the employee's health, disability, and life insurance premiums, as well as amounts paid into the employee's retirement program. In addition, many employers compensate full-time employees for time not worked during holidays, illnesses, vacations, and absences related to military obligations, pregnancy, bereavement, and so forth. The amounts of these various employee benefits are calculated on the basis of contractual arrangements with employees and/or their collective bargaining units.

Some employers offer their employees what are called **flexible benefits plans**, under which each employee receives some minimum coverage in medical insurance and pension contributions, plus additional benefit "credits" that they use for additional benefits of their choice, such as additional vacation time, more health insurance, or payments for child care. These plans are sometimes called **cafeteria-style benefit plans** because they offer a menu of options. As suggested by the discussion of Electronics Incorporated at the beginning of the chapter, the implementation of such plans places additional demands on an organization's payroll data processing system, because the system employed to determine each employee's benefit allocation must be flexible enough to allow for many different possibilities.

Updating Employee Records

Each employee's record in the employee data base must be updated on the basis of data indicating the current period's employee activity, payroll, and benefits. First, the time and attendance records in the data base are updated for the current period's time and attendance data. If employee output or performance data (such as units produced or sales volume) are used in computing gross pay, these data will also be posted to corresponding fields in the employee record. Second, each employee's payroll master record is updated by increasing the year-to-date and quarter-to-date totals of gross pay, individual payroll deduction and employer-paid benefit amounts, and net pay by the corresponding amounts for the current payroll period.

Payroll Disbursement

Most employees are paid either by check or by direct deposit of the net pay amount in a bank account designated by the employee. In the latter case the employee generally receives a facsimile of a paycheck indicating the amount deposited together with the earnings statement. The paychecks (or facsimiles) and earnings statements may be distributed to employees by supervisory personnel or through the organization's internal mail service.

If employees are paid through direct deposit, the payroll system must generate a series of payroll deposit files, one for each bank through which payroll deposits are made. Each of these files will contain a record for each of the employees whose accounts are maintained at that bank. Each record will include the employee's Social Security number, name, bank account number, and net pay amount to be deposited. Each of these files is transmitted electronically to the corresponding bank, which will then deposit the net pay amounts in each employee's bank account.

Employee paychecks are generally not drawn on the organization's regular bank account. Instead, for control purposes a separate payroll bank account is used. Therefore when the payroll is prepared, a check must be drawn on the organization's regular bank account to transfer the total net pay into the payroll bank account. After the payroll register is prepared and cross-footed to verify the accuracy of the payroll calculations, this check is drawn and deposited in the payroll bank account. Employee direct deposits and paychecks are then charged against this account. Theoretically, the organization's payroll bank account should have a zero balance both at the beginning and end of this process; this makes it easier to detect any possible errors or irregularities in the processing of employee paychecks.

Accounting for Compensation Costs

Personnel compensation costs represent one of the largest costs (often *the* largest cost) of doing business. Therefore it is important to keep track of how these costs contribute to the organization's various objectives and operations. This task is the responsibility of the cost accounting function. The primary basis for accounting for compensation costs consists of job time tickets and similar records detailing how each employee's time on the job has been distributed among various production jobs, projects, contracts, or clients. As explained in Chapter 18, job time tickets result in the charging of direct labor costs to specific production orders in process. Similarly, job accounting input data on professional staff personnel indicate how their compensation costs should be charged to such things as a research and development project, a project to design and implement a new information system, a sales promotion campaign, a construction project, a government contract, or a contract to provide professional services to an outside client, to name just a few possible examples.

Once the correct allocation of compensation costs has been calculated, summary journal entries are prepared to recognize the allocation. The first entry credits the payroll control account for the gross pay of all employees during the payroll period and debits this total to various expense and inventory accounts. For example, direct labor costs are debited to the work-in-process inventory account. The second entry credits various liability accounts associated with employer-paid benefits, including payroll tax obligations and liabilities for insurance premiums, retirement plan contributions, vacation pay, and so forth. The debit portion of this journal entry allocates the total credit to the same expense and inventory accounts as the first entry; in fact, these two entries are often combined.

In addition to the allocation of compensation costs to general ledger accounts by means of a journal entry, the cost accounting system also allocates these same costs in other ways for other purposes. For example, for purposes of measuring product costs as a basis for setting prices, direct labor and related compensation costs are allocated to specific production orders. Also, for management control purposes employee compensation costs are allocated to departments, contracts, and other cost centers. For example, the direct labor costs associated with each employee are charged to the factory department in which that employee works. This provides a basis for management to measure and evaluate the performance of factory supervisors in controlling costs within their departments.

Similar journal entries and cost allocations are prepared to allocate compensation costs associated with indirect factory labor, professional staff personnel, sales personnel, supervisory personnel, and so forth. From these cost allocations the cost accounting function prepares weekly or monthly reports analyzing compensation costs by department, project, contract, and the like. These reports generally compare actual costs during the current period with costs for prior periods and/or to budgeted or standard costs, and they provide a useful tool for management control of compensation costs.

General Ledger The final step in payroll cycle data processing is the posting of summary accounting journal entries to the general ledger. Several journal entries are required, as mentioned in previous sections. First, the payroll preparation process generates a journal entry that summarizes the preparation of employee payrolls, including the calculation of payroll deductions and the preparation of employee paychecks. An example of this journal entry follows.

Payroll Control	$80,545.00	
Federal Income Tax Withholdings Payable		$13,930.80
FICA Tax Withholdings Payable		6,040.90
State Income Tax Withholdings Payable		4,856.25
Group Insurance Premiums Payable		2,296.65
Retirement Fund Contributions Payable		3,027.25
Savings Bond Deductions Payable		1,173.40
Union Dues Deductions Payable		749.75
Cash		48,470.00

The debit to the payroll control account represents the total gross pay of all employees, while the credit to cash represents the total net pay. The various liability accounts shown here represent the most common payroll deductions. Periodically, separate checks are prepared and issued to pay each of these liabilities.

Second, the cost accounting process generates journal entries that summarize the distribution of total compensation costs to various expense and inventory accounts. For example, the amount debited to the payroll control account in the previous entry would be allocated as follows:

Work-in-Process Inventory	$24,849.65	
Manufacturing Overhead	14,274.80	
General and Administrative Expense	23,365.45	
Selling Expense	18,055.10	
Payroll Control		$80,545.00

Each of the accounts debited in this entry is a control account, which means that corresponding to each of these accounts there is a subsidiary ledger providing a more detailed breakdown of costs and expenses. Specifically, the work-in-process inventory subsidiary ledger shows how direct labor costs are charged to individual production orders in process. The manufacturing overhead subsidiary ledger shows how indirect factory labor costs are broken down into such categories as materials handling labor, maintenance labor, and supervisory salaries. The general and administrative expense subsidiary ledger shows how expenditures for administrative compensation are broken down into such categories as clerical wages, professional staff salaries, and managerial salaries. Finally, the selling expense subsidiary ledger shows how compensation costs associated with the selling function are broken down into such categories as sales salaries, sales commissions, clerical wages, and managerial salaries.

The amount credited to the payroll control account should be exactly equal to the amount debited to this account in the previous entry.

If these amounts are not equal, an error has occurred either in calculating payrolls or in payroll cost distribution. It is important to pinpoint the source of any such error and correct it before employee paychecks are distributed. This form of internal check is called a **zero balance check** because the balance of the payroll control account should be zero after these two journal entries are posted.

The cost accounting process must also allocate the total of all employer-paid benefits to the same set of expense and inventory control accounts as in the previous journal entry. For example:

Work-in-Process Inventory	$7,026.52	
Manufacturing Overhead	4,036.36	
General and Administrative Expense	6,606.84	
Selling Expense	5,105.28	
FICA Taxes Payable		$6,040.90
State Unemployment Taxes Payable		4,027.25
Federal Unemployment Taxes Payable		966.54
Group Insurance Premiums Payable		2,296.65
Retirement Fund Contributions Payable		3,027.25
Liability for Vacation Pay		6,417.10

In this example the total debit amount is allocated to the four expense and inventory accounts in exactly the same proportion as in the previous entry. With respect to the credit amounts, the credit to FICA Taxes Payable is equal to the credit to FICA Tax Withholdings Payable in the first journal entry, since the FICA tax is levied in an equal amount on both the employer and employee. The federal and state unemployment taxes are levied on the employer based on a percentage of gross pay set by legislation; these amounts go into a fund that is used to provide financial assistance to qualified persons who become temporarily unemployed. In this example the amounts of group insurance premiums and retirement fund contributions are identical to the corresponding amounts withheld from the employee's payroll, indicating that this employer has a policy of matching, dollar for dollar, the employee's contributions to these programs. As with payroll deductions, separate checks are periodically prepared and issued to pay each of these liabilities. Finally, the liability for vacation pay is based on the number of days that the employee is entitled to be compensated while absent from work for vacations, holidays, illnesses, and so on, in proportion to the total number of days in the work year. The vacation pay liability is effectively "paid" when the employee is compensated for one or more days of absence from work.

Payroll Service Bureaus

As mentioned earlier, there are few variations in the way that employee payrolls are processed in various industries. However, one important variation that deserves mention is that many companies do not process their own payrolls but, instead, contract with independent payroll processing service bureaus. According to one survey, about 35% of organizations use this approach.[4] The payroll service bureau maintains payroll master file records for client employees, receives employee activity records from the client at the end of each pay period, and processes these data to prepare the client's employee paychecks and earnings statements, together with payroll summary reports.

The popularity of payroll services bureaus, especially with smaller businesses, can be attributed to the increasing complexity of federal and state legislation affecting payrolls, payroll deductions, and payroll tax filings. Payroll service bureaus maintain a trained staff of specialists who are familiar with the applicable laws and regulations and are prepared to make any necessary changes in their payroll systems to reflect the frequent changes in these laws and regulations. In addition, in comparison to a small business, a service bureau is generally better prepared to deal with such problems as equipment failure, loss of file data, absence of key employees, or catastrophic events such as fire or flood.

There are some disadvantages to using payroll service bureaus. First, because the payroll data are physically maintained at the service bureau site, the client has less control over its payroll data, which raises a concern for the security of that data. Second, if the client requests a special report—for example, to provide employee information for management control purposes—the service bureau charges a separate fee for this service. Third, the service bureau may be slow to respond to client requests for special reports or other customized services. Before contracting the services of a payroll service bureau, an organization must carefully consider whether the advantages are sufficient to offset these disadvantages.

THE PERSONNEL/ PAYROLL DATA PROCESSING SYSTEM

The personnel/payroll data processing system consists of two closely related systems. First is the personnel data processing system, which emphasizes the collection, processing, storage, and reporting of data and information relating to an organization's human resources. Second is the payroll data processing system, which focuses on the determination of employee compensation and the preparation of paychecks. These systems execute the basic personnel/payroll cycle functions and procedures described in the previous section. In many companies these two data processing systems are fully integrated, while in many others they are not. This section describes and illustrates the use of computer-based systems to process personnel and payroll data, with emphasis on methods of data capture, preliminary data processing procedures, data base updating, and reporting. Internal control objec-

---

[4] Michael J. Kavanagh, Hal G. Gueutal, and Scott I. Tannenbaum, *Human Resource Information Systems: Development and Application* (Boston: PWS-KENT, 1990): 301.

tives and procedures associated with personnel and payroll data processing are also explained.

Data Capture Within the personnel/payroll cycle, data on two key transaction records must be captured in machine-readable form. The first is the **personnel change record,** which documents any change in one or more employee attributes, such as job title, department, training programs completed, added skills and qualifications, performance assessments, wage rate or salary, payroll withholding status, employment status (new hire, unpaid leave, or separation), and so forth. The second basic transaction record is the employee activity record. For employees paid an hourly wage, employee activity records indicate the number of hours that the employee spent on the job each day during the most recent payroll period and the allocation of those hours among the various jobs to which the employee was assigned. For salaried employees, time and attendance data are generally not captured on a regular basis, since gross compensation per payroll period is a fixed amount. However, as mentioned earlier in the chapter, many salaried personnel must report the distribution of their total job time among projects, contracts, clients, and so forth. For employees who are paid sales commissions or other special forms of compensation, the employee activity record must indicate the dollar sales volume or other factors upon which compensation is based. This section describes ways in which these transaction records may be captured in machine-readable form.

Personnel change records originate either with the employee (such as for changes in voluntary payroll deductions or payroll withholding status) or with line supervisory personnel. The content of a personnel change record varies with the type of change but will generally include the employee number and name, the effective change date, and details of the change. These data are generally keyed into the computer system from on-line terminals. The traditional approach is to first record the data manually on "personnel change" documents and to then transmit these to a data entry department to be keyed into the system. It is increasingly common for these data to be keyed in directly by supervisory personnel or by authorized personnel staff employees at the time the personnel change record is created.

Special forms are generally used by salaried employees for reporting job time distribution data. For example, programmers are commonly required to prepare daily time sheets to record their hours worked on specific projects, programs, and tasks (coding, testing, etc.). Such forms are often filled out manually by the employee and collected in a batch to be keyed into the system by data entry personnel. In more contemporary systems each employee enters his or her job time data directly into the computer, using an on-line data entry terminal that presents an image of the form on the display screen.

For sales personnel paid on a commission basis, the data needed to calculate gross compensation may be captured automatically as a by-product of sales order processing. Similarly, the data required to calculate other forms of incentive compensation are often available in other information systems within the organization and may be captured automatically through some type of interface with the payroll data processing system.

For hourly employees there are two distinct employee activity records: the job time record and the time and attendance record. The capture of factory job time data in machine-readable form is discussed in Chapter 18 and is not discussed further here. However, the reader may wish to refer to Fig. 18.9 for an illustration of how bar coding may be used to capture such data automatically.

Time and attendance data for hourly employees are generally entered into the computer in one of two ways. The first way is to use employee clock cards, like the one illustrated in Fig. 19.3, as source documents for batch data entry. At the end of each pay period the clock cards are collected, and the total time worked is manually computed and recorded on each card. The batch of clock cards is then transmitted to a data entry department, where the employee number and time worked are keyed in for each employee. These records are then stored on a temporary file to await payroll processing.

So that manual computations and keying of clock card data are avoided, special data collection devices may be used to capture time and attendance data automatically. For example, employees may punch in and out of work by inserting an identification badge into a badge reader that records the employee number, date, and time (see Focus 19.1). These records are then accumulated on an input file that is

19.1 FOCUS

Electronic Timekeeping at Scott Paper

When Scott Paper, a leading manufacturer and marketer of sanitary tissue paper products, replaced traditional time clocks with an automated time and attendance system at its largest plant, in Mobile, Alabama, it gained unexpected savings. Now instead of collecting time cards by hand from the twenty-five hundred employees, making calculations manually, and then keying the numbers into the payroll system, Scott collects the time and attendance data by bar code readers. The data are calculated electronically and are fed automatically into the payroll system. In addition to tracking straight time, overtime, holiday pay, and so on, the system is programmed to take into account many very complex work rules and schedules. The system has

processed to update payroll files and generate paychecks at the end of each payroll period. This approach is often used in a factory environment, but it may be used for clerical employees as well.

Preliminary Data Processing Procedures

This section describes the preliminary steps involved in processing personnel change transactions and employee time and attendance transactions.

The processing of personnel change transactions takes place in two steps, as illustrated in the systems flowchart in Fig. 19.4. The first step begins with the submission of a recommended personnel change from an on-line terminal, as described previously in the section on data capture. As this data entry occurs, the system performs various edit checks to verify the accuracy of the data, including field checks, validity checks, range checks, and reasonableness tests. Possible errors identified by these edit checks are flagged for immediate review and correction by the terminal operator. After passing these checks, the personnel change transaction is entered into the human resources information system, but it is not processed directly to update the affected portions of the employee data base. Instead, it is assigned a status code of "recommended" or "approval pending" and recorded on a transaction file with other pending personnel change records.

On a regular basis a senior personnel manager (someone who has the authority to approve personnel changes) will access this transaction file from an on-line terminal and review each recommended personnel change. When the senior personnel manager decides that a recom-

---

dramatically reduced the burden on payroll and accounting resources. What's more, this straightforward (even unglamorous) form of automation has paid for itself in a single year.

All twenty-five hundred workers are expected to be on the system by June 1992. Transactions are validated immediately, and files are updated in background mode, which frees readers for efficient input. Any bottleneck caused by a data processing lag time would be noticeable immediately, because 45% of the clocking in and out occurs in three 2-minute periods during the workday.

The new electronic timekeeping system enables workers to go straight to their work areas to clock in instead of congregating in sometimes distant "clock alleys." Reporting directly to their work area gives employees more chance to talk with the operators, engineers, and mechanics coming off shift. This contact encourages a more interactive work style. In addition, the accuracy of the payroll information is excellent. There are fewer errors in the paychecks, and far less administrative time is spent checking and correcting.

Source: From Claire Barth, "Automating Time and Attendance," *Management Accounting* (June 1992):14–15. Reprinted with permission of the Institute of Management Accountants.

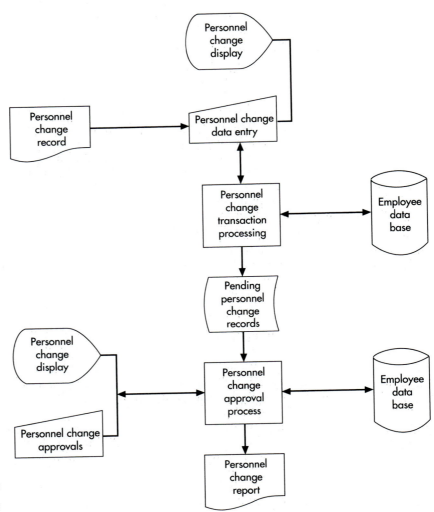

Figure 19.4
Data entry and processing of personnel change transactions

mended personnel change should be approved, he or she will enter a change in the status code to "approved" and indicate the effective date. Before processing this change, the system will examine the identity of the person approving the change and perform a compatibility test to ensure that this person has the authority to approve the personnel change. If so, the system will change the status code to "approved" and append the effective date and the manager's identity code to the change record. When the effective date arrives, the system will automatically update the appropriate records in the employee data base.

This approval procedure for personnel change transactions is very important for purposes of internal control owing to the nature of these transactions, which include changes in wage rates, salaries, commission rates, payroll deductions, employment status, job grade or rank, and related factors that affect the organization's financial and legal relationships with its employees. Thus the risk of possible fraudulent transactions is high, as is the organization's financial exposure in the event that erroneous or fraudulent transactions are actually processed. By separating responsibility for the recommendation and approval steps, and by limiting the number of people who are authorized to approve permanent changes in the employee data base, an organization can more effectively protect itself against these additional risks and exposures.

One other important internal control procedure is indicated in Fig. 19.4. As pending personnel change transactions are reviewed and dispensed with by the senior personnel manager, the human resources information system should prepare a series of personnel change reports indicating the status and disposition of each pending personnel change. A separate report is prepared for each department within the organization, and a copy of each department's report is transmitted to the departmental supervisor. Additional copies are prepared for personnel or other staff employees responsible for recommending personnel change transactions. Supervisory and staff personnel who receive these reports should review them carefully to verify that the details of each listed transaction are consistent with the original personnel changes that they recommended. This provides additional protection against the risks of unauthorized personnel change transactions.

Employee time and attendance records are generally accumulated on temporary files during the payroll period, to be processed in one large batch at the end of the payroll period. Sort, merge, and edit procedures similar to those employed in preliminary processing of batches of sales order transactions (see Fig. 16.8) are generally used. Because payroll processing is invariably performed sequentially by employee number, one essential step is to sort the time and attendance records into sequential order. If a central payroll department processes payrolls for several locations, it is efficient to merge the time and attendance files from each location into a single transaction file.

Edit checks performed on each time and attendance record include a field check for numeric data in the employee number and hours worked fields, a validity check of the employee number, and a limit check of hours worked. A count of the number of employee records for each department is also made, for comparison with the correct departmental employee counts maintained on the employee data base. Hash totals of employee numbers and hours worked may also be tallied, to be checked against like totals after subsequent payroll runs. For factory employees the computer may also reconcile the time worked data obtained from clock cards with the time worked data obtained from job time tickets. Any discrepancies identified by these various tests must be investigated and corrected prior to regular payroll processing. Control is facilitated by preparing printed listings of employees and hours worked by department, to be distributed to departmental supervisors for their review.

Data Base Update   Once employee records have been updated for personnel change transactions, and once employee time and attendance data have been cap-
tured in machine-readable form and validated by edit programs, the
next step is payroll processing. This includes calculating employee
payrolls, preparing paychecks, and updating the payroll-related portions of the employee data base. The update portion of payroll processing involves appending each employee's current period time and
attendance data and earnings data to the data base and modifying the
accumulated quarter-to-date and year-to-date totals of gross pay, net
pay, and all payroll deductions for each employee.

This section describes the basic content and structure of the employee data base, with emphasis on those parts of the data base that are
most directly related to payroll processing. Next, payroll processing
procedures are explained, including the process of updating the employee data base to reflect the effects of payroll processing. Batch
processing procedures are stressed, but on-line processing procedures
are also briefly explained.

The Employee Data Base. In many organizations a payroll processing
system organized around a payroll data base operates under the control
of the Accounting Department, while a separate human resources
information system organized around a personnel data base operates
under the control of the Personnel Department. Recall, for example,
that this is precisely the situation encountered by Lisa Jackson at
Electronics Incorporated. According to a 1988 survey, 70% of companies operate separate payroll and human resources information systems,
though the trend is definitely toward integration of these two systems.[5]
Integration of these systems is quite logical, since each of the data
bases is organized around the same entity—the employee. The integrated data base is simply referred to as the employee data base.

An example of the content and organization of an employee data
base appears in Fig. 19.5. This data base is organized as a tree structure
with the employee master record at the root. Shown at the top of the
figure by record name only (without data contents) are seven records
that contain personnel details about each employee. Shown at the
bottom, below the employee master record, are four records that
contain data required for payroll processing and cost accounting.

Each of the personnel detail records shown is a repeating group; that
is, there is a one-to-many relationship between the employee master
record and each one of these seven detail record types. For example,
for each employee there will be one or more "formal education detail"
records, each containing the name of a secondary school, college, or
university attended by the employee, the dates attended, the major

---

[5] As reported in Michael J. Kavanagh, Hal G. Gueutal, and Scott I. Tannenbaum,
Human Resource Information Systems: Development and Application (Boston: PWS-
KENT, 1990), Chapter 10.

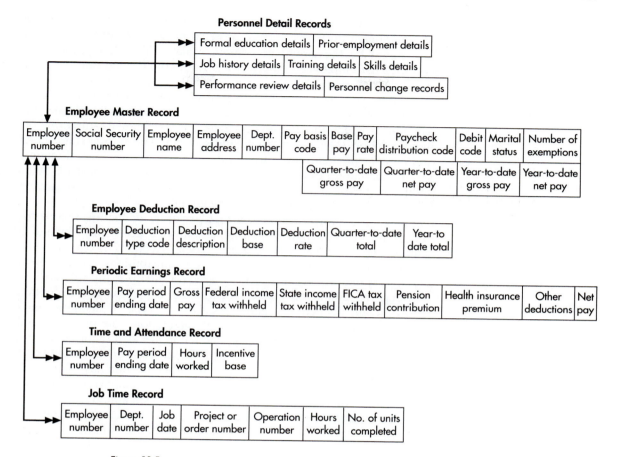

Figure 19.5
A sample employee data base

field of study, and the name and date granted of any degree earned by the employee. Similarly, prior-employment records list details about each job the employee held prior to this one; job history records list details about each position the employee held within this organization; training records list details about each training program the employee has completed while employed with the organization; skills records list details about all employment-related skills possessed by the employee; performance review records list details about each performance assessment that the employee has received while employed with the organization; and personnel change records list the details of each personnel change transaction relating to the employee. Each of these detail records includes the employee number, which links it to the appropriate employee master record. Since the primary focus of our discussion here is payroll processing, the specific data content of these various personnel detail records is not shown.

Within the employee master record there are several fields that require further explanation. The pay basis code indicates whether the employee is paid on an hourly, salaried, or other basis. The "base pay" field indicates the amount of the employee's annual pay that is not contingent on hours worked or performance measures; generally, this would be the employee's annual salary. The "pay rate" field specifies the employee's hourly wage rate, commission rate, or other incentive pay rate. The paycheck distribution code indicates whether the employee's paycheck is delivered directly to the employee or is deposited in the employee's bank account. The debit code indicates the account to which the employee's gross pay is charged—direct labor, indirect labor, sales commission, and so forth. The marital status code and number of exemptions are required for computing federal income tax withholdings. Finally, the quarter-to-date and year-to-date fields show the employee's cumulative gross and net pay since the beginning of the current quarter and year, respectively.

For each employee there will be a separate deduction record for each type of deduction from that employee's gross pay, including federal and state tax withholdings, Social Security taxes, life and health insurance premiums, pension fund contributions, savings bond purchases, and union dues. Thus there is a one-to-many relationship between the employee master record and the employee deduction record. Each deduction record specifies the type of deduction and (where applicable) the basis or rate of calculation. The quarterly and year-to-date totals of each payroll deduction are also recorded here.

Each periodic earnings record lists the amount of the employee's gross pay, net pay, and all payroll deductions for one payroll period. Essentially, these are the data that appear on the employee's earnings statement accompanying each paycheck. For each employee there are multiple earnings records in the data base, one for each payroll period.

Each time and attendance record indicates the number of hours worked by a wage-earning employee during a particular payroll period. For salaried employees this record would simply indicate the employee's status (full-time, half-time, on leave, etc.). For employees paid on an incentive basis, the "incentive base" field would specify the value of whatever factor the incentive calculation is based on, such as dollar sales or units of production in excess of quota.

Finally, each job time record indicates the number of hours that the employee worked on each specific job or project during each pay period.

As is the case at many companies, the payroll and personnel data bases at Electronics Incorporated are separately maintained, as mentioned earlier. The Personnel Department maintains a personnel master file that is linked to a series of personnel detail records such as those shown at the top of Fig. 19.5, while the Accounting Department maintains an employee payroll master file that is linked to a series of payroll detail records such as those shown at the bottom of Fig. 19.5. This arrangement has caused a number of problems for EI. One problem is that some redundant data items are maintained in the two master files (such as name and address, pay details, marital status, and details about the employee's benefits and related payroll deductions). While the amount of wasted storage space is relatively small, the greater problem is that data items that appear in both files and should have identical values occasionally do not agree, which forces someone to track down the error. Often these errors are caused by data processing delays, since both master files are updated weekly but at different times during the week. Another problem is that on-line access to the two data bases has been limited for two reasons: a shortage of display terminals and an archaic inquiry processing system that provides good security but is not user-friendly. In turn, this leads to delays in responding to employee inquiries and change requests, as personnel staff employees who have difficulty accessing the computer system instead try to manually extract the necessary information from paper documents maintained in filing cabinets.

To begin to address these problems, Lisa Jackson arranged to meet with Grace Healy, EI's Chief Information Officer. At the beginning of their meeting Grace told Lisa that a proposal had been made three years earlier to resolve these problems. The proposal would have integrated EI's personnel and payroll master files and all of the related detail records. In addition, the batch updating process would have been replaced with an on-line system incorporating a user-friendly software interface that would enable users from many locations to retrieve or update information in the data base. This proposal had been strongly resisted by EI's Payroll Supervisor and its Controller, who contended that the plan would threaten the security and integrity of the payroll files by making these files accessible to many different users, some of whom might find a way to break the system's security codes and make unauthorized changes in payroll data. In the end the Controller's arguments had carried the day, and the personnel and payroll systems had remained unchanged.

However, Grace was pleased that Lisa had raised these issues and suggested that the time might be right to put the proposal forward again. First, EI's former controller had retired six months earlier, and his replacement seemed more receptive to change. Second, more secure software interfaces were now commercially available. Grace was also enthusiastic about Lisa's suggestions that EI implement flexible benefits, incentive compensation, and a skills inventory information system. According to Grace, while these plans were not feasible given the current state of EI's personnel and payroll systems, the development of an integrated system would allow Lisa to implement her ideas with little difficulty. In short, after learning that an obsolete information system could interfere with her plans to move EI's personnel functions in a new strategic direction, Lisa now discovered that the implementation of new information technology could actually facilitate her plans. She left her meeting with Grace feeling much more positive about her future at EI.

Batch Processing. For two reasons it is natural for payroll processing to be performed in batch mode. First, it is standard practice to prepare the essential products of payroll processing—employee paychecks and earnings statements—only at the end of each pay period. Second, the activity ratio in payroll processing is generally close to 100%, which makes sequential batch processing much more efficient than on-line processing.

A computer-based batch processing system for payroll processing is shown in Fig. 19.6. Note that all personnel change transactions, including new hires and terminations, must be processed to update the employee data base prior to payroll processing. In addition, transaction data editing and correction procedures must be completed prior to the final payroll processing run, because it would not be appropriate to reject the transaction records of any employee who is entitled to a paycheck. For convenience it is assumed here that the payroll transactions input includes both time and attendance records, upon which the

Figure 19.6
Batch processing of employee payrolls

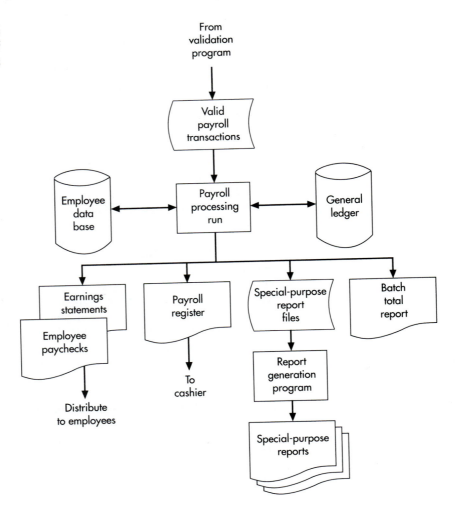

calculation of payrolls is based, and job time records, upon which the distribution of compensation costs to general ledger accounts is based.

Processing occurs in employee number sequence. For each employee the payroll master record and the time and attendance record are read and processed to calculate the employee's gross pay. Then each of the employee's deduction records are read, and the amount of each payroll deduction is determined. Next, all payroll deductions are summed, and the total is subtracted from gross pay to obtain net pay. Cumulative quarter-to-date and year-to-date totals of gross pay, deductions, and net pay for the employee are computed and posted to the employee's payroll master and deduction records in the employee data base. Details of each employee payroll are printed on the payroll register report, and employee paychecks and earnings statements are printed. Each employee's time and attendance record and job time record are appended to the employee data base, along with an earnings record for the current payroll period.

As each payroll transaction is processed, the system must determine the general ledger account or accounts to which each employee's compensation cost should be charged. This determination is based on the job time record and/or the debit code in the employee master record. As payroll processing proceeds, the system maintains running totals of amounts debited to each account affected. At the conclusion of the run these totals are the basis for the journal entry summarizing the cost distribution for the entire payroll. From the column totals from the payroll register, the journal entry summarizing the credit distribution (e.g., net pay plus liabilities for payroll withholdings) is also obtained. These summary journal entries are then posted to the general ledger. In addition, the journal entries and other batch totals are printed on a summary batch total report.

As payroll processing proceeds, any employee information required for special-purpose reports is recorded on a temporary disk file. At the conclusion of the process each of these special-purpose report files is processed by a report generation program to print the related report. Government agencies require many of these reports, including quarterly and annual federal, state, and local income tax reports; Social Security tax reports; employee W-2 (annual tax withholdings) forms; equal employment opportunity (EEO) compliance reports; and employee pension benefits reports.

Another category of special-purpose payroll reports involves those employees paid on a direct-deposit basis. Pay data for these employees are written onto a series of files, one for each bank into which direct deposits are made. In addition, a facsimile (nonnegotiable copy) of the paycheck, rather than an actual check, is printed for each employee. At the conclusion of payroll processing, a printout of the direct-deposit file for each bank is generated, and a copy of each file and its printout are transmitted to the appropriate bank to effect the necessary funds transfers.

On-Line Processing. As discussed earlier, on-line processing of personnel change transactions is common (see Fig. 19.4). When entered, these transactions are often given an effective date that differs from the input date. This means that a programmed routine must be activated each day to review all approved personnel change transactions that exist within the employee data base and to compare their effective date with the current date. For each transaction for which these dates match, the system will modify the related fields in the employee master record and/or other affected records.

On-line processing of employee payrolls is unusual but sometimes necessary. For example, it is needed when an error is made in an employee paycheck that requires a replacement check to be generated outside the regular payroll process. It is also needed for a new employee who should have received a first paycheck but didn't because of a delay in updating the payroll files. Ideally, the payroll system will be flawless so that situations of this type never arise. Of course, in the real world these situations do arise, and the payroll system must be able to deal with them. From a systems standpoint this is not too difficult; the system must be able to interface with an on-line user to obtain the necessary data, perform all of the same calculations and record updates described earlier in the section on batch processing, and, if necessary, reverse the effects of any errors in the general ledger accounts. The more critical issue here is to ensure that internal controls are in place to prevent any possible abuse of this special procedure. Such controls should include limiting the number of persons who have the authority to process such special transactions, using password access controls to prevent unauthorized users from initiating such transactions, and requiring that all such transactions be subject to special approval before they are executed.

Control Objectives and Procedures

Within each accounting cycle, internal control procedures should be designed to ensure that specific objectives are met. Therefore, when one examines internal controls within the personnel/payroll cycle, it is useful to begin by delineating internal control objectives for the personnel/payroll function. Then the set of control procedures that will achieve each objective may be identified. This approach is followed here.

Internal control procedures within the personnel/payroll cycle must be designed to ensure that the following objectives are met.

1. All personnel and payroll transactions are properly authorized on the basis of established criteria.

2. All employees are assigned to productive work suited to their capabilities, and they carry out that work effectively and efficiently.

3. All valid payroll and personnel change transactions are accurately recorded and processed.

4. Accurate employee personnel and payroll master file records are maintained.

5. All disbursements for employee compensation are properly made to or on behalf of the appropriate employees.

Numerous internal control procedures have been described in earlier sections of this chapter. Our goal in this section is to associate these procedures with the five internal control objectives listed here and to identify any other control procedures necessary to achieve each objective.

Proper authorization procedures must be employed with respect to personnel change transactions (including new hires and terminations), employee activity transactions, and inquiries into the employee data base. These procedures are important because of certain risks that are inherent in the payroll area, including the insertion of fictitious employee records into the payroll files; preservation of the records of terminated employees in the payroll files in order to misappropriate their paychecks; falsification of wage rates, salaries, or commission rates; and fraudulent inflation of hours worked, units of piecework produced, or other bases for pay calculations. In addition, it is important to protect the privacy and confidentiality of employee personnel and payroll information by preventing unauthorized access to that information.

The review and approval of personnel change transactions is the responsibility of supervisory employees within the Personnel Department. An important control procedure here is that all personnel changes should be approved by an employee other than the person recommending the change. The approval procedure may involve simply reading and signing a transaction document. However, it is becoming more common for transaction approvals to be performed through an on-line information system, as described earlier in this chapter. In this case authorization procedures are enforced by having the system verify the validity of the user's account number and password and check the compatibility of each transaction request with the level of authority assigned to that user. If personnel change transactions are entered by a data entry department, the data entry clerks should check that the transaction documentation originated from, and was approved by, the Personnel Department. In either case the system should generate a set of reports listing all personnel changes processed for each department within the organization. These reports should be reviewed by departmental supervisors and by a senior personnel staff employee who can recognize any unauthorized change transactions.

Employee time and attendance records are generally collected automatically from a time clock or a badge reader. Job time records are sometimes captured automatically as well but are often prepared manually by each employee. In any case all employee activity records should be reviewed and approved by departmental supervisors in order to detect any obvious discrepancies. Finally, the privacy of employee data should be protected by limiting access to the employee data base to authorized personnel only and by enforcing these restrictions using a system of password access controls.

The assignment of employees to work tasks and the evaluation of employee performance are important obligations of departmental supervisors. Both careful observation of employees at work and periodic review of quantitative performance measures are essential. Formal reports evaluating employee performance should be prepared regularly, and supervisors should hold a conference with each employee to review these evaluations. As employee performance is invariably reflected in departmental performance, regular evaluation of departmental and supervisory performance is also an important element of control. Computer systems can enhance the effectiveness with which supervisors carry out this task by providing more complete and timely information on employee productivity and performance.

Checking the accuracy of payroll transaction input and processing is of critical importance because of the sheer complexity of payroll processing. Legal and tax requirements are already extensive, and changes in these requirements continue to occur. These complexities increase the risks of errors in payroll calculations and related processes. In addition, there are the usual risks of incorrect or falsified payroll and personnel change transaction input, including inflated hours worked data and fraudulent wage or salary increases. Authorization procedures can prevent or detect some incorrect input data, but these procedures are not foolproof. Hence, additional procedures should be employed to check the accuracy with which payroll and personnel change transactions are recorded and processed.

Several techniques for this purpose have already been mentioned. For example, badge readers may be used to automatically capture employee time and attendance data in machine-readable form. The payroll processing system should automatically reconcile time and attendance data with employee job time records. For payroll change transactions that are entered from on-line terminals, the data entry software should employ prompting or preformatting to simplify the data entry process. All personnel change transaction data and employee activity data should be subjected to edit checks to determine the validity of employee numbers and the reasonableness of such data items as changes in employee compensation, hours worked per pay period, and units of production or dollar sales volume in excess of quota. Data entry procedures should also include redundant data checks or closed-loop verification to ensure that personnel and payroll file change transactions are not accidentally posted to the wrong employee file records.

Since payroll processing is invariably performed in batch mode, batch totals are an important technique for ensuring accurate transaction processing. One important batch total is a count of the number of employees scheduled to receive paychecks each pay period; from the employee data base this total can be determined in advance of payroll processing and then compared with the actual number of paychecks generated by the system. Other important batch totals include the sum of all salary increases, wage rate increases, and dollar sales volume for computing sales commissions. Hash totals of hours worked and other transaction data might also be utilized. These various batch totals should be prepared during the early stages of transaction processing and checked against comparable batch totals generated by the system at each subsequent stage of processing. In addition, cross-footing of the payroll register and zero balancing of the general ledger payroll control account provide two final checks on the accuracy of payroll processing.

The accuracy of payroll processing is further enhanced by two other control procedures that occur outside the payroll processing cycle. First, a separate payroll bank account should be used, and this account should be reconciled following each payroll period in order to detect possible discrepancies in payroll disbursements. Second, internal audit personnel should occasionally review a sample of payroll processing output on a surprise basis and verify the accuracy of all payroll calculations.

The maintenance of accurate personnel and payroll records involves protecting the employee data base against contamination from erroneous or fraudulent transaction input, using the techniques just described, and securing the employee data base against such threats as fire, flood, sabotage, and unauthorized access. For example, one large organization recently lost 120,000 payroll records through the actions of a disgruntled employee who planted a computer virus in the payroll system.[6]

A variety of techniques are employed to protect the security of the employee data base. First, internal and external file labels should be used to ensure that the data base is not inadvertently erased or processed by the wrong program. Second, a backup copy of the employee data base should be prepared after each payroll run, and backup copies of all payroll and personnel change transaction files should also be saved. Then, if the data base is damaged in any way, a current copy can be restored by processing the backup transaction files against the last backup copy of the data base. It is critically important to store all backup files in a secure off-site location, since fires, floods, or sabotage may damage everything stored in an organization's primary data processing location. Finally, on-line access to the employee data base must be restricted through an access control system utilizing account numbers, passwords, and compatibility tests of all transactions submitted by on-line users.

The disbursement of employee compensation is also sensitive from a control standpoint. Risks include theft of paychecks or pay envelopes, preparation of paychecks for fictitious or terminated employees, unauthorized use of blank paycheck forms, and misappropriation of unclaimed wages.

---

[6] As reported in Kavanagh, Gueutal, and Tannenbaum, *Human Resource Information Systems*, 307.

If possible, all employee earnings should be disbursed by check rather than cash. Distribution by mail or by direct deposit in employee bank accounts is preferable to hand distribution. If paychecks are physically distributed to employees, this should be done by each employee's immediate supervisor, rather than by payroll or personnel staff employees. Access to blank payroll check forms should be restricted. Payroll checks should be sequentially prenumbered, and all checks should be strictly accounted for as part of the payroll bank reconciliation process.

Special control procedures are necessary for handling unclaimed paychecks. If paychecks are distributed by hand to employees, unclaimed paychecks for terminated or absent employees will be fairly common. Even if paychecks are distributed by mail, some may occasionally be returned for lack of a forwarding address. In any event an unclaimed paycheck indicates the possibility of manipulation. When a paycheck is unclaimed, a responsible employee should verify the paycheck's validity by tracing its preparation to the original employee activity records and by checking the payroll data against the employee data base. Further attempts should be made to distribute such paychecks to the proper persons. If these are unsuccessful, the paychecks should be locked up for safekeeping and eventually destroyed.

Reporting   Personnel and payroll data capture, data processing, data base updating, and internal control are all of critical importance to ensure that personnel/payroll cycle activities are carried out effectively. However, from a management perspective the reports generated by the human resources information system are also of prime importance. Payroll processing is characterized by a heavy volume of scheduled reports; some are required for internal purposes, and others are needed to meet external reporting requirements, especially those imposed by various government agencies. Personnel administrators and other managers also make use of demand reports generated by means of inquiry processing, decision support systems, expert systems, or analysis of data downloaded to a personal computer. Several examples of the content and utilization of such reports are described in this section.

The payroll register is one example of a scheduled report prepared by most payroll data processing systems to meet internal needs. This report lists detailed payroll data for each employee during a specific pay period. Often the payroll register is accompanied by a separate deduction register, which details the miscellaneous payroll deductions of each employee. These reports provide useful reference information for payroll accountants, supervisors, and personnel administrators. Sample payroll and deduction registers are shown in Fig. 19.7.

Another example of a scheduled report used for internal management purposes is the employee performance report. This report provides detailed information on productivity, efficiency, absenteeism or tardiness, quality of work, supervisory ratings, and other performance measures for each employee. Some employee performance reports

ELECTRONICS INCORPORATED					PAYROLL REGISTER				Period Ended 12/3/93
					Deductions				
Employee Number	Employee Name	Hours Worked	Pay Rate	Gross Pay	Federal Tax Withheld	FICA Tax Withheld	State Tax Withheld	Miscellaneous	Net Pay
375439871	Allred, Lawrence	40.0	$6.25	$250.00	$35.60	$18.75	$16.25	$27.60	$151.80
365402872	Barrett, Charlene	43.6	$6.50	$295.10	$42.40	$22.13	$19.18	$40.15	$171.24
345529104	Curtis, George	40.0	$6.75	$270.00	$39.20	$20.25	$17.55	$27.90	$165.10
365577682	Evans, Mary	44.2	$7.00	$324.10	$46.60	$24.31	$21.07	$29.62	$202.50

ELECTRONICS INCORPORATED		DEDUCTION REGISTER					Period Ended 12/3/93
		Miscellaneous Deductions					Total Miscellaneous Deductions
Employee Number	Employee Name	Health Insurance	Life Insurance	Retirement Fund	Union Dues	Savings Bond	
375439871	Allred, Lawrence	$10.40	$5.50	$7.50	$4.20	$0.00	$27.60
365402872	Barrett, Charlene	$11.60	$5.50	$8.85	$4.20	$10.00	$40.15
345529104	Curtis, George	$10.40	$5.20	$8.10	$4.20	$0.00	$27.90
365577682	Evans, Mary	$10.20	$5.50	$9.72	$4.20	$0.00	$29.62

Figure 19.7
Payroll and deduction registers

compare actual performance with a predetermined standard. For example, in a manufacturing company that uses standard costing, the productivity of factory employees might be evaluated in comparison to predetermined labor time standards, as illustrated in Fig. 18.15. To evaluate the performance of supervisory personnel, the information system should prepare reports that aggregate the performance measures of all employees within each department.

In addition to employee performance reports, departmental supervisors and personnel administrators need regular reports on the status of employees and positions within the organization. One such report is the **work force inventory**, which simply lists all employees assigned to each department, together with selected reference information such as job title, age, length of service, EEO classification, wage rate or salary, highest degree attained, recent performance ratings, and current address and telephone number. A summary version of this report, called a **work force profile**, provides descriptive statistics about the work force, such as the average age and length of service of employees by department, the number of employees by EEO classification in each department, and the average level of education attained by employees within each department.

A similar report that lists all authorized positions within the organization, broken down by department, is called a **position control report**. For each position this report lists the job qualifications required, the amount budgeted for employee compensation, and the position status (filled or vacant). For each position that has been filled, the report lists details about the employee, including name, age, length of service, sex, race, and actual compensation.

Business organizations must prepare several other scheduled reports to fulfill external reporting requirements. The federal government and most state governments require employers to withhold employee income taxes from payrolls and remit the withholdings at specified times. The same applies to Social Security and unemployment taxes. Periodically, employers must file reports with the appropriate governmental body detailing their compliance. For example, employers must file regular reports with the Internal Revenue Service detailing their liability for federal income and Social Security taxes withheld and reporting the deposit of these taxes in an approved federal bank. By January 31 of each year, employers must furnish each employee with a Form W-2 (Wage and Tax Statement) summarizing the total wages or salary paid to the employee and the totals withheld for Social Security taxes and federal, state, and local income taxes.

Numerous other federal and state government agencies require that employers adhere to certain record-keeping and reporting requirements as a means of documenting their compliance with various laws and government regulations. These include minimum wage, overtime, and equal pay standards under the Fair Labor Standards Act, record-keeping requirements on accidents and occupational diseases under the Occupational Safety and Health Act (OSHA), reporting requirements for employee pension and other benefit plans under the Employee Retirement Income Security Act (ERISA), and record-keeping requirements on minority hiring and work force composition under EEO regulations. A sample portion of a required EEO report appears in Fig. 19.8. The personnel and payroll data processing systems must be designed to maintain the necessary data and to report the required information for such reports, in the specified format, at regular intervals or upon request.

Inquiry processing is frequently employed by personnel administrators and others needing access to personnel information. For example, suppose that officials at the American Broadcasting Company (ABC) are approached by agents of the EEO Commission who request data on numbers of employees in various job positions broken down by EEO classification. To respond to this request, ABC officials would use an inquiry processing system to search the employee data base, key on the job position code and EEO classification fields, and tally the number of employees in each EEO category within each job position. For another example, suppose that a division manager at Exxon Corporation is seeking an employee for an important assignment in Venezuela. To perform the assignment, the employee must be an expert

Section D—Employment Data

Employment at this establishment—Report all permanent full-time or part-time employees including apprentices and on-the-job trainees unless specifically excluded as set forth in the instructions. Enter the appropriate figures on all lines and in all columns. Blank spaces will be considered zeros.

Job Categories		Overall Totals (Sum of Columns B–K) A	Male					Female				
			White (Not of Hispanic Origin) B	Black (Not of Hispanic Origin) C	Hispanic D	Asian or Pacific Islander E	American Indian or Alaskan Native F	White (Not of Hispanic Origin) G	Black (Not of Hispanic Origin) H	Hispanic I	Asian or Pacific Islander J	American Indian or Alaskan Native K
Officials and managers	1	1306	695	8	3	2	1	571	13	7	4	2
Professionals	2	121	45	3	1	1		67	2	1	1	
Technicians	3	74	45	1	1	3		22			2	
Sales workers	4	33	16	1	1	1		13			1	
Office and clerical	5	3460	390	35	9	7	1	2772	139	39	55	13
Craft workers (skilled)	6	12	8	2	1		1					
Operatives (semiskilled)	7	45	31	3	1	4	2	4				
Laborers (unskilled)	8	1	1									
Service workers	9	90	64	8	1		1	14	2			
Total	10	5142	1295	61	18	18	6	3463	156	47	63	15
Total employment reported in previous EEO-1 report	11	4630	1166	55	15	16	5	3117	144	42	55	15
(The trainees below should also be included in the figures for the appropriate occupational categories above.)												
Formal on-the-job trainees — White collar	12	42	18	2	1			16	3	1	1	
Formal on-the-job trainees — Production	13	8	5	1	2							

Figure 19.8
Sample EEO report

petroleum geologist with managerial experience and the ability to speak fluent Spanish. Inquiry processing would be employed to search Exxon's employee data base, keying on these three attributes, to identify all employees meeting these criteria and to prepare a report listing the name of each employee, current position and location, and other relevant qualifications.

To facilitate the identification of employees with particular combinations of skills, many organizations use a **skills inventory system**. To implement such a system, a standardized list of all relevant employment-related skills must first be developed. These skills include educational qualifications, experience, professional certifications, foreign language proficiency, and so forth. Then each individual skill is assigned a code number. The complete list of skill codes and descriptions forms the organization's **skills index**. Next, the skills each employee possesses must be determined. Finally, the appropriate skill codes must be appended to each employee record in the data base. The data base may then easily be searched to identify all employees possessing any combination of skills. A skills inventory system is especially useful in organizations that employ a large number of professionals, such as management consulting firms, engineering firms, law firms, and accounting firms.

When Lisa Jackson first joined Electronics Incorporated, one of her goals was to develop a skills inventory system. However, she soon discovered that doing this for EI's work force of 3000 employees would be an enormous task requiring more resources than could be spared by either the personnel staff or the MIS Department. However, Grace Healy suggested that Lisa begin by developing a prototype system for employees within one particular function or area of the company. Lisa selected the research and engineering function, which employs 400 professionals in various product development activities that are critical to EI's success. A task force was formed with representatives from the Personnel, Engineering, and MIS departments, and work began on identifying and indexing relevant research and engineering skills. Within four months the prototype system was operational, and plans were being made to extend the system to EI's managerial personnel.

A common application of decision support systems is to assist business managers and labor negotiators in contract negotiations with labor unions. Such negotiations often require management to make complex trade-offs among such factors as wage rates, overtime premiums, working conditions, paid vacations and holidays, and contributions to employee benefit plans. A decision support system may be used to answer what-if questions concerning the cost implications of alternative contract proposals. One approach is to simulate the effect of each proposal on total compensation for union employees under various assumptions about future production volume.

These various examples assume the existence of a computer-based human resources information system utilizing an integrated data base that includes both payroll and personnel information on employees plus information on positions within the organization, job applicants, and other human resources information. However, in many organizations these various systems are not fully integrated. In addition, some systems, especially payroll, may be fully computerized, while others relating to personnel and human resources are not. This may make it difficult to pull together all the information required to prepare some of the more sophisticated human resources analyses. Under these circumstances downloading of information from the payroll data base to a personal computer may provide a starting point for the development of useful personnel reporting applications. This approach was recently followed very successfully by the human resources department of a major metropolitan newspaper (see Focus 19.2).

For another example of downloading, consider a large engineering research firm that wishes to analyze the causes of employee turnover. This project requires data on employees who voluntarily left the firm, including attributes that might affect turnover, such as location, supervisor, professional specialty, educational qualifications, professional certifications, job assignments, length of service, compensation (including recent pay raises), and performance ratings. These data can be downloaded from the firm's employee data base to a personal computer file. Then a statistical technique such as regression analysis may be used to identify factors that are most highly correlated with employee turnover. An extension of this analysis is to use the resulting regression model to predict which of the firm's current employees are most likely to voluntarily terminate their employment in the near future. Similar analyses could be performed to identify factors that are correlated with productivity, quality, and other job performance measures.

An example of the use of an expert system in human resource management is provided by Extejt and Lynn, who describe how a large bank in Cleveland developed an expert system to assist in the selection of job candidates for a management trainee program.[7] Three experts in recruiting who had consistently recommended candidates who evolved into excellent employees were queried about the decision rules they used in selecting candidates. These rules were converted to "if–then" format and entered into an expert system shell. The resulting expert system program was provided to campus recruiters in a portable laptop computer. After each candidate interview the recruiter would respond to a series of questions about the candidate from the expert system, which would then make a recommendation on the candidate.

These examples illustrate how the power of the computer can substantially improve the quality and timeliness of the information available to personnel managers. Scheduled management reports can provide large volumes of information for reference purposes and also highlight and summarize this information according to various deci-

---

[7] Marian M. Extejt and Marc P. Lynn, "Expert Systems as Human Resource Management Decision Tools," *Journal of Systems Management* (November 1988): 10–15.

19.2 FOCUS

Human Resource Information Management Using PC/FOCUS

At a major metropolitan daily newspaper, the Human Resources (HR) Department faced a major dilemma. With seven professional and three clerical employees HR handled recruitment, training and development, EEO compliance, salary and benefits administration, position tracking, and various other personnel functions for an organization of 2700 employees.

For many years all of these functions had been performed manually, despite the fact that computers were applied in many other areas of the newspaper's operations, including payroll. The payroll system had just undergone a major overhaul, with the promise that HR applications would also be automated. But implementation of the new system had fallen behind schedule, and development of the HR applications had been put on hold to ensure that the payroll system could be completed on time. Even after it became operational, the payroll system was inundated with problems, and it had become obvious that HR would have a long wait before development efforts could go forward on its many needed applications.

sion-relevant criteria. Other scheduled reports help personnel managers fulfill their obligations to provide information required for compliance with various government laws and regulations. Demand reports can provide specific information tailored to a particular management need and can assist management in analyzing this information. A well-designed system for personnel and payroll data processing uses all of these reporting techniques to enhance the effectiveness of the personnel management function.

CASE CONCLUSION: IMPROVING PERSONNEL INFORMATION SYSTEMS AT ELECTRONICS INCORPORATED

Lisa Jackson was very pleased when Grace Healy's proposal to integrate EI's personnel and payroll data bases was approved with the support of the company's new controller. However, six months later she was beginning to get frustrated with the slow rate of progress on the project. When she inquired about the delay, Lisa learned that there were over 400 data items in EI's personnel and payroll data bases, and almost 20% of them were redundant; that is, the same item of data was stored in both data bases. For many of the redundant items data names or other attributes were not consistent between the two systems. Hence, much time had been consumed in developing standardized data definitions. Next, an overall data base schema had been developed,

At this point a decision was made to try to automate HR's position-tracking system on a PC using a fourth-generation data base management system called PC/FOCUS. The position-tracking system consisted of two main files, one containing employee information, the other containing information on job positions. Much of the data required to create these files was downloaded from the mainframe payroll system. HR staff were responsible for entering data on new employees, new positions, and employee position changes into the system. The system produced quarterly reports showing the number of authorized, budgeted positions within each department, their status (filled or vacant), and the incumbent's name, sex, and race. Other reports detailed employee activity by department, analyzed hiring decisions in terms of the race and sex of applicants and the individual hired, and provided summaries of employee counts by sex, race, and EEO category. While the manual system required two people working full-time for two weeks to produce these reports, the new system required only one person working two days.

After the position-tracking system was successfully implemented, HR used PC/FOCUS to automate several other functions. They included a salary administration application dealing with job history and salary history information for nonunion employees, an application to maintain information on the dependents of employees covered by supplemental life insurance, a salary planning application, and a system for tracking job applicants. Thus while the newspaper's programming staff continued to work out the bugs in the new payroll system, the HR staff was able to use a PC to resolve many of its own pressing information processing needs.

Source: Adapted from Sonja Hunn, "A PC/Mainframe Team to HR's Rescue," *Personnel* (August 1989):37–42.

and work had begun on converting the actual data. At this stage many inconsistencies had been discovered in the values of identical data items in the two data bases, and several weeks had been required to clean up the data. Finally, work was now underway to modify the data names in all of the programs used by EI to process payroll and personnel data to make them consistent with the new standardized data definitions. In addition, several on-line terminals were being acquired, and work was underway to develop on-line data entry and inquiry software that would be user-friendly and yet highly secure. These steps would be followed by a testing and conversion process and training sessions to instruct EI staff personnel in using the new software. The project manager has assured Lisa that the new system will be operational within three months.

Shortly after the integration project began, Lisa had appointed separate task forces to develop recommendations on how to implement a flexible benefits program and an incentive compensation plan. The flexible benefits task force began by holding a series of meetings with employees representing all of EI's departments to learn what kinds of options the employees would prefer. Once the general outline of a new flexible benefits program became clear, this task force also began meeting with the systems development group to make sure that the program would be compatible with the new system. Lisa had just received the final recommendations of the flexible benefits task force, and she was eager to obtain top management's approval of the program and proceed with its implementation. However, the program could not be implemented until the new system was up and running, and Lisa could not be certain of when that would occur.

Meanwhile, the incentive compensation task force had begun by examining what kinds of performance measures were currently used by EI managers in evaluating and rewarding employee performance. As an aid in this analysis, an attempt was made to create a personal computer file containing performance data on each employee by downloading compensation data and performance information from EI's payroll and personnel data bases. The task force soon discovered that other important employee performance measures resided on EI's marketing and production data bases. Once the personal computer files were complete, a series of meetings were scheduled with EI supervisory personnel to review the data and discuss various ways to implement an incentive compensation plan. These meetings had raised the issue of group incentive schemes, which the task force was now exploring. Meetings had also begun between this task force and the systems development group to establish how the new system should be designed to accommodate an incentive compensation plan. At this point Lisa was not sure when this task force would provide its recommendations. However, it was becoming clear to her that any new incentive compensation plan would place strong demands on EI's information systems. In particular, strong interfaces would be required between EI's integrated personnel/payroll system and several other EI systems in order to capture the necessary employee performance data.

One bright spot for Lisa was EI's new skills inventory system. Research and engineering managers had become enthusiastic users of the new system, and several enhancements were planned. The system had already been extended to include EI's managerial and supervisory personnel and would soon cover all administrative staff employees. The only problem with this system was that a decision would soon have to be made on whether to continue to run it on EI's personal computer network or to consolidate it with the new integrated personnel/payroll system. Lisa had received conflicting advice on this question and had not decided which approach she favored. As she pondered this issue, Lisa also reflected on the irony of her current position. After deliberately avoiding all contact with computers since early in her university studies, Lisa had now concluded that an understanding of modern information technology had become crucial to her own success and career advancement in her chosen field. ■

SUMMARY

Personnel/payroll cycle activities include hiring, training, assigning, compensating, evaluating, and discharging employees. Related data processing activities include recording employee activity, processing employee payrolls, preparing and distributing paychecks, maintaining employee records, and preparing numerous scheduled and demand reports describing various aspects of the work force. The focal point of these data processing activities is the maintenance of an employee data base that includes payroll, personnel, and employment history information.

Payroll data processing is generally accomplished with batch processing. Because the processing of payrolls involves a large volume of records, many computations, and extensive reporting requirements, it was one of the earliest applications of computers in business. The payroll data processing system must be designed to capture data on employee activity, calculate employee compensation and payroll deductions, prepare employee paychecks, and generate a variety of reports to fulfill reporting requirements imposed by assorted government agencies. The system must incorporate internal controls that ensure proper authorization of all transactions, facilitate effective supervision of employees, protect the accuracy of all transaction and master file data, and secure the distribution of paychecks to employees.

Increasingly, many companies are integrating the payroll data processing system with the personnel information system to form an integrated human resources information system. These systems generally use an on-line interface for data entry and inquiry processing. Integrated systems facilitate the implementation of such progressive human resource management programs as flexible benefits and incentive compensation. In addition, integrated systems can more easily generate a variety of scheduled and demand reports that aid departmental supervisors, personnel administrators, and management executives in the effective management of human resources.

KEY TERMS

Define the following terms.

personnel/payroll cycle	payroll register	work force inventory
personnel cycle	flexible benefits plan	work force profile
payroll cycle	cafeteria-style benefits plan	position control report
position control file	zero balance check	skills inventory system
applicant file	personnel change record	skills index
employee clock card	deduction register	

DISCUSSION QUESTIONS

19.1 As this chapter points out, many companies operate their payroll and personnel information systems separately, though the trend is toward integration of these systems. Discuss the reasons why these systems are separate in so many companies. What reasons are there for integrating these two systems?

19.2 You are involved in implementing a new employee performance evaluation system at the Curtis Manufacturing Company. The system will provide each factory supervisor with monthly reports containing detailed employee performance data. The supervisor of the Finishing Department, Joe Waller, has indicated that he does not need this information. Waller feels that he can get all the information he needs to evaluate the employees in his department simply by observing their behavior. How would you try to persuade Waller that the new information system could be useful to him?

19.3 Some accountants have suggested the establishment of human resource accounting systems. Under such systems investments in employee hiring and training would be accounted for as assets—that is, debited to an asset account, allocated to specific employees, amortized as an expense over the employee's expected period of employment, and charged off as a loss if the employee resigned or was discharged. Do you think that human resource accounting systems are a good idea?

19.4 At the conclusion of a recent audit, external auditors for the Donovan Manufacturing Company recommended that production job time tickets be reconciled with employee clock cards prior to payroll data processing. The company had not previously followed this procedure, and the Payroll Supervisor described the suggested procedure as "an unnecessary waste of time." Assume that you are an assistant controller assigned to prepare a recommendation to the company's Controller concerning whether or not to implement this suggestion. What would you recommend, and why?

Problems

19.1 Kids Choice Corporation is a manufacturer and distributor of children's toys. Within the past three years the company's sales volume has declined as several important distributors have dropped the Kids Choice product line. In response the company's top management has just ordered every department within the company to reevaluate its operations, identify possible problems that may be contributing to the company's loss of business, and prepare recommendations for improvement.

You have been asked to evaluate the employee compensation and benefits program at Kids Choice. You have learned that all Kids Choice employees are paid either an hourly wage or a salary. The corporation's employee benefits program is modest in scope, and employees have few options in selecting benefit plans. Personnel staff employees are often behind in approving personnel and payroll transactions for data entry, and errors are frequently found in personnel records. When asked about the company's compensation system, several employees complain about errors in their paychecks and indicate that they must check their paychecks carefully before depositing them. In addition, many employees complain that pay raises seem to be determined subjectively and that they are in the dark about how management evaluates their performance.

Required

Could Kids Choice Corporation's compensation and benefits system, and the data processing operations that support it, have anything to do with the decline in its competitive fortunes? Describe several ways in which this system might be improved.

19.2 What internal controls in a payroll data processing system would provide the best protection against the following errors or manipulations?

a. Because of an inadvertent data entry error, an employee's wage rate was overstated on the payroll master file.

b. A fictitious employee payroll record was entered into the payroll master file.

c. Because of an inadvertent data entry error, an employee's time worked for one day was recorded as 80 instead of 8.

d. Using an on-line terminal, a computer operator entered a payroll transaction that increased her own salary by 50%.

e. A company's cashier pocketed and cashed the unclaimed paychecks of terminated employees.

f. A factory employee punched a friend's clock card in at 1:00 P.M. and out at 5:00 P.M. while the friend spent the afternoon playing golf.

g. A programmer obtained the disk containing the current payroll master file from the file storage area and modified the file to increase his monthly salary.

h. Several job time records were lost before they were entered into the system; as a result, several hundred dollars in labor costs were not charged to a job.

i. A computer operator making an error correction entry using the console accidentally erased a portion of the payroll master file.

j. A large portion of the payroll master file was destroyed when the disk containing the file was used as a scratch file for another application.

19.3 Prepare a record layout for each of the following payroll transactions. The records will be inputs to a computer application that updates an employee data base like the one shown in Fig. 19.5.

a. Adding an employee payroll record for a newly hired employee

b. Changing an existing employee's number of exemptions

c. Adding a deduction record for an employee who has authorized a monthly savings bond deduction

d. Changing an employee's regular pay rate

19.4 Manufacturing executives at the Iowa Manufacturing Company are considering the implementation of an incentive compensation system for production employees. Incentive bonuses would be paid for all units produced in excess of the standard quantity per hour. There would be different bonus rates per unit for each production operation, but these rates have yet to be determined. The company utilizes computerized production and payroll data processing systems built around data bases identical to those illustrated in Figs. 18.11 and 19.5.

Required

For this new system, additional items of data may have to be added to one or both of these data bases. Identify any additional data items that will be required, and indicate how the two data bases should be modified to accommodate the new incentive system.

19.5 The Internal Audit Department of Manor Company conducts audits in the company's several

plants on a regular basis. The Internal Audit Department is expected to perform operational audits. A team of internal auditors was assigned to review the Payroll Department of the Galena plant. The internal audit consisted of (1) various tests to verify the numerical accuracy of the Payroll Department's records and (2) the determination of the procedures used to process the payroll.

The internal audit team found that all numerical items were accurate. The proper hourly rates were used and the wages and deductions were calculated correctly. The payroll register was properly footed, totaled, and posted.

Various plant personnel were interviewed to ascertain the payroll procedures being used in the department. The audit team's findings were as follows:

■ The payroll clerk receives the time cards from the various department supervisors at the end of each pay period, checks the employee's hourly rate against information provided by the Personnel Department, and records the regular and overtime hours for each employee.

■ The payroll clerk sends the time cards to the plant's Data Processing Department for compilation and processing.

■ The Data Processing Department returns the time cards with the printed checks and payroll register to the payroll clerk upon completion of the processing.

■ The payroll clerk verifies the hourly rate and hours worked for each employee by comparing the detail in the payroll register with the time cards.

■ If errors are found, the payroll clerk voids the computer-generated check, prepares another check for the correct amount, and adjusts the payroll register accordingly.

■ The payroll clerk obtains the plant signature plate from the Accounting Department and signs the payroll checks.

■ An employee of the Personnel Department picks up the checks and holds them until they are delivered to the department supervisors for distribution to the employees.

Required

Using the findings of the internal audit team, identify the shortcomings in the payroll procedures used in the Payroll Department of the Galena plant, and suggest corrective action the internal audit team should recommend. (CMA Examination)

19.6 Your company is in the process of automating

the input to its payroll system and converting its payroll files and processes to be run on data base management software. Presently, employee time worked data are recorded on clock cards such as the one shown in Fig. 19.3. The new system will collect these data automatically as employees enter badges into badge readers when they arrive at their work sites.

As a first step in the application design, you are to diagram the data structure reflected in the clock card. In addition to fields for the actual data shown in Fig. 19.3, include fields for the following data items that are blank on this clock card: daily totals of regular time and overtime, period totals for regular time and overtime, and name of the person who approved the hours and signed the card. However, do not include fields for the pay rate and the payroll dollar calculations that are shown on the right side of the card. Your data structure diagram should use a format similar to that in Fig. 19.5. Note that the data base will contain only the variable data on the clock card, not the constant data.

19.7 You are a systems analyst at the Barden Manufacturing Company. Barden's Production Manager has recently noticed that overtime hours and costs have been much higher during the past three months than in the three months previous to that period. To assist the Production Manager in investigating this matter, you have been asked to prepare a report analyzing overtime hours and costs by department over the past six months.

Barden uses an employee data base like the one illustrated in Fig. 19.5. Barden pays its factory employees weekly, so that overtime represents any hours in excess of 40 per pay period. To prepare your report, you will download selected information from the employee data base to your personal computer and then format it so that it may be easily understood and interpreted.

Required

a. To perform your analysis, what data should you download from the employee data base to your personal computer?

b. Briefly describe how you should process this data to prepare your report.

c. Design a report format that presents the required detail and summary information in an effective manner.

19.8 The Vane Corporation is a manufacturing concern that has been in business for 18 years. During this period the company has grown from a very small family-owned operation to a medium-sized manufacturing concern with several departments. Despite this growth a substantial number of the procedures employed by Vane have been in effect since the business was started. Just recently Vane has computerized its payroll function.

The payroll function operates in the following manner. Each worker picks up a weekly time card on Monday morning and writes in his or her name and identification number. These blank cards are kept near the factory entrance. The workers write on the time card the time of their daily arrival and departure. On the following Monday the factory foremen collect the completed time cards for the previous week and send them to data processing.

In data processing the time cards are used to prepare the weekly time file. This file is processed with the master payroll file, which is maintained on magnetic tape according to worker identification number. The checks are written by the computer on the regular checking account and imprinted with the treasurer's signature. After the payroll file is updated and the checks are prepared, the checks are sent to the factory foremen, who distribute them to the workers or hold them for the workers to pick up later if they are absent.

The foremen notify data processing of new employees and terminations. Any changes in hourly pay rate or any other changes affecting payroll are usually communicated to data processing by the foremen.

The workers also complete a job time ticket for each individual job they work on each day. The job time tickets are collected daily and sent to cost accounting where they are used to prepare a cost distribution analysis.

Further analysis of the payroll function reveals the following information.

■ A worker's gross wages never exceed $300 per week.

■ Raises never exceed $0.55 per hour for the factory workers.

■ No more than 20 hours of overtime is allowed each week.

■ The factory employs 150 workers in ten departments.

The payroll function has not been operating smoothly for some time, but even more problems have surfaced since the payroll was computerized.

The foremen have indicated that they would like a weekly report indicating worker tardiness, absenteeism, and idle time, so they can determine the amount of productive time lost and the reason for the lost time. The following errors and inconsistencies have been encountered the past few pay periods:

- A worker's paycheck was not processed properly because he had transposed two numbers in his identification number when he filled out his time card.
- A worker was issued a check for $1531.80 when it should have been $153.81.
- One worker's paycheck was not written, and this error was not detected until the paychecks for that department were distributed by the foreman.
- Part of the master payroll file was destroyed when the tape reel was inadvertently mounted on the wrong tape drive and used as a scratch tape. Data processing attempted to reestablish the destroyed portion from original source documents and other records.
- One worker received a paycheck for an amount considerably higher than he should have. Further investigation revealed that 84 had been keyed in instead of 48 for hours worked.
- Several records on the master payroll file were skipped and not included on the updated master payroll file. This was not detected for several pay periods.
- In processing nonroutine changes, a computer operator included a pay rate increase for one of his friends in the factory. This was discovered by chance by another employee.

Required

Identify the control weaknesses in the payroll procedure and in the computer processing as it is now conducted by the Vane Corporation. Recommend the changes necessary to correct the system. Arrange your answer in the following format.

(CMA Examination)

Control Weaknesses	Recommendations

19.9 Arlington Industries manufactures and sells engine parts for large industrial equipment. The company employs over one thousand workers for three shifts, and most employees work overtime when necessary. Arlington has had a major growth in its production and has purchased a mainframe computer to handle order processing, inventory management, production planning, distribution operations, and accounting applications. Michael Cromley, President of Arlington, suspects that there may be internal control weaknesses due to the quick implementation of the computer system. Cromley recently hired Kathleen Luddy as the Internal Control Accountant.

Cromley asked Luddy to review the payroll processing system first. Luddy has reviewed the payroll process, interviewed individuals involved, and compiled the flowchart displayed in Fig. 19.9. Additional information concerning payroll processing follows.

The Personnel Department determines the wage rate of all employees at Arlington. Personnel starts the process by sending an authorization form for adding an employee to the payroll coordinator, Marjorie Adams. After Adams inputs this information into the system, the computer automatically determines the overtime and shift differential rates for the individual, updating the payroll master file.

Arlington uses an external service to provide monthly payroll tax updates. The company receives a magnetic tape every month, which the Data Processing Department installs to update the payroll master file for tax calculations.

Employees at Arlington use a time clock to record the hours worked. Every Monday morning Adams collects the previous week's time cards from the card bin, leaves the new week's time cards, and begins the computerized processing of payroll information in order to produce paychecks the following Friday. Adams reviews the time cards to ensure that the hours worked are correctly totaled; the system will determine whether overtime has been worked or a shift differential is required.

All the other processes displayed on the flowchart are performed by Adams. The system automatically assigns a sequential number to each payroll check produced. The checks are stored in a box next to the computer printer to provide immediate access. After the checks are printed, Adams uses an automatic check-signing machine to sign the checks with an authorized signature plate that Adams keeps locked in a safe.

After the check processing is completed, Adams distributes the checks to the employees, leaving the checks for the second- and third-shift employees with the appropriate shift supervisor. Adams then notifies the Data Processing Department that she is finished with her weekly processing, and they make

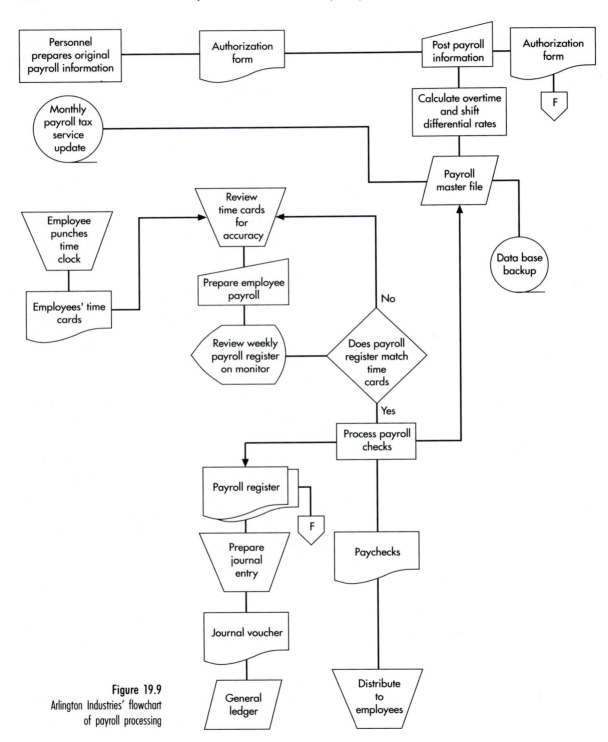

Figure 19.9
Arlington Industries' flowchart of payroll processing

a backup of the payroll master file to magnetic tape for storage on the tape shelves in the computer room.

Required

By referring to the information described in the problem and the flowchart in Fig. 19.9, identify and describe the following:

a. Five different areas in Arlington Industries' payroll processing system where the system controls are inadequate

b. Two different areas in Arlington Industries' payroll processing system where the system controls are satisfactory

(CMA Examination)

19.10 The Sharpesville Insurance Company utilizes a computer-based system with disk file storage. Among the files it maintains on disk are a salesperson payroll master, sequenced by salesperson number, and a policyholders master, sequenced by policy number.

Each salesperson's monthly gross pay is equal to $500 plus commission. Each salesperson's commission is calculated as 5% of all premiums collected during the first year of the policy from policyholders who purchased from the salesperson and 1% of all premiums collected during the next four years from those policyholders.

Each day the policyholders' master file is updated for new policies sold and premium payments received on outstanding policies. All premium payments are collected on a monthly basis. At the end of each month the policyholders' master and salespersons' payroll master are processed to compute the salespersons' payrolls and print their paychecks and earnings statements. Other outputs from this processing run are a printed payroll register, a summary report, and a temporary disk file containing a list of all policyholders who did not pay their last monthly premium. The disk file is subsequently processed to prepare a printed report on delinquent policyholders.

Required

a. What data must be contained in each policyholder master record in order for that file to be used as described in generating salespersons payroll data? (Do not mention policyholder master data that are not used in generating salespersons payroll data.)

b. Prepare a systems flowchart of the monthly payroll processing run described.

c. Assume that the processing you illustrated in part b is done sequentially. What operations must then be performed on the policyholders master file prior to the run?

d. What accounting journal entry would be accumulated in the run and printed out as part of the summary information? (Show accounts debited and accounts credited.)

e. Prepare a macroflowchart of the monthly payroll processing program. The flowchart should include (1) separate input and output symbols for each file processed in the run; (2) decision symbols for all decisions necessary to accomplish sequential processing, to determine whether or not to include each policyholder on the listing of policyholders behind on premium payments, and to determine the appropriate rate to be used in calculating the salesperson's commission; and (3) a single processing step representing calculation of net pay and all processing steps necessary to accumulate gross pay.

19.11 Rose Publishing Company devotes the bulk of its work to the development of high school and college texts. The Printing Division has several production departments and employs 400 persons, of which 95% are hourly rated production workers. Production workers may work on several projects in one day. They are paid weekly based on total hours worked.

A manual time card system is used to collect data on time worked. Each employee punches in and out when entering or leaving the plant. The Timekeeping Department audits the time cards daily and prepares input sheets for the computerized functions of the payroll system.

Currently, a daily report of the previous day's clock card information by department is sent to each departmental supervisor in the Printing Division for verification and approval. Any changes are made directly on the report, signed by the supervisor, and returned to the Timekeeping Department. The altered report serves as the input authorization for changes to the system. Because of the volume and frequency of reports, this report-changing procedure is the most expensive process in the system.

Timekeeping submits the corrected hourly data to General Accounting and Cost Accounting for further processing. General Accounting maintains the payroll system that determines weekly payroll; prepares weekly checks; summarizes data for monthly, quarterly, and annual reports; and generates W-2 forms. A weekly and monthly payroll distribution report is prepared by the Cost Accounting Department that shows the labor costs by department.

Competition in college textbook publishing has increased steadily in the past three years. While Rose has maintained its sales volume, profits have declined. Direct labor cost is believed to be the basic cause of this decline in profits, but insufficient detail on labor utilization is available to pinpoint the suspected inefficiencies. Chuck Hutchins, a systems consultant, was engaged to analyze the current system and to make recommendations for improving data collection and processing procedures. Excerpts from the report that Hutchins prepared appear in Table 19.1.

Required

a. Compared with the traditional clock card system, what are the advantages and disadvantages of the recommended system of electronically recording the entry to and exit from the plant?

b. Identify the items to be included in the individual employee's master file.

c. The TALC system allows the employee's departmental supervisor and the Personnel Department to examine the data contained in an individual employee's master file.

   1. Discuss the extent of the information each should be allowed to examine.

   2. Describe the safeguards that may be installed to prevent unauthorized access to the data.

d. The recommended system allows both the departmental supervisors and the project managers to obtain current labor distribution data on a limited basis. The limitations mentioned can lead to a conflict between a departmental supervisor and a project manager.

   1. Discuss the reasons for the specified limitations.

   2. Recommend a solution for the possible conflict that could arise if a departmental supervisor and a project manager do not agree.

(CMA Examination)

Table 19.1
Excerpts from Hutchins's report

An integrated time and attendance labor cost (TALC) system should be developed. Features of this system would include direct data entry; labor cost distribution by project as well as department; on-line access to time and attendance data for verification, correction, and update; and creation and maintenance of individual employee work history files for long-term analysis.

The TALC system should incorporate uniquely encoded employee badges that would be used to electronically record entry to and exit from the plant directly into the data system.

Labor cost records should be maintained at the employee level, showing the time worked in the department by project. Thus labor cost can be fully analyzed. Responsibility for correct and timely entry must reside with the departmental supervisors and must be verified by project managers on a daily basis because projects involve several departments.

On-line terminals should be available in each department for direct data entry. Access to the system will be limited to authorized users through a coded entry (password) system. Departmental supervisors will be allowed to inspect, correct, verify, and update only time and attendance information for employees in their respective departments. Project managers may access information recorded for their projects only, and exceptions to such data must be certified outside the system and entered by the affected supervisor.

Appropriate data should be maintained at the employee level to allow verification of employee personnel files and individual work history by department and project. Access to employee master file data should be limited to the Personnel Department. Work history data will be made available for analysis only at the project or departmental level and only to departmental supervisors and project managers for whom an employee works.

CASE 19.1: ANYCOMPANY, INC.—AN ONGOING COMPREHENSIVE CASE

One of the best ways to learn is to immediately apply what you have studied. The purpose of this case is to allow you to do that. You will select a local company that you can work with. At the end of most chapters you will find an assignment that will have you apply what you have learned using the company you have selected as a reference. This case, then, may become an ongoing case study that you will work on throughout the term.

Select a local company and obtain permission to study its personnel/payroll information system. Answer the following questions about its system.

1. Who are the individuals responsible for maintaining personnel records, recommending personnel change transactions, approving personnel change transactions, recording employee activity, supervising the processing of employee payrolls, distributing employee paychecks, and reporting to government agencies to satisfy legal and tax requirements? Prepare a partial organization chart, and identify where these individuals are located on this chart.

2. What documents are used in the system? Obtain a sample copy of each document.

3. What master files are maintained in the system? What is the data content of each master file? Prepare (or obtain copies of) record layouts for each master file.

4. For each master file, explain how it is updated. Identify each of the different types of transactions that cause the file to be updated. What is the data content of each transaction record? Describe how these transaction data are captured in machine-readable form for entry into the company's computer system. Prepare (or obtain copies of) record layouts for each transaction record.

5. If the company uses a data base management system, prepare (or obtain a copy of) a schema diagram identifying the linkages among the various master files within the system.

6. Prepare (or obtain copies of) system flowcharts for each of the major master file update processes. For each process, indicate whether the company uses batch processing, on-line processing, or a combination of these.

7. Describe internal control procedures employed by the company in this system. Do you feel that the company's internal controls are satisfactory?

8. Identify and obtain sample copies of reports that are prepared by the system. For each report, identify the file or files from which the information originates. Indicate the frequency with which each report is prepared and whether it is prepared on the mainframe computer or a personal computer. Identify who receives each report and how it is used. Evaluate the content and format of each report.

9. Describe how accounting transaction information that originates in this system is transmitted to the company's general ledger system.

CASE 19.2: DARWIN DEPARTMENT STORE

The Darwin Department Store pays all of its employees on a salaried basis. Payroll processing is done by computer, and the payroll master file is maintained on disk. At periodic intervals during a month batches of payroll file change transactions are entered into the system by Personnel Department staff using an on-line terminal and then are posted to the payroll master file. This run produces a printed report listing all of the file changes processed.

The payroll run takes place on the last day of each month. Because all employees are paid a fixed salary, there is no transaction input. This run produces printed employee paychecks and earnings statements, a printed summary report, and a payroll register file recorded on disk. The payroll register file is subsequently processed to prepare a printed payroll register report.

1. Explain what is meant by "payroll file change transactions." Give four examples of such transactions that might occur in the context of this application.

2. Prepare a systems flowchart of the computer processes described.

3. List the components of the hardware configuration needed to accomplish all phases of the processing described.

4. The "summary report" that is generated by the payroll run includes accounting journal entries. What are these journal entries? (Indicate accounts debited and accounts credited.)

5. Describe a comprehensive set of control policies and procedures for this payroll data processing application. Identify the control objectives, and relate each control policy or procedure to a specific control objective. Explain the functioning of each control policy or procedure within the specific context of this payroll data processing application.

6. Suppose that Darwin decides to pay its sales personnel on a commission basis. This would require some modifications to this system. Describe the changes that would be required in (a) the payroll master file, (b) the payroll run, and (c) internal control procedures.

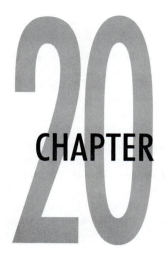

CHAPTER

The Financial Management and Financial Reporting Cycles

LEARNING OBJECTIVES

After studying this chapter, you should be able to:

- Describe the key activities and data processing operations included in the financial management and financial reporting cycles.
- Describe the decision responsibilities and information requirements of financial management.
- Give several examples of the information provided to financial management by the accounting information system.
- Flowchart data and information flows in the financial management and financial reporting cycles.
- Evaluate and recommend control policies and procedures for the financial management and financial reporting cycles.

INTEGRATIVE CASE: ELECTRONICS INCORPORATED

Tony Gonzales, Chief Financial Officer (CFO) at Electronics Incorporated, is having a bad day. First, he meets with Kevin Robinson, EI's new Controller, to discuss what could be done to speed up the preparation of the company's quarterly financial report. Tony is scheduled to present EI's quarterly financial results to Wall Street security analysts next Wednesday, and he is beginning to worry that there will be nothing to present. According to Kevin, the volume of transactions at the end of this quarter has been higher than usual, and EI's general ledger system has been temporarily overwhelmed. Kevin assured Tony that everything is now on track and that preliminary results will be available by Monday morning.

Next, Tony has lunch with Grace Healy, EI's Chief Information Officer. Grace is upset that her request for $2.5 million to upgrade and expand EI's computer facilities has been denied by the Capital Investments Committee, which Tony chairs. Tony points out that this project ranked below several others on the net present value–to–investment index that EI uses in ranking proposed capital investment projects. Grace's response is that the estimated benefits for these other projects have been improperly inflated, and she challenges Tony to investigate these projects after 12 months to determine whether the estimated benefits have been realized. Grace also asserts that the benefits from upgraded computer facilities are more tangible, in that EI's other operating units would be willing to pay for the improved services they would receive.

Later, Tony receives a call from an officer at the Dayton National Bank, who advises him that EI's account is close to being overdrawn. Apparently, collections on account have been lower than expected over the past two weeks, and some short-term borrowing will be required. As Tony hastily schedules a meeting with bank officials to arrange an emergency extension of EI's line of credit, he is very concerned about what this is likely to cost.

While driving downtown to meet with bank officials, Tony thinks of some questions that he wishes he had asked Grace about ways to improve EI's information systems. These questions are:

1. How can the accounting closing process be completed more promptly?

2. Can a system be developed to report on the success of capital investment projects 12 months after their implementation?

3. Can information be generated to support her claim that EI's other operating units would be willing to pay for the services they receive from the Information Systems Department?

4. Can a system be developed to provide better forecasts of cash flows?

What would you suggest to Tony about how EI's information systems might be improved to address these issues? ∎

INTRODUCTION

The financial management cycle is a recurring set of management activities and related data processing operations directed at securing a steady flow of financial resources into and through an organization. Closely related to the financial management cycle is the financial reporting cycle, which is the accounting cycle that processes all the economic transactions of an organization to prepare financial statements and other reports analyzing the financial status and performance of the organization and its various operating units. The economic transactions that originate in the revenue cycle, the procurement cycle, the production cycle, the personnel/payroll cycle, and the financial management cycle all become input to the financial reporting cycle. Thus in addition to its central role in supporting the financial management function, the financial reporting cycle integrates all of the other accounting cycles that we have studied in the previous four chapters.

Financial management activities include establishing credit policies, managing the collection of receivables, arranging sources of capital funds for the organization, maintaining relationships with investors and creditors, planning capital expenditures, planning and controlling cash flows, and securing appropriate insurance coverage. Related data processing operations include processing cash receipts and disbursements, maintaining accounting records, budgeting cash flows and operating results, preparing financial statements, and developing information to assist management in evaluating the financial performance of managers, divisions, investments, and so forth. The information system that supports the financial management function through data processing operations and financial reporting processes is referred to here as the financial information system.

The focus of this chapter is on financial information systems. Financial information is any information concerning the flow of funds through an organization. Virtually all activities and decisions within an organization have some effect on the organization's finances. The financial management function and the related systems that generate financial information are thus vital to effective business management. This chapter begins by describing the decision responsibilities and information requirements of the financial management function. This establishes the kinds of information that must be produced by information systems designed to serve financial managers. The next section describes in general terms the basic functions and procedures that must be performed within the financial reporting cycle and other data processing cycles related to the financial management function. These procedures generate the raw data that are the source of a substantial volume of financial information. The remainder of the chapter describes and illustrates how these various financial data processing activities are accomplished using modern information technology.

THE FINANCIAL MANAGEMENT FUNCTION

For an understanding of the decision-making responsibilities and related information requirements of financial managers it is useful to begin by examining the organization structure of the financial management function within a typical business entity. In an organizational sense the financial management function includes the Treasurer, who is responsible for administration of the finance function, and the Controller, who administers the accounting function. In many businesses the Treasurer and the Controller are combined organizationally under the au-

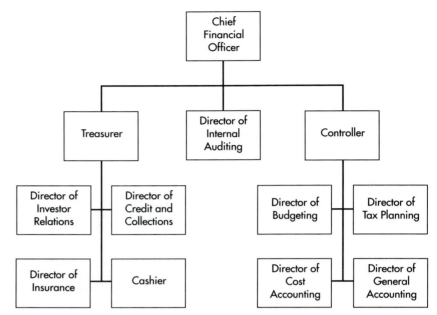

Figure 20.1
Organization structure for financial management

thority of a top financial executive, often called the **Chief Financial Officer** (CFO) or Executive Vice-President for Finance. An example of an organization structure of this type is shown in Fig. 20.1.

As Fig. 20.1 indicates, it is common for the Director of Internal Auditing to also report to the CFO; this structure is consistent with the need for the internal audit function to be organizationally independent of the accounting function. However, the internal auditing function is discussed in Chapters 12 and 15 and is therefore not discussed further here. This section focuses on the role of the CFO, the Treasurer, the Controller, and the various staff functions reporting to the Treasurer and Controller.

The Chief Financial Officer   The CFO is responsible both for administering the functions under his or her authority and for making decisions and recommendations about the most important aspects of the finance function. These latter tasks include decisions about long-term financing, dividend policy, capital expenditures, and resource allocation within the firm. Another important responsibility of the CFO involves monitoring, analyzing, and reporting on the firm's operating performance.

Decisions about long-term financing are made infrequently in most business organizations, perhaps only once every few years. Each major decision in this area, however, will have a significant impact on the firm's success and growth over an extended period of time. Perhaps the most important strategic decision involves selecting the best mix of debt and equity financing in order to gain the advantages of financial leverage while minimizing financial risk and interest charges. Once this selection has been established, decisions must be made about the best sources of long-term debt and equity financing and about the timing and marketing of new security issues. Selecting the sources of long-term financing involves choosing among such alternatives as bonds, common stock, preferred stock, and other financial instruments. Planning the timing of financing involves determining when entry into the capital markets can be achieved on terms most favorable to the firm. Dividend policy is also closely related to long-term financing, because another source of long-term funds is retained earnings that are not paid out as dividends.

Much of the information required for decisions on long-term financing is external information concerning, for example, the state of the economy and its impact on stock and bond prices, interest rates, and the capital markets generally. Internally generated information useful for decision making in this area includes long-term past and future information regarding the firm's financial position and earnings performance. Basic financial statements generated by the accounting function, including the balance sheet, income statement, and statement of cash flows, provide a perspective on past trends and present conditions. Major plans developed by top executives, and the financial projections generated on the basis of such plans, are also an important source of information.

The CFO is also deeply involved in the planning and control of capital expenditures, which include expenditures for the acquisition of property, plant, equipment and other assets having a long-term benefit to the firm. Planning capital expenditures includes determining the total amount that the firm will spend on capital expenditures for each year or quarter and deciding among alternative capital investments. These decisions establish how the firm's financial resources will be allocated among its divisions, functions, and other operating units and are thus crucial to the firm's growth and success. Controlling capital expenditures involves establishing policies for granting approval of expenditure requests, verifying that each expenditure is properly made to acquire the designated resources, confirming that these resources are being employed as specified in the expenditure request, and evaluating the actual return on the invested capital relative to the estimated return.

The information required for capital expenditure planning consists primarily of estimates of cash inflows and outflows associated with alternative capital investments, along with an evaluation of the risks and uncertainties affecting each alternative. The discounted cash flow technique should be applied to cash flow estimates to determine the net present value of each alternative investment, and this provides a basis for ranking the various alternatives.[1] The availability of funds for

---

[1] For an extensive treatment of capital budgeting and cash flow discounting, see Harold Bierman, Jr., and Seymour Smidt, *The Capital Budgeting Decision*, 7th ed. (New York: Macmillan, 1988).

capital expenditures may be estimated on the basis of sales forecasts and earnings projections. For purposes of controlling capital expenditures the required information includes the formal request for authorization of the expenditure, indicating the costs associated with the purchase, the expected benefits, and the projected revenues or cost savings. A record of all vital data relating to each capital asset acquired should be prepared when the asset is put into service and should be maintained for as long as the asset is owned and used. Other control information may be obtained from follow-up studies that evaluate the accuracy of the original cost and benefit estimates.

The CFO must continuously monitor the firm's operating results, including the costs, revenues, and earnings generated by its various operating units, and its overall cash flows. This task requires the preparation of annual operating budgets for departments, divisions, and other operating units within the firm and the establishment of systems of financial reporting that generate comparisons of each unit's actual financial performance with its operating budget. The CFO must then analyze these reports to recognize actual or potential problems and to identify likely sources and solutions for these problems. The CFO is also responsible for reporting each unit's operating results to its managers and for helping each operating manager interpret his or her unit's results and understand how to improve them. In addition, the CFO is responsible for reporting the firm's financial results to the investment community and for keeping stockholders, security analysts, and external investors apprised of significant developments affecting the firm's financial condition and performance. Finally, the CFO must ensure that the firm's external financial reports adhere to the standards and regulatory requirements of the Securities and Exchange Commission (SEC), the Financial Accounting Standards Board (FASB), and other applicable regulatory bodies.

To perform these analysis and reporting tasks effectively, the CFO must receive, on a regular basis, internal information on the financial performance of the firm and its operating units. This information includes monthly financial statements for the firm and its major divisions and monthly reports comparing actual and budgeted financial performance for each significant operating unit. In addition, the CFO must have access to the detailed financial data underlying these reports in order to better analyze existing trends and conditions and better understand the implications of the firm's financial results. Finally, in order to develop an appropriate perspective for understanding the firm's financial performance, the CFO also needs external information on current economic, industry, and market conditions.[2]

---

[2] For additional discussion of the CFO's role, see Carlos Cantu, "A CEO's Perspective: The Role of the CFO," *Financial Executive* (July/August 1991): 30–31.

The Treasurer The Treasurer's responsibilities include managing working capital and short-term cash flows, advising the CFO on long-term financing decisions, capital structure, and the firm's participation in the capital markets (as just described), and administering the various treasurership staff functions.

Working capital management involves monitoring accounts receivable and establishing procedures to speed collections on account, monitoring inventory balances and establishing procedures to minimize the costs of holding and ordering inventories while minimizing the risk of inventory stockouts, and monitoring accounts payable balances to ensure that they are paid on a timely basis and that cash discounts are taken whenever it is cost-effective to do so. Cash management involves making decisions about the investment of cash balances in excess of short-term cash requirements and about the timing and sources of short-term cash borrowing. Alternatives for short-term cash investment include U.S. Treasury bills, bank certificates of deposit, and commercial paper. Alternative sources of short-term borrowing include trade credit, commercial bank unsecured credit, and secured loans using inventories or accounts receivable as collateral.

Effective management of cash and working capital requires both external and internal information. Internal information on receivables, inventories, and payables is essential for making decisions on working capital management, and external information on customers and suppliers may be useful as well. Decisions on investing idle cash should be based on information about the nature, yield, and maturity dates of various alternative investments. Decisions on the best sources of short-term borrowing require information about the options available in the financial markets. The timing of these investment and borrowing decisions depends primarily on internal information concerning when excess cash balances will be available or when short-term borrowing will be required. Short-term cash budgets that project weekly or monthly cash flows for the immediate future are the primary source of such information. These budgets may be supplemented by revenue projections generated from accounts receivable data and by cash outflow projections generated from accounts payable and purchase commitments data.

The importance of budgeting short-term cash flows is exemplified by the problem encountered by Tony Gonzales at Electronics Incorporated. Apparently, EI's bank account was close to being overdrawn because of an unexpected shortfall in cash receipts. With a cash budgeting system in place, Tony would receive a daily report containing estimated and actual cash receipts each day over the next few weeks. Any impending cash shortage would be immediately apparent. This would allow Tony to take steps that might speed collections on account, slow cash disbursements, and/or make favorable arrangements for short-term borrowing, if necessary.

Modern information technology is enabling banks to offer new services that enhance a company's ability to manage its short-term cash flows. For example, Harry D. LeTourneau, Executive Vice-President of NationsBank in Charlotte, North Carolina, describes a service called automated target balance management. Under this service the company specifies a target balance for its bank account. Then on a daily basis the bank's automated system will compare the company's actual balance with its target balance. If the actual balance exceeds the target balance, the excess is automatically invested in a portfolio of short-term financial instruments. If the actual balance falls below the target balance, a portion of the short-term investment portfolio is liquidated to cover the difference. If necessary, the system will automatically charge the company's short-term line of credit to make up any remaining deficiency in the target balance.[3] This system significantly reduces the time spent by treasury staff personnel in monitoring short-term cash flows to avoid temporary shortfalls in the company's cash balance.

The Treasurership Staff Functions

The separation of treasurership staff functions into investor relations, credit and collections, insurance, and cashier, as shown in Fig. 20.1, is representative of the way in which these responsibilities are functionally allocated in many large business organizations. The primary responsibilities of each of these staff functions are briefly reviewed here.

The Director of Investor Relations administers the process of communicating the firm's financial results to the investment community, including not only the firm's own stockholders but also security analysts, stock exchanges through which the firm's securities are traded, investment bankers through whom new debt and equity securities are issued, and the SEC, which regulates the securities markets. To fulfill this responsibility, the Director must maintain a data base of information on current firm stockholders and stockholder transactions and must maintain contact with other key persons in the investment community. Like the CFO, the Director of Investor Relations must receive regular information on the financial performance of the firm plus external information on current economic trends and conditions.

The Director of Credit and Collections is responsible for developing and administering policies on the granting of credit and the collection of accounts. Credit-granting policies, credit limits, and collection procedures must be tight enough to avoid tying up funds in accounts receivable unnecessarily, since these funds could be profitably invested elsewhere. On the other hand, credit policies and procedures must be loose enough to avoid the loss of sales and customers. The Director of Credit and Collections must find the optimal trade-off between these two conflicting objectives.

---

[3] Harry D. LeTourneau, "What to Expect from Your Bank," *Financial Executive* (May/June 1992): 23–26.

Some of the information requirements of the credit and collection function are external. For example, the Director needs information on the creditworthiness of new customers in order to decide whether, and to what limit, to extend credit to them. Primary external sources of credit information include Dun & Bradstreet, which provides credit reports and ratings on business firms, and local credit bureaus, which provide credit reports on individuals. Much internal information should also be available to assist in credit decisions. Records of the payment history of a customer are useful in making decisions on whether to extend further credit. Information on current past-due balances is also relevant to the credit-granting decision and to the decision of whether to initiate special collection procedures. Reports analyzing customer accounts written off as uncollectible are useful in the establishment of credit-granting policies.

The Director of Insurance is responsible for identifying and evaluating potential losses to the firm that are insurable, selecting the appropriate mix of insurance coverage and other methods for dealing with these risks, obtaining insurance coverage on terms favorable to the firm, and administering the firm's various insurance contracts. This function is sometimes referred to as the risk management function. The Director of Insurance needs both external and internal information for decision making. External information requirements include knowledge of the characteristics and costs of various types of available insurance coverage. Internal information requirements include estimates of potential losses that would result from physical damage to assets, disability or death of key employees, criminal action, and fraud or negligence on the part of employees. While accounting records provide useful information for estimating potential losses from physical damage to assets, information systems often do not provide sufficient information to develop accurate estimates of the size and likelihood of potential losses from the other types of insurable risks. In order to administer the organization's insurance programs, the Director of Insurance needs information concerning payment of premiums, execution of new insurance contracts in accordance with established policies, maintenance and funding of reserves for self-insurance, and reporting and collection of claims.

The Cashier establishes and maintains banking arrangements for the organization. This function encompasses selecting the firm's banks and banking locations; establishing bank accounts; negotiating the terms and conditions relating to those accounts; utilizing lockbox accounts for the collection of customer remittances; establishing policies and procedures relating to electronic funds transfers for employee payrolls, customer remittances, and supplier payments; and arranging a line of bank credit to cover short-term borrowing requirements. The Cashier is also responsible for endorsing, depositing, and maintaining a record of cash receipts; reviewing and approving disbursement authorizations; signing and distributing checks; and maintaining a record of cash disbursements. To carry out these responsibilities, the Cashier needs internal information on cash receipt and disbursement transactions, and on bank deposits and related bank transactions initiated by the firm, plus bank statements that provide details about transactions and balances relating to all of the firm's bank accounts.

The Controller   The Controller's responsibilities include designing systems to efficiently process large volumes of accounting transaction data, ensuring that effective internal controls are in place throughout the organization, preparing and interpreting financial information used by management to evaluate the economic performance of the business organization and of individual managers within the organization, assessing the financial implications of alternative management plans and strategies, and administering the various controllership staff functions located under his or her authority.

Little more need be said about the functions of designing accounting systems, internal controls, and financial reports, since these topics have been a focal point of this book, especially throughout Part 5. Nonetheless, we will add two points. First, a key part of these responsibilities is to ensure compliance with a myriad of laws, regulations, and standards, including the financial reporting standards of the SEC and FASB, tax legislation enforced by the IRS, internal control standards promulgated by the Foreign Corrupt Practices Act, and pension fund accounting requirements under the Employee Retirement Income Security Act (ERISA). Second, to fulfill these responsibilities effectively, the Controller must be adept at working with other people, because accounting systems, internal controls, and financial reports cross virtually all organizational boundaries and affect the work experiences of supervisors, managers, and executives throughout the organization.

Another important part of the Controller's role is to serve as a financial consultant to top management and to other managers within the organization. In this role the Controller must address a variety of questions. For example, what caused the company's net income to increase (or decrease)? Why did certain key financial ratios increase (or decrease) in the company's recent financial statements, and what does it mean for the company's financial health and future prospects? How should top management interpret and evaluate the financial performance of the firm's operating divisions? What steps should the company take to improve its earnings, reduce its taxes, improve its key financial ratios, reduce its costs, and improve its cash flows? What would be the effect on the company's production costs if a new manufacturing process were implemented? What if a new sales commission plan were adopted? What if the company lowered its prices? To address questions like these, the Controller must have a thorough understanding of the company's financial strengths and weaknesses and of its position within the industries that it serves and the economy as a whole; and the Controller must be very proficient at preparing, analyzing, and interpreting financial information.

The Controllership Staff Functions

The separation of controllership staff functions into budgeting, tax planning, cost accounting, and general accounting, as shown in Fig. 20.1, is representative of the way in which these responsibilities are functionally allocated in many large business organizations. The primary responsibilities of each of these staff functions are briefly reviewed here.

The Director of Budgeting is responsible for preparing three kinds of budgets. First, as explained in Chapter 2, are the operating budgets for each organizational unit that delineate the unit's projected revenues and expenses over the next 12 months. The operating budget serves as a standard for evaluating the performance of unit managers. To prepare the operating budget, the Director of Budgeting needs information about each unit's projected level of activity. To obtain this information, the Director begins by working with sales managers to determine projected sales volume. The Director then works with production planners and other managers throughout the organization to determine the level of operating expenses that must be incurred to support the projected sales volume.

From the operating budget and its implications for cash collections and expenditures the Director of Budgeting prepares a **cash budget** that specifies the timing of the organization's operating cash inflows and outflows. In addition, the Director works with operating managers to develop cash flow estimates to support requests for capital expenditures and participates in the process of prioritizing these requests. After final decisions have been made on capital expenditures, the Director of Budgeting prepares a **capital expenditures budget** that specifies the total cash inflows and outflows associated with all ongoing capital investment projects. This budget must be combined with the organization's operating cash budget to determine overall cash flows and related financing requirements. Thus the Director of Budgeting plays an important role in assisting management to plan and control the organization's operating, investment, and financing activities.

The Director of Tax Planning makes recommendations on how the organization can minimize its tax liabilities, and administers the organization's tax reporting activities to ensure compliance with all applicable laws and regulations. The Director must advise the Controller and other top executives about the tax effects of alternative management decisions. When the organization is involved in a large transaction that has a significant tax effect, the Director must assist management in executing the transaction in a way that minimizes adverse tax consequences. The Director is also responsible for preparation and submission of federal, state, and local tax returns.

The Director of Cost Accounting supervises those accounting activities directly relating to manufacturing operations. This function includes the determination of standard costs for materials, labor, and overhead for each of the company's products. It also includes the establishment of accounting systems to record and process accounting data on manufacturing work in progress and to generate reports comparing actual and standard production costs for each manufacturing department, for each product, and so on. While the cost accounting function is most highly developed in manufacturing companies, comparable functions exist in companies outside the manufacturing sector. For example, the importance of cost accounting is now recognized by companies in the retail, health care, transportation, and financial services industries as the need to measure and control costs becomes more acute throughout our economy.

The Director of General Accounting is responsible for supervising the routine operating functions of the Accounting Department, including accounts receivable, inventory, accounts payable, payroll, and general ledger. This function includes establishing systems for processing accounting data and maintaining accounting records in each of these areas. It also includes establishing internal control procedures and monitoring the execution of those procedures. Finally, it includes generating routine operating reports such as accounts receivable aging schedules, cash flow commitments schedules, payroll registers, operating budgets, cash disbursements registers, and so forth. The Director of General Accounting must monitor these activities on a continuous basis to ensure that they are performed promptly and effectively.

Summary

The CFO, Treasurer, and treasurer's staff are primarily *users* of accounting information, much like managers in the areas of marketing, production, and human resource administration. In contrast, the Controller and controller's staff are primarily responsible for *producing* accounting information. This does not imply that the controllership function is somehow less important. As we have pointed out numerous times throughout Part 5, the quality of an organization's accounting information systems is often crucial for its success. In addition, accounting personnel are important participants in organizational decision making because they can understand and explain the accounting information that is often essential in making sound decisions. This is especially true in business organizations, where the goals—maximizing profits, providing the best value to customers, increasing shareholder wealth—are basically of a financial nature.

In summary, the financial management, marketing, production, and human resource management functions provide the four pillars of management for any organization. The accounting function is not only an important subset of financial management but also a crucial part of all of the management functions because of its role in processing data to support and control operating activities, and in generating information to support management decision making.

THE FINANCIAL MANAGEMENT AND FINANCIAL REPORTING CYCLES: BASIC FUNCTIONS AND PROCEDURES

This section reviews, at a very general level, the basic functions and procedures that are performed in four key data processing cycles relating to the finance and accounting functions. They are the cash receipts cycle, the cash disbursements cycle, the capital expenditures cycle, and the financial reporting cycle. Each discussion begins with a diagram of the key steps in the cycle, followed by a more detailed discussion of each step. The setting assumed in these discussions is a typical manufacturing company, though (in contrast to the revenue and procurement cycles) there are fewer variations in the functions and procedures performed in these cycles across different types of business organizations.

The Cash Receipts Cycle

The steps in the cash receipts cycle include receiving and recording cash receipts, depositing cash receipts in a bank account, posting individual receipts to customer accounts, and posting total receipts to the general ledger. This process is illustrated in Fig. 20.2. The key functions and procedures performed within each of these steps are now described in detail.

Receiving and Recording Cash Receipts. A business organization may receive cash from its customers in several different ways, including over the counter, as in a retail establishment; by check through the mail; by check through a bank lockbox account; or electronically through a bank-managed electronic funds transfer (EFT) network.

A vital tool for recording and controlling over-the-counter cash receipts transactions is the cash register. Because this method of receiving cash exposes a company to a significant risk of theft and human error, it is important to establish procedures to ensure that these transactions are accurately recorded. Cash registers automatically create an internal record of each transaction and issue a printed customer receipt for each sale. Many also employ scanners to accurately capture inventory and price data, and microcomputers to accurately compute sales taxes and transaction totals. Many also utilize a screen or window in which the amount of each sale is displayed; this facilitates the supervision of cash register operators. Another important supervisory control procedure is reconciliation of the cash register record of total cash receipts to the actual amount of cash on hand in each register. In addition, the total of cash receipts from all registers should be reconciled to the total daily cash sales balance obtained from processing customer sales slips or invoices.

When a company receives checks by mail, mailroom personnel are required to list and total all checks received, often using an adding machine tape. The checks are sent to the Cashier's department for endorsement and deposit in the bank. The batch total accumulated in the mailroom provides an important means of verifying the accuracy of the deposit. This is an example of the use of segregation of duties to achieve effective internal control. Mailroom personnel are precluded from theft because they do not have the authority to endorse checks.

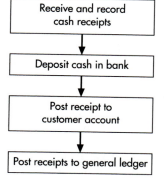

Figure 20.2
Basic cash receipts processing functions and procedures

But the Cashier, who does have this authority, is precluded from theft because an independent record of all checks received is prepared before the checks are sent to the Cashier.

When a bank lockbox account is used, customers are advised to mail their payments on account to a post office box rented by the company. Several times each day bank personnel pick up these customer payments and immediately deposit the customer checks into the company's bank account. The bank then provides the company with a record of all deposited receipts.

With EFT, companies or individuals making payment provide instructions to the bank to transfer funds out of their account and into the payee's account. Instructions may be transmitted by wire, telex, or direct computer-to-computer links. EFT's may also be preauthorized to permit automatic payment of recurring bills, such as mortgage payments, utility bills, or insurance premiums. As with lockbox accounts, the bank provides the payee with a record of all payments received and deposited in the payee's account; this is done at least once daily. In essence, these techniques combine the steps of receiving and recording cash and depositing it in the bank.

Depositing Cash in the Bank. The vast majority of business organizations utilize a bank account to facilitate the recording and control of cash receipts and disbursements. Effective control requires that cash receipts be deposited in the bank promptly following their receipt.

When cash is received over the counter, all cash receipts should be deposited *in full* in a bank account at least once each day. This means that employees who receive cash should not have the authority to make refunds or other payments out of cash receipts. There are two reasons for this procedure. First, it enables supervisory or audit personnel to directly reconcile bank deposits to records of cash register receipts and/or cash sales, which provides greater assurance that all cash received will be recorded and deposited. Second, it minimizes the substantial risks of theft and human error to which any organization is exposed whenever cash payments are made from cash receipts. When a retail store has a policy of paying cash refunds to customers who return merchandise, this should be handled by a "customer service" function that is separate from the store's regular checkout counters.

When checks are received by mail, the Cashier's department generally endorses the checks and prepares the bank deposit. Checks are endorsed "for deposit only" to ensure that all checks received are deposited. Before the deposit is made, an independent party should verify that the total on the bank deposit slip is equal to the total recorded by mailroom personnel.

Whenever cash or checks are physically transmitted to the bank, a printed receipt for the deposit is provided by the bank teller. So that the internal control loop is closed, this receipt should be compared with the predetermined total of receipts to be deposited. This should be done by an employee who was not involved in the process of receiving or depositing the cash or checks.

Post Receipts to Customer Accounts. Each customer payment on account should be accompanied by a **remittance advice**, which is a record that indicates the customer's account number, the amount remitted, and the invoices or statement to which the payment applies. The remittance advice may be a copy of the customer invoice or statement, a preprinted remittance form generated by the payee's computer and mailed to the customer along with the bill, or (for EFT remittances) an electronic record. On the basis of the remittance advice the payee posts the remittance to the appropriate customer account by subtracting the amount received from the outstanding account balance. If the open-invoice method is used (see Chapter 16), each remittance should be matched to its corresponding invoice in the customer file. In addition, if the customer has a credit limit, the "credit available" field must be recomputed by subtracting the updated account balance from the credit limit.

During the process of posting remittances to customer accounts it is customary to check the payment status of all open customer accounts. A common procedure is to report this information in the form of an **accounts receivable aging schedule**, which classifies all remaining unpaid invoices (or account balances) as current, 1–30 days past due, 31–60 days past due, and so on, and lists each amount due in one of several report columns according to its aging category. File totals for each aging category are accumulated and printed at the end of the aging schedule. This report is provided to the Director of Credit and Collections, who uses it to evaluate the effectiveness of current credit policies and to identify customers for whom credit privileges should be rescinded and/or for whom special collection procedures should be initiated. In the event that account write-offs become necessary, they should be initiated in the Credit Department after all attempts to collect the account have proved unsuccessful.

Post Total Receipts to General Ledger. After cash has been received, recorded, and deposited in the bank, and customer accounts have been credited where appropriate, the final step in the cash receipts cycle is the posting of a summary journal entry to the general ledger accounts. In the case of cash sales over the counter the amount of the journal entry is based on the bank deposit slip and the corresponding records of cash register receipts. The accounting journal entry follows.

Cash (debit)	$21,764.54
Sales Revenue (credit)	$21,764.54

When this journal entry is posted to the general ledger, the balance of both the cash account and the sales revenue account are increased.

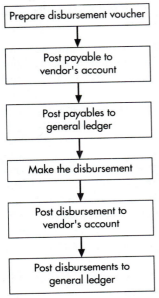

Figure 20.3
Basic cash disbursements processing functions and procedures

In the case of cash received on account, the amount of the journal entry will be equal to the total of all customer checks and/or electronic remittances deposited to the company's bank account. The journal entry follows.

Cash (debit)	$45,467.12	
Accounts Receivable (credit)		$45,467.12

This journal entry increases the balance of the cash account in the general ledger and decreases the balance of the accounts receivable control account. For verification of the accuracy of the process of posting customer remittances the updated balances of all individual customer accounts receivable should be summed, and this sum should be compared with the new balance of the accounts receivable control account.

While cash sales and customer remittances on account form the vast majority of cash receipts in a typical business organization, there are also some less routine sources of cash receipts. They include receipts of principal or interest on notes receivable, receipts from the sale of capital assets, and miscellaneous income from dividends, interest, or rentals. As with routine cash receipts, these should be deposited in full in the company's bank account to establish proper control.

Though the cash receipts cycle occurs on a daily basis, there is one other important control procedure that is generally performed on a monthly basis: the preparation of a bank reconciliation. This process is initiated when the bank sends the company a statement indicating the beginning and ending bank account balances for the period and listing all receipts, checks processed, and other transactions during the period. This must be reconciled to the company's own record of cash on deposit in the account. As part of this process, the bank statement listing of deposits should be compared with the corresponding deposit slips, with an adjustment for deposits made after the date of the bank statement. The bank reconciliation should reveal any errors or irregularities in processing cash receipts that may not have been detected by other internal control procedures.

The Cash Disbursements Cycle   The steps in the cash disbursements cycle include preparing the disbursement voucher, posting each payables transaction to the vendor's account, posting total payables to the general ledger, making the disbursement, posting each disbursement to the vendor's account, and posting total disbursements to the general ledger. This process is illustrated in Fig. 20.3. The key functions and procedures performed within each of these steps are now described in detail.

Preparing the Disbursement Voucher. As explained in Chapter 17, vendor invoices are approved for payment by accounts payable personnel who, in the case of inventory purchases, compare each vendor invoice with the corresponding purchase order and receiving report to verify that the items were ordered, received, and properly billed. For purchases of other assets or of services, accounts payable personnel verify that payment of the vendor invoice has been authorized by a supervisor or manager who has the appropriate authority. At the conclusion of this process a disbursement voucher is prepared that documents the authorization to pay one or more invoices received from a specific vendor. An example of a disbursement voucher appears in Fig. 20.4.

As shown, the disbursement voucher identifies the vendor; lists the invoice number, date, and gross amount of one or more of the vendor's invoices that are to be paid; and breaks down the gross amount of each invoice into amounts for purchase returns and allowances, purchase discounts, and the net amount to be disbursed. In addition, each voucher details the general ledger account or accounts to which the net disbursement is to be debited; this breakdown is labeled the **debit distribution**.

The process of matching vendor invoices with purchase orders and receiving reports is a prime candidate for automation. For example, Deeb and Brown describe how this process was automated at the American Sterilizer Company (AMSCO), a diversified manufacturer.

Figure 20.4
Disbursement voucher

ELECTRONICS INCORPORATED 3001 Dryden Rd. Dayton, OH 45439		Voucher No.: 16123	

Date Entered: 11/17/93

Prepared by: *BC*

Vendor No.: 65432

Remit to:
Avalon Electronics
1401 East Broad St.
Columbus, OH 43213

Debit Distribution

Account No.	Amount
00-140	$996.75
22-145	308.15
20-638	192.44

Vendor Invoice		Invoice Amount	Returns & Allowances	Purchase Discount	Net Remittance
Number	Date				
5386	11/03/93	$984.50	$98.45	$17.72	$868.33
5467	11/05/93	641.85	0.00	12.84	629.01
Voucher Totals:		$1626.35	$98.45	$30.56	$1497.34

As vendor invoice data are entered into the system, an on-line purchasing file is accessed to verify the purchase order number and compare the invoice price with the purchase order price. In addition, quantities invoiced are matched against quantities received according to an authorized packing slip (receiving report) record. The system also sets the payment date after first determining whether it is cost-effective to pay the invoice in time to receive a purchase discount. Finally, the system compares each invoice with all previously approved invoices to avoid duplicate payments. Deeb and Brown report that this system has decreased AMSCO's operating costs, reduced duplicate payments, and improved its cash control.[4]

Posting the Payable to the Vendor's Account. The preparation of the disbursement voucher represents formal recognition of an account payable to the vendor. As noted in Chapter 17, this function requires that the vendor's account payable be updated. Updating is done by appending the voucher and the related invoices to the vendor file and by increasing the amount in the "balance-due" field in the vendor file by the net amount of the disbursement voucher.

Posting Payables Transactions to the General Ledger. At the same time that individual vendor accounts are updated, an overall accounting journal entry must be prepared and posted to the general ledger. This entry credits the accounts payable control account and debits the account or accounts indicated in the debit distribution. This was illustrated in Chapter 17 in the context of inventory purchases. The difference here is that many more asset and expense accounts might be involved, since payables are recognized for the purchase of services, inventories, and other assets. Extending the example from Fig. 20.4, the journal entry would be as follows:

Raw Materials Inventory (debit)	$996.75	
Supplies (debit)	308.15	
Maintenance and Repairs Expense (debit)	192.44	
Accounts Payable (credit)		$1497.34

If a large batch of disbursement vouchers are processed together, the accounts debited in this entry are a composite of the debit distributions from each individual voucher and will usually include many different asset and expense accounts.

Making the Disbursement. On a regular basis, such as daily or weekly, the vouchers due for payment are retrieved, and a disbursement is made to settle each voucher payable. Before the disbursement is made, data on supporting documents such as the vendor invoice, receiving report, and purchase order should be reviewed to verify that they properly

---

[4] Michael J. Deeb and Eugene A. Brown, "Automating Accounts Payable at AMSCO," *Management Accounting* (January 1990): 28–30.

match the data on the voucher. Once this is verified, the disbursement is initiated either by (1) manually preparing and signing a check, (2) instructing the data processing system to generate a check, or (3) instructing the data processing system to initiate an electronic funds transfer transaction that will transfer the necessary funds to the vendor's bank account. At this time all supporting documents should be marked "paid" to avoid duplicate disbursements based on the same supporting documents. All checks are then mailed to the appropriate vendors, together with a remittance advice. A copy of the voucher, with the debit distribution blocked out, could serve as a remittance advice.

In a typical business organization not all cash disbursements are handled through the use of the disbursement vouchering and accounts payable process. There are other routine cash disbursements that are generated by data processing systems that employ a separate set of procedures and controls. One obvious example is payroll disbursements, which are described in detail in Chapter 19. Two other examples are cash dividend payments to shareholders, which are generally made once each quarter, and interest payments to holders of bonds issued by the company, which are generally made semiannually. For control purposes these disbursement systems generally employ separate bank accounts established specifically for a single purpose, as described in Chapter 19 in the context of payroll.

In addition, many firms find it convenient to be able to make some small cash disbursements in cash rather than by check or EFT. In such cases a petty cash fund may be established from which such disbursements can be made. Use of an imprest system for maintaining such funds provides control over the cash disbursed in this manner. Under this system the amount of the fund is set at some designated amount, such as $100. A petty cash fund custodian is made solely responsible for the fund; this person should not have any other cash-handling or recording functions. The appointed individual must prepare a petty cash voucher for each disbursement made from the fund and obtain the signature of the payee on the voucher. The fund custodian retains these vouchers so that at any given time the total amount of the vouchers plus the cash remaining in the fund should equal the designated amount of the fund. An internal auditor may periodically make surprise counts of the fund to verify this condition.

When the amount of the petty cash fund is low, the fund custodian presents all petty cash vouchers to the Accounts Payable Department. On the basis of these supporting documents, a disbursement voucher is prepared authorizing replenishment of the fund in the exact amount of the total of all the petty cash vouchers. A check is then prepared and cashed to effect the replenishment. Petty cash vouchers must be marked "paid" at this time to prevent their reuse. Furthermore, the unexpended balance of the fund should be verified at this time. The replenishment check should bring the fund balance up to its designated level.

Posting the Disbursement to the Vendor's Account.   When a disbursement is made to pay a vendor on account, the vendor record must be updated. This is done by appending the disbursement record to the vendor file and by decreasing the amount in the ''balance-due'' field in the vendor's account payable record by the amount of the disbursement.

For disbursements not related to accounts payable there is an update process analogous to the updating of the vendor's account. For example, payroll disbursements cause each employee's payroll account to be updated, dividend disbursements cause each shareholder's record to be updated, and interest payments to bondholders cause each bondholder's record to be updated.

Posting Disbursements to the General Ledger.   At the conclusion of the disbursement cycle, a summary journal entry is prepared reflecting all disbursements made to vendors, and this entry is posted to the general ledger. An example of this accounting journal entry follows.

Accounts Payable (debit) $39,634.50
Cash (credit) $39,634.50

Cash disbursements to pay dividends or interest would take exactly the same form, except that the debits would be to ''Dividends Payable'' and ''Interest Expense,'' respectively.

As with cash receipts, the preparation of the bank reconciliation provides a final control check on the cash disbursements process. As part of the reconciliation procedure, all canceled checks should be examined to verify that they were endorsed by the proper payee. EFT transactions should also be verified. All checks issued should be accounted for as either canceled, outstanding, or voided. This process is facilitated by the sequential prenumbering of checks. The bank statement may include certain direct charges, such as bank service fees, that require recognition by the firm through an accounting journal entry. Separate bank reconciliations should also be performed on accounts used for payroll, dividends, and bond interest. The objective of the bank reconciliation process is to provide assurance that all cash transactions have been properly processed and accounted for and, if this is not the case, to identify any errors and irregularities so that they can be corrected or otherwise dealt with as necessary.

The Capital Expenditures Cycle   The steps in the capital expenditures cycle include authorization of the capital expenditure, acquisition and installation of the capital asset, updating of asset records, and posting the transaction to the general ledger. This process is illustrated in Fig. 20.5. The key functions and procedures performed within each of these steps are now described in detail.

Authorizing the Capital Expenditure.   In most large organizations capital expenditures are authorized in one of two ways, depending on their size.

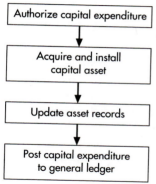

Figure 20.5
Basic capital expenditures processing functions and procedures

Large capital expenditures are first recommended by a supervisor or manager, who provides details about projected cash flows and other costs and benefits of the proposed expenditure. All such recommendations are then reviewed by a senior executive and/or an executive committee, which ranks them in order of priority and decides which ones will be approved. For smaller capital expenditures (e.g., those costing $10,000 or less) supervisory or managerial personnel are authorized to acquire the assets directly out of their departmental budgets, without going through the formal approval process. In either case the output of this process is a document of some kind that provides formal authorization to acquire a particular capital asset.

As suggested in the case of Electronics Incorporated, there is an inherent flaw in the process of approving large capital expenditure requests based on cash flow projections developed by the managers who are recommending the expenditures. As Grace Healy pointed out to Tony Gonzales, many managers have a tendency to inflate their cash flow projections in order to increase the likelihood that their recommendations will be approved. The solution to this problem is easy to identify but difficult to implement. A system is needed that can collect data on the actual cash flows associated with each capital investment project and report to top management on how these compare with the original projections. Top management could then confront, and perhaps penalize, those supervisors or managers whose cash flow estimates turned out to be substantially overstated. In turn, this would encourage more accurate cash flow projections. In practice, however, it is often difficult to trace specific cash flows to a particular capital investment project, because account coding methods are generally not precise enough. This provides a challenge for accounting information systems at EI and other large organizations.

Acquiring and Installing the Asset. The capital investment authorization process generally provides authorization to acquire a particular type of asset but does not specify the exact model or vendor. In an attempt to acquire the best value for their capital expenditures, most large organizations invite several competing vendors to provide bids. Each vendor prepares a proposal specifying exactly what assets and related services it will provide and at what cost. The capital investments committee reviews these proposals and selects the best one. If the project requires an ongoing relationship with the vendor, a formal contract should also be prepared to delineate the responsibilities and expectations of both parties.

Once a vendor has been selected, the acquisition of the asset may be handled through the regular purchasing process, as described in Chapter 17. Specifically, a formal purchase order is prepared, receipt of the asset is formally documented using a receiving report, the vendor invoice is compared with the purchase order and receiving report to verify its accuracy, and a disbursement voucher is used to authorize payment to the vendor. In many cases installing the asset may be complex and time-consuming. Therefore an installation report should be prepared to document the successful installation and operation of the asset prior to approval of a final payment to the vendor.

Updating Capital Asset Records.   Every organization should maintain a file containing records for each of its capital assets. Each of these records should contain an identifying number for the asset, plus its description, serial number, and location; the name and address of the vendor; the acquisition and installation cost; and all depreciation charges. In accounting terms this file might be referred to as the property and equipment subsidiary ledger. As with other subsidiary ledgers, the sum of the individual asset cost amounts in all of the asset records must be equal to the total of the property and equipment control account in the general ledger. When a new asset is acquired and installed, a new asset record should be created and added to the capital asset file. The acquisition contract, purchase order, receiving report, disbursement voucher, and installation report should provide the necessary data to support the creation of the asset record.

The capital asset file is an important source of information for control purposes. From the asset's serial number and location, as recorded in this file, an inventory of capital assets should be taken on a regular basis to verify that each asset is still in place and operating effectively. All transfers of an asset from one location to another should be authorized and documented, with the resulting documentation serving as a basis for recording such transfers in the capital asset file. Periodic reconciliation of the capital asset file with its corresponding general ledger control account is also a necessary control procedure. The capital asset records are also a useful source of information for insurance purposes. Finally, when it is decided that a capital asset has outlived its usefulness and is retired, this decision should be approved by a designated manager; and the documentation of this approval should be used as the basis for removing the asset record from the capital asset file.

General Ledger.   After the capital asset has been successfully installed and the capital asset record has been created, an accounting journal entry should be prepared to recognize the asset acquisition, and this entry should be posted to the general ledger. The form of this journal entry is as follows:

Property and Equipment (debit)	$52,000.00	
Accounts Payable (credit)		$52,000.00

The amount debited to the property and equipment account represents the total cost of acquiring and installing the asset. Note that asset acquisitions are generally processed together with other purchase and accounts payable transactions, so this journal entry would represent only one part of the accounts payable debit distribution posted to the general ledger, as described earlier in the section on the cash disbursements cycle. However, large and expensive assets that are purchased on a long-term contract might be processed separately, with the credit portion of this journal entry made to a long-term liability account.

The Financial Reporting Cycle

The financial reporting cycle brings together all of the other accounting cycles that we have studied throughout Part 5 of the book. It begins with a series of steps that are common to virtually all of these accounting cycles:

1. Capturing data on business transactions
2. Updating one or more data bases or master files for the effects of each transaction (note that accountants refer to this step as *posting* the transaction to the *subsidiary ledger*)
3. Preparing journal entries summarizing the accounting effects of these transactions
4. Posting these accounting journal entries to the general ledger

These steps occur on a daily basis. In addition, the financial reporting cycle encompasses several steps that take place at the end of each accounting period, after data on all business transactions during the period have been captured and processed to update the general ledger:

5. Preparing a trial balance
6. Preparing adjusting and closing journal entries and posting them to the general ledger
7. Preparing financial statements, including the balance sheet, income statement, and statement of cash flows

Figure 20.6 presents an overview of the financial reporting cycle. Note that all of the subsidiary accounting cycles that we have previously discussed are represented in the top half of this diagram. In each case the business process that generates transactions is identified, as is the data base that both supports the business process and serves as an accounting subsidiary ledger. Notice in this diagram how all of these subsidiary accounting cycles funnel accounting transaction data (in the form of journal entries) to the general ledger. The general ledger, then, is the ultimate accounting data base and is the focal point of any accounting system.

Several other aspects of this diagram require further explanation. First, note that the vast majority of all business transactions originate from one of the eight business processes listed at the top of the diagram starting from the left. However, there are other business events and processes that generate nonroutine transactions that do not fall into any of these eight categories; this is reflected by the inclusion of the "other events and processes" box in the upper right corner. Some examples of these nonroutine transactions are purchase or sale of investment securities, issuance or retirement of debt instruments, issuance or repurchase of equity securities, issuance of stock dividends, and recording the effects of changes in accounting principles or estimates. These nonroutine transactions must be separately recorded by

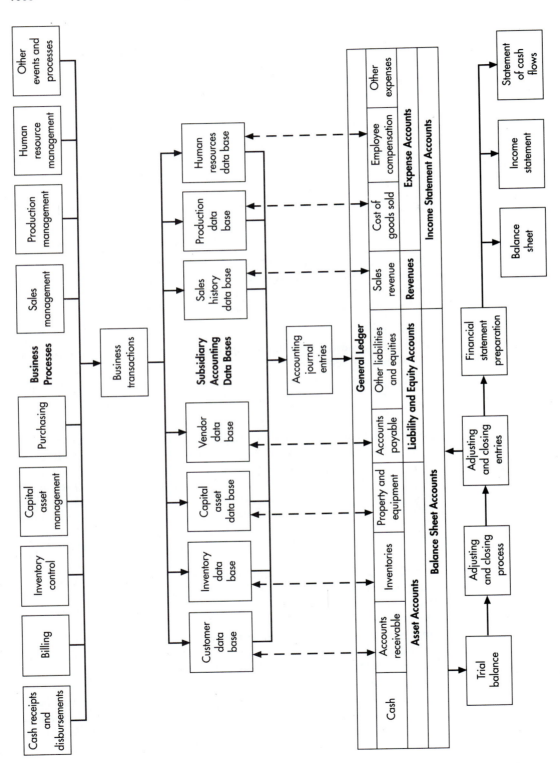

Figure 20.6

The financial reporting cycle

accounting personnel. Since they generally do not affect any of the seven key subsidiary accounting data bases shown in the diagram, these transactions are posted directly to the general ledger accounts.

Next, note the structure of the general ledger and its relationship to the various subsidiary accounting data bases. As shown, the general ledger consists of various accounts and account categories. The categories—assets, liabilities, equities, revenues, and expenses—should be familiar to any student who has completed an introductory accounting course. But note how many of the most important general ledger accounts correspond to a specific subsidiary accounting data base, as reflected by the dashed vertical lines. Each of these lines signifies that a periodic reconciliation of the general ledger control account to its corresponding subsidiary accounting data base is a key part of the accounting process. At a minimum this reconciliation should be performed at the end of each month, just prior to the closing process.

Finally, the steps shown at the bottom of the diagram occur at the conclusion of the accounting period (monthly, quarterly, and annually). Together, these steps are referred to as the "closing process." The key functions and procedures performed within each of these steps are now described in detail.

Balancing the General Ledger.   At the end of the accounting period, accounting personnel must make sure that all routine and nonroutine accounting transactions have been recorded and posted to the appropriate general ledger accounts. Then the ending balance of each individual general ledger account must be determined by taking its beginning balance, adding the amount of all transactions that increase the balance, and subtracting the amount of all transactions that reduce the balance. Following this step a **trial balance** is prepared; this is a report that lists all of the general ledger accounts with their balances shown in one of two columns, depending on whether the account has a debit or a credit balance. The totals of these two columns are then computed and should agree, since a central feature of the accounting equation is that debits and credits must always be equal.

The preparation of the trial balance is an important control procedure in any accounting system. Obviously, if the trial balance does not balance, an error has been made in recording or posting one or more accounting transactions, and all such errors must be identified and corrected before the accounting process continues. In addition, accounting personnel should review the trial balance carefully to verify that all pertinent accounting transactions have been recorded and posted to the general ledger. After any additional transactions or error corrections are recorded and posted to the general ledger, a new balance must be computed for the accounts affected, and a new trial balance generated. This process will continue until the accountant is certain that the trial balance is correct.

Adjusting and Closing Entries.   Under the accrual accounting system used by modern business organizations, the recognition of revenues and expenses does not generally correspond to the collection and disbursement of cash. For example, when capital assets are purchased, the amount paid is not immediately expensed; instead, it is debited to an asset account. Then at the end of each subsequent accounting period a special accounting journal entry called an **adjusting entry** is made to charge a portion of the asset's cost to depreciation expense for that period. This is but one example of the variety of adjusting entries that must be made at the end of each accounting period to recognize items of revenue or expense for which the actual cash inflow or outflow occurs at some previous or subsequent point in time. In general, there are four categories of events that must be recognized using adjusting entries:

1. Expenses incurred but not yet paid, such as income and property taxes, wages and salaries, interest, and utilities

2. Expiration of the value of expenses paid in advance, including depreciation of capital assets, supplies inventories consumed, and prepaid insurance premiums

3. Revenues earned but not yet collected, such as interest revenue

4. Revenues collected in advance that are earned over time, such as rental revenue and magazine subscription fees

In addition, there are some adjusting entries that do not fit into these standard categories, such as an adjustment of the inventory accounts to record the results of a physical inventory or the elimination of profits and account balances arising from transactions with subsidiary companies.

At the end of each accounting period, after the trial balance has been finalized, accounting personnel must identify and prepare all necessary adjusting journal entries. This process is simplified by the fact that for most companies the adjusting entries that are made in one accounting period are similar, and sometimes identical, to the adjusting entries made in prior periods. So the accountant should begin this process by referring to the adjusting entries of prior periods and then make any changes in these that are required for the current period. Once all adjusting entries have been prepared, they must be posted to the general ledger, and a new balance must be computed for the general ledger accounts affected.

After adjusting entries have been prepared and processed, a series of **closing entries** are prepared to zero out all revenue and expense account balances and to transfer the resulting net credit or debit (net income or loss) to the retained earnings account. These represent the final set of accounting journal entries posted to the general ledger in any accounting period. After they are posted, the balance of each income statement account is zero, while the balance of each balance sheet account is equal to its beginning balance for the subsequent accounting period.

The adjusting and closing process should be routine but often is not. For example, recall that Electronics Incorporated experienced an unexpected delay in the preparation of its quarterly financial report.

When Tony Gonzales pressed Kevin Robinson, EI's Controller, to explain the reasons for the delay, Kevin indicated that the computer had "crashed" during the month-end batch run in which all journal entries accumulated during the month are posted to the general ledger. After this problem had been resolved and a preliminary trial balance prepared, Kevin noticed that no journal entry had been recorded for the issuance of stock options to corporate executives. While preparing and submitting this journal entry, Kevin assigned an assistant to prepare the month-end adjusting entries. Subsequently, he discovered that some necessary adjusting entries were missing, and he had to scramble to prepare them. Together, these three problems caused a delay of more than one week in generating the quarterly financial report, which arrived on Tony's desk on the afternoon prior to his scheduled presentation to Wall Street security analysts. After listening to this explanation, Tony wondered whether there might be a way to automate the adjusting and closing process to minimize the likelihood of future delays.

Preparation of Financial Statements. The culmination of the financial reporting process is the preparation of the standard financial statements reflecting the firm's financial position and results of operations. The balances in the revenue and expense accounts prior to the processing of closing entries are the basis for preparation of the income statement, which calculates the firm's net income by subtracting total expenses from total revenues. After closing entries are processed and the correct ending balance in the retained earnings account is determined, the balances of the asset, liability, and equity accounts are the basis for preparation of the balance sheet. From the information in these statements, plus other information about the firm's investment and financing transactions, the statement of cash flows is prepared. These are the three primary financial statements of any business organization. They provide essential information for managers, lenders, and investors about the firm's financial status, performance, and future prospects.

Most large business organizations prepare financial statements for internal use on a monthly basis. Corporate financial reports are issued to shareholders, investors, and other external parties on a quarterly and annual basis, and they include the three basic financial statements plus footnotes and a narrative analysis by top management. For corporations whose shares are publicly traded in the securities markets the quarterly financial report is subject to audit review, while the annual financial report is subject to a full audit. These audits are conducted by independent certified public accountants, who issue a separate audit opinion on the financial statements. The auditor's opinion is published as part of the corporate financial report. Before they issue their opinion, auditors will sometimes require that a company record additional adjusting journal entries to improve the accuracy and fairness of presentation of the published financial statements. Thus the audit opinion adds credibility to the published corporate financial report.

THE FINANCIAL INFORMATION SYSTEM

To briefly summarize the previous section, there are three data processing systems within the financial management cycle: the cash receipts system, the cash disbursements system, and the capital expenditures system. The central data processing system within.the financial reporting cycle is the general ledger system. Together, these four data processing systems constitute the financial information system. By carrying out the basic functions and procedures explained in the previous section, these systems maintain the organization's financial records and produce the financial information that is required to manage the organization effectively. This section describes and illustrates the use of computer-based systems to process financial data and generate information for financial management. Consistent with the format of previous chapters, the material is presented in five subsections dealing with data capture, preliminary data processing procedures, data base updating, control objectives and procedures, and reporting information to management.

Data Capture

This section describes methods of capturing, in machine-readable form, transaction data on cash receipts from customers; capital asset acquisitions, improvements, and retirements; and accounting journal entries. Transaction data relating to cash disbursements are entered into the system as vendor invoices are received and approved, as described in Chapter 17.

One way of entering cash receipts data into the computer is by means of on-line keying from remittance advice source documents. This process requires keying in the customer account number, invoice number or numbers, amount remitted, and date received. Transaction dates and other data about the original transactions would already be stored in the seller's customer data base, accessible via the customer account number. The date that the remittance data is keyed into the system and the identity of the person keying in the data are entered into the remittance record automatically by the system.

There are several alternative methods by which remittance data may be captured automatically in machine-readable form. For example, utility companies, department stores, and credit card issuers use turnaround documents printed in machine-readable form, which are mailed to the customer with the bill and then returned with the customer's payment as a remittance advice. In retail establishments that use point-of-sale devices, cash receipts data are captured automatically by these devices when they record collections from customers for merchandise purchased. A third alternative is to request that customers send their payments to a bank lockbox service, which in turn will transmit the cash receipts data in machine-readable form from the bank's computer to the seller's computer.

A relatively new approach to capturing remittance data in machine-readable form is image processing, or imaging. This is particularly well suited to processing large remittances that cover dozens, perhaps hundreds, of invoices. For example, Pfizer, Inc., developed an imaging system to help its accounts receivable function process multipage remittance documents, some of which are hundreds of pages long and contain thousands of lines of data such as invoice numbers, store numbers, dates, and amounts. This system uses an optical scanner that reads each remittance page's image according to a predefined customer profile that is stored in the computer. The customer profile specifies how each customer formats its remittance advice data. The scanner digitizes the data and stores it in a temporary file for subsequent review and processing. This system cut Pfizer's remittance processing work load in half, and enables accounts receivable operators to work on handling exceptions while the system processes routine cases automatically.[5]

As described earlier in the chapter, electronic funds transfer also entails the automatic capture of remittance data, in the form of records transmitted from the EFT network to the seller's computer. For example, Deere and Company and Mellon Bank have developed an effective system for handling EFT remittances from Deere's network of 3400 independent dealers, under which dealers use a computer terminal or push-button telephone to initiate a debit to their account for credit to Deere.[6] PPG Industries receives electronic remittances totaling close to a half billion dollars annually from General Motors, its biggest customer.[7] Cummins Engine has recently implemented such a system for handling remittances from its largest customers (see Focus 20.1).

Capital asset acquisition and improvement transaction records include such data as asset number, transaction date, acquisition cost, installation cost, asset description, location, depreciation method, and useful life. Although these data input requirements are extensive, most companies generally do not have a large number of asset acquisitions and improvements at one time. Therefore it is not essential that capital asset acquisition data be automatically captured in machine-readable form. In most cases these data are keyed into the system by accounting staff personnel using on-line terminals. Data on the disposal of capital assets through retirement or sale are also entered into the system in this manner.

With respect to data capture, accounting journal entries fall into one of three categories. First, summary journal entry records for routine transactions involving billing, accounts payable, inventory, production operations, payroll, and cash receipts and disbursements are created automatically as a by-product of computer processing; and they are posted directly to the general ledger, as depicted in Figs. 16.10, 16.11, 17.11, 18.12, 18.13, 18.14, and 19.6. Second, recurring journal entries

---

[5] William N. Ruisi, "Tomorrow's Technology Simplifies Today's Remittance Processing," *Business Credit* (January 1992): 8–9.

[6] The Globecon Group, Ltd., *Electronic Data Interchange and Corporate Trade Payments* (Morristown, N.J.: Financial Executives Research Foundation, 1988), 55–56.

[7] *Ibid.*, 47.

20.1

FOCUS

EDI at Cummins Engine

In the mid-1980s Cummins Engine decided to pursue the productivity benefits of electronic data interchange (EDI) as an important element of its business strategy. Cummins is a major producer of diesel engines, components, and power systems for heavy-duty trucks and industrial machinery. Its primary U.S. cus- tomers are truck and equipment manufacturers and a nationwide network of distributors. In this situation EDI provides immediate benefit, since the majority of the detail is exchanged with relatively few (a hundred or so) trading partners.

By mid-1989 Cummins was ready to start tackling implemen- tation with its 32 distributors, all of whom were already exchanging data, in private formats, with Cummins's main computer. Because the distributors already had access to its computer, Cummins decided to have them transmit the remittance detail in ANSI 820 format directly to the accounts receivable system,

of a routine nature are generated and posted automatically by the computer; these include month-end adjusting and closing entries, reversing entries made at the beginning of each accounting period, and most journal entries associated with the preparation of consolidated financial statements. Third, entries for nonroutine transactions such as asset retirements, new bond or stock issues, accounts receivable write- offs, and investments in debt or equity securities, as well as certain nonroutine month-end adjusting entries, are keyed in by accounting staff personnel using on-line terminals.

Preliminary Data Processing Procedures

This section describes the preliminary steps involved in processing cash receipt transaction records, capital asset transaction records, and accounting journal entry records. With respect to cash disbursement transaction records, preliminary data processing procedures employed in reviewing and approving vendor invoices for payment are described in Chapter 17.

Preliminary data processing procedures for cash receipt transactions are depicted in Fig. 20.7. This flowchart shows remittance records originating in many of the ways described in the previous section, though not all of these data capture methods would necessarily be used by a single company. For all remittances received by mail, the amount received must be checked prior to processing to verify that it agrees with the amount indicated on the remittance advice document. If remittance records originate from more than one source, the first step in processing is to merge the separate remittance input files into a

rather than send it via a bank. They continued to transfer the funds as a separate automated clearing house (ACH) payment through existing bank procedures.

To get the full benefits from financial EDI transactions, value (funds) must be transferred as well as the details provided about what items are being paid. Such electronic funds transfer (EFT) between a buyer and a seller is performed by a financial intermediary, usually a bank, which adds a level of complexity to the payment order/remittance advance (820) transaction. Major

banks can integrate the EFT and EDI aspects of the transaction in a single data flow and can serve as a buffer between trading partners with differing needs for high-tech and low-tech (paper) data exchange methods by converting data between the various formats.

Over a 14-month period Cummins Engine's credit group went from "novice" to "expert" in receiving electronic remittance advice and payment orders from outside customers, distributors, and banks. Three key benefits of EDI are reduced cost, improved accuracy, and increased timeli-

ness, much of which result simply from not rekeying data, as it is generally accepted that 70% of computer input is output from another computer. The benefits to the Credit Department have been multiplied throughout the company, since Cummins has also implemented EDI in a variety of manufacturing and financial applications.

Source: From Martha M. Heidkamp, "Reaping the Benefits of Financial EDI," *Management Accounting* (May 1991): 39–43. Reprinted with permission of the Institute of Management Accountants.

single remittance transaction data file. Each remittance input file should have a control record indicating its source, the number of records, the total dollar amount of remittances, and perhaps a hash total of the customer account numbers.

On a periodic basis, such as once each day, the merged remittance transaction data file is processed by an edit program. This program performs various edit checks on the data, including field checks for numeric data in all numeric fields, check digit verification or other validity checks of the customer account number, a range check on the receipt date, a limit check on the amount received, and a completeness test of each record. Any transactions rejected by these edit checks are listed on an error report and on a temporary disk file. They should be promptly examined, and corrections should be entered using an on-line terminal. The corrected records are then written onto the next day's remittance transaction data file.

All transactions passing the edit checks are written onto a temporary disk file and printed in a daily remittance listing. Batch totals are computed and checked against those in each input file control record, and a batch total report is printed. The input file is then sorted by account number in preparation for processing to update the customer data base.

For capital asset transaction data preliminary data processing procedures are performed by an on-line data entry program that interacts with accounting personnel as they enter data. A simplified data entry technique such as preformatting or prompting should be used. The

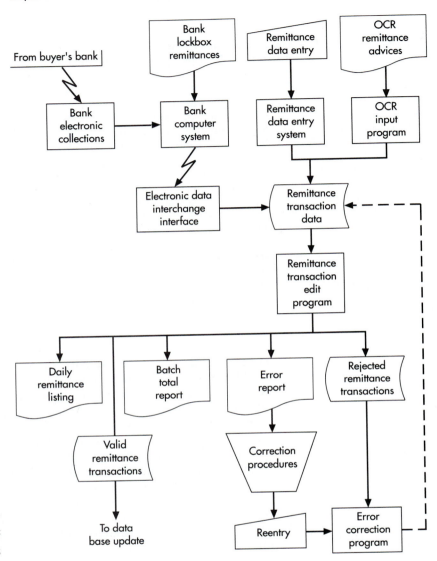

Figure 20.7
Preliminary processing of cash receipts transactions

system performs various edit checks on the input data and displays a message requesting confirmation or correction of any questionable data. At the conclusion of the data entry process, a printed listing of all transaction data is prepared for review by supervisory personnel. The capital asset transaction records may be processed to update the capital asset data base at this time, or they may be stored on a temporary input file to be processed subsequently by a data base update program.

Preliminary data processing procedures employed for routine accounting journal entry transactions differ from those used for nonroutine journal entries. Routine entries generated as a by-product of other accounting processes are often processed directly to update the general ledger, without any intervening data processing steps. An alternative approach is to record such entries on a temporary disk file, where they are first subject to review, adjustment, and approval by an accounting supervisor and are then processed in a batch to update the general ledger.

Nonroutine accounting journal entry transactions entered from on-line terminals are particularly sensitive from an internal control standpoint and should be rigorously controlled. Access controls, including passwords and compatibility tests, should be used to ensure that such transactions are entered only by authorized personnel. Prompting or preformatting should be used to facilitate the data entry process. All such transactions should be subject to edit checks, including a validity check of account numbers, a redundant data check or closed-loop verification on account number and account name, a reasonable test of transaction amounts, and a sign check of account balances after the transaction is posted. In addition, all transactions entered in this way that involve large dollar amounts should be flagged for subsequent review and approval by accounting supervisory personnel. Finally, a printed listing of all such transactions should be prepared for supervisory review.

Data Base Update

After these various transaction records have been captured in machine-readable form and subjected to preliminary data processing procedures, the next step is to process them to update their respective data bases. Cash receipt transactions are processed to update customer records within the marketing data base (see Fig. 16.9), while cash disbursement transactions are processed to update vendor records within the purchasing data base (see Fig. 17.8). Capital asset acquisition, improvement, and retirement transactions are processed to update the capital assets data base, whose content and structure are described in this section. Finally, accounting journal entries are processed to update general ledger records within the accounting data base, which is also described in this section.

This section begins by describing and illustrating batch processing procedures employed to update the accounts receivable master file for cash receipt transactions and to process cash disbursements and update the accounts payable master file. On-line processing is generally not used for these transactions, because real-time processing and continuously current data bases offer little comparative advantage over batch processing. Then following a description of the capital assets data base, on-line processing methods to update this data base for capital asset transactions are explained. The section concludes by describing the accounting data base and explaining the procedures used in processing accounting journal entry transactions to update general ledger records within this data base.

Cash Receipts Processing. Figure 20.8 is a systems flowchart depicting batch processing of cash receipt transactions to update customer accounts receivable records. Cash receipt transactions are generally pro-

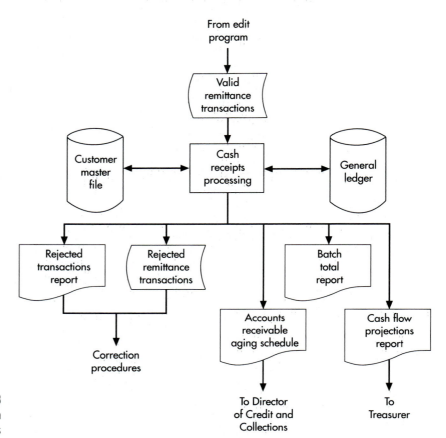

Figure 20.8
Batch processing of cash receipts transactions

cessed on a regular basis, as frequently as once daily in large companies. The input to this process consists of the validated remittance transaction file produced by the edit program shown in Fig. 20.7. An initial step in the update run is to perform those additional validity checks on each remittance record that require a comparison of transaction data to master file data. These procedures include checking that the account number on each transaction record matches one on a master file record; if the open-invoice method is used, matching each invoice paid per the remittance record with an outstanding invoice record in the customer file; checking that the total amount received does not exceed the customer's balance due; and checking that the customer has not deducted a cash discount from the remittance when the payment receipt date is past the allowable discount date. Any transactions not meeting these tests are listed on an error report and written on a separate transaction file, to be dealt with through special correction procedures.

For receipt transactions that pass these validity checks, the program updates the current balance, invoice status (open vs. paid), and credit available fields in the customer master file, as described earlier in the chapter. On a weekly or monthly basis an accounts receivable aging schedule is prepared and provided to the Director of Credit and Collections for use in establishing and administering the company's credit policies, also as described earlier. In addition, data needed for the summary journal entry, the batch total report, and the cash flow projections report are accumulated by the program during the run. Paid invoice records are usually retained in the customer file for some period of time to provide sales history data but are eventually deleted from the data base.

At the conclusion of this run, the summary journal entry (debit cash, credit accounts receivable) is posted to the general ledger, and a batch total report is printed. Once each week, or at the request of the Treasurer, a cash receipt projections report is prepared. For this report a projected collection date is estimated for each outstanding invoice. Then the system maintains a running total of forecasted remittance amounts by projected collection date as the run proceeds. The final report lists the total estimated collections for each of the next 30 to 60 days and is furnished to the Treasurer for use in short-term budgeting of cash flows.

Cash Disbursements Processing. Figure 20.9 is a systems flowchart showing batch processing of cash disbursements. This process takes place at least once each week. The process begins by scanning each record in the vendor master file to identify all disbursement vouchers that have been approved for payment and for which payment is due prior to the next scheduled disbursement processing run. A record of each voucher to be paid is written onto a temporary disk file, and the status of the voucher record in the vendor file is changed from "open" to "paid." For each vendor the amounts of all vouchers to be paid are summed to determine the total payment to that vendor, and this amount is subtracted from the accounts payable balance in the vendor's record. This process is repeated for each vendor, resulting in the creation of a temporary disk file containing records of all vouchers to be paid.

Next, this file becomes input to a cash disbursements processing program. For each vendor this program prepares a remittance advice record listing the invoice number and net amount of all vendor invoices being paid (these data are extracted from the voucher records), and it shows the total remittance as the sum of the net amount of each invoice paid. If the disbursement is to be made by check, the check and remittance advice documents are then printed. If the disbursement is to be made by electronic funds transfer, then the payment record is recorded on a temporary file of electronic disbursement transactions. A record of each disbursement is printed on a cash disbursements register. This program also maintains running totals of the amounts disbursed, the number of checks written, the number of vendor invoices and vouchers paid, and any other totals required to prepare the summary journal entry and batch total report.

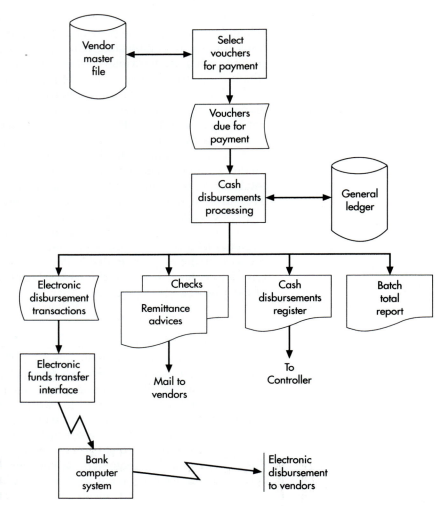

Figure 20.9
Batch processing of cash disbursements transactions

At the conclusion of the cash disbursements run the summary journal entry (debit accounts payable, credit cash) is posted to the general ledger, and a batch total report is printed. The checks and remittance advices are assembled for mailing to vendors, and the cash disbursements register is delivered to the Controller. The file of electronic disbursements is processed by an electronic funds transfer interface program, which transmits the disbursement records to the bank's computer. The bank then charges the company's account for the total of all electronic disbursements and uses the EFT network to initiate credits to the bank accounts of the various vendors. Notification of payment is also sent to each vendor through the EFT network.

The Capital Assets Information System.   The capital assets information system captures data on capital asset transactions, maintains a data base on the organization's stock of capital assets, and provides information about past activity relating to these assets and their current status. The heart of this information system is a capital assets data base containing details about each asset, including its description, location, acquisition data, depreciation records, improvement records, and maintenance records. A simplified example of the data content and structure of a capital assets data base appears in Fig. 20.10.

The capital assets data base shown in Fig. 20.10 is organized as a tree structure. The asset master record is the root, and this is linked in a one-to-many relationship with three different types of transaction records. The asset number field serves as the primary key that links these records. In addition to descriptive data about the asset, the asset master record contains several items of accounting data, including the depreciation method code, estimated useful life, salvage value, total cost, accumulated depreciation, and current net book value. Each improvement record lists the date, total cost, and description of any significant improvements made to the asset, together with a reference number indicating the vendor invoice or work order that provides additional details. Each depreciation record contains details about the depreciation charge on the asset for each year since its date of acquisition. Each maintenance record contains descriptive details plus cost data relating to all repair and maintenance services performed on the asset. The capital asset data base is the central repository of data on all of the organization's capital assets and is a useful source of reference information for general accounting, capital budgeting, insurance administration, and tax planning.

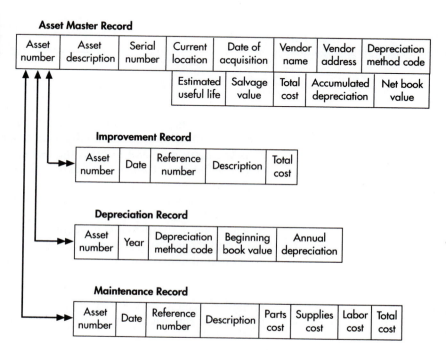

Figure 20.10
Key elements of the capital assets data base

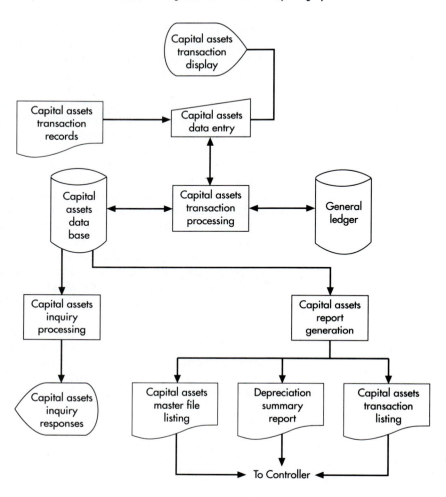

Figure 20.11
Capital assets information system

The systems flowchart in Fig. 20.11 presents an overview of the capital assets information system. In this system capital assets acquisition, improvement, and other transactions are entered by accounting personnel from on-line terminals. The transaction processing system edits the input data and informs the terminal operator of any potential errors. After each transaction passes all edit checks, it is processed to update the capital assets data base. For newly acquired assets, an asset number is assigned, and a new asset master record is created containing all of the data items indicated in Fig. 20.10. For asset improvement transactions, an improvement record is created and added to the data base, and the cost of the improvement is added to the asset's total cost. Asset maintenance transactions cause a new maintenance record to be added to the data base, with no adjustments made to the asset master record. For asset disposal transactions, the asset master record and all related transactions are removed from the data base. Depreciation transaction records are generally created automatically as part of the adjusting and closing process at the end of each accounting period. For each depreciation record the amount of accumulated depreciation in the asset master is increased by the depreciation amount, while the net book value is decreased by this amount.

As an alternative to updating the capital assets data base directly for capital assets transactions, they may be recorded in a temporary file for subsequent review by an accounting supervisor. The supervisor would periodically log on to the system, request a display of all new asset transaction records, review each record in conjunction with its supporting documents, and enter an approval code. At the conclusion of this review process each approved transaction would be processed to update the data base.

As it processes each capital assets transaction, the system generates a journal entry reflecting the accounting effects of the transaction. These journal entries are posted directly to the appropriate general ledger accounts at the same time that the capital assets data base is updated.

If accounting, engineering, or production personnel need immediate access to details about a particular capital asset, an inquiry processing system is used to retrieve the requested data from the capital assets data base and display it on the user's terminal. In addition, there is a report generation processor that regularly scans the capital assets data base and prepares various standard reports for the Controller or other accounting personnel. Three such reports are shown in Fig. 20.11. The capital assets master file listing serves as a useful reference; if printed in sequential order by asset location, it can also serve as a basis for taking a physical inventory of capital assets to verify their existence, location, and condition. The depreciation summary report analyzes current depreciation expense charges by type of asset, by department, and by division. The capital assets transaction listing enumerates all asset transactions processed during the most recent month and should be reviewed by the Controller or Director of General Accounting to ensure that no unauthorized transactions have been processed.

The Accounting Data Base. The overall structure of the accounting data base is illustrated in Fig. 20.12. The central record in this data base is the general ledger master record, the primary key for which is the general ledger account number. As explained in the discussion of the chart of accounts in Chapter 2, the general ledger account number generally incorporates two or more subcodes. Thus, when incorporated into a data base, it becomes a concatenated key consisting of two or more fields (see Chapter 7). In this example the key consists of three fields: the account number, which identifies the primary nature of the account (e.g., cash, accounts payable, sales revenue, maintenance expense); the unit number, which identifies the organizational location (division, plant, sales office) to which the account belongs; and the department number, which indicates the functional department to which the account belongs (engineering, purchasing, personnel). The

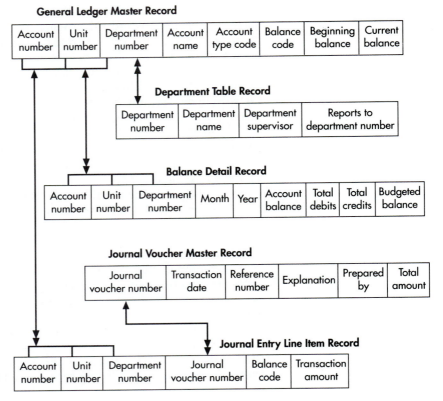

Figure 20.12
Key elements of the accounting data base

remainder of the general ledger master record consists of the account name, the account type code (e.g., asset, liability, expense), the balance code indicating whether the normal balance is a debit or credit, the account balance at the beginning of the current accounting period, and the current account balance.

The department number field links the general ledger to a department table that provides additional details about each department, including the department name, supervisor's name, and the number of the department to which this supervisor reports in the organizational hierarchy. Each department table record is associated with one or more general ledger master records. This linkage is useful, for example, in generating reports listing all expenses incurred within specific departments or all expenses incurred within all departments reporting to a particular manager.

Also associated with each general ledger master record is a set of balance detail records. Each balance detail record indicates the account balance, the budgeted balance, and the total debits and total credits posted to the account for a specific month. Thus there will be at least 12 balance detail records for each general ledger master record (e.g., one for each month in the current year). Many organizations retain balance detail records in the accounting data base for one or more prior years so that comparative financial reports may be prepared. There are also balance detail records in the data base for each remaining month in the current year, though these only contain budgeted balance data.

The remainder of the accounting data base consists of journal voucher records. As explained in Chapter 16 (see Fig. 16.5), the journal voucher is a record of an accounting journal entry. Its primary key is the journal voucher number. The journal voucher master record contains the transaction date, a narrative explanation of the journal entry, the identity of the person who prepared the entry, and the total dollar amount of debits and credits. It also includes a reference number—for example, to a source document or transaction batch number—which is essential to maintain the audit trail linking general ledger summary data to the original source documents.

In addition, each journal voucher includes two or more line item records indicating the specific accounts debited and credited. Each of these journal entry line item records includes the journal voucher number (providing a link to the journal voucher master record), general ledger account number, balance code (indicating whether this account is being debited or credited), and the dollar amount. Of course, the total of all debit amounts should equal the total of all credit amounts, and this total is also included in the journal voucher master record as a form of internal check. Finally, each journal voucher line item record is also linked to a specific general ledger master record through the general ledger account number. In this way every general ledger master record is linked to every accounting journal entry affecting that general ledger account.

One familiar type of accounting record that seems to be missing from Fig. 20.12 is the journal. Recall from Chapter 2 (and from your introductory accounting course) that accounting journal entries are initially recorded in journals showing the accounts debited and credited. For repetitive transactions (sales, cash receipts, cash disbursements) specialized journals are used, while a general journal is used to record summary journal entries from the specialized journals plus other nonroutine journal entries. So if Fig. 20.12 represents the key elements of the accounting data base, where are these journals? The answer is related to the distinction between logical and physical records and the ability of data base technology to provide links between them (see Chapter 7). Here the journals are *logical* records that are not *physically* stored in any single location in the data base. However, using a few simple data base processing steps, the system can manipulate the physical records that do exist in the data base to create other records (in this case, journals) that are part of some users' logical view of the data base. For example, to create a sales journal for February 3, 1994, the system can scan the sales invoice records within the marketing data base (see Fig. 16.9), identify all sales that took place on that date, retrieve all relevant data related to each of these sales, format that data as a sales journal, and display or print it for the accountant's use. To create a general journal, the system would perform a similar series of operations on the journal voucher records illustrated in Fig. 20.12. Thus, as far as the accounting user is concerned, these journals do exist in the data base and are available for reference as needed. In computer science terminology the process by which a journal is generated is *transparent* to the user; that is, the user can see the journal but cannot see the processing steps that the system executed in preparing the journal.

Another interesting aspect of Fig. 20.12 is the treatment of budget data. Most modern organizations use budgeting in financial planning and control. Here each balance detail record contains a budgeted balance field, which represents either the budgeted monthly closing balance of the account (for balance sheet accounts) or the budgeted monthly total of revenue or expense (for income statement accounts). By keying on the department number, the unit number, and the month, the system can generate an operating budget for any department within any organizational unit for any designated month. To generate a performance report for a prior month, it would follow the same steps, except that the system would retrieve the actual account balance data in addition to the budgeted data.

The disadvantage of this method of handling budget data is that the budgeted amounts are fixed rather than flexible. A **flexible budget** is one where the budgeted amounts vary depending on some measure of organizational activity. For example, the amount budgeted to operate a maintenance department should be higher if 200 service calls are received each month than if only 100 calls are received. To implement a flexible budget for operating expenses, the data base must include formulas for computing the budgeted amount of each expense item. These formulas are based on the idea that costs and expenses may be classified as either fixed or variable. A **fixed cost** is one that does not vary with the level of activity; for example, the salary of the supervisor of a production department will not vary as the number of units produced increases or decreases. A **variable cost** is one that varies in proportion to the level of activity; for example, the cost of direct materials used in producing a product will vary in proportion to the number of units produced. Some costs contain both fixed and variable components; for example, the portion of maintenance costs that is associated with equipment depreciation is fixed, while the portion associated with maintenance labor is variable.

A typical formula for establishing flexible budget amounts involves multiplying the variable rate of the cost or expense item times a rate base (or measure of activity) and then adding an estimate of the fixed portion of the cost or expense for the period. For example, monthly indirect labor costs for a factory department might be budgeted as

$$\$1000 + (\$0.10) \times \text{(number of direct labor hours)},$$

where $1000 represents the fixed portion and $0.10 represents the variable rate per direct labor hour (the rate base). In the accounting

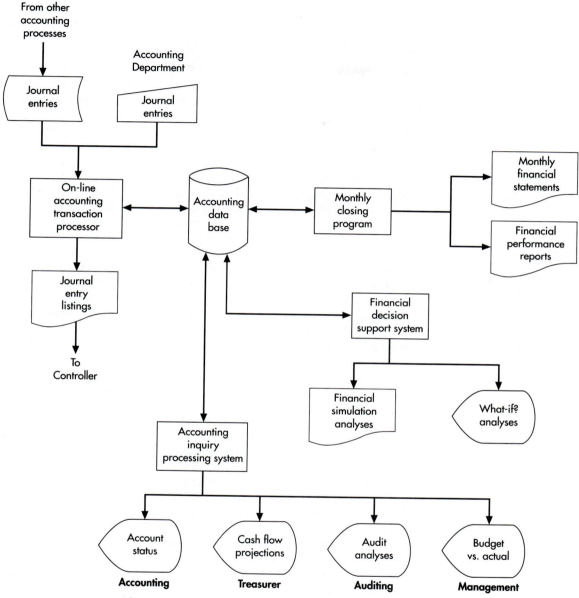

Figure 20.13
On-line general ledger
accounting system

data base, then, the balance detail record for this department's indirect labor account would contain separate fields for the budgeted monthly fixed cost, the budgeted variable cost rate, and a code indicating the rate base by which the variable cost rate is multiplied.

General Ledger Processing. The systems flowchart in Fig. 20.13 depicts an on-line system for general ledger processing. As explained earlier in the chapter and shown in the flowchart, summary accounting journal entries are entered into this system as a by-product of other accounting processes, such as billing, disbursement voucher preparation, and payroll. Journal entries for nonroutine transactions and month-end adjustments are entered by Accounting Department personnel using on-line terminals. All of these entries are processed as they occur by an on-line accounting transaction processor. This program checks for possible errors in each journal entry transaction and then posts each debit and credit to the designated general ledger accounts in the accounting data base. On a periodic basis, at least once daily, the system generates a printed listing of all journal entries processed and transmits this printout to the Controller for reference and control purposes.

Also apparent from the flowchart is the fact that the accounting data base is an important source of information for a variety of purposes. At the end of each month the monthly closing program generates routine adjusting and closing entries and posts these to the general ledger accounts. Then a report generation subroutine within this program prepares the company's balance sheet, income statement, and statement of cash flows. By keying on the unit number, this program can also prepare separate financial statements for the company's divisions or subsidiary companies. In addition, a separate report generation subroutine retrieves budgeted and actual revenue and expense data from the data base and prepares financial performance reports comparing budgeted and actual financial results for each department and organizational location.

The accounting data base also interfaces with financial decision support system programs and with accounting inquiry processing programs. These programs retrieve financial information for accounting and auditing staff personnel and prepare a variety of analyses of this information to assist management in financial decision making. Some examples of reports and analyses that may be obtained in this manner are described in the later section on reporting.

Accounting journal entries could be processed in a batch mode. For example, at Electronics Incorporated as summary journal entries are generated by other system processes, they are recorded on a temporary disk file. Other journal entries for nonroutine transactions are entered into the system from on-line terminals located in the accounting department and are also stored on this temporary disk file. Twice each month the accumulated batch of journal entries is processed to update the general ledger accounts. Although batch processing might provide greater processing efficiency than on-line processing, the obvious disadvantage is that EI's accounting data base is up to date only twice each month, immediately following the batch run. In addition, any delays in the month-end batch run will probably delay the closing process as a whole, as happened at EI. In response to this problem Tony Gonzales inquired about how other companies handled this matter, and he discovered that there is a strong trend to replace batch systems with on-line systems that post all accounting journal entries directly to the general ledger as they are captured within the system.

Tony has decided to push for the implementation of such an approach in EI's general ledger processing system.

Control Objectives and Procedures

Within each accounting cycle, internal control procedures should be designed to ensure that specific objectives are met. Therefore in examining internal controls within the financial management and financial reporting cycles, one should begin by delineating internal control objectives and then identify the set of control procedures that should achieve each objective. This approach is followed here.

Internal control procedures within the financial management and financial reporting cycles must be designed to ensure that the following objectives are met.

1. All cash receipts, cash disbursements, capital asset transactions, and accounting journal entries are properly authorized on the basis of established criteria.
2. Cash and capital assets are properly safeguarded.
3. All valid cash, capital asset, and accounting transactions are accurately recorded and processed.
4. Accurate accounts receivable, accounts payable, capital asset, and general ledger records are maintained.
5. Cash and capital assets are prudently and productively used.

Numerous internal control procedures have been described in earlier sections of this chapter. Our goal in this section is to associate these procedures with the five internal control objectives listed and to identify any other control procedures necessary to achieve each objective. To support this presentation, we give an overview of the control procedures employed to achieve each objective in Table 20.1

A responsible official, such as the Cashier, should be in charge of authorizing the deposit of cash receipts in the bank. At least once each day, all checks and currency received should be transmitted to the Cashier, who endorses all checks, prepares a deposit slip, and deposits the entire amount in the bank. Before preparing the deposit, the Cashier should verify that all checks are stamped "for deposit only" and that cash register receipts have been reconciled with the register's internal record of cash received.

Cash disbursement authorization procedures are the responsibility of the Accounts Payable Department, based on a comparison of vendor invoices with purchase orders and receiving reports or on a review of vendor invoices for proper approvals by responsible officials. Cash disbursements in excess of a certain amount (such as $10,000) are often subject to separate review and approval by a senior official. Accounts payable personnel document each payment authorization by preparing a disbursement voucher, which in turn is reviewed by the Cashier prior to issuing a check. Following this review the Cashier uses a check-signing machine with a signature plate to imprint his or her signature on each check; this authorizes the bank to process the check.

Control Objective	Related Control Procedures
Proper authorization of cash receipts, cash disbursements, capital asset transactions, and accounting journal entries	Bank deposit prepared by a responsible official, such as the Cashier Cash disbursement approval based on comparison of vendor invoice with related purchase order and receiving report Special approval for large cash disbursements Access to EFT facilities limited to authorized persons Special procedures for authorizing sales returns and allowances, bad debt write-offs, and purchase returns and allowances Management review and approval of capital asset acquisitions Preparation of journal voucher records to authorize journal entries Access control procedures for on-line transaction data entry
Safeguarding of cash and capital assets	Accurate records of cash on hand and of cash receipts and disbursements Use of a checking account, together with sequentially prenumbered checks and regular reconciliation of bank account balances Daily deposit of all cash receipts in the bank Limited access to blank checks Mail room listing of checks received by mail Reconciliation of cash received with amount recorded on cash register tape Proper use of imprest petty cash funds Separation of recording, authorization, and custodial functions Plant security measures to restrict physical access to plant assets Assignment of responsiblity and accountability for each capital asset Proper approval and documentation of all capital asset acquisitions, transfers, and disposals Maintenance of adequate casualty insurance coverage
Accurate recording and processing of cash, capital asset, and accounting transactions	Effective assignment of responsibility for recording and processing each type of transaction Use of simplified accounting transaction data entry procedures, or of automated capture of accounting transaction data Edit checks of accounting transaction data entry
Maintaining accurate records of accounts receivable, accounts payable, capital assets, and general ledger accounts	Maintenance of the security and integrity of the accounting data base and of other related data bases using (1) file labels, (2) file backup procedures, (3) off-site storage of backup files, (4) effective access control procedures, and (5) compatibility tests Regular reconciliation of subsidiary ledger totals with general ledger control account balances Regular verification of subsidiary ledger data through comparisons with external data, including bank account statements, account confirmations, and capital asset inventories Separation of recording, authorization, and custodial functions
Prudent and productive use of cash and capital assets	Effective cash budgeting Earn cash discounts offered for prompt payment of supplier invoices Effective monitoring of collections of accounts receivable Assignment of responsibility and accountability for each capital asset Incorporation of asset-related measures into managerial performance reports

Table 20.1
Overview of financial information system control objectives and procedures

The processing of cash receipts and disbursements by electronic funds transfer requires that special attention be paid to internal control. Before committing an organization to the use of EFT, its management must obtain assurance that the bank's computer system and EFT network interface are secure from unauthorized intervention and are subject to regular audits designed to monitor their security. Access to the system should be controlled through the use of account numbers and passwords. A limited number of responsible management officials, such as the Cashier, Controller, and Treasurer, should be authorized to use the system. Each disbursement record should include a code identifying the person who initially authorized the disbursement; this person would generally be the accounts payable clerk who approves vendor invoices for payment. A separate person, such as the Cashier, should be responsible for reviewing all authorized disbursements and issuing final approval before they are released to the EFT network. For special transactions, such as all disbursements in excess of $10,000, an additional authorization code should be required. Before transactions are processed, the network software should review each transaction record for the presence of the proper authorization codes. The EFT network should also employ data transmission controls such as parity checking, echo checking, and data encryption.

Special procedures should be employed for authorizing sales returns and allowances, bad debt write-offs, and purchase returns and allowances. In each case authorization should be the responsibility of a designated official who is organizationally independent of the persons responsible for maintaining accounts receivable and accounts payable records. To initiate such a transaction, this official accesses the accounting information system from an on-line terminal and creates a record that lists the details of the transaction, stipulates the reasons for it, and documents its approval. The system must be programmed to review this record and verify that the necessary approvals are present before posting the transaction to the accounts receivable or payable records.

Authorization of capital asset acquisitions is a managerial responsibility. As explained earlier, lower-level managers are generally authorized to purchase capital assets costing up to a specified dollar amount. The purchase of assets costing more than that amount must be authorized by top executives. In each case approval must be based on an explicit analysis of the costs and benefits of acquiring the asset. In addition, asset improvement, maintenance, and retirement transactions should be authorized and documented by a designated official.

The creation of a journal voucher record effectively authorizes a journal entry. With respect to journal voucher records prepared automatically as a by-product of billing, cost accounting, accounts payable, and other accounting processes, authorization is regulated by the controls built into these other processes. To control journal voucher records for nonroutine transactions entered into the system directly from on-line terminals, only a limited number of accounting staff personnel should be authorized to enter such records. Before posting journal entries to the general ledger, the transaction processing system should check each journal voucher record to verify that a valid authorization code is present.

With respect to capital asset transactions, journal vouchers, sales returns and allowances, bad debt write-offs, purchase returns and allowances, and any other accounting transactions entered into the system through on-line terminals, on-line access controls are a crucial part of the authorization process. In particular, for each authorized system user, the access control matrix stipulates exactly what kinds of transactions that user is authorized to initiate (see Chapter 13). Each time an on-line user enters a transaction, the system enforces access control by performing a compatibility test, which involves checking the access control matrix to verify that this user has the authority to enter this type of transaction. Additional control is provided by having the system prepare printouts listing all accounting transactions entered through on-line terminals. These printouts are transmitted to the Controller, who should verify that each listed transaction is proper and has been appropriately authorized.

The objective of safeguarding cash entails a variety of procedures, many of which were explained earlier in this chapter. Most important are procedures designed to capture and maintain accurate records of all cash receipts and disbursements and to provide accountability for the cash amounts recorded. To provide for maximum accountability for cash receipts, an organization should have a policy that all checks and currency received each day are deposited intact in the bank. To the extent possible, given the nature of the business, the handling of money within the organization should be minimized. A checking account should be used so that all cash transactions are recorded in both company and bank records. Checks should be sequentially prenum-

20.2 FOCUS

An Information Revolution in Banking

According to Harry D. LeTourneau, Executive Vice-President of NationsBank in Charlotte, North Carolina, the banking industry is in transition. Major investments in information technology have recently been made to provide better service to banking customers. For example, banks used to view cash management as float management. However, in the 1990s cash management is increasingly viewed as information management. Banks are putting more information and activity on-line to provide customers with quicker access to vital financial data. Other changes will occur as new products are developed and service costs are reduced.

At a recent Treasurers Conference sponsored by the Financial Executives Institute, LeTourneau described several new banking products and services that are coming into

bered, and the Cashier or another designated official should regularly verify that all checks are properly accounted for. Access to blank checks should be restricted to minimize the risk that fraudulent checks will be prepared. To protect companies from fraudulent checks, some banks will accept a file from their customers that lists the number and amount of all outstanding checks and will not process any customer check that is not on that list (see Focus 20.2). Mail room listings of cash receipts should be reconciled with bank deposits, and cash register records of cash receipts should be reconciled with the amount of cash in the register. A bank reconciliation should be prepared each month to verify that the company's cash records are consistent with those of the bank. Petty cash funds should be no larger than necessary and should be controlled using the imprest system.

Separation of recording, custodial, and authorization functions is another important aspect of internal control for purposes of safeguarding cash. Cash receipts are generally *recorded* by mail room personnel, by retail sales personnel utilizing cash registers, and by a computer-based system that maintains accounts receivable records. Deposit of cash receipts in the bank is generally *authorized* by the Cashier, through the endorsement process, while *custody* of cash receipts is the responsibility of a third party who physically transmits them to the bank for deposit. Cash disbursements are generally *authorized* by accounts payable personnel as they create disbursement vouchers and are *recorded* by a computer-based system that maintains accounts payable and cash disbursement records. These functions must be organizationally independent of the *custodial* function of preparing, sign-

---

greater use in the 1990s. One such service, referred to as "Surepay" by NationsBank, is a daily account reconciliation. With this service companies transmit their outstanding check files to the bank. The bank then matches up incoming debits on the basis of check numbers and amounts, generates exception information, transmits this information on-line to the company, and requests payment instructions. NationsBank presently offers its Surepay service to commercial accounts, but it is expensive. LeTourneau believes that NationsBank is finding ways to reduce the cost of the Surepay service and to demonstrate its value to customers. For example, he states:

Surepay will eliminate the situation we encountered last year when someone in our Raleigh, North Carolina, operation was screening a large check. This was the third time the check was screened because it was so large, and the person looking at it said she thought that particu-lar company's checks always had a perforated edge at the top, but this check was flat. We called the company—a major oil firm—to verify the check, and, sure enough, it was fraudulent. That employee saved us and our customer $8 to $10 million. Obviously, we need greater reliability in authorizing check payments, and that's what Surepay will provide.

Source: Adapted from Harry D. LeTourneau, "What to Expect from Your Bank," *Financial Executive* (May/June 1992): 23.

ing, and distributing checks, which is generally performed by the Cashier. Internal control is further enhanced by having the bank reconciliation prepared by someone who is organizationally independent of the recording, authorization, and custodial functions.

Procedures for safeguarding capital assets include plant security measures that restrict access to facilities to authorized personnel at authorized times; assignment of accountability for each capital asset to a specific manager; approval and documentation of all capital asset acquisitions, transfers, and disposals; and maintenance of adequate casualty insurance coverage on all facilities and equipment. In addition, a periodic physical inventory should be taken of all assets on hand. Traditionally, the physical inventory is based on a printout listing all capital assets records in sequence by their location. A more efficient approach is to attach bar-coded tags to all assets and to use a bar code reader to automatically capture the required physical inventory data.[8]

The third control objective is to ensure that all valid cash, capital assets, and accounting transactions are accurately recorded and processed. Effective control here begins with the assignment of responsibility for recording these transactions to qualified employees who can effectively perform all necessary data entry, review, and reconciliation procedures. For example, mail room personnel must compare the amount of each receipt with the accompanying remittance advice. Accounts payable personnel must reconcile each vendor invoice with the related purchase order and receiving report. To provide these employees with extra incentive to record and process all transactions correctly, the system captures the identity of the person initiating each transaction or batch of transactions.

A variety of procedures should be employed to control the accuracy of accounting transaction data as they are entered into the system and processed. Prompting or preformatting can be used to facilitate the data entry process, and redundant data checks or closed-loop verification may be used to ensure that all transactions are posted to the appropriate master file records. The accuracy of specific transaction data items should be checked using validity checks, field checks, range checks, reasonableness tests, completeness tests, and so forth. Limit checks can be used to flag large transactions for additional review and special approval. Each journal voucher record should be checked to verify that total debits and total credits are equal. Whenever batch processing is used, particularly in processing cash receipts and disbursements, batch totals should be prepared in the initial stages of transaction processing and then reconciled to corresponding batch totals generated by the computer during subsequent processing steps.

---

[8] See Suzanne Ekman, "Bar Coding Fixed Asset Inventories," *Management Accounting* (December 1992): 58–61.

Finally, automatic capture of accounting transaction data as a by-product of other accounting processes helps to ensure input data accuracy.

The fourth control objective is to ensure that accurate accounts receivable, accounts payable, capital assets, and general ledger records are maintained. The focal point here is maintaining the integrity of the various data bases that contain these records. For this purpose a number of data security controls are used, including internal and external file labels, proper file backup procedures, and off-site storage of backup files. Also of critical importance are the access control procedures described earlier in this section. In addition, the computer should be programmed to frequently reconcile the accounts receivable, accounts payable, and capital assets subsidiary ledgers with the corresponding general ledger control accounts and to continuously maintain a balanced general ledger. Regular comparisons of these various accounting records to actual values are facilitated by using the computer to prepare bank reconciliations, accounts receivable and accounts payable confirmations, and departmental capital assets listings. Finally, as explained earlier, the responsibility for maintaining these records should be organizationally independent of the functions of authorizing the related transactions and maintaining custody of the related assets.

The fifth control objective is to ensure that cash and capital assets are prudently and productively used. Management controls designed to ensure that cash is used prudently and productively begin with cash budgeting procedures that provide precise estimates of cash inflows and outflows based on current receivables, payables, purchase commitments, and other anticipated receipts and obligations. An effective budgeting system helps management ensure that sufficient cash is available to take advantage of cash discounts for prompt payment offered by suppliers, to plan capital asset acquisitions and other major expenditures at the most advantageous times, to arrange for any necessary short- and intermediate-term borrowing at the best possible terms, and to invest any excess cash balances to earn the best available returns. These aims are further enhanced by programming the accounts payable system to pay all vendor invoices in time to earn any cash discounts offered for prompt payment and by designing the accounts receivable system to monitor collections and promptly report on any customer accounts needing attention because of slow payment.

The prudent and productive use of capital assets is enhanced by assigning responsibility and accountability for each asset to appropriate supervisory and managerial personnel. An important part of this responsibility is recommending (and justifying) replacement of equipment and facilities when necessary. The capital assets information system should continuously monitor and report on the need for preventive maintenance, repairs, and replacement of all facilities and equipment. As a way of providing management incentives for productive asset utilization, departmental performance reports should incorporate asset-related measures. For example, each manager's financial accounts should be charged with depreciation expense and repairs and maintenance expense on the capital assets within their departments. In addition, financial performance should be evaluated by use of such criteria as return on assets or return on investment, which incorporate measures of asset value.

Reporting   Accounting data capture, data processing, data base updating, and internal control are all of critical importance to ensure that financial management and financial reporting cycle activities are carried out effectively. However, from a management perspective the reports generated by the financial information system are also of prime importance. Scheduled reports, demand reports, and triggered reports all facilitate financial management activities. Numerous examples of such reports are identified in Figs. 20.8, 20.9, 20.11, and 20.13. The content and utilization of several financial management reports are described in this section.

The number of scheduled financial reports mentioned in earlier sections of this chapter is too large to permit a full description of each one here. The general nature and purpose of most of these reports is evident from the brief descriptions already given. Of course, the content and format of three well-known scheduled financial reports—the balance sheet, income statement, and statement of cash flows—should already be familiar to most readers. Examples of two other scheduled financial reports that are used for internal management purposes are illustrated and described more fully here.

The cash disbursements register is a list of all payments, by check or EFT, made by the daily cash disbursements processing procedure (see Fig. 20.9). It is sometimes referred to as a check register, but the growth of EFT as a means of payment has made this label obsolete. For each disbursement this report lists vendor information; disbursement details, such as method of payment and check number or vendor bank account number; gross disbursement voucher amount; cash discount; and net amount disbursed. At the end of the report, the total gross, discount, and net amounts are printed, along with a breakdown of the net amount by disbursement mode (check or EFT). An example of a cash disbursements register appears in Fig. 20.14. This report is useful to the Controller for reference purposes and is a key part of the audit trail for cash disbursement transactions.

Departmental financial performance reports are generated monthly, at the conclusion of the general ledger closing and financial statement preparation process (see Fig. 20.13). These reports compare actual and budgeted financial performance for each organizational unit within the entity. The type of information included in these performance reports depends on the type of organizational unit and its level in the organizational hierarchy. At the lowest level, production, service, and administrative departments are evaluated as cost centers, and their performance reports compare actual and budgeted costs. An example of such a report for a factory production department appears in Fig. 20.15.

BLACKWELL INDUSTRIES
CASH DISBURSEMENTS REGISTER

Date: July 15, 1994

Time: 10:38:09

Voucher No.	Vendor No.	Vendor Name	Disbursed by		Accounts Payable dr.	Purchase Discount cr.	Cash cr.
38729	632845	National Supply	Check #	10451	$ 512.67	$ 10.25	$ 502.42
38730	176413	Ross Mfg. Co.	Check #	10452	95.07	.95	94.12
38731	415242	Northern Metals	EFT #5437-6410922		742.72	14.85	727.87
38732	366021	Webster Bros.	EFT #4712-2867715		4208.18	84.16	4124.02
38733	618775	ABX Distributors	Check #	10453	825.30	8.25	817.05

Figure 20.14
Cash disbursements register

Sales departments are evaluated as revenue centers, and their performance reports generally compare actual sales to sales quotas or forecasts (see Table 16.1). Product lines and service departments that charge operating departments for services performed are evaluated as profit centers, and their performance reports compare actual and budgeted revenues, expenses, and net profits. Plants, divisions, and other autonomous operating units are evaluated as investment centers, and their financial performance reports consist of a set of standard financial statements encompassing assets, liabilities, revenues, expenses, and profits. Financial reports such as these provide information of critical importance in evaluating the performance of departmental supervisors, managers, and executives.

Performance reporting is a crucial function of the accounting information system, because the information used in evaluating managerial

Figure 20.15
Financial performance report for a cost center

ELECTRONICS INCORPORATED
OPERATING PERFORMANCE SUMMARY

Department #473, Assembly

Supervisor: Oscar Nagursky

Cost Item	Month Ending 10/31/94			Cumulative Year to Date		
	Budget	Actual	Over (Under) Budget	Budget	Actual	Over (Under) Budget
Controllable overhead						
Indirect labor	$4,750	$4,608	$(142)	$46,500	$46,240	$(260)
Idle time	250	304	54	2,400	2,510	110
Tools and supplies	880	856	(24)	8,600	8,510	(90)
Maintenance	750	802	52	7,250	8,190	940
Rework	120	70	(50)	1,150	900	(250)
Miscellaneous	200	230	30	1,900	1,850	(50)
Total controllable overhead	$6,950	$6,870	$(80)	$67,800	$68,200	$ 400
Direct labor	$13,200	$13,256	$56	$130,000	$131,920	$1920

performance has a significant effect on managerial incentives and behavior. This point was driven home to EI's Tony Gonzales when he attended a dinner meeting of financial executives at which the speaker discussed how her company had changed its end-user services (EUS) department from a cost center to a profit center, with commensurate changes in the accounting and performance reporting systems. According to the speaker, the EUS department was now much more sensitive to user needs. In addition, EUS was able to expand its capacity by spending the "profits" it earned through charging other departments for its services, rather than by competing with other departments for a larger share of the company's operating budget. Tony immediately recognized that a similar approach might be beneficial for EI, which currently treated its Information Systems Department (ISD) as a cost center. This would address Grace Healy's claim that EI's other operating units would be willing to pay for ISD services, and it would provide a more rational basis for determining the amount of capital resources that should be allocated to the ISD. The following morning Tony asked Kevin Robinson to study how EI would need to modify its accounting systems in order to prepare performance reports that would treat the ISD as a profit center.

As indicated in Figs. 20.11 and 20.13, inquiry processing is often employed to extract useful administrative and management information from various financial data bases. For example, accounting staff personnel frequently must examine the current status of a specific account or transaction in response to a request from management, a customer, or a supplier. Internal or external auditors may want to retrieve information regarding financial trends or relationships in order to determine which accounts require more extensive audit scrutiny. Management may desire interim reports comparing actual and budgeted costs for specific executives or projects. The Treasurer may wish to retrieve information useful in monitoring corporate cash flows on a daily or even hourly basis. An inquiry processing system that can respond to these and other similar requests on a timely basis is an essential component of any modern financial information system.

Triggered reports may also be employed in financial information systems. One example that would have been especially useful to Tony Gonzales is a report identifying prospective cash flow shortfalls. As sales, purchases, cash receipts, and cash disbursements transactions are processed, the system would update cash flow projections incorporated into the cash budget. If the cash flow effects of these various transactions deviate from expectations, causing the organization to face an unanticipated shortage of cash, the budgeting system would be programmed to promptly generate a revised cash budget report highlighting the prospective shortfall. This triggered report would then be provided to the CFO or Treasurer, who could initiate any necessary corrective steps on a timely basis.

Financial performance reports for departments or projects might also be triggered under special conditions. Under normal conditions these reports are usually prepared on a monthly basis. However, if production costs in a factory department suddenly began to exceed standards by more than some preset average (such as 10%), the system could be programmed to prepare an interim financial performance report for management's immediate attention. Similarly, if actual costs suddenly began to exceed budgeted costs for a marketing research project, a software development project, or a product development project, the system could prepare an interim analysis of project costs for management's attention. These are good examples of the ways an information system can be designed to support application of the principle of management by exception.

An expert system may be used to assist financial executives in managing the organization's investment portfolio. Such a system would employ knowledge bases on current economic conditions and on the general suitability of various categories of investments (for example, Treasury bills or blue-chip stocks). The economic conditions knowledge base would be continuously updated to reflect current economic trends. The system would interact with a designated financial executive who specified the organization's investment goals. From these specifications and its knowledge bases the expert system would prepare recommendations as to the proportions of the investment portfolio that should be allocated to each investment category. This system might be integrated with the organization's cash budgeting system so that factors associated with investment timing could be taken into account.[9]

Decision support systems are commonly used by management in the analysis of financial information to support decision making. Even before the advent of microcomputers in the early 1980s some firms were using mainframe-based decision support systems that employed financial planning models. As the use of microcomputers in business organizations became widespread, financial planning emerged as one of the most popular uses of microcomputer spreadsheet packages, graphics packages, and statistical modeling programs. In a typical application, a portion of the financial data base, including selected budget data, is downloaded to a personal computer file. A decision support system is used to simulate the company's operations and related cash flows over the next 6 to 18 months. Such a system normally includes a what-if capability that enables the user to examine the possible effects of changes in key financial policies, conditions, or assumptions underlying the model. For example, the user might wish to examine what would happen to cash flows or other key operating variables if a major customer failed, or if product prices were reduced

---

[9] A similar system designed to support investment analysis by an individual investor is described in Barry Shane, Mitchel Fry, and Reuben Toro, "The Design of an Investment Portfolio Selection Decision Support System Using Two Expert Systems and a Consulting System," *Journal of Management Information Systems* (Spring 1987): 79–92.

by 5%, or if sales of a new product fell 20% below projections. The decision support system simulates the company's operations under the revised conditions and prepares a report analyzing the projected effects on the specified variables.

Esmark, Inc., utilizes a decision support system in evaluating corporate mergers and acquisitions. This system utilizes a data base containing financial statements for all of the company's divisions and a model that consolidates these statements and generates three-year financial statement projections. When a prospective merger candidate is being evaluated, its historical financial data are loaded into the data base. A related model then generates financial projections for the merger candidate based on different assumptions about growth rates, capital investment levels, and profits. Next, the consolidation model is used to prepare combined financial statement projections (including the merger candidate) as a way of evaluating the impact of the prospective merger on Esmark's overall operations. This model can also be used to explore the effects of different methods of financing the acquisition of the subsidiary company and to analyze the effects of different methods of accounting for the acquisition.[10]

These examples illustrate how the power of computers can substantially improve the quality of the financial information available to support management decision making. Scheduled reports can provide large volumes of information for reference purposes and also summarize this information according to various decision-relevant criteria. Triggered reports can highlight information about specific conditions or transactions that call for prompt management attention. Demand reports can provide specific information relevant to a particular management purpose. A well-designed financial information system uses all of these tools to enhance the effectiveness of the financial management function.

CASE CONCLUSION: IMPROVING FINANCIAL INFORMATION SYSTEMS AT ELECTRONICS INCORPORATED

In the six months following his "bad day" at Electronics Incorporated, Tony Gonzales has made significant progress in addressing the problems and issues that had given him such difficulty. First, EI's most recent quarterly financial results are now on his desk, one full week before he is scheduled to present them to a group of security analysts. Five months earlier he had persuaded Grace Healy to assign two of her top systems staff personnel to convert EI's general ledger system to a full on-line system. The new system was implemented last month, and it has handled this month's closing process very smoothly. By posting all accounting journal entry transactions directly to the affected accounts immediately as they are generated by other accounting pro-

---

[10] As described in Germain Boer, *Decision Support Systems for Management Accountants* (Montvale, N.J.: National Association of Accountants, 1987), 40.

cesses or entered from on-line terminals, the new system keeps the general ledger up to date on a continuous basis. In addition, a module was added to the system that automates the preparation and processing of month-end adjusting and closing entries. The development team is presently working on a user interface that will enable managers to access the new system to obtain an up-to-the-minute financial performance report for their departments.

Second, Tony has arranged for this development team to start working on a new cash budgeting system as soon as they complete work on the general ledger system. This new system will be integrated with the general ledger system and will maintain EI's cash flow budget on a continuous basis, updated for daily collections, expenditures, and changes in cash flow projections. Cash budget reports will be available at any time on request and will also be triggered automatically by prospective cash flow shortages. Since this new system will not be implemented for several months, Tony has asked his assistant, Dennis McKinney, to develop an alternative system to download cash flow data to a spreadsheet program and generate a similar cash flow report. Dennis has been able to do this, though the system is cumbersome because it requires data from so many different data bases, including customer accounts, open purchase orders, vendor accounts, and the new general ledger. Tony has asked Dennis to generate this "stopgap" report for him once each week and hopes that it will be satisfactory until the new mainframe system can be implemented.

Third, Kevin Robinson has prepared a proposal to treat EI's Information Systems Department as a profit center. This would require that EI's accounting and budgeting systems be modified to permit an internal transfer pricing scheme for computer services. Under this scheme each operating manager would receive an expanded operating budget but would also have this budget charged for the cost of computer services received from ISD. These charges would be treated as revenues to ISD. This would permit the development of monthly profit and loss statements for ISD, and they would replace the old ISD financial performance reports that analyze actual versus budgeted costs. In addition, ISD would be allowed to reinvest a portion of its departmental profits to acquire new hardware, software, and other resources needed to serve the operating departments. As a result, ISD would no longer be competing with the operating departments for capital investment funds. Grace Healy has endorsed this proposal with enthusiasm and is assisting Tony and Kevin in selling the plan to EI's operating managers.

Finally, in response to Grace's challenge, Tony has Dennis working to develop a "postaudit" plan for all capital projects approved by EI's Capital Investments Committee. The idea is that every capital project should be subject to an annual review for a period of three years from its initial approval. The review would attempt to assess whether the actual returns on the project were consistent with the projected benefits. Dennis has suggested that every proposed capital investment project be accompanied by a financial schedule delineating how the project would affect the operating results of the related organizational unit. These schedules could then be stored in a capital investments data base and used as a basis of comparison to actual operating results for subsequent years. Tony likes this idea, but he has encountered resistance to it among many operating managers, who feel that it would underrate the importance of the intangible benefits that often flow from a capital investment project. Tony is hopeful that he can refine the proposal to overcome this objection.

As he reflects on the progress of his new initiatives over the past six months, Tony begins to realize that EI's information system has played a central role in each one. It occurs to him that virtually all new developments in accounting and finance over the course of his entire career have been closely linked to improvements in information technology. In fact, much the same thing could be said about new developments in marketing, manufacturing, human resource management, and most other areas of business. Effective utilization of information technology is essential to the success of virtually all modern business organizations, Tony concludes, and this is likely to become even more true in the future than it is now. ∎

SUMMARY

Financial management cycle activities include arranging sources of capital funds for the organization, maintaining relationships with investors and creditors, planning capital expenditures, establishing credit and collection policies, securing appropriate insurance coverage, planning and controlling cash flows, and evaluating the financial performance of managers and organizational units. Related data processing operations include recording the receipt and disbursement of cash, maintaining records of capital assets, maintaining general accounting records, and preparing budgets, financial performance reports, and financial statements. The accounting information system plays a central role in carrying out these data processing operations and in supplying financial information to management.

The processing of cash receipts and cash disbursements transactions is generally accomplished using batch processing. On-line processing is much more common for the maintenance of capital asset records and general ledger records. These various systems must be designed to efficiently capture accounting transaction data on cash receipts, cash disbursements, capital asset acquisitions, improvements and retirements, and journal entries. In addition, data bases dealing with capital assets and general ledger accounts must be maintained. Internal controls must be in place to ensure that all of these transactions are properly authorized and accurately processed, to safeguard cash and capital assets and ensure that they are productively used, and to maintain the integrity of the capital assets and general ledger accounting data bases. Finally, these systems must be able to generate a wide variety of scheduled, demand, and triggered reports that will enhance the effectiveness of the financial management process.

KEY TERMS   Define the following terms.

financial management cycle
financial reporting cycle
financial information system
Treasurer
Controller
Chief Financial Officer
cash budget

capital expenditures budget
remittance advice
accounts receivable aging
    schedule
debit distribution
trial balance
adjusting entry

closing entries
cash receipt
    projections report
flexible budget
fixed cost
variable cost
cash disbursements register

DISCUSSION QUESTIONS

20.1 Discuss the similarities and differences between business organizations and nonprofit organizations with respect to the design of financial information systems.

20.2 Cite as many examples as you can of information processing interfaces (or interactions) between two or more of the following information subsystems of a typical business organization: marketing, purchasing, production, personnel, and finance.

20.3 Discuss the similarities and differences between the functions of the Treasurer and the Controller. Must these functions be separated, or could one executive effectively fill both roles?

20.4 The Consumer Manufacturing Company is considering a major reorganization in which the Marketing Departments at its various divisions would be consolidated into a worldwide marketing organization. Currently, these marketing departments are evaluated as revenue centers—that is, by

comparing actual sales with sales quotas. After the reorganization the new marketing organization would be evaluated as a profit center. Discuss the implications of this change in the performance reporting and evaluation system.

20.5 Blackwell Industries is a large manufacturing company. On a daily basis, its accounting system processes hundreds of accounting journal entries. After the journal entry records are captured in machine-readable form, they are stored on a temporary disk file and then processed to update the general ledger in a large batch every Friday afternoon and on the last day of each month. It has been suggested that Blackwell convert its general ledger update system to on-line processing, under which each accounting journal entry would be processed to update the general ledger immediately as it is entered into the system. Discuss the relative advantages and disadvantages of this suggestion.

PROBLEMS

20.1 Kids Choice Corporation is a manufacturer and distributor of children's toys. Within the past three years the company's sales volume has declined as several important distributors have dropped the Kids Choice product line. In response the company's top management has just ordered every department in the company to reevaluate its operations, identify possible problems that may be contributing to the company's loss of business, and prepare recommendations for improvement.

You have been asked to evaluate the financial information system at Kids Choice. You have learned that cash receipts transactions are processed twice each month and that any of these transactions that fail edit checks are resubmitted to the next processing run. Several customers have complained that their accounts are not correct. In addition, you have learned that virtually all organizational units within the company are treated as cost centers and receive monthly performance reports comparing actual and budgeted costs. Finally, the capital expenditures budget is allocated among organizational units in proportion to the size of each unit's operating budget, and there is no reporting on the prospective or actual costs and benefits of specific capital assets acquisitions.

Required

Could Kids Choice Corporation's financial information system and the data processing operations that support it have anything to do with the decline in its competitive fortunes? Describe several ways in which this system might be improved.

20.2 What internal controls in a cash receipts data processing system would provide the best protection against the following errors or manipulations?

a. Several checks received through the mail were stolen by personnel in the mail room and endorsed for deposit into the account of a fictitious company.

b. The Cashier has stolen company funds; instead of endorsing checks received for deposit, the Cashier cashes them and keeps the cash without recording its receipt.

c. Due to an error in keying in a customer's account number, a remittance was inadvertently posted to the wrong account in the customer data base.

d. Due to a bug in the cash receipts processing program, several records in the customer data base were inadvertently destroyed and could not be reconstructed.

e. Sales personnel in a retail organization have stolen cash and covered it up by not recording cash sales.

f. A company lost a large customer payment remitted through electronic funds transfer owing to lax internal controls in the EFT network.

g. A mathematical error was made in the summary journal entry posted to the general ledger to reflect one day's batch of customer remittances; no errors were made in posting individual remittances to specific customer accounts.

20.3 What internal controls in a cash disbursements data processing system would provide the best protection against the following errors or manipulations?

a. A clerical employee obtained a batch of blank company checks and wrote a large check payable to a fictitious company.

b. The accounts payable control account in the general ledger data base became overstated over a period of several months due to numerous errors made in keying in summary journal entries for cash disbursements.

c. A fictitious invoice was received for goods that were never ordered or delivered, entered into the accounts payable data base, and then paid on its designated due date.

d. After a check was prepared in payment of a vendor invoice, the invoice was inadvertently left in the accounts payable data base; and a second check in payment of the same invoice was prepared and mailed on the following day.

e. A vendor was overpaid for goods ordered and received, due to the overstatement of item prices on the vendor's invoice.

f. The petty cash fund custodian "borrowed" a portion of the fund for her personal use.

20.4 What internal controls in a capital assets data processing system would provide the best protection against the following errors or manipulations?

a. Acquisition of a capital asset for which no worthwhile use exists within the firm

b. A report by a department supervisor that an asset in the factory has been scrapped, when actually the supervisor has removed it and taken it home

c. A large overstatement of the property and equipment control account in the general ledger data base after several errors are made in updating the account over a period of years

d. Inaccurate charging of depreciation to departments because several items of equipment are no longer located in the departments where they were originally installed

e. Unauthorized use of a capital asset by an employee for personal reasons unrelated to employment

f. Payment of insurance and property taxes on assets no longer owned by the company

g. Continued ownership of obsolete or otherwise nonproductive assets.

20.5 Your company has just acquired a data base management system, and one of its first applications will be to accounts payable and cash disbursements processing. A disbursement voucher form identical to the one in Fig. 20.4 is used. You are to diagram the data structure of the disbursement voucher as a first step in the application design. Use a format similar to that in Fig. 20.10 or 20.12. Note that the data base will contain only the variable data on the disbursement voucher, not the constant data.

20.6 The Able Manufacturing Company maintains a budget master file on disk. At the end of each month this file is processed by computer together with the general ledger, also maintained on disk, to generate performance reports for all production departments. The format of each report is identical to that shown in Fig. 20.15, except that direct labor costs are not included.

The budgeted amount of each overhead expense item for each month is computed as $(a + bx)$, where a is the fixed amount of that expense item per month, b is the variable rate of that expense item, and x is the value of the base to which the variable rate is applied. The rate base for each expense item is one of the three different rate bases used: direct labor cost, direct labor hours, and machine hours. The value of each of these three bases for the current month is entered into the system at the beginning of processing.

Required

What specific data elements must be included in each overhead expense record of (a) the budget master file and (b) the general ledger in order for these files to be used as described in generating performance reports for production departments?

20.7 Culp Electronics Company processes disbursement authorizations on-line as vendor invoices are matched with receiving reports, purchase orders, and other supporting documents in the Accounting Department. Each disbursement authorization is entered via a data terminal and processed to update the accounts payable master file. The debit portion of the entry is processed to update the general ledger and either the materials inventory master file (for inventory purchases) or the fixed asset master file (for asset purchases).

For each disbursement authorization relating to an inventory purchase the following data are entered: the vendor account number; amount due; discount rate; due date; and for each item purchased, the part number, price, and quantity.

Required

Considering only disbursement authorizations relating to inventory purchases, describe several means by which the system could be programmed to check the accuracy and validity of the input data. Relate your answer specifically to the data items mentioned.

20.8 The Rock Island Brewery recently acquired a new computer system that will utilize magnetic disk storage for all files. Its previous computer system used magnetic tape storage for all data files. You are involved in designing a computer application that will process disbursement vouchers approved for payment. Once each day data entry clerks will enter data from voucher documents into the system, using on-line keyboards. The data will be recorded on one or more temporary disk files.

Once all the data have been entered, separate voucher files will be merged, the combined file will be sorted by vendor account number, and a listing of all vouchers entered that day will be printed for distribution to the Controller. The voucher file will then be processed to update the accounts payable master file. During this run any vouchers already on the master file that are due for payment on the current date will be deleted from the file, and a check and remittance advice for those vouchers will be printed. Details of each paid voucher will also be listed on a cash disbursements register, which will be provided to the Controller. During this run summary journal entries will be accumulated, and these entries will be posted to the general ledger master file. A batch total report containing these summary journal entries and other batch totals will be printed at the conclusion of this run.

Required

a. Prepare a systems flowchart of the data processing system described.

b. What accounting journal entries will be generated during these data processing operations?

c. What are the most significant advantages of having the accounts payable and general ledger master files stored on disk rather than on tape?

20.9 Walker Corporation is a wholesaler that sells hardware and building materials to retail outlets in the East and Midwest. Walker maintains its customer accounts in a marketing data base like the one illustrated in Fig. 16.9. Walker's customers pay by the invoice and return a copy of the invoice with each payment to serve as a remittance advice. Walker updates its customer accounts using the open-invoice method; that is, each customer payment is matched against an outstanding invoice. Walker processes customer remittances by accumulating the invoice/remittance advice documents in batches of 50 and transmitting these batches to a data entry department. There data entry clerks key the remittance transaction records into a minicomputer system, which records them on a temporary disk file. At the end of each day all of these temporary files are merged and processed on Walker's mainframe computer system to update the customer records.

Required

a. Prepare a systems flowchart of all data processing operations described.

b. List the data items that should be included in the remittance transaction record. Which of these items would be keyed into each record by the operator, and which entered into the record directly by the system? Prepare a record layout for the remittance transaction record.

c. What batch totals should be prepared and checked during this process?

d. What edit checks should be performed on the remittance input data (1) as it is keyed in, when there is no access to the corresponding customer file data, and (2) as it is processed by the update program, when input data can be compared with customer file data?

e. A systems analyst has suggested that Walker eliminate its batch update run and replace it with an on-line update process where the customer file is accessed and updated directly as the data are being keyed in by data entry clerks. What would be the advantages and disadvantages of this approach?

20.10 You are a systems analyst at Zollinger Corporation. You have recently been assigned to assist Zollinger's Treasurer by developing a system that will project operating cash flows over the next 30 days. Your system will download selected data from various mainframe data bases to a personal computer, which will process the data and prepare the report. These data bases are the marketing data base, which is like the one shown in Fig. 16.9 and includes data on open customer invoices that will be used to forecast cash receipts; the purchasing data base (see Fig. 17.8), which includes data on open purchase orders and vendor invoices due for payment that will be used to forecast cash disbursements; and the employee data base (see Fig. 19.5), which includes data on employee time, attendance, and wage rates or salaries (to simplify the problem, ignore incentive pay), which will be used to forecast the weekly payroll disbursement. All the data you will need to obtain from these data bases are updated on a continuous basis.

Required

a. To prepare the report, what data should you download from each of these data bases?

b. Briefly describe how you should process these data to prepare the report.

c. Design a report format that presents the required information in an effective manner. (*Hint:* Refer to Table 17.1 for an example of a similar report.)

20.11 The Darwin Department Store maintains its customer accounts by computer. Once each day data on all receipts of customer payments on account are keyed into the system by data entry clerks. Data on nonroutine customer file changes and other adjustments to customer accounts are also keyed in at this time. All of these transactions are recorded on a temporary disk file. After all the transactions have been entered, they are sorted by customer account number and processed to update the accounts receivable master file, which is maintained on disk. Output of this update run includes a printed report listing error transactions and summary information and a printed report listing all past-due accounts.

Required

a. What data should be included on each cash receipt input record?

b. Give two specific examples of the "nonroutine customer file changes and other adjustments" referred to.

c. Prepare a systems flowchart of all computer processes described.

d. Describe a comprehensive set of control policies and procedures for this cash receipts processing application. Identify the control objectives, and relate each control policy or procedure to a specific control objective. Explain the functioning of each control policy or procedure within the specific context of this cash receipts processing application.

20.12 Down and Out is a nonprofit organization that raises funds for, organizes, and carries out community service projects in various Eastern cities. Down and Out's revenues consist of charitable contributions from individuals and businesses plus grants and awards from government entities and foundations. Each item of revenue may be either *restricted* to a particular project or *unrestricted*. Unrestricted revenues are allocated among projects by Down and Out's Board of Directors. The organization's expenditures include items such as advertising, postage, travel, salaries, rent, utilities, office supplies, and office equipment. Each expenditure is classified, according to its purpose, into one of four categories: solicitation of revenues, delivery of services, administrative expenses, and capital investments.

Down and Out has a centralized accounting system that maintains accounting records for each of its divisions (cities) and service projects. This system is built around a general ledger master file, which consists of a header file containing static (nonchanging) information for each account in the chart of accounts, and a balance file. Each balance file record contains the amount budgeted for the year, the actual amount received or spent, and the total outstanding commitment (amount committed but not yet dispensed) for each expense account. The general ledger master file is regularly updated using a general ledger transaction file containing data on revenue, expenditure, and commitment transactions.

Down and Out's accounting system operates as follows:

■ As funds received are processed, a general ledger transaction record is created specifying the account number and amount received, and posted to the general ledger master file.

■ Purchase orders are issued for all expenditures except salaries. Each time a purchase order is issued, the general ledger account to which the expenditure will be assigned must be identified.

■ When purchase orders are batch processed, a general ledger transaction record is created for each purchase order, indicating the account number and amount. These transaction records are then processed to update the general ledger master file, which results in the commitment balance in the general ledger balance file being increased by the amount of the purchase order.

■ Each time a purchase order is filled, a supplier invoice is received and approved for payment. As part of this process, the purchase order number and general ledger account number are identified.

■ When supplier invoices are batch processed for payment, additional general ledger transaction records are created indicating the account number and expenditure amount. These records are then processed to update the general ledger master file, which reduces the commitment balance and increases the actual expense balance in the general ledger balance file.

■ Annual salaries for staff personnel are set by the Board of Directors prior the start of the fiscal year, and the commitments balances for all salaries accounts are set accordingly. As salaries are paid, these commitments balances are reduced and the actual expense balances increased.

■ At the end of each month, budget reports are generated for each project, listing:

1. the amount budgeted for every revenue and expense account.

2. the actual amount of revenue or expense for the year-to-date for each account.

3. the total outstanding commitment amount (expense accounts only).

4. for revenue accounts, the variances between the amount budgeted and the amount received for the year-to-date.

5. for expense accounts, the variance between the amount budgeted for the year-to-date and the sum of the actual and committed expenditures.

6. budgeted and actual totals of revenue, expenses, commitments, and net project variance for the year-to-date.

Required

a. Identify the primary key for the general ledger files.

b. Prepare record layouts for the general ledger master and transaction files.

c. Design a report format for the monthly budget report.

(SMAC Examination, adapted)

20.13 Alichem is a chemical producer that has been in business for three years. Ed Caz was hired as Controller two months ago. Recently, when copies of the completed purchase orders arrived in the Accounting Department, Caz learned that the Processing Department was replacing some large machines. Caz had not approved these purchase orders. By questioning Sharon Price, Director of Purchasing, he learned that the orders had not been forwarded to him for approval. He discovered that, while the Purchasing Department negotiates and orders all direct materials and processing supplies, the procedure differs for the purchase of fixed assets. When fixed assets are to be acquired, the Purchasing Department issues and records a blank, prenumbered purchase order to the requesting user department. The user department handles its own purchasing arrangements. Through additional inquiries, Caz was able to identify the current procedures followed for fixed asset acquisition; these procedures are presented in the first column of Table 20.2.

Caz believes that the acquisition procedure should be more efficiently distributed over the functions, thus providing the automatic implementation of new controls. Furthermore, he believes that a management group should review and approve requests for fixed assets before an order is placed. In a manner similar to the description of the current procedures, Caz prepared the description of his proposed procedures presented in the second column of Table 20.2.

Required

a. Identify the strengths or improvements of Caz's proposed procedures for fixed asset acquisition over the current procedures.

b. Identify and explain what further modifications, controls, or applications could be incorporated into the proposed procedures for fixed asset administration.

(CMA Examination)

20.14 The Baby Bear Toy Manufacturing Company uses a computerized general ledger accounting system to prepare its monthly trial balance. On a weekly basis the company updates its general ledger master file by processing it on a Record Interface Transactions Program together with an accounts receivable interface file, an accounts payable interface file, a payroll interface file, and a fixed asset interface file. All of these files are stored on magnetic disks.

The Record Interface Transactions Program generates accounting journal entries, creates records in the general ledger transaction file, and updates the general ledger master file. The updated general ledger master file and the general ledger transaction file are each copied onto backup magnetic tapes by the programs Copy General Ledger Master File and Copy General Ledger Transaction File, respectively. At the end of each month the Print Trial Balance Program accesses the general ledger master file to generate a trial balance.

Required

a. What file organization would you suggest be used for the general ledger master file and for the magnetic tape copy of the general ledger transaction file? Support your recommendation.

b. Draw a systems flow chart representing the system exactly as it is described.

c. In the general ledger system as described, an important procedure has not been included to properly generate the monthly financial statements. Identify this procedure, and describe what files and programs would be necessary to include the missing procedure.

(SMAC Examination, adapted)

20.15 VBR Company has recently installed a new computer system that has on-line, real-time capability. Cathode ray tube terminals are used for data entry and inquiry. A new cash receipts and accounts receivable file maintenance system has been designed and implemented for use with this new equipment. All programs have been written and tested, and the new system is being run in parallel with the old system. After two weeks of parallel operation, no differences have been observed between the two systems other than keypunch errors on the old system.

Al Brand, Data Processing Manager, is enthusiastic about the new equipment and system. He reveals that the system was designed, coded,

Current Procedures	Proposed Procedures
User Department	**User Department**
Need determined; decision and approval to acquire made internally	Determine need
Vendor bids requested and obtained for type and model of asset selected	Obtain bids and select best vendor in consultation with Purchasing as necessary
Blank, prenumbered purchase order requested from Purchasing Department	Prepare purchase request that includes type and model, bids, and justification
	Management Review
Purchasing Department	Review justification
Issue and log blank, prenumbered purchase order to user	Assure that asset meets goals and objectives of the business and department
	Verify that request is within existing guidelines
	Approve or reject assset request
User Department	
Select best bid and place order	**Purchasing Department**
Prepare purchase order and distribute copies as follows:	Receive approved requisition
Original and copy to vendor	Prepare prenumbered purchase order and place order with selected vendor
File copy for Receiving Department	Negotiate financing with vendor, if necessary
File copy for Accounting Department	Assume responsibility to follow up if delivery is delayed and distribute copies as follows:
File copy retained for user department	Original and copy to vendor
	File copy for Receiving Department
	File copy for Accounting Department
	File copy for Purchasing Department
Receiving Department	
Asset arrives at Receiving Department's dock	**Receiving Department**
Receiving notifies Accounting so that Accounting can verify that correct asset has been received and can issue brass tag number	Asset arrives
	Prepare a receiving report including visible condition of asset upon receipt; copy sent to Accounting Department
Asset delivered to user department after verifications or returned to vendor if there is a problem	Match original of receiving report with purchase order copy and file
	Deliver asset to user
Send invoice to Accounting if packed with asset	Deliver copy of receiving report and invoice, if received with asset, to Accounting
User Department	**User Department**
User receives, installs, and tests the asset or receives notification of return	Receive, install, and test asset
	Accept or reject asset
If asset malfunctions upon or shortly after installation, user deals with vendor and attempts to delay payment	Prepare and send copy of acceptance report to Accounting and Purchasing indicating acceptance or rejection
	Asset returned to vendor if rejected
Accounting Department	**Purchasing Department**
Verify asset; issue and record brass tag number	Receive acceptance report from user department
Receive and match invoice to purchase order copy	Deal with vendor if asset rejected or fails shortly after installation
Forward invoice to Controller for approval	
Payment approved by Controller	**Accounting Department**
Check prepared and asset recorded unless user requests a delay of payment	Match accounting copies of purchase order, receiving report, acceptance report with invoice
	If all reports are acceptable, prepare payment approval or else keep matched documents in open-invoice file
Check mailed	Controller or delegate approves invoice for payment
Brass tagging of asset is verified	Issue and mail check
	Record asset
	Issue brass tagging number and verify that asset is tagged

Table 20.2
Procedures for Alichem

compiled, debugged, and tested by programmers utilizing an on-line CRT terminal installed specifically for around-the-clock use by the programming staff; he claimed that this access to the computer saved one-third in programming elapsed time. All files, including accounts receivable, are on-line at all times as the firm moves toward a full data base mode. All programs, new and old, are available at all times for recall into memory for scheduled operating use or for program maintenance. Program documentation and actual tests confirm that data entry edits in the new system include all conventional data error and validity checks appropriate to the system.

Inquiries have confirmed that the new system conforms precisely to the flowcharts, a portion of which are shown in Fig. 20.16. A turnaround copy of the invoice is used as a remittance advice (R/A) by 99% of the customers; if the R/A is missing, the cashier applies the payment to a selected invoice. Sales terms are net 60 days, but payment patterns are sporadic. Statements are not mailed to customers. Late payments are commonplace and are not

vigorously pursued. VBR does not have a bad debt problem because bad debt losses average only 0.5% of sales.

Before authorizing the termination of the old system, Cal Darden, the Controller, has requested a review of the internal control features that have been designed for the new system. Security against unauthorized access and fraudulent actions, assurance of the integrity of the files, and protection of the firm's assets should be provided by the internal controls.

Required

a. Describe how fraud by lapping of accounts receivable could be committed in the new system, and discuss how it could be prevented.

b. Consider both the description of VBR Company's new system and the systems flowchart presented. Describe any other defects that exist in the system. Suggest how each other defect you identified could be corrected.

(CMA Examination)

CASE 20.1: ANYCOMPANY, INC.—AN ONGOING COMPREHENSIVE CASE

One of the best ways to learn is to immediately apply what you have studied. The purpose of this case is to allow you to do that. You will select a local company that you can work with. At the end of most chapters you will find an assignment that will have you apply what you have learned using the company you have selected as a reference. This case, then, may become an ongoing case study that you work on throughout the term.

Select a local company and obtain permission to study its financial information system. Answer the following questions about its system.

1. Who are the individuals responsible for maintaining capital assets records and general ledger records; processing cash receipts and cash disbursements transactions; approving capital asset acquisitions, improvements, and retirements; and preparing financial reports? Prepare a partial organization chart, and identify where these individuals are located on this chart.

2. What documents are used in the system? Obtain a sample copy of each document.

3. What master files are maintained in the system? What is the data content of each master file? Prepare (or obtain copies of) record layouts for each file.

4. For each master file, explain how it is updated. Identify each of the different types of transactions that cause the file to be updated. What is the data content of each transaction record? Describe how these transaction data are captured in machine-readable form for entry into the company's computer system. Prepare (or obtain copies of) record layouts for each transaction record.

5. If the company uses a data base management system, prepare (or obtain a copy of) a schema diagram identifying the linkages among the various records within the capital assets and general ledger data bases.

6. Prepare (or obtain copies of) system flowcharts for each of the major master file update processes.

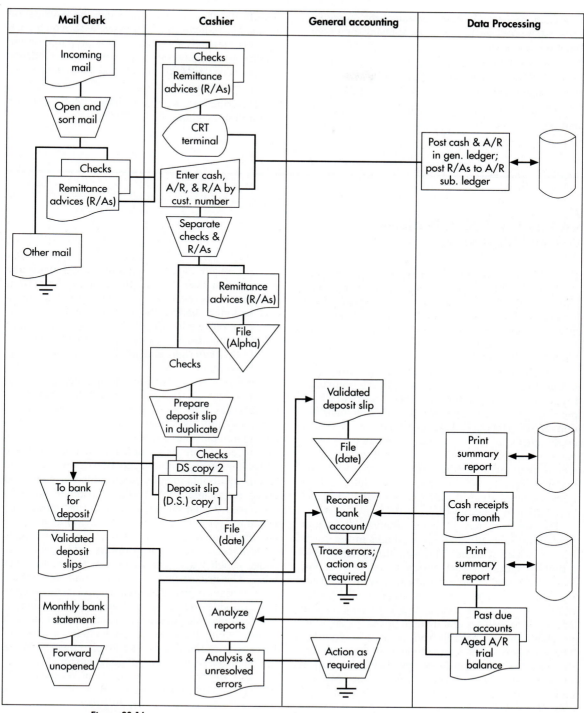

Figure 20.16
Computer system at VBR Company

For each process, indicate whether the company uses batch processing, on-line processing, or a combination of these.

7.   Describe internal control procedures employed by the company in these systems. Do you feel that the company's internal controls are satisfactory?

8.   Identify and obtain sample copies of reports that are prepared by the system. For each report, identify the file or files from which the information originates. Indicate the frequency with which each report is prepared and whether it is prepared on the mainframe computer or a personal computer. Identify who receives each report and how it is used. Evaluate the content and format of each report.

9.   Describe how accounting journal entry data are captured in machine-readable form.

CASE 20.2: TRANSINTERNATIONAL DISTRIBUTION COMPANY

The Transinternational Distribution Company (TDC) is an importing and exporting company operating in 10 different countries with its head office located in Vancouver, Canada. The company primarily imports products produced in third-world countries and distributes them in Canada, the United States and Western Europe.

All sales are on account and customers are billed in Canadian dollars, U.S. dollars, British pounds or French francs, depending upon the country in which the sale occurs. Because of the worldwide distribution of its products, TDC conducts an extensive credit check of potential new customers. A trial basis is used for the initial six-month period, after which customers' credit terms are reviewed and updated yearly. All accounts receivable, collections, and cash deposit functions are handled by the head office in Vancouver.

The company has a unique situation because of the federal sales tax and import duties in the countries in which it deals. This situation gives rise to different prices for each product that is sold. For example, a product sold in Canada may be taxed at a very low rate, may be tax-exempt in the United States, and may be taxed at a very high rate in France. The result is that invoice prices for the same product can vary greatly from country to country. The company must keep abreast of these pricing variances so that it can supply timely information on product prices to its salespeople in the different countries in which it deals.

As a result of the company's continuous and rapid growth over the past three years, the current sales, accounts receivable, and cash receipts system can no longer handle the volumes and the differences in currencies. The President of TDC has asked you to outline a system that would efficiently handle this situation and produce management by exception reports.

Your preliminary systems design includes a customer master file that has customer number as its primary key and includes data on the customer's name and address, credit status, credit limit, salesperson number, current account balance, and codes for currency type and credit terms. Each of these codes links each customer record to a separate table giving additional details about the currency and credit terms applicable to that customer. In addition, your design includes an inventory master file keyed to product stock number that contains typical inventory file data plus a pricing code, which links each inventory record to a pricing table, and a tax code, which links each inventory record to a tax table. The pricing table provides details about how each product is priced in each country, while the tax table provides details about sales taxes and import duties applicable to sales of each product in each country. Finally, your design includes a sales invoice master file that has an invoice header record that is linked to the corresponding customer record, and one or more invoice line item records, each linked to its corresponding inventory record. All of these records are stored on disk files.

Your preliminary design also includes eight computer runs that perform the following operations.

- *Run #1:* Accepts data on new customer accounts keyed in by data entry clerks from approved customer forms prepared by the Credit Department.

- *Run #2:* Accepts customer order data keyed in by data entry clerks who are reading from copies of sales order documents that have been mailed to Vancouver by salespeople. This run enters each order into a sales order transaction file.

- *Run #3:* At the each of each day this run processes the complete sales order transaction file for the day, together with the customer master file, the inventory master file, and their related tables, to create sales invoice records. Each invoice record includes prices, currencies, credit terms, sales taxes, and import duties applicable to the customer. Each new sales invoice record is appended to the master file of outstanding sales invoices. Six copies of each new invoice are printed, and two of these copies are transmitted to the Shipping Department to initiate shipment to the customer. This run also updates the account balance in each customer record and the balance on hand in each inventory record. Finally, this run prints a daily invoice summary register listing summary data on each invoice.

- *Run #4:* Accepts cash receipts data keyed in by data entry clerks reading from remittance advice documents. This run updates the customer master file and sales invoice master file for the payments received. Fully paid invoices are purged from the master file of outstanding sales invoices and written onto a separate sales invoice history master file. This run also writes each cash receipt transaction record onto a temporary disk file. Near the end of each day, after all cash receipt records have been keyed in, this temporary file is processed by a report generator to print a daily cash receipts journal.

- *Run #5:* Once each month the customer master file and outstanding sales invoice master file are processed to prepare a monthly customer statement for each customer having either a non-zero account balance or one or more transactions during the prior month.

- *Run #6:* Once each month the customer master file and outstanding sales invoice master file are processed to prepare a report of accounts over the credit limit.

- *Run #7:* Once each month the customer master file and outstanding sales invoice master file are processed to prepare a report of overdue accounts by due date.

- *Run #8:* Once each month the customer master file and outstanding sales invoice master file are processed to prepare an accounts receivable aged trial balance.

1. Prepare a data base schema diagram showing each of the master file records and tables described, including their primary keys and partial data contents, plus the linkages between the various files.

2. Prepare a systems flowchart of each of the computer runs described. To simplify your flowchart, treat the various table files as part of their corresponding master files (e.g., do not show the table files separately in your flowcharts).

3. For each of the first four computer runs, prepare an outline listing (a) important internal control objectives associated with the run and (b) key internal control policies and procedures directed at achieving each objective.

4. From which of these runs will accounting journal entries be generated as a by-product? In each case, which accounts will be debited and credited?

5. Prepare report layouts reflecting your preliminary design for the (a) daily invoice summary register, (b) daily cash receipts journal, (c) monthly customer statement, (d) accounts over the credit limit report, (e) overdue accounts by due date report, and (f) accounts receivable aged trial balance. (SMAC Examination, adapted)

APPENDIX: COMPREHENSIVE CASES

CASE A.1: F & C CONSTRUCTION[1]

Frank, owner of F & C Construction, has the opportunity to bid on a job that includes remodeling two existing auto dealership offices and constructing a new office. This job would give F & C Construction a chance to move into a new market and expand its customer base. Frank is excited about the possibilities of making this move; however, to operate in this market, Frank will need to prepare formal business reports. Additionally, he is concerned about his ability to bid competitively and track the increased number of jobs this opportunity would provide.

---

[1] This case, authored by Martha M. Eining of the University of Utah and Gail Lynn Cook of Syracuse University, appeared in the Spring 1993 issue of the *Journal of Accounting Case Research*. The case requirements have been modified to match the structure and content of this book. Reprinted from the *Journal of Accounting Case Research* with the permission of Captus Press Inc., North York, Ontario, Canada, and the Accounting Education Resource Centre of The University of Lethbridge, Lethbridge, Alberta, Canada.

Note: The purpose of this case is to provide an opportunity to apply the concepts of information systems to a business enterprise that is based on a real-world situation. F & C Construction is a typical example of a small-business record-keeping system. For many companies this type of system works—at year-end the company has made money. The owner of this company recognizes the benefits to be gained from a formal information system in assisting him with a controlled expansion plan.

Background

F & C Construction is a small, sole proprietorship. The owner, Frank, started his construction company approximately two years ago. Business is increasing at a steady pace. Currently, jobs range in size from small (kitchen countertop replacements, wooden decks) to large (additions to homes). His customers are individual homeowners.

Advertising is predominantly by word of mouth. The company logo is on both company trucks, and a placard is placed in a high-visibility location at job sites. Business cards are posted on bulletin boards in local stores and handed out at every opportunity. Satisfied customers and suppliers have made many referrals. F & C Construction is known for high standards of workmanship, using quality materials, and a no-surprises billing policy. (If Frank forgets to include a charge in the estimate, it is not added on at a later date. If the customer and Frank negotiate a change in the planned work, the bill is modified accordingly.)

The company currently employs Frank and two construction workers. Frank and his two workers are licensed to do general contracting work only; therefore, any plumbing or electrical work associated with a job is subcontracted out. Caren, Frank's wife, does the bookkeeping on a part-time basis. A tax accountant is retained as a financial advisor and for filing all necessary tax documents.

F & C Construction is run out of an office in Frank's home. A telephone answering machine takes calls whenever Frank and Caren are both away from the office. F & C Construction's physical assets include two pickup trucks, an assortment of large and small tools, and an inventory of supplies (screws, nuts, bolts, spackle, etc.) that is stored in a shed or on the trucks.

Sales

When a potential customer calls to request a bid on a job, an appointment is scheduled. Frank does all of the bidding for F & C Construction. A formal proposal (Fig. 1) is completed and submitted to the customer. If the customer accepts the proposal, it is signed and becomes a legal contract. The customer keeps one copy, and F & C Construction retains the other copy. The contract also serves as the accounts receivable record since it includes a schedule of payments and a work schedule. To date, due to the limited size of the business, keeping track of receivables due from customers has not been a problem.

The proposal indicates the customer's name, address, phone number, where the work is to be done, a description of the job, terms of the agreement, and a payment schedule. Payments are required as follows:

- *Large jobs:* Payments are broken down by the following major sections; one-half of the amount owed for the section is due when work begins on that section, and the remainder is due when the work is completed.

  1. Subcontractor fees
  2. Framing
  3. Roofing
  4. Siding
  5. Sheetrock
  6. Trim

- *Small jobs:* One-half of the payment is due up front and the remainder is due at completion.

Cash Receipts

Payments are recorded on the contract or a separate sheet of paper attached to the contract when received. Frank immediately makes out a deposit slip, in duplicate, and brings the deposit to the bank. One copy of the deposit slip is retained, and the other goes to the bank with the cash/check. Caren records all deposits in the check register (Fig. 2). The date the deposit was made, the customer name, the check number, and the amount of the deposit are recorded. Monthly, Caren does the bank reconciliation.

Purchases

As materials, supplies, and tools are needed, they are purchased from local suppliers. Since Frank deals with these suppliers on a regular basis, he mentally compares prices to obtain the best price for the quality products needed. If the purchase is a small dollar amount, Frank usually pays cash. (*Note:* When I asked Frank how he handled receipts for cash purchases, he told me he threw the cash register receipt on the dashboard of whichever truck he was driving, and at month-end he or Caren collected them so Caren could do the bookkeeping.)

If the purchase is for a large dollar amount, Frank charges the purchase. He has a line of credit with all of his major suppliers who bill on a monthly basis. The charge slips are accumulated along with cash register receipts on the dashboards of the trucks and collected monthly for payment and recording purposes. When an invoice is received, Caren matches it with the charge slip(s).

Occasionally, a special tool is needed to complete a job. In these instances, Frank rents the tool from a local tool rental company. The procedure for rentals is the same as that for credit purchases. If a piece of equipment is rented more than two or three times, it is purchased.

Cash Disbursements

F & C Construction has one checking account that is separate from Frank and Caren's personal checking account. Both Frank and Caren write checks to pay bills, meet payroll, and pay tax obligations. When a check is written, the payee, date, amount, and explanation for the check are recorded on the check stub, which remains in the check register (Fig. 2). All bills are paid by the fifteenth of the month to avoid finance charges. At month-end, Caren updates the check register and ledger book. Cash disbursements are tracked (spread) by category.

Payroll

When a subcontractor is used, jobs are awarded based on bids, and a standard subcontractor agreement (Fig. 3) is executed. Subcontractor fees are collected by F & C Construction according to the payment schedule above. Subcontractors are paid when they have completed their job, unless it is a big job and the subcontractor needs some money up front.

FROM F&C Construction	PROPOSAL	Proposal No.
		Sheet No.
		Date

Proposal Submitted To	Work To Be Performed At
Name _____ Street _____ City _____ State _____ Telephone Number _____	Street _____ City _____ State _____ Date of Plans _____ Architect _____

We hereby propose to furnish all the materials and perform all the labor necessary for the completion of

All material is guaranteed to be as specified, and the above work to be performed in accordance with the drawings and specifications submitted for above work and completed in a substantial workmanlike manner for the sum of

$\hspace{6cm}$ Dollars ($ \hspace{2cm}$).

with payments to be made as follows:

_____

_____

Any alteration or deviation from above specifications involving extra costs, will be executed only upon written orders, and will become an extra charge over and above the estimate. All agreements contingent upon strikes, accidents or delays beyond our control. Owner to carry fire, tornado and other necessary insurance upon above work. Workmen's Compensation and Public Liability Insurance on above work to be taken out by _____

Respectfully submitted _____

Per _____

Note—This proposal may be withdrawn by us if not accepted within _____ days

ACCEPTANCE OF PROPOSAL

The above prices, specifications and conditions are satisfactory and are hereby accepted. You are authorized to do the work as specified. Payment will be made as outlined above.

_____

Accepted _____ Signature _____

Date _____ Signature _____

Figure 1 Proposal form

A-3

CHECK REGISTER			1	2	3	4
	Date	Paid to/Received from	Check #	Account #	Amount	Total
1						
2						
3						
4						
5						
6						
7						
8						
9						
10						
11						
12						
13						
14						
15						
16						
17						
18						
19						
20						
21						
22						
23						
24						
25						
26						
27						
28						
29						
30						

Figure 2
Check register form

Time cards (Fig. 4) are kept for each of the construction workers. Workers fill out the time card daily to track hours worked. Frank approves the time cards, and workers are paid by check on a weekly basis. Caren uses the time cards to update the payroll register (Fig. 5). Most of this information—name, address, Social Security number, earnings, and withholdings—is necessary for tax purposes.

Frank pays himself a salary on a weekly basis. He writes a check and records the amount on the check stub. This information is then used by Caren to update the ledger book. Caren is not paid.

Quarterly and Yearly Procedures

On a quarterly basis, Caren brings the ledger book up to date and gives it to the accountant, who prepares quarterly financial statements that are used to prepare payroll tax forms. All forms and payments are filed on a timely basis by Caren.

At year-end, a federal tax form 1099 is filed for each subcontractor and construction worker. This form reports the amount paid to subcontractors and workers by federal ID number or Social Security number. The information needed to file each 1099 is available on the

**THIS FORM IS VALID IN ALL
50 STATES — USE THE SECTION
BELOW IN
STATE OF CALIFORNIA ONLY**

"NOTICE TO OWNER"
(Section 7019–Contractors License Law)

Under the Mechanics' Lien Law, any contractor, subcontractor, laborer, materialman or other person who helps to improve your property and is not paid for his labor, services or material, has a right to enforce his claim against your property.

Under the law, you may protect yourself against such claims by filing, before commencing such work or improvement, an original contract for the work of improvement or a modification thereof, in the office of the county recorder of the county where the property is situated and requiring that a contractor's payment bond be recorded in such office. Said bond shall be in an amount not less than fifty percent (50%) of the contract price and shall, in addition to any conditions for the performance of the contract, be conditioned for the payment in full of the claims of all persons furnishing labor, sevices, equipment or materials for the work described in said contract.

STATE OF CALIFORNIA ONLY

Contractors are required by law to be licensed and regulated by the Contractors' State License Board. Any question concerning a contractor may be referred to the Registrar of the Board, whose address is:

Contractors' State License Board
1020 N Street
Sacramento, California 95814

STANDARD SUBCONTRACT AGREEMENT

FOR $ _____
THE TOTAL CONTRACT AMOUNT
between

_____

and

_____

_____

for

_____

_____

Dated _____ 19 ___

ARCHITECTS

Figure 3
Subcontract agreement form
(front side)

SUBCONTRACT AGREEMENT

THIS AGREEMENT, made this_____day of_____A.D. 19____,
by and between_____hereinafter called the
Contractor, and_____hereinafter called the
Subcontractor.

For the consideration hereinafter named, the Subcontractor agrees with the Contractor, as follows:

ARTICLE 1. WORK: The Subcontractor agrees to furnish all material and perform all work necessary to complete_____

At:_____
     <u>ADDRESS</u>   CITY   COUNTY   STATE

For:_____
     <u>OWNER OR OWNERS</u>

according to the general conditions of the contract, as per the drawings and specifications, and amendments and/or changes to either (details thereof to be supplied as needed) prepared and identified by_____, Architect, and to the full satisfaction of said Architect.

ARTICLE 2. TIME: The Subcontractor agrees to promptly begin work as soon as notified by the Contractor, and to complete the work as follows:

ARTICLE 3. EXTRAS: No deviations from the work specified in the contract will be permitted or paid for unless a written extra work or change order is first agreed upon and signed as required.

ARTICLE 4. ASSIGNMENT: No assignment of this Subcontract agreement is permitted without prior written permission from the Contractor.

ARTICLE 5. INSURANCE: The Subcontractor agrees to obtain and pay for the following insurance coverages: Workmen's Compensation, Public Liability, Property Damage, and any other insurance coverage which may be necessary as required by the Owner, Contractor, or State Law.

ARTICLE 6. TAXES: The Subcontractor agrees to pay any and all Federal, State, or Local Taxes which are, or may be, assessed upon the material and labor which he furnishes under this contract.

IN CONSIDERATION WHEREOF, the Contractor agrees that he will pay the Subcontractor, in_____
_____payments, the sum of_____
_____Dollars($_____)
for materials and work, said amount to be paid as follows:_____percent (_____%) of all labor
and material which has been fixed in place by the Subcontractor, to be paid on or about the_____
of the following month, except the final payment, which the Contractor shall pay to the Subcontractor within
_____days after the Subcontractor shall have completed his work to the full satisfaction of the Architect or Owner.

The Contractor and the Subcontractor for themselves, their successors, executors, administrators and assigns, hereby agree to the full performance of the covenants herein contained.

IN WITNESS WHEREOF, they have executed this agreement the day and year first above written.

_____
WITNESS

_____
WITNESS

Tops Form No. 3461–Revised
Litho in U.S.A

_____
SUBCONTRACTOR
_____
BY
_____
STATE LICENSE NO.
_____
CONTRACTOR
_____
BY
_____
STATE LICENSE NO.

SPECIAL CALIFORNIA NOTICE CLAUSE ON REVERSE SIDE

WEEKLY TIME CARD							FROM			TO		
(This card must be forwarded to Payroll Department before payment is made)												

Employee _____ Badge No. _____

Address _____ Plant No. _____

Position _____ S.S. Acct. No. _____ Dept. No. _____

Name of Employer _____

	A.M.		P.M.		OVERTIME		EXTRA		TOTAL HOURS			COMPUTATION OF EARNINGS & DEDUCTIONS	
	In	Out	In	Out	In	Out	In	Out	Regular	Overtime	Extra		
MON												Regular Time	
												Overtime	
TUE												Extra Time	
WED												Total Earnings	
THU												S.S.	
FRI												Fed.	
SAT												State	
SUN												Local	

I, the undersigned, certify that the records indicated above were my true and accurate working hours for the payroll period.

Total Hours _____

Total Deductions _____

Net Pay _____

Signature _____

Stock Form No. 883
The Colonial Co., Brooklyn, NY 11230

Figure 4
Weekly time card form

subcontractor agreements or in the payroll account for the workers. The accountant also prepares the income tax return.

Future

Frank expects F & C Construction to continue to grow. The local economy is good, and individual homeowners are investing in home improvements. Frank also wants to expand into the remodeling and office construction areas. This expansion will require competitive bidding and formal reporting, perhaps to meet bonding company requirements. Improvements to the formal information system are needed to support the expected growth and allow Frank to continue doing the actual construction work.

Required

The requirements for this case are divided to coincide with the major sections of the book. In addition, the appropriate chapters are also identified.

Part 1: Conceptual Foundations of Accounting Information Systems

1. (Chapter 1)   Identify the information system that is currently in place for F & C Construction. What

are the major deficiencies in the current information system? In general, what kinds of accounting information would be important to a small construction company?

2. (Chapter 2)   Explain the transaction processing system that F & C Construction is currently using. Make sure to include a description of the input, storage, processing, and output.

3. (Chapter 3)   Prepare document flowcharts to illustrate the current cycles presented for F & C Construction.

Part 2: The Technology of Information Systems

4. (Chapter 5)   Considering the type of company and the number of employees, develop a proposal for the type of computer hardware and software that should be purchased to create a computerized information system. Include a discussion of the concepts of a personal information system for Frank. Determine approximate costs for the items that you propose (you can use information from computer magazines and computer catalogs).

5. (Chapter 7)   Discuss how the use of a data base system could improve the information available to

Frank and Caren. In this type of small company, what problems would be encountered with the implementation and maintenance of a data base system? What role would (or should) their accountant play in the development of a data base system?

Part 3: The Systems Development Process

6. (Chapter 8) Evaluate the feasibility of computerizing F & C Construction. Since you were given no dollar amount in the case, just consider the items that you would include in this type of analysis (separate them into costs of computerizing and benefits of computerizing). Make sure that you consider items that could be quantified as well as those that are qualitative. From the description of the company, indicate for which of these items you believe you could find information. What would you do about items for which you could find no information?

7. (Chapter 8) Consider the behavioral implications of computerizing F & C Construction. How do you think Frank will react to computerization? Who will actually do the daily computer tasks? Will computerization make Frank and Caren's daily work easier or more complex?

8. (Chapter 9) Develop a plan to determine, in detail, the information needs for F & C Construction. Be sure to take into consideration the fact that Frank wants to expand the business. From the information in the case, indicate the most important information needs for F & C Construction.

9. (Chapter 10) From the information needs discussed in Requirement 8, design one of the reports that would be needed for F & C Construction.

10. (Chapter 10) Design the input forms and screens needed to capture the data for producing the report designed in Requirement 10.

11. (Chapter 11) Assuming that F & C Construction has decided to computerize, discuss the pros and cons of buying off-the-shelf packages versus developing their own software programs.

Part 4: Control and Audit of Accounting Information Systems

12. (Chapter 12) Identify the internal control weaknesses in the current operation of F & C Construction. For each control, offer possible solutions to the weakness. This will be easier if you provide the information by the cycles discussed in the case.

13. (Chapter 13) Assuming that F & C Construction computerizes, set up a system of internal controls over the computer function.

Part 5: Accounting Information Systems and Applications

14. (Chapter 18) If you did not complete the document flowcharts for all cycles in Part 1, then you should develop a document flowchart of the production cycle for the current operation of F & C Construction.

15. (Chapter 18) Specifically identify the information needed for the production cycle. Develop documentation to show how this output would be provided.

16. (Chapter 18) Assume (if you did not already complete this activity) that F & C Construction has chosen to computerize. Develop a new systems flowchart that will describe the flow of documents and information in a computerized environment for the production cycle.

17. (Chapter 18) Identify the internal control objectives that should be established for F & C Construction's production cycle. Assuming that F & C Construction will computerize its production cycle, describe several internal control policies and procedures that should be established to achieve *each* of these objectives.

18. (Chapter 19) If you did not complete the document flowcharts for all cycles in Part 1, then you should develop a document flowchart of the payroll cycle for the current operation of F & C Construction.

19. (Chapter 19) Specifically identify the information needed for the payroll cycle. Develop documentation to show how this output would be provided.

20. (Chapter 19) Assume (if you did not already complete this activity) that F & C Construction has chosen to computerize. Develop a new systems flowchart that will describe the flow of documents and information in a computerized environment for the payroll cycle.

21. (Chapter 19) Identify the internal control objectives that should be established for F & C Construction's payroll cycle. Assuming that F & C Construction will computerize its payroll cycle, describe several internal control policies and procedures that should be established to achieve *each* of these objectives.

												WEEK ENDING			
NAME	MARRIED SINGLE	EXEMPTIONS	HOURS							TOTAL HOURS	RATE	EARNINGS			
			Sun.	Mon.	Tues.	Wed.	Thurs.	Fri.	Sat.			Regular	Overtime	Other	
1										Reg.					
										O.T.					
2										Reg.					
										O.T.					
3										Reg.					
										O.T.					
4										Reg.					
										O.T.					
5										Reg.					
										O.T.					
6										Reg.					
										O.T.					
7										Reg.					
										O.T.					
8										Reg.					
										O.T.					
9										Reg.					
										O.T.					
10										Reg.					
										O.T.					
11										Reg.					
										O.T.					
12										Reg.					
										O.T.					
13										Reg.					
										O.T.					
14										Reg.					
										O.T.					
15										Reg.					
										O.T.					
Totals															

Figure 5
Payroll register form

_____ 19_____

	Total Wages	DEDUCTIONS						Net Pay	Total Wages	CUMULATIVE TOTALS					
		Soc. Sec.	U.S. With. Tax	State With. Tax							Soc. Sec.	U.S. With. Tax	State With. Tax			
1																
2																
3																
4																
5																
6																
7																
8																
9																
10																
11																
12																
13																
14																
15																

CASE A.2: CACTUS SPINE COUNTRY CLUB[1]

Cactus Spine Golf Course is a private country club located outside Las Vegas. It currently provides its members with an 18-hole golf course, driving range, Golf Shop, and restaurant. Recently a committee was formed to examine the feasibility of expanding member services. In particular, they were interested in developing plans to design and finance a swimming pool complex for the property. Members currently pay for recreational services as they use them. In addition, they pay an initiation fee upon joining the club and an annual fee of $1200 that is due and payable on the anniversary date of membership.

Organization Structure

Figure 1 shows the structure of the Cactus Spine Country Club. The club is governed by a Board of Directors that is elected from the membership. The Board appoints a qualified member to the position of Financial Secretary for a two-year period. Although the Board of Directors is not compensated, the Financial Secretary receives a monthly stipend for services rendered to the Club.

John Parr is the new Club Manager. He was hired two months ago after the retirement of Jerry Putter, who held the position for 10 years. John came to the club highly recommended and with considerable experience. John reports to the Board of Directors. He also works closely with the Financial Secretary, Mary Adams, and Joan Peters, his personal secretary.

Tom Birdie, Golf Pro, reports directly to John Parr. Tom oversees the maintenance of the course and the operations of the Golf Shop. He manages 30–45 full- and part-time employees, including Harry Eagle, Golf Shop Manager, and John Greene, Maintenance Manager. Sally Jones also reports directly to John Parr. As Restaurant Manager, she supervises 10–20 full- and part-time staff members. There is a fairly high turnover in

these areas since many employees are hired on a temporary basis for peak demand periods.

The Accounting Department is headed by Fran Smith, a long-time employee. Two accounting clerks and the Club Cashier report to Fran. In addition, several full-time golf shop employees are cross-trained in cashier and accounting duties. These people are used to maintain the 7-day staffing needs in the Cashier and Accounting departments and to further fill in during longer summer days.

The Golf Shop

Harry Eagle maintains a small inventory of quality athletic apparel and golf equipment in the Golf Shop. He and his staff also maintain a supply of related accessories and a cooler with cold beverages and snacks that can be heated in the microwave by golfers waiting to tee off. Golf reservations are made at the Golf Shop either by phone or in person. They are recorded manually on a daily reservation sheet (Fig. 2) that is preprinted with the available tee times. Up to four people can sign up for one tee time. Members usually sign up in pairs or foursomes. When checking in for their reservation, members sign the daily reservation sheet. The clerk on duty then distributes the key for the mandatory electric cart and records the cart number next to the signature of the party responsible for the key. The members' signatures authorize that the greens fee be charged to their account. Greens fees include the use of one electric cart per two golfers. Fees for a guest can be charged to the member's account or they can be paid in cash. The guest column on the reservation sheet is used to record the few cash payments. These cash payments also are rung into the cash register.

All golf lessons, food, clothing, equipment, and accessory sales are recorded on the cash register whether they are cash or credit purchases. Prenumbered sales invoices also are prepared in triplicate when members charge items at the Golf Shop (except for the greens fees). Members receive the original invoice. At the end of each day, Harry Eagle takes the daily reservation sheet, cash register tape, duplicate invoices, and cash to the Cashier in the Accounting Department.

[1] This case was prepared by Carol F. Venable, School of Accountancy, San Diego State University, as a basis for classroom discussion rather than to illustrate effective or ineffective handling of an accounting system. Copyright 1993 by Carol F. Venable. Reprinted with permission.

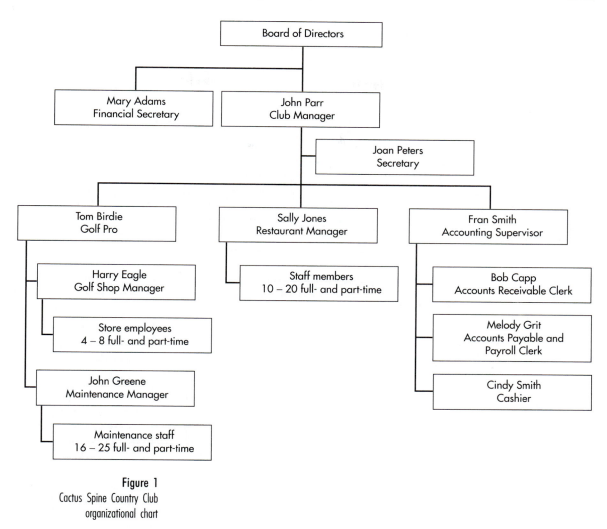

Figure 1
Cactus Spine Country Club
organizational chart

Cash Handling and Accounts Receivable Processing for the Golf Shop

When the Club Cashier receives the daily reservation sheet, cash register tape, invoices, and cash from the Golf Shop, the amounts from the register tape are compared to the charge invoices and the collected cash. These amounts are recorded by the Cashier on the cash drawer summary sheet (Fig. 3). Harry, or his representative, then signs the cash drawer summary sheet to transfer the amounts collected. The Cashier combines these funds with those that were collected from the restaurant and prepares a daily bank deposit for all cash sales. This deposit is separate from the one that is prepared to deposit the payments on account that arrive in the mail. All deposits are made by John Parr's secretary. The Cashier turns over the daily reservation sheet and one copy of the charge invoices to the Accounts Receivable Clerk, who enters the amounts in the accounting system. Posted invoices and the daily reservation sheet are maintained in a file in chronological order in the Accounts Receivable Department. The second copy of the invoice is attached to the cash drawer summary sheet and filed in the Cashier's file. At one time, the second copy was sent to the member with the monthly statement, but this procedure was deleted

Reservation Sheet For _____

Time	Name	Signature	ID #	Cart	Guest
0545					
0600					
0615					
0630					
0645					
0700					
0715					
0730					

Figure 2
Daily reservation sheet

when the accounting records were automated. Members who question an item on their statement can obtain a copy of the invoice from the Accounting Department.

Restaurant and Catering Services

Sally Jones, Restaurant Manager, supervises 10–20 full- and part-time individuals who provide breakfast, lunch, and light dinner services. She also arranges for outside catering when the club plans large, formal events or when club members want to utilize the facilities for private parties. Members may charge their daily purchases or pay cash. The daily sales procedures are similar to those that are used in the Golf Shop. The restaurant opens daily one-half hour before sunrise. It

	Register Cash Sales	Register Credit Sales	For Office Use
GOLF SHOP CASH DRAWER SUMMARY SHEET			Date
Greens Fees			
Lessons			
Food			
Clothing			
Equipment			
Golf Accessories			
Other			
Totals Per Register Tape			
Plus Beginning Bank _____ Received by		For Cashier's Use	
End of Shift Cash Out Requirement			
Cash Delivered to Cashier _____ Delivered by		For Cashier's Use _____ Received by	
Cash Over/(Short)			
DR Cash	_____	For GJ Use	
CR Cash Sales Accts	_____	_____	
CR Other Accts	_____	Recorded by	
DR/CR Cash Over(Short)	_____		

Figure 3
Cash drawer summary sheet

closes at 7 P.M. in the summer and at 4 P.M. in the winter.

Members may rent restaurant and meeting room facilities for private parties. All catering services for private parties must be arranged through Sally Jones. If a private caterer is used in place of or in addition to the regular staff, the club is billed directly and Sally charges the catering fees to the member's account. This is in addition to the rental fee that is charged for using the facilities. The rental fee has remained stable for a number of years. Several private parties are held each month, and the facilities are usually fully booked during holiday and graduation periods. Sally Jones prepares a party charge slip in triplicate for billing members' accounts for room rentals, food, services, and private catering fees. After the event, she mails the original to the member, keeps a copy, and sends another to the Accounts Receivable Clerk.

Incoming Mail and Purchasing

John Parr's secretary, Joan Peters, opens all the mail and prepares a daily cash receipts prelist. She forwards the prelist, the checks, and the remittance advices to the Cashier. She also handles all correspondence and prepares purchase orders (Fig. 4) for the approval of John Parr. Department heads must submit purchase requisitions to her before any purchase orders are prepared. When bills arrive, she attaches a copy of the appropriate purchase order and forwards it to the Accounts Payable Clerk after the Club Manager has reviewed and initialed the bill. Catering bills are handled separately. These are forwarded to Sally Jones, who authorizes payment by initialing the invoice and forwarding it to the Accounts Payable Clerk. The Accounts Payable Clerk inputs all bills to the accounts payable system. The Accounting Department Supervisor reviews the accounts payable listing and authorizes payment. The Accounts Payable Clerk then prints the checks, which must be signed by the Financial Secretary before being mailed. All accounts payable records are maintained in the Accounting Department.

The Current Accounting System

Fran Smith is the head of the Accounting Department. She started with the club 10 years ago as a clerk in the Golf Shop. After taking several night school courses in accounting, she was promoted to Accounts Receivable Clerk 4 years ago. Fran then was promoted to her current position after the untimely death of the Head Accountant 3 years ago. Fran carefully has maintained the same procedures that were started before her promotion. However, there is no formal documentation for the current accounting system.

The current accounting system was installed by the former Head Accountant. It consists of a small IBM personal computer with a simple general ledger package that has accounts payable and accounts receivable modules. The system was designed so that the Head Accountant made all general journal entries. One clerk is responsible for maintaining the accounts receivable records. Another clerk is responsible for accounts payable records. This second clerk also is responsible for preparing, distributing, collecting, and reviewing time sheets and time cards. Once a week the payroll items are sent to an outside payroll service that prepares the checks and payroll records. The number of employees fluctuates depending on the season of the year. Many temporary employees are hired during summer and holiday periods. Paychecks must be picked up in person from the Cashier.

The Cashier, Cynthia Smith, is responsible for safeguarding all monies. Incoming receipts are deposited intact with separate bank deposit slips for cash sales, mail receipts, and other cashier-generated monies. Remittance advices are forwarded to the Accounts Receivable Clerk with the prelist. Daily deposits are recorded on a cash receipts report, a copy of which goes to Mary Adams at the end of the month. Since members are provided with check-cashing privileges, Cynthia must replenish the amount of cash in the club safe twice a week. In addition to her other duties at the end of the day, she prepares the beginning bank for each cash register. The Accounting Department Supervisor acts as Cashier when Cynthia Smith is away from the cashier's cage. They each maintain a separate cash drawer. At the end of the day, all paperwork and monies must balance on the reconciliation sheet.

The Accounts Receivable Clerk also is responsible for entering the annual fee into the billing system so that it will be included on the member's bill. Although it is an annual fee, members are allowed to pay it in three monthly installments. The clerk keeps a manual card file which indicates when each member's installment is to be entered into the billing system. The clerk dates and then initials the card when the amount is posted into the automated system.

Responsibilities of the Financial Secretary

Mary Adams is responsible for monitoring the financial position of the club. On a monthly basis, Mary receives a financial report detailing overall income and expenses. She reviews the results and presents the report at the

<table>
<tr><td colspan="3">

Cactus
Spine
Country
Club

</td><td colspan="2">

SEND INVOICE TO:

ACCOUNTING DEPARTMENT
123 Prickly Pear Lane
Cacti, NV 12345

(123) 123-1234

</td><td>

PURCHASE
ORDER NO. 1332

This number must
appear on all
documents and
packages.

</td></tr>
</table>

Vendor				Ship to:	
Date	Ship by Date	Ship Via		Freight Terms	Special Terms
Quantity	Product Number	Description—Color Code		Unit Cost	Unit

PURCHASE CONDITIONS

1. Acknowledgment required.
2. Vendor is responsible for extra freight on partial shipments.
3. No substitutions without prior approval.
4. Our purchase order number must appear on all documents and packages.

PR File No. _____

Purchasing Agent

Figure 4
Purchase order

Board of Directors meeting. Mary spends approximately 5 hours per week working at the club. She signs all checks, and she receives reports which indicate the members who are in arrears. Mary is responsible for monitoring and contacting delinquent members before they are turned over to the Board of Directors for further action. She also receives copies of the validated bank deposit slips, the monthly bank statement, and a copy of the cash receipts report, which itemizes the daily deposits. She reconciles these records.

Discussion at the Last Board Meeting

At the last board meeting, Mary reported the financial results for the previous month and noted that operating expenses again had exceeded operating revenues. Mary also reported that she and John Parr had reviewed the financial statements for the past year. They both agreed that the club must increase its revenues in the near future. Expenses have risen at a steady pace over the past six months. They recommended that an immediate 10 percent across-the-board increase in prices be approved by the Board. John reported that the club must soon upgrade its maintenance equipment. He currently is working with Tom Birdie and the Equipment Custodian in inventorying and examining the condition of the maintenance equipment and electric golf carts. He stated that equipment records were incomplete.

During the meeting, John noted that the annual club dues were less than those at comparable facilities, but he refrained from making a recommendation to increase these dues. John also recommended hiring a firm to examine the accounting system and to make recommendations for its improvement. He explained that his requests to the Accounting Department for departmental reports cannot always be handled by the current system. Although some reports have been manually prepared, the department doesn't have the time to compile others. He also noted that the Accounting Department Supervisor, Fran Smith, didn't appear to understand all of his concerns about the operations of the accounting system. After considering the reports by John and Mary, the Board decided to hire outside consultants. The Board wants a review of current operations and recommendations for upgrading the accounting system.

Required

The requirements for this case are divided to coincide with the major sections of the book. In addition, the appropriate chapters are also identified.

Part 1: Conceptual Foundations of Accounting Information Systems

1. (Chapter 1)　　Discuss whether the Board of Directors should follow the recommendation for an immediate 10% price increase. What effect would a price increase have on demand? What are the external and internal factors that could be negatively affecting the financial operations of the club?

2. (Chapter 2)　　Does the current system produce sufficient reports for decision making? Recommend three reports, and explain why they would be useful to management.

3. (Chapter 3)　　Prepare a flowchart of the purchasing and accounts payable procedures.

Part 2: The Technology of Information Systems

4. (Chapter 4 or 5)　　Should the club upgrade its computer system? Identify the areas that should be upgraded? Discuss the benefits that would be gained from upgrading the system.

5. (Chapter 6)　　Design a network configuration for Cactus Spine Country Club. Why did you choose to include certain functions on the network?

6. (Chapter 7)　　The company wants to create a new-member master file that can be used for automatic billing when membership fees are due. The club plans to retain the same three-month installment payment plan. Prepare a three-column work sheet that identifies (a) the field names in the new-member master file, (b) the field type (alphabetic, numeric, alphanumeric, date, monetary), and (c) the positions (the number of characters in the field).

Part 3: The Systems Development Process

7. (Chapter 8)　　Identify the areas within the club where there may be resistance to changing the system. Discuss why there could be resistance, and recommend some ways to avoid potential problems.

8. (Chapter 9)　　Consider the various strategies for determining information system requirements, and suggest which strategies would be appropriate for this company. What are the factors that affect the level of uncertainty in this company?

9. (Chapter 10)　　Design a sales invoice for the Golf Shop.

10. (Chapter 11)　　Should the club continue to use outsourcing for its payroll? Consider the costs and benefits.

Part 4: Control and Audit of Accounting Information Systems

11. (Chapter 12)　　Assess the costs and benefits of using part-time and temporary employees. Does the use of these employees increase control risks? Does cross-training of employees benefit the club, and does this increase any risks?

12. (Chapter 13)　　Assume that a thief broke into the Accounting Department looking for money. After finding none, he vandalized the department. Records were destroyed, and the computer was stolen. What activities should be listed in a disaster recovery plan to help the department recover from this event?

13. (Chapter 14) Distinguish between management fraud and employee fraud, and identify individuals and/or situations where this could occur within the country club.

14. (Chapter 15) Prepare an input controls matrix using the same format as given in the chapter, but replace the field names with those that would be in the new-member master file (see Requirement 6). Place checks in the cells of the matrix that represent input controls you might expect to find for each field.

Part 5: Accounting Information Systems and Applications

15. (Chapter 16) Design a party charge slip that can be used for multiple purposes: (a) to reserve a room and book a party, and (b) to later bill for the party costs.

16. (Chapter 17) Identify the internal control strengths and weaknesses of and recommend improvements to the purchasing and accounts payable functions. Use the following format to prepare your answer.

Item Number	Description	Recommendations to Correct Weaknesses
Strengths		
Weaknesses		

17. (Chapter 19) List the activities that the Payroll Clerk must perform before the completed time sheets and time cards are sent to the outside payroll service. Does anything need to be done after the paychecks are received from the outside payroll service?

18. (Chapter 20) Identify the internal control weaknesses of and recommend improvements for the control of fixed assets. Use the following format to prepare your answer.

Item Number	Nature of Weakness	Recommendation to Correct Weakness

CASE A.3: VIDEOS TONITE[1]

Videos Tonite is a family business that is owned and operated by Bob and Mary Smithson. The business consists of two video rental stores in a suburban area of Chicago. Their daughter, Barbara, is a full-time employee who eventually will take over the business when Bob and Mary reach retirement age in a few years. Each store is open for business from 10 A.M. until 8 P.M., Monday through Saturday, and from noon until 5 P.M. on Sunday. There are four part-time employees at each location. The three family members divide their time between the two stores so that new employees are scheduled to work with a family member.

Videos Tonite rents the most popular movies. Each store has approximately 2000 videos in stock, and there

are 10 video machines (VCRs) that are available for rent. Bob orders all merchandise, and he has been quite successful in assessing the video rental market. Recently at the urging of his suppliers, Bob added a small line of new videos for sale. The videos seem to be selling well. He has placed two restocking orders since adding this merchandise. Each store also offers bagged popcorn and candy that is restocked on Monday and Friday of each week by the popcorn company supplier. The supplier leaves a delivery slip after each restocking, and the company sends an invoice every two weeks.

Membership Terms

Videos Tonite rents only to members of the Videos Tonite Rental Club. A person becomes a member by filling out an application and paying a $75 deposit. The company requires the application information and deposit because the store originally experienced problems with cassettes and machines being stolen by customers. New customers now receive a customer number, which

---

[1] This case was prepared by Carol F. Venable, School of Accountancy, San Diego State University, as a basis for classroom discussion rather than to illustrate effective or ineffective handling of an accounting system. Copyright 1993 by Carol F. Venable. Reprinted with permission.

"VIDEOS TONITE" CUSTOMER DEPOSIT LOG					
Date Received	Customer Number	Name	Address	Date Returned	Check Number

Figure 1
Customer deposit log

is recorded on their application and used on all subsequent transactions. Once a customer has rented items and promptly returned them six times, the customer can request that the $75 deposit be returned. Refund request forms are kept at the counter. A customer deposit log (Fig. 1) is used to maintain a record of the deposits and refunds. Mary designed the log and had it printed at a local printer, because there was a problem tracking deposit returns when they first initiated the deposit policy. All deposit refunds are made by check. If the original deposit has been returned and a customer does not respond to return requests, Bob will use the services of a collection agency. The collection agency has been successful in tracking down the few customers who move from the area.

Rental Procedures

Each rental cassette and VCR has its own identification number and checkout card. All of the VCRs and rental videos are kept behind the counter. When club members want to check out a movie or VCR, they select its checkout card from the display rack and give the card to a clerk on duty. The clerk selects the video, writes the customer number on the checkout card, and places the checkout card in the video slot. The clerk then pulls the customer card (Fig. 2) from the customer file and enters the rental information. Customers may purchase an op-

tional damage waiver by paying an additional 20 cents on each video rental. If they take this option, the clerk puts a check in the fee waiver column on the customer card. Customers are charged $65 for a damaged or lost video if they have not taken out the separate damage waiver. The customer card is stored in the checkout file box. When a video is returned, the checkout card must be put back on the correct display rack. The customer card is then put back in the customer file after the clerk puts a checkmark next to the item that was returned. When a customer card is full, a new one is prepared and the old one is destroyed. A club member may also reserve a movie or machine by calling the store and having the clerk pull the checkout card, video, and customer card and hold them for the customer behind the counter.

When Videos Tonite first opened, the checkout system was adequate. Now, however, there are approximately 1500 club members at each store. Bob estimates that about 30 percent are regular customers. Another 40 percent come in less often, but they still rent videos on a regular basis. Two of the biggest problems are lost or misplaced cards and lengthy lines of customers waiting for service, especially during peak hours. Additional problems include an inability to determine which movies and VCRs are available for rental, movies not being annotated with a checkmark on the member's card after

CUSTOMER CARD			
Number:		Name:	
Phone:		Deposit: Yes No	
Date	Item No.	Description	Fee Waiver

Figure 2
Customer card

a return, and members' finding out that the movies they reserved have been checked out to someone else. Bob and Barbara go through the checkout box periodically to find overdue rentals and misfiled cards. When the store is busy, cards sometimes get piled up behind the counter before they are filed.

Accounting Procedures

The company only has a few suppliers. When invoices for merchandise are received, Bob checks that the invoice contains only those items that he actually received. Since Bob does all the ordering and unpacking, it is easy for him to keep track of the incoming merchandise. The invoice then goes to Mary, who prepares and signs all the checks. In fact, Mary does all of the bookkeeping. There are no formal financial statements. At the end of the year, Mary takes the records to their tax preparer. She uses columnar paper to maintain the equivalent of a cash receipts journal and an expenditures journal. Mary also prepares and keeps records for the payroll. At the end of each month, she carefully totals her work sheets and reconciles her records to the bank

statement. Bob and Mary sit down at the end of each month to review the work sheets and their bank balances. They must manage their cash flows and plan for major purchases and improvements because there are several slow rental seasons during the year.

All sales are recorded on a cash register. In addition, a prenumbered sales invoice is prepared in duplicate when a new member pays a deposit or when a customer pays for a damaged video or VCR. The original is given to the member, and the copy goes in the cash register. At the end of the day, these invoices and the money in the cash register are bagged and put in the floor safe. Before each store opens, Mary opens the bag and prepares the bank deposit. Because the register drawer starts with $35 in change each day, Mary calculates and records the day's sales revenue by subtracting the $35 and the amounts recorded on the invoices. She checks for missing invoices, and she makes sure that the total amount recorded on the register agrees with the amount in the sales drawer. She records the information on a daily sales sheet (Fig. 3) that is later consolidated on columnar paper. There is seldom a shortage or overage.

```
┌─────────────────────────────────────────────────────────┐
│                      VIDEOS TONITE                        │
│                   DAILY SALES SHEET                       │
│                                                           │
│   Location:_____      Date:_____    │
├──────────────────────────────────────┬──────────────────┤
│   Cash total at end of day:          │   $              │
├──────────────────────────────────────┼──────────────────┤
│   Less beginning bank:               │   $              │
├──────────────────────────────────────┼──────────────────┤
│   Amount deposited to bank:          │   $              │
├──────────────────────────────────────┼──────────────────┤
│   Less damage deposits:              │   $              │
├──────────────────────────────────────┼──────────────────┤
│   Less payments for damaged items:   │   $              │
├──────────────────────────────────────┼──────────────────┤
│   Less other payments (itemize below):│  $              │
├──────────────────────────────────────┼──────────────────┤
│   Daily sales revenue:               │   $              │
├──────────────────────────────────────┴──────────────────┤
│   Invoice numbers used:                                   │
├───────────────────────────────────────────────────────────┤
│   Description of other payments:                          │
│                                                           │
└───────────────────────────────────────────────────────────┘
```

Figure 3
Daily sales sheet

The duplicate invoices for damage deposits are attached to the application form and stored in the application file in alphabetical order. The duplicate invoices for payments of damaged goods are attached to the daily sales sheet.

Expansion Possibilities

Last month one of Bob's old college buddies, Doug Alano, offered to sell Bob his two video stores that are known as Adventures in Video. These stores are located in nearby suburbs and they have done well since they opened. The stores are being offered for sale because Doug's doctor recommended that he take an early retirement due to the onset of a serious illness. Although Doug's two stores have many operating procedures that are similar to Videos Tonite, they cater to several additional market segments with different products and service policies. In addition to daily rentals of popular current releases, which are targeted to residents in the immediate vicinity of the stores, there are specialty rental sections for foreign language and classic films. These specialty films target several market segments, and the two stores draw customers from the entire metropolitan area. These customers willingly pay a pre-

mium price to rent foreign and classic films, and they expect special services since they travel greater distances. Doug offers a variable rental period rate and variable fees. He has two full-time managers, Janet Wilson and Ricardo Hernandez, who oversee the foreign language and classic film stock and maintain a phone reservation system. Current membership is estimated to be at 12,000. Of the 9500 videos in stock, approximately 1500 are foreign language videos.

Bob, Mary, and Barbara are excited about this expansion opportunity. Mary, however, is worried because she already has her hands full with the records from the two stores. She says that doubling her work load would keep her tied to paperwork all day. They asked their tax accountant for advice. After examining the sales proposal and the tax records of Adventures in Video, he noted that it appeared to be a good financial opportunity to expand in the video business. He suggested, however, that their ability to manage the additional facilities might require some reorganization. He suggested that Bob, Mary, and Barbara speak with a consultant about automating the records and procedures. They agree that they must do something, but they aren't sure what approach to take.

Required

The requirements for this case are divided to coincide with the major sections of the book. In addition, the appropriate chapters are also identified.

Part 1: Conceptual Foundations of Accounting Information Systems

1. (Chapter 1) Discuss whether Bob and Mary have adequately monitored their business. Do they need monthly financial statements? How centralized or de-centralized are the decision-making processes?

2. (Chapter 1) Prepare an organizational chart for the current operations.

3. (Chapter 2) Develop a coding scheme to identify the items that are rented to customers.

4. (Chapter 3) Prepare flowcharts that describe the new-customer deposit procedures and the video rental procedures.

Part 2: The Technology of Information Systems

5. (Chapter 4 or 5) What types of hardware and software could be used in the day-to-day operations of Videos Tonite?

6. (Chapter 6) Could Videos Tonite use a network system in its current stores? Could one be used if it expands? Describe the system you would recommend.

7. (Chapter 7) Assume that the company will use a relational data base to maintain its rental information. Prepare four relational tables for its rental invoice data. Include a rental invoice table, a member table, a line item table, and an inventory table. Enter three hypothetical entries into each table.

Part 3: The Systems Development Process

8. (Chapters 8 and 9) Should Bob and Mary computerize their current operations? What aspects of their business should be computerized? Identify the costs and benefits of computerization. (Dollar values are not necessary.)

9. (Chapter 8) Assume that the company has decided to expand. Identify four systems development projects that should be undertaken now and in the future. Prepare a master plan that specifies what the systems will consist of, how they will be developed, and where the information system is headed. Prioritize the projects, and describe the criteria used for prioritization. Limit your plan to two typewritten pages.

10. (Chapter 9) Consider the various strategies for determining information system requirements, and suggest which strategies would be appropriate for this com-

pany. What are the factors that affect the level of uncertainty in this company?

11. (Chapter 10) How could the job responsibilities change for Bob, Mary and Barbara if they purchase Adventures in Video? What other personnel changes might be necessary? What type of training would be needed?

Part 4: Control and Audit of Accounting Information Systems

12. (Chapter 12) Identify the internal control weaknesses of and recommend improvements in the new-customer deposit procedures. Use the following format to prepare your answer. If you prepared a flowchart for Requirement 4, cross-reference your list to it.

Item Number	Nature of Weakness	Recommendation to Correct Weakness

13. (Chapter 13 or 14) Assume that Mary and Bob decide to computerize their customer records and their rental video inventory. Identify four potential threats to this new information system, and make recommendations to minimize these threats.

14. (Chapter 15) Consider the four types of audits discussed in Chapter 15. Select the two that you feel are most needed by this company, and provide the rationale for your decision.

Part 5: Accounting Information Systems and Applications

15. (Chapter 16) Identify the internal control weaknesses of and recommend improvements in the video rental procedures. Use the following format to prepare your answer. If you prepared a flowchart for Requirement 4, cross-reference your list to it.

Item Number	Nature of Weakness	Recommendation to Correct Weakness

16. (Chapter 17) Identify the internal control weaknesses of and recommend improvements in the purchasing of new resale videos and in the purchasing of bagged

popcorn and candy. Use the following format to prepare your answer.

Item Number	Nature of Weakness	Recommendation to Correct Weakness

17. (Chapter 19)   Mary prepares the payroll manually. Assume that Mary prepares a work schedule one week in advance, although no description of the current timekeeping or payroll system is provided. Design a simple system for timekeeping that meets the internal control objectives for a payroll system. Provide a brief narrative and a copy of any documents that are necessary.

18. (Chapter 20)   Assess the cash-handling procedures and the use of the daily sales sheet. Determine whether the daily sales sheet (a) provides sufficient information for managerial decision making and (b) accurately reflects the company's revenues for external reporting purposes.

CASE A.4: THE WOODEN NICKEL[1]

Background

The Wooden Nickel is a small retail clothing store located in Stillwater, Oklahoma, across the street from Oklahoma State University. The store was opened in 1976 by K. Cohlmia and is run as a sole proprietorship. The store specializes in casual clothing and caters to the upscale university student market. Stillwater has approximately 35,000 residents, so the 18,000 students at the university have a tremendous impact on all retail stores in town.

The Wooden Nickel divides its inventory into a men's department and a women's department. K. strives to provide the type of clothing that is not found in discount outlets. In fact, the store is the only authorized supplier of Polo products in the city and surrounding area.

At the current time, all accounting is done manually. The store's business can be divided into two cycles: (1) spring and summer and (2) fall and winter. Because of the cyclical nature of the business, it is often necessary to borrow to cover the outlay for purchases. This is then repaid as quickly as the revenue from the sales cycle permits. K. negotiates with local banks to cover this need on a yearly basis. There are currently nine employees (job descriptions are presented in Fig. 1).

The store has a display area which covers the entire front of a renovated older building. There is one centrally located electronic cash register which is used for all sales. The back of the building is divided into a large office and a merchandise storage area. K. uses the office for all of his ownership duties. The bookkeeper also uses this office and the managers use it whenever the need arises. In addition, the safe is located in the office. There is a rear entrance near the storage area where goods can be unloaded.

Sales (Revenue) Cycle

Regular Sales   The Wooden Nickel has yearly sales of between $700,000 and $800,000. The store generates from 50 to 70 sales tickets each day, with an average of 2 items per ticket. The daily sales process is discussed in detail below. While the majority of the customers pay by cash, check, or credit card, they do have approximately 500 charge customers. Historically, K. has allowed only customers he knows personally to open charge accounts. The store has no established policy for charge customers.

When a customer wishes to make a sale, the customer can give the merchandise to any available salesclerk or take it to the cash register station. The salesclerk completes two copies of a prenumbered sales ticket. If a bank card is being used, a three-part bank card receipt is also completed. The transaction is then entered into the cash register by transaction type:

- Cash key: The sales ticket is validated on the back with the date and amount.

---

[1] This case was prepared by Patrick Dorr, School of Accounting, Oklahoma State University, and by Martha M. Eining, University of Utah, as a basis for classroom discussion rather than to illustrate effective or ineffective handling of an accounting system. Reprinted with permission.

```
┌─────────────────────────────────────────┐
│ Owner (K)                                │
│ Budgeting and purchasing                 │
│ Advertising                              │
│ Writing and controlling checks           │
│ Payroll                                  │
│ Bank statement reconciliation            │
│ Credit card process                      │
└─────────────────────────────────────────┘
  ┌───────────────────────────────────────────────┐
  │ Manager, Women's                               │
  │ Department (Melanie)                           │
  │ Supervises salesclerks                         │
  │ Prepares work schedules                        │
  │ Merchandising                                  │
  │ Assists with buying for women's department     │
  │ Sales as needed                                │
  │ Handles alterations                            │
  └───────────────────────────────────────────────┘
   ┌──────────────────────────────────────────────┐
   │ Manager, Men's                               │
   │ Department (Jay)                             │
   │ Supervises salesclerks                       │
   │ Prepares work schedules                      │
   │ Merchandising                                │
   │ Assists with buying for men's department     │
   │ Sales as needed                              │
   │ Handles all vendor returns                   │
   │ Deposits to bank                             │
   └──────────────────────────────────────────────┘
    ┌────────────────────────────────────────────────────────┐
    │ Bookkeeper (Kim)                                        │
    │ Prepares daily deposits                                 │
    │ Posts accounts receivables                              │
    │ Prepares statements for customer accounts monthly       │
    │ Receiving                                               │
    │ Makes inventory tags                                    │
    │ Filing                                                  │
    │ Sales as needed                                         │
    └────────────────────────────────────────────────────────┘
     ┌──────────────────────────────────────────────────────────────────┐
     │ Salesclerks                                                       │
     │ (5–6)                                                             │
     │ All sales functions (are not specifically assigned to a department)│
     │ Assist with merchandising and inventory tagging                   │
     │ General housekeeping duties                                       │
     └──────────────────────────────────────────────────────────────────┘
```

Figure 1
Job descriptions

- Credit key/charge account: The sales ticket is validated as above.
- Check key: The sales ticket and the check are validated.
- Bank card key: Bank card receipt is validated.

The first copy of the sales ticket (and bank card receipt if applicable) is given to the customer. The second copy is placed in the cash register. The third copy of the bank card receipt is filed by date in the back office. The top copy of the sales ticket is presented in Fig. 2, and the bank card receipt is presented in Fig. 3.

Layaway Sales   When a customer chooses to put an item on layaway, a special layaway form is completed (see Fig. 4). A minimum down payment of 25% is required to hold the merchandise. The balance is due in three equal payments over the next three months. The sale is entered using the layaway key on the register, and the form is validated with the date and amount. The cash deposit is included in the daily sales and handled as described in the sales cycle.

Sales Returns   The store's policy is never to give a cash refund when the item was paid for by cash or check.

48598

WOODEN NICKEL

225 S. Knoblock

Stillwater, Oklahoma 74074

377-8808

_____ 19_____

Customer _____

_____

Sold by	Cash	Charge	On Acct.	Paid Out	
Qty.	Description			Price	Amount	
No Cash Refunds					
			Sales Tax		
			Total		

Figure 2
Example sales ticket

Instead, it issues a credit for the merchandise that has been returned. A three-part sales ticket is prepared and marked as a return. If the original sale was made on account, only two copies are prepared. If the merchandise was purchased on a credit card, then the refund is made through the credit card. In this case, a bank card credit receipt must also be prepared.

The sales return transaction is entered using the sales return key on the register. After the ticket is validated, the original is given to the customer, the duplicate is placed in the cash register, and the third copy is placed in a credit file which is kept near the cash register. The bookkeeper uses the second copy of credit account returns to post the transaction to the accounts receivable subsidiary cards. Even though the amount of the sales return is actually a credit, it is kept in the accounts receivable card to avoid the necessity of setting up an accounts payable file.

When the customer returns to use the credit to purchase an item, the credit is verified with the copy which has been placed in the credit file. This copy is then validated and put in the cash register. It is used by the bookkeeper to offset the balance in the accounts receivable subsidiary card.

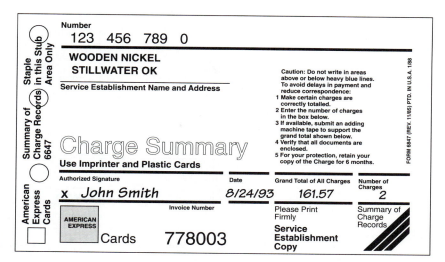

Figure 3
Example bank card receipt

Cash Receipts   The owner or one of the store managers opens the mail daily and separates the checks or receipts. The manager prepares a sales ticket for each receipt and then enters the checks into the register using the accounts receivable key. The sales ticket is validated with the date and amount. The checks are placed in the drawer and included in the daily deposit. The bookkeeper posts the collections from the information on the sales ticket to the individual account receivable cards. The same procedure is used for layaway payments.

End-of-Day Activity   At the end of the day, one of the store managers rings out the register and reconciles the money and bank card receipts in the cash drawer with the total on the register tape. The cash register tape indicates totals by transaction type. Figure 5 presents an example of the cash register tape. The penciled notations on the tape were made by the manager when balancing to the cash drawer. The information from the cash register tape is entered into the daily receipts reconciliation (see Fig. 6). One hundred dollars is kept in the cash register drawer and becomes the next day's beginning balance. The manager then places all other money, copies of sales ticket and bank card receipts, the register tape, and the reconciliation in the safe overnight.

The following morning, the bookkeeper retrieves all the items from the safe. The bookkeeper reconciles the register tape with the checks, cash, and bank card receipts from the previous day. A daily deposit is then prepared by the bookkeeper. The manager delivers the deposit to the bank.

Finally, the bookkeeper uses the sales tickets to post credit sales to the accounts receivable subsidiary cards.

Daily sales amounts from the daily receipts reconciliation are entered into the sales journal at this time. Figure 7 provides an overview of the daily sales register. All paper documentation is then stored in a file cabinet.

Purchasing (Procurement) Cycle

Purchasing   The owner plans the budget, breaking the total amount down into retail dollars available for each department based on projected sales. He takes 8 to 10 buying trips per year. While on each trip he comes in contact with at least 40 vendors who provide him with their own purchase orders. He uses these purchase orders to make notations on what items he would like to order, constantly trying to maintain a running total so he doesn't exceed the department's budgeted amount. The actual ordering is not done until the owner returns to the store and reviews the purchase orders. He then places the order by sending a copy of the completed purchase order to the vendor. A duplicate copy of the purchase order is filed by vendor.

Receiving   All shipments are sent via UPS. Shipments will typically arrive and be unloaded through the back entrance. However, sometimes they will be delivered through the front. The bookkeeper or owner unpacks the goods and compares the units received with the packing list accompanying the shipment. If any discrepancies exist (i.e., errors in amounts shipped), they are noted on the packing list and then discussed by phone with the vendor. The same procedure is used if any of the merchandise is damaged. The vendor then issues a return authorization. This must be received before the merchandise is returned.

LAYAWAY MERCHANDISE IDENTIFICATION TICKET

Date _____   No.   1931

Name _____

Address _____

City _____

Telephone _____ Clerk No. _____

Qty.	Description	Price
	LAYAWAY	

—Agreement—

Sub Total	
Tax	
Layaway Fee	
Total	
Deposit	
Balance	

Payments of $_____
To Be Made Every ☐ MO.
                  ☐ WK.
Failure to make payment
for 30 days will cause
merchandise to be re-
placed in stock and the
customer forfeiting all previous payments.
Date_____
Customer's
Signature_____

Date	Old Balance	Amount Paid	New Balance
	LAYAWAY		

Location_____ No. of Packages_____

No Exchanges or Cash Refunds
Customer's Identification Stub

Figure 4
Example layaway form

The packing list is kept in an open file until the invoice is received. Any information about discrepancies and/or damaged goods is transferred to the invoice when it is received and the invoice is adjusted accordingly. The packing list is then used by the bookkeeper to make inventory tags. The salesclerks attach the tags to the merchandise in their spare time.

Cash Disbursements   When the vendor's invoice is received, the packing list is pulled and checked for dis-crepancies. Any problems are handled by phone; the two documents are stapled together and filed by due date. Most invoices carry a 2/10, net 30 discount. About 10% of the men's clothing vendors and 90% of the women's vendors offer cash discounts of 2%–8%. This cycle is summarized in the flowchart in Fig. 9.

All checks are prenumbered and controlled by the owner. On the tenth of each month he pulls all the invoices, issues the checks, and mails them. All other bills are paid by the owner on the fifteenth of each month. He also keeps track of the payroll, which is paid on the first and sixteenth of the month. He enters all amounts to the check register (see Fig. 8).

Periodic Procedures

The bookkeeper prepares customer statements by making a copy of the accounts receivable subsidiary cards illustrated in Fig. 10. These are mailed to customers at the end of each month. At this point there is no real effort to track accounts receivable balances, and no interest is charged on accounts.

The owner reconciles the bank statement and takes care of all bank card activity. A periodic inventory is completed on January 1 and July 1. All available employees assist with the inventory.

An outside accountant is retained to assist with taxes and preparation of any financial reports which may be needed. The store currently maintains a daily sales register, a check register, and a file of accounts receivable subsidiary cards. No other books are being maintained.

Required

The requirements for this case are divided to coincide with the major sections of the book. In addition, the appropriate chapters are also identified.

Part 1: Conceptual Foundations of Accounting Information Systems

1. (Chapter 1) Identify the deficiencies in the current information system for the Wooden Nickel. Discuss the information that you think would be most important for internal decision making and for external needs.

2. (Chapter 2) Develop and describe coding schemes for tracking inventory in the Wooden Nickel.

3. (Chapter 3) Develop a data flow diagram for the sales cycle of the Wooden Nickel.

4. (Chapter 3) Prepare document flowcharts to illustrate the current cycles presented for the Wooden Nickel. Use the example presented for the cash disbursements cycle as a guide.

Part 2: The Technology of Information Systems

5. (Chapter 4) To what extent should the Wooden Nickel computerize? What items should be considered in the decision to computerize? Include a discussion of the type of computer hardware and the type of end-user software that you would suggest to the owner. Make sure that you justify your suggestions.

6. (Chapter 5) Develop a proposal for K. to use microcomputers to support his decision-making process. What should be provided? What would you suggest differently for the two store managers?

NET SL	0031	
W/TAX	2189.33	
ITEMS	0065	
NO SLE	0012	
TRAIN	0000	
	0.00	
CASH	0031	
	330.98	
CHECK	0018	
	1097.03	
CHARG	0003	
	285.82	
CARD	0006	
	410.67	
LAYAWY	0002	
	164.69	
GC RED	0000	
	0.00	
LAY RA	0003	
	69.86	
PO	0000	
	0.00	
RA	0001	
	30.00	
MARK	0000	
	0.00	
VOID	0000	
	0.00	
RETURN	0000	
	0.00	
CREDIT	0000	
	0.00	
TAX	128.83	

Figure 5
Example cash register tape totals

Figure 6   Example daily receipts reconciliation

WOODEN NICKEL

DAILY RECEIPTS RECONCILIATION
DATE 10-17

Cash	330.98	
Checks	1097.03	
Deposit total	1428.01	
Private charges		
Rec. on acct.		30.00
Layaways		164.69
Layaways rec. on acct.		69.86
W.N. charge cards		285.82
Visa/Mastercard		410.67
Discover Card		
Am. Express Card		
Paid outs		

7. (Chapter 6)   Describe and discuss different possibilities for using data communications at the Wooden Nickel. For example, should it have a network? If so, what kind? Should it use a point-of-sale system? In your discussion, include both the positive and negative aspects of each choice.

8. (Chapter 7)   Discuss how the use of a data base system could improve the information available to the owner and managers of the Wooden Nickel. What problems would be encountered with the implementation of a data base system?

Part 3: The Systems Development Process

9. (Chapter 8)   Prepare a feasibility analysis for the computerization of the Wooden Nickel. Be sure to consider the number of transactions and the needs of the store. You should also include both the quantifiable and the nonquantifiable items.

10. (Chapter 9)   Develop a plan to determine, in detail, the information needs for the Wooden Nickel. On the basis of the information in the case, indicate the most important information needs for the Wooden Nickel.

11. (Chapter 10)   From the information needs discussed in requirement 1, design one of the reports that would be needed for the wooden Nickel.

12. (Chapter 10)   Design the input forms and screens needed to capture the information for the report designed in Requirement 12.

13. (Chapter 11)   Develop a plan for K. to follow to purchase hardware and software. Include all items that he should consider in choosing vendors.

14. (Chapter 11)   How could the Wooden Nickel take advantage of reengineering? Consider the sales cycle. How could this cycle be reengineered?

Part 4: Control and Audit of Accounting Information Systems

15. (Chapter 12)   Identify the internal control weaknesses in the current operation of the Wooden Nickel. For each weakness, offer possible solutions. This will be easier if you provide the information by the cycles discussed in the case.

16. (Chapter 12)   How can the Wooden Nickel achieve adequate segregation of duties considering the size of the company?

17. (Chapter 13)   Assuming that the Wooden Nickel computerizes, set up a system of internal controls over the computer function.

Part 5: Accounting Information Systems and Applications

18. (Chapter 16)   If you did not complete the document flowcharts for all cycles in Part 1, then you should develop a document flowchart of the sales (revenue) cycle for the current operation of the Wooden Nickel.

19. (Chapter 16)   Specifically identify the information needed for the revenue cycle. Develop documentation to show how this output would be provided.

20. (Chapter 16)   Assume (if you did not already complete this activity) that the Wooden Nickel has chosen to computerize. Develop a new systems flowchart that will describe the flow of documents and information in a computerized environment for the revenue cycle.

21. (Chapter 16)   Identify the internal control objectives that should be established for the Wooden Nickel's revenue cycle. Assuming that the Wooden Nickel will computerize its revenue cycle, describe several internal control policies and procedures that should be established to achieve *each* of these objectives.

Figure 7 Daily sales register

Date	Sales*1	Sales Tax	Charges*	Rec/Acct	Layaway*	Layaway Rec/Acct	Cash Refund	Freight	Deposit	Bank Card*
10-17	2189.33	128.83	285.82	30.00	164.69	69.86			1428.01	410.67

* All figures include sales taxes. This is because the information from the cash register tape includes sales taxes.

1. Sales = cash (and check) receipts − receipts on account − layaway receipts + charge sales + layaway sales + bank card sales.

Date	Chk Number	Description	Purchases	Freight	Advert-ising	Selling Expense	Repairs	Rent	Wages	Misc Dr Cr
10-10	2946	Polimer Supply	286.70							
10-10	2947	B. Distributer	1049.21							
10-15	2948	DK Advertising			216.00					

Figure 8 Check register

Cash Disbursements
(Owner and Manager)

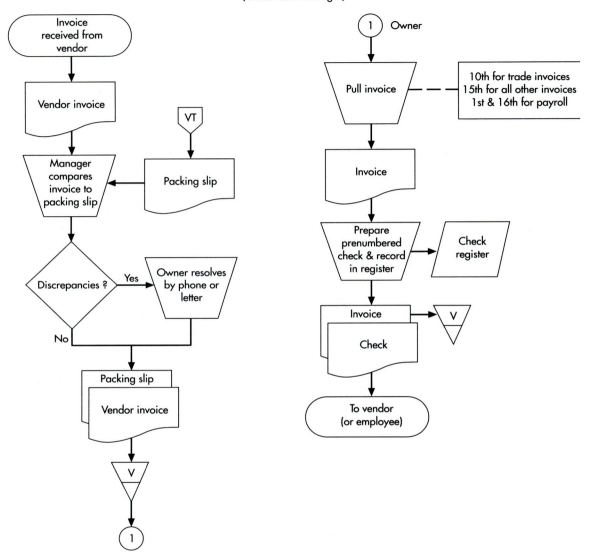

Files: V= vendor, by due date

Figure 9   Flowchart of cash disbursement cycle

22. (Chapter 17)   If you did not complete the document flowcharts for all cycles in Part 1, then you should develop a document flowchart of the procurement cycle for the current operation of the Wooden Nickel.

23. (Chapter 17)   Specifically identify the informa-

tion needed for the procurement cycle. Develop documentation to show how this output would be provided.

24. (Chapter 17)   Assume (if you did not already complete this activity) that the Wooden Nickel has chosen to computerize. Develop a new systems flowchart

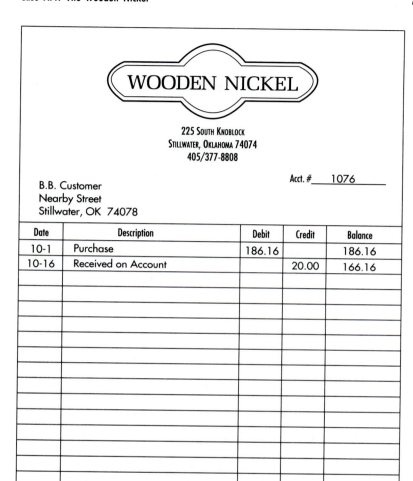

Figure 10
Example accounts receivable
subsidiary card

that will describe the flow of documents and information in a computerized environment for the procurement cycle.

25. (Chapter 17)   Identify the internal control objectives that should be established for the Wooden Nickel's procurement cycle. Assuming that the Wooden Nickel will computerize its procurement cycle, describe several internal control policies and procedures that should be established to achieve *each* of these objectives.

GLOSSARY

Access Time. The time required to transfer data to or from a storage device.

Accounting Cycle. The activities corresponding to an organization's major accounting transactions. There are five major accounting cycles: acquisition and cash disbursements; payroll and personnel; sales and collection; capital acquisition and repayment; and inventory and warehousing.

Accounting Information System (AIS). The human and capital resources within an organization that are responsible for (1) the preparation of financial information and (2) the preparation of information obtained from collecting and processing company transactions. The AIS is a subset of the management information system.

Ad Hoc Queries. Nonrepetitive requests for reports or answers to specific questions about the contents of the system's data files.

Address. The unique identifier of a computer storage location.

Administrative Controls. The plan of organization and all methods and procedures that are concerned with operational efficiency and adherence to managerial policies.

APL. An acronym for A Programming Language, a mathematically structured programming language developed by IBM. APL is often utilized on real-time and time-sharing computer systems.

Application. The problem or data processing task to which a computer's processing power is applied. **Applications Software** are the programs that perform the data or information processing tasks required by the user (i.e., accounts receivable and payable, inventory control, payroll, etc.).

Application Controls. Controls that relate to the data inputs, files, programs, and outputs of a specific computer application, rather than the computer system in general. *Contrast with* General Controls.

Application Generator. An application that produces a set of programs to accomplish a specific set of tasks based on user specifications.

Application Programmer. A person who formulates a logical model, or user view, of the data to be processed and then writes an application program using a programming language.

Arithmetic-Logic Unit. The portion of the CPU that executes arithmetic calculations and logic comparisons.

Arithmetic Processor. A microprocessor that can complete arithmetic computations up to 200 times faster than a regular microprocessor.

Artificial Intelligence (AI). A field of study in which researchers are attempting to develop computers that have the ability to reason, think, and learn like a human being.

ASCII. An acronym for American Standard Code for Informational Interchange, a standard seven-bit code that facilitates the interchange of data between data processing, data communications, and related equipment. Also known as the ASCII character set.

Assembler. A special program that converts a symbolic language program to a machine language.

Assembler Language. A programming language in which each machine-level instruction is represented by mnemonic characters that bear some relation to the instruc-

tion. It is also referred to as a symbolic language.

Asynchronous Transmission. Data transmission in which each character is transmitted separately. A start bit is required before and after each individual character because the interval of time between transmission of characters can vary. *Contrast with* Synchronous Transmission.

Attribute. A characteristic of interest in a file or data base; the different individual properties of an entity. Examples of attributes are employee number, pay rate, name, and address.

Audio Response Unit. A hardware device that converts computer output into spoken output (e.g., telephone directory assistance).

Audit Hook. A concurrent audit technique that embeds audit routines into application software to flag certain kinds of transactions that might be indicative of fraud.

Audit Log. A log, kept on magnetic tape or disk, of all computer system transactions that have audit significance.

Audit Trail. A traceable path of a transaction through a data processing system, from source documents to final output.

Automated Flowcharting Program. A program that interprets the source code of a program and generates a flowchart of the logic used by the program.

Backup File. A duplicate copy of a current file.

Bar Code. A special identification label found on most merchandise. The code includes vertical lines of differing widths that represent binary information that is read by an optical scanner.

Batch Processing. The accumulation of transaction records into groups or batches for processing

1

at some regular interval such as daily or weekly. The records are usually sorted into some sequence (such as numerical or alphabetical) before processing.

Batch Total. A sum of the instances of a numerical item, calculated for a batch of documents. This total is calculated prior to processing the batch and is compared with machine-generated totals at each subsequent processing step to verify that the data were processed correctly.

Baud Rate. The speed with which data are electronically transferred from one location to another. In many data communications transmissions it is equal to one bit per second.

BBS. An acronym for a bulletin board system. A BBS is an information and message-passing center accessed by users with telecommunications devices such as modems.

Biometric Identification. A method of identifying people by using unique physical characteristics, such as fingerprints, voice patterns, retina prints, signature dynamics, or the way people type certain groups of characters.

Bit. A binary digit, which is the smallest storage location in a computer. A bit may be either "on" or "off," or "magnetized" or "nonmagnetized." A combination of bits (usually eight) is used to represent a single character of data.

Bus. The path for moving data, instructions, or other signals between the various components of the CPU. The bus can be in the form of a cable or in the form of the connecting paths within a microcomputer chip.

Business Cycle. A reoccurring set of business transactions or events that occur in organizations. The five major business cycles are the revenue, procurement, production, personnel payroll, and

financial management and reporting.

Bus Network. A type of network organization where all devices are attached to a main channel called a bus. Each network device can access the other devices by sending a message to its address. Each device reads the address of all messages sent on the bus and responds to the messages sent to it.

Bus Size. The number of bits that can, at one time, be transmitted from one location in the computer to another.

Byte. A group of adjacent bits that is treated as a single unit by the computer. The most common size for a byte is eight bits. An eight-bit byte can be used to represent an alphabetic, numeric, or special character, or two numeric characters can be "packed" into a single eight-bit byte.

Canned Software. Programs written by computer manufacturers or software development companies for sale on the open market to a broad range of users with similar needs.

CASE. An acronym for computer-aided software engineering. This type of software is used by analysts to document and manage a systems development effort.

Cathode Ray Tube (CRT). Another name for the monitor on a computer. Sometimes terminals are referred to as CRTs as well.

CD ROM. A storage device that uses laser optics rather than magnetic storage devices for reading data. Although CD ROM disks are "read-only," the disks are useful for storing large volumes of data (roughly 600 megabytes per disk).

Centralized System. Data processing is done at a centralized processing center. User terminals are linked to the centralized host computer so that users can send data to the host computer for

processing and access data as needed.

Central Processing Unit (CPU). The hardware that contains the circuits that control the interpretation and execution of instructions and that serves as the principal data processing device. Its major components are the arithmetic-logic unit, the memory, and the control unit.

Channel. (1) A path that electronic signals follow when traveling between electronic devices. (2) A hardware device that acts as a communication interface between the CPU and input/output devices.

Character. A letter, numeric digit, or other symbol used for representing data to be processed by a computer.

Check Digit Verification. The edit check in which a check digit is recalculated to verify that an error has not been made. This calculation can be made only on a data item that has a check digit.

Checkpoint. Any one of a series of points during a long processing run at which an exact copy of all the data values and status indicators of a program is captured. Should a system failure occur, the system could be backed up to the most recent checkpoint and processing could begin again at the checkpoint rather than at the beginning of the program.

Client/Server. An arrangement of a LAN where information requested by a user is first processed as much as possible by the server and then transmitted to the user. *Contrast with* File Server.

Closed-Loop Verification. An input validation method in which data that have just been entered into the system are sent back to the sending device so that the user can verify that the correct data have been entered.

Coaxial Cable. A group of copper or aluminum wires that have been wrapped and shielded to reduce interference. The cables are used to transmit electronic messages between hardware devices.

Coding. (1) Assigning numbers, letters, or other symbols according to a systematic plan so that a user can determine the classifications to which a particular item belongs. (2) Writing program instructions that direct a computer to perform a specific data processing task.

Communications Channel. The line, or link, between the sender and the receiver in a data communications network.

Communications Network. An information system consisting of one or more computers, a number of other hardware devices, and communication channels all linked together into a network.

Communications Software. A program that controls the transmission of data electronically over communications lines.

Compatibility Test. A procedure for checking a password to determine whether its user is authorized to initiate the type of transaction or inquiry he or she is attempting to initiate.

Compensating Controls. Control procedures that will compensate for the deficiency in other controls.

Compiler. A program that converts all high-level language commands into machine language commands before any commands are executed. *Contrast with* Interpreter.

Completeness Test. An on-line data entry control in which the computer checks to see whether all of the data required for a particular transaction have been entered by the user.

Computer Configuration Flowchart. A type of flowchart that shows the different hardware devices in a computer system.

Computer Console. A hardware device that computer operators use to interact with large computer systems.

Computer Crime. Any illegal act for which knowledge of a computer is essential for the crime's perpetration, investigation, or prosecution.

Computer-Integrated Manufacturing. A manufacturing approach in which much of the manufacturing process is performed and monitored by computerized equipment, in part through the use of robotics and real-time data collection on manufacturing activities.

Computer Output Microfilm (COM). A hardware device that uses a photographic process to record computer output on photosensitive film in microscopic form.

Computer Programming. The process of writing software programs to accomplish a specific task or set of tasks.

Computer Security. All of the policies, procedures, tools, and other means of safeguarding information systems from unauthorized access or alteration and from intentional or unintentional damage or theft.

Computer System. The input/output devices, data storage devices, CPU, and other peripheral devices that are connected together. The software necessary to operate the computer is also considered a part of the system.

Computer System Flowchart. A type of flowchart that shows the inputs to a computer system or program, the program modules that process the data, and the output from the system.

Computer Virus. A segment of executable code that attaches itself to an application program or some other executable system component. When the hidden program is triggered, it makes unauthorized alterations to the way a system operates.

Concatenated Key. The combination of two fields in a data base table that together become a unique identifier or key field.

Concentrator. A communications device that combines signals from several sources and sends them over a single line. The concentrator also performs such tasks as data formatting, data validation, and data backup.

Conceptual Systems Design. A phase of the systems development life cycle in which the systems designer proposes a systems design without considering the physical restrictions of particular hardware and software.

Concurrent Audit Technique. A software routine that continuously monitors an information system as it processes live data in order to collect, evaluate, and report to the auditor information about the system's reliability.

Concurrent Update Control. A control that locks out one user to protect individual records from potential errors that could occur if two users attempted to update the same record simultaneously.

Configuration. (1) For a network a configuration is the entire interrelated set of hardware. (2) For a microcomputer the configuration references the complete internal and external components of the computer, including peripherals.

Context Diagram. The highest level of a data flow diagram. It provides a summary-level view of a system. It shows the data processing system, the inputs and outputs of the system, and the external entities that are the sources and destinations of the system's inputs and outputs.

Continuous and Intermittent Simulation (CIS). A concurrent audit technique that embeds an audit module into a data base management system rather than into the application software.

Control Unit. The CPU component that interprets program instructions and controls and coordinates the system's input,

output, and storage devices.

Corrective Controls. The procedures established to remedy problems that are discovered through detective controls.

Cross-Footing Balance Test. A procedure in which work sheet data are totaled both across and down and then the total of the horizontal totals is compared with the total of the vertical totals to make sure that the work sheet balances.

Custom Software. Computer software that is developed and written in-house to meet the unique needs of a particular company.

Data. Characters that are accepted as input to an information system for further storing and processing. After processing, the data become information.

Data Base. A set of interrelated, centrally controlled data files that are stored with as little data redundancy as possible. A data base consolidates many records previously stored in separate files into a common pool of data records and serves a variety of users and data processing applications.

Data Base Administrator. The person responsible for coordinating, controlling, and managing the data in the data base.

Data Base Management System (DBMS). The specialized computer program that manages and controls the data and interfaces between the data and the application programs.

Data Base Query Language. An easy-to-use programming language that lets the user ask questions about the data stored in a data base.

Data Base Retrieval System (DBRS). The public data bases, or electronic libraries, that contain millions of items of data that can be retrieved, reviewed, and analyzed for a fee.

Data Communications. The transmis-

sion of data from a point of origin to a point of destination.

Data Definition Language (DDL). A data base management system language that ties the logical and physical views of the data together. It is used to create the data base, to describe the schema and subschema, to describe the records and fields in the data base, and to specify any security limitations or constraints imposed on the data base.

Data Destination. A component of data flow diagrams that represents an entity outside of the system that receives data produced by the system.

Data Dictionary/Directory. An ordered collection of data elements that is essentially a centralized source of data about data. For each data element used in the organization, there is a record in the data dictionary that contains data about that data element.

Data Diddling. Changing data before it enters, as it enters, or after it has already been entered into the system. The change can be made to delete data, to change data, or to add data to the system.

Data Encryption. The translation of data into a secret code for storage or data transmission purposes. Encryption is particularly important when confidential data are being transmitted from remote terminals, because data transmission lines can be electronically monitored without the user's knowledge.

Data Flow Diagram. A diagram that concentrates on identifying the types of data and their flow through various types of processing. The physical nature of the data (e.g., physical document, electronic) is ignored; the diagram simply identifies the content of the data, the source, and the destination.

Data Independence. A data organization approach in which the data and the application programs

that use the data are independent. Thus one may be changed without affecting the other.

Data Leakage. The unauthorized copying of company data, often without leaving any indication that it was copied.

Data Manipulation Language (DML). A data base management system language that is used to update, replace, store, retrieve, insert, delete, sort, and otherwise manipulate the records and data items in the data base.

Data Processing Center. The room that houses a company's computer system (the hardware, software, and people who operate the system).

Data Processing Cycle. The operations performed on data in computer-based systems in order to generate meaningful and relevant information. The data processing cycle has four stages: data input, data processing, data storage, and information output.

Data Query Language (DQL). A high-level, English-like command language that is used to interrogate a data base. Most DQLs contain a fairly powerful set of commands that are easy to use yet provide a great deal of flexibility.

Data Redundancy. The storage of the same item of data in two or more files within an organization.

Data Source. A component of a data flow diagram that represents a source of data outside the system being modeled.

Data Store. A component of a data flow diagram that represents the storage of data within a system.

Data Value. The actual value stored in a field. It describes a particular attribute of an entity.

Debugging. The process of checking for errors in a computer program and correcting the errors that are discovered.

Decentralized System. An information

processing system that has an independent CPU and a data processing manager at each location.

Decision Support System (DSS). An interactive computer system designed to help with the decision-making process by providing access to a computer-based data base or decision-making model.

Desktop Publishing (DTP). The software that provides an end user with the ability to design, develop, and produce professional-quality printed documents containing text, charts, pictures, graphs, spreadsheets, photographs, and illustrations.

Detective Controls. Controls designed to discover control problems soon after they arise.

Diagnostic Messages. Messages that inform the programmer of syntax errors.

Direct Access. An access method that allows the computer to access a particular record without reading any other records. Since each storage location on a direct-access storage device has a unique address, the computer can find the record needed as long as it has the record's address.

Direct-Access Storage Device (DASD). A storage device (such as a disk drive) that can directly access individual storage locations to store or retrieve data.

Direct Conversion. An approach to converting from one system to another in which the old system is altogether discontinued, after which the new system is started (also known as "burning the bridges" or "crash conversion").

Disaster Recovery Plan. A plan that prepares a company to recover its data processing capacity as smoothly and quickly as possible in response to any emergency that could disable the computer system.

Distributed Data Processing (DDP). A

system in which computers are set up at remote locations and then linked to a centralized mainframe computer.

Documentation. Written material consisting of instructions to operators, descriptions of procedures, and other descriptive material. Documentation may be classified into three basic categories: administrative, systems, and operating.

Document Flowchart. A diagram illustrating the flow of documents through the different departments and functions of an organization.

Downloading. The transmission of data or software maintained on a large host (mainframe) computer to a personal computer for use by an individual working at the personal computer.

Downsizing. The shift of data processing and problem solving from mainframes to smaller computer systems. Downsizing saves money and allows the end user to be more involved in the processing of the data.

Eavesdropping. The act in which a computer user observes transmissions intended for someone else. One way unauthorized individuals can intercept signals is by setting up a wiretap.

Echo Check. A hardware control that verifies transmitted data by having the receiving device send the message back to the sending device so that the message received can be compared with the message sent.

Edit Check. An accuracy check performed by an edit program.

Edit Program. A computer program that verifies the validity and accuracy of input data.

Electronic Data Interchange (EDI). The use of computerized communication to exchange business data electronically in order to process transactions.

Electronic Data Processing (EDP). The processing of data utilizing a computer system. Little or no

human intervention is necessary while data are being processed.

Electronic Funds Transfer (EFT). The transfer of funds between two or more organizations or individuals using computers and other automated technology.

Electronic Mail (E-Mail). A system that allows a person to use a computer to send a message to another person.

Electronic Vaulting. The electronic transmission of backup copies of data to a physically different location. Electronic vaulting permits on-line access to backup data when necessary.

Embedded Audit Module. A special portion of an application program that keeps track of items of interest to auditors, such as any unauthorized attempts to access the data files.

End-User Computing (EUC). The creation, control, and implementation by end users of their own information system.

End-User System (EUS). An information system developed by the users themselves rather than professionals in the IS department, to meet their own operational and managerial information needs. An EUS draws upon the information in existing corporate data bases to meet users' information needs.

Entity. The item about which information is stored in a record. Examples of an entity include an employee, an inventory item, and a customer account.

Error Message. A message from the computer indicating that it has encountered a mistake or malfunction.

Ethernet. A bus configuration that allows LAN devices to put messages on the network and to take them off. In addition, ethernet regulates "traffic" on the network.

Executive Information System (EIS). An information system designed to provide executives with the needed information to make stra-

tegic plans, to control and operate the company, to monitor business conditions in general, and to identify business problems and opportunities.

Expert System (ES). A computerized information system that allows nonexperts to make decisions about a particular problem that are comparable to those of experts in the area.

Fault Tolerance. The capability of a system to continue performing its functions in the presence of a hardware failure.

Feasibility Study. An investigation to determine whether the development of a new application or system is practical. This is one of the first steps in the systems evaluation and selection process.

Femtosecond. One-quadrillionth of a second.

Fiber Optics Cable. A data transmission cable consisting of thousands of tiny filaments of glass or plastic.

Field. The part of a data record that contains the data value for a particular attribute. All records of a particular type usually have their fields in the same order. For example, the first field in all accounts receivable records may be reserved for the customer account number.

Field Check. An edit check in which the characters in a field are examined to make sure that they are of the correct field type (e.g., numeric data in numeric fields).

File. A set of logically related records, such as the payroll records of all employees.

File Access. The way the computer finds or retrieves each record it has stored.

File Maintenance. The periodic processing of transaction files against a master file. This maintenance, which is the most common task in virtually all data processing systems, includes record additions, deletions, updates, and changes. After file

maintenance, the master file will contain the most current information.

File Organization. The way data are stored on the physical storage media. File organization may be either sequential or direct (random, nonsequential, or relative).

File Server. An arrangement in a LAN where an entire file is sent to the user and then processed by the user, not the server. *Contrast with* Client/Server.

Flat File. A file structure in which every record is identical to every other record in terms of attributes and field lengths.

Flexible Manufacturing System (FMS). A system in which a computer is used to automate and integrate the performance of all major production tasks within a factory, including production planning, stock control, materials handling, machine scheduling and operation, and quality control.

Floppy Disk. A 5 $^1/_4$-inch or 3 $^1/_2$-inch diskette.

Flowchart. A diagrammatical representation of the flow of information and the sequence of operations in a process or system.

Flowcharting Symbols. A set of objects that are used in flowcharts to show how and where data move. Each symbol has a special meaning that is easily conveyed by its shape.

Fourth-Generation Languages (4GLs). High-level, application, or user-oriented languages that are easy to learn and do not require the user to understand the details of the computer.

Front-End Processor (FEP). A dedicated communications computer that is connected to a host CPU. It handles the communications tasks so that the CPU can spend its time processing data.

Gantt Chart. A bar graph used for project planning and control. Project activities are shown on the left, and units of time are shown across the top. The time

period over which each activity is expected to be performed is represented with a horizontal bar on the graph.

Gateway. A communications interface device that allows a local area network to be connected to external networks and to communicate with external mainframes and data bases.

General Controls. Controls that relate to all or many computerized accounting activities, such as those relating to the plan of organization of data processing activities and the separation of incompatible functions. *Contrast with* Application Controls.

Generalized Audit Software Package (GASP). A software package that performs audit tests on the data files of a company.

Gigabyte. One billion characters of data.

Grandfather-Father-Son Concept. A method for maintaining backup copies of files on magnetic tape or disk. The three most current copies of the data are retained, with the son being the most recent.

Graphical User Interface (GUI). An operating environment in which the user selects commands, starts programs, or lists files by pointing to pictorial representations (icons) with a mouse. A Macintosh computer, Microsoft's Windows, and IBM's OS/2 are all GUI environments.

Groupware. Software that combines the power of computer networks with the immediacy and personal touch of the face-to-face brainstorming session. Groupware lets users hold computer conferences, decide when to hold a meeting, make a calendar for a department, collectively brainstorm on creative endeavors, manage projects, and design products.

Hacking. Unauthorized access to and use of computer systems, usually by means of a personal computer and telecommunications networks.

Hard Disk. A magnetic storage disk made of rigid material and enclosed in a sealed unit to cut down on the chances of the magnetic medium's being damaged by foreign particles. A hard disk has a much faster access time and greater storage capacity than a floppy disk.

Hardware. The physical equipment, or machinery, that is used in a computer system.

Hash Total. A total generated from values for a field that would not usually be totaled, such as customer account numbers. It is usually generated manually from source documents prior to input and compared with machine-generated totals at each subsequent processing step. Any discrepancy may indicate a loss of records or errors in data transcription or processing.

Hierarchical Network. A variation of the star network. The configuration looks like a hierarchical organization chart.

Hierarchical Organization Structure. An organizational structure created by subdividing organizational goals and tasks into a graded series of lower-level goals and tasks.

Hybrid Network. A combination of both star and ring network configurations.

Image Processing. The use of scanning and photographic techniques to capture the exact image of a document. The scanning device converts the text and pictures into a digitized electronic code that can be displayed on a computer monitor and stored on laser optical disks.

Implementation. The process of installing a computer. It includes selecting and installing the equipment, training personnel, establishing operating policies, and getting the software onto the system and functioning properly.

Implementation Plan. A written plan that outlines how the new system will be implemented. The plan includes a timetable for completion, the name of the person responsible for each activity, cost estimates, and task milestones.

Indexed-Sequential-Access Method (ISAM). A file organization and access approach in which records are stored in sequential order by their primary key on a direct-access storage device. An index file is created that allows the file to be accessed and updated randomly.

Index File. A master file of record identifiers and corresponding storage locations.

Information. Data that have been processed and organized into output that is meaningful to the person who receives it. Information can be mandatory, essential, or discretionary.

Information Center (IC). A department or division in a company with the purpose of facilitating, coordinating, and controlling end-user activities and support.

Information Processing. The process of turning data into information. This process has four stages: data input, data processing, data storage, and information output.

Information System. An organized way of collecting, processing, managing, and reporting information so that an organization can achieve its objectives and goals. A formal information system has an explicit responsibility to produce information. In contrast, an informal information system is one that arises out of a need that is not satisfied by a formal channel. It operates without a formal assignment of responsibility.

Initial Investigation. A preliminary investigation to determine whether a proposed new system is both needed and possible.

Input. Data entered into the computer system either from an external storage device or from the keyboard of the computer.

Input Controls Matrix. A matrix that shows the control procedures applied to each field of an input record.

Input Device. Hardware used to enter data into the computer system.

Input/Output-Bound System. A system that can process data faster than it can receive input and send output. Consequently, the processor has to wait on the I/O devices.

Input Validation Routine. A computer program or routine designed to check the validity or accuracy of input data.

Inquiry Processing. The processing of user information queries by searching master files for the desired information and then organizing the information into an appropriate response.

Integrated Circuits. Small silicon chips that contain the circuitry used by the computer.

Integrated Services Digital Network (ISDN). An extensive digital network with built-in intelligence to permit all types of data (voice, data, images, facsimile, video, etc.) to be sent over the same line.

Integrated Test Facility. A testing technique in which a dummy company or division is introduced into the company's computer system. Test transactions may then be conducted on these fictitious master records without affecting the real master records. These test transactions may be processed along with the real transactions, and the employees of the computer facility need not be aware that testing is being done.

Interface. The common boundary between two pieces of hardware or between two computer systems. It is the point at which the two systems communicate with each other.

Internal Control. The controls within a business organization that ensure that information is processed correctly.

Interpreter. A program that, one statement at a time, translates the source language into machine code and then executes it. *Contrast with* Compiler.

Journal Voucher. A form that is used to summarize a group of transactions. For example, a group of documents would be gathered and their total entered on the journal voucher.

Key-to-Disk Encoder. A device allowing several keying stations to be linked to a minicomputer that has an attached disk memory. Data may be entered simultaneously from each of the keying stations and pooled on the disk file.

Key-to-Tape Encoder. A device for keying in data and recording the data on magnetic tape.

Kilobyte (K). A unit equal to 1024 bytes of memory capacity; usually expressed in terms of 1000 characters of memory. That is, 64K represents approximately 64,000 characters of memory.

Kiting. A fraud scheme where the perpetrator covers up a theft of cash by creating cash through the transfer of money between banks.

Language Translator. A software program that is used to convert instructions written in a programming language into machine language. There are three types: assemblers, compilers, and translators.

LAN Interface. The hardware device that interfaces between the local area network (LAN) cable and the hardware devices (computers, printers, etc.) connected to the LAN.

Lapping. Concealing a cash shortage by means of a series of delays in posting collections to accounts.

Light Pen. A pencil-shaped device that uses photoelectric circuitry to enter data through the video display terminal of the computer system. Its principal use is in graphics applications.

Limit Check. An edit check to ensure that a numerical amount in a record does not exceed some predetermined limit.

Local Area Network (LAN). A network that links together microcomputers, disk drives, word processors, printers, and other equipment that is located within a limited geographical area, such as one building.

Logical Model. A description of a system that focuses on the essential activities and flow of information in the system, irrespective of how the flow is actually accomplished.

Logical View. The manner in which users conceptually organize, view, and understand the relationships among data items. *Contrast with* Physical View.

Logic Time Bomb. A program that lies idle until some specified circumstance or a particular time triggers it. Once triggered, the bomb sabotages the system by destroying programs or data.

Logistics Management. The planning and control of the physical flow of materials through an organization, through purchasing, inventory management, and production management.

Machine-Independent Language. A programming language that can be used on many different types of computer platforms. The language is not dependent upon the type of computer being used.

Machine Language. A binary code that can be interpreted by the internal circuity of the computer.

Macro. (1) A series of keystrokes or commands that can be given a name, stored, and activated each time the keystrokes must be repeated. (2) A programming command.

Magnetic Disk. A magnetic storage medium consisting of one or more flat, round disks with a magnetic surface on which data can be written.

Magnetic Ink Character Recognition (MICR). The recognition of characters printed by a machine that uses a special magnetic ink.

Magnetic Tape. A secondary storage medium that is about a half inch wide and has a magnetic surface on which data can be stored. The most popular types are seven-track and nine-track tapes.

Mainframe Computer. (1) Same as CPU. (2) A large-sized digital computer, typically with a separate stand-alone CPU. It is larger than a minicomputer.

Main Memory. The internal memory directly controlled by the CPU, which usually consists of the ROM and RAM of the computer.

Management Information System. The set of human and capital resources within an organization that is responsible for collecting and processing data so that all levels of management have the information they need to plan and control the activities of the organization.

Manufacturing Resource Planning. A comprehensive, computerized planning and control system for manufacturing operations. It is an enhancement of materials requirements planning that incorporates capacity planning for factory work centers and scheduling of production operations.

Mapping Program. A program activated during regular processing that provides information about which portions of the application program were not executed.

Masquerading. The process whereby a perpetrator gains access to a system by pretending to be an authorized user. This approach requires that the perpetrator know the legitimate user's identification numbers and passwords.

Master File. A permanent file of records that reflects the current status of relevant business items such as inventory and accounts receivable. The master file is updated with the latest transactions from the current transaction file.

Master Plan. A document specifying the overall information system plan of an organization.

Megabyte (M). One million characters of data.

Megahertz (MHz). One million computer cycles per second.

Memory Unit. The part of the CPU where data and instructions are stored internally.

Menu. A list of computer commands or options that is displayed by a program. The user chooses the option that will cause the desired action to take place.

Message. (1) The data transmitted over a data communication system. (2) The instructions that are given to an object in object-oriented languages.

Microcomputer. A small computer system anywhere from a "computer on a chip" to a system that covers a desktop. Often called a personal or desktop computer, this type of computer usually sells for less than $5000.

Microprocessor. A large-scale or very large scale integrated circuit on a silicon chip. Some of the more common microprocessors in use are the 8088, 8086, 80286, 80386, 80486, pentium (80586), Z80, 68000, and 8080.

Microsecond. One-millionth of a second.

Millisecond. One-thousandth of a second.

Minicomputer. A digital computer that usually is larger than a microcomputer but smaller than a mainframe computer. It has a higher performance, a more powerful instruction set, higher prices, more input/output capability, a greater variety of programming languages, and a more powerful operating system than a microcomputer does. However, it has fewer of these features than a mainframe computer does.

MIPS. Millions of instructions per second; a way of measuring CPU speed.

Modem. Stands for modulator/demodulator; a communications device that converts the computer's digital signals into analog signals that can be sent over phone lines. The modem can be internal (mounted on a board within the computer) or external (a freestanding unit).

Modular Conversion. An approach for converting from an old system to a new system in which parts of the old system are gradually replaced by the new until the old system has been entirely replaced by the new.

Monitor. (1) A video display unit or CRT. (2) Software that controls how a system operates.

Motherboard. The main circuit board of a microcomputer. It usually contains the memory, the CPU, and the input/output circuitry.

Mouse. A small device that is connected to a computer, usually by a cord. When the user moves the mouse, the movement is translated into a movement of the screen's cursor; the user issues a command by pressing a button on the mouse when the cursor is positioned on the desired command.

MS-DOS. An acronym for Microsoft/Disk Operating System, the operating system used by IBM and many IBM-compatible microcomputers.

Multidrop Line. A communications channel configuration in which most terminals are linked together, with only one or a few terminals linked directly to the CPU.

Multiplexor. A communications device that combines signals from several sources and sends them out over a single line. Multiplexors can also split the signals back into the individual messages.

Multiprocessing. The simultaneous execution of two or more tasks, usually by two or more processing units that are part of the same system.

Multiprogramming. A programming method in which execution switches back and forth between two or more programs so that the processing unit seems to be executing them simultaneously.

Nanosecond. One-billionth of a second.

Network. (1) A group of interconnected computers and terminals; a series of locations tied together by communications channels. (2) A data structure involving relationships among multiple record types.

Object-Oriented Language. A programming language in which the user selects objects instead of writing procedural code. Each object can then be modified, reused, or copied. The objects are sent messages telling them what to do.

Object-Oriented Programming (OOP). Programming a computer using an object-oriented language. The programmer uses objects to create a program instead of writing procedural code. Each object is sent a message telling it what to do.

Object Program. A compiled or assembled machine-level program that can be executed by the computer. The source program and the translator are inputs to the computer translation process, and the output is the machine-executable object program.

On-Line Device. A hardware device that is connected directly to the CPU by cable or telephone line (e.g., CRT terminal, disk drive).

On-Line Processing. A method of

processing in which individual transactions are processed as they occur and from their point of origin, rather than having them accumulate to be processed in batches. On-line processing requires the use of on-line data entry terminals and direct-access file storage media so that each master record can be accessed directly.

On-Line, Real-Time Processing. A method of processing in which the computer system processes data immediately after it is captured and provides updated information to the user on a timely basis. On-line, real-time processing usually entails one of two forms of processing: on-line updating and inquiry processing.

Operating Environment. A software program that runs on top of the operating system to provide the system with desirable enhancements. For example, Microsoft's Windows is an operating environment that runs on top of DOS.

Operating System. A software program that controls the overall operation of a computer system. Its functions include controlling the execution of computer programs, scheduling, debugging, assigning storage areas, managing data, and controlling input and output.

Operations and Maintenance Phase. The last phase of the systems development life cycle, in which follow-up studies are conducted to detect and correct design deficiencies. Minor modifications will be made as problems arise in the new system.

Optical Character Recognition (OCR). The use of light-sensitive hardware devices to convert characters readable by humans into computer input. Since OCR readers can read only certain items, a special machine-readable font must be used.

Optical Disk. A mass storage medium that is capable of storing billions of bits. Lasers are used to write to and read from an optical disk.

Output. The information produced by a system. Output is typically produced for the use of a particular individual or group of users.

Outsourcing. Hiring an outside company to handle all or part of the data processing activities.

Parallel Conversion. A systems conversion approach in which the new and old systems are run simultaneously until the organization is assured that the new system is functioning correctly.

Parallel Interface. A way of connecting peripherals (like a printer) to a computer. Data are transferred simultaneously along several parallel cables at the same time.

Parallel Processing. A method of processing in which two or more processing tasks are performed simultaneously within a single CPU.

Parallel Port. A communications interface that allows data to be transmitted a whole character (eight bits) at a time. *Contrast with* Serial Port.

Parallel Simulation. An approach auditors use to detect unauthorized program changes and data processing accuracy. The auditor writes his or her own version of a program and then reprocesses data. The outputs of the auditor's program and the client's program are compared to verify that they are the same.

Parity Bit. An extra bit added to a byte, character, or word. The parity bit is magnetized as needed to ensure that there is always an odd (or even) number of magnetized bits. The computer uses the odd (or even) parity scheme to check the accuracy of each item of data.

Parity Checking. A checking process in which a computer reads or receives a set of characters and sums the number of 1 bits in each character to verify that it is an even (or odd) number. If it is not, the character contains an error.

Password. A series of letters, numbers, or both that must be entered in order to access and use system resources. Password use helps prevent unauthorized tampering with hardware, software, and the organization's data.

Payroll Register. A listing of payroll data for each employee for the current payroll period.

Peripherals. The hardware devices (such as those used for input, output, processing, and data communications) that are connected to the CPU.

Personal Information System. A type of information system where individuals use a personal computer, data they have created and stored themselves, and corporate data to meet their own personal information needs.

Physical Access. The ability to physically use computer equipment.

Physical Model. The description of physical aspects of a data base (e.g., field and file sizes, storage and access methods, security procedures).

Physical Systems Design. The phase of the systems development life cycle in which the designer specifies the hardware, software, and procedures for delivering the conceptual systems design.

Physical View. The way data are physically arranged and stored on disks, tapes, and other storage media. EDP personnel use this view to make efficient use of storage and processing resources. *Contrast with* Logical View.

Picosecond. One-trillionth of a second.

Piggybacking. A method of fraud in which a perpetrator latches onto a legitimate user who is logging into a system. The legitimate user unknowingly carries the perpetrator with him as he is allowed into the system.

Pixel. The smallest particle of information that appears on a monitor's screen. The greater the number of pixels displayed, the better the monitor's resolution is.

Plotter. A hard copy output device that produces drawings and other graphical output by moving an ink pen across a page.

Point-of-Sale (POS) Recorder (Terminal). An electronic device that functions as both a terminal and a cash register. It is commonly used in retail stores to record sales information at the time of the sale and to perform other data processing functions.

Point-to-Point Line. A communications channel configuration that uses a separate line between each terminal and the central computer.

Postimplementation Review. A review made after a new system has been operating for a brief period. The purposes of this review are to ensure that the new system is meeting its planned objectives, to identify the adequacy of system standards, and to review system controls.

Preformatting. An on-line data entry control in which the computer displays a form on the screen and the user fills in the blanks in the form as needed.

Preventive Controls. A control system that places restrictions on and requires documentation of employee activities so as to reduce the occurrence of errors and deviations. Because preventive controls operate from within the process being controlled, they are perhaps the type of control most consistent with the original meaning of the term *internal control*.

Primary Key. A unique identification code assigned to each record within a system. The primary key is the key used most frequently to distinguish, order,

and reference records.

Procedure-Oriented Language. A high-level language such as COBOL or FORTRAN in which the programmer must specify the logic necessary to accomplish a specific task.

Program. A set of instructions that can be executed by a computer.

Program Flowchart. A diagrammatical representation of the logic and sequence of processes used in a computer program.

Program Generators. Computer programs designed to speed up the process of writing programs. The user specifies certain information, such as what the screen layouts should look like and what processing procedures need to be performed, and the program generates program instructions.

Program Tracing. A technique used to obtain detailed knowledge of the logic of an application program, as well as to test the program's compliance with its control specifications.

Programming Language. The language the programmer uses to write a computer program (e.g., COBOL, BASIC, Pascal, LOGO).

Project Development Plan. A proposal to develop a particular computer system application. It contains an analysis of the requirements and expectations of the proposed application.

Project Management Software. A software program that is used to plan, schedule, track, control, and evaluate projects to ensure that they are completed within the budget and on time.

Project Development Team. A group of people consisting of specialists, management, and users who develop a project's plan and direct the steps of the systems life cycle. The team monitors costs, progress, and employees and gives status reports to top management and to the steering committee.

Protocol. The set of rules governing the exchange of data between two systems or components of a system.

Prototype. A systems design technique in which a simplified working model, or prototype, of an information system is developed.

Pseudocode. An informal design language oriented toward structured programming. It uses English language phrases to describe the processing logic of a computer program.

Public Data Bases. Electronic libraries containing millions of items of data that can be reviewed, retrieved, analyzed, and saved by the general public.

Query. A request for specific information from a computer. Queries are often used with a data base management system to extract data from the data base.

Query Languages. Languages used to process data files and to obtain quick responses to questions about those files.

Random Access Memory (RAM). A temporary storage location for computer instructions and data. RAM may have data both written to it and read from it.

Random Surveillance. A way of detecting fraud by having auditors periodically audit the system and test system controls. Informing employees that the auditors will conduct random surveillance is a deterrent to computer crime.

Range Check. An edit check designed to verify that a data item falls within a certain predetermined range of acceptable values.

Read-Only Memory (ROM). The internal CPU memory that can be read but usually cannot be changed.

Real-Time Notification. A variation of the embedded audit module in which the auditor is notified of each transaction as it occurs by means of a message printed on the auditor's terminal.

Real-Time System. A system that is able to respond to an inquiry or provide data fast enough to make the information meaningful to the user. Real-time systems are usually designed for very fast response.

Reasonableness Test. An edit check of the logical correctness of relationships among the values of data items on an input record and the corresponding file record. For example, a journal entry that debits inventory and credits wages payable is not reasonable.

Record. A set of logically related data items that describe specific attributes of an entity, such as all payroll data relating to a single employee.

Record Count. A total of the number of input documents in a process or the number of records processed in a run.

Record Layout. A document that illustrates the arrangement of items of data in input, output, and file records.

Recovery Procedures. A set of procedures that are followed if the computer quits in the middle of processing a batch of data. The procedures allow the user to recover from hardware or software failures.

Redundant Data Check. An edit check that requires the inclusion of two identifiers in each input record (e.g., the customer's account number and the first five letters of the customer's name). If these input values do not match those on the record, the record will not be updated.

Reengineering. The thorough analysis and complete redesign of all business processes and information systems to achieve dramatic performance improvements. Reengineering seeks to reduce a company to its essential business processes.

Relational Data Base. A data base model in which all data elements are logically viewed as being stored in the form of two-dimensional tables called relations. These tables are, in effect, flat files where each row represents a unique entity or record. Each column represents a field where the record's attributes are stored. The tables serve as the building blocks from which data relationships can be created.

Remittance Advice. An enclosure included with a customer's payment that indicates the invoices, statements, or other items paid.

Report Generators. Computer programs designed to make report writing easier and faster.

Report Writers. Software that lets a user specify the data elements to be printed. The report writer searches the data base, extracts the desired items, and prints them out in the user-specified format.

Reprocessing. An approach auditors use to detect unauthorized program changes. The auditor verifies the integrity of an application program and then saves it for future use. At subsequent intervals, and on a surprise basis, the auditor uses the previously verified version of the program to reprocess data that have been processed by the version used by the company. The output of the two runs is compared and discrepancies are investigated.

Requirements Costing. A system evaluation method in which a list is made of all of the required features of the desired system. If a proposed system does not have a desired feature, the cost of developing or purchasing that feature is added to the basic cost of the system. This method allows different systems to be evaluated on the basis of the costs of providing the required features.

Resolution. A term used to describe the density and overall quality of the video display on a terminal or monitor.

Response Time. The amount of time that elapses between making a query and receiving a response.

Ring Network. A configuration in which the data communications channels form a loop or circular pattern when the local processors are linked together. *Contrast with* Star Network.

Rollback. A process whereby a log of all preupdate values is prepared for each record that is updated within a particular interval. If there is a system failure, the records can be restored to the preupdate values and the processing started over.

Round Down. A fraud technique used in financial institutions that pay interest. The programmer instructs the computer to round down all interest calculations to two decimal places. The fraction of a cent that was rounded down on each calculation is put into the programmer's own account.

Sabotage. An intentional act to destroy a system or some of its components.

Salami Technique. A fraud technique where tiny slices of money are stolen from many different accounts.

Scanning Routine. A software routine that searches a program for the occurrence of a particular variable name or other combinations of characters.

SCARF (System Control Audit Review File). A concurrent audit technique that embeds audit modules into application software to continuously monitor all transaction activity and collect data on transactions having special audit significance.

Scavenging. The unauthorized access to confidential information by searching corporate records. Scavenging methods range from searching trash cans for printouts or carbon copies of confidential information to scanning the contents of computer memory.

Schema. A description of the types of data elements that are in the data base, the relationships among the data elements, and the structure or overall logical model used to organize and describe the data.

Secondary Key. A field that can be used to identify records in a file. Unlike the primary key, it does not provide a unique identification.

Secondary Storage. Storage media, such as magnetic disks or magnetic tape, on which data that are not currently needed by the computer can be stored. Also referred to as auxiliary storage.

Semiconductor. A tiny silicon chip upon which a number of miniature circuits have been inscribed.

Separation of Duties. The separation of assigned duties and responsibilities in such a way that no single employee can both perpetrate and conceal errors or irregularities.

Sequence Check. An edit check that determines whether a batch of input data is in the proper numerical or alphabetical sequence.

Sequential-Access Method (SAM). An access method that requires data items to be accessed in the same order in which they were written.

Sequential File. A way of storing numeric or alphabetical records according to a key. For example, customer numbers can range from 00001 to 99999. To access a sequential file record, the system starts at the beginning of the file and reads each record until the desired record is located.

Serial Interface. A way of connecting peripherals (like a printer) to a computer. Data are transferred along a single cable one bit at a time.

Serial Port. A communications interface that allows data to be sent only one bit at a time. *Contrast with* Parallel Port.

Server. A high-capacity computer that contains the network software to handle communications, storage, and resource-sharing needs of other computers in the network. The server also contains the application software and data common to all users.

Service Bureau. An organization that provides data processing services on its own equipment to users for a fee.

Sign Check. An edit check that verifies that the data in a field have the appropriate arithmetic sign.

Snapshot. An audit technique that records the content of both a transaction record and a related master file record before and after each processing step.

Software. A computer program that gives instructions to the CPU. Also used to refer to programming languages and computer systems documentation.

Source Code or Program. A computer program written in a source language such as BASIC, COBOL, or assembly language. The source program is translated into the object (machine language) program by a translation program such as a compiler or assembler.

Source Data Automation (SDA). The collection of transaction data in machine-readable form at the time and place of origin. Examples of SDA devices are optical scanners and automated teller machines.

Source Document. A document containing the initial record of a transaction that takes place. Examples of source documents, which are usually recorded on preprinted forms, include sales invoices, purchase orders, and employee time cards.

Star Network. A configuration in which there is a centralized real-time computer system to which all other computer systems are linked. *Contrast with* Ring Network.

Steering Committee. An executive-level committee to plan and oversee the IS function. The committee typically consists of management from the systems department, the controller, and other management affected by the information systems function.

Storage. Placement of data in internal memory or on a medium such as magnetic disk or magnetic tape, from which they can later be retrieved.

Structure Chart. A document showing the hierarchical organization of computer program modules. The idea is that each module should be able to be developed and tested independently of the other processing modules.

Structured Programming. A modular approach to programming in which each module performs a specific function, stands alone, and is coordinated by a control module. Also referred to as "GOTOless" programming because modular design makes GOTO statements unnecessary.

Structured Walk-Through. A formal review process in program design in which one or more programmers walk through the logic and code of another programmer to detect weaknesses and errors in program design.

Subschema. (1) A subset of the schema that includes only those data items used in a particular application program or by a particular user. (2) The way the user defines the data and the data relationships.

Subsystem. A smaller system that is a part of the entire information system. Each subsystem performs a specific function that is important to and supports the system of which it is a part.

Supercomputer. A very large, high-speed computer used by businesses and organizations that have high-volume needs.

Superzapping. The use of a special system program to bypass regular system controls to perform unauthorized acts. A superzap utility was originally written to handle emergencies, such as restoring a system that has crashed.

Suspense File. A file containing records that have been identified as erroneous or are of uncertain status.

Switched Line. A regular dial-up telephone line. The charges for line use are usually based on the amount of time used and the length of line used.

Symbolic Language. A language in which each machine instruction is represented by symbols that bear some relation to the instruction. For example, the symbol A might represent the Add command.

Synchronous Transmission. Data transmission in which start and stop bits are required only at the beginning and end of a block of characters. *Contrast with* Asynchronous Transmission.

Syntax. The rules of grammar and structure that govern the use of a programming language.

Syntax Errors. Errors that result from using the programming language improperly or from incorrectly typing the source program.

System. (1) An entity consisting of two or more components or subsystems that interact to achieve a goal. (2) The equipment and programs that make up a complete computer installation. (3) The programs and related procedures that perform a single task on a computer.

System Flowchart. A diagrammatical representation that shows the flow of data through a series of operations in an automated data processing system. It shows how data are captured and input into the system, the processes that operate on the data, and system outputs.

Systems Analysis. (1) A rigorous and systematic approach to decision making, characterized by a comprehensive definition of available alternatives and an exhaustive analysis of the merits of each alternative as a basis for choosing the best alternative. (2) Examination of the user information requirements within an organization in order to establish objectives and specifications for the design of an information system.

Systems Approach. A way of handling systems change by recognizing that every system must have an objective, a set of components, and a set of inter-relationships among the components. The systems approach proceeds step by step, with a thorough exploration of all implications and alternatives at each step.

Systems Concept. A systems analysis principle that states that alternative courses of action within a system must be evaluated from the standpoint of the system as a whole rather than that of any single subsystem or set of subsystems.

Systems Design. The process of preparing detailed specifications for the development of a new information system.

Systems Development Life Cycle. Five procedures and steps that a company goes through when it decides to design and implement a new information system. The five steps are systems analysis, conceptual design, physical design, implementation and conversion, and operation and maintenance.

Systems Software. Software that interfaces between the hardware and the application program. Systems software can be classified as operating systems, data base management systems, utility programs, language translators, and communications software.

Systems Survey. The systematic gathering of facts relating to the existing information system. This task is generally carried out by a systems analyst.

Tagging. An audit procedure in which certain records are marked with a special code before processing. During processing all data relating to the marked records are captured and saved so that they can be verified later by the auditors.

Tape Drive. The device that controls the movement of the magnetic tape and that reads and writes on the tape.

Tape File Protection Ring. A circular plastic ring that determines when a tape file can be written on. When the ring is inserted on a reel of magnetic tape, data can be written on the tape. If the ring is removed, the data on the tape cannot be overwritten with new information.

Telecommunications System. An information system that uses data communications technology.

Teleconferencing. The linking of different people in different locations electronically or through telecommunications so that they can confer.

Terabytes. One-trillion characters of memory.

Terminal. An input/output device for entering or receiving data directly from the computer. Also referred to as cathode ray tube (CRT) or visual display terminal (VDT).

Terrestrial Microwave System. A microwave data transmission system that utilizes transmission facilities located on the earth instead of on satellites.

Test Data. Data that have been specially developed to test the accuracy and completeness of a computer program. The results from the test data are compared with hand-calculated results to verify that the program operates properly.

Test Data Generator. A program that takes the specifications describing the logic characteristics of the program to be tested and automatically generates a set of test data that can be used to check the logic of the program.

Throughput. The total amount of useful work performed by a computer system during a given period of time.

Time-Sharing. The use of small slices of CPU time from a large mainframe computer by a number of small users, for a fee.

TIPS. Trillions of instructions per second; a way of measuring CPU speed.

Token Ring. A LAN configuration that forms a closed loop. A token is passed around the ring to indicate that a device is free to send or receive a message.

Transaction File. A relatively temporary data file containing transaction data that are typically used to update a master file.

Transaction Log. A detailed record of every transaction entered in a system through data entry.

Transaction Processing. A process that begins with capturing transaction data and ends with an informational output.

Trapdoor. A set of computer instructions that allows a user to bypass the system's normal controls.

Tree. A data structure or logical data model in which relationships among data items are expressed in the form of a hierarchical structure.

Trojan Horse. A set of unauthorized computer instructions in an authorized and otherwise properly functioning program. It performs some illegal act at a preappointed time or under a predetermined set of conditions.

Turnaround Document. A document readable by humans which is prepared by the computer as output, sent outside the system, and then returned as input into the computer. An example is a

utility bill.

Turnkey System. A system that is delivered to customers ready (theoretically) to be turned on. A turnkey system supplier buys hardware, writes applications software that is tailored both to that equipment and to the specific needs of its customers, and then markets the entire system.

Uninterruptible Power System. An alternative power supply device that protects against the loss of power and fluctuations in the power level.

Universal Product Code (UPC). A machine-readable code that is read by optical scanners. The code consists of a series of bar codes and is printed on most products sold in grocery stores.

UNIX. A flexible and widely used operating system for 16-bit machines.

Updating. Changing stored data to reflect more recent events (e.g., changing the account receivable balance because of a recent sale or collection).

Users. All the people that interact with the system. Users are people who record data, manage the system, and control the system's security. Those who use information from the system are end users.

Utility Program. A set of prewritten programs that perform a variety of file and data handling tasks (e.g., sorting or merging files) and other housekeeping chores.

Validity Check. An edit test in which an identification number or transaction code is compared to a table of valid identification numbers or codes maintained in computer memory.

Value-Added Network (VAN). A public network that adds value to the data communications process by handling the difficult task of in-

terfacing with the multiple types of hardware and software used by different companies.

Value Chain. The linking together of all the primary and support activities in a business. Value is added as a product passes through the chain.

Value of Information. Value of information = benefit − cost.

Value System. The combination of several value chains into one system. A value system includes the value chains of a company, its suppliers, its distributors, and its customers.

Very Large Scale Integration (VLSI). A process in which a large number (1000 or more) of integrated circuits are placed on one chip.

Virtual Memory (Storage). On-line secondary storage that is used as an extension of primary memory, thus giving the appearance of a larger, virtually unlimited amount of internal memory. Pages of data or program instructions are swapped back and forth between secondary and primary storage as needed.

Voice Input. A data input unit that recognizes human voices and converts spoken messages into machine-readable input.

Voice Mail (V-Mail). A service that converts voice messages into computer data and stores them so that they can be retrieved later by the person for whom they were intended.

Voucher. A document that summarizes the data relating to a disbursement and represents final authorization of payment.

Walk-Through. A meeting, attended by those associated with a project, in which a detailed review of systems procedures and/or program logic is carried out in a step-by-step manner.

WATS Line. An acronym for wide

area telephone service line; a phone line for which the customer pays both a fixed charge and an additional charge that varies directly with the amount of extra use.

Wide Area Network (WAN). A telecommunications network that covers a large geographic area anywhere from a few cities to the whole globe. A WAN uses telephone lines, cables, microwaves, or satellites to connect a wide variety of hardware devices in many different locations.

Wiretap. A device for listening (eavesdropping) on an unprotected communications line.

Word. A group of bytes moved and processed by a computer. The most common size for large computers is 32 bits; for smaller computers it is 16 bits.

Worm. Similar to a virus, except that it is a program rather than a code segment hidden in a host program. A worm also copies itself and actively transmits itself directly to other systems.

WORM. An acronym for write-once, read-many. For example, an optical disk can be written on once but later read many times.

Zero Balance Check. An internal check that requires the balance of the payroll control account to be zero after all entries to it have been made.

REFERENCES

Chapter 1

Abramson, David H. "The Future of Accounting: Scenarios for 1996." *Journal of Accountancy* (October 1986):120–124.

Ackoff, R. L. "Management Misinformation Systems." *Management Science* (December 1, 1967):147–156.

Breden, Denise, and Robert Demichiel. *Inflation and Managerial Decision Making*. Montvale, N.J.: National Association of Accountants, 1985.

Davis, Gordon B. "Commentary on Information Systems." *Accounting Horizons* (March 1987):75–79.

Davis, Gordon B., and Margrethe H. Olson. *Management Information Systems: Conceptual Foundations, Structure, and Development*. 2nd ed. New York: McGraw-Hill, 1985.

Douglas, Patricia P., and Teresa K. Beed. *Presenting Accounting Information to Management*. Montvale, N.J.: National Association of Accountants, 1986.

Dreyfuss, Joel, and Brenton Schlender. "Today's Leaders Look to Tomorrow." *Fortune* (March 26, 1990):30–31, 68–72, 149–150.

Foust, Dean. "Uncle Sam Can't Keep Track of His Trillions." *Business Week* (September 2, 1991): 72–73.

Gelfond, Susan. "The Computer Age Dawns in the Corner Office." *Business Week* (June 27, 1988):84–86.

Hodge, Bartow; Robert A. Fleck, Jr.; and C. Brian Honess. *Management Information Systems*. Reston, Va.: Reston Publishing, 1984.

Joseph, Gilbert W. "Why Study Accounting Information Systems?" *Journal of Systems Management* (September 1987):24–26.

Kirkpatrick, David. "From Desk to Neck: The PC as Fashion." *Fortune* (January 13, 1992):79.

Lynch, David. "MIS: Conceptual Framework, Criticisms, and Major Requirements for Success." *Journal of Business Communication* (Winter 1984):19–31.

Margolis, Nell, and Ellis Booker.

"Taming the Health Care Cost Monster." *Computerworld* (August 3, 1992):1, 14–15.

Meyer, N. D. "Integrating Information Systems and Corporate Strategy." *Financial Executive* (September/October 1989):37–41.

Mock, Theodore J.; Barry E. Cushing; Gordon B. Davis; Miklos A. Vasarhelyi; Clinton E. White, Jr.; and Joseph W. Wilkinson. "Report of the AAA Committee on Contemporary Approaches to Teaching Accounting Information Systems." *Journal of Information Systems* (Spring 1987):127–156.

Platenic, Suzanne. "Building Tomorrow's Bottom Line." *Beyond Computing* (Premier Issue 1992):15–19.

Porter, M. E., and V. E. Millar. "How Information Gives You Competitive Advantage." *Harvard Business Review* (July/August 1985):149–160.

Roussey, Robert S. "The CPA in the Information Age: Today and Tomorrow." *Journal of Accountancy* (October 1986):94–107.

Sass, C. Joseph, and Teresa A. Keefe. "MIS for Strategic Planning and a Competitive Edge." *Journal of Systems Management* (June 1988):14–17.

Wilder, Clinton. "Value Judgement." *Computerworld* (March 2, 1992):69–70.

Whitmore, Sam. Editorial, "Futuristic MIT Project Could Yield Timely Gems." *PC Week* (March 2, 1992):68.

Zachary, G. Pascal. "Computer Data Overload Limits Productivity Gains." *Wall Street Journal* (November 11, 1991):B1.

Chapter 2

Boer, Germain. *Classifying and Coding for Accounting Operations*. Montvale, N.J.: National Association of Accountants, 1987.

Daly, James. "Insurer Sees Future in Imaging Strategy." *Computerworld* (January 6, 1992):41.

Diamond, Susan Z. *Records Management: A Practical Guide*. New York: American Manage-

ment Association, 1983.

Kabak, Irwin, and Thomas J. Beam. "Two-Dimensional Accounting: A New Management Demand." *Industrial Management* 32 (6)(November/December 1990):25–29.

Pelton, Charles. "IS Operations Make for a Healthy Cash Flow." *InformationWEEK* (December 11, 1989):33, 36.

Roderick, Richard M. "Redesigning an Accounting Department for Corporate and Personal Goals." *Management Accounting* (February 1984):56–60.

Chapter 3

Aktas, A. Ziya. *Structured Analysis and Design of Information Systems*. Englewood Cliffs, N.J.: Prentice-Hall, 1987.

American National Standard Institute. *Flowchart Symbols and Their Usage in Information Processing*. Publication No. ANSI X3.5. New York: American National Standards Institute, 1970.

Bohm, C., and G. Jacopini. "Flow Diagrams, Turing Machines and Languages with Only Two Formation Rules." *Communications of the ACM* 9 (5)(1966):366–371.

DeMarco, Tom. *Structured Analysis and System Specification*. Englewood Cliffs, N.J.: Prentice-Hall, 1979.

Egyhazy, Csaba J. "Technical Software Development Tools." *Journal of Systems Management* (January 1985):8–13.

Faye, David, and Theodore J. Mock. "How to Prepare Better Accounting Systems Flowcharts." *Practical Accountant* (November 1986):106–118.

Kievit, K., and M. Martin. "Systems Analysis Tools—Who's Using Them? *Journal of Systems Management* (July 1989):26–30.

Laudeman, Max. "Document Flowcharts for Internal Control." *Journal of Systems Management* (March 1980):22–30.

Li, David H. "Control Flowcharting: An Introduction." *Internal Auditor* (June 1983):26–29.

McMenamin, Stephen M., and John

F. Palmer. *Essential Systems Analysis,* Englewood Cliffs, N.J.: Yourdon Press, 1984.

Quinn, Juanita C. "Flow Chart Eases Planning Process for Hospitals." *Health Care Strategic Management* (April 1991):16–18.

Chapter 4

Alpert, Mark. "Building a Better Bar Code." *Fortune* (June 15, 1992):101.

Avery, Susan. "Bar Coding: How Did We Ever Get Along Without It?" *Purchasing* (April 5, 1990):82–85.

Cafasso, Rosemary. "Users Eyeball OS/2 Slimdown Plan." *Computerworld* (November 2, 1992):37–38.

Capron, H. L. *Computers: Tools for an Information Age.* 2nd ed. Menlo Park, Calif.: Benjamin/Cummings, 1990.

Currid, Cheryl. "Intel's Pentium Will Keep Competing Clone Makers on Their Toes." *InfoWorld* (November 2, 1992):58.

Dalette, Denise, and John Schneidawind. "Computers That 'Hear' Taking Jobs." *USA Today* (March 6–8, 1992):1A–2A.

Gantz, John. "Pen Computers Will Usher in the Next PC Revolution." *InfoWorld* (December 30, 1991/January 6, 1992):107.

Hof, Robert D. "Inside Intel: It's Moving at Double-Time to Head Off Competitors." *Business Week* (June 1, 1992):86–94.

Johnson, Maryfran. "Wherever You Go, They Will Follow." *Computerworld* (July 15, 1991):19.

Kaplan, Michael. "Tracking Technologies." *Beyond Computing* (August/September, 1992):50–55.

Keller, John J. "Computers Get Powerful 'Hearing' Aids: Improved Methods of Voice Recognition." *Wall Street Journal* (April 7, 1992):B1.

Kirchner, Jake. "GAO Tells a $970,000 Horror Story." *Computerworld* (December 3, 1979):12.

Lee, Yvonne. "Portables Expected to Eclipse Desktop PC Sales." *InfoWorld* (October 28, 1991):112.

Owen, Darrel E. "SMR Forum: Information Systems Organizations—Keeping Pace with the Pressures." *Sloan Management Review* (Spring 1986):59–68.

Paddock, Harold E. "Voice Input a Reality." *Internal Auditor* (December 1983):23–26.

Rockart, J. F., and M. S. Scott-Morton. "Implications of Changes in Information Technology for Corporate Strategy." *Interfaces* (January/February 1984):84–95.

Sadhwani, Arjan T., and Thomas Tyson. "Does Your Firm Need Bar Coding?" *Management Accounting* (April 1990):45–48.

Saffo, Paul. "Future Tense." *InfoWorld* (December 9, 1991):66.

"Soon, the 64-Bit Chip Will Jog Huge Memories." *Wall Street Journal* (March 23, 1992):B1.

"Teaching Computers to Tell a 'G' from a 'C.' *Business Week* (December 7, 1992):118.

Chapter 5

Booker, Ellis. "Pizza Hut: Making It Great with Imaging, EDI." *Computerworld* (January 27, 1992):67,72.

———. "Sears Selects Compuadd for $53M POS Project." *Computerworld* (January 13, 1992):7.

Bulkeley, William F. "Technology, Economics, and Ego Conspire to Make Software Difficult to Use." *Wall Street Journal* (May 20, 1991):R7–R8.

Cangemi, Michael P., and Robert D. Watson. "How Auditors Can Use Computers." *Practical Accountant* (March 1989):25–31.

Coale, Kristi, and Laurie Flynn. "The PC Has Its Whole Future Ahead of It." *InfoWorld* (August 12, 1991):46–50.

"Computers: The New Look." *Business Week* (November 30, 1987):112–123.

Coughlan, Francie. "Putting Pizzazz into Presentations." *PC Week* (July 20, 1992):93, 97.

"DTP Publishing Tools Add Power, Cut Costs." *PC Week* (September 21, 1992):123, 126.

Elliot, Lance B. "AI Crime Busters." *AI Expert* (January 1992):11.

Elliston, James. "Image Processing: Bright Picture for the Future." *Management Accounting* (August 1991):23–26.

Fitzgerald, Michael. "Laptops Make Sales Force Shine." *Computerworld* (August 12, 1991):35.

———. "Mission Impossible." *Computerworld* (July 20, 1992):87.

Francett, Barbara. "AI (Quietly) Goes Mainstream." *Computerworld* (July 29, 1991):59–66.

Kakhsaz, Ali R. "Getting the Picture on Document Image Management." *Journal of Accountancy* (December 1991):74–78.

Keefe, Patricia. "Penney Cashes in on Leading Edge." *Computerworld* (June 20, 1988):1, 62–64.

King, Julia. "Buck Bangers." *Computerworld* (December 23, 1991):16.

———. "Users Help Alaska Air Group Soar." *Computerworld* (December 23, 1991/January 2, 1992):16.

Kleinschrod, Walter A. "Taking Stock of Accounting Software." *Today's Office* (June 1990):8–13.

Lu, Cary. "Personal Computing." *INC.* (October 1991):OG6–OG20.

McSharry, Thomas P., Jr. "Tool of the Trade." *New Accountant* (November 1986):10–12.

Marshall, Patrick. "Personal Information Managers: Names and Notes at Your Fingertips." *InfoWorld* (June 3, 1991):65–77.

Miller, Robert. "Accounting Software Saves Dollars and Makes Sense." *Today's Office* (July 1991):19–22.

Millman, Howard. "PC-Based Accounting Software Sparks Interest in Downsizing." *Computerworld* (February 24, 1992):76.

Murphy, John A. "Personal Information Managers: Putting Your Thoughts on Disk." *Today's Office* (February 1991):30–33.

Nash, Kim S. "Signing On-Line Yields Productivity Benefits." *Computerworld* (November 18, 1991):29, 37.

Needle, Sheldon. "What's New in Accounting Software?" *Journal of Accountancy* (October 1991): 77–82.

"PC Buyer's Guide." *USA Today* (May 26, 1992):5B.

"Product Spotlight." *Computerworld* (February 24, 1992):77.

Richardson, Rick. "Computer Literacy vs. Tech Smarts." *New Accountant* (January 1992):16–17.

Rockart, John F., and Lauren S. Flannery. "The Management of End User Computing." *Communications of the ACM* (October 1983):776–784.

Romney, Marshall B., and James V. Hansen. *An Introduction to Mi-*

crocomputers and Their Controls. Altamonte Springs, Fla.: Institute of Internal Auditors, 1985.

Romney, Marshall B., and Kevin D. Stocks. "Microcomputer Controls." Internal Auditor (June 1985):18–22.

———. "How to Buy a Small Computer System." Journal of Accountancy (July 1985):46–60.

Sadler, Jeanne. "Small Businesses Tap into the Power of Computers." Wall Street Journal (July 1991):B1.

Schiff, Jonathan B. "Towards the Paperless Audit." Internal Auditor (June 1989):30–35.

Schlender, Brenton R. "The Future of the PC." Fortune (August 26, 1991):40–54.

Schneidawind, John, and Kathy Rebello. "IBM Sparked Revolution at Work, Home." USA Today (August 12, 1991):1B–2B.

Schwartz, Evan I. "Software Even a CFO Could Love." Business Week (November 2, 1992):132–137.

Schwartz, Evan I., and James B. Treece. "Smart Programs Go To Work." Business Week (March 2, 1992):97–105.

Seymour, Jim. "Left Unchecked, Spreadsheets Can Be a What-If Disaster." PC Week (August 21, 1984):37.

Tong, Hoo-Min D., and Amar Gupta. "The Personal Computer." Scientific American (September 1982):87–105.

Waller, Thomas C., and Rebecca A. Gallun. "Microcomputer Literacy Requirements in the Accounting Industry." Journal of Accounting Education 3 (Fall 1985):31–40.

Wilder, Clinton. "Users: Downsizing Gain Is Worth the Pain." Computerworld (October 14, 1991):4.

Wolfe, Christopher; Craig Bain; and Wally McPheters. "Microcomputer Productivity in the Internal Audit Function: A Case Study." Ohio CPA Journal (Spring 1989):12–16.

Chapter 6

Alper, Alan, and James Daly. "Penney Cashes in on Leading Edge." Computerworld (June 20, 1988):1, 62–66.

"At the Pump: A Special Report." Wall Street Journal (May 21, 1992):1.

Booker, Ellis. "Motorola to Provide Remote E-Mail." Computerworld (November 4, 1991):18.

———. "United Shift to Unix Heats Up." Computerworld (November 18, 1992):6.

Caldwell, Bo. "Gearing Up to Integrate Voice and Data." InfoWorld (January 13, 1992):S67–70.

Caron, Jeremiah. "Pocket Modems Useful Solution for Travelers." Computerworld (December 16, 1991):110.

Currid, Cheryl. "The Old Crystal Ball Could Start Giving Off Some New Signals." InfoWorld (December 30, 1991/January 6, 1992):42.

Dern, Daniel. "E-Mail Integration: Taking on New Roles." InfoWorld (February 24, 1992):41, 44.

Fitzgerald, Michael. "GUI Revs PCs at Big Six Firm." Computerworld (January 13, 1992):1, 101.

Flynn, Laurie. "Hotels Speed Reservations with PC Network Linking." InfoWorld (November 11, 1991):S72.

Glass, Brett. "2400-Baud Modems." PC World (September 1991):228, 229, 232, 233.

Horwitt, Elisabeth. "GE Telecom to Impose Order on Corporatewide LAN Chaos." Computerworld (January 13, 1992):1, 101.

Jenks, Andrew. "Groupware Fosters Shared Info, Ideas." USA Today (October 21, 1991):10E.

LaPolla, Stephanie. "St. Paul Insures Its LANs by Preparing Managers." PC Week (February 10, 1992):S/14.

Markoff, John. "A System to Speed Airline Travel." New York Times (September 6, 1989).

———. "Computer Conversation Is Changing Human Contact." New York Times (May 13, 1990).

"May I Take Your Order?" Computerworld (October 7, 1991):29.

Molta, Dave. "Save Time, Energy, and Money: Consolidate Your Servers." Network Computing (August 1991):85–86.

Nash, Jim. "Niagra Mohawk Looks to Tap the Power of Networking." Computerworld (February 25, 1991):52.

Pastore, Richard. "Insurer Puts LAN Skills on Sale." Computerworld (May 6, 1991):45.

Radding, Alan. "Small Wagers Can Pay Off, But Don't Bet the

Farm." Computerworld (November 20, 1989):85–91.

Romney, Marshall B., and James V. Hansen. An Introduction to Microcomputers and Their Controls. Altamonte Springs, Fla.: Institute of Internal Auditors, 1985.

Schatz, W. "EDI: Putting the Muscle in Commerce and Industry." Datamation (March 15, 1988):56–64.

Scott, Karyl. "NetWare on Downsizing Fast Track." InfoWorld (February 10, 1992):S61–S64.

Verity, John W.; Peter Coy; and Jeffrey Rothfeder. "Special Report: Taming the Wild Network." Business Week (October 8, 1990):142–148.

Wagoner, Kathleen P., and Mary M. Ruprecht. End-User Computing. Cincinnati: South-Western, 1993.

Wallace, Bob. "National Fuel Gas Migrates SCADA Net to LAN Platform." Network World (April 15, 1991):24.

Wilder, Clinton. "Users: Downsizing Gain Is Worth the Pain." Computerworld (October 13, 1991):4.

———. "Codex Goes Paperless with EDI." Computerworld (January 13, 1992):6.

Zarowin, Stanley. "A Guide to Updating Telecommunications." Journal of Accountancy (December 1991):68–70, 73.

Chapter 7

Ambrosio, Johanna. "UPS 'Dials' Up Fast Data on Deliveries." Computerworld (September 14, 1992):79.

Baker, Sharon. "University Scientists Crack High-Tech Welfare Data Shell." Computerworld (May 22, 1989):18.

Baum, David. "Au Bon Pain Gains Quick Access to Sales Data." InfoWorld (August 10, 1992):46.

Bozman, Jean S. "Coke Plans to Add Life with Relational Database Move." Computerworld (January 13, 1992):35.

Daly, James. "Stumped? Ask Your Mac." Computerworld (March 9, 1992):37.

Hamilton, Rosemary. "Chase Banks on 'Info' Access." Computerworld (January 27 1992):6.

Levick, Diane. "A New Weapon for Car Insurers: Database Allows Companies to Check Drivers' Records." New York Newsday

(February 20, 1990):49.

Nolan, Richard L. "Computer Databases: The Future Is Now." *Harvard Business Review* (September/October 1973):98–114.

Richman, Tom. "Mrs. Fields' Secret Ingredient." *Inc.* (October 1987):65–72.

Smith, James F., and Amer Mufti. "Using the Relational Database." *Management Accounting* (October 1985):43–54.

Chapter 8

Anthes, Gary H. "Planning Spells Results at MCI." *Computerworld* (January 27, 1992):31.

Booker, Ellis. "IS Trailblazing Puts Retailer on Top." *Computerworld* (February 12, 1990):69, 73.

Booker, Ellis, and Michael Fitzgerald. "Retailers Try EDI Hard Sell." *Computerworld* (July 9, 1990):1, 8.

Bozman, Jean S. "Red Cross Revamp Slowly Takes Shape." *Computerworld* (June 8, 1992):63.

Coy, Peter, and Chuck Hawkins. "The New Realism in Office Systems." *Business Week* (June 15, 1992):128–132.

Gibson, Cyrus F., and Richard L. Nolan. "Managing the Four Stages of EDP Growth." *Harvard Business Review* (January/February 1974):76–88.

Hamilton, Rosemary. "Met Life Finds Dividend in Automation System." *Computerworld* (January 6, 1992):41.

Janus, Susan. "Managers Face a Crisis in Systems Development." *PC Week* (January 2, 1989):1, 8.

Laplante, Alice. "For IS, Quality Is 'Job None.'" *Computerworld* (January 6, 1992):57–59.

Nash, Kim S. "Trucking Firm Seeks Faster Dispatching." *Computerworld* (January 2, 1991):33.

Nolan, Richard L. "Managing the Crises in Data Processing." *Harvard Business Review* (March/April 1979):115–126.

———. "Managing Information Systems by Committee." *Harvard Business Review* (July/August 1982):72–79.

Ryan, Alan J. "Banks Assess IS' Worth." *Computerworld* (October 7, 1991):113–116.

Smith, Geoffrey. "The Computer System That Nearly Hospitalized an Insurer." *Business Week* (June 15, 1992):133.

Wexler, Joanie M. "Bell Atlantic Revamping Infrastructure." *Computerworld* (May 18, 1992):15.

Wilde, Cande. "Staying Aligned: Five Tales." *Computerworld* (May 25, 1992):78.

Chapter 9

Anthony, Robert N. *Planning and Control Systems: A Framework for Analysis.* Boston: Graduate School of Business Administration, Harvard University, 1965.

Booker, Ellis. "IS Trailblazing Puts Retailer on Top." *Computerworld* (February 12, 1990):69, 73.

Davis, Gordon B., and Malcolm C. Monroe. "The Problem of Information Requirements for Computer Applications." *Accounting Horizons* (December 1987):105–109.

Dykman, Charlene A., and Ruth Robbins. "Organizational Success Through Effective Systems Analysis." *Journal of Systems Management* (July 1991):6–8.

Gabel, David. "A Yen for Just-in-Time Decisions Aids Sony's Drive for Coprocessing." *Computerworld* (April 10, 1989):SR/5.

Keen, Peter G. W., and Michael S. Scott Morton. *Decision Support Systems: An Organizational Perspective.* Reading, Mass.: Addison-Wesley, 1978.

Lem, Robert. "The Choice Is Yours." *Computerworld* (November 18, 1991):85–86.

Marenghi, Catherine. "Nashua Keeps Quality Flame Burning in Customer Service." *Computerworld* (January 6, 1992):61.

Munro, Malcolm C. "Identifying Critical Information for Strategic Management." *In Strategic Planning and Management Handbook,* edited by William R. King and David I. Cleland, pp. 406–421. New York: Van Nostrand Reinhold, 1987.

Naumann, J. David; G. B. Davis; and J. D. McKeen. "Determining Information Requirements: A Contingency Method for Selection of a Requirements Assurance Strategy." *Journal of Systems and Software* 1:227.

Rothfeder, Jeffrey. "Using the Law to Rein in Computer Runaways." *Business Week* (April 3, 1989):70–76.

Ryan, Alan J. "Banks Assess IS' Worth." *Computerworld* (October 7, 1991):113–116.

———. "D & B Scores Contracts." *Computerworld* (May 13, 1991): 29.

"U.S. Sprint Readies for Its Run into the 90's." *IBM Update* (March/April 1989):8.

Chapter 10

Anthes, Gary H. "Triumph over a Taxing Project." *Computerworld* (November 4, 1991):65–69.

Boar, Bernard. "Application Prototyping: A Life Cycle Perspective." *Journal of Systems Management* (February 1986):25–31.

Bronsema, Gloria S., and Peter G. W. Keen. "Education Intervention and Implementation in MIS." *Sloan Management Review* (Summer 1983):35–43.

Canning, Richard G. "Strategies for Introducing New Systems." *EDP Analyzer* (July 1985):1–12.

Chubb, Timothy D. "Why Computer Systems Conversions Are Tricky." *Management Accounting* (September 1983):36–41.

Cushing, Barry E. "Pricing Internal Computer Services: The Basic Issues." *Management Accounting* (April 1976):47–50.

Cutler, William. "Survey Finds Maintenance Problem Still Escalating." *Computerworld* (January 27, 1986):31, 34.

———. "Creating Foundation of Easy-Care Code." *Computerworld* (July 25, 1988):56–57.

Desanctis, Gerardine, and James F. Courtney. "Toward Friendly User MIS Implementation." *Communications of the ACM* (October 1983):732–738.

Gullo, Karen. "Stopping Runaways in Their Tracks." *Information Week* (November 13, 1989):63–70.

Gremillion, Lee L., and Philip Pyburn. "Breaking the Systems Development Bottleneck." *Harvard Business Review* (March/April 1983):130–137.

Kauber, Peter G. "Prototyping: Not a Method but a Philosophy." *Journal of Systems Management* (September 1985):28–33.

McFarlan, F. Warren. "Information Technology Changes the Way You Compete." *Harvard Business Review* (May/June

1984):98–103.

Milner, David. "Integrated Approach to Systems Development." *Data Processing* (April 1985):13–18.

Plasket, Richard L. "Project Management: New Technology Enhances Old Concepts." *Journal of Systems Management* (June 1986):6–10.

Rifkin, Glen, and Mitch Betts. "Strategic Systems Plan Gone Awry." *Computerworld* (March 14, 1988):1, 104–105.

Schneidawind, John. "Getting the Bugs Out." *USA Today* (August 29, 1991):1–2.

Schneider, Dan. "The Feasibility of Converting to an Open Systems Architecture." *Journal of Systems Management* (June 1991):28–30.

Sumner, Mary, and Jerry Sitek. "Are Structured Methods for Systems Analysis and Design Being Used?" *Journal of Systems Management* (June 1986):18–23.

Chapter 11

Banker, Rajiv D., and Robert J. Kaufmann. "Reuse and Productivity in Integrated Computer-Aided Software Engineering: An Empirical Study." *MIS Quarterly* (September 1991): 375–398.

Coy, Peter. "The New Realism in Office Systems." *Business Week* (June 15, 1992):128–133.

Halper, Mark. "Weather Drives Burpee to Outsourcing." *Computerworld* (October 12, 1992):77, 80.

Hammer, Michael. "Reengineering Work: Don't Automate, Obliterate." *Harvard Business Review* (July/August 1990):104–112.

———. "Making the Quantum Leap." *Beyond Computing* (March/April 1992):10–14.

Henkoff, Ronald. "Make Your Office More Productive." *Fortune* (February 25, 1991): 72–84.

Janson, Jennifer L. "Firms Tighten Belts by Outsourcing Operations." *PC Week* (February 10, 1992):S/15.

King, Julia. "Rip It Up!" *Computerworld* (July 15, 1991):55–56.

Kirkpatrick, David. "Why Not Farm Out Your Computing?" *Fortune* (September 23, 1991):103–112.

Kleinschrod, Walter A. "Outsourcing: Weighing the Issues."

Beyond Computing (October/November 1992):44–50.

Margolis, Nell. "Outsourcing Could be $21B Niche by 1996." *Computerworld* (September 30, 1991):72.

Port, Otis, et al. "The Software Trap: Automate—Or Else." *Business Week* (May 9, 1988):142–154.

Platenic, Suzanne. "Should I or Shouldn't I?" *Beyond Computing* (Premiere Issue 1992):25–30.

Wilder, Clinton. "Giant Firms Join Outsourcing Parade." *Computerworld* (September 30, 1991):1, 91.

———. "Banking Giant Buys into Outsourcing." *Computerworld* (November 11, 1991):1, 108.

———. "Measuring the Payoff from Re-Engineering." *Computerworld* (November 18, 1991):65.

———. "80% Satisfied with Outsourcing, Survey Says." *Computerworld* (January 27, 1992):77.

Chapter 12

American Institute of Certified Public Accountants. *Statement on Auditing Standards No. 1–69.* New York: AICPA, 1992.

Arthur Andersen and Company. *A Guide for Studying and Evaluating Internal Accounting Controls.* Chicago: Arthur Andersen, 1978.

Carmichael, Douglas R. "The Auditor's New Guide to Errors, Irregularities and Illegal Acts." *Journal of Accountancy* (September 1988):40–48.

Committee of Sponsoring Organizations of the Treadway Commission. *Internal Control—Integrated Framework.* New York: Committee of Sponsoring Organizations of the Treadway Commission, 1992.

Coughlan, John W. "The Fairfax Embezzlement." *Management Accounting* (May 1983):32–39.

Cushing, Barry E. "A Mathematical Approach to the Analysis and Design of Internal Control Systems." *Accounting Review* (January 1974):24–41.

Davia, H. R.; P. C. Coggins; J. C. Wideman; and J. T. Kastantin. *Management Accountant's Guide to Fraud Discovery and Control.* New York: Wiley, 1992.

Dumaine, Brian. "Beating Bolder

Corporate Crooks." *Fortune* (April 25, 1988):193–202.

Eichen, Susan P., and Mary Ann Domurachi. "Designing Internal Control Systems for Appropriate Management Control." *Corporate Accounting* (Fall 1986):20–28.

Ellentuck, Elmer I. "How to Minimize Employee Fraud: A Checklist." *Practical Accountant* (March/April 1972):30–37.

Elliott, Robert K., and John J. Willingham. *Management Fraud: Detection and Deterrence.* New York: Petrocelli Books, 1980.

Foreign Corrupt Practices Act of 1977. U.S. Code, 1976 edition, Supplement II, Title 15, Selection 78. Washington, D.C.: U.S. Government Printing Office, 1979.

Goldstein, Leslie M. "Favorite Frauds." *Internal Auditor* (August 1992):35–39.

Gurry, E. J. "Locating Potential Irregularities." *Journal of Accountancy* (September 1975):111–114.

Hogg, Joseph D. "How Much Does an Error Cost—And How Much Does It Cost to Prevent It?" *Internal Auditor* (August 1992):67–69.

Levy, Marvin M. "Financial Fraud: Schemes and Indicia." *Journal of Accountancy* (August 1985):78–87.

Mack, Kenneth. "Computer Fraud and Fidelity Bonding." *CPA Journal* (October 1982):18–23.

Mautz, Robert K.; Walter G. Kell; Michael W. Maher; Alan G. Merten; Raymond R. Reilly; Dennis G. Severance; and Bernard J. White. *Internal Control in U.S. Corporations: The State of the Art.* New York: Financial Executives Research Foundation, 1980.

Mautz, R. K., and James Winjum. *Criteria for Management Control Systems.* New York: Financial Executives Research Foundation, 1981.

Monk, Harold L., Jr. and Kay W. Tatum. "Applying SAS No. 55 in Audits of Small Business." *Journal of Accountancy* (November 1988):40–56.

Price Waterhouse & Company. *Guide to Accounting Controls: Establishing, Evaluating and Monitoring Control Systems.* New York: Price Waterhouse & Company, 1979.

Chapter 13

American Institute of Certified Public Accountants. *Audit and Control Considerations in an On-line Environment.* New York: AICPA, 1983.

———. *Statements on Auditing Standards No. 1–69.* New York: AICPA, 1992.

Baker, Richard H. *Computer Security Handbook.* 2nd ed. Blue Ridge Summit, Pa.: TAB Books, 1991.

Buss, Martin D. J., and Lynn M. Salerno. "Common Sense and Computer Security." *Harvard Business Review* (March/April 1984):112–121.

Canning, Richard G. "Information Security and Privacy." *EDP Analyzer* (February 1986):1–11.

Cerullo, Michael J., and Virginia Cerullo. "Microcomputer Controls." *National Public Accountant* (May 1991):28–33.

Crossman, Trevor D. "Taking the Measure of Programmer Productivity." *Datamation* (May 1979): 144–147.

Cushing, Barry E. "Pricing Internal Computer Services: The Basic Issues." *Management Accounting* (April 1976):47–50.

Dascher, Paul E., and W. Ken Harmon. "Assessing Microcomputer Risks and Controls for Clients." *CPA Journal* (May 1984):36–41.

Doedjak, Tina. "Controlling and Auditing Microcomputer Data Security." *EDPACS* (April 1992): 4–9.

Drury, D., and J. Bates. *Data Processing Chargeback Systems: Theory and Practice.* Hamilton, Ontario: Society of Management Accountants of Canada, 1979.

Forgione, Dana, and Alan Blankley. "Microcomputer Security and Control." *Journal of Accountancy* (June 1990):83–90.

Gaston, S. J. *Controlling and Auditing Small Computer Systems.* Toronto: Canadian Institute of Chartered Accountants, 1986.

Goldstein, Andy. "Operating Systems Offer Security Features to Control Computer Access." *Computer Technology Review* (Winter 1993):191–199.

Gove, Ronald A. "EDI Security." *EDPACS* (December 1990):1–8.

Guldentops, Eric. "Security and Control in Electronic Funds Transfer: The SWIFT Case."

EDPACS (April 1991):1–11.

Hanson, James V., and Ned C. Hill. "Control and Audit of Electronic Data Interchange." *MIS Quarterly* (December 1989):403–413.

Hoffman, Michael J. "DP Cost Allocation: A Management Perspective." *Journal of Systems Management* (January 1984):16–19.

Institute of Internal Auditors Research Foundation. *Systems Auditability and Control Report.* Altamonte Springs, Fla.: Institute of Internal Auditors Research Foundation, 1991.

Kelley, Neil D. "The Economics of Uninterruptible Power." *Infosystems* (September 1980):55–64.

Kleinberg, Eugene R. "Strategies for Effective Microcomputer Management." *Journal of Information Systems Management* (Winter 1986):27–35.

Luke, Larry R. "Password Security Systems." *EDPACS* (October 1984):1–6.

Mautz, Robert K.; Alan G. Merten; and Dennis G. Severance. *Senior Management Control of Computer-Based Information Systems.* Morristown, N.J.: Financial Executives Research Foundation, 1983.

Murphy, Michael A., and Xenia Ley Parker. *Handbook of EDP Auditing.* 2nd ed. Boston: Warren, Gorham & Lamont, 1989.

Norris, Daniel M., and Elaine Waples. "Control of Electronic Data Interchange Systems." *Journal of Systems Management* (March 1989):21–25.

Parker, Robert. "Access Control Software: What It Will and Will Not Do." *EDPACS* (February 1991):1–8.

Paroby, Stephen M.; John G. Baab; and Lewis Kramer. "Controlling Your Computer." *Corporate Accounting* (Spring 1987):34–41.

Phillips, Mark. "Planning Speeds Bank's Recovery from Fire." *Disaster Recovery Journal* (January/February/March 1992):56–58.

Rogers, Michael. "A Data Survival Guide." *Disaster Recovery Journal* (April/May/June 1992):14–16.

St. Clair, Linda. "Security for Small Computer Systems." *EDPACS* (November 1983):1–10.

Vahtera, Pauli. "Electronic Data Interchange: The Auditor's Slant." *EDPACS* (November 1991):1–14.

Wright, Benjamin. "Controlling EDI." *Management Accounting* (August 1991):46–49.

Zmud, Robert W. "Design Alternatives for Organizing Information Systems Activities." *MIS Quarterly* (June 1984):79–93.

Chapter 14

Albrecht, W. Steve; Marshall B. Romney; *et al. How to Detect and Prevent Business Fraud.* Englewood Cliffs, N.J.: Prentice-Hall, 1982.

Albrecht, W. Steve; Marshall B. Romney; and Keith Howe. *Deterring Fraud: The Internal Auditor's Perspective.* Altamonte Springs, Fla. Institute of Internal Auditors, 1984.

Alexander, Michael. "Prison Term for First U.S. Hacker-Law Convict." *Computerworld* (February 20, 1989):1, 12.

———. "Hacker Stereotypes Changing." *Computerworld* (April 3, 1989):101.

———. "Strong Scruples Can Curb Computer Crime." *Computerworld* (April 3, 1989):100.

———. "Biometric System Use Widening." *Computerworld* (January 8, 1990):16.

———. "Computer Crime: Ugly Secret for Business." *Computerworld* (March 12, 1990):1, 104.

Allen, Brandt. "Embezzler's Guide to the Computer." *Harvard Business Review* (July/August 1975):79–89.

———. "The Biggest Computer Frauds: Lessons for CPAs." *Journal of Accountancy* (May 1977):52–62.

Atkins, William. "Jesse James at the Terminal." *Harvard Business Review* (July/August 1985):82–87.

Bloombecker, Buck. "Computer Ethics for Cynics." *Computerworld* (February 29, 1988):17–18.

———. *Spectacular Computer Crimes.* Homewood, Ill.: Dow-Jones–Irwin, 1990.

Bologna, Jack. "Internal Security: Issues and Answers." *Office Administration and Automation* (July 1985):33–37.

Booker, Ellis. "Retinal Scanners Eye-Dentify Inmates." *Computerworld* (March 23, 1992):28.

Bozman, Jean S. "Bell Tolls for the Shadow Hawk." *Computerworld*

(August 15, 1988):104.

———. "Airline Hurt by Faulty Fare Estimation." *Computerworld* (September 19, 1988): 2.

Burrough, Bryan. "The Embezzler David L. Miller Stole from His Employers and Isn't in Prison." *Wall Street Journal* (September 19, 1986):1.

Churbuck, David. "Desktop Forgery." *Forbes* (November 27, 1989):246–254.

Cole, Patrick. "Are ATMs Easy Targets for Crooks?" *Business Week* (March 6, 1989):30.

Davis, Fred. "Could the Repo Man Grab Your Invaluable Software?" *PC Week* (November 12, 1990):266.

Elmer-DeWitt, Philip. "Surveying the Data Diddlers." *Time* (February 17, 1986):95.

Enyart, Bob. "Software Security System Thwarts Attack on Data." *PC Week* (April 10, 1989):37–38.

Finch, Peter. "Confessions of a Compulsive High-Roller." *Business Week* (July 29, 1991):78–79.

Gerber, Barry. "Sometimes 'Abort, Retry' Means 'Network Virus.'" *PC Week* (April 2,1990):57.

Goldberg, Jeff. "Computerized Breaking and Entering." *OMNI* (September 1990):18.

Hafner, K. M. "Is Your Computer Secure?" *Business Week* (August 1, 1988):65–72.

Hafner, Katie, and John Markoff. *Cyberpunk.* New York: Simon and Schuster, 1991.

Hoffer, Jeffrey A., and Detmar A. Straub, Jr. "The 9 to 5 Underground: Are You Policing Computer Crimes?" *Sloan Management Review* (Summer 1989):35–43.

Honon, Patrick. "Avoiding Virus Hysteria." *Personal Computing* (May 1989):85.

Information Protection Review **2** (1) Deloitte & Touche, 1–6.

Keefe, Patricia. "Doing Away with Hard Disks." *Computerworld* (March 12, 1990):39.

McAfee, John. "The Virus Cure." *Datamation* (February 15, 1989):30–31.

Mason, Janet. "Crackdown on Software Pirates." *Computerworld* (February 5, 1990):107–115.

Menkus, Belden. "Eight Factors Contributing to Computer Fraud." *Internal Auditor* (Octo-

ber 1990):71–74.

Nabut, Martin. "Inside Crimes Threaten Corporate Well-Being." *Computerworld* (June 3, 1987):25–26.

Romney, Marshall B.; David Cherrington; and W. Steve Albrecht. "Red-Flagging the White-Collar Criminal." *Management Accounting* (March 1980):51–57.

———. "Auditors and the Detection of Fraud." *Journal of Accountancy* (May 1980):63–69.

———. "The Role of Management in Reducing Fraud." *Financial Executive* (March 1981):28–34.

Russell, Harold F. *Foozles and Frauds.* Altamonte Springs, Fla.: Institute of Internal Auditors, 1977.

Savage, J. A. "Computer Time Bomb Defused: Felon Nailed." *Computerworld* (September 26, 1988):2.

Savage, J. W. "System Bugs Breed $635 Tax Oversight." *Computerworld* (April 4, 1988): 1, 4.

"University of Oregon Settles Suit Brought by Software Publishers." *Wall Street Journal* (August 23, 1991):B2.

Wells, J. T. "Six Common Myths About Fraud." *Journal of Accountancy* (February 1990):82–88.

Whiteside, Thomas. *Computer Capers,* New York: Crowell, 1978.

Chapter 15

Adams, Donald L. "Alternatives to Computer Audit Software." *Journal of Accountancy* (November 1975):54–57.

American Institute of Certified Public Accountants. *Computer-Assisted Audit Techniques.* New York: AICPA, 1979.

———. *Audit and Control Considerations in an On-Line Environment.* New York: AICPA, 1983.

———. *Statements on Auditing Standards No. 1–69.* New York: AICPA, 1992.

Arens, Alvin, A., and James K. Loebbecke. *Auditing: An Integrated Approach.* 5th ed. Englewood Cliffs, N.J.: Prentice-Hall, 1991.

Borthick, A. Faye. "Audit Implications of Information Systems." *CPA Journal* (April 1986):40–46.

Brown, Carol E., and David S. Murphy. "The Use of Auditing Expert Systems in Public Ac-

counting." *Journal of Information Systems* (Fall 1990):63–72.

Cerullo, Michael J., and John C. Corless. "Auditing Computer Systems." *CPA Journal* (September 1984):18–33.

Committee on Basic Auditing Concepts. *A Statement of Basic Auditing Concepts.* Sarasota, Fla.: American Accounting Association, 1973.

Cunninghame, Don. "Using the Application Charge Control Audit as a Management Control." *EDPACS* (September 1992):1–7.

Doediak, Tina. "Controlling and Auditing Microcomputer Data Security." *EDPACS* (April 1992):4–9.

Gaston, S. J. *Controlling and Auditing Small Computer Systems.* Toronto: Canadian Institute of Chartered Accountants, 1986.

Gliezner, Shmuel. "The Dummy Entity, a Valuable Audit Tool." *EDPACS* (June 1985):1–20.

Hanson, James V., and Ned C. Hill. "Control and Audit of Electronic Data Interchange." *MIS Quarterly* (December 1989):403–413.

Institute of Internal Auditors. *Standards for the Professional Practice of Internal Auditing.* Altamonte Springs, Fla.: Institute of Internal Auditors, 1978.

Institute of Internal Auditors Research Foundation. *Systems Auditability and Control Report.* Altamonte Springs, Fla.: Institute of Internal Auditors Research Foundation, 1991.

Khandeker, Jayawant G., and Maria L. Langer. "Personal Computers: An Audit Perspective." *Internal Auditor* (October 1990):55–61.

Lamond, Bruce J. "An Auditing Approach to Disaster Recovery." *Internal Auditor* (October 1990):33–48.

Leinicke, Linda Marie; W. Max Rexroad; and Jon D. Ward. "Computer Fraud Auditing: It Works." *Internal Auditor* (August 1990):26–33.

Loebbecke, James K.; John F. Mullarkey; and George R. Zuber. "Auditing in a Computer Environment." *Journal of Accountancy* (January 1983):68–78.

Lovata, Linda M. "The Utilization of Generalized Audit Software." *Auditing: A Journal of Practice*

& Theory (Fall 1988):72–86.

Murphy, Michael A., and Xenia Ley Parker. *Handbook of EDP Auditing.* 2nd ed. Boston: Warren, Gorham & Lamont, 1989.

Perry, William E. "Planning for Audit Software Use." *Journal of Accounting and EDP* (Winter 1986):234–240.

Perry, William E. "Planning for Audit Software Use." *Journal of Accounting and EDP* (Winter 1986):234–240.

Robertson, Jack C. *Auditing.* 7th ed. Homewood, Ill.: BPI Irwin, 1993.

Skudrna, Vincent J., and Frank J. Lackner. "The Implementation of Concurrent Audit Techniques in Advanced EDP Systems." *EDPACS* (April 1984):1–9.

Sriram, Ram S., and Glenn E. Sumners. "Understanding Concurrent Audit Techniques." *EDPACS* (July 1992):1–8.

Temkin, Robert H. "Automating Auditing: Auditing Will Never Be the Same." *Corporate Accounting* (Fall 1986):56–59.

Vahtera, Pauli. "Electronic Data Interchange: The Auditor's Slant." *EDPACS* (November 1991):1–14.

Vasarhelyi, Miklos A. "Audit Automation: Online Technology and Auditing." *CPA Journal* (April 1985):10–17.

Vasarhelyi, Miklos A., and Fern B. Halper. "The Continuous Audit of Online Systems." *Auditing: A Journal of Practice & Theory* (Spring 1991):110–125.

Weber, Ron. "An Audit Perspective of Operating System Security." *Journal of Accountancy* (September 1975):97–100.

———. *EDP Auditing: Conceptual Foundations and Practice.* 2nd ed. New York: McGraw-Hill, 1988.

Yarberry, William A. "Auditing the Change Control System." *EDPACS* (June 1984):1–5.

Chapter 16

Bentz, William F., and Robert F. Lusch. "Now You Can Control Your Product's Market Performance." *Management Accounting* (January 1980):17–25.

Byers, C. R., and L. J. Morris. "Enhancing Sales Force Productivity with a Relational DBMS." *Journal of Systems Management* (January 1991):13–17.

Cash, James I., Jr., and Benn R. Konsynski. "IS Redraws Competitive Boundaries." *Harvard Business Review* (March/April 1985):134–142.

Cathey, Jack M. "Electronic Data Interchange: What a Controller Should Know." *Management Accounting* (November 1991):47–51.

Devlin, B. A., and P. T. Murphy. "An Architecture for a Business and Information System." *IBM Systems Journal* **27** (1) (1988):60–80.

Garrett, Gary C., and William M. Barnes. "Evaluating Automated Order Processing Systems." *Journal of Accounting and EDP* (Spring 1985):41–46.

Gensch, Dennis H.; Nicola Aversa; and Steven P. Moore. "A Choice-Modeling Market Information System That Enabled ABB Electric to Expand Its Market Share." *Interfaces* (January/February 1990):6–25.

Glisson, L. Milton; William D. Cooper; and Gwendolyn Highsmith-Quick. "The Ins and Outs of Shipping Documents." *CPA Journal* (November 1991):66–69.

Goslar, Martin D. "Capability Criteria for Marketing Decision Support Systems." *Journal of Management Information Systems* (Summer 1986):81–95.

Henderson, Frederick A. "EBDI: A Radical Approach to Paper Work." *Corporate Accounting* (Winter 1988):40–45.

Higby, Mary A., and Badie N. Farah. "The Status of Marketing Information Systems, Decision Support Systems and Expert Systems in the Marketing Function of U.S. Firms." *Information & Management* (January 1991):29–35.

Hughes, G. David. "Computerized Sales Management." *Harvard Business Review* (March/April 1983):102–112.

Huguet, James, and Anne Berlack. "Bring Your Salespeople On-Line." *Sales & Marketing Management* (August 1991):44–48.

Institute of Internal Auditors Research Foundation. *Systems Auditability and Control Report. Module 6: Business Systems.* Altamonte Springs, Fla.: Institute of Internal Auditors Research Foundation, 1991.

Jackson, Barbara B., and Benson P.

Shapiro. "New Way to Make Product Line Decisions." *Harvard Business Review* (May/June 1979):139–149.

McLeod, Raymond, Jr., and John C. Rogers. "Marketing Information Systems: Their Current Status in *Fortune* 1000 Companies." *Journal of Management Information Systems* (Spring 1985):57–75.

Schatz, Willie. "EDI: Putting the Muscle in Commerce & Industry." *Datamation* (March 15, 1988):56–64.

Steinberg, Margery, and Richard E. Plank. "Expert Systems: The Integrative Sales Management Tool of the Future." *Journal of the Academy of Marketing Science* (Summer 1987):55–62.

Strassmann, Paul. "Productivity and Strategic Advantage Through Information Systems." *Fortune* (December 5, 1988):198–212.

Sviokla, John J. "An Examination of the Impact of Expert Systems on the Firm: The Case of XCON." *MIS Quarterly* (June 1990):127–140.

Walsh, Myles, and Frank O'Neill. "Downloading: Data Center Mainframe to PCs in the Real World." *Journal of Systems Management* (August 1986):24–29.

Chapter 17

Avery, Susan. "Bar Coding: How Did We Ever Get Along Without It?" *Purchasing* (April 5, 1990):82–89.

Bernard, Paul. "Managing Vendor Performance." *Production and Inventory Management Journal* (First Quarter 1989):1–8.

Biggs, Joseph R., and Ellen J. Long. "Gaining the Competitive Edge with MRP/MRP II." *Management Accounting* (May 1988):27–32.

Carter, Joseph R. "Implementing Supplier Bar Codes." *Production and Inventory Management Journal* (Fourth Quarter 1991):42–47.

Carter, Joseph R., and Lawrence D. Fredendall. "The Dollars and Sense of Electronic Data Interchange." *Production and Inventory Management Journal* (Second Quarter 1990):22–26.

Closs, David J. "Designing Computerized Inventory Management Systems." *Journal of Accounting* and EDP (Summer 1985):22–29.

Deis, Paul. "Using an MRP System for Financial Decision Support." Journal of Accounting and EDP (Winter 1986):38–48.

Dillard, Jesse F.; Kamesh Ramakrishna; and B. Chandrasekaran. "Knowledge-Based Decision Support Systems for Military Procurement." In Barry G. Silverman, ed., Expert Systems for Business. Reading, Mass.: Addison-Wesley, 1987, pp. 120–139.

Evans-Correia, Kate. "Caterpillar Digs into EDI Purchasing." Purchasing (August 15, 1991):91–95.

Forbes, Robert S.; Douglas F. Jones; and Steven T. Marty. "Managerial Accounting and Vendor Relations for JIT: A Case Study." Production and Inventory Management Journal (First Quarter 1989):76–81.

Freeland, James R. "A Survey of Just-in-Time Purchasing Practices in the United States." Production and Inventory Management Journal (Second Quarter 1991):43–50.

Gessford, John Evans. Modern Information Systems Designed for Decision Support. Reading, Mass.: Addison-Wesley, 1980.

Globecon Group, Ltd. Electronic Data Interchange and Corporate Trade Payments. Morristown, N.J.: Financial Executive Research Foundation, 1988.

Giunipero, Larry C. "Motivating and Monitoring JIT Supplier Performance." Journal of Purchasing and Materials Management (Summer 1990):19–24.

Hammer, Michael. "Reengineering Work: Don't Automate, Obliterate." Harvard Business Review (July/August 1990):104–112.

Hillier, Frederick S., and Gerald J. Lieberman. Introduction to Operations Research. 5th ed. New York: McGraw-Hill, 1990.

Inman, R. Anthony. "Quality Certification of Suppliers by JIT Manufacturing Firms." Production and Inventory Management Journal (Second Quarter 1990):58–61.

Institute of Internal Auditors Research Foundation. Systems Auditability and Control Report. Module 6: Business Systems. Altamonte Springs, Fla.: Institute of Internal Auditors Research Foundation, 1991.

Kim, Il-Woon, and Arjan T. Sadhwani. "Is Your Inventory Really All There?" Management Accounting (July 1991):37–40.

Krajewski, Lee J.: Barry E. King; Larry P. Ritzman; and Danny S. Wong. "Kanban, MRP, and Shaping the Manufacturing Environment." Management Science (January 1987):39–57.

Mecimore, Charles D., and James K. Weeks. Techniques in Inventory Management and Control. Montvale, N.J.: National Association of Accountants, 1987.

Miller, Jeffrey G., and Linda G. Sprague. "Behind the Growth in Materials Requirement Planning." Harvard Business Review (September/October 1975):83–91.

Nakano, Jinichiro, and Robert W. Hall. "Management Specs for Stockless Production." Harvard Business Review (May/June 1983):84–91.

Patton, Joseph D., Jr., and Herbert C. Feldman. "Designing a Cost-Effective Service Parts Inventory Management System." Journal of Accounting and EDP (Spring 1986):45–50.

Porter, Anne Millen. "Supplier Evaluation Revisited." Purchasing (October 24, 1991):58–68.

Raia, Ernest. "JIT Delivery: Redefining 'On-Time.'" Purchasing (September 13, 1990):64–76.

Ramasesh, Ranga V. "Recasting the Traditional Inventory Model to Implement Just-in-Time Purchasing." Production and Inventory Management Journal (First Quarter 1990):71–75.

Robinson, Michael A., and John E. Timmerman. "How Vendor Analysis Supports JIT Manufacturing." Management Accounting (December 1987):20–24.

Sadhwani, Arjan T., and M. H. Sarhan. "Electronic Systems Enhance JIT Operations." Management Accounting (December 1987):25–30.

Sadhwani, Arjan T.; M. H. Sarhan; and Dayal Kiringoda. "Just-in-Time: An Inventory System Whose Time Has Come." Management Accounting (December 1985):36–44.

Sadhwani, Arjan T., and Thomas Tyson. "Does Your Firm Need Bar Coding?" Management Accounting (April 1990):45–48.

———. Financial Managers' Guide to Selecting and Implementing Bar Codes. Montvale, N.J.: National Association of Accountants, 1990.

Sauers, Dale G. "Analyzing Inventory Systems." Management Accounting (May 1986):30–36.

Schatz, Willie. "EDI: Putting the Muscle in Commerce and Industry." Datamation (March 15, 1988):56–64.

Stundza, Tom. "Can Supplier Ratings be Standardized?" Purchasing (November 8, 1990):60–64.

Vollmann, Thomas E.; William L. Berry; and D. Clay Whybark. Manufacturing Planning and Control Systems. 3rd ed. Homewood, Ill.: Irwin, 1992.

Waples, Elaine, and Daniel M. Norris. "Just-in-Time Production and the Financial Audit." Production and Inventory Management Journal (Fourth Quarter 1989):25–27.

Zimmerman, Susan. "Sold on EDI." Purchasing (May 17, 1990):86–87.

Chapter 18

Attaran, Mohsen. "The Automated Factory: Justification and Implementation." Business Horizons (May/June 1989):80–86.

Baker, Gordon L.; William A. Clark, Jr.; Jonathan J. Frund; and Richard E. Wendell. "Production Planning and Cost Analysis on a Microcomputer." Interfaces (July/August 1987):53–60.

Beischel, Mark E., and K. Richard Smith. "Linking the Shop Floor to the Top Floor." Management Accounting (October 1991):25–29.

Bennett, Earl D., and Sarah A. Reed. CIM Implementation Process: A Case Study. Montvale, N.J.: National Association of Accountants, 1991.

Biggs, Joseph R., and Ellen J. Long. "Gaining the Competitive Edge with MRP/MRP II." Management Accounting (May 1988):27–32.

Cooper, Robin, and Robert S. Kaplan. "How Cost Accounting Systematically Distorts Product Costs." In William J. Bruns, Jr., and Robert S. Kaplan, eds., Accounting and Management: Field Study Perspectives. Boston: Harvard Business School Press, 1987, pp. 204–228.

Dangerfield, Byron J., and John S. Morris. "Flexibility of Relational Data Bases in Manufacturing Applications." *Production and Inventory Management Journal* (Second Quarter 1990):69–73.

Doll, William J., and Mark A. Vonderembse. "Forging a Partnership to Achieve Competitive Advantage: The CIM Challenge." *MIS Quarterly* (June 1987):205–220.

Ettlie, John E., and Stacy A. Reifeis. "Integrating Design and Manufacturing to Deploy Advanced Manufacturing Technology." *Interfaces* (November/December 1987):63–74.

Foster, George, and Charles T. Horngren. "JIT: Cost Accounting and Cost Management Issues." *Management Accounting* (June 1987):19–25.

Green, F. B.; Felix Amenkhienan; and George Johnson. "Performance Measures and JIT." *Management Accounting* (February 1991):50–53.

Harris, Ellen. "The Impact of JIT Production on Product Costing Information Systems." *Production and Inventory Management Journal* (First Quarter 1990):44–48.

Hohner, Gregory J. "Manufacturing Cell Design of Factory Floor Local Area Networks: Focus on Connectivity." *Production and Inventory Management Journal* (Third Quarter 1989):18–24.

Horngren, Charles T., and George Foster. *Cost Accounting: A Managerial Emphasis.* 7th ed. Englewood Cliffs, N.J.: Prentice-Hall, 1991.

Howell, Robert A.; James D. Brown; Stephen R. Soucy; and Allen H. Seed. *Management Accounting in the New Manufacturing Environment.* Montvale, N.J.: National Association of Accountants, 1987.

Inman, R. Anthony. "Flexible Manufacturing Systems: Issues and Implementation." *Industrial Management* (July/August 1991):7–11.

Institute of Internal Auditors Research Foundation. *Systems Auditability and Control Reports. Module 6: Business Systems.* Altamonte Springs, Fla.: Institute of Internal Auditors Research Foundation, 1991, Chapter 6.

Kathawala, Yunus. "Expert Systems: Implications for Operations Management." *Industrial Management & Data Systems* **90** (6)(1990):12–16.

Keegan, Daniel P.; Robert G. Eiler; and Joseph V. Anania. "An Advanced Cost Management System for the Factory of the Future." *Management Accounting* (December 1988):31–37.

McKinnon, Sharon M., and William J. Bruns, Jr. "What Production Managers Really Want to Know." *Management Accounting* (January 1993):29–35.

McNair C. J.; William Mosconi; and Thomas Norris. *Meeting the Technology Challenge: Cost Accounting in a JIT Environment.* Montvale, N.J.: National Association of Accountants, 1988.

Morse, Wayne J.; Harold P. Roth; and Kay M. Poston. *Measuring, Planning, and Controlling Quality Costs.* Montvale, N.J.: National Association of Accountants, 1987.

Myers, M. Scott. "Let JIT Mend Your Split Culture." *Industrial Management* (March/April 1988):11–18.

Needle, Sheldon. "Microcomputer-Based Manufacturing Software." *Journal of Accountancy* (June 1990):75–80.

Novin, Adel M. "Applying Overhead: How to Find the Right Bases and Rates." *Management Accounting* (March 1992):40–43.

Ochs, Robert, and John Bicheno. "Activity-Based Cost Management Linked to Manufacturing Strategy." *Industrial Management* (January/February 1991):11–16.

Ormsby, Joseph G.; Susan Y. Ormsby; and Carl R. Ruthstrom. "MRP-II Implementation: A Case Study." *Production and Inventory Management Journal* (Fourth Quarter 1990):77–81.

O'Rourke, J. Tracy. "The Common Sense of CIM." *Industrial Management & Data Systems* **90** (7)(1990):3–8.

Parekh, Rajen. "Capacity/Inventory Planning Using a Spreadsheet." *Production and Inventory Management Journal* (First Quarter 1990):1–3.

Patell, James M. "Adapting a Cost Accounting System to Just-in-Time Manufacturing: The Hewlett-Packard Personal Office Computer Division." In William J. Bruns, Jr., and Robert S. Kaplan, eds., *Accounting and Management: Field Study Perspectives.* Boston: Harvard Business School Press, 1987, pp. 229–267.

Ross, David F. "The Role of Information in Implementing MRP-II Systems." *Production and Inventory Management Journal* (Third Quarter 1989):49–52.

Sadhwani, Arjan T., and Thomas Tyson. *Financial Managers' Guide to Selecting and Implementing Bar Codes.* Montvale, N.J.: National Association of Accountants, 1990.

Schatz, Willie. "Making CIM Work." *Datamation* (December 1, 1988):18–21.

Sena, James A., and Lawrence Murphy Smith. "Designing and Implementing an Integrated Job Cost Accounting System." *Journal of Information Systems* (Fall 1986):102–112.

Stec, Stanley F. "Manufacturing Control Through Bar Coding at Target Products." *Management Accounting* (April 1988):47.

Stephens, Charlotte S.; William N. Ledbetter; and James L. Eddy. "The Best of Both Worlds: A Mainframe- and Microcomputer-Based MRP-II System." *Production and Inventory Management Journal* (Third Quarter 1990):35–40.

Tyson, Thomas, and Arjan T. Sadhwani. "Bar Codes Speed Factory Floor Reporting." *Management Accounting* (April 1988):41–46.

Vickery, Adrian R. "Design of a Manufacturing Data Base for Management Use." *Computers & Industrial Engineering* **7** (1983):225–240.

Vollmann, Thomas E.; William L. Berry; and D. Clay Whybark. *Manufacturing Planning and Control Systems.* 3rd ed. Homewood, Ill.: Irwin, 1992.

Wetherbe, James C., and Scott Conrad. "What MIS Executives Need to Know About Robotics." *Journal of Systems Management* (May 1983):38–42.

Chapter 19

Barth, Claire. "Automating Time and Attendance." *Management Accounting* (June 1992):14–15.

Butler, Stephen A., and Michael W. Maher. *Management Incentive Compensation Plans.* Montvale, N.J.: National Association of Accountants, 1986.

Davey, Bruce W., and Larry S. Jacobson, eds. *Computerizing Human Resource Management.* Alexandria, Va.: International Personnel Management Association, 1987.

Desanctis, Gerardine. "Human Resource Information Systems: A Current Assessment." *MIS Quarterly* (March 1986):15–27.

Diers, Cynthia D. "Personnel Computing: Make the HRIS More Effective." *Personnel Journal* (May 1990):92–94.

Duff, Kenneth. "HR-Link: An HRIS from Apple Canada." *Personnel* (May 1990):6–14.

Dugan, Margot. "Meeting a Competitive Challenge: Upgrading Computer Resources at Grumman Data Systems." *Industrial Management* (September/October 1990):21–23.

Extejt, Marian M., and Marc P. Lynn. "Expert Systems as Human Resource Management Decision Tools." *Journal of Systems Management* (November 1988):10–15.

Fisher, Cynthia D.; Lyle F. Schoenfeldt; and James B. Shaw. *Human Resource Management.* Boston: Houghton Mifflin, 1990.

Hunn, Sonja. "A PC/Mainframe Team to HR's Rescue." *Personnel* (August 1989):37–42.

Institute of Internal Auditors Research Foundation. *Systems Auditability and Control Report. Module 6: Business Systems.* Alamonte Springs, Fla.: Institute of Internal Auditors Research Foundation, 1991.

Ivancevich, John M. *Human Resource Management: Foundations of Personnel.* 5th ed. Homewood, Ill.: Irwin, 1992.

Kavanagh, Michael J.; Hal G. Gueutal; and Scott I. Tannenbaum. *Human Resource Information Systems: Development and Application.* Boston: PWS-Kent, 1990.

Knapp, Jeffrey. "Trends in HR Management Systems." *Personnel* (April 1990):56–61.

Maxwell, Barbara S. "Improving the Quality of HRIS Data." *Personnel* (April 1989):48–58.

Merens, Michele. "Beware the Increasing Complexities of Payroll." *Management Accounting* (October 1991):42–44.

Murlis, Helen, and Derek Pritchard. "The Computerized Way to Evaluate Jobs." *Personnel Management* (April 1991):48–53.

Palmer, John. "Information Technology at Your Service." *Personnel Management* (June 1991):57–60.

Pederson, R. Brian. "Weyerhaeuser: Streamlining Payroll." *Management Accounting* (October 1991):38–41.

Perry, Stephen G. "The PC-Based HRIS." *Personnel Administrator* (February 1988):60–63.

Pollard, John R. "HRIS: Time Is of the Essence." *Personnel Journal* (November 1990):42–44.

Rocco, Jerry. "Computers Track High-Potential Managers." *HR Magazine* (August 1991):66–68.

Rock, Milton L., and Lance A. Berger. *The Compensation Handbook.* 3rd ed. New York: McGraw-Hill, 1991.

Rosenberg, Stephen. "Flexibility in Installing a Large-Scale HRIS: New York City's Experience." *Personnel Administrator* (December 1985):39–46.

Salam, D. J., and L. K. Price. *Principles of Payroll Administration.* Paramus, N.J.: Prentice-Hall Information Services, 1988.

Tinsley, Dillard B. "Computers Facilitate HR Function." *Personnel* (February 1990):32–35.

Chapter 20

Bierman, Harold, Jr., and Seymour Smidt. *The Capital Budgeting Decision.* 7th ed. New York: Macmillan, 1988.

Boer, Germain. *Decision Support Systems for Management Accountants.* Montvale, N.J.: National Association of Accountants, 1987.

Boris, Larry. "People vs. Machine: A Case for Automated Tracking Systems." *Credit World* (May/June 1992):23–27.

Cantu, Carlos. "A CEO's Perspective: The Role of the CFO." *Financial Executive* (July/August 1991):30–31.

Culbertson, William Y. "Expert Systems in Finance." *Corporate Accounting* (Spring 1987):47–50.

Deeb, Michael J., and Eugene A. Brown. "Automating Accounts Payable at AMSCO." *Management Accounting* (January 1990):28–30.

Douglas, Patricia P. "Reporting Accounting Information to Top Management." *Corporate Accounting* (Summer 1987):38–45.

Douglas, Patricia P., and Teresa K. Beed. *Presenting Accounting Information to Management.* Montvale, N.J.: National Association of Accountants, 1986.

Earl, Michael J., and Eng S. Ong. "Treasury Management Information Systems and the Contribution of Information Technology." *Information & Management* (April 1987):209–217.

Ekman, Suzanne. "Bar Coding Fixed Asset Inventories." *Management Accounting* (December 1992):58–61.

Globecon Group, Ltd. *Electronic Data Interchange and Corporate Trade Payments.* Morristown, N.J.: Financial Executives Research Foundation, 1988.

Golden, Charles W., and Mary R. Golden. "Beyond 'What If': A Risk-Oriented Capital Budgeting Model." *Journal of Information Systems* (Spring 1987):53–64.

Heidkamp, Martha M. "Reaping the Benefits of Financial EDI." *Management Accounting* (May 1991):39–43.

Hobart, Bridgette A. "Improve Your Bottom Line: Fixed Asset Management." *Management Accounting* (September 1991):54–58.

LeTourneau, Harry D. "What to Expect from Your Bank." *Financial Executive* (May/June 1992):23–26.

McDowell, Robert L.; Elizabeth E. McHugh; and Sharon L. Hakeman. *The Impact of Business Systems Technologies on the Financial Function.* Montvale, N.J.: National Association of Accountants, 1988.

Potter, Douglas A. *Automated Accounting Systems and Procedures Handbook.* New York: Wiley,

1991.

Ruisi, William N. "Tomorrow's Technology Simplifies Today's Remittance Processing." *Business Credit* (January 1992):8–9.

Ryan, Bruce J. "DEC's Decentralized Financial System Puts Strategy Above Controls." *Financial Executive* (July/August 1989):42–46.

Shane, Barry; Mitchell Fry; and Reuben Toro. "The Design of an Investment Portfolio Selection Decision Support System Using Two Expert Systems and a Consulting System." *Journal of Management Information Systems* (Spring 1987):79–92.

Stout, David E.; Matthew J. Liberatore; and Thomas F. Monahan. "Decision Support Software for Capital Budgeting." *Management Accounting* (July 1991):50–53.

Willson, James D., and James P. Colford. "The New Controller— With Five Redefined Chores." *Financial Executive* (March/April 1991):22–27.

INDEX

4GL 173–178, 204, 418
acceptance test 452
access control matrix 606, 831, 1032
access controls 250, 604–607, 911, 965, 1017, 1032
access restriction 668
access time 157, 160–162, 308
accountant 26, 28, 61, 100, 101, 146–147, 201, 204–206, 301, 527–530, 674, 693, 1011
  role in changing information system 346–347
accounting controls 528–530, 563–565, 704
accounting cycles 20–21, 551, 785, 987, 1007
accounting data base 1007–1009, 1023–1028
accounting information system (AIS) 14–20, 25–26, 32–36, 53, 931
accounting software 211–212, 477
accounting system 530, 550–558
accounts receivable 280, 302, 651, 765–767, 1017
accounts receivable aging schedule 999, 1019
actual overhead rates 903, 904
ad hoc queries 176
ad hoc reports 204, 433
ad hoc users 311
ADA 173
add-ins 216
adjusting entries 1009–1011
administrative controls 528, 529, 707
administrative documentation 611, 714, 725, 728
aggression 359–360
ALGOL 172
allocation base 597–598, 916
analog 249, 253, 273
APL 172
Apple-DOS 180
applicant file 938
application controls 581–582, 615–633, 697, 731
application files 301, 305
application generators 177
application programmers 311, 584, 660
application software 170, 182–183, 211, 475–480
arithmetic and logic unit 155–156
artificial intelligence (AI) 229–232
assembler 171, 182
asynchronous transmission 254–255
attributes 62–63, 73, 317–319
audio response units 168–169, 280
audio teleconferencing 276
audit 542, 670, 697–742, 1011, 1031
audit committee 538–539, 565
audit evidence 694, 700–701, 720–721
audit hook 722–723
audit log 722–724

audit planning 698–700, 742
audit results 701–702
audit software 213–214, 716, 733, 736–741
audit trail 56, 313, 440, 546, 724, 1036
audit work, scope and objectives of 695–698
auditing 201, 674, 693–742
auditing process 698–702, 732
authorization 439, 542–545, 552–553, 588–589, 662, 786, 842–843, 963–964, 1031
automated decision table programs 717
automated flowcharting programs 717
automated system 7, 9, 360
avoidance 360

back order 763, 779
back-end (or lower) CASE tools 415, 416
backlog 195, 207, 270, 474, 872
backup file 66, 603, 610, 707, 787, 965
balance-forward method 766, 769
bandwidths 255, 267
banking systems 278–279
bar codes 165–167, 826, 844, 891
BASIC 172, 173
batch processing 74–77, 718
  in financial management reporting cycle 1017–1020
  in personnel/payroll cycle 959–961
  in procurement cycle 835–838
  in production cycle 899–904
  in sales order processing system 779–781
batch totals 126–127, 548, 617–619, 628–629,
  in financial management reporting cycle 1019
  in personnel/payroll cycle 964–967
  in procurement cycle 824, 836–837
  in production cycle 894
  in sales order processing system 771–773, 781
baud rate 249–250
behavioral aspects of change 356–362
benchmark problem 485
bill of lading 763, 770
bill of materials 868, 872–873, 893–894
billing 764–765
bits 156–159, 169, 254
blanket order 816
block code 79
bottom-up approach 354
boundary 11, 107
broadband 256
budget 83, 995–996, 1026–1028
bulletin board system (BBS) 273
business cycles 20–21, 53–54
business organization 21–25
business processes 409, 503–510, 1007
bus network 264
byte 156–158, 254

C 172
cables 169, 257–258, 267
CAD/CAM systems 153, 869–871, 906–907
cafeteria-style benefit plans 945
canned software 477–480
capital assets information system 1020–1023
capital budgeting 369
capital budgeting model 366
capital expenditures budget 995
capital expenditures cycle 1004–1007
CASE 414–419
CASE encyclopedia 415
CASE tools 414–419, 498
cash budget 991, 995, 1038
cash disbursements cycle 1000–1004
cash disbursements processing 1019–1020
cash disbursements register 1019–1020, 1036
cash flow commitments report 846–847
cash receipt projections report 1019
cash receipts cycle 997–1000
cash receipts processing 1017–1019
CD ROM 153, 161–162
cellular radio 259
central processing unit (CPU) 147–148, 155–159, 250
centralized data processing system 247
centralized network 261
centralized organization 24
chain 73
character 63, 156
chart of accounts 80–82, 539
check digit verification 619–620, 629, 775
checkpoint 603, 728
Chief Financial Officer (CFO) 988–990
Chief Information Officer (CIO) 582–583
children 315
client/server 268–269
closed loop verification 624, 633, 785, 831, 910
closing entries 56, 1009–1011
coaxial cable 258, 267
coding 78–86, 127, 435, 444, 448
cold site 614
collusion 545–546
common carriers 271
communication interface devices 267–268
communications channel 248, 250, 252–260
communications interface devices 248–250, 267–268
communications network 246, 252–253, 261–274
communications software 182, 248, 250–252, 272
compact disk 161
compatibility test 606, 788, 845, 1032
compensating controls 587, 704–705
compensation costs 946–947
compilers 173, 174

completeness test 623, 625, 629
complex network 316, 331
compliance audit 697–698
computer
  central processing unit 155–159
  classifications of 150–155
  history of 147–150
  input devices 162–168
  output devices 168–170
  secondary storage devices and media
    159–162
  software 170–183
  speed measurements of 157–158
  storage measurements of 156–157
computer audit software 716, 730–741
computer conferencing 276
computer configuration flowcharts 121–124
computer consultants 672
computer crime 647, 651–653, 660, 672–673
computer fraud 645–676
computer instructions fraud 655
computer languages 170–179, 397, 444
computer operations 586–587, 595–596,
  616, 742
computer output microfilm (COM) 169–170
computer program 170, 302, 443
computer programming 170
computer security 646–647, 705–708
computer security officer 671
computer services, internal pricing of
  596–600
computer system flowcharts 121, 125–127
computer virus 659,
computer-aided design (CAD) 869–871, 907
computer-aided manufacturing (CAM)
  870–871, 907
computer-aided programming tools 415
computer-aided software engineering
  (CASE) 414–419
computer-based message systems 274–277
computer-based system 6–9
computer-integrated manufacturing (CIM)
  874–877, 906
concatenated key 321, 1023
concealment of assets 650–651
conceptual data modeling 330
conceptual design 330–332, 349, 409–414,
conceptual design specifications 411–412
conceptual systems design report 412–414
concurrent audit techniques 720–724
concurrent update controls 602, 728
constraints 11, 352–354
context diagram 109–110
contingency theory 402
continuous and intermittent simulation
  (CIS) 723–724
control 11, 13, 206, 209, 356, 439, 496,
  527–542, 742, 962
control account 55, 767–768, 947–949, 1000
control concepts 527–537
control environment 530, 537–542
control flowcharts 121
control objectives and procedures 542–550
  in financial management and reporting
    cycle 1029–1036
  in personnel/payroll cycle 962–966

control objectives and procedures (cont.):
  in procurement cycle 841–845
  in production cycle 908–912
  in sales order processing system 785–788
control of errors and exceptions 626–628
control risk 560, 699
control totals 75–76, 454, 548, 781
control unit 155–156
controlled growth approach 210
controller 662, 987, 994–995
controlling site access 600, 616
controls and standards design 439–440
conversion 171, 349, 440–455, 626
conversion of assets 650–651
conversion phase 349
corrective controls 534
cost accounting 884, 995–996
CP/M 180
CPU time 597–598
credit limit 762, 779, 992
cross-footing balance test 618
cryptography 602
custom software 475–477
customized CASE package 416
cycle
  business and accounting 20–21
  capital expenditures 1004–1006
  cash disbursements 1000–1004
  cash receipts 997–1000
  financial reporting 986–1042
  financial management 986–1042
  personnel/payroll 929–975
  procurement 806–853
  production 864–920
  revenue 754–795
cycle billing 769
cycle counting 844–845

data 2–4, 302, 507, 669
data base 63–65, 216–217, 263, 301
  employee 956–959
  marketing 776–779
  production 896–899
  purchasing 831–835
data base administrator (DBA) 302–304,
  310–311, 583
data base approach 65, 301–308
data base design 329–332, 434–435
data base management system (DBMS)
  181, 216, 302, 308–314, 602
data base query languages 176
data base systems 65, 301–334, 779
data base update
  in financial management and reporting
    cycle 1017–1029
  in personnel/payroll cycle 956–962
  in procurement cycle 831–841
  in production cycle 895–908
  in sales order processing system 776–785
data bus 158
data capture
  in financial management and reporting
    cycle 1012–1014
  in personnel/payroll cycle 951–953
  in procurement cycle 824–827
  in production cycle 890–891

data capture (cont.):
  in sales order processing system 771–774
data communications 148, 247
  applications 274–284
  channels 252–260
  hardware 249–250
  model 248–249
  network organization 261–265
  network types 266–274
  software 250–252
data communications networks 246,
  266–274
data compatibility 305
data conversion 454–455
data definition language (DDL) 308, 327
data dependence 304
data destinations 103
data dictionary 106, 311–313, 602
data diddling 657
data encryption 602, 668, 707
data files 301, 601–604, 655, 728–731
data flow 103–108, 118
data flow diagram (DFD) 102–112, 397
data fraud 655
data inconsistencies 304, 306
data independence 306
data input 58–61
data integration 304
data leakage 657
data maintenance 66, 76
data manipulation language (DML) 309,
  327
data ownership 306, 666
data preparation 148, 163, 619
data preparation devices 148, 163
data processing 9, 66–77, 261
data processing center 151, 493, 496
data processing cycle 9, 58–78, 997
data query language (DQL) 309
data redundancy 263, 304, 306, 320, 334
data repository 415–418
data security 251, 787
data sharing 305
data sources 102–103, 393–395
data storage 61–66, 434
data stores 103–107
data transmission 251
data transmission controls 607–609, 617
data values 62, 910
DBMS functions and users 310–311
DBMS languages and interfaces 308–310
DDP network configurations 264–265
debit distribution 1001–1003, 1006
debugging 181, 446
decentralized organization 24
decentralized system 261–262
decision room 228–229
decision support system (DSS) 14–15, 177,
  214, 226–229, 1039–1040
decision table 128–130, 717
deduction register 966
demand reports 433, 788, 793, 966
design considerations 81–82, 329–332,
  410–412
desktop organizer 225–226
desktop publishing (DTP) 219–221, 654

detailed reports 85
detective controls 534, 560
deterring computer fraud 664–674
developing software programs 443–448
diagnostic messages 173
digital 158, 249, 253, 273, 275
direct access 67, 70, 71, 160
direct access processing 70–74
direct conversion 453
disaster recovery 612–615
disaster recovery plan 613–617, 707, 728
disbursement voucher 819, 1000–1003
discretionary information 18
diskette 159, 161, 670–671
distributed data processing (DDP) 247–248, 261–265, 607
divisional organization structure 21, 23
document flowcharts 106, 121, 564
documentation 101–102, 121, 208, 355, 364, 395, 406, 418, 452, 611–612, 617, 817–818
documents 77, 224, 436, 546
download 155
downloading 201, 214, 790
downsizing 151, 266, 346, 494
duplex 255–256
duplicate processing 306

eavesdropping 607, 658
echo check 608
economic feasibility 365–369
economic order quantity 809
edit check 621–626, 629, 775
edit program 621–622, 629, 716, 727, 775, 836
electronic data interchange (EDI) 163, 282–284, 609, 764, 780, 819, 827–830, 1014–1015
electronic funds transfer (EFT) 279, 609, 997–998, 1013, 1015, 1019–1020, 1030
electronic mail (E-mail) 247, 274–275
electronic spreadsheet 198, 214–216
electronic vaulting 603
embedded audit modules 720
embezzlement 527, 545, 552, 553, 558
employee clock card 940, 952
employee data base 956–959
employee fraud 552, 556, 649–650
employee training 665–666
end-user computing (EUC) 196–198
 benefits of 206–207
 controlling 209–211
 use 205–206
 managing 209–211
 risks of 207–209
 skill levels of 204–205
end-user development 205–206
end-user software 211–232
end-user system (EUS) 16
end-users 11, 175, 204, 211
enforced vacations 666–667
enterprise information system 197
entity 5, 62, 63, 103, 331, 415
environment 11, 402–403, 537–538,
error detection and control 251, 436, 448, 785
essential information 18–19

ethernet 269
evaluating design alternatives 410–411
exception reports 13, 76, 433, 735, 911
execution time 157
executive information system (EIS) 15, 501
executive support system 15
expected loss 559, 564
expediting 876, 912
expert system (ES) 15–16, 179, 229–232, 791–792, 971, 1039
exposure 527, 559, 564, 610, 716
external fraud 649–650
external influences 538, 541–542
external information requirements 17–18, 993
external label 601, 626, 630
external users 16–18, 77

facsimile (FAX) transmission 203, 274
fault tolerance 612
feasibility analysis 363–369, 398
feasibility study 363, 398–399, 412
feedback 10, 361, 535
feedback control 534–535
feedforward control 535
fiber optics cable 258
fidelity bond 541, 611
field check 622, 629, 775
fields 63, 312
file 58, 63, 65–85, 107, 120, 154–155, 251, 268, 367
file access 67–68
file design 434–435
file maintenance 10, 66, 778
file maintenance controls 624–626, 628
file organization 67–68
file transmission 251
file-oriented approach 301–308
file-server 268
financial accounting 16
financial audit 697, 731–741
financial information system 987, 1012–1040
financial cycle functions and procedures 997–1011
financial management cycle 556–558, 986, 1012
financial management function 987–996
financial modeling system 177
financial reporting cycle 986, 1007–1011
financial statements, preparation of 1011
financial total 618
finished products 877, 883–884
firm infrastructure 28
fixed cost 495, 1026
flat file 317–318
flexible benefits plans 945
flexible budget 1026
flexible manufacturing systems (FMS) 870–871
flexible pricing 599
floppy disk 161
flowchart 111–128, 397, 628, 892, 1014
flowchart symbols 113–119
flowcharting template 115

Foreign Corrupt Practices Act 529–530, 563–565
forensic accountant 674
form 77, 436–437
formal information systems 7, 933
forms design 436–438
FORTRAN 172
fourth generation languages (4GL) 173–178, 418
framework for studying decision making 404–405
fraud 556, 645–674,
fraud hot line 671–672
fraud perpetrators 648, 660, 663, 672–674
fraud process 650–651
fraudulent financial reporting 649–650
front-end (or upper) CASE tools 414–415, 416
front-end processor (FEP) 250
full costing 598
full-duplex channels 255
functional organizational structure 21, 23

Gantt charts 442–443, 590
gateway 267
General Accounting Office (GAO) 693, 732–733
general authorization 543
general controls 581–582, 600–615
general journal 55, 1025–1026
general ledger 55, 315, 625, 767–768, 820–824, 884–887, 947–949, 1006–1007, 1009–1011
general ledger processing 1027–1029
generalized audit software (GAS) 731–732, 735
Generalized Audit Software Package (GASP) 213
gigabyte 156–157
goal conflict 24, 352
goal congruence 24, 352
grandfather-father-son concept 603
graphical user interface (GUI) 181, 268, 307
graphics languages 177
graphics software 221–222
group codes 79
group decision support software (GDSS) 228
group information system 197
groupware 205, 229, 277

hacking 658
half-duplex 255
hard copy 169
hard disk 161, 218
hardware 147–170, 183, 249–250, 480
hash total 618, 629, 955
header label 601, 608, 630
hierarchical network 264
hierarchical program design 445
hierarchical structure 22, 131, 314
high-level languages 171–173, 309
HIPO chart 131–132
hiring and firing practices 664
history file 66, 832
hot site 614

human resources 28, 932–939, 956, 966
hybrid network 265

icon 164, 178, 181
image processing 222–225, 509
impact printers 169
impersonation 657
implementation and conversion phase 332, 349, 440–455
implementation plan 441–443
implementation team 441, 442
imprest system 558, 1003, 1033
income tax software 212–213
independent check 547–550
index file 72
indexed file organization 72
indexed–sequential–access method (ISAM) 72
inference engine 230
informal information system 7
information 1, 3–9, 12–23, 25–38, 399
information center (IC) 210
information interfaces 11
information output 58, 77–78
information processing 9, 197, 703
information systems 2–35
   accountant's role in changing 346–347
   and adding value 26–29
   and organizational structure 21–25
   components of 9–12
   defined 6–9
   objectives and constraints 352–354
   operational audits of 741–743
   people who plan, manage, and develop 350–352
   plans for 355
   reasons for change in 345–347
   strategies for 354
   types of 12–16
   why study? 25–26
information systems audits 697, 702–731
information systems function 582–600
information systems responsibilities 582–587
information systems steering committee 351–352
inherent risk 560, 698–699, 701
initial investigation 347, 389–391
initial outlay costs 367, 369
input 10, 58–61,
input devices 148, 162–163
input controls matrix 726
input design 435–436
input fraud 654–655
input medium 148
input validation routines 620–623, 628, 783
input/output bound 162
inquiry processing 76, 783, 790, 846, 915, 1023, 1038
instructions 11, 170, 444, 655
integrated (or customized) CASE package 416–418
integrated services digital network (ISDN) 273–274
integrated software 35, 215
integrated test facility (ITF) 721
integration 6, 65, 304, 354

internal auditing 540, 695–698
internal check 547–548, 940, 949, 1025
internal control 121, 527, 555, 558–565, 666
internal control flowcharts 121
internal control structure 530, 537, 539
internal frauds 649–650
internal information requirements 18–20, 993
internal labels 601
internal pricing of computer services 596–600
internal rate of return 369
internal users 17–19, 76–78
interpreter 173, 182
interview 393–394
inventory accounting 818–819
inventory availability 762–763, 768, 770
inventory receipts 817–818, 826, 830, 835–836
inverted file 72, 73
inverted lists 72, 73

job order costing 884, 887
job time ticket 882, 899, 940
JOIN 323
journal voucher 55–56, 765, 767, 820, 1025–1026, 1031
joystick 164
just–in–time (JIT) system 811–812, 826, 873–874

key 67, 583
   primary 67, 68, 72, 321, 331
   secondary 68, 73
key verification 619, 629, 724
key–to–disk encoder 163
key–to–tape encoder 163
kilobyte 156–157
kiting 651
knowledge base 229–231, 1039
knowledge base management system 230
knowledge engineering 229

laissez–faire approach 210
LAN interface 267
language translators 182
lapping 651, 666
leased lines 255
ledger 55, 58, 79, 333, 544
legal feasibility 365
light pens 164, 826
limit check 622–623, 629, 1034
line count 618, 629
line–sharing device 260
linked list 72–73
LISP 173
local area network (LAN) 248, 266–271, 450, 659, 669
logic errors 173, 417, 447
logic time bomb 657
logical access control 604–607, 617, 706–707
logical data structures 314
logical file organization 67
logical model 314, 396–397, 418
logical view 102, 303, 329
lower CASE tools 415–416

machine independent languages 172
machine language 171, 173, 179, 182
machine vision 167
macro 215
macroinstructions 171
magnetic disks 118, 160–161, 603
magnetic ink character recognition (MICR) 164, 165
magnetic stripe 167
magnetic tape 159–160, 602–603, 655
mainframe computers 150–152, 162, 481, 605
management accounting 17
management audit 697
management by exception 85, 1039
management control 404, 530–533, 589–600
management cycle 13, 556–558
management fraud 649–650
management information system (MIS) 13–14
managing disgruntled employees 664–665
mandatory information 18
manual information systems 7
manufacturing resource planning (MRP–II) 873
many–to–many 315–316, 331
mapping programs 717
market pricing 599
marketing management function 756–761
masquerading 657
master files 65–71, 301, 624–626, 630–633
master plan 355
materiality 701
materials requirements planning (MRP) 810, 873
materials requisition 881–884, 897–900, 910–911
megabyte 156–157
megahertz 157, 159
message 178, 274–277, 266
microcomputer 153–155, 198–203, 248, 481
   hardware 158–159
   software 211–232
microfilm 169–170, 432
microprocessor 158
microsecond 157
millisecond 157
mini–company test 721
minicomputers 152, 449, 481
MIPS (millions of instructions per second) 157
models 314, 396, 397, 415
modem 249, 253, 273
modified canned software 478–479
modular conversion 454
modules 438, 445, 448
monopolist approach 209
motherboard 158
mouse 164
move ticket 883, 890, 899, 901, 911
MS–DOS 180
multiattribute search file organization 72–74
multidrop lines 260
multiple factor base 598
multiplexor 250
multiprogramming 181, 586

nanosecond 157–158
narrative description 101, 109, 119
narrowband 255
natural languages 174–175, 229
net present value 369, 989
network 229, 314–316, 333, 780
network management 250
network server 268
network software 268
network switching 264
node 261, 314, 442
non-operational or throwaway prototypes 499
nonimpact printers 169
nonskilled end users 204
numerical control 440, 870–871, 906

object 178, 415
object oriented language 178–179
object oriented programming (OOP) 178
object program 171
observation 395, 398, 700, 706, 727, 729
office automation (OA) 16, 219
off-line devices 155
on-line data entry controls 623–624, 628
on-line devices 155
on-line processing 76–77, 720, 724
    in personnel/payroll cycle 962
    in procurement cycle 838–841
    in production cycle 904–908
    in sales order processing system 781–784
on-line real-time processing 76, 1017
on-line testing 720
on-line updating 76–77
one-to-many 315, 331, 777–778, 956, 1021
open requisitions report 846
open-invoice method 765, 999
open-to-buy (OTB) control system 822
operating costs 367–368
operating documentation 611, 714, 728
operating environment 181
operating system (OS) 150, 180–181, 263, 311, 596
operational audit 697, 741–743
operational control 404
operational documents 77
operational feasibility 364
operational prototypes 499
operations list 868, 872, 894, 897, 906
opportunity (for fraud) 587–588, 662–663
optical character recognition (OCR) 164, 165, 435, 773
optical disk 161–162, 223, 434
order release 890, 892–894, 898, 909
organization structure 23, 450, 505, 538, 756
organizational codes 82–85
organizational independence 543, 553–554, 556–557, 587–588
organizational structure 21, 23–24, 82, 450, 757, 867, 932, 988
OS/2 180
outbound activities 26
output 10, 77–78, 148, 655–656
output controls 626, 628
output devices 168–170
output design 432–434

output fraud 655–656
output medium 148, 168
outsourcing 490–496
overdue deliveries report 836, 838, 850

packing slip 763
parallel conversion 453–454
parallel interface 169
parallel processing 151, 453–454
parallel simulation 692, 713
parallel transmission 253–254
parent 314, 778
parity bit 608
parity checking 608–609
PASCAL 172
password 605–607, 706–708
payback period 369
payroll cycle 937
payroll disbursement 946
payroll preparation 943–945
payroll registers 944
payroll service bureaus 949–950
PC-DOS 180
performance evaluation 362, 591–593, 757, 937
performance report 83, 534–535, 884, 907
peripherals 147, 151, 154–155
personal computer controls 609–611, 617
personal digital assistant (PDA) 154
personal identification numbers (PIN) 279
personal information system 197
personnel administration and training 449–451
personnel change record 951, 953, 957
personnel cycle 937, 938–940
personnel executives 932–933
personnel management function 932–937
personnel policies and practices 540–541, 610, 708, 741–742
personnel staff functions 933–936
personnel/payroll cycle 20, 555–556, 930–950
    functions and procedures 937–950
personnel/payroll data processing system 950–972
PERT 442, 590
phase-in conversion 454
physical design 332, 349, 440
physical design phase 349
physical model 396
physical systems design 412, 432–440
physical systems design report 440, 458
physical view 102, 302–304
PICK 180
picosecond 157
piggybacking 657
pixel 168
PL/1 173
planning 13, 404, 441–443, 612–614
planning and managing systems development 350–356
plotter 169
point scoring 485, 488
point-of-sale (POS) 30, 165
point-to-point lines 260
pointer 72, 315
position control file 938

position control report 968
post-implementation review 455–456
post-implementation review report 456
predetermined overhead rates 903
preformatting 623, 831, 844
preliminary data processing procedures
    in financial management and reporting cycle 1014–1017
    in personnel/payroll cycle 953–955
    in procurement cycle 828–831
    in production cycle 892–895
    in sales order processing system 774–776
preparing design specifications 411–412
pressure (for fraud) 660–662
preventive controls 533, 560, 603
preventive maintenance 612, 707
primary activities 27
primary key 67, 68, 72, 321, 331
primary memory 155, 156, 158, 181
printers 124, 164, 169–170, 266–267, 788
private branch exchange (PBX) 273
procedures 11, 252
procedures design 439
procedures manuals 11, 393, 451, 538
process costing 887
processes 105–106
processing capability 263
processing of test data 452, 718–720
processor 10–11, 124, 158–159
processor fraud 655
procurement cycle 20, 552–554, 807, 813–824
production cycle 20, 554–555, 865, 877–889
production data base 871, 880, 891–918
production executives 867–868
production information system 889–918
production management function 867–877
production operations 882–883
production order 879
production planning 872–875, 877–880
production scheduling 872, 880–881, 907
profitability analysis 756–759
program dependence 304–305
program design 438–439, 445
program development 435, 438, 444, 708–710
program flowcharts 113, 127
program logic 119, 452, 717
program modification 710–713
program tracing 717
programmer/analyst performance evaluation 591–593
programming languages 170, 217, 444, 498, 717
PROJECT 322–324
project controls 593–595, 616
project development plan 355, 590, 593
project management software 226
project milestones 593, 742
project team 352, 354, 387, 392, 406
projection 360
PROLOG 173
prompting 623, 831, 844, 964
proper control of sensitive data 669
proposal to conduct systems analysis 391
protecting personal computers 609–611
protocol 252

prototype 435, 496, 511
prototyping 403, 474, 496–503
pseudocode 130
public data bases 182, 272–273
purchase order 815–816
purchase requisition 813–814
purchasing 19, 28, 506–509, 606, 625, 790, 808
purchasing and inventory data processing system 824–851
purchasing and inventory management function 808–813
purchasing data base 831–835, 836–839, 844, 896, 1017

queries 78, 176, 322–323
questionnaires 394–395, 700

Radio Frequency Identification 167
random access memory (RAM) 155
random surveillance 670
randomizing 72
range check 622, 629, 632, 775, 895
rationalization (of fraud) 663–664
re-engineering 346, 474, 503–510
read only memory (ROM) 155, 161
real-time notification 723
real-time processing 76, 1017
reasonable assurance 528–529, 532, 558, 564, 701
reasonableness test 622, 632, 828, 895
receiving report 507, 543, 700, 817
record 63–64, 67–69, 302–303, 312, 435
record count 618–619, 629
record layout 302, 435, 736
redundant data checks 622–624, 775, 895, 910, 964
relational data base 317–329, 332
relations 319, 322–323, 332
reliability 19, 26, 256, 264, 561
reliability analysis 561–563
remittance advice 999, 1003, 1012–1014
remote batch processing 75
reorder point 809–810, 822, 825, 840
repeating group 315, 778, 956
report file 66, 961
report generators 176–177
report writers 309–310
reporting
    in financial management and reporting cycle 1036–1040
    in personnel/payroll cycle 966–972
    in procurement cycle 845–851
    in production cycle 912–918
    in sales order processing system 788–793
reports 14, 77, 305, 433
reprocessing technique 713
request for systems development 389, 391
requests for proposals (RFP) 480–483
requirements costing 488
requirements definition 329–330, 503
resolution 168, 869
responsibility accounting 82–85, 535, 540
retail sales systems 279–280
revenue cycle 22, 38, 54–58, 552, 755, 761–771
ring network 265

risk 207, 527, 540, 552, 555, 558–561, 563–564, 581
robotics 871
rollback 604, 607
root 314, 896, 956, 1021
rotation of duties 540, 666–667
round-down technique 656
router 268
routing sheet 868
RPG 173

sabotage 359, 613, 647
safeguarding of assets 528, 546–547, 695
salami technique 656
sales analysis 758–759
sales invoice 54, 318–327, 764–765, 777–780
sales order 280–281, 761
sales order preparation 761–762
sales order processing systems 280–281
satellite 259, 277, 509
scanners 164–165, 826, 840, 911, 997
scanning routines 717
SCARF 722, 724
scavenging 658
scheduled reports 433, 788–789, 845, 912, 966, 968, 1036
scheduling feasibility 365
schema 303, 304, 331
scope 14, 391, 399
screen design 436–438
secondary key 68, 73
secondary storage 148, 159–162, 181
security 251, 307, 646, 665, 705–708, 787
security measures 11, 449, 665
segregation of duties 543–546, 552, 587–589, 610, 666, 787, 997
SELECT 322–323
self-checking digit 620
semiconductor 155, 231
semiskilled end users 204
semistructured decisions 405
sequence check 621, 629, 895
sequence codes 79
sequential access 67, 72, 159
sequential file 68, 72
sequential file processing 68–70
serial interface 169, 249
serial transmission 169, 253–254
server 266–270
service bureau 273, 613, 949–950
service order 769–770
shipping 763–764
shipping order 763–764, 770, 780–782, 786–787
sign check 622, 625, 632
simple network 315–316
simplex 255
simulation analysis 485
single factor base 597
site access 600–601, 616
site license 266
site preparation 449
skilled end users 205
skills index 970
skills inventory system 970
smart cards 167, 826

snapshot technique 721
social system 449
software 170–183, 211–232, 250–252, 268, 306–307, 368, 414, 443–448, 474–480, 731–741
software piracy 210, 657
source data 333, 586, 615, 618–622, 629, 724–728
source data automation (SDA) 61, 76, 163, 164–168, 186, 261
source data controls 619–620, 628, 724–728
source document 59
source program 171, 173, 712, 717
special-purpose analyses 433
specialized journal 55
specific authorization 528–529, 543
spreadsheets 198, 214–216
standardized data 306
standards design 439–440
star network 266
steering committee 351–352, 391, 398, 410–412, 441, 585
stock status report 789, 838, 845–846
stored data 10, 66, 223, 415, 601–604
strategic planning 404, 416
stratified sampling 740
structured decisions 405
structured English 130–131
structured programming 178, 445
structured systems analysis 397
subschema 304, 308, 311
subsidiary ledger 55, 56, 65
subsystems 5, 6, 11–12, 14, 354, 550
summary reports 84, 740, 781, 849, 1023
supercomputer 150–151
superzapping 657
support activities 27–28
suspense file 66
switched line 255
symbolic languages 171–172
synchronous transmission 254–255
syntax errors 129, 173, 447
system 5–6, 38, 352, 449
    operation and maintenance 455–458
    financial information 1012–1040
    personnel/payroll 950–972
    production information 889–918
    purchasing and inventory 824–851
    sales order processing 771–793
system downtime 612, 617
system review 704–705, 709, 712, 714, 725, 727–728
system's boundaries 391
systems acquisition 412, 475–490
systems analysis 127, 130, 209, 347–349, 354–355, 387–408, 587
systems analysis phase 347, 407
systems analysts 347, 351, 359, 362, 396, 585, 592
systems approach 354
systems concept 6
systems development 343–373, 502
    life cycle 347–349, 474
    organization of 584–585
    planning and managing 350–356
systems documentation 101, 611, 714, 728
systems flowcharts 102, 113, 121, 127

systems implementation 440–455
systems maintenance 455–458
systems operation 455–458
systems project controls 593–595
systems software 170, 179–182, 287, 307, 584, 672
systems survey 347, 392–398
systems survey report 398

table file 66
tagging 722
tape file protection ring 602
technical feasibility 364
technical system 449
technology 26, 28, 32, 34, 35, 196
teleconferencing 276
telephone lines 257, 668
telephone networks 273
template 215, 791
terabyte 157
terrestrial microwave 258
test data generator 718
testing software programs 443–448
testing systems 208, 451–452, 502
tests of controls 704–705, 709
theft of assets 650–651
threats 527, 540, 546, 559, 564, 602
threats to information systems 647
throughput 162, 596, 913
throwaway prototypes 499
time-sharing 273
TIPS 157
token ring 270
top-down approach 354, 397
touch-sensitive 164
trailer label 601, 609, 626, 631
transaction 8, 53, 65–71, 74–77, 81, 119
transaction file 65, 626–627, 629–631, 736–739, 953, 1018

transaction log 603, 624, 787
transaction processing 53–59, 930
transaction processing cycles 53–54
transaction processing systems 14, 196, 543, 1021
transaction trail 546
transcription error 550
transposition error 549
trap door 656
treasurer 987, 991–992
tree 314–316, 317, 331, 332
trial balance 56, 213–214, 1009
triggered exception reports 433
triggered reports 845, 850–851, 912
trojan horse 656
turnaround document 60, 163, 165, 620, 891
turnkey systems 477

uninterruptible power system 612
unit pricing 598
universal product code (UPC) 165–167, 774
UNIX 180
unstructured decisions 405
upper CASE tools 414
user interface 226–227, 230, 783
users 11, 16, 77, 100–101, 310–311, 360–362, 406
utility programs 181, 710

validity check 622, 739, 828, 895, 955, 1018
value activities 26, 28
value chain 26, 28–29
value of information 4–5
value system 29
value-added network (VAN) 272–273
variable cost 1026–1027

vendor invoice 819–820
vendor performance report 847, 851
vendor records 820, 832–833, 838
vendor selection 480
video conferencing 276
video display terminals 164, 168
videodisk 162
virtual memory 181
virus 659, 668–671, 707, 965
visual display terminal (VDT) 163
voice input 168
voice mail (V-mail) 275–276
voiceband 255
volume label 601
voucher 55, 56, 557–558, 635, 765, 819

walk-through 439, 452
wall clock time (WCT) 597
WATS line 255
white collar criminals 648, 660
wide-area network (WAN) 271–272
Windows NT 180
wiretap 658
word 5, 158, 159, 168
word processing 16, 198, 218–219, 417
work force inventory 967
work force profile 967
worm (virus) 659
WORM (write once, read many) 161
WYSIWYG 220

XENIX 180
zero balance check 949